MW01044835

The Scholarship Book 2003

The Complete Guide to Private-Sector Scholarships, Fellowships, Grants and Loans for the Undergraduate

NATIONAL SCHOLARSHIP RESEARCH SERVICE

Prentice Hall Press

ISSN 1528-9079

Notice

Our editors and proofreaders have made every effort to ensure that the e-mail addresses, Web sites, and phone numbers used were accurate and current at the time this book went to print. We recognize, however, that the electronic media is ever changing and, therefore, we advise that you preview this information before sharing it with others.

Printed in the United States of America

10 9 8 7 6 5 4 3 2 1

ISBN 0-7352-0367-9

Prentice Hall Press **Paramus, NJ 07652**

http://www.phpress.com

Contents

Introduction

The information in *THE SCHOLARSHIP BOOK 2003* was compiled from the database of the largest private sector financial aid research service in the world. Located in Santa Rosa, California, NATIONAL SCHOLARSHIP RESEARCH SERVICE (NSRS)™ began tracking private sector scholarships in the late 1970s, using a specialized computer system. As awards increased and research uncovered new sources for today's students, the addition of the INTERNATIONAL SCHOLARSHIP RESEARCH SERVICE (ISRS) doubled the size of this independently developed database. Prospective college students and present undergraduates will find the information in this book valuable in directing their applications and broadening their prospects for scholarship selection.

THE FACTS

According to the Association of Fund Raising Counsel, more than 80 percent of the grant applications that went to more than 44,000 foundations in the United States were either misdirected or filled out improperly. Many scholarships, fellowships, grants, loans, and internships go unclaimed each year—not because students do not qualify, but because they don't know that the money is available. In 1997, NSRS surveyed the private sector scholarship sources and the results found that 3.5 percent or almost 1 billion dollars of these private sector monies went undistributed. There is a great need to organize this "paper-chase" of information into a workable source for today's student. Utilizing the data collected in this book, students will have a broad base of information to convert to their advantage. The monies are there. Apply for them!

PRIVATE SECTOR FUNDS

Philanthropy in the United States is alive and well. These funds, which totaled $58.67 billion in 1982, increased to a whopping $329.91 billion in 1997. Of that amount, nearly 15 percent (or $49.49 billion) goes into the United States educational system, making the private sector the leader in funding at 55 percent of the available scholarships, fellowships, grants, and loans domestically. An additional $30-plus billion is dispersed by other countries worldwide.

And that amount increases daily. The interest alone on a properly invested $2 million is easily $100,000 annually. Private sector resources for higher education are as varied as the awards themselves.

Many scholarships are renewable. You simply sign for them year after year. Most allow you to "piggy-back" several individual scholarships. The average undergraduate scholarship is $5,000 per year, ranging from a low of $100 to a high of $25,000. Graduate-level fellowships range from $10,000 to over $60,000.

INVESTIGATE THE POSSIBILITIES

Don't think you can't apply because you earn too much money; **80 percent of the private sector does not require a financial statement or proof of need.** Don't think that application deadlines occur only in the fall; **private sector deadlines are passing daily** because often they are set to coincide with the tax year or organizational meeting dates. Don't believe that grades are the only consideration for an award; many application questions deal with personal, occupational, and educational background; organizational affiliation; talent, or ethnic origins; **90 percent are not concerned with grades.** Don't be concerned with age; many organizations are interested in the re-entry student and the mid-career development student. **In fact age is not a restriction,** especially since 1 out of 2 students are now over the age of 25. This is a big jump from 3 years ago when 1 out of 4 were over 25. This is because many students are going back to school after starting families or changing careers as we shift from the industrial wave to the high-tech wave. The Business and Professional Women's Foundation awards hundreds of scholarships to applicants who must be older than 25 or even 35. There is a scholarship at the California state colleges for students over the age of 60 for life-long learning.

PLAN TO COMPETE AND QUALIFY

The plan is simple—use this book and every other resource you can find. Inquire at your institution's financial aid office about government assistance and private endowments at the school. If you are a high school student in any year, begin by writing to ten or more schools. Select a range of institutions that interest you, both large and small, public and private. Request the application materials and school catalogs—many private endowments are available in the forms of scholarships and fellowships bequeathed by alumni and are listed in the school catalog under financial aid. A significant number of these go unclaimed because qualified students do not know they exist! The information is available, but the commitment and determination to find it belongs to the individual.

The private sector is easily accessed with this book. The student can use the tables provided to cross-reference the scholarships applicable to his or her personal background and educational goals. Choose as many as you qualify for, and request application forms and any pertinent materials. Some have specific requirements for applicants such as a personal interview, the submission of an essay or related work, or a promise to work for the company on completion of study and/or the earning of a degree. Others may have paid internships or work advancement programs. Still others may simply require that you fill out an application form.

The money is there. Many go unclaimed. Even the most common scholarship source, such as Rotary, Lions, Elks, Zonta, etc., are complaining that students are not requesting their scholarship application forms, nor applying. Students who do not take the time to inquire lose every advantage. The opportunity to advance to a graduate degree will widen many avenues for your future, and the rewards are incalculable. Information is merely a passage waiting to be used. The resources to achieve your goals are available to you; you need only pursue them.

Just for Fun: A Potpourri of Scholarships

Note: Most of the following sources are detailed in this book. Just find them in the alphabetical index in the back of the book, and look up their record numbers for details. Those not listed either are for graduate or international study only, or the sources wished not to appear in this book, primarily because they are at a particular school.

- Your tuition troubles could be gone with the wind! If you are a lineal descendant of a worthy Confederate soldier, contact the **United Daughters of the Confederacy** about their $400 to $1,500 scholarships.
- If you or your parents are actively involved in Harness Racing, you just might hitch yourself to one of the **Harness Tracks of America** scholarships worth $2,500 to $3,000.
- You could lace up a scholarship of up to $2,000 for undergraduate study if you are a dependent child of a worker in the footwear industry. It's a patent idea from **Two/Ten International Footwear Foundation**.
- Jen unu mil pundo nun EK! (Here's a thousand pounds—now go!) If you understood that you might be eligible for a **Norwich Jubilee Esperanto Foundation** scholarship paying $500 to study Esperanto in the United Kingdom.
- For students whose ancestors put their John Hancocks on the Declaration of Independence, scholarships worth $1,200 to $2,000 are given by **Descendants of the Signers of the Declaration of Independence.**

TOP INTERNATIONAL SCHOLARSHIPS FOR NON-U.S. STUDENTS

- Like sushi? Then you may want to contact the **Association of International Education** in Japan. Programs of six months to one year are offered to international undergraduate and graduate students to pursue studies in Japan.
- Want to study somewhere between the Statue of Liberty and the Golden Gate Bridge? The **American Association of University Women Educational Foundation** offers non-U.S. citizens the opportunity to pursue full-time study or research in the U.S. Must be female graduate or postgraduate students.
- If you have ever written a letter to a friend about your experience in a foreign country, then you should contact **World of Knowledge.** This was one of their past contests, and new ones are created each year for international graduate students who will be attending college in the U.S.
- Danish citizens wishing to study in the U.K. should contact the **Anglo-Danish Society.** Awards of up to 175 pounds/month are given for up to six months of study.
- Students in various European countries can apply to the **Netherlands Organization for International Cooperation in Higher Education.** Grants are given for study in the Netherlands.
- Students of Mongolian heritage who are citizens of Mongolia, the People's Republic of China, and the former Soviet Union can receive a scholarship from the **Mongolia Society.** Awards allow students to pursue studies in the U.S.

TOP INTERNATIONAL SCHOLARSHIPS FOR U.S. STUDENTS

- Ever wondered what school is like in another country? College students may apply to the **Rotary Foundation of Rotary International** for the opportunity to study in a foreign country. Both student's home country and country of intended study must have Rotary Clubs.
- Gesundheit! U.S. citizens who are sophomores or juniors in high school don't even have to know what that means if they join **Youth for Understanding International Exchange** to Germany. Students with a minimum 3.0 GPA live with a host family in Germany, and there is no language requirement.
- **Zeta Phi Beta Sorority Educational Foundation** provides $500-$1,000 to U.S. undergraduate and graduate students planning to study abroad. Awards also given to foreign students wishing to study in the U.S.

- Ever wondered what living with an international family would be like? High school students wishing to attend secondary school in another country should contact **AFS Intercultural Programs.** Students from fifty different countries live with host families in this international exchange.
- You'll be smashing plates you're so excited when you hear from the **Cyprus Children's Fund.** They award scholarships to U.S. citizens and U.S. residents of Greek or Greek Cypriot heritage who wish to pursue studies in Greece or Cyprus. Greek and Cyprus citizens may receive awards to study in the U.S.
- The **Youth Foundation, Inc.** offers scholarships for a U.S. undergraduate's junior year abroad. Selection is based on character, need, scholastic achievement, objective, motivation, potential for leadership, and good citizenship.
- Want to get away? Various scholarships are awarded by the **Institute for the International Education of Students** for studying abroad in many different countries. Organization encourages students with a wide variety of interests and abilities and who represent a wide range of social and economic backgrounds.

TOP CELEBRITY SCHOLARSHIPS

- The cost of college doesn't go for the price of peanuts these days, so **The Scripps Howard Foundation** is offering the **Charles M. Schultz Award.** $2,500 for an outstanding college cartoonist working at a college newspaper or magazine. Don't be a Blockhead! Apply!
- "Average yet creative" is the punchline for junior telecommunications majors at Ball State University. **The David Letterman Telecommunications Scholarship Program** could pay your way to graduation if you are an average student with a very creative mind.
- Don't make a big production out of the high cost of filmmaking! All it takes is "Forty Acres and a Mule"! **Spike Lee** and **Columbia Pictures** offer production fellowships to students in their second or third year of graduate study at the New York University Tisch School of Film. Two $5,000 fellowships are awarded per year to graduates rolling in action in production, filmmaking, and acting. Contact Tisch School of Film.
- This is certainly one house with high equity! Morehouse College received $1 million dollars from celebrity Oprah Winfrey to establish the **Oprah Winfrey Endowed Scholarship Fund.** Contact Morehouse College.
- Is the cost of college a dramatization? The right stage for you could be **Debbie Allen** and **Phylicia Rashad's** applause for their father in the **Dr. Andrew Allen Creative Arts Scholarship** of $15,000. A command performance is requested from undergraduate juniors and seniors at Howard University who portray excellence in drama, song, and dance.
- Are you between the ages of 17 and 22 living in the Golden State or the Lone Star State? If you are a Mexican-American resident of California or Texas and in an undergraduate program, you may just strike gold with the **Vikki Carr Scholarship** of up to $3,000!
- College costs driving you up the wall? Go ahead and dance on the ceiling! **Lionel Richie** has made students of Tuskegee University lighter than air with his $500,000 donation for an endowment in the business school at Tuskegee. Contact Tuskegee University.
- Well Hee-Haw, Y'all! Miniere's Network offers the **Minnie Pearl Scholarships** to financially needy high school seniors who have a significant bilateral hearing loss, good grades, and who have been accepted for enrollment by an accredited university, college, or technical school.

TOP CORPORATE SCHOLARSHIPS

- How sweet it is! **Sara Lee Corporation** employees and their children can apply for a student loan of up to $2,500 for study at an accredited institution.
- Would you like fries with that? **McDonald's** scholarships are served to New York Tri-State residents planning to attend their first year of college full-time. Must be U.S. citizens/permanent residents and show evidence of either community service or employment.

- Are you a high school senior searching for college tuition? You CAN go to school with help from the **American National Can Company** scholarship program. These scholarships are available for undergraduate study to dependents of company employees.
- Want to "bank" on your college education? If you are a high school senior and are a dependent of a **Citibank** employee, you can receive a scholarship of up to $5,000 for undergraduate study.
- Don't be derailed by the cost of a college education! The **Union Pacific Railroad** offers an Employee Dependent Scholarship Program to high school seniors in the top 1/4 of their class.

TOP SCHOLARSHIPS FOR WOMEN

- The **California Junior Miss Program** scholarship competition is open to girls in their junior year of high school who are U.S. citizens and California residents. Winner receives $15,000 for books, fees, and tuition at any college in the world.
- Fore! The **Women's Western Golf Foundation** has $2,000/year awaiting female high school seniors who are U.S. citizens and who have high academic standing, financial need, and an involvement with golf—skill is NOT a criterion!
- You don't need to see it to believe it! The **National Federation of the Blind** (Hermione Grant Calhoun Scholarship) offers $3,000 to legally blind women who are undergraduate or graduate students studying in any field.
- For women re-entry students, the **Jeanette Rankin Foundation** awards $1,000 to the winning woman aged 35 or older who is a U.S. citizen enrolled in a program of voc-tech training or in an undergraduate program.
- Are you a female undergraduate in the field of science or social science? If so, you can apply to the **Association for Women in Science Educational Foundation's** *Dr. Vicki L. Schechtman Scholarship.* Award for U.S. citizens with a minimum 3.0 GPA, and may be used for tuition, books, housing, research, equipment, etc.
- Don't beat around the bush. Contact the **Landscape Architecture Foundation** (Harriett Barnhart Wimmer Scholarship), which offers $1,000 to women who have demonstrated excellent design ability in landscape architecture, have sensitivity to the environment, and who are going into their final year of undergraduate study.
- For modern-day Rosie the Riveters, the **Society of Women Engineers** (General Electric Foundation Scholarship) offers $1,000 to women who are U.S. citizens studying engineering or computer science. Must be high school seniors entering an accredited school as freshmen.
- The **Astraea National Lesbian Action Foundation** (Margot Karle Scholarship) gives $500 to women students whose career path or extracurricular activities demonstrate political or social commitment to fighting for the civil rights of gays and lesbians.
- Love to fly? The **International Society of Women Airline Pilots** (ISA International Career Scholarship) offers $500-$1,500 to women throughout the world who are pursuing careers as airline pilots and have at least 750 hours of flight experience.

TOP SCHOLARSHIPS FOR MEN

- The **Phi Kappa Theta National Foundation** (Scholarship Program) offers undergraduate scholarships to members of the Phi Kappa Theta fraternity. Five scholarships are awarded based on financial need.
- Male opera singers who are from the land down under may apply for the *Sir Robert Askin Operatic Travelling Scholarship* offered by **Arts Management P/L.** Australian citizenship is required, and you must be between the ages of 18-30.
- Do you belong to the NAACP? The **NAACP National Office** offers the *Willems Scholarship* for male members of the NAACP studying engineering, chemistry, physics, or mathematics. Undergraduates receive $2,000, and the graduate award is $3,000.

- American males of Anglo-Saxon or German descent should contact the **Maud Glover Folsom Foundation, Inc.** which offers $2,500 to those under age 35. For use in prep school, high school, college, and advanced education.
- The **Boys & Girls Clubs of San Diego** (Spence Reese Scholarship Fund) offer scholarships to male high school students planning a career in medicine, law, engineering, or political science. Preference to students who live within a 250-mile radius of San Diego. Boys Club affiliation is not required.
- Your prayers have been answered! The **Elmer O. & Ida Preston Educational Trust** (Grants and Loans) offers an award that is half-grant and half-loan to male residents of Iowa who are pursuing a collegiate or professional study at an Iowa college or university. Applicants must be planning on a career in Christian ministry and must provide a recommendation from a minister commenting on the student's potential.
- Strike! The **Young American Bowling Alliance** offers the *Chuck Hall Star of Tomorrow Scholarship* of $4,000 to male students who are amateur bowlers and members of ABC or YABA up to age 21. Must be a high school senior or an undergraduate attending college.
- The **Raymond J. Harris Education Trust** offers scholarships of various amounts to Christian males for use at nine Philadelphia area colleges. Students must be studying medicine, law, engineering, dentistry, or agriculture.
- Fill your financial cavities with funds from the **American Dental Hygienists Association.** They have several scholarships designated for under-represented groups in that field, specifically minorities and men.

TOP SCHOLARSHIPS FOR MINORITIES

- The **Council on International Educational Exchange** offers *Bailey Minority Scholarships* of $500 for minorities studying in any field. Awards are for study, work, volunteer, and home-stay programs almost anywhere in the world.
- Minority undergraduates with at least a 3.0 GPA desiring to spend a semester or summer studying in a participating foreign university and who demonstrate leadership potential and extracurricular involvement in multicultural or international issues may qualify for *International Scholarships for Minorities* from the **American Institute for Foreign Study.** There is one scholarship that consists of full program fees and transportation, and there are also five semester scholarships of $1,000.
- The **Jackie Robinson Foundation** offers scholarships of $5,000 per year for four years to minority high school seniors who are college-bound. The program includes counseling, assistance in obtaining summer jobs, and permanent employment after graduation.
- Ethnic minorities with disabilities and ethnic minorities with disabilities who are gifted and talented meet the criteria for *Stanley E. Jackson Scholarship Awards* of $500 from the **Foundation for Exceptional Children.**
- Women of color who are interested in the fields of sports, physical education, and other sports-related careers have the opportunity to receive *Jackie Joyner-Kersee/Zina Garrison Minority Scholarships* of $4,000-$5,000 from the **Women's Sports Foundation.**
- High school seniors have new windows of opportunity with the **Gates Millennium Scholars Program.** School faculty may nominate African American, Native American, Hispanic, and Asian American students planning to enter college. Awards are based on academic performance in math and science, school activities, leadership potential, and need. Must be U.S. citizen.
- Disadvantaged and/or minority students entering a program leading to a B.A. or M.A. in architecture may have the ability to receive scholarships from the *Minority/Disadvantaged Scholarship Program* offered by the **American Institute of Architects/American Architectural Foundation.**
- The **American Association of Law Libraries** offers a *George A. Straight Minority Stipend Grant* of $3,500 to a minority group member who is a college graduate with library experience and is working toward an advanced degree that could further his or her law library career.

TOP RELIGIOUS SCHOLARSHIPS

- The **David and Dovetta Wilson Scholarship Fund** offers scholarships of $1,000 to college-bound high school seniors who are U.S. citizens and are selected for their academic achievement, involvement in the community, and religious activities.
- The **Memorial Foundation for Jewish Culture** offers an *International Scholarship Program for Community Service,* which is open to any individual, regardless of country of origin, for undergraduate study that leads to careers in the Rabbinate, Jewish education, social work, or religious functionaries outside the U.S., Israel, and Canada. Must commit to serve in a community of need for three years.
- Scholarships are being offered to high school graduates who are from the southeastern U.S. and who wish to study ministry, missionary work, or social work by **The Heath Education Fund.**
- The **American Foundation for the Blind** offers a *Gladys C. Anderson Memorial Scholarship* of $1,000 to a woman who is legally blind and studying religious or classical music at the college level. A sample performance tape of voice or instrumental selection is required.
- **Women of the Evangelical Lutheran Church in America** offers *Belmer-Flora Prince Scholarships* for women who are ELCA members planning on studying for ELCA service abroad that does not lead to a church-certified profession. Women must be U.S. citizens, over the age of 21, and have experienced an interruption in schooling for at least two years since high school.
- The *Leonard M. Perryman Communications Scholarship for Ethnic Minority Students* of $2,500 is offered by the **United Methodist Church** to an ethnic minority undergraduate junior or senior who is enrolled in an accredited school of communications or journalism. The student must have a Christian faith and be pursuing a career in religious communications.
- The **Presbyterian Church (U.S.A.)** offers its members scholarships if they are high school seniors planning to pursue full-time studies at participating colleges. Must be U.S. citizens/permanent residents and show financial need.
- The *David W. Self* and *Richard S. Smith* scholarship funds offer scholarships to undergraduate students who are members of the **United Methodist Church** and planning careers in the ministry or other religious careers.

TOP KINDERGARTEN TO 12TH-GRADE SCHOLARSHIPS

- Students in grades 7-12 have the opportunity to win up to $5,000 from **Alliance for Young Artists and Writers, Inc.** All that is required is the ability to demonstrate a talent in art, photography, writing, or interdisciplines. Cash grants are awarded and can be used for any field of study.
- Have you ever had the desire to fly? The **Stephen M. Price Foundation** is giving boys and girls between the ages of 14 and 16 who are economically disadvantaged and reside in the area of Jacksonville, Florida, the opportunity to earn a private pilot's license.
- The **Veterans of Foreign Wars of the United States** have an annual *Voice of Democracy Audio-Essay Scholarship Contest.* The contest is open to students in tenth, eleventh, and twelfth grades who attend public, private, and parochial high schools. Awards range from $1,000 to $20,000.
- It has become easier for needy students in Washington to attend private schools. The **Washington Scholarship Fund** is offering up to $1,700 per year to students in grades K-12.
- **AFS Intercultural Programs** has created the *International Exchange Student Program* to give high school students the opportunity to study abroad for a semester or a year with financial assistance. Students live with host families and attend local secondary schools.
- Students between the ages of 6 and 21 and who have moderate to profound hearing loss are being given the opportunity to win scholarships by the **Alexander Graham Bell Association for the Deaf.** In order to qualify, students must use speech and residual hearing and/or speechreading as a primary form of communication.
- The **John Edgar Thomson Foundation** is offering financial assistance to the daughters of deceased railroad workers between the ages of infancy and 22 depending on whether or not a higher education is sought.

- Scholarships and awards can be earned by students who participate in a sewing, knitting, or crocheting competition. **The National Make It Yourself with Wool Competition** involves creating a wool garment from a current pattern. The fabric must contain at least 60% wool.
- Students in grades 4-12 can enter an essay competition and possibly receive an award to help with full to partial tuition to Space Camp. This competition was created by the **U.S. Space Camp Foundation.**

TOP TRAVEL SCHOLARSHIPS

- Have you completed two years of university coursework or the equivalent in professional experience? If so, the **Rotary Foundation of Rotary International** is offering to pay up to $23,000/year for you to travel and study internationally.
- If you are a female athlete and you enjoy to travel, then here is the perfect opportunity for you. The **Women's Sports Foundation** is giving up to $1,500 to individual athletes and up to $3,000 to teams. These grants are available for training, coaching, equipment, and travel.
- **Woods Hole Oceanographic Institute** is awarding a $3,900 stipend and possible travel allowance to students who have completed their junior year of college or are beginning graduate school. They must be studying in any field of science with an interest in oceanography. The students will travel to Woods Hole, MA, and study there for twelve weeks during the summer.
- Do you ever feel the need to escape to a foreign country for a few months? If you are a minority student with a 2.0 GPA or higher, you just might qualify to spend the summer abroad. **Youth for Understanding International Exchange** chooses forty students every year to spend a summer in select countries where they will live with host families.
- Have you ever wondered what it would be like to live in a castle? The **Giacomo Leopardi Center** is offering to pay the tuition and travel expenses for the first three hundred students who apply. The school is located in Italy and it teaches the Italian language and culture.
- High school sophomores, juniors, and seniors are being given the opportunity to spend two or three weeks at sites in North or Central America by the **Earthwatch Student Challenge Awards.** This gives them the opportunity to have an intimate look at the world of science and state-of-the-art technology.

TOP ARTS SCHOLARSHIPS

- Action! **The Christophers** offers a film and video contest for college students to create an image expressing an annual topic. Awards are based on ability to capture theme, artistic/professional proficiency, and adherence to rules.
- Calling all Americans! The **Ladies Auxiliary to the Veterans of Foreign Wars of the United States** gives high school students an opportunity to express their patriotism through art. Annual awards are given for works on paper or canvas in a variety of styles.
- Are you a drama geek? The **Princess Grace Foundation** offers scholarships for students under age 25 in acting, directing, and design at U.S. schools.
- Want to see how Buzz and Woody came to life? **Pixar Animation Studios** offers summer internships for college and university students to obtain "hands on" experience in animation.
- Playwrights and composers should submit an original full-length play or musical to the **Stanley Drama Award Competition.** Work must not have been professionally produced or received tradebook publication.
- High school seniors and 17- to 18-year-olds in the creative and performing arts should contact **The National Foundation for Advancement in the Arts** to enter their talent contest. Areas include dance, jazz, music, photography, theatre, visual arts, voice, and writing.

TOP ATHLETIC SCHOLARSHIPS

- Fore! U.S. high school seniors who have served as a caddie at a WGA member club may apply for a scholarship from the **Western Golf Association.** Must be in the top 25% of your class, have outstanding personal character, and demonstrate financial need.
- The **Francis Ouimet Scholarship Fund** offers scholarships to Massachusetts residents who have worked as golf caddies, in pro shops, or as superintendents of operations at a Massachusetts golf course.
- NCAA student-athletes can receive scholarships from the **National Collegiate Athletic Association** for graduate or undergraduate study, depending on GPA and financial need. Must be nominated by a faculty athletics representative at your school.
- Do you want to be the next Picaboo Street? The **Women's Sports Foundation** provides financial assistance to female athletes and women pursuing sports-related careers.
- Kansas students who have participated in high school athletics may apply to the **American Legion of Kansas** for their scholarship to be used at any Kansas college, university, or trade school.
- Whoa! The **National Horseshoe Pitchers Association** gives awards to students under age 18 who compete in a horseshoe pitching league.
- The **Community Foundation of Western Massachusetts** offers scholarships to graduating seniors of Gateway Regional High School in Huntington, MA, and Longmeadow High School in Longmeadow, MA. Must have a strong interest in and have excelled in athletics.
- Caddies at New Jersey golf clubs can receive undergraduate scholarships from the **New Jersey State Golf Association.** Awards based on scholastic achievement, financial need, and length of service as a caddie.
- The **Aromando Family Educational Foundation** offers scholarships to aspiring teachers and theologians of Italian ancestry who are practicing Roman Catholics with a minimum 3.0 GPA. Must have at least two varsity letters in one or more high school sanctioned athletic or extracurricular programs.

TOP AVIATION SCHOLARSHIPS

- Love to fly? Scholarships are being made available for students studying in the fields of aviation and aerospace by the **Ninety-Nines, Inc. International.** Eligibility requirements vary.
- Calling all Amelia Earharts! The **International Society of Women Airline Pilots** offers scholarships to women who are interested in pursuing careers in flying the world's airlines. Applicants must have a U.S. FAA Commercial Pilot Certificate with an Instrument Rating and a First Class medical. They also must have 750 flight hours.
- Undergraduate juniors and seniors who have scholastic plans leading to future participation in the aerospace sciences and technologies have the ability to win the *Dr. Robert H. Goddard Space Science and Engineering Scholarship* from the **National Space Club.**
- Do you prefer the business end of aviation? Then contact the **Aviation Distributors and Manufacturers Association International.** They offer scholarships to students pursuing careers in aviation management or as professional pilots.
- Do you prefer whirlybirds? The **Vertical Flight Foundation** is giving scholarships to undergraduate and graduate students who have proven interests in pursuing careers in some aspect of helicopter or vertical flight. The scholarships are up to $2,000.
- The Eagle has landed! Minority graduate students who are studying in the fields of science and engineering qualify for **National Aeronautics and Space Administration Scholarships** if they are considering a career in space science and/or aerospace technology.
- Stand at attention! CAP cadets pursuing studies in Ground and Air Training for FAA private pilot licenses qualify for a $2,100 *Major Gen. Lucas V. Beau Flight Scholarship* which is being offered by the **Civil Air Patrol.**

- Do you copy, 10-4? The **Aircraft Electronics Association Educational Foundation** offers scholarships to students who are studying avionics and/or aircraft repair and who are attending post-secondary institutions, including technical schools.
- Are you a daredevil? The **EAA Aviation Foundation** offers two *Aviation Achievement Scholarships* of $500 and up annually to individuals who are active in sport aviation. The scholarships are to be used in order to further the recipients' aviation education training.

Sample Time-Saving Form Letter Requesting Application Information

Use this sample letter as a guide to create a general letter requesting information. Photocopy your letter and address the envelopes for mailing. Include the name of the scholarship you are applying for with the address on the envelope, so they will know which scholarship(s) you are requesting. Because this information is on the envelope, which you have to personally address anyway, it is not necessary to also include it on the letter. Just make sure your name and address are included, and photocopy the same request to be mailed to all the different sources, keeping it as generic as possible. It isn't time to introduce yourself until you send in the application. Enclosing a self-addressed, stamped envelope may give you a speedier response. Remember to apply well in advance of the deadlines. You should keep a calendar to keep track of them.

Date

Scholarship Program Office

Dear Scholarship Director:

Please send me application forms for any scholarships or fellowships that you might offer. I am enclosing a self-addressed, stamped envelope for your convenience in replying.

Sincerely,

Your name
Address
Phone Number

The Plan

Once you have written to scholarship sources for complete information, you might consider starting three financial aid boxes to maintain your information. You might call them "Government Funding," "School Endowments," and "Private Sector."

The Government Funding Box

Put all information from state and federal programs in this box.

Remember:
Dept. of Education 800/4FED-AID.
800/433-3243

The Coordinating Board for your state is in your phone book under "Government" or call your school.

The School Endowments Box

The college catalog's financial aid section will usually list the endowments and scholarships from alumni and local businesses. Put the catalogs in this box.

The Private Sector Box

This box should contain material you have gleaned from this book and/or from your own research.

The Search

Believe it or not, just about everything about you will come into play in your search for scholarships—your ancestry, religion, place of birth and residence, parent's union or corporate affiliation, your interest in a particular field, or simply by filling out the applicatio—can all be eligibility factors.

Using the tables in this book, the average student will find at least 20 to over 100 different private sector scholarship sources. Next, write to them and ask for their scholarship applications and requirements. *The letter can be a general request for information "form" letter that can be photocopied, but you should be specific about the name of the scholarship you are inquiring about on the envelope. For example, The Cassidy Endowment for Education (XYZ Scholarship).*

Write to each source as far in advance of their scholarship deadline as possible, and don't forget to send a self-addressed, stamped envelope—it not only expedites their reply, it is polite and shows that you care about applying and some organizations do require one.

Remember, on the outside of the envelope, list the name of the specific scholarship you are inquiring about. That way the person opening the mail will know where to direct your inquiry. Replies to these letters should be sorted into the appropriate boxes.

THE GOVERNMENT BOX

Please, please fill out the Free Application for Federal Student Aid (FAFSA) from the federal government. You can get a FAFSA from any high school, junior college, college, university or phone 800/4FED-AID (800/433-3243) or *http://www.fafsa.ed.gov* for web access. Note, the nice thing about this phone number is that you can track your information regarding it being processed and to what schools it was sent to per your request and when. At the very least these state and federal forms are the beginning of your scholarship profile at the financial aid office at the school. Most of the schools are now using these forms for their private endowment-based scholarship. So, even if you do not receive government funding, you will be ready to apply for loans from various outside school sources, such as banks, and the school-based programs, such as school endowments, scholarships, fellowships, grants, loans, college work study, athletic, military ROTC, etc. *So the FAFSA is a must, no matter what!*

On a quiet Saturday or when you have time, sit down and review the information. In the "Government" box, you will find that the state and federal forms are very similar, asking a multitude of questions regarding income, assets, and expenses. Don't automatically exclude yourself from state and federal funding thinking that you or your family make too much money. These programs vary tremendously from state to state and the federal programs have changed quite a bit. For example, there is no longer a $32,500 limit on the amount parents can earn in order to qualify for a student loan; but since that limit has been raised to $45,000, there will be less federal money to go around, so be sure to get in line quickly.

A bit of good news in the student loan arena is that the federal government no longer will consider the value of your house or farm in determining the amount of aid for which you qualify. I cannot stress enough the importance of filing the FAFSA, so please do it no matter what!

THE SCHOOL ENDOWMENTS BOX

You will usually find a list of endowments from alumni listed in the financial aid section of the college catalog. Often endowments to schools are not advertised and may go unclaimed. For example, at a small school like the University of San Francisco, the total endowments average $20 million to $30 million per year. At Ivy League schools, endowments range from $100 million to $200+ million each year. Of those endowments, 10 percent to 15 percent go to the financial aid office in the form of scholarships, fellowships, grants, and loans.

You will discover that sources in the "School Endowments" box are really just other forms of private sector scholarships. The difference is that endowment money is given directly to the school and is administered exclusively by the school's financial aid office, so you must deal directly with the college. You'll find that the myths I talked about earlier also apply to these private endowments—again, don't exclude yourself because of those old clichés regarding your grades, financial status, deadlines, or age.

THE PRIVATE SECTOR BOX

With your "Private Sector" box, you will find that once you have seen one or two forms, you have pretty much seen them all. Usually they are one or two pages asking where you are going to school, what you are going to major in, and why you think you deserve the scholarship. Some scholarship sources require that you join their organization. If the organization relates to your field of study, you should strongly consider joining because it will keep you informed (via newsletters, magazine, etc.) about developments in that field.

Some scholarship organizations may want you to promise that you will work for them for a period of time. The Dow Jones Newspaper Fund offers up to $80,000 in scholarships annually for journalism and mass communications students. In addition, a two-week intensive course (equivalent to advanced editing courses at most journalism departments) is followed by summer employment at a newspaper—interns receive a weekly salary. This could even yield a permanent job for the student.

Source: Discover Card Tribute Award (Scholarship)
American Association of School Administrators
P.O. Box 9338
Arlington, VA 22219

Telephone: 703/875-0708

Amount(s): $2,500–$25,000

Deadline(s): January

Area(s): All fields of study

Description: Open to high school juniors whose freshman and sophomore GPA was at least 2.75. Award is based on ***financial*** merit, not on financial need. Applicants must have achievement in 3 of these 4 areas: special talent, leadership, obstacles overcome, and community service.

Information: A total of 9 scholarships are available in each of the fifty states. Write to above address for an application or check Web site.

Include scholarship name as well as organization name & address on envelope.

Call if you don't receive application by a month or so before deadline or check if there is a Web site.

Don't request info too late! Write at least a month before deadline for an application.

Different foundations have different definitions of need, academic achievement, etc. Don't rule yourself out until you have exact descriptions from the foundations themselves.

Don't forget to include contact name if given.

The Essay

Most organizations awarding scholarships require an essay as part of the application process. The essay is the most important part of the private sector scholarship search.

The following excerpt from the University of California at Los Angeles (UCLA) application material emphasizes the importance of the essay and contains good advice no matter where you are going to college:

> *The essay is an important part of your application for admission and for scholarships.*
>
> *For these purposes, the University seeks information that will distinguish you from other applicants. You may wish, therefore, to write about your experiences, achievements, and goals. You might, for example, discuss an important life experience and what you learned from it. You might also describe unusual circumstances, challenges, or hardships you have faced. School activities and experiences are also topics to discuss in your essay but they do not need to be the focus.*

Rather than listing activities, describe your level of achievement in areas you have pursued—including employment or volunteer activities—and the personal qualities revealed by the time and effort you have devoted to them.

Also, discuss your interest in your intended field of study. If you have a disability, you may also include a description of its impact on your experiences, goals, and aspirations.

The University seeks information about any exceptional achievements such as activities, honors, awards, employment, or volunteer work that demonstrates your motivation, achievement, leadership, and commitment.

Make sure your essay is neatly typed, is well written, and does not contain grammatical errors or misspelled words.

The Application

When filling out scholarship application forms, be complete, concise, and creative. People who read these applications want to know the real you, not just your name. Scholarship applications should clearly emphasize your ambitions, motivations, and what makes you different from everyone else. Be original!

Your application should be neatly handwritten or typewritten, and neatness counts. I had a complaint from one foundation about a student who had an excellent background and qualifications but used a crayon to fill out the application.

Once your essay is finished, make a master file of it and other supporting items. Photocopy your essay and attach it to each application. If requested, also include: a resume or curriculum vitae, extracurricular activities sheet (usually one page), transcripts, SAT or ACT scores, letters of recommendation (usually one each from a teacher, employer, and friend) outlining your moral character, and if there are any newspaper articles, etc., about you, it is a good idea to include them, as well.

Application Checklist

The following supporting documents may be requested with your application. I suggest you make a master file for these documents and photocopy them. You can then just pull a copy from your file and attach it to the application upon request.

- ❑ 1. Include your essay.
- ❑ 2. Include extracurricular activities sheet, or
- ❑ 3. Include curriculum vitae if in college, or resume if you are in the job market.
- ❑ 4. Include transcripts.
- ❑ 5. Include SAT or ACT scores.
- ❑ 6. Include letters of recommendation.
- ❑ 7. Include any newspaper articles, etc., about yourself (if you have any).

You might also include your photograph, whether it's a high school picture or a snapshot of you working at your favorite hobby. This helps the selection committee feel a little closer to you. Instead of just seeing a name, they will have a face to match it.

Mail your applications early, at least a month before the deadline.

The Calendar

I also find it helpful to keep a calendar with deadlines circled so you can stay organized. You can hang it above your three scholarship boxes so it is easily visible. Each application should have its own file. On the outside of the file, you might rate your chances of getting the scholarship on a scale of 1 to 10.

If a scholarship application deadline has passed, save it for the next year. If you are turned down for a scholarship, don't worry. Some organizations want to see if you will apply a second time. The important point is to stay motivated and be persistent.

Calendar

Sun	M	T	W	Th	F	Sat
1	2	3	4	5	6	7
8	9	10	11	12	13	14
15	16	17	18	19	20	21
22	23	24	25	26	27	28
29	30	31				

Government Box

Endowment Box

Private Sector Box

Box With Master Files 1–7.

IMPORTANT NOTE

Every effort has been made to supply you with the most accurate and up-to-date information possible, but—even as this book goes to print—awards are being added and application requirements are being changed by sponsoring organizations. Such circumstances are beyond our control.

Since the information we have supplied may not reflect the current status of any particular award program you are interested in, you should use this book only as a guide. Contact the source of the award for current application information.

SCHOLARSHIP SEARCH SCAMS

If they guarantee a scholarship or if the information is free, buyer beware! Think about it. The decision for scholarship selection is decided only by the scholarship organization itself, not by someone selling you the information. And, most of these online organizations with free information on the World Wide Web are just selling your very personal information to mailing houses. It's like Grandma used to say, *"Nothing is free, and you get what you pay for!"*

A disturbing number of scholarship-sponsoring organizations have reported in recent months that they are receiving a high volume of inquiries from students who are *unqualified* for the awards about which they are asking.

Because of the number of these types of reports, we are investigating the origins of the misguided inquiries. Most often we find that someone has taken only names and addresses from our scholarship books and is selling the information—a general listing of scholarships available in a particular field of study—to students without regard to the student's qualifications. Most of these "operations" make no effort to match the student's educational goals and personal background with the requirements of the scholarships.

Lastly, if any scholarship service is so-called FREE or guarantees a scholarship, savings bond, or a fountain pen, "buyer beware!" If it sounds too good to be true, then it probably is. Since it is solely at the discretion of the scholarship-sponsoring organizations to choose their scholarship recipients each year, these scholarship search scams cannot guarantee that users of their service will get a scholarship. Use this book to accurately cross-match scholarship sources for which you are eligible and avoid those scholarship search scams who merely copy information from our books.

How to Use This Book

Each award, book, and resource listed has a record number preceding it. All of our indexes are based on these record numbers.

Here is a short guide to finding the information you need:

SCHOLARSHIP AND AWARD LISTINGS

Each listing contains a very condensed description of the award, its eligibility requirements, deadline dates, and where to get more information or an application.

You will notice a large "General" section. These are awards that do not usually specify a particular field of study in their eligibility requirements. You need to use the indexes provided and read each listing carefully to see if you might qualify for one of these awards.

Use the information we have provided only as a guide. Write to the source for a complete description of qualifications.

HELPFUL PUBLICATIONS

This section contains a selection of books and pamphlets that we consider helpful to the student. These publications are excellent sources of information on a wide variety of college and financial aid subjects.

If you discover a publication you find particularly helpful, let us know so we can share the information with others.

CAREER INFORMATION

This is a list of organizations that can help you decide where to study, give you information on job opportunities available in your field of study, and much more. We encourage you to write to these organizations for information.

ALPHABETICAL INDEX

A to Z, this index lists the reference number of every award, book, and career organization included in this book.

LEGEND FOR "QUICK FIND INDEX" AND "FIELD OF STUDY" INDEX:

D = Dependent
DIS = Disabled
DEC = Deceased
NOT D = Not Dependent
G = for Graduate Study only

Examples:

Choose Fireman if you are a Fireman.
Choose **Fireman-D-DIS** if you are a **dependent** of a **disabled** Fireman.
Choose **Fireman-D-DEC** if you are a **dependent** of a **deceased** Fireman.
Choose **Fireman-NOT D** if you are a **dependent** of a fireman but are **not** a fireman yourself.
Choose **Fireman-G** if you are a **graduate** student who is a fireman.

B = Booklet source in "Helpful Publications" section.
C = Career source in "Career Information" section.

Scholarships and Award Listings

SCHOOL OF BUSINESS

1—AMERICAN HEALTH AND BEAUTY AIDS INSTITUTE (Fred Luster, Sr. Education Foundation Scholarships for College-Bound High School Seniors)

401 North Michigan Avenue
Chicago IL 60611-4267
312/644-6610
AMOUNT: $250 and $500
DEADLINE(S): APR 15
FIELD(S): Chemistry, Business, or Engineering

For college-bound high school seniors who will be enrolled as a college freshman in a four-year college majoring in chemistry, business, or engineering. 3.0 GPA required.

Send two letters of recommendation (one from a school official) and high school transcript. Scholastic record, school activities, and extracurricular activities considered.

2—AMERICAN INDIAN SCIENCE AND ENGINEERING SOCIETY (Burlington Northern Santa Fe Pacific Foundation Scholarships)

P.O. Box 9828
Albuquerque NM 87119-9828
505/765-1052
FAX: 505/765-5608
E-mail: scholarships@aises.org
Internet: http://www.aises.org/scholarships
AMOUNT: $2,500/year
DEADLINE(S): MAR 31
FIELD(S): Business; Education; Science; Engineering; Health Administration

Open to high school seniors who are at least 1/4 American Indian. Must reside in KS, OK, CO, AZ, NM, MN, ND, OR, SD, WA, MT, or San Bernardino County, CA (Burlington Northern and Santa Fe Pacific service areas). Must demonstrate financial need.

5 awards annually. Renewable up to 4 years. See Web site or contact Patricia Browne for an application.

3—BEDDING PLANTS FOUNDATION, INC. (Harold Bettinger Memorial Scholarship)

P.O. Box 280
East Lansing MI 48826-0280
517/333-4617
FAX: 517/333-4494
E-mail: BPFI@aol.com
Internet: http://www.bpfi.org
AMOUNT: $1,000
DEADLINE(S): MAY 15
FIELD(S): Horticulture AND Business/Marketing

Open to graduate and undergraduate students already attending a four-year college/university who have either a horticulture major with business/marketing emphasis OR a business/marketing major with horticulture emphasis. Cash award, with checks issued jointly in name of recipient and college/institution he or she will attend for current year. Must submit references and transcripts.

1 award annually. See Web site or send printed self-addressed mailing label (or self-addressed, stamped envelope) to BPFI after January 1 for an application. Recipient will be notified.

4—BEDDING PLANTS FOUNDATION, INC. (Jerry Wilmot Scholarship)

P.O. Box 280
East Lansing MI 48826-0280
517/333-4617
FAX: 517/333-4494
E-mail: BPFI@aol.com
Internet: http://www.bpfi.org
AMOUNT: $2,000
DEADLINE(S): MAY 15
FIELD(S): Horticulture AND Business/Finance; Garden Center Management

Open to undergraduate students already attending a four-year college/university who either have a major in horticulture with business/finance emphasis OR have a major in business/finance with horticulture emphasis. Should wish to pursue a career in garden center management. Cash award, with checks issued jointly in name of recipient and college/institution he or she will attend for current year. Must submit references and transcripts.

1 award annually. See Web site or send printed self-addressed mailing label (or self-addressed, stamped envelope) to BPFI after January 1 for an application. Recipient will be notified.

5—CAREER OPPORTUNITIES FOR YOUTH, INC. (Collegiate Scholarship Program)

P.O. Box 996
Manhattan Beach CA 90266
310/535-4838
AMOUNT: $250 to $1,000
DEADLINE(S): SEP 30
FIELD(S): Engineering, Science, Mathematics, Computer Science, Business Administration, Education, Nursing

For students of Latino/Hispanic background residing in the Southern California area who have completed at least one semester/quarter of study at an accredited four-year university. Must have a cumulative GPA of 2.5 or higher.

Priority will be given to students who demonstrate financial need. Send SASE to above location for details.

6—CELANESE CANADA, INC. (Scholarships)

AUCC; 350 Albert Street, Suite 600
Ottawa Ontario K1R 1B1 CANADA
613/563-1236; FAX: 613/563-9745
E-mail: awards@aucc.ca
Internet: http://www.aucc.ca
AMOUNT: $1,500
DEADLINE(S): JUL 2
FIELD(S): Mechanical and Chemical Engineering; Chemistry; Business Administration and Commerce

Open to Canadian citizens/permanent residents for their final year of an undergraduate program in one of above fields. Must attend a college/university which is a member, or affiliated to a member, of the Association of Universities and Colleges of Canada. Candidates are expected to have achieved a high level of academic excellence as well as to have exhibited superior intellectual ability and judgment. In some cases, study in certain province/school is required.

APPLICATIONS ARE BY NOMINATION ONLY. Not renewable. See Web site or contact AUCC for nomination procedures.

7—CHICAGO ROOFING CONTRACTORS ASSOCIATION (Scholarship)

4415 W. Harrison Street, #322
Hillside IL 60162
708/449-3340
FAX: 708/449-0837
E-mail: crcainfo@crca.org
Internet: http://www.crca.org
AMOUNT: $2,000
DEADLINE(S): Varies
FIELD(S): Business; Engineering; Architecture; Liberal Arts; Sciences

Open to high school seniors who reside in one of the eight counties in Northern Illinois: Cook, DuPage, Lake, Kane, Kendall, DeKalb, McHenry, or Will. Must be accepted as a full-time student in a four-year college/university to pursue a degree in one of the above fields. Must be U.S. citizen. Based on academic achievements, extracurricular activites, and community involvement.

Renewable. Contact CRCA for an application.

8—COUNCIL OF ENERGY RESOURCE TRIBE (CERT)

1999 Broadway, Suite 2600
Denver CO 80202
303/282-7576
AMOUNT: $1,000 per year
DEADLINE(S): JUL 1
FIELD(S): Science, Engineering, or Business

Only for applicants who are members of the T.R.I.B.E.S. program their senior year in high school. TRIBES enrollment is limited to ensure a quality experience for each student. To qualify for TRIBES, students must be graduating seniors, plan to attend a college in the fall, and be interested in business, engineering, science, or related fields. Indian students who wish to attend TRIBES may contact CERT for information and an application.

9—CUBAN AMERICAN NATIONAL FOUNDATION (The Mas Family Scholarships)

7300 NW 3 Terrace
Miami FL 33122
305/592-7768
FAX: 305/592-7889
E-mail: canfnet.org
Internet: http://www.canfnet.org
AMOUNT: Individually negotiated
DEADLINE(S): MAR 15
FIELD(S): Engineering, Business, International Relations, Economics, Communications, Journalism

For Cuban-Americans students, graduates and undergraduates, born in Cuba or direct descendants of those who left Cuba. Must be in top 10% of high school class or maintain a 3.5 GPA in college.

10,000 awards/year. Recipients may reapply for subsequent years. Financial need considered along with academic success, SAT and GRE scores, and leadership potential. Essays and proof of Cuban descent required.

10—EMPIRE COLLEGE (Dean's Scholarship)

3035 Cleveland Avenue
Santa Rosa CA 95403
707/546-4000
FAX: 707/546-4058
AMOUNT: $250-$1,500
DEADLINE(S): APR 15
FIELD(S): Accounting; Secretarial; Legal; Medical (Clinical and Administrative); Travel and Tourism; General Business; Computer Assembly; Network Assembly/Administration

Open to high school seniors who plan to attend Empire College. Must be U.S. citizen.

10 awards annually. Contact Ms. Mary Farha for an application.

11—HILLSDALE COLLEGE (Freedom as Vocation Scholarship)

33 E. College Street
Hillsdale MI 49242-1298
517/437-7341
Internet: http://www.hillsdale.edu
AMOUNT: Varies
DEADLINE(S): None
FIELD(S): Business; History; Political Science; Economics

Open to Hillsdale College undergraduates who maintain a minimum 3.0 GPA and commit to a series of courses in the above fields. Student must rank in top 20% of class and top 10% of test scores. Must possess excellent communications, public speaking, and leadership skills and demonstrate outstanding character and citizenship. Financial need NOT a factor.

Renewable. No application process; students are selected. See Web site for details.

12—JC PENNEY (Scholarship Program)

Corporate Headquarters
Plano TX 75023
972/431-1347
Internet: http://www.jcpenneyinc.com
AMOUNT: $1,500
DEADLINE(S): Varies
FIELD(S): Business; Merchandising; Retail Studies; Information Systems

For undergraduates in above fields. Must be dependent children of or associates who are employed at JC Penney both at the time of applying for the scholarships and at the time of awarding the scholarships-or can be dependents of deceased/retired associates having three continuous years of service.

128 one-time awards. Current recipients may reapply as long as the scholarship program is offered at their school. The campuses which offer this scholarship are the 32 colleges where JC Penney recruits new management trainees-campuses reevaluated each year. Contact your (participating) school for an application or visit your local JC Penney store.

13—JOHNSON AND WALES UNIVERSITY (Annual Johnson and Wales University National High School Recipe Contest)

8 Abbott Place
Providence RI 02903
401/598-2345
AMOUNT: $1,000 to $5,000
DEADLINE(S): JAN 31
FIELD(S): Business, Hospitality, Technology, Culinary Arts

For students planning to attend Johnson & Wales University, Providence, Rhode Island.

Write to above address for detailed description.

14—JOHNSON AND WALES UNIVERSITY (Gilbane Building Company Eagle Scout Scholarship)

8 Abbott Place
Providence RI 02903
401/598-2345
AMOUNT: $1,200
DEADLINE(S): None
FIELD(S): Business, Hospitality, Technology, Culinary Arts

For students attending Johnson & Wales University, Providence, Rhode Island. Must be Eagle Scouts.

Send letter of recommendation and transcript to above address.

15—JOHNSON AND WALES UNIVERSITY (National High School Entrepreneur of the Year Contest)

8 Abbott Place
Providence RI 02903
401/598-2345
AMOUNT: $1,000 to $10,000
DEADLINE(S): DEC 27
FIELD(S): Business, Hospitality, Technology, Culinary Arts

For students attending Johnson & Wales University, Providence, Rhode Island.

Send for detailed description to above address.

16—JOHNSON AND WALES UNIVERSITY (Scholarships)

8 Abbott Place
Providence RI 02903
401/598-2345
AMOUNT: $200 to $10,000
DEADLINE(S): None
FIELD(S): Business, Hospitality, Technology, Culinary Arts

For students attending Johnson & Wales University, Providence, Rhode Island.

Renewable for four years. Write for complete information.

17—JUNIATA COLLEGE (Anna Groninger Smith Memorial Scholarship)

Financial Aid Office
Huntingdon PA 16652
814/641-3603
FAX: 814/641-3355
E-mail: clarkec@juniata.edu
AMOUNT: $4,000 (max.)
DEADLINE(S): APR 1
FIELD(S): Business

Open to females in business studies applying to Juniata College. Must demonstrate financial need and fill out government FAFSA form.

Contact Cynthia G. Clarke, Research Specialist, for an application or enrollment information. See your financial aid office for FAFSA.

18—LAGRANT FOUNDATION (Scholarships)

911 Wilshire Boulevard, Suite 2150
Los Angeles CA 90017-3450
323/469-8680
FAX: 323/469-8683
Internet: http://www.lagrant foundation.org
AMOUNT: $2,000
DEADLINE(S): MAR 31
FIELD(S): Communications or Business

Applicant must be a U.S. citizen and a member of one of the following ethnic groups: African American, Asian Pacific American, Hispanic, or Native American.

Applicant must be a high-school senior, planning to attend a four-year accredited institution and planning to carry a total of 12 units or more per quarter/semester

Applicant must have a minimum of 2.5 GPA and MUST declare one of the following majors in their first year of college: public relations, marketing, or advertising.

19—LEAGUE OF UNITED LATIN AMERICAN CITIZENS (General Electric/LULAC Scholarship Program)

2000 L Street NW, #610
Washington DC 20036
202/835-9646
FAX: 202/835-9685
Internet: http://www.lulac.org/
AMOUNT: $5,000
DEADLINE(S): JUL 15
FIELD(S): Business; Engineering

Open to minority students who are enrolled as business or engineering majors leading to a bachelor's degree at accredited colleges/universities in the U.S. and will be college sophomores in the fall of application year. Recipients may be offered temporary summer or internship positions with GE businesses; however the students are under no obligation to accept GE employment.

2 awards annually. Send self-addressed, stamped envelope for an application.

20—NATIONAL ITALIAN AMERICAN FOUNDATION (George L. Graziado Fellowship for Business)

1860 19th Street NW
Washington DC 20009
202/530-5315
AMOUNT: $2,500 and $5,000
DEADLINE(S): MAY 30
FIELD(S): Business and Management

Open to undergraduate American students of Italian ancestry studying at the George L. Graziado School of Business and Management at Pepperdine University, California.

2 awards given. Academic merit, financial need, and community service are considered. Contact organization for application and details.

21—NATIONAL ITALIAN AMERICAN FOUNDATION (Norman R. Peterson Scholarship)

1860 19th Street NW
Washington DC 20009
202/530-5315
AMOUNT: One is $5,000; one is $2,500
DEADLINE(S): MAY 31
FIELD(S): Business/Finance/Economics

For undergraduate American students from the midwest (Michigan-based) of Italian ancestry for study at John Cabot University in Rome.

For information contact Francesca Gleason, Director of Admissions at 011-39-6-687-8881.

22—NATIVE AMERICAN SCHOLARSHIP FUND, INC. (Scholarships)

8200 Mountain Road NE, Suite 203
Albuquerque NM 87110
505/262-2351
FAX: 505/262-0543
E-mail: NScholarsh@aol.com
AMOUNT: Varies
DEADLINE(S): MAR 15; APR 15; SEP 15
FIELD(S): Math; Engineering; Science; Business; Education; Computer Science

Open to American Indians or Alaskan Natives (1/4 degree or more) enrolled as members of a federally recognized, state recognized, or terminated tribe. For graduate or undergraduate study at an accredited four-year college or university.

208 awards annually. Contact Lucille Kelley, Director of Recruitment, for an application.

23—PROJECT CAMBIO FOUNDATION (Project Cambio Scholarship)

P.O. Box 3004-227
Corvallis OR 97339
503/929-6108
AMOUNT: $1,000
DEADLINE(S): APR 1
FIELD(S): Business

Scholarships available for women of Hispanic descent. Applicants should be interested in pursuing a change in career or advancement after being out of the job market.

24—SAN FRANCISCO REGIONAL MANAGEMENT ASSOCIATION (Frank Figueroa Memorial Scholarship)

605 North Arrowhead Avenue, Suite 101
San Bernardino CA 92401
AMOUNT: $1,000
DEADLINE(S): JUN 30
FIELD(S): Public Administration

Available to students who are currently enrolled or accepted to an M.P.A. (Masters of Public Administration) program at an accredited California, Arizona, Nevada, or Hawaii institution. Must submit resume, transcript, and essay.

25—SOCIETY OF SATELLITE PROFESSIONALS INTERNATIONAL (SSPI Scholarships)

225 Reinekers Lane, Suite 600
Alexandria VA 22314
703/857-3717

FAX: 703/857-6335
E-mail: neworbit@aol.com;
Internet: http://www.sspi.org
AMOUNT: $1,500 to $4,000
DEADLINE(S): DEC 1
FIELD(S): Satellites as related to communications, domestic and international telecommunications policy, remote sensing, journalism, law, meteorology, energy, navigation, business, government, and broadcasting services

Various scholarships for students studying in the above fields.

Access Web site for details and applications or send a self-addressed, stamped envelope (SASE) for a complete listing.

26—SRP/NAVAJO GENERATING STATION (Navajo Scholarship)

P.O. Box 850
Page AZ 86040
520/645-6539
FAX: 520/645-7295
E-mail: ljdawave@srp.gov
AMOUNT: Based on need
DEADLINE(S): APR 30
FIELD(S): Engineering, Environmental Studies, Business, Business Management, Health, Education

Scholarships for full-time students who hold membership in the Navajo Tribe and who are pursuing a degree in a field of study recognized as significant to the Navajo Naiton, Salt River Project, or the Navajo Generating Station, such as those listed above. Must be junior or senior, have and maintain a GPA of 3.0

Average of 15 awards per year. Inquire of Linda Dawavendewa at above location.

27—TYSON FOUNDATION, INC. (Alabama Scholarship Program)

2210 W. Oaklawn
Springdale AR 72762-6999
501/290-4995
AMOUNT: Varies (according to need)
DEADLINE(S): FEB 28
FIELD(S): Business; Agriculture; Engineering; Computer Science; Nursing

Open to residents of the general areas of Albertville, Ashland, Blountsville, Gadsden, Heflin, or Oxford, Alabama, who are U.S. citizens and live in the vicinity of a Tyson facility. Must be pursuing full-time undergraduate study at an accredited U.S. institution and demonstrate financial need. Must also be employed part-time and/or summers to help fund education.

Renewable up to 8 semesters or 12 trimesters as long as student meets criteria. Contact Tyson Foundation for an application no later than last day of February; deadline to return application is April 20.

28—TYSON FOUNDATION, INC. (Arkansas Scholarship Program)

2210 W. Oaklawn
Springdale AR 72762-6999
501/290-4955
AMOUNT: Varies (according to need)
DEADLINE(S): FEB 28
FIELD(S): Business; Agriculture; Engineering; Computer Science; Nursing

Open to Arkansas residents who are U.S. citizens pursuing full-time undergraduate study at an accredited U.S. institution. Must demonstrate financial need and be employed part-time and/or summers to help fund education.

Renewable up to 8 semesters or 12 trimesters as long as student meets criteria. Contact Tyson Foundation for an application no later than last day of February; deadline to return application is April 20.

29—TYSON FOUNDATION, INC. (Florida Scholarship Program)

2210 Oaklawn
Springdale AR 72762-6999
501/290-4995
AMOUNT: Varies (according to need)
DEADLINE(S): FEB 28
FIELD(S): Business; Agriculture; Engineering; Computer Science; Nursing

Open to residents of the general area of Jacksonville, Florida, who are U.S. citizens and live in the vicinity of a Tyson facility. Must be pursuing full-time undergraduate study in an accredited U.S. institution and demonstrate financial need. Must also be employed part-time and/or summers to help fund education.

Renewable up to 8 semesters or 12 trimesters as long as student meets criteria. Contact Tyson Foundation for an application no later than last day of February; deadline to return application is April 20.

30—TYSON FOUNDATION, INC. (Georgia Scholarship Program)

2210 Oaklawn
Springdale AR 72762-6999
501/290-4995
AMOUNT: Varies (according to need)
DEADLINE(S): FEB 28
FIELD(S): Business; Agriculture; Engineering; Computer Science; Nursing

Open to residents of the general areas of Cumming, Buena Vista, Dawson, or Vienna, Georgia, who are U.S. citizens and live in the vicinity of a Tyson facility. Must be pursuing full-time undergraduate study in an accredited U.S. institution and demonstrate financial need. Must also be employed part-time and/or summers to help fund education.

Renewable up to 8 semesters or 12 trimesters as long as student meets criteria. Contact Tyson Foundation for an application no later than last day of February; deadline to return application is April 20.

31—TYSON FOUNDATION, INC. (Illinois Scholarship Program)

2210 Oaklawn
Springdale AR 72762-6999
501/290-4995
AMOUNT: Varies (according to need)
DEADLINE(S): FEB 28
FIELD(S): Business; Agriculture; Engineering; Computer Science; Nursing

Open to residents of the general area of Chicago, Illinois, who are U.S. citizens and live in the vicinity of a Tyson facility. Must be pursuing full-time undergraduate study in an accredited U.S. institution and demonstrate financial need. Must also be employed part-time and/or summers to help fund education.

Renewable up to 8 semesters or 12 trimesters as long as student meets criteria. Contact Tyson Foundation for an application no later than last day of February; deadline to return application is April 20.

32—TYSON FOUNDATION, INC. (Indiana Scholarship Program)

2210 Oaklawn
Springdale AR 72762-6999
501/290-4995
AMOUNT: Varies (according to need)
DEADLINE(S): FEB 28
FIELD(S): Business; Agriculture; Engineering; Computer Science; Nursing

Open to residents of the general areas of Portland or Corydon, Indiana, who are U.S. citizens and live in the vicinity of a Tyson facility. Must be pursuing full-time undergraduate study at an accredited U.S. institution and demonstrate financial need. Must also be employed part-time and/or summers to help fund education.

Renewable up to 8 semesters or 12 trimesters as long as student meets criteria. Contact Tyson Foundation for an application no later than last day of February; deadline to return application is April 20.

33—TYSON FOUNDATION, INC. (Mississippi Scholarship Program)

2210 Oaklawn
Springdale AR 72762-6999
501/290-4995

AMOUNT: Varies (according to need)
DEADLINE(S): FEB 28
FIELD(S): Business; Agriculture; Engineering; Computer Science; Nursing

Open to residents of the general areas of Cleveland, Jackson, Forest, or Vicksburg, Mississippi, who are U.S. citizens and live in the vicinity of a Tyson facility. Must be pursuing full-time undergraduate study in an accredited U.S. institution and demonstrate financial need. Must also be employed part-time and/or summers to help fund education.

Renewable up to 8 semesters or 12 trimesters as long as student meets criteria. Contact Tyson Foundation for an application no later than last day of February; deadline to return application is April 20.

34—TYSON FOUNDATION, INC. (Missouri Scholarship Program)

2210 Oaklawn
Springdale AR 72762-6999
501/290-4995

AMOUNT: Varies (according to need)
DEADLINE(S): FEB 28
FIELD(S): Business; Agriculture; Engineering; Computer Science; Nursing

Open to residents of the general areas of Dexter, Monett, Neosho, Noel, or Sedalia, Missouri, who are U.S. citizens and live in the vicinity of a Tyson facility. Must be pursuing full-time undergraduate study in an accredited U.S. institution and demonstrate financial need. Must also be employed part-time and/or summers to help fund education.

Renewable up to 8 semesters or 12 trimesters as long as student meets criteria. Contact Tyson Foundation for an application no later than last day of February; deadline to return application is April 20.

35—TYSON FOUNDATION, INC. (North Carolina Scholarship Program)

2210 Oaklawn
Springdale AR 72762-6999
501/290-4995

AMOUNT: Varies (according to need)
DEADLINE(S): FEB 28
FIELD(S): Business; Agriculture; Engineering; Computer Science; Nursing

Open to residents of the general areas of Creswell, Monroe, Sanford, or Wilkesboro, North Carolina, who are U.S. citizens and live in the vicinity of a Tyson facility. Must be pursuing full-time undergraduate study in an accredited U.S. institution and demonstrate financial need. Must also be employed part-time and/or summers to help fund education.

Renewable up to 8 semesters or 12 trimesters as long as student meets criteria. Contact Tyson Foundation for an application no later than the last day of February; deadline to return application is April 20.

36—TYSON FOUNDATION, INC. (Oklahoma Scholarship Program)

2210 Oaklawn
Springdale AR 72762-6999
501/290-4995

AMOUNT: Varies (according to need)
DEADLINE(S): FEB 28
FIELD(S): Business; Agriculture; Engineering; Computer Science; Nursing

Open to residents of the general areas of Broken Bow or Stillwell, Oklahoma, who are U.S. citizens and live in the vicinity of a Tyson facility. Must be pursuing full-time undergraduate study in an accredited U.S. institution and demonstrate financial need. Must also be employed part-time and/or summers to help fund education.

Renewable up to 8 semesters or 12 trimesters as long as student meets criteria. Contact Tyson Foundation for an application no later than last day of February; deadline to return application is April 20.

37—TYSON FOUNDATION, INC. (Pennsylvania Scholarship Program)

2210 Oaklawn
Springdale AR 72762-6999
501/290-4995

AMOUNT: Varies (according to need)
DEADLINE(S): FEB 28
FIELD(S): Business; Agriculture; Engineering; Computer Science; Nursing

Open to residents of the general area of New Holland, Pennsylvania, who are U.S. citizens and live in the vicinity of a Tyson facility. Must be pursuing full-time undergraduate study in an accredited U.S. institution and demonstrate financial need. Must also be employed part-time and/or summers to help fund education.

Renewable up to 8 semesters or 12 trimesters as long as student meets criteria. Contact Tyson Foundation for an application no later than last day of February; deadline to return application is April 20.

38—TYSON FOUNDATION, INC. (Tennessee Scholarship Program)

2210 Oaklawn
Springdale AR 72762-6999
501/290-4995

AMOUNT: Varies (according to need)
DEADLINE(S): FEB 28
FIELD(S): Business; Agriculture; Engineering; Computer Science; Nursing

Open to residents of the general areas of Shelbyville or Union City, Tennessee, who are U.S. citizens and live in the vicinity of a Tyson facility. Must be pursuing full-time undergraduate study in an accredited U.S. institution and demonstrate financial need. Must also be employed part-time and/or summers to help fund education.

Renewable up to 8 semesters or 12 trimesters as long as student meets criteria. Contact Tyson Foundation for an application no later than last day of February; deadline to return application is April 20.

39—TYSON FOUNDATION, INC. (Texas Scholarship Program)

2210 Oaklawn
Springdale AR 72762-6999
501/290-4995

AMOUNT: Varies (according to need)
DEADLINE(S): FEB 28
FIELD(S): Business; Agriculture; Engineering; Computer Science; Nursing

Open to residents of the general areas of Carthage, Center, or Seguin, Texas, who are U.S. citizens and live in the vicinity of a Tyson facility. Must be pursuing full-time undergraduate study in an accredited U.S. institution and demonstrate financial need. Must also be employed part-time and/or summers to help fund education.

Renewable up to 8 semesters or 12 trimesters as long as student meets criteria. Contact Tyson Foundation for an application no later than last day of February; deadline to return application is April 20.

40—TYSON FOUNDATION, INC. (Virginia Scholarship Program)

2210 Oaklawn
Springdale AR 72762-6999
501/290-4995
AMOUNT: Varies (according to need)
DEADLINE(S): FEB 28
FIELD(S): Business; Agriculture; Engineering; Computer Science; Nursing

Open to residents of the general areas of Glen Allen, Harrisonburg, or Temperanceville, Virginia, who are U.S. citizens and live in the vicinity of a Tyson facility. Must be pursuing full-time undergraduate study in an accredited U.S. institution and demonstrate financial need. Must also be employed part-time and/or summers to help fund education.

Renewable up to 8 semesters or 12 trimesters as long as student meets criteria. Contact Tyson Foundation for an application no later than last day of February; deadline to return application is April 20.

41—UNIVERSITY OF NEWCASTLE/AUSTRALIA (Bachelor of Management Undergraduate Scholarship for International Students)

Student Administration Unit, Student Services Centre, Univ. of Newcastle, Callaghan NSW 2308
AUSTRALIA
+61-(02)-4921-6541
FAX: +61-(02)-4960-1766
E-mail: scholarships@newcastle.edu.au
Internet: http://www.newcastle.edu.au/services/ousr/stuadmin/schol/index.htm
AMOUNT: Full tuition for 1 year or one-third reduction in tuition for 3 years
DEADLINE(S): NOV 1
FIELD(S): Hotel Management

Scholarship for undergraduate international students majoring in hotel management at the Faculty of Central Coast.

See Web site or contact organization for details.

42—WOMEN GROCERS OF AMERICA (Mary Macey Scholarships)

1825 Samuel Morse Drive
Reston VA 20190-5317
703/437-5300
FAX: 703/437-7768
E-mail: wga@nationalgrocers.org
Internet: http://www.nationalgrocers.org
AMOUNT: $1,000 (minimum)
DEADLINE(S): JUN 1
FIELD(S): Food Marketing/Management; Food Service Technology; Business Administration as related to the Grocery Industry

For students with a minimum 2.0 GPA attending a U.S. college/university. Must be entering sophomores or continuing students in good standing in a 2-year associate degree or 4-year degree-granting institution or a graduate program, planning a career in the grocery industry. Financial need NOT considered.

2+ awards annually. Renewable. See Web site or contact Anne Wintersteen at the above address for an application.

43—WOMEN IN DEFENSE (HORIZONS Scholarship Foundation)

NDIA
2111 Wilson Boulevard, Suite 400
Arlington VA 22201-3061
703/247-2552
FAX: 703/522-1820
E-mail: cbanks@mciworld.com
Internet: http://www.ndia.org/wid/
AMOUNT: $500+
DEADLINE(S): NOV 1; JUL 1
FIELD(S): Engineering; Computer Science; Physics; Math; Business; Law; International Relations; Political Science; Operations Research; Economics; National Security/Defense

Open to women employed/planning careers in defense/national security areas. Must be currently enrolled full- or part-time at an accredited college/university at the graduate or undergraduate junior/senior level. Must have a minimum 3.25 GPA, demonstrate financial need, and be U.S. citizen. Based on academic achievement, work experience, objectives, and recommendations.

Renewable. See Web site or MUST send self-addressed, stamped envelope to Courtney Banks for application.

44—WOODROW WILSON NATIONAL FELLOWSHIP FOUNDATION/U.S. DEPARTMENTS OF COMMERCE AND AGRICULTURE (Fellowships)

CN 5329
Princeton NJ 08543-5329
609/452-7007
FAX: 609/452-0066
E-mail: richard@woodrow.org
Internet: http://www.woodrow.org
AMOUNT: Varies
DEADLINE(S): Varies
FIELD(S): Commerce; Agriculture

Open to minority students in the U.S. who are interested in careers in commerce or agriculture.

See Web site or contact WWNFF for an application.

45—ZONTA INTERNATIONAL FOUNDATION (Jane M. Klausman Women in Business Scholarships)

557 West Randolph Street
Chicago IL 60661-2206
312/930-5848
FAX: 312/930-0951
E-mail: zontafdtn@zonta.org
Internet: http://www.zonta.org
AMOUNT: $4,000
DEADLINE(S): Varies
FIELD(S): Business

The program is designed to encourage women to enter careers and to seek leadership positions in business-related fields in their communities and throughout the world.

Applicants must be enrolled in their second or third year of an undergraduate business-related degree program

46—ZONTA INTERNATIONAL FOUNDATION (Young Women in Public Affairs Award)

557 West Randolph Street
Chicago IL 60661-2206
312/930-5848
FAX: 312/930-0951
E-mail: zontafdtn@zonta.org
Internet: http://www.zonta.org
AMOUNT: $1,000
DEADLINE(S): Varies
FIELD(S): Public Affairs

Zonta International YWPA Program (Young Women in Public Affairs) was established in 1990 to encourage secondary-school women, 21 years of age or younger, to pursue careers and leadership positions in social policy-making, government, and volunteer organizations. The Zonta International Foundation awards $500 U.S. to each district winner and $1,000 U.S. to the international winner.

BUSINESS ADMINISTRATION

47—ACCOUNTING/NET (Account For Your Future Scholarship Program)

600 Stewart Street, Suite 1101
Seattle WA 98101
206/441-8285
Internet: http://www.accounting students.com
AMOUNT: $1,000
DEADLINE(S): JUN 1
FIELD(S): Accounting

Scholarships for outstanding accounting students, undergraduate and graduate, sponsored by AccountingNet, John Wiley & Sons, and KPMG. Applications are accepted ONLY online.

3 awards annually. See Web site for details.

48—AIR FORCE RESERVE OFFICER TRAINING CORPS (AFROTC Scholarships)

551 E. Maxwell Boulevard
Maxwell AFB AL 36112-6106
334/953-7783
AMOUNT: Full tuition, books, and fees for all 4 years of college
DEADLINE(S): DEC 1
FIELD(S): Science; Engineering; Business; Political Science; Psychology; Geography; Foreign Studies; Foreign Language

Competitive scholarships based on individual merit to high school seniors and graduates who have not completed any full-time college work. Must be a U.S. citizen between the ages of 17-27. Must also have GPA of 2.5 or above, be in top 40% of class, and complete Applicant Fitness Test. Cannot be a single parent. Your college/university must offer AFROTC.

2,300 awards annually. Contact above address for application packet.

49—AIRCRAFT ELECTRONICS ASSOCIATION EDUCATIONAL FOUNDATION (Scholarships)

P.O. Box 1963
Independence MO 64055
816/373-6565
FAX: 816/478-3100
Internet: http://aeaavnews.org
AMOUNT: $1,000-$16,000
DEADLINE(S): Varies
FIELD(S): Avionics; Aircraft Repair

Various scholarships for high school and college students attending postsecondary institutions, including technical schools. Some are for study in Canada or Europe as well as the U.S.

25 programs. See Web site or contact AEA for specific details and applications.

50—AIRPORTS COUNCIL INTERNATIONAL (Scholarships)

Southern Illinois University
at Carbondale
Carbondale IL 62901
618/453-8898
AMOUNT: $2,500
DEADLINE(S): NOV 1
FIELD(S): Airport Management or Airport Administration

Scholarships for undergraduates enrolled in an accredited college or university focusing on a career in airport management. Must have at least a 3.0 GPA. Must reside and attend school in either the U.S., Canada, Saipan, Bermuda, U.S. Virgin Islands, or Guam.

4 awards yearly. Write ATTN: Aviation Management and Flight Dept., College of Technical Careers, at above address.

51—AMERICAN ALLIANCE FOR HEALTH, PHYSICAL EDUCATION, RECREATION & DANCE

1900 Association Drive
Reston VA 20191
703/476-3400 or 800/213-7193
E-mail: webmaster@aahperd.org
Internet: http://www.aahperd.org
AMOUNT: Varies
DEADLINE(S): Varies
FIELD(S): Health Education, Leisure and Recreation, Girls and Women in Sports, Sport and Physical Education, Dance

This organization has six national sub-organizations specializing in the above fields. Some have grants and fellowships for both individuals and group projects. The Web site has the details for each group.

Visit Web site for details or write to above address for details.

52—AMERICAN ASSOCIATION OF ADVERTISING AGENCIES, INC. (Multicultural Advertising Internship Program)

405 Lexington Avenue
New York NY 10174-1801
212/682-2500 or 800/676-9333
FAX: 212/573-8968
E-mail: rhonda@aaaa.org
Internet: http://www.commercepark.com/AAAA/maip/
AMOUNT: $350/wk. + partial exp. and travel
DEADLINE(S): JAN 30
FIELD(S): Advertising; Marketing; Public Relations

A ten-week summer internship for minorities (African-American, Native American, Hispanic, or Asian) working in the advertising business. Must be U.S. citizen or permanent resident.

Write, call, or access Web site for application and information.

53—AMERICAN ASSOCIATION OF ADVERTISING AGENCIES, INC. (Multicultural Advertising Internship Program)

405 Lexington Avenue, 18th Floor
New York NY 10174-1801
212/682-2500 or 800/676-9333
FAX: 212/573-8968
E-mail: tiffany@aaaa.org
Internet: http://www.aaaa.org
AMOUNT: $350/week + partial expenses and travel
DEADLINE(S): JAN 22
FIELD(S): Advertising; Marketing; Public Relations

Ten-week summer internship in the U.S. is open to African-Americans, Native Americans, Hispanics, or Asians interested in a career in advertising. Must be U.S. citizen/permanent resident, have a minimum 3.0 GPA, and be a college junior, senior, or graduate student. Internships help students gain practical work experience and prepare them for entry-level positions. Scholarship program is also available for selected creative finishing schools.

75-100 awards annually. See Web site or contact AAAA for an application.

54—AMERICAN ASSOCIATION OF AIRPORT EXECUTIVES (Scholarships)

4212 King Street
Alexandria VA 22302
703/824-0500
FAX: 703/820-1395
Internet: http://www.airportnet.org
AMOUNT: $1,000
DEADLINE(S): MAY 15
FIELD(S): Airport Management or Airport Administration

Scholarships for undergraduates who have reached junior standing or higher through graduate school. Selection based on scholastic achievement, financial need, and extracurricular/community activities. Must be focusing on a career in airport management and have at least a 3.0 GPA.

10 awards yearly. Each university may submit one student's application only. APPLY THROUGH YOUR UNIVERSITY.

55—AMERICAN ASSOCIATION OF HISPANIC CERTIFIED PUBLIC ACCOUNTANTS (Scholarships)

100 N. Main Street, Suite 406
San Antonio TX 78205
203/255-7003
FAX: 203/259-2872
E-mail: AAHCPA@netscape.net
Internet: http://www.aahcpa.org

AMOUNT: Varies
DEADLINE(S): SEP 15
FIELD(S): Accounting

Undergraduates must be of Hispanic descent and have completed or be enrolled in an intermediate-level accounting course. Graduate students must be of Hispanic descent and be enrolled in a program with an accounting emphasis or be in the last year of a 5-year accounting program. All applicants must have a minimum overall 3.0 GPA and be U.S. citizens. Must submit official transcripts, a letter of recommendation, copy of class schedule, and an essay along with application.

10-40 awards annually. Contact the AAHCPA Scholarship Committee for an application packet.

56—AMERICAN HEALTH AND BEAUTY AIDS INSTITUTE (Fred Luster, Sr. Education Foundation Scholarships for College-Bound High School Seniors)

401 North Michigan Avenue
Chicago IL 60611-4267
312/644-6610

AMOUNT: $250 and $500
DEADLINE(S): APR 15
FIELD(S): Chemistry, Business, or Engineering

For college-bound high school seniors who will be enrolled as a college freshman in a four-year college majoring in chemistry, business, or engineering. 3.0 GPA required.

Send two letters of recommendation (one from a school official) and high school transcript. Scholastic record, school activities, and extracurricular activities considered.

57—AMERICAN HOTEL FOUNDATION (American Express Card Scholarship Program)

1201 New York Avenue NW,
Suite 600
Washington DC 20005-3931
202/289-3181
FAX: 202/289-3199
E-mail: ahf@ahma.com
Internet: http://www.ei-ahma.org

AMOUNT: Up to $2,000
DEADLINE(S): MAR 1
FIELD(S): Hospitality/Hotel Management

For full-time (20 hours/week min.) American Hotel & Motel Association (AH&MA)-member property employees and their dependents enrolled in academic classes to enhance their professional development in the hospitality management field. For use at specified schools, either two-year or four-year, or for tuition assistance for distance learning courses and professional certification programs offered through the Educational Institute of AH&MA.

Check Web site for list of eligible schools. Applications (document #620) available via Fax-on-Demand: 1-800-701-7725. Input document number(s) you are requesting and your fax number.

58—AMERICAN HOTEL FOUNDATION (Ecolab Scholarship Program)

1201 New York Avenue NW,
Suite 600
Washington DC 20005-3931
202/289-3181
FAX: 202/289-3199
E-mail: ahf@ahma.com
Internet: http://www.ei-ahma.org

AMOUNT: $1,000
DEADLINE(S): JUN 1
FIELD(S): Hospitality/Hotel Management

For students pursuing an A.A. or B.A. degree in hospitality or hotel management on a full-time basis (minimum 12 hours).

12 annual awards. Applications (document #630) are available through Fax-on-Demand at 1-800-701-7725. The requested information will be faxed to you momentarily.

59—AMERICAN HOTEL FOUNDATION (Hyatt Hotel Fund for Minority Lodging Management Students)

1201 New York Avenue NW,
Suite 600
Washington DC 20005-3931
202/289-3181
FAX: 202/289-3199
E-mail: ahf@ahma.com
Internet: http://www.ei-ahma.org

AMOUNT: $2,000
DEADLINE(S): None
FIELD(S): Hospitality/Hotel Management

For minority students pursuing an undergraduate degree in hospitality or hotel management on a full-time basis (minimum 12 hours). For use at specified schools. Recipients are nominated by their colleges. Criteria are academic performance, hospitality work experience extracurricular involvement, career goals, and financial needs.

Check Web site for list of eligible schools. Inquire at your dean's office for consideration of the nomination.

60—AMERICAN INSTITUTE OF POLISH CULTURE (Scholarships)

1440 79th Street Causeway,
Suite 117
Miami FL 33141
305/864-2349
FAX: 305/865-5150
E-mail: info@ampolinstitute.org
Internet: http://www.ampolinstitute.org

AMOUNT: $1,000
DEADLINE(S): FEB 15
FIELD(S): Journalism; Public Relations; Communications

Awards are to encourage young Americans of Polish descent to pursue the above professions. Can be used for full-time study at any accredited American college. Criteria for selection include achievement, talent, and involvement in public life.

$25 processing fee. Renewable. Send self-addressed, stamped envelope to Mrs. Harriet Irsay for an application.

61—AMERICAN INTERCONTINENTAL UNIVERSITY (Emilio Pucci Scholarships)

Admissions Committee
3330 Peachtree Road NE
Atlanta GA 30326
404/812-8192 or
1-888/248-7392

AMOUNT: $1,800 (deducted from tuition over 6 quarters)
DEADLINE(S): None
FIELD(S): Fashion Design; Fashion Marketing; Interior Design; Commercial Art; Business Administration; Video Production

Scholarships are for high school seniors who are interested in either a 2-year or 4-year program at one of the campuses of the American Intercontinental University:

Atlanta, GA; Los Angeles, CA; London, UK; or Dubai, United Arab Emirates. Scholarship is applied toward tuition.

Write for applications and complete information.

62—AMERICAN PLANNING ASSOCIATION (Minority Scholarship and Fellowship Programs)

122 South Michigan Avenue,
Suite 1600
Chicago IL 60605
312/431-9100
FAX: 312/431-9985

AMOUNT: $2,000-$5,000 (grads); $2,500 (undergrads)
DEADLINE(S): MAY 14
FIELD(S): Urban Planning, Community Development, Environmental Sciences, Public Administration, Transportation, or Urban Studies

Scholarships for African-Americans, Hispanics, or Native American students pursing undergraduate degrees in the U.S. in the above fields. Must have completed first year. Fellowships for graduate students. Programs must be approved by the Planning Accreditation Board. U.S. citizenship.

Call or write for complete information.

63—AMERICAN PUBLIC TRANSIT ASSOCIATION (Transit Hall of Fame Scholarships)

1201 New York Avenue
Washington DC 20005
FAX: 202/898-4029
E-mail: dfoth@apta.com
Internet: http://www.apta.com

AMOUNT: $2,500 or more
DEADLINE(S): None
FIELD(S): Transit-related fields of study

For college juniors, seniors, or graduate students enrolled in a degree program in a fully accredited institution who demonstrates an interest in entering the transit industry. Criteria include interest in the transit field, financial need, leadership characteristics, scholastic achievement, citizenship extracurricular activities, and essay, and a brief in-person or telephone interview. Must be nominated by an APTF representative who can oversee an internship program.

Write to above address to inquire about how to be nominated and other information.

64—AMERICAN SOCIETY OF TRAVEL AGENTS (ASTA) FOUNDATION (Student Scholarships)

1101 King Street
Alexandria VA 22314
703/739-2782
FAX: 703/684-8319
E-mail: myriaml@astahq.com
Internet: http://www.astanet.com

AMOUNT: $200-$3,000
DEADLINE(S): JUN; JUL; DEC
FIELD(S): Travel; Tourism; Hospitality

Various undergraduate and graduate scholarships are available to U.S. and Canadian citizens, permanent residents, and legal aliens. Must have a minimum 2.5 GPA and submit proof of enrollment in travel and tourism courses. Must also submit official statement of tuition amount, letter of recommendation, transcripts, and other specific requirements for individual awards. Financial need usually NOT considered.

30-50 awards annually. Renewable. See Web site or contact Myriam Lechuga, Manager, for an application and specific award details. Research funds also available to individuals researching travel and tourism topic.

65—AMERICAN SOCIETY OF TRAVEL AGENTS (ASTA) FOUNDATION, INC. (Fernando R. Ayuso Award)

1101 King Street
Alexandria VA 22314
703/739-2782
FAX: 703/684-8319
E-mail: myriaml@astahq.com
Internet: http://www.astanet.com

AMOUNT: Travel, registration, and accommodations
DEADLINE(S): JUL 28
FIELD(S): Travel and Tourism

Open to U.S. citizens with 2 years' credit at accredited college/university to attend the International Travel Fair of Madrid, Spain. Must be involved in professional capacity in travel industry for 2 years or have been engaged in study of travel/tourism at college/university level for 2 years. Must submit letter of recommendation and 500-word essay in both Spanish and English on "How Travel Industry Can Serve to Promote Understanding Between Different Cultures."

See Web site or contact Myriam Lechuga for an application.

66—AMERICAN SOCIETY OF WOMEN ACCOUNTANTS (Scholarships)

60 Revere Drive, Suite 500
Northbrook IL 60062
800/326-2163 or 847/205-1029
FAX: 847/480-9282
Internet: http://www.aswa.org/scholarship.html

AMOUNT: $4,000 (1); $3,000 (2); $2,000 (4)
DEADLINE(S): Varies
FIELD(S): Accounting

Scholarships for female accounting majors who are either full- or part-time students. Must have completed a minimum of 60 semester hours or 90 quarter hours and be enrolled in an accredited college, university, or professional school of accounting (which is designated to award a post-baccalaureate Certificate of Accounting). Membership in ASWA not required.

Applications must be made through the local chapter. Call ASWA for the name of a local chapter.

67—APICS EDUCATION AND RESEARCH FOUNDATION (Donald W. Fogarty International Student Paper Competition)

5301 Shawnee Road
Alexandria VA 22312
800/444-2742
Internet: http://www.apics.org

AMOUNT: $100-$1,700+
DEADLINE(S): MAY 15 (submit papers to a local APICS chapter)
FIELD(S): Production/Operations Management; Resource Management

Awards offered for winning papers on the subject of production and operations management or resource management, including inventory issues. Open to full-time or part-time undergraduate or graduate students; NOT for high school students. Financial need is NOT a factor.

Up to 180 awards annually. For complete information, please call APICS customer service at the above 800 number to request a D.W.F. International Student Paper Competition Manual (item #01002) and the name of a local APICS chapter.

68—ASSOCIATION FOR WOMEN IN SCIENCE EDUCATIONAL FOUNDATION (Ruth Satter Memorial Award)

1200 New York Avenue NW,
Suite 650
Washington DC 20005
202/326-8940 or 800/886-AWIS
E-mail: awis@awis.org
Internet: http://www.awis.org

AMOUNT: $1,000
DEADLINE(S): JAN 16
FIELD(S): Various Sciences and Social Sciences

Scholarships for female doctoral students who have interrupted their education three years or more to raise a family. Summary page, description of research project, resume, references, transcripts, biographical sketch, and proof of eligibility from department head required. U.S. citizens may attend any graduate institution; noncitizens must be enrolled in U.S. institutions.

See Web site or write to above address for more information or an application.

69—ASSOCIATION OF CERTIFIED FRAUD EXAMINERS (Scholarships)

The Gregor Building
716 West Avenue
Austin TX 78701
800/245-3321 or 512/478-9070
FAX: 512/478-9297
E-mail: acfe@tpoint.net
Internet: http://www.cfenet.com

AMOUNT: $500
DEADLINE(S): MAY 15
FIELD(S): Accounting and/or criminal justice

Scholarships for full-time graduate or undergraduate students majoring in accounting or criminal justice degree programs. Awards are based on overall academic achievement, three letters of recommendation, and an original 250-word essay explaining why the applicant deserves the award and how fraud awareness will affect his or her professional career development. Also required is a letter of recommendation from a Certified Fraud Examiner or a local CFE Chapter.

Contact organization for applications and further details.

70—AVIATION DISTRIBUTORS AND MANUFACTURERS ASSOCIATION INTERNATIONAL (ADMA International Scholarship Fund)

1900 Arch Street
Philadelphia PA 19103-1498
215/564-3484
FAX: 215/564-2175
E-mail: assnhqt@netaxs.com

AMOUNT: Varies
DEADLINE(S): MAR 15
FIELD(S): Aviation Management; Professional Pilot

Open to students seeking a career in aviation management or as a professional pilot. Emphasis may be in general aviation, airway science management, aviation maintenance, flight engineering, or airway a/c systems management.

Applicants must be studying in the aviation field in a four-year school having an aviation program. Write for complete information.

71—AYN RAND INSTITUTE (Atlas Shrugged Essay Competition)

Dept. DB, 4640 Admiralty Way, Suite 406
Marina del Rey CA 90292
E-mail: essay@aynrand.org
Internet: http://www.aynrand.org/contests/

AMOUNT: $5,000 (1st prize); $3,000 (2nd); $1,000 (3rd)
DEADLINE(S): FEB 15
FIELD(S): Business

Open to students enrolled in a graduate or undergraduate business degree program who write a 1,000-1,200-word essay on Ayn Rand's *Atlas Shrugged.* Essays judged on style and content and must demonstrate an outstanding grasp of the philosophy meaning of *Atlas Shrugged.*

See Web site or contact your Business Ethics professor for guidelines-do NOT write to above address. Winners announced May 1.

72—BEDDING PLANTS FOUNDATION, INC. (Ed Markham International Scholarship)

P.O. Box 280
East Lansing MI 48826-0280
517/333-4617
FAX: 517/333-4494
E-mail: BPFI@aol.com
Internet: http://www.bpfi.org

AMOUNT: $1,000
DEADLINE(S): MAY 15
FIELD(S): Horticulture AND International Business

Open to graduate and undergraduate students already attending a four-year college/university who are majoring in horticulture or related field. Should wish to further understanding of domestic and international marketing through international horticulturally related study, work, or travel. Cash award, with checks issued jointly in name of recipient and college/institution he or she will attend for current year. Must submit references and transcripts.

1 award annually. See Web site or send printed self-addressed mailing label (or self-addressed, stamped envelope) to BPFI after January 1 for an application. Recipient will be notified.

73—BEDDING PLANTS FOUNDATION, INC. (Harold Bettinger Memorial Scholarship)

P.O. Box 280
East Lansing MI 48826-0280
517/333-4617
FAX: 517/333-4494
E-mail: BPFI@aol.com
Internet: http://www.bpfi.org

AMOUNT: $1,000
DEADLINE(S): MAY 15
FIELD(S): Horticulture AND Business/Marketing

Open to graduate and undergraduate students already attending a four-year college/university who have either a horticulture major with business/marketing emphasis OR a business/marketing major with horticulture emphasis. Cash award, with checks issued jointly in name of recipient and college/institution he or she will attend for current year. Must submit references and transcripts.

1 award annually. See Web site or send printed self-addressed mailing label (or self-addressed, stamped envelope) to BPFI after January 1 for an application. Recipient will be notified.

74—BEDDING PLANTS FOUNDATION, INC. (Jerry Wilmot Scholarship)

P.O. Box 280
East Lansing MI 48826-0280
517/333-4617
FAX: 517/333-4494
E-mail: BPFI@aol.com
Internet: http://www.bpfi.org

AMOUNT: $2,000
DEADLINE(S): MAY 15
FIELD(S): Horticulture AND Business/Finance; Garden Center Management

Open to undergraduate students already attending a four-year college/university who either have a major in horticulture with business/finance emphasis OR have a major in business/finance with horticulture emphasis. Should wish to pursue a career in garden center management. Cash award, with checks issued jointly in name of recipient and college/institution he or she will attend for current year. Must submit references and transcripts.

1 award annually. See Web site or send printed self-addressed mailing label (or self-addressed, stamped envelope) to BPFI after January 1 for an application. Recipient will be notified.

75—BLUES HEAVEN FOUNDATION, INC. (Muddy Waters Scholarship)

2120 S. Michigan Avenue
Chicago IL 60616
312/808-1286
AMOUNT: $2,000
DEADLINE(S): APR 30
FIELD(S): Music; Music Education; African-American Studies; Folklore; Performing Arts; Arts Management; Journalism; Radio/TV/Film

Scholarship is made on a competitive basis with consideration given to scholastic achievement, concentration of studies, and financial need. Applicant must have full-time enrollment status in a Chicago area college/university in at least their first year of undergraduate studies or a graduate program. Scholastic aptitude extracurricular involvement, grade point average, and financial need are all considered.

Contact Blues Heaven Foundation, Inc. to receive an application between February and April.

76—BUENA VISTA COLLEGE NETWORK (Internships in Film Marketing)

3900 W. Alameda Avenue
Burbank CA 91505-4316
818/567-5000
E-mail: College_Network@studio.disney.com
AMOUNT: Varies
DEADLINE(S): None
FIELD(S): Fields of study related to the motion picture industry, including marketing and promotion

Internships for full-time college students age 18 and up interested in a career in a facet of the motion picture industry. Must have unlimited access to computer with modem and transportation, be able to work 4-6 hours per week and 2-3 weekends per month. Attend film openings and sneak previews. Evaluate various aspects via an interactive computer system. Compensation ranges from $30 to $60/month. Possible school credit.

Access Web site by writing "Buena Vista College Network" from Yahoo. Available in most states and parts of Canada. Details, an interactive application, and E-mail access are located on Web site.

77—CANADIAN RECREATIONAL CANOEING ASSOCIATION (Bill Mason Memorial Scholarship Fund)

446 Main Street W.
P.O. Box 398
Merrickville Ontario K0G 1N0 CANADA
613/269-2910
FAX: 613/269-2908
Internet: http://www.crca.ca/bill.html
AMOUNT: $1,000
DEADLINE(S): OCT 15
FIELD(S): Outdoor Recreation; Environmental Studies

Scholarship is a tribute to Bill Mason, a Canadian recognized at home and abroad as a canoeist, environmentalist, artist, filmmaker, photographer, and public speaker. Applicant must be a full-time student at a Canadian university or college. Must be planning a career related to the above fields, be a Canadian citizen, maintain a B+ average, and be a second-year student or higher. Financial need must be demonstrated. Background in canoeing/kayaking is an asset.

Scholarship is paid in two installments: $700 by Nov. 10, and $300 after receipt of May 15 progress report.

78—CAREER OPPORTUNITIES FOR YOUTH, INC. (Collegiate Scholarship Program)

P.O. Box 996
Manhattan Beach CA 90266
310/535-4838
AMOUNT: $250 to $1,000
DEADLINE(S): SEP 30
FIELD(S): Engineering, Science, Mathematics, Computer Science, Business Administration, Education, Nursing

For students of Latino/Hispanic background residing in the Southern California area who have completed at least one semester/quarter of study at an accredited four-year university. Must have a cumulative GPA of 2.5 or higher.

Priority will be given to students who demonstrate financial need. Send SASE to above location for details.

79—CELANESE CANADA, INC. (Scholarships)

AUCC; 350 Albert Street, Suite 600
Ottawa Ontario K1R 1B1 CANADA
613/563-1236; FAX: 613/563-9745
E-mail: awards@aucc.ca
Internet: http://www.aucc.ca
AMOUNT: $1,500
DEADLINE(S): JUL 2
FIELD(S): Mechanical and Chemical Engineering; Chemistry; Business Administration and Commerce

Open to Canadian citizens/permanent residents for their final year of an undergraduate program in one of above fields. Must attend a college/university which is a member, or affiliated to a member, of the Association of Universities and Colleges of Canada. Candidates are expected to have achieved a high level of academic excellence as well as to have exhibited superior intellectual ability and judgment. In some cases, study in certain province/school is required.

APPLICATIONS ARE BY NOMINATION ONLY. Not renewable. See Web site or contact AUCC for nomination procedures.

80—CITY UNIVERSITY (Scholarships in Actuarial Science)

International Office, City University, Northampton Square
London EC1V 0HB ENGLAND UK
+44 (0) 171 477 8019
FAX: +44 (0) 171 477 8562
E-mail: international@city.ac.uk
Internet: http://www.britcoun.org/eis/profiles/cityuniversity/cituschp.htm
AMOUNT: 1,000 pounds/year
DEADLINE(S): Varies
FIELD(S): Actuarial Science

Scholarships for undergraduate students from non-European Union countries who are pursuing studies in actuarial science, the study of statistics as related to insurance services. For use at City University in London.

Selection based on academic merit. Renewable for term of course. Program is through the British Council. Contact Karen Jones at University for details.

81—CLUB MANAGERS ASSOCIATION OF AMERICA

1733 King Street
Alexandria VA 22314
703/739-9500
AMOUNT: $1,000-$2,000
DEADLINE(S): MAY 1
FIELD(S): Management of clubs

Grants for sophomores, juniors, and seniors specializing in club management at an accredited college or university. Should have 2.5 or better GPA. Awards are not based solely on need.

Send SASE to above location for details.

82—COLORADO RESTAURANT ASSOCIATION (Scholarship Education Fund)

430 E. 7th Avenue
Denver CO 80203
800/522-2972 or 303/830-2972
FAX: 303/830-2973

E-mail: info@coloradorestaurant.com
Internet: http://www.colorado restaurant.com
AMOUNT: $500-$2,500
DEADLINE(S): MAR 20
FIELD(S): Foodservice; Hospitality

Open to junior and senior level college students enrolled in a two- or four-year degree program in foodservice and hospitality related fields at a Colorado college/university.

Contact CRA for an application.

83—COLORADO SOCIETY OF CPAs EDUCATIONAL FOUNDATION (Gordon Scheer Scholarship)

7979 E. Tufts Avenue, #500
Denver CO 80237-2843
303/773-2877 or 800/523-9082
Internet: http://www.cocpa.org
AMOUNT: $1,250
DEADLINE(S): JUN 30
FIELD(S): Accounting

For undergraduates who have completed intermediate accounting, have a 3.5 or better GPA, and are majoring in accounting at a Colorado college or university offering accredited accounting majors.

Renewable with reapplication. See Web site or contact Gena Mantz at above location for an application.

84—COLORADO SOCIETY OF CPAs EDUCATIONAL FOUNDATION (Scholarships for Ethnically Diverse High School Seniors)

7979 E. Tufts Avenue, #500
Denver CO 80237-2843
303/773-2877 or 800/523-9082
Internet: http://www.cocpa.org
AMOUNT: $1,000
DEADLINE(S): MAR 1
FIELD(S): Accounting

Open to ethnically diverse high school seniors in Colorado schools who intend to major in accounting at Colorado colleges/universities which offer accredited accounting programs. Must have at least a 3.0 GPA and be African American, Hispanic, Asian-American, American Indian, or Pacific Islander.

See Web site or contact Gena Mantz at above location for an application.

85—COLORADO SOCIETY OF CPAs EDUCATIONAL FOUNDATION (Scholarships for Undergraduates and Graduates)

7979 E. Tufts Avenue, #500
Denver CO 80237-2843
303/773-2877 or 800/523-9082
Internet: http://www.cocpa.org
AMOUNT: $1,000
DEADLINE(S): JUN 30; NOV 30
FIELD(S): Accounting

For undergraduates and graduates who have completed intermediate accounting, have a 3.0 or better GPA, and are majoring in accounting at a Colorado college/university offering accredited accounting majors. Financial need considered.

Scholarships are renewable with reapplication. See Web site or contact Gena Mantz at above location for an application.

86—COLORADO SOCIETY OF CPAs EDUCATIONAL FOUNDATION (Scholarships for Ethnically Diverse Undergraduates and Graduates)

7979 E. Tufts Avenue, #500
Denver CO 80237-2843
303/773-2877 or 800/523-9082
Internet: http://www.cocpa.org
AMOUNT: $1,000
DEADLINE(S): JUN 30
FIELD(S): Accounting

For ethnically diverse undergraduates and graduates who have completed intermediate accounting, have 3.0 or better GPA, and are majoring in accounting at a Colorado college/university offering accredited accounting majors. Must be African American, Hispanic, Asian-American, American Indian, or Pacific Islander. Financial need considered.

Renewable with reapplication. See Web site or contact Gena Mantz at above location for an application.

87—COMMUNITY FOUNDATION OF WESTERN MASSACHUSETTS (Joseph Bonfitto Scholarship)

1500 Main Street
P.O. Box 15769
Springfield MA 01115
413/732-2858
AMOUNT: $2,000
DEADLINE(S): APR 15
FIELD(S): Creative Design; Advertising; Art

Open to graduating seniors of Agawam High School in Massachusetts who are pursuing a career through higher education in one of the above areas of study. Based on financial need, academic merit, and extracurricular activities. Must submit transcripts and fill out government FAFSA form.

1 award annually. Renewable with reapplication. Send self-addressed, stamped envelope to Community Foundation for an application and contact your financial aid office for FAFSA. Notification is in June.

88—CONFERENCE OF MINORITY PUBLIC ADMINISTRATORS (Scholarships and Travel Grants)

P.O. Box 3010
Fort Worth TX 76113
817/871-8325
Internet: http://www.compa.org
AMOUNT: $400 (travel grants); up to $1,500 (academic year)
DEADLINE(S): Varies
FIELD(S): Public administration/public affairs

COMPA offers two academic scholarships, at least five travel grants, and a $1,000 gift to the college that has the largest number of student registrants at its annual conference. Travel grants are for attending the conference. For minorities and women pursuing full-time education in the above fields and committed to excellence in public service and administration in city, county, state, and federal governments.

Contact Edwin Cook at above location for details.

89—CONTRACT MANAGEMENT INSTITUTE (Scholarships)

1912 Woodford Road
Vienna VA 22182
703/448-9231
E-mail: info@ncmahq.org
Internet: http://www.ncmahq.org/cmi/scholar.html
AMOUNT: Varies
DEADLINE(S): Varies
FIELD(S): Business: Contract Management specialty

Scholarships for undergraduate and graduate students enrolled in a business-oriented curriculum who intend to enter into the Contract Management field. Available from each of the eight NMCA regions. One program, the Martin L. Kaufman Memorial Scholarship, is for business students who intend to enter the military service of the U.S. upon graduation.

Inquire of organization for details.

90—COOPERATIVE ASSOCIATION OF STATES FOR SCHOLARSHIPS (CASS) (Scholarships)

c/o Commonwealth Liaison
Unit 310 The Garrison
St. Michael BARBADOS
809/436-8754

AMOUNT: Varies
DEADLINE(S): None
FIELD(S): Business application/computer science

Scholarships for economically disadvantaged deaf youth, ages 17-25, with strong leadership potential and an interest in computer science/business applications. Must be from Barbados, St. Kitts/Nevis, Grenada, St. Vincent, Antigua/Barbuda, St. Lucia, Dominica, or Jamaica.

Write to E. Caribbean Reg. Coordinator (CASS) at above address.

91—CUBAN AMERICAN NATIONAL FOUNDATION (The Mas Family Scholarships)

7300 NW 3 Terrace
Miami FL 33122
305/592-7768
FAX: 305/592-7889
E-mail: canfnet.org
Internet: http://www.canfnet.org

AMOUNT: Individually negotiated
DEADLINE(S): MAR 15
FIELD(S): Engineering, Business, International Relations, Economics, Communications, Journalism

For Cuban-Americans students, graduates and undergraduates, born in Cuba or direct descendants of those who left Cuba. Must be in top 10% of high school class or maintain a 3.5 GPA in college.

10,000 awards/year. Recipients may reapply for subsequent years. Financial need considered along with academic success, SAT and GRE scores, and leadership potential. Essays and proof of Cuban descent required.

92—EAA AVIATION FOUNDATION (Scholarship Program)

P.O. Box 3065
Oshkosh WI 54903-3065
920/426-6815 or 888/EAA-EAA9 or 888/322-3229
E-mail: education@eaa.org
Internet: http://www.eaa.org

AMOUNT: $500-$5,000
DEADLINE(S): MAY 1
FIELD(S): Aviation

Six different scholarship programs open to well-rounded individuals involved in school and community activities as well as aviation. Applicant's academic records should verify his/her ability to complete educational activity for which scholarship is requested. For all but one scholarship, students must major in aviation. Financial need considered in some programs. One scholarship includes tuition, books, fees, etc. at the Fox Valley Technical College in Wisconsin.

Renewable. $5 application fee. Contact EAA for an application (one application covers all of the scholarship programs).

93—EDUCATIONAL FOUNDATION FOR WOMEN IN ACCOUNTING (Women in Transition and Women at Risk Scholarships)

P.O. Box 1925
Southeastern PA 19399-1925
610/407-9229
Internet: http://www.efwa.org/laurels.htm

AMOUNT: $4,000 (transition); $2,000 (at risk)
DEADLINE(S): APR 30
FIELD(S): Accounting

Open to women who, either through divorce or death of a spouse, have become the sole source of support for themselves and their family and wish to pursue a bachelor's degree in accounting. Based on commitment and need. Must submit transcripts, letters of reference, evidence of leadership potential, statement of employment history, statement of need, and statement of both professional and personal goals/objectives.

Renewable. See Web site or contact Alexandra Miller, WIT Committee Chair, for an application. Selection made by June 15.

94—EMPIRE COLLEGE (Dean's Scholarship)

3035 Cleveland Avenue
Santa Rosa CA 95403
707/546-4000
FAX: 707/546-4058

AMOUNT: $250-$1,500
DEADLINE(S): APR 15
FIELD(S): Accounting; Secretarial; Legal; Medical (Clinical and Administrative); Travel and Tourism; General Business; Computer Assembly; Network Assembly/Administration

Open to high school seniors who plan to attend Empire College. Must be U.S. citizen.

10 awards annually. Contact Ms. Mary Farha for an application.

95—EPILEPSY FOUNDATION OF AMERICA (Behavioral Sciences Student Fellowships)

4351 Garden City Drive
Landover MD 20785-2267
301/459-3700 or 800/EFA-1000
TDD: 800/332-2070
FAX: 301/577-2684
Internet: http://www.epilepsy foundation.org

AMOUNT: $2,000
DEADLINE(S): FEB 1
FIELD(S): Epilepsy Research/Practice; Sociology; Social Work; Psychology; Anthropology; Nursing; Economics; Vocational Rehabilitation; Counseling; Political Science

Three-month fellowships awarded to undergraduate and graduate students in above fields for work on a project during the summer or other free period. Students propose an epilepsy-related study or training project to be carried out at a U.S. institution of their choice. A preceptor must accept responsibility for supervision of the student and the project.

Contact EFA for an application. Notification by June 1.

96—ERNST & YOUNG (Mike Smith Memorial Scholarship)

Private Bag 3105
Hamilton NEW ZEALAND
07 8562889 ext. 8964, 6732
FAX: 07 8384370
E-mail: rgty_dbc

AMOUNT: $1,200
DEADLINE(S): None given
FIELD(S): Management with emphasis in Accounting

For a third-year candidate pursuing a degree of Bachelor of Management studies in the following year with Accounting as the major discipline.

Contact "The Scholarships Administrator, University of Waikato" at above address. Successful applicant may also be offered employment with Ernst & Young following tenure of the award.

97—FASHION GROUP INTERNATIONAL OF GREATER WASHINGTON DC (Scholarships)

P.O. Box 71055
Chevy Chase MD 20813-1055
212/593-1715 (in New York)
Internet: http://fgi.org/washington.htm

AMOUNT: Up to $2,500
DEADLINE(S): APR 1
FIELD(S): Fashion-related areas

Scholarships for students majoring in fashion-related fields. Must be permanent residents of the Greater Metropolitan Washington DC area. Must either graduate from high school in June and/or have been admitted to an accredited institution or be enrolled in a university or college as an undergraduate or graduate student.

Application form and details are available on Web site or contact organization for further information.

98—FLORIDA DEPT. OF EDUCATION (Ethics In Business Scholarship Program)

Student Financial Assist.; 255 Collins
Tallahassee FL 32399-0400
850/487-0049 or 888/827-2004
E-mail: OSFABF@mail.doe.state.fl.us
Internet: http://www.firn.edu/doe

AMOUNT: Varies
DEADLINE(S): Varies
FIELD(S): Business

Provides assistance to undergraduate students who enroll at community colleges and eligible private Florida colleges and universities. Applications and award procedures are determined by each sector representative.

Contact your school's financial aid office or Florida Department of Education for more information.

99—FONDATION MARCEL HICTER-COUNCIL OF EUROPE (Travel Bursary System)

Rue Cornet de Grez 14
B-1210 Brussells BELGIUM
+32/2 219 9886
FAX: +32/2 217 3572
E-mail: fond.hicter@glo.be

AMOUNT: 5,000 FRF (max.)
DEADLINE(S): None
FIELD(S): Cultural Management

Open to students of European nationality who wish to pursue undergraduate or graduate studies in a European country that signed the European cultural convention. Financial need NOT a factor.

100 awards annually. Contact Isabelle Piette for an application.

100—FUND FOR AMERICAN STUDIES (Institutes on Political Journalism; Business & Government Affairs & Comparative Political & Economic Systems)

1526 18th Street NW
Washington DC 20036
202/986-0384 or 800/741-6964
Internet: http://www.dcinternships.com

AMOUNT: Up to $2,975
DEADLINE(S): JAN 31 (early decision); MAR 15 (general application deadline)
FIELD(S): Political Science; Economics; Journalism; Business Administration

The Fund for American Studies, in conjunction with Georgetown University, sponsors summer institutes that include internships, courses for credit, site briefings, and dialogues with policy leaders. Scholarships are available to sophomores and juniors to cover the cost of the program.

Approximately 100 awards per year. For Fund's programs only. Call, check Web site, or write for complete information.

101—GEORGE HARDING SCHOLARSHIP FUND

22344 Long Boulevard
Dearborn MI 48124
313/225-2798

AMOUNT: $750
DEADLINE(S): Ongoing
FIELD(S): Business Administration/Finance

Scholarships for Michigan residents who are full-time students enrolled in four-year Michigan colleges or universities and pursuing finance-related degrees. To be used only for the senior year of college or first year of graduate school.

Write to Richard E. Gardner, Trustee, at above address for details.

102—GOLDEN GATE RESTAURANT ASSOCIATION (Scholarship Foundation Awards)

720 Market Street, Suite 200
San Francisco CA 94102
415/781-5348
FAX: 415/781-3925
E-mail: AdministrationCoordinator@ggra.org

AMOUNT: $500-$2,500
DEADLINE(S): MAR 31
FIELD(S): Foodservice Industry

Open to California residents who are undergrads majoring in foodservice at a college/university. Category I awards require students to be full-time and have graduated from high school in the San Francisco Bay Area; Category II requires students to be full-time, have completed at least one semester, and have a minimum 2.75 GPA; and Category III requires students to be part-time, working in the foodservice/hospitality industry 20 hours/week, and have a minimum 2.75 GPA.

Contact Matthew Bass, GGRASF Administration Coordinator, for an application.

103—GOVERNMENT FINANCE OFFICERS ASSOCIATION (Frank L. Greathouse Government Accounting Scholarship)

180 N. Michigan Avenue, Suite 800
Chicago IL 60601-7476
312/977-9700

AMOUNT: $2,000
DEADLINE(S): FEB 12
FIELD(S): Finance

Scholarships for senior, full-time undergraduates preparing for a career in state or local government finance. Must be a citizen or permanent resident of the U.S. or Canada. Criteria include career/educational goals, GPA, and letters of recommendation.

Winner is invited to attend Annual Conference (at Government Finance Officers Association's expense) where award is presented. Çontact John Wiley at above address for an application/more information.

104—HILLSDALE COLLEGE (Freedom as Vocation Scholarship)

33 E. College Street
Hillsdale MI 49242-1298
517/437-7341
Internet: http://www.hillsdale.edu

AMOUNT: Varies
DEADLINE(S): None
FIELD(S): Business; History; Political Science; Economics

Open to Hillsdale College undergraduates who maintain a minimum 3.0 GPA and commit to a series of courses in the above fields. Student must rank in top 20% of class and top 10% of test scores. Must possess excellent communications, public speaking, and leadership skills and demonstrate outstanding character and citizenship. Financial need NOT a factor.

Renewable. No application process; students are selected. See Web site for details.

105—HISPANIC COLLEGE FUND (Scholarships for Hispanic Students)

One Thomas Circle NW, Suite 375
Washington DC 20005
202/296-5400
FAX: 202/296-3774
E-mail: Hispanic.Fund@Internet MCI.com
Internet: http://hispanicfund.org

AMOUNT: Varies
DEADLINE(S): APR 15

FIELD(S): Most college majors leading to a career in business

Scholarships for deserving Hispanic college students pursuing a higher education in a major leading to a business career and who are full-time students at accredited institutions. U.S. citizenship. Must demonstrate financial need.

Contact above organization for details or visit Web site for application.

106—HOSPITALITY FINANCIAL AND TECHNOLOGY PROFESSIONALS (Scholarships)

11709 Boulder Lane, Suite 110
Austin TX 78726
800/646-4387
Internet: http://www.hftp.org

AMOUNT: $1,000-$1,500
DEADLINE(S): JUL 15
FIELD(S): Accounting or hospitality management

For students majoring in either accounting or hospitality management at an accredited college or university.

Applications must come through an IAHA local chapter president. Send SASE for details.

107—INDEPENDENT ACCOUNTANTS INTERNATIONAL EDUCATIONAL FOUNDATION, INC. (Robert Kaufman Memorial Scholarship Award)

9200 S. Dadeland Boulevard, Suite 510
Miami FL 33156
305/670-0580
Internet: http://www.accountants.org

AMOUNT: $250-$2,500
DEADLINE(S): FEB 28
FIELD(S): Accounting

Open to students who are pursuing or planning to pursue an education in accounting at recognized academic institutions throughout the world. Must demonstrate financial need for larger sums; not required for $250 honorary textbook award.

Up to 20 awards annually. See Web site ONLY for complete information.

108—INSTITUT D'ETUDES POLITIQUES DE PARIS (US Sciences Po Alumni Association Scholarships)

27 rue Saint Guillaume
75337 Paris Cedex 07 FRANCE
331/4549-5047
FAX: 331/4544-1252
Internet: http://sciencespo.org/bourses.htm

AMOUNT: $5,000 (max.)
DEADLINE(S): Varies
FIELD(S): European Studies; Political Science; Economics; Finance

Open to U.S. citizens who will pursue undergraduate, graduate, or postgraduate studies at IEP Paris, either through admission to the school or through an exchange program with an accredited U.S. school. Must have sufficient fluency in French to meet instructional requirements. Must submit cover letter, resume, and brief essay. Award may be used to cover educational costs and related expenses, including fees, round-trip airfare to Paris, textbooks, and school supplies.

See Web site or contact Mr. P. Cauchy, Director of International Student Services, for an application.

109—INSTITUTE FOR HUMANE STUDIES (Koch Summer Fellow Program)

3401 N. Fairfax Drive, Suite 440
Arlington VA 22201-4432
703/993-4880 or 800/697-8799
FAX: 703/993-4890
E-mail: ihs@gmu.edu
Internet: http://www.TheIHS.org

AMOUNT: $1,500 + airfare and housing
DEADLINE(S): FEB 15
FIELD(S): Economics; Public Policy; Law; Government; Politics

Open to undergraduates and graduates to build skills and gain experience by participating in an 8-week summer internship program. Includes two week-long seminars, the internship, and research and writing projects with professionals. Must submit college transcripts, essays, and application. Financial need NOT a factor.

32 awards annually. Not renewable. Apply online or contact IHS for an application.

110—INSTITUTE FOR HUMANE STUDIES (Summer Seminars Program)

3401 N. Fairfax Drive, Suite 440
Arlington VA 22201-4432
703/993-4880 or 800/697-8799
FAX: 703/993-4890
E-mail: ihs@gmu.edu
Internet: http://www.TheIHS.org

AMOUNT: Free summer seminars, including room/board, lectures, seminar materials, and books
DEADLINE(S): MAR
FIELD(S): Social Sciences; Humanities; Law; Journalism; Public Policy; Education; Film; Writing; Economics; Philosophy

Open to college students, recent graduates, and graduate students who share an interest in learning and exchanging ideas about the scope of individual rights, free markets, the rule of law, peace, and tolerance.

See Web site for seminar information or to apply online or contact IHS for an application.

111—INSTITUTE FOR OPERATIONS RESEARCH AND THE MANAGEMENT SCIENCES (INFORMS Summer Internship Directory)

P.O. Box 64794
Baltimore MD 21264-4794
800/4INFORMS
FAX: 410/684-2963
E-mail: jps@informs.org
Internet: http://www.informs.org/INTERN/

AMOUNT: Varies
DEADLINE(S): Varies
FIELD(S): Fields related to information management: business management, engineering, mathematics

A Web site listing of summer internships in the field of operations research and management sciences. Both applicants and employers can register online.

Access Web site for list.

112—INSTITUTE OF CHARTERED ACCOUNTANTS OF NEW ZEALAND (Coopers & Lybrand Peter Barr Research Fellowship)

Cigna House, 40 Mercer Street
P.O. Box 11 342
Wellington NEW ZEALAND
64-4-474 7840
FAX: 64-4-473 6303

AMOUNT: Up to $10,000
DEADLINE(S): SEP 30
FIELD(S): Accounting

Fellowship offers financial assistance for projects that will benefit the accountancy profession in New Zealand. Open primarily to members of the Institute (other memberships considered).

Write for complete information.

113—INSTITUTE OF INTERNATIONAL EDUCATION (National Security Education Program-Undergraduate Scholarships)

1400 K Street NW, 6th Floor
Washington DC 20005-2403

202/326-7697 or
800/618-NSEP (6737)
E-mail: nsep@iie.org
Internet: http://www.iie.org/nsep/
AMOUNT: Varies: up to $8,000/semester
DEADLINE(S): FEB 8
FIELD(S): Open to all majors; preference to applied sciences, engineering, business, economics, math, computer science, international affairs, political science, history, and the policy sciences.

For study abroad OUTSIDE the U.S., Canada, Australia, New Zealand, and Western Europe. For study in areas deemed critical to U.S. national security. Applications available on U.S. campuses from August through early December. Or contact organization for details.

Inquire at above location for details.

114—INTERNATIONAL ASSOCIATION OF FIRE CHIEFS FOUNDATION (Scholarship Program)

1257 Wiltshire Road
York PA 17403
717/854-9083
AMOUNT: $250-$4,000
DEADLINE(S): AUG 15
FIELD(S): Business and Urban Administration, Fire Science

Open to members of a fire service of a state, county, provincial, municipal, community, industrial, or federal fire department.

Renewable. Write for complete information.

115—INTERNATIONAL FACILITY MANAGEMENT ASSOCIATION (Student Scholarships)

1 E. Greenway Plaza, Suite 1100
Houston TX 77046-0194
Internet: http://www.ifma.org
AMOUNT: $1,000-$5,000
DEADLINE(S): MAY 31
FIELD(S): Facility Management

Open to full-time graduate and junior or senior level undergraduate students who are enrolled in a facility management or related program. Graduates must have a minimum 3.0 GPA; undergrads must have a minimum 2.75 GPA. Students may not be employed full-time as a facility management professional. Must submit official transcripts, letter of professional intent, and two appraisals.

See Web site or contact IFMA Foundation for an application.

116—INTERNATIONAL RADIO AND TELEVISION SOCIETY FOUNDATION (Summer Fellowship Program)

420 Lexington Avenue, Suite 1714
New York NY 10170
212/867-6650
FAX: 212/867-6653
Internet: http://www.irts.org
AMOUNT: Housing, stipend, and travel
DEADLINE(S): NOV 12
FIELD(S): Broadcasting; Communications; Sales; Marketing

Nine-week summer fellowship program in New York City is open to outstanding full-time undergraduate juniors and seniors with a demonstrated interest in a career in communications. Financial need NOT a factor.

20-25 awards annually. Not renewable. See Web site or contact Maria DeLeon-Fisher at IRTS for an application.

117—JAMES FORD BELL FOUNDATION (Summer Internship Program)

2925 Dean Parkway, Suite 811
Minneapolis MN 55416
612/285-5435
FAX: 612/285-5437
E-mail: famphiladv@uswest.net
AMOUNT: $4,000 for 3 months
DEADLINE(S): APR 30
FIELD(S): Business/Public Administration; Public Policy; Organization Leadership; Nonprofit Management

Interns spend the summer with organizations selected by the Foundation; the organizations select interns from master's degree programs in above or related fields and college seniors with strong interest in nonprofit work. Internships normally in the Twin Cities area.

Contact Foundation for a list of internship opportunities in February and March ONLY; students should request position list, not an application for the program itself (only organizations apply for the program).

118—JC PENNEY (Scholarship Program)

Corporate Headquarters
Plano TX 75023
972/431-1347
Internet: http://www.jcpenneyinc.com
AMOUNT: $1,500
DEADLINE(S): Varies
FIELD(S): Business; Merchandising; Retail Studies; Information Systems

For undergraduates in above fields. Must be dependent children of or associates who are employed at JC Penney both at the time of applying for the scholarships and at the time of awarding the scholarships-or can be dependents of deceased/retired associates having three continuous years of service.

128 one-time awards. Current recipients may reapply as long as the scholarship program is offered at their school. The campuses which offer this scholarship are the 32 colleges where JC Penney recruits new management trainees-campuses reevaluated each year. Contact your (participating) school for an application or visit your local JC Penney store.

119—JOHN RANKIN FUND (Travel Scholarships in Accounting or Law)

Trustees of the John Rankin Fund,
c/o Jonathan Stone Esq., The Hall
East Ilsley, Newbury RG20 7LW
Written Inquiry
AMOUNT: 5,000 pounds
DEADLINE(S): MAR 31
FIELD(S): Accounting, Law

A biannual award for either a law or accounting student, barrister, solicitor, or qualified accountant to study abroad. Applicant must be under 26 on Oct. 1 of the year of application.

Write to organization for information.

120—JOHNSON AND WALES UNIVERSITY (Annual Johnson and Wales University National High School Recipe Contest)

8 Abbott Place
Providence RI 02903
401/598-2345
AMOUNT: $1,000 to $5,000
DEADLINE(S): JAN 31
FIELD(S): Business, Hospitality, Technology, Culinary Arts

For students planning to attend Johnson & Wales University, Providence, Rhode Island.

Write to above address for detailed description.

121—JOHNSON AND WALES UNIVERSITY (Gilbane Building Company Eagle Scout Scholarship)

8 Abbott Place
Providence RI 02903
401/598-2345
AMOUNT: $1,200
DEADLINE(S): None

FIELD(S): Business, Hospitality, Technology, Culinary Arts

For students attending Johnson & Wales University, Providence, Rhode Island. Must be Eagle Scouts.

Send letter of recommendation and transcript to above address.

122—JOHNSON AND WALES UNIVERSITY (National High School Entrepreneur of the Year Contest)

8 Abbott Place
Providence RI 02903
401/598-2345
AMOUNT: $1,000 to $10,000
DEADLINE(S): DEC 27
FIELD(S): Business, Hospitality, Technology, Culinary Arts

For students attending Johnson & Wales University, Providence, Rhode Island.

Send for detailed description to above address.

123—KARLA SCHERER FOUNDATION (Scholarships)

737 N. Michigan Avenue, Suite 2330
Chicago IL 60611
312/943-9191
AMOUNT: Varies
DEADLINE(S): MAR 1
FIELD(S): Finance; Economics

Open to women who plan to pursue careers in finance and/or economics in the private manufacturing-based sector. For undergraduate or graduate study at any accredited institution. Send letter stating what school you attend or plan to attend, the courses you plan to take, and how you will use your education in your chosen career.

Renewable. With application request, please include above information as well as a self-addressed, stamped envelope to assure a prompt response.

124—KOSCIUSZKO FOUNDATION (Summer Sessions in Poland and Rome)

15 E. 65th Street
New York NY 10021-6595
212/734-2130
FAX: 212/628-4552
E-mail: thekf@pegasusnet.com
Internet: http://www.kosciuszko foundation.org
AMOUNT: Varies
DEADLINE(S): Varies
FIELD(S): Polish Studies; History; Literature; Art; Economics; Social Studies; Language; Culture

Open to undergraduate and graduate students, graduating high school students who are 18 or older, and persons of any age who are not enrolled in a college/university program. Study programs are offered in Poland and Rome from mid-June through the end of August in above fields. Must be U.S. citizen/permanent resident.

See Web site or send a self-addressed, stamped envelope to Addy Tymczyszyn, Summer Studies Abroad Coordinator, for an application.

125—LADY ALLEN OF HURTWOOD MEMORIAL TRUST (Travel Grants)

21 Aspull Common
Leigh Lancs WN7 3PB ENGLAND
01942-674895
AMOUNT: Up to 1,000 pounds sterling
DEADLINE(S): JAN 15
FIELD(S): Welfare and Education of Children

A travel grant to those whose proposed project will directly benefit their work with children. People working with children and young people may apply, particularly those working with disabled and disadvantaged children. Successful candidates must write up an account of the work which the scholarship has funded. GRANTS ARE NOT FOR ACADEMIC STUDY; ONLY QUALIFIED INDIVIDUALS MAY APPLY.

Contact Dorothy E. Whitaker, Trustee, for application forms—available between May and December each year.

126—LONDON SCHOOL OF ECONOMICS AND POLITICAL SCIENCE (Scholarships)

Scholarships Office; Houghton Street
London WC2A 2AE ENGLAND UK
+44 (0) 171 955 7162/7155
FAX: +44 (0) 171 831 1684
E-mail: scholarships@lse.ac.uk
Internet: http://www.lse.ac.uk/index/EDUCATE/CONTACTS.HTM or http://www.lse.ac.uk/index/restore/GRADUATE/Financial/text/funding.htm or http://www.britcoun.org/eis/profiles/lse/lseschp.htm
AMOUNT: Varies with award
DEADLINE(S): Varies
FIELD(S): Economics; Accounting; Finance; Political Science; International Relations

Various scholarships, awards, and prizes are available to international students. Several are for students from specific countries, and some are limited to certain fields of study. Some include all expenses, and others pay partial expenses. For undergraduates and graduate students.

Accessing LSE's Web site and using their "search" option, write in "scholarships," and a vast array of programs will appear.

127—LOUISIANA STATE UNIVERSITY AT SHREVEPORT (College of Business Administration Scholarships)

Dean's Office; One University Place
Shreveport LA 71115-2399
318/797-5363
FAX: 318/797-5366
E-mail: finaid@pilot.lsus.edu
Internet: http://www.lsus.edu
AMOUNT: Varies
DEADLINE(S): Varies
FIELD(S): Business Administration

A number of scholarships are funded for business students enrolled at various levels at LSUS.

Contact the Dean's Office in the College of Business Administration at LSUS for details on specific scholarships.

128—MEXICAN AMERICAN GROCERS ASSOCIATION (Scholarships)

405 N. San Fernando Road
Los Angeles CA 90031
213/227-1565
FAX: 213/227-6935
AMOUNT: Varies
DEADLINE(S): JUL 31
FIELD(S): Business

Scholarships for Hispanic college students who are at least college sophomores. Must have 2.5 GPA or above, be U.S. citizen or permanent resident, and demonstrate financial need.

Send a self-addressed, stamped envelope to Jackie Solis at above address for further information.

129—MIDWAY COLLEGE (Institutional Aid Program)

Financial Aid Office
Midway KY 40347
606/846-4421
AMOUNT: Varies
DEADLINE(S): MAR 1
FIELD(S): Nursing; Paralegal; Education; Psychology; Biology; Equine Studies; Liberal Studies; Business Administration

Scholarships and grants are open to women who are accepted for enrollment at Midway College. Awards support undergraduate study in the above areas.

80 awards annually. Contact Midway College's Financial Aid Office for an application.

130—NATIONAL AIR TRANSPORTATION ASSOCIATION FOUNDATION (John W. Godwin, Jr., Memorial Scholarship Fund)

4226 King Street
Alexandria VA 22302
808/808-NATA or 703/845-9000
FAX: 703/845-8176

AMOUNT: $2,500
DEADLINE(S): None
FIELD(S): Flight training

Scholarship for flight training for any certificate and/or flight rating issued by the FAA, at any NATA-Member company offering flight training. Must accumulate a minimum of 15 dual or solo flight hours each calendar month.

Contact organization for details.

131—NATIONAL AIR TRANSPORTATION ASSOCIATION FOUNDATION (The Pioneers of Flight Scholarship)

4226 King Street
Alexandria VA 22302
703/845-9000
FAX: 703/845-8176

AMOUNT: $2,500
DEADLINE(S): None
FIELD(S): General aviation

Scholarship for college students who are in the sophomore or junior year at the time of application intending to pursue full-time study at an accredited four-year college or university and can demonstrate an interest in pursuing a career in general aviation.

Must be nominated by an NATA Regular or Associate Member company.

132—NATIONAL ASSOCIATION OF WATER COMPANIES-NEW JERSEY CHAPTER (Scholarship)

Elizabethtown Water Co.
600 South Avenue
Westfield NJ 07091
908/654-1234
FAX: 908/232-2719

AMOUNT: $2,500
DEADLINE(S): APR 1
FIELD(S): Business Administration; Biology; Chemistry; Engineering Communications

For U.S. citizens who have lived in NJ at least 5 years and plan a career in the investor-owned water utility industry in disciplines such as those above. Must be undergrad or graduate student in a two- or four-year NJ college or university.

GPA of 3.0 or better required. Contact Gail P. Brady for complete information.

133—NATIONAL CUSTOMS BROKERS & FORWARDERS ASSN OF AMERICA INC. (NCBFAA Scholarship)

1200 18th Street NW, Suite 901
Washington DC 20036
202/466-0222

AMOUNT: $5,000
DEADLINE(S): FEB 1
FIELD(S): International Business-Customs Brokerage or Freight Forwarding

Open to family members and employees of regular NCBFAA members who are interested in a career in customs brokerage or freight forwarding. Applicants must have a 2.0 or better GPA and submit a 1,000- to 1,500-word essay.

Write for complete information.

134—NATIONAL ITALIAN AMERICAN FOUNDATION (Assunta Luchetti Martino Scholarship for International Studies)

1860 19th Street NW
Washington DC 20009-5599
202/530-5315

AMOUNT: $1,000
DEADLINE(S): MAY 31
FIELD(S): International studies

For undergraduates of Italian ancestry who are pursuing degrees in international studies.

Considerations are academic merit, financial need, and commmunity service. Write for application and further information.

135—NATIONAL ITALIAN AMERICAN FOUNDATION (Bolla Wines Scholarship)

1860 19th Street NW
Washington DC 20009-5599
202/530-5315

AMOUNT: $1,000
DEADLINE(S): MAY 31
FIELD(S): International studies-emphasis on Italian business or Italian-American history.

For undergraduate or graduate students of Italian heritage with a GPA of 3.0+ and a background in international studies. Must write an essay on "The Importance of Italy in Today's Business World." (3 pages, double spaced, typed.)

Community service and financial need considered. Write for appliacation and details.

136—NATIONAL ITALIAN AMERICAN FOUNDATION (George L. Graziado Fellowship for Business)

1860 19th Street NW
Washington DC 20009-5599
202/530-5315

AMOUNT: $2,500 and $5,000
DEADLINE(S): MAY 30
FIELD(S): Business and Management

Open to undergraduate American students of Italian ancestry studying at the George L. Graziado School of Business and Management at Pepperdine University, California.

2 awards given. Academic merit, financial need, and community service are considered. Contact organization for application and details.

137—NATIONAL ITALIAN AMERICAN FOUNDATION (Merrill Lynch Scholarship)

1860 19th Street NW
Washington DC 20009-5599
202/530-5315

AMOUNT: $1,000
DEADLINE(S): MAY 31
FIELD(S): Business

For undergraduates of Italian ancestry who are pursuing degrees in business and are residents of the state of New York.

Considerations are academic merit, financial need, and commmunity service. Write for application and further information.

138—NATIONAL ITALIAN AMERICAN FOUNDATION (The Vennera Noto Scholarship)

1860 19th Street NW
Washington DC 20009-5599
202/530-5315

AMOUNT: $2,000
DEADLINE(S): MAY 31
FIELD(S): Business administration

For undergraduates of Italian ancestry who are business majors.

Considerations are academic merit, financial need, and commmunity service. Write for application and further information.

139—NATIONAL SOCIETY DAUGHTERS OF THE AMERICAN REVOLUTION (Enid Hall Griswold Memorial Scholarship)

1776 D Street NW
Washington DC 20006-5392
202/628-1776
Internet: http://www.dar.org
AMOUNT: $1,000
DEADLINE(S): FEB 15
FIELD(S): History; Political Science; Government; Economics

Open to undergraduate juniors and seniors (US citizens) attending an accredited U.S. college or university. Awards are placed on deposit with school. Awards are judged on academic excellence, commitment to field of study, and need. Affiliation with DAR not required.

Not renewable. See Web site or send a self-addressed, stamped envelope for an application or more information.

140—NATIONAL SOCIETY OF ACCOUNTANTS SCHOLARSHIP FOUNDATION (NSA Annual Awards)

1010 North Fairfax Street
Alexandria VA 22314-1574
703/549-6400
FAX: 703/549-2984
E-mail: snoell@mindspring.com
Internet: http://www.nsacct.org
AMOUNT: $500-$1,000
DEADLINE(S): MAR 10
FIELD(S): Accounting

Open to undergraduate accounting students in an accredited two- or four-year college in the U.S. who are U.S. or Canadian citizens. Must maintain an overall GPA of 3.0. Selection based on academic attainment, leadership ability, and financial need. Payment by Foundation is made directly to your college/university.

30 awards annually. See Web site or contact Susan Noell, Foundation Director, for an application.

141—NATIONAL SOCIETY OF ACCOUNTANTS SCHOLARSHIP FOUNDATION (Stanley H. Stearman Scholarship Award)

1010 North Fairfax Street
Alexandria VA 22314-1574
703/549-6400
FAX: 703/549-2984
E-mail: snoell@mindspring.com
Internet: http://www.nsacct.org
AMOUNT: $2,000/year
DEADLINE(S): MAR 10
FIELD(S): Accounting

For U.S. or Canadian citizens in undergraduate or graduate programs in the U.S. who have a minimum 3.0 GPA. Must be the spouse, child, grandchild, niece, nephew, or son/daughter-in-law of an active or deceased NSA member who have held membership for at least one year. Must include letter of intent, outlining reasons for seeking award, intended career objective, and how this award would be used to accomplish that objective.

1 award annually. Renewable up to 3 years. See Web site or contact Susan Noell, Foundation Director, for an application.

142—NATIONAL TOURISM FOUNDATION (NTF Scholarships)

P.O. Box 3071
Lexington KY 40596-3071
800/682-8886
FAX: 606/226-4414
Internet: http://www.ntaonline.com
AMOUNT: $500-$5,000
DEADLINE(S): APR 15
FIELD(S): Travel and Tourism

Various scholarships for full-time students at two- or four-year colleges/universities in North America who are entering their junior or senior year of study. Must be a strong academic performer and have at least a 3.0 GPA. Degree emphasis must be in a travel- and tourism-related field, such as hotel management, restaurant management, or tourism. Letters of recommendation, resume, college transcript, and an essay are required.

See Web site for additional requirements of each individual scholarship. Students may apply for more than one award, but may only receive one. Send a self-addressed, stamped envelope to above address for an application.

143—NAVAL HISTORICAL CENTER (Internship Program)

Washington Navy Yard
901 M Street SE
Washington DC 20374-5060
202/433-6901
FAX: 202/433-8200
E-mail: efurgol@nhc.navy.mil
Internet: http://www.history.navy.mil
AMOUNT: $400 possible honoraria; otherwise, unpaid
DEADLINE(S): None
FIELD(S): Education; History; Public Relations; Design

Registered students of colleges/universities and graduates thereof are eligible for this program, which must be a minimum of 3 weeks, full- or part-time. Four specialities available: Curator, Education, Public Relations, and Design. Interns receive orientation and assist in their departments, and must complete individual project which contributes to Center. Must submit a letter of recommendation, unofficial transcript, and writing sample of not less than 1,000 words.

Contact Dr. Edward M. Furgol, Curator, for an application.

144—NEW YORK CITY DEPT. CITYWIDE ADMINISTRATIVE SERVICES (Urban Fellows Program)

1 Centre Street, 24th Floor
New York NY 10007
212/487-5600
FAX: 212/487-5720
AMOUNT: $18,000 stipend
DEADLINE(S): JAN 20
FIELD(S): Public Administration; Urban Planning; Government; Public Service; Urban Affairs

Fellowship program provides one academic year (9 months) of full-time work experience in urban government. Open to graduating college seniors and recent college graduates. U.S. citizenship required.

Write for complete information.

145—NEW YORK CITY DEPT. OF CITYWIDE ADMINISTRATIVE SERVICES (Government Scholars Internship Program)

1 Centre Street, 24th Floor
New York NY 10007
212/487-5600
FAX: 212/487-5720
AMOUNT: $3,000 stipend
DEADLINE(S): JAN 13
FIELD(S): Public Administration; Urban Planning; Government; Public Service; Urban Affairs

10-week summer intern program open to undergraduate sophomores, juniors, and seniors. Program provides students with unique opportunity to learn about NY City government. Internships available in virtually every city agency and mayoral office.

Write to New York City Fellowship Programs at above address for complete information.

146—NEW YORK STATE HIGHER EDUCATION SERVICES CORPORATION (N.Y. State Regents Professional/Health Care Opportunity Scholarships)

Cultural Education Center, Room 5C64
Albany NY 12230

518/486-1319
Internet: http://www.hesc.com
AMOUNT: $1,000-$10,000/year
DEADLINE(S): Varies
FIELD(S): Medicine and dentistry and related fields, architecture, nursing, psychology, audiology, landscape architecture, social work, chiropractic, law, pharmacy, accounting, speech language pathology

For NY state residents who are economically disadvantaged and members of a minority group underrepresented in the chosen profession and attending school in NY state. Some programs carry a service obligation in New York for each year of support. For U.S. citizens or qualifying noncitizens.

Medical/dental scholarships require one year of professional work in NY.

147—NEW YORK STATE SENATE (Legislative Fellows Program; R. J. Roth Journalism Fellowship; R. A. Wiebe Public Service Fellowship)

NYS Senate Student Programs Office, 90 South Swan Street, Rm. 401
Albany NY 12247
518/455-2611
FAX: 518/432-5470
E-mail: students@senate.state.ny.us
AMOUNT: $25,000 stipend (not a scholarship)
DEADLINE(S): MAY (first Friday)
FIELD(S): Political Science; Government; Public Service; Journalism; Public Relations

One-year programs for U.S. citizens who are grad students and residents of New York state or enrolled in accredited programs in New York state. Fellows work as regular legislative staff members of the office to which they are assigned. The Roth Fellowship is for communications/journalism majors, and undergrads may be considered for this program.

14 fellowships per year. Fellowships take place at the New York State Legislative Office. Write for complete information.

148—NEW YORK STATE THEATRE INSTITUTE (Internships in Theatrical Production)

155 River Street
Troy NY 12180
518/274-3573; E-mail: nysti@crisny.org
Internet: http://www.crisny.org/not-for-profit/nysti/int.htm
AMOUNT: None
DEADLINE(S): None
FIELD(S): Fields of study related to theatrical production, including box office and PR

Internships for college students, high school seniors, and educators-in-residence interested in developing skills in above fields. Unpaid, but college credit is earned. Located at Russell Sage College in Troy, NY. Gain experience in box office, costumes, education, electrics, music, stage management, scenery, properties, performance, and public relations. Interns come from all over the world.

Must be associated with an accredited institution. See Web site for more information. Call Ms. Arlene Leff, Intern Director at above location. Include your postal mailing address.

149—NINETY-NINES, SAN FERNANDO VALLEY CHAPTER/VAN NUYS AIRPORT (Aviation Career Scholarships)

P.O. Box 8160
Van Nuys CA 91409
818/989-0081
AMOUNT: $3,000
DEADLINE(S): MAY 1
FIELD(S): Aviation Careers

For men and women of the greater Los Angeles area pursuing careers as professional pilots, flight instructors, mechanics, or other aviation career specialists. Applicants must be at least 21 years of age and U.S. citizens.

3 awards annually. Send self-addressed, stamped, business-sized envelope to above address for application after January 1.

150—OPERA AMERICA (Fellowship Program)

1156 15th Street NW, Suite 810
Washington DC 20005
202/293-4466
FAX: 202/393-0735
AMOUNT: $1,200/month + transportation and housing
DEADLINE(S): MAY 7
FIELD(S): General or Artistic Administration, Technical Direction, or Production Management

Open to opera personnel, individuals entering opera administration from other disciplines, and graduates of arts administration or technical/production training programs who are committed to a career in opera in North America.

Must be U.S. or Canadian citizen or legal resident lawfully eligible to receive stipend.

151—PRESIDENT'S COMMISSION ON WHITE HOUSE FELLOWSHIPS

712 Jackson Place NW
Washington DC 20503
202/395-4522
FAX: 202/395-6179
E-mail: almanac@ace.esusda.gov
AMOUNT: Wage (up to GS-14 Step 3; approximately $65,000 in 1995)
DEADLINE(S): DEC 1
FIELD(S): Public Service; Government; Community Involvement; Leadership

Mid-career professionals spend one year as special assistants to senior executive branch officials in Washington. Highly competitive. Nonpartisan; no age or educational requirements. Fellowship year runs September 1 through August 31.

1,200 candidates applying for 11 to 19 fellowships each year. Write for complete information.

152—PRESS CLUB OF DALLAS FOUNDATION (Scholarship)

400 N. Olive
Dallas TX 75201
214/740-9988
AMOUNT: $1,000-$3,000
DEADLINE(S): APR 15
FIELD(S): Journalism and Public Relations

Open to students who are at least sophomore level in undergraduate studies or working toward a masters degree in the above fields in a Texas college or university. This scholarship is renewable by reapplication.

Write to Carol Wortham at the above address for complete information.

153—ROYAL THAI EMBASSY, OFFICE OF EDUCATIONAL AFFAIRS (Revenue Dept. Scholarships for Thai Students)

1906 23rd Street NW
Washington DC 20008
202/667-9111 or 202/667-8010
FAX: 202/265-7239
AMOUNT: Varies
DEADLINE(S): APR
FIELD(S): Computer Science (Telecommunications), Law, Economics, Finance, Business Administration

Scholarships for students under age 35 from Thailand who have been accepted to study in the U.S or U.K. for the needs of the Revenue Dept., Ministry of Finance. Must pursue any level degree in one of the above fields.

Selections are based on academic records, employment history, and advisor recommendations.

154—SCOTTISH RITE CHARITABLE FOUNDATION (Bursaries for College Students)

Roeher Institute, Kinsmen Bldg.
4700 Keele Street
North York Ontario M3J 1P3
CANADA
416/661-9611
TDD: 416/661-2023
FAX: 416/661-5701
E-mail: mail@aacl.org
Internet: http://www.aacl.org
AMOUNT: $2,000 (max.)
DEADLINE(S): JUL 1
FIELD(S): Human Services; Intellectual Disability; Special Education; DSW

Open to Canadian citizens/landed immigrants accepted into a full-time undergraduate college program in a Canadian college/university. Must submit outline of intended study, transcripts, community involvement, and letters of reference from supervisors. Financial need NOT a factor.

3 awards annually. Must be recommended by a Provincial Association of the Canadian Association for Community Living. Contact your provincial association for details.

155—SOIL AND WATER CONSERVATION SOCIETY (SWCS Internships)

7515 N.E. Ankeny Road
Ankeny IA 50021-9764
515/289-2331 or 800/THE-SOIL
FAX: 515/289-1227
E-mail: charliep@swcs.org
Internet: http://www.swcs.org
AMOUNT: Varies—most are uncompensated
DEADLINE(S): Varies
FIELD(S): Journalism, marketing, database management, meeting planning, public policy research, environmental education, landscape architecture

Internships for undergraduates and graduates to gain experience in the above fields as they relate to soil and water conservation issues. Internship openings vary through the year in duration, compensation, and objective. SWCS will coordinate particulars with your academic advisor.

Contact SWCS for internship availability at any time during the year or see Web site for jobs page.

156—SONOMA CHAMBOLLE-MUSIGNY SISTER CITIES, INC. (Henri Cardinaux Memorial Scholarship)

Chamson Scholarship Committee
P.O. Box 1633
Sonoma CA 95476-1633
707/939-1344
FAX: 707/939-1344
E-mail: Baileysci@vom.com
AMOUNT: up to $1,500 (travel + expenses)
DEADLINE(S): JUL 15
FIELD(S): Culinary Arts; Wine Industry; Art; Architecture; Music; History; Fashion

Hands-on experience working in above or similar fields and living with a family in small French village in Burgundy or other French city. Must be Sonoma County, CA, resident at least 18 years of age and be able to communicate in French. Transcripts, employer recommendation, photograph, and essay (stating why, where, and when) required.

1 award. Nonrenewable. Also offers opportunity for candidate in Chambolle-Musigny to obtain work experience and cultural exposure in Sonoma, CA.

157—SPACE COAST CREDIT UNION (Four-Year Scholarships)

Marketing Dept.
P.O. Box 2470
Melbourne FL 32902
Internet: http://www.sccu.com/scholarship/
AMOUNT: $1,250/year
DEADLINE(S): APR 15
FIELD(S): Computer Science, Business (Finance, Economics, Human Resources, Industrial Relations, Marketing)

Must be graduating from a high school in Brevard, Volusia, Flagler, or Indian River counties, be a member of SCCU, have a minimum GPA of 3.0, be planning to attend a four-year Florida institution of higher education, and write a 200-word essay on the topic "Why credit unions are valuable to society."

2 annual awards. For membership information or an application, see our Web page or write to the above address.

158—SPACE COAST CREDIT UNION (Two-Year Scholarships)

Marketing Dept.
P.O. Box 2470
Melbourne FL 32902
Internet: http://www.sccu.com/scholarship/
AMOUNT: $750/year, two years; $1,000 bonus if go on for Bachelor's
DEADLINE(S): APR 15
FIELD(S): Math, Economics, Science, Computer Science, Marketing, Journalism, Political Science

Must be graduating from a high school in Brevard, Volusia, Flagler, or Indian River counties, be a member of SCCU, have a minimum 3.0 GPA, planning to attend a two-year Florida institution of higher education for an associates degree, and be willing to write a 200-word essay on the topic "Why credit unions are valuable to society."

4 annual awards. Students going on to complete a four-year degree could be eligible for a bonus scholarship of $1,000 for the next two years. For membership information or an application, see our Web page or write to the above address.

159—SRP/NAVAJO GENERATING STATION (Navajo Scholarship)

P.O. Box 850
Page AZ 86040
520/645-6539
FAX: 520/645-7295
E-mail: ljdawave@srp.gov
AMOUNT: Based on need
DEADLINE(S): APR 30
FIELD(S): Engineering, Environmental Studies, Business, Business Management, Health, Education

Scholarships for full-time students who hold membership in the Navajo Tribe and who are pursuing a degree in a field of study recognized as significant to the Navajo Naiton, Salt River Project, or the Navajo Generating Station, such as those listed above. Must be junior or senior, have and maintain a GPA of 3.0

Average of 15 awards per year. Inquire of Linda Dawavendewa at above location.

160—STATE FARM COMPANIES FOUNDATION (Exceptional Student Fellowship)

One State Farm Plaza, SC-3
Bloomington IL 61710-0001
309/766-2039/2161
E-mail: Nancy.Lynn.gr3o@statefarm.com
Internet: http://www.statefarm.com
AMOUNT: $3,000 (nominating institution receives $250)
DEADLINE(S): FEB 15
FIELD(S): Accounting; Business Administration; Actuarial Science;

Computer Science; Economics; Finance; Insurance/Risk Management; Investments; Management; Marketing; Mathematics; Statistics

For U.S. citizens who are full-time juniors or seniors when they apply. Must demonstrate significant leadership in extracurricular activities, have minimum 3.6 GPA, and attend accredited U.S. college/university. Must be nominated by dean, department head, professor, or academic advisor.

50 awards annually. Not renewable. See Web site, visit your financial aid office, or write to above address for an application.

161—STATE NEWS (Scholarships)

Michigan State University
343 Student Services
E. Lansing MI 48824-1113
E-mail: recruiter@statenews.com
Internet: http://statenews.com/scholarship/

AMOUNT: $2,000/year for 4 years + job
DEADLINE(S): FEB 5
FIELD(S): Journalism; Advertising

Open to high school seniors who will start at MSU in the fall. Must have an above-average GPA and have demonstrated a strong interest in high school journalism or advertising through their newspapers and yearbooks. Recipients work in paying positions at *The State News* after the first semester of their freshman year, either in the newsroom or in the advertising department. State News pay will be in addition to the scholarship. May major in any academic program.

2 awards annually. See Web site or contact Ben Schwartz, *State News* General Manager, for an application.

162—STATISTICS NEW ZEALAND (Pacific Islands Scholarship)

EEO Co-ordinator
P.O. Box 2922
Wellington NEW ZEALAND
04/495-4643
FAX: 04/495-4817
E-mail: anisiata_soagia-pritchard@stats.govt.nz

AMOUNT: $3,500/year + travel
DEADLINE(S): OCT 31
FIELD(S): Statistics; Mathematics; Demography; Economics; Geography; Quantitative Social Sciences

Open to all indigenous people of Pacific Islands descent who are residents in New Zealand and who wish to study for an undergraduate tertiary qualification at a New Zealand university. Recipient must spend 6-10 weeks of vacation break in employment with Statistics New Zealand. Based on relevance of course of study; academic ability; language, community involvement, and culture; and personal attributes, including potential leadership qualities. References required.

1 award annually. Renewable up to 3 years. Contact Anisiata Soagia-Pritchard, EEO Coordinator, for an application. Notification in December.

163—STUDENT CONSERVATION ASSOCIATION (SCA Resource Assistant Program)

P.O. Box 550
Charlestown NH 03603
603/543-1700
FAX: 603/543-1828
E-mail: internships@sca-inc.org
Internet: http://www.sca-inc.org

AMOUNT: $1,180-$4,725
DEADLINE(S): Varies
FIELD(S): Environment and related fields

Must be 18 and U.S. citizen; need not be student. Fields: Ag, archaeology, anthro, botany, caves, civil/env engineering, env education, fisheries, forests, herpetology, history, living hist/roleplaying, visitor services, landscape arch/env design, paleontology, recreation/resource/range mgmt, trail maintenance/constrctn, wildlife mgmt, geology, hydrology, library/museums, surveying...

900 positions in U.S. and Canada. Send $1 for postage for application; outside U.S./Canada, send $20.

164—THE AMERICAN ASSOCIATION OF ATTORNEY-CERTIFIED PUBLIC ACCOUNTANTS FOUNDATION (Student Writing Competition)

24196 Alicia Parkway, Suite K
Mission Viejo CA 92691
800/CPA-ATTY
FAX: 714/768-7062

AMOUNT: $250-$1,500
DEADLINE(S): APR 1
FIELD(S): Accounting; Law

Essay contest for accounting and/or law students.

Contact organization for current topics and rules.

165—THE ART INSTITUTES INTERNATIONAL (Evelyn Keedy Memorial Scholarship)

300 Sixth Avenue, Suite 800
Pittsburgh PA 15222-2598
412/562-9800
FAX: 412/562-9802
E-mail: webadmin@aii.edu
Internet: http://www.aii.edu

AMOUNT: 2 years full tuition
DEADLINE(S): MAY 1
FIELD(S): Various fields in the creative and applied arts: video production, broadcasting, culinary arts, fashion design, Web site administration, etc.

Scholarships at 12 different locations nationwide in various fields described above. For graduating high school seniors admitted to an Arts Institutes International School, the New York Restaurant School, or NCPT. Transcripts, letters of recommendation, and resume must be submitted with application.

See Web site or contact AII for more information.

166—TRANSPORTATION CLUBS INTERNATIONAL (Charlotte Woods Memorial Scholarship)

P.O. Box 1072
Glen Alpine NC 28628
206/549-2251

AMOUNT: $1,000
DEADLINE(S): MAY 31
FIELD(S): Transportation Logistics; Traffic Management

Open to TCI members or their dependents enrolled at an accredited college or university in a program in transportation, traffic management, or related area and considering a career in transportation.

Type an essay of not more than 200 words on why you have chosen transportation or an allied field as a career path. Include your objectives. Financial need is also considered. Send SASE (business size) for complete information and application.

167—TRANSPORTATION CLUBS INTERNATIONAL (Ginger & Fred Deines Canada Scholarships)

P.O. Box 1072
Glen Alpine NC 28628
206/549-2251

AMOUNT: $500 and/or $1,000
DEADLINE(S): MAY 31
FIELD(S): Transportation Logistics; Traffic Management

For a student of Canadian nationality and enrolled in a school in Canada or U.S. in a degree or vocational program in the above or related areas.

Type an essay of not more than 200 words on why you have chosen transportation or an allied field as a career path. Include your objectives. Send an SASE for further details.

168—TRANSPORTATION CLUBS INTERNATIONAL (Ginger & Fred Deines Mexico Scholarships)

P.O. Box 1072
Glen Alpine NC 28688
206/549-2251

AMOUNT: $500 and/or $1,000
DEADLINE(S): May 31
FIELD(S): Transportation; Traffic Management

Open to students of Mexican nationality who are enrolled in a Mexican or U.S. institution of higher learning in a degree or vocational program in the above or related areas.

Type an essay of not more than 200 words on why you have chosen transportation or an allied field as a career path. Include your objectives. Send SASE for complete information.

169—TRANSPORTATION CLUBS INTERNATIONAL (Hooper Memorial Scholarships)

P.O. Box 1072
Glen Alpine NC 28628
206/549-2251

AMOUNT: $1,500
DEADLINE(S): MAY 31
FIELD(S): Transportation Logistics; Traffic Management

For students enrolled in an accredited college or university in a degree or vocational program in transportation logistics, traffic management, or related fields and preparing for a career in transportation.

Type an essay of not more than 200 words on why you have chosen transportation or an allied field as a career. Include your objectives. Financial need is considered. Send SASE (business size) for complete information.

170—TRAVEL AND TOURISM RESEARCH ASSOCIATION (Awards for Projects)

546 East Main Street
Lexington KY 40508
606/226-4344
FAX: 606/226-4355
Internet: http://www.ttra.com

AMOUNT: $700-$1,000
DEADLINE(S): MAR 1
FIELD(S): Travel and tourism and related fields

3 awards for undergraduate, graduate, and doctoral students in the area of travel and tourism research. Awards for outstanding papers and dissertations.

Visit Web site and/or send SASE to above location for details.

171—U.S. DEPARTMENT OF TRANSPORTATION (Dwight D. Eisenhower Transportation Fellowship Program)

4600 N. Fairfax Drive, Suite 800
Arlington VA 22203
703/235-0538
FAX: 703/235-0593
Internet: http://www.nhi.fhwa.dot.gov

AMOUNT: Varies
DEADLINE(S): FEB 15
FIELD(S): Transportation

Open to graduate students and undergraduate juniors and seniors to pursue studies or research in any area of the U.S. transportation industry. Must be U.S. citizen. Objectives of program are to attract the nation's brightest minds to the field of transportation, to enhance the careers of transportation professionals by encouraging them to seek advanced degrees, and to retain top talent in the U.S. transportation industry.

See Web site or contact Universities and Grants Programs at the Dept. of Transportation for an application and specific details on each of the six award programs.

172—U.S. DEPT. OF HEALTH & HUMAN SERVICES (Indian Health Service Health Professions Scholarship Program)

Twinbrook Metro Plaza, Suite 100
12300 Twinbrook Parkway
Rockville MD 20852
301/443-0234
FAX: 301/443-4815
Internet: http://www:ihs.gov/Recruitment/DHPS/SP/SBTOC3.asp

AMOUNT: Tuition + fees and monthly stipend of $938.
DEADLINE(S): APR 1
FIELD(S): Health professions, accounting, social work

Open to Native Americans or Alaska natives who are graduate students or college juniors or seniors in a program leading to a career in a fields listed above. U.S. citizenship required. Renewable annually with reapplication.

Scholarship recipients must intend to serve the Indian people. They incur a one-year service obligation to the IHS for each year of support for a minimum of two years. Write for complete information.

173—UNITED STATES DEPARTMENT OF AGRICULTURE (1890 National Scholars Program)

14th & Independence Avenue SW
Room 301-W; Whitten Bldg.
Washington DC 20250-9600
202/720-6905
E-mail: usda-m@fie.com
Internet: http://web.fie.com/htdoc/fed/agr/ars/edu/prog/mti/agrpgaak.htm

AMOUNT: Tuition, employment/benefits, use of pc/software, fees, books, room/board
DEADLINE(S): JAN 15
FIELD(S): Agriculture, Food, or Natural Resource Sciences

For U.S. citizens, high school grad/GED, GPA 3.0+, verbal/math SAT 1000+, composite score 21+ ACT, first-year college student, and attend participating school.

34+ scholarships/yr/4 years. Send applications to U.S.D.A. Liaison officer at the 1890 Institution of your choice (see Web page for complete list).

174—UNIVERSITY OF NORTH TEXAS (Merchandising and Hospitality Scholarships)

Dean, School of Merchandising/Hospitality Management
P.O. Box 311100
Denton TX 76203-1100
817/565-2436
Internet: http://www.unt.edu/scholarships/smhm.htm

AMOUNT: Varies
DEADLINE(S): Varies
FIELD(S): Business: Merchandising and Hospitality Management

Several scholarships for students in the above fields are offered at the University of North Texas. Specialties and eligibility requirements vary.

See Web site for more information. Contact school for details.

175—UNIVERSITY OF OKLAHOMA-H.H. HERBERT SCHOOL OF JOURNALISM AND MASS COMMUNICATION (Undergraduate Scholarships)

860 Van Vleet Oval, Room 101
Norman OK 73019
405/325-2721

AMOUNT: $5,000/year

DEADLINE(S): FEB
FIELD(S): Journalism: Print or Broadcast, Advertising, Electronic Media, News Communication, Professional Writing, Public Relations

For undergraduate students studying in the above fields who plan to attend the University of Oklahoma. Interview is part of acceptance process.

Contact David Dary at above location for details.

176—UNIVERSITY OF WAIKATO (International Management Programme Scholarship)

Private Bag 3105
Hamilton ZEW ZEALAND
07 8562889 ext. 8964 or 6732
FAX: 07 8384370
E-mail: rgty_dbc
AMOUNT: Varies (individually coordinated)
DEADLINE(S): MAY
FIELD(S): International Management Studies

For overseas travel in connection with studies in the International Management Programme within the degree of Bachelor of Management Studies. For students who have completed at least two years of study toward the degree.

For details, contact the Scholarships Administrator, University of Waikato, at above address.

177—UTA ALUMNI ASSOCIATION (Daniel Kauth Scholarship)

University of Texas at Arlington
Box 19457
Arlington TX 76019
Internet: http://www.uta.edu/alumni/scholar.htm
AMOUNT: $250
DEADLINE(S): Varies
FIELD(S): Marketing

For full-time students at the University of Texas at Arlington who are majoring in marketing. Must submit transcript and letter stating career goals, future commitment to UTA, and financial need.

1 award annually. Contact UTA Alumni Association for an application.

178—W.E. UPJOHN INSTITUTE FOR EMPLOYMENT RESEARCH (Grant)

300 South Westnedge Avenue
Kalamazoo MI 49007-4686
616/343-5541
FAX: 616/343-7310
E-mail: webmaster@we.upjohninst.org
Internet: http://www.upjohninst.org
AMOUNT: Up to $45,000 + $25,000 to conduct surveys/assemble data
DEADLINE(S): JAN 26
FIELD(S): Employment Relationships, Low Wages/Public Policy, Social Insurance

Grants are for proposals that will lead to a book that contributes to the Institute's research program. Proposals evaluated on contribution to important policy issues/professional literature, technical merit, professional qualifications, likelihood of timely completion of project, cost effectiveness, and consistency with Institute's interests. Must submit 8 copies of both a 3-page summary and curriculum vitae. Subset of applicants will then submit 15-page proposal.

Fax and e-mail submissions will not be accepted. See Web site for details or write to above address.

179—WOMEN IN DEFENSE (HORIZONS Scholarship Foundation)

NDIA
2111 Wilson Boulevard, Suite 400
Arlington VA 22201-3061
703/247-2552
FAX: 703/522-1820
E-mail: cbanks@mciworld.com
Internet: http://www.ndia.org/wid/
AMOUNT: $500+
DEADLINE(S): NOV 1; JUL 1
FIELD(S): Engineering; Computer Science; Physics; Math; Business; Law; International Relations; Political Science; Operations Research; Economics; National Security/Defense

Open to women employed/planning careers in defense/national security areas. Must be currently enrolled full- or part-time at an accredited college/university at the graduate or undergraduate junior/senior level. Must have a minimum 3.25 GPA, demonstrate financial need, and be U.S. citizen. Based on academic achievement, work experience, objectives, and recommendations.

Renewable. See Web site or MUST send self-addressed, stamped envelope to Courtney Banks for application.

180—WOMEN'S SPORTS FOUNDATION (Jackie Joyner-Kersee and Zina Garrison Minority Internships)

Eisenhower Park
East Meadow NY 11554
800/227-3988
FAX: 516/542-4716
E-mail: WoSport@aol.com
Internet: http://www.lifetimetv.com/WoSport
AMOUNT: $4,000-$5,000
DEADLINE(S): Ongoing
FIELD(S): Sports-related fields

Provides women of color an opportunity to gain experience in a sports-related career and interact in the sports community. May be undergraduates, college graduates, graduate students, or women in a career change. Internships are located at the Women's Sports Foundation in East Meadow, New York.

4-6 awards annually. See Web site or write to above address for details.

181—WORLD LEISURE AND RECREATION ASSOCIATION (Scholarships)

WLRA Secretariat; Site 81C Comp 0
Okanagan Falls BC V0H 1R0
CANADA
250/497-6578
E-mail: secretariat@worldleisure.org
Internet: http://www.worldleisure.org
AMOUNT: Varies
DEADLINE(S): FEB 1
FIELD(S): Recreation and Leisure Studies

Scholarships intended to allow college seniors or graduate students in recreation or leisure services programs to attend international meetings/conferences or conventions, thereby gaining a broader perspective of world leisure and recreation.

See Web site or contact WLRA for an application.

182—WYOMING TRUCKING ASSOCIATION (Scholarships)

P.O. Box 1909
Casper WY 82602
Written Inquiry
AMOUNT: $250-$300
DEADLINE(S): MAR 1
FIELD(S): Transportation Industry

For Wyoming high school graduates enrolled in a Wyoming college, approved trade school, or the University of Wyoming. Must be pursuing a course of study which will result in a career in the transportation industry in Wyoming, including but not limited to: safety, environmental science, diesel mechanics, truck driving, vocational trades, business management, sales management, computer skills, accounting, office procedures, and management.

1-10 awards annually. Write to WYTA for an application.

183—Y'S MEN INTERNATIONAL-U.S. AREA (Alexander Scholarship Loan Fund)

12405 W. Lewis Avenue
Avondale AZ 85323-6518
Written Inquiry
AMOUNT: $1,000-$1,500/year
DEADLINE(S): MAY 30; OCT 30
FIELD(S): Business Administration; Youth Leadership

Open to U.S. citizens/permanent residents with a strong desire to pursue professional YMCA service. Must be YMCA staff pursuing undergraduate or graduate study and demonstrate financial need. Repayment of loan is waived if recipient enters YMCA employment after graduation.

Send self-addressed, business-sized envelope plus $1 for postage and handling to above address for an application.

SCHOOL OF EDUCATION

184—ALPHA DELTA KAPPA (International Teacher Education Scholarship)

1615 W. 92nd Street
Kansas City MO 64114
816/363-5525 or 800/247-2311
FAX: 816/363-4010
E-mail: alphadeltakappa@worldnet.att.net
Internet: http://www.alphadeltakappa.org
AMOUNT: Varies
DEADLINE(S): JAN 1
FIELD(S): Education

Open to young women from foreign countries to study in the U.S. Must be an unmarried woman with no dependents and between 20 to 35 years of age. Must also be a non-U.S. citizen residing outside the U.S. and maintain that residency status from the time of application to the awarding of the scholarship. Must plan to enter the teaching profession or be engaged in the teaching profession and shall have completed at least one year of college. Doctoral studies not eligible.

7 awards annually. Contact Alpha Delta Kappa after August 1 for an application.

185—AMERICAN INDIAN SCIENCE AND ENGINEERING SOCIETY (Burlington Northern Santa Fe Pacific Foundation Scholarships)

P.O. Box 9828
Albuquerque NM 87119-9828
505/765-1052
FAX: 505/765-5608
E-mail: scholarships@aises.org
Internet: http://www.aises.org/scholarships
AMOUNT: $2,500/year
DEADLINE(S): MAR 31
FIELD(S): Business; Education; Science; Engineering; Health Administration

Open to high school seniors who are at least 1/4 American Indian. Must reside in KS, OK, CO, AZ, NM, MN, ND, OR, SD, WA, MT, or San Bernardino County, CA (Burlington Northern and Santa Fe Pacific service areas). Must demonstrate financial need.

5 awards annually. Renewable up to 4 years. See Web site or contact Patricia Browne for an application.

186—ARCTIC INSTITUTE OF NORTH AMERICA (Jim Bourque Scholarship)

Univ. of Calgary
2500 University Drive NW
Calgary Alberta T2N 1N4
CANADA
403/220-7515
FAX: 403/282-4609
E-mail: smccaffe@ucalgary.ca
Internet: http://www.ucalgary.ca/UofC/Others/AINA/scholar/scholar.html
AMOUNT: $1,000
DEADLINE(S): JUL 15
FIELD(S): Education; Environmental Studies; Traditional Knowledge; Telecommunications

Open to Canadian Aboriginal students who intend to take, or are enrolled in, post-secondary training in above fields. There is no application; applicants must submit description of program and reasons for choice, transcript, letter of recommendation, statement of financial need, and proof of enrollment or application to a postsecondary institution.

See Web site or contact AINA for details. Award announced on August 1.

187—CALIFORNIA MATHEMATICS COUNCIL (Scholarship)

CMC-SS Scholarship Committee
1500 North Verdugo Road
Glendale CA 91208-2894
E-mail: sjkolpas@sprintmail.com
AMOUNT: $100-$1000
DEADLINE(S): JAN 31
FIELD(S): Education

Scholarships will be presented for students who are studying elementary education or secondary education. Only applicants who teach, reside, or go to school in Southern California will be considered.

187A—CHARLES E. SAAK TRUST (Educational Grants)

Wells Fargo Bank
8405 N. Fresno Street, Suite 210
Fresno CA 93720
Written Inquiry
AMOUNT: Varies
DEADLINE(S): MAR 31
FIELD(S): Education; Dentistry

Undergraduate grants for residents of the Porterville-Poplar area of Tulare County, California. Must carry a minimum of 12 units, have at least a 2.0 GPA, be under age 21, and demonstrate financial need.

Approximately 100 awards per year. Renewable with reapplication. Write for complete information.

188—CONTINENTAL SOCIETY DAUGHTERS OF INDIAN WARS (Scholarship)

Route 2, Box 184
Locust Grove OK 74352
918/479-5670
AMOUNT: $1,000
DEADLINE(S): JUN 15
FIELD(S): Education; Social Work; Social Service

Open to Native American, certified tribal members with plans to work on a reservation. Must be an undergraduate junior or senior accepted to or already attending an accredited college/university, be carrying at least eight semester hours, and have a minimum 3.0 GPA. Must be U.S. citizen and demonstrate financial need.

1 award annually. Renewable. Contact Mrs. Ronald Jacobs for an application.

189—GRACE FOUNDATION (Scholarship Trust Fund)

P.O. Box 924
Menlo Park CA 94026-0924
Written Inquiry
AMOUNT: $1,000-$4,000
DEADLINE(S): JAN 31
FIELD(S): Ministry; Medicine; Teaching; Social Service

Open to students from developing countries in Asia/Southeast Asia to pursue full-time study at an accredited college/university. For training future Christian ministers and professional workers in above fields. Must have completed one or more years of college in or near their native country, be a strong Christian, have a minimum 3.0 GPA, and demonstrate financial need.

Renewable up to 4 years with maintenance of 3.0 GPA. Applications available between September 1 and October 31.

190—IDAHO STATE BOARD OF EDUCATION (Education Incentive Loan Forgiveness)

P.O. Box 83720
Boise ID 83720-0037
208/334-2270

AMOUNT: Varies
DEADLINE(S): Varies
FIELD(S): Education; Nursing

Open to Idaho residents who have graduated from an Idaho high school within two years, ranking within the top 15% of graduating class or having earned a minimum 3.0 GPA. Must enroll as a full-time student in an Idaho college/university, pursuing a program of study toward an Idaho teaching certificate or licensure by the Board of Nursing as a registered nurse. Must plan to pursue career within Idaho for a minimum of two years.

Renewable. Contact the financial aid office of the Idaho public college/university you plan to attend for an application and deadlines.

191—INSTITUTE FOR HUMANE STUDIES (Summer Seminars Program)

3401 N. Fairfax Drive, Suite 440
Arlington VA 22201-4432
703/993-4880 or 800/697-8799
FAX: 703/993-4890
E-mail: ihs@gmu.edu
Internet: http://www.TheIHS.org

AMOUNT: Free summer seminars, including room/board, lectures, seminar materials, and books
DEADLINE(S): MAR
FIELD(S): Social Sciences; Humanities; Law; Journalism; Public Policy; Education; Film; Writing; Economics; Philosophy

Open to college students, recent graduates, and graduate students who share an interest in learning and exchanging ideas about the scope of individual rights, free markets, the rule of law, peace, and tolerance.

See Web site for seminar information or to apply online or contact IHS for an application.

192—KOSCIUSZKO FOUNDATION (UNESCO Teaching in Poland Program)

15 E. 65th Street
New York NY 10021-6595
212/734-2130
FAX: 212/628-4552
E-mail: thekf@pegasusnet.com
Internet: http://www.kosciuszko foundation.org

AMOUNT: $1,000-$5,000
DEADLINE(S): JAN 29
FIELD(S): Education

Open to American teachers, university faculty, university, college, and high school students over the age of 18 who wish to apply for teaching and teaching assistant positions. This is an educational and cultural summer exchange program that takes place at six locations in Poland during the month of July.

See Web site or send a self-addressed, stamped envelope to the Cultural Department for an application.

193—LOUISIANA OFFICE OF STUDENT FINANCIAL ASSISTANCE (Tuition Opportunity Program for Students-Teacher Awards)

P.O. Box 91202
Baton Rouge LA 70821-9202
800/259-5626 ext. 1012
FAX: 225/922-0790
E-mail: custserv@osfa.state.la.us;
Internet: http://www.osfa.state.la.us

AMOUNT: $4,000/year (education majors); $6,000/year (math/chemistry majors)
DEADLINE(S): JUL 1
FIELD(S): Education; Math; Chemistry

Open to Louisiana residents pursuing undergraduate or graduate study at a Louisiana public or LAICU private postsecondary institution. Must major in one of above fields leading to teacher certification. Loans are forgiven by working as a certified teacher in Louisiana one year for each year loan is received. Must be U.S. citizen with a minimum 3.0 GPA. Financial need NOT a factor.

90 awards annually. Renewable. Apply by completing Free Application for Federal Student Aid (FAFSA) and Teacher Award application. Contact Public Information Rep.

194—MIDWAY COLLEGE (Institutional Aid Program)

Financial Aid Office
Midway KY 40347
606/846-4421

AMOUNT: Varies
DEADLINE(S): MAR 1
FIELD(S): Nursing; Paralegal; Education; Psychology; Biology; Equine Studies; Liberal Studies; Business Administration

Scholarships and grants are open to women who are accepted for enrollment at Midway College. Awards support undergraduate study in the above areas.

80 awards annually. Contact Midway College's Financial Aid Office for an application.

195—NAACP NATIONAL OFFICE (Sutton Education Scholarship)

4805 Mount Hope Drive
Baltimore MD 21215
410/620-5372 or 877/NAACP-98
E-mail: education@naacp.org;
Internet: http://www.naacp.org/work/education/eduscholarship.shtml

AMOUNT: $1,000 undergrads; $2,000 grads
DEADLINE(S): APR 30
FIELD(S): Education

Open to NAACP members majoring in the above area. Undergrads must have GPA of 2.5+; graduates' GPAs must be 3.0+. Renewable if the required GPA is maintained.

Financial need must be established. Write for complete information. Include a legal size, self-addressed, stamped envelope.

196—NATIONAL JUNIOR CLASSICAL LEAGUE (Scholarships)

National Junior Classical League
Club, Miami University
Oxford OH 45056
513/529-7741
Fax: 513/529-7742
E-mail: info@aclclassics.org;
Internet: http://www.aclclassics.org or http://www.njcl.org

AMOUNT: $500-$1,500
DEADLINE(S): May 1
FIELD(S): Education

Open to NJCL members who are high school seniors and plan to study Classics (though Classics major is not required). Preference will be given to a student who plans to pursue a teaching career in the Classics (also not a requirement).

197—NATIVE AMERICAN SCHOLARSHIP FUND, INC. (Scholarships)

8200 Mountain Road, NE, Suite 203
Albuquerque NM 87110
505/262-2351

FAX: 505/262-0543
E-mail: NScholarsh@aol.com
AMOUNT: Varies
DEADLINE(S): MAR 15; APR 15; SEP 15
FIELD(S): Math; Engineering; Science; Business; Education; Computer Science

Open to American Indians or Alaskan Natives (1/4 degree or more) enrolled as members of a federally recognized, state recognized, or terminated tribe. For graduate or undergraduate study at an accredited four-year college or university.

208 awards annually. Contact Lucille Kelley, Director of Recruitment, for an application.

198—NAVAL HISTORICAL CENTER (Internship Program)

Washington Navy Yard
901 M Street SE
Washington DC 20374-5060
202/433-6901
FAX: 202/433-8200
E-mail: efurgol@nhc.navy.mil
Internet: http://www.history.navy.mil
AMOUNT: $400 possible honoraria; otherwise, unpaid
DEADLINE(S): None
FIELD(S): Education; History; Public Relations; Design

Registered students of colleges/universities and graduates thereof are eligible for this program, which must be a minimum of 3 weeks, full- or part-time. Four specialties available: Curator, Education, Public Relations, and Design. Interns receive orientation and assist in their departments, and must complete individual project which contributes to Center. Must submit a letter of recommendation, unofficial transcript, and writing sample of not less than 1,000 words.

199—NEW ZEALAND FEDERATION OF UNIVERSITY WOMEN-WAIKATO BRANCH (Kahurangi Maori Language Award)

P.O. Box 7065
Hamilton
New Zealand
07/855-3776
AMOUNT: $1,000
DEADLINE(S): MAR 15
FIELD(S): Education; Maori Studies

Open to Maori women who are full-time students enrolled for a third or fourth year at the University of Waikato School of Education or the Department of Maori Studies. Must be fluent in or studying the Maori language for a Bachelor of Education degree or Diploma of Teaching.

Contact the Convenor, NAFUW, Waikato Branch for an application.

EDUCATION

200—ADELPHI UNIVERSITY (Athletic Grants)

1 South Avenue
Garden City NY 11530
516/877-3080
Internet: http://www.adelphi.edu/finaid/awards.html
AMOUNT: $2,000-$13,000
DEADLINE(S): FEB 15
FIELD(S): Any major, but must demonstrate exceptional ability in athletics

Various scholarships for full-time students at Adelphi University who demonstrate excellence in athletics. Must continue to participate in the University's athletic teams and maintain 2.0 GPA overall to maintain scholarship.

See Web site for further information; contact school to apply.

201—ALASKA COMMISSION ON POST-SECONDARY EDUCATION (Alaska Teacher Scholarship Loan Program)

3030 Vintage Boulevard
Juneau AK 99801
907/465-6741
FAX: 907/465-5316
E-mail: ftolbert@educ.state.ak.us
AMOUNT: Up to $7,500/year, with $37,500 lifetime maximum
DEADLINE(S): MAY 1 (nominations from school superintendents)
FIELD(S): Elementary or Secondary Education

Loans for Alaska high school graduates from rural areas who intend to teach in rural areas. Students are nominated by their rural schools. Employment as a teacher in a rural area in Alaska can result in up to 100% forgiveness of the loan. For use in both Alaska and elsewhere.

75-100 awards per year. Contact ACPE for details and the qualifications of a "rural" resident.

202—AMERICAN ALLIANCE FOR HEALTH, PHYSICAL EDUCATION, RECREATION & DANCE

1900 Association Drive
Reston VA 20191
703/476-3400 or 800/213-7193
E-mail: webmaster@aahperd.org
Internet: http://www.aahperd.org
AMOUNT: Varies
DEADLINE(S): Varies
FIELD(S): Health Education, Leisure and Recreation, Girls and Women in Sports, Sport and Physical Education, Dance

This organization has six national sub-organizations specializing in the above fields. Some have grants and fellowships for both individuals and group projects. The Web site has the details for each group.

Visit Web site for details or write to above address for details.

203—AMERICAN FOUNDATION FOR THE BLIND (Delta Gamma Foundation Memorial Scholarship)

11 Penn Plaza, Suite 300
New York NY 10001
212/502-7661
FAX: 212/502-7771
E-mail: juliet@afb.org
Internet: http://www.afb.org
AMOUNT: $1,000
DEADLINE(S): APR 30
FIELD(S): Rehabilitation/Education of Visually Impaired/Blind

Open to legally blind undergraduate and graduate students of good character who have exhibited academic excellence and are studying in field of rehabilitation/education of persons who are blind or visually impaired. Must be U.S. citizen. Must submit evidence of legal blindness; official transcripts; proof of college/university acceptance; three letters of recommendation; and typewritten statement describing goals, work experience, activities, and how money will be used.

1 award annually. See Web site or contact Julie Tucker at AFB for an application.

204—AMERICAN INDIAN SCIENCE AND ENGINEERING SOCIETY (Burlington Northern Santa Fe Pacific Foundation Scholarships)

P.O. Box 9828
Albuquerque NM 87119-9828
505/765-1052
FAX: 505/765-5608
E-mail: scholarships@aises.org
Internet: http://www.aises.org/scholarships
AMOUNT: $2,500/year

DEADLINE(S): MAR 31
FIELD(S): Business; Education; Science; Engineering; Health Administration

Open to high school seniors who are at least 1/4 American Indian. Must reside in KS, OK, CO, AZ, NM, MN, ND, OR, SD, WA, MT, or San Bernardino County, CA (Burlington Northern and Santa Fe Pacific service areas). Must demonstrate financial need.

5 awards annually. Renewable up to 4 years. See Web site or contact Patricia Browne for an application.

205—AMERICAN SPEECH-LANGUAGE HEARING FOUNDATION (Young Scholars Award for Minority Students)

10801 Rockville Pike
Rockville MD 20852
301/897-5700 ext. 4203
FAX 301/571-0457
Internet: http://www.asha.org
AMOUNT: $2,000
DEADLINE(S): JUN 6
FIELD(S): Speech-Language Pathology; Audiology

Open to racial/ethnic college seniors who are U.S. citizens accepted for graduate study in speech-language pathology or audiology.

Contact Gina Smolka for an application after February 1.

206—ARCTIC INSTITUTE OF NORTH AMERICA (Jim Bourque Scholarship)

Univ. of Calgary
2500 University Drive NW
Calgary Alberta T2N 1N4
CANADA
403/220-7515
FAX: 403/282-4609
E-mail: smccaffe@ucalgary.ca
Internet: http://www.ucalgary.ca/UofC/Others/AINA/scholar/scholar.html
AMOUNT: $1,000
DEADLINE(S): JUL 15
FIELD(S): Education; Environmental Studies; Traditional Knowledge; Telecommunications

Open to Canadian Aboriginal students who intend to take, or are enrolled in, postsecondary training in above fields. There is no application; applicants must submit description of program and reasons for choice, transcript, letter of recommendation, statement of financial need, and proof of enrollment or application to a postsecondary institution.

See Web site or contact AINA for details. Award announced on August 1.

207—AROMANDO FAMILY EDUCATIONAL FOUNDATION (Aromando and Mauriello Memorial Awards)

207 Route 541; R.D.#7
Medford NJ 08055
609/654-2397
E-mail: jha0227@netzero.net
AMOUNT: $200 (min.)
DEADLINE(S): DEC 1
FIELD(S): Elementary/Special Education; Theology (Priest/Nun)

Open to high school seniors/grads accepted to or attending any college/university full-time and majoring in teaching (elementary or special education) or for religious service (to become priest or nun). Must be an American of Italian heritage and a practicing Roman Catholic with a minimum 3.0 GPA. Must have received at least two varsity letters in one or more high-school sanctioned athletic or extracurricular programs. Financial need NOT a factor.

Send self-addressed, stamped, legal-size envelope for an application.

208—ASSOCIATION FOR EDUCATION AND REHABILITATION OF THE BLIND AND VISUALLY IMPAIRED (William and Dorothy Ferrell Scholarship)

4600 Duke Street, #430
P.O. Box 22397
Alexandria VA 22304
703/823-9690
FAX: 703/823-9695
E-mail: aer@aerbvi.org
Internet: http://www.aerbvi.org
AMOUNT: $500
DEADLINE(S): APR 15 (of even-numbered years)
FIELD(S): Fields of study related to the blind/visually impaired

Scholarships for students who are legally blind, pursuing postsecondary education in a field related to services for the blind or visually impaired. Financial need NOT a factor.

2 awards annually. See Web site or contact Carolyn Sharp at above address for details.

209—ASSOCIATION FOR EDUCATION AND REHABILITATION OF THE BLIND AND VISUALLY IMPAIRED (Telesensory Scholarship)

4600 Duke Street, #430
P.O. Box 22397
Alexandria VA 22304
703/823-9690
FAX: 703/823-9695
E-mail: aer@aerbvi.org
Internet: http://www.aerbvi.org
AMOUNT: $1,000
DEADLINE(S): APR 15 (of even-numbered years)
FIELD(S): Fields of study related to the blind/visually impaired

Scholarships for students who are members of AER pursuing postsecondary education in a field related to services for the blind or visually impaired. Must become an AER member before applying. Financial need NOT a factor.

1 award annually. For membership information or an application, see Web site or contact Carolyn Sharp at above address.

210—B.M. WOLTMAN FOUNDATION (Lutheran Scholarships for Students of the Ministry and Teaching)

7900 U.S. 290 E.
Austin TX 78724
512/926-4272
AMOUNT: $500-$2,500
DEADLINE(S): Varies
FIELD(S): Theology (Lutheran Ministry); Teacher Education (Lutheran Schools)

Scholarships for undergrads and graduate students studying for careers in the Lutheran ministry or for teaching in a Lutheran school. For Texas residents attending, or planning to attend, any college in Texas.

45 awards. Renewable. Send for details.

211—BLUES HEAVEN FOUNDATION, INC. (Muddy Waters Scholarship)

2120 S. Michigan Avenue
Chicago IL 60616
312/808-1286
AMOUNT: $2,000
DEADLINE(S): APR 30
FIELD(S): Music; Music Education; African-American Studies; Folklore; Performing Arts; Arts Management; Journalism; Radio/TV/Film

Scholarship is made on a competitive basis with consideration given to scholastic achievement, concentration of studies, and financial need. Applicant must have full-time enrollment status in a Chicago area college/university in at least their first year of undergraduate studies or a graduate program. Scholastic aptitude extracurricular involvement, grade point average, and financial need are all considered.

Contact Blues Heaven Foundation, Inc. to receive an application between February and April.

212—CALIFORNIA GRANGE FOUNDATION (Deaf Activities Scholarships)

Pat Avila, 2101 Stockton Boulevard
Sacramento CA 95817
Written Inquiry

AMOUNT: Varies
DEADLINE(S): APR 1
FIELD(S): Course work that will be of benefit to the deaf community

Scholarships students entering, continuing, or returning to college to pursue studies that will benefit the deaf community.

Write for information after Feb. 1 of each year.

213—CALIFORNIA SCHOOL LIBRARY ASSOCIATION (Leadership for Diversity Scholarship)

CSLA Office, 1499 Old Bayshore Highway, Suite 142
Burlingame CA 94010
415/692-2350
FAX: 415/692-4956

AMOUNT: $1,000
DEADLINE(S): JUN 1
FIELD(S): School librarian/media teacher

Scholarship for a member of a traditionally underrepresented group enrolled in a California accredited library media teacher credential program. Must intend to work as a library media teacher in a California school library media center for a minimum of three years.

Financial need considered. Send SASE for details to above organization.

214—CALIFORNIA STUDENT AID COMMISSION (Assumption Program of Loans for Education-APLE)

P.O. Box 419026
Rancho Cordova CA 95741-9026
916/526-7590
FAX: 916/526-8002
E-mail: custsvcs@csac.ca.gov
Internet: http://www.csac.ca.gov

AMOUNT: Up to $11,000
DEADLINE(S): JUN 30
FIELD(S): Elementary/Secondary Education

Assumes loan debt for students pursuing K-12 teaching career, in exchange for teaching service. For California resident attending school in California, having completed 60 semester units undergrad study and continuing to be enrolled for at least 10 semester units/equivalent through end of each term. Must provide four consecutive years teaching in CA K-12 public school in designated-subject shortage area, or in school serving many low-income students.

Up to 4,500 awards annually. Must be nominated by participating colleges or school districts with approved teacher preparation programs. Contact the APLE Coordinator at your school or above address.

215—CALIFORNIA STUDENT AID COMMISSION (Child Development Teacher Grants)

P.O. Box 419026
Rancho Cordova CA 95741-9026
916/526-7590
TDD: 916/526-7542
FAX: 916/526-8002
E-mail: custsvcs@csac.ca.gov
Internet: http://www.csac.ca.gov

AMOUNT: $1,000 (2-year colleges); $2,000 (4-year colleges)
DEADLINE(S): None given
FIELD(S): Early Childhood Education

For California residents attending California public/private 2- or 4-year institutions who plan to teach/supervise at a licensed children's center. Must have financial need and at least "C" average. Must be pursuing child development permit at the teacher, site supervisor, or program director level. In return, students must teach full-time in licensed CA children's center for one year for each year of assistance.

Up to 100 grants annually. Renewable for an additional year. For more information, contact your financial aid or early childhood education office, or the California Student Aid Commission.

216—CAREER OPPORTUNITIES FOR YOUTH, INC. (Collegiate Scholarship Program)

P.O. Box 996
Manhattan Beach CA 90266
310/535-4838

AMOUNT: $250 to $1,000
DEADLINE(S): SEP 30
FIELD(S): Engineering, Science, Mathematics, Computer Science, Business Administration, Education, Nursing

For students of Latino/Hispanic background residing in the Southern California area who have completed at least one semester/quarter of study at an accredited four-year university. Must have a cumulative GPA of 2.5 or higher.

Priority will be given to students who demonstrate financial need. Send SASE to above location for details.

217—CIVIL AIR PATROL (CAP Undergraduate Scholarships)

Civil Air Patrol
National Headquarters
Maxwell AFB AL 36112-6332
334/953-5315

AMOUNT: $750
DEADLINE(S): JAN 31
FIELD(S): Humanities; Science; Engineering; Education

Open to CAP members who have received the Billy Mitchell Award or the senior rating in Level II of the senior training program. For undergraduate study in the above areas.

Write for complete information.

218—COMMUNITY FOUNDATION OF WESTERN MASSACHUSETTS (Nate McKinney Memorial Scholarship)

1500 Main Street
P.O. Box 15769
Springfield MA 01115
413/732-2858

AMOUNT: $1,000
DEADLINE(S): APR 15
FIELD(S): Music; Athletics; Science

Open to graduating seniors of Gateway Regional High School in Huntington, Massachusetts. Recipient must excel academically, demonstrate good citizenship, and have a strong interest in at least two of the following areas: music, science, and athletics. Based on financial need, academic merit, and extracurricular activities. Must submit transcripts and fill out government FAFSA form.

1 award annually. Renewable up to 4 years with reapplication. Contact Community Foundation for an application and your financial aid office for FAFSA. Notification is in June.

219—CONTINENTAL SOCIETY DAUGHTERS OF INDIAN WARS (Scholarship)

Route 2, Box 184
Locust Grove OK 74352
918/479-5670

AMOUNT: $1,000
DEADLINE(S): JUN 15
FIELD(S): Education; Social Work; Social Service

Open to Native American, certified tribal members with plans to work on a reservation. Must be an undergraduate junior or senior accepted to or already attending an accredited college/university, be carrying at least eight semester hours, and have a minimum 3.0 GPA. Must be U.S. citizen and demonstrate financial need.

1 award annually. Renewable. Contact Mrs. Ronald Jacobs for an application.

220—EASTER SEAL SOCIETY OF IOWA, INC. (Scholarships and Awards)

P.O. Box 4002
Des Moines IA 50333-4002
515/289-1933
AMOUNT: $400-$600
DEADLINE(S): APR 15
FIELD(S): Physical Rehabilitation, Mental Rehabilitation, and related areas

Open ONLY to Iowa residents who are full-time undergraduate sophomores, juniors, seniors, or graduate students at accredited institutions planning a career in the broad field of rehabilitation. Must indicate financial need and be in top 40% of their class.

6 scholarships per year. Must reapply each year.

221—F.J. CONNELL MUSIC SCHOLARSHIP TRUST

1187 Simcoe Street
Moose Jaw Saskatchewan S6H 3J5
CANADA
306/694-2045
AMOUNT: $750 (Canadian)
DEADLINE(S): OCT 1
FIELD(S): Music

For students studying any aspect of music, such as education, performance, composition, history, etc. Must have completed the equivalent of one year of full-time music studies and be planning a professional career in music. No citizenship or residency requirements, but recipients will usually be Canadians.

Contact above location for details.

222—FOUNDATION FOR EXCEPTIONAL CHILDREN (Minigrant Awards for Teachers)

1920 Association Drive
Reston VA 22091
703/620-1054
AMOUNT: Up to $500
DEADLINE(S): MAR 1
FIELD(S): Education projects for gifted children or for those with disabilities

Minigrant awards for innovative education-related projects benefiting gifted children or children or youth with disabilities. Only for teachers employed by public or nonprofit institutions.

Apply to Minigrant Committee at above location.

223—FOUNDATION FOR TECHNOLOGY EDUCATION (Hearlihy/FTE Grant)

1914 Association Drive, Suite 201
Reston VA 20191-1539
Phone/FAX: 804/559-4226
E-mail: thughes@pen.k12.va.us
Internet: http://www.iteawww.org
AMOUNT: $2,000
DEADLINE(S): DEC 1
FIELD(S): Technology education

Grant for a technology teacher (K-12). Purpose is to recognize and encourage the integration of a quality technology education program within the school curriculum.

Access Web site or contact above organization for details.

224—FOUNDATION FOR TECHNOLOGY EDUCATION (Litherland/FTE Scholarship)

1914 Association Drive, Suite 201
Reston VA 20191-1539
Phone/FAX: 804/559-4226
E-mail: thughes@pen.k12.va.us
Internet: http://www.iteawww.org
AMOUNT: $1,000
DEADLINE(S): DEC 1
FIELD(S): Technology Education Teacher Preparation

Scholarship for an undergraduate student majoring in the above field. Based upon interest in teaching, academic ability, need, and faculty recommendation. Must not be a senior by application deadline and must be a current, full-time undergraduate. Minimum GPA of 2.5 required.

Must be a member of the International Technology Education Association. Membership may be enclosed with scholarship application.

225—FOUNDATION FOR TECHNOLOGY EDUCATION (Undergraduate Scholarship)

1914 Association Drive, Suite 201
Reston VA 20191-1539
Phone/FAX: 804/559-4226
E-mail: thughes@pen.k12.va.us
Internet: http://www.iteawww.org
AMOUNT: $1,000
DEADLINE(S): DEC 1
FIELD(S): Technology Education Teacher Preparation

Scholarship for an undergraduate student majoring in the above field. Based upon interest in teaching, academic ability, need, and faculty recommendation. Must not be a senior by application deadline and must be a current, full-time undergraduate. Minimum GPA of 2.5 required.

Must be a member of the International Technology Education Association. Membership may be enclosed with scholarship application.

226—FRANCIS NATHANIEL AND KATHERYN PADGETT KENNEDY FOUNDATION (Scholarships for Southern Baptists)

933 Sunset Drive
Greenwood SC 29646
803/942-1400
AMOUNT: $400-$1,000
DEADLINE(S): MAY 15
FIELD(S): Theology (in preparation for the ministry or missionary work) or Christian education

Scholarships for college-bound high school seniors and undergraduates who are active members of the a church of the National Baptist Convention. Must be planning a career as a Southern Baptist minister, foreign missionary, or in Christian education.

Send SASE for details.

227—FREEDOM FROM RELIGION FOUNDATION (Student Essay Contest)

P.O. Box 750
Madison WI 53701
608/256-5800
Internet: http://www.infidels.org/org/ffrf
AMOUNT: $1,000; $500; $250
DEADLINE(S): JUL 15
FIELD(S): Humanities; English; Education; Philosophy; Science

Essay contest on topics related to church-state entanglement in public schools or growing up a "freethinker" in religious-oriented society. Topics change yearly, but all are on general theme of maintaining separation of church and state. New topics available in February. For high school seniors and currently enrolled college/technical students. Must be U.S. citizen.

Send SASE to address above for complete information. Please indicate whether wanting information for college competition or high school. Information will be sent when new topics are announced each February. See Web site for details.

228—GENERAL FEDERATION OF WOMEN'S CLUBS OF MASSACHUSETTS (Newtonville Woman's Club Scholarship)

245 Dutton Road, Box 679
Sudbury MA 01776-0679
508/229-2023
AMOUNT: $600
DEADLINE(S): MAR 1
FIELD(S): Education/Teaching

For high school seniors in Massachusetts who will enroll in a four-year accredited college or university in a teacher training program that leads to certification to teach. Letter of endorsement from sponsoring GFWC of MA club, personal letter stating need and pertinent information, letter of recommendation from a high school department head or career counselor, transcripts, and personal interview required with application.

At least one scholarship annually. For more information or an application, send a self-addressed, stamped envelope to Marilyn Perry, Scholarship Chairman, at above address.

229—GRACE FOUNDATION (Scholarship Trust Fund)

P.O. Box 924
Menlo Park CA 94026-0924
Written Inquiry
AMOUNT: $1,000-$4,000
DEADLINE(S): JAN 31
FIELD(S): Ministry; Medicine; Teaching; Social Service

Open to students from developing countries in Asia/Southeast Asia to pursue full-time study at an accredited college/university. For training future Christian ministers and professional workers in above fields. Must have completed one or more years of college in or near their native country, be a strong Christian, have a minimum 3.0 GPA, and demonstrate financial need.

Renewable up to 4 years with maintenance of 3.0 GPA. Applications available between September 1 and October 31.

230—IDAHO STATE BOARD OF EDUCATION (Education Incentive Loan Forgiveness)

P.O. Box 83720
Boise ID 83720-0037
208/334-2270
AMOUNT: Varies
DEADLINE(S): Varies
FIELD(S): Education; Nursing

Open to Idaho residents who have graduated from an Idaho high school within two years, ranking within the top 15% of graduating class or having earned a minimum 3.0 GPA. Must enroll as a full-time student in an Idaho college/university, pursuing a program of study toward an Idaho teaching certificate or licensure by the Board of Nursing as a registered nurse. Must plan to pursue career within Idaho for a minimum of two years.

Renewable. Contact the financial aid office of the Idaho public college/university you plan to attend for an application and deadlines.

231—ILLINOIS STUDENT ASSISTANCE COMMISSION (David A. DeBolt Teacher Shortage Scholarship Program)

1755 Lake Cook Road
Deerfield IL 60015-5209
800/899-ISAC
Internet: http://www.isac1.org
AMOUNT: Tuition, fees, room/board or $5,000
DEADLINE(S): MAY 1
FIELD(S): Education-Teacher Training

Scholarships and loans for Illinois students planning to teach at approved Illinois preschools, elementary schools, or secondary schools in a designated teacher shortage discipline.

300 annual awards. Illinois residency and U.S. citizenship required. Access Web site or write for complete information.

232—ILLINOIS STUDENT ASSISTANCE COMMISSION (Minority Teachers of Illinois Scholarship Program)

1755 Lake Cook Road
Deerfield IL 60015-5209
800/899-ISAC
Internet: http://www.isac1.org
AMOUNT: Tuition, fees, room/board or $5,000
DEADLINE(S): MAY 1
FIELD(S): Education-Teacher Training

Scholarships and loans for Illinois students planning to teach at approved Illinois preschools, elementary schools, or secondary schools.

400 annual awards. Illinois residency and U.S. citizenship required. Access Web site or write for complete information.

233—ILLINOIS STUDENT ASSISTANCE COMMISSION (Special Education Teacher Tuition Waiver Program)

1755 Lake Cook Road
Deerfield IL 60015-5209
800/899-ISAC
Internet: http://www.isac1.org
AMOUNT: Tuition and fees
DEADLINE(S): FEB 15
FIELD(S): Special Education Teacher Training

Waiver of tuition and fees for Illinois students seeking initial certification in special education and who attend Illinois public universities.

300 annual awards. Illinois residency and U.S. citizenship required. Access Web site or write for complete information.

234—INSTITUTE FOR HUMANE STUDIES (Summer Seminars Program)

3401 N. Fairfax Drive, Suite 440
Arlington VA 22201-4432
703/993-4880 or 800/697-8799
FAX: 703/993-4890
E-mail: ihs@gmu.edu
Internet: http://www.TheIHS.org
AMOUNT: Free summer seminars, including room/board, lectures, seminar materials, and books
DEADLINE(S): MAR
FIELD(S): Social Sciences; Humanities; Law; Journalism; Public Policy; Education; Film; Writing; Economics; Philosophy

Open to college students, recent graduates, and graduate students who share an interest in learning and exchanging ideas about the scope of individual rights, free markets, the rule of law, peace, and tolerance.

See Web site for seminar information or to apply online or contact IHS for an application.

235—INTERNATIONAL ORDER OF ALHAMBRA (Scholarship Grants)

Supreme Office
4200 Leeds Avenue
Baltimore MD 21229-5496
410/242-0660
FAX: 410/536-5729
AMOUNT: $400 (max.)
DEADLINE(S): JAN 1; JUL 1
FIELD(S): Special Education

Open to students entering at least their junior or senior year of college in preparation for placement in special education, including teacher training for work with the mentally and physically disabled. Tenable at any accredited public/private college/university where student will earn a minimum of 3 credit hours during semester. With completed application, student must submit letter from school confirming enrollment/major. Graduate and postgraduate awards also available.

Contact the Supreme Office for an application.

236—INTERNATIONAL READING ASSOCIATION (Albert J. Harris Award)

800 Barksdale Road
P.O. Box 8139
Newark DE 19714-8139
302/731-1600 ext. 226
FAX: 302/731-1057
E-mail: gkeating@reading.org

AMOUNT: $500
DEADLINE(S): SEP 15
FIELD(S): Reading Disabilities

This prize recognizes outstanding published works (single- or joint-authored research-based articles) on the topics of reading disabilities and the prevention, assessment, or instruction of learners experiencing difficulty learning to read. Publications that have appeared in a refereed professional journal or monograph from June of the previous year to June of the current year are eligible, and may be submitted by the author or anyone else. IRA membership NOT required.

1 award annually. Contact Gail Keating, Projects Manager, Division of Research and Policy, at above address for guidelines.

237—INTERNATIONAL READING ASSOCIATION (Dina Feitelson Research Award)

800 Barksdale Road
P.O. Box 8139
Newark DE 19714-8139
302/731-1600 ext. 226
FAX: 302/731-1057
E-mail: gkeating@reading.org

AMOUNT: $500
DEADLINE(S): SEP 15
FIELD(S): Beginning Reading

This prize is to recognize an outstanding empirical study, or a literacy- or reading-related topic published in a refereed journal. Article must have been published between June of the previous year and June of the current year, and may be submitted by the author or anyone else. IRA membership is NOT required.

1 award annually. Contact Gail Keating, Projects Manager, Division of Research and Policy, at above address for guidelines.

238—INTERNATIONAL READING ASSOCIATION (Elva Knight Research Grant)

800 Barksdale Road
P.O. Box 8139
Newark DE 19714-8139
302/731-1600 ext. 226
FAX: 302/731-1057
E-mail: gkeating@reading.org

AMOUNT: $5,000 max.
DEADLINE(S): OCT 15
FIELD(S): Reading/Literacy Research

Grant is to assist researcher in a reading and literacy project. Research is defined as inquiry that addresses significant questions about literacy instruction and practice. Open to IRA members worldwide. Projects should be completed within two years.

1 award annually to researcher outside the U.S./Canada, 1 to a teacher-initiated research project, and up to 5 additional grants. For membership information, use extension 267. For guidelines, contact Gail Keating, Projects Manager, Division of Research and Policy, at above address.

239—INTERNATIONAL READING ASSOCIATION (Nila Banton Smith Research Dissemination Support Grant)

800 Barksdale Road
P.O. Box 8139
Newark DE 19714-8139
302/731-1600 ext. 226
FAX: 302/731-1057
E-mail: gkeating@reading.org

AMOUNT: $5,000
DEADLINE(S): OCT 15
FIELD(S): Reading/Literacy Research

Purpose of this award is to facilitate the dissemination of literacy research to the educational community. Open to all IRA members worldwide.

1 award annually. For membership information, use extension 267. For guidelines, contact Gail Keating, Projects Manager, Division of Research and Policy, at above address.

240—INTERNATIONAL READING ASSOCIATION (Teacher as Researcher Grant)

800 Barksdale Road
P.O. Box 8139
Newark DE 19714-8139
302/731-1600 ext. 226
FAX: 302/731-1057
E-mail: gkeating@reading.org

AMOUNT: $1,000-$5,000
DEADLINE(S): OCT 15
FIELD(S): Reading/Literacy Instruction

Award is to support teachers in their inquiries about literacy learning and instruction. IRA members who are practicing K-12 teachers with full-time teaching responsibilities (includes librarians, Title 1 teachers, classroom, and resource teachers) may apply.

Several awards annually. For membership information, use extension 267. For guidelines, contact Gail Keating, Projects Manager, Division of Research and Policy, at above address.

241—JAMES MADISON MEMORIAL FELLOWSHIP FOUNDATION (Fellowships)

2000 K Street NW, Suite 303
Washington DC 20006
202/653-8700
FAX: 202/653-6045
Internet: http://www.jamesmadison.com

AMOUNT: Tuition, fees, books, and room/board
DEADLINE(S): MAR 1
FIELD(S): Education: American History, American Government, Social Studies

Open to U.S. citizens/nationals who are teachers, or planning to become teachers, in above fields at the secondary school level. Must currently possess a bachelor's degree, or plan to receive one no later than August 31. Fellows must teach above subjects in grades 7-12 for no less than one year for each full year of study under the fellowship. Proposed graduate study should contain substantial constitutional coursework.

See Web site or contact Foundation for an application.

242—JEWISH VOCATIONAL SERVICE (Academic Scholarship Program)

One S. Franklin Street
Chicago IL 60606
312/357-4500
FAX: 312/855-3282
TTY: 312/855-3282
E-mail: jvschicago@jon.cjfny.org

AMOUNT: $5,000 (max.)
DEADLINE(S): MAR 1
FIELD(S): "Helping" Professions; Mathematics; Engineering; Sciences; Communications (at Univ IL only); Law (certain schools in IL only)

Open to Jewish men and women legally domiciled in the greater Chicago metropolitan area, who are identified as having promise for significant contributions in their chosen careers, and are in need of financial assistance for full-time academic programs in above areas. Must have entered undergraduate junior year in career programs requiring no postgrad education, be in graduate/professional school, or be in a vo-tech training program. Interview required.

Renewable. Contact JVS for an application between December 1 and February 15.

243—JEWISH WELFARE BOARD (Scholarships)

15 E. 26th Street
New York NY 10010
212/532-4949
AMOUNT: $1,000-$4,000
DEADLINE(S): FEB 1
FIELD(S): Social work, adult education, early childhood education, health education, physical education, cultural studies, Jewish education

Scholarships for Jewish college juniors or seniors pursuing careers in the above fields. Must be committed to the work of the YMHA, YWHA, or Jewish community centers. Must do a year of field work in a Jewish community center.

Renewable. Contact organization for details.

244—KANSAS BOARD OF REGENTS (Kansas Teacher Scholarship)

700 SW Harrison Street, Suite 1410
Topeka KS 66603-3760
785/296-3518
AMOUNT: $5,000/year
DEADLINE(S): APR 1
FIELD(S): Education

For Kansas residents committed to teaching in Kansas. Preference given to students who will teach in special education, secondary science, and vocational/practical arts. May change annually. Graduate work can be funded if it is required for initial certification. If recipient does not teach in Kansas, the scholarship converts to a loan with 15% interest. Must complete the FAFSA.

$10 application fee. Renewable for 4 years (or 5 if a 5-year program). Contact Kansas Board of Regents for an application. See your financial aid office for the FAFSA.

245—LADY ALLEN OF HURTWOOD MEMORIAL TRUST (Travel Grants)

21 Aspull Common
Leigh Lancs WN7 3PB ENGLAND
01942-674895
AMOUNT: Up to 1,000 pounds sterling
DEADLINE(S): JAN 15
FIELD(S): Welfare and Education of Children

A travel grant to those whose proposed project will directly benefit their work with children. People working with children and young people may apply, particularly those working with disabled and disadvantaged children. Successful candidates must write up an account of the work which the scholarship has funded. GRANTS ARE NOT FOR ACADEMIC STUDY; ONLY QUALIFIED INDIVIDUALS MAY APPLY.

Contact Dorothy E. Whitaker, Trustee, for application forms-available between May and December each year.

246—LOUISIANA OFFICE OF STUDENT FINANCIAL ASSISTANCE (Tuition Opportunity Program for Students-Teacher Awards)

P.O. Box 91202
Baton Rouge LA 70821-9202
800/259-5626 ext. 1012
FAX: 225/922-0790
E-mail: custserv@osfa.state.la.us;
Internet: http://www.osfa.state.la.us
AMOUNT: $4,000/year (education majors); $6,000/year (math/chemistry majors)
DEADLINE(S): JUL 1
FIELD(S): Education; Math; Chemistry

Open to Louisiana residents pursuing undergraduate or graduate study at a Louisiana public or LAICU private post-secondary institution. Must major in one of above fields leading to teacher certification. Loans are forgiven by working as a certified teacher in Louisiana one year for each year loan is received. Must be U.S. citizen with a minimum 3.0 GPA. Financial need NOT a factor.

90 awards annually. Renewable. Apply by completing Free Application for Federal Student Aid (FAFSA) and Teacher Award application. Contact Public Information Rep.

247—MIDWAY COLLEGE (Institutional Aid Program)

Financial Aid Office
Midway KY 40347
606/846-4421
AMOUNT: Varies
DEADLINE(S): MAR 1
FIELD(S): Nursing; Paralegal; Education; Psychology; Biology; Equine Studies; Liberal Studies; Business Administration

Scholarships and grants are open to women who are accepted for enrollment at Midway College. Awards support undergraduate study in the above areas.

80 awards annually. Contact Midway College's Financial Aid Office for an application.

248—NATIONAL ASSOCIATION OF AMERICAN BUSINESS CLUBS (AMBUCS Scholarships for Therapists)

P.O. Box 5127
High Point NC 27262
910/869-2166
FAX: 910/887-8451
E-mail: ambucs@ambucs.com;
Internet: http://www.ambucs.com
AMOUNT: $500-$6,000
DEADLINE(S): APR 15
FIELD(S): Physical Therapy, Music Therapy, Occupational Therapy, Speech-Language Pathology, Audiology, Rehabilitation, Recreation Therapy, and related areas

Open to undergraduate juniors and seniors or graduate students who have good scholastic standing and plan to enter the fields listed above. GPA of 3.0 or better (4.0 scale) and U.S. citizenship required. Must demonstrate financial need.

Renewable. Please include a self-addressed stamped envelope (SASE); applications are mailed in December; incomplete applications will not be considered.

249—NATIONAL CLEARINGHOUSE FOR PROFESSIONS IN SPECIAL EDUCATION (Various Financial Aid Sources)

NCPSE, 1920 Association Drive
Reston VA 20191-1589
800/641-7824 or 783/264-9476
or TTY: 703/264-9480
E-mail: ncpse@cec.sped.org
Internet: http://www.cec.sped.org/ncpse.htm
AMOUNT: Varies
DEADLINE(S): Varies
FIELD(S): Special education

A listing of financial aid resources through the U.S. Dept. of Education, Office of Special education Programs for training professionals in the field of special education. Funds are available through certain colleges and universities. Applicants may be eligible to have all or part of their college tuition paid and receive an annual stipend.

For listing of of colleges and universities who have received these funds, contact NCPSE for information. State your level in college, the states in which you are interested, and the specialty areas in which you would like to concentrate.

250—NATIONAL FEDERATION OF THE BLIND (Educator of Tomorrow Award)

805 Fifth Avenue
Grinnell IA 50112
515/236-3366
AMOUNT: $3,000
DEADLINE(S): MAR 31
FIELD(S): Education: Elementary, Secondary, and Postsecondary

For legally blind students pursuing or planning to pursue a full-time postsecondary course of study in the U.S.. Based on academic excellence, service to the community, and financial need. Membership NOT required.

1 award annually. Renewable. Contact Mrs. Peggy Elliot, Scholarship Committee Chairman, for an application.

251—NATIONAL SCHOOL SUPPLY AND EQUIPMENT ASSOCIATION-EDUCATION EXCELLENCE FOUNDATION (Be Your Best! Teacher Scholarships)

8300 Colesville Road, Suite 250
Silver Spring MD 20910
301/495-0240 or 800/395-5550
FAX: 301/495-3330
Internet: http://www.nssea.org
AMOUNT: $500
DEADLINE(S): JUN 30
FIELD(S): Teacher education

Scholarships for teachers who can demonstrate a need for professional development.

20 awards to be made.

252—NATIONAL STRENGTH AND CONDITIONING ASSOCIATION (Challenge Scholarships)

P.O. Box 9908
Colorado Springs CO 80932-0908
719/632-6722
FAX: 719/632-6722
E-mail: nsca@usa.net
Internet: http://www.colosoft.com/nsca
AMOUNT: $1,000
DEADLINE(S): MAR 1
FIELD(S): Body Strength and Conditioning

Open to National Strength and Conditioning Association members to pursue undergraduate or graduate study in fields related to body strength and conditioning.

Contact NSCA for an application or membership information.

253—NATIVE AMERICAN SCHOLARSHIP FUND, INC. (Scholarships)

8200 Mountain Road NE, Suite 203
Albuquerque NM 87110
505/262-2351
FAX: 505/262-0543
E-mail: NScholarsh@aol.com
AMOUNT: Varies
DEADLINE(S): MAR 15; APR 15; SEP 15
FIELD(S): Math; Engineering; Science; Business; Education; Computer Science

Open to American Indians or Alaskan Natives (1/4 degree or more) enrolled as members of a federally recognized, state recognized, or terminated tribe. For graduate or undergraduate study at an accredited four-year college or university.

208 awards annually. Contact Lucille Kelley, Director of Recruitment, for an application.

254—NATURAL SCIENCES AND ENGINEERING RESEARCH COUNCIL OF CANADA (Undergraduate Student Research Awards in Small Universities)

350 Albert Street
Ottawa Ontario K1A 1H5 CANADA
613/995-5992
FAX: 613/992-5337
E-mail: schol@nserc.ca
Internet: http://www.nserc.ca/programs/usrasmen.htm
AMOUNT: $3,600 (max.)
DEADLINE(S): Varies
FIELD(S): Natural Sciences; Engineering

Research awards for Canadian citizens/permanent residents attending eligible institutions, and who have no more than 6 and no fewer than 2 academic terms remaining to complete bachelor's degree. Cumulative GPA of at least 2nd class (B). Must be doing full-time in research and development activities during award tenure.

Students in health sciences not eligible. Students with BAs and who are studying for a second may apply.

255—NAVAL HISTORICAL CENTER (Internship Program)

Washington Navy Yard
901 M Street, SE
Washington DC 20374-5060
202/433-6901
FAX: 202/433-8200
E-mail: efurgol@nhc.navy.mil
Internet: http://www.history.navy.mil
AMOUNT: $400 possible honoraria; otherwise, unpaid
DEADLINE(S): None
FIELD(S): Education; History; Public Relations; Design

Registered students of colleges/universities and graduates thereof are eligible for this program, which must be a minimum of 3 weeks, full- or part-time. Four specialties available: Curator, Education, Public Relations, and Design. Interns receive orientation and assist in their departments, and must complete individual project which contributes to Center. Must submit a letter of recommendation, unofficial transcript, and writing sample of not less than 1,000 words.

Contact Dr. Edward M. Furgol, Curator, for an application.

256—NEW ZEALAND FEDERATION OF UNIVERSITY WOMEN-WAIKATO BRANCH (Kahurangi Maori Language Award)

P.O. Box 7065
Hamilton NEW ZEALAND
07/855-3776
AMOUNT: $1,000
DEADLINE(S): MAR 15
FIELD(S): Education; Maori Studies

Open to Maori women who are full-time students enrolled for a third or fourth year at the University of Waikato School of Education or the Department of Maori Studies. Must be fluent in or studying the Maori language for a Bachelor of Education degree or Diploma of Teaching.

Contact the Convenor, NAFUW, Waikato Branch for an application.

257—NEW ZEALAND FEDERATION OF UNIVERSITY WOMEN-WAIKATO BRANCH (Kahurangi Maori Language Award)

P.O. Box 7065
Hamilton NEW ZEALAND
07/855-3776
AMOUNT: $1,000
DEADLINE(S): MAR 15
FIELD(S): Education; Maori Studies

Open to Maori women who are full-time students enrolled for a third or fourth year at the University of Waikato School of Education or the Department of Maori Studies. Must be fluent in or studying the Maori language for a Bachelor of Education degree or Diploma of Teaching.

Contact the Convenor, NAFUW, Waikato Branch for an application.

258—NORTH CAROLINA DEPARTMENT OF PUBLIC INSTRUCTION (Scholarship Loan Program for Prospective Teachers)

301 N. Wilmington Street
Raleigh NC 27601-2825
919/715-1120
AMOUNT: Up to $2,500/year
DEADLINE(S): FEB
FIELD(S): Education: Teaching, school psychology and counseling, speech/language impaired, audiology, library/media services

For NC residents planning to teach in NC public schools. At least 3.0 high school GPA required; must maintain 2.5 GPA during freshman year and 3.0 cumulative thereafter. Recipients are obligated to teach one year in an NC public school for each year of assistance. Those who do not fulfill their teaching obligation are required to repay the loan plus interest.

200 awards per year. For full-time students. Applications available in Dec. from high school counselors and college and univerwity departments of education.

259—NORTH CAROLINA DEPT. OF PUBLIC INSTRUCTION (Teacher Assistant Scholarship Loan)

301 N. Wilmington Street
Raleigh NC 27601-2825
919/715-1120
AMOUNT: Up to $1,200/yr
DEADLINE(S): JAN
FIELD(S): Education: Teaching, school psychology or counseling, speech/language impaired, audiology, library/media services

For NC residents employed as K-12 teaching assistants in public schools who wish to pursue teacher licensure. Must either hold a BA degree or have completed general college courses prerequisite to admission to degree program and be admitted to an approved teacher education program at a four-year institution. Two-year community college early childhood education program is acceptable.

Must remain employed as teaching assistant while pursuing licensure and teach one year in an NC public school for each year of assistance received. Applications available in Sept. from local school superintendent.

260—PHI DELTA KAPPA (Scholarship Grants for Prospective Educators)

408 N. Union Street
P.O. Box 789
Bloomington IN 47402-0789
812/339-1156
FAX: 812/339-0018
E-mail: headquarters@PDKintl.org
Internet: http://www.PDKintl.org
AMOUNT: $1,000-$5,000
DEADLINE(S): JAN 31
FIELD(S): Education/Teaching Career

Undergraduate scholarships for high school seniors who plan to pursue a college major in education and to become teachers.

51 annual awards.

261—PHI DELTA KAPPA, INC. (Scholarship Grants for Prospective Educators)

408 N. Union Street
P.O. Box 789
Bloomington IN 47402-0789
812/339-1156
FAX: 812/339-0018
E-mail: headquarters@pdkimtl.org
Internet: http://www.pdkimtl.org
AMOUNT: $1,000 (45); $2,000 (1); $5,000 (1); $4,000 (1)
DEADLINE(S): JAN 15
FIELD(S): Education/Teacher Training

Open to high school seniors who plan to pursue careers as teachers or educators. Based on scholastic achievement, school/community activities, recommendations, and an essay. Must be U.S. or Canadian citizen or legal resident. Financial need NOT considered.

53 awards annually. See Web site or send self-addressed, stamped envelope to Shari Bradley at above address for an application.

262—PHILADELPHIA COLLEGE OF BIBLE (Scholarships, Grants, and Loans)

Financial Aid Dept.
200 Manor Avenue
Langhorne PA 19047
800/366-0049
Internet: http://www.pcb.edu
AMOUNT: Varies
DEADLINE(S): Varies
FIELD(S): Fields of study relating to Christian education

Various scholarships, loans, and grants are available to students attending this undergraduate Bible college in Phila-delphia, PA. High school seniors, transfer students, and others may apply. Some programs are for students with outstanding academic achievement, musical talent, or leaderships skills. Some are for dependents of Christian workers, missionaries, or alumni. Some are based on financial need.

Access Web site for details and/or send SASE to school for further information.

263—PI LAMBDA THETA (Distinguished Student Scholar Award for Education Majors)

P.O. Box 6626
Bloomington IN 47401-5599
812/339-3411
FAX: 812/339-3462
E-mail: pam@pilambda.org
Internet: http://www.pilambda.org
AMOUNT: $500
DEADLINE(S): NOV 1
FIELD(S): Education

Award for an outstanding undergraduate student who is an education major and is at least a second-semester sophomore. Membership in Pi Lambda Theta not required. GPA of 3.5 required. Must demonstrate leadership potential and a strong dedication to the field of education. Nomination must be made by a college/university instructor, professor, or supervisor.

Contact above location for details.

264—PI LAMBDA THETA (Thelma Jean Brown Classroom Teacher Award)

P.O. Box 6626
Bloomington IN 47401-5599
812/339-3411
FAX: 812/339-3462
E-mail: pam@pilambda.org
Internet: http://www.pilambda.org
AMOUNT: $500
DEADLINE(S): FEB 10
FIELD(S): Classroom Teacher, K-12

Award for an outstanding classroom teacher in grades K-12 in a public or parochial school which is not exceptionally well supported financially. Must demonstrate ability to build supportive and effective relationships with students, parents, and co-workers and an exceptional commitment to teaching. Nomination must be made by a Pi Lambda Theta member in good standing.

Contact above location for details.

265—PILOT INTERNATIONAL FOUNDATION (PIF/Lifeline Scholarship)

P.O. Box 5600
Macon GA 31208-5600
Written Inquiries
AMOUNT: Varies
DEADLINE(S): MAR 1
FIELD(S): Disabilities/Brain-related Disorders

This program assists ADULT students re-entering the job market, preparing for a second career, or improving their professional skills for an established career. Applicants must be preparing for, or already involved in, careers working with people with disabilities/brain-related disorders. GPA of 3.5 or more is required.

Must be sponsored by a Pilot Club in your home town, or in the city in which your college or university is located. Send a self-addressed, stamped envelope for complete information.

266—PILOT INTERNATIONAL FOUNDATION (Ruby Newhall Memorial Scholarship)

P.O. Box 5600
Macon, GA 31208-5600
Written Inquiries
AMOUNT: Varies
DEADLINE(S): MAR 15
FIELD(S): Disabilities/Brain-related disorders

For international students who have studied in the U.S. for at least one year, and who intend to return to their home country six months after graduation. Applicants must be full-time students majoring in a field related to human health and welfare, and have a GPA of 3.5 or more.

Applicants must be sponsored by a Pilot Club in their home town, or in the city in which their college or university is located. Send a self-addressed, stamped envelope for complete information.

267—PILOT INTERNATIONAL FOUNDATION (The Pilot International Scholarship Program)

P.O. Box 5600
Macon GA 31208-5600
Written Inquiries
AMOUNT: Varies
DEADLINE(S): MAR 1
FIELD(S): Disabilities/Brain-related disorders

This program provides assistance to undergraduate students preparing for careers working directly with people with disabilities or training those who will. GPA of 3.5 or greater required.

Applicants must be sponsored by a Pilot Club in their home town, or in the city in which their college or university is located. Send a self-addressed, stamped envelope for complete information.

268—ROEHER INSTITUTE (Bursaries for College Students)

Kinsman Bldg.; York University
4700 Keele Street
North York Ontario M3J 1P3
CANADA
416/661-9611
AMOUNT: Up to $2,000
DEADLINE(S): JUL 1
FIELD(S): Intellectual Disability

Open to students enrolled full-time in Canadian community colleges who are recommended by the provincial association for the mentally challenged in their province. Must be Canadian citizen or legal resident.

Contact Provincial Association or address above for complete information.

269—SCOTTISH RITE CHARITABLE FOUNDATION (Bursaries for College Students)

Roeher Institute, Kinsmen Bldg.;
4700 Keele Street
North York Ontario M3J 1P3
CANADA
416/661-9611; TDD: 416/661-2023
FAX: 416/661-5701
E-mail: mail@aacl.org
Internet: http://www.aacl.org
AMOUNT: $2,000 (max.)
DEADLINE(S): JUL 1
FIELD(S): Human Services; Intellectual Disability; Special Education; DSW

Open to Canadian citizens/landed immigrants accepted into a full-time undergraduate college program in a Canadian college/university. Must submit outline of intended study, transcripts, community involvement, and letters of reference from supervisors. Financial need NOT a factor.

3 awards annually. Must be recommended by a Provincial Association of the Canadian Association for Community Living. Contact your provincial association for details.

270—SRP/NAVAJO GENERATING STATION (Navajo Scholarship)

P.O. Box 850
Page AZ 86040
520/645-6539
FAX: 520/645-7295
E-mail: ljdawave@srp.gov
AMOUNT: Based on need
DEADLINE(S): APR 30
FIELD(S): Engineering, Environmental Studies, Business, Business Management, Health, Education

Scholarships for full-time students who hold membership in the Navajo Tribe and who are pursuing a degree in a field of study recognized as significant to the Navajo Naiton, Salt River Project, or the Navajo Generating Station, such as those listed above. Must be junior or senior, have and maintain a GPA of 3.0

Average of 15 awards per year. Inquire of Linda Dawavendewa at above location.

271—STATE STUDENT ASSISTANCE COMMISSION OF INDIANA (Scholarships for Special Education Teachers and Physical/Occupational Therapists)

150 W. Market Street, 5th Floor
Indianapolis IN 46204
317/232-2350
FAX: 317/232-3260
E-mail: grants@ssaci.in.us
Internet: http://www.ai.org/ssaci/
AMOUNT: $1,000
DEADLINE(S): Varies (with college)
FIELD(S): Special Education; Physical and Occupational Therapy

Open to Indiana residents pursuing full-time undergraduate or graduate study in special education or physical or occupational therapy at an Indiana college/university. Must be U.S. citizen, have a minimum 2.0 GPA, and demonstrate financial need.

See Web site or contact SSACI for an application.

272—TENNESSEE STUDENT ASSISTANCE CORPORATION (TSAC Minority Teaching Fellows Program)

404 James Robertson Parkway
Nashville TN 37243-0820
615/532-3499 or 800/447-1523
FAX: 615/741-5555
AMOUNT: $5,000/year (max. $20,000)
DEADLINE(S): APR 15
FIELD(S): Education

For minority Tennessee residents who are attending Tennessee institutions and studying to be teachers. Entering freshmen must have at least a 2.75 high school GPA, and continuing college students must have a minimum 2.5 college GPA. Must also be in top 25% of class or have at least 18 ACT or 850 SAT. Recipients must agree to teach at a K-12 level Tennessee public school one year for each year the award is received.

Apply at your high school guidance office, college financial aid office, or contact Michael C. Roberts, Student Aid Compliance Administrator, at above address.

273—THE AMERICAN CLASSICAL LEAGUE (Ed Phinney Commemorative Scholarship)

Miami University
Oxford OH 45056
513/529-7741
FAX: 513/529-7742
E-mail: AmericanClassicalLeague @muohio.edu or a.c.l@mich.edu
Internet: http://www.umich.edu/~acleague/phinney.html

AMOUNT: Up to $500
DEADLINE(S): JAN 15
FIELD(S): Teachers or teacher candidates in the classics (Latin and/or Greek)

Scholarships of up to $500 to apply to first-time attendance at the League's institute OR up to $500 to cover cost of other activities that serve to enhance a teacher's skills in the classroom in the classics OR up to $150 for purchase of materials from the ACL Teaching and Materials Resource Center. Memberships required except for first-time attendance at institute.

Send request for information to above address.

274—THE COUNCIL FOR EXCEPTIONAL CHILDREN (Black Caucus Scholarship)

1920 Association Drive
Reston VA 20191-1589
Internet: http://www.cec.sped.org

AMOUNT: $500
DEADLINE(S): DEC 2
FIELD(S): Special education

Scholarship for a student pursuing a degree in Special Education and who is of African American background. Must be U.S. or Canadian citizen. Must be a student member of the Council for Exceptional Children. Minimum GPA of 2.5 required.

Write to Coordinator of Student Activities at above address or visit Web site for further information. Application is on Web site.

275—THE COUNCIL FOR EXCEPTIONAL CHILDREN (Ethnic Diversity Scholarship)

1920 Association Drive
Reston VA 20191-1589
Internet: http://www.cec.sped.org

AMOUNT: $500
DEADLINE(S): DEC 2
FIELD(S): Special education

Scholarship for a student pursuing a degree in Special Education and who is a member of one of these groups: African American, American Indian, Alaska Native, or Native Canadian, Hispanic, Asian, or Pacific Islander. Must be U.S. or Canadian citizen. Must be a student member of the Council for Exceptional Children. Minimum GPA of 2.5 required.

Write to Coordinator of Student Activities at above address or visit Web site for further information. Application is on Web site.

276—THE WALT DISNEY COMPANY (American Teacher Awards)

P.O. Box 9805
Calabasas CA 91372

AMOUNT: $2,500 (36 awards); $25,000 (Outstanding Teacher of the Year)
DEADLINE(S): FEB 15
FIELD(S): Teachers: Athletic Coach, Early Childhood, English, Foreign Language/ESL, General Elementary, Mathematics, Performing Arts, Physical Education/Health, Science, Social Studies, Visual Arts, Voc/Tech Education

Awards for K-12 teachers in the above fields.

Teachers, or anyone who knows a great teacher, can write for applications at the above address.

277—UNIVERSITY OF NORTH TEXAS (Scholarships for Elementary and Secondary Education Majors)

P.O. Box 311337
Denton TX 76203-1337
940/565-2992 (Elem.) or 940/565-2826 (Secondary)
Internet: http://www.unt.edu/scholarships/gelem.htm AND http://www.unt.edu/scholarships/teacher.htm

AMOUNT: Varies
DEADLINE(S): Varies
FIELD(S): Education: Elementary and Secondary Teaching

Several scholarships for students in the teacher education departments at the University of North Texas. Eligibility requirements vary.

See Web site for more information. Write to either Dept. of Elementary, Early Childhood, and Reading Education OR Dept. of Teacher Education and Administration/Secondary Education for details.

278—UNIVERSITY OF WYOMING (Superior Students in Education Scholarship)

College of Education
Undergraduate Studies Office
McWhinnie Hall, Room 100
P.O. Box 3374
Laramie WY 82071-3374
307/766-2533

AMOUNT: Varies
DEADLINE(S): OCT
FIELD(S): Education

For Wyoming high school graduates who have demonstrated high scholastic achievement and qualities of leadership and who plan to teach in Wyoming public schools. May attend the University of Wyoming or any community college in the state and major in education. Based on residency, ACT scores, grades, courses taken, school activities, letters of recommendation, and student responses to prepared questions. Must maintain a 2.5 GPA to remain in program.

16 awards annually. Renewable up to ten semesters (no more than five may be at a community college). Contact the University of Wyoming's College of Education Undergraduate Studies Office for an application.

279—WOMEN'S SPORTS FOUNDATION (Jackie Joyner-Kersee and Zina Garrison Minority Internships)

Eisenhower Park
East Meadow NY 11554
800/227-3988
FAX: 516/542-4716
E-mail: WoSport@aol.com
Internet: http://www.lifetimetv.com/WoSport

AMOUNT: $4,000-$5,000
DEADLINE(S): Ongoing
FIELD(S): Sports-related fields

Provides women of color an opportunity to gain experience in a sports-related career and interact in the sports community. May be undergraduates, college graduates, graduate students, or women in a career change. Internships are located at the Women's Sports Foundation in East Meadow, New York.

4-6 awards annually. See Web site or write to above address for details.

280—WORLD LEISURE AND RECREATION ASSOCIATION (Scholarships)

WLRA Secretariat; Site 81C Comp 0
Okanagan Falls BC V0H 1R0
CANADA
250/497-6578
E-mail: secretariat@worldleisure.org
Internet: http://www.worldleisure.org
AMOUNT: Varies
DEADLINE(S): FEB 1
FIELD(S): Recreation and Leisure Studies

Scholarships intended to allow college seniors or graduate students in recreation or leisure services programs to attend international meetings/conferences or conventions, thereby gaining a broader perspective of world leisure and recreation.

See Web site or contact WLRA for an application.

281—Y'S MEN INTERNATIONAL-U.S. AREA (Alexander Scholarship Loan Fund)

12405 W. Lewis Avenue
Avondale AZ 85323-6518
Written Inquiry
AMOUNT: $1,000-$1,500/year
DEADLINE(S): MAY 30; OCT 30
FIELD(S): Business Administration; Youth Leadership

Open to U.S. citizens/permanent residents with a strong desire to pursue professional YMCA service. Must be YMCA staff pursuing undergraduate or graduate study and demonstrate financial need. Repayment of loan is waived if recipient enters YMCA employment after graduation.

Send self-addressed, business-sized envelope plus $1 for postage and handling to above address for an application.

282—ZETA PHI BETA SORORITY EDUCATIONAL FOUNDATION (Isabel M. Herson Scholarship in Education)

1734 New Hampshire Avenue NW
Washington DC 20009
Internet: http://www.zpb1920.org/nefforms.htm
AMOUNT: $500-$1,000
DEADLINE(S): FEB 1
FIELD(S): Elementary and Secondary Education

Open to graduate and undergraduate level students enrolled in a degree program in either elementary or secondary education. Award is for full-time study for one academic year (Fall-Spring). Must submit proof of enrollment.

Send self-addressed, stamped envelope to above address between September 1 and December 15 for an application.

SCHOOL OF ENGINEERING

283—AIR FORCE RESERVE OFFICER TRAINING CORPS (AFROTC Scholarships)

551 E. Maxwell Boulevard
Maxwell AFB AL 36112-6106
334/953-7783
AMOUNT: Full tuition, books, and fees for all 4 years of college
DEADLINE(S): DEC 1
FIELD(S): Science; Engineering; Business; Political Science; Psychology; Geography; Foreign Studies; Foreign Language

Competitive scholarships based on individual merit to high school seniors and graduates who have not completed any full-time college work. Must be a U.S. citizen between the ages of 17-27. Must also have GPA of 2.5 or above, be in top 40% of class, and complete Applicant Fitness Test. Cannot be a single parent. Your college/university must offer AFROTC.

2,300 awards annually. Contact above address for application packet.

284—AMERICAN FOUNDATION FOR THE BLIND (Paul W. Ruckes Scholarship)

11 Penn Plaza, Suite 300
New York NY 10001
212/502-7661
FAX: 212/502-7771
E-mail: juliet@afb.org
Internet: http://www.afb.org
AMOUNT: $1,000
DEADLINE(S): APR 30
FIELD(S): Engineering; Computer/Physical/Life Sciences

Open to legally blind and visually impaired undergraduate and graduate students pursuing a degree in one of above fields. Must be U.S. citizen. Must submit written documentation of visual impairment from ophthalmologist or optometrist (need not be legally blind); official transcripts; proof of college/university acceptance; three letters of recommendation; and typewritten statement describing goals, work experience extracurricular activities, and how monies will be used.

1 award annually. See Web site or contact Julie Tucker at AFB for an application.

285—AMERICAN HEALTH AND BEAUTY AIDS INSTITUTE (Fred Luster, Sr. Education Foundation Scholarships for College-Bound High School Seniors)

401 North Michigan Avenue
Chicago IL 60611-4267
312/644-6610
AMOUNT: $250 and $500
DEADLINE(S): APR 15
FIELD(S): Chemistry, Business, or Engineering

For college-bound high school seniors who will be enrolled as a college freshman in a four-year college majoring in chemistry, business, or engineering. 3.0 GPA required.

Send two letters of recommendation (one from a school official) and high school transcript. Scholastic record, school activities, and extracurricular activities considered.

286—AMERICAN INDIAN SCIENCE AND ENGINEERING SOCIETY (A.T. Anderson Memorial Scholarship)

P.O. Box 9828
Albuquerque NM 87119-9828
505/765-1052
FAX: 505/765-5608
E-mail: scholarships@aises.org
Internet: http://www.aises.org/scholarships
AMOUNT: $1,000-$2,000
DEADLINE(S): JUN 15
FIELD(S): Medicine; Natural Resources; Science; Engineering

Open to undergraduate and graduate students who are at least 1/4 American Indian or recognized as member of a tribe. Must be member of AISES ($10 fee), enrolled full-time at an accredited institution, and demonstrate financial need.

Renewable. See Web site or contact Patricia Browne for an application and/or membership information.

287—AMERICAN INDIAN SCIENCE AND ENGINEERING SOCIETY (Burlington Northern Santa Fe Pacific Foundation Scholarships)

P.O. Box 9828
Albuquerque NM 87119-9828
505/765-1052
FAX: 505/765-5608
E-mail: scholarships@aises.org
Internet: http://www.aises.org/scholarships
AMOUNT: $2,500/year

DEADLINE(S): MAR 31
FIELD(S): Business; Education; Science; Engineering; Health Administration

Open to high school seniors who are at least 1/4 American Indian. Must reside in KS, OK, CO, AZ, NM, MN, ND, OR, SD, WA, MT, or San Bernardino County, CA (Burlington Northern and Santa Fe Pacific service areas). Must demonstrate financial need.

5 awards annually. Renewable up to 4 years. See Web site or contact Patricia Browne for an application.

288—AMERICAN RADIO RELAY LEAGUE FOUNDATION (The Henry Broughton, K2AE Memorial Scholarship)

225 Main Street
Newington CT 06111
860/594-0200
FAX: 860/594-0259
Internet: http://www.arrl.org/
AMOUNT: $1,000
DEADLINE(S): FEB 1
FIELD(S): Engineering; Science

For radio amateurs with a general class license whose home residence is within 70 miles of Schenectady, New York. For study leading to a bachelor's degree at an accredited four-year college/university.

1+ awards annually. Contact ARRL for an application.

289—AMERICAN SOCIETY OF ENGINEERS OF INDIAN ORIGIN (Undergraduate Scholarship Programs)

P.O. Box 49494
Atlanta GA 30359-1494
770/451-2299
Internet: http://www.iasf.org/asei.htm
AMOUNT: Up to $1,000
DEADLINE(S): AUG 15
FIELD(S): Engineering Fields: Architecture, Computer Technology, Geotechnical or Geoenvironmental Engineering, and allied sciences

Several scholarships for undergraduate engineering students in the above fields who were born in India or who are Indian by ancestry or relation. For study in the U.S. Some programs have residency requirements in certain states.

Contact Dr. Narsi Narasimhan at above location for applications and details.

290—AMERICAN SOCIETY OF NAVAL ENGINEERS SCHOLARSHIP

1452 Duke Street
Alexandria VA 22314-3458
703/836-6727
Internet: http://www.navalengineers.org
AMOUNT: Up to $3,500
DEADLINE(S): FEB
FIELD(S): Engineering

Application must be for support for the last year of a full-time or co-op undergraduate program or for one year of full-time graduate study leading to a designated engineering or physical science degree in an accredited college or university. A scholarship will not be awarded to a doctoral candidate or to a person already having an advanced degree.

291—AMERICAN WATER WORKS ASSOCIATION (Holly A. Cornell Scholarship)

Annette Carabetta
Scholarship Coordinator
6666 West Quincy Avenue
Denver CO 80235
303/347-6206
FAX: 303/794-6303
E-mail: acarabetta@awwa.org
AMOUNT: $5,000
DEADLINE(S): Mid JAN
FIELD(S): Engineering

Female and/or minority (as defined by the U.S. Equal Employment Opportunity Commission) U.S. citizens who are currently Master's degree students and anticipate completion of the requirements for a Master's degree in engineering Students who have been accepted into graduate school but have not yet begun graduate study are encouraged to apply.

292—ASSOCIATION OF CALIFORNIA WATER AGENCIES (ACWA)

910 K Street, Suite 100
Sacramento CA 95814
916/441-4545
Internet: http://www.acwanet.com
AMOUNT: $1500
DEADLINE(S): APR 1
FIELD(S): Engineering

ACWA's awards are not based solely on scholastic achievement but also on the individual's commitment and motivation to their chosen field. Financial need will also be considered. Must submit at least two letters of recommendation.

293—ASSOCIATION OF STATE DAM SAFETY OFFICIALS (Scholarship)

450 Old Vine Street, Second Floor
Lexington KY 40507
606/257-5140
Internet: http://www.damsafety.org
AMOUNT: $5000
DEADLINE(S): FEB 2
FIELD(S): Engineering

Successful recipients must be U.S. citizens enrolled as juniors or seniors in an accredited civil engineering program. Must demonstrate an interest in a career in hydraulics, hydrology, or geotechnical disciplines. Minimum 3.0 GPA.

294—ASSOCIATED WESTERN UNIVERSITIES, INC. (AWU Undergraduate Student Fellowships)

4190 S. Highland Drive, Suite 211
Salt Lake City UT 84124-2600
801/273-8900
FAX: 801/277-5632
E-mail: info@awu.org
Internet: http://www.awu.org
AMOUNT: $300/week stipend + possible travel allowance
DEADLINE(S): FEB 1
FIELD(S): Science; Mathematics; Engineering; Technology

Eight- to sixteen-week fellowships.

295—NATIONAL AIR AND SPACE MUSEUM (Verville Fellowship)

955 L'Enfant Plaza, Suite 700
Washington DC 20560
202/287-3271
Internet: http://www.nasm.edu
AMOUNT: $35,000
DEADLINE(S): JAN 15
FIELD(S): Engineering

Nine- to twelve-month in-residence fellowship candidates who provide a critical approach to trends and accomplishments in aviation or space history. Good writing skills required. Advanced degree is not required.

Scholarships are open to undergraduates enrolled in accredited institutions and who have completed at least one year of college by start of fellowship. Based on academic performance/class standing, career goals, recommendations, and compatibility of scientific interests/abilities with needs/resources of host facility. Citizenship restrictions may apply for some facilities.

500+ awards annually. Renewable. See Web site or contact AWU for an application and list of participating laboratories.

296—ASSOCIATION FOR WOMEN IN SCIENCE EDUCATIONAL FOUNDATION (Ruth Satter Memorial Award)

1200 New York Avenue NW,
Suite 650
Washington DC 20005
202/326-8940 or 800/886-AWIS
E-mail: awis@awis.org
Internet: http://www.awis.org

AMOUNT: $1,000
DEADLINE(S): JAN 16
FIELD(S): Various Sciences and Social Sciences

Scholarships for female doctoral students who have interrupted their education three years or more to raise a family. Summary page, description of research project, resume, references, transcripts, biographical sketch, and proof of eligibility from department head required. U.S. citizens may attend any graduate institution; noncitizens must be enrolled in U.S. institutions.

See Web site or write to above address for more information or an application.

297—ASTRONAUT SCHOLARSHIP FOUNDATION (Scholarships)

Exec. Director
6225 Vectorspace Boulevard
Titusville FL 32780
321/269-6119
FAX: 321/267-3970
E-mail: MercurySvn@aol.com
Internet: http://www.astronaut scholarship.org/guidelines.html

AMOUNT: Varies
DEADLINE(S): Varies
FIELD(S): Engineering and Physical Sciences (Medical Research ok, but NOT Professional Medicine)

Open to juniors, seniors, and graduate students at a select group of schools. Must be U.S. citizen with the intention to pursue research or advance field of study upon completion of final degree. Special consideration given to students who have shown initiative, creativity, excellence, and/or resourcefulness in their field. Must be NOMINATED by faculty or staff.

See Web site for list of eligible schools. Contact Howard Benedict, Executive Director, for details.

298—AT&T BELL LABORATORIES (Summer Research Program for Minorities and Women)

101 Crawfords Corner Road
Holmdel NJ 07733-3030
Written Inquiry

AMOUNT: Salary + travel and living expences for summer
DEADLINE(S): DEC 1
FIELD(S): Engineering; Math; Sciences; Computer Science

Program offers minority students and women students technical employment experience at Bell Laboratories. Students should have completed their third year of study at an accredited college or university. U.S. citizen or permanent resident.

Selection is based partially on academic achievement and personal motivation. Write special programs manager-SRP for complete information.

299—B.F. GOODRICH (Collegiate Inventors Program)

c/o Inventure Place
221 South Broadway Street
Akron OH 44308-1505
330/849-6887
Internet: http://www.invent.org/bfg/bfghome.html

AMOUNT: $7,500 (graduate); $3,000 (undergraduate)
DEADLINE(S): JUN 1
FIELD(S): Engineering

Competition is open to U.S. graduate and undergraduate students studying full time. Applicants should submit an original invention or idea that has not been made public. Applications are available online in PDF format.

300—BARRY GOLDWATER SCHOLARSHIP AND EXCELLENCE IN EDUCATION FOUNDATION (Scholarships)

6225 Brandon Avenue, Suite 315
Springfield VA 22150-2519
703/756-6012
FAX: 703/756-6015
E-mail: GOLDH2o@erols.com
Internet: http://www.act.org/goldwater

AMOUNT: $7,500/year (max.)
DEADLINE(S): FEB 1
FIELD(S): Math; Natural Sciences; Engineering

Open to college sophomores and juniors with a minimum 3.0 GPA. Must be U.S. citizen, resident alien, or American national pursuing a degree at an accredited institution in math, natural sciences, or engineering disciplines that contribute to technological advances.

300 awards annually. See Web site or contact your Goldwater Faculty Representative on campus. Students must be nominated by their institution and cannot apply on their own.

301—BOYS AND GIRLS CLUBS OF SAN DIEGO (Spence Reese Scholarship Fund)

1761 Hotel Circle So., Suite 123
San Diego CA 92108
619/298-3520

AMOUNT: $2,000/year
DEADLINE(S): MAY 15
FIELD(S): Medicine; Law; Engineering; Political Science

Open to male high school seniors planning a career in one of the above fields. Must be residents of Imperial, Riverside, Orange, San Diego, or Los Angeles counties in California. Boys and Girls Club affiliation NOT required.

$10 application fee. Renewable up to 4 years. Send a self-addressed, stamped envelope to Boys and Girls Club for an application after January 1.

302—BRITISH COLUMBIA PARAPLEGIC FOUNDATION (C.W. Deans Memorial Scholarship)

780 SW Marine Drive
Vancouver BC V6P 5Y7 CANADA
604/324-3611
FAX: 604/324-3671

AMOUNT: Varies
DEADLINE(S): JUL 31
FIELD(S): Engineering

Open to spinal cord injured engineering students for beginning or continuing study at a university in British Columbia. Considerations include academic standing and financial need. Must be member of the British Columbia Paraplegic Assn.

Canadian citizen, legal resident, or resident of British Columbia. Write for complete information.

303—BROOKHAVEN WOMEN IN SCIENCE (Renate W. Chasman Scholarship)

P.O. Box 183
Upton NY 11973-5000
E-mail: pam@bnl.gov

AMOUNT: $2,000
DEADLINE(S): APR 1
FIELD(S): Natural Sciences; Engineering; Mathematics

Open ONLY to women who are residents of the boroughs of Brooklyn or Queens or the counties of Nassau or Suffolk in New York who are reentering school after a period of study. For juniors, seniors, or first-year graduate students.

1 award annually. Not renewable. Contact Pam Mansfield at above location for an application. Phone calls are NOT accepted.

304—CAREER OPPORTUNITIES FOR YOUTH, INC. (Collegiate Scholarship Program)

P.O. Box 996
Manhattan Beach CA 90266
310/535-4838
AMOUNT: $250 to $1,000
DEADLINE(S): SEP 30
FIELD(S): Engineering, Science, Mathematics, Computer Science, Business Administration, Education, Nursing

For students of Latino/Hispanic background residing in the Southern California area who have completed at least one semester/quarter of study at an accredited four-year university. Must have a cumulative GPA of 2.5 or higher.

Priority will be given to students who demonstrate financial need. Send SASE to above location for details.

305—CHICAGO ENGINEERS' FOUNDATION (Engineering Incentive Awards)

Union League Club of Chicago
65 W. Jackson Boulevard
Chicago IL 60604-3598
312/435-5961 or 312/427-7800
FAX: 312/427-9177
E-mail: commdept@ulcc.org
Internet: http://www.ulcc.org/chicago.htm
AMOUNT: Varies
DEADLINE(S): Varies
FIELD(S): Engineering

Open to Chicago-area high school seniors who have been admitted to an accredited college/university engineering program. Selections are made on the basis of academic excellence.

26 awards annually. Contact ULCC for an application.

306—CHICAGO ROOFING CONTRACTORS ASSOCIATION (Scholarship)

4415 W. Harrison Street, #322
Hillside IL 60162
708/449-3340
FAX: 708/449-0837
E-mail: crcainfo@crca.org
Internet: http://www.crca.org
AMOUNT: $2,000
DEADLINE(S): Varies
FIELD(S): Business; Engineering; Architecture; Liberal Arts; Sciences

Open to high school seniors who reside in one of the eight counties in Northern Illinois: Cook, DuPage, Lake, Kane, Kendall, DeKalb, McHenry, or Will. Must be accepted as a full-time student in a four-year college/university to pursue a degree in one of the above fields. Must be U.S. citizen. Based on academic achievements, extracurricular activities, and community involvement.

Renewable. Contact CRCA for an application.

307—CITY UNIVERSITY (Scholarships in Engineering)

International Office, City University, Northampton Square
London EC1V 0HB ENGLAND UK
+44 (0) 171 477 8019
FAX: +44 (0) 171 477 8562
E-mail: international@city.ac.uk
Internet: http://www.britcoun.org/eis/profiles/cityuniversity/cituschp.htm
AMOUNT: 950 pounds/year
DEADLINE(S): Varies
FIELD(S): Engineering

Scholarships for undergraduate students from non-European Union countries who are pursuing studies in engineering. For use at City University in London.

Selection based on academic merit. Renewable for term of course. Program is through the British Council. Contact Karen Jones at University for details.

308—CIVIL AIR PATROL (CAP Undergraduate Scholarships)

Civil Air Patrol
National Headquarters
Maxwell AFB AL 36112-6332
334/953-5315
AMOUNT: $750
DEADLINE(S): JAN 31
FIELD(S): Humanities; Science; Engineering; Education

Open to CAP members who have received the Billy Mitchell Award or the senior rating in Level II of the senior training program. For undergraduate study in the above areas.

Write for complete information.

309—COMMUNITY FOUNDATION OF WESTERN MASSACHUSETTS (James L. Shriver Scholarship)

1500 Main Street
P.O. Box 15769
Springfield MA 01115
413/732-2858
AMOUNT: $750
DEADLINE(S): APR 15
FIELD(S): Technical Fields

Open to residents of Western Massachusetts to pursue technical careers through college, trade, or technical school. Based on financial need, academic merit, and extracurricular activities. Must submit transcripts and fill out government FAFSA form.

1 award annually. Renewable with reapplication. Contact Community Foundation for an application and your financial aid office for FAFSA. Notification is in June.

310—COMMUNITY FOUNDATION SILICON VALLEY (Valley Scholars Program)

111 W. Saint John Street, Suite 230
San Jose CA 95113
408/278-0270
FAX: 408/278-0280
Internet: http://www.cfsv.org
AMOUNT: $20,000 (over 4 years of college)
DEADLINE(S): Varies (early spring)
FIELD(S): Science and/or math

A scholarship program for public high school students in the Silicon Valley (San Mateo and Santa Clara counties and Fremont Union High school District, California) who have demonstrated enthusiasm and aptitude for science and math. Must be U.S. citizen or permanent resident.

Up to 20 students are selected each year. Each Valley Scholar receives financial support, guidance through the college admission process, and a mentor whose interests match their own. Students may apply during their sophomore year of high school and must be academically outstanding.

311—CONSULTING ENGINEERS COUNCIL OF NEW JERSEY (Louis Goldberg Scholarship Fund)

66 Morris Avenue
Springfield NJ 07081
973/564-5848
FAX: 973/564-7480
AMOUNT: $1,000
DEADLINE(S): JAN 1
FIELD(S): Engineering or Land Surveying

Open to undergraduate students who have completed at least two years of study (or fifth year in a five-year program) at an ABET-accredited college or university in New Jersey, are in top half of their class, and are considering a career as a consulting engineer or land surveyor. Must be U.S. citizen.

Recipients will be eligible for American Consulting Engineers Council national scholarships of $2,000 to $5,000. Write for complete information.

312—CONSULTING ENGINEERS COUNCIL OF PA (Scholarship)

2040 Linglestown Road, Suite 200
Harrisburg PA 17110
717/540-6811
Internet: http://www.cecpa.org

AMOUNT: $2,000
DEADLINE(S): DEC
FIELD(S): Engineering

For engineering students entering their senior or fifth year (in a five-year program). Must be enrolled in an accredited engineering school in Pennsylvania. Winners will go on to compete at the national level.

313—COUNCIL OF ENERGY RESOURCE TRIBE (CERT)

1999 Broadway, Suite 2600
Denver CO 80202
303/282-7576

AMOUNT: $1,000 per year
DEADLINE(S): JUL 1
FIELD(S): Science, Engineering, or Business

Only for applicants who are members of the T.R.I.B.E.S. program their senior year in high school. TRIBES enrollment is limited to ensure a quality experience for each student. To qualify for TRIBES, students must be graduating seniors, plan to attend a college in the fall, and be interested in business, engineering, science, or related fields. Indian students who wish to attend TRIBES may contact CERT for information and an application.

314—CUBAN AMERICAN NATIONAL FOUNDATION (The Mas Family Scholarships)

7300 NW 3 Terrace
Miami FL 33122
305/592-7768
FAX: 305/592-7889
E-mail: canfnet.org
Internet: http://www.canfnet.org

AMOUNT: Individually negotiated
DEADLINE(S): MAR 15
FIELD(S): Engineering, Business, International Relations, Economics, Communications, Journalism

For Cuban-Americans students, graduates and undergraduates, born in Cuba or direct descendants of those who left Cuba. Must be in top 10% of high school class or maintain a 3.5 GPA in college.

10,000 awards/year. Recipients may reapply for subsequent years. Financial need considered along with academic success, SAT and GRE scores, and leadership potential. Essays and proof of Cuban descent required.

315—DE MONTFORT UNIVERSITY (Carlton Laser Services, Ltd. Bursaries)

Secretary, De Montfort University
Global Education Trust
De Montfort University
The Gateway, Leicester LE1 9BH
ENGLAND UK
Internet: http://www.eng.dmu.ac.uk/CLSbursaries.html

AMOUNT: 1,200 pounds
DEADLINE(S): Varies
FIELD(S): Engineering

Bursaries for selected potential engineering students to assist with cost of study at De Montfort University. Must intend to take up a career in Leicestershire-based industry and be below age 21.

Write to Secretary for information pack.

316—GENERAL LEARNING COMMUNICATIONS (DuPont Challenge Science Essay Awards Program)

900 Skokie Boulevard, Suite 200
Northbrook IL 60062-4028
847/205-3000
FAX: 847/564-8197
Internet: http://www.glcomm.com/dupont

AMOUNT: $1,500 (max.)
DEADLINE(S): JAN 28
FIELD(S): Science and Technology

Annual essay competition open to students in grades 7-12 in the U.S. and Canada. Cash awards for first, second, and honorable mention. First-place essayists in each of two divisions, their science teacher, and a parent of each receive a trip to the Space Center Houston/NASA at the end of April.

102 awards annually. See Web site or contact your science teacher or GLC for official entry blank.

317—GEORGE BIRD GRINNELL AMERICAN INDIAN CHILDREN'S FUND (Al Qoyawayma Award)

11602 Montague Ct.
Potomac MD 20854
301/424-2440
FAX: 301/424-8281
E-mail: Grinnell_Fund@MSN.com

AMOUNT: $1,000
DEADLINE(S): JUN 1
FIELD(S): Science; Engineering

Open to Native American undergraduate and graduate students majoring in science or engineering and who have demonstrated an outstanding interest and skill in any one of the arts. Must be American Indian/Alaska Native (documented with Certified Degree of Indian Blood), be enrolled in college/university, be able to demonstrate commitment to serving community or other tribal nations, and document financial need.

Contact Dr. Paula M. Mintzies, President, for an application after January 1.

318—GERBER SCIENTIFIC, INC. (H. Joseph Gerber Vision Scholarship Program)

83 Gerber Road West
South Windsor CT 06074
860/648-8027
Internet: http://www.gerberscientific.com

AMOUNT: Varies
DEADLINE(S): MAR 15
FIELD(S): Engineering, Mathematics, Computer Science, Natural Sciences

Scholarship program for high school seniors in Connecticut.

50 scholarships to be awarded.

319—H. FLETCHER BROWN FUND (Scholarships)

c/o PNC Bank, Trust Dept.
P.O. Box 791
Wilmington DE 19899
302/429-1186

AMOUNT: Varies
DEADLINE(S): APR 15
FIELD(S): Medicine; Dentistry; Law; Engineering; Chemistry

Open to U.S. citizens born in Delaware and still residing in Delaware. For 4 years of study (undergrad or grad) leading to a degree that enables applicant to practice in chosen field.

Scholarships are based on need, scholastic achievement, and good moral character. Applications available in February. Write for complete information.

320—H. FLETCHER BROWN TRUST (Scholarships)

222 Delaware Avenue, 16th Floor
Wilmington DE 19899

302/429-1338
AMOUNT: Varies
DEADLINE(S): APR 9
FIELD(S): Chemistry; Engineering; Law; Medicine; Dentistry

Open to financially needy native-born DELAWARE residents ONLY who are pursuing an undergraduate degree. Must have minimum 1,000 SAT score and rank in upper 20% of class. Interview required.

Send self-addressed, stamped envelope to Donald Drois, Account Administrator, PNC Bank, at above address for an application.

321—ILLUMINATING ENGINEERING SOCIETY OF NORTH AMERICA (Robert W. Thunen Memorial Scholarships)

Golden Gate Section
P.O. Box 77527
San Francisco CA 94107-1527
E-mail: riverfield@juno.com
AMOUNT: $2,500
DEADLINE(S): APR 1
FIELD(S): Illumination (Architectural, Commercial, Residential, Airport, Navigational, Theatrical, TV, Agricultural, Vision, etc.)

Open to full-time undergraduate juniors and seniors and graduate students in an accredited four-year college/university located in Northern California or Nevada, Oregon, or Washington. Must submit statement of purpose (with respect to lighting education) and three letters of recommendation.

2+ awards annually. Contact Heide M. Kawahata, Chair, for an application. Awards announced by May 3.

322—INSTITUTE OF INTERNATIONAL EDUCATION (National Security Education Program-Undergraduate Scholarships)

1400 K Street NW, 6th Floor
Washington DC 20005-2403
202/326-7697 or
800/618-NSEP (6737)
E-mail: nsep@iie.org
Internet: http://www.iie.org/nsep/
AMOUNT: Varies: up to $8,000/semester
DEADLINE(S): FEB 8
FIELD(S): Open to all majors; preference to applied sciences, engineering, business, economics, math, computer science, international affairs, political science, history, and the policy sciences.

For study abroad OUTSIDE the U.S., Canada, Australia, New Zealand, and Western Europe. For study in areas deemed critical to U.S. national security. Applications available on U.S. campuses from August through early December. Or contact organization for details.

Inquire at above location for details.

323—INSTITUTION OF ELECTRICAL ENGINEERS (Scholarships for Women)

Savoy Place
London WC2R 0BL ENGLAND
0171 240 1871 ext. 2211/2235
FAX: 0171 497 3609
E-mail: scholarships@iee.org.uk
Internet: http://www.iee.org.uk/Awards/ugwom.htm
AMOUNT: 750 pounds/year
DEADLINE(S): JUN 15
FIELD(S): Engineering

Scholarships for women residing in the United Kingdom and pursuing degrees in engineering.

Candidates must be undertaking mathematics and physics "A" level or Scottish Higher examinations. Renewable for the entire period of an IEE-accredited course. Check Web site or contact organization for application details.

324—INSTITUTION OF ELECTRICAL ENGINEERS (Undergraduate Scholarships)

Savoy Place
London WC2R 0BL ENGLAND
0171 240 1871 Ext. 2211/2235
FAX: 0171 497 3609
E-mail: scholarships@iee.org.uk
Internet: http://www.iee.org.uk/Awards/ugsum.htm
AMOUNT: 750-1,000 pounds/year
DEADLINE(S): JUN 30; SEP 30
FIELD(S): Engineering

Scholarships for residents of the United Kingdom and pursuing degree in various engineering specialties. Criteria vary, including academic excellence and financial need.

Check Web site or contact organization for application details.

325—JEWISH FEDERATION OF METROPOLITAN CHICAGO (Academic Scholarship Program for Studies in the Sciences)

One South Franklin Street
Chicago IL 60606
Written Inquiry
AMOUNT: Varies
DEADLINE(S): MAR 1
FIELD(S): Mathematics, Engineering, or Science

Scholarships for college juniors, seniors, and graduate students who are Jewish and are residents of Chicago, IL and Cook County.

Academic achievement and financial need are considered. Applications accepted after Dec. 1.

326—JOHNSON AND WALES UNIVERSITY (Annual Johnson and Wales University National High School Recipe Contest)

8 Abbott Place
Providence RI 02903
401/598-2345
AMOUNT: $1,000 to $5,000
DEADLINE(S): JAN 31
FIELD(S): Business, Hospitality, Technology, Culinary Arts

For students planning to attend Johnson & Wales University, Providence, Rhode Island.

Write to above address for detailed description.

327—JOHNSON AND WALES UNIVERSITY (Gilbane Building Company Eagle Scout Scholarship)

8 Abbott Place
Providence RI 02903
401/598-2345
AMOUNT: $1,200
DEADLINE(S): None
FIELD(S): Business, Hospitality, Technology, Culinary Arts

For students attending Johnson & Wales University, Providence, Rhode Island. Must be Eagle Scouts.

Send letter of recommendation and transcript to above address.

328—JOHNSON AND WALES UNIVERSITY (National High School Entrepreneur of the Year Contest)

8 Abbott Place
Providence RI 02903
401/598-2345
AMOUNT: $1,000 to $10,000
DEADLINE(S): DEC 27
FIELD(S): Business, Hospitality, Technology, Culinary Arts

For students attending Johnson & Wales University, Providence, Rhode Island.

Send for detailed description to above address.

329—JOHNSON AND WALES UNIVERSITY (Scholarships)

8 Abbott Place
Providence RI 02903
401/598-2345
AMOUNT: $200 to $10,000
DEADLINE(S): None
FIELD(S): Business, Hospitality, Technology, Culinary Arts

For students attending Johnson & Wales University, Providence, Rhode Island.

Renewable for four years. Write for complete information.

330—JOSEPH BLAZEK FOUNDATION (Scholarships)

8 S. Michigan Avenue
Chicago IL 60603
312/236-3882
AMOUNT: $1,000/year
DEADLINE(S): MAR 15
FIELD(S): Science; Chemistry; Engineering; Mathematics; Physics

Open to residents of Cook County, Illinois, who are high school seniors planning to study at a four-year college/university.

Renewable. Contact Foundation for an application.

331—KOREAN-AMERICAN SCIENTISTS AND ENGINEERS ASSOCIATION (KSEA Scholarships)

1952 Gallows Road, Suite 300
Vienna VA 22182
703/748-1221
FAX: 703/748-1331
E-mail: admin@ksea.org
Internet: http://www.ksea.org
AMOUNT: $1,000
DEADLINE(S): FEB 28
FIELD(S): Science, Engineering, or Medicine

Scholarships to encourage Korean-American students to study in a science, engineering, or pre-med discipline and to recognize high-performing students. Must have graduated from a high school in the U.S.

5 to 8 awards yearly. Must be a student member of KSEA or a child of a member.

332—LEAGUE OF UNITED LATIN AMERICAN CITIZENS (General Electric/LULAC Scholarship Program)

2000 L Street NW, #610
Washington DC 20036
202/835-9646
FAX: 202/835-9685
Internet: http://www.lulac.org/
AMOUNT: $5,000
DEADLINE(S): JUL 15
FIELD(S): Business; Engineering

Open to minority students who are enrolled as business or engineering majors leading to a bachelor's degree at accredited colleges/universities in the U.S. and will be college sophomores in the fall of application year. Recipients may be offered temporary summer or internship positions with GE businesses; however the students are under no obligation to accept GE employment.

2 awards annually. Send self-addressed, stamped envelope for an application.

333—LEAGUE OF UNITED LATIN AMERICAN CITIZENS (General Motors Corporation/LULAC Scholarship Program)

2000 L Street NW, #610
Washington DC 20036
202/835-9646
FAX: 202/835-9685
Internet: http://www.lulac.org/
AMOUNT: $2,000
DEADLINE(S): JUL 15
FIELD(S): Engineering

Open to minority students with career interests in engineering. Must be enrolled or planning to enroll as an engineering major leading to a bachelor's degree at a college/university approved by LULAC and GM. Program is intended to assist and encourage outstanding minority students in completing their college education.

20 awards annually. Send self-addressed, stamped envelope for an application.

334—LOS ANGELES COUNCIL OF BLACK PROFESSIONAL ENGINEERS (Al-Ben Scholarship)

P.O. Box 881029
Los Angeles CA 90009
310/635-7734
E-mail: secy1@lablackengineers.org
Internet: http://www.lablackengineers.org/scholarships.html
AMOUNT: Varies
DEADLINE(S): Varies
FIELD(S): Engineering; Mathematics; Computer Studies; Applied Scientific Studies

Open to technically inclined precollege and undergraduate students enrolled in one of the above fields. Must be of African American, Native American, or Hispanic ancestry. Preference given to students attending college in Southern California or who are Southern California residents.

See Web site to download an application.

335—MARYLAND HIGHER EDUCATION COMMISSION (Maryland Science and Technology Scholarship Program)

16 Francis Street
Annapolis Park MD 21401
410/974-5370 or 800/974-1024
E-mail: ssamail@mhec.state.md.us
Internet: http://www.mhec.state.md.us/SSA/stech_qa.htm
AMOUNT: $3,000/year (BA); $1,000/year (AA)
DEADLINE(S): None
FIELD(S): Computer Science; Engineering; Technology

Scholarships for college-bound Maryland high school seniors who will major in one of the above fields and who are accepted to an eligible associate or bachelor's degree program in Maryland. The deadline was not known at this writing, so check for deadline date. Must agree to work in the state after graduation in a related field, one year for each year of assistance received.

Must maintain a 3.0 GPA.

336—NAACP NATIONAL OFFICE (NAACP Willems Scholarship)

4805 Mount Hope Drive
Baltimore MD 21215
401/358-8900
AMOUNT: $2,000 undergrads; $3,000 grads
DEADLINE(S): APR 30
FIELD(S): Engineering; Chemistry; Physics; Mathematics

Open to NAACP male members majoring in one of the above areas. Undergrads must have GPA of 2.5+; graduates' GPAs must be 3.0+. Renewable if the required GPA is maintained.

Financial need must be established. Two letters of recommendation typed on letterhead from teachers or professors in the major field of specialization. Write for complete information. Include a legal size, self-addressed, stamped envelope.

337—NATIONAL AERONAUTICS AND SPACE ADMINISTRATION (ACCESS Internships)

Stennis Space Center, Bldg. 1100
Bay Saint Louis MS 39529

228/688-2079
E-mail: covington.pamela@ssc.nasa.gov
AMOUNT: Internship only
DEADLINE(S): None
FIELD(S): Aeronautics/Aerospace; Astronomy; Chemistry; Physics; Engineering; Math; Earth, Life, Materials, Computer, and Physical Sciences

Nine- to ten-week summer internships are open to undergraduates with physical or learning disabilities who maintain a minimum 3.0 GPA and are U.S. citizens. Purpose is to increase the number of students with disabilities pursuing technical degrees related to NASA's mission and to provide on-site experience. Internship takes place at the Stennis Space Center in Mississippi.

Contact Pam Covington for an application.

338—NATIONAL FEDERATION OF THE BLIND (Frank Walton Horn Memorial Scholarship)

805 Fifth Avenue
Grinnell IA 50112
515/236-3366
AMOUNT: $3,000
DEADLINE(S): MAR 31
FIELD(S): Architecture; Engineering

Open to legally blind students pursuing or planning to pursue a full-time postsecondary course of study in the U.S. Based on academic excellence, service to the community, and financial need. Membership NOT required.

1 award annually. Renewable. Contact Mrs. Peggy Elliot, Scholarship Committee Chairman, for an application.

339—NATIONAL FEDERATION OF THE BLIND (Howard Brown Rickard Scholarship)

805 Fifth Avenue
Grinnell IA 50112
515/236-3366
AMOUNT: $3,000
DEADLINE(S): MAR 31
FIELD(S): Law; Medicine; Engineering; Architecture; Natural Sciences

For legally blind students pursuing or planning to pursue a full-time postsecondary course of study in the U.S.. Based on academic excellence, service to the community, and financial need. Membership NOT required.

1 award annually. Renewable. Contact Mrs. Peggy Elliot, Scholarship Committee Chairman, for an application.

340—NATIONAL SCIENCE FOUNDATION (Graduate Research Fellowships)

Oak Ridge Associated Universities
P.O. Box 3010
702 South Illinois Avenue, Suite B-102
Oak Ridge TN 37831
423/241-4300
E-mail: nsfgrfp@orau.gov
Internet: http://www.fastlane.nsf.gov
AMOUNT: $15,000 annual stipend plus tuition and fees
DEADLINE(S): NOV
FIELD(S): Science, Mathematics, and Engineering

Fellowships are awarded for graduate study in fields supported by the NSF, including the mathematical, physical, biological, behavioral, and social sciences; engineering; the history of science and the philosophy of science; and for research-based Ph.D. degrees in science education. In most cases, an individual has three opportunities to apply: during the senior year of college, the first year of graduate school, and the beginning of the second year of graduate school. Applicants must be U.S. citizens.

341—NATIONAL SCIENCES AND ENGINEERING RESEARCH COUNCIL OF CANADA (Undergraduate Scholarships)

Scholarships/Fellowships Division
350 Albert Street
Ottawa Ontario K1A 1H5 CANADA
613/996-2009
FAX: 613/996-2589
E-mail: schol@nserc.ca
Internet: http://www.nserc.ca
AMOUNT: Up to $3,600
DEADLINE(S): Varies
FIELD(S): Natural Sciences, Engineering, Biology, or Chemistry

Open to Canadian citizens or permanent residents working towards degrees in science or engineering. Academic excellence and research aptitude are considerations.

Write for complete information.

342—NATIONAL SOCIETY OF BLACK ENGINEERS (Scholarships)

1454 Duke Street
Alexandria VA 22314
703/549-2207
FAX: 703/683-5312
E-mail: nsbehq@nsbe.org
Internet: http://www.nsbe.org
AMOUNT: Varies
DEADLINE(S): Varies
FIELD(S): Engineering and engineering technologies

Programs for black and other ethnic minorities in the fields of engineering and the engineering technologies. Organization offers pre-college programs, scholarships, career fairs, a journal, a newsletter, etc.

Contact organization for details.

343—NATIONAL SPACE CLUB (Dr. Robert H. Goddard Scholarship)

2000 L Street NW, Suite 710
Washington DC 20036-4907
202/973-8661
AMOUNT: $10,000
DEADLINE(S): JAN 8
FIELD(S): Science and Engineering

Open to undergraduate juniors and seniors and graduate students who have scholastic plans leading to future participation in the aerospace sciences and technology. Must be U.S. citizen. Award based on transcript, letters of recommendation, accomplishments, scholastic plans, and proven past research and participation in space-related science and engineering. Personal need is considered, but is not controlling.

Renewable. Send a self-addressed, stamped envelope for more information.

344—NATIONAL SPACE CLUB (Dr. Robert H. Goddard Historical Essay Award)

2000 L Street NW, Suite 710
Washington DC 20036-4907
202/973-8661
AMOUNT: $1,000 + plaque
DEADLINE(S): DEC 4
FIELD(S): Aerospace History

Essay competition open to any U.S. citizen on a topic dealing with any significant aspect of the historical development of rocketry and astronautics. Essays should not exceed 5,000 words and should be fully documented. Will be judged on originality and scholarship.

Previous winners not eligible. Send self-addressed, stamped envelope for complete information.

345—NATIONAL TECHNICAL ASSOCIATION, INC. (Scholarship Competitions for Minorities and Women in Science and Engineering)

5810 Kingstowne Ctr., #120221
Alexandria VA 22315-5711

E-mail: ntamfj1@aol.com
Internet: http://www.huenet.com/nta
AMOUNT: $500-$5,000
DEADLINE(S): Varies
FIELD(S): Science; Mathematics; Engineering; Applied Technology

Scholarship competitions for minorities and women pursuing degrees in the above fields. Additional scholarships are available through local chapters of NTA.

See Web site or write to above address for details and for locations of local chapters.

346—NATIVE AMERICAN SCHOLARSHIP FUND, INC. (Scholarships)

8200 Mountain Road NE, Suite 203
Albuquerque NM 87110
505/262-2351
FAX: 505/262-0543
E-mail: NScholarsh@aol.com
AMOUNT: Varies
DEADLINE(S): MAR 15; APR 15; SEP 15
FIELD(S): Math; Engineering; Science; Business; Education; Computer Science

Open to American Indians or Alaskan Natives (1/4 degree or more) enrolled as members of a federally recognized, state recognized, or terminated tribe. For graduate or undergraduate study at an accredited four-year college or university.

208 awards annually. Contact Lucille Kelley, Director of Recruitment, for an application.

347—NEW ZEALAND FEDERATION OF UNIVERSITY WOMEN-WAIKATO BRANCH (Kahurangi Maori Language Award)

P.O. Box 7065
Hamilton NEW ZEALAND
07/855-3776
AMOUNT: $1,000
DEADLINE(S): MAR 15
FIELD(S): Education; Maori Studies

Open to Maori women who are full-time students enrolled for a third or fourth year at the University of Waikato School of Education or the Department of Maori Studies. Must be fluent in or studying the Maori language for a Bachelor of Education degree or Diploma of Teaching.

Contact the Convenor, NAFUW, Waikato Branch for an application.

348—NATURAL SCIENCES AND ENGINEERING RESEARCH COUNCIL OF CANADA (Undergraduate Student Research Awards in Industry)

350 Albert Street
Ottawa Ontario K1A 1H5 CANADA
613/995-5992
FAX: 613/992-5337
E-mail: schol@nserc.ca
Internet: http://www.nserc.ca/programs/usrainen.htm
AMOUNT: $3,600 (max.)
DEADLINE(S): Varies
FIELD(S): Natural Sciences; Engineering

Tenable in approved Canadian industrial organizations. For Canadian citizens or permanent residents, who have no more than 4 academic terms remaining to complete bachelor's degree. Cumulative GPA of at least second class (B). Recipients must be employed full-time in research and development activities during award tenure. Travel allowance may be granted.

Students in health sciences not eligible. Those already holding a bachelor's and studying for a second may apply, but those holding higher degrees in the natural sciences or engineering may not.

349—OAK RIDGE INSTITUTE FOR SCIENCE AND EDUCATION (ORISE Education and Training Programs)

P.O. Box 117
Oak Ridge TN 37831-0117
Internet: http://www.orau.gov/orise/educ.htm
AMOUNT: Varies
DEADLINE(S): Varies
FIELD(S): Engineering; Aeronautics; Computer Science; Technology; Earth Science; Environmental Studies; Biology; Chemistry; Physics; Medical Research

Numerous programs funded by the U.S. Department of Energy are offered for undergraduate students through postgraduate researchers. Includes fellowship and internship opportunities throughout the U.S.. Some have citizenship restrictions. Travel may be included.

See Web site or write for a catalog of specific programs and requirements.

350—OFFICE OF NAVAL RESEARCH (NSAP-Naval Science Awards Program)

ONR 353; 800 N. Quincy Street
Arlington VA 22217-5660
800/422-6727 or 703/696-5787
E-mail: thurmab@onrhq.onr.navy.mil
Internet: http://www.onr.navy.mil or http://www.jshs.org
AMOUNT: $2,000-$20,000
DEADLINE(S): Varies (established by individual regional, state, and district science fairs)
FIELD(S): Science; Engineering

For high school students (grades 9-12) who participate in a regional/district/state science fair. Winners can participate in Junior Science and Humanities Symposia (JSHS) Program. Awards also offered in each of 14 categories at International Science and Engineering Fair (ISEF), sponsored by Science Service, Inc. Must be U.S. citizen or permanent resident.

24 awards annually. Renewable. See Web site or contact Mrs. Barbara M. Thurman (Project Officer) at address above for complete information on NSAP, ISEF, and JSHS.

351—QUEEN'S UNIVERSITY OF BELFAST (Industrial Scholarships)

Training and Employment Agency
Management Development Division
9-21 Adelaide Street
Belfast BT2 8DT
NORTHERN IRELAND UK
+44 (0) 1232 245133
Internet: http://www.icbl.qub.ac.uk/prospectus/funding/scholars.htm
AMOUNT: Varies
DEADLINE(S): Varies
FIELD(S): Engineering: Aeronautical, Electrical and Electronic, Mechanical, and Manufacturing

Scholarships in Northern Ireland for study in the above fields.

Contact the University at the address shown for complete information.

352—RAYMOND J. HARRIS EDUCATION TRUST

P.O. Box 7899
Philadelphia PA 19101-7899
Written Inquiry
AMOUNT: Varies
DEADLINE(S): FEB 1
FIELD(S): Medicine, Law, Engineering, Dentistry, or Agriculture

Scholarships for Christian men to obtain a professional education in medicine, law, engineering, dentistry, or agriculture at nine Philadelphia area colleges.

Contact Mellon Bank, N.A. at above location for details and the names of the nine colleges.

353—ROBERT SCHRECK MEMORIAL FUND (Grants)

c/o Texas Commerce Bank, Trust Dept.
P.O. Drawer 140
El Paso TX 79980

915/546-6515
AMOUNT: $500-$1500
DEADLINE(S): JUL 15; NOV 15
FIELD(S): Medicine; Veterinary Medicine; Physics; Chemistry; Architecture; Engineering; Episcopal Clergy

Grants to undergraduate juniors or seniors or graduate students who have been residents of El Paso County for at least two years. Must be U.S. citizen or legal resident and have a high grade point average. Financial need is a consideration.

Write for complete information.

354—ROBOTIC INDUSTRIES ASSOCIATION (RIA Robotics Scholarship Competition)

900 Victors Way
P.O. Box 3724
Ann Arbor MI 48106
734/994-6088
FAX: 734/994-3338
E-mail: mlehtinen@robotics.org
Internet: http://www.robotics.org
AMOUNT: $1,000
DEADLINE(S): DEC 10
FIELD(S): Robotics

Competition is for undergraduate students attending school in North America. Students must submit a paper that poses a technical problem and offers a solution that involves robotics. Team entries are allowed. Financial need NOT a factor.

3 awards annually. Not renewable. See Web site or contact Marcy Lehtinen at RIA for full guidelines and past winners.

355—SAN DIEGO AEROSPACE MUSEUM (Bill Gibbs Scholarship)

Education Dept.
2001 Pan American Plaza
San Diego CA 92101
619/234-8291 ext. 19
FAX: 619/233-4526
Internet: http://aerospacemuseum.org/Scholastic.HTML
AMOUNT: Varies
DEADLINE(S): Varies
FIELD(S): Aerospace: math, physics, science, or engineering

For students who are residents of San Diego County, California, who have an aerospace career interest who have been accepted to a four-year college or university in a degree program relating to math, physics, science, or engineering.

Call or write museum for further information.

356—SCIENCE SERVICE (Discovery Young Scientist Challenge)

1719 N Street NW
Washington DC 20036
202/785-2255
FAX: 202/785-1243
E-mail: dkruft@sciserv.org
Internet: http://www.sciserv.org
AMOUNT: Varies
DEADLINE(S): JUN
FIELD(S): Science; Math; Engineering

Open to middle schoolers (5th-8th grades) who win their regional or state science fair. Enables students to participate in a national science competition that emphasizes the student's ability to communicate about science. Must be U.S. citizen and be nominated by the fair director in order to apply.

Contact Danielle Kruft at Science Service for DYSC nomination procedures.

357—SCIENCE SERVICE (Intel International Science and Engineering Fair)

1719 N Street NW
Washington DC 20036
202/785-2255
FAX: 202/785-1243
E-mail: jkim@sciserv.org
Internet: http://www.sciserv.org
AMOUNT: Varies (totaling $2 million)
DEADLINE(S): DEC 1
FIELD(S): Science; Math; Engineering

Open to high school students (grades 9-12) who participate in this worldwide science competition. Scholarships, internships with noted scientists, and travel and equipment grants are awarded.

Contact Jinny Kim at Science Service for official ISEF entry book. Sponsored by the Intel Corporation.

358—SCIENCE SERVICE (Intel Science Talent Search)

1719 N Street NW
Washington DC 20036
202/785-2255
FAX: 202/785-1243
E-mail: cmdroms@sciserv.org
Internet: http://www.sciserv.org
AMOUNT: $100,000 (1st place); $75,000 (2nd); $50,000 (3rd); $25,000 (4th-6th); $20,000 (7th-10th); 30 at $5,000; 300 at $1,000; 40 laptops
DEADLINE(S): DEC 1
FIELD(S): Science; Math; Engineering

Open to high school seniors who submit a report of an independent research project in science, math, or engineering. Must include transcripts, SAT scores, and official entry form. Forty finalists are invited to Washington, DC, to participate in competition. Purpose is to encourage students to pursue careers in science and engineering.

40 awards annually. Contact Courtney Droms at Science Service for official STS entry book. Sponsored by the Intel Corporation.

359—SIEMENS WESTINGHOUSE (Science and Technology Competition)

186 Wood Avenue S.
Iselin NJ 08830
877/822-5233
E-mail: foundation@sc.siemens.com
Internet: http://www.siemens-foundation.org
AMOUNT: $120,000 (max.)
DEADLINE(S): Varies
FIELD(S): Biology; Physical Sciences; Mathematics; Physics; Chemistry; Computer Science; Environmental Science

Open to U.S. high school seniors to pursue independent science research projects, working individually or in teams of 2 or 3 to develop and test their own ideas. May work with one of the universities/laboratories that serve as Siemens' partners. Students from the 50 states, DC, and Territories may compete in one of six geographic areas. Individual and team national prize winners receive a second scholarship award to be applied to undergraduate or graduate education.

See Web site or contact Siemens Foundation for details.

360—SOCIETY FOR THE ADVANCEMENT OF MATERIAL & PROCESS ENGINEERING (SAMPE Undergraduate Award)

5300 Forge Road
Whitemarsh MD 21162
Internet: http://www.sampe.org
AMOUNT: $750-$3,000
DEADLINE(S): FEB 1
FIELD(S): Engineering

Engineering students with a minimum 3.3 GPA who are freshman, sophomore, and junior members of SAMPE Student Chapters are eligible. Include letter of recommendation from SAMPE advisor and transcripts.

361—SOCIETY OF AUTOMOTIVE ENGINEERS (Penn State Erie-Behrend College/SAE Scholarship)

400 Commonwealth Drive
Warrendale PA 15096-0001
724/772-4047
E-mail: connie@sae.org
Internet: http://www.sae.org/students/schlrshp.htm
AMOUNT: $500-$1,000
DEADLINE(S): DEC 1
FIELD(S): Engineering

Applicants must be incoming freshmen accepted into a Penn State-Behrend engineering or engineering technology program.

$5 application fee. 1 award annually. See Web site or contact Connie Harnish, SAE Educational Relations Division, for an application. Notification is in June.

362—SOCIETY OF AUTOMOTIVE ENGINEERS (Penn State Univ (PSES)/SAE Scholarship)

400 Commonwealth Drive
Warrendale PA 15096-0001
724/772-4047
E-mail: connie@sae.org
Internet: http://www.sae.org/students/schlrshp.htm
AMOUNT: $2,500
DEADLINE(S): DEC 1
FIELD(S): Engineering; Computer Science

Applicants must be accepted at the University Park Campus of Penn State University and pursue a major in the College of Engineering.

$5 application fee. 1 award annually. Renewable for 3 years. See Web site or contact Connie Harnish, SAE Educational Relations Division, for an application. Notification is in June.

363—SOCIETY OF AUTOMOTIVE ENGINEERS (Purdue Univ/Dean's Engineering Scholar/SAE Scholarship)

400 Commonwealth Drive
Warrendale PA 15096-0001
724/772-4047
E-mail: connie@sae.org
Internet: http://www.sae.org/students/schlrshp.htm
AMOUNT: $1,250
DEADLINE(S): DEC 1
FIELD(S): Engineering; Computer Science

Applicants must be accepted at Purdue's West Lafayette Campus in Indiana. Most winners have an SAT score above 1300 and are in the top 5% of their high school class. Excellent applicants will automatically be considered for other Dean's Engineering Scholar Awards.

$5 application fee. 1 award annually. See Web site or contact Connie Harnish, SAE Educational Relations Division, for an application. Notification is in June.

364—SOCIETY OF AUTOMOTIVE ENGINEERS (Rochester Institute of Technology/SAE Scholarship)

400 Commonwealth Drive
Warrendale PA 15096-0001
724/772-4047
E-mail: connie@sae.org
Internet: http://www.sae.org/students/schlrshp.htm
AMOUNT: $5,000
DEADLINE(S): DEC 1
FIELD(S): Engineering; Computer Science

Applicants must be incoming freshmen and enrolled at the Rochester Institute of Technology in New York. Awards based on academic credentials and leadership potential. A personal interview is recommended. Must maintain 3.0 GPA for renewal.

$5 application fee. 25 awards annually. Renewable up to 3 years. See Web site or contact Connie Harnish, SAE Educational Relations Division, for an application. Notification is in June.

365—SOCIETY OF AUTOMOTIVE ENGINEERS (SAE Long-Term Member Sponsored Scholarships)

400 Commonwealth Drive
Warrendale PA 15096-0001
724/772-4047
E-mail: connie@sae.org
Internet: http://www.sae.org/students/schlrshp.htm
AMOUNT: $1,000
DEADLINE(S): DEC 1
FIELD(S): Engineering

Applicant must be in their senior year of undergraduate engineering, student member of SAE, and nominated by the SAE Faculty Advisor, Section Chair, or Vice Chair for Student Activities. Must show demonstration of leadership and support of SAE, the SAE collegiate chapter on campus, and the local SAE section.

2-3 awards annually. See Web site or contact Connie Harnish, SAE Educational Relations Division, for nomination information. Notification is in June.

366—SOCIETY OF AUTOMOTIVE ENGINEERS (SUNY-Stony Brook/SAE Scholarship)

400 Commonwealth Drive
Warrendale PA 15096-0001
724/772-4047
E-mail: connie@sae.org
Internet: http://www.sae.org/students/schlrshp.htm
AMOUNT: $1,000
DEADLINE(S): DEC 1
FIELD(S): Engineering; Computer Science

Incoming freshmen admitted directly to SUNY-Stony Brook may apply. Based on academic achievement and demonstrated motivation for a career as a professional engineer. Must maintain a 3.0 GPA for renewal.

$5 application fee. 4 awards annually. Renewable up to 4 years. See Web site or contact Connie Harnish, SAE Educational Relations Division, for an application. Notification is in June.

367—SOCIETY OF AUTOMOTIVE ENGINEERS (SUNY-Alfred/Vernon Gleasman/SAE Scholarship)

400 Commonwealth Drive
Warrendale PA 15096-0001
724/772-4047
E-mail: connie@sae.org
Internet: http://www.sae.org/students/schlrshp.htm
AMOUNT: $500
DEADLINE(S): DEC 1
FIELD(S): Engineering

For incoming freshmen and transfer students academically prepared to pursue an Associate in Applied Science and/or Bachelor's in Engineering Technologies at SUNY-Alfred. Preference given to students enrolling in Mechanical Engineering Technology.

$5 application fee. 1 award annually. See Web site or contact Connie Harnish, SAE Educational Relations Division, for an application. Notification is in June.

368—SOCIETY OF AUTOMOTIVE ENGINEERS (SUNY-New Paltz/SAE Scholarship)

400 Commonwealth Drive
Warrendale PA 15096-0001
724/772-4047

E-mail: connie@sae.org
Internet: http://www.sae.org/students/schlrshp.htm
AMOUNT: $1,500
DEADLINE(S): DEC 1
FIELD(S): Engineering; Computer Science

Applicants must be incoming freshmen accepted for study at SUNY-New Paltz. Minimum high school average of 90 (100 point scale) in a college preparatory program and a 1300 SAT combined score (30 ACT composite) are required. Must maintain 3.0 GPA for renewal.

$5 application fee. 1 award annually. Renewable for 5 years. See Web site or contact Connie Harnish, SAE Educational Relations Division, for an application. Notification is in June.

369—SOCIETY OF AUTOMOTIVE ENGINEERS (Stevens Institute of Technology/SAE Scholarship)

400 Commonwealth Drive
Warrendale PA 15096-0001
724/772-4047 or 201/216-5194
E-mail: connie@sae.org
Internet: http://www.sae.org/students/schlrshp.htm
AMOUNT: $6,000+/year
DEADLINE(S): DEC 1
FIELD(S): Engineering; Computer Science

For incoming freshmen at Stevens Institute of Technology in New Jersey. Recipients must maintain a "B" average for this scholarship to continue past freshman year. Additional financial aid, up to $12,000/year, awarded on the basis of need as indicated by the Free Application for Federal Student Aid (FAFSA) and the Stevens Financial Aid Application (file both by March 1).

$5 application fee. 2 four-year awards annually. See Web site or contact Connie Harnish, SAE Educational Relations Division, for an application. Notification is in June.

370—SOCIETY OF AUTOMOTIVE ENGINEERS (Univ Pittsburgh/SAE Scholarship)

400 Commonwealth Drive
Warrendale PA 15096-0001
724/772-4047
E-mail: connie@sae.org
Internet: http://www.sae.org/students/schlrshp.htm
AMOUNT: $1,000/year
DEADLINE(S): DEC 1
FIELD(S): Engineering; Computer Science

Must be a freshman applicant at the University of Pittsburgh with a 1250 SAT score and high school class rank in the top 10%. Must be U.S. citizen or permanent resident. Must maintain 3.0 GPA for renewal.

$5 application fee. 1 award annually. Renewable for 3 years. See Web site or contact Connie Harnish, SAE Educational Relations Division, for an application. Notification is in June.

371—SOCIETY OF AUTOMOTIVE ENGINEERS (Univ Southern California/SAE Scholarship)

400 Commonwealth Drive
Warrendale PA 15096-0001
724/772-4047
E-mail: connie@sae.org
Internet: http://www.sae.org/students/schlrshp.htm
AMOUNT: $4,000
DEADLINE(S): DEC 1
FIELD(S): Engineering; Computer Science

Applicants must be incoming freshmen who have been admitted to the University of Southern California in Los Angeles. Awarded based on the academic merit of the student. Must maintain 3.0 GPA for renewal.

$5 application fee. 2 awards annually. Renewable up to 4 years. See Web site or contact Connie Harnish, SAE Educational Relations Division, for an application. Notification is in June.

372—SOCIETY OF AUTOMOTIVE ENGINEERS (Univ Texas-Austin/SAE Scholarship)

400 Commonwealth Drive
Warrendale PA 15096-0001
724/772-4047
E-mail: connie@sae.org
Internet: http://www.sae.org/students/schlrshp.htm
AMOUNT: $3,000
DEADLINE(S): DEC 1
FIELD(S): Engineering; Computer Science

For incoming freshmen at the University of Texas at Austin. Selection is based on high school grades and SAT (1350 minimum) or ACT (31 minimum) scores. Recipients must not accept other scholarships from UT (except National Merit). Must maintain GPA of 3.25 for renewal.

$5 application fee. 2 awards annually. Renewable 3 more years. See Web site or contact Connie Harnish, SAE Educational Relations Division, for an application. SAT/ACT scores must be sent to UT by Febrary 1. Notification is in June.

373—SOCIETY OF AUTOMOTIVE ENGINEERS (Univ Toledo/SAE Scholarship)

400 Commonwealth Drive
Warrendale PA 15096-0001
724/772-4047 or 800/5-TOLEDO
E-mail: connie@sae.org
Internet: http://www.sae.org/students/schlrshp.htm
AMOUNT: $1,000
DEADLINE(S): DEC 1
FIELD(S): Engineering; Computer Science

Applicants must be U.S. citizens who are incoming freshmen at the University of Toledo in Ohio. Must maintain 3.0 GPA for renewal.

$5 application fee. 1 award annually. Renewable 3 more years. See Web site or contact Connie Harnish, SAE Educational Relations Division, for an application. Notification is in June. For admissions info, write to University of Toledo, Office of Admissions, 2801 West Bancroft, Toledo, OH 43606.

374—SOCIETY OF AUTOMOTIVE ENGINEERS (Wayne State Univ/College of Engineering/Dean's/SAE Scholarship)

400 Commonwealth Drive
Warrendale PA 15096-0001
724/772-4047 or 313/577-3780
E-mail: connie@sae.org
Internet: http://www.sae.org/students/schlrshp.htm
AMOUNT: $1,500
DEADLINE(S): DEC 1
FIELD(S): Engineering; Computer Science

For high school seniors and/or transfer students planning to attend Wayne State University in Michigan. Must have 3.5 GPA, be a U.S. citizen, and maintain full-time enrollment status. Selection also based on ACT/SAT scores. Award is based solely on merit, NOT financial need. Must maintain minimum 3.0 GPA for renewal.

1 four-year award annually. See Web site or contact Connie Harnish, SAE Educational Relations Division, for an application. Or write to Dr. Gerald Thompkins, Assistant Dean of Student Affairs, Wayne State University, College of Engineering, 5050 Anthony Wayne Drive, Detroit, MI 48202. Notification is in June.

375—SOCIETY OF AUTOMOTIVE ENGINEERS (Washington Univ/SAE Scholarship)

400 Commonwealth Drive
Warrendale PA 15096-0001
724/772-4047
E-mail: connie@sae.org
Internet: http://www.sae.org/students/schlrshp.htm

AMOUNT: $3,000
DEADLINE(S): DEC 1
FIELD(S): Engineering; Computer Science

Applicants must be incoming freshmen to the School of Engineering and Applied Science at Washington University in St. Louis, Missouri. Selection based on demonstrated academic achievement and leadership ability, contribution to school and community, and potential for professional achievement.

$5 application fee. Several awards annually. Renewable up to 4 years. See Web site or contact Connie Harnish, SAE Educational Relations Division, for an application. Notification is in June.

376—SOCIETY OF AUTOMOTIVE ENGINEERS (Western Michigan Univ/SAE Scholarship)

400 Commonwealth Drive
Warrendale PA 15096-0001
724/772-4047
E-mail: connie@sae.org
Internet: http://www.sae.org/students/schlrshp.htm

AMOUNT: $5,000-$10,000 (over a 4-year period)
DEADLINE(S): DEC 1
FIELD(S): Engineering; Computer Science

Applicants must be residents of Michigan who are incoming freshmen at Western Michigan University. Award based on appropriateness of high school courses to preparation for engineering technology education, admission GPA, and ACT scores. Must maintain 2.5 GPA for renewal.

$5 application fee. 2 four-year awards annually. See Web site or contact Connie Harnish, SAE Educational Relations Division, for an application. Notification is in June.

377—SOCIETY OF AUTOMOTIVE ENGINEERS (West Virginia Univ/SAE Scholarship)

400 Commonwealth Drive
Warrendale PA 15096-0001
724/772-404
E-mail: connie@sae.org
Internet: http://www.sae.org/students/schlrshp.htm

AMOUNT: $1,000
DEADLINE(S): DEC 1
FIELD(S): Engineering; Computer Science

Applicants must be incoming freshmen pursuing a degree in the College of Engineering and Mineral Resources at West Virginia University.

$5 application fee. 1 award annually. See Web site or contact Connie Harnish, SAE Educational Relations Division, for an application. Notification is in June.

378—SOCIETY OF AUTOMOTIVE ENGINEERS (Wichita State Univ/SAE Scholarship)

400 Commonwealth Drive
Warrendale PA 15096-0001
724/772-4047
E-mail: connie@sae.org
Internet: http://www.sae.org/students/schlrshp.htm

AMOUNT: $1,500
DEADLINE(S): DEC 1
FIELD(S): Engineering; Computer Science

Applicants must be incoming freshmen at Wichita State University in Kansas. Selection based on academic and leadership achievement. Must maintain 3.0 GPA for renewal.

$5 application fee. 1 award annually. Renewable for 3 years. See Web site or contact Connie Harnish, SAE Educational Relations Division, for an application. Notification is in June.

379—SOCIETY OF AUTOMOTIVE ENGINEERS (Widener Univ/SAE Scholarship)

400 Commonwealth Drive
Warrendale PA 15096-0001
724/772-4047
E-mail: connie@sae.org
Internet: http://www.sae.org/students/schlrshp.htm

AMOUNT: $5,000
DEADLINE(S): DEC 1
FIELD(S): Engineering; Computer Science

Applicants must be new freshmen at Widener University near Philadelphia, Pennsylvania. Must maintain 3.0 GPA for renewal.

$5 application fee. 2 four-year awards annually. See Web site or contact Connie Harnish, SAE Educational Relations Division, for an application. Notification is in June.

380—SOCIETY OF AUTOMOTIVE ENGINEERS (Wright State Univ/SAE Scholarship)

400 Commonwealth Drive
Warrendale PA 15096-0001
724/772-4047
E-mail: connie@sae.org
Internet: http://www.sae.org/students/schlrshp.htm

AMOUNT: $1,000
DEADLINE(S): DEC 1
FIELD(S): Engineering; Computer Science

Applicants must be freshmen at Wright State University in Dayton, Ohio. Award based on scholarship and achievement. Applicant may also be considered for other university scholarships based on merit and achievement.

$5 application fee. 1 award annually. Not renewable. See Web site or contact Connie Harnish, SAE Educational Relations Division, for an application. Notification is in June.

380A—SOCIETY OF AUTOMOTIVE ENGINEERS (Yanmar/SAE Scholarship)

400 Commonwealth Drive
Warrendale PA 15096-0001
724/772-4047
E-mail: connie@sae.org
Internet: http://www.sae.org/students/schlrshp.htm

AMOUNT: $2,000 ($1,000/year)
DEADLINE(S): APR 1
FIELD(S): Engineering, as related to the Conservation of Energy in Transportation, Agriculture and Construction, and Power Generation

For graduate students and undergraduates in their senior year who are citizens of North America (U.S./Canada/Mexico). Based on previous scholastic performance with additional consideration given for special study or honors in the field of award, and for leadership achievement related to engineering or science. Emphasis will be placed on research or study related to the internal combustion engine.

1 award annually. See Web site or contact Connie Harnish, SAE Educational Relations Division, for an application. Notification is in June.

381—SOCIETY OF HISPANIC PROFESSIONAL ENGINEERS FOUNDATION (SHPE Scholarships)

5400 E. Olympic Boulevard,
Suite 210
Los Angeles CA 90022
323/888-2080

AMOUNT: $500-$3,000
DEADLINE(S): APR 15
FIELD(S): Engineering; Science

Open to deserving students of Hispanic descent who are seeking careers in engineering or science. For full-time undergraduate or graduate study at a college or university. Based on academic achievement and financial need.

Send self-addressed, stamped envelope to above address for an application.

382—SOCIETY OF PETROLEUM ENGINEERS (Gus Archie Memorial Scholarship)

P.O. Box 833836
Richardson TX 75083-3836
972/952-9315
FAX: 972/952-9435
E-mail: twhipple@spelink.spe.org
Internet: http://www.spe.org

AMOUNT: $4,000/year
DEADLINE(S): MAY
FIELD(S): Petroleum Engineering

For students who are pursuing an undergraduate degree in petroleum engineering.

1 to 2 awards per year. Renewable. Financial need a factor but not primary. Contact Tom Whipple at above address for an application.

383—SOCIETY OF WOMEN ENGINEERS (3M Company Scholarships)

120 Wall Street, 11th Floor
New York NY 10005-3902
800/666-ISWE or 212/509-9577
FAX: 212/509-0224
E-mail: hq@swe.org
Internet: http://www.swe.org

AMOUNT: $1,050
DEADLINE(S): MAY 15
FIELD(S): Engineering

Open to women who are entering freshmen in a college/university with an ABET-accredited program or in a SWE-approved school. Must be U.S. citizen. Preference is given to chemical, electrical, industrial, and mechanical engineering majors.

3 awards annually. Send a self-addressed, stamped envelope to SWE for an application. Recipients are notified in September.

384—SOCIETY OF WOMEN ENGINEERS (Anne Maureen Whitney Barrow Memorial Scholarship)

120 Wall Street, 11th Floor
New York NY 10005-3902
800/666-ISWE or 212/509-9577
FAX: 212/509-0224
E-mail: hq@swe.org
Internet: http://www.swe.org

AMOUNT: $5,000
DEADLINE(S): MAY 15
FIELD(S): Engineering

Open to women who are incoming freshmen in a college/university with an ABET-accredited program or in a SWE-approved school.

1 award every 4 years. Renewable for 3 years. Send a self-addressed, stamped envelope to SWE for an application. Recipient is notified in September.

385—SOCIETY OF WOMEN ENGINEERS (B.K. Krenzer Memorial Re-entry Scholarship)

120 Wall Street, 11th Floor
New York NY 10005-3902
800/666-ISWE or 212/509-9577
FAX: 212/509-0224
E-mail: hq@swe.org
Internet: http://www.swe.org

AMOUNT: $1,000
DEADLINE(S): MAY 15
FIELD(S): Engineering; Computer Science

For women who have been out of the engineering job market as well as out of school for a minimum of two years. For any year undergraduate or graduate study, full- or part-time, at a college/university with an ABET-accredited program or in a SWE-approved school. Must have a minimum 3.5 GPA. Preference is given to degreed engineers desiring to return to the work-force following a period of temporary retirement.

1 award annually. Send a self-addressed, stamped envelope to SWE for an application. Recipient is notified in September.

386—SOCIETY OF WOMEN ENGINEERS (Central Intelligence Agency Scholarship)

120 Wall Street, 11th Floor
New York NY 10005-3902
800/666-ISWE or 212/509-9577
FAX: 212/509-0224
E-mail: hq@swe.org
Internet: http://www.swe.org

AMOUNT: $1,000
DEADLINE(S): FEB 1
FIELD(S): Electrical Engineering; Computer Science

Open to entering sophomores at a college/university with an ABET-accredited program or in a SWE-approved school. Must have a minimum 3.5 GPA and be a U.S. citizen.

1 award annually. Send a self-addressed, stamped envelope to SWE for an application. Recipient is notified in May.

387—SOCIETY OF WOMEN ENGINEERS (Chrysler Corporation Re-entry Scholarship)

120 Wall Street, 11th Floor
New York NY 10005-3902
800/666-ISWE or 212/509-9577
FAX: 212/509-0224
E-mail: hq@swe.org
Internet: http://www.swe.org

AMOUNT: $2,000
DEADLINE(S): MAY 15
FIELD(S): Engineering; Computer Science

For women who have been out of the engineering job market as well as out of school for a minimum of two years. For any level of study at a college/university with an ABET-accredited program or in a SWE-approved school. Must have a minimum 3.5 GPA.

1 award annually. Send a self-addressed, stamped envelope to SWE for an application. Recipient is notified in September.

388—SOCIETY OF WOMEN ENGINEERS (Chrysler Corporation Scholarships)

120 Wall Street, 11th Floor
New York NY 10005-3902
800/666-ISWE or 212/509-9577
FAX: 212/509-0224
E-mail: hq@swe.org
Internet: http://www.swe.org

AMOUNT: $1,500
DEADLINE(S): MAY 15
FIELD(S): Engineering; Computer Science

Open to women who are entering freshmen in a college/university with an ABET-accredited program or in a SWE-approved school.

2 awards annually. Send a self-addressed, stamped envelope to SWE for an application. Recipients are notified in September.

389—SOCIETY OF WOMEN ENGINEERS (Chrysler Corporation Scholarship)

120 Wall Street, 11th Floor
New York NY 10005-3902
800/666-ISWE or 212/509-9577
FAX: 212/509-0224
E-mail: hq@swe.org
Internet: http://www.swe.org

AMOUNT: $1,750
DEADLINE(S): FEB 1
FIELD(S): Engineering; Computer Science

Open to women who are entering sophomores, juniors, or seniors in a college/university with an ABET-accredited program or in a SWE-approved school. Must be a member of an underrepresented group in the engineering or computer science field. Must have a minimum 3.5 GPA.

1 award annually. Send a self-addressed, stamped envelope to SWE for an application. Recipient is notified in May.

390—SOCIETY OF WOMEN ENGINEERS (Chevron Scholarships)

120 Wall Street, 11th Floor
New York NY 10005-3902
800/666-ISWE or 212/509-9577
FAX: 212/509-0224
E-mail: hq@swe.org
Internet: http://www.swe.org

AMOUNT: $2,000
DEADLINE(S): FEB 1
FIELD(S): Chemical, Civil, and Petroleum Engineering

Open to entering sophomores and juniors at a college/university with an ABET-accredited program or in a SWE-approved school. Must have a minimum 3.5 GPA and be majoring in one of the above fields.

2 awards annually. Send a self-addressed, stamped envelope to SWE for an application. Recipients are notified in May.

391—SOCIETY OF WOMEN ENGINEERS (David Sarnoff Research Center Scholarship)

120 Wall Street, 11th Floor
New York NY 10005-3902
800/666-ISWE or 212/509-9577
FAX: 212/509-0224
E-mail: hq@swe.org
Internet: http://www.swe.org

AMOUNT: $1,500
DEADLINE(S): FEB 1
FIELD(S): Engineering; Computer Science

Open to women who are entering juniors at a college/university with an ABET-accredited program or in a SWE-approved school. Must have a minimum 3.5 GPA and be a U.S. citizen.

1 award annually. Send a self-addressed, stamped envelope to SWE for an application. Recipient is notified in May.

392—SOCIETY OF WOMEN ENGINEERS (GTE Foundation Scholarships)

120 Wall Street, 11th Floor
New York NY 10005-3902
800/666-ISWE or 212/509-9577
FAX: 212/509-0224
E-mail: hq@swe.org
Internet: http://www.swe.org

AMOUNT: $1,000
DEADLINE(S): FEB 1
FIELD(S): Electrical Engineering; Computer Science

Open to women who are entering sophomores or juniors at a college/university with an ABET-accredited program or in a SWE-approved school. Must have a minimum 3.5 GPA.

9 awards annually. Send a self-addressed, stamped envelope to SWE for an application. Recipients are notified in May.

393—SOCIETY OF WOMEN ENGINEERS (General Motors Foundation Scholarships)

120 Wall Street, 11th Floor
New York NY 10005-3902
800/666-ISWE or 212/509-9577
FAX: 212/509-0224
E-mail: hq@swe.org
Internet: http://www.swe.org

AMOUNT: $1,500 + $500 travel grant
DEADLINE(S): FEB 1
FIELD(S): Engineering: Mechanical, Electrical, Chemical, Industrial, Materials, Automotive, Manufacturing, Technology

For women entering as juniors at a college/university with ABET-accredited program or in SWE-approved school. Must exhibit career interest in automotive industry or manufacturing environment. Must have minimum 3.5 GPA and demonstrate leadership by holding position of responsibility in student organization. Travel grant available to recipients to attend SWE National Convention and Student Conference.

2 awards annually. Renewable senior year. Send self-addressed, stamped envelope to SWE for application. Recipients notified in May.

394—SOCIETY OF WOMEN ENGINEERS (Ivy Parker Memorial Scholarship)

120 Wall Street, 11th Floor
New York NY 10005-3902
800/666-ISWE or 212/509-9577
FAX: 212/509-0224
E-mail: hq@swe.org
Internet: http://www.swe.org

AMOUNT: $2,000
DEADLINE(S): FEB 1
FIELD(S): Engineering; Computer Science

Open to women who are entering sophomores or juniors at a college/university with an ABET-accredited program or in a SWE-approved school. Must have a minimum 3.5 GPA and demonstrate financial need.

1 award annually. Send a self-addressed, stamped envelope to SWE for an application. Recipient is notified in May.

395—SOCIETY OF WOMEN ENGINEERS (Judith Resnick Memorial Scholarship)

120 Wall Street, 11th Floor
New York NY 10005-3902
800/666-ISWE or 212/509-9577
FAX: 212/509-0224
E-mail: hq@swe.org
Internet: http://www.swe.org

AMOUNT: $2,000
DEADLINE(S): FEB 1
FIELD(S): Aerospace; Aeronautical/Astronautical Engineering

Open to women who are entering seniors at a college/university with an ABET-accredited program or in a SWE-approved school. Must have a minimum 3.5 GPA and be an active SWE Student Member. This award is in memory of astronaut Judith Resnik, who lost her life aboard the space shuttle Challenger.

1 award annually. Send a self-addressed, stamped envelope to SWE for an application. Recipient is notified in May.

396—SOCIETY OF WOMEN ENGINEERS (Lillian Moller Gilbreth Scholarship)

120 Wall Street, 11th Floor
New York NY 10005-3902
800/666-ISWE or 212/509-9577
FAX: 212/509-0224
E-mail: hq@swe.org
Internet: http://www.swe.org
AMOUNT: $5,000
DEADLINE(S): FEB 1
FIELD(S): Engineering; Computer Science

Open to women who are entering juniors or seniors at a college/university with an ABET-accredited program or in a SWE-approved school. Must have a minimum 3.5 GPA and demonstrate oustanding achievement and potential.

1 award annually. Send a self-addressed, stamped envelope to SWE for an application. Recipient is notified in May.

397—SOCIETY OF WOMEN ENGINEERS (Lockheed-Martin Corporation Scholarships)

120 Wall Street, 11th Floor
New York NY 10005-3902
800/666-ISWE or 212/509-9577
FAX: 212/509-0224
E-mail: hq@swe.org
Internet: http://www.swe.org
AMOUNT: $3,000
DEADLINE(S): MAY 15
FIELD(S): Engineering

Open to women who are entering freshmen in a college/university with an ABET-accredited program or in a SWE-approved school.

2 awards annually. Send a self-addressed, stamped envelope to SWE for an application. Recipients are notified in September.

398—SOCIETY OF WOMEN ENGINEERS (Lockheed-Martin Fort Worth Scholarships)

120 Wall Street, 11th Floor
New York NY 10005-3902
800/666-ISWE or 212/509-9577
FAX: 212/509-0224
E-mail: hq@swe.org
Internet: http://www.swe.org
AMOUNT: $1,000
DEADLINE(S): FEB 1
FIELD(S): Electrical and Mechanical Engineering

Open to women who are entering juniors at a college/university with an ABET-accredited program or in a SWE-approved school. Must have a minimum 3.5 GPA.

2 awards annually. Send a self-addressed, stamped envelope to SWE for an application. Recipients are notified in May.

399—SOCIETY OF WOMEN ENGINEERS (MASWE Memorial Scholarships)

120 Wall Street, 11th Floor
New York NY 10005-3902
800/666-ISWE or 212/509-9577
FAX: 212/509-0224
E-mail: hq@swe.org
Internet: http://www.swe.org
AMOUNT: $1,000-$2,000
DEADLINE(S): FEB 1
FIELD(S): Engineering; Computer Science

Open to women who are entering sophomores, juniors, or seniors at a college/university with an ABET-accredited program or in a SWE-approved school. Must have a minimum 3.5 GPA, show outstanding scholarship, and demonstrate financial need.

3 awards annually. Send a self-addressed, stamped envelope to SWE for an application. Recipients are notified in May.

400—SOCIETY OF WOMEN ENGINEERS (Northrop Corporation Founders Scholarship)

120 Wall Street, 11th Floor
New York NY 10005-3902
800/666-ISWE or 212/509-9577
FAX 212/509-0224
E-mail: hq@swe.org
Internet: http://www.swe.org
AMOUNT: $1,000
DEADLINE(S): FEB 1
FIELD(S): Engineering

Open to women who are entering sophomores at a college/university with an ABET-accredited program or in a SWE-approved school. Must have a minimum 3.5 GPA, be a U.S. citizen, and be a current SWE Student Member.

1 award annually. Send a self-addressed, stamped envelope to SWE for an application. Recipient is notified in May.

401—SOCIETY OF WOMEN ENGINEERS (Northrop Grumman Scholarships)

120 Wall Street, 11th Floor
New York NY 10005-3902
800/666-ISWE or 212/509-9577
FAX: 212/509-0224
E-mail: hq@swe.org
Internet: http://www.swe.org
AMOUNT: $1,000-$1,500
DEADLINE(S): MAY 15
FIELD(S): Engineering; Computer Science

Open to women who are entering freshmen in a college/university with an ABET-accredited program or in a SWE-approved school.

3 awards annually. Send a self-addressed, stamped envelope to SWE for an application. Recipients are notified in September.

402—SOCIETY OF WOMEN ENGINEERS (Olive Lynn Salembier Scholarship)

120 Wall Street, 11th Floor
New York NY 10005-3902
800/666-ISWE or 212/509-9577
FAX: 212/509-0224
E-mail: hq@swe.org
Internet: http://www.swe.org
AMOUNT: $2,000
DEADLINE(S): MAY 15
FIELD(S): Engineering; Computer Science

For women who have been out of the engineering job market as well as out of school for a minimum of two years. For any year undergraduate or graduate study, full- or part-time, at a college/university with an ABET-accredited program or in a SWE-approved school. Must have a minimum 3.5 GPA.

1 award annually. Send a self-addressed, stamped envelope to SWE for an application. Recipient is notified in September.

403—SOCIETY OF WOMEN ENGINEERS (Rockwell Corporation Scholarships)

120 Wall Street, 11th Floor
New York NY 10005-3902
800/666-ISWE or 212/509-9577
FAX: 212/509-0224
E-mail: hq@swe.org
Internet: http://www.swe.org
AMOUNT: $3,000
DEADLINE(S): FEB 1
FIELD(S): Engineering; Computer Science

Open to minority women who are entering juniors at a college/university with an ABET-accredited program or in a SWE-approved school. Must demonstrate leadership ability and have a minimum 3.5 GPA.

2 awards annually. Send a self-addressed, stamped envelope to SWE for an application. Recipients are notified in May.

404—SOCIETY OF WOMEN ENGINEERS (Stone and Webster Scholarships)

120 Wall Street, 11th Floor
New York NY 10005-3902
800/666-ISWE or 212/509-9577
FAX: 212/509-0224
E-mail: hq@swe.org
Internet: http://www.swe.org

AMOUNT: $1,000-$1,500
DEADLINE(S): FEB 1
FIELD(S): Engineering; Computer Science

Open to women who are entering sophomores, juniors, or seniors at a college/university with an ABET-accredited program or in a SWE-approved school. Must have a minimum 3.5 GPA.

4 awards annually. Send a self-addressed, stamped envelope to SWE for an application. Recipients are notified in May.

405—SRP/NAVAJO GENERATING STATION (Navajo Scholarship)

P.O. Box 850
Page AZ 86040
520/645-6539
FAX: 520/645-7295
E-mail: ljdawave@srp.gov

AMOUNT: Based on need
DEADLINE(S): APR 30
FIELD(S): Engineering, Environmental Studies, Business, Business Management, Health, Education

Scholarships for full-time students who hold membership in the Navajo Tribe and who are pursuing a degree in a field of study recognized as significant to the Navajo Naiton, Salt River Project, or the Navajo Generating Station, such as those listed above. Must be junior or senior, have and maintain a GPA of 3.0

Average of 15 awards per year. Inquire of Linda Dawavendewa at above location.

406—TAU BETA PI ASSOCIATION, INC. (Undergraduate Scholarships)

P.O. Box 2697
Knoxville TN 37901-2697
423/546-4578

AMOUNT: $2,000
DEADLINE(S): JAN 15
FIELD(S): Engineering

For members of Tau Beta Pi to use for their senior year of full-time undergraduate study. Membership is not by application-only by collegiate chapter invitation and initiation. Reference letters are required to apply for scholarship.

9 awards annually. Not renewable. Write for complete information.

407—TEXAS SOCIETY OF PROFESSIONAL ENGINEERS (Scholarships)

Austin TX 78768
512/472-9286 or 800/580-8973
Internet: http://www.tspe.org

AMOUNT: Varies
DEADLINE(S): JAN 30
FIELD(S): Engineering (Math, Sciences)

Scholarships for graduating high school seniors who are Texas residents planning to attend Texas engineering colleges

Contact organization for details. Application is on Web site.

408—THE BRITISH COUNCIL (Scholarships for Citizens of Mexico)

10 Spring Gardens
London SW1A 2BN ENGLAND UK
+44 (0) 171 930 8466
FAX: +44 (0) 161 957 7188
E-mail: education.enquiries@britcoun.org
Internet: http://www.britcoun.org/mexico/mexschol.htm

AMOUNT: Varies
DEADLINE(S): Varies
FIELD(S): Social Sciences, Applied Sciences, Technology

The British Council in Mexico offers approximately 100 scholarships per year in the above fields for undergraduates and graduates to study in the United Kingdom. Good level of English language retired.

The Web site listed here gives more details. For more information, contact: leticia.magana@bc-mexico.sprint.com. or contact organization in London.

409—THE DAPHNE JACKSON MEMORIAL FELLOWSHIPS TRUST (Fellowships in Science/Engineering)

School of Physical Sciences
Dept. of Physics, University of Surrey
Guildford, Surrey GU2 5XH
ENGLAND UK
01483 259166
FAX: 01483 259501
E-mail: J.Woolley@surrey.ac.uk
Internet: http://www.sst.ph.ic.ac.uk/trust/

AMOUNT: Varies
DEADLINE(S): Varies
FIELD(S): Science or Engineering, including Information Sciences

Fellowships to enable well-qualified and highly motivated scientists and engineers to return to appropriate careers following a career break due to family commitments. May be used on a flexible, part-time basis. Tenable at various U.K. universities.

See Web site and/or contact organization for details.

410—THE NORWAY-AMERICA ASSOCIATION (The Norwegian Marshall Fund)

Drammensveien 20C
N-0255 Oslo 2 NORWAY
011 47-22-44-76-83

AMOUNT: Up to $5,000
DEADLINE(S): Varies
FIELD(S): All fields of study

The Marshall Fund was established in 1977 as a token of Norway's gratitude to the U.S. for support after World War Two. Objective is to promote research in Norway by Americans in science and humanities. For U.S. citizens.

Contact above location for further information.

411—TYSON FOUNDATION, INC. (Alabama Scholarship Program)

2210 W. Oaklawn
Springdale AR 72762-6999
501/290-4995

AMOUNT: Varies (according to need)
DEADLINE(S): FEB 28
FIELD(S): Business; Agriculture; Engineering; Computer Science; Nursing

Open to residents of the general areas of Albertville, Ashland, Blountsville, Gadsden, Heflin, or Oxford, Alabama, who are U.S. citizens and live in the vicinity of a Tyson facility. Must be pursuing full-time undergraduate study at an accredited U.S. institution and demonstrate financial need. Must also be employed part-time and/or summers to help fund education.

Renewable up to 8 semesters or 12 trimesters as long as student meets criteria. Contact Tyson Foundation for an application no later than last day of February; deadline to return application is April 20.

412—TYSON FOUNDATION, INC. (Arkansas Scholarship Program)

2210 W. Oaklawn
Springdale AR 72762-6999
501/290-4955

AMOUNT: Varies (according to need)
DEADLINE(S): FEB 28
FIELD(S): Business; Agriculture; Engineering; Computer Science; Nursing

Open to Arkansas residents who are U.S. citizens pursuing full-time undergraduate study at an accredited U.S. institution. Must demonstrate financial need and be employed part-time and/or summers to help fund education.

Renewable up to 8 semesters or 12 trimesters as long as student meets criteria. Contact Tyson Foundation for an application no later than last day of February; deadline to return application is April 20.

413—TYSON FOUNDATION, INC. (Florida Scholarship Program)

2210 Oaklawn
Springdale AR 72762-6999
501/290-4995

AMOUNT: Varies (according to need)
DEADLINE(S): FEB 28
FIELD(S): Business; Agriculture; Engineering; Computer Science; Nursing

Open to residents of the general area of Jacksonville, Florida, who are U.S. citizens and live in the vicinity of a Tyson facility. Must be pursuing full-time undergraduate study in an accredited U.S. institution and demonstrate financial need. Must also be employed part-time and/or summers to help fund education.

Renewable up to 8 semesters or 12 trimesters as long as student meets criteria. Contact Tyson Foundation for an application no later than last day of February; deadline to return application is April 20.

414—TYSON FOUNDATION, INC. (Georgia Scholarship Program)

2210 Oaklawn
Springdale AR 72762-6999
501/290-4995

AMOUNT: Varies (according to need)
DEADLINE(S): FEB 28
FIELD(S): Business; Agriculture; Engineering; Computer Science; Nursing

Open to residents of the general areas of Cumming, Buena Vista, Dawson, or Vienna, Georgia, who are U.S. citizens and live in the vicinity of a Tyson facility. Must be pursuing full-time undergraduate study in an accredited U.S. institution and demonstrate financial need. Must also be employed part-time and/or summers to help fund education.

Renewable up to 8 semesters or 12 trimesters as long as student meets criteria. Contact Tyson Foundation for an application no later than last day of February; deadline to return application is April 20.

415—TYSON FOUNDATION, INC. (Illinois Scholarship Program)

2210 Oaklawn
Springdale AR 72762-6999
501/290-4995

AMOUNT: Varies (according to need)
DEADLINE(S): FEB 28
FIELD(S): Business; Agriculture; Engineering; Computer Science; Nursing

Open to residents of the general area of Chicago, Illinois, who are U.S. citizens and live in the vicinity of a Tyson facility. Must be pursuing full-time undergraduate study in an accredited U.S. institution and demonstrate financial need. Must also be employed part-time and/or summers to help fund education.

Renewable up to 8 semesters or 12 trimesters as long as student meets criteria. Contact Tyson Foundation for an application no later than last day of February; deadline to return application is April 20.

416—TYSON FOUNDATION, INC. (Indiana Scholarship Program)

2210 Oaklawn
Springdale AR 72762-6999
501/290-4995

AMOUNT: Varies (according to need)
DEADLINE(S): FEB 28
FIELD(S): Business; Agriculture; Engineering; Computer Science; Nursing

Open to residents of the general areas of Portland or Corydon, Indiana, who are U.S. citizens and live in the vicinity of a Tyson facility. Must be pursuing full-time undergraduate study at an accredited U.S. institution and demonstrate financial need. Must also be employed part-time and/or summers to help fund education.

Renewable up to 8 semesters or 12 trimesters as long as student meets criteria. Contact Tyson Foundation for an application no later than last day of February; deadline to return application is April 20.

417—TYSON FOUNDATION, INC. (Mississippi Scholarship Program)

2210 Oaklawn
Springdale AR 72762-6999
501/290-4995

AMOUNT: Varies (according to need)
DEADLINE(S): FEB 28
FIELD(S): Business; Agriculture; Engineering; Computer Science; Nursing

Open to residents of the general areas of Cleveland, Jackson, Forest, or Vicksburg, Mississippi, who are U.S. citizens and live in the vicinity of a Tyson facility. Must be pursuing full-time undergraduate study in an accredited U.S. institution and demonstrate financial need. Must also be employed part-time and/or summers to help fund education.

Renewable up to 8 semesters or 12 trimesters as long as student meets criteria. Contact Tyson Foundation for an application no later than last day of February; deadline to return application is April 20.

418—TYSON FOUNDATION, INC. (Missouri Scholarship Program)

2210 Oaklawn
Springdale AR 72762-6999
501/290-4995

AMOUNT: Varies (according to need)
DEADLINE(S): FEB 28
FIELD(S): Business; Agriculture; Engineering; Computer Science; Nursing

Open to residents of the general areas of Dexter, Monett, Neosho, Noel, or Sedalia, Missouri, who are U.S. citizens and live in the vicinity of a Tyson facility. Must be pursuing full-time undergraduate study in an accredited U.S. institution and demonstrate financial need. Must also be employed part-time and/or summers to help fund education.

Renewable up to 8 semesters or 12 trimesters as long as student meets criteria. Contact Tyson Foundation for an application no later than last day of February; deadline to return application is April 20.

419—TYSON FOUNDATION, INC. (North Carolina Scholarship Program)

2210 Oaklawn
Springdale AR 72762-6999
501/290-4995

AMOUNT: Varies (according to need)
DEADLINE(S): FEB 28

FIELD(S): Business; Agriculture; Engineering; Computer Science; Nursing

Open to residents of the general areas of Creswell, Monroe, Sanford, or Wilkesboro, North Carolina, who are U.S. citizens and live in the vicinity of a Tyson facility. Must be pursuing full-time undergraduate study in an accredited U.S. institution and demonstrate financial need. Must also be employed part-time and/or summers to help fund education.

Renewable up to 8 semesters or 12 trimesters as long as student meets criteria. Contact Tyson Foundation for an application no later than the last day of February; deadline to return application is April 20.

420—TYSON FOUNDATION, INC. (Oklahoma Scholarship Program)

2210 Oaklawn
Springdale AR 72762-6999
501/290-4995
AMOUNT: Varies (according to need)
DEADLINE(S): FEB 28
FIELD(S): Business; Agriculture; Engineering; Computer Science; Nursing

Open to residents of the general areas of Broken Bow or Stillwell, Oklahoma, who are U.S. citizens and live in the vicinity of a Tyson facility. Must be pursuing full-time undergraduate study in an accredited U.S. institution and demonstrate financial need. Must also be employed part-time and/or summers to help fund education.

Renewable up to 8 semesters or 12 trimesters as long as student meets criteria. Contact Tyson Foundation for an application no later than last day of February; deadline to return application is April 20.

421—TYSON FOUNDATION, INC. (Pennsylvania Scholarship Program)

2210 Oaklawn
Springdale AR 72762-6999
501/290-4995
AMOUNT: Varies (according to need)
DEADLINE(S): FEB 28
FIELD(S): Business; Agriculture; Engineering; Computer Science; Nursing

Open to residents of the general area of New Holland, Pennsylvania, who are U.S. citizens and live in the vicinity of a Tyson facility. Must be pursuing full-time undergraduate study in an accredited U.S. institution and demonstrate financial need. Must also be employed part-time and/or summers to help fund education.

Renewable up to 8 semesters or 12 trimesters as long as student meets criteria. Contact Tyson Foundation for an application no later than last day of February; deadline to return application is April 20.

422—TYSON FOUNDATION, INC. (Tennessee Scholarship Program)

2210 Oaklawn
Springdale AR 72762-6999
501/290-4995
AMOUNT: Varies (according to need)
DEADLINE(S): FEB 28
FIELD(S): Business; Agriculture; Engineering; Computer Science; Nursing

Open to residents of the general areas of Shelbyville or Union City, Tennessee, who are U.S. citizens and live in the vicinity of a Tyson facility. Must be pursuing full-time undergraduate study in an accredited U.S. institution and demonstrate financial need. Must also be employed part-time and/or summers to help fund education.

Renewable up to 8 semesters or 12 trimesters as long as student meets criteria. Contact Tyson Foundation for an application no later than last day of February; deadline to return application is April 20.

423—TYSON FOUNDATION, INC. (Texas Scholarship Program)

2210 Oaklawn
Springdale AR 72762-6999
501/290-4995
AMOUNT: Varies (according to need)
DEADLINE(S): FEB 28
FIELD(S): Business; Agriculture; Engineering; Computer Science; Nursing

Open to residents of the general areas of Carthage, Center, or Seguin, Texas, who are U.S. citizens and live in the vicinity of a Tyson facility. Must be pursuing full-time undergraduate study in an accredited U.S. institution and demonstrate financial need. Must also be employed part-time and/or summers to help fund education.

Renewable up to 8 semesters or 12 trimesters as long as student meets criteria. Contact Tyson Foundation for an application no later than last day of February; deadline to return application is April 20.

424—TYSON FOUNDATION, INC. (Virginia Scholarship Program)

2210 Oaklawn
Springdale AR 72762-6999
501/290-4995
AMOUNT: Varies (according to need)
DEADLINE(S): FEB 28
FIELD(S): Business; Agriculture; Engineering; Computer Science; Nursing

Open to residents of the general areas of Glen Allen, Harrisonburg, or Temperanceville, Virginia, who are U.S. citizens and live in the vicinity of a Tyson facility. Must be pursuing full-time undergraduate study in an accredited U.S. institution and demonstrate financial need. Must also be employed part-time and/or summers to help fund education.

Renewable up to 8 semesters or 12 trimesters as long as student meets criteria. Contact Tyson Foundation for an application no later than last day of February; deadline to return application is April 20.

425—U.S. DEPARTMENT OF DEFENSE (High School Apprenticeship Program)

U.S. Army Cold Regions Research and Engineering Laboratory
72 Lyme Road
Hanover NH 03755
603/646-4500; DSN: 220-4500
FAX: 603/646-4693
Internet: http://www.acq.osd.mil/ddre/edugate/s-aindx.html
AMOUNT: Internship
DEADLINE(S): None specified
FIELD(S): Sciences and Engineering

A teacher must recommend you for these three competitive high school apprenticeships with our Laboratory. High school students from New Hampshire who are at least 16 and who have completed their junior year in high school are eligible. Should have interest and ability in science, engineering, or mathematics.

Applications are available from participating local high school guidance counselors. Contact Susan Koh at the above address for more information.

426—U.S. DEPARTMENT OF DEFENSE (SEAP Science and Engineering Apprenticeship Program)

707 22nd Street NW
Washington DC 20052
202/994-2234
FAX: 202/994-2459
Internet: http://www.acq.osd.mil/ddre/edugate/ceeindx.htm/#A010
AMOUNT: $1,400 (min.)
DEADLINE(S): JAN 26
FIELD(S): Science; Engineering

Eight-week summer apprenticeships throughout the U.S. are available to high school students who are U.S. citizens planning careers in science or engineering. Based on grades, science/math courses taken, scores on standardized tests, areas of interest, teacher recommendations, and personal student statement. Students responsible for transportation to and from site.

See Web site or contact M. Phillips for an application. Refer to Code #A010.

427—UNIVERSITY OF MARYLAND (John B. and Ida Slaughter Endowed Scholarship in Science, Technology, and the Black Community)

2169 Lefrak Hall
College Park MD 20742-7225
301/405-1158
FAX: 301/314-986
Internet: http://www.bsos.umd.edu/aasp/scholarship.html

AMOUNT: Varies (in-state tuition costs)
DEADLINE(S): MAR
FIELD(S): Science and Technology AND African-American Studies

Open to African-Americans who are U.S. residents with a minimum 2.8 GPA. Must be accepted to or enrolled at UMCP for freshmen year and must submit letter of recommendation from high school counselor or UMCP faculty member. Should have an interest in applying science and technology to the problems of the Black community. Essay required.

Renewable. Contact the Center for Minorities in Science and Engineering at UMCP for an application.

428—UNIVERSITY OF WALES-SCHOOL OF ELECTRONIC ENGINEERING and COMPUTER SYSTEMS (Undergraduate Scholarships)

Dean Street
Bangor, Gwynedd
LL57 1UT WALES UK
+44 (0)01248 382686
FAX: +44(0)012248 361429
E-mail: admissions@sees.bangor.ac.uk
Internet: http://www.sees.bangor.ac.uk/courses.html

AMOUNT: 1,000 pounds
DEADLINE(S): None
FIELD(S): Electronic Engineering and Computer Systems

Undergraduate scholarships in the above fields in Bangor, North Wales.

Runners-up receive 50-pound book tokens. Contact school for details.

429—WOMEN IN DEFENSE (HORIZONS Scholarship Foundation)

NDIA
2111 Wilson Boulevard, Suite 400
Arlington VA 22201-3061
703/247-2552
FAX: 703/522-1820
E-mail: cbanks@mciworld.com
Internet: http://www.ndia.org/wid/

AMOUNT: $500+
DEADLINE(S): NOV 1; JUL 1
FIELD(S): Engineering; Computer Science; Physics; Math; Business; Law; International Relations; Political Science; Operations Research; Economics; National Security/Defense

Open to women employed/planning careers in defense/national security areas. Must be currently enrolled full- or part-time at an accredited college/university at the graduate or undergraduate junior/senior level. Must have a minimum 3.25 GPA, demonstrate financial need, and be U.S. citizen. Based on academic achievement, work experience, objectives, and recommendations.

Renewable. See Web site or MUST send self-addressed, stamped envelope to Courtney Banks for application.

430—WOODROW WILSON NATIONAL FELLOWSHIP FOUNDATION (Leadership Program for Teachers)

CN 5281
Princeton NJ 08543-5281
609/452-7007
FAX: 609/452-0066
E-mail: marchioni@woodrow.org OR irish@woodrow.org
Internet: http://www.woodrow.org

AMOUNT: Varies
DEADLINE(S): Varies
FIELD(S): Science; Mathematics

WWLPT offers summer institutes for middle and high school teachers in science and mathematics. One- and two-week teacher outreach, TORCH Institutes, are held in the summer throughout the U.S.

See Web site or contact WWNFF for an application.

431—WOODS HOLE OCEANOGRAPHIC INSTITUTION (Traineeships in Oceanography for Minority Group Undergraduates)

360 Woods Hole Road
Woods Hole MA 02543-1541
508/289-2219
FAX: 508/457-2188
E-mail: mgately@whoi.edu
Internet: http://www.whoi.edu

AMOUNT: Varies
DEADLINE(S): FEB 16
FIELD(S): Physical/Natural Sciences, Mathematics, Engineering

For minority undergraduates enrolled in U.S. colleges/universities who have completed at least two semesters. These awards provide training and research experience for students with interests in the above fields. Traineeships may be awarded for a ten- to- twelve-week period in the summer or for a semester during the academic year.

Renewable. For an application/more information, contact the Education Office, Clark Laboratory 223, MS #31, at above address.

432—XEROX TECHNICAL MINORITY SCHOLARSHIP (School-Year Tuition)

907 Culver Road
Rochester NY 14609
Internet: www.xerox.com/employment

AMOUNT: Up to $5,000 (varies according to tuition and academic excellence)
DEADLINE(S): SEP 15
FIELD(S): Various engineering and science disciplines

Scholarships for minorities enrolled full-time in a technical degree program at the bachelor level or above. Must be African-American, Native American, Hispanic, or Asian. Recipient may not have tuition or related expenses covered by other scholarships or grants.

If above requirements are met, obtain application from Web site or address above. Your financial aid office must fill out the bottom half of the form. Send completed application, your resume and a cover letter to Xerox Technical Minority Scholarship Program at above address.

433—XEROX TECHNICAL MINORITY SCHOLARSHIP (Summer Employment Program)

Xerox Square
Rochester NY 14644
Written Inquiry

AMOUNT: Up to $5,000 (varies according to tuition and academic excellence)
DEADLINE(S): SEP 15
FIELD(S): Engineering and Science Disciplines

Scholarships for minorities enrolled in a technical degree program at the bachelor level or above. Must be African-American, Native American, Hispanic, or Asian. Xerox will match your skills with a sponsoring organization that will offer a meaningful summer work experience complimenting your academic learning.

If above requirements are met, send your resume and a cover letter to Xerox Corporation Corporate Employment and College Relations Technical Minority Scholarship Program.

AERONAUTICS

434—AERO CLUB OF NEW ENGLAND (Aviation Scholarships)

ACONE Education Committee
4 Thomas Road
Danvers MA 01923
978/263-7793
E-mail: jbuckaroo@mindspring.com
Internet: http://www.acone.org
AMOUNT: $500-$2,500
DEADLINE(S): MAR 30
FIELD(S): Aviation and Related Fields

Several scholarships with varying specifications for eligibility for New England residents to be used at FAA-approved flight schools in New England states.

Information and applications are on Web site above.

435—AIR FORCE RESERVE OFFICER TRAINING CORPS (AFROTC Scholarships)

551 E. Maxwell Boulevard
Maxwell AFB AL 36112-6106
334/953-7783
AMOUNT: Full tuition, books, and fees for all 4 years of college
DEADLINE(S): DEC 1
FIELD(S): Science; Engineering; Business; Political Science; Psychology; Geography; Foreign Studies; Foreign Language

Competitive scholarships based on individual merit to high school seniors and graduates who have not completed any full-time college work. Must be a U.S. citizen between the ages of 17-27. Must also have GPA of 2.5 or above, be in top 40% of class, and complete Applicant Fitness Test. Cannot be a single parent. Your college/university must offer AFROTC.

2,300 awards annually. Contact above address for application packet.

436—AIR FORCE RESERVE OFFICER TRAINING CORPS (AFROTC Scholarships)

551 E. Maxwell Boulevard
Maxwell AFB AL 36112-6106
334/953-7783
AMOUNT: Full tuition, books, and fees for all 4 years of college
DEADLINE(S): DEC 1
FIELD(S): Science; Engineering; Business; Political Science; Psychology; Geography; Foreign Studies; Foreign Language

Competitive scholarships based on individual merit to high school seniors and graduates who have not completed any full-time college work. Must be a U.S. citizen between the ages of 17-27. Must also have GPA of 2.5 or above, be in top 40% of class, and complete Applicant Fitness Test. Cannot be a single parent. Your college/university must offer AFROTC.

2,300 awards annually. Contact above address for application packet.

437—AMERICAN INSTITUTE OF AERONAUTICS AND ASTRONAUTICS (Undergraduate Scholarships)

1801 Alexander Bell Drive, Suite 500
Reston VA 20191-4344
800/639-AIAA; 703/264-7630
FAX: 703/264-7551
E-mail: rayc@aiaa.org
Internet: http://www.aiaa.org
AMOUNT: $2,000
DEADLINE(S): JAN 31
FIELD(S): Science, Engineering, Aeronautics, Astronautics

For students who have completed at least one academic semester or quarter of full-time college work in the area of science or engineering encompassed by the technical activities of the AIAA. Must have GPA of at least 3.0, be currently enrolled in accredited college or university. Membership in AIAA not required to apply but must become one before receiving a scholarship award.

Students who receive these awards are eligible for yearly continuation until completion of senior year upon submission of application, career essay, transcripts and 2 letters of recommendation from college professor.

438—ASSOCIATED WESTERN UNIVERSITIES, INC. (AWU Undergraduate Student Fellowships)

4190 S. Highland Drive, Suite 211
Salt Lake City UT 84124-2600
801/273-8900
FAX: 801/277-5632
E-mail: info@awu.org
Internet: http://www.awu.org
AMOUNT: $300/week stipend + possible travel allowance
DEADLINE(S): FEB 1
FIELD(S): Science; Mathematics; Engineering; Technology

Eight- to sixteen-week fellowships.

439—ASTRONAUT SCHOLARSHIP FOUNDATION (Scholarships)

Exec. Director
6225 Vectorspace Boulevard
Titusville FL 32780
321/269-6119
FAX: 321/267-3970
E-mail: MercurySvn@aol.com
Internet: http://www.astronautscholarship.org/guidelines.html
AMOUNT: Varies
DEADLINE(S): Varies
FIELD(S): Engineering and Physical Sciences (Medical Research ok, but NOT Professional Medicine)

Open to juniors, seniors, and graduate students at a select group of schools. Must be U.S. citizen with the intention to pursue research or advance field of study upon completion of final degree. Special consideration given to students who have shown initiative, creativity, excellence, and/or resourcefulness in their field. Must be NOMINATED by faculty or staff.

See Web site for list of eligible schools. Contact Howard Benedict, Executive Director, for details.

440—AVIATION COUNCIL OF PENNSYLVANIA (Scholarships)

3111 Arcadia Avenue
Allentown PA 18103
610/797-1133
FAX: 610/797-8238
AMOUNT: $1,000
DEADLINE(S): JUL 31
FIELD(S): Aviation Maintenance, Aviation Management, or Pilot Training

Scholarships for individuals in the above fields who are residents of Pennsylvania but can attend school outside Pennsylvania.

Up to 4 awards yearly.

441—AVIATION DISTRIBUTORS AND MANUFACTURERS ASSOCIATION INTERNATIONAL (ADMA International Scholarship Fund)

1900 Arch Street
Philadelphia PA 19103-1498

215/564-3484
FAX: 215/564-2175
E-mail: assnhqt@netaxs.com
AMOUNT: Varies
DEADLINE(S): MAR 15
FIELD(S): Aviation Management; Professional Pilot

Open to students seeking a career in aviation management or as a professional pilot. Emphasis may be in general aviation, airway science management, aviation maintenance, flight engineering, or airway a/c systems management.

Applicants must be studying in the aviation field in a four-year school having an aviation program. Write for complete information.

442—AVIATION INSURANCE ASSOCIATION (Scholarship)

Aviation Technology Department
1 Purdue Airport
West Lafayette IN 47906-3398
765/494-5782
AMOUNT: $1,000
DEADLINE(S): FEB 28
FIELD(S): Aviation

Scholarships for aviation students who have completed at least 30 college credits, 15 of which are in aviation. Must have GPA of at least 2.5 and be a U.S. citizen.

Write to Professor Bernard Wulle at Purdue University at above address for application and details.

443—CIVIL AIR PATROL (Major Gen. Lucas V. Beau Flight Scholarship)

Civil Air Patrol National HQ,
HQ CAP/CFR
105 South Hansell Street; Bldg. 714
Maxwell AFB AL 36112-6332
334/953-4238
FAX: 334-953-6699
E-mail: cpr@capnhq.gov
Internet: http://www.capnhq.gov/nhq/cp/cp.htm
AMOUNT: $2,100
DEADLINE(S): MAR 1
FIELD(S): Ground and Air Training for FAA private pilot licensing

Open to CAP cadets pursuing undergraduate studies in the above field. 5 awards annually.

See Web site or write for complete information.

444—EAA AVIATION FOUNDATION (Scholarship Program)

P.O. Box 3065
Oshkosh WI 54903-3065
920/426-6815 or 888/EAA-EAA9 or 888/322-3229
E-mail: education@eaa.org
Internet: http://www.eaa.org
AMOUNT: $500-$5,000
DEADLINE(S): MAY 1
FIELD(S): Aviation

Six different scholarship programs open to well-rounded individuals involved in school and community activities as well as aviation. Applicant's academic records should verify his/her ability to complete educational activity for which scholarship is requested. For all but one scholarship, students must major in aviation. Financial need considered in some programs. One scholarship includes tuition, books, fees, etc. at the Fox Valley Technical College in Wisconsin.

Renewable. $5 application fee. Contact EAA for an application (one application covers all of the scholarship programs).

445—ILLINOIS PILOTS ASSOCIATION (IPA Memorial Scholarship)

40 West Apache Lane
Huntley IL 60142
Internet: http://www.illinoispilots.com/
AMOUNT: $500
DEADLINE(S): APR 1
FIELD(S): Aviation

Scholarships for individuals majoring in an aviation-oriented curriculum who are residents of Illinois and attending a college or university in Illinois.

Check Web site or write for details.

446—INSTITUTION OF ELECTRICAL ENGINEERS (Scholarships for Women)

Savoy Place
London WC2R 0BL ENGLAND
0171 240 1871 ext. 2211/2235
FAX: 0171 497 3609
E-mail: scholarships@iee.org.uk
Internet: http://www.iee.org.uk/Awards/ugwom.htm
AMOUNT: 750 pounds/year
DEADLINE(S): JUN 15
FIELD(S): Engineering

Scholarships for women residing in the United Kingdom and pursuing degrees in engineering.

Candidates must be undertaking mathematics and physics "A" level or Scottish Higher examinations. Renewable for the entire period of an IEE-accredited course. Check Web site or contact organization for application details.

447—INSTITUTION OF ELECTRICAL ENGINEERS (Undergraduate Scholarships)

Savoy Place
London WC2R 0BL ENGLAND
0171 240 1871 ext. 2211/2235
FAX: 0171 497 3609
E-mail: scholarships@iee.org.uk
Internet: http://www.iee.org.uk/Awards/ugsum.htm
AMOUNT: 750-1,000 pounds/year
DEADLINE(S): JUN 30; SEP 30
FIELD(S): Engineering

Scholarships for residents of the United Kingdom and pursuing degree in various engineering specialties. Criteria vary, including academic excellence and financial need.

Check Web site or contact organization for application details.

448—INTERNATIONAL SOCIETY OF WOMEN AIRLINE PILOTS (ISA Career Scholarship)

2250 E. Tropicana Avenue,
Suite 19-395
Las Vegas NV 89119-6594
E-mail: wame@swbell.net
Internet: http://www.iswap.org/scholarship.html
AMOUNT: Varies
DEADLINE(S): APR 15
FIELD(S): Airline Pilot Advanced Ratings

Open to women whose goals are to fly the world's airlines. For advanced pilot ratings, such as the U.S. FAA ATP certificate or equivalent.

Applicants must have a U.S. FAA Commercial Pilot Certificate with an Instrument Rating and a First Class medical certificate (or equivalent). Also must have a minimum of 750 flight hours. Personal interview is required. Check Web site or write for more information and application.

449—INTERNATIONAL SOCIETY OF WOMEN AIRLINE PILOTS (Fiorenze De Bernardi Merit Award.)

2250 E. Tropicana Avenue,
Suite 19-395
Las Vegas NV 89119-6541
E-mail: wame@swbell.net
Internet: http://www.iswap.org/scholarship.html
AMOUNT: Varies
DEADLINE(S): APR 15
FIELD(S): Airline Pilot Training

A merit scholarship for women throughout the world who are pursuing airline pilot careers. Selection based on need, demonstrated dedication to career goal, work history, experience, and recommendations.

To aid pilots with CFI, CFII, MEI, or any equivalents. Must have a U.S.FAA Commercial Pilot Certificate with an Instrument Rating and a First Class medical certificate (or equivalent). Candidates must have a minimum of 250 flight hours. Personal interview required. Check Web site or write for more information and application.

450—INTERNATIONAL SOCIETY OF WOMEN AIRLINE PILOTS (Holly Mullins Memorial Scholarship)

2250 E. Tropicana Avenue,
Suite 19-395
Las Vegas NV 89119-6594
E-mail: wame@swbell.net
Internet: http://www.iswap.org/scholarship.html

AMOUNT: Varies
DEADLINE(S): APR 15
FIELD(S): Airline Pilot Training

A merit scholarship for women who are single mothers and pursuing airline pilot careers. Selection is based on need, demonstrated dedication to career goal, work history experience, and recommendations.

To aid pilots with CFI, CRII, MEI, or any equivalents. Must have a U.S.FAA Commercial Pilot Certificate with an Instrument Rating and a First Class medical certificate (or equivalent). Additionally, candidates must have a minimum of 750 flight hours. Check Web site or write for more information and application.

451—INTERNATIONAL SOCIETY OF WOMEN AIRLINE PILOTS (ISA Airline Scholarship)

2250 E. Tropicana Avenue,
Suite 19-395
Las Vegas NV 89119-6594
E-mail: wame@swbell.net
Internet: http://www.iswap.org/scholarship.html

AMOUNT: Varies
DEADLINE(S): APR 15
FIELD(S): Flight Engineering and Type Ratings

For women seeking careers in aviation and need Flight Engineer Certificates and Type Ratings on 727, 737, 747, 757, and DC-10 aircraft. For Flight Engineers, 1,000 hours flight time and a current FE written required. For Type Rating scholarship, an ATP Certificate and a current FE written.

Check Web site or write for more information and application.

452—LOS ANGELES COUNCIL OF BLACK PROFESSIONAL ENGINEERS (Al-Ben Scholarship)

P.O. Box 881029
Los Angeles CA 90009
310/635-7734
E-mail: secy1@lablackengineers.org
Internet: http://www.lablackengineers.org/scholarships.html

AMOUNT: Varies
DEADLINE(S): Varies
FIELD(S): Engineering; Mathematics; Computer Studies; Applied Scientific Studies

Open to technically inclined precollege and undergraduate students enrolled in one of the above fields. Must be of African American, Native American, or Hispanic ancestry. Preference given to students attending college in Southern California or who are Southern California residents.

See Web site to download an application.

453—MARYLAND HIGHER EDUCATION COMMISSION (Maryland Science and Technology Scholarship Program)

16 Francis Street
Annapolis Park MD 21401
410/974-5370 or 800/974-1024
E-mail: ssamail@mhec.state.md.us
Internet: http://www.mhec.state.md.us/SSA/stech_qa.htm

AMOUNT: $3,000/year (BA); $1,000/year (AA)
DEADLINE(S): None
FIELD(S): Computer Science; Engineering; Technology

Scholarships for college-bound Maryland high school seniors who will major in one of the above fields and who are accepted to an eligible associate or bachelor's degree program in Maryland. The deadline was not known at this writing, so check for deadline date. Must agree to work in the state after graduation in a related field, one year for each year of assistance received.

Must maintain a 3.0 GPA.

454—NATIONAL AERONAUTICS AND SPACE ADMINISTRATION (ACCESS Internships)

Stennis Space Center, Bldg. 1100
Bay Saint Louis MS 39529
228/688-2079
E-mail: covington.pamela@ssc.nasa.gov

AMOUNT: Internship only
DEADLINE(S): None
FIELD(S): Aeronautics/Aerospace; Astronomy; Chemistry; Physics; Engineering; Math; Earth, Life, Materials, Computer, and Physical Sciences

Nine- to ten-week summer internships are open to undergraduates with physical or learning disabilities who maintain a minimum 3.0 GPA and are U.S. citizens. Purpose is to increase the number of students with disabilities pursuing technical degrees related to NASA's mission and to provide on-site experience. Internship takes place at the Stennis Space Center in Mississippi.

Contact Pam Covington for an application.

455—NATIONAL AIR TRANSPORTATION ASSOCIATION FOUNDATION (John W. Godwin, Jr., Memorial Scholarship Fund)

4226 King Street
Alexandria VA 22302
808/808-NATA or 703/845-9000
FAX: 703/845-8176

AMOUNT: $2,500
DEADLINE(S): None
FIELD(S): Flight training

Scholarship for flight training for any certificate and/or flight rating issued by the FAA, at any NATA-Member company offering flight training. Must accumulate a minimum of 15 dual or solo flight hours each calendar month.

Contact organization for details.

456—NATIONAL AIR TRANSPORTATION ASSOCIATION FOUNDATION (The Pioneers of Flight Scholarship)

4226 King Street
Alexandria VA 22302
703/845-9000
FAX: 703/845-8176

AMOUNT: $2,500
DEADLINE(S): None
FIELD(S): General aviation

Scholarship for college students who are in the sophomore or junior year at the time of application intending to pursue full-time study at an accredited four-year college or university and can demonstrate an interest in pursuing a career in general aviation.

Must be nominated by an NATA Regular or Associate Member company.

457—NATIONAL BUSINESS AVIATION ASSOCIATION (Indiana Business Aviation Association PDP Scholarships)

1200 Eighteenth Street NW,
Suite 400
Washington DC 20036-2527
202/783-9353
FAX: 202/331-8364
E-mail: jevans@nbaa.org
Internet: http://www.nbaa.org/scholarships/

AMOUNT: $1,150
DEADLINE(S): AUG 31
FIELD(S): Aviation-related curricula

Valid only for students enrolled at institutions that are NBAA and University Aviation Association (UAA) members. Open to college sophomores, juniors, or seniors who will be continuing in school the following academic year in an aviation-related baccalaureate or graduate program at these specific member institutions. Must be U.S. citizen and have 3.0 or better GPA.

4 awards per year. Check Web site or contact NBAA for complete information and application.

458—NATIONAL BUSINESS AVIATION ASSOCIATION (Lawrence Ginocchio Aviation Scholarship)

1200 Eighteenth Street NW,
Suite 400
Washington DC 20036-2527
202/783-9353
FAX: 202/331-8364
E-mail: jevans@nbaa.org
Internet: http://www.nbaa.org/scholarships/

AMOUNT: $5,000
DEADLINE(S): AUG 22
FIELD(S): Aviation-related curricula

Valid only for students enrolled at institutions that are NBAA and University Aviation Association (UAA) members. Open to college sophomores, juniors, or seniors who will be continuing in school the following academic year in an aviation-related baccalaureate or graduate program at these specific member institutions. Must be U.S. citizen and have 3.0 or better GPA.

5 awards per year. Check Web site or contact NBAA for complete information and application.

459—NATIONAL GAY PILOTS ASSOCIATION (Pilot Scholarships)

13140 Coit Road, Suite 320, LB 120
Dallas TX 75240
972/233-9107 ext. 203
FAX: 972/490-4219
E-mail: ngpa@ngpa.org
Internet: http://www.ngpa.org

AMOUNT: $2,000
DEADLINE(S): APR 30
FIELD(S): Pilot Training and Related Fields in Aerospace, Aerodynamics, Engineering, Airport Management, etc.

Scholarships for tuition or flight training costs for student pilots enrolled at a college or university offering an accredited aviation curriculum in the above fields. Also for flight training costs in a professional pilot training program at any training facility certified by the FAA. Not for training for a Private Pilot license. Send SASE for application or visit Web site for further instructions.

For applicants who can provide evidence of volunteering in any group that supports the gay/lesbian community and their rights.

460—NATIONAL SCIENCES AND ENGINEERING RESEARCH COUNCIL OF CANADA (Undergraduate Scholarships)

Scholarships/Fellowships Division
350 Albert Street
Ottawa Ontario K1A 1H5 CANADA
613/996-2009
FAX: 613/996-2589
E-mail: schol@nserc.ca
Internet: http://www.nserc.ca

AMOUNT: Up to $3,600
DEADLINE(S): Varies
FIELD(S): Natural Sciences, Engineering, Biology, or Chemistry

Open to Canadian citizens or permanent residents working towards degrees in science or engineering. Academic excellence and research aptitude are considerations.

Write for complete information.

461—NATIONAL SOCIETY OF BLACK ENGINEERS (Scholarships)

1454 Duke Street
Alexandria VA 22314
703/549-2207
FAX: 703/683-5312
E-mail: nsbehq@nsbe.org
Internet: http://www.nsbe.org

AMOUNT: Varies
DEADLINE(S): Varies
FIELD(S): Engineering and engineering technologies

Programs for black and other ethnic minorities in the fields of engineering and the engineering technologies. Organization offers precollege programs, scholarships, career fairs, a journal, a newsletter, etc.

Contact organization for details.

462—NATURAL SCIENCES AND ENGINEERING RESEARCH COUNCIL OF CANADA (Undergraduate Student Research Awards in Small Universities)

350 Albert Street
Ottawa Ontario K1A 1H5 CANADA
613/995-5992
FAX: 613/992-5337
E-mail: schol@nserc.ca
Internet: http://www.nserc.ca/programs/usrasmen.htm

AMOUNT: $3,600 (max.)
DEADLINE(S): Varies
FIELD(S): Natural Sciences; Engineering

Research awards for Canadian citizens/permanent residents attending eligible institutions, and who have no more than 6 and no fewer than 2 academic terms remaining to complete bachelor's degree. Cumulative GPA of at least 2nd class (B). Must be doing full-time in research and development activities during award tenure.

Students in health sciences not eligible. Students with BAs and who are studying for a second may apply.

463—NINETY-NINES, INC. (Amelia Earhart Memorial Scholarships)

Box 965, 7100 Terminal Drive
Oklahoma City OK 73159-0965
800/994-1929 or 405/685-7969
FAX: 405/685-7985
E-mail: 99s@ninety-nines.org
Internet: http://www.ninety-nines.org

AMOUNT: Varies
DEADLINE(S): DEC 31
FIELD(S): Advanced Aviation Ratings

Scholarships for female licensed pilots who are members of the 99s, Inc.

15-20 awards annually. Financial need considered. Contact Liz Rousch at above address for application and/or membership information.

464—NINETY-NINES, SAN FERNANDO VALLEY CHAPTER/VAN NUYS AIRPORT (Aviation Career Scholarships)

P.O. Box 8160
Van Nuys CA 91409

818/989-0081
AMOUNT: $3,000
DEADLINE(S): MAY 1
FIELD(S): Aviation Careers

For men and women of the greater Los Angeles area pursuing careers as professional pilots, flight instructors, mechanics, or other aviation career specialists. Applicants must be at least 21 years of age and U.S. citizens.

3 awards annually. Send self-addressed, stamped, business-sized envelope to above address for application after January 1.

465—OAK RIDGE INSTITUTE FOR SCIENCE AND EDUCATION (ORISE Education and Training Programs)

P.O. Box 117
Oak Ridge TN 37831-0117
Internet: http://www.orau.gov/orise/educ.htm
AMOUNT: Varies
DEADLINE(S): Varies
FIELD(S): Engineering; Aeronautics; Computer Science; Technology; Earth Science; Environmental Studies; Biology; Chemistry; Physics; Medical Research

Numerous programs funded by the U.S. Department of Energy are offered for undergraduate students through postgraduate researchers. Includes fellowship and internship opportunities throughout the U.S.. Some have citizenship restrictions. Travel may be included.

See Web site or write for a catalog of specific programs and requirements.

466—QUEEN'S UNIVERSITY OF BELFAST (Industrial Scholarships)

Training and Employment Agency, Management Development Division, 9-21 Adelaide Street
Belfast BT2 8DT Northern Ireland UK
+44 (0) 1232 245133
Internet: http://www.icbl.qub.ac.uk/prospectus/funding/scholars.htm
AMOUNT: Varies
DEADLINE(S): Varies
FIELD(S): Engineering: Aeronautical, Electrical and Electronic, Mechanical, and Manufacturing

Scholarships in Northern Ireland for study in the above fields.

Contact the University at the address shown for complete information.

467—SAN DIEGO AEROSPACE MUSEUM (Bill Gibbs Scholarship)

Education Dept.
2001 Pan American Plaza
San Diego CA 92101
619/234-8291 ext. 19
FAX: 619/233-4526
Internet: http://aerospacemuseum.org/Scholastic.HTML
AMOUNT: Varies
DEADLINE(S): Varies
FIELD(S): Aerospace: math, physics, science, or engineering

For students who are residents of San Diego County, California, who have an aerospace career interest who have been accepted to a four-year college or university in a degree program relating to math, physics, science, or engineering.

Call or write museum for further information.

468—THE DAPHNE JACKSON MEMORIAL FELLOWSHIPS TRUST (Fellowships in Science/Engineering)

School of Physical Sciences, Dept. of Physics, University of Surrey
Guildford, Surrey GU2 5XH
ENGLAND UK
01483 259166
FAX: 01483 259501
E-mail: J.Woolley@surrey.ac.uk
Internet: http://www.sst.ph.ic.ac.uk/trust/
AMOUNT: Varies
DEADLINE(S): Varies
FIELD(S): Science or engineering, including information sciences

Fellowships to enable well-qualified and highly motivated scientists and engineers to return to appropriate careers following a career break due to family commitments. May be used on a flexible, part-time basis. Tenable at various U.K. universities.

See Web site and/or contact organization for details.

469—THE FRASCA FAMILY/UNIVERSITY AVIATION ASSOCIATION (The Joseph Frasca Excellence in Aviation Scholarship)

c/o College of Applied Sciences and Art, Southern Illinois University
Carbondale IL 62901-6623
618/453-8898
AMOUNT: $1,000
DEADLINE(S): JUN 3
FIELD(S): Aviation Maintenance or Flight Training

Scholarships for college juniors or seniors currently enrolled in a University Aviation Association (UAA)-affiliated institution and pursuing a career in one of the above fields. Minimum GPA of 3.0. Must show membership in a flight-related organization.

2 awards yearly.

470—THE ART INSTITUTES INTERNATIONAL (Evelyn Keedy Memorial Scholarship)

300 Sixth Avenue, Suite 800
Pittsburgh PA 15222-2598
412/562-9800
FAX: 412/562-9802
E-mail: webadmin@aii.edu
Internet: http://www.aii.edu
AMOUNT: 2 years full tuition
DEADLINE(S): MAY 1
FIELD(S): Various fields in the creative and applied arts: video production, broadcasting, culinary arts, fashion design, Web site administration, etc.

Scholarships at 12 different locations nationwide in various fields described above. For graduating high school seniors admitted to an Arts Institutes International School, the New York Restaurant School, or NCPT. Transcripts, letters of recommendation, and resume must be submitted with application.

See Web site or contact AII for more information.

471—VERTICAL FLIGHT FOUNDATION (AHS Vertical Flight Foundation Engineering Scholarships)

217 N. Washington Street
Alexandria VA 22314-2520
703/684-6777
FAX: 703/739-9279
E-mail: staff@vtol.org
Internet: http://www.vtol.org/vff.html
AMOUNT: $2,000-$4,000
DEADLINE(S): FEB 1
FIELD(S): Engineering in vertical flight area

These merit-based awards, from the American Helicopter Society, are open to undergraduate juniors and seniors and graduate students pursuing full-time studies in vertical flight at accredited schools of engineering. Must submit transcripts and references. Scholarships awarded to student once as an undergraduate senior, once as a master's student, and once as a Ph.D. student. Financial need NOT a factor.

3 to 8 awards annually. See Web site or contact VFF for an application.

472—VIRGINIA AVIATION AND SPACE EDUCATION FORUM (Aviation Scholarship)

c/o Virginia Department of Aviation
5702 Gulfstream Road
Richmond VA 23250-2422

804/236-3624
FAX: 804/236-3625
E-mail: director@doav.state.va.us
Internet: www.doav.state.va.us/
AMOUNT: $1,000
DEADLINE(S): FEB 14
FIELD(S): Aviation-related programs

Scholarships for high school seniors planning a career in aviation who are residents of Virginia who have been accepted and are enrolled in an accredited college. Must have at least a 3.5 GPA.

Contact above location or access Web site for application and details of eligibility requirements.

ARCHITECTURE

473—AIR FORCE RESERVE OFFICER TRAINING CORPS (AFROTC Scholarships)

551 E. Maxwell Boulevard
Maxwell AFB AL 36112-6106
334/953-7783
AMOUNT: Full tuition, books, and fees for all 4 years of college
DEADLINE(S): DEC 1
FIELD(S): Science; Engineering; Business; Political Science; Psychology; Geography; Foreign Studies; Foreign Language

Competitive scholarships based on individual merit to high school seniors and graduates who have not completed any full-time college work. Must be a U.S. citizen between the ages of 17-27. Must also have GPA of 2.5 or above, be in top 40% of class, and complete Applicant Fitness Test. Cannot be a single parent. Your college/university must offer AFROTC.

2,300 awards annually. Contact above address for application packet.

474—AMERICAN INSTITUTE OF ARCHITECTS/AMERICAN ARCHITECTURAL FOUNDATION (Scholarship For First Professional Degree Candidates)

1735 New York Avenue NW
Washington DC 20006-5292
202/626-7511
FAX: 202/626-7420
E-mail: mfelber@archfoundation.org
Internet: http://www.archfoundation.org/scholarships/index.htm
AMOUNT: $500-$2,500
DEADLINE(S): FEB
FIELD(S): Architecture

Open to undergraduate students in their final two years or graduate students pursuing their master's degree in architecture. Awards tenable at accredited institutions in the U.S. and Canada.

Applications available ONLY through the office of the dean or department head at an NAAB or RAIC school of architecture. Contact Mary Felber at AIA/AAF for more information.

475—AMERICAN INSTITUTE OF ARCHITECTS/AMERICAN ARCHITECTURAL FOUNDATION (Fellowship For Advanced Study or Research)

1735 New York Avenue NW
Washington DC 20006-5292
202/626-7511
FAX: 202/626-7420
E-mail: mfelber@archfoundation.org
Internet: http://www.archfoundation.org/scholarships/index.htm
AMOUNT: $1,000-$2,000
DEADLINE(S): FEB 15
FIELD(S): Architecture

Open to architects (either BArch or MArch) to pursue an advanced degree or conduct research in architecture or a closely related field of study. Funding is based on the merits of a project proposal and not given for tuition assistance. See Web site or contact Mary Felber at AIA/AAF for more information.

476—AMERICAN INSTITUTE OF ARCHITECTS/AMERICAN HOSPITAL ASSOCIATION (AIA/AHA Graduate Fellowships in Health Facilities Planning and Design)

1735 New York Avenue NW
Washington DC 20006
202/626-7511
FAX: 202/626-7420
E-mail: jbarry@aia.org
Internet: http://www.archfoundation.org/scholarships/index.htm
AMOUNT: $27,000 (total fund)
DEADLINE(S): JAN 31
FIELD(S): Architecture-Health Facilities

For graduate students, or those in last year of undergraduate work in architecture, who are U.S. or Canadian citizens for coursework or independent study.

2 awards annually. See Web site or contact Jennifer Barry at above address for complete information and application.

477—AMERICAN INSTITUTE OF ARCHITECTS, NEW YORK CHAPTER (Douglas Haskell Award)

200 Lexington Avenue, 6th Floor
New York NY 10016
212/683-0023 ext. 14
FAX: 212/696-5022
E-mail: info@aiany.org
Internet: http://www.aiany.org/nyfoundation/scholarships.html
AMOUNT: $2,000 (minimum)
DEADLINE(S): MAR 21
FIELD(S): Architectural Writing

Awards to encourage fine writing on architecture and related design subjects and to foster regard for intelligent criticism among future professionals. For students enrolled in a professional architecture or related program, such as art history, interior design, urban studies, and landscape architecture. Submit a news story, an essay or feature article, book review, or journal accompanied by a 100-word statement describing the purpose of the piece.

Check Web site or contact AIANY at above location for complete information.

478—AMERICAN PLANNING ASSOCIATION (Minority Scholarship and Fellowship Programs)

122 South Michigan Avenue, Suite 1600
Chicago IL 60605
312/431-9100
FAX: 312/431-9985
AMOUNT: $2,000-$5,000 (grads); $2,500 (undergrads)
DEADLINE(S): MAY 14
FIELD(S): Urban Planning, Community Development, Environmental Sciences, Public Administration, Transportation, or Urban Studies

Scholarships for African-Americans, Hispanics, or Native American students pursuing undergraduate degrees in the U.S. in the above fields. Must have completed first year. Fellowships for graduate students. Programs must be approved by the Planning Accreditation Board. U.S. citizenship.

Call or write for complete information.

479—AMERICAN SOCIETY OF ENGINEERS OF INDIAN ORIGIN (Undergraduate Scholarship Programs)

P.O. Box 49494
Atlanta GA 30359-1494
770/451-2299
Internet: http://www.iasf.org/asei.htm
AMOUNT: Up to $1,000
DEADLINE(S): AUG 15
FIELD(S): Engineering Fields: Architecture, Computer Technology,

Geotechnical or Geoenvironmental Engineering, and allied sciences

Several scholarships for undergraduate engineering students in the above fields who were born in India or who are Indian by ancestry or relation. For study in the U.S. Some programs have residency requirements in certain states.

Contact Dr. Narsi Narasimhan at above location for applications and details.

480—ASSOCIATED WESTERN UNIVERSITIES, INC. (AWU Undergraduate Student Fellowships)

4190 S. Highland Drive, Suite 211
Salt Lake City UT 84124-2600
801/273-8900
FAX: 801/277-5632
E-mail: info@awu.org
Internet: http://www.awu.org

AMOUNT: $300/week stipend + possible travel allowance
DEADLINE(S): FEB 1
FIELD(S): Science; Mathematics; Engineering; Technology

Eight- to sixteen-week fellowships.

481—BRITISH COLUMBIA HERITAGE TRUST (Scholarships)

P.O. Box 9818 Stn Prov Govt.
Victoria BC V8W 9W3 CANADA
250/356-1433
FAX: 250/356-7796
E-mail: heritage@tbc.gov.bc.ca

AMOUNT: $5,000
DEADLINE(S): FEB 1
FIELD(S): British Columbia History; Architecture; Archaeology; Archival Management

Open to graduate students who are Canadian citizens or permanent residents. Criteria are scholarly record and academic performance, educational and career objectives, and proposed program of study.

Write for complete information.

482—CHICAGO ROOFING CONTRACTORS ASSOCIATION (Scholarship)

4415 W. Harrison Street, #322
Hillside IL 60162
708/449-3340
FAX: 708/449-0837
E-mail: crcainfo@crca.org
Internet: http://www.crca.org

AMOUNT: $2,000
DEADLINE(S): Varies
FIELD(S): Business; Engineering; Architecture; Liberal Arts; Sciences

Open to high school seniors who reside in one of the eight counties in Northern Illinois: Cook, DuPage, Lake, Kane, Kendall, DeKalb, McHenry, or Will. Must be accepted as a full-time student in a four-year college/university to pursue a degree in one of the above fields. Must be U.S. citizen. Based on academic achievements, extracurricular activities, and community involvement.

Renewable. Contact CRCA for an application.

483—FLORIDA FEDERATION OF GARDEN CLUBS, INC. (FFGC Scholarships for College Students)

6065 21st Street SW
Vero Beach FL 32968-9427
561/778-1023
Internet: http://www.ffgc.org

AMOUNT: $1,500-$3,500
DEADLINE(S): MAY 1
FIELD(S): Ecology; Environmental Issues; Land Management; City Planning; Environmental Control; Horticulture; Landscape Design; Conservation; Botany; Forestry; Marine Biology; Floriculture; Agriculture

Various scholarships for Florida residents with a "B" average or better enrolled full-time as a junior, senior, or graduate student at a Florida college or university.

See Web site or contact Melba Campbell at FFGC for an application.

484—FLORIDA FEDERATION OF GARDEN CLUBS, INC. (FFGC Scholarships for High School Students)

6065 21st Street SW
Vero Beach FL 32968-9427
561/778-1023
Internet: http://www.ffgc.org

AMOUNT: $1,500
DEADLINE(S): MAY 1
FIELD(S): Ecology; Environmental Issues; Land Management; City Planning; Environmental Control; Horticulture; Landscape Design; Conservation; Botany; Forestry; Marine Biology; Floriculture; Agriculture

Scholarships for Florida residents with a "B" average or better who will be incoming freshmen at a Florida college or university.

See Web site or contact Melba Campbell at FFGC for an application.

485—GRAHAM FOUNDATION FOR ADVANCED STUDIES IN THE FINE ARTS (Research Grants)

Four West Burton Place
Chicago IL 60610
312/787-4071
Internet: http://www.grahamfoundation.org

AMOUNT: $10,000-$25,000
DEADLINE(S): JAN 15; JUL 15
FIELD(S): Architecture

Research grants open to individuals and institutions for specific projects relating to contemporary architecture planning. Grants do not support study or research in pursuit of an academic degree no scholarships available.

Write for more information.

486—HISPANIC COLLEGE FUND (Scholarships for Hispanic Students)

One Thomas Circle NW, Suite 375
Washington DC 20005
202/296-5400
FAX: 202/296-3774
E-mail: Hispanic.Fund@InternetMCI.com
Internet: http://hispanicfund.org

AMOUNT: Varies
DEADLINE(S): APR 15
FIELD(S): Most college majors leading to a career in business

Scholarships for deserving Hispanic college students pursuing a higher education in a major leading to a business career and who are full-time students at accredited institutions. U.S. citizenship. Must demonstrate financial need.

Contact above organization for details or visit Web site for application.

487—INSTITUTION OF ELECTRICAL ENGINEERS (Scholarships for Women)

Savoy Place
London WC2R 0BL ENGLAND
0171 240 1871 ext. 2211/2235
FAX: 0171 497 3609
E-mail: scholarships@iee.org.uk
Internet: http://www.iee.org.uk/Awards/ugwom.htm

AMOUNT: 750 pounds/year
DEADLINE(S): JUN 15
FIELD(S): Engineering

Scholarships for women residing in the United Kingdom and pursuing degrees in engineering.

Candidates must be undertaking mathematics and physics "A" level or Scottish Higher examinations. Renewable for the entire period of an IEE-accredited course. Check Web site or contact organization for application details.

488—IRISH ARTS COUNCIL (Awards and Opportunities)

70 Merrion Square
Dublin 2 IRELAND
Tel: +353 1 618 0200
FAX: +353 1 661 0349/676 1302
E-mail: info@artscouncil.ie
Internet: http://www.artscouncil.ie
AMOUNT: Varies (with program)
DEADLINE(S): Varies (with program)
FIELD(S): Creative Arts; Visual Arts; Performing Arts

Numerous programs open to young and established artists who are Irish citizens or legal residents. Purpose is to assist in pursuit of talents and recognize achievements.

See Web site or contact above address for an application.

489—LANDSCAPE ARCHITECTURE FOUNDATION (Edith H. Henderson Scholarship)

636 Eye Street NW
Washington DC 20001-3736
202/898-2444
FAX: 202/898-1185
E-mail: msippel@asla.org
Internet: http://www.asla.org
AMOUNT: $1,000
DEADLINE(S): APR 1
FIELD(S): Landscape Architecture

Scholarship available to any landscape architecture student who has in the past or is participating in a class in public speaking or creative writing. Must write a 200- to 400-word typed review of Edith H. Henderson's book Edith Henderson's Home Landscape Companion.

Locate the book in a library or call 800-787-2665 or 800-241-0113 to order. Be sure and state that you are a landscape architect student applying for the Henderson scholarship.

490—LANDSCAPE ARCHITECTURE FOUNDATION (LAF/CLASS Fund Scholarships)

636 Eye Street NW
Washington DC 20001-3736
202/898-2444
FAX: 202/898-1185
E-mail: msippel@asla.org
Internet: http://www.asla.org
AMOUNT: $500-$2,000
DEADLINE(S): APR 1
FIELD(S): Landscape Architecture or Ornamental Horticulture

Scholarships and internships for students enrolled in certain California colleges: California Polytechnic Institute (Pomona or San Luis Obispo), UCLA, and UC-Davis who show promise and a commitment to landscape architecture as a profession.

Access Web site for complete information.

491—LOS ANGELES COUNCIL OF BLACK PROFESSIONAL ENGINEERS (Al-Ben Scholarship)

P.O. Box 881029
Los Angeles CA 90009
310/635-7734
E-mail: secy1@lablackengineers.org
Internet: http://www.lablackengineers.org/scholarships.html
AMOUNT: Varies
DEADLINE(S): Varies
FIELD(S): Engineering; Mathematics; Computer Studies; Applied Scientific Studies

Open to technically inclined precollege and undergraduate students enrolled in one of the above fields. Must be of African American, Native American, or Hispanic ancestry. Preference given to students attending college in Southern California or who are Southern California residents.

See Web site to download an application.

492—NATIONAL GARDEN CLUBS, INC. (Scholarships)

4401 Magnolia Avenue
St. Louis MO 63110-3492
314/776-7574
FAX: 314/776-5108
E-mail: renee_blaschke@juno.com
Internet: http://www.gardenclub.org
AMOUNT: $3,500
DEADLINE(S): MAR 1
FIELD(S): Horticulture, Floriculture, Landscape Design, City Planning, Land Management, and allied subjects.

Open to juniors, seniors, and graduate students who are U.S. citizens and are studying any of the above or related subjects. Student must have the endorsement of the state in which he/she resides permanently. Applications will be forwarded to the National State Chairman and judged on a national level.

30-35 scholarships are awarded. Write to the above address for complete information.

493—NATIONAL FEDERATION OF THE BLIND (Frank Walton Horn Memorial Scholarship)

805 Fifth Avenue
Grinnell IA 50112
515/236-3366
AMOUNT: $3,000
DEADLINE(S): MAR 31
FIELD(S): Architecture; Engineering

Open to legally blind students pursuing or planning to pursue a full-time postsecondary course of study in the U.S. Based on academic excellence, service to the community, and financial need. Membership NOT required.

1 award annually. Renewable. Contact Mrs. Peggy Elliot, Scholarship Committee Chairman, for an application.

494—NATIONAL FEDERATION OF THE BLIND (Howard Brown Rickard Scholarship)

805 Fifth Avenue
Grinnell IA 50112
515/236-3366
AMOUNT: $3,000
DEADLINE(S): MAR 31
FIELD(S): Law; Medicine; Engineering; Architecture; Natural Sciences

For legally blind students pursuing or planning to pursue a full-time postsecondary course of study in the U.S.. Based on academic excellence, service to the community, and financial need. Membership NOT required.

1 award annually. Renewable. Contact Mrs. Peggy Elliot, Scholarship Committee Chairman, for an application.

495—NATIONAL SOCIETY OF BLACK ENGINEERS (Scholarships)

1454 Duke Street
Alexandria VA 22314
703/549-2207
FAX: 703/683-5312
E-mail: nsbehq@nsbe.org
Internet: http://www.nsbe.org
AMOUNT: Varies
DEADLINE(S): Varies
FIELD(S): Engineering and engineering technologies

Programs for black and other ethnic minorities in the fields of engineering and the engineering technologies. Organization offers precollege programs, scholarships, career fairs, a journal, a newsletter, etc.

Contact organization for details.

496—NATIONAL STONE, SAND & GRAVEL ASSOCIATION (NSSGA Quarry Engineering Scholarships)

2101 Wilson Boulevard, Suite 100
Arlington VA 22201
800/342-1415 or 703/525-8788
FAX: 703/525-7782
E-mail: info@nssga.org
Internet: http://www.nssga.org

AMOUNT: $2,000; $1,000; $600 + award to school department
DEADLINE(S): APR 15
FIELD(S): Landscape Architecture

Contest in which undergraduate landscape architecture students work with a local rock quarry to produce a reclamation proposal.

See Web site or write for complete information and application.

497—NEW YORK CITY DEPT. CITYWIDE ADMINISTRATIVE SERVICES (Urban Fellows Program)

1 Centre Street, 24th Floor
New York NY 10007
212/487-5600
FAX: 212/487-5720

AMOUNT: $18,000 stipend
DEADLINE(S): JAN 20
FIELD(S): Public Administration; Urban Planning; Government; Public Service; Urban Affairs

Fellowship program provides one academic year (9 months) of full-time work experience in urban government. Open to graduating college seniors and recent college graduates. U.S. citizenship required.

Write for complete information.

498—NEW YORK CITY DEPT. OF CITYWIDE ADMINISTRATIVE SERVICES (Government Scholars Internship Program)

1 Centre Street, 24th Floor
New York NY 10007
212/487-5600
FAX: 212/487-5720

AMOUNT: $3,000 stipend
DEADLINE(S): JAN 13
FIELD(S): Public Administration; Urban Planning; Government; Public Service; Urban Affairs

10-week summer intern program open to undergraduate sophomores, juniors, and seniors. Program provides students with unique opportunity to learn about NY City government. Internships available in virtually every city agency and mayoral office.

Write to New York City Fellowship Programs at above address for complete information.

499—NEW YORK STATE HIGHER EDUCATION SERVICES CORPORATION (N.Y. State Regents Professional/Health Care Opportunity Scholarships)

Cultural Education Center, Room 5C64
Albany NY 12230
518/486-1319
Internet: http://www.hesc.com

AMOUNT: $1,000-$10,000/year
DEADLINE(S): Varies
FIELD(S): Medicine and dentistry and related fields, architecture, nursing, psychology, audiology, landscape architecture, social work, chiropractic, law, pharmacy, accounting, speech language pathology

For NY state residents who are economically disadvantaged and members of a minority group underrepresented in the chosen profession and attending school in NY state. Some programs carry a service obligation in New York for each year of support. For U.S. citizens or qualifying noncitizens.

Medical/dental scholarships require one year of professional work in NY.

500—PERMANENT GROUP (Marten Bequest Travelling Scholarships)

35 Clarence Street
Sydney NSW 2000 AUSTRALIA
+61 (02) 8295-8191
FAX: +61 (02) 8295-8695
E-mail: linda.ingaldo@permanentgroup.com.au
Internet: http://www.permanentgroup.com.au/

AMOUNT: Aus. $18,000
DEADLINE(S): OCT 25
FIELD(S): Art; Performing Arts; Creative Writing

Open to native-born Australians aged 21-35 (17-35 ballet) who are of outstanding ability and promise in one or more categories of the Arts. The scholarships are intended to augment a scholar's own resources toward a cultural education and may be used for study, maintenance, and travel either in Australia or overseas. Categories are: instrumental music, painting, singing, sculpture, architecture, ballet, prose, poetry, and acting.

6 scholarships granted in each of 9 categories which rotate in 2 groups on an annual basis. Contact Linda Ingaldo for more information and entry form.

501—ROBERT SCHRECK MEMORIAL FUND (Grants)

c/o Texas Commerce Bank, Trust Dept.
P.O. Drawer 140
El Paso TX 79980
915/546-6515

AMOUNT: $500-$1,500
DEADLINE(S): JUL 15; NOV 15
FIELD(S): Medicine; Veterinary Medicine; Physics; Chemistry; Architecture; Engineering; Episcopal Clergy

Grants to undergraduate juniors or seniors or graduate students who have been residents of El Paso County for at least two years. Must be U.S. citizen or legal resident and have a high grade point average. Financial need is a consideration.

Write for complete information.

502—SKIDMORE, OWINGS & MERRILL FOUNDATION (Interior Architecture Traveling Fellowship Program)

224 S. Michigan Avenue,
Suite 1000
Chicago IL 60604
312/554-9090 or 312/427-4202
FAX: 312/360-4545
E-mail: SOMFoundation@som.com
Internet: http://www.som.com/html/som_foundation.html

AMOUNT: $7,500
DEADLINE(S): Varies (consult with school)
FIELD(S): Architecture or Interior Design

For a student graduating with a B.A. or M.A. degree from an accredited U.S. architectural or FIDER school. It will allow the Fellow to visit buildings and settings that are central to his or her area of interest and study.

Must submit portfolio and a proposed travel itinerary, etc. See Web site or contact SOM Foundation at above address for complete information.

503—SMITHSONIAN INSTITUTION-COOPER-HEWITT, NATIONAL DESIGN MUSEUM (Peter Krueger Summer Internships)

2 E. 91st Street
New York NY 10128
212/849-8380
FAX: 212/860-6909
E-mail: edu@ch.si.edu
Internet: http://www.si.edu/ndm/
AMOUNT: $2,500 stipend
DEADLINE(S): MAR 15
FIELD(S): Art History; Architectural History; Museum Studies; Museum Education; Design

This ten-week (June-August) internship is open to college students considering a career in one of the above fields as well as graduate students who have not yet completed their M.A. degree. Interns are assigned to specific curatorial, education, or administrative departments where they will assist on special research or exhibition projects, as well as participate in daily museum activities. Housing NOT provided.

To apply, submit resume, transcript, 2 letters of recommendation, and 1- to 2-page essay on interest. Contact the Intern Coordinator for details. Notification by April 30.

504—SOIL AND WATER CONSERVATION SOCIETY

7515 N.E. Ankeny Road
Ankeny IA 50021-9764
515/289-2331 or 800/THE-SOIL
FAX: 515/289-1227
E-mail: charliep@swcs.org
Internet: http://www.swcs.org
AMOUNT: Varies—most are uncompensated
DEADLINE(S): Varies
FIELD(S): Journalism, marketing, database management, meeting planning, public policy research, environmental education, landscape architecture

Internships for undergraduates and graduates to gain experience in the above fields as they relate to soil and water conservation issues. Internship openings vary through the year in duration, compensation, and objective. SWCS will coordinate particulars with your academic advisor.

Contact SWCS for internship availability at any time during the year or see Web site for jobs page.

505—SONOMA CHAMBOLLE-MUSIGNY SISTER CITIES, INC. (Henri Cardinaux Memorial Scholarship)

Chamson Scholarship Committee
P.O. Box 1633
Sonoma CA 95476-1633
707/939-1344
FAX: 707/939-1344
E-mail: Baileysci@vom.com
AMOUNT: Up to $1,500 (travel + expenses)
DEADLINE(S): JUL 15
FIELD(S): Culinary Arts; Wine Industry; Art; Architecture; Music; History; Fashion

Hands-on experience working in above or similar fields and living with a family in small French village in Burgundy or other French city. Must be Sonoma County, CA, resident at least 18 years of age and be able to communicate in French. Transcripts, employer recommendation, photograph, and essay (stating why, where, and when) required.

1 award. Nonrenewable. Also offers opportunity for candidate in Chambolle-Musigny to obtain work experience and cultural exposure in Sonoma, CA.

506—STUDENT CONSERVATION ASSOCIATION (SCA Resource Assistant Program)

P.O. Box 550
Charlestown NH 03603
603/543-1700
FAX: 603/543-1828
E-mail: internships@sca-inc.org
Internet: http://www.sca-inc.org
AMOUNT: $1,180-$4,725
DEADLINE(S): Varies
FIELD(S): Environment and related fields

Must be 18 and U.S. citizen; need not be student. Fields: Agriculture, Archaeology, anthropology, botany, caves, civil/environmental engineering, environmental education, fisheries, forests, herpetology, history, living history/roleplaying, visitor services, landscape architecture/environmental design, paleontology, recreation/ resource/ range management, trail maintenance/construction, wildlife management, geology, hydrology, library/museums, surveying...

900 positions in U.S. and Canada. Send $1 for postage for application; outside U.S./Canada, send $20.

507—THE DAPHNE JACKSON MEMORIAL FELLOWSHIPS TRUST (Fellowships in Science/Engineering)

School of Physical Sciences
Dept. of Physics, University of Surrey
Guildford, Surrey GU2 5XH
ENGLAND UK
01483 259166
FAX: 01483 259501
E-mail: J.Woolley@surrey.ac.uk
Internet: http://www.sst.ph.ic.ac.uk/trust/
AMOUNT: Varies
DEADLINE(S): Varies
FIELD(S): Science or Engineering, including Information Sciences

Fellowships to enable well-qualified and highly motivated scientists and engineers to return to appropriate careers following a career break due to family commitments. May be used on a flexible, part-time basis. Tenable at various U.K. universities.

See Web site and/or contact organization for details.

508—UNIVERSITIES OF GLASGOW AND STRATHCLYDE (Scholarships in Naval Architecture, Ocean Engineering, and Marine Engineering)

Henry Dyer Bldg.
100 Montrose Street
Glasgow G4 0LZ
SCOTLAND UK
+44 0141 548 3875
FAX: +44 0141 552 2879
E-mail: s.craufurd@na-me.ac.uk
Internet: http://www.na-me.ac.uk
AMOUNT: 500-1,000 pounds per annum
DEADLINE(S): mid-JAN
FIELD(S): Naval Architecture; Ocean/Offshore Engineering; Marine Engineering

Scholarships for students entering to study in the above fields. Up to 10 bursaries are available, varying in amount. Awards based on merit and performance at an interview. In the second and third years of the course, student may compete for a number of Lloyd's Register Sponsorships, which provide substantial annual bursaries and paid summer employment/training within an organization.

See Web site for further information on the combined programs from these 2 universities. Contact Simon Craufurd, Recruitment Officer, at the above address for information and application forms.

509—UNIVERSITY OF ILLINOIS AT URBANA-CHAMPAIGN (Lydia E. Parker Bates Scholarship)

620 East John Street
Champaign IL 61820
217/333-0100
Internet: http://www.uiuc.edu/
AMOUNT: Up to $1,000

DEADLINE(S): MAR 15

FIELD(S): Art, Architecture, Landscape Architecture, Urban Planning, Dance, Theater, and all related subjects except Music

Open to undergraduate students in the College of Fine and Applied Arts who are attending the University of Illinois at Urbana-Champaign. Must demonstrate financial need and have 2.85 GPA. Complete the Free Application for Federal Student Aid with UIUC admission application.

175 awards per year. Recipients must carry at least 12 credit hours per semester. Contact office of student financial aid for application.

510—WAVERLY COMMUNITY HOUSE INC. (F. Lammot Belin Arts Scholarships)

Scholarships Selection Committee
P.O. Box 142
Waverly PA 18471
570/586-8191
FAX: 570/586-0185
E-mail: info@waverlycomm.com
Internet: http://www.waverlycomm.com

AMOUNT: $10,000

DEADLINE(S): DEC 15

FIELD(S): Painting; Sculpture; Music; Drama; Dance; Literature; Architecture; Photography

Applicants must have resided in the Abington or Pocono regions of Northeastern Pennsylvania. They must furnish proof of exceptional ability in their chosen field but no formal training in any academic or professional program.

U.S. citizenship required. Finalists must appear in person before the selection committee. See Web site or write for complete information.

511—WEBB INSTITUTE (Naval Architecture Scholarships)

298 Crescent Beach Road
Glen Cove NY 11542-1398
516/671-2213
FAX: 516/674-9838
E-mail: admissions@webb-institute.edu
Internet: http://www.webb-institute.edu

AMOUNT: Full tuition for 4 years

DEADLINE(S): FEB 15

FIELD(S): Naval Architecture; Marine Engineering

Open to high school students aged 16-24 who are in the top 10% of their class and have a minimum 3.2 GPA. Based on college boards, SAT scores, demonstrated interest in above areas, and an interview. Must be U.S. citizen. Tenable at the Webb Institute.

20-25 awards annually. Contact Webb Institute for an application.

512—WESTERN EUROPEAN ARCHITECTURE FOUNDATION (Gabriel Prize for Architecture)

c/o The Boston Society of Architects
52 Broad Street
Boston MA 02109-4301

AMOUNT: $15,000

DEADLINE(S): DEC

FIELD(S): Architecture

Supports all travel and study costs for a period of three months in France, during which time the student will study architectural environments in France or its immediate spheres of influence, between 1630 and 1930. Students record their interpretive studies in freehand and perspective drawings.

513—INTERNATIONAL SOCIETY OF WOMEN AIRLINE PILOTS (ISA Career Scholarship)

2250 E. Tropicana Avenue, Suite 19-395
Las Vegas NV 89119-6594
E-mail: wame@swbell.net
Internet: http://www.iswap.org/scholarship.html

AMOUNT: Varies

DEADLINE(S): APR 15

FIELD(S): Airline Pilot Advanced Ratings

Open to women whose goals are to fly the world's airlines. For advanced pilot ratings, such as the U.S. FAA ATP certificate or equivalent.

Applicants must have a U.S. FAA Commercial Pilot Certificate with an Instrument Rating and a First Class medical certificate (or equivalent). Also must have a minimum of 750 flight hours. Personal interview is required. Check Web site or write for more information and application.

514—XEROX TECHNICAL MINORITY SCHOLARSHIP (Summer Employment Program)

Xerox Square
Rochester NY 14644
Written Inquiry

AMOUNT: Up to $5,000 (varies according to tuition and academic excellence)

DEADLINE(S): SEP 15

FIELD(S): Engineering and Science Disciplines

Scholarships for minorities enrolled in a technical degree program at the bachelor level or above. Must be African-American, Native American, Hispanic, or Asian. Xerox will match your skills with a sponsoring organization that will offer a meaningful summer work experience complimenting your academic learning.

If above requirements are met, send your resume and a cover letter to Xerox Corporation Corporate Employment and College Relations Technical Minority Scholarship Program.

CIVIL ENGINEERING

515—AIR FORCE RESERVE OFFICER TRAINING CORPS (AFROTC Scholarships)

551 E. Maxwell Boulevard
Maxwell AFB AL 36112-6106
334/953-7783

AMOUNT: Full tuition, books, and fees for all 4 years of college

DEADLINE(S): DEC 1

FIELD(S): Science; Engineering; Business; Political Science; Psychology; Geography; Foreign Studies; Foreign Language

Competitive scholarships based on individual merit to high school seniors and graduates who have not completed any full-time college work. Must be a U.S. citizen between the ages of 17-27. Must also have GPA of 2.5 or above, be in top 40% of class, and complete Applicant Fitness Test. Cannot be a single parent. Your college/university must offer AFROTC.

2,300 awards annually. Contact above address for application packet.

516—AMERICAN SOCIETY OF CIVIL ENGINEERS (Arthur S. Tuttle Memorial Scholarship)

Student Services
1801 Alexander Bell Drive
Reston VA 20191-4400
800/548-2723 or 703/295-6000
FAX: 703/295-6222
E-mail: student@asce.org
Internet: http://www.asce.org/about/stud_scholar.cfm

AMOUNT: $2,000

DEADLINE(S): FEB 7

FIELD(S): Civil Engineering

Award is for the first year of formal graduate tuition; undergraduates should apply during their senior year. Must a member of ASCE (Membership applications may be submitted along with scholarship applications).

See Web site or contact ASCE for an application between October and February.

517—AMERICAN SOCIETY OF CIVIL ENGINEERS (B. Charles Tiney Memorial Student Chapter Scholarship)

Student Services
1801 Alexander Bell Drive
Reston VA 20191-4400
800/548-2723 or 703/295-6000
FAX: 703/295-6222
E-mail: student@asce.org
Internet: http://www.asce.org/about/stud_scholar.cfm
AMOUNT: $2,000
DEADLINE(S): FEB 7
FIELD(S): Civil Engineering

Open to undergraduate freshmen, sophomores, and juniors who are ASCE National Student Members (NSM applications may be submitted along with scholarship applications). To be used toward tuition.

12 awards annually. See Web site or contact ASCE for an application between October and February.

518—AMERICAN SOCIETY OF CIVIL ENGINEERS (O.H. Ammann Research Fellowship in Structural Engineering)

Student Services
1801 Alexander Bell Drive
Reston VA 20191-4400
800/548-2723 or 703/295-6000
FAX: 703/295-6222
E-mail: student@asce.org
Internet: http://www.asce.org/about/stud_scholar.cfm
AMOUNT: $5,000
DEADLINE(S): FEB 24
FIELD(S): Structural Engineering

For ASCE members in any grade to create new knowledge in the field of structural design and construction. Membership application may be submitted along with fellowship application.

1 award annually. See Web site or contact ASCE for an application between October and February.

519—AMERICAN SOCIETY OF CIVIL ENGINEERS (Samuel Fletcher Tapman Student Chapter/Club Scholarships)

Student Services
1801 Alexander Bell Drive
Reston VA 20191-4400
800/548-2723 or 703/295-6000
FAX: 703/295-6222
E-mail: student@asce.org
Internet: http://www.asce.org/about/stud_scholar.cfm
AMOUNT: $2,000
DEADLINE(S): FEB 7
FIELD(S): Civil Engineering

Open to undergraduate freshmen, sophomores, and juniors who are ASCE National Student Members (NSM applications may be submitted along with scholarship applications). To be used toward tuition.

12 awards annually. See Web site or contact ASCE for an application between October and February.

520—ASSOCIATED BUILDERS AND CONTRACTORS SCHOLARSHIP PROGRAM

1300 N. 17th Street, 8th Floor
Rosslyn VA 22209
703/812-2008
FAX: 703/812-8235
E-mail: hess@abc.org
Internet: http://www.abc.org
AMOUNT: $2,500
DEADLINE(S): APR 1
FIELD(S): Construction

Open to undergrads enrolled in an accredited 4-year degree program who have completed at least 1 year of study in construction (other than a design discipline). Must have at least 1 full year remaining subsequent to application deadline. If an ABC student chapter exists at the college or institution, student must be a member.

Approximately 4 scholarships per year. See Web site or contact ABC for complete information and application.

521—ASSOCIATED WESTERN UNIVERSITIES, INC. (AWU Undergraduate Student Fellowships)

4190 S. Highland Drive, Suite 211
Salt Lake City UT 84124-2600
801/273-8900
FAX: 801/277-5632
E-mail: info@awu.org
Internet: http://www.awu.org
AMOUNT: $300/week stipend + possible travel allowance
DEADLINE(S): FEB 1
FIELD(S): Science; Mathematics; Engineering; Technology

Eight- to sixteen-week fellowships.

522—BROOKHAVEN WOMEN IN SCIENCE (Renate W. Chasman Scholarship)

P.O. Box 183
Upton NY 11973-5000
E-mail: pam@bnl.gov
AMOUNT: $2,000
DEADLINE(S): APR 1
FIELD(S): Natural Sciences; Engineering; Mathematics

Open ONLY to women who are residents of the boroughs of Brooklyn or Queens or the counties of Nassau or Suffolk in New York who are reentering school after a period of study. For juniors, seniors, or first-year graduate students.

1 award annually. Not renewable. Contact Pam Mansfield at above location for an application. Phone calls are NOT accepted.

523—INSTITUTION OF ELECTRICAL ENGINEERS (Scholarships for Women)

Savoy Place
London WC2R 0BL ENGLAND
0171 240 1871 ext. 2211/2235
FAX: 0171 497 3609
E-mail: scholarships@iee.org.uk
Internet: http://www.iee.org.uk/Awards/ugwom.htm
AMOUNT: 750 pounds/year
DEADLINE(S): JUN 15
FIELD(S): Engineering

Scholarships for women residing in the United Kingdom and pursuing degrees in engineering.

Candidates must be undertaking mathematics and physics "A" level or Scottish Higher examinations. Renewable for the entire period of an IEE-accredited course. Check Web site or contact organization for application details.

524—LOS ANGELES COUNCIL OF BLACK PROFESSIONAL ENGINEERS (Al-Ben Scholarship)

P.O. Box 881029
Los Angeles CA 90009
310/635-7734
E-mail: secy1@lablackengineers.org
Internet: http://www.lablackengineers.org/scholarships.html
AMOUNT: Varies
DEADLINE(S): Varies
FIELD(S): Engineering; Mathematics; Computer Studies; Applied Scientific Studies

Open to technically inclined precollege and undergraduate students enrolled in one of the above fields. Must be of African

American, Native American, or Hispanic ancestry. Preference given to students attending college in Southern California or who are Southern California residents.

See Web site to download an application.

525—MARYLAND HIGHER EDUCATION COMMISSION (Maryland Science and Technology Scholarship Program)

16 Francis Street
Annapolis Park MD 21401
410/974-5370 or 800/974-1024
E-mail: ssamail@mhec.state.md.us
Internet: http://www.mhec.state.md.us/SSA/stech_qa.htm

AMOUNT: $3,000/year (BA); $1,000/year (AA)
DEADLINE(S): None
FIELD(S): Computer Science; Engineering; Technology

Scholarships for college-bound Maryland high school seniors who will major in one of the above fields and who are accepted to an eligible associate or bachelor's degree program in Maryland. The deadline was not known at this writing, so check for deadline date. Must agree to work in the state after graduation in a related field, one year for each year of assistance received.

Must maintain a 3.0 GPA.

526—MIDWEST ROOFING CONTRACTORS ASSOCIATION (Construction Industry Scholarships)

4840 West 15th Street, Suite 1000
Lawrence KS 66049-3876
800/497-6722
FAX: 785/843-7555
E-mail: mrca@mrca.org
Internet: http://www.mrca.org

AMOUNT: Varies
DEADLINE(S): JUN 20
FIELD(S): Construction

Applicants must be pursuing or planning to pursue a curriculum at an accredited university, college, community college, vocational, or trade school that will lead to a career in the construction industry. Three letters of recommendation required.

Contact MRCA for an application.

527—NATIONAL ASSOCIATION OF WATER COMPANIES-NEW JERSEY CHAPTER (Scholarship)

Elizabethtown Water Co.,
600 South Avenue
Westfield NJ 07091
908/654-123491
FAX: 908/232-2719

AMOUNT: $2,500
DEADLINE(S): APR 1
FIELD(S): Business Administration; Biology; Chemistry; Engineering Communications

For U.S. citizens who have lived in NJ at least 5 years and plan a career in the investor-owned water utility industry in disciplines such as those above. Must be undergrad or graduate student in a two- or four-year NJ college or university.

GPA of 3.0 or better required. Contact Gail P. Brady for complete information.

528—NATIONAL ASSOCIATION OF WOMEN IN CONSTRUCTION (Founders' Scholarship Foundation Awards)

327 South Adams
Fort Worth TX 76104
817/877-5551 or 800/552-3506
FAX: 817/877-0324
Internet: http://www.nawic.org

AMOUNT: $500-$2,000
DEADLINE(S): FEB 1
FIELD(S): Construction-related fields

Open to full-time students (men or women) enrolled in a construction-related program leading to an associate's or bachelor's degree. Applicants should be in at least their first year of college and have at least 1 year remaining.

Awards committee considers grades, interest in construction, extracurricular activities, employment experience, financial need, and evaluation by academic advisor. Applications available after October 15. Write or access Web site for further information.

529—NATIONAL SOCIETY OF BLACK ENGINEERS (Scholarships)

1454 Duke Street
Alexandria VA 22314
703/549-2207
FAX: 703/683-5312
E-mail: nsbehq@nsbe.org
Internet: http://www.nsbe.org

AMOUNT: Varies
DEADLINE(S): Varies
FIELD(S): Engineering and engineering technologies

Programs for black and other ethnic minorities in the fields of engineering and the engineering technologies. Organization offers precollege programs, scholarships, career fairs, a journal, a newsletter, etc.

Contact organization for details.

530—OAK RIDGE INSTITUTE FOR SCIENCE AND EDUCATION (ORISE Education and Training Programs)

P.O. Box 117
Oak Ridge TN 37831-0117
Internet: http://www.orau.gov/orise/educ.htm

AMOUNT: Varies
DEADLINE(S): Varies
FIELD(S): Engineering; Aeronautics; Computer Science; Technology; Earth Science; Environmental Studies; Biology; Chemistry; Physics; Medical Research

Numerous programs funded by the U.S. Department of Energy are offered for undergraduate students through postgraduate researchers. Includes fellowship and internship opportunities throughout the U.S. Some have citizenship restrictions. Travel may be included.

See Web site or write for a catalog of specific programs and requirements.

531—QUEEN'S UNIVERSITY OF BELFAST (Industrial Scholarships)

Training and Employment Agency,
Management Development Division,
9-21 Adelaide Street
Belfast BT2 8DT Northern Ireland UK
+44 (0) 1232 245133
Internet: http://www.icbl.qub.ac.uk/prospectus/funding/scholars.htm

AMOUNT: Varies
DEADLINE(S): Varies
FIELD(S): Engineering: Aeronautical, Electrical and Electronic, Mechanical, and Manufacturing

Scholarships in Northern Ireland for study in the above fields.

Contact the University at the address shown for complete information.

532—STUDENT CONSERVATION ASSOCIATION (SCA Resource Assistant Program)

P.O. Box 550
Charlestown NH 03603
603/543-1700
FAX: 603/543-1828
E-mail: internships@sca-inc.org
Internet: http://www.sca-inc.org

AMOUNT: $1,180-$4,725
DEADLINE(S): Varies
FIELD(S): Environment and related fields

Must be 18 and U.S. citizen; need not be student.

900 positions in U.S. and Canada. Send $1 for postage for application; outside U.S./Canada, send $20. Fields: Agriculture, Archaeology, anthropology, botany, caves, civil/environmental engineering, environmental education, fisheries, forests, herpetology, history, living history/roleplaying, visitor services, landscape architecture/environmental design, paleontology, recreation/resource/range management, trail maintenance/construction, wildlife management, geology, hydrology, library/museums, surveying...

533—THE DAPHNE JACKSON MEMORIAL FELLOWSHIPS TRUST (Fellowships in Science/Engineering)

School of Physical Sciences,
Dept. of Physics, University of Surrey
Guildford, Surrey GU2 5XH
ENGLAND UK
01483 259166
FAX: 01483 259501
E-mail: J.Woolley@surrey.ac.uk
Internet: http://www.sst.ph.ic.ac.uk/trust/

AMOUNT: Varies
DEADLINE(S): Varies
FIELD(S): Science or Engineering, including Information Sciences

Fellowships to enable well-qualified and highly motivated scientists and engineers to return to appropriate careers following a career break due to family commitments. May be used on a flexible, part-time basis. Tenable at various U.K. universities.

See Web site and/or contact organization for details.

534—INTERNATIONAL SOCIETY OF WOMEN AIRLINE PILOTS (ISA Career Scholarship)

2250 E. Tropicana Avenue,
Suite 19-395
Las Vegas NV 89119-6594
E-mail: wame@swbell.net
Internet: http://www.iswap.org/scholarship.html

AMOUNT: Varies
DEADLINE(S): APR 15
FIELD(S): Airline Pilot Advanced Ratings

Open to women whose goals are to fly the world's airlines. For advanced pilot ratings, such as the U.S. FAA ATP certificate or equivalent.

Applicants must have a U.S. FAA Commercial Pilot Certificate with an Instrument Rating and a First Class medical certificate (or equivalent). Also must have a minimum of 750 flight hours. Personal interview is required. Check Web site or write for more information and application.

535—XEROX TECHNICAL MINORITY SCHOLARSHIP (Summer Employment Program)

Xerox Square
Rochester NY 14644
Written Inquiry

AMOUNT: Up to $5,000 (varies according to tuition and academic excellence)
DEADLINE(S): SEP 15
FIELD(S): Engineering and Science Disciplines

Scholarships for minorities enrolled in a technical degree program at the bachelor level or above. Must be African-American, Native American, Hispanic, or Asian. Xerox will match your skills with a sponsoring organization that will offer a meaningful summer work experience complimenting your academic learning.

If above requirements are met, send your resume and a cover letter to Xerox Corporation Corporate Employment and College Relations Technical Minority Scholarship Program.

COMPUTER SCIENCE

536—AIR FORCE RESERVE OFFICER TRAINING CORPS (AFROTC Scholarships)

551 E. Maxwell Boulevard
Maxwell AFB AL 36112-6106
334/953-7783

AMOUNT: Full tuition, books, and fees for all 4 years of college
DEADLINE(S): DEC 1
FIELD(S): Science; Engineering; Business; Political Science; Psychology; Geography; Foreign Studies; Foreign Language

Competitive scholarships based on individual merit to high school seniors and graduates who have not completed any full-time college work. Must be a U.S. citizen between the ages of 17-27. Must also have GPA of 2.5 or above, be in top 40% of class, and complete Applicant Fitness Test. Cannot be a single parent. Your college/university must offer AFROTC.

2,300 awards annually. Contact above address for application packet.

537—ALICE L. HALTOM EDUCATIONAL FUND

Toni MacKain-Bremner
P. O. Box 1794
Houston TX 77251
281/514-6062
E-mail: toni.mackain@compaq.com
Internet: http://www.alhef.org

AMOUNT: $1,000-$2,000
DEADLINE(S): MAY 1
FIELD(S): Information and Records Management

For students who are actively pursuing an education for a career in information and records management. Applicants must submit a completed scholarship application form provided by the Trust Administration. Three letters of recommendation are required from employers, instructors, or individuals. A copy of the most current, official school transcript must be provided.

538—AMERICAN FOUNDATION FOR THE BLIND (Paul W. Ruckes Scholarship)

11 Penn Plaza, Suite 300
New York NY 10001
212/502-7661
FAX: 212/502-7771
E-mail: juliet@afb.org
Internet: http://www.afb.org

AMOUNT: $1,000
DEADLINE(S): APR 30
FIELD(S): Engineering; Computer/Physical/Life Sciences

Open to legally blind and visually impaired undergraduate and graduate students pursuing a degree in one of above fields. Must be U.S. citizen. Must submit written documentation of visual impairment from ophthalmologist or optometrist (need not be legally blind); official transcripts; proof of college/university acceptance; three letters of recommendation; and typewritten statement describing goals, work experience extracurricular activities, and how monies will be used.

1 award annually. See Web site or contact Julie Tucker at AFB for an application.

539—AMERICAN RADIO RELAY LEAGUE FOUNDATION (The PHD ARA Scholarship)

225 Main Street
Newington CT 06111
860/594-0200
FAX: 860/594-0259
Internet: http://www.arrl.org/

AMOUNT: $1,000

DEADLINE(S): FEB 1
FIELD(S): Journalism; Computer Science; Electronic Engineering

For undergraduate or graduate students who are residents of the ARRL Midwest Division (IA, KS, MO, NE) who hold any class of radio amateur license-or student may be the child of a deceased radio amateur.

1 award annually. See Web site or contact ARRL for an application.

540—AMERICAN SOCIETY OF ENGINEERS OF INDIAN ORIGIN (Undergraduate Scholarship Programs)

P.O. Box 49494
Atlanta GA 30359-1494
770/451-2299
Internet: http://www.iasf.org/asei.htm

AMOUNT: Up to $1,000
DEADLINE(S): AUG 15
FIELD(S): Engineering Fields: Architecture, Computer Technology, Geotechnical or Geoenvironmental Engineering, and allied sciences

Several scholarships for undergraduate engineering students in the above fields who were born in India or who are Indian by ancestry or relation. For study in the U.S. Some programs have residency requirements in certain states.

Contact Dr. Narsi Narasimhan at above location for applications and details.

541—ARMED FORCES COMMUNICATIONS AND ELECTRONICS ASSOCIATION (AFCEA ROTC Scholarships)

4400 Fair Lakes Court
FairFAX: VA 22033-3899
800/336-4583 ext. 6147 or
703/631-6100
Internet: http://www.afcea.org/awards/scholarships.htm

AMOUNT: $2,000
DEADLINE(S): APR 1
FIELD(S): Electrical Engineering, Electronics, Computer Science, Computer or Aerospace Engineering, Physics, Mathematics

Scholarships in the above fields for ROTC students working toward a degree in an accredited four-year college or university in the U.S.

Must be nominated by Professors of Military Science, Naval Science, or Aerospace Studies. Contact the commander of each ROTC unit at your school.

542—ARMED FORCES COMMUNICATIONS AND ELECTRONICS ASSOCIATION (General Emmett Paige Scholarships for Military Personnel, Veterans, and Their Dependents)

4400 Fair Lakes Court
FairFAX: VA 22033-3899
800/336-4583 ext. 6147 or
703/631-6100
Internet: http://www.afcea.org/awards/scholarships.htm

AMOUNT: $2,000
DEADLINE(S): MAR 1
FIELD(S): Electrical Engineering, Electronics, Computer Science, Computer or Aerospace Engineering, Physics, Mathematics

Scholarships in the above fields for persons on active duty in a military service or veterans and to their spouses or dependents who are working toward a degree in an accredited four-year college or university in the U.S. Must have GPA of 3.4 or more.

Check Web site or contact AFCEA for information and application.

543—ARMED FORCES COMMUNICATIONS AND ELECTRONICS ASSOCIATION (General John A. Wickham Scholarships)

4400 Fair Lakes Court
FairFAX: VA 22033-3899
800/336-4583 ext. 6149 or
703/631-6149
Internet: http://www.afcea.org/awards/scholarships.htm

AMOUNT: $2,000
DEADLINE(S): MAY 1
FIELD(S): Electrical Engineering, Electronics, Computer Science, Computer or Aerospace Engineering, Physics, Mathematics

Scholarships in the above fields for persons working toward degrees in accredited four-year colleges or universities in the U.S. Must have GPA of 3.4 or more.

Check Web site or contact AFCEA for information and application.

544—ASSOCIATED WESTERN UNIVERSITIES, INC. (AWU Undergraduate Student Fellowships)

4190 S. Highland Drive, Suite 211
Salt Lake City UT 84124-2600
801/273-8900
FAX: 801/277-5632
E-mail: info@awu.org
Internet: http://www.awu.org

AMOUNT: $300/week stipend + possible travel allowance
DEADLINE(S): FEB 1
FIELD(S): Science; Mathematics; Engineering; Technology

Eight- to sixteen-week fellowships.

545—ASSOCIATION FOR COMPUTING MACHINERY (Listing of Internships and Summer Jobs)

1515 Broadway, 17th Floor
New York NY 10036
800/342-6626 or
+1-212/869-7440 (global)
FAX: +1-212/944-1318;
E-mail: summer_intern@acm.org
Internet: http://www.acm.org/student/internships.html

AMOUNT: Varies
DEADLINE(S): Varies
FIELD(S): Computer science

A listing on the Internet of several internships and summer employment in the field of computer science at various companies and colleges in the U.S., Canada, and elsewhere. Each one has its own requirements.

Access Web site for details.

546—AMERICAN PLANNING ASSOCIATION (Minority Scholarship and Fellowship Programs)

122 South Michigan Avenue,
Suite 1600
Chicago IL 60605
312/431-9100
FAX: 312/431-9985

AMOUNT: $2,000-$5,000 (grads); $2,500 (undergrads)
DEADLINE(S): MAY 14
FIELD(S): Urban Planning, Community Development, Environmental Sciences, Public Administration, Transportation, or Urban Studies

Scholarships for African-Americans, Hispanics, or Native American students pursuing undergraduate degrees in the U.S. in the above fields. Must have completed first year. Fellowships for graduate students. Programs must be approved by the Planning Accreditation Board. U.S. citizenship.

Call or write for complete information.

547—ASTRONAUT SCHOLARSHIP FOUNDATION (Scholarships)

Exec. Director
6225 Vectorspace Boulevard
Titusville FL 32780
321/269-6119
FAX: 321/267-3970
E-mail: MercurySvn@aol.com;
Internet: http://www.astronaut scholarship.org/guidelines.html

AMOUNT: Varies
DEADLINE(S): Varies
FIELD(S): Engineering and Physical Sciences (Medical Research ok, but NOT Professional Medicine)

Open to juniors, seniors, and graduate students at a select group of schools. Must be U.S. citizen with the intention to pursue research or advance field of study upon completion of final degree. Special consideration given to students who have shown initiative, creativity, excellence, and/or resourcefulness in their field. Must be NOMINATED by faculty or staff.

See Web site for list of eligible schools. Contact Howard Benedict, Executive Director, for details.

548—AT&T BELL LABORATORIES (Summer Research Program for Minorities and Women)

101 Crawfords Corner Road
Holmdel NJ 07733-3030
Written Inquiry

AMOUNT: Salary + travel and living expenses for summer
DEADLINE(S): DEC 1
FIELD(S): Engineering; Math; Sciences; Computer Science

Program offers minority students and women students technical employment experience at Bell Laboratories. Students should have completed their third year of study at an accredited college or university. U.S. citizen or permanent resident.

Selection is based partially on academic achievement and personal motivation. Write special programs manager-SRP for complete information.

549—BROOKHAVEN WOMEN IN SCIENCE (Renate W. Chasman Scholarship)

P.O. Box 183
Upton NY 11973-5000
E-mail: pam@bnl.gov

AMOUNT: $2,000
DEADLINE(S): APR 1
FIELD(S): Natural Sciences; Engineering; Mathematics

Open ONLY to women who are residents of the boroughs of Brooklyn or Queens or the counties of Nassau or Suffolk in New York who are reentering school after a period of study. For juniors, seniors, or first-year graduate students.

1 award annually. Not renewable. Contact Pam Mansfield at above location for an application. Phone calls are NOT accepted.

550—CANADIAN BUREAU OF INTERNATIONAL EDUCATION (Lucent Global Science Scholars)

220 Laurier Ave. W., Suite 1100
Ottawa, Ontario K1P 5Z9 CANADA
613/237-4820 ext. 234
FAX: 613/237-1073
E-mail: smealanson@cbie.ca
Internet: http://www.cbie.ca

AMOUNT: $5,000 U.S. + internship
DEADLINE: MAR 15
FIELD(S): Engineering, Computer Science

Open to full-time students who are in their first year at a Canadian university and majoring in a computer-related field. Students will attend a week-long summit with other winners at the Lucent/Bell Labs headquarters in New Jersey and complete a paid summer internship, probably at Lucent Canada.

Applicants must be in high academic standing, eligible to work in Canada, and competent in English.

See Web site or contact CBIE for more details and an application form.

551—CAREER OPPORTUNITIES FOR YOUTH, INC. (Collegiate Scholarship Program)

P.O. Box 996
Manhattan Beach CA 90266
310/535-4838

AMOUNT: $250 to $1,000
DEADLINE(S): SEP 30
FIELD(S): Engineering, Science, Mathematics, Computer Science, Business Administration, Education, Nursing

For students of Latino/Hispanic background residing in the Southern California area who have completed at least one semester/quarter of study at an accredited four-year university. Must have a cumulative GPA of 2.5 or higher.

Priority will be given to students who demonstrate financial need. Send SASE to above location for details.

552—COOPERATIVE ASSOCIATION OF STATES FOR SCHOLARSHIPS (CASS) (Scholarships)

c/o Commonwealth Liaison
Unit 310 The Garrison
St. Michael BARBADOS
809/436-8754

AMOUNT: Varies
DEADLINE(S): None
FIELD(S): Business application/computer science

Scholarships for economically disadvantaged deaf youth, ages 17-25, with strong leadership potential and an interest in computer science/business applications. Must be from Barbados, St. Kitts/Nevis, Grenada, St. Vincent, Antigua/Barbuda, St. Lucia, Dominica, or Jamaica.

Write to E. Caribbean Reg. Coordinator (CASS) at above address.

553—DATA PROCESSING MANAGEMENT ASSOCIATION (Bert A. Monaghan Scholarship Fund)

Michel C. Gleis, Secretary/Treasurer
5522 Cantaloupe Avenue
Van Nuys CA 91401

AMOUNT: $1,000
DEADLINE(S): NOV 30
FIELD(S): Computer Science

Fund provides for students with demonstrated financial need who wish to pursue a career in the computer science field.

554—FRAUNHOFER CENTER FOR RESEARCH IN COMPUTER GRAPHICS (Student and Scholar Exchange Programs)

321 S. Main Street
Providence RI 02903
401/453-6363 ext. 100
FAX: 401/453-0444
E-mail: info@crcg.edu
Internet: http://www.crcg.edu/Education/exchange.html

AMOUNT: Stipend for living expenses; transportation costs reimbursed
DEADLINE(S): None
FIELD(S): Computer Graphics

Educational exchanges between U.S. and Europe for participants to become involved in the new information society. In the U.S., sites are in Rhode Island. In

Europe, the Technical University of Darmstadt in Germany is the main site. Students conducting thesis research or practicums can stay for up to six months. Summer students normally stay for ten to twelve weeks.

Europeans apply to Dr. Joachim Rix, Dept. of Industrial Applications at above company, Rundeturmstr. 6, D-64283 Darmstadt, Germany.

Phone: (+49) 6151 155 220
FAX: (+49) 6151 155 299

U.S. students apply to Sheri Mulcahey at above address.

555—GERBER SCIENTIFIC, INC. (H. Joseph Gerber Vision Scholarship Program)

83 Gerber Road West
South Windsor CT 06074
860/648-8027
Internet: http://www.gerberscientific.com

AMOUNT: Varies
DEADLINE(S): MAR 15
FIELD(S): Engineering, Mathematics, Computer Science, Natural Sciences

Scholarship program for high school seniors in Connecticut.

Fifty scholarships to be awarded.

556—HISPANIC COLLEGE FUND (Scholarships for Hispanic Students)

One Thomas Circle NW, Suite 375
Washington DC 20005
202/296-5400
FAX: 202/296-3774
E-mail: Hispanic.Fund@InternetMCI.com
Internet: http://hispanicfund.org

AMOUNT: Varies
DEADLINE(S): APR 15
FIELD(S): Most college majors leading to a career in business

Scholarships for deserving Hispanic college students pursuing a higher education in a major leading to a business career and who are full-time students at accredited institutions. U.S. citizenship. Must demonstrate financial need.

Contact above organization for details or visit Web site for application.

557—IEEE COMPUTER SOCIETY (Richard Merwin Student Scholarship)

1730 Massachusetts Avenue NW
Washington DC 20036-1992
202/371-1013
FAX: 202/778-0884
Internet: http://www.computer.org/students/scholarship.htm

AMOUNT: $3,000
DEADLINE(S): MAY 31
FIELD(S): Computer Science, Computer Engineering, or Electrical Engineering

Scholarships for active leaders in student branch chapters of the IEEE Computer Society who show promise in their academic and professional efforts.

Four awards. Contact above address or Web site for details.

558—INSTITUTE FOR OPERATIONS RESEARCH AND THE MANAGEMENT SCIENCES (INFORMS Summer Internship Directory)

P.O. Box 64794
Baltimore MD 21264-4794
800/4INFORMS
FAX: 410/684-2963
E-mail: jps@informs.org
Internet: http://www.informs.org/INTERN/

AMOUNT: Varies
DEADLINE(S): Varies
FIELD(S): Fields related to information management: business management, engineering, mathematics

A Web site listing of summer internships in the field of operations research and management sciences. Both applicants and employers can register online.

Access Web site for list.

559—INSTITUTE OF INTERNATIONAL EDUCATION (National Security Education Program-Undergraduate Scholarships)

1400 K Street NW, 6th Floor
Washington DC 20005-2403
202/326-7697 or
800/618-NSEP (6737)
E-mail: nsep@iie.org
Internet: http://www.iie.org/nsep/

AMOUNT: Varies: up to $8,000/semester
DEADLINE(S): FEB 8
FIELD(S): Open to all majors; preference to applied sciences, engineering, business, economics, math, computer science, international affairs, political science, history, and the policy sciences.

For study abroad OUTSIDE the U.S., Canada, Australia, New Zealand, and Western Europe. For study in areas deemed critical to U.S. national security. Applications available on U.S. campuses from August through early December. Or contact organization for details.

Inquire at above location for details.

560—INSTITUTION OF ELECTRICAL ENGINEERS (Scholarships for Women)

Savoy Place
London WC2R 0BL ENGLAND
0171 240 1871 ext. 2211/2235
FAX: 0171 497 3609
E-mail: scholarships@iee.org.uk
Internet: http://www.iee.org.uk/Awards/ugwom.htm

AMOUNT: 750 pounds/year
DEADLINE(S): JUN 15
FIELD(S): Engineering

Scholarships for women residing in the United Kingdom and pursuing degrees in engineering.

Candidates must be undertaking mathematics and physics "A" level or Scottish Higher examinations. Renewable for the entire period of an IEE-accredited course. Check Web site or contact organization for application details.

561—JOHNSON AND WALES UNIVERSITY (Annual Johnson and Wales University National High School Recipe Contest)

8 Abbott Place
Providence RI 02903
401/598-2345

AMOUNT: $1,000 to $5,000
DEADLINE(S): JAN 31
FIELD(S): Business, Hospitality, Technology, Culinary Arts

For students planning to attend Johnson & Wales University, Providence, Rhode Island.

Write to above address for detailed description.

562—JOHNSON AND WALES UNIVERSITY (Gilbane Building Company Eagle Scout Scholarship)

8 Abbott Place
Providence RI 02903
401/598-2345

AMOUNT: $1,200
DEADLINE(S): None
FIELD(S): Business, Hospitality, Technology, Culinary Arts

For students attending Johnson & Wales University, Providence, Rhode Island. Must be Eagle Scouts.

Send letter of recommendation and transcript to above address.

563—JOHNSON AND WALES UNIVERSITY (National High School Entrepreneur of the Year Contest)

8 Abbott Place
Providence RI 02903
401/598-2345
AMOUNT: $1,000 to $10,000
DEADLINE(S): DEC 27
FIELD(S): Business, Hospitality, Technology, Culinary Arts

For students attending Johnson & Wales University, Providence, Rhode Island.

Send for detailed description to above address.

564—JOHNSON AND WALES UNIVERSITY (Scholarships)

8 Abbott Place
Providence RI 02903
401/598-2345
AMOUNT: $200 to $10,000
DEADLINE(S): None
FIELD(S): Business, Hospitality, Technology, Culinary Arts

For students attending Johnson & Wales University, Providence, Rhode Island.

Renewable for four years. Write for complete information.

565—JUNIATA COLLEGE (John & Irene Dale Information Technology Scholarships)

Office of Student Financial Aid Planning; 1700 Moore Street
Huntingdon PA 16652
814/641-3142
FAX: 814/641-5311
E-mail: cramerr@juniata.edu
Internet: http://www.juniata.edu/
AMOUNT: $3,000
DEADLINE(S): MAR 1
FIELD(S): Information Technology

Open to students applying to Juniata College with a major of information technology.

Contact Randy Rennell, Director of Student Financial Planning, for an application or enrollment information.

566—LOS ANGELES COUNCIL OF BLACK PROFESSIONAL ENGINEERS (Al-Ben Scholarship)

P.O. Box 881029
Los Angeles CA 90009
310/635-7734
E-mail: secy1@lablackengineers.org
Internet: http://www.lablackengineers.org/scholarships.html
AMOUNT: Varies
DEADLINE(S): Varies
FIELD(S): Engineering; Mathematics; Computer Studies; Applied Scientific Studies

Open to technically inclined precollege and undergraduate students enrolled in one of the above fields. Must be of African American, Native American, or Hispanic ancestry. Preference given to students attending college in Southern California or who are Southern California residents.

See Web site to download an application.

567—MARYLAND HIGHER EDUCATION COMMISSION (Maryland Science and Technology Scholarship Program)

16 Francis Street
Annapolis Park MD 21401
410/974-5370 or 800/974-1024
E-mail: ssamail@mhec.state.md.us
Internet: http://www.mhec.state.md.us/SSA/stech_qa.htm
AMOUNT: $3,000/year (BA); $1,000/year (AA)
DEADLINE(S): None
FIELD(S): Computer Science; Engineering; Technology

Scholarships for college-bound Maryland high school seniors who will major in one of the above fields and who are accepted to an eligible associate or bachelor's degree program in Maryland. The deadline was not known at this writing, so check for deadline date. Must agree to work in the state after graduation in a related field, one year for each year of assistance received.

Must maintain a 3.0 GPA.

568—MICROSOFT CORPORATION (National Minority and/or Women's Scholarships)

One Microsoft Way
Redmond WA 98052-8303
E-mail: scholar@microsoft.com
Internet: http://www.microsoft.com/college/scholarships/
AMOUNT: Tuition for 1 year
DEADLINE(S): JAN 31
FIELD(S): Computer Science, Computer Engineering, or a related technical discipline, such as Math or Physics

Full tuition scholarships awarded for 1 academic year to women and minorities (African Americans, Hispanics, or Native Americans) enrolled full-time in the above fields with a demonstrated interest in computers and making satisfactory progress towards a degree. Awards are made through designated schools and are not transferable to other institutions.

See Web site above for details.

569—MICROSOFT CORPORATION (Summer Internships)

One Microsoft Way
Redmond WA 98052-8303
425/882-8080
E-mail: scholar@microsoft.com
Internet: http://www.microsoft.com/college/scholarships/
AMOUNT: Varies
DEADLINE(S): None
FIELD(S): Computer Science, Computer Engineering, or a related technical discipline, such as Math or Physics

Summer internships for individuals with a deep passion for technological advancement. Must commit to a 12-week minimum. Includes transportation, shipping costs, and shared cost of housing. Competitive compensation offered.

Check Web site above for details.

570—NAACP NATIONAL OFFICE (Louis Stokes Science & Technology Award)

4805 Mount Hope Drive
Baltimore MD 21215
410/620-5372 or 877/NAACP-98
E-mail: education@naacp.org
Internet: http://www.naacp.org/work/education/eduscholarship.shtml
AMOUNT: $2,000
DEADLINE(S): APR 30
FIELD(S): Engineering, Science, Computer Science, or Mathematics

Open to incoming freshmen who are members of NAACP majoring in one of the above areas.

Financial need must be established. Write for complete information. Include a legal size, self-addressed, stamped envelope.

571—NATIONAL AERONAUTICS AND SPACE ADMINISTRATION (ACCESS Internships)

Stennis Space Center, Bldg. 1100
Bay Saint Louis MS 39529

228/688-2079
E-mail: covington.pamela@ssc.nasa.gov
AMOUNT: Internship only
DEADLINE(S): None
FIELD(S): Aeronautics/Aerospace; Astronomy; Chemistry; Physics; Engineering; Math; Earth, Life, Materials, Computer, and Physical Sciences

Nine- to ten-week summer internships are open to undergraduates with physical or learning disabilities who maintain a minimum 3.0 GPA and are U.S. citizens. Purpose is to increase the number of students with disabilities pursuing technical degrees related to NASA's mission and to provide on-site experience. Internship takes place at the Stennis Space Center in Mississippi.

Contact Pam Covington for an application.

572—NATIONAL FEDERATION OF THE BLIND (Computer Science Scholarship)

805 Fifth Avenue
Grinnell IA 50112
641/236-3366
Internet: http://www.nfb.org/
AMOUNT: $3,000
DEADLINE(S): MAR 31
FIELD(S): Computer Science

For legally blind students pursuing or planning to pursue a full-time postsecondary course of study in the US. Based on academic excellence, service to the community, and financial need. Membership NOT required.

1 award annually. Renewable. Contact Mrs. Peggy Elliot, Scholarship Committee Chairman, for an application.

573—NATIONAL SCIENCES AND ENGINEERING RESEARCH COUNCIL OF CANADA (Undergraduate Scholarships)

Scholarships/Fellowships Division
350 Albert Street
Ottawa Ontario K1A 1H5 CANADA
613/996-2009
FAX: 613/996-2589
E-mail: schol@nserc.ca
Internet: http://www.nserc.ca
AMOUNT: Up to $3,600
DEADLINE(S): Varies
FIELD(S): Natural Sciences, Engineering, Biology, or Chemistry

Open to Canadian citizens or permanent residents working towards degrees in science or engineering. Academic excellence and research aptitude are considerations.

Write for complete information.

574—NATIONAL SOCIETY OF BLACK ENGINEERS (Scholarships)

1454 Duke Street
Alexandria VA 22314
703/549-2207
FAX: 703/683-5312
E-mail: nsbehq@nsbe.org
Internet: http://www.nsbe.org
AMOUNT: Varies
DEADLINE(S): Varies
FIELD(S): Engineering and engineering technologies

Programs for black and other ethnic minorities in the fields of engineering and the engineering technologies. Organization offers precollege programs, scholarships, career fairs, a journal, a newsletter, etc.

Contact organization for details.

575—OAK RIDGE INSTITUTE FOR SCIENCE AND EDUCATION (ORISE Education and Training Programs)

P.O. Box 117
Oak Ridge TN 37831-0117
Internet: http://www.orau.gov/orise/educ.htm
AMOUNT: Varies
DEADLINE(S): Varies
FIELD(S): Engineering; Aeronautics; Computer Science; Technology; Earth Science; Environmental Studies; Biology; Chemistry; Physics; Medical Research

Numerous programs funded by the U.S. Department of Energy are offered for undergraduate students through postgraduate researchers. Includes fellowship and internship opportunities throughout the U.S. Some have citizenship restrictions. Travel may be included.

See Web site or write for a catalog of specific programs and requirements.

576—QUEEN'S UNIVERSITY OF BELFAST (Industrial Scholarships)

Training and Employment Agency, Management Development Division,
9-21 Adelaide Street
Belfast BT2 8DT Northern Ireland UK
+44 (0) 1232 245133
Internet: http://www.icbl.qub.ac.uk/prospectus/funding/scholars.htm
AMOUNT: Varies
DEADLINE(S): Varies
FIELD(S): Engineering: Aeronautical, Electrical and Electronic, Mechanical, and Manufacturing

Scholarships in Northern Ireland for study in the above fields.

Contact the University at the address shown for complete information.

577—ROBOTIC INDUSTRIES ASSOCIATION (RIA Robotics Scholarship Competition)

900 Victors Way
P.O. Box 3724
Ann Arbor MI 48106
734/994-6088
FAX: 734/994-3338
E-mail: mlehtinen@robotics.org
Internet: http://www.robotics.org
AMOUNT: $1,000
DEADLINE(S): DEC 10
FIELD(S): Robotics

Competition is for undergraduate students attending school in North America. Students must submit a paper that poses a technical problem and offers a solution that involves robotics. Team entries are allowed. Financial need NOT a factor.

3 awards annually. Not renewable. See Web site or contact Marcy Lehtinen at RIA for full guidelines and past winners.

578—ROYAL THAI EMBASSY, OFFICE OF EDUCATIONAL AFFAIRS (Revenue Dept. Scholarships for Thai Students)

1906 23rd Street NW
Washington DC 20008
202/667-9111 or 202/667-8010
FAX: 202/265-7239
AMOUNT: Varies
DEADLINE(S): APR
FIELD(S): Computer Science (Telecommunications), Law, Economics, Finance, Business Administration

Scholarships for students under age 35 from Thailand who have been accepted to study in the U.S. or U.K. for the needs of the Revenue Dept., Ministry of Finance. Must pursue any level degree in one of the above fields.

Selections are based on academic records, employment history, and advisor recommendations.

579—SIEMENS WESTINGHOUSE (Science and Technology Competition)

186 Wood Avenue S.
Iselin NJ 08830
877/822-5233
E-mail: foundation@sc.siemens.com
Internet: http://www.siemens-foundation.org
AMOUNT: $120,000 (max.)

DEADLINE(S): Varies
FIELD(S): Biology; Physical Sciences; Mathematics; Physics; Chemistry; Computer Science; Environmental Science

Open to U.S. high school seniors to pursue independent science research projects, working individually or in teams of 2 or 3 to develop and test their own ideas. May work with one of the universities/laboratories that serve as Siemens' partners. Students from the 50 states, DC, and Territories may compete in one of six geographic areas. Individual and team national prize winners receive a second scholarship award to be applied to undergraduate or graduate education.

See Web site or contact Siemens Foundation for details.

580—SOCIETY OF WOMEN ENGINEERS (Admiral Grace Murray Hopper Scholarships)

230 E. Ohio Street, Suite 400
Chicago, IL 60611-3265
312/596-5223
FAX: 312/644-8557
E-mail: hq@swe.org
Internet: http://www.swe.org
AMOUNT: $1,000
DEADLINE(S): MAY 15
FIELD(S): Engineering; Computer Science; Computer Engineering

Open to women who are entering freshmen at a college/university with an ABET-accredited program or in a SWE-approved school. Must be studying computer engineering or computer science in any form of a four-year program.

5 awards annually. See Web site or send a self-addressed, stamped envelope to SWE for an application. Recipients are notified in September.

581—SOCIETY OF WOMEN ENGINEERS (Microsoft Corporation Scholarships)

230 E. Ohio Street, Suite 400
Chicago IL 60611-3265
312/596-5223
FAX: 312/644-8557
E-mail: hq@swe.org
Internet: http://www.swe.org
AMOUNT: $2,500
DEADLINE(S): FEB 1
FIELD(S): Computer Science; Computer Engineering

Open to women who are entering sophomores, juniors, or seniors or graduate students at a college/university with an ABET-accredited program or in a SWE-approved school. Must have a minimum 3.5 GPA.

2 awards annually. See Web site or send a self-addressed, stamped envelope to SWE for an application. Recipients are notified in May.

582—SPACE COAST CREDIT UNION (Four-Year Scholarships)

Marketing Dept.
P.O. Box 2470
Melbourne FL 32902
Internet: http://www.sccu.com/scholarship/
AMOUNT: $1,250/year
DEADLINE(S): APR 15
FIELD(S): Computer Science, Business (Finance, Economics, Human Resources, Industrial Relations, Marketing)

Must be graduating from a high school in Brevard, Volusia, Flagler, or Indian River counties, be a member of SCCU, have a minimum GPA of 3.0, be planning to attend a four-year Florida institution of higher education, and write a 200-word essay on the topic "Why credit unions are valuable to society."

Two annual awards. For membership information or an application, see our Web page or write to the above address.

583—SPACE COAST CREDIT UNION (Two-Year Scholarships)

Marketing Dept.
P.O. Box 2470
Melbourne FL 32902
Internet: http://www.sccu.com/scholarship/
AMOUNT: $750/year, two years; $1,000 bonus if go on for Bachelor's
DEADLINE(S): APR 15
FIELD(S): Math, Economics, Science, Computer Science, Marketing, Journalism, Political Science

Must be graduating from a high school in Brevard, Volusia, Flagler, or Indian River counties, be a member of SCCU, have a minimum 3.0 GPA, planning to attend a two-year Florida institution of higher education for an associates degree, and be willing to write a 200-word essay on the topic "Why credit unions are valuable to society."

Four annual awards. Students going on to complete a four-year degree could be eligible for a bonus scholarship of $1,000 for the next two years. For membership information or an application, see our Web page or write to the above address.

584—STATE FARM COMPANIES FOUNDATION (Exceptional Student Fellowship)

One State Farm Plaza; SC-3
Bloomington IL 61710-0001
309/766-2039/2161
E-mail: Nancy.Lynn.gr3o@statefarm.com
Internet: http://www.statefarm.com
AMOUNT: $3,000 (nominating institution receives $250)
DEADLINE(S): FEB 15
FIELD(S): Accounting; Business Administration; Actuarial Science; Computer Science; Economics; Finance; Insurance/Risk Management; Investments; Management; Marketing; Mathematics; Statistics

For U.S. citizens who are full-time juniors or seniors when they apply. Must demonstrate significant leadership in extracurricular activities, have minimum 3.6 GPA, and attend accredited U.S. college/university. Must be nominated by dean, department head, professor, or academic advisor.

50 awards annually. Not renewable. See Web site, visit your financial aid office, or write to above address for an application.

585—THE DAPHNE JACKSON MEMORIAL FELLOWSHIPS TRUST (Fellowships in Science/Engineering)

School of Physical Sciences,
Dept. of Physics, University of Surrey
Guildford, Surrey GU2 5XH
ENGLAND UK
01483 259166
FAX: 01483 259501
E-mail: J.Woolley@surrey.ac.uk
Internet: http://www.sst.ph.ic.ac.uk/trust/
AMOUNT: Varies
DEADLINE(S): Varies
FIELD(S): Science or engineering, including information sciences

Fellowships to enable well-qualified and highly motivated scientists and engineers to return to appropriate careers following a career break due to family commitments. May be used on a flexible, part-time basis. Tenable at various U.K. universities.

See Web site and/or contact organization for details.

586—TYSON FOUNDATION, INC. (Alabama Scholarship Program)

2210 W. Oaklawn
Springdale AR 72762-6999

501/290-4995
AMOUNT: Varies (according to need)
DEADLINE(S): FEB 28
FIELD(S): Business; Agriculture; Engineering; Computer Science; Nursing

Open to residents of the general areas of Albertville, Ashland, Blountsville, Gadsden, Heflin, or Oxford, Alabama, who are U.S. citizens and live in the vicinity of a Tyson facility. Must be pursuing full-time undergraduate study at an accredited U.S. institution and demonstrate financial need. Must also be employed part-time and/or summers to help fund education.

Renewable up to 8 semesters or 12 trimesters as long as student meets criteria. Contact Tyson Foundation for an application no later than last day of February; deadline to return application is April 20.

587—TYSON FOUNDATION, INC. (Arkansas Scholarship Program)

2210 W. Oaklawn
Springdale AR 72762-6999
501/290-4955
AMOUNT: Varies (according to need)
DEADLINE(S): FEB 28
FIELD(S): Business; Agriculture; Engineering; Computer Science; Nursing

Open to Arkansas residents who are U.S. citizens pursuing full-time undergraduate study at an accredited U.S. institution. Must demonstrate financial need and be employed part-time and/or summers to help fund education.

Renewable up to 8 semesters or 12 trimesters as long as student meets criteria. Contact Tyson Foundation for an application no later than last day of February; deadline to return application is April 20.

588—TYSON FOUNDATION, INC. (California Scholarship Program)

2210 W. Oaklawn
Springdale AR 72762-6999
501/290-4995
FAX: 501/290-7984
E-mail: coments@tysonfoundation.org
Internet: http://www.tysonfoundation.org
AMOUNT: Varies (according to need)
DEADLINE(S): FEB 28 (to request application); APR 20 (to apply)
FIELD(S): Business; Agriculture; Engineering; Computer Science; Nursing; Biology; Chemistry

Open to residents of Modesto, California, who are U.S. citizens and live in the vicinity of a Tyson facility. Must be pursuing full-time undergraduate study at an accredited U.S. institution and demonstrate financial need. Must also be employed part-time and/or summers to help fund education.

Renewable up to 8 semesters or 12 trimesters as long as student meets criteria. Contact Tyson Foundation to see if area of residence qualifies and for an application.

589—TYSON FOUNDATION, INC. (Florida Scholarship Program)

2210 Oaklawn
Springdale AR 72762-6999
501/290-4995
AMOUNT: Varies (according to need)
DEADLINE(S): FEB 28
FIELD(S): Business; Agriculture; Engineering; Computer Science; Nursing

Open to residents of the general area of Jacksonville, Florida, who are U.S. citizens and live in the vicinity of a Tyson facility. Must be pursuing full-time undergraduate study in an accredited U.S. institution and demonstrate financial need. Must also be employed part-time and/or summers to help fund education.

Renewable up to 8 semesters or 12 trimesters as long as student meets criteria. Contact Tyson Foundation for an application no later than last day of February; deadline to return application is April 20.

590—TYSON FOUNDATION, INC. (Georgia Scholarship Program)

2210 Oaklawn
Springdale AR 72762-6999
501/290-4995
AMOUNT: Varies (according to need)
DEADLINE(S): FEB 28
FIELD(S): Business; Agriculture; Engineering; Computer Science; Nursing

Open to residents of the general areas of Cumming, Buena Vista, Dawson, or Vienna, Georgia, who are U.S. citizens and live in the vicinity of a Tyson facility. Must be pursuing full-time undergraduate study in an accredited U.S. institution and demonstrate financial need. Must also be employed part-time and/or summers to help fund education.

Renewable up to 8 semesters or 12 trimesters as long as student meets criteria. Contact Tyson Foundation for an application no later than last day of February; deadline to return application is April 20.

591—TYSON FOUNDATION, INC. (Illinois Scholarship Program)

2210 Oaklawn
Springdale AR 72762-6999
501/290-4995
AMOUNT: Varies (according to need)
DEADLINE(S): FEB 28
FIELD(S): Business; Agriculture; Engineering; Computer Science; Nursing

Open to residents of the general area of Chicago, Illinois, who are U.S. citizens and live in the vicinity of a Tyson facility. Must be pursuing full-time undergraduate study in an accredited U.S. institution and demonstrate financial need. Must also be employed part-time and/or summers to help fund education.

Renewable up to 8 semesters or 12 trimesters as long as student meets criteria. Contact Tyson Foundation for an application no later than last day of February; deadline to return application is April 20.

592—TYSON FOUNDATION, INC. (Indiana Scholarship Program)

2210 Oaklawn
Springdale AR 72762-6999
501/290-4995
AMOUNT: Varies (according to need)
DEADLINE(S): FEB 28
FIELD(S): Business; Agriculture; Engineering; Computer Science; Nursing

Open to residents of the general areas of Portland or Corydon, Indiana, who are U.S. citizens and live in the vicinity of a Tyson facility. Must be pursuing full-time undergraduate study at an accredited U.S. institution and demonstrate financial need. Must also be employed part-time and/or summers to help fund education.

Renewable up to 8 semesters or 12 trimesters as long as student meets criteria. Contact Tyson Foundation for an application no later than last day of February; deadline to return application is April 20.

593—TYSON FOUNDATION, INC. (Mississippi Scholarship Program)

2210 Oaklawn
Springdale AR 72762-6999
501/290-4995
AMOUNT: Varies (according to need)
DEADLINE(S): FEB 28
FIELD(S): Business; Agriculture; Engineering; Computer Science; Nursing

Open to residents of the general areas of Cleveland, Jackson, Forest, or Vicksburg, Mississippi, who are U.S. citizens and live in the vicinity of a Tyson facility. Must be pursuing full-time undergraduate study in an accredited U.S. institution and demonstrate financial need. Must also be employed part-time and/or summers to help fund education.

Renewable up to 8 semesters or 12 trimesters as long as student meets criteria. Contact Tyson Foundation for an application no later than last day of February; deadline to return application is April 20.

594—TYSON FOUNDATION, INC. (Missouri Scholarship Program)

2210 Oaklawn
Springdale AR 72762-6999
501/290-4995
AMOUNT: Varies (according to need)
DEADLINE(S): FEB 28
FIELD(S): Business; Agriculture; Engineering; Computer Science; Nursing

Open to residents of the general areas of Dexter, Monett, Neosho, Noel, or Sedalia, Missouri, who are U.S. citizens and live in the vicinity of a Tyson facility. Must be pursuing full-time undergraduate study in an accredited U.S. institution and demonstrate financial need. Must also be employed part-time and/or summers to help fund education.

Renewable up to 8 semesters or 12 trimesters as long as student meets criteria. Contact Tyson Foundation for an application no later than last day of February; deadline to return application is April 20.

595—TYSON FOUNDATION, INC. (North Carolina Scholarship Program)

2210 Oaklawn
Springdale AR 72762-6999
501/290-4995
AMOUNT: Varies (according to need)
DEADLINE(S): FEB 28
FIELD(S): Business; Agriculture; Engineering; Computer Science; Nursing

Open to residents of the general areas of Creswell, Monroe, Sanford, or Wilkesboro, North Carolina, who are U.S. citizens and live in the vicinity of a Tyson facility. Must be pursuing full-time undergraduate study in an accredited U.S. institution and demonstrate financial need. Must also be employed part-time and/or summers to help fund education.

Renewable up to 8 semesters or 12 trimesters as long as student meets criteria. Contact Tyson Foundation for an application no later than the last day of February; deadline to return application is April 20.

596—TYSON FOUNDATION, INC. (Oklahoma Scholarship Program)

2210 Oaklawn
Springdale AR 72762-6999
501/290-4995
AMOUNT: Varies (according to need)
DEADLINE(S): FEB 28
FIELD(S): Business; Agriculture; Engineering; Computer Science; Nursing

Open to residents of the general areas of Broken Bow or Stillwell, Oklahoma, who are U.S. citizens and live in the vicinity of a Tyson facility. Must be pursuing full-time undergraduate study in an accredited U.S. institution and demonstrate financial need. Must also be employed part-time and/or summers to help fund education.

Renewable up to 8 semesters or 12 trimesters as long as student meets criteria. Contact Tyson Foundation for an application no later than last day of February; deadline to return application is April 20.

597—TYSON FOUNDATION, INC. (Pennsylvania Scholarship Program)

2210 Oaklawn
Springdale AR 72762-6999
501/290-4995
AMOUNT: Varies (according to need)
DEADLINE(S): FEB 28
FIELD(S): Business; Agriculture; Engineering; Computer Science; Nursing

Open to residents of the general area of New Holland, Pennsylvania, who are U.S. citizens and live in the vicinity of a Tyson facility. Must be pursuing full-time undergraduate study in an accredited U.S. institution and demonstrate financial need. Must also be employed part-time and/or summers to help fund education.

Renewable up to 8 semesters or 12 trimesters as long as student meets criteria. Contact Tyson Foundation for an application no later than last day of February; deadline to return application is April 20.

598—TYSON FOUNDATION, INC. (Tennessee Scholarship Program)

2210 Oaklawn
Springdale AR 72762-6999
501/290-4995
AMOUNT: Varies (according to need)
DEADLINE(S): FEB 28
FIELD(S): Business; Agriculture; Engineering; Computer Science; Nursing

Open to residents of the general areas of Shelbyville or Union City, Tennessee, who are U.S. citizens and live in the vicinity of a Tyson facility. Must be pursuing full-time undergraduate study in an accredited U.S. institution and demonstrate financial need. Must also be employed part-time and/or summers to help fund education.

Renewable up to 8 semesters or 12 trimesters as long as student meets criteria. Contact Tyson Foundation for an application no later than last day of February; deadline to return application is April 20.

599—TYSON FOUNDATION, INC. (Texas Scholarship Program)

2210 Oaklawn
Springdale AR 72762-6999
501/290-4995
AMOUNT: Varies (according to need)
DEADLINE(S): FEB 28
FIELD(S): Business; Agriculture; Engineering; Computer Science; Nursing

Open to residents of the general areas of Carthage, Center, or Seguin, Texas, who are U.S. citizens and live in the vicinity of a Tyson facility. Must be pursuing full-time undergraduate study in an accredited U.S. institution and demonstrate financial need. Must also be employed part-time and/or summers to help fund education.

Renewable up to 8 semesters or 12 trimesters as long as student meets criteria. Contact Tyson Foundation for an application no later than last day of February; deadline to return application is April 20.

600—TYSON FOUNDATION, INC. (Virginia Scholarship Program)

2210 Oaklawn
Springdale AR 72762-6999
501/290-4995
AMOUNT: Varies (according to need)
DEADLINE(S): FEB 28
FIELD(S): Business; Agriculture; Engineering; Computer Science; Nursing

Open to residents of the general areas of Glen Allen, Harrisonburg, or Temperanceville, Virginia, who are U.S. citizens and live in the vicinity of a Tyson facility. Must be pursuing full-time undergraduate study in an accredited U.S. institution and demonstrate financial need.

Must also be employed part-time and/or summers to help fund education.

Renewable up to 8 semesters or 12 trimesters as long as student meets criteria. Contact Tyson Foundation for an application no later than last day of February; deadline to return application is April 20.

601—U.S. DEPT. OF HEALTH & HUMAN SERVICES (Indian Health Service Health Professions Scholarship Program)

Twinbrook Metro Plaza, Suite 100
12300 Twinbrook Parkway
Rockville MD 20852
301/443-0234
FAX: 301/443-4815
Internet: http://www:ihs.gov/Recruitment/DHPS/SP/SBTOC3.asp
AMOUNT: Tuition + fees and monthly stipend of $938.
DEADLINE(S): APR 1
FIELD(S): Health professions, accounting, social work

Open to Native Americans or Alaska natives who are graduate students or college juniors or seniors in a program leading to a career in a fields listed above. U.S. citizenship required. Renewable annually with reapplication.

Scholarship recipients must intend to serve the Indian people. They incur a one-year service obligation to the IHS for each year of support for a minimum of two years. Write for complete information.

602—U.S. ENVIRONMENTAL PROTECTION AGENCY-NATIONAL NETWORK FOR ENVIRONMENTAL MANAGEMENT STUDIES (Fellowships)

1200 Pennsylvania Avenue NW; Mailcode 1704A
Washington DC 20460
202/564-0452;
E-mail: jojokian.sheri@epa.gov
Internet: http://www.epa.gov/enviroed/students.html
AMOUNT: Varies
DEADLINE(S): DEC
FIELD(S): Environmental Policies, Regulations, and Law; Environmental Management and Administration; Environmental Science; Public Relations and Communications; Computer Programming and Development

Fellowships are open to undergraduate and graduate students working on research projects in the above fields, either full-time during the summer or part-time during the school year. Must be U.S. citizen or legal resident. Financial need NOT a factor.

65+ awards annually. Not renewable. See Web site or contact the Career Service Center of participating universities for an application.

603—UNIVERSITY OF MARYLAND (John B. and Ida Slaughter Endowed Scholarship in Science, Technology, and the Black Community)

2169 Lefrak Hall
College Park MD 20742-7225
301/405-1158
FAX: 301/314-986
Internet: http://www.bsos.umd.edu/aasp/scholarship.html
AMOUNT: Varies (in-state tuition costs)
DEADLINE(S): MAR
FIELD(S): Science and Technology AND African-American Studies

Open to African-Americans who are U.S. residents with a minimum 2.8 GPA. Must be accepted to or enrolled at UMCP for freshmen year and must submit letter of recommendation from high school counselor or UMCP faculty member. Should have an interest in applying science and technology to the problems of the Black community. Essay required.

Renewable. Contact the Center for Minorities in Science and Engineering at UMCP for an application.

604—WOMEN IN DEFENSE (HORIZONS Scholarship Foundation)

NDIA
2111 Wilson Boulevard, Suite 400
Arlington VA 22201-3061
703/247-2552
FAX: 703/522-1820
E-mail: cbanks@mciworld.com
Internet: http://www.ndia.org/wid/
AMOUNT: $500+
DEADLINE(S): NOV 1; JUL 1
FIELD(S): Engineering; Computer Science; Physics; Math; Business; Law; International Relations; Political Science; Operations Research; Economics; National Security/Defense

Open to women employed/planning careers in defense/national security areas. Must be currently enrolled full- or part-time at an accredited college/university at the graduate or undergraduate junior/senior level. Must have a minimum 3.25 GPA, demonstrate financial need, and be U.S. citizen. Based on academic achievement, work experience, objectives, and recommendations.

Renewable. See Web site or MUST send self-addressed, stamped envelope to Courtney Banks for application.

605—INTERNATIONAL SOCIETY OF WOMEN AIRLINE PILOTS (ISA Career Scholarship)

2250 E. Tropicana Avenue, Suite 19-395
Las Vegas NV 89119-6594
E-mail: wame@swbell.net
Internet: http://www.iswap.org/scholarship.html
AMOUNT: Varies
DEADLINE(S): APR 15
FIELD(S): Airline Pilot Advanced Ratings

Open to women whose goals are to fly the world's airlines. For advanced pilot ratings, such as the U.S. FAA ATP certificate or equivalent.

Applicants must have a U.S. FAA Commercial Pilot Certificate with an Instrument Rating and a First Class medical certificate (or equivalent). Also must have a minimum of 750 flight hours. Personal interview is required. Check Web site or write for more information and application.

606—XEROX TECHNICAL MINORITY SCHOLARSHIP (Summer Employment Program)

Xerox Square
Rochester NY 14644
Written Inquiry
AMOUNT: Up to $5,000 (varies according to tuition and academic excellence)
DEADLINE(S): SEP 15
FIELD(S): Engineering and Science Disciplines

Scholarships for minorities enrolled in a technical degree program at the bachelor level or above. Must be African-American, Native American, Hispanic, or Asian. Xerox will match your skills with a sponsoring organization that will offer a meaningful summer work experience complimenting your academic learning.

If above requirements are met, send your resume and a cover letter to Xerox Corporation Corporate Employment and College Relations Technical Minority Scholarship Program.

ELECTRICAL ENGINEERING

607—AIR FORCE RESERVE OFFICER TRAINING CORPS (AFROTC Scholarships)

551 E. Maxwell Boulevard
Maxwell AFB AL 36112-6106
334/953-7783

AMOUNT: Full tuition, books, and fees for all 4 years of college
DEADLINE(S): DEC 1
FIELD(S): Science; Engineering; Business; Political Science; Psychology; Geography; Foreign Studies; Foreign Language

Competitive scholarships based on individual merit to high school seniors and graduates who have not completed any full-time college work. Must be a U.S. citizen between the ages of 17-27. Must also have GPA of 2.5 or above, be in top 40% of class, and complete Applicant Fitness Test. Cannot be a single parent. Your college/university must offer AFROTC.

2,300 awards annually. Contact above address for application packet.

608—AMERICAN RADIO RELAY LEAGUE FOUNDATION (Scholarships)

225 Main Street
Newington CT 06111
860/594-0200
FAX: 860/594-0259
Internet: http://www.arrl.org/

AMOUNT: $500-5,000
DEADLINE(S): FEB 1
FIELD(S): Electronics, Communications, and related fields

Various scholarship funds available for undergraduate or graduate students who reside and/or attend school in various ARRL Divisions.

See Web site or contact ARRL for an application.

609—AMERICAN RADIO RELAY LEAGUE FOUNDATION (The PHD ARA Scholarship)

225 Main Street
Newington CT 06111
860/594-0200
FAX: 860/594-0259
Internet: http://www.arrl.org/

AMOUNT: $1,000
DEADLINE(S): FEB 1
FIELD(S): Journalism; Computer Science; Electronic Engineering

For undergraduate or graduate students who are residents of the ARRL Midwest Division (IA, KS, MO, NE) who hold any class of radio amateur license-or student may be the child of a deceased radio amateur.

1 award annually. See Web site or contact ARRL for an application.

610—AMERICAN RADIO RELAY LEAGUE FOUNDATION (The Henry Broughton, K2AE Memorial Scholarship)

225 Main Street
Newington CT 06111
860/594-0200
FAX: 860/594-0259
Internet: http://www.arrl.org/

AMOUNT: $1,000
DEADLINE(S): FEB 1
FIELD(S): Engineering; Science

For radio amateurs with a general class license whose home residence is within 70 miles of Schenectady, New York. For study leading to a bachelor's degree at an accredited four-year college/university.

1+ awards annually. Contact ARRL for an application.

611—AMERICAN SOCIETY OF ENGINEERS OF INDIAN ORIGIN (Undergraduate Scholarship Programs)

P.O. Box 49494
Atlanta GA 30359-1494
770/451-2299
Internet: http://www.iasf.org/asei.htm

AMOUNT: Up to $1,000
DEADLINE(S): AUG 15
FIELD(S): Engineering Fields: Architecture, Computer Technology, Geotechnical or Geoenvironmental Engineering, and allied sciences

Several scholarships for undergraduate engineering students in the above fields who were born in India or who are Indian by ancestry or relation. For study in the U.S. Some programs have residency requirements in certain states.

Contact Dr. Narsi Narasimhan at above location for applications and details.

612—ARMED FORCES COMMUNICATIONS AND ELECTRONICS ASSOCIATION (AFCEA ROTC Scholarships)

4400 Fair Lakes Court
FairFAX: VA 22033-3899
800/336-4583 ext. 6147 or
703/631-6100
Internet: http://www.afcea.org/awards/scholarships.htm

AMOUNT: $2,000
DEADLINE(S): APR 1
FIELD(S): Electrical Engineering, Electronics, Computer Science, Computer or Aerospace Engineering, Physics, Mathematics

Scholarships in the above fields for ROTC students working toward a degree in an accredited four-year college or university in the U.S.

Must be nominated by Professors of Military Science, Naval Science, or Aerospace Studies. Contact the commander of each ROTC unit at your school.

613—ARMED FORCES COMMUNICATIONS AND ELECTRONICS ASSOCIATION (AFCEA ROTC Scholarships)

4400 Fair Lakes Court
FairFAX: VA 22033-3899
800/336-4583 ext. 6147 or
703/631-6100
Internet:
http://www.afcea.org/awards/scholarships.htm

AMOUNT: $2,000
DEADLINE(S): APR 1
FIELD(S): Electrical Engineering, Electronics, Computer Science, Computer or Aerospace Engineering, Physics, Mathematics

Scholarships in the above fields for ROTC students working toward a degree in an accredited four-year college or university in the U.S.

Must be nominated by Professors of Military Science, Naval Science, or Aerospace Studies. Contact the commander of each ROTC unit at your school.

614—ARMED FORCES COMMUNICATIONS AND ELECTRONICS ASSOCIATION (General John A. Wickham Scholarships)

4400 Fair Lakes Court
FairFAX: VA 22033-3899
800/336-4583 ext. 6149 or
703/631-6149
Internet: http://www.afcea.org/awards/scholarships.htm

AMOUNT: $2,000
DEADLINE(S): MAY 1
FIELD(S): Electrical Engineering, Electronics, Computer Science, Computer or Aerospace Engineering, Physics, Mathematics

Scholarships in the above fields for persons working toward degrees in accredited four-year colleges or universities in the U.S. Must have GPA of 3.4 or more.

Check Web site or contact AFCEA for information and application.

615—ASSOCIATED WESTERN UNIVERSITIES, INC. (AWU Undergraduate Student Fellowships)

4190 S. Highland Drive, Suite 211
Salt Lake City UT 84124-2600
801/273-8900
FAX: 801/277-5632
E-mail: info@awu.org
Internet: http://www.awu.org
AMOUNT: $300/week stipend + possible travel allowance
DEADLINE(S): FEB 1
FIELD(S): Science; Mathematics; Engineering; Technology

Eight- to sixteen-week fellowships.

616—ASSOCIATION FOR COMPUTING MACHINERY (Listing of Internships and Summer Jobs)

1515 Broadway, 17th Floor
New York NY 10036
800/342-6626 or
+1-212/869-7440 (global)
FAX: +1-212/944-1318;
E-mail: summer_intern@acm.org
Internet: http://www.acm.org/student/internships.html
AMOUNT: Varies
DEADLINE(S): Varies
FIELD(S): Computer science

A listing on the Internet of several internships and summer employment in the field of computer science at various companies and colleges in the U.S., Canada, and elsewhere. Each one has its own requirements.

Access Web site for details.

617—AT&T BELL LABORATORIES (Summer Research Program for Minorities and Women)

101 Crawfords Corner Road
Holmdel, NJ 07733-3030
Written Inquiry
AMOUNT: Salary + travel and living expenses for summer
DEADLINE(S): DEC 1
FIELD(S): Engineering; Math; Sciences; Computer Science

Program offers minority students and women students technical employment experience at Bell Laboratories. Students should have completed their third year of study at an accredited college or university. U.S. citizen or permanent resident.

Selection is based partially on academic achievement and personal motivation. Write special programs manager-SRP for complete information.

618—BROOKHAVEN WOMEN IN SCIENCE (Renate W. Chasman Scholarship)

P.O. Box 183
Upton NY 11973-5000
E-mail: pam@bnl.gov
AMOUNT: $2,000
DEADLINE(S): APR 1
FIELD(S): Natural Sciences; Engineering; Mathematics

Open ONLY to women who are residents of the boroughs of Brooklyn or Queens or the counties of Nassau or Suffolk in New York who are reentering school after a period of study. For juniors, seniors, or first-year graduate students.

1 award annually. Not renewable. Contact Pam Mansfield at above location for an application. Phone calls are NOT accepted.

619—FRAWNHOFER CENTER FOR RESEARCH IN COMPUTER GRAPHICS (Student and Scholar Exchange Programs)

321 S. Main Street
Providence RI 02903
401/453-6363 ext. 100
FAX: 401/453-0444
E-mail: info@crcg.edu
Internet: http://www.crcg.edu/Education/exchange.html
AMOUNT: Stipend for living expenses; transportation costs reimbursed
DEADLINE(S): None
FIELD(S): Computer Graphics

Educational exchanges between U.S. and Europe for participants to become involved in the new information society. In the U.S., sites are in Rhode Island. In Europe, the Technical University of Darmstadt in Germany is the main site. Students conducting thesis research or practicums can stay for up to six months. Summer students normally stay for ten to twelve weeks.

Europeans apply to Dr. Joachim Rix, Dept. of Industrial Applications at above company, Rundeturmstr. 6, D-64283 Darmstadt, Germany.

Phone: (+49) 6151 155 220
FAX: (+49) 6151 155 299

U.S. students apply to Sheri Mulcahey at above address.

620—GREAT LAKES COMMISSION (Carol A. Ratza Memorial Scholarship)

400 Fourth Street
Ann Arbor MI 48103-4816
E-mail: mdonahue@glc.org
Internet: http://www.glc.org
AMOUNT: $500
DEADLINE(S): MAR 28
FIELD(S): Electronic Communications Technology

Open to high school seniors and returning students enrolled full-time at a Great Lakes college/university (IL, IN, MI, MN, NY, OH, PA, WI, Ontario, Quebec). Must have a demonstrated interest in the environmental or economic applications of electronic communications technology, exhibit academic excellence, and have a sincere appreciation for the Great Lakes and their protection. Must submit resume, transcripts, recommendations, and essay or Web page on Great Lakes issue.

See Web site or contact Dr. Michael J. Donahue, President/CEO, for an application. Recipient announced by May 1.

621—HISPANIC COLLEGE FUND (Scholarships for Hispanic Students)

One Thomas Circle NW, Suite 375
Washington DC 20005
202/296-5400
FAX: 202/296-3774
E-mail: Hispanic.Fund@Internet MCI.com
Internet: http://hispanicfund.org
AMOUNT: Varies
DEADLINE(S): APR 15
FIELD(S): Most college majors leading to a career in business

Scholarships for deserving Hispanic college students pursuing a higher education in a major leading to a business career and who are full-time students at accredited institutions. U.S. citizenship. Must demonstrate financial need.

Contact above organization for details or visit Web site for application.

622—IEEE COMPUTER SOCIETY (Richard Merwin Student Scholarship)

1730 Massachusetts Avenue NW
Washington DC 20036-1992
202/371-1013
FAX: 202/778-0884
Internet: http://www.computer.org/students/scholrship.htm
AMOUNT: $3,000
DEADLINE(S): MAY 31
FIELD(S): Computer Science, Computer Engineering, or Electrical Engineering

Scholarships for active leaders in student branch chapters of the IEEE Computer Society who show promise in their academic and professional efforts.

Four awards. Contact above address or Web site for details.

623—INSTITUTE FOR OPERATIONS RESEARCH AND THE MANAGEMENT SCIENCES (INFORMS Summer Internship Directory)

P.O. Box 64794
Baltimore MD 21264-4794
800/4INFORMS
FAX: 410/684-2963
E-mail: jps@informs.org
Internet: http://www.informs.org/INTERN/
AMOUNT: Varies
DEADLINE(S): Varies
FIELD(S): Fields related to information management: business management, engineering, mathematics

A Web site listing of summer internships in the field of operations research and management sciences. Both applicants and employers can register online.

Access Web site for list.

624—INSTITUTION OF ELECTRICAL ENGINEERS (Jubilee Scholarships & Faraday Lecture Scholarship)

Savoy Place
London WC2R 0BL ENGLAND
+44-020-7344-8458
FAX: +44-020-7497-3609
E-mail: scholarships@iee.org.uk
Internet: http://www.iee.org.uk/EduCareers/Awards/
AMOUNT: 750 pounds/year
DEADLINE(S): JUN 30
FIELD(S): Electrical, Electronic, Manufacturing, or Related Engineering

Scholarships for students currently residing in the United Kingdom in the above engineering fields.

12 awards available. Renewable for the entire period of an IEE-accredited course. Check Web site or contact organization for application details.

625—INSTITUTION OF ELECTRICAL ENGINEERS (Scholarships for Women)

Savoy Place
London WC2R 0BL ENGLAND
0171 240 1871 ext. 2211/2235
FAX: 0171 497 3609
E-mail: scholarships@iee.org.uk
Internet: http://www.iee.org.uk/Awards/ugwom.htm
AMOUNT: 750 pounds/year
DEADLINE(S): JUN 15
FIELD(S): Engineering

Scholarships for women residing in the United Kingdom and pursuing degrees in engineering.

Candidates must be undertaking mathematics and physics "A" level or Scottish Higher examinations. Renewable for the entire period of an IEE-accredited course. Check Web site or contact organization for application details.

626—LOS ANGELES COUNCIL OF BLACK PROFESSIONAL ENGINEERS (Al-Ben Scholarship)

P.O. Box 881029
Los Angeles CA 90009
310/635-7734
E-mail: secy1@lablackengineers.org
Internet: http://www.lablackengineers.org/scholarships.html
AMOUNT: Varies
DEADLINE(S): Varies
FIELD(S): Engineering; Mathematics; Computer Studies; Applied Scientific Studies

Open to technically inclined precollege and undergraduate students enrolled in one of the above fields. Must be of African American, Native American, or Hispanic ancestry. Preference given to students attending college in Southern California or who are Southern California residents.

See Web site to download an application.

627—MARYLAND HIGHER EDUCATION COMMISSION (Maryland Science and Technology Scholarship Program)

16 Francis Street
Annapolis Park MD 21401
410/974-5370 or 800/974-1024
E-mail: ssamail@mhec.state.md.us
Internet: http://www.mhec.state.md.us/SSA/stech_qa.htm
AMOUNT: $3,000/year (BA); $1,000/year (AA)
DEADLINE(S): None
FIELD(S): Computer Science; Engineering; Technology

Scholarships for college-bound Maryland high school seniors who will major in one of the above fields and who are accepted to an eligible associate or bachelor's degree program in Maryland. The deadline was not known at this writing, so check for deadline date. Must agree to work in the state after graduation in a related field, one year for each year of assistance received.

Must maintain a 3.0 GPA.

628—MICROSOFT CORPORATION (National Minority and/or Women's Scholarships)

One Microsoft Way
Redmond WA 98052-8303
E-mail: scholar@microsoft.com
Internet: http://www.microsoft.com/college/scholarships/
AMOUNT: Tuition for 1 year
DEADLINE(S): JAN 31
FIELD(S): Computer Science, Computer Engineering, or a related technical discipline, such as Math or Physics

Full tuition scholarships awarded for 1 academic year to women and minorities (African-Americans, Hispanics, or Native Americans) enrolled full-time in the above fields with a demonstrated interest in computers and making satisfactory progress towards a degree. Awards are made through designated schools and are not transferable to other institutions.

See Web site above for details.

629—MICROSOFT CORPORATION (Summer Internships)

One Microsoft Way
Redmond WA 98052-8303
425/882-8080
E-mail: scholar@microsoft.com
Internet: http://www.microsoft.com/college/scholarships/
AMOUNT: Varies
DEADLINE(S): None
FIELD(S): Computer Science, Computer Engineering, or a related technical discipline, such as Math or Physics

Summer internships for individuals with a deep passion for technological advancement. Must commit to a 12-week minimum. Includes transportation, shipping costs, and shared cost of housing. Competitive compensation offered.

Check Web site above for details.

630—NATIONAL SCIENCES AND ENGINEERING RESEARCH COUNCIL OF CANADA (Undergraduate Scholarships)

Scholarships/Fellowships Division
350 Albert Street
Ottawa Ontario K1A 1H5 CANADA
613/996-2009
FAX: 613/996-2589
E-mail: schol@nserc.ca
Internet: http://www.nserc.ca
AMOUNT: Up to $3,600
DEADLINE(S): Varies

FIELD(S): Natural Sciences, Engineering, Biology, or Chemistry

Open to Canadian citizens or permanent residents working towards degrees in science or engineering. Academic excellence and research aptitude are considerations.

Write for complete information.

631—NATIONAL SOCIETY OF BLACK ENGINEERS (Scholarships)

1454 Duke Street
Alexandria VA 22314
703/549-2207
FAX: 703/683-5312
E-mail: nsbehq@nsbe.org
Internet: http://www.nsbe.org

AMOUNT: Varies
DEADLINE(S): Varies
FIELD(S): Engineering and engineering technologies

Programs for black and other ethnic minorities in the fields of engineering and the engineering technologies. Organization offers precollege programs, scholarships, career fairs, a journal, a newsletter, etc.

Contact organization for details.

632—QUEEN'S UNIVERSITY OF BELFAST (Industrial Scholarships)

Training and Employment Agency,
Management Development Division,
9-21 Adelaide Street
Belfast BT2 8DT Northern Ireland UK
+44 (0) 1232 245133
Internet: http://www.icbl.qub.ac.uk/prospectus/funding/scholars.htm

AMOUNT: Varies
DEADLINE(S): Varies
FIELD(S): Engineering: Aeronautical, Electrical and Electronic, Mechanical, and Manufacturing

Scholarships in Northern Ireland for study in the above fields.

Contact the University at the address shown for complete information.

633—ROYAL THAI EMBASSY, OFFICE OF EDUCATIONAL AFFAIRS (Revenue Dept. Scholarships for Thai Students)

1906 23rd Street NW
Washington DC 20008
202/667-9111 or 202/667-8010
FAX: 202/265-7239

AMOUNT: Varies
DEADLINE(S): APR
FIELD(S): Computer Science (Telecommunications), Law, Economics, Finance, Business Administration

Scholarships for students under age 35 from Thailand who have been accepted to study in the U.S. or U.K. for the needs of the Revenue Dept., Ministry of Finance. Must pursue any level degree in one of the above fields.

Selections are based on academic records, employment history, and advisor recommendations.

634—THE DAPHNE JACKSON MEMORIAL FELLOWSHIPS TRUST (Fellowships in Science/Engineering)

School of Physical Sciences,
Dept. of Physics, University of Surrey
Guildford, Surrey GU2 5XH
ENGLAND UK
01483 259166
FAX: 01483 259501
E-mail: J.Woolley@surrey.ac.uk
Internet: http://www.sst.ph.ic.ac.uk/trust/

AMOUNT: Varies
DEADLINE(S): Varies
FIELD(S): Science or Engineering, including Information Sciences

Fellowships to enable well-qualified and highly motivated scientists and engineers to return to appropriate careers following a career break due to family commitments. May be used on a flexible, part-time basis. Tenable at various U.K. universities.

See Web site and/or contact organization for details.

635—UNIVERSITY OF MARYLAND (John B. and Ida Slaughter Endowed Scholarship in Science, Technology, and the Black Community)

2169 Lefrak Hall
College Park MD 20742-7225
301/405-1158
FAX: 301/314-986
Internet: http://www.bsos.umd.edu/aasp/scholarship.html

AMOUNT: Varies (in-state tuition costs)
DEADLINE(S): MAR
FIELD(S): Science and Technology AND African-American Studies

Open to African-Americans who are U.S. residents with a minimum 2.8 GPA. Must be accepted to or enrolled at UMCP for freshmen year and must submit letter of recommendation from high school counselor or UMCP faculty member. Should have an interest in applying science and technology to the problems of the Black community. Essay required.

Renewable. Contact the Center for Minorities in Science and Engineering at UMCP for an application.

636—INTERNATIONAL SOCIETY OF WOMEN AIRLINE PILOTS (ISA Career Scholarship)

2250 E. Tropicana Avenue,
Suite 19-395
Las Vegas NV 89119-6594
E-mail: wame@swbell.net
Internet: http://www.iswap.org/scholarship.html

AMOUNT: Varies
DEADLINE(S): APR 15
FIELD(S): Airline Pilot Advanced Ratings

Open to women whose goals are to fly the world's airlines. For advanced pilot ratings, such as the U.S. FAA ATP certificate or equivalent.

Applicants must have a U.S. FAA Commercial Pilot Certificate with an Instrument Rating and a First Class medical certificate (or equivalent). Also must have a minimum of 750 flight hours. Personal interview is required. Check Web site or write for more information and application.

637—WOMEN'S INTERNATIONAL NETWORK OF UTILITY PROFESSIONALS (Julia Kiene & Lyle Mamer Fellowships)

P.O. Box 335
White's Creek TN 37189
615/876-5444
E-mail: winup@aol.com
Internet: http://winup.org (no www).

AMOUNT: $1,000 to $2,000
DEADLINE(S): MAR 1
FIELD(S): Energy; Utilities and related fields listed below

Open to graduate students or graduating college seniors pursuing an advanced degree in any phase of energy, including communications, education, electric utilities, electrical engineering, electric home appliances/equipment manufacturing, marketing research, etc.

The college or university selected by applicant must be accredited and approved by the WINUP Fellowship Committee. See Web site or send SASE to above location for complete information.

638—XEROX TECHNICAL MINORITY SCHOLARSHIP (Summer Employment Program)

Xerox Square
Rochester NY 14644
Written Inquiry
AMOUNT: Up to $5,000 (varies according to tuition and academic excellence)
DEADLINE(S): SEP 15
FIELD(S): Engineering and Science Disciplines

Scholarships for minorities enrolled in a technical degree program at the bachelor level or above. Must be African-American, Native American, Hispanic, or Asian. Xerox will match your skills with a sponsoring organization that will offer a meaningful summer work experience complimenting your academic learning.

If above requirements are met, send your resume and a cover letter to Xerox Corporation Corporate Employment and College Relations Technical Minority Scholarship Program.

ENGINEERING TECHNOLOGY

639—AIR FORCE RESERVE OFFICER TRAINING CORPS (AFROTC Scholarships)

551 E. Maxwell Boulevard
Maxwell AFB AL 36112-6106
334/953-7783
AMOUNT: Full tuition, books, and fees for all 4 years of college
DEADLINE(S): DEC 1
FIELD(S): Science; Engineering; Business; Political Science; Psychology; Geography; Foreign Studies; Foreign Language

Competitive scholarships based on individual merit to high school seniors and graduates who have not completed any full-time college work. Must be a U.S. citizen between the ages of 17-27. Must also have GPA of 2.5 or above, be in top 40% of class, and complete Applicant Fitness Test. Cannot be a single parent. Your college/university must offer AFROTC.

2,300 awards annually. Contact above address for application packet.

640—AMERICAN CHEMICAL SOCIETY (Minority Scholars Program)

1155 Sixteenth Street NW
Washington, DC 20036
202/872-6250 or 800/227-5558
FAX: 202/776-8003
E-mail: r_hughes@acs.org
Internet: http://www.acs.org
AMOUNT: Up to $3,000
DEADLINE(S): FEB 15
FIELD(S): Chemistry; Biochemistry; Chemical Engineering; Chemical Technology

Open to (a) high school seniors who will enter college in the coming year, (b) college students currently/planning to pursue full time study, (c) community college graduates/transfer students pursuing a bachelor's, and (d) community college freshmen. Awarded on the basis of merit and financial need to African-American, Hispanic, and American Indian students with outstanding academic records combined with strong interest in chemistry. Must be U.S. citizen/permanent resident.

See Web site or contact ACS for an application.

641—AMERICAN INDIAN SCIENCE AND ENGINEERING SOCIETY (EPA Tribal Lands Environmental Science Scholarship)

P.O. Box 9828
Albuquerque NM 87119-9828
505/765-1052
FAX: 505/765-5608
E-mail: scholarships@aises.org
Internet: http://www.aises.org/scholarships/index.html
AMOUNT: $4,000
DEADLINE(S): JUN 15
FIELD(S): Biochemistry; Biology; Chemical Engineering; Chemistry; Entomology; Environmental Economics/Science; Hydrology; Environmental Studies

Open to American Indian college juniors, seniors, and graduate students enrolled full-time at an accredited institution. Must demonstrate financial need and be a member of AISES ($10 fee). Certificate of Indian blood NOT required.

Not renewable. See Web site for more information and/or an application.

642—AMERICAN SOCIETY FOR PHOTOGRAMMETRY AND REMOTE SENSING (Robert E. Altenhofen Memorial Scholarship)

5410 Grosvenor Lane, Suite 210
Bethesda MD 20814-2160
301/493-0290
FAX: 301/493-0208
E-mail: asprs@asprs.org
Internet: http://www.asprs.org
AMOUNT: $2,000 + certificate
DEADLINE(S): DEC 2
FIELD(S): Photogrammetry

Open to undergraduate and graduate students who are student or active members of ASPRS and are attending an accredited college/university. Purpose is to encourage and commend students who display exceptional interest and ability in the theoretical aspects of photogrammetry. Must submit courses taken/grades, faculty references, study plans, and relevant reports. Upon completion of award period, must submit final report of scholastic accomplishments.

See Web site or contact ASPRS for an application or membership information.

643—AMERICAN SOCIETY FOR PHOTOGRAMMETRY AND REMOTE SENSING (Space Imaging Award for Application of Digital Landsat TM Data)

5410 Grosvenor Lane, Suite 210
Bethesda MD 20814-2160
301/493-0290
FAX: 301/493-0208
E-mail: asprs@asprs.org
Internet: http://www.asprs.org
AMOUNT: Data valued up to $4,000 + plaque
DEADLINE(S): DEC 2
FIELD(S): Remote Sensing

Open to undergraduate and graduate students enrolled full-time at an accredited college/university with image processing facilities appropriate for conducting proposed work. Must be ASPRS member. Purpose is to support remote sensing education and stimulate development of applications of digital Landsat Thematic Mapper TM data. Must submit brief proposal and demonstrate research capability. Upon completion of award period, must submit written report of project.

See Web site or contact ASPRS for an application or membership information.

644—AMERICAN SOCIETY FOR PHOTOGRAMMETRY AND REMOTE SENSING (William A. Fischer Memorial Scholarship)

5410 Grosvenor Lane, Suite 210
Bethesda MD 20814-2160
301/493-0290
FAX: 301/493-0208
E-mail: asprs@asprs.org
Internet: http://www.asprs.org
AMOUNT: $2,000 + certificate
DEADLINE(S): DEC 2

FIELD(S): Remote Sensing

Open to current or prospective graduate students enrolled full-time at an accredited college/university with image processing facilities appropriate for conducting proposed work. Must be ASPRS member. Purpose is to support remote sensing education and stimulate new and innovative use of remote sensing data/techniques to the natural, cultural, and agricultural resources of the Earth. May need to submit samples of technical papers or research reports to demonstrate research capability. Upon completion of award period, must submit written report of project.

See Web site or contact ASPRS for an application or membership information.

645—AMERICAN SOCIETY OF HEATING, REFRIGERATING, AND AIR-CONDITIONING ENGINEERS (ASHRAE Scholarship Program)

1791 Tullie Circle, NE
Atlanta GA 30329
404/636-8400
FAX: 404/321-5478
Internet: http://www.ashrae.org

AMOUNT: $3,000
DEADLINE(S): DEC 1
FIELD(S): Heating, Ventilation, Air-Conditioning & Refrigeration (HVAC&R)

Open to engineering undergraduate students planning a career in HVAC&R. Must have completed a full semester or quarter of college study and be currently enrolled full-time in an ABET-accredited program with at least one full year of undergraduate study remaining. Minimum 3.0 GPA, letters of recommendation, transcripts, and financial need are required. Awards teneable at accredited institutions.

6 awards annually. Not renewable. Contact Lois Benedict at above address for an application.

646—AMERICAN SOCIETY OF HEATING, REFRIGERATING, AND AIR-CONDITIONING ENGINEERS (Reuben Trane Scholarships)

1791 Tullie Circle, NE
Atlanta GA 30329-2305
404/636-8400
FAX: 404/321-5478
Internet: http://www.ashrae.org

AMOUNT: $5,000
DEADLINE(S): DEC 1
FIELD(S): Heating, Ventilation, Air-Conditioning & Refrigeration (HVAC&R)

Open to engineering undergraduate students planning a career in HVAC&R. Must have completed a full semester or quarter of college, be currently enrolled full-time in an ABET-accredited program with at least two full years of undergraduate study remaining. Minimum 3.0 GPA required. Must demonstrate financial need and leadership abilities. For eligibility in second year, student must remain full-time with GPA of 3.0 or higher. Awards tenable at accredited institutions.

4 two-year awards annually. Contact Lois Benedict at above address for an application.

647—AMERICAN SOCIETY OF HEATING, REFRIGERATING, AND AIR-CONDITIONING ENGINEERS (ASHRAE Engineering Technology Scholarships)

1791 Tullie Circle, NE
Atlanta GA 30329
404/636-8400
FAX: 404/321-5478
Internet: http://www.ashrae.org

AMOUNT: $3,000
DEADLINE(S): MAY 1
FIELD(S): Engineering Technology

For full-time students in a two-year associates degree or ABET-accredited bachelor's degree engineering technology program with one full year of study remaining. Must have GPA of 3.0 or higher and demonstrate financial need. Letters of recommendation and transcripts are required.

2 awards annually. Not renewable. Contact Lois Benedict at above address for an application.

648—AMERICAN WATER RESOURCES ASSOCIATION (Richard A. Herbert Memorial Scholarships)

4 West Federal Street
Middleburg VA 20118-1626
540/687-8390
FAX: 540/687-8395
E-mail: info@awra.org
Internet: http://www.awra.org//student/herbert.html

AMOUNT: $1,000 + complimentary AWRA membership
DEADLINE(S): APR 26
FIELD(S): Water Resources and related fields

For full-time undergraduates working towards first degree and for graduates. Based on academic performance, including cumulative GPA, relevance of curriculum to water resources, and leadership in extracurricular activities related to water resources. Quality and relevance of research is also considered from graduate students. Transcripts, letters of reference, and summary of academic interests/achievements, extracurricular interests, and career goals required (2-page limit).

2 awards annually: 1 undergrad and 1 graduate. Recipients announced in the summer. Contact AWRA Student Activities Committee, for an application.

649—AMERICAN WELDING SOCIETY (Scholarships)

550 NW LeJeune Road
Miami FL 33126
800/443-9353, ext. 461 or 305/445-6628
FAX: 305/443-7559
Internet: http://www.aws.org

AMOUNT: $2,500-$3,000
DEADLINE(S): JAN 15
FIELD(S): Welding Engineering and Technology

AWS has nine different scholarship programs for U.S. citizens pursuing undergraduate study at an accredited U.S. institution. Two programs are also for Canadian citizens studying at Canadian institutions. Must be at least 18 years of age with a high school diploma or equivalent and a minimum 2.0 GPA. Some programs require financial need. Must submit two letters of reference, brief biography, transcript, proposed curriculum, and verification of enrollment/employment.

Renewable up to 4 years. Contact AWS for details on specific scholarships. Awards announced in February.

650—ASSOCIATED WESTERN UNIVERSITIES, INC. (AWU Undergraduate Student Fellowships)

4190 S. Highland Drive, Suite 211
Salt Lake City UT 84124-2600
801/273-8900
FAX: 801/277-5632
E-mail: info@awu.org
Internet: http://www.awu.org

AMOUNT: $300/week stipend + possible travel allowance
DEADLINE(S): FEB 1
FIELD(S): Science; Mathematics; Engineering; Technology

Eight- to sixteen-week fellowships.

651—AT&T BELL LABORATORIES (Summer Research Program for Minorities and Women)

101 Crawfords Corner Road
Holmdel NJ 07733-3030
Written Inquiry

AMOUNT: Salary + travel and living expenses for summer
DEADLINE(S): DEC 1
FIELD(S): Engineering; Math; Sciences; Computer Science

Program offers minority students and women students technical employment experience at Bell Laboratories. Students should have completed their third year of study at an accredited college or university. U.S. citizen or permanent resident.

Selection is based partially on academic achievement and personal motivation. Write special programs manager-SRP for complete information.

652—AUTOMOTIVE HALL OF FAME (Educational Fund)

21400 Oakwood Boulevard
Dearborn MI 48124-4078
313/240-4000
FAX: 313/240-8641
Internet: http://www.automotivehall offame.org

AMOUNT: $250-$2,000
DEADLINE(S): MAY 30
FIELD(S): Automotive-Related Careers

Open to full-time undergraduate and graduate students who have a sincere interest in pursuing an automotive career upon graduation from college. Must be at least a college freshman at a 4-year institution or a high school senior for an 18-month or 2-year program. Must be attending or accepted into an accredited college, university, or trade school in the U.S. Transcripts and letters of recommendation required. Financial need considered but not necessary.

12+ awards annually. Renewable. See Web site or send self-addressed, stamped envelope for an application. Recipients notified mid-September.

653—BARRY GOLDWATER SCHOLARSHIP AND EXCELLENCE IN EDUCATION FOUNDATION (Scholarships)

6225 Brandon Avenue, Suite 315
Springfield VA 22150-2519
703/756-6012
FAX: 703/756-6015
E-mail: GOLDH2o@erols.com
Internet: http://www.act.org/goldwater

AMOUNT: $7,500/year (max.)
DEADLINE(S): FEB 1
FIELD(S): Math; Natural Sciences; Engineering

Open to college sophomores and juniors with a minimum 3.0 GPA. Must be U.S. citizen, resident alien, or American national pursuing a degree at an accredited institution in math, natural sciences, or engineering disciplines that contribute to technological advances.

300 awards annually. See Web site or contact your Goldwater Faculty Representative on campus. Students must be nominated by their institution and cannot apply on their own.

654—BROOKHAVEN WOMEN IN SCIENCE (Renate W. Chasman Scholarship)

P.O. Box 183
Upton NY 11973-5000
E-mail: pam@bnl.gov

AMOUNT: $2,000
DEADLINE(S): APR 1
FIELD(S): Natural Sciences; Engineering; Mathematics

Open ONLY to women who are residents of the boroughs of Brooklyn or Queens or the counties of Nassau or Suffolk in New York who are reentering school after a period of study. For juniors, seniors, or first-year graduate students.

1 award annually. Not renewable. Contact Pam Mansfield at above location for an application. Phone calls are NOT accepted.

655—CANADIAN RECREATIONAL CANOEING ASSOCIATION (Bill Mason Memorial Scholarship Fund)

446 Main Street W.
P.O. Box 398
Merrickville Ontario K0G 1N0 CANADA
613/269-2910
FAX: 613/269-2908
Internet: http://www.crca.ca/bill.html

AMOUNT: $1,000
DEADLINE(S): OCT 15
FIELD(S): Outdoor Recreation; Environmental Studies

Scholarship is a tribute to Bill Mason, a Canadian recognized at home and abroad as a canoeist, environmentalist, artist, filmmaker, photographer, and public speaker. Applicant must be a full-time student at a Canadian university or college. Must be planning a career related to the above fields, be a Canadian citizen, maintain a B+ average, and be a second-year student or higher. Financial need must be demonstrated. Background in canoeing/kayaking is an asset.

Scholarship is paid in two installments: $700 by Nov. 10, and $300 after receipt of May 15 progress report.

656—CANADIAN SOCIETY FOR CHEMICAL ENGINEERING (Edmonton Chemical Engineering Scholarship)

130 Slater Street, Suite 550
Ottawa Ontario KIP 6E2 CANADA
613/232-6252 or 888/542-2242
FAX: 613/232-5862
E-mail: lhuskins@cheminst.ca
Internet: http://www.chemeng.ca/

AMOUNT: $1,000 + certificate + travel expenses to attend conference
DEADLINE(S): APR 30
FIELD(S): Chemical Engineering

For undergraduates in chemical engineering entering the second, third, fourth, or fifth year of studies at a Canadian university. Offered to a student who has demonstrated leadership qualities and provided contributions to the CSChE via participation in student chapters, and above average academic performance. Must be members of CSChE. Letter of application should document contributions to Society and should be accompanied by a transcript and two letters of support.

1 award annually. Contact the Program Manager, Awards, for an application.

657—CANADIAN SOCIETY FOR CHEMICAL ENGINEERING (Sarina Chemical Engineering Scholarship)

130 Slater Street, Suite 550
Ottawa Ontario KIP 6E2 CANADA
613/232-6252 or 888-542/2242
FAX: 613/232-5862
E-mail: lhuskins@cheminst.ca
Internet: http://www.chemeng.ca/

AMOUNT: $1,000 + certificate + travel expenses to attend conference
DEADLINE(S): APR 30
FIELD(S): Chemical Engineering

For undergraduate students about to enter their final year of studies at a Canadian university. Offered to student who has achieved academic excellence as well as demonstrated contributions to CSChE, such as participation in student chapters. Must be members of CSChE. Letter of application (6 copies) should include evidence of contributions to the Society as well as academic transcript (1 original and 5 copies), and two letters of reference.

1 award annually. Contact the Program Manager, Awards, for an application.

658—CANADIAN SOCIETY FOR CHEMICAL ENGINEERING (SNC/LAVALIN Plant Competition)

130 Slater Street, Suite 550
Ottawa Ontario KIP 6E2 CANADA
613/232-6252 or 888/542-2242
FAX: 613/232-5862
E-mail: lhuskins@cheminst.ca
Internet: http://www.chemeng.ca/

AMOUNT: $1,000 + certificate + subscription to Canadian Journal of Chemical Engineering
DEADLINE(S): MAY 15
FIELD(S): Chemical Engineering

Competition for individuals and groups (6 individuals max.) of undergraduate students registered in chemical engineering programs in Canadian universities. Entries should include summary/flowsheet of process, copy of final report submitted to university, list of students who performed work with their addresses and phone numbers, name of collaborating organization and engineers who assisted students, and a brief description of assistance provided by that organization.

1 award annually. Contact the Program Manager, Awards, for an application.

659—CELANESE CANADA, INC. (Scholarships)

AUCC; 350 Albert Street, Suite 600
Ottawa Ontario K1R 1B1 CANADA
613/563-1236; FAX: 613/563-9745
E-mail: awards@aucc.ca
Internet: http://www.aucc.ca

AMOUNT: $1,500
DEADLINE(S): JUL 2
FIELD(S): Mechanical and Chemical Engineering; Chemistry; Business Administration and Commerce

Open to Canadian citizens/permanent residents for their final year of an undergraduate program in one of above fields. Must attend a college/university which is a member, or affiliated to a member, of the Association of Universities and Colleges of Canada. Candidates are expected to have achieved a high level of academic excellence as well as to have exhibited superior intellectual ability and judgment. In some cases, study in certain province/school is required.

APPLICATIONS ARE BY NOMINATION ONLY. Not renewable. See Web site or contact AUCC for nomination procedures.

660—COMMUNITY FOUNDATION OF WESTERN MASSACHUSETTS (James L. Shriver Scholarship)

1500 Main Street
P.O. Box 15769
Springfield MA 01115
413/732-2858

AMOUNT: $750
DEADLINE(S): APR 15
FIELD(S): Technical Fields

Open to residents of Western Massachusetts to pursue technical careers through college, trade, or technical school. Based on financial need, academic merit, and extracurricular activities. Must submit transcripts and fill out government FAFSA form.

1 award annually. Renewable with reapplication. Contact Community Foundation for an application and your financial aid office for FAFSA. Notification is in June.

661—GENERAL LEARNING COMMUNICATIONS (DuPont Challenge Science Essay Awards Program)

900 Skokie Boulevard, Suite 200
Northbrook IL 60062-4028
847/205-3000
FAX: 847/564-8197
Internet: http://www.glcomm.com/dupont

AMOUNT: $1,500 (max.)
DEADLINE(S): JAN 28
FIELD(S): Science and Technology

Annual essay competition open to students in grades 7-12 in the U.S. and Canada. Cash awards for first, second, and honorable mention. First-place essayists in each of two divisions, their science teacher, and a parent of each receive a trip to the Space Center Houston/NASA at the end of April.

102 awards annually. See Web site or contact your science teacher or GLC for official entry blank.

662—GLOBAL AUTOMOTIVE AFTERMARKET SYMPOSIUM (Scholarship)

4050 Pennsylvania; Suite 225
Kansas City MO 64111
816/523-8118
FAX: 816/523-7293
Internet: http://awda.org/

AMOUNT: $1,000 + matching grant after graduation
DEADLINE(S): FEB 28
FIELD(S): Automotive Aftermarket: various aspects

Funded by a variety of trade associations, this scholarship is for students pursuing careers in the automotive aftermarket. Must be a graduating high school senior. Matching bonus awarded for working in the field for at least 6 months after graduation. Must be enrolled on a college-level program or a vocational NATEF-accredited automotive technician program.

Contact Automotive Warehouse Distributors Association at the above address or access the Web site for more information.

663—GREAT LAKES COMMISSION (Carol A. Ratza Memorial Scholarship)

400 Fourth Street
Ann Arbor MI 48103-4816
E-mail: mdonahue@glc.org
Internet: http://www.glc.org

AMOUNT: $500
DEADLINE(S): MAR 28
FIELD(S): Electronic Communications Technology

Open to high school seniors and returning students enrolled full-time at a Great Lakes college/university (IL, IN, MI, MN, NY, OH, PA, WI, Ontario, Quebec). Must have a demonstrated interest in the environmental or economic applications of electronic communications technology, exhibit academic excellence, and have a sincere appreciation for the Great Lakes and their protection. Must submit resume, transcripts, recommendations, and essay or Web page on Great Lakes issue.

See Web site or contact Dr. Michael J. Donahue, President/CEO, for an application. Recipient announced by May 1.

664—HISPANIC COLLEGE FUND (Scholarships for Hispanic Students)

One Thomas Circle NW, Suite 375
Washington DC 20005
202/296-5400
FAX: 202/296-3774
E-mail: Hispanic.Fund@InternetMCI.com
Internet: http://hispanicfund.org

AMOUNT: Varies
DEADLINE(S): APR 15
FIELD(S): Most college majors leading to a career in business

Scholarships for deserving Hispanic college students pursuing a higher education in a major leading to a business career and who are full-time students at accredited institutions. U.S. citizenship. Must demonstrate financial need.

Contact above organization for details or visit Web site for application.

665—HOBART INSTITUTE OF WELDING TECHNOLOGY (Scholarships)

400 Trade Square East
Troy OH 45373
800/332-9448 or 937/332-5090
FAX: 937/332-5200
E-mail: hiwt@welding.org
Internet: http://www.welding.org

AMOUNT: $6,725
DEADLINE(S): APR 1; AUG 1; DEC 1
FIELD(S): Structural Welding

Open to undergraduates and technical school students in a structural welding program at the Hobart Institute of Welding Technology. Must have graduated from high school within the past seven years, or have obtained a GED equivalent during that time. Based on an essay, grades, and references; financial need NOT a factor.

3 awards annually. See Web site or send self-addressed, stamped envelope to above address for an application.

666—INSTITUTE FOR OPERATIONS RESEARCH AND THE MANAGEMENT SCIENCES (INFORMS Summer Internship Directory)

P.O. Box 64794
Baltimore MD 21264-4794
800/4INFORMS
FAX: 410/684-2963
E-mail: jps@informs.org
Internet: http://www.informs.org/INTERN/

AMOUNT: Varies
DEADLINE(S): Varies
FIELD(S): Fields related to information management: business management, engineering, mathematics

A Web site listing of summer internships in the field of operations research and management sciences. Both applicants and employers can register online.

Access Web site for list.

667—INSTITUTE OF INDUSTRIAL ENGINEERS (Dwight D. Gardner Scholarship and A.O. Putnam Scholarships)

25 Technology Park
Norcross GA 30092
770/449-0461 or 800/494-0460
FAX: 770/441-3295
E-mail: srichards@iienet.org
Internet: http://www.iienet.org

AMOUNT: $2,000 (Gardner); $600 (Putnam)
DEADLINE(S): NOV 15
FIELD(S): Industrial Engineering

Undergraduate scholarships for active IIE members with at least three semester (5 quarters) of study remaining at an accredited college or university in the U.S. and its territories, Canada, or Mexico. A GPA of 3.4 or better is required. The Putnam Scholarship is for students pursuing an interest in management consulting within the field of industrial engineering.

Do not apply directly for these scholarships. Student must be nominated by their department head or faculty advisor. Nomination forms are sent to each school at the beginning of the fall term or they can be found on the Web site.

668—INSTITUTE OF INDUSTRIAL ENGINEERS (IIE Council of Fellows Undergraduate Scholarships)

25 Technology Park
Norcross GA 30092-2988
770/449-0461 or 800/494-0460
FAX: 770/441-3295
E-mail: srichards@iienet.org
Internet: http://www.iienet.org

AMOUNT: $400
DEADLINE(S): NOV 15
FIELD(S): Industrial Engineering

Undergraduate scholarships for active IIE members with at least three semester (5 quarters) of study remaining at an accredited college or university in the U.S. and its territories, Canada, or Mexico. A GPA of 3.4 or better is required. Scholarship is intended to reward outstanding academic scholarship and leadership.

Contact the organization at address above to receive application.

669—INSTITUTE OF INDUSTRIAL ENGINEERS (United Parcel Service Scholarships for Female and Minority Students)

25 Technology Park
Norcross GA 30092-2988
770/449-0461 or 800/494-0460
FAX: 770/441-3295
E-mail: srichards@iienet.org
Internet: http://www.iienet.org

AMOUNT: $4,000 (each)
DEADLINE(S): NOV 15
FIELD(S): Industrial Engineering

Graduate and undergraduate scholarships for active IIE members with at least three semesters (5 quarters) of study remaining at an accredited college or university in the U.S. and its territories, Canada, or Mexico. A GPA of 3.4 or better is required. One is for a minority student, and one is for a female.

Do not apply directly for these scholarships. Student must be nominated by their department head or faculty advisor. Nomination forms are sent to each school at the beginning of the fall term or they can be found on the Web site.

670—INSTITUTION OF ELECTRICAL ENGINEERS (Jubilee Scholarships & Faraday Lecture Scholarship)

Savoy Place
London WC2R 0BL ENGLAND
+44-020-7344-8458
FAX: +44-020-7497-3609
E-mail: scholarships@iee.org.uk
Internet: http://www.iee.org.uk/EduCareers/Awards/

AMOUNT: 750 pounds/year
DEADLINE(S): JUN 30
FIELD(S): Electrical, Electronic, Manufacturing, or Related Engineering

Scholarships for students currently residing in the United Kingdom in the above engineering fields.

12 awards available. Renewable for the entire period of an IEE-accredited course. Check Web site or contact organization for application details.

671—INSTITUTION OF ELECTRICAL ENGINEERS (Scholarships for Women)

Savoy Place
London WC2R 0BL ENGLAND
0171 240 1871 ext. 2211/2235
FAX: 0171 497 3609
E-mail: scholarships@iee.org.uk
Internet: http://www.iee.org.uk/Awards/ugwom.htm

AMOUNT: 750 pounds/year
DEADLINE(S): JUN 15
FIELD(S): Engineering

Scholarships for women residing in the United Kingdom and pursuing degrees in engineering.

Candidates must be undertaking mathematics and physics "A" level or Scottish Higher examinations. Renewable for the entire period of an IEE-accredited course. Check Web site or contact organization for application details.

672—INTERNATIONAL SOCIETY OF EXPLOSIVES ENGINEERS (McDowell/Nelson/Bob Hermiah/Paul Muehl Combined Scholarship Program)

30325 Bainbridge Road
Cleveland OH 44139
440/349-4400
FAX: 440/349-3788
Internet: http://www.isee.org
AMOUNT: Varies
DEADLINE(S): MAY 31
FIELD(S): Explosives

Open to students pursuing their first associate, undergraduate, or graduate degree as full-time students at an accredited college/university. Must be in the process of applying or be already accepted for college admission. Must have a minimum 2.9 GPA and demonstrate financial need. Funds will be sent directly to the educational institution.

Renewable. See Web site or contact ISEE for an application.

673—JAMES F. LINCOLN ARC WELDING FOUNDATION (Award Program)

P.O. Box 17188
Cleveland OH 44117
216/481-4300
Internet: http://www.jflf.org
AMOUNT: Varies
DEADLINE(S): MAY 1
FIELD(S): Arc Welding and Engineering Design

Open to high school students, college undergraduates, and graduate students, and to professionals working in the fields of arc welding and engineering design. Various programs are available.

See Web site or send self-addressed, stamped envelope to Roy Morrow, President, at above address.

674—LOS ANGELES COUNCIL OF BLACK PROFESSIONAL ENGINEERS (Al-Ben Scholarship)

P.O. Box 881029
Los Angeles CA 90009
310/635-7734
E-mail: secy1@lablackengineers.org
Internet: http://www.lablackengineers.org/scholarships.html
AMOUNT: Varies
DEADLINE(S): Varies
FIELD(S): Engineering; Mathematics; Computer Studies; Applied Scientific Studies

Open to technically inclined precollege and undergraduate students enrolled in one of the above fields. Must be of African American, Native American, or Hispanic ancestry. Preference given to students attending college in Southern California or who are Southern California residents.

See Web site to download an application.

675—MICROSOFT CORPORATION (National Minority and/or Women's Scholarships)

One Microsoft Way
Redmond WA 98052-8303
E-mail: scholar@microsoft.com
Internet: http://www.microsoft.com/college/scholarships/
AMOUNT: Tuition for 1 year
DEADLINE(S): JAN 31
FIELD(S): Computer Science, Computer Engineering, or a related technical discipline, such as Math or Physics

Full tuition scholarships awarded for 1 academic year to women and minorities (African-Americans, Hispanics, or Native Americans) enrolled full-time in the above fields with a demonstrated interest in computers and making satisfactory progress towards a degree. Awards are made through designated schools and are not transferable to other institutions.

See Web site above for details.

676—MICROSOFT CORPORATION (Summer Internships)

One Microsoft Way
Redmond WA 98052-8303
425/882-8080
E-mail: scholar@microsoft.com
Internet: http://www.microsoft.com/college/scholarships/
AMOUNT: Varies
DEADLINE(S): None
FIELD(S): Computer Science, Computer Engineering, or a related technical discipline, such as Math or Physics

Summer internships for individuals with a deep passion for technological advancement. Must commit to a 12-week minimum. Includes transportation, shipping costs, and shared cost of housing. Competitive compensation offered.

Check Web site above for details.

677—MARYLAND HIGHER EDUCATION COMMISSION (Maryland Science and Technology Scholarship Program)

16 Francis Street
Annapolis Park MD 21401
410/974-5370 or 800/974-1024
E-mail: ssamail@mhec.state.md.us
Internet: http://www.mhec.state.md.us/SSA/stech_qa.htm
AMOUNT: $3,000/year (BA); $1,000/year (AA)
DEADLINE(S): None
FIELD(S): Computer Science; Engineering; Technology

Scholarships for college-bound Maryland high school seniors who will major in one of the above fields and who are accepted to an eligible associate or bachelor's degree program in Maryland. The deadline was not known at this writing, so check for deadline date. Must agree to work in the state after graduation in a related field, one year for each year of assistance received.

Must maintain a 3.0 GPA.

678—NATIONAL ASSOCIATION OF PLUMBING-HEATING-COOLING CONTRACTORS (Delta Faucet Company Scholarship Program)

P.O. Box 6808
Falls Church VA 22040
703/237-8100 or 800/533-7694
FAX: 703/237-7442
Internet: http://www.phccweb.org/foundation/
AMOUNT: $2,500
DEADLINE(S): JUN 1
FIELD(S): Plumbing; Heating; Cooling

Open to undergraduates enrolled in a p-h-c related major at an accredited four-year college/university. Must be sponsored by an active member of the PHCC National Association who has maintained that status for at least the two-year period prior to date of application.

6 awards annually. Not renewable. See Web site or contact NAPHCC for an application or to search for PHCC members in your area for sponsorship.

679—NATIONAL ASSOCIATION OF PLUMBING-HEATING-COOLING CONTRACTORS (Educational Foundation Scholarship Program)

P.O. Box 6808
Falls Church VA 22040
703/237-8100 or 800/533-7694
FAX: 703/237-7442
Internet: http://www.phccweb.org/foundation/

AMOUNT: $3,000/year
DEADLINE(S): MAY 1
FIELD(S): Plumbing; Heating; Cooling

Open to undergraduates enrolled in a p-h-c related major at an accredited four-year college/university. Must be sponsored by an active member of the PHCC National Association who has maintained that status for at least the two-year period prior to date of application. Must submit academic information, letters of recommendation, and maintain a "C" average or better throughout period for which scholarship is awarded.

4 awards annually. Renewable up to 4 years. See Web site or contact NAPHCC for an application or to search for PHCC members in your area for sponsorship.

680—NATIONAL ASSOCIATION OF WATER COMPANIES-NEW JERSEY CHAPTER (Scholarship)

Elizabethtown Water Co.
600 South Avenue
Westfield NJ 070
908/654-1234
FAX: 908/232-2719

AMOUNT: $2,500
DEADLINE(S): APR 1
FIELD(S): Business Administration; Biology; Chemistry; Engineering Communications

For U.S. citizens who have lived in NJ at least 5 years and plan a career in the investor-owned water utility industry in disciplines such as those above. Must be undergrad or graduate student in a two- or four-year NJ college or university.

GPA of 3.0 or better required. Contact Gail P. Brady for complete information.

681—NATIONAL SCIENCES AND ENGINEERING RESEARCH COUNCIL OF CANADA (Undergraduate Scholarships)

Scholarships/Fellowships Division;
350 Albert Street
Ottawa Ontario K1A 1H5 CANADA
613/996-2009
FAX: 613/996-2589
E-mail: schol@nserc.ca
Internet: http://www.nserc.ca

AMOUNT: Up to $3,600
DEADLINE(S): Varies
FIELD(S): Natural Sciences, Engineering, Biology, or Chemistry

Open to Canadian citizens or permanent residents working towards degrees in science or engineering. Academic excellence and research aptitude are considerations.

Write for complete information.

682—NATIONAL SOCIETY OF BLACK ENGINEERS (Scholarships)

1454 Duke Street
Alexandria VA 22314
703/549-2207
FAX: 703/683-5312
E-mail: nsbehq@nsbe.org
Internet: http://www.nsbe.org

AMOUNT: Varies
DEADLINE(S): Varies
FIELD(S): Engineering and engineering technologies

Programs for black and other ethnic minorities in the fields of engineering and the engineering technologies. Organization offers precollege programs, scholarships, career fairs, a journal, a newsletter, etc.

Contact organization for details.

683—NAVY RECRUITING COMMAND (Armed Forces Health Professions Scholarships)

Chief
5722 Integrity Drive
Millington, TN 38054
888/633-9674
Internet: http://www.navy.com

AMOUNT: average of $1,058/month stipend + tuition, fees, books, lab fees, etc.
DEADLINE(S): Applications taken year-around
FIELD(S): Medicine, Dentistry, Optometry, Physical Therapy, Pharmacology, Health Care Administration, Industrial Hygiene, etc.

Open to U.S. citizens enrolled or accepted for enrollment in any of the above fields at an accredited institution in the U.S. or Puerto Rico. Must qualify for appointment as a Navy officer and sign a contractual agreement. Must be between the ages of 18 and 40 for some programs and have a GPA around 3.0.

See Web site, contact local Navy Recruiting Office, or contact the above address.

684—OAK RIDGE INSTITUTE FOR SCIENCE AND EDUCATION (ORISE Education and Training Programs)

P.O. Box 117
Oak Ridge TN 37831-0117
Internet: http://www.orau.gov/orise/educ.htm

AMOUNT: Varies
DEADLINE(S): Varies
FIELD(S): Engineering; Aeronautics; Computer Science; Technology; Earth Science; Environmental Studies; Biology; Chemistry; Physics; Medical Research

Numerous programs funded by the U.S. Department of Energy are offered for undergraduate students through postgraduate researchers. Includes fellowship and internship opportunities throughout the U.S. Some have citizenship restrictions. Travel may be included.

See Web site or write for a catalog of specific programs and requirements.

685—QUEEN'S UNIVERSITY OF BELFAST (Industrial Scholarships)

Training and Employment Agency,
Management Development Division
9-21 Adelaide Street
Belfast BT2 8DT Northern Ireland UK
+44 (0) 1232 245133
Internet: http://www.icbl.qub.ac.uk/prospectus/funding/scholars.htm

AMOUNT: Varies
DEADLINE(S): Varies
FIELD(S): Engineering: Aeronautical, Electrical and Electronic, Mechanical, and Manufacturing

Scholarships in Northern Ireland for study in the above fields.

Contact the University at the address shown for complete information.

686—ROBOTIC INDUSTRIES ASSOCIATION (RIA Robotics Scholarship Competition)

900 Victors Way
P.O. Box 3724
Ann Arbor MI 48106
734/994-6088
FAX: 734/994-3338
E-mail: mlehtinen@robotics.org
Internet: http://www.robotics.org

AMOUNT: $1,000
DEADLINE(S): DEC 10
FIELD(S): Robotics

Competition is for undergraduate students attending school in North America. Students must submit a paper that poses a technical problem and offers a solution that involves robotics. Team entries are allowed. Financial need NOT a factor.

3 awards annually. Not renewable. See Web site or contact Marcy Lehtinen at RIA for full guidelines and past winners.

687—SOCIETY FOR IMAGING SCIENCE AND TECHNOLOGY (Raymond Davis Scholarship)

7003 Kilworth Lane
Springfield VA 22151
703/642-9090
FAX: 703/642-9094
E-mail: info@imaging.org
Internet: http://www.imaging.org

AMOUNT: $1,000
DEADLINE(S): DEC 15
FIELD(S): Photographic/Imaging Science or Engineering

Scholarships for undergraduate juniors or seniors or graduate students for full-time continuing studies in the theory or practice of photographic or imaging science or engineering, including research in the theory or practice of image formation by radiant energy.

Check the Web site or write for complete information and application.

688—SOCIETY OF MANUFACTURING ENGINEERING EDUCATION FOUNDATION (Scholarships and Fellowship)

One SME Drive
P.O. Box 930
Dearborn MI 48121-0930
313/271-1500 or 800/733-4763
FAX: 313/271-2861
E-mail: monzcyn@sme.org
Internet: http://www.sme.org/foundation

AMOUNT: $600-$20,000
DEADLINE(S): FEB 1
FIELD(S): Manufacturing Engineering/Technology; Industrial Engineering

Twenty-eight scholarship programs and one fellowship are available annually to high school, undergraduate, and graduate students. Minimum GPA varies with each scholarship. Financial need NOT a factor.

See Web site or contact Cindy Monzon at SME for an application.

689—SOCIETY OF SATELLITE PROFESSIONALS INTERNATIONAL (SSPI Scholarships)

225 Reinekers Lane, Suite 600
Alexandria VA 22314
703/857-3717
FAX: 703/857-6335
E-mail: neworbit@aol.com;
Internet: http://www.sspi.org

AMOUNT: $1,500 to $4,000
DEADLINE(S): DEC 1
FIELD(S): Satellites as related to communications, domestic and international telecommunications policy, remote sensing, journalism, law, meteorology, energy, navigation, business, government, and broadcasting services

Various scholarships for students studying in the above fields.

Access Web site for details and applications or send a self-addressed, stamped envelope (SASE) for a complete listing.

690—SOCIETY OF WOMEN ENGINEERS (DuPont Company Scholarship)

230 E. Ohio Street, Suite 400
Chicago IL 60611-3265
312/596-5223
FAX: 312/644-8557 or
FAX: 212/509-0224
E-mail: hq@swe.org
Internet: http://www.swe.org

AMOUNT: $2,000
DEADLINE(S): MAY 15
FIELD(S): Chemical Engineering; Mechanical Engineering

Open to women who are entering freshmen in a college/university in the eastern U.S. who have an ABET-accredited program or in an eastern SWE-approved school. Must have a 3.0 GPA on 4.0 scale.

2 awards every year. See Web site or send a self-addressed, stamped envelope to SWE for an application. Recipient is notified in September.

691—STUDENT CONSERVATION ASSOCIATION (SCA Resource Assistant Program)

P.O. Box 550
Charlestown NH 03603
603/543-1700
FAX: 603/543-1828
E-mail: internships@sca-inc.org
Internet: http://www.sca-inc.org

AMOUNT: $1,180-$4,725
DEADLINE(S): Varies
FIELD(S): Environment and related fields

Must be 18 and U.S. citizen; need not be student.

900 positions in U.S. and Canada. Send $1 for postage for application; outside U.S./Canada, send $20. Fields: Agriculture, Archaeology, anthropology, botany, caves, civil/environmental engineering, environmental education, fisheries, forests, herpetology, history, living history/roleplaying, visitor services, landscape architecture/environmental design, paleontology, recreation/resource/range management, trail maintenance/construction, wildlife management, geology, hydrology, library/museums, surveying...

692—THE ART INSTITUTES INTERNATIONAL (Evelyn Keedy Memorial Scholarship)

300 Sixth Avenue, Suite 800
Pittsburgh PA 15222-2598
412/562-9800
FAX: 412/562-9802
E-mail: webadmin@aii.edu
Internet: http://www.aii.edu

AMOUNT: 2 years full tuition
DEADLINE(S): MAY 1
FIELD(S): Various fields in the creative and applied arts: video production, broadcasting, culinary arts, fashion design, Web site administration, etc.

Scholarships at 12 different locations nationwide in various fields described above. For graduating high school seniors admitted to an Arts Institutes International School, the New York Restaurant School, or NCPT. Transcripts, letters of recommendation, and resume must be submitted with application.

See Web site or contact AII for more information.

693—THE DAPHNE JACKSON MEMORIAL FELLOWSHIPS TRUST (Fellowships in Science/Engineering)

School of Physical Sciences,
Dept. of Physics, University of Surrey
Guildford, Surrey GU2 5XH
ENGLAND UK
01483 259166
FAX: 01483 259501
E-mail: J.Woolley@surrey.ac.uk
Internet: http://www.sst.ph.ic.ac.uk/trust/

AMOUNT: Varies
DEADLINE(S): Varies
FIELD(S): Science or Engineering, including Information Sciences

Fellowships to enable well-qualified and highly motivated scientists and engineers to return to appropriate careers following a career break due to family commitments. May be used on a flexible, part-time basis. Tenable at various U.K. universities.

See Web site and/or contact organization for details.

694—THE INTERNATIONAL SOCIETY FOR OPTICAL ENGINEERING (Scholarships and Grants)

P.O. Box 10
Bellingham WA 98227
360/676-3290
FAX: 360/647-1445
E-mail: scholarships@spie.org
Internet: http://www.spie.org
AMOUNT: $500-$7,000
DEADLINE(S): FEB 7
FIELD(S): Optics; Optical Science and Engineering

Open to college students at all levels for study of optical or optoelectronic applied science and engineering. May be awarded to students in community colleges or technical institutes and to undergraduate and graduate students at colleges and universities.

Write to the SPIE Scholarship Committee or visit Web site (address above) for complete information.

695—THE ART INSTITUTES INTERNATIONAL (Evelyn Keedy Memorial Scholarship)

300 Sixth Avenue, Suite 800
Pittsburgh PA 15222-2598
412/562-9800
FAX: 412/562-9802
E-mail: webadmin@aii.edu
Internet: http://www.aii.edu
AMOUNT: 2 years full tuition
DEADLINE(S): MAY 1
FIELD(S): Various fields in the creative and applied arts: video production, broadcasting, culinary arts, fashion design, Web site administration, etc.

Scholarships at 12 different locations nationwide in various fields described above. For graduating high school seniors admitted to an Arts Institutes International School, the New York Restaurant School, or NCPT. Transcripts, letters of recommendation, and resume must be submitted with application.

See Web site or contact AII for more information.

696—UNIVERSAL TECHNICAL INSTITUTE (Joe Gibbs National High School Competition)

3121 W. Weldon Avenue
Phoenix AZ 85017
800/859-1202 or 888/884-3678 or 602/264-4164
Internet: http://www.uticorp.com/utiedu/national.html
AMOUNT: $5,000 (max.)
DEADLINE(S): Varies
FIELD(S): Technical (Auto/Truck Mechanics or HVAC)

Competition for high school seniors pursuing careers as technicians in the above areas. Winners will receive scholarships valued from $500 to $5,000 for use at UTI, which has campuses in Arizona, Illinois, and Texas. Awards are based on a written test of technical skills to be taken at various sites in the U.S. Awards also are given to schools by students finishing in the top 10%.

Nearly $400,000 will be awarded in the Auto/Truck competition, and over $100,000 in the HVAC/R competition. Call, check Web site, or write for details.

697—UNIVERSITY OF MARYLAND (John B. and Ida Slaughter Endowed Scholarship in Science, Technology, and the Black Community)

2169 Lefrak Hall
College Park MD 20742-7225
301/405-1158
FAX: 301/314-986
Internet: http://www.bsos.umd.edu/aasp/scholarship.html
AMOUNT: Varies (in-state tuition costs)
DEADLINE(S): MAR
FIELD(S): Science and Technology AND African-American Studies

Open to African-Americans who are U.S. residents with a minimum 2.8 GPA. Must be accepted to or enrolled at UMCP for freshmen year and must submit letter of recommendation from high school counselor or UMCP faculty member. Should have an interest in applying science and technology to the problems of the Black community. Essay required.

Renewable. Contact the Center for Minorities in Science and Engineering at UMCP for an application.

698—WATER ENVIRONMENT FEDERATION (Canham Graduate Studies Scholarships)

601 Wythe Street
Alexandria VA 22314-1994
703/684-2477 or 800/666-0206
FAX: 703/645-2492
Internet: http://www.wef.org
AMOUNT: $2,000-$2,500
DEADLINE(S): MAR 1
FIELD(S): Water Environment; Water Pollution Control and related fields

Open to graduate students in water environment programs. Must be member of the Water Environment Federation (nominal fee) and commit to working in the environmental field for 2 years following the completion of studies.

2 awards annually. Contact the organization or see Web site for details and application-go to "Membership Benefits" then to "WEF Distinguished Honors and Awards."

699—WOMEN'S AUXILIARY TO THE AMERICAN INSTITUTE OF MINING, METALLURGICAL, AND PETROLEUM ENGINEERS (WAAIME Scholarship Loan Fund)

Three Park Avenue, Suite 17B
New York NY 10016-5998
212/419-7673
FAX: 212/419-7680
E-mail: waaimeny@juno.com
Internet: http://www.aimeny.org
AMOUNT: Varies
DEADLINE(S): MAR 15
FIELD(S): Earth Sciences, as related to the Minerals Industry

Open to undergraduate juniors and seniors and graduate students, whose majors relate to an interest in the minerals industry. Eligible applicants receive a scholarship loan for all or part of their education. Recipients repay only 50%, with no interest charges. Repayment begins by six months after graduation and should be completed within six years.

See Web site or contact WAAIME at above address for an application.

700—WYOMING TRUCKING ASSOCIATION (Scholarships)

P.O. Box 1909
Casper WY 82602
Written Inquiry
AMOUNT: $250-$300
DEADLINE(S): MAR 1
FIELD(S): Transportation Industry

For Wyoming high school graduates enrolled in a Wyoming college, approved trade school, or the University of Wyoming. Must be pursuing a course of study which will result in a career in the transportation industry in Wyoming, including but not limited to: safety, environmental science, diesel mechanics, truck driving, vocational trades, business management, sales management, computer skills, accounting, office procedures, and management.

1-10 awards annually. Write to WYTA for an application.

701—INTERNATIONAL SOCIETY OF WOMEN AIRLINE PILOTS (ISA Career Scholarship)

2250 E. Tropicana Avenue,
Suite 19-395
Las Vegas NV 89119-6594
E-mail: wame@swbell.net
Internet: http://www.iswap.org/scholarship.html

AMOUNT: Varies
DEADLINE(S): APR 15
FIELD(S): Airline Pilot Advanced Ratings

Open to women whose goals are to fly the world's airlines. For advanced pilot ratings, such as the U.S. FAA ATP certificate or equivalent.

Applicants must have a U.S. FAA Commercial Pilot Certificate with an Instrument Rating and a First Class medical certificate (or equivalent). Also must have a minimum of 750 flight hours. Personal interview is required. Check Web site or write for more information and application.

702—XEROX TECHNICAL MINORITY SCHOLARSHIP (Summer Employment Program)

Xerox Square
Rochester NY 14644
Written Inquiry

AMOUNT: Up to $5,000 (varies according to tuition and academic excellence)
DEADLINE(S): SEP 15
FIELD(S): Engineering and Science Disciplines

Scholarships for minorities enrolled in a technical degree program at the bachelor level or above. Must be African-American, Native American, Hispanic, or Asian. Xerox will match your skills with a sponsoring organization that will offer a meaningful summer work experience complimenting your academic learning.

If above requirements are met, send your resume and a cover letter to Xerox Corporation Corporate Employment and College Relations Technical Minority Scholarship Program.

MECHANICAL ENGINEERING

703—AIR FORCE RESERVE OFFICER TRAINING CORPS (AFROTC Scholarships)

551 E. Maxwell Boulevard
Maxwell AFB AL 36112-6106
334/953-7783

AMOUNT: Full tuition, books, and fees for all 4 years of college
DEADLINE(S): DEC 1
FIELD(S): Science; Engineering; Business; Political Science; Psychology; Geography; Foreign Studies; Foreign Language

Competitive scholarships based on individual merit to high school seniors and graduates who have not completed any full-time college work. Must be a U.S. citizen between the ages of 17-27. Must also have GPA of 2.5 or above, be in top 40% of class, and complete Applicant Fitness Test. Cannot be a single parent. Your college/university must offer AFROTC.

2,300 awards annually. Contact above address for application packet.

704—AMERICAN SOCIETY OF ENGINEERS OF INDIAN ORIGIN (Undergraduate Scholarship Programs)

P.O. Box 49494
Atlanta GA 30359-1494
770/451-2299
Internet: http://www.iasf.org/asei.htm

AMOUNT: Up to $1,000
DEADLINE(S): AUG 15
FIELD(S): Engineering Fields: Architecture, Computer Technology, Geotechnical or Geoenvironmental Engineering, and allied sciences

Several scholarships for undergraduate engineering students in the above fields who were born in India or who are Indian by ancestry or relation. For study in the U.S. Some programs have residency requirements in certain states.

Contact Dr. Narsi Narasimhan at above location for applications and details.

705—AMERICAN SOCIETY OF MECHANICAL ENGINEERS (ASME Student Loans)

Three Park Avenue
New York NY 10016-5990
212/591-8131
FAX: 212/591-7143
E-mail: oluwanifiset@asme.org
Internet: http://www.asme.org/education/enged/aid/index.htm

AMOUNT: $3,000
DEADLINE(S): APR 15; OCT 15
FIELD(S): Mechanical Engineering

Loans for ASME student members who are undergraduate or graduate students in a mechanical engineering or related program. Must be citizens or residents of the U.S., Canada, or Mexico. Loans are 1% below the Stafford loan rate. Financial need is considered.

Contact ASME at above address or see Web site for an application or membership information.

706—AMERICAN SOCIETY OF MECHANICAL ENGINEERS (Frank William and Dorothy Given Miller Scholarship)

Three Park Avenue
New York NY 10016-5990
212/591-8131
FAX: 212/591-7143
E-mail: oluwanifiset@asme.org
Internet: http://www.asme.org/education/enged/aid/index.htm

AMOUNT: $2,000
DEADLINE(S): MAR 15
FIELD(S): Mechanical Engineering

For ASME student members in their junior or senior undergraduate year in mechanical engineering or related program. Must be U.S.citizen or North American resident. Financial need NOT considered.

2 awards annually. Not renewable. Contact Nellie Malave at above address for an application or membership information.

707—AMERICAN SOCIETY OF MECHANICAL ENGINEERS (Garland Duncan Scholarship)

Three Park Avenue
New York NY 10016-5990
212/705-8131
FAX: 212/705-7143
E-mail: oluwanifiset@asme.org
Internet: http://www.asme.org/education/enged/aid/index.htm

AMOUNT: $3,000
DEADLINE(S): MAR 15
FIELD(S): Mechanical Engineering

For ASME student members in their junior or senior undergraduate years studying mechanical engineering or a related program. Must demonstrate financial need.

3 awards annually. Contact ASME at above address or see Web site for an application or membership information.

708—AMERICAN SOCIETY OF MECHANICAL ENGINEERS (Kenneth Andrew Roe Scholarship)

Three Park Avenue
New York NY 10016-5990
212/591-8131
FAX: 212/591-7143

E-mail: oluwanifiset@asme.org
Internet: http://www.asme.org/education/enged/aid/index.htm
AMOUNT: $10,000
DEADLINE(S): MAR 15
FIELD(S): Mechanical Engineering

Open to ASME student members in their junior or senior undergraduate years studying mechanical engineering or related program. Must be U.S. citizen or North American resident. Financial need considered.

1 award annually. Contact ASME at above address or see Web site for an application or membership information.

709—AMERICAN SOCIETY OF MECHANICAL ENGINEERS (Melvin R. Green Scholarship)

Three Park Avenue
New York NY 10016-5990
212/591-8131
FAX: 212/591-7143
E-mail: oluwanifiset@asme.org
Internet: http://www.asme.org/education/enged/aid/index.htm
AMOUNT: $3,500
DEADLINE(S): MAR 15
FIELD(S): Mechanical Engineering

For ASME student members who are in their junior or senior undergraduate years studying mechanical engineering or a related program. Financial need NOT considered.

2 awards annually. Contact ASME at above address or see Web site for an application or membership information.

710—AMERICAN SOCIETY OF MECHANICAL ENGINEERS AUXILIARY INC. (F.W. Beichley Scholarship)

Three Park Avenue
New York NY 10016-5990
212/591-8131
FAX: 212/591-7143
E-mail: oluwanifiset@asme.org
Internet: http://www.asme.org/education/enged/aid/index.htm
AMOUNT: $2,000
DEADLINE(S): MAR 15
FIELD(S): Mechanical Engineering

For junior and senior undergraduate students who are student members of ASME, studying mechanical engineering or a related program. Must demonstrate financial need.

1 award annually. Contact ASME at above address or see Web site for an application or membership information.

711—ASM INTERNATIONAL FOUNDATION (Undergraduate Scholarships)

Scholarship Program;
9639 Kinsman Road
Materials Park OH 44073-0002
440/338-5151
FAX: 440/338-4643
E-mail: asmif@po.asm-intl.org
Internet: http://www.asm-intl.org/
AMOUNT: $500 to full tuition
DEADLINE(S): MAY 1
FIELD(S): Metallurgy; Materials Science

For undergraduate students majoring in metallurgy/materials. For citizens of the U.S, Canada, or Mexico who are enrolled in a recognized college or university in one of those countries. Must be a student member of ASM. Some awards have more specific requirements.

See Web site or write to ASM for membership information or more details and application.

712—ASSOCIATED WESTERN UNIVERSITIES, INC. (AWU Undergraduate Student Fellowships)

4190 S. Highland Drive, Suite 211
Salt Lake City UT 84124-2600
801/273-8900
FAX: 801/277-5632
E-mail: info@awu.org
Internet: http://www.awu.org
AMOUNT: $300/week stipend + possible travel allowance
DEADLINE(S): FEB 1
FIELD(S): Science; Mathematics; Engineering; Technology

Eight- to sixteen-week fellowships.

713—AT&T BELL LABORATORIES (Summer Research Program for Minorities and Women)

101 Crawfords Corner Road
Holmdel, NJ 07733-3030
Written Inquiry
AMOUNT: Salary + travel and living expenses for summer
DEADLINE(S): DEC 1
FIELD(S): Engineering; Math; Sciences; Computer Science

Program offers minority students and women students technical employment experience at Bell Laboratories. Students should have completed their third year of study at an accredited college or university. U.S. citizen or permanent resident.

Selection is based partially on academic achievement and personal motivation. Write special programs manager-SRP for complete information.

714—CELANESE CANADA, INC. (Scholarships)

AUCC; 350 Albert Street, Suite 600
Ottawa Ontario K1R 1B1 CANADA
613/563-1236; FAX: 613/563-9745
E-mail: awards@aucc.ca
Internet: http://www.aucc.ca
AMOUNT: $1,500
DEADLINE(S): JUL 2
FIELD(S): Mechanical and Chemical Engineering; Chemistry; Business Administration and Commerce

Open to Canadian citizens/permanent residents for their final year of an undergraduate program in one of above fields. Must attend a college/university which is a member, or affiliated to a member, of the Association of Universities and Colleges of Canada. Candidates are expected to have achieved a high level of academic excellence as well as to have exhibited superior intellectual ability and judgment. In some cases, study in certain province/school is required.

APPLICATIONS ARE BY NOMINATION ONLY. Not renewable. See Web site or contact AUCC for nomination procedures.

715—BROOKHAVEN WOMEN IN SCIENCE (Renate W. Chasman Scholarship)

P.O. Box 183
Upton NY 11973-5000
E-mail: pam@bnl.gov
AMOUNT: $2,000
DEADLINE(S): APR 1
FIELD(S): Natural Sciences; Engineering; Mathematics

Open ONLY to women who are residents of the boroughs of Brooklyn or Queens or the counties of Nassau or Suffolk in New York who are reentering school after a period of study. For juniors, seniors, or first-year graduate students.

1 award annually. Not renewable. Contact Pam Mansfield at above location for an application. Phone calls are NOT accepted.

716—INSTITUTION OF ELECTRICAL ENGINEERS (Jubilee Scholarships & Faraday Lecture Scholarship)

Savoy Place
London WC2R 0BL ENGLAND
+44-020-7344-8458

FAX: +44-020-7497-3609
E-mail: scholarships@iee.org.uk
Internet: http://www.iee.org.uk/EduCareers/Awards/
AMOUNT: 750 pounds/year
DEADLINE(S): JUN 30
FIELD(S): Electrical, Electronic, Manufacturing, or Related Engineering

Scholarships for students currently residing in the United Kingdom in the above engineering fields.

12 awards available. Renewable for the entire period of an IEE-accredited course. Check Web site or contact organization for application details.

717—INSTITUTION OF ELECTRICAL ENGINEERS (Scholarships for Women)

Savoy Place
London WC2R 0BL ENGLAND
0171 240 1871 ext. 2211/2235
FAX: 0171 497 3609
E-mail: scholarships@iee.org.uk
Internet: http://www.iee.org.uk/Awards/ugwom.htm
AMOUNT: 750 pounds/year
DEADLINE(S): JUN 15
FIELD(S): Engineering

Scholarships for women residing in the United Kingdom and pursuing degrees in engineering.

Candidates must be undertaking mathematics and physics "A" level or Scottish Higher examinations. Renewable for the entire period of an IEE-accredited course. Check Web site or contact organization for application details.

718—INSTITUTION OF MECHANICAL ENGINEERS (James Clayton Undergraduate Scholarships)

Educational Svs., Northgate Avenue
Bury St. Edmunds
Suffolk IP32 6BN ENGLAND UK
+44(01284) 718617
FAX: +44(01284) 724471
E-mail: k_frost@imeche.org.uk
Internet: http://www.imeche.org.uk
AMOUNT: 500 pounds sterling/year, up to 4 years
DEADLINE(S): JUN 30
FIELD(S): Mechanical Engineering

For U.K. residents still undertaking full-time secondary education and expecting to commence their degree in the next academic session. Must be accepted into an accredited course and expect to obtain "A" level grades. Recipients must become members of the IMechE and maintain membership throughout course.

Up to 20 awards annually. Check Web site or contact IMechE for an application.

719—INSTITUTION OF MECHANICAL ENGINEERS (Various Grants and Scholarships)

Educational Svs.; Northgate Avenue
Bury St. Edmunds
Suffolk IP32 6BN ENGLAND UK
+44(01284) 718617
FAX: +44(01284) 724471
E-mail: k_frost@imeche.org.uk
Internet: http://www.imeche.org.uk
AMOUNT: Varies
DEADLINE(S): JUN 30 (scholarships); varies (grants)
FIELD(S): Mechanical Engineering

Grants for study or research in mechanical engineering or a related science. Some require membership or student membership in the Institution of Mechanical Engineers. Some require U.K. residency. Grants are normally for periods of less than one year.

See Web site or contact IMechE for details.

720—INSTITUTION OF MINING AND METALLURGY (Centenary Scholarship)

Hallam Court; 77 Hallam Street
London W1W 5BS ENGLAND
+44 207-580-3802
FAX: +44 207-436-5388
Internet: http://www.imm.org.uk
AMOUNT: 500 pounds sterling
DEADLINE(S): MAR 15
FIELD(S): Mining/Metallurgy

Open to first or second year undergraduates who are student membership of the institution. To be used for projects, visits, etc. in furtherance of applicants' career development. Based on academic excellence and scholarship, NOT financial need.

Contact Carol MacKenzie at above address for an application or membership information.

721—INSTITUTION OF MINING AND METALLURGY (Stanley Elmore Fellowship Fund)

Hallam Court; 77 Hallam Street
London W1W 5BS ENGLAND
+44 207-580-3802
FAX: +44 207-436-5388
Internet: http://www.imm.org.uk
AMOUNT: Up to 14,000 pounds sterling
DEADLINE(S): MAR 15
FIELD(S): Mining; Metallurgy

Fellowships tenable at a United Kingdom university for research into all branches of extractive metallurgy and mineral processing, and in special cases, for expenditure related to such research. Based on academic excellence and scholarship, NOT financial need. Preference given to IMM members.

Contact Carol MacKenzie at above address for an application.

722—LOS ANGELES COUNCIL OF BLACK PROFESSIONAL ENGINEERS (Al-Ben Scholarship)

P.O. Box 881029
Los Angeles CA 90009
310/635-7734
E-mail: secy1@lablackengineers.org
Internet: http://www.lablackengineers.org/scholarships.html
AMOUNT: Varies
DEADLINE(S): Varies
FIELD(S): Engineering; Mathematics; Computer Studies; Applied Scientific Studies

Open to technically inclined precollege and undergraduate students enrolled in one of the above fields. Must be of African American, Native American, or Hispanic ancestry. Preference given to students attending college in Southern California or who are Southern California residents.

See Web site to download an application.

723—MARYLAND HIGHER EDUCATION COMMISSION (Maryland Science and Technology Scholarship Program)

16 Francis Street
Annapolis Park MD 21401
410/974-5370 or 800/974-1024
E-mail: ssamail@mhec.state.md.us
Internet: http://www.mhec.state.md.us/SSA/stech_qa.htm
AMOUNT: $3,000/year (BA); $1,000/year (AA)
DEADLINE(S): None
FIELD(S): Computer Science; Engineering; Technology

Scholarships for college-bound Maryland high school seniors who will major in one of the above fields and who are accepted to an eligible associate or bachelor's degree program in Maryland. The deadline was not known at this writing, so check for deadline date. Must agree to work in the state after graduation in a related field, one year for each year of assistance received.

Must maintain a 3.0 GPA.

724—NATIONAL AERONAUTICS AND SPACE ADMINISTRATION (ACCESS Internships)

Stennis Space Center, Bldg. 1100
Bay Saint Louis MS 39529
228/688-2079
E-mail: covington.pamela@ssc.nasa.gov

AMOUNT: Internship only
DEADLINE(S): None
FIELD(S): Aeronautics/Aerospace; Astronomy; Chemistry; Physics; Engineering; Math; Earth, Life, Materials, Computer, and Physical Sciences

Nine- to ten-week summer internships are open to undergraduates with physical or learning disabilities who maintain a minimum 3.0 GPA and are U.S. citizens. Purpose is to increase the number of students with disabilities pursuing technical degrees related to NASA's mission and to provide on-site experience. Internship takes place at the Stennis Space Center in Mississippi.

Contact Pam Covington for an application.

725—NATIONAL ASSOCIATION OF WATER COMPANIES-NEW JERSEY CHAPTER (Scholarship)

Elizabethtown Water Co.
600 South Avenue
Westfield NJ 07091
908/654-1234
FAX: 908/232-2719

AMOUNT: $2,500
DEADLINE(S): APR 1
FIELD(S): Business Administration; Biology; Chemistry; Engineering Communications

For U.S. citizens who have lived in NJ at least 5 years and plan a career in the investor-owned water utility industry in disciplines such as those above. Must be undergrad or graduate student in a two- or four-year NJ college or university.

GPA of 3.0 or better required. Contact Gail P. Brady for complete information.

726—NATIONAL SOCIETY OF BLACK ENGINEERS (Scholarships)

1454 Duke Street
Alexandria VA 22314
703/549-2207
FAX: 703/683-5312
E-mail: nsbehq@nsbe.org
Internet: http://www.nsbe.org

AMOUNT: Varies
DEADLINE(S): Varies
FIELD(S): Engineering and engineering technologies

Programs for black and other ethnic minorities in the fields of engineering and the engineering technologies. Organization offers precollege programs, scholarships, career fairs, a journal, a newsletter, etc.

Contact organization for details.

727—NATIONAL STONE, SAND & GRAVEL ASSOCIATION (NSSGA Quarry Engineering Scholarships)

2101 Wilson Boulevard, Suite 100
Arlington VA 22201
800/342-1415 or 703/525-8788
FAX: 703/525-7782
E-mail: info@nssga.org
Internet: http://www.nssga.org

AMOUNT: $2,500
DEADLINE(S): APR 30
FIELD(S): Quarry Engineering

Open to students intending to pursue a career in the aggregate industry and who are enrolled in an undergraduate program working toward this objective.

10 awards annually. Employment in industry a plus. See Web site or write for complete information and application.

728—QUEEN'S UNIVERSITY OF BELFAST (Industrial Scholarships)

Training and Employment Agency,
Management Development Division,
9-21 Adelaide Street
Belfast BT2 8DT Northern Ireland UK
+44 (0) 1232 245133
Internet: http://www.icbl.qub.ac.uk/prospectus/funding/scholars.htm

AMOUNT: Varies
DEADLINE(S): Varies
FIELD(S): Engineering: Aeronautical, Electrical and Electronic, Mechanical, and Manufacturing

Scholarships in Northern Ireland for study in the above fields.

Contact the University at the address shown for complete information.

729—ROBOTIC INDUSTRIES ASSOCIATION (RIA Robotics Scholarship Competition)

900 Victors Way
P.O. Box 3724
Ann Arbor MI 48106
734/994-6088
FAX: 734/994-3338
E-mail: mlehtinen@robotics.org
Internet: http://www.robotics.org

AMOUNT: $1,000
DEADLINE(S): DEC 10
FIELD(S): Robotics

Competition is for undergraduate students attending school in North America. Students must submit a paper that poses a technical problem and offers a solution that involves robotics. Team entries are allowed. Financial need NOT a factor.

3 awards annually. Not renewable. See Web site or contact Marcy Lehtinen at RIA for full guidelines and past winners.

730—SOCIETY OF SATELLITE PROFESSIONALS INTERNATIONAL (SSPI Scholarships)

225 Reinekers Lane, Suite 600
Alexandria VA 22314
703/857-3717
FAX: 703/857-6335
E-mail: neworbit@aol.com;
Internet: http://www.sspi.org

AMOUNT: $1,500 to $4,000
DEADLINE(S): DEC 1
FIELD(S): Satellites as related to Communications, Domestic and International Telecommunications Policy, Remote Sensing, Journalism, Law, Meteorology, Energy, Navigation, Business, Government, and Broadcasting Services.

Various scholarships for students studying in the above fields.

Access Web site for details and applications or send a self-addressed, stamped envelope (SASE) for a complete listing.

731—THE DAPHNE JACKSON MEMORIAL FELLOWSHIPS TRUST (Fellowships in Science/Engineering)

School of Physical Sciences,
Dept. of Physics, University of Surrey
Guildford, Surrey GU2 5XH
ENGLAND UK
01483 259166
FAX: 01483 259501

E-mail: J.Woolley@surrey.ac.uk
Internet: http://www.sst.ph.ic.ac.uk/trust/
AMOUNT: Varies
DEADLINE(S): Varies
FIELD(S): Science or Engineering, including Information Sciences

Fellowships to enable well-qualified and highly motivated scientists and engineers to return to appropriate careers following a career break due to family commitments. May be used on a flexible, part-time basis. Tenable at various U.K. universities.

See Web site and/or contact organization for details.

732—THE ART INSTITUTES INTERNATIONAL (Evelyn Keedy Memorial Scholarship)

300 Sixth Avenue, Suite 800
Pittsburgh PA 15222-2598
412/562-9800
FAX: 412/562-9802
E-mail: webadmin@aii.edu
Internet: http://www.aii.edu
AMOUNT: 2 years full tuition
DEADLINE(S): MAY 1
FIELD(S): Various fields in the creative and applied arts: video production, broadcasting, culinary arts, fashion design, Web site administration, etc.

Scholarships at 12 different locations nationwide in various fields described above. For graduating high school seniors admitted to an Arts Institutes International School, the New York Restaurant School, or NCPT. Transcripts, letters of recommendation, and resume must be submitted with application.

See Web site or contact AII for more information.

733—WEBB INSTITUTE (Naval Architecture Scholarships)

298 Crescent Beach Road
Glen Cove NY 11542-1398
516/671-2213
FAX: 516/674-9838
E-mail: admissions@webb-institute.edu
Internet: http://www.webb-institute.edu
AMOUNT: Full tuition for 4 years
DEADLINE(S): FEB 15
FIELD(S): Naval Architecture; Marine Engineering

Open to high school students aged 16-24 who are in the top 10% of their class and have a minimum 3.2 GPA. Based on college boards, SAT scores, demonstrated interest in above areas, and an interview. Must be U.S. citizen. Tenable at the Webb Institute.

20-25 awards annually. Contact Webb Institute for an application.

734—WESTERN EUROPEAN ARCHITECTURE FOUNDATION (Gabriel Prize for Architecture)

c/o The Boston Society of Architects
52 Broad Street
Boston MA 02109-4301
AMOUNT: $15,000
DEADLINE(S): DEC
FIELD(S): Architecture

Supports all travel and study costs for a period of three months in France, during which time the student will study architectural environments in France or its immediate spheres of influence, between 1630 and 1930. Students record their interpretive studies in freehand and perspective drawings.

735—WOMEN'S AUXILIARY TO THE AMERICAN INSTITUTE OF MINING, METALLURGICAL, AND PETROLEUM ENGINEERS (WAAIME Scholarship Loan Fund)

Three Park Avenue, Suite 17B
New York NY 10016-5998
212/419-7673
FAX: 212/419-7680
E-mail: waaimeny@juno.com
Internet: http://www.aimeny.org
AMOUNT: Varies
DEADLINE(S): MAR 15
FIELD(S): Earth Sciences, as related to the Minerals Industry

Open to undergraduate juniors and seniors and graduate students, whose majors relate to an interest in the minerals industry. Eligible applicants receive a scholarship loan for all or part of their education. Recipients repay only 50%, with no interest charges. Repayment begins by six months after graduation and should be completed within six years.

See Web site or contact WAAIME at above address for an application.

736—INTERNATIONAL SOCIETY OF WOMEN AIRLINE PILOTS (ISA Career Scholarship)

2250 E. Tropicana Avenue, Suite 19-395
Las Vegas NV 89119-6594
E-mail: wame@swbell.net
Internet: http://www.iswap.org/scholarship.html
AMOUNT: Varies
DEADLINE(S): APR 15
FIELD(S): Airline Pilot Advanced Ratings

Open to women whose goals are to fly the world's airlines. For advanced pilot ratings, such as the U.S. FAA ATP certificate or equivalent.

Applicants must have a U.S. FAA Commercial Pilot Certificate with an Instrument Rating and a First Class medical certificate (or equivalent). Also must have a minimum of 750 flight hours. Personal interview is required. Check Web site or write for more information and application.

737—XEROX TECHNICAL MINORITY SCHOLARSHIP (Summer Employment Program)

Xerox Square
Rochester NY 14644
Written Inquiry
AMOUNT: Up to $5,000 (varies according to tuition and academic excellence)
DEADLINE(S): SEP 15
FIELD(S): Engineering and Science Disciplines

Scholarships for minorities enrolled in a technical degree program at the bachelor level or above. Must be African-American, Native American, Hispanic, or Asian. Xerox will match your skills with a sponsoring organization that will offer a meaningful summer work experience complimenting your academic learning.

If above requirements are met, send your resume and a cover letter to Xerox Corporation Corporate Employment and College Relations Technical Minority Scholarship Program.

SCHOOL OF HUMANITIES

738—AMERICAN BAR FOUNDATION (Montgomery Summer Research Fellowships for Minority Undergraduate Students)

750 N. Lake Shore Drive
Chicago IL 60611
312/988-6500
FAX: 312/988-6579

E-mail: fellowships@abfn.org
Internet: http://www.abf-sociolegal.org
AMOUNT: $3,600 stipend
DEADLINE(S): MAR 1
FIELD(S): Social Sciences; Humanities; Law

Summer research opportunity open to sophomore and junior undergraduates who are Native American, African-American, Mexican, Puerto Rican, or other minority. Must be U.S. citizen or permanent resident and have at least a 3.0 GPA. Students are assigned a mentor and participate in seminars; must also work at the Foundation's office in Chicago for 35 hours per week for 10 weeks. Essay, transcripts, and letter of recommendation required.

4 awards annually; announced in April. See Web site or contact ABF for an application.

739—CHICAGO ROOFING CONTRACTORS ASSOCIATION (Scholarship)

4415 W. Harrison Street, #322
Hillside IL 60162
708/449-3340
FAX: 708/449-0837
E-mail: crcainfo@crca.org
Internet: http://www.crca.org
AMOUNT: $2,000
DEADLINE(S): Varies
FIELD(S): Business; Engineering; Architecture; Liberal Arts; Sciences

Open to high school seniors who reside in one of the eight counties in Northern Illinois: Cook, DuPage, Lake, Kane, Kendall, DeKalb, McHenry, or Will. Must be accepted as a full-time student in a four-year college/university to pursue a degree in one of the above fields. Must be U.S. citizen. Based on academic achievements extracurricular activities, and community involvement.

Renewable. Contact CRCA for an application.

740—CIVIL AIR PATROL (CAP Undergraduate Scholarships)

Civil Air Patrol
National Headquarters
Maxwell AFB AL 36112-6332
334/953-5315
AMOUNT: $750
DEADLINE(S): JAN 31
FIELD(S): Humanities; Science; Engineering; Education

Open to CAP members who have received the Billy Mitchell Award or the senior rating in Level II of the senior training program. For undergraduate study in the above areas.

Write for complete information.

741—COLLEGE MISERICORDIA (Presidential Scholarships)

301 Lake Street
Dallas PA 18612-1098
800/852-7675
Internet: http://www.miseri.edu
AMOUNT: Full or part tuition
DEADLINE(S): MAR 1
FIELD(S): Prelaw or the humanities

Scholarships for incoming freshmen to this coeducational Catholic college in Pennsylvania. High school senior applicants must rank in the upper 20% of their classes and have achieved SAT or ACT scores in the 8th percentile or better.

Obtain applications from the Admissions Office.

742—FREEDOM FROM RELIGION FOUNDATION (Student Essay Contest)

P.O. Box 750
Madison WI 53701
608/256-5800
Internet: http://www.infidels.org/org/ffrf
AMOUNT: $1,000; $500; $250
DEADLINE(S): JUL 15
FIELD(S): Humanities; English; Education; Philosophy; Science

Essay contest on topics related to church-state entanglement in public schools or growing up a "freethinker" in religious-oriented society. Topics change yearly, but all are on general theme of maintaining separation of church and state. New topics available in February. For high school seniors and currently enrolled college/technical students. Must be U.S. citizen.

Send SASE to address above for complete information. Please indicate whether wanting information for college competition or high school. Information will be sent when new topics are announced each February. See Web site for details.

743—HIGHER EDUCATION PROGRAMS (Javits Fellowship Board)

U.S. Department of Education
1990 K Street NW, 6th Floor
Washington DC 20006-8521
202/502-7700
E-mail: OPE_Javits_Program@ed.gov
Internet: http://www.ed.gov/offices/OPE/HEP/iegps/javits.html
AMOUNT: $10,000-$18,000
DEADLINE(S): NOV 30
FIELD(S): Arts, Humanities, and Social Sciences

Fellowships can be offered to individuals who at the time of application have not yet completed their first full year of doctoral or MFA study or are entering graduate school for the first time in the next academic year. Students who have already received a Ph.D. or M.F.A., or received a Javits fellowship in previous years, are not eligible.

744—INSTITUTE FOR HUMANE STUDIES (Humane Studies Fellowship)

3301 N. FairFAX: Drive; Suite 440
Arlington VA 22201-4432
703/993-4880 or 800/697-8799
FAX: 703/993-4890
E-mail: ihs@gmu.edu
Internet: http://www.TheIHS.org
AMOUNT: $12,000 (max.)
DEADLINE(S): DEC
FIELD(S): Social Sciences; Liberal Arts; Law; Humanities; Jurisprudence; Journalism

Open to graduate and advanced undergraduate or law students pursuing degrees at any accredited domestic or foreign college/university. Based on academic performance, demonstrated interest in the classical liberal tradition, and potential to contribute to the advancement of a free society.

90 awards annually. Apply online or contact IHS for an application.

745—INSTITUTE FOR HUMANE STUDIES (Summer Seminars Program)

3301 N. FairFAX: Drive, Suite 440
Arlington VA 22201-4432
703/993-4880 or 800/697-8799
FAX: 703/993-4890
E-mail: ihs@gmu.edu
Internet: http://www.TheIHS.org
AMOUNT: Free summer seminars, including room/board, lectures, seminar materials, and books
DEADLINE(S): MAR
FIELD(S): Social Sciences; Humanities; Law; Journalism; Public Policy; Education; Film; Writing; Economics; Philosophy

Open to college students, recent graduates, and graduate students who share an interest in learning and exchanging ideas about the scope of individual rights, free markets, the rule of law, peace, and tolerance.

See Web site for seminar information or to apply online or contact IHS for an application.

746—MIDWAY COLLEGE (Institutional Aid Program)

Financial Aid Office
Midway KY 40347
606/846-4421

AMOUNT: Varies
DEADLINE(S): MAR 1
FIELD(S): Nursing; Paralegal; Education; Psychology; Biology; Equine Studies; Liberal Studies; Business Administration

Scholarships and grants are open to women who are accepted for enrollment at Midway College. Awards support undergraduate study in the above areas.

80 awards annually. Contact Midway College's Financial Aid Office for an application.

747—NATIONAL FEDERATION OF THE BLIND (Humanities Scholarship)

805 5th Avenue
Grinnell IA 50112
641/236-3369
Internet: http://www.nfb.org

AMOUNT: $3,000
DEADLINE(S): MAR 31
FIELD(S): Humanities (Art, English, Foreign Languages, History, Philosophy, Religion)

Open to legally blind students pursuing or planning to pursue a full-time postsecondary education in the US. Scholarships are awarded on basis of academic excellence, service to the community, and financial need. Must include transcripts and two letters of recommendation. Membership NOT required.

1 award annually. Renewable. Contact Mrs. Peggy Elliot, Scholarship Committee Chair, for an application.

748—NATIONAL ITALIAN AMERICAN FOUNDATION (Scholarship Program)

1860 19th Street NW
Washington DC 20009
202/387-0600
FAX: 202/387-0800
E-mail: scholarships@niaf.org
Internet; http://www.niaf@org/scholarships

AMOUNT: $2,000-$5,000 per year (renewable)
DEADLINE(S): APR 30
FIELD(S): Humanities; Area Studies Foreign Language

140 scholarships awarded annually to undergraduate, graduate, and doctoral students of Italian-American descent in any field of study, or to students from any ethnic background majoring or minoring in Italian language, Italian studies, Italian American studies, or a related field. Applications can only be submitted online. See Web site for application and more information on requirements.

749—NORTH CAROLINA STATE UNIVERSITY (Thomas Jefferson Scholarship in Agriculture and Humanities)

115 Patterson Hall, Box 7642
Raleigh NC 27695-7642
Written Inquiry

AMOUNT: $1,000
DEADLINE(S): MAR
FIELD(S): Agriculture AND Humanities

Open to first-year undergraduate students with a double major in agriculture and humanities who attend or plan to attend North Carolina State University.

750—PEW YOUNGER SCHOLARS PROGRAM (Graduate Fellowships)

G-123 Hesburgh Library
University of Notre Dame
Notre Dame IN 46556
219/631-4531
FAX: 219/631-8721
E-mail: Karen.M.Heinig.2@nd.edu
Internet: http://www.nd.edu/~pesp/pew/PYSPHistory.html

AMOUNT: $13,000
DEADLINE(S): NOV 30
FIELD(S): Social Sciences, Humanities, Theology

Program is for use at any Christian undergraduate school and most seminaries. Check with organization to see if your school qualifies. Apply during senior year. Recipients may enter a competition in which ten students will be awarded a $39,000 ($13,000/year) fellowship for three years of dissertation study. For use at top-ranked Ph.D. programs at outstanding universities.

NOT for study in medicine, law business, performing arts, fine arts, or the pastorate. Check Web site and/or organization for details.

751—ROSE HILL COLLEGE (Louella Robinson Memorial Scholarship)

P.O. Box 3126
Aiken SC 29802-3126
800/684-3769
FAX: 803/641-0240
E-mail: rosehill@rosehill.edu
Internet: http://www.rosehill.edu

AMOUNT: $10,000/year for four years
DEADLINE(S): Varies
FIELD(S): Liberal arts and humanities curricula

For undergraduate residents of Indian River County, Florida, to attend Rose Hill College in Aiken, South Carolina. The school offers a liberal arts education and follows the Great Books curriculum, a program of reading and seminars.

One annual award. Applicants must meet entry requirements of RHC. Contact above location for details.

752—ROSE HILL COLLEGE (Scholarships for Children of Eastern Orthodox Priests/Deacons)

P.O. Box 3126
Aiken SC 29802-3126
800/684-3769
FAX: 803/641-0240
E-mail: rosehill@rosehill.edu
Internet: http://www.rosehill.edu

AMOUNT: Full scholarship: $10,000/year for four years
DEADLINE(S): Varies
FIELD(S): Liberal Arts and Humanities Curricula

For undergraduates who are children of Eastern Orthodox Christan priests or deacons to attend Rose Hill College in Aiken, South Carolina. The school offers a liberal arts education and follows the Great Books Curriculum, a program of reading and seminars.

6-10 annual awards. Applicants must meet entry requirements of RHC. Contact above location for details.

753—ROSE HILL COLLEGE (Scholarships for the Homeschooled)

P.O. Box 3126
Aiken SC 29802-3126
800/684-3769
FAX: 803/641-0240
E-mail: rosehill@rosehill.edu
Internet: http://www.resehill.edu

AMOUNT: Full scholarship: $10,000/year for four years
DEADLINE(S): Varies

FIELD(S): Liberal Arts and Humanities Curricula

For undergraduates who have been homeschooled for three of the last five years of their high school education. For use at Rose Hill College in Aiken, South Carolina. The school offers a liberal arts education and follows the Great Books Curriculum, a program of reading and seminars. Scholarships will be awarded primarily on the basis of an essay which the student will be asked to write.

Four annual awards. Applicants must meet entry requirements of RHC. Contact above location for details.

754—SIGUROUR NORDAL INSTITUTE (Snorri Sturluson Icelandic Fellowships)

P.O. Box 1220
121 Reykjavik ICELAND
354/562-6050
FAX: 354/562-6263
E-mail: postur@mrn.stjr.is
Internet: http://www.mrn.stjr.is
AMOUNT: Varies (based on travel and living expenses)
DEADLINE(S): OCT 31
FIELD(S): Humanities

Open to writers, translators, and scholars (not to university students) in the field of humanities from outside Iceland, to enable them to stay in Iceland for a period of at least three months, in order to improve their knowledge of the Icelandic language, culture, and society. Preference given to candidate from Eastern or Southern Europe, Asia, Africa, Latin America, or Oceania. At conclusion, fellows must submit report on how grant was spent.

1 award annually. To apply, submit account of purpose and period of stay in Iceland, as well as details of education and publications. Snorri Sturluson was a famous Icelandic author.

755—UNITARIAN UNIVERSALIST ASSN. (Stanfield/D'Orlando Art Scholarship)

25 Beacon Street
Boston MA 02108
617/742-7025; FAX: 617/742-7025
E-mail: stanfield@uua.org
Internet: http://www.uua.org/info/application.pdf
AMOUNT: Varies
DEADLINE(S): FEB 15
FIELD(S): Art

Art scholarships for graduate or undergraduate fine art students. Applicants must be Unitarian Universalists. Limited to the study of painting, drawing, photography, and/or sculpture. Criteria for recipient include an active relationship with Unitarian Universalism, financial need, and enrollment in an accredited institution. Contact Patricia Frevert for details.

No phone calls please.

756—WOODROW WILSON NATIONAL FELLOWSHIP FOUNDATION (Andrew W. Mellon Fellowships)

CN 5329
Princeton NJ 08543-5329
800/899-9963
FAX: 609/452-0066
E-mail: mellon@woodrow.org;
Internet: http://www.woodrow.org/mellon
AMOUNT: Tuition and stipend of $17,500
DEADLINE(S): MID DEC
FIELD(S): Humanistic Studies

The Fellowship is for one year only and cannot be deferred. Mellon Fellows are expected to carry a full course load during the nine-month academic year of the Fellowship. Fellows may not accept supplementary awards or employment, including teaching assistantships. Members of underrepresented groups are particularly encouraged to apply.

AREA STUDIES

757—AIR FORCE RESERVE OFFICER TRAINING CORPS (AFROTC Scholarships)

551 E. Maxwell Boulevard
Maxwell AFB AL 36112-6106
334/953-7783
AMOUNT: Full tuition, books, and fees for all 4 years of college
DEADLINE(S): DEC 1
FIELD(S): Science; Engineering; Business; Political Science; Psychology; Geography; Foreign Studies; Foreign Language

Competitive scholarships based on individual merit to high school seniors and graduates who have not completed any full-time college work. Must be a U.S. citizen between the ages of 17-27. Must also have GPA of 2.5 or above, be in top 40% of class, and complete Applicant Fitness Test. Cannot be a single parent. Your college/university must offer AFROTC.

2,300 awards annually. Contact above address for application packet.

758—ALLIANCE FOR YOUNG ARTISTS AND WRITERS, INC./AMERICAN MUSEUM OF NATURAL HISTORY (Young Naturalist Awards)

Scholastic, Inc.
555 Broadway
New York NY 10012-3999
212/343-6582 or
800-SCHOLASTIC
FAX: 212/343-4885
E-mail: A&WGeneralinfo@scholastic.com
Internet: http://www.amnh.org/youngnaturalistawards
AMOUNT: Up to $2,500 + trip to New York to visit AMNH
DEADLINE(S): JAN
FIELD(S): Natural Sciences

For all students in grades 7-12 currently enrolled in a public or nonpublic school in the U.S., Canada, U.S. territories, or U.S.-sponsored schools abroad. Program focuses on finding and rewarding excellence in biology, earth science, astronomy, and cultural studies. Students are encouraged to perform observation-based projects that require creativity, inquiry, and critical analysis. Specific topics vary annually.

48 awards annually. See Web site for application.

759—AMERICAN ASSOCIATION OF TEACHERS OF FRENCH (National French Contest)

Sidney L. Teitelbaum
Box 32030
Sarasota FL 34239
FAX: 914/364-9820
AMOUNT: Varies
DEADLINE(S): Varies
FIELD(S): French Language; French Studies

Le Grand Concours, or National French Contest, is a French event in the form of a 60-minute national examination to help stimulate further interest in the teaching and learning of French and to help identify and reward achievement on the part of both students and teachers.

Not a scholarship. Winners receive trips, medals, and books. Write for complete information or ask your French teacher. All students of French, from FLES through senior high school, are eligible. In addition, students studying French on overseas campuses, with a private tutor exclusive of any formal classroom instruction in French, or via Homeschooling, are all eligible for awards.

760—AMERICAN ASSOCIATION OF TEACHERS OF ITALIAN (College Essay Contest)

Cal State University
Chico-Foreign Language Department
Chico CA 95929
Written Inquiries

AMOUNT: $100-$300
DEADLINE(S): JUN 15
FIELD(S): Italian Language; Italian Studies

Not a scholarship. Prize given on a competitive basis to essays written in Italian by college students on a prescribed topic. Contest open to undergraduate students at accredited colleges and universities in North America. Essay in Italian language on topic pertaining to literature or culture.

Write to Prof. Eugenio Frongia at address above for complete information.

761—AMERICAN BAR FOUNDATION (Montgomery Summer Research Fellowships for Minority Undergraduate Students)

750 N. Lake Shore Drive
Chicago IL 60611
312/988-6500
FAX: 312/988-6579
E-mail: fellowships@abfn.org
Internet: http://www.abf-sociolegal.org

AMOUNT: $3,600 stipend
DEADLINE(S): MAR 1
FIELD(S): Social Sciences; Humanities; Law

Summer research opportunity open to sophomore and junior undergraduates who are Native American, African-American, Mexican, Puerto Rican, or other minority. Must be U.S.citizen or permanent resident and have at least a 3.0 GPA. Students are assigned a mentor and participate in seminars; must also work at the Foundation's office in Chicago for 35 hours per week for 10 weeks. Essay, transcripts, and letter of recommendation required.

4 awards annually; announced in April. See Web site or contact ABF for an application.

762—THE AMERICAN CLASSICAL LEAGUE (Ed Phinney Commemorative Scholarship)

Miami University
Oxford OH 45056
513/529-7741
FAX: 513/529-7742
E-mail: AmericanClassicalLeague@muohio.edu or a.c.l@mich.edu
Internet: http://www.umich.edu/~acleague/phinney.html

AMOUNT: Up to $500
DEADLINE(S): JAN 15
FIELD(S): Teachers or teacher candidates in the classics (Latin and/or Greek)

Scholarships of up to $500 to apply to first-time attendance at the League's institute OR up to $500 to cover cost of other activities that serve to enhance a teacher's skills in the classroom in the classics OR up to $150 for purchase of materials from the ACL Teaching and Materials Resource Center. Memberships required except for first-time attendance at institute.

Send request for information to above address.

763—AMERICAN PLANNING ASSOCIATION (Minority Scholarship and Fellowship Programs)

122 South Michigan Avenue, Suite 1600
Chicago IL 60605
312/431-9100
FAX: 312/431-9985

AMOUNT: $2,000-$5,000 (grads); $2,500 (undergrads)
DEADLINE(S): MAY 14
FIELD(S): Urban Planning, Community Development, Environmental Sciences, Public Administration, Transportation, or Urban Studies

Scholarships for African-Americans, Hispanics, or Native American students pursing undergraduate degrees in the U.S. in the above fields. Must have completed first year. Fellowships for graduate students. Programs must be approved by the Planning Accreditation Board. U.S. citizenship.

Call or write for complete information.

764—ARCTIC INSTITUTE OF NORTH AMERICA (Jim Bourque Scholarship)

Univ. of Calgary
2500 University Drive NW
Calgary Alberta T2N 1N4
CANADA
403/220-7515
FAX: 403/282-4609
E-mail: smccaffe@ucalgary.ca
Internet: http://www.ucalgary.ca/UofC/Others/AINA/scholar/scholar.html

AMOUNT: $1,000
DEADLINE(S): JUL 15
FIELD(S): Education; Environmental Studies; Traditional Knowledge; Telecommunications

Open to Canadian Aboriginal students who intend to take, or are enrolled in, post-secondary training in above fields. There is no application; applicants must submit description of program and reasons for choice, transcript, letter of recommendation, statement of financial need, and proof of enrollment or application to a postsecondary institution.

See Web site or contact AINA for details. Award announced on August 1.

765—ARCTIC INSTITUTE OF NORTH AMERICA (Northern Scientific Training Program Grants)

Univ. of Calgary
2500 University Drive NW
Calgary Alberta T2N 1N4
CANADA
403/220-7515
FAX: 403/282-4609
E-mail: hills@geo.ucalgary.ca
Internet: http://www.ucalgary.ca/UofC/Others/AINA/scholar/scholar.html

AMOUNT: Varies
DEADLINE(S): NOV
FIELD(S): Northern Canadian and Arctic Studies

Open to Canadian citizens/permanent residents enrolled in a Canadian university who are either graduate students or senior undergraduates entering final year and intending to undertake honor's thesis based on northern research which will be continued in subsequent graduate study. Grant helps pay for transportation and living costs to enable students to obtain practical fieldwork experience in Canada's North or in the northern parts of the other seven arctic countries.

See Web site or contact Dr. Leonard Hills at AINA for details.

766—ASSOCIATION FOR THE STUDY OF AFRO-AMERICAN LIFE & HISTORY, INC. (Afro-American Life and History Essay Contest)

1407 Fourteenth St. NW
Washington DC 20005-3704
202/667-2822

AMOUNT: $500
DEADLINE(S): JAN 15
FIELD(S): Afro American

Award is available to students interested in African-American studies. May be applied to either graduate or undergraduate work. Applicants must be in their first two years of study.

767—ASSOCIATION FOR WOMEN IN PSYCHOLOGY/AMERICAN PSYCHOLOGICAL ASSOCIATION DIVISION 35 (Annual Student Research Prize)

SUNY Fredonia
Fredonia NY 14063
716/673-3893
Internet: http://www.apa.org/divisions/div35/div35awpr.html

AMOUNT: $200
DEADLINE(S): APR
FIELD(S): Women's Issues

Undergraduate and graduate students may submit research papers relevant in some way to women's lives. Research can be either basic or applied. Entries should be of approximately journal length and written in APA style.

Send four copies of the paper and a self-addressed, stamped, postcard and business-sized envelope to Ingrid Johnston-Robledo, Ph.D., Department of Psychology, at the above address.

768—BLUES HEAVEN FOUNDATION, INC. (Muddy Waters Scholarship)

2120 S. Michigan Avenue
Chicago IL 60616
312/808-1286

AMOUNT: $2,000
DEADLINE(S): APR 30
FIELD(S): Music; Music Education; African-American Studies; Folklore; Performing Arts; Arts Management; Journalism; Radio/TV/Film

Scholarship is made on a competitive basis with consideration given to scholastic achievement, concentration of studies, and financial need. Applicant must have full-time enrollment status in a Chicago area college/university in at least their first year of undergraduate studies or a graduate program. Scholastic aptitude extracurricular involvement, grade point average, and financial need are all considered.

Contact Blues Heaven Foundation, Inc. to receive an application between February and April.

769—BRITISH ACADEMY (Sir Ernest Cassel Educational Trust)

10 Carlton House
Islington, London SWIY 5AH
ENGLAND UK
020 7969 5217
FAX: 020 7969 5414
E-mail: grants@britac.ac.uk
Internet: http://www.britac.ac.uk/funding/guide/cetf.html

AMOUNT: Up to 5,000 pounds per annum
DEADLINE(S): FEB; APR; SEP; NOV (end of ea. month)
FIELD(S): Language, literature, or civilization of any country

The British Academy administers funds on behalf of the Sir Ernest Cassel Educational Trust to support travel costs related to a research project. Research Grants Department Awards are particularly aimed at recent postdoctoral scholars.

Obtain application from the Research Grants Department.

770—BRITISH COLUMBIA HERITAGE TRUST (Scholarships)

P.O. Box 9818, Stn Prov Govt.
Victoria BC V8W 9W3 CANADA
250/356-1433
FAX: 250/356-7796
E-mail: heritage@tbc.gov.bc.ca

AMOUNT: $5,000
DEADLINE(S): FEB 1
FIELD(S): British Columbia History; Architecture; Archaeology; Archival Management

Open to graduate students who are Canadian citizens or permanent residents. Criteria are scholarly record and academic performance, educational and career objectives, and proposed program of study.

Write for complete information.

771—CANADIAN INSTITUTE OF UKRAINIAN STUDIES (Leo J. Krysa Family Undergraduate Scholarship)

352 Athabasca Hall; Univ. of Alberta
Edmonton Alberta T6G 2E8
CANADA
E-mail: cius@gpu.srv.ualberta.ca
Internet: http://www.ualberta.ca/~cius/cius-grants.htm

AMOUNT: $3,500 (max.)
DEADLINE(S): Varies
FIELD(S): Ukrainian Studies

For a student in the faculty of Arts or Education about to enter the final year of study in pursuit of an undergraduate degree. Applicants' programs must emphasize Ukrainian and/or Ukrainian-Canadian studies, through a combination of Ukrainian and East European or Canadian courses. Candidates must be Canadian citizens/permanent residents and use the 8-month scholarship at any Canadian university.

1 award annually. Not renewable. Contact above address for an application.

772—UCLA CENTER FOR 17TH- AND 18TH-CENTURY STUDIES (Fellowships)

UCLA
310 Royce Hall
Los Angeles CA 90095-1404
310/206-8552
FAX: 310/206-8577
E-mail: c1718cs@humnet.ucla.edu
Internet; http://www.humnet.ucla.edu/humnet/C1718CS/Postd.htm#Ahm Get

AMOUNT: $1,000-$18,400
DEADLINE(S): Varies
FIELD(S): British Literature/History (17th and 18th Centuries)

Undergraduate stipends, graduate assistantships, and postdoctoral fellowships are for advanced study and research regarding British literature and history of the 17th and 18th centuries.

Contact the Center for current year's theme and an application.

773—CENTER FOR CHINESE STUDIES (Research Grant Program)

20 Chungshan S. Road
Taipei Taiwan 10001 R.O.C.
886-2-2314-7321
FAX: 886-2-2371-2126
E-mail: ccsgrant@msg.ncl.edu.tw
Internet: http://ccs.ncl.edu.tw/res_e_2.html

AMOUNT: NT $25,000-55,000
DEADLINE(S): APR 30
FIELD(S): Chinese Studies

Grants for foreign professors, associate professors, assistant professors, and doctoral candidates. Intended for research in the Republic of China. Can be used in Chinese studies-related departments of colleges, universities, or research institutions. Must be non-Chinese.

774—CENTER FOR CROSS-CULTURAL STUDY (Tuition Awards for Study in Sevill, Spain)

446 Main Street
Amherst MA 01002-2314

413/256-0011 or 800/377-2621
FAX: 413/256-1968
E-mail: cccs@crocker.com
Internet: http://www.cccs.com
AMOUNT: $500
DEADLINE(S): Varies
FIELD(S): Study of Spanish and Spanish Culture

Partial tuition assistance is available at this facility in Spain. Applicants must submit an original essay in Spanish, between 2 or 3 double-spaced, typed pages. Also required as a short description in English of your experience with the Spanish language and culture and a faculty recommendation.

Awards are for one semester or academic year programs in Seville. Contact organization for specific details regarding the essays.

775—CENTRE FOR INDEPENDENT STUDIES (Liberty and Society Scholarship)

P.O. Box 92
St. Leonards NSW 1590
Sydney AUSTRALIA
02 612 9438 4377
FAX: 02 612 9439 7310
E-mail: jlindsay@cis.org.au
Internet: http://www.cis.org.au
AMOUNT: Approx. $1,000
DEADLINE(S): Varies
FIELD(S): Classical Liberalism

For undergraduate and graduate students under the age of 30 who have good university results to attend weekend seminars in Sydney, Australia. Preference is given to people from the Oceania region.

Visit Web site for an application.

776—CHRISTIAN A. JOHNSON ENDEAVOR FOUNDATION (Native American Fellows)

John F. Kennedy School of Government, Harvard University
79 John F. Kennedy Street
Cambridge MA 02138
617/495-1152
FAX: 617/496-3900
Internet: http://www.ksg.harvard.edu/hpaied/index.htm
AMOUNT: Varies
DEADLINE(S): MAY 1
FIELD(S): American Indian Affairs

Fellowships for students of Native American ancestry who attend a John F. Kennedy School of Government degree program. Applicant, parent, or grandparent must hold membership in a federally or state-recognized tribe, band, or other organized group of Native Americans. Must be committed to a career in American Indian affairs. Awards based on merit and need.

Renewable, based on renomination and availability of funds. To apply, contact John F. Kennedy School of Government at above address.

777—DUMBARTON OAKS (The Bliss Prize Fellowship in Byzantine Studies)

1703 32nd Street NW
Washington DC 20007-2961
202/339-6410
Internet: http://www.doaks.org/Blissprize.html
AMOUNT: Graduate school tuition and living expenses plus summer travel expenses
DEADLINE(S): NOV 1 (nominations due OCT 15)
FIELD(S): Byzantine Studies

Open to outstanding college seniors who plan to enter the field of Byzantine studies. Must be in last year of studies or already hold BA and have completed at least one year of Greek by January of senior year. Restricted to candidates currently enrolled or recent graduates of U.S. or Canadian universities/colleges. Students must be nominated by their advisors.

Contact Dumbarton Oaks for complete information.

778—EMBASSY OF JAPAN (Monbusho Scholarship Program for Japanese Studies)

1155 21st Street NW
Washington DC 20036
202/238-6700
E-mail: eojjicc@erolscom
Internet: http://www.embjapan.org
AMOUNT: 142,500 yen per month
DEADLINE(S): APR 1
FIELD(S): Japanese Language and/or Cultural Studies

The Japanese Government Ministry of Education, Science, and Culture (Monbusho) offers scholarships for foreign students to study for one to two years in Japan. Program offers intensive Japanese language instruction, but applicant must already speak Japanese.

All sixteen Japanese consulates in the U.S. accept and review applications. Deadlines vary. For information and application materials, contact the nearest consulate-general of Japan or the Embassy of Japan in Washington.

779—EMBASSY OF THE CZECH REPUBLIC (Scholarships for Czechs Living Abroad)

3900 Spring of Freedom Street NW
Washington DC 20008
202/274-9103
FAX: 202/363-6308
E-mail: con_washington@embassy.mzv.cz
Internet: http://www.mzv.cz/washington
AMOUNT: Varies
DEADLINE(S): APR 30
FIELD(S): Czech Language and Literature, History, Theology, and/or Ethnography

Scholarships for undergraduate and graduate citizens of the Czech Republic who are living in the U.S. The ideal applicant should use his/her knowledge for the benefit of the Czech community abroad.

20 annual awards. For a maximum of two semesters of study. See Web site or write/call for further information.

780—FOUNDATION FOR THE ADVANCEMENT OF MESOAMERICAN STUDIES, INC. (Research Grants)

268 S. Suncoast Boulevard
Crystal River FL 34429
352/795-5990
FAX: 352/795-1970
E-mail: famsi@famsi.org
Internet: http://www.famsi.org
AMOUNT: $10,000 (max.)
DEADLINE(S): SEP 30
FIELD(S): Archaeology, Art History, Epigraphy, Linguistics, Ethnography, Sociology

Open to undergraduates, graduates, and postgraduates to pursue research or scholarly works with potential for significant contributions to the understanding of ancient Mesoamerican cultures and continuities thereof among the indigenous cultures in modern Mesoamerica (Mexico, Belize, Guatemala, Honduras, and El Salvador). The foundation encourages interdisciplinary projects.

30-35 awards annually. Renewable. See Web site for an application.

781—GERMAN ACADEMIC EXCHANGE SERVICE (DAAD Programs)

871 U.N. Plaza
New York NY 10017
212/758-3223
FAX: 212/755-5780

E-mail: daadny@daad.org
Internet: http://www.daad.org
AMOUNT: Varies (with program)
DEADLINE(S): Varies (with program)
FIELD(S): Varies (with program)

Grants are available to faculty and full-time students who are citizens or permanent residents of the U.S. or Canada. Programs are for study in Germany in a variety of fields.

See Web site or contact DAAD Programs Administrator for an application.

782—GIACOMO LEOPARDI CENTER (Scholarships for Italian Language Study in Italy)

Via Castello
61020 Belforte all'Isauro ITALY
39 0722 726000
FAX: 39 0722 726010
E-mail: centroleopardi@wnt.it
Internet: http://www.italian.org/
AMOUNT: Cost of tuition (about $750)
DEADLINE(S): Varies
FIELD(S): Italian language and literature

The Center is in a castle built in the late Middle Ages. The castle is the site of school for teaching the Italian language and culture. Students are lodged in rooms in the Castle. Scholarships are for the first 300 to apply, and they are for tuition only. Students still must pay for food and lodging.

Ten scholarships covering the cost of an Italian Language and Culture course. Most details are found on the Web site.

783—HILLEL: THE FOUNDATION FOR JEWISH CAMPUS LIFE (Steinhardt Jewish Campus Service Corps)

1640 Rhode Island Avenue NW
Washington, DC 20036
202/857-6559; FAX:202/857-6626
E-mail: mgruenwald@hillel.org
Internet: http://www.hillel.org
AMOUNT: One-year fellowship
DEADLINE(S): MAR
FIELD(S): Student Leadership

Open to college seniors and recent college graduates with leadership skills and ability to create dynamic and innovative engagement strategies designed to reach Jewish college students. Must possess commitment to service; willingness to use time, abilities, and talents to enhance lives of others; and dedication to strengthening Jewish identity among students with whom they work. Corps fellows get to know interests and concerns of students and build programs and activities to match.

See Web site or contact Melanie Sasson Gruenwald or Rachel Gurshman for an application.

784—INSTITUT D'ETUDES FRANCAISES D'AVIGNON (Scholarships for Summer Study in Avignon, France)

Bryn Mawr College
Bryn Mawr PA 19010-2899
610/526-5083
FAX: 610/526-7479
E-mail: avignon@brynmawr.edu
Internet: http://www.brynmawr.edu/Adm/academic/special/avignon/details.html
AMOUNT: Varies
DEADLINE(S): MAR 15
FIELD(S): French-related studies

Scholarships based on academic excellence and financial need for a six-week summer study program in Avignon, France. Program is offered to male and female students from other colleges as well as Bryn Mawr. For graduates and undergraduates who have completed three years of college-level French or equivalent.

Contact the Director of the Institute for application information.

785—INSTITUTE FOR HUMANE STUDIES (Humane Studies Fellowship)

3301 N. FairFAX: Drive; Suite 440
Arlington VA 22201-4432
703/993-4880 or 800/697-8799
FAX: 703/993-4890
E-mail: ihs@gmu.edu
Internet: http://www.TheIHS.org
AMOUNT: $12,000 (max.)
DEADLINE(S): DEC
FIELD(S): Social Sciences; Liberal Arts; Law; Humanities; Jurisprudence; Journalism

Open to graduate and advanced undergraduate or law students pursuing degrees at any accredited domestic or foreign college/university. Based on academic performance, demonstrated interest in the classical liberal tradition, and potential to contribute to the advancement of a free society.

90 awards annually. Apply online or contact IHS for an application.

786—INTERNATIONAL INSTITUTE FOR POPULATION SCIENCES (Short-Term Training Programmes for Indian Officials and Foreign Nationals)

Govandi Station Road
Deonar, Mumbai-400 088,
Maharashtra INDIA
(091) 22-5563254/55/56
FAX: (091) 22-5563257
E-mail: iips@bom3.vsnl.net.in
Internet: http://www.unescap.org/pop/popin/profiles/india/welcome.htm
AMOUNT: Varies
DEADLINE(S): Varies
FIELD(S): Population Studies

These courses range from 2 weeks to 3 months. One program is for personnel working in the Population Research Centers, Medical Colleges, Health and Family Welfare Departments, Universities, etc. of India or for Senior Officials of the Planning Departments of various States of India. Another is for officials of foreign countries. The expenses of such training programs are borne by sponsoring agencies.

Not renewable. Contact the Director of IIPS for an application.

787—JAMES MADISON MEMORIAL FELLOWSHIP FOUNDATION (Fellowships)

2000 K Street NW, Suite 303
Washington DC 20006
202/653-8700
FAX: 202/653-6045
Internet: http://www.jamesmadison.com
AMOUNT: Tuition, fees, books, and room/board
DEADLINE(S): MAR 1
FIELD(S): Education: American History, American Government, Social Studies

Open to U.S. citizens/nationals who are teachers, or planning to become teachers, in above fields at the secondary school level. Must currently possess a bachelor's degree, or plan to receive one no later than August 31. Fellows must teach above subjects in grades 7-12 for no less than one year for each full year of study under the fellowship. Proposed graduate study should contain substantial constitutional coursework.

See Web site or contact Foundation for an application.

788—JAPANESE AMERICAN CITIZENS LEAGUE (Yoshiko Tanaka Memorial Scholarship)

1765 Sutter Street
San Francisco CA 94115
415/921-5225

FAX: 415/931-4671
E-mail: jacl@jacl.org
Internet: http://www.jacl.org
AMOUNT: $1,000-$5,000
DEADLINE(S): APR 1
FIELD(S): Japanese Language/Culture; U.S.-Japan Relations

Open to JACL members and their children only. For undergraduate students with an interest in Japanese language, culture, or the enhancement of U.S.-Japan relations and who are planning to attend a college, university, trade school, business school, or any other institution of higher learning. Must submit personal statement, letters of recommendation, and transcripts. Financial need NOT a factor.

For membership information or an application, send a self-addressed, stamped envelope to above address, stating your level of study. Applications available October 1 through March 20; recipients notified in July.

789—JAPANESE GOVERNMENT (Monbusho Japanese Studies Scholarships)

350 S. Grand Avenue, Suite 1700
Los Angeles CA 90071
213/617-6700 ext. 338
FAX: 213/617-6728
Internet: http://embjapan.org/la
AMOUNT: Tuition + $1,400-$1,800/month
DEADLINE(S): MAR
FIELD(S): Japanese Studies and closely related fields

For undergraduate students aged 18-30 years who major/minor in above fields and who wish to study in Japan. Intermediate Japanese proficiency is required. Scholarship is for one year and includes round-trip airfare, one-time arrival allowance, partly subsidized housing expenses, and partly subsidized medical expenses.

For further information or an application, contact Mr. Cory Crocker at the Japan Information and Culture Center, Consulate General of Japan, at above address.

790—JEWISH WELFARE BOARD (Scholarships)

15 E. 26th Street
New York NY 10010
212/532-4949
AMOUNT: $1,000-$4,000
DEADLINE(S): FEB 1
FIELD(S): Social work, adult education, early childhood education, health education, physical education, cultural studies, Jewish education

Scholarships for Jewish college juniors or seniors pursuing careers in the above fields. Must be committed to the work of the YMHA, YWHA, or Jewish community centers. Must do a year of field work in a Jewish community center.

Renewable. Contact organization for details.

791—JUNIATA COLLEGE (Baker Peace Scholarship)

Office of Student Financial Planning,
1700 Moore Street
Huntingdon PA 16652
814/641-3142
FAX: 814/641-5311
AMOUNT: $1,000-$2,000
DEADLINE(S): FEB 1
FIELD(S): Peace and Conflict Studies; International Affairs

Open to incoming freshman at Juniata College who rank in the upper 20% of their high school class, have above average SAT scores, and demonstrate an interest in peace-related issues. Must submit 1,000-word essay on designated topic, two letters of recommendation, and maintain a minimum 3.0 GPA.

Renewable up to 4 years. Contact Randy Rennell, director of student financial planning, for an application.

792—KOSCIUSZKO FOUNDATION (Summer Sessions in Poland and Rome)

15 E. 65th Street
New York NY 10021-6595
212/734-2130
FAX: 212/628-4552
E-mail: thekf@pegasusnet.com;
Internet: http://www.kosciuszko foundation.org
AMOUNT: Varies
DEADLINE(S): Varies
FIELD(S): Polish Studies; History; Literature; Art; Economics; Social Studies; Language; Culture

Open to undergraduate and graduate students, graduating high school students who are 18 or older, and persons of any age who are not enrolled in a college/university program. Study programs are offered in Poland and Rome from mid-June through the end of August in above fields. Must be U.S. citizen/permanent resident.

See Web site or send a self-addressed, stamped envelope to Addy Tymczyszyn, Summer Studies Abroad Coordinator, for an application.

793—KOSCIUSZKO FOUNDATION (Year Abroad Program)

15 E. 65th Street
New York NY 10021-6595
212/734-2130; FAX: 212/628-4552
E-mail: thekf@aol.com
Internet: http://www.kosciuszko foundation.org
AMOUNT: Tuition, housing, and monthly stipend
DEADLINE(S): JAN 16
FIELD(S): Polish Studies

Open to American students who wish to study Polish language, history, literature, and culture for credit at the undergraduate level. Must be enrolled at a U.S. college/university entering junior or senior year or be enrolled in a master's or doctoral program (except dissertation level). Must have a minimum 3.0 GPA and be U.S. citizen/permanent resident. Based on academics, goals, and interest in Polish subjects or involvement in Polish American community.

$50 application fee (1 application is valid for 2 years). See Web site or send a self-addressed, stamped envelope to Addy Tymczyszyn for an application. Notification in late spring.

794—MEMORIAL FOUNDATION FOR JEWISH CULTURE (International Scholarship Program for Community Service)

15 East 26th Street, Room 1703
New York NY 10010
212/889-9080
Internet: http://www.mfjc.org/index.htm
AMOUNT: Varies
DEADLINE(S): NOV 30
FIELD(S): Jewish Studies

Open to any individual regardless of country of origin for undergrad study that leads to careers in the Rabbinate, Jewish education, social work, or as religious functionaries in Diaspora Jewish communities outside the U.S., Israel, and Canada.

Must commit to serve in a community of need for 3 years. Those planning to serve in the U.S., Canada, or Israel are excluded from this program. Write for complete information.

795—MEMORIAL FOUNDATION FOR JEWISH CULTURE (Soviet Jewry Community Service Scholarship Program)

15 East 26th Street; Room 1703
New York NY 10010
212/889-9080
Internet: http://www.mfjc.org/index.htm
AMOUNT: Not specified
DEADLINE(S): NOV 30
FIELD(S): Jewish studies

Open to Jews from the former Soviet Union enrolled or planning to enroll in recognized institutions of higher Jewish learning. Must agree to serve a community of Soviet Jews anywhere in the world for a minimum of three years.

Grants are to help prepare well-qualified Soviet Jews to serve in the FSU. Write for complete information.

796—MINISTRY OF EDUCATION OF THE REPUBLIC OF CHINA (Scholarships for Foreign Students)

5 South Chung-Shan Road
Taipei; Taiwan REPUBLIC OF CHINA
(86) (02) 356-5696
FAX: (86) (02) 397-6778
E-mail; emic@moe.edu.cn
Internet: http://www.moe.edu.cn
AMOUNT: NT$25,000 (per month)
DEADLINE(S): Varies (inquire of school)
FIELD(S): Chinese studies or language

Undergraduate and graduate scholarships are available to foreign students wishing to study in Taiwan. Must have already studied in R.O.C. for at least one term. Must study full time.

Scholarships are for 6-12 months. 300 awards per year. Write for complete information or please contact colleges directly.

797—MINISTRY OF EDUCATION, SCIENCE, AND CULTURE (Icelandic Studies Scholarships)

Solvholsgata 4
Reykjavik IS-150 ICELAND
354/560-9500
FAX: 354/562-3068
E-mail: postur@mrn.stjr.is
Internet: http://www.mrn.stjr.is
AMOUNT: Registration fees plus stipend
DEADLINE(S): Varies
FIELD(S): Icelandic Studies

Eight-month scholarship is open to students at any level of study to pursue studies in Icelandic language, literature, and history at the University of Iceland.

Contact Ministry of Education for an application.

798—THE MORRIS K. UDALL FOUNDATION

110 South Church Ave., Suite 3350,
Tucson AZ 85701
520/670-5529
FAX: 520/670-5530
Internet: http://www.udall.gov/
AMOUNT: Up to $5,000
DEADLINE(S): FEB 15
FIELD(S): Health Care

Scholarships available to two groups: 1) college sophomores and juniors who have outstanding potential in the study of the environment and related fields and 2)Native American or Alaska Natives in fields related to health care or tribal policy.

799—NATIONAL ITALIAN AMERICAN FOUNDATION (Scholarship Program)

1860 19th Street NW
Washington DC 20009
202/387-0600
FAX:202/387-0800
E-mail: scholarships@niaf.org
Internet: http://www.niaf.org/scholarships
AMOUNT: $2,500-$5,000 per year (renewable)
DEADLINE(S): APR 30
FIELD(S): Humanities, Area Studies, Foreign Language

140 scholarships awarded annually to undergraduate, graduate, and doctoral students of Italian-American descent in any field of study, or to students from any ethnic background majoring or minoring in Italian language, Italian studies, Italian American studies, or a related field. Selection based on academic merit, financial need, and community service. Applications can only be submitted online. See web site for application and more information on requirements. Last year, NIAF granted approximately 140 scholarships.

800—NATIONAL WOMEN'S STUDIES ASSOCIATION (Graduate Scholarship in Lesbian Studies)

7100 Baltimore Avenue, Suite 301
College Park MD 20740
301/403-0525
Internet: http://www.nwsa.org/scholarship.htm
AMOUNT: $500
DEADLINE(S): JAN 31
FIELD(S): Lesbian Studies

The NWSA Scholarship in Lesbian Studies will be awarded to a student who will be doing research or writing a Master's thesis or Ph.D. dissertation in Lesbian studies. Preference will be given to NWSA members.

801—NATIONAL WOMEN'S STUDIES ASSOCIATION (Graduate Scholarship in Women's Studies)

7100 Baltimore Avenue
Suite 301
College Park MD 20740
301/403-0525
Internet http://www.nwsa.org/scholarship.htm
AMOUNT: $500-$1,000
DEADLINE(S): JAN 31
FIELD(S): Women's Studies

Open to any student who will be engaged in the research or writing stages of a Master's Thesis or Ph.D. Dissertation in the interdisciplinary field of women's studies. The research project must be on women and must enhance the NWSA mission. Applicants must be members of NWSA at the time of application.

802—NEW ZEALAND FEDERATION OF UNIVERSITY WOMEN-WAIKATO BRANCH (Kahurangi Maori Language Award)

P.O. Box 7065
Hamilton NEW ZEALAND
07/855-3776
AMOUNT: $1,000
DEADLINE(S): MAR 15
FIELD(S): Education; Maori Studies

Open to Maori women who are full-time students enrolled for a third or fourth year at the University of Waikato School of Education or the Department of Maori Studies. Must be fluent in or studying the Maori language for a Bachelor of Education degree or Diploma of Teaching.

Contact the Convenor, NAFUW, Waikato Branch for an application.

803—NORWEGIAN INFORMATION SERVICE (Norwegian Emigration Fund of 1975)

825 Third Avenue, 38th Floor
New York NY 10022-7584
212/421-7333
AMOUNT: Varies (NOK 5,000 to NOK 70,000)

DEADLINE(S): FEB 1
FIELD(S): History of Norwegian emigration and relations between the U.S. and Norway

Purpose of the fund is to award scholarships to Americans for advanced or specialized studies in Norway of subjects dealing with emigration history and relations between Norway and the U.S.

Must be U.S. citizen or resident. U.S. institutions may also be eligible. Write for complete information.

804—PHOENIX INDIAN MEDICAL CENTER AUXILIARY

Indian Health Career Awards
4212 North 16th Street
Phoenix AZ 85016
602/263-1576
AMOUNT: Up to $700
Deadlines: SEP 15, NOV 15
FIELD(S): Human Health

For students majoring in Human Health related fields. Each year, the Foundation awards undergraduate scholarships of up to $5,000 to American juniors and seniors in fields related to the environment, and to Native Americans and Alaska Natives in fields related to health care or tribal policy.

805—SMITHSONIAN INSTITUTION (Minority Student Internship Program)

Office of Fellowships
750 9th Street NW, Suite 9300
Washington DC 20560-0902
202/275-0655
FAX: 202/275-0489
E-mail: siofg@ofg.si.edu
Internet: http://www.si.edu/research+study
AMOUNT: $350/week + possible travel expenses
DEADLINE(S): Varies
FIELD(S): Humanities; Environmental and Cultural Studies; Natural History; Earth Science; Art History; Biology

Ten-week, full-time internships in residence at the Smithsonian are open to U.S. minority students who wish to participate in research or museum-related activities in above and related fields. Must be undergraduates or beginning graduate students with a minimum 3.0 GPA. Must submit essay, resume, and official transcript.

Contact the Office of Fellowships or see Web site for an application.

806—SMITHSONIAN INSTITUTION-FREER/SACKLER GALLERIES (Dick Louie Memorial Internship for Americans of Asian Descent)

Education Dept.
Washington DC 20560-0707
202/357-4880; TTY: 202/786-2374
Internet: http://www.asia.si.edu
AMOUNT: Stipend
DEADLINE(S): Varies
FIELD(S): Asian Art; Art History; Museum Studies

This summer internship is an opportunity for high school students of Asian descent to gain practical experience in a museum setting. Must be entering or completing senior year of high school, and must live and attend high school in the Washington metropolitan area.

Contact the Internship Coordinator for an application.

807—SONOMA CHAMBOLLE-MUSIGNY SISTER CITIES, INC. (Henri Cardinaux Memorial Scholarship)

Chamson Scholarship Committee
P.O. Box 1633
Sonoma CA 95476-1633
707/939-1344
FAX: 707/939-1344
E-mail: Baileysci@vom.com
AMOUNT: Up to $1,500 (travel + expenses)
DEADLINE(S): JUL 15
FIELD(S): Culinary Arts; Wine Industry; Art; Architecture; Music; History; Fashion

Hands-on experience working in above or similar fields and living with a family in small French village in Burgundy or other French city. Must be Sonoma County, CA, resident at least 18 years of age and be able to communicate in French. Transcripts, employer recommendation, photograph, and essay (stating why, where, and when) required.

1 award. Nonrenewable. Also offers opportunity for candidate in Chambolle-Musigny to obtain work experience and cultural exposure in Sonoma, CA.

808—SONS OF NORWAY FOUNDATION (King Olav V Norwegian-American Heritage Fund)

1455 West Lake Street
Minneapolis MN 55408
612/827-3611
AMOUNT: $250-$3,000
DEADLINE(S): MAR 1
FIELD(S): Norwegian Studies

For U.S. citizens 18 or older who have demonstrated a keen and sincere interest in the Norwegian heritage. Must be enrolled in a recognized educational institution and be studying such topics as arts, crafts, literature, history, music, folklore, etc. of Norway.

Financial need is a consideration but it is secondary to scholarship. 12 awards per year.

809—SONS OF NORWAY FOUNDATION (King Olav V Norwegian-American Heritage Fund)

1455 West Lake Street
Minneapolis MN 55408
Written Inquiry
AMOUNT: $250-$3,000
DEADLINE(S): MAR 1
FIELD(S): American Studies

For Norwegian citizens 18 or older who have demonstrated a keen and sincere interest in the heritage of the United States. Must be enrolled in a recognized educational institution and be studying such topics as arts, crafts, literature, history, music, folklore, etc. of the U.S.

Financial need is a consideration but it is secondary to scholarship. 12 awards per year.

810—STATISTICS NEW ZEALAND (Pacific Islands Scholarship)

EEO Co-ordinator
P.O. Box 2922
Wellington NEW ZEALAND
04/495-4643
FAX: 04/495-4817
E-mail: anisiata_soagia-pritchard@stats.govt.nz
AMOUNT: $3,500/year + travel
DEADLINE(S): OCT 31
FIELD(S): Statistics; Mathematics; Demography; Economics; Geography; Quantitative Social Sciences

Open to all indigenous people of Pacific Islands descent who are resident in New Zealand and who wish to study for an undergraduate tertiary qualification at a New Zealand university. Recipient must spend 6-10 weeks of vacation break in employment with Statistics New Zealand. Based on relevance of course of study; academic ability; language, community involvement, and culture; and personal attributes, including potential leadership qualities. References required.

1 award annually. Renewable up to 3 years. Contact Anisiata Soagia-Pritchard, EEO Coordinator, for an application. Notification in December.

811—THE LEMMERMANN FOUNDATION (Fondazione Lemmermann Scholarship Awards)

c/o Studio Associato Romanelli
via Cosseria, 5
00192 Roma ITALY
(06) 324.30.23
FAX: (06) 322.17.88
E-mail: lemmermann@mail.nexus.it
Internet: http://www.lemmermann.nexus.it/lemmermann/

AMOUNT: 750 euro per month
DEADLINE(S): MAR 15; SEP 30
FIELD(S): Italian/Roman studies in the subject areas of literature, archaeology, history of art

For university students who need to study in Rome to carry out research and prepare their theses concerning Rome and the Roman culture from the period Pre-Roman to present-day time in the subject areas above.

Contact above organization for details. Access Web site for application form.

812—U.S. INSTITUTE OF PEACE (National Peace Essay Contest)

1200 17th Street NW, Suite 200
Washington DC 20036
202/457-1700
FAX: 202/429-6063
E-mail: essay_contest@usip.org
Internet: http://www.usip.org

AMOUNT: $1,000-$10,000
DEADLINE(S): JAN
FIELD(S): Political Science; U.S. History

1,500-word essay contest for high school students on the U.S. response to international conflict. No restrictions as to citizenship/residency.

Not renewable. See Web site or contact USIP for specific guidelines.

813—UNIVERSITY OF MARYLAND (John B. and Ida Slaughter Endowed Scholarship in Science, Technology, and the Black Community)

2169 Lefrak Hall
College Park MD 20742-7225
301/405-1158
FAX: 301/314-986
Internet: http://www.bsos.umd.edu/aasp/scholarship.html

AMOUNT: Varies (in-state tuition costs)
DEADLINE(S): MAR
FIELD(S): Science and Technology AND African-American Studies

Open to African-Americans who are U.S. residents with a minimum 2.8 GPA. Must be accepted to or enrolled at UMCP for freshmen year and must submit letter of recommendation from high school counselor or UMCP faculty member. Should have an interest in applying science and technology to the problems of the Black community. Essay required.

Renewable. Contact the Center for Minorities in Science and Engineering at UMCP for an application.

814—UNIVERSITY OF WAIKATO, NEW ZEALAND (Rewi Alley Scholarship in Modern Chinese Studies)

The Postgraduate Studies and Scholarships Office, B Block Annex
Private Bag 3105
Hamilton NEW ZEALAND
07 856 2889 ext. 8964 or 6732
FAX: 07 838 4370
E-mail: scholarships@wakato.ac.nz
Internet: http://www.waikato.ac.nz

AMOUNT: $400
DEADLINE(S): AUG 31
FIELD(S): Study of China

For study and research on China at a New Zealand university or other approved institution.

Contact Scholarships Administrator, University of Waikato, at above location.

ART

815—ACADEMY OF CANADIAN CINEMA AND TELEVISION (Internship; National Apprenticeship Training Program)

172 King Street East
Toronto Ontario M5A 1J3 CANADA
800/644-5194
FAX: 416/366/8454
E-mail: cmaloney@academy.ca
Internet: http://www.academy.ca/Academy/About/GeneralACCTInfo.html

AMOUNT: $300 per week for 12 weeks
DEADLINE(S): FEB
FIELD(S): Film and Television Production and Management

Program designed to provide hands-on professional training to students in their graduating year from film and/or television diploma/degree programs. Must be Canadian citizen or landed immigrant studying full-time in Canada.

Six awards per year. Contact Christine Maloney for complete information.

816—ACADEMY OF MOTION PICTURE ARTS AND SCIENCES (Student Academy Awards)

8949 Wilshire Boulevard
Beverly Hills CA 90211-1972
310/247-3000 Ext. 130;
FAX:310/859-9351
E-mail: rmiller@oscars.org
Internet: http://www.oscars.org/saa/index.html

AMOUNT: $1,000, $1,500, and $2,000
DEADLINE(S): APR 1
FIELD(S): Film production: alternative, animation, documentary, or dramatic

Student academy awards competition is open to students enrolled at a U.S. college, university, film school, or art school. The film must have been made in a teacher-student relationship. No professional may be involved in the production.

Up to five awards each year. Award may not be used for educational purposes. Contact Richard Miller at above location or access Web site for complete information.

817—ADELPHI UNIVERSITY (Talent Awards)

1 South Avenue
Garden City NY 11530
516/877-3080 or 800/ADELPHI
Internet: http://www.ecampus.adelphi.edu/finaid/au_scholarships_grants.cfm#art

AMOUNT: $1,000-$7,000
DEADLINE(S): FEB 15
FIELD(S): Theater, Dance, Art, or Music

Various scholarships for full-time students at Adelphi University in the above fields. Must document financial need-fill out a FAFSA form. Must maintain 3.0 GPA in major and 2.5 overall to maintain scholarship.

See Web site for further information; contact school to apply.

818—ALLIANCE FOR YOUNG ARTISTS AND WRITERS, INC. (Scholastic Art and Writing Awards)

Scholastic, Inc.
555 Broadway
New York NY 10012-3999
212/343-6582 or 800-SCHOLASTIC
FAX: 212/343-4885
E-mail: A&Wgeneralinfo@scholastic.com
Internet: http://www.scholastic.com/artandwriting/about.htm
AMOUNT: Varies
DEADLINE(S): Varies (upon location)
FIELD(S): Art; Writing

For all students in grades 7-12 currently enrolled in a public or nonpublic school in the U.S., Canada, U.S. territories, or U.S.-sponsored schools abroad. Awards are available in 10 writing categories and 16 art categories. Publishing opportunities may be available for winning students in both art and writing categories.

1,000+ awards annually.

819—ALVIN M. BENTLEY FOUNDATION (Scholarship Program)

College of Literature, Science, and the Arts
The University of Michigan
500 S. State Street, #2522
Ann Arbor MI 48109
517/729-9040
FAX: 517/723-2454
E-mail: lsascholarship@umich.edu
AMOUNT: $7,500-$10,000 per year
DEADLINE(S): None
FIELD(S): Literature; Science; Arts

Open to Michigan residents applying as freshmen to the University of Michigan's College of Literature, Science, and the Arts. Based on academic excellence and extracurricular activities. Must be nominated; there are no separate applications. Candidates are chosen from U of M applications received from Michigan resident freshmen.

820—AMERICA-ISRAEL CULTURAL FOUNDATION (Sharett Scholarship Program)

51 E. 42nd Street, #400
New York NY 10017
212/557-1600
FAX: 212/557-1611
E-mail: usaaicf@aol.com
Internet: http://www.aicf.webnet.org/involved_overview.html
AMOUNT: Varies
DEADLINE(S): MAR 15
FIELD(S): Music, Dance, Theater, Visual Arts, Film and Television

Scholarships are for one year of study and are renewable.

800 scholarships per year. Write for complete information.

821—AMERICAN HISTORICAL ASSOCIATION (John E. O'Connor Film Award)

400 A Street SE
Washington DC 20003
E-mail: aha@theaha.org
Internet: http://www.theaha.org
AMOUNT: Varies
DEADLINE(S): Varies
FIELD(S): Filmmaking

This honorific award seeks to recognize outstanding interpretations of history through the medium of film or video. Films and videos may provide unique perspectives on the past using techniques that are different from those employed by the author of a book. The production should reflect such imaginative use of the medium.

822—AMERICAN INDIAN ARTS COUNCIL, INC.

Scholarship Committee
725 Preston Forest Shopping Center, Suite B
Dallas, TX 75230
(214) 891-9640
AMOUNT: $250-$1,000
Deadlines: MAR 1 and SEP 15
FIELD(S): Fine Arts

The Academic Scholarship Fund was created to encourage excellence in the study of fine arts, traditional/tribal arts, performing arts, visual arts, creative writing, communications arts, and arts administration by Native American students enrolled in institutions of higher learning. Need official tribal documentation, a 2.5 GPA, and a major in one of the Fine Arts.

823—AMERICAN INSTITUTE OF ARCHITECTS, NEW YORK CHAPTER (Douglas Haskell Award)

200 Lexington Avenue, 6th Floor
New York NY 10016
212/683-0023 ext. 14
FAX: 212/696-5022
E-mail: info@aiany.org
Internet: http://www.aiany.org/nyfoundation/scholarships.html
AMOUNT: $2,000 (minimum)
DEADLINE(S): MAR 21
FIELD(S): Architectural Writing

Awards to encourage fine writing on architecture and related design subjects and to foster regard for intelligent criticism among future professionals. For students enrolled in a professional architecture or related program, such as art history, interior design, urban studies, and landscape architecture. Submit a news story, an essay or feature article, book review, or journal accompanied by a 100-word statement describing the purpose of the piece.

Check Web site or contact AIANY at above location for complete information.

824—AMERICAN INTERCONTINENTAL UNIVERSITY (Emilio Pucci Scholarships)

Admissions Committee
3330 Peachtree Road NE
Atlanta GA 30326
404/812-8192 or 1-888/248-7392
AMOUNT: $1,800 (deducted from tuition over 6 quarters)
DEADLINE(S): None
FIELD(S): Fashion Design; Fashion Marketing; Interior Design; Commercial Art; Business Administration; Video Production

Scholarships are for high school seniors who are interested in either a 2-year or 4-year program at one of the campuses of the American Intercontinental University: Atlanta, GA; Los Angeles, CA; London, UK; or Dubai, United Arab Emirates. Scholarship is applied toward tuition.

Write for applications and complete information.

825—AMERICAN INTERCONTINENTAL UNIVERSITY (Emilio Pucci Scholarships)

Admissions Committee
3330 Peachtree Road NE
Atlanta GA 30326
404/812-8192 or 1-888/248-7392
AMOUNT: $1,800
DEADLINE(S): None
FIELD(S): Fashion Design; Fashion Marketing; Interior Design; Commercial Art; Video Production; Business Administration

Scholarships are for high school juniors or seniors who are interested in studying in the above fields at one of the campuses of the American Intercontinental University: Atlanta, GA; Los Angeles, CA; London, UK; or Dubai, United Arab Emirates.

Write or call for applications and complete information.

826—AMERICAN MOTHERS, INC. (Gertrude Fogelson Cultural and Creative Arts Awards)

1296 E. 21st Street
Brooklyn NY 11201
718/253-5676
AMOUNT: Up to $1,000
DEADLINE(S): JAN 1 (annually)
FIELD(S): Visual Arts, Creative Writing, and Vocal Music

An award to encourage and honor mothers in artistic pursuits.

Write to Alice Miller at above address for details.

827—AMERICAN SOCIETY OF INTERIOR DESIGNERS (Scholarship and Awards Program)

608 Massachusetts Avenue NE
Washington DC 20002-6006
202/546-3480
E-mail: education@asid.org
Internet: http://www.asid.org
AMOUNT: $750-$3,000
DEADLINE(S): MAR
FIELD(S): Interior Design

Several awards available to both undergraduates and graduate students studying the field of interior design. Portfolios and research papers are common submission material. Scholarships will be awarded on the basis of academic/creative accomplishment.

828—ART INSTITUTE OF CHICAGO (Student Academy Awards)

Columbus Drive at Jackson Boulevard
Chicago IL 60603
312/443-3735
Internet: http://www.oscars.org/saa
AMOUNT: Up to $2,000
DEADLINE(S): APR
FIELD(S): Filmmaking

The purpose of the Student Academy Awards competition is to support and encourage filmmakers with no previous professional experience who are enrolled in accredited colleges and universities. While professional advice may be requested and given during the making of student films, as a full-time student, the Academy believes that professional camera persons, directors, editors, and writers should not play any major role in the production of such films.

829—ASIFA (Helen Victoria Haynes World Peace Storyboard and Animation Contest)

c/o Donna Morse, School of Communications, Lake Superior Hall, Grand Valley State University
Allendale MI 49401
E-mail: HaynesWorldPeace@aol.com
Internet: http://www.swcp.com/animate/contest.htm
AMOUNT: $500 + software and ASIFA conference registration
DEADLINE(S): APR
FIELD(S): Animation; Cartooning

For high school and college students to design, draw, and mount a storyboard for an animated short for the Annual ASIFA/Central Conference and Retreat. The storyboard should depict your vision of how to achieve World Peace.

2 prize packages: 1 for high school students and 1 for college students. See Web site for official rules or contact Mary Lou Haynes at above address for more information.

830—BLUES HEAVEN FOUNDATION, INC. (Muddy Waters Scholarship)

2120 S. Michigan Avenue
Chicago IL 60616
312/808-1286
AMOUNT: $2,000
DEADLINE(S): APR 30
FIELD(S): Music; Music Education; African-American Studies; Folklore; Performing Arts; Arts Management; Journalism; Radio/TV/Film

Scholarship is made on a competitive basis with consideration given to scholastic achievement, concentration of studies, and financial need. Applicant must have full-time enrollment status in a Chicago area college/university in at least their first year of undergraduate studies or a graduate program. Scholastic aptitude extracurricular involvement, grade point average, and financial need are all considered.

Contact Blues Heaven Foundation, Inc. to receive an application between February and April.

831—BUENA VISTA COLLEGE NETWORK (Internships in Film Marketing)

3900 W. Alameda Avenue
Burbank CA 91505-4316
818/567-5000
E-mail: College_Network@studio.disney.com
AMOUNT: Varies
DEADLINE(S): None
FIELD(S): Fields of study related to the motion picture industry, including marketing and promotion

Internships for full-time college students age 18 and up interested in a career in a facet of the motion picture industry. Must have unlimited access to computer with modem and transportation, be able to work 4-6 hours per week and 2-3 weekends per month. Attend film openings and sneak previews. Evaluate various aspects via an interactive computer system. Compensation ranges from $30 to $60/month. Possible school credit.

Access Web site by writing "Buena Vista College Network" from Yahoo. Available in most states and parts of Canada. Details, an interactive application, and E-mail access are located on Web site.

832—CANADIAN PRINTING INDUSTRIES ASSN. (Scholarship Trust Fund)

75 Albert Street, Suite 906
Ottawa Ontario K1P 5E7 CANADA
613/236-7208; 800/267-7280
FAX: 613/236-8169
E-mail: Dominique@cpia-aci.ca
Internet: http://www.cpia-aci.ca/b-schol.html
AMOUNT: Canadian $1,250 per year
DEADLINE(S): JUN 30
FIELD(S): Printing; Graphic Arts

Open to undergraduates enrolled in their first year as a full-time student in a recognized Canadian 2-year, 3-year, or 4-year colleges or universities who are interested in a career in printing or graphic arts. Must maintain at least a B average. Part-time students and design or art majors are not eligible.

50 awards per year. Renewable. Write Dominique Laliberte, director of finance, for complete information.

833—CHARLES AND LUCILLE KING FAMILY FOUNDATION (Scholarships)

366 Madison Avenue, 10th Floor
New York NY 10017
212/682-2913
E-mail: info@kingfoundation.org
Internet: http://www.kingfoundation.org
AMOUNT: $2,500 (max.)
DEADLINE(S): APR 15
FIELD(S): Film; Television

Open to juniors, seniors, and graduate students who are majoring in television or film at four-year universities. Must demonstrate academic ability, financial need, and professional potential. Must submit transcripts, three letters of recommendation, and a typed personal statement.

Renewable. See your financial aid office or contact Foundation for an application.

834—COMMUNITY FOUNDATION OF WESTERN MASSACHUSETTS (Joseph Bonfitto Scholarship)

1500 Main Street
P.O. Box 15769
Springfield MA 01115
413/732-2858

AMOUNT: $2,000
DEADLINE(S): APR 15
FIELD(S): Creative Design; Advertising; Art

Open to graduating seniors of Agawam High School in Massachusetts who are pursuing a career through higher education in one of the above areas of study. Based on financial need, academic merit, and extracurricular activities. Must submit transcripts and fill out government FAFSA form.

1 award annually. Renewable with reapplication. Send self-addressed, stamped envelope to Community Foundation for an application and contact your financial aid office for FAFSA. Notification is in June.

835—COUNCIL FOR BASIC EDUCATION (Chinese Culture Fellowship)

1319 F. Street NW, Suite 900
Washington D.C. 20004
202/347-4171
FAX: 202/347-5047
E-mail: info@c-b-e.org
Internet: http://www.c-b-e.org/index.htm

AMOUNT: $1,000
DEADLINE(S): JUN
FIELD(S): Chinese Culture and Chinese Artistic Resources in New York City

Fellowships available to teams of two teachers (K-12)—one art teacher and one humanities teacher—to develop an interdisciplinary project that can be used to broaden the appreciation and understanding of Chinese culture and Chinese artistic resources in New York City. Teachers use web-based technology and make their material available to teachers nationally and internationally. A total of ten teachers or five teams will receive the award for six weeks of independent study during the summer.

Contact organization for details.

836—DISTRICT OF COLUMBIA COMMISSION ON THE ARTS and HUMANITIES (Grants)

410 Eighth Street NW, 5th Floor
Washington DC 20004
202/724-5613; TDD: 202/727-3148
FAX: 202/727-4135
Internet: http://www.dcarts.dc.gov/main.shtm

AMOUNT: Varies
DEADLINE(S): Varies
FIELD(S): Media, Visual Arts, Crafts

Applicants for grants must be professional artists and residents of Washington DC for at least one year prior to submitting application. Awards intended to generate art endeavors within the Washington DC community.

Open also to art organizations that train, exhibit, or perform within DC. Write for complete information.

837—EDFUND (Student Photography Contest)

Student Services
P.O. Box 419045
Rancho Cordova, CA 95741-9045
877/2EDFUND
Internet: http://www.edfund.org/photocontest/

AMOUNT: $1,000
DEADLINE(S): APR 30
FIELD(S): Photography

Open to all students presently enrolled in any university, college, community college, business, technology or trade school. Only black-and-white prints will be accepted. See Web site for details on submission and theme. Students may be at any point in their academic career.

838—ELIZABETH GREENSHIELDS FOUNDATION (Grants)

1814 Sherbrooke Street W., Suite 1
Montreal Quebec H3H 1E4
CANADA
514/937-9225
FAX: 514/937-0141
E-mail: egreen@total.net

AMOUNT: Canadian $10,000
DEADLINE(S): None
FIELD(S): Painting; Drawing; Printmaking; Sculpture

Grants are to aid artists in the early stages of their careers. Work must be representational or figurative. Applicants must have started or completed art school training and/or must demonstrate, through past work and future plans, a commitment to making art a lifetime career. Funds may be used for any art-related purpose: study, travel, studio rental, purchase of materials, etc.

45-55 awards annually. Contact Micheline Leduc, Administrator, for an application.

839—FASHION GROUP INTERNATIONAL OF GREATER WASHINGTON DC (Scholarships)

P.O. Box 71055
Chevy Chase MD 20813-1055
212/593-1715 (in New York)
Internet:
http://www.fgi.org/washington.htm

AMOUNT: Up to $2,500
DEADLINE(S): APR 1
FIELD(S): Fashion-related areas

Scholarships for students majoring in fashion-related fields. Must be permanent residents of the Greater Metropolitan Washington DC area. Must either graduate from high school in June and/or have been admitted to an accredited institution or be enrolled in a university or college as an undergraduate or graduate student.

Application form and details are available on Web site or contact organization for further information.

840—FIVE WINGS ARTS COUNCIL (Artist Mentor Scholarships for Students)

200 First Street NE
Staples MN 56479
218/894-5485
FAX: 218/894-3045
E-mail: mturner@ncscmn.org
Internet: http://www.fwac.org

AMOUNT: Up to $500
DEADLINE(S): OCT 15
FIELD(S): Literary Arts; Visual Arts; Music; Theater; Media Arts; Dance

Open to rural high school students in grades 9-12 who are enrolled in an independent school district within the counties of Cass, Crow Wing, Morrison, Todd, and Wadena, Minnesota. Each recipient is matched with a qualified mentor who will establish a study schedule with student. Award is based on creative potential, accomplishments in art, maturity, and personal motivation.

10 awards annually. Contact Mark Turner, Director, for details.

841—FLORIDA DEPARTMENT OF STATE-ARTS COUNCIL (Individual Artists' Fellowships)

Division Cultural Affairs; The Capitol
Tallahassee FL 32399-0250
850/487-2980
TT: 850/488-5779
FAX: 850/922-5259
Internet: http://www.dos.state.fl.us/dca/fellow.html

AMOUNT: $5,000
DEADLINE(S): JAN 14
FIELD(S): Dance; Folklife/Traditional Arts; Interdisciplinary; Literature (children's literature, fiction, poetry); Media Arts; Music/Composition; Theater; Visual Arts and Crafts

Open to legal residents of Florida who are creative artists of at least 18 years of age. May NOT be enrolled in any undergraduate or graduate degree-seeking program during fellowship period.

38 awards annually. Renewable with reapplication after four years since date of previous award. Contact Florida Arts Council for information packet. Notification during summer.

842—FOUNDATION OF LEXOGRAPHIC TECHNICAL ASSOCIATION (Flexographic Scholarship)

900 Marconi Avenue
Ronkonkoma NY 11779
516/737-6020
FAX: 516/737-6813
E-mail: education@flexography.org
Internet: http://www.fta-ffta.org

AMOUNT: $2,000
DEADLINE(S): Varies
FIELD(S): Graphic Communication-Flexography

Must have a GPA of at least 3.0 and be going to a school offering flexography as a course of study. Must be a high school senior going to college (proof required), or a college sophomore, junior, or senior.

Nineteen awards per year. Renewable.

843—GEORGE BIRD GRINNELL AMERICAN INDIAN CHILDREN'S FUND (Al Qoyawayma Award)

11602 Montague Court
Potomac MD 20854
301/424-2440
FAX: 301/424-8281
E-mail: Grinnell_Fund@MSN.com

AMOUNT: $1,000
DEADLINE(S): JUN 1
FIELD(S): Science; Engineering

Open to Native American undergraduate and graduate students majoring in science or engineering and who have demonstrated an outstanding interest and skill in any one of the arts. Must be American Indian/Alaska Native (documented with Certified Degree of Indian Blood), be enrolled in college/university, be able to demonstrate commitment to serving community or other tribal nations, and document financial need.

Contact Dr. Paula M. Mintzies, President, for an application after January 1.

844—HANDWEAVERS GUILD OF AMERICA, INC. (HGA and Dendel Scholarships)

Two Executive Concourse, Suite 201
3327 Duluth Highway
Duluth GA 30096-3301
770/495-7702
FAX: 770/495-7703
E-mail: weavespindye@compuserve.com
Internet: http://www.weavespindye.org

AMOUNT: Varies
DEADLINE(S): MAR 15
FIELD(S): Fiber Arts

Open to students enrolled in accredited undergraduate or graduate programs in the U.S.,its possessions, and Canada. Awards are for furthering education in the field of fiber arts, including training for research, textile history, and conservation. Based on artistic merit rather than on financial need. HGA Scholarship is restricted to tuition; Dendel Scholarship may also be used for materials or travel. Must submit transcripts and slides.

Contact HGA for an application. Awards made in June; money must be spent within one year of issue date, and written report on money use must be submitted.

845—HAROLD HYAM WINGATE FOUNDATION (Wingate Scholarships)

20-22 Stukeley Street, 2nd Floo
London WC2B 5LR ENGLAND UK
0171 465 1521
E-mail: clark@wingate.org.uk
Internet: http://www.wingate.org.uk/

AMOUNT: Up to 10,000 pounds/year
DEADLINE(S): FEB 1
FIELD(S): Creative Works

Financial support for individuals of great potential or proven excellence to develop original work of intellectual, scientific, artistic, social, or environmental value, and to outstanding talented musicians. Not for taught courses or for leading to professional qualifications, or for electives or for completing courses already begun or for a higher degree. For citizens of the United Kingdom or other Commonwealth countries, Ireland, Israel, or of European countries.

Must be age 24 or older. May be held for up to three years. Contact Faith Clark, administrator, for additional information. Application, details, and examples of previous awards available on Web site.

846—HAYSTACK MOUNTAIN SCHOOL OF CRAFTS (Scholarship Program)

Admissions Office
P.O. Box 518
Deer Isle ME 04627
207/348-2306
FAX: 207/348-2307
E-mail: haystack@haystack-mtn.org
Internet: http://www.haystack-mtn.org

AMOUNT: $500-$1,000
DEADLINE(S): MAR 25
FIELD(S): Crafts

Open to technical assistants and work-study students in graphics, ceramics, weaving, jewelry, glass, blacksmithing, fabric, or wood. Tenable for one of the six two- to three-week summer sessions at Haystack Mountain School. One year of graduate study or equivalent experience is required for TA applicants.

100 scholarships awarded annually. Must be 18 years of age or older.

847—ILLINOIS ARTS COUNCIL (Artists Fellowship Awards)

100 W. Randolph, Suite 10-500
Chicago IL 60601-3298
312/814-6750
E-mail: rose@arts.state.il.us
Internet: http://www.state.il.us/agency/iac/Guidelines/Fellowships/afa02pdf.pdf

AMOUNT: $7,000
DEADLINE(S): Varies
FIELD(S): Choreography, Crafts, Ethnic and Folk Arts, Interdisciplinary/Performance Art, Media Arts, Music Composition, Photography, Playwriting/Screenwriting, Poetry, Prose, and Visual Arts

The Artists Fellowship Program is the agency's major program for individual artist support. These awards are given annually to Illinois artists of exceptional talent in recognition of their outstanding work and commitment within the arts. Awards are made based upon the quality of the works submitted and the evolving professional accomplishments of the applicant.

848—INSTITUTE FOR HUMANE STUDIES (Summer Seminars Program)

3401 N. FairFAX: Drive, Suite 440
Arlington VA 22201-4432
703/993-4880 or 800/697-8799
FAX: 703/993-4890
E-mail: ihs@gmu.edu
Internet: http://www.TheIHS.org
AMOUNT: Free summer seminars, including room/board, lectures, seminar materials, and books
DEADLINE(S): MAR
FIELD(S): Social Sciences; Humanities; Law; Journalism; Public Policy; Education; Film; Writing; Economics; Philosophy

Open to college students, recent graduates, and graduate students who share an interest in learning and exchanging ideas about the scope of individual rights, free markets, the rule of law, peace, and tolerance.

See Web site for seminar information or to apply online or contact IHS for an application.

849—INSTITUTE OF INTERNATIONAL EDUCATION (Cintas Fellowship)

809 United Nations Plaza
New York NY 10017-3580
E-mail: cintas@iie.org
Internet: http://www.iie.org/cintas
AMOUNT: $10,000
DEADLINE(S): APR
FIELD(S): Fine Arts

Acknowledges outstanding creative accomplishments and encourages the further development of creative talents in the fields of architecture, literature, music composition, and the visual arts and photography. For artists of Cuban citizenship or direct descent who do not live in Cuba.

850—INTERMEDIA ARTS (Artist Opportunities)

2822 Lyndale Avenue S.
Minneapolis MN 55408
612/871-4444; FAX: 612/871-6927
E-mail: info@intermediaarts.org
Internet: http://www.intermediaarts.org
AMOUNT: Varies
DEADLINE(S): Varies
FIELD(S): Art

Projects, fellowships, and sponsorships are available to U.S. artists at all levels. Some have geographic restrictions and other criteria.

See Web site or contact Intermedia Arts for an information booklet.

851—IRISH ARTS COUNCIL (Awards and Opportunities)

70 Merrion Square
Dublin 2 IRELAND
+353 1 618 0200
FAX: +353 1 661 0349/676 1302
E-mail: info@artscouncil.ie
Internet: http://www.artscouncil.ie
AMOUNT: Varies (with program)
DEADLINE(S): Varies (with program)
FIELD(S): Creative Arts; Visual Arts; Performing Arts

Numerous programs open to young and established artists who are Irish citizens or legal residents. Purpose is to assist in pursuit of talents and recognize achievements.

See Web site or contact above address for an application.

852—JOHN K. and THIRZA F. DAVENPORT FOUNDATION (Scholarships in the Arts)

20 North Main Street
South Yarmouth MA 02664-3143
508/398-2293
FAX: 508/394-6765
Internet: http://www.davenportrealty.com/pdf/foundationapplication.pdf
AMOUNT: Varies
DEADLINE(S): JUL 15
FIELD(S): Theatre, Music, Art

For Barnstable County, Massachusetts residents in their last two years of undergraduate or graduate (preferred) study in visual or performing arts. Must demonstrate financial need.

6-8 awards annually. Renewable. Contact Mrs. Chris M. Walsh for more information.

853—KATE NEAL KINLEY MEMORIAL FELLOWSHIP

Chairperson, Kate Neal Kinley Memorial Fellowship Committee
University of Illinois, College of Fine & Applied Arts
115 Architecture Building
608 East Lorado Taft Drive
Champaign IL 61820
217/333-1661
AMOUNT: Up to $7,000
DEADLINE(S): JAN
FIELD(S): Fine Arts

For one-year of advanced study in the fine arts (architecture, art, or music) in the U.S. or overseas. Applicant must demonstrate a superior understanding in their field of study based on grades and submitted work.

854—KOSCIUSZKO FOUNDATION (Summer Sessions in Poland and Rome)

15 E. 65th Street
New York NY 10021-6595
212/734-2130
FAX: 212/628-4552
E-mail: thekf@pegasusnet.com;
Internet: http://www.kosciuszkofoundation.org
AMOUNT: Varies
DEADLINE(S): Varies
FIELD(S): Polish Studies; History; Literature; Art; Economics; Social Studies; Language; Culture

Open to undergraduate and graduate students, graduating high school students who are 18 or older, and persons of any age who are not enrolled in a college/university program. Study programs are offered in Poland and Rome from mid-June through the end of August in above fields. Must be U.S. citizen/permanent resident.

See Web site or send a self-addressed, stamped envelope to Addy Tymczyszyn, Summer Studies Abroad Coordinator, for an application.

855—LADIES AUXILIARY TO THE VETERANS OF FOREIGN WARS OF THE UNITED STATES (Young American Creative Patriotic Art Awards)

406 West 34th Street
Kansas City MO 64111
816/561-8655
FAX: 816/931-4753
Internet: http://www.ladiesauxvfw.com
AMOUNT: $10,000-first, $5,000-second, $2,500-third
DEADLINE(S): FEB 15
FIELD(S): Art

An opportunity for high school students to display their artistic talents and to demonstrate their American patriotism while at the same time being eligible to compete for educational funds. Art must be on paper or canvas. Watercolor, pencil, pastel, charcoal, tempera, crayon, acrylic, pen-and-ink, or oil may be used.

856—LIBERACE FOUNDATION FOR THE PERFORMING AND CREATIVE ARTS (Scholarship Fund)

1775 East Tropicana Avenue
Las Vegas NV 89119-6529
702/798-5595; FAX: 702/798-7386
E-mail: foundation@liberace.org
Internet: http://www.liberace.org

AMOUNT: Varies
DEADLINE(S): MAR 15
FIELD(S): Music; Theater; Dance; Visual Arts

Provides grants to accredited INSTITUTIONS that offer training in above fields. Grants are to be used exclusively for scholarship assistance to talented and deserving students. Recipients should be promising and deserving upperclassmen (junior, senior, graduate) enrolled in a course of study leading up to a career in the arts.

NO DIRECT-TO-STUDENT GRANTS ARE MADE. Student's school must apply on their behalf. See Web site or write to above address for details.

857—LIGHT WORK (Artist-in-Residence Program)

316 Waverly Avenue
Syracuse NY 13244
315/443-1300
FAX: 315/443-9516
E-mail: cdlight@syearedu
Internet: http://www.lightwork.org/residency/resinfo.html

AMOUNT: $2,000 stipend
DEADLINE(S): None
FIELD(S): Photography

Career support for mid-career professional artists from around the world working with photography or digital imaging. Residency is for one month, and financial need is NOT considered.

12-15 awards annually. Not renewable. There is no application form or deadline. Artists interested in applying should send a letter of intent, current resume, statement about their work, and slides of their most recent work or current project.

858—MEMPHIS COLLEGE OF ART (Portfolio Awards)

Overton Park
1930 Poplar Avenue
Memphis TN 38104-2764
800/727-1088
E-mail: admissions@mca.edu
Internet: http://www.mca.edu/index.cfm

AMOUNT: Half tuition
DEADLINE(S): Varies (NOV 15 through JUL 31)
FIELD(S): Visual Arts

Awards are given to excellent visual art portfolios submitted by either high school students or transfer students. Awards to be used for full-time enrollment at Memphis College of Art. International students are welcome.

Two half-tuition scholarships are awarded annually based on excellence and irrespective of need. Additional aid is available based on need.

859—METROPOLITAN MUSEUM OF ART (Internships)

1000 Fifth Avenue
New York NY 10028-0198
212/570-3710
E-mail: mmainterns@metmuseum.org
Internet: http://www.metmuseum.org/education/er_internship.asp

AMOUNT: $2,500-$20,000 for certain longer programs
DEADLINE(S): JAN; FEB
FIELD(S): Art History

Internships for undergraduates and graduates who intend to pursue careers in art museums. Programs vary in length and requirements. Interns work in curatorial, education, conservation, administration, or library department of museum. Some require demonstration of economic need. Duration ranges from nine weeks to ten months. Volunteer positions also available.

860—MINNESOTA STATE ARTS BOARD (Grants Program)

Park Square Court
400 Sibley Street; Suite 200
St. Paul MN 55101-1928
651/215-1600 or 800/8MN-ARTS
FAX: 651/215-1602
E-mail: msab@arts.state.mn.us
Internet: http://www.arts.state.mn.us/index.html

AMOUNT: $8,000 (fellowships); $500-$1,500 (grants)
DEADLINE(S): AUG (Visual Arts); SEP (Music and Dance); OCT (Literature and Theater)
FIELD(S): Literature; Music; Theater; Dance; Visual Arts

Fellowships and career opportunity grants are open to professional artists who are residents of Minnesota. Grants may NOT be used for support of tuition or work toward any degree.

Contact MSAB for an application.

861—NATIONAL COWBOY HALL OF FAME (John F. & Anna Lee Stacey Scholarship Fund for Art Education)

1700 Northeast 63rd Street
Oklahoma City OK 73111
Internet: http://www.cowboyhalloffame.org

AMOUNT: $5,000
DEADLINE(S): FEB
FIELD(S): Painting

Scholarships for students in the U.S. and abroad who are serious in their study of conservative art, namely, painting and drawing. The recipient may use the funds granted in any way he or she wishes to further art education along conservative lines.

862—NATIONAL FOUNDATION FOR ADVANCEMENT IN THE ARTS (Arts Recognition and Talent Search)

800 Brickell Avenue
Miami FL 33131
800/970-ARTS or 305/377-1140
FAX: 305/377-1149
E-mail: info@nfaa.org
Internet: http://www.ARTSawards.org

AMOUNT: $100-$3,000
DEADLINE(S): OCT 1
FIELD(S): Creative and Performing Arts

Talent contest for high school seniors and 17- to 18-year-olds in dance, jazz, music, photography, theatre, visual arts, voice, and writing. Except for those applying in Music/Jazz, applicants must be U.S. citizens or permanent residents. May apply in more than one category, but only one financial award will be given to any individual, and a fee is required for each category in which student applies.

$35 application fee ($25 if apply by June 1); fee may be waived if you are unable to meet this requirement). 400 awards annually. Not renewable. Contact NFAA for an application packet.

863—NATIONAL GARDEN CLUBS, INC. (Scholarships)

4401 Magnolia Avenue
St. Louis MO 63110-3492
314/776-7574

FAX: 314/776-5108
E-mail: renee_blaschke@juno.com
Internet: http://www.gardenclub.org
AMOUNT: $3,500
DEADLINE(S): MAR 1
FIELD(S): Horticulture, Floriculture, Landscape Design, City Planning, Land Management, and allied subjects.

Open to juniors, seniors, and graduate students who are U.S. citizens and are studying any of the above or related subjects. Student must have the endorsement of the state in which he/she resides permanently. Applications will be forwarded to the National State Chairman and judged on a national level.

30-35 scholarships are awarded. Write to the above address for complete information.

864—NATIONAL LEAGUE OF AMERICAN PEN WOMEN, INC. (Scholarships for Mature Women)

1300 Seventeenth Street NW
Washington DC 20036
202/785-1997
Internet: http://www.cooper.edu/admin/career_services/fellowships/mature.html
AMOUNT: $1,000
DEADLINE(S): JAN 15 (even-numbered years)
FIELD(S): Art; Music; Creative Writing

The National League of American Pen Women gives three $1,000 grants in even-numbered years to women aged 35 and over.

Send SASE for details at the above address.

865—NATIONAL PTA (Reflections Program)

330 N. Wabash Avenue; Suite 2100
Chicago IL 60611-3690
800/307-4PTA or 312/670-6782
FAX: 312/670-6783
E-mail: info@pta.org
Internet: http://www.pta.org
AMOUNT: Varies
DEADLINE(S): Varies
FIELD(S): Literature; Musical Composition; Photography; Visual Arts

Open to students in preschool through grade twelve to express themselves and to receive positive recognition for their artistic efforts. Young artists can get involved in the Reflections Program of their local PTA or PTSA. Any PTA/PTSA in good standing can sponsor a Reflections Program. Rules and deadlines differ from PTA to PTA and from state to state.

Contact your state PTA office for information about the Reflections Program in your area.

866—NATIONAL SCULPTURE SOCIETY (Awards & Scholarships)

1177 Avenue of the Americas
New York NY 10036
212/764-5645
Internet: http://www.nationalsculpture.org/
AMOUNT: Up to $1,000
DEADLINE(S): APR
FIELD(S): Sculpture

For students of figurative or representational sculpture. Young artists are also eligible for the National Sculpture competition through this society, including prizes given for a figure modeling competition and other Young Sculptor Awards given based on jurying of slides. See Web site for other scholarship opportunities.

867—NAVAL HISTORICAL CENTER (Internship Program)

Washington Navy Yard
901 M Street, SE
Washington DC 20374-5060
202/433-6901
FAX: 202/433-8200
E-mail: efurgol@nhc.navy.mil
Internet: http://www.history.navy.mil
AMOUNT: $400 possible honoraria; otherwise, unpaid
DEADLINE(S): None
FIELD(S): Education; History; Public Relations; Design

Registered students of colleges/universities and graduates thereof are eligible for this program, which must be a minimum of 3 weeks, full- or part-time. Four specialities available: Curator, Education, Public Relations, and Design. Interns receive orientation and assist in their departments, and must complete individual project which contributes to Center. Must submit a letter of recommendation, unofficial transcript, and writing sample of not less than 1,000 words.

Contact Dr. Edward M. Furgol, Curator, for an application.

868—NEW YORK STATE THEATRE INSTITUTE (Internships in Theatrical Production)

155 River Street
Troy NY 12180
518/274-3573
E-mail: nysti@crisny.org
Internet: http://www.crisny.org/not-for-profit/nysti/int.htm
AMOUNT: None
DEADLINE(S): None
FIELD(S): Fields of study related to theatrical production, including box office and PR

Internships for college students, high school seniors, and educators-in-residence interested in developing skills in above fields. Unpaid, but college credit is earned. Located at Russell Sage College in Troy, NY. Gain experience in box office, costumes, education, electrics, music, stage management, scenery, properties, performance, and public relations. Interns come from all over the world.

Must be associated with an accredited institution. See Web site for more information. Call Ms. Arlene Leff, Intern Director at above location. Include your postal mailing address.

869—NOVA SCOTIA COLLEGE OF ART AND DESIGN (Scholarships)

5163 Duke Street
HaliFAX: Nova Scotia B3J 3J6
CANADA
902/494-8129
FAX: 902/425-2987
E-mail: ann@nscad.ns.ca
Internet: http://www.nscad.ns.ca
AMOUNT: $450-$13,500
DEADLINE(S): Varies
FIELD(S): Art; Fine Arts

The Nova Scotia College of Art and Design administers a number of scholarships and bursary awards that acknowledge high achievement and special promise. Awards restricted to students accepted to or officially registered at the college.

Contact L. Ann Read, Student Services, at above address for school catalog and details on specific scholarships.

870—OUTDOOR WRITERS ASSOCIATION OF AMERICA (OWAA Scholarship Awards)

121 Hickory Street
Missoula MT 59801
406/728-7434
FAX: 406/728-7445
E-mail: owaaa@montana.com
Internet: http://www.owaa.org
AMOUNT: $2,500-$3,500
DEADLINE(S): MAR 1
FIELD(S): Outdoor Communications: Print, Film, Art, Broadcasting, etc.

Open to junior and senior undergraduates and graduate students in above fields. Must attend an accredited school of journalism or mass communications that has registered with OWAA as a scholarship program participant. Based on career goals in outdoor communications, examples of work, letters of recommendation, and academic achievement. Must be U.S. or Canadian citizen/permanent resident.

3+ awards annually. Contact your school or send a self-addressed, stamped envelope to Steve Wagner, Executive Director, for guidelines.

871—PERMANENT GROUP (Portia Geach Memorial Award)

Level 3, 35 Clarence Street
Sydney NSW 2000 AUSTRALIA
(02)8295 8316
FAX: (02)8295 8496
E-mail: gabrielle.steinhoff@permanentgroup.com.au
Internet: http://www.permanentgroup.com.au/
AMOUNT: Aus. $18,000
DEADLINE(S): AUG 28
FIELD(S): Portrait Painting

Award for a female painter who is an Australia resident, either Australian-born or British-born. Portrait is to be of a person distinguished in arts, letters, or sciences; self-portraits are accepted.

$30 entry fee per painting. Contact Gabrielle Steinhoff, trust administrator, for more information/entry form.

872—PIXAR ANIMATION STUDIOS (Summer Internships)

1200 Park Avenue
Emeryville CA 94608
FAX: 510/725-3151
E-mail: hr@pixar.com
Internet: http://www.pixar.com
AMOUNT: Varies
DEADLINE(S): MAR
FIELD(S): Animation

Summer internships offer "hands on" experience for currently enrolled college/university students, based on departmental needs. Send a resume with name/address/phone, position, work experience/education, internships, and hardware/software experience. Must also submit reels: VHS (NTSC or PAL) or 3/4" (NTSC), 5 minutes in length starting with most recent work, music optional-visual skills nicer, and credit list explaining your reel and software used.

See Web site for details/available positions.

873—PRINT AND GRAPHICS FOUNDATION (Scholarship)

200 Deer Run Road
Sewickley PA 15143-2600
412/741-6860
E-mail: pgsf@gatf.org
Internet: http://www.gatf.org
AMOUNT: $500-$1,000
DEADLINE(S): APR
FIELD(S): Printing

For students pursuing careers in graphic communications, printing, or publishing.

874—RHYTHM and HUES STUDIOS (Computer Graphics Scholarship)

5404 Jandy Place
Los Angeles CA 90066
310/448-7500
E-mail: scholarship@rhythm.com
Internet: http://www.rhythm.com/recruiting/scholarship/index.html
AMOUNT: $1,000-$4,000
DEADLINE(S): Mid JUN
FIELD(S): Computer Modeling; Computer Character Animation; Digital Cinematography

Open to all students enrolled full-time in an accredited undergraduate or graduate degree program within six months of the deadline. Entries should include cover sheet stating name, address, phone, SSN, school, major, faculty advisor name/ address/phone, and category under which entry is being submitted. Also include photocopy of current student ID and typewritten description of entry, including hardware/software used.

1 award in modeling, 1 in animation, and 3 in cinematography; 1 $4,000 grant also goes to each winner's academic department. Contact Rhythm and Hues Studios for more information.

875—RIPON COLLEGE (Performance/Recognition Tuition Scholarships)

Admissions Office
300 Seward Street
P.O. Box 248
Ripon WI 54971
920/748-8101
E-mail: adminfo@ripon.edu
Internet: http://www.ripon.edu
AMOUNT: $5,000-$10,000/year
DEADLINE(S): MAR 1
FIELD(S): Music; Forensics; Art; Theater

Open to undergraduate and graduate students attending or planning to attend Ripon College. Purpose is to recognize and encourage academic potential and accomplishment in above fields. Interview, audition, or nomination may be required.

Renewable. Contact Office of Admission for an application.

876—ROSE HILL COLLEGE (Louella Robinson Memorial Scholarship)

P.O. Box 3126
Aiken SC 29802-3126
800/684-3769
FAX: 803/641-0240
E-mail: rosehill@rosehill.edu
Internet: http://www.rosehill.edu
AMOUNT: $10,000/year for four years
DEADLINE(S): Varies
FIELD(S): Liberal arts and humanities curricula

For undergraduate residents of Indian River County, Florida, to attend Rose Hill College in Aiken, South Carolina. The school offers a liberal arts education and follows the Great Books curriculum, a program of reading and seminars.

One annual award. Applicants must meet entry requirements of RHC. Contact above location for details.

877—ROSE HILL COLLEGE (Scholarships for Children of Eastern Orthodox Priests/Deacons)

P.O. Box 3126
Aiken SC 29802-3126
800/684-3769
FAX: 803/641-0240
E-mail: rosehill@rosehill.edu
Internet: http://www.rosehill.edu
AMOUNT: Full scholarship: $10,000/year for four years
DEADLINE(S): Varies
FIELD(S): Liberal Arts and Humanities Curricula

For undergraduates who are children of Eastern Orthodox Christan priests or deacons to attend Rose Hill College in Aiken, South Carolina. The school offers a liberal arts education and follows the Great Books Curriculum, a program of reading and seminars.

6-10 annual awards. Applicants must meet entry requirements of RHC. Contact above location for details.

878—ROSE HILL COLLEGE (Scholarships for the Homeschooled)

P.O. Box 3126
Aiken SC 29802-3126
800/684-3769

FAX: 803/641-0240
E-mail: rosehill@rosehill.edu
Internet: http://www.resehill.edu
AMOUNT: Full scholarship: $10,000/year for four years
DEADLINE(S): Varies
FIELD(S): Liberal Arts and Humanities Curricula

For undergraduates who have been homeschooled for three of the last five years of their high school education. For use at Rose Hill College in Aiken, South Carolina. The school offers a liberal arts education and follows the Great Books Curriculum, a program of reading and seminars. Scholarships will be awarded primarily on the basis of an essay which the student will be asked to write.

Four annual awards. Applicants must meet entry requirements of RHC. Contact above location for details.

879—SMITHSONIAN INSTITUTION (Minority Student Internship Program)

Office of Fellowships
750 9th Street NW, Suite 9300
Washington DC 20560-0902
202/275-0655
FAX: 202/275-0489
E-mail: siofg@ofg.si.edu
Internet: http://www.si.edu/research+study
AMOUNT: $350/week + possible travel expenses
DEADLINE(S): Varies
FIELD(S): Humanities; Environmental and Cultural Studies; Natural History; Earth Science; Art History; Biology

Ten-week, full-time internships in residence at the Smithsonian are open to U.S. minority students who wish to participate in research or museum-related activities in above and related fields. Must be undergraduates or beginning graduate students with a minimum 3.0 GPA. Must submit essay, resume, and official transcript.

Contact the Office of Fellowships or see Web site for an application.

880—SMITHSONIAN INSTITUTION-COOPER-HEWITT, NATIONAL DESIGN MUSEUM (Peter Krueger Summer Internships)

2 E. 91st Street
New York NY 10128-6990
212/849-8380
FAX: 212/860-6909
E-mail: edu@ch.si.edu
Internet: http://www.si.edu/ndm/
AMOUNT: $2,500 stipend
DEADLINE(S): MAR 15
FIELD(S): Art History; Architectural History; Museum Studies; Museum Education; Design

This ten-week (June-August) internship is open to college students considering a career in one of the above fields as well as graduate students who have not yet completed their M.A. degree. Interns are assigned to specific curatorial, education, or administrative departments where they will assist on special research or exhibition projects, as well as participate in daily museum activities. Housing NOT provided.

To apply, submit resume, transcript, 2 letters of recommendation, and 1- to 2-page essay on interest. Contact the Intern Coordinator for details. Notification by April 30.

881—SMITHSONIAN INSTITUTION-COOPER-HEWITT, NATIONAL DESIGN MUSEUM (Summer Internships)

Education Dept.
2 E. 91st Street
New York NY 10128-6990
212/849-8404
AMOUNT: $2,500 stipend
DEADLINE(S): MAR 31
FIELD(S): Design and Applied Arts; Exhibition Development; Library Services; Collections Management; Museum Registration; Museum Education

This ten-week summer internship (June-August) is open to those who have completed at least two years of college who wish to gain experience at Cooper-Hewitt in such museum operations as research in above fields.

Contact the Internship Coordinator for an application.

882—SMITHSONIAN INSTITUTION-FREER/SACKLER GALLERIES (Dick Louie Memorial Internship for Americans of Asian Descent)

Education Dept.
Washington DC 20560-0707
202/357-4880; TTY: 202/786-2374
Internet: http://www.asia.si.edu
AMOUNT: Stipend
DEADLINE(S): Varies
FIELD(S): Asian Art; Art History; Museum Studies

This summer internship is an opportunity for high school students of Asian descent to gain practical experience in a museum setting. Must be entering or completing senior year of high school, and must live and attend high school in the Washington metropolitan area.

Contact the Internship Coordinator for an application.

883—SOCIETY FOR TECHNICAL COMMUNICATION (Undergraduate Scholarships)

901 N. Stuart Street, Suite 904
Arlington VA 22203
703/522-4114
FAX: 703/522-2075
E-mail: stc@stcva.org
Internet: http://www.stcva.org/scholarships.html
AMOUNT: $2,000
DEADLINE(S): FEB 15
FIELD(S): Technical Communication

Open to full-time undergraduate students who have completed at least one year of study and are enrolled in an accredited 2- or 4-year degree program for career in any area of technical communication: technical writing, editing, graphic design, multimedia art, etc.

Awards tenable at recognized colleges and universities in U.S. and Canada. Fourteen awards per year—7 undergraduate and seven graduate. See Web site and/or write for complete information.

884—SOCIETY OF ILLUSTRATORS (Student Scholarship Competition)

128 E. 63rd Street
New York NY 10021
212/838-2560
FAX: 212/838-2561
AMOUNT: Varies
DEADLINE(S): FEB 1
FIELD(S): Illustration; Cartooning; Animation; Graphic Design

Cash awards are given to selected college-level art students who enter an annual juried exhibition.

Chairmen of college-level art programs should request, on school letterhead, the "Call for Entries" for the Student Scholarship Competition. Individual student inquiries will NOT be honored.

885—SOLOMON R. GUGGENHEIM MUSEUM (Internship Programs)

1071 Fifth Avenue
New York NY 10128-0173
212/423-3526
E-mail: education@guggenheim.org
AMOUNT: Varies (some positions nonpaid)
DEADLINE(S): FEB 15 (Summer); MAY 15 (Fall); NOV 1 (Spring)

FIELD(S): Art Administration; Art History

Various internships, which offer practical museum training experience, are available for undergraduates, recent graduates, and graduate students in art history, administration, conservation, education, and related fields. Location varies, including New York, Italy, and Spain. Housing NOT included. Cover letter, resume, transcripts, letters of recommendation, list of foreign languages/relevant coursework, and essay (less than 500 words, describing interest) required.

Contact the Internship Coordinator, Education Department, at the Museum for details of each internship and application procedures.

886—SONOMA CHAMBOLLE-MUSIGNY SISTER CITIES, INC. (Henri Cardinaux Memorial Scholarship)

Chamson Scholarship Committee
P.O. Box 1633
Sonoma CA 95476-1633
707/939-1344
FAX: 707/939-1344
E-mail: Baileysci@vom.com

AMOUNT: Up to $1,500 (travel + expenses)
DEADLINE(S): JUL 15
FIELD(S): Culinary Arts; Wine Industry; Art; Architecture; Music; History; Fashion

Hands-on experience working in above or similar fields and living with a family in small French village in Burgundy or other French city. Must be Sonoma County, CA, resident at least 18 years of age and be able to communicate in French. Transcripts, employer recommendation, photograph, and essay (stating why, where, and when) required.

1 award. Nonrenewable. Also offers opportunity for candidate in Chambolle-Musigny to obtain work experience and cultural exposure in Sonoma, CA.

887—TELETOON (Animation Scholarship Award Competition)

BCE Place
787 Bay Street
P.O. Box 787
Toronto Ontario M5J 2T3 CANADA
416/956-2060
E-mail: pascaleg@teletoon.com
Internet: http://www.teletoon.com

AMOUNT: $1,500-$4,000
DEADLINE(S): MAY 14
FIELD(S): Animation

For young Canadian talent to pursue studies and embark on career in animation. Based on whose work best embodies development and promotion of original animated content and those who become innovators in their field. Additional grand prize goes to student for overall commitment, creativity, accomplishment, and passion for animation. Entrance Scholarships for high schools students, Continuing Ed Scholarships for college, and Most Promising Student for graduating college students.

10 awards annually. See Web site or contact Teletoon for official rules.

888—THE ART INSTITUTES INTERNATIONAL (Evelyn Keedy Memorial Scholarship)

300 Sixth Avenue, Suite 800
Pittsburgh PA 15222-2598
412/562-9800
FAX: 412/562-9802
E-mail: webadmin@aii.edu
Internet: http://www.aii.edu

AMOUNT: 2 years full tuition
DEADLINE(S): MAY 1
FIELD(S): Various fields in the creative and applied arts: video production, broadcasting, culinary arts, fashion design, Web site administration, etc.

Scholarships at 12 different locations nationwide in various fields described above. For graduating high school seniors admitted to an Arts Institutes International School, the New York Restaurant School, or NCPT. Transcripts, letters of recommendation, and resume must be submitted with application.

See Web site or contact AII for more information.

889—THE CHRISTOPHERS (Video Contest)

12 East 48th Street
New York NY 10017
212/759-4050
FAX: 212/838-5073
E-mail: youth-coordinator@christophers.org
Internet: http://www.christophers.org

AMOUNT: $3,000 (first prize); $2,000 (second); $1,000 (third); 5 $1,000 honorable mentions + all winners aired nationwide on TV series "Christopher Closeup"
DEADLINE(S): MID JUN
FIELD(S): Film and Video

Contest for college students in good standing to use any style or format to create on film or video an image expressing the annual theme in five minutes or less. Entries must be submitted on 3/4" VHS cassette ONLY, labeled with entry title, length, name, and address of entrant. Official entry form must be included. Contest judged on ability to capture theme, artistic/technical proficiency, and adherence to rules.

Winners notified in September. See Web site for an official entry form and/or current year's theme.

890—THE LEMMERMANN FOUNDATION (Fondazione Lemmermann Scholarship Awards)

c/o Studio Associato Romanelli
via Cosseria, 5
00192 Roma ITALY
(06) 324.30.23
FAX: (06) 322.17.88
E-mail: lemmermann@mail.nexus.it
Internet: http://www.lemmermann.nexus.it/lemmermann/

AMOUNT: 750 euro per month
DEADLINE(S): MAR 15; SEP 30
FIELD(S): Italian/Roman studies in the subject areas of literature, archaeology, history of art

For university students who need to study in Rome to carry out research and prepare their theses concerning Rome and the Roman culture from the period Pre-Roman to present-day time in the subject areas above.

Contact above organization for details. Access Web site for application form.

891—THE REUTER FOUNDATION (The Peter Sullivan Memorial Fellowships for News Graphics Journalists)

The Director, 85 Fleet Street
London EC4P 4AJ ENGLAND
(+44) 20 7542 7015
E-mail: rtrfoundation@easynet.co.uk

AMOUNT: Travel, tuition, and living allowance
DEADLINE(S): SEP 30
FIELD(S): Journalism-news graphics

Fellowships for working, full-time news graphics journalists with at least five years experience. The three-month program offers an opportunity for talented news graphic journalists and designers to create a university study plan suited to their individual needs. Must be fluent in either Spanish or English.

Access Web site or write for application details. Application form is on Web site.

892—THE WALT DISNEY COMPANY (American Teacher Awards)

P.O. Box 9805
Calabasas CA 91372
AMOUNT: $2,500 (36 awards); $25,000 (Outstanding Teacher of the Year)
DEADLINE(S): FEB 15
FIELD(S): Teachers: Athletic Coach, Early Childhood, English, Foreign Language/ESL, General Elementary, Mathematics, Performing Arts, Physical Education/Health, Science, Social Studies, Visual Arts, Vo-Tech Education

Awards for K-12 teachers in the above fields.

Teachers, or anyone who knows a great teacher, can write for applications at the above address.

893—UNITARIAN UNIVERSALIST ASSOCIATION (Musicians' Network Scholarships)

4190 Front Street
San Diego CA 92103
Written Inquiry
AMOUNT: $100-$700
DEADLINE(S): VARIES
FIELD(S): Art, Poetry, Music

Financial aid to undergraduate students in the above fields. Must be active with the Unitarian Universalist Association.

Renewable. Write for complete information.

894—UNIVERSITY FILM ANd VIDEO ASSOCIATION (Carole Fielding Student Grants)

Professor Robert Johnson
Framington State College
100 State Street
Framington MA 01701
Internet: http://www.uvfa.org
AMOUNT: $1,000 to $4,000
DEADLINE(S): JAN 1
FIELD(S): Film, video, multi-media production

Open to undergraduate/graduate students. Categories are narrative, experimental, animation, documentary, multi-media. Applicant must be sponsored by a faculty member who is an active member of the University Film and Video Association.

Write to the above address for application and complete details.

895—UNIVERSITY FILM AND VIDEO FOUNDATION (Kodak Scholarship Endowment Fund)

SMPTE
595 W. Hartsdale Avenue
White Plains NY 10607
Internet: http://www.kodak.com
AMOUNT: $5,000 (max.)
DEADLINE(S): Varies (spring)
FIELD(S): Cinematography

Open to junior, senior, and graduate-level students of cinematography at U.S. colleges and universities offering four-year degree programs in motion picture filmmaking (BA, BFA, MA, or MFA). Nomination requires endorsement of the applicant's school's faculty/administration as to the outstanding potential and cinematographic ability of the student. School must conduct portfolio review to nominate up to two candidates.

896—UNIVERSITY OF ILLINOIS AT URBANA-CHAMPAIGN (Lydia E. Parker Bates Scholarship)

620 East John Street
Champaign IL 61820
217/333-0100
Internet: http://www.uiuc.edu/
AMOUNT: Up to $1,000
DEADLINE(S): MAR 15
FIELD(S): Art, Architecture, Landscape Architecture, Urban Planning, Dance, Theater, and all related subjects except Music.

Open to undergraduate students in the College of Fine and Applied Arts who are attending the University of Illinois at Urbana-Champaign. Must demonstrate financial need and have 2.85 GPA. Complete the Free Application for Federal Student Aid with UIUC admission application.

175 awards per year. Recipients must carry at least 12 credit hours per semester. Contact office of student financial aid for application.

897—VIRGINIA MUSEUM OF FINE ARTS (Fellowships)

2800 Grove Avenue
Richmond VA 23221-2466
804/204-2661
Internet: http://vmfa.state.va.us
AMOUNT: $4,000 (undergrads-max.); $6,000 (grads); $8,000 (professionals)
DEADLINE(S): MAR 1
FIELD(S): Crafts; Drawing; Filmmaking; Painting; Photography; Printmaking; Sculpture; Video; Art History (graduate only)

Open to Virginia residents of at least one year who are U.S. citizens or legal residents. Fellowships are available to undergraduates, graduates, and professional artists. Financial need is considered.

Contact VMFA for an application.

898—WHITTIER COLLEGE (Talent Scholarship)

13406 E. Philadelphia Street
Whittier CA 90608
562/907-4285
FAX: 562/464-4560
E-mail: admission@whittier.edu
Internet: http://www.whittier.edu
AMOUNT: $5,000-$10,000
DEADLINE(S): FEB 1
FIELD(S): Art, Music, Theater

Eligibility based on portfolio or audition submissions judged by music, art, or theater department.

Write above address for complete information.

899—WOMEN'S STUDIO WORKSHOP (Fellowship Grants)

P.O. Box 489
New York NY 12472
845/658-9133
FAX: 845/658-9031
E-mail: wsw@ulster.net
Internet: http://www.wsworkshop.org/
AMOUNT: Tuition
DEADLINE(S): MAR 15; NOV 1
FIELD(S): Visual Arts

WSW Fellowship Grants are designed to provide concentrated work time for artists to explore new ideas in a dynamic and supportive community of women artists. WSW welcomes applications from emerging artists.

The facilities feature complete studios in intaglio, silkscreen, hand papermaking, photography, letterpress, and clay (a new addition to the WSW Fellowship program). Two- to six-week sessions are available each year from September through June.

900—WORLDSTUDIO FOUNDATION (Scholarship Program)

225 Varick Street, 9th Floor
New York NY 10014
212/366-1317
FAX: 212/807-0024
E-mail: scholarships@worldstudio.org
Internet: http://www.worldstudio.org
AMOUNT: $1,000-$5,000
DEADLINE(S): APR 27
FIELD(S): Visual arts

Worldstudio Foundation provides scholarships to minority and economically disadvantaged students who are studying the design/architecture/arts disciplines in American colleges and universities. These fields include architecture, arts, fashion design, filmmaking, graphics/graphic arts/printing, interior design, landscape architecture.

Application Requirements: application, essay, financial need analysis, photo, portfolio, references, self-addressed stamped envelope, transcript.

ENGLISH LANGUAGE AND LITERATURE

901—ACADEMY OF MOTION PICTURE ARTS AND SCIENCES (Nicholl Fellowships in Screenwriting)

8949 Wilshire Boulevard
Beverly Hills CA 90211-1972
310/247-3000
E-mail: nicholl@oscars.org
Internet: http://www.oscars.org/nicholl

AMOUNT: $30,000
DEADLINE(S): MAY 1
FIELD(S): Screenwriting

Academy awards competition is open to any screenwriter who has not sold any form of a screenplay for more than $5,000. Screenplays must be originally written in English.

Up to 5 awards annually. Send self-addressed, stamped, business-sized envelope after January 1 to AMPAS for an application.

902—ALLIANCE FOR YOUNG ARTISTS AND WRITERS, INC. (Scholastic Art and Writing Awards)

Scholastic, Inc.
555 Broadway
New York NY 10012-3999
212/343-6582 or 800-SCHOLASTIC
FAX: 212/343-4885
E-mail: A&Wgeneralinfo@scholastic.com
Internet: http://www.scholastic.com/artandwriting/about.htm

AMOUNT: Varies
DEADLINE(S): Varies (upon location)
FIELD(S): Art; Writing

For all students in grades 7-12 currently enrolled in a public or nonpublic school in the U.S., Canada, U.S. territories, or U.S.-sponsored schools abroad. Awards are available in 10 writing categories and 16 art categories. Publishing opportunities may be available for winning students in both art and writing categories.

1,000+ awards annually.

903—ALVIN M. BENTLEY FOUNDATION (Scholarship Program)

College of Literature, Science, and the Arts
The University of Michigan
500 S. State Street, #2522
Ann Arbor MI 48109
517/729-9040
FAX: 517/723-2454
E-mail: lsascholarship@umich.edu

AMOUNT: $7,500-$10,000 per year
DEADLINE(S): None
FIELD(S): Literature; Science; Arts

Open to Michigan residents applying as freshmen to the University of Michigan's College of Literature, Science, and the Arts. Based on academic excellence and extracurricular activities. Must be nominated; there are no separate applications. Candidates are chosen from U of M applications received from Michigan resident freshmen.

904—ATLANTA ASSOCIATION OF BLACK JOURNALISTS (Clayton Competition)

Scholarship Committee
P.O. Box 54128
Atlanta GA 303308

AMOUNT: $1,000
DEADLINE(S):MAR 1
FIELD(S): Journalism, Mass Communications, English, Public Relations

For African American College Students. Must be enrolled in college or university in the state of Georgia. Must write an assay.

905—AMERICAN ASSOCIATION OF LAW LIBRARIES (Type I Scholarships: Library Degree for Law School Graduates)

53 W. Jackson Boulevard, Suite 940
Chicago IL 60604
312/939-4764 ext. 10
FAX: 312/431-1097
E-mail: rshaevel@aall.org
Internet: http://www.aallnet.org

AMOUNT: Varies
DEADLINE(S): APR 1
FIELD(S): Law Librarianship

Open to law school graduates working towards a degree in an accredited library school. Preference given to those with meaningful law library experience and to AALL members. Must demonstrate financial need.

1 award annually. See Web site or contact Rachel Shaevel, Membership Coordinator, for an application.

906—AMERICAN FOUNDATION FOR THE BLIND (R. L. Gillette Scholarships)

11 Penn Plaza, Suite 300
New York NY 10001
212/502-7661
FAX: 212/502-7771
E-mail: afbinfo@afb.org
Internet: http://www.afb.org

AMOUNT: $1,000
DEADLINE(S): APR
FIELD(S): Literature; Music

Open to legally blind women enrolled in a four-year undergraduate degree program in literature or music. Must be U.S.citizen. Must submit evidence of legal blindness; official transcripts; proof of college/university acceptance; three letters of recommendation; performance tape (30 minutes max.) or creative writing sample; and typewritten statement describing educational and personal goals, work experience, extracurricular activities, and how monies will be used.

2 awards annually. See Web site or contact Julie Tucker at AFB for an application.

907—AMERICAN LEGION (National High School Oratorical Contest)

American Legion Headquarters
P.O. Box 1055
Indianapolis IN 46206
317/630-1249
E-mail: mbuss@legion.org
Internet: http://www.legion.org

AMOUNT: $14,000-$18,000 (national); $1,500 (quarter finalist); $1,500 (each state winner)
DEADLINE(S): Varies
FIELD(S): English Language/Literature

Competition open to high school students (grades 9-12). Undergraduate scholarship awards go to the winners.

Applicants must be U.S. citizens or lawful permanent residents.

908—AMERICAN LIBRARY ASSOCIATION (The Bound to Stay Bound Books Scholarship)

50 E. Huron
Chicago IL 60611
800/545-2433

FAX: 312/440-9374
E-mail: lmays@ala.org
Internet: http://www.ala.org
AMOUNT: $6,000
DEADLINE(S): MAR 1
FIELD(S): Library Science

Provides financial assistance in the form of three $6,000 annual awards for the education of men and women who intend to pursue an M.L.S. or advanced degree and who plan to work in the area of library service to children. This work may be serving children up to and including the age of 14 in any type library. The Scholarship is made possible by the ALSC through the generous contributions of Bound to Stay Bound Books, Incorporated.

Must use on-line application.

909—AMERICAN LIBRARY ASSOCIATION (The Frederic G. Melcher Scholarship)

50 E. Huron
Chicago IL 60611
800/545-2433
FAX: 312/440-9374
E-mail: lmays@ala.org
Internet: http://www.ala.org
AMOUNT: $6,000
FIELD(S): MAR 1
FIELD(S): Library Science

Provides financial assistance for the professional education of men and women who intend to pursue an M.L.S. degree and who plan to work in children's librarianship. This work may be serving children up to and including the age of 14 in any type of library. Two $6,000 scholarships are awarded annually. The scholarship is made possible by ALSC through generous contributions from librarians, professional associates, friends, and others in the book world, as tribute to Frederic G. Melcher, a great leader in promoting better books for children.

Must use on-line application.

910—AMERICAN MOTHERS, INC. (Gertrude Fogelson Cultural and Creative Arts Awards)

1296 E. 21st Street
Brooklyn NY 11201
718/253-5676
AMOUNT: Up to $1,000
DEADLINE(S): JAN 1 (annually)
FIELD(S): Visual Arts, Creative Writing, and Vocal Music

An award to encourage and honor mothers in artistic pursuits.

Write to Alice Miller at above address for details.

911—AMY LOWELL POETRY TRAVELLING SCHOLARSHIP TRUST (Scholarship)

Exchange Place
Boston MA 02109-2891
AMOUNT: $37,000
DEADLINE(S): OCT. 15
DEADLINE(S): JAN 31
FIELD(S): Literature/English/Writing

The Amy Lowell Poetry Travelling Scholarship awards a scholarship each year to a poet of American birth. Upon acceptance, the recipient agrees to spend one year outside the continent of North America in a place deemed by the recipient suitable to advance the art of poetry. At the end of the year, the recipient shall submit at least three poems for consideration by the trust's committee. Application request deadline 10/1. Application submission deadline 10/15.

912—AMERICAN PLANNING ASSOCIATION (Minority Scholarship and Fellowship Programs)

122 South Michigan Avenue, Suite 1600
Chicago IL 60605
312/431-9100
FAX: 312/431-9985
AMOUNT: $2,000-$5,000 (grads); $2,500 (undergrads)
DEADLINE(S): MAY 14
FIELD(S): Urban Planning, Community Development, Environmental Sciences, Public Administration, Transportation, or Urban Studies

Scholarships for African-Americans, Hispanics, or Native American students pursuing undergraduate degrees in the U.S. in the above fields. Must have completed first year. Fellowships for graduate students. Programs must be approved by the Planning Accreditation Board. U.S. citizenship.

Call or write for complete information.

913—ASSOCIATION FOR LIBRARY and INFORMATION SCIENCE EDUCATION (Alise Research Grants Program)

471 Park Avenue
State College, PA 16803
814/238-0254
AMOUNT: $2,500
DEADLINE(S): OCT 1
FIELD(S): Library Science

Grants are to help support research costs. Open to members of the Association for Library and Information Science.

For membership information or an application, write to above address.

914—BACKPACKER MAGAZINE (Outdoor Scholarship Program)

135 N. Sixth Street
Emmaus, PA 18098
Internet: http://backpacker.com/scholarship
AMOUNT: $1,000
DEADLINE(S): MAR 31
FIELD(S): Writing

Available to students who have demonstrated a commitment to and aptitude for addressing outdoor-related issues and topics through writing. Must be: enrolled as a full-time student in a four-year college or university; have a B (3.0) average or better; entering your junior or senior year

915—BEVERLY HILLS THEATRE GUILD (Julie Harris Playwright Award Competition)

2815 N. Beachwood Drive
Los Angeles CA 90068-1923
323/465-2703
AMOUNT: $5,000 (first prize); $2,000 (second); $1,000 (third)
DEADLINE(S): NOV 1
FIELD(S): Playwriting

Annual competition of full-length (90 minutes) unproduced, unpublished plays. Must be U.S. itizen. Co-authorship is allowed. Musicals, short one-act plays, adaptations, translations, and plays having won other competitions or entered in previous BHTG competitions are not eligible.

Send a self-addressed, stamped envelope for an application. Entries accepted August 1 to November 1.

916—BLUES HEAVEN FOUNDATION, INC. (Muddy Waters Scholarship)

2120 S. Michigan Avenue
Chicago IL 60616
312/808-1286
AMOUNT: $2,000
DEADLINE(S): APR 30
FIELD(S): Music; Music Education; African-American Studies; Folklore; Performing Arts; Arts Management; Journalism; Radio/TV/Film

Scholarship is made on a competitive basis with consideration given to scholastic achievement, concentration of studies, and financial need. Applicant must have full-time enrollment status in a Chicago area college/university in at least their first year of undergraduate studies or a graduate program. Scholastic aptitude extracurricular involvement, grade point average, and financial need are all considered.

Contact Blues Heaven Foundation, Inc. to receive an application between February and April.

917—BRITISH ACADEMY (Sir Ernest Cassel Educational Trust)

10 Carlton House
Islington, London SWIY 5AH
ENGLAND UK
020 7969 5217
FAX: 020 7969 5414
E-mail: grants@britac.ac.uk
Internet: http://www.britac.ac.uk/funding/guide/cetf.html

AMOUNT: Up to 5,000 pounds per annum
DEADLINE(S): FEB; APR; SEP; NOV (end of ea. month)
FIELD(S): Language, literature, or civilization of any country

The British Academy administers funds on behalf of the Sir Ernest Cassel Educational Trust to support travel costs related to a research project. Research Grants Department Awards are particularly aimed at recent postdoctoral scholars.

Obtain application from the Research Grants Department.

918—BUENA VISTA COLLEGE NETWORK (Internships in Film Marketing)

3900 W. Alameda Avenue
Burbank CA 91505-4316
818/567-5000
E-mail: College_Network@studio.disney.com

AMOUNT: Varies
DEADLINE(S): None
FIELD(S): Fields of study related to the motion picture industry, including marketing and promotion

Internships for full-time college students age 18 and up interested in a career in a facet of the motion picture industry. Must have unlimited access to computer with modem and transportation, be able to work 4-6 hours per week and 2-3 weekends per month. Attend film openings and sneak previews. Evaluate various aspects via an interactive computer system. Compensation ranges from $30 to $60/month. Possible school credit.

Access Web site by writing "Buena Vista College Network" from Yahoo. Available in most states and parts of Canada. Details, an interactive application, and E-mail access are located on Web site.

919—CASE WESTERN RESERVE UNIVERSITY (Marc A. Klein

Playwriting Award
Department of Theater Arts
10900 Euclid Avenue
Cleveland, OH 44106-7077

AMOUNT: $1,000
Deadline: MAY
FIELD(S): Playwriting

The award carries a cash prize and the play receives a full mainstage production by Case Western Reserve University's Department of Theater Arts.

920—CATHOLIC LIBRARY ASSOCIATION (World Book, Inc., Award)

100 North Street; Suite 224
Pittsfield MA 01201-5109
413/443-2CLA
FAX: 413/442-2CLA
E-mail: cla@vgernet.net
Internet: http://www.cathla.org

AMOUNT: $1,500
DEADLINE(S): MAR 15
FIELD(S): Library Science

Open to members of the National Catholic Library Association who are interested in gaining added proficiency in school or children's librarianship. Must submit report describing program of study (workshops, seminars, summer sessions, sabbaticals, etc.), including statement of expenses (tuition, room/board, and travel) relative to program of study. Grant is NOT given for library science degree.

1-3 awards annually. See Web site or send self-addressed, stamped envelope for an application. Awards announced at annual convention during Easter Week.

921—UCLA CENTER FOR 17TH- AND 18TH-CENTURY STUDIES (Fellowships)

UCLA
310 Royce Hall
Los Angeles CA 90095-1404
310/206-8552
FAX: 310/206-8577
E-mail: c1718cs@humnet.ucla.edu
Internet; http://www.humnet.ucla.edu/humnet/C1718CS/Postd.htm#Ahm Get

AMOUNT: $1,000-$18,400
DEADLINE(S): Varies
FIELD(S): British Literature/History (17th and 18th Centuries)

Undergraduate stipends, graduate assistantships, and postdoctoral fellowships are for advanced study and research regarding British literature and history of the 17th and 18th centuries.

Contact the Center for current year's theme and an application.

922—CHICAGO TRIBUNE (Nelson Algren Awards)

Editorial Dept.
435 N. Michigan Avenue
Chicago IL 60611-4041
Written Inquiry

AMOUNT: $5,000 (first prize); $1,500 (3 runners-up)
DEADLINE(S): FEB
FIELD(S): Fiction Writing

Open to Americans who submit unpublished short fiction. Stories must be typed and double-spaced, between 2,500 and 10,000 words. Manuscripts will not be returned. Authors' names should not appear on the manuscript. Author should enclose a cover sheet with name, address, phone, and title of entry.

923—COUNCIL FOR BASIC EDUCATION (Chinese Culture Fellowship)

1319 F. Street NW, Suite 900
Washington, D.C. 20004
202/347-4171
FAX: 202/347-5047
E-mail: info@c-b-e.org
Internet: http://www.c-b-e.org/index.htm

AMOUNT: $1,000
DEADLINE(S): JUN
FIELD(S): Chinese Culture and Chinese Artistic Resources in New York City

Fellowships available to teams of two teachers (K-12)-one art teacher and one humanities teacher-to develop an interdisciplinary project that can be used to broaden the appreciation and understanding of Chinese culture and Chinese artistic resources in New York City. Teachers use web-based technology and make their material available to teachers nationally and internationally. A total of ten teachers or five teams will receive the award for six weeks of independent study during the summer.

Contact organization for details.

924—COUNCIL FOR THE ADVANCEMENT OF SCIENCE WRITING, INC. (Nate Haseltine Fellowships)

P.O. Box 404
Greenlawn NY 11740
516/757-5664
AMOUNT: $1,000-$2,000
DEADLINE(S): JUN 1
FIELD(S): Science writing, journalism/communications

Available for master's and doctoral candidates on the basis of academic achievement, quality of writing and commitment to a writing career.

925—DISTRICT OF COLUMBIA COMMISSION ON THE ARTS and HUMANITIES (Grants)

410 Eighth Street NW, 5th Floor
Washington DC 20004
202/724-5613; TDD: 202/727-3148
FAX: 202/727-4135
Internet: http://www.dcarts.dc.gov/main.shtm
AMOUNT: Varies
DEADLINE(S): Varies
FIELD(S): Media, Visual Arts, Crafts

Applicants for grants must be professional artists and residents of Washington DC for at least one year prior to submitting application. Awards intended to generate art endeavors within the Washington DC community.

Open also to art organizations that train, exhibit, or perform within DC. Write for complete information.

926—FIVE WINGS ARTS COUNCIL (Artist Mentor Scholarships for Students)

200 First Street NE
Staples MN 56479
218/894-5485
FAX: 218/894-3045
E-mail: mturner@ncscmn.org
Internet: http://www.fwac.org
AMOUNT: Up to $500
DEADLINE(S): OCT 15
FIELD(S): Literary Arts; Visual Arts; Music; Theater; Media Arts; Dance

Open to rural high school students in grades 9-12 who are enrolled in an independent school district within the counties of Cass, Crow Wing, Morrison, Todd, and Wadena, Minnesota. Each recipient is matched with a qualified mentor who will establish a study schedule with student. Award is based on creative potential, accomplishments in art, maturity, and personal motivation.

10 awards annually. Contact Mark Turner, Director, for details.

927—FLORIDA DEPARTMENT OF STATE-ARTS COUNCIL (Individual Artists' Fellowships)

Division Cultural Affairs; The Capitol
Tallahassee FL 32399-0250
850/487-2980
TT: 850/488-5779
FAX: 850/922-5259
Internet: http://www.dos.state.fl.us/dca/fellow.html
AMOUNT: $5,000
DEADLINE(S): JAN 14
FIELD(S): Dance; Folklife/Traditional Arts; Interdisciplinary; Literature (children's literature, fiction, poetry); Media Arts; Music/Composition; Theater; Visual Arts and Crafts

Open to legal residents of Florida who are creative artists of at least 18 years of age. May NOT be enrolled in any undergraduate or graduate degree-seeking program during fellowship period.

38 awards annually. Renewable with reapplication after four years since date of previous award. Contact Florida Arts Council for information packet. Notification during summer.

928—FOREST ROBERTS THEATRE (Mildred and Albert Panowski Playwriting Award)

Northern Michigan Univ.
1401 Presque Isle Avenue
Marquette MI 49855-5364
906/227-2553
Internet: http://www.nmu.edu/theatre
AMOUNT: $2,000
DEADLINE(S): Varies
FIELD(S): Playwriting

This competition is open to any playwright, but only one play per playwright may be entered. Entries must be original, full-length plays not previously produced or published. May be co-authored, based upon factual material, or an adaptation. Scripts must be typewritten or word processed and securely bound within a cover or folder and clearly identified.

929—FREEDOM FORUM JOURNALISM SCHOLARSHIP (Rachel Marquez Frankel Scholarship Fund)

The Freedom Forum World Center
1101 Wilson Boulevard
Arlington, VA 22209
703/528-0800
AMOUNT: $2500
DEADLINE(S): JAN 31
FIELD(S): Communications

Undergraduates studying journalism or mass communications.

930—FREEDOM FROM RELIGION FOUNDATION (Student Essay Contest)

P.O. Box 750
Madison WI 53701
608/256-5800
Internet: http://www.infidels.org/org/ffrf
AMOUNT: $1,000; $500; $250
DEADLINE(S): JUL 15
FIELD(S): Humanities; English; Education; Philosophy; Science

Essay contest on topics related to church-state entanglement in public schools or growing up a "freethinker" in religious-oriented society. Topics change yearly, but all are on general theme of maintaining separation of church and state. New topics available in February. For high school seniors and currently enrolled college/technical students. Must be U.S. citizen.

Send SASE to address above for complete information. Please indicate whether wanting information for college competition or high school. Information will be sent when new topics are announced each February. See Web site for details.

931—GENERAL LEARNING COMMUNICATIONS (DuPont Challenge Science Essay Awards Program)

900 Skokie Boulevard, Suite 200
Northbrook IL 60062-4028
847/205-3000
FAX: 847/564-8197
Internet: http://www.glcomm.com/dupont
AMOUNT: $1,500 (max.)
DEADLINE(S): JAN 28
FIELD(S): Science and Technology

Annual essay competition open to students in grades 7-12 in the U.S. and Canada. Cash awards for first, second, and honorable mention. First-place essayists in each of two divisions, their science teacher, and a parent of each receive a trip to the Space Center Houston/NASA at the end of April.

102 awards annually. See Web site or contact your science teacher or GLC for official entry blank.

932—GEORGE MASON UNIVERSITY (Associated Writing Programs Award Series; St. Martin's Press Award)

Tallwood House, Mail Stop 1E3
FairFAX: VA 22030
703/993-4301
FAX: 703/993-4302
E-mail: awp@gmu.edu
Internet: http://web.gmu.edu/departments/awp/

AMOUNT: $2,000 honorarium; (AWP); $10,000 advance against royalties (St. Martin's Press)
DEADLINE(S): JAN 1 (through FEB 28-postmark)
FIELD(S): Writing: poetry, short fiction, creative nonfiction and novels

AWP competition is for book-length manuscripts in poetry, short fiction, and creative nonfiction; St. Martin's Press Young Writers Award is for a novel whose author is 32 years of age or younger. Open to authors writing in English, regardless of their nationality or residence.

Novel manuscripts will be judged and published by St. Martin's Press. All genres require a handling fee of $10 for AWP members and $15 for nonmembers. Contact above address or Web site for details.

933—GEORGE MASON UNIVERSITY (Mary Roberts Rinehart Awards)

English Dept.; MSN 3E4
4400 University Drive
FairFAX: VA 22030-4444
703/993-1180
FAX: 703/993-1161
E-mail: bgompert@gmu.edu

AMOUNT: $2,000
DEADLINE(S): NOV 30
FIELD(S): Creative Writing

Grants are given to unpublished writers to complete previously unpublished works of fiction, poetry, biography, autobiography, or history with a strong narrative quality. Need not be U.S. citizen, but works must be in English, and awards are in U.S. dollars. Submitted samples of a nominee's writing may be up to 30 pages in length for all categories. Financial need NOT considered.

3 awards annually. Candidates must be nominated by writing program faculty member or a sponsoring writer, agent, or editor. Contact William Miller at address above for complete information.

934—GEORGE WASHINGTON UNIVERSITY (George McCandlish Fellowship in American Literature)

Graduate Studies English Dept.
Washington DC 20052
202/676-6180

AMOUNT: $2,500+18hrs tuition
DEADLINE(S):Varies
FIELD(S): American Literature

Graduate fellowship to the most promising student enrolling in a graduate degree program (M.A. or Ph.D.) in American literature. For study at George Washington University. Must have grade point average of 3.25 or better.

935—GEORGIA LIBRARY ASSOCIATION ADMINISTRATIVE SERVICES (Hubbard Scholarship Fund)

4290 Paces Ferry Road
Atlanta GA 30309-2955
710/801-5330

AMOUNT: $3,000
DEADLINE(S): MAY 1
FIELD(S): Library Science

For graduating seniors and graduates of accredited colleges who have been accepted into an ALA-accredited degree program. Must be ready to begin study in fall term of award year and intend to complete degree requirements within two years. Recipients agree to work (following graduation) for one year in a library or library-related capacity in Georgia OR to pay back a prorated amount of the award within three years (with interest).

Contact GLA for an application.

936—GERMAN MARSHALL FUND OF THE UNITED STATES (Peter Weitz Prize)

Julianne Smith, Program Officer
11 Dupont Circle N.W., Suite 750
Washington, DC 20036
202-238-4003
FAX: 202-265-1662
E-mail: jsmith@gmfus.org
Internet: http://www.gmfus.org

AMOUNT: $5,000-$10,000
DEADLINE(S): LATE FEB
FIELD(S): Journalism

Rewards excellence and originality in reporting and analyzing European and transatlantic affairs. senior prize to U.S.- or Europe based journalist covering European issues for American newspapers and magazines. $5,000 young journalist prize to U.S.-based journalists who are U.S. citizens and under 35.

937—GOLDEN KEY NATIONAL HONOR SOCIETY (Literary Contest)

1189 Ponce de Leon Avenue
Atlanta GA 30306-4624
800/377-2401 or 404/377-2400
E-mail: mboone@gknhs.gsu.edu

AMOUNT: $1,000
DEADLINE(S): APR 1
FIELD(S): Non-Fiction; Poetry; Fiction; Newswriting

Open to Golden Key student members who submit original, unpublished works of nonfiction or poetry that do not exceed 1,000 words. First-prize winners are published in CONCEPTS magazine.

3 first-prize awards annually. Contact the Editor for guidelines.

938—HAROLD HYAM WINGATE FOUNDATION (Wingate Scholarships)

2nd Floor, 20-22 Stukeley Street
London WC2B 5LR ENGLAND UK
0171 465 1521
E-mail: clark@wingate.org.uk
Internet: http://www.wingate.org.uk/

AMOUNT: Up to 10,000 pounds/year
DEADLINE(S): FEB 1
FIELD(S): Creative Works

Financial support for individuals of great potential or proven excellence to develop original work of intellectual, scientific, artistic, social, or environmental value, and to outstanding talented musicians. Not for taught courses or for leading to professional qualifications, or for electives or for completing courses already begun or for a higher degree. For citizens of the United Kingdom or other Commonwealth countries, Ireland, Israel, or of European countries.

Must be age 24 or older. May be held for up to three years. Contact Faith Clark, administrator, for additional information. Application, details, and examples of previous awards available on Web site.

939—IAPA (Scholarship Fund for young journalists and journalism school graduates)

1801 SW 3rd Avenue
Miami, FL 33129

AMOUNT: Varies
DEADLINE(S): DEC 31
FIELD(S): Journalism

Journalists or journalism school seniors or graduates between 21 and 35 years of age with a good command of the language they are to use. Students must have completed their degree before beginning the scholarship year. Write for complete information.

940—ILLINOIS ARTS COUNCIL (Artists Fellowship Awards)

100 W. Randolph, Suite 10-500
Chicago IL 60601-3298
312/814-6750
E-mail: rose@arts.state.il.us
Internet: http://www.state.il.us/agency/iac/Guidelines/Fellowships/afa02pdf.pdf

AMOUNT: $7,000
DEADLINE(S): Varies
FIELD(S): Choreography, Crafts, Ethnic and Folk Arts, Interdisciplinary/Performance Art, Media Arts, Music Composition, Photography, Playwriting/Screenwriting, Poetry, Prose, and Visual Arts

The Artists Fellowship Program is the agency's major program for individual artist support. These awards are given annually to Illinois artists of exceptional talent in recognition of their outstanding work and commitment within the arts. Awards are made based upon the quality of the works submitted and the evolving professional accomplishments of the applicant.

941—INSTITUTE FOR HUMANE STUDIES (Humane Studies Fellowship)

3301 N. FairFAX: Drive, Suite 440
Arlington VA 22201-4432
703/993-4880 or 800/697-8799
FAX: 703/993-4890
E-mail: ihs@gmu.edu
Internet: http://www.TheIHS.org

AMOUNT: $12,000 (max.)
DEADLINE(S): DEC
FIELD(S): Social Sciences; Liberal Arts; Law; Humanities; Jurisprudence; Journalism

Open to graduate and advanced undergraduate or law students pursuing degrees at any accredited domestic or foreign college/university. Based on academic performance, demonstrated interest in the classical liberal tradition, and potential to contribute to the advancement of a free society.

90 awards annually. Apply online or contact IHS for an application.

942—INSTITUTE FOR HUMANE STUDIES (Summer Seminars Program)

3401 N. FairFAX: Drive; Suite 440
Arlington VA 22201-4432
703/993-4880 or 800/697-8799
FAX: 703/993-4890
E-mail: ihs@gmu.edu
Internet: http://www.TheIHS.org

AMOUNT: Free summer seminars, including room/board, lectures, seminar materials, and books
DEADLINE(S): MAR
FIELD(S): Social Sciences; Humanities; Law; Journalism; Public Policy; Education; Film; Writing; Economics; Philosophy

Open to college students, recent graduates, and graduate students who share an interest in learning and exchanging ideas about the scope of individual rights, free markets, the rule of law, peace, and tolerance.

See Web site for seminar information or to apply online or contact IHS for an application.

943—IOWA SCHOOL OF LETTERS (The John Simmons Short Fiction Award)

Univ Iowa; 102 Dey House
507 N. Clinton Street
Iowa City IA 52242-1000
319/335-2000

AMOUNT: Winners' manuscripts will be published by University of Iowa under standard press contract
DEADLINE(S): Varies (AUG 1-SEP 30)
FIELD(S): Creative Writing: Fiction

Any writer who has not previously published a volume of prose fiction is eligible to enter the competition. The manuscript must be a collection of short stories of at least 150 typewritten pages. Writers who have published a volume of poetry are eligible. Revised manuscripts which have been previously entered may be resubmitted.

Send a self-addressed, stamped envelope to Connie Brothers at above address for guidelines.

944—IRISH ARTS COUNCIL (Awards and Opportunities)

70 Merrion Square
Dublin 2 IRELAND
Tel: +353 1 618 0200
FAX: +353 1 661 0349/676 1302
E-mail: info@artscouncil.ie
Internet: http://www.artscouncil.ie

AMOUNT: Varies (with program)
DEADLINE(S): Varies (with program)
FIELD(S): Creative Arts; Visual Arts; Performing Arts

Numerous programs open to young and established artists who are Irish citizens or legal residents. Purpose is to assist in pursuit of talents and recognize achievements.

See Web site or contact above address for an application.

945—KAPLAN/NEWSWEEK ("My Turn" Essay Contest)

Kaplan, Inc.
Community Outreach Director
888 7th Avenue
New York, NY 10106
800/KAP-TEST
Internet: http://www.kaplan.com

AMOUNT: $1,000-$10,000
DEADLINE(S): MAR 31
FIELD(S): Writing/journalism

Essay should be based on personal opinion or experience essay on topic chosen by student. Applicant must be high school senior or college freshman.

Essays must be original and factually accurate and are judged on effectiveness, creativity, insight, organization and development, consistent use of language, variety in sentence structure and vocabulary, use of proper grammar, spelling and punctuation

946—KOSCIUSZKO FOUNDATION (Summer Sessions in Poland and Rome)

15 E. 65th Street
New York NY 10021-6595
212/734-2130
FAX: 212/628-4552
E-mail: thekf@pegasusnet.com;
Internet: http://www.kosciuszkofoundation.org

AMOUNT: Varies
DEADLINE(S): Varies
FIELD(S): Polish Studies; History; Literature; Art; Economics; Social Studies; Language; Culture

Open to undergraduate and graduate students, graduating high school students who are 18 or older, and persons of any age who are not enrolled in a college/university program. Study programs are offered in Poland and Rome from mid-June through the end of August in above fields. Must be U.S. citizen/permanent resident.

See Web site or send a self-addressed, stamped envelope to Addy Tymczyszyn, Summer Studies Abroad Coordinator, for an application.

947—LOUISIANA STATE UNIVERSITY AT SHREVEPORT (H.J. Sachs English Scholarship)

Bronson Hall
Shreveport LA 71115-2399
318/797-5371
Internet: http://www.lsus.edu
AMOUNT: $600
DEADLINE(S): Varies
FIELD(S): English

This stipend is awarded for one academic year to either an English major or an English education major at LSUS. The recipient is chosen on the basis of academic merit, character, and need.

Contact the Dean's Office in the College of Liberal Arts at LSUS for an application.

948—LOUISIANA STATE UNIVERSITY AT SHREVEPORT (Walter O. Bigby Scholarship)

Bronson Hall
Shreveport LA 71115-2399
318/797-5371
Internet: http://www.lsus.edu
AMOUNT: Up to $500/semester
DEADLINE(S): Varies
FIELD(S): Political Science; English; History; Law

Recipient must be entering the junior or senior year at LSUS with a major in political science, English, or history; may also be enrolled in some other Liberal Arts degree program if preparing to enter law school.

Contact the Dean's Office in the College of Liberal Arts at LSU.S.for an application.

949—MIAMI INTERNATIONAL PRESS CLUB (Scholarship Program)

c/o Laura Englebright
625 Candia Avenue
Florida Gables FL 33134
305/444-0345
AMOUNT: $500
DEADLINE(S): JUN 1
FIELD(S): Journalism; Communications

South Florida residents (Dade County) who are deserving high school seniors or college students are eligible for these undergraduate scholarships tenable at any accredited college or university. Renewable.

950—MICHAEL KANIN PLAYWRITING AWARDS PROGRAM KC/ACTF

The Kennedy Center
Washington, DC 20566
AMOUNT: Varies
DEADLINE(S): DEC
FIELD(S): Playwriting

For student playwrights, organized by the American College Theater Festival, The Kennedy Center.

951—THE MICHIGAN OUTDOOR WRITERS ASSOCIATION (Scholarship)

Attn: Bob Holzhei
MOWA Scholarship Committee
3601 Avery, St. Johns, MI 48879
517/224-3465
E-mail: scholarship@mioutdoorwriters.org
AMOUNT: $1,000
DEADLINE(S): JAN
FIELD(S): Journalism/writing

Must be Michigan resident for at least five years, enrolled at a Michigan college or university.

The deadline for receiving applications is January 25. Letters of support and proofs of performance (copies of VCR samples or outdoor communications and class assignments) must be submitted with the application.

952—MILL MOUNTAIN THEATRE (NEW PLAY COMPETITION)

Center in the Square
Roanoke, VA 24011-1437
540/342-5749
FAX: 540/342-5745
E-mail: outreach@millmountain.org
Internet: http://www.millmountain.org
AMOUNT: $500-$1,000
DEADLINE(S): JAN 1
FIELD(S): Playwriting

Award open to any playwright living in the U.S. Must submit one unproduced, unpublished theatrical script in English. Script must be agent-submitted or recommended by a director, literary manager, or dramaturgy. Must also submit author's biography, history of play, and brief synopsis of scenes. Submission dates are October 1 to January 1.

953—MINNESOTA STATE ARTS BOARD (Grants Program)

Park Square Court
400 Sibley Street; Suite 200
St. Paul MN 55101-1928
651/215-1600 or 800/8MN-ARTS
FAX: 651/215-1602
E-mail: msab@arts.state.mn.us
Internet: http://www.arts.state.mn.us/index.html
AMOUNT: $8,000 (fellowships); $500-$1,500 (grants)
DEADLINE(S): AUG (Visual Arts); SEP (Music and Dance); OCT (Literature and Theater)
FIELD(S): Literature; Music; Theater; Dance; Visual Arts

Fellowships and career opportunity grants are open to professional artists who are residents of Minnesota. Grants may NOT be used for support of tuition or work toward any degree.

Contact MSAB for an application.

954—NATIONAL ENDOWMENT FOR THE ARTS (Fellowships for Creative Writers)

Nancy Hanks Center
1100 Pennsylvania Avenue, NW
Washington, DC 20506-0001
AMOUNT: $20,000
DEADLINE(S): Mid MAR
FIELD(S): Creative Writing

Fellowships enable recipients to set aside time for writing, research, travel, and general career advancement. The Endowment's support of a project may extend for up to two years.

955—NATIONAL FEDERATION OF STATE POETRY SOCIETIES (Edna Meudt Memorial Scholarship Fund)

c/o Madelyn Eastlund
310 S. Adams Street
Beverly Hills, Fl 34465
Written Request
AMOUNT: $500
DEADLINE(S): FEB 1
FIELD(S): Poetry

Any junior or senior of an accredited university or college will be eligible for consideration based on the following: 1) submission of a completed application; 2) submission of 10 original poems, single-spaced, 1-page limit, 50-character-per-line limit, 40-line-per-poem limit; and 3) the 10-poem manuscript must be titled. Financial need NOT a factor. Winning manuscripts are published by NFSPS, and each recipient will receive 75 copies and can read at annual convention.

2 awards annually. Send a self-addressed, stamped, business-sized envelope to NFSPS for an application. Award recipients announced after April 1.

956—INSTITUTE FOR HUMANE STUDIES (Humane Studies Fellowship)

3301 N. FairFAX: Drive; Suite 440
Arlington VA 22201-4432
703/993-4880 or 800/697-8799
FAX: 703/993-4890
E-mail: ihs@gmu.edu
Internet: http://www.TheIHS.org
AMOUNT: $12,000 (max.)
DEADLINE(S): DEC
FIELD(S): Social Sciences; Liberal Arts; Law; Humanities; Jurisprudence; Journalism

Open to graduate and advanced undergraduate or law students pursuing degrees at any accredited domestic or foreign college/university. Based on academic performance, demonstrated interest in the classical liberal tradition, and potential to contribute to the advancement of a free society.

90 awards annually. Apply online or contact IHS for an application.

957—NATIONAL FOUNDATION FOR ADVANCEMENT IN THE ARTS (Arts Recognition and Talent Search)

800 Brickell Avenue
Miami FL 33131
800/970-ARTS or 305/377-1140
FAX: 305/377-1149
E-mail: info@nfaa.org
Internet: http://www.ARTSawards.org
AMOUNT: $100-$3,000
DEADLINE(S): OCT 1
FIELD(S): Creative and Performing Arts

Talent contest for high school seniors and 17- to 18-year-olds in dance, jazz, music, photography, theatre, visual arts, voice, and writing. Except for those applying in Music/Jazz, applicants must be U.S. citizens or permanent residents. May apply in more than one category, but only one financial award will be given to any individual, and a fee is required for each category in which student applies.

$35 application fee ($25 if apply by June 1); fee may be waived if you are unable to meet this requirement). 400 awards annually. Not renewable. Contact NFAA for an application packet.

958—NATIONAL LEAGUE OF AMERICAN PEN WOMEN, INC. (Scholarships for Mature Women)

1300 Seventeenth Street NW
Washington DC 20036
202/785-1997
Internet: http://www.cooper.edu/admin/career_services/fellowships/mature.html
AMOUNT: $1,000
DEADLINE(S): JAN 15 (even-numbered years)
FIELD(S): Art; Music; Creative Writing

The National League of American Pen Women gives three $1,000 grants in even-numbered years to women aged 35 and over.

Send SASE for details at the above address.

959—NATIONAL SPEAKERS ASSOCIATION (NSA Scholarship)

1500 S. Priest Drive
Tempe AZ 85281
480/968-2552
FAX: 480/968-0911
E-mail: Information@nsaspeaker.org
Internet: http://www.nsaspeaker.org
AMOUNT: $4,000
DEADLINE(S): JUN 1
FIELD(S): Speech

For college juniors, seniors, and graduate students who are majoring or minoring in speech. Must be full-time student with above-average academic record. Applicant should be a well-rounded student, capable of leadership, with the potential to make an impact using oral communication skills. Must submit official transcript, 500-word essay on career objectives, and letter of recommendation from speech teacher/department head along with application (7 copies each).

960—NATIONAL SPEAKERS ASSOCIATION (Outstanding Professor Awards)

1500 S. Priest Drive
Tempe AZ 85281
480/968-2552
FAX: 480/968-0911
E-mail: Information@nsaspeaker.org
Internet: http://www.nsaspeaker.org
AMOUNT: $2,000
DEADLINE(S): JUN 1
FIELD(S): Speech/Communications

Open to full-time faculty members in the Department of Speech Communication of accredited U.S. colleges or universities. Nominations to be forwarded through department head and should include vitae and two letters of recommendation from students. Must show commitment through effective teaching courses in public speaking, presentations, etc. and/or through research in same areas.

961—NATIONAL WRITERS ASSOCIATION FOUNDATION (Scholarship)

3140 S. Peoria; #295
Aurora CO 80014
303/841-0246
FAX: 303/841-2607
E-mail: sandywrter@aol.com
Internet: http://www.nationalwriters.com
AMOUNT: $1,000
DEADLINE(S): DEC 31
FIELD(S): Writing

Scholarship for career support. Financial need must be demonstrated.

1 award annually. See Web site or contact Sandy Whelchel for an application.

962—NORTH CAROLINA DEPARTMENT OF PUBLIC INSTRUCTION (Scholarship Loan Program for Prospective Teachers)

301 N. Wilmington Street
Raleigh NC 27601-2825
919/715-1120
AMOUNT: Up to $2,500/year
DEADLINE(S): FEB
FIELD(S): Education: Teaching, school psychology and counseling, speech/language impaired, audiology, library/media services

For NC residents planning to teach in NC public schools. At least 3.0 high school GPA required; must maintain 2.5 GPA during freshman year and 3.0 cumulative thereafter. Recipients are obligated to teach one year in an NC public school for each year of assistance. Those who do not fulfill their teaching obligation are required to repay the loan plus interest.

200 awards per year. For full-time students. Applications available in Dec. from high school counselors and college and university departments of education.

963—NORTH CAROLINA DEPT. OF PUBLIC INSTRUCTION (Teacher Assistant Scholarship Loan)

301 N. Wilmington Street
Raleigh NC 27601-2825
919/715-1120
AMOUNT: Up to $1,200/yr
DEADLINE(S): JAN
FIELD(S): Education: Teaching, school psychology or counseling, speech/language impaired, audiology, library/media services

For NC residents employed as K-12 teaching assistants in public schools who wish to pursue teacher licensure. Must either hold a BA degree or have completed general college courses prerequisite to admission to degree program and be admitted to an approved teacher education program at a four-year institution. Two-year community college early childhood education program is acceptable.

Must remain employed as teaching assistant while pursuing licensure and teach one year in an NC public school for each year of assistance received. Applications available in Sept. from local school superintendent.

964—PERMANENT GROUP (Kathleen Mitchell Award)

Level 3, 35 Clarence Street
Sydney NSW 2000 AUSTRALIA
(02)8295 8316
FAX: (02)8295 8496
Internet: http://www.permanentgroup.com.au
AMOUNT: Aus. $5,000
DEADLINE(S): JAN 31
FIELD(S): Novel Writing

Award for female Australian residents who were Australian-born or British-born. Novels must have been published while the author is under 30 years of age and during the two years prior to the deadline. "For the advancement, improvement, and betterment of Australian literature, to improve the educational style of such authors, and to provide them with additional amounts and thus enable them to improve their literary efforts."

Contact Claudia Crosariol, Projects Administrator, for more information/entry form.

965—PERMANENT GROUP (Miles Franklin Literary Award)

Level 3 35 Clarence Street
Sydney NSW 2000 AUSTRALIA
(02)8295 8316
FAX: (02)8295 8496
Internet: http://www.permanentgroup.com.au
AMOUNT: Aus. $28,000
DEADLINE(S): JAN 31
FIELD(S): Novel/Playwriting

Annual award for the best book on some aspect of Australian life published in the 12-month period prior to the award deadline each year. If no novel is worthy of the award, a play will be chosen. More than one entry may be submitted by each author; a novel/play written by two or more authors in collaboration is also eligible.

Winner announced in May or June. Contact Claudia Crosariol, Projects Administrator, for complete information/entry form.

966—PHILLIPS EXETER ACADEMY (George Bennett Fellowship in Writing)

20 Main Street
Exeter, NH 03833-2460
Internet: http://www.exeter.edu/english/bennett.html
AMOUNT: $6,000 plus housing
DEADLINE(S): Varies
FIELD(S): Writing

For someone who is or intends to become a professional writer, and has a manuscript in progress.

967—PLAYWRIGHTS' CENTER (Many Voices Residency and Collaboration Grants Programs)

2301 East Franklin Avenue
Minneapolis MN 55406-1099
612/332-7481
FAX: 612/332-6037
E-mail: pwcenter@mtn.org
Internet: http://www.pwcenter.org
AMOUNT: $200-$2,000 stipend + tuition to a Center class
DEADLINE(S): JUL 1
FIELD(S): Playwriting

Residencies for minority individuals interested in becoming playwrights who live in Minnesota or within a 100-mile radius of the Twin Cities at the time of application whose work demonstrates exceptional artistic merit and potential. Award recipients will spend an 8- to 9-month residency at the Center, have a one-on-one mentorship with a playwright, and other opportunities to develop their craft.

Collaboration grants are for culturally diverse teams of 2 or more writers to create new theater pieces. Awards range from $200 to $2,000. Send a self-addressed, stamped envelope to above address for an application.

968—PLAYWRIGHTS' CENTER (McKnight Fellowships)

2301 East Franklin Avenue
Minneapolis MN 55406-1099
612/332-7481
FAX: 612/332-6037
E-mail: info@pwcenter.org
Internet: http://www.pwcenter.org
AMOUNT: $25,000
DEADLINE(S): FEB 1
FIELD(S): Playwriting

For MN playwrights whose work has had a significant impact on the contemporary theater. One work must have been fully produced by professional theater. Eligible playwrights must be nominated by a theater professional.

2 awards annually. Professionals wishing to nominate a playwright should contact the Center in early Fall.

969—POETRY SOCIETY OF AMERICA (George Bogin Memorial Award)

15 Gramercy Park
New York NY 10003
212/254-9628
FAX: 212/673-2352
Internet: http://www.poetrysociety.org
AMOUNT: $500
DEADLINE(S): DEC
FIELD(S): Poetry

Prizes for the best selections of four or five poems that reflect the encounter of the ordinary and the extraordinary, use language in an original way, and take a stand against oppression in any of its forms.

970—POETRY SOCIETY OF AMERICA (Robert H. Winner Memorial Award)

15 Gramercy Park
New York NY 10003
212/254-9628
Internet: http://www.poetrysociety.org
AMOUNT: $2,500
DEADLINE(S): DEC 21
FIELD(S): Poetry

For poets over 40 years of age who have not published or who have no more than one book. This award acknowledges original work done in midlife by someone who has not had substantial recognition. Send a brief but cohesive manuscript of up to 10 poems or 20 pages. Poems entered here may be submitted to other contests as well. Please include date of birth on cover page.

$5 entry fee for nonmembers. Contact PSA for submission guidelines.

971—POETRY SOCIETY OF AMERICA (Shelley Memorial Award)

15 Gramercy Park
New York NY 10003
212/254-9628
Internet: http://www.poetrysociety.org
AMOUNT: $6,000-$9,000
DEADLINE(S): DEC
FIELD(S): Poetry

This contest (NOT scholarship) is open to both PSA members and nonmembers. All submissions must be unpublished on the date of entry and not scheduled for publication by the date of the PSA awards ceremony held in the spring.

$5 entry fee for nonmembers. Contact PSA for submission guidelines.

972—PRINCESS GRACE FOUNDATION-USA (Grants for Young Playwrights)

150 E. 58th Street; 21stFloor
New York NY 10155
212/317-1470
FAX: 212/317-1473
E-mail: pgus@pgfusa.com
Internet: http://www.pgfusa.com

AMOUNT: $7,500 + 10-week residency at New Dramatists, Inc., New York City and other benefits
DEADLINE(S): MAR 31
FIELD(S): Playwriting

Grant is for ten-week residency in New York for emerging playwrights who are U.S. citizens/permanent residents. Awards based primarily on artistic quality of submitted play, appropriateness of activities to individual's artistic growth, and potential future excellence. Script will be included in New Dramatists' lending library, be distributed to catalogue subscribers for one year, and possibly be published through the Dramatists' Play Service.

1 award annually. See Web site or contact Ms. Toby E. Boshak, Executive Director, for an application.

973—RAGDALE FOUNDATION (Frances Shaw Fellowship)

1260 N. Green Bay Road
Lake Forest IL 60045-1106
847/234-1063
FAX: 847/234-1075
E-mail: ragdaleevents@aol.com
Internet: http://www.ragdale.ord

AMOUNT: 2-month residency plus travel expense
DEADLINE(S): FEB 1
FIELD(S): Creative Writing

Writing residency for women who have begun to write seriously after the age of 55. U.S. citizenship required, and financial need must be demonstrated.

1 award annually. Not renewable. Contact Sylvia Brown at above address for details.

974—RIPON COLLEGE (Performance/Recognition Tuition Scholarships)

Admissions Office
300 Seward Street
P.O. Box 248
Ripon WI 54971
920/748-8101
E-mail: adminfo@ripon.edu
Internet: http://www.ripon.edu

AMOUNT: $5,000-$10,000/year
DEADLINE(S): MAR 1
FIELD(S): Music; Forensics; Art; Theater

Open to undergraduate and graduate students attending or planning to attend Ripon College. Purpose is to recognize and encourage academic potential and accomplishment in above fields. Interview, audition, or nomination may be required.

Renewable. Contact Office of Admission for an application.

975—ROSE HILL COLLEGE (Louella Robinson Memorial Scholarship)

P.O. Box 3126
Aiken SC 29802-3126
800/684-3769
FAX: 803/641-0240
E-mail: rosehill@rosehill.edu
Internet: http://www.rosehill.edu

AMOUNT: $10,000/year for four years
DEADLINE(S): Varies
FIELD(S): Liberal arts and humanities curricula

For undergraduate residents of Indian River County, Florida, to attend Rose Hill College in Aiken, South Carolina. The school offers a liberal arts education and follows the Great Books curriculum, a program of reading and seminars.

One annual award. Applicants must meet entry requirements of RHC. Contact above location for details.

976—ROSE HILL COLLEGE (Scholarships for Children of Eastern Orthodox Priests/Deacons)

P.O. Box 3126
Aiken SC 29802-3126
800/684-3769
FAX: 803/641-0240
E-mail: rosehill@rosehill.edu
Internet: http://www.rosehill.edu

AMOUNT: Full scholarship: $10,000/year for four years
DEADLINE(S): Varies
FIELD(S): Liberal Arts and Humanities Curricula

For undergraduates who are children of Eastern Orthodox Christan priests or deacons to attend Rose Hill College in Aiken, South Carolina. The school offers a liberal arts education and follows the Great Books Curriculum, a program of reading and seminars.

6-10 annual awards. Applicants must meet entry requirements of RHC. Contact above location for details.

977—ROSE HILL COLLEGE (Scholarships for the Homeschooled)

P.O. Box 3126
Aiken SC 29802-3126
800/684-3769
FAX: 803/641-0240
E-mail: rosehill@rosehill.edu
Internet: http://www.resehill.edu

AMOUNT: Full scholarship: $10,000/year for four years
DEADLINE(S): Varies
FIELD(S): Liberal Arts and Humanities Curricula

For undergraduates who have been homeschooled for three of the last five years of their high school education. For use at Rose Hill College in Aiken, South Carolina. The school offers a liberal arts education and follows the Great Books Curriculum, a program of reading and seminars. Scholarships will be awarded primarily on the basis of an essay which the student will be asked to write.

Four annual awards. Applicants must meet entry requirements of RHC. Contact above location for details.

978—SAN DIEGO PRESS CLUB FOUNDATION (Scholarship)

2454 Heritage Park Row
San Diego CA 92110
619/299-5747;
E-mail: sdpressc@cts.com;
Internet: http://www.sddt.com/~pressclub

AMOUNT: $1,500
DEADLINE(S): JUL 1
FIELD(S): Journalism

Awards are for San Diego County residents only who pursue a career in journalism or a related field, such as English. Two scholarships available: community college and four-year college and university.

979—SPECIAL LIBRARIES ASSOCIATION (SLA Scholarship Program)

1700 Eighteenth Street NW
Washington DC 20009-2508

202/234-4700
FAX: 202/265-9317
E-mail: sla@sla.org
Internet: http://www.sla.org
AMOUNT: $6,000
DEADLINE(S): OCT 31
FIELD(S): Library Science

Open to college graduates or college seniors with an interest in special librarianship. Scholarship is for graduate study in librarianship leading to a master's degree at a recognized school of library or information science.

Applicants must submit evidence of financial need. Write for complete information.

980—STANFORD UNIVERSITY (Creative Writing Fellowships)

Stanford University
Stanford, CA 94305-2087
Internet: http://www.stanford.edu/dept/english/cw/
AMOUNT: $41,000
DEADLINE(S): DEC
FIELD(S): Creative Writing

For poets and creative writers (fiction) to spend two years at Stanford in the Creative Writing Program.

981—STANLEY DRAMA AWARD (Playwriting/Musical Awards Competition)

Dept of Theatre
Wagner College
One Campus Road
Staten Island NY 10301
718/390-3325
AMOUNT: $2,000
DEADLINE(S): OCT 1
FIELD(S): Playwriting; Music Composition

Annual award for an original full-length play or musical which has not been professionally produced or received trade book publication. Must submit musical works on cassette tape with book and lyrics. A series of 2-3 thematically related one-act plays will also be considered. When submitting scripts, send self-addressed, stamped envelope large enough to accommodate the script.

Contact the Department of Theater at Wagner College for complete information.

982—STUDENT CONSERVATION ASSOCIATION (SCA Resource Assistant Program)

P.O. Box 550
Charlestown NH 03603
603/543-1700
FAX: 603/543-1828
E-mail: internships@sca-inc.org
Internet: http://www.sca-inc.org
AMOUNT: $1,180-$4,725
DEADLINE(S): Varies
FIELD(S): Environment and related fields

Must be 18 and U.S. citizen; need not be student. Fields: Agriculture, Archaeology, anthropology, botany, caves, civil/environmental engineering, environmental education, fisheries, forests, herpetology, history, living history/roleplaying, visitor services, landscape architecture/environmental design, paleontology, recreation/resource/range management, trail maintenance/ construction, wildlife management, geology, hydrology, library/museums, surveying...

900 positions in U.S. and Canada. Send $1 for postage for application; outside U.S./Canada, send $20.

983—THE ASSOCIATION FOR WOMEN IN COMMUNICATIONS (Scholarship)

c/o Reuters America
1333 H Street NW
5th Floor
Washington DC 20005
202/256-0866
E-mail: susan.heavey@reuters.com
AMOUNT: $1,000
DEADLINE(S): MAR 15
FIELD(S): Journalism

Current sophomore or junior female student attending a Washington, DC-area university or college studying communications, advertising, journalism, public relations, marketing, graphic arts, or a related field with an overall GPA of 3.0 or higher

984—THE JOHN F. KENNEDY CENTER FOR THE PERFORMING ARTS (Awards, Fellowships, and Scholarships)

The Kennedy Center
2700 F Street NW
Washington DC 20566-0001
202/416-8857
FAX: 202/416-8802
E-mail: skshaffer@kennedy-center.org
Internet: http://www.kennedy-center.org/actf
AMOUNT: Varies
DEADLINE(S): Varies
FIELD(S): Playwriting, Stage Design, and Acting

Various scholarships and awards in the above fields.

Contact organization for a booklet, "The Kennedy Center American College Theater Festival," for details and/or visit Web site.

985—THE LEMMERMANN FOUNDATION (Fondazione Lemmermann Scholarship Awards)

c/o Studio Associato Romanelli
via Cosseria, 5
00192 Roma ITALY
(06) 324.30.23
FAX: (06) 322.17.88
E-mail: lemmermann@mail.nexus.it
Internet:
http://www.lemmermann.nexus.it/lemmermann/
AMOUNT: 750 euro per month
DEADLINE(S): MAR 15; SEP 30
FIELD(S): Italian/Roman studies in the subject areas of literature, archaeology, history of art

For university students who need to study in Rome to carry out research and prepare their theses concerning Rome and the Roman culture from the period Pre-Roman to present day time in the subject areas above.

Contact above organization for details. Access Web site for application form.

986—THE WALT DISNEY COMPANY (American Teacher Awards)

P.O. Box 9805
Calabasas CA 91372
AMOUNT: $2,500 (36 awards); $25,000 (Outstanding Teacher of the Year)
DEADLINE(S): FEB 15
FIELD(S): Teachers: Athletic Coach, Early Childhood, English, Foreign Language/ESL, General Elementary, Mathematics, Performing Arts, Physical Education/Health, Science, Social Studies, Visual Arts, Vo-Tech Education

Awards for K-12 teachers in the above fields.

Teachers, or anyone who knows a great teacher, can write for applications at the above address.

987—UNIVERSITY OF NEW MEXICO (Mary McDonald Scholarship)

Office of Financial Aid
Albuquerque NM 87131
AMOUNT: Varies
DEADLINE(S): MAR 1
FIELD(S): English

For University of New Mexico students majoring in English. Must be nominated by faculty.

988—U.S. INSTITUTE OF PEACE (National Peace Essay Contest)

1200 17th Street NW; Suite 200
Washington DC 20036
202/457-1700
FAX: 202/429-6063
E-mail: essay_contest@usip.org
Internet: http://www.usip.org

AMOUNT: $1,000-$10,000
DEADLINE(S): JAN
FIELD(S): Political Science; U.S. History

1,500-word essay contest for high school students on the U.S. response to international conflict. No restrictions as to citizenship/residency.

Not renewable. See Web site or contact USIP for specific guidelines.

989—UNITARIAN UNIVERSALIST ASSOCIATION (Musicians' Network Scholarships)

4190 Front Street
San Diego CA 92103
Written Inquiry

AMOUNT: $100-$700
DEADLINE(S): VARIES
FIELD(S): Art, Poetry, Music

Financial aid to undergraduate students in the above fields. Must be active with the Unitarian Universalist Association.

Renewable. Write for complete information.

990—UNIVERSITY FILM and VIDEO ASSOCIATION (Carole Fielding Student Grants)

Professor Robert Johnson
Framington State College
100 State Street
Framington MA 01701
Internet: http://www.uvfa.org

AMOUNT: $1,000 to $4,000
DEADLINE(S): JAN 1
FIELD(S): Film, video, multi-media production

Open to undergraduate/graduate students. Categories are narrative, experimental, animation, documentary, multimedia. Applicant must be sponsored by a faculty member who is an active member of the University Film and Video Association.

Write to the above address for application and complete details.

991—UNIVERSITY OF ILLINOIS AT URBANA-CHAMPAIGN (Lydia E. Parker Bates Scholarship)

620 East John Street
Champaign IL 61820
217/333-0100
Internet: http://www.uiuc.edu/

AMOUNT: Up to $1,000
DEADLINE(S): MAR 15
FIELD(S): Art, Architecture, Landscape Architecture, Urban Planning, Dance, Theater, and all related subjects except Music.

Open to undergraduate students in the College of Fine and Applied Arts who are attending the University of Illinois at Urbana-Champaign. Must demonstrate financial need and have 2.85 GPA. Complete the Free Application for Federal Student Aid with UIUC admission application.

175 awards per year. Recipients must carry at least 12 credit hours per semester. Contact office of student financial aid for application.

FOREIGN LANGUAGE

992—AIR FORCE RESERVE OFFICER TRAINING CORPS (AFROTC Scholarships)

551 E. Maxwell Boulevard
Maxwell AFB AL 36112-6106
334/953-7783

AMOUNT: Full tuition, books, and fees for all 4 years of college
DEADLINE(S): DEC 1
FIELD(S): Science; Engineering; Business; Political Science; Psychology; Geography; Foreign Studies; Foreign Language

Competitive scholarships based on individual merit to high school seniors and graduates who have not completed any full-time college work. Must be a U.S. citizen between the ages of 17-27. Must also have GPA of 2.5 or above, be in top 40% of class, and complete Applicant Fitness Test. Cannot be a single parent. Your college/university must offer AFROTC.

2,300 awards annually. Contact above address for application packet.

993—AMERICAN ASSOCIATION OF TEACHERS OF FRENCH (National French Contest)

Sidney L. Teitelbaum; Box 32030
Sarasota FL 34239
FAX: 941/364-9820

AMOUNT: Varies
DEADLINE(S): Varies
FIELD(S): French Language; French Studies

Le Grand Concours, or National French Contest, is a French event in the form of a 60-minute national examination to help stimulate further interest in the teaching and learning of French and to help identify and reward achievement on the part of both students and teachers.

Not a scholarship. Winners receive trips, medals, and books. Write for complete information or ask your French teacher. All students of French, from FLES through senior high school, are eligible. In addition, students studying French on overseas campuses, with a private tutor exclusive of any formal classroom instruction in French, or via Homeschooling, are all eligible for awards.

994—AMERICAN ASSOCIATION OF TEACHERS OF GERMAN (National AATG/PAD Awards)

112 Haddontowne Court #104
Cherry Hill NJ 08034
856/795-5553
FAX: 856/795-4398
Internet: http://www.aatg.org

AMOUNT: Costs of study trip
DEADLINE(S): DEC 1 (deadline for teachers to order test)
FIELD(S): German Language

This summer-study trip award to Germany is open to high school students who study German. U.S. citizenship or permanent residency is required.

995—AMERICAN ASSOCIATION OF TEACHERS OF ITALIAN (College Essay Contest)

Cal State University, Chico
Foreign Language Department
Chico CA 95929
Written Inquiries

AMOUNT: $100-$300
DEADLINE(S): JUN 15
FIELD(S): Italian Language; Italian Studies

Not a scholarship. Prize given on a competitive basis to essays written in Italian by college students on a prescribed topic. Contest open to undergraduate students at accredited colleges and universities in North America. Essay in Italian language on topic pertaining to literature or culture.

Write to Prof. Eugenio Frongia at address above for complete information.

996—AMERICAN INSTITUTE OF INDIAN STUDIES (Language Program)

1130 E. 59th Street
Chicago IL 60637
773/702-8638
E-mail: aiis@uchicago.edu
Internet: http://ccat.sas.upenn.edu/aiis/

AMOUNT: $3,000 + travel
DEADLINE(S): JAN 31
FIELD(S): Languages of India

Fellowships for classes held in India for U.S. citizens who have a minimum of 2 years, or 240 hours, of classroom instruction in a language of India: Hindi, Bengali, Tamil, or Telugu.

10 awards annually. Contact AIIS for an application.

997—BNAI ZION FOUNDATION, INC. (Scholarship)

Scholarship Director
Bnai Zion/Brith Abraham
136 East 39th Street
New York NY 10016
212/725-1211
FAX: 212/679-1109

AMOUNT: $100
DEADLINE(S): APR 15
FIELD(S): Hebrew

Scholarships are available for students wishing to pursue the language of Hebrew in American institutions. Must demonstrate excellence in Hebrew study.

998—BRITISH ACADEMY (Sir Ernest Cassel Educational Trust)

10 Carlton House
Islington, London SWIY 5AH
ENGLAND UK
020 7969 5217
FAX: 020 7969 5414
E-mail: grants@britac.ac.uk
Internet: http://www.britac.ac.uk/funding/guide/cetf.html

AMOUNT: Up to 5,000 pounds per annum
DEADLINE(S): FEB; APR; SEP; NOV (end of ea. month)
FIELD(S): Language, literature, or civilization of any country

The British Academy administers funds on behalf of the Sir Ernest Cassel Educational Trust to support travel costs related to a research project. Research Grants Department Awards are particularly aimed at recent postdoctoral scholars.

Obtain application from the Research Grants Department.

999—CEMANAHUAC EDUCATIONAL COMMUNITY (Scholarships for Teachers of Spanish)

Cemanahuac Educational Community
Apartado 5-21
Cuernavace, Morelos MEXICO
(52-77) 318-6407
FAX: (52-77) 312-5418
E-mail: 74052.2570@compuserve.com;
Internet: http://www.cemanahuac.com/

AMOUNT: Varies
DEADLINE(S): Varies
FIELD(S): Spanish language

Scholarships for U.S. teachers of Spanish are available through the American Association of Teachers of Spanish and Portuguese (610/363-7005) and the American Council on the Teaching of Foreign Languages (914/963-8830) for use at Cemanahuac in Mexico. And, 50+ U.S. school systems have arranged with Cemanahuac for reduced rates for educators struggling to meet the needs of children and their families from a Hispanic background. Contact Cemanahuac for list of districts.

Contact organization for details, and contact AATSP and ACTFL for scholarship possibilities.

1000—CENTER FOR ARABIC STUDY ABROAD (CASA Fellowships)

Johns Hopkins Univ.
1619 Massachusetts Avenue, NW
Washington DC 20036-1983
202/663-5750
E-mail: CASA@mail.jhuwash.jhu.edu
Internet: http://www.sais-jhu.edu/languages/CASA

AMOUNT: Tuition, allowance, and airfare
DEADLINE(S): DEC 31
FIELD(S): Advanced Arabic Language Training

Fellowships for summer and full-year intensive Arabic training at the American University in Cairo, Egypt. Open to graduate students and a limited number of undergraduates. A minimum two years of Arabic study is required. Must be U.S. citizen/permanent resident.

20 awards annually. Contact D. Whaley, Program Administrator, for an application.

1001—CENTRO DE IDIOMAS DEL SURESTE A.C. (Intensive Spanish Scholarship)

Calle 14 #106 X 25 Colonia Mexico
Merida Yucatan 97128 MEXICO
1152-99-26-11-55
FAX: 1152-99-26-90-20
Internet: http://www.cisyucatan.com.mx

AMOUNT: Varies
DEADLINE(S): Varies (45 days before enrollment)
FIELD(S): Spanish Language

Scholarships for Spanish language study at CIS, open to students currently enrolled in an undergraduate or graduate program. No citizenship requirements. Preference given to students with financial need.

Renewable. Contact Chloe C. Pacheco at CIS for an application.

1002—COLUMBIA UNIVERSITY (Donald Keene Center of Japanese Culture Scholarship)

507 Kent Hall
New York NY 10027
212/854-5036
FAX: 212/854-4019
E-mail: donald-keene-center@columbia.edu;
Internet: http://www.columbia.edu/cu/ealac/dkc

AMOUNT: $2,500
DEADLINE(S): Feb 15
FIELD(S): Japanese

The Donald Keene Center of Japanese Culture at Columbia University annually awards two $2,500 Japan-U.S. Friendship Commission Prizes for the Translation of Japanese Literature. One prize is given for the best translation of a modern work of literature and the other for the best classical literary translation. Translators of any nationality are welcome to apply. To qualify, works must be book-length translations of Japanese literary works: novels, collections of short stories, literary essays, memoirs, drama, or poetry.

1003—GERMAN ACADEMIC EXCHANGE SERVICE (DAAD Programs)

871 United States Plaza
New York NY 10017
212/758-3223
FAX: 212/755-5780
E-mail: daadny@daad.org

Internet: http://www.daad.org
AMOUNT: Varies (with program)
DEADLINE(S): Varies (with program)
FIELD(S): Varies (with program)

Grants are available to faculty and full-time students who are citizens or permanent residents of the U.S. or Canada. Programs are for study in Germany in a variety of fields.

See Web site or contact DAAD Programs Administrator for an application.

1004—GIACOMO LEOPARDI CENTER (Scholarships for Italian Language Study in Italy)

Via Castello
61020 Belforte all'Isauro ITALY
39 0722 726000
FAX: 39 0722 726010
E-mail: centroleopardi@wnt.it
Internet: http://www.italian.org/
AMOUNT: Cost of tuition (about $750)
DEADLINE(S): Varies
FIELD(S): Italian language and literature

The Center is in a castle built in the late Middle Ages. The castle is the site of school for teaching the Italian language and culture. Students are lodged in rooms in the Castle. Scholarships are for the first 300 to apply, and they are for tuition only. Students still must pay for food and lodging.

Ten scholarships covering the cost of an Italian Language and Culture course. Most details are found on the Web site.

1005—INSTITUT D'ETUDES FRANCAISES D'AVIGNON (Scholarships for Summer Study in Avignon, France)

Bryn Mawr College
Bryn Mawr PA 19010-2899
610/526-5083
FAX: 610/526-7479
E-mail: avignon@brynmawr.edu
Internet: http://www.brynmawr.edu/Adm/academic/special/avignon/details.html
AMOUNT: Varies
DEADLINE(S): MAR 15
FIELD(S): French-related studies

Scholarships based on academic excellence and financial need for a six-week summer study program in Avignon, France. Program is offered to male and female students from other colleges as well as Bryn Mawr. For graduates and undergraduates who have completed three years of college-level French or equivalent.

Contact the Director of the Institute for application information.

1006—INSTITUTE OF INTERNATIONAL EDUCATION (National Security Education Program Undergraduate Scholarship)

809 United Nations Place
New York NY 10017
212/984-5388
FAX: 212/984-5393
E-mail: csanders@iie.org
Internet: http://www.iie.org/nsep/
AMOUNT: Varies: up to $6,000
DEADLINE(S): Varies
FIELD(S): Foreign Language

Scholarships are available to enable recipients to pursue serious study abroad in critical world areas that do NOT include Western Europe, Canada, Australia, or New Zealand.

A foreign language component must be included in every applicant's study abroad proposal. Check with NSEP representative at your local campus or write or call above location for complete information.

1007—JAPANESE AMERICAN CITIZENS LEAGUE (Yoshiko Tanaka Memorial Scholarship)

1765 Sutter Street
San Francisco CA 94115
415/921-5225
FAX: 415/931-4671
E-mail: jacl@jacl.org
Internet: http://www.jacl.org
AMOUNT: $1,000-$5,000
DEADLINE(S): APR 1
FIELD(S): Japanese Language/Culture; U.S.-Japan Relations

Open to JACL members and their children only. For undergraduate students with an interest in Japanese language, culture, or the enhancement of U.S.-Japan relations and who are planning to attend a college, university, trade school, business school, or any other institution of higher learning. Must submit personal statement, letters of recommendation, and transcripts. Financial need NOT a factor.

For membership information or an application, send a self-addressed, stamped envelope to above address, stating your level of study. Applications available October 1 through March 20; recipients notified in July.

1008—KOSCIUSZKO FOUNDATION (Summer Sessions in Poland and Rome)

15 E. 65th Street
New York NY 10021-6595
212/734-2130
FAX: 212/628-4552
E-mail: thekf@pegasusnet.com;
Internet: http://www.kosciuszkofoundation.org
AMOUNT: Varies
DEADLINE(S): Varies
FIELD(S): Polish Studies; History; Literature; Art; Economics; Social Studies; Language; Culture

Open to undergraduate and graduate students, graduating high school students who are 18 or older, and persons of any age who are not enrolled in a college/university program. Study programs are offered in Poland and Rome from mid-June through the end of August in above fields. Must be U.S. citizen/permanent resident.

See Web site or send a self-addressed, stamped envelope to Addy Tymczyszyn, Summer Studies Abroad Coordinator, for an application.

1009—NATIONAL ITALIAN AMERICAN FOUNDATION (Scholarship Program)

1860 19th Street NW
Washington DC. 20009
202/387-0600
FAX:202/387-0800
E-mail: scholarships@niaf.org
Internet: http://www.niaf@org/scholarships
AMOUNT: $2,000-$5,000 per year (renewable)
DEADLINE(S): APR 30
FIELD(S): Humanities, Area Studies, Foreign Language

140 scholarships awarded annually to undergraduate, graduate, and doctoral students of Italian-American descent in any field of study, or to students from any ethnic background majoring or minoring in Italian language, Italian studies, Italian American studies, or a related field. Applications can only be submitted online. See Web site for application and more information on requirements.

1010—NEW ZEALAND FEDERATION OF UNIVERSITY WOMEN-WAIKATO BRANCH (Kahurangi Maori Language Award)

P.O. Box 7065
Hamilton NEW ZEALAND
07/855-3776
AMOUNT: $1,000
DEADLINE(S): MAR 15
FIELD(S): Education; Maori Studies

Open to Maori women who are full-time students enrolled for a third or fourth year at the University of Waikato School of Education or the Department of Maori

Studies. Must be fluent in or studying the Maori language for a Bachelor of Education degree or Diploma of Teaching.

Contact the Convenor, NAFUW, Waikato Branch for an application.

1011—NORWICH JUBILEE ESPERANTO FOUNDATION (Travel Grants)

37 Granville Court
Oxford OX3 0HS ENGLAND
01865-245509
AMOUNT: 1,000 pounds sterling (max.)
DEADLINE(S): None
FIELD(S): Esperanto

Travel grants open to those who speak Esperanto and wish to improve their use of the language through travel in the UK. Candidates must be under the age of 26 and be able to lecture in Esperanto.

1012—SONOMA CHAMBOLLE-MUSIGNY SISTER CITIES, INC. (Henri Cardinaux Memorial Scholarship)

Chamson Scholarship Committee
P.O. Box 1633
Sonoma CA 95476-1633
707/939-1344
FAX: 707/939-1344
E-mail: Baileysci@vom.com
AMOUNT: Up to $1,500 (travel + expenses)
DEADLINE(S): JUL 15
FIELD(S): Culinary Arts; Wine Industry; Art; Architecture; Music; History; Fashion

Hands-on experience working in above or similar fields and living with a family in small French village in Burgundy or other French city. Must be Sonoma County, CA, resident at least 18 years of age and be able to communicate in French. Transcripts, employer recommendation, photograph, and essay (stating why, where, and when) required.

1 award. Nonrenewable. Also offers opportunity for candidate in Chambolle-Musigny to obtain work experience and cultural exposure in Sonoma, CA.

1013—SOUTHEAST MISSOURI STATE UNIVERSITY (Constance Rowe French Scholarship)

One University Plaza
Cape Girardeau MO 63701
573/651-2476
Internet: http://www.2.semo.edu/foreignlang/SCH-FR.HTML
AMOUNT: Up to full tuition and fees
DEADLINE(S): Varies
FIELD(S): French or Education with a French minor

Scholarships for French majors or Education majors with a French minor at Southeast Missouri State University. Awarded for study in a French-speaking country for the summer after the sophomore year, either semester of the junior year, or for the summer after the junior year. Financial need may be considered.

Contact Dr. Daniel A. MacLeay at the University for more information. His E-mail contact point is accessible at the Web site listed.

1014—SOUTHEAST MISSOURI STATE UNIVERSITY (Frances and Cornelius Crowley Scholarship)

One University Plaza
Cape Girardeau MO 63701
573/651-2000
E-mail: djedan@semo.edu
Internet: http://www2.semo.edu/foreignlang/sch-sn.html
AMOUNT: Varies
DEADLINE(S): Varies
FIELD(S): Spanish Language

Scholarships for full-time students who are members of the Spanish club at Southeast Missouri State University. Must have a 2.8 or higher GPA overall, 3.0 Spanish GPA. Applicants must compose an assigned essay.

1015—SOUTHEAST MISSOURI STATE UNIVERSITY (German Scholarship)

One University Plaza
Cape Girardeau MO 63701
573/651-2000
E-mail: djedan@semo.edu
Internet: http://www2.semo.edu/foreignlang/sch-gn.html
AMOUNT: Varies
DEADLINE(S): Varies
FIELD(S): German language

Scholarships for full-time students who are German majors at Southeast Missouri State University. Awarded for overseas study purposes. Must have a 2.5 or higher GPA.

Contact Dr. Dieter Jedan at the University for more information. His E-mail contact point is accessible at the Web site listed.

1016—SUOMI-SEURA/FINLAND SOCIETY

Mariankatu 8
00170 Helsinki FINLAND
358-9-6841210
Internet: http://www.suomi-seura.fi/english
AMOUNT: EUR 340
DEADLINE(S): Spring
FIELD(S): Seminar on Finnish Language and Culture

Grant and travel grant to students from outside Europe.

Applicants must be of Finnish descent.

1017—THE AMERICAN CLASSICAL LEAGUE (Ed Phinney Commemorative Scholarship)

Miami University
Oxford OH 45056
513/529-7741
FAX: 513/529-7742
E-mail: AmericanClassicalLeague@muohio.edu or a.c.l@mich.edu
Internet: http://www.umich.edu/~acleague/phinney.html
AMOUNT: Up to $500
DEADLINE(S): JAN 15
FIELD(S): Teachers or teacher candidates in the classics (Latin and/or Greek)

Scholarships of up to $500 to apply to first-time attendance at the League's institute OR up to $500 to cover cost of other activities that serve to enhance a teacher's skills in the classroom in the classics OR up to $150 for purchase of materials from the ACL Teaching and Materials Resource Center. Memberships required except for first-time attendance at institute.

Send request for information to above address.

1018—THE BRITISH COUNCIL (Bursaries/Scholarships for Residents of Myanmar (Burma) in English Language Classes)

78 Kanna Road
P.O. Box 638
Yangon MYANMAR (BURMA)
(00 950 1) 254 658
FAX: (00 950 1) 245 345
E-mail: admin@bc-burma.bcouncil.org
Internet: http://www.britcoun.org/burma
AMOUNT: Varies
DEADLINE(S): Varies
FIELD(S): English Language

The British Council's Teaching Centre in Rangoon has an extensive program in teaching the English language.

The Web site listed here gives more details; the British council lists hundreds of educational programs worldwide on its Web site.

1019—THE CENTER FOR CROSS-CULTURAL STUDY (Tuition Awards for Study in Seville, Spain)

446 Main Street
Amherst MA 01002-2314
413/256-0011 or 800/377-2621
FAX: 413/256-1968
E-mail: cccs@crocker.com
Internet: http://www.cccs.com
AMOUNT: $500
DEADLINE(S): Varies
FIELD(S): Study of Spanish and Spanish Culture

Partial tuition assistance is available at this facility in Spain. Applicants must submit an original essay in Spanish, between 2 or 3 double-spaced, typed pages. Also required as a short description in English of your experience with the Spanish language and culture and a faculty recommendation.

Awards are for one semester or academic year programs in Seville. Contact organization for specific details regarding the essays.

1020—THE WALT DISNEY COMPANY (American Teacher Awards)

P.O. Box 9805
Calabasas CA 91372
AMOUNT: $2,500 (36 awards); $25,000 (Outstanding Teacher of the Year)
DEADLINE(S): FEB 15
FIELD(S): Teachers: Athletic Coach, Early Childhood, English, Foreign Language/ESL, General Elementary, Mathematics, Performing Arts, Physical Education/Health, Science, Social Studies, Visual Arts, Vo-Tech Education

Awards for K-12 teachers in the above fields.

Teachers, or anyone who knows a great teacher, can write for applications at the above address.

1021—UNIVERSITY OF ROCHESTER (Mildred R. Burton Summer Study Grants/Scholarships for Summer Language Study)

Box 270251
Rochester NY 14627-0251
585/275-4251
Internet: http://www.rochester.edu/College/MLC/burton.html
AMOUNT: Varies
DEADLINE(S): Varies
FIELD(S): Foreign Language

Scholarships for undergraduate students to complete an approved course of summer language study in a country where that language is spoken. Preference will be given to University of Rochester students who intend to study in a program run by the University if such a program is available in the language the student wishes to study. Must have completed at least one year of foreign language study at U.R. and graduate students in the Dept. of Modern Languages and Cultures.

Based on merit and need. Applications are available from the Dept. of Modern Languages and Cultures.

PERFORMING ARTS

1022—ACADEMY OF TELEVISION ARTS AND SCIENCES COLLEGE (Television Awards)

Hap Lovejoy, Educational Programs and Services Administrator
Academy of Television Arts and Sciences
5220 Lankershim Boulevard
North Hollywood CA 91601
818/754-2830
FAX: 818/761-8524
E-mail: collegeawards@emmys.com/foundation
Internet: http://www.emmys.com/foundation
AMOUNT: $500-$2,000
DEADLINE(S): DEC 12
FIELD(S): Arts, Communications, Filmmaking, Journalism, Performing Arts, Photojournalism, TV/Radio Broadcasting

The academy confers three awards in each of the following categories: comedy, drama, music programs, documentary, news, sports, magazine shows, traditional animation, and nontraditional animation. Submit tape of original production.

1023—ACADEMY OF VOCAL ARTS (Scholarships)

1920 Spruce Street
Philadelphia PA 19103-6685
215/735-1685
FAX: 215/732-2189
Internet: http://www.avaopera.com
AMOUNT: Full Tuition
DEADLINE(S): JAN
FIELD(S): Vocal Music; Operatic Acting

Tenable only at the Academy Of Vocal Arts. Open to unusually gifted singers with at least four years college vocal training or equivalent. College degree recommended. Award includes full tuition scholarships and complete training in voice, operatic acting, and repertoire. Merit-based fellowships for additional expenses are also available. Winners are selected in Spring competitive auditions. Total student enrollment limited to 30.

Contact the Academy of Vocal Arts for an application.

1024—ADELPHI UNIVERSITY (Talent Awards)

1 South Avenue
Garden City NY 11530
516/877-3080 or 800/ADELPHI
Internet: http://www.ecampus.adelphi.edu/finaid/au_scholarships_grants.cfm#art
AMOUNT: $1,000-$7,000
DEADLINE(S): FEB 15
FIELD(S): Theater, Dance, Art, or Music

Various scholarships for full-time students at Adelphi University in the above fields. Must document financial need-fill out a FAFSA form. Must maintain 3.0 GPA in major and 2.5 overall to maintain scholarship.

See Web site for further information; contact school to apply.

1025—ALVIN M. BENTLEY FOUNDATION (Scholarship Program)

College of Literature, Science, and the Arts
The University of Michigan
500 S. State Street, #2522
Ann Arbor MI 48109
517/729-9040
FAX: 517/723-2454
E-mail: lsascholarship@umich.edu
AMOUNT: $7,500-$10,000 per year
DEADLINE(S): None
FIELD(S): Literature; Science; Arts

Open to Michigan residents applying as freshmen to the University of Michigan's College of Literature, Science, and the Arts. Based on academic excellence and extracurricular activities. Must be nominated; there are no separate applications. Candidates are chosen from U of M applications received from Michigan resident freshmen.

1026—AMERICA-ISRAEL CULTURAL FOUNDATION (Sharett Scholarship Program)

51 E. 42nd Street, #400
New York NY 10017
212/557-1600
FAX: 212/557-1611
E-mail: usaaicf@aol.com
Internet: http://www.aicf.webnet.org/involved_overview.html
AMOUNT: Varies
DEADLINE(S): MAR 15
FIELD(S): Music, Dance, Theater, Visual Arts, Film and Television

Scholarships are for one year of study and are renewable.

800 scholarships per year. Write for complete information.

1027—AMERICAN ACCORDION MUSICOLOGICAL SOCIETY (Contest)

322 Haddon Avenue
Westmont NJ 08108
856/858-1212
Internet: http://www.aamsaccordionfest.com
AMOUNT: $1,000 (max)
DEADLINE(S): SEP 10
FIELD(S): Music Composition for Accordion

Annual competition open to amateur or professional music composers who write a serious piece music (of six minutes or more) for the accordion.

Write for complete information.

1028—AMERICAN ALLIANCE FOR HEALTH, PHYSICAL EDUCATION, RECREATION & DANCE

1900 Association Drive
Reston VA 20191
703/476-3400 or 800/213-7193;
E-mail: webmaster@aahperd.org
Internet: http://www.aahperd.org
AMOUNT: Varies
DEADLINE(S): Varies
FIELD(S): Health Education, Leisure and Recreation, Girls and Women in Sports, Sport and Physical Education, Dance

This organization has six national suborganizations specializing in the above fields. Some have grants and fellowships for both individuals and group projects. The Web site has the details for each group.

Visit Web site for details or write to above address for details.

1029—AMERICAN FOUNDATION FOR THE BLIND (Gladys C. Anderson Memorial Scholarship)

11 Penn Plaza; Suite 300
New York NY 10001
212/502-7600
FAX: 212/502-7777
E-mail: afbinfo@afb.org
Internet: http://www.afb.org
AMOUNT: $1,000
DEADLINE(S): Varies
FIELD(S): Religious/Classical Music

Open to legally blind women studying religious or classical music at the college level. Must be U.S. citizen. Must submit evidence of legal blindness; official transcripts; proof of college/university acceptance; three letters of recommendation; performance tape of voice/instrumental selection (30 minutes max.); and typewritten statement describing educational and personal goals, work experience, extracurricular activities, and how scholarship monies will be used.

1 award annually. See Web site or contact the AFB for an application.

1030—AMERICAN FOUNDATION FOR THE BLIND (R. L. Gillette Scholarships)

11 Penn Plaza; Suite 300
New York NY 10001
212/502-7661
FAX: 212/502-7771
E-mail: afbinfo@afb.org
Internet: http://www.afb.org
AMOUNT: $1,000
DEADLINE(S): APR
FIELD(S): Literature; Music

Open to legally blind women enrolled in a four-year undergraduate degree program in literature or music. Must be U.S.citizen. Must submit evidence of legal blindness; official transcripts; proof of college/university acceptance; three letters of recommendation; performance tape (30 minutes max.) or creative writing sample; and typewritten statement describing educational and personal goals, work experience, extracurricular activities, and how monies will be used.

2 awards annually. See Web site or contact Julie Tucker at AFB for an application.

1031—AMERICAN GUILD OF ORGANISTS (National Competition in Organ Improvisation)

475 Riverside Drive; Suite 1260
New York NY 10115
212/870-2310
FAX: 212/870-2163
E-mail: info@agohq.org
Internet: http://www.agohq.org
AMOUNT: $2,000 (first prize); $1,000 (second); $500 (third)
DEADLINE(S): VARIES
FIELD(S): Organ Performance

Biannual competition seeks to further the art of improvisation in organ performance by recognizing and rewarding superior performers in the field. Membership in AGO required. Open to all members, including student members.

$35 registration fee. Contact AGO for membership information or an application.

1032—AMERICAN GUILD OF ORGANISTS (National Young Artists Competition)

475 Riverside Drive; Suite 1260
New York NY 10115
212/870-2310
FAX: 212/870-2163
E-mail: info@agohq.org
Internet: http://www.agohq.org
AMOUNT: $2,000 (first prize); $1,500 (second); $750 (third)
DEADLINE(S): Varies
FIELD(S): Organ Performance

Competition for organists between the ages of 22 and 32. Must be members of AGO.

Contact AGO for membership information or an application.

1033—AMERICAN GUILD OF ORGANISTS (Regional Competitions for Young Organists)

475 Riverside Drive; Suite 1260
New York NY 10115
212/870-2310
FAX: 212/870-2163
E-mail: info@agohq.org
Internet: http://www.agohq.org
AMOUNT: $1,000 (first prize); $500 (second)
DEADLINE(S): VARIES
FIELD(S): Organ Performance

Biannual competition for young people up to age 23 in nine different regions of the US. Membership NOT required.

$25 registration fee. Contact AGO for an application.

1034—AMERICAN STRING TEACHERS ASSOCIATION (ASTA) (Merle J. Isaac Composition Competition)

4153 Chain Bridge Road
FairFAX: VA 22030
703/279-2113
FAX: 703/279-2114
E-mail: asta@astaweb.com
Internet: http://www.astaweb.com
AMOUNT: Up to $1,000
DEADLINE(S): MAY 1
FIELD(S): Music composition

Applicant must submit an original composition that is unpublished and has never been submitted for publication, suitable for String Orchestra. Entries for middle school/junior high and high school level full orchestra will be accepted. Manuscripts will be judged on score analysis and a live performance.

See Web site for details of rules.

1035—AMERICAN STRING TEACHERS ASSOCIATION (ASTA) (Solo Competitions)

4153 Chain Bridge Road
FairFAX: VA 22030
703/279-2113
FAX: 703/279-2114
E-mail: asta@astaweb.com
Internet: http://www.astaweb.com
AMOUNT: Up to $4,500
DEADLINE(S): Varies
FIELD(S): Music (Strings): Violin, Viola, Cello, Double Bass, Classical Guitar, and Harp

Participants must be ASTA members or current students of ASTA members. Involves state competitions which lead to national competition. Two age groups: Junior Division-under 19 and Senior Division-19-25. Application fees required. For U.S. and Canadian citizens/legal residents.

Details of rules and various deadlines are on Web site above. List of state solo competition chairpersons is on Web site.

1036—PERMANENT GROUP Lady Mollie Askin Ballet Trust Scholarship

Permanent, Level 3
35 Clarence Street
Sydney NSW 2000 AUSTRALIA
(02)8295 8316
FAX: (02) 8295 8496
E-mail: Gabrielle.Steinhoff@permanentgroup.com.au
Internet: http://www.permanentgroup.com.au
AMOUNT: Aus. $15,000
DEADLINE(S): APR 18
FIELD(S): Ballet

"For the furtherance of culture and advancement of education in Australia and elsewhere to be awarded by the Trustees to Australian citizens who shall be adjudged of outstanding ability and promise in ballet." Must be between ages of 17 and 30 at deadline. Award may be used for study, maintenance, and travel either in Australia or overseas. Must submit proof of citizenship, curriculum vitae, references, summary of aims/activities, VHS w/ 2 pieces, and 5 photographs of positions.

Winner announced in June or July. Contact Gabrielle Steinhoff, Trust Administrator, for more information/entry form.

1037—ASSOCIATED BOARD OF THE ROYAL SCHOOLS OF MUSIC (Scholarships)

Administrative Asst.
International Administration
14 Bedford Square
London, ENGLAND WC1B 3JG
0171-636 5400
E-mail: abrsm@abrsm.ac.uk
Internet: http://www.abrsm.ac.uk
AMOUNT: Varies
DEADLINE(S): DEC
FIELD(S): Music Performance

Awarded to students who demonstrate outstanding musical promise. Must first apply to the Royal School of Music of applicant's choice. Scholarships are awarded on a competitive basis.

1038—ARTS MANAGEMENT P/L (Sir Robert Askin Operatic Travelling Scholarship)

Permanent, Level 3
35 Clarence Street
Sydney NSW 2000 AUSTRALIA
(02)8295 8316
FAX: (02) 8295 8496
E-mail: Gabrielle.Steinhoff@permanentgroup.com.au
Internet: http://www.permanentgroup.com.au
AMOUNT: Aus. $15,000
DEADLINE(S): SEP 25
FIELD(S): Opera Singing

For male Australian citizens between the ages of 18 and 30. Entrants should submit a photo, reviews, and an audio tape comprising three contrasting works (including period up to Mozart in original language and one work in English). Must include summary of proposed aims/activities, including names of teachers/institutions, travel plans, and dates. Must include proof of citizenship, curriculum vitae, and at least three references.

Contact Gabriella Steinhoff, Trust Administrator, for more information/entry form.

1039—ASSOCIATED MALE CHORUSES OF AMERICA (Scholarships)

5 Bayswater Avenue
Richmond Hill Ontario L4E 2L4
CANADA
905/773-7438
E-mail: trmusic@aci.on.ca
Internet: http://www.amcofa.org
AMOUNT: $500 or more
DEADLINE(S): MAR 1
FIELD(S): Music: Voice/Choral or Instrumental

Six awards/year. Scholarships for music majors, both male and female, enrolled as full-time college students in Bachelor's Degree programs. Student must be sponsored by a member chorus of the AMCA. List of member choruses available online. May reapply.

Applications and details are online at above Web site OR send self-addressed, stamped envelope (at rate appropriate for Canada) to Tom Rayner, AMCA Scholarship Chair, at above E-mail or postal address for detailed information and application. However, applications will not be available until October 1. Include your regular mail address.

1040—BEEBE FUND (Frank Huntington Beebe Fund for Musicians)

Secretary
290 Huntington Avenue
Boston MA 02115
617/585-1267
AMOUNT: $12,000
DEADLINE(S): DEC
FIELD(S): Music Performance

For junior and senior musicians who wish to study music and performance abroad, usually in Europe. Applications available beginning October 1. Award typically covers transportation, room and board, and tuition.

1041—BLUES HEAVEN FOUNDATION, INC. (Muddy Waters Scholarship)

2120 S. Michigan Avenue
Chicago IL 60616
312/808-1286
AMOUNT: $2,000

DEADLINE(S): APR 30
FIELD(S): Music; Music Education; African-American Studies; Folklore; Performing Arts; Arts Management; Journalism; Radio/TV/Film

Scholarship is made on a competitive basis with consideration given to scholastic achievement, concentration of studies, and financial need. Applicant must have full-time enrollment status in a Chicago area college/university in at least their first year of undergraduate studies or a graduate program. Scholastic aptitude extracurricular involvement, grade point average, and financial need are all considered.

Contact Blues Heaven Foundation, Inc. to receive an application between February and April.

1042—BUENA VISTA COLLEGE NETWORK (Internships in Film Marketing)

3900 W. Alameda Avenue
Burbank CA 91505-4316
818/567-5000
E-mail: College_Network@studio.disney.com
AMOUNT: Varies
DEADLINE(S): None
FIELD(S): Fields of study related to the motion picture industry, including marketing and promotion

Internships for full-time college students age 18 and up interested in a career in a facet of the motion picture industry. Must have unlimited access to computer with modem and transportation, be able to work 4-6 hours per week and 2-3 weekends per month. Attend film openings and sneak previews. Evaluate various aspects via an interactive computer system. Compensation ranges from $30 to $60/month. Possible school credit.

Access Web site by writing "Buena Vista College Network" from Yahoo. Available in most states and parts of Canada. Details, an interactive application, and E-mail access are located on Web site.

1043—CHAMBER MUSIC AMERICA (Gruber Foundation Award/Heidi Castleman Award for Excellence in Chamber Music Teaching)

305 Seventh Avenue
New York NY 10001
212/242-2022
E-mail: info@chamber-music.org
Internet: http://www.chamber-music.org
AMOUNT: $1,000
DEADLINE(S): DEC
FIELD(S): Chamber Music

Awards to honor teachers' efforts to involved students ages 6 to 18 in performing chamber music. Must be a music educator responsible for a chamber music program in elementary or high school.

Contact CMA for an application after August 1.

1044—CHOPIN FOUNDATION OF THE UNITED STATES, INC. (Scholarship Program for Young Pianists)

1440 79th St. Causeway, Suite 117
Miami FL 33141
305/868-0624
FAX: 305/865-5150
E-mail: info@choin.org
Internet: http://www.chopin.org
AMOUNT: $1,000/year up to 4 years
DEADLINE(S): FEB 15
FIELD(S): Music: piano

Scholarship program for pianists 14 to 17 years old who demonstrate an affinity for the interpretation of Chopin's music. The pianist is supported and encouraged throughout four years of preparation to qualify for the American Naitonal Chopin Piano Competition held in Miami, FL, every 5 years. The winners of this competition are sent to the International Chopin Piano Competition in Warsaw, Poland.

10 scholarships annually. For U.S. citizens or legal residents whose field of study is music and whose major is piano. $25. registration fee. Must be a full-time student. Submit references, audio tape, and formal application which is available at the above Web site or write for details.

1045—COLBURN-PLEDGE MUSIC SCHOLARSHIP FOUNDATION (Scholarships for Texas String Instrument Students)

101 Cardinal Avenue
San Antonio TX 78209
Written Inquiry
AMOUNT: Varies
DEADLINE(S): APR
FIELD(S): Music: String instruments

Awards for Texas residents studying a string instrument-violin, viola, cello, bass-in classical music with the intention of becoming a professional musician and in need of financial aid. Applicants can be in junior high, high school, or college. Texas residents may attend out-of-state music schools and/or music camps. Auditions of selected applicants are held in San Antonio around June 1.

Write for detailed information.

1046—COLUMBIA UNIVERSITY (Joseph H. Bearns Prize in Music)

Attn: Bearns Prize Committee
Columbia University
Department of Music
2960 Broadway
621 Dodge Hall, MC #1813
New York NY 10027
AMOUNT: Up to $6,000
DEADLINE(S): MAR
FIELD(S): Music Composition

Awarded to two young American composers, one award in orchestral, choral, etc. and one in soli, quartet, sextet, etc. Prizes are open to composers between the ages of 18 and 25. Submissions must be original compositions.

1047—COMMUNITY FOUNDATION OF WESTERN MASSACHUSETTS (Nate McKinney Memorial Scholarship)

1500 Main Street
P.O. Box 15769
Springfield MA 01115
413/732-2858
AMOUNT: $1,000
DEADLINE(S): APR 15
FIELD(S): Music; Athletics; Science

Open to graduating seniors of Gateway Regional High School in Huntington, Massachusetts. Recipient must excel academically, demonstrate good citizenship, and have a strong interest in at least two of the following areas: music, science, and athletics. Based on financial need, academic merit, and extracurricular activities. Must submit transcripts and fill out government FAFSA form.

1 award annually. Renewable up to 4 years with reapplication. Contact Community Foundation for an application and your financial aid office for FAFSA. Notification is in June.

1048—CONCORSO INTERNAZIONALE DI VIOLINO (Premio N. Paganini)

Comune di Genova; Via Sottoripa
16124 Genova ITALY
0039-010-5574215
FAX: 0039-010-2469272
E-mail: violinopaganini@commune.genova.it
Internet: http://www.comune.genova.it/turismo/paganini/welcome.htm
AMOUNT: 1,200 to 12,000 EURO
DEADLINE(S): MAY 31
FIELD(S): Violin

Contest for violinists of any nationality who are between the ages of 16 and 33.

100 euro entrance fee. See Web site or contact above address for official rules.

1049—CONCORSO INTERNAZIONALE PER QUARTETTO D'ARCHI (Premio Paolo Borciani)

Teatro Municipale Valli
Piazza Martiri del 7 luglio
42100 Reggio Emilia ITALY
39/0522/458811
FAX: 39/0522/458822
E-mail: premioboraiani@iteatre.re.it

AMOUNT: 36,000,000 Italian Lira (first prize); 26,000,000 IL (second prize); 12,000,000 IL (third prize)-All receive medal and diploma
DEADLINE(S): JAN 31
FIELD(S): String Quartets

This competition, which takes place in June at above address, is open to string quartets of all nationalities whose members are younger than 35 years of age; the total age of the ensemble shall not exceed 120 years in June of contest year. Biography, photos, reference letters, tape recordings, and birth certificates required. Participating quartets receive free room and board.

Entry fee. Contact above address for competition guidelines and application procedures.

1050—CONCORSO PIANISTICO INTERNAZIONALE (International Piano Competition)

Via Paradiso 6
20038 Seregno (Milan) ITALY
Phone/FAX: +39/0362/222.914
E-mail: pozzoli@concorsopozzoli.it
Internet: http://www.concorsopozzoli.it

AMOUNT: Varies
DEADLINE(S): MAY 31
FIELD(S): Piano

International piano competition for persons age 32 and older held every two years. Open to persons of all nationalities.

For details access Web site and/or send for booklet which explains in detail the prizes and requirements.

1051—CONCOURS CLARA HASKIL (International Piano Competition)

Rue de Conseil 31;
Case postale 234
CH-1800 Vevey 1 SWITZERLAND
41-21-922 67 04
FAX: 41-21-922 67 34
Internet: http://www.regart.ch/clara-haskil

AMOUNT: CHF 20, 000
DEADLINE(S): MAY 31
FIELD(S): Piano

Competition for pianists of all nationalities who are not more than 27 years of age. Traveling expenses are the responsibility of the candidate, as is accommodation; however, competition office can supply addresses of welcoming families (generally free of charge). Must submit three good-quality, black and white, 9x15cm photographs for brochure along with completed application form.

CHF 250-entry fee. Contact Clara Haskil for brochure detailing timetable, programme, and regulations.

1052—CONCOURS GEZA ANDA (International Piano Competition)

Bleicherweg 18
CH-8002 Zurich SWITZERLAND
0041/1/205 14 23
FAX: 0041/1/205 14 29
E-mail: info@gezaanda.ch
Internet: http://www.gezaanda.ch

AMOUNT: CHF 60,000
DEADLINE(S): MAR 1
FIELD(S): Piano

Pianists under 31 years of age from any nation may participate in the triennial June competition. Competition is divided into four rounds: Audition, Recital, Mozart Piano Concerto with orchestra, and Piano Concerto with orchestra. Applications must be accompanied by a curriculum vitae, certificate of birth (photocopy), and two photographs (suitable for publication). The Jury will select candidates for audition on the basis of written applications.

Application fee of CH 300-required. Travel and accommodation expenses not included. Contact Concours Geza Anda for an application packet.

1053—CONTEMPORARY RECORD SOCIETY (CRS Competitions)

724 Winchester Road
Broomall PA 19008
610/544-5920
FAX: 610/544-5921
E-mail: crsnews@erols.com
Internet: http://www.erols.com/crsnews

AMOUNT: VARIES
DEADLINE(S): FEB 5
FIELD(S): Music

All musicians are accepted for consideration for a recording grant.

$50 application fee. Renewable. Contact Caroline Hunt at CRS for an application.

1054—COUNCIL FOR BASIC EDUCATION (Chinese Culture Fellowship)

1319 F. Street NW, Suite 900
Washington, D.C. 20004
202/347-4171
FAX: 202/347-5047
E-mail: info@c-b-e.org
Internet: http://www.c-b-e.org/index.htm

AMOUNT: $1,000
DEADLINE(S): JUN
FIELD(S): Chinese Culture and Chinese Artistic Resources in New York City

Fellowships available to teams of two teachers (K-12)-one art teacher and one humanities teacher-to develop an interdisciplinary project that can be used to broaden the appreciation and understanding of Chinese culture and Chinese artistic resources in New York City. Teachers use web-based technology and make their material available to teachers nationally and internationally. A total of ten teachers or five teams will receive the award for six weeks of independent study during the summer.

Contact organization for details.

1055—CURTIS INSTITUTE OF MUSIC (Tuition Scholarships)

Admissions Office
1726 Locust Street
Philadelphia PA 19103-6187
215/893-5262
FAX: 215/893-7900@ADR
E-mail:admissions@curtis.edu
Internet: http://www.curtis.edu

AMOUNT: Full tuition
DEADLINE(S): DEC 16
FIELD(S): Music, Voice, Opera

Full-tuition scholarships open to students in the above areas who are accepted for full-time study at the Curtis Institute of Music. (Opera is for master of music only.)

Scholarships are renewable. Write or see Web site for complete information.

1056—DELTA OMICRON (Triennial Composition Competition for Solo Piano)

12297 W. Tennessee Place
Lakewood CO 80228-3325

E-mail: DOExecSec@aol.com
Internet: http://deltaomicron.people.virginia.edu
Written Inquiry
AMOUNT: $500 + premiere performance at Conference
DEADLINE(S): MAR
FIELD(S): Music composition competition

Award for solo piano composition with a time length from seven to ten minutes. No music fraternity affiliation required.

Prior publication or performance not allowed. Entry fee of $10 is required. Contact Judith Eidson at above address for details.

1057—DELTA OMICRON INTERNATIONAL MUSIC FRATERNITY (Triennial Composition Competition for Sacred Choral Anthem for Three- or Four-Part Voices)

12297 W. Tennessee Pl.
Lakewood CO 80228-3325
E-mail: DOExecSec@aol.com
Internet: http://deltaomicron.people.virginia.edu
Written Inquiry
AMOUNT: $500 and premiere
DEADLINE(S): MAR
FIELD(S): Music Composition

Sacred choral anthem for 3- or 4-part voices; SSA, SAB, or SATB with keyboard accompaniment or a capella with optional obligato. Competition open to composers of college age or over. No music fraternity affiliation required.

Prior publication or public performance of entry is NOT allowed. Entry fee of $10 is required. Contact Judith Eidson at above address for complete information.

1058—DISTRICT OF COLUMBIA COMMISSION ON THE ARTS AND HUMANITIES (Grants)

410 Eighth Street NW, 5th Floor
Washington DC 20004
202/724-5613; TDD: 202/727-3148
FAX: 202/727-4135
Internet: http://www.dcarts.dc.gov/main.shtm
AMOUNT: Varies
DEADLINE(S): Varies
FIELD(S): Media, Visual Arts, Crafts

Applicants for grants must be professional artists and residents of Washington DC for at least one year prior to submitting application. Awards intended to generate art endeavors within the Washington DC community.

Open also to art organizations that train, exhibit, or perform within DC. Write for complete information.

1059—DIXIE COLLEGE (Music Scholarships)

225 South 700 East
St. George UT 84770
435/652-7802 (vocal) or
435/652-7996 (strings) or
435/652-7997 (brass, woodwinds, percussion) or
435/652-7803 (flute, piano)
E-mail: kim@cc.dixie.edu
Internet: http://dsc.dixie.edu/music
AMOUNT: Varies
DEADLINE(S): MAR 1
FIELD(S): Music

Scholarships at Dixie College in St. George, Utah, for music students. Available for music majors and minors, and some are for nonmajors/minors who participate in ensembles. Available for both vocal and instrumental. Auditions required.

See Web site for audition details. Request scholarship forms from your high school counselor or from the Dixie College Financial Aid Office at 435/652-7575.

1060—DONNA REED FOUNDATION (Performing Arts Scholarships)

1305 Broadway
Denison IA 51442
Internet: http://www.donnareed.org
AMOUNT: $500-$4,000
DEADLINE(S): APR 1
FIELD(S): Performing Arts

Award to recognize, encourage, and support individuals who demonstrate excellence and a high level of interest in the performing arts. Must be a citizen or permanent resident of the United States or one of its official territories. Finalists will attend Donna Reed Performing Arts Workshop Program and perform in the final competition. All expenses to the Workshop will be paid by the foundation.

1061—EASTERN KENTUCKY UNIVERSITY (Music Scholarships)

Dr. Robert James, Chair
Dept. of Music
521 Lancaster Avenue
Richmond KY 40475-3102
859/622-1341
FAX: 859/622-3266
E-mail: rob.james@eku.edu
nternet: http://www.music.eku.edu
AMOUNT: Varies
DEADLINE(S): Varies
FIELD(S): Music

Scholarships for talented young instrument or voice musicians preparing themselves for careers in music or music education. Must audition for scholarship. Application (on Web site) is due at least two weeks prior to the desired audition date.

Scholarship recipients are required to participate in performing ensembles and maintain a GPA of 2.5 to retain scholarship.

1062—F.J. CONNELL MUSIC SCHOLARSHIP TRUST

1187 Simcoe Street
Moose Jaw Saskatchewan S6H 3J5
CANADA
306/694-2045
AMOUNT: $750 (Canadian)
DEADLINE(S): OCT 1
FIELD(S): Music

For students studying any aspect of music, such as education, performance, composition, history, etc. Must have completed the equivalent of one year of full-time music studies and be planning a professional career in music. No citizenship or residency requirements, but recipients will usually be Canadians.

Contact above location for details.

1063—FELLOWSHIP OF UNITED METHODISTS IN MUSIC AND WORSHIP ARTS (Scholarships)

P.O. Box 24787
Nashville TN 37202-787
800/952-8977
FAX: 615/749-6874
Internet: http://hometown.aol.com/fummwa
AMOUNT: VARIES
DEADLINE(S): MAR 1
FIELD(S): Music; Theology

Open to college-bound high school seniors and undergraduates who are active members of the United Methodist church. Based on talent, leadership ability, and potential for success.

4 awards annually. Renewable. Contact Fellowship for an application.

1064—FIVE WINGS ARTS COUNCIL (Artist Mentor Scholarships for Students)

200 First Street NE
Staples MN 56479
218/894-5485
FAX: 218/894-3045
E-mail: mturner@ncscmn.org
Internet: http://www.fwac.org

AMOUNT: Up to $500
DEADLINE(S): OCT 15
FIELD(S): Literary Arts; Visual Arts; Music; Theater; Media Arts; Dance

Open to rural high school students in grades 9-12 who are enrolled in an independent school district within the counties of Cass, Crow Wing, Morrison, Todd, and Wadena, Minnesota. Each recipient is matched with a qualified mentor who will establish a study schedule with student. Award is based on creative potential, accomplishments in art, maturity, and personal motivation.

10 awards annually. Contact Mark Turner, Director, for details.

1065—FLORIDA DEPARTMENT OF STATE-ARTS COUNCIL (Individual Artists' Fellowships)

Division Cultural Affairs; The Capitol
Tallahassee FL 32399-0250
850/487-2980
TTD: 850/488-5779
FAX: 850/922-5259
Internet: http://www.dos.state.fl.us/dca/fellow.html

AMOUNT: $5,000
DEADLINE(S): JAN 14
FIELD(S): Dance; Folklife/Traditional Arts; Interdisciplinary; Literature (children's literature, fiction, poetry); Media Arts; Music/Composition; Theater; Visual Arts and Crafts

Open to legal residents of Florida who are creative artists of at least 18 years of age. May NOT be enrolled in any undergraduate or graduate degree-seeking program during fellowship period.

38 awards annually. Renewable with reapplication after four years since date of previous award. Contact Florida Arts Council for information packet. Notification during summer.

1066—FONDATION DES ETATS-UNIS (Harriet Hale Woolley Scholarships)

The Director
Fondation des Etats-Unis
15, boulevard Jourdan
75690 Paris Cedex 14, FRANCE
01 53 80 68 80

AMOUNT: $8,500 French francs
DEADLINE(S): JAN
FIELD(S): Fine Arts

Available to female graduates of American colleges. Must have evidence of artistic or musical accomplishment. This graduate-level study in Paris will focus on visual fine arts or music.

1067—FRANCIS CHAGRIN FUND (Grants)

Francis House; Francis Street
London SWIP 1DE ENGLAND
0207 828 9696
FAX: 0207 931 9928
E-mail: spnm@spnm.org.uk
Internet: http://www.spnm.org.uk

AMOUNT: 250 pounds sterling (max.)
DEADLINE(S): None
FIELD(S): Music Composition

For British composers or composers resident in the UK. The fund considers applications for: 1) reproduction of scores and parts by photocopying or other reprographic means; 2) covering and binding of scores and parts; and 3) reproduction of tapes for use in performance. Financial need is NOT considered. Applications are considered monthly.

Not renewable. Contact Jo-Anne Naish at above address for an application.

1068—FRIBOURG FESTIVAL OF SACRED MUSIC (International Competition in Composition of Sacred Music)

P.O. Box 292
CH-1701 Fribourg SWITZERLAND
Written Inquiry

AMOUNT: first prize: Sw. Fr. 8,000; second prize: Sw. Fr. 2,000; third prize: 1,000.
DEADLINE(S): JUL 28 (odd-numbered years)
FIELD(S): Composition of Sacred Music

Biannual competition to encourage creation of original musical works taking their inspiration from sacred texts in the Christian tradition. Open to musical composers of all ages and nationalities. Composition must be original and never have been performed, not even partially. A work usually is of 20 minutes in duration, according to given theme. Composer must send 6 copies of score and bio-data. Jury of composers selects winners.

Contact Nicole Renevey, Administrator, at above address for technical restrictions of music piece. NOT A SCHOLARSHIP.

1069—GENERAL FEDERATION OF WOMEN'S CLUBS OF MASSACHUSETTS (Music Scholarship)

245 Dutton Road, Box 679
Sudbury MA 01776-0679
978/443-4569
FAX: 978/443-1617

AMOUNT: $500
DEADLINE(S): FEB 1
FIELD(S): Piano, Instrument, Music Education, or Music Therapy

Competitive scholarships for seniors in Massachusetts high schools. Letter of endorsement from sponsoring GFWC of MA club, letter of recommendation from either a high school principal or music teacher, transcripts, and personal audition (two short pieces contrasting in nature) required with application.

For more information or an application, send a self-addressed, stamped envelope to Alyce Burke, Coordinator, Arts Department, at above address.

1070—GENERAL FEDERATION OF WOMEN'S CLUBS OF MASSACHUSETTS (Dorchester Women's Club Scholarship)

245 Dutton Road, Box 679
Sudbury MA 01776-0679
978/443-4569
FAX: 978/443-1617

AMOUNT: $500
DEADLINE(S): FEB 1
FIELD(S): Voice

For undergraduates enrolled in a four-year accredited college, university, or school of music. Letter of endorsement from sponsoring GFWC of MA club, personal letter stating your need and other pertinent information, letter of recommendation from college department head or music professor, and transcripts required with application.

At least one scholarship annually. For more information or an application, send self-addressed, stamped envelope to Alyce Burke, Coordinator, Arts Department, at above address.

1071—GEORGE BIRD GRINNELL AMERICAN INDIAN CHILDREN'S FUND (Al Qoyawayma Award)

11602 Montague Court
Potomac MD 20854
301/424-2440
FAX: 301/424-8281
E-mail: Grinnell_Fund@MSN.com

AMOUNT: $1,000
DEADLINE(S): JUN 1

FIELD(S): Science; Engineering

Open to Native American undergraduate and graduate students majoring in science or engineering and who have demonstrated an outstanding interest and skill in any one of the arts. Must be American Indian/Alaska Native (documented with Certified Degree of Indian Blood), be enrolled in college/university, be able to demonstrate commitment to serving community or other tribal nations, and document financial need.

Contact Dr. Paula M. Mintzies, President, for an application after January 1.

1072—GLENN MILLER BIRTHPLACE SOCIETY (Scholarship Program)

107 E. Main
Clarinda IA 51632
PHONE/FAX: 712/542-2461
Internet: http://www.glennmiller.org

AMOUNT: $900-$2,200
DEADLINE(S): MAR 15
FIELD(S): Music Performance (Instrumental and Vocal)

Competitions open to high school seniors and undergraduate freshmen who intend to make music a central part of their future life (music major NOT required). Audition tape and refundable $25 appearance fee required with application. Finalists perform at Clarinda's Glenn Miller Festival in June, where checks are presented to the winners.

4 awards annually. Send self-addressed, stamped envelope for an application. Notification by May 15.

1073—GOLDEN KEY NATIONAL HONOR SOCIETY (Performing Arts Showcase)

1189 Ponce de Leon Avenue NE
Atlanta GA 30306-4624
800/377-2401 or 404/377-2400
E-mail: mboone@goldenkey.gsu.edu
Internet:http://goldenkey.gsu.edu

AMOUNT: $1,000
DEADLINE(S): MAR
FIELD(S): Voice; Dance; Dramatic Interpretation; Original Musical Composition (Instrumental/Voice); Instrumental Performance; Film Making

Open to Golden Key student members and alumni. Award includes the chance to perform at the Golden Key International Convention in each of above categories.

To enter, send your videotaped performance to above address. Contact Michelle Boone for complete information.

1074—GUSTAVU.S.ADOLPHU.S.COLLEGE (Anderson Theatre and Dance Scholarships)

Office of Admission
800 West College Avenue
St. Peter MN 56082
507/933-7676 or 800/GUSTAVUS
E-mail: admission@gustavus.edu
Internet: http://www.gustavus.edu

AMOUNT: $500-$2,000
DEADLINE(S): JAN 1
FIELD(S): Theatre and/or Dance

Scholarships tenable at Gustavus Adolphus College, St. Peter, Minnesota, for students pursuing studies in theatre and/or dance. Students may be enrolled in any major. For renewal, recipient must participate in a departmental project and maintain a 3.0 GPA.

Contact college for details.

1075—GUSTAVUS ADOLPHUS COLLEGE (The Jussi Bjorling Music Scholarships)

Office of Admission
800 West College Avenue
St. Peter MN 56082
507/933-7676 or 800/GUSTAVUS
E-mail: admission@gustavus.edu
Internet: http://www.gustavus.edu/

AMOUNT: Up to $2,000
DEADLINE(S): JAN 15
FIELD(S): Music

Scholarships tenable at Gustavus Adolphus College, St. Peter, Minnesota, for students pursuing studies and participation in music. Recipients may be of any major, but are required to participate in a performing ensemble and take private lessons.

25-30 awards per year. Renewable. Contact college for details.

1076—HAROLD HYAM WINGATE FOUNDATION (Wingate Scholarships)

2nd Floor, 20-22 Stukeley Street
London WC2B 5LR ENGLAND UK
0171 465 1521
E-mail: clark@wingate.org.uk
Internet: http://www.wingate.org.uk/

AMOUNT: Up to 10,000 pounds/year
DEADLINE(S): FEB 1
FIELD(S): Creative Works

Financial support for individuals of great potential or proven excellence to develop original work of intellectual, scientific, artistic, social, or environmental value, and to outstanding talented musicians. Not for taught courses or for leading to professional qualifications, or for electives or for completing courses already begun or for a higher degree. For citizens of the United Kingdom or other Commonwealth countries, Ireland, Israel, or of European countries.

Must be age 24 or older. May be held for up to three years. Contact Faith Clark, administrator, for additional information. Application, details, and examples of previous awards available on Web site.

1077—HATTORI FOUNDATION FOR YOUNG MUSICIANS (Awards for Young Soloists)

72 E. Leopold Road
London SW19 7JQ ENGLAND UK
0208 944 5319
FAX: 0208 946 6970

AMOUNT: 1,000 pounds sterling (max.)
DEADLINE(S): April
FIELD(S): Music Performance (Instrumental)

Awards for British nationals or foreign nationals who are UK residents. Must be aged 15-20 or 21-27 and show promise of an international career as a soloist. Course fees and instrument purchase are not funded. Financial need is NOT a factor.

10 awards annually. Renewable. Contact the foundation for details.

1078—ILLINOIS ARTS COUNCIL (Artists Fellowship Awards)

100 W. Randolph, Suite 10-500
Chicago IL 60601-3298
312/814-6750
E-mail: rose@arts.state.il.us
Internet: http://www.state.il.us/agency/iac/Guidelines/Fellowships/afa02pdf.pdf

AMOUNT: $7,000
DEADLINE(S): Varies
FIELD(S): Choreography, Crafts, Ethnic and Folk Arts, Interdisciplinary/Performance Art, Media Arts, Music Composition, Photography, Playwriting/Screenwriting, Poetry, Prose, and Visual Arts

The Artists Fellowship Program is the agency's major program for individual artist support. These awards are given annually to Illinois artists of exceptional talent in recognition of their outstanding work and commitment within the arts. Awards are made based upon the quality of the works submitted and the evolving professional accomplishments of the applicant.

1079—INDIANA STATE UNIVERSITY (Music Scholarships)

Department of Music
Terre Haute IN 47809
812/237-3009
FAX: 812/237-2771
Internet: http://www.indstate.edu/music/scholar.html
AMOUNT: Varies
DEADLINE(S): Varies
FIELD(S): Music

Various scholarships for music students at Indiana State University. Requirements and specialties vary. See Web site for details.

On Web site, send E-mail to Dr. Todd Sullivan for details, or call or write for further information. Dates for auditions are available from the office of the Dept. of Music. Some scholarships are through the University, and several are from private donors.

1080—INDIANA UNIVERSITY SCHOOL OF MUSIC (Music Scholarships)

School of Music, Admissions
MU101, 1201 E. 3rd Street
Bloomington IN 47405-2200
812/855-1352
FAX: 812/856-6086
E-mail: musicfa@indiana.edu
Internet: http://www.music.indiana.edu
AMOUNT: Varies
DEADLINE(S): Varies
FIELD(S): Music

Several scholarships are available in the Indiana University Dept. of Music. All undergraduate music majors must audition prior to admission and study a classical instrument. Music minors need not audition.

A listing of the scholarships is on the Web site as well as the various deadlines dates for the university as well as for the audition dates for the music department. Deadlines begin as early as Nov. 11 for applying to the department, and auditions occur as early as December.

1081—ARTS INTERNATIONAL (Fund For Performing Arts)

251 Park Avenue South, 5th Floor
New York NY 10010-7302
212/674-9744
FAX: 212/674-9092
Internet: http://www.artsinternational.org
AMOUNT: VARIES
DEADLINE(S): SEP; JAN; MAY
FIELD(S): Performing Arts

Grants to support U.S. artists at international festivals and exhibitions. The festival must take place outside the U.S. and be international in scope with representation from at least two countries outside the host country or have a U.S. theme with representation from at least three U.S. performing artists or groups.

Must be open to the general public. Call for details.

1082—INTERNATIONALER MUSIKWETTBEWERB (International Music Competition of the Ard Munich)

Bayerischer Rundfunk
D-80300 Munchen GERMANY
0049(0)89 5900 2471
FAX: 0049(0)89 5900 3573
E-mail: ard.conc@br-mail.de:
Internet: http://www.ard-musikwettbewerb.de
AMOUNT: 20,000 DM (first prize); 14,000 DM (second); 10,000 DM (third)
DEADLINE(S): APR
FIELD(S): Piano; Violin; Horn; Organ

For outstanding young musicians, aged 17-30, who are at concert standard. Performance is evaluated on technique, musical presentation, artistic personality, and voice and tonal quality.

Contact Nicole Braun or Ingeborg Krause at above address for official rules and entry form.

1083—INTERNATIONAL TRUMPET GUILD (Conference Scholarships)

241 East Main Street, #247
Westfield MA 01086-1633
413/564-0337
FAX: 413/568-1913
E-mail: competitions@trumpetguild.org
Internet: http://www.trumpetguild.org
AMOUNT: $200 + waive Conference registration fee
DEADLINE(S): FEB 15
FIELD(S): Trumpet

Music competition for trumpet players under age 25 to enable them to attend ITG's annual conference. Must be a student member of the International Trumpet Guild by the deadline. Must submit the appropriate taped audition to the current scholarship competition chair. Generally, the student's trumpet playing must be at a relatively advanced level in order to play the repertoire.

See Web site for membership information and audition requirements.

1084—INTERNATIONAL TRUMPET GUILD (Competitions)

241 East Main Street, #247
Westfield MA 01086-1633
413/564-0337
FAX: 413/568-1913
E-mail: competitions@trumpetguild.org
Internet: http://www.trumpetguild.org
AMOUNT: VARIES + waive Conference registration fee
DEADLINE(S): FEB 15
FIELD(S): Trumpet

Performance competitions in three categories: solo, jazz, and mock orchestra. Entrants must be under age 25 to enable them to attend ITG's annual conference. Must be a student member of the International Trumpet Guild by the deadline.

See Web site for membership information and audition requirements.

1085—IRISH ARTS COUNCIL (Awards and Opportunities)

70 Merrion Square
Dublin 2 IRELAND
Tel: +353 1 618 0200
FAX: +353 1 661 0349/676 1302
E-mail: info@artscouncil.ie
Internet: http://www.artscouncil.ie
AMOUNT: Varies (with program)
DEADLINE(S): Varies (with program)
FIELD(S): Creative Arts; Visual Arts; Performing Arts

Numerous programs open to young and established artists who are Irish citizens or legal residents. Purpose is to assist in pursuit of talents and recognize achievements.

See Web site or contact above address for an application.

1086—JACOB'S PILLOW DANCE FESTIVAL (Scholarships)

P.O. Box 287
Lee MA 02138
413/637-1322
FAX: 413/243-4744
E-mail: info@jacobspillow.org
Internet: http://www.jacobspillow.org
AMOUNT: Varies
DEADLINE(S): APR 5
FIELD(S): Dance

Preprofessional dance training for 16-year-old dancers at the School at Jacob's Pillow. Must demonstrate financial need.

Not renewable. Contact J.R. Glover for an application.

1087—JOHN K. and THIRZA F. DAVENPORT FOUNDATION (Scholarships in the Arts)

20 North Main Street
South Yarmouth MA 02664-3143
508/398-2293
FAX: 508/394-6765
Internet: http://www.davenportrealty.com/pdf/foundationapplication.pdf
AMOUNT: Varies
DEADLINE(S): JUL 15
FIELD(S): Theatre, Music, Art

For Barnstable County, Massachusetts residents in their last two years of undergraduate or graduate (preferred) study in visual or performing arts. Must demonstrate financial need.

6-8 awards annually. Renewable. Contact Mrs. Chris M. Walsh for more information.

1088—KATHLEEN FERRIER MEMORIAL FUND (Kathleen Ferrier Awards)

52 Rosebank Holyport Road
London SW6 6LY ENGLAND
0171/381-0985 (telephone and FAX)
E-mail: info@ferrierawards.org.uk
Internet: http://www.ferrierawards.org.uk
AMOUNT: 17,500 pounds sterling
DEADLINE(S): MAR 1 (applications available in JAN)
FIELD(S): Singing Competition

Competitive annual awards are open to British singers (and those from the Commonwealth and the Republic of Ireland) who are over 21 but not over the age of 28 on the day of the final auditions.

Write to Administrator at above address for complete information.

1089—KOSCIUSZKO FOUNDATION (Chopin Piano Competition)

15 E. 65th Street
New York NY 10021-6595
212/734-2130
FAX: 212/628-4552
E-mail: thekf@aol.com
Internet: http://www.kosciuszkofoundation.org
AMOUNT: $5,000 (first place)
DEADLINE(S): MAR
FIELD(S): Piano

Open to U.S. citizens/permanent residents and international full-time students with valid student visas. Must be between the ages of 16 and 22 as of April in contest year. Preliminaries are held in the spring in Chicago, Houston, and New York City, with finals in New York City. Must have ready a program of 60-75 minutes, including Chopin and other required composers. Must also submit biography/curriculum vitae, letters of recommendation, proof of age, and photo.

$35 application fee. See Web site or send a self-addressed, stamped envelope to the Cultural Department for an application after December 1.

1090—KOSCIUSZKO FOUNDATION (Marcella Sembrich Voice Competition)

15 E. 65th Street
New York NY 10021-6595
212/734-2130
FAX: 212/628-4552
E-mail: thekf@aol.com
Internet: http://www.kosciuszkofoundation.org
AMOUNT: $1,000 (max.) + travel to various domestic and international recitals
DEADLINE(S): DEC
FIELD(S): Voice

This voice competition is held every third year and is open to students between the ages of 18 and 35 who are U.S. citizens or full-time international students in the U.S. with valid visas who wish to pursue a career in voice.

See Web site or send a self-addressed, stamped envelope to the Cultural Department for an application.

1091—LIBERACE FOUNDATION FOR THE PERFORMING AND CREATIVE ARTS (Scholarship Fund)

1775 East Tropicana Avenue
Las Vegas NV 89119-6529
702/798-5595; FAX: 702/798-7386
E-mail: foundation@liberace.org
Internet: http://www.liberace.org
AMOUNT: Varies
DEADLINE(S): MAR 15
FIELD(S): Music; Theater; Dance; Visual Arts

Provides grants to accredited INSTITUTIONS that offer training in above fields. Grants are to be used exclusively for scholarship assistance to talented and deserving students. Recipients should be promising and deserving upperclassmen (junior, senior, graduate) enrolled in a course of study leading up to a career in the arts.

NO DIRECT-TO-STUDENT GRANTS ARE MADE. Student's school must apply on their behalf. See Web site or write to above address for details.

1092—LIEDERKRANZ FOUNDATION, INC. (Scholarship Awards)

6 East 87th Street
New York NY 10128
212/534-0880
AMOUNT: $1,000-$5,000
DEADLINE(S): NOV 15
FIELD(S): Vocal Music

Awards can be used anywhere. Age limit for General Voice 20-35 years old, and limit for Wagnerian Voice is 25-45 years. There is a $35 application fee.

14-18 scholarships annually. NOT renewable. Send a self-addressed stamped envelope to the address above for application regulations, audition schedules, and other details.

1093—LOREN L. ZACHARY SOCIETY FOR THE PERFORMING ARTS (National Vocal Competition for Young Opera Singers)

2250 Gloaming Way
Beverly Hills CA 90210
310/276-2731
FAX: 310/275-8245
AMOUNT: $10,000 (first prize); min. of $1,000 (finalists)
DEADLINE(S): JAN (NY); MAR (LA); MAY (final competition)
FIELD(S): Opera Singing

Annual vocal competition open to young (aged 21-33 females; 21-35 males) Opera singers. The competition is geared toward finding employment for them in European Opera houses. Financial assistance is only possible through participation in the audition program. Financial need NOT considered.

$35 application fee. 10 awards annually. Send self-addressed, stamped envelope to Mrs. Nedra Zachary at address above for an application.

1094—MARTIN MUSICAL SCHOLARSHIP FUND (Scholarships)

Lawn Cottage, 23a Brackley Road
Beckenham, Kent BR3 1RB
ENGLAND
PHONE/FAX: 0181-658-9432
AMOUNT: Up to 2,000 pounds sterling
DEADLINE(S): DEC 1
FIELD(S): Instrumental Music

Scholarships are administered by the London Philharmonic Orchestra. For applicants of exceptional talent under age 25. Awards are for study at any approved institution in England for non-U.K. citizens; citizens of the U.K. may study anywhere. Candidates must be studying for a career as either soloist, chamber musician, or orchestral player. Additional programs are for viola players, violinists, and wood wind performers.

Not open to organists, singers, composers, or for academic studies. Awards are valid for two years. Auditions are held in London the January following the December deadline date. Registration fee of 10 pounds. Write for complete information.

1095—MENDELSSOHN SCHOLARSHIP FOUNDATION (Composers Scholarships)

c/o Royal Academy of Music
Marylebone Road
London NW1 5HT England
Written Inquiry
AMOUNT: 5,000 pounds sterling
DEADLINE(S): March
FIELD(S): Musical Composition

Open to composers of any nationality under the age of 30 who are residents (for at least 3 years) in the UK or Ireland. For further studies in composition.

Contact Miss Jean Shannon at address above for complete information.

1096—MERCYHURST COLLEGE (D'Angelo Young Artists Competition)

Executive Director
501 East 38th Street
Erie PA 16546
814/824-2394
AMOUNT: Up to $10,000
DEADLINE(S): JAN
FIELD(S): Performance Art

For international musicians who demonstrate the ability to embark on a performance career in voice, strings, or piano. Undergraduates must be between the ages of 18 and 30.

1097—MERCYHURST COLLEGE D'ANGELO SCHOOL OF MUSIC (Scholarships)

501 E. 38th Street
Erie PA 16546
814/824-2394
FAX: 814/824-3332
E-mail: Ryan@mercyhurst.edu
Internet: http://www.mercyhurst.edu
AMOUNT: Up to $10,000
DEADLINE(S): None
FIELD(S): Music

For music students who wish to attend the D'Angelo School of Music At Mercyhurst College in Erie, Pennsylvania. Audition required.

Renewable for four years. Contact Rebecca Ryan for an application.

1098—MINNESOTA STATE ARTS BOARD (Grants Program)

Park Square Court
400 Sibley Street, Suite 200
St. Paul MN 55101-1928
651/215-1600 or 800/8MN-ARTS
FAX: 651/215-1602
E-mail: msab@arts.state.mn.us
Internet: http://www.arts.state.mn.us/index.html
AMOUNT: $8,000 (fellowships); $500-$1,500 (grants)
DEADLINE(S): AUG (Visual Arts); SEP (Music and Dance); OCT (Literature and Theater)
FIELD(S): Literature; Music; Theater; Dance; Visual Arts

Fellowships and career opportunity grants are open to professional artists who are residents of Minnesota. Grants may NOT be used for support of tuition or work toward any degree.

Contact MSAB for an application.

1099—MUSIC ACADEMY OF THE WEST (Scholarships)

1070 Fairway Road
Santa Barbara CA 93108-2899
805/969-4726
FAX: 805/969-0686
E-mail: catalog@musicacademy.org
Internet: http://www.musicacademy.org
AMOUNT: Tuition, room and board
DEADLINE(S): Varies
FIELD(S): Music

Scholarships for this eight-week summer session for musicians age 16 and up. Maximum age for vocalists is 32. Student must pay transportation and limited fees. Deadlines run from January 3 through Feb 28, depending on instrument. Audition dates are set up throughout the U.S.

Access Web site for details and application, or write for information.

1100—McCORD CAREER CENTER (Level II McCord Medical/Music Scholarship)

Healdsburg High School
1024 Prince Street
Healdsburg CA 95448
707/431-3473
E-mail: career@husd.com
AMOUNT: Varies
DEADLINE(S): APR 15
FIELD(S): Medicine; Music

For graduates of Healdsburg High School who are planning a career in music or medicine. Must be enrolled full-time at a college/university as an undergraduate junior or senior in the fall, or earning an advanced degree in graduate or medical school, or entering into a vocational/certificate program. Transcripts, proof of attendance, and an essay are required.

Contact the McCord Career Center at Healdsburg High School for an application.

1101—NATIONAL ASSOCIATION OF TEACHERS OF SINGING (Artist Awards Competition)

6406 Merrill Rd, Suite B
Jacksonville FL 32277
904/744-9022
FAX: 904/744-9033
E-mail: WmVessels@aol.com
Internet: http://www.nats.org
AMOUNT: Varies
DEADLINE(S): Varies
FIELD(S): Singing

Purpose of the program is to select young singers who are ready for professional careers and to encourage them to carry on the tradition of fine singing. Selection based on present accomplishments rather than future potential. Applicants should be between 21 and 35 years old and have studied with a NATS teacher or a member of NATS.

Contact NATS for an application.

1102—NATIONAL FEDERATION OF MUSIC CLUBS (Competitions and Awards)

1336 North Delaware Street
Indianapolis IN 46202-2481
317/638-4003
Internet: http://www.nfmc-music.org/
AMOUNT: Varies
DEADLINE(S): Varies
FIELD(S): Music Performance

Several monetary awards available for students' voice, piano, composition, accompanying instruments, and music education. Apply through Web site.

1103—NATIONAL FOUNDATION FOR ADVANCEMENT IN THE ARTS (Arts Recognition and Talent Search)

800 Brickell Avenue
Miami FL 33131
800/970-ARTS or 305/377-1140
FAX: 305/377-1149
E-mail: info@nfaa.org
Internet: http://www.ARTSawards.org

AMOUNT: $100-$3,000
DEADLINE(S): OCT 1
FIELD(S): Creative and Performing Arts

Talent contest for high school seniors and 17- to 18-year-olds in dance, jazz, music, photography, theatre, visual arts, voice, and writing. Except for those applying in Music/Jazz, applicants must be U.S. citizens or permanent residents. May apply in more than one category, but only one financial award will be given to any individual, and a fee is required for each category in which student applies.

$35 application fee ($25 if apply by June 1); fee may be waived if you are unable to meet this requirement). 400 awards annually. Not renewable. Contact NFAA for an application packet.

1104—NATIONAL GUILD OF COMMUNITY SCHOOLS OF THE ARTS (Young Composers Awards)

40 N. Van Brunt Street; Suite 32
P.O. Box 8018
Englewood NJ 07631
201/871-3337
FAX: 201/871-7639
E-mail: info@natguild.org
Internet: http://www.nationalguild.org

AMOUNT: Sr. Category $1,000 (first place), $500 (second); Jr. Category $500 (first), $250 (second)
DEADLINE(S): Varies (early Spring)
FIELD(S): Music Composition

Competition open to students aged 13-18 (as of June 30 of award year) who are enrolled in a public or private secondary school, recognized musical school, or engaged in private study of music with an established teacher in the U.S. or Canada. Two categories are ages 13-15 and 16-18. Must be U.S. or Canadian citizen/legal resident.

Write to above address for an application.

1105—NATIONAL LEAGUE OF AMERICAN PEN WOMEN, INC. (Scholarships for Mature Women)

1300 Seventeenth Street NW
Washington DC 20036
202/785-1997
Internet: http://www.cooper.edu/admin/career_services/fellowships/mature.html

AMOUNT: $1,000
DEADLINE(S): JAN 15 (even-numbered years)
FIELD(S): Art; Music; Creative Writing

The National League of American Pen Women gives three $1,000 grants in even-numbered years to women aged 35 and over.

Send SASE for details at the above address.

1106—NATIONAL PTA (Reflections Program)

330 N. Wabash Avenue; Suite 2100
Chicago IL 60611-3690
800/307-4PTA or 312/670-6782
FAX: 312/670-6783
E-mail: info@pta.org
Internet: http://www.pta.org

AMOUNT: Varies
DEADLINE(S): Varies
FIELD(S): Literature; Musical Composition; Photography; Visual Arts

Open to students in preschool through grade twelve to express themselves and to receive positive recognition for their artistic efforts. Young artists can get involved in the Reflections Program of their local PTA or PTSA. Any PTA/PTSA in good standing can sponsor a Reflections Program. Rules and deadlines differ from PTA to PTA and from state to state.

Contact your state PTA office for information about the Reflections Program in your area.

1107—NEW JERSEY STATE OPERA (International Vocal Competition)

Robert Treat Center
50 Park Pl., 10th Floor
Newark NJ 07102
973/623-5757
FAX: 973/623-5761

AMOUNT: $10,000 total
DEADLINE(S): Varies
FIELD(S): Opera singing

Professional opera singers between the ages of 22 and 34 can apply for this international competition.

Renewable yearly. Contact Mrs. Judy Marrasce at above address for information.

1108—NEW YORK STATE THEATRE INSTITUTE (Internships in Theatrical Production)

155 River Street
Troy NY 12180
518/274-3573
E-mail: nysti@crisny.org
Internet: http://www.crisny.org/not-for-profit/nysti/int.htm

AMOUNT: None
DEADLINE(S): None
FIELD(S): Fields of study related to theatrical production, including box office and PR

Internships for college students, high school seniors, and educators-in-residence interested in developing skills in above fields. Unpaid, but college credit is earned. Located at Russell Sage College in Troy, NY. Gain experience in box office, costumes, education, electrics, music, stage management, scenery, properties, performance, and public relations. Interns come from all over the world.

Must be associated with an accredited institution. See Web site for more information. Call Ms. Arlene Leff, Intern Director at above location. Include your postal mailing address.

1109—OMAHA SYMPHONY GUILD (International New Music Competition)

1605 Howard Street
Omaha NE 68102-2705
402/342-3836
FAX: 402/342-3819
E-mail: kimmet@omahasymphony.org
Internet: http://www.omahasymphony.org

AMOUNT: $3,000
DEADLINE(S): APR 15
FIELD(S): Musical Composition

For composers aged 25 or above to enter a composition of 20 minutes in length or less. Composition is scored for chamber orchestra or ensemble. Work must be previously unpublished and not performed by a professional orchestra.

$30 entry fee. 1 award annually. Not renewable. Contact Kimberly Mettenbrink for application procedures.

1110—OPERA AMERICA (Fellowship Program)

1156 15th Street NW, Suite 810
Washington DC 20005
202/293-4466
FAX: 202/393-0735

AMOUNT: $1,200/month + transportation and housing
DEADLINE(S): MAY 7
FIELD(S): General or Artistic Administration, Technical Direction, or Production Management

Open to opera personnel, individuals entering opera administration from other disciplines, and graduates of arts administration or technical/production training programs who are committed to a career in opera in North America.

Must be U.S. or Canadian citizen or legal resident lawfully eligible to receive stipend.

1111—ORCHESTRA SONOMA GUILD (Scholarship)

6040 Della Court
Rohnert Park CA 49428
Written Inquiry
E-mail: RubyCh@ap.net

AMOUNT: $350 (first); $100 (second)
DEADLINE(S): MAY
FIELD(S): Music

Scholarships for youth in grades 5 through 12 and who excel in music. Applicants not selected may re-apply until they win first place.

Send self-addressed, stamped envelope to Ruby Chroninger, Secretary, at above address for application and details. Recommendations from private or school music teacher and audition tape with two contrasting pieces required.

1112—ORGAN HISTORICAL SOCIETY (E. Power Biggs Fellowship)

P.O. Box 26811
Richmond VA 23261
804/353-9226

AMOUNT: Funding of attendance at Annual Convention
DEADLINE(S): DEC 31
FIELD(S): Historic Pipe Organs

Fellowships are to encourage students and others to become involved in the appreciation of historic pipe organs by funding their attendance at the OHS Annual Convention.

3-4 awards annually. Contact Robert Zanca, Biggs Committee Chair, for an application.

1113—PHILADELPHIA COLLEGE OF BIBLE (Scholarships, Grants, and Loans)

Financial Aid Dept
200 Manor Avenue
Langhorne PA 19047
800/366-0049
Internet: http://www.pcb.edu

AMOUNT: Varies
DEADLINE(S): Varies
FIELD(S): Fields of study relating to Christian education

Various scholarships, loans, and grants are available to students attending this undergraduate Bible college in Philadelphia, PA. High school seniors, transfer students, and others may apply. Some programs are for students with outstanding academic achievement, musical talent, or leaderships skills. Some are for dependents of Christian workers, missionaries, or alumni. Some are based on financial need.

Access Web site for details and/or send SASE to school for further information.

1114—PRINCESS GRACE FOUNDATION-USA (Drama Scholarships and Fellowships)

150 East 58th Street
21st Floor
New York NY 10155
212/317-1470
FAX: 212/317-1473
E-mail: pgfusa@pgfusa.com
Internet: http://www.pgfusa.com

AMOUNT: Varies
DEADLINE(S): Varies
FIELD(S): Theater/Drama/Dance/Film

Scholarships for students age 25 or under in acting, directing, and design (scenic, lighting, and costume design in their last year of professional training at a nonprofit school or organization in the U.S. Also fellowships for salary assistance for an apprentice or new member age 30 or younger in a theater company. New members must have joined the company within the past two years.

Must be nominated by the artistic director of a theater company or by the dean or department chair of a professional school in theater. Do not apply to Foundation. U.S. citizenship or legal residency required. Write or access Web site for further information.

1115—QUEEN ELISABETH INTERNATIONAL MUSIC COMPETITION OF BELGIUM

20 Rue Au Laines
B-1000 Brussels BELGIUM
32 2 513 00 99
FAX: 32 2 514 32 97
E-mail: info@queen-elisabeth-competition.be
Internet: http://www.queen-elisabeth-competition.be

AMOUNT: 1.250-12.400 euro
DEADLINE(S): JAN 15
FIELD(S): Singing

Categories: opera, oratio, and lied. Open to singers of all nationalities who are under 32 years of age. Applications must include certified copy of birth certificate, proof of nationality, curriculum vitae, a list with main repertoire, and three photographs, including one b&w glossy. During actual participation in concert, host family may accommodate singers free of charge. Semi-finalists not from Belgium are entitled to 50% reimbursement of travelling expenses.

Contact Mr. Michel-Etienne Van Neste for an application.

1116—QUEEN MARIE JOSE (International Musical Prize Contest)

Box 19, CH-1252 Meinier
Geneva SWITZERLAND
Internet: http://musnov1.unige.ch/prixrmj/

AMOUNT: 10,000 Swiss francs
DEADLINE(S): MAY 31
FIELD(S): Music Composition

This competition is open to composers of all nationalities without age limit. It is designed to award a new work never performed before and is given every other year.

Not renewable. See Web site or write for yearly subject and official rules.

1117—QUEEN SONJA INTERNATIONAL MUSIC COMPETITION (Voice Competition)

P.O. Box 5190 Majorstuen
0302 Oslo NORWAY
+47/23367067,
FAX: +47/22463630
E-mail: Sonja@nmh.no

AMOUNT: $30,000 approximate total prize money
DEADLINE(S): MAR 15
FIELD(S): Voice

Applicants must be between the ages of 17 and 31. In addition to cash awards for the 4 finalists (places 1-4) the Board of Directors will endeavor to provide them with solo engagements in Norway.

Write to above address for complete information and conditions for applications. NO SCHOLARSHIPS ARE GIVEN.

1118—RIPON COLLEGE (Performance/Recognition Tuition Scholarships)

Admissions Office
300 Seward Street
P.O. Box 248
Ripon WI 54971
920/748-8101
E-mail: adminfo@ripon.edu
Internet: http://www.ripon.edu
AMOUNT: $5,000-$10,000/year
DEADLINE(S): MAR 1
FIELD(S): Music; Forensics; Art; Theater

Open to undergraduate and graduate students attending or planning to attend Ripon College. Purpose is to recognize and encourage academic potential and accomplishment in above fields. Interview, audition, or nomination may be required.

Renewable. Contact Office of Admission for an application.

1119—ROYAL PHILHARMONIC SOCIETY (Julius Isserlis Scholarship)

10 Stratford Place
London W1C 1BA ENGLAND
44 0 20 7491 8110
FAX: 44 0 20 7493 7463
E-mail:admin@royalphilharmonicsociety.org.uk
Internet: http://www.royalphilharmonicsociety.org.uk
AMOUNT: 12,500 pounds sterling per year for two years
DEADLINE(S): Varies
FIELD(S): Music, Performing Arts (various categories)

Scholarship awarded by competition to enable music students in varying performance categories and nationalities to study outside of Great Britain. Applicants MUST permanently reside in the United Kingdom and be between the ages of 15 and 25.

Competition is held every two years. The next award is offered in 2003. Write to General Administrator at the above address for complete information.

1120—RYAN DAVIES MEMORIAL FUND (Grants)

1 Squire Court; The Marina
Swansea, WALES UK SA1 3XB
PHONE/FAX: 011-44-1792-301500
AMOUNT: Up to $2,500 each
DEADLINE(S): MAY 30
FIELD(S): Performing Arts

Grants to assist performing artists (up to age 30) in any level of study up through postgraduate. Must be of Welsh extraction and demonstrate financial need.

8 awards annually. Contact the secretary, at address above for complete information.

1121—SAN ANGELO SYMPHONY SOCIETY (Sorantin Young Artist Award)

P.O. Box 5922
San Angelo TX 76902
915/658-5877
FAX: 915/653-1045
Internet: http://www.sanangelosymphony.org
AMOUNT: $3,000 (winner); $1,000 (3 others); $500 (runners-up)
DEADLINE(S): OCT 15
FIELD(S): Music: Voice, Instrumental, Piano

A competition open to instrumentalists who have not reached their 28th birthdays by November 22 and to vocalists who have not reached their 31st birthdays by November 22. Provides opportunity for a cash award with the symphony orchestra.

Contact the San Angelo Symphony Society for an application.

1122—SAN FRANCISCO CONSERVATORY OF MUSIC (Various Scholarships)

1201 Ortega Street
San Francisco CA 94122-4498
415/759-3431
FAX: 415/759-3499
E-mail: admit@sfcm.edu
Internet: http://www.sfcm.edu
AMOUNT: Varies
DEADLINE(S): Varies
FIELD(S): Music

A variety of scholarships for music students attending the San Francisco Conservatory of Music. Graduate assistantships are available for full-time candidates for Master of Music degree.

See Web site or write for detailed information.

1123—SKIDMORE COLLEGE (Filene Music Scholarships)

Music Department
815 North Broadway
Saratoga Springs NY 12866-1632
Internet:www.skidmore.edu/academics/music/scholarships/Schlrshp.htm
AMOUNT: $6,000/year
DEADLINE(S): FEB 1
FIELD(S): Music

Scholarships for talented young instrument or voice musicians based on musical excellence as revealed by a competition. Must submit a cassette performance tape by Feb. 1. Filene scholars need not major in music; however, recipients are expected to continue to develop their skills through private instruction in the Music Department each semester and top participate in department ensembles. Final round of competitions is in April and is done in person.

Four scholarships per year. U.S. citizens and permanent residents will receive additional assistance to meet financial need if it exceeds $6,000 in a given academic year. Renewable if student continues in good academic standing and receives the recommendation of the Dept. of Music.

1024—SMITHSONIAN INSTITUTION (Minority Student Internship Program)

Office of Fellowships
750 9th Street NW, Suite 9300
Washington DC 20560-0902
202/275-0655
FAX: 202/275-0489
E-mail: siofg@ofg.si.edu
Internet: http://www.si.edu/research+study
AMOUNT: $350/week + possible travel expenses
DEADLINE(S): Varies
FIELD(S): Humanities; Environmental and Cultural Studies; Natural History; Earth Science; Art History; Biology

Ten-week, full-time internships in residence at the Smithsonian are open to U.S. minority students who wish to participate in research or museum-related activities in above and related fields. Must be undergraduates or beginning graduate students with a minimum 3.0 GPA. Must submit essay, resume, and official transcript.

Contact the Office of Fellowships or see Web site for an application.

1025—SONOMA CHAMBOLLE-MUSIGNY SISTER CITIES, INC. (Henri Cardinaux Memorial Scholarship)

Chamson Scholarship Committee
P.O. Box 1633
Sonoma CA 95476-1633
707/939-1344
FAX: 707/939-1344
E-mail: Baileysci@vom.com
AMOUNT: Up to $1,500 (travel + expenses)
DEADLINE(S): JUL 15

FIELD(S): Culinary Arts; Wine Industry; Art; Architecture; Music; History; Fashion

Hands-on experience working in above or similar fields and living with a family in small French village in Burgundy or other French city. Must be Sonoma County, CA, resident at least 18 years of age and be able to communicate in French. Transcripts, employer recommendation, photograph, and essay (stating why, where, and when) required.

1 award. Nonrenewable. Also offers opportunity for candidate in Chambolle-Musigny to obtain work experience and cultural exposure in Sonoma, CA.

1126—SOUTHERN ILLINOIS UNIVERSITY (Music Scholarships)

School of Music, Mailcode 4302
Carbondale IL 62901-4302
618/53-MUSIC (536-8742)
FAX: 618/453-5808
Internet: http://www.siu.edu/departments/cola/music001/scholar.html

AMOUNT: Varies
DEADLINE(S): APR 15
FIELD(S): Music

Several music scholarships are available for freshmen and transfer students at Southern Illinois University. An audition is required, usually held in February and March. A taped audition can be arranged.

See Web site and/or contact Dr. Daniel Mellado for more information.

1127—STEPHEN ARLEN MEMORIAL FUND (Grant Award)

English Nat'l Opera
London Coliseum; St. Martin's Lane
London WC2N 4ES ENGLAND
020 7845 9355
FAX: 020 7845 9274
E-mail: SAMFund@eno.org

AMOUNT: 3,000 pounds sterling
DEADLINE(S): FEB 28
FIELD(S): Opera; Ballet; Drama; Music

Grant is made annually to an artist under 30 years of age who has completed formal training and now wishes to pursue a career in the arts. Awarded to artist proposing an independent project rather than to fund further training. Must be United Kingdom resident.

Contact The Secretary at above address for an application.

1128—STUDENT CONSERVATION ASSOCIATION (SCA Resource Assistant Program)

P.O. Box 550
Charlestown NH 03603
603/543-1700
FAX: 603/543-1828
E-mail: internships@sca-inc.org
Internet: http://www.sca-inc.org

AMOUNT: $1,180-$4,725
DEADLINE(S): Varies
FIELD(S): Environment and related fields

Must be 18 and U.S. citizen; need not be student. Fields: Agriculture, Archaeology, anthropology, botany, caves, civil/environmental engineering, environmental education, fisheries, forests, herpetology, history, living history/roleplaying, visitor services, landscape architecture/environmental design, paleontology, recreation/ resource/ range management, trail maintenance/construction, wildlife management, geology, hydrology, library/museums, surveying...

900 positions in U.S. and Canada. Send $1 for postage for application; outside U.S./Canada, send $20.

1129—SUZUKI ASSOCIATION OF THE AMERICAS (Music Teacher Scholarships)

P.O. Box 17310
Boulder CO 80308
303/444-0948
FAX: 303/444-0984
E-mail: Suzuki@rmi.net
Internet: http://www.suzukiassociation.org

AMOUNT: $225-$600
DEADLINE(S): FEB 1
FIELD(S): Teaching: Music

Scholarships for music teachers and prospective music teachers who are full-time college students. Membership in above organization for a minimum of six months prior to application required. Visit Web site for details.

Request membership information or application from above location.

1130—THE BAGBY FOUNDATION FOR THE MUSICAL ARTS, INC. (Musical Study Grants)

501 Fifth Avenue, Suite 1401
New York NY 10017
212/986-6094

AMOUNT: $2,000-$6,000
DEADLINE(S): Ongoing
FIELD(S): Music

Musical study grants based on talent and need.

Send a letter to above location outlining financial need.

1131—THE DONNA REED FOUNDATION (National Scholarships)

1305 Broadway
Denison IA 51442
712/263-3334
FAX: 712/263-8026
E-mail: info@donnareed.org
Internet: http://www.donnareed.org

AMOUNT: $4,000 (5 awards); $500 (for each of 10 finalists)
DEADLINE(S): MAR 15
FIELD(S): Performing Arts: Acting, Vocal, Instrumental, Musical Theater or Dance

Scholarships for high school seniors in the performing arts listed above. May be used at an accredited university or an approved program of instruction. Involves a competition.

Five awards, ten finalists. Contact Foundation or access Web site for application details.

1132—THE DONNA REED FOUNDATION (Performing Arts Scholarships for Iowa High School Seniors)

1305 Broadway
Denison IA 51442
712/263-3334
FAX: 712/263-8026
E-mail: info@donnareed.org
Internet: http://www.donnareed.org

AMOUNT: $1,000
DEADLINE(S): MAR 15
FIELD(S): Performing Arts: Acting, Vocal, Instrumental, Musical Theater or Dance

Scholarships for high school seniors who are residents of Iowa and pursuing an education in the performing arts listed above. May be used at an accredited university or an approved program of instruction. Involves a competition.

Five awards. Contact Foundation or access Web site for application details.

1133—THE DONNA REED FOUNDATION (Performing Arts Scholarships for Crawford County, Iowa, High School Seniors)

1305 Broadway
Denison IA 51442

712/263-3334
FAX: 712/263-8026
E-mail: info@donnareed.org
Internet: http://www.donnareed.org
AMOUNT: $500
DEADLINE(S): MAR 15
FIELD(S): Performing Arts: Acting, Vocal, Instrumental, Musical Theater or Dance

Scholarships for high school seniors who are residents of Crawford County, Iowa, and pursuing an education in the performing arts listed above. May be used at an accredited university or an approved program of instruction. Involves a competition.

Five awards. Contact Foundation or access Web site for application details.

1134—THE JOHN F. KENNEDY CENTER FOR THE PERFORMING ARTS (Awards, Fellowships, and Scholarships)

The Kennedy Center
2700 F Street NW
Washington DC 20566-0001
202/416-8857
FAX: 202/416-8802
E-mail: skshaffer@kennedy-center.org
Internet: http://www.kennedy-center.org/actf
AMOUNT: Varies
DEADLINE(S): Varies
FIELD(S): Playwriting, Stage Design, and Acting

Various scholarships and awards in the above fields.

Contact organization for a booklet, "The Kennedy Center American College Theater Festival," for details and/or visit Web site.

1135—THE KUN SHOULDER REST, INC. (Listing of Music Competitions)

200 MacLaren Street
Ottawa Ontario CANADA K2P 0L6
+1 (613) 232-1861
FAX: +1 (613) 232-9771
E-mail: kun@kunrest.com
Internet: http://www.kunrest.com
AMOUNT: Varies
DEADLINE(S): Varies
FIELD(S): Music: Various instruments and voice

This manufacturer of shoulder rests for violinists offers a listing of international competitions in various types of music, primarily for (but not limited to) players of stringed instruments.

The listing is available on the Web site above, or a list can be requested of the company.

1136—THE MR. HOLLAND'S OPUS FOUNDATION (The Melody Program)

15125 Ventura Boulevard, Suite 204
Sherman Oaks CA 91403
818/787-6787
FAX: 818/784-6788
E-mail: info@mhopus.org
Internet: http://www.mhopus.org
AMOUNT: A musical instrument
DEADLINE(S): None
FIELD(S): Instrumental Music

Founded by actor Richard Dreyfus, composer Michael Kamen, and director Stephen Herek, all of whom were involved in the film with the same name as this group, the program provides used and/or new instruments to schools and individuals who are financially limited. Targets qualified K-12 school music programs in need of assistance. The students must have completed at least three years of continuous group or private study and must have performed with school and/or community ensembles or provided accompaniment for same.

Send SASE (self-addressed stamped envelope (55 cents postage) for application or access Web site, which has an application as well as more details. Recommendations and cassette performance tape required.

1137—THE MR. HOLLAND'S OPUS FOUNDATION (The Special Projects Program)

15125 Ventura Blvd., Suite 204
Sherman Oaks CA 91403
818/787-6787
FAX: 818/784-6788
E-mail: info@mhopus.org;
Internet: http://www.mhopus.org
AMOUNT: A musical instrument
DEADLINE(S): None
FIELD(S): Instrumental Music

Founded by actor Richard Dreyfuss, composer Michael Kamen, and director Stephen Herek, all of whom were involved in the film with the same name as this group, the program provides used and/or new instruments to schools and individuals who are financially limited. Targets community schools of the arts, hospitals, music therapy programs, after-school music programs, and youth symphonies in need of assistance. The students must have completed at least three years of continuous group or private study and must have performed with school and/or community ensembles or provided accompaniment for same.

Send SASE (self-addressed stamped envelope (55 cents postage) for application, or access Web site, which has an application as well as more details. Recommendations and cassette performance tape required.

1138—THE NATIONAL ASSOCIATION OF NEGRO MUSICIANS, INC. (Brantley Choral Arranging Competition)

P.O. Box 2024
Gardena CA 90247
773/779-1325 or 213/756-5354
Internet: http://www.edtech.morehouse.edu/cgrimes/brantley.htm
AMOUNT: $500
DEADLINE(S): APR 30
FIELD(S): Music: Choral Arrangement

An annual competition for African-Americans talented in music arrangement. The work must be a choral arrangement of a Negro spiritual. Should be between 3-5 minutes in length. Arranger's name must not appear on the score—use a "nom de plume." See more information on Web site.

There is a $25 entrance fee. For specific details, contact organization. Send scores, fees and info. To Byron J. Smith, coordinator, to address above.

1139—THE NATIONAL ASSOCIATION OF NEGRO MUSICIANS, INC. (Scholarship Competitions)

8120-B Prairie Park Place
Chicago IL 60619-4808
773/779-1325
Internet: http://www.edtech.morehouse.edu/cgrimes/scholars.htm
AMOUNT: $1,500 (first); $1,000 (second); $750 (third); $500 (fourth); $250 (fifth)
DEADLINE(S): Varies
FIELD(S): Music: organ, winds, piano, voice, or strings

An annual competition for African-Americans talented in music performance in the above areas. For ages 18-30. Contestants must be sponsored by a local branch in good standing. Competition involves local, regional, and national events. Winners proceed to next level. Contact organization for location of your nearest branch. Specialty rotates yearly. 1999-winds; 2000-piano; 2001-voice; 2002-

strings; 2003-organ, etc. Not for professional musicians.

See Web site for further information. There is a $5 fee for the local competitions.

1140—THE WALT DISNEY COMPANY (American Teacher Awards)

P.O. Box 9805
Calabasas CA 91372

AMOUNT: $2,500 (36 awards); $25,000 (Outstanding Teacher of the Year)
DEADLINE(S): FEB 15
FIELD(S): Teachers: Athletic Coach, Early Childhood, English, Foreign Language/ESL, General Elementary, Mathematics, Performing Arts, Physical Education/Health, Science, Social Studies, Visual Arts, Voc/Tech Education

Awards for K-12 teachers in the above fields.

Teachers, or anyone who knows a great teacher, can write for applications at the above address.

1141—THELONIOUS MONK INSTITUTE OF JAZZ (International Jazz Instrument Competition)

5225 Wisconsin Avenue NW
Washington DC 20015
202/364-7272
FAX: 202/364-0176
E-mail: info@monkinst.org
Internet: http://www.monkinstitute.org

AMOUNT: $20,000 (first); $10,000 (second); $5,000 (third); $1,000 (additional finalists)
DEADLINE(S): AUG 5
FIELD(S): Music: Jazz instrument

Competition for the world's most promising young musicians to receive college-level training by America's jazz masters, worldwide recognition, and performance opportunities. Musicians under contract with a major label are not eligible. Decisions based on audiotape presentation and application.

Application is on Web site or contact above organization for current information regarding application. Instructions for audiotape selections are very specific.

1142—THELONIOUS MONK INSTITUTE OF JAZZ (International Jazz Composers Competition)

5225 Wisconsin Avenue NW
Washington DC 20001
202/364-7272
FAX: 202/364-0176
E-mail: info@monkinst.org
Internet: http://www.monkinstitute.org

AMOUNT: $10,000 grand prize
DEADLINE(S): AUG 5
FIELD(S): Music: Composition for Jazz Instrument

Competition presented by the Thelonious Monk Institute of Jazz and BMI to reward excellence in jazz composition. Composition to be written for trumpet. Can be written for up to five instruments with trumpet being the featured instrument. Solos for trumpet okay. Composers must not have had their jazz compositions recorded on a major label or recorded by a major jazz artist.

Application is on Web site or contact above organization for current information regarding application. Instructions for audiotape selections are very specific.

1143—UNITARIAN UNIVERSALIST ASSOCIATION (Musicians' Network Scholarships)

4190 Front Street
San Diego CA 92103
Written Inquiry

AMOUNT: $100-$700
DEADLINE(S): VARIES
FIELD(S): Art, Poetry, Music

Financial aid to undergraduate students in the above fields. Must be active with the Unitarian Universalist Association.

Renewable. Write for complete information.

1144—UNIVERSITY FILM AND VIDEO ASSOCIATION (Carole Fielding Student Grants)

Professor Robert Johnson
Framington State College
100 State Street
Framington MA 01701
Internet: http://www.uvfa.org

AMOUNT: $1,000 to $4,000
DEADLINE(S): JAN 1
FIELD(S): Film, video, multi-media production

Open to undergraduate/graduate students. Categories are narrative, experimental, animation, documentary, multimedia. Applicant must be sponsored by a faculty member who is an active member of the University Film and Video Association.

Write to the above address for application and complete details.

1145—UNIVERSITY OF ILLINOIS AT URBANA-CHAMPAIGN (Lydia E. Parker Bates Scholarship)

620 East John Street
Champaign IL 61820
217/333-0100
Internet: http://www.uiuc.edu/

AMOUNT: Up to $1,000
DEADLINE(S): MAR 15
FIELD(S): Art, Architecture, Landscape Architecture, Urban Planning, Dance, Theater, and all related subjects except Music.

Open to undergraduate students in the College of Fine and Applied Arts who are attending the University of Illinois at Urbana-Champaign. Must demonstrate financial need and have 2.85 GPA. Complete the Free Application for Federal Student Aid with UIUC admission application.

175 awards per year. Recipients must carry at least 12 credit hours per semester. Contact office of student financial aid for application.

1146—UNIVERSITY OF NORTH TEXAS (Music Scholarships)

College of Music
P.O. Box 311367
Denton TX 76203-1367
940/565-2791
FAX: 940/565-2002
E-mail: undergrad@music.unt.edu
Internet: http://www.unt.edu/scholarships

AMOUNT: Varies
DEADLINE(S): MAY 1
FIELD(S): Music

Several scholarships for music students are offered at the University of North Texas. Specialties and eligibility requirements vary.

See Web site for more information. Contact school for details.

1147—UNIVERSITY OF TEXAS AT EL PASO (Music Scholarships)

Department of Music
Fox Fine Arts Center, Room 301
500 West University Avenue
El Paso TX 79968-0552
915/747-5606
FAX: 915/747-5023
E-mail: music@utep.edu
Internet: http://www.utep.edu

AMOUNT: Varies
DEADLINE(S): MAR 1

FIELD(S): Music

Several music scholarships are available at the University of Texas at El Paso. Virtually all members of large ensembles receive a service award of some type, while more serious students may audition for a music scholarship. Auditions are usually held in March or April.

See Web site and/or contact Dr. Ron Hufstader, chair, for more information.

1148—UTA ALUMNI ASSOCIATION (Sue and Art Mosby Scholarship Endowment in Music)

University of Texas at Arlington
Box 19457
Arlington TX 76019
817/272-2594
FAX: 817/272-2597
E-mail: alumni@uta.edu
Internet: http://www.uta.edu/alumni/scholar.htm

AMOUNT: $500
DEADLINE(S): Varies
FIELD(S): Music

Must be a full-time student in good standing at the University of Texas at Arlington. Must demonstrate financial need and musical ability with potential to complete UTA degree. Audition required.

1 award annually. Contact UTA Alumni Association for an application.

1149—UNIVERSITY OF ILLINOIS AT URBANA-CHAMPAIGN (Lydia E. Parker Bates Scholarship)

620 East John Street
Champaign IL 61820
217/333-0100
Internet: http://www.uiuc.edu/

AMOUNT: Up to $1,000
DEADLINE(S): MAR 15
FIELD(S): Art, Architecture, Landscape Architecture, Urban Planning, Dance, Theater, and all related subjects except Music.

Open to undergraduate students in the College of Fine and Applied Arts who are attending the University of Illinois at Urbana-Champaign. Must demonstrate financial need and have 2.85 GPA. Complete the Free Application for Federal Student Aid with UIUC admission application.

175 awards per year. Recipients must carry at least 12 credit hours per semester. Contact office of student financial aid for application.

1150—WAMSO (Young Artist Competition)

1111 Nicollet Mall
Minneapolis MN 55403
612/371-5654
Fax: 612/371-7176
Internet: http://www.wamso.org

AMOUNT: $3,000 first prize in addition to $2,250 WAMSO Achievement Award and performance with MN Orchestra, $2,500 second prize, $1,000 third prize, as well as a grand prize which is awarded at the discretion of the music director of the orchestra.
DEADLINE(S): SEPT 23
FIELD(S): Piano and Orchestral Instruments

Competition offers 4 prizes and possible scholarships to high school and college students in schools in IN, IA, MN, MO, NE, SD, WI, and the Canadian provinces of Manitoba and Ontario. Entrants may not have passed their 26th birthday on date of competition (which is usually held in January).

1151—WHITTIER COLLEGE (Talent Scholarship)

13406 E. Philadelphia Street
Whittier CA 90608
562/907-4285
FAX: 562/464-4560
E-mail: admission@whittier.edu
Internet: http://www.whittier.edu

AMOUNT: $5,000-$10,000
DEADLINE(S): FEB 1
FIELD(S): Art, Music, Theater

Eligibility based on portfolio or audition submissions judged by music, art, or theater department.

Write above address for complete information.

1152—WITTENBERG UNIVERSITY (Music Scholarship Funds)

P.O. Box 720
Springfield OH 45501-0720
937/327-7340 or 800/677-7347
FAX: 937/327-7558
E-mail: Music@wittenberg.edu
Internet: http://www.wittenberg.edu/academics/music/scholaid.shtml

AMOUNT: $600-half tuition
DEADLINE(S): MAR 15
FIELD(S): Music

Scholarships for music majors and minors and also for students who continue to study and participate in music ensembles while pursuing non-music degrees. Interested students must complete application to the University and be accepted and participate in an audition by March 19.

Request a Music Audition Packet for instructions. See Web site for more information, and write to: Music Department, Wittenberg University, at above address.

PHILOSOPHY

1153—AMERICAN JEWISH LEAGUE FOR ISRAEL (Scholarship)

130 East 59th Street, 14th Floor
New York NY 10022
212/371-1583
E-mail: ajlimlk@aol.com

AMOUNT: Varies
DEADLINE(S): MAY
FIELD(S): Religion

This merit-based scholarship provides tuition for U.S. undergraduate or graduate students to study at one of the participating universities in Israel.

1154—B.M. WOLTMAN FOUNDATION (Lutheran Scholarships for Students of the Ministry and Teaching)

7900 U.S. 290 E.
Austin TX 78724
512/926-4272

AMOUNT: $500-$2,500
DEADLINE(S): Varies
FIELD(S): Theology (Lutheran Ministry); Teacher Education (Lutheran Schools)

Scholarships for undergrads and graduate students studying for careers in the Lutheran ministry or for teaching in a Lutheran school. For Texas residents attending, or planning to attend, any college in Texas.

45 awards. Renewable. Send for details.

1155—CHRISTIAN CHURCH-DISCIPLES OF CHRIST (Katherine J. Schutze Memorial and Edwin G. and Lauretta M. Michael Scholarship)

P.O. Box 1986
Indianapolis IN 46206-1986
317/635-3100
FAX: 317/635-4426
E-mail: cwebb@dhm.disciples.org

AMOUNT: Varies
DEADLINE(S): MAR 15
FIELD(S): Theology

Open to Christian Church (Disciples of Christ) members who are female seminary students preparing for the ordained ministry. Must be enrolled as a full-time student in an accredited school or seminary, have an above average GPA (minimum C+), and demonstrate financial need. Must submit transcripts and references. Schutze scholarship is open to all women who meet above criteria; Michael Scholarship is for minister's wives only.

Renewable. Contact Division of Homeland Ministries at above address for an application.

1156—CHRISTIAN CHURCH-DISCIPLES OF CHRIST (Rowley/Ministerial Education Scholarship)

P.O. Box 1986
Indianapolis IN 46206-1986
317/635-3100
FAX: 317/635-4426
E-mail: cwebb@dhm.disciples.org
AMOUNT: Varies
DEADLINE(S): MAR 15
FIELD(S): Theology

Open to Christian Church (Disciples of Christ) members who are seminary students preparing for the ordained ministry. Must be enrolled as a full-time student in an accredited school or seminary, have an above average GPA (minimum C+), and demonstrate financial need. Must submit transcripts and references.

Renewable. Contact Division of Homeland Ministries at above address for an application.

1157—CHRISTIAN CHURCH-DISCIPLES OF CHRIST (Star Supporter Scholarship/Loan)

P.O. Box 1986
Indianapolis IN 46206-1986
317/635-3100
FAX: 317/635-4426
E-mail: cwebb@dhm.disciples.org
AMOUNT: $2,000
DEADLINE(S): MAR 15
FIELD(S): Theology

Open to Christian Church (Disciples of Christ) members who are Black/Afro-American students preparing for the ordained ministry. Must be enrolled as a full-time student at an accredited school or seminary, have an above average GPA (minimum C+), and demonstrate financial need. Must submit transcripts and references. Three years of service in a full-time professional ministry will repay the scholarship/loan.

100 awards annually. Renewable. Contact Division of Homeland Ministries at above address for an application.

1158—CLEM JAUNICH EDUCATION TRUST (Scholarships)

7801 E. Bushlake Road; Suite 260
Bloomington MN 55439
612/546-1555
AMOUNT: $750-$3,000
DEADLINE(S): JUL 1
FIELD(S): Theology; Medicine

Open to students who have attended public or parochial school in the Delano (MN) school district or currently reside within 7 miles of the city of Delano MN. Awards support undergraduate or graduate study in theology or medicine.

4-6 awards annually. Contact Joseph Abrahams for an application.

1159—CYNTHIA E. AND CLARA H. HOLLIS FOUNDATION

100 Summer Street
Boston MA 02110
Written Inquiry
AMOUNT: Varies
DEADLINE(S): APR 1
FIELD(S): Nursing, Social Work, Dental or Medical Technology, and Religion

Scholarships for Massachusetts with preference given to students in the above fields. For undergraduates, graduates, vo-tech, and adult education. Must demonstrate financial need.

Send SASE to Walter E. Palmer, Esq., 35 Harvard Street, Brookline, MA 02146 for application details. Scholarship forms are also available from the rector of All Saints Church, Brookline High School, and St. Mary's High School, all in Brookline, Massachusetts.

1160—EMBASSY OF THE CZECH REPUBLIC (Scholarships for Czechs Living Abroad)

3900 Spring of Freedom Street NW
Washington DC 20008
202/274-9103
FAX: 202/363-6308
E-mail: con_washington@embassy.mzv.cz
Internet: http://www.mzv.cz/washington
AMOUNT: Varies
DEADLINE(S): APR 30
FIELD(S): Czech Language and Literature, History, Theology, and/or Ethnography

Scholarships for undergraduate and graduate citizens of the Czech Republic who are living in the U.S. The ideal applicant should use his/her knowledge for the benefit of the Czech community abroad.

20 annual awards. For a maximum of two semesters of study. See Web site or write/call for further information.

1161—FRANCIS NATHANIEL AND KATHERYN PADGETT KENNEDY FOUNDATION (Scholarships for Southern Baptists)

933 Sunset Drive
Greenwood SC 29646
803/942-1400
AMOUNT: $400-$1,000
DEADLINE(S): MAY 15
FIELD(S): Theology (in preparation for the ministry or missionary work) or Christian education

Scholarships for college-bound high school seniors and undergraduates who are active members of the a church of the National Baptist Convention. Must be planning a career as a Southern Baptist minister, foreign missionary, or in Christian education.

Send SASE for details.

1162—FRANKS FOUNDATION (Scholarships)

P.O. Box 3168
Portland OR 97208-3168
503/275-5929
FAX: 503/275-4177
E-mail: marlyn.norquist@usbank.com
AMOUNT: Varies
DEADLINE(S): MAR 1
FIELD(S): Nursing; Theology

Open to Oregon residents from Deschutes, Crook, Jefferson, Harney, Lake, Grant, and Klamath Counties. Must be a full-time undergraduate or graduate student at a 2- or 4-year public, private, or nonprofit postsecondary institution eligible for Fed Title IV financial aid. Must have a minimum 2.5 GPA and demonstrate financial need.

20-25 awards annually. Renewable. Contact Marlyn Norquist for an application.

1163—FREEDOM FROM RELIGION FOUNDATION (Student Essay Contest)

P.O. Box 750
Madison WI 53701
608/256-5800
Internet: http://www.infidels.org/org/ffrf
AMOUNT: $1,000; $500; $250
DEADLINE(S): JUL 15

FIELD(S): Humanities; English; Education; Philosophy; Science

Essay contest on topics related to church-state entanglement in public schools or growing up a "freethinker" in religious-oriented society. Topics change yearly, but all are on general theme of maintaining separation of church and state. New topics available in February. For high school seniors and currently enrolled college/technical students. Must be U.S. citizen.

Send SASE to address above for complete information. Please indicate whether wanting information for college competition or high school. Information will be sent when new topics are announced each February. See Web site for details.

1164—GRAND AVENUE PRESBYTERIAN CHURCH (Davis Foute Eagleton Memorial Student Loan Fund)

Secretary
1601 N. Travis Street
Sherman TX 75092-3761
903/893-7428
E-mail: Snyder@texoma.net

AMOUNT: Varies
DEADLINE(S): AUG 15 (fall); DEC 15 (spring)
FIELD(S): Theology; Christian Service

Open to full-time students of any Christian denomination in an accredited seminary, college, or university who desire to prepare for career in parish ministry, chaplain ministry, or other Christian service. Loans made in following priority: Members of Grand Avenue Presbyterian Church, current Austin College students/alumni, Presbyterians in Pres. schools, Presbyterians in other schools, non-Presbyterians in Presbyterian schools, and Presbyterians in graduate religion studies.

Contact Susan G. Snyder, Secretary, DFE Board, for an application.

1165—INSTITUTE FOR HUMANE STUDIES (Humane Studies Fellowship)

3301 N. FairFAX: Drive; Suite 440
Arlington VA 22201-4432
703/993-4880 or 800/697-8799
FAX: 703/993-4890
E-mail: ihs@gmu.edu
Internet: http://www.TheIHS.org

AMOUNT: $12,000 (max.)
DEADLINE(S): DEC
FIELD(S): Social Sciences; Liberal Arts; Law; Humanities; Jurisprudence; Journalism

Open to graduate and advanced undergraduate or law students pursuing degrees at any accredited domestic or foreign college/university. Based on academic performance, demonstrated interest in the classical liberal tradition, and potential to contribute to the advancement of a free society.

90 awards annually. Apply online or contact IHS for an application.

1166—INSTITUTE FOR HUMANE STUDIES (Summer Seminars Program)

3401 N. FairFAX: Drive, Suite 440
Arlington VA 22201-4432
703/993-4880 or 800/697-8799
FAX: 703/993-4890
E-mail: ihs@gmu.edu
Internet: http://www.TheIHS.org

AMOUNT: Free summer seminars, including room/board, lectures, seminar materials, and books
DEADLINE(S): MAR
FIELD(S): Social Sciences; Humanities; Law; Journalism; Public Policy; Education; Film; Writing; Economics; Philosophy

Open to college students, recent graduates, and graduate students who share an interest in learning and exchanging ideas about the scope of individual rights, free markets, the rule of law, peace, and tolerance.

See Web site for seminar information or to apply online or contact IHS for an application.

1167—J. HUGH and EARLE W. FELLOWS MEMORIAL FUND (Scholarship Loans)

Pensacola Junior College
President
1000 College Boulevard
Pensacola FL 32504-8998
904/484-1700
Internet: http://www.pjc.cc.fl.us/

AMOUNT: Each is negotiated individually
DEADLINE(S): None
FIELD(S): Medicine; Nursing; Medical Technology; Theology (Episcopal)

Open to bona fide residents of the Florida counties of Escambia, Santa Rosa, Okaloosa, or Walton. For undergraduate study in the fields listed above. U.S. citizenship required.

Loans are interest-free until graduation. Write for complete information.

1168—MONSIGNOR JOSEPH M. LUDDY SCHOLARSHIP FOUNDATION, INC.

The Skills Group
341 Science Park Road, Suite #6
State College PA 16803
814/238-3245

AMOUNT: Varies
DEADLINE(S): SEP
FIELD(S): Religion

For male residents of Blair County, PA, either current or past, who plan to attend a graduate program in social work or who are pursuing a career as a Roman Catholic priest.

1169—PEW YOUNGER SCHOLARS PROGRAM (Graduate Fellowships)

G-123 Hesburgh Library
University of Notre Dame
Notre Dame IN 46556
219/631-4531
FAX: 219/631-8721
E-mail: Karen.M.Heinig.2@nd.edu
Internet: http://www.nd.edu/~pesp/pew/PYSPHistory.html

AMOUNT: $13,000
DEADLINE(S): NOV 30
FIELD(S): Social Sciences, Humanities, Theology

Program is for use at any Christian undergraduate school and most seminaries. Check with organization to see if your school qualifies. Apply during senior year. Recipients may enter a competition in which ten students will be awarded a $39,000 ($13,000/year) fellowship for three years of dissertation study. For use at top-ranked Ph.D. programs at outstanding universities.

NOT for study in medicine, law business, performing arts, fine arts, or the pastorate. Check Web site and/or organization for details.

1170—PHILADELPHIA COLLEGE OF BIBLE (Scholarships, Grants, and Loans)

Financial Aid Dept
200 Manor Avenue
Langhorne PA 19047
800/366-0049
Internet: http://www.pcb.edu

AMOUNT: Varies
DEADLINE(S): Varies
FIELD(S): Fields of study relating to Christian education

Various scholarships, loans, and grants are available to students attending this undergraduate Bible college in Philadelphia,

PA. High school seniors, transfer students, and others may apply. Some programs are for students with outstanding academic achievement, musical talent, or leaderships skills. Some are for dependents of Christian workers, missionaries, or alumni. Some are based on financial need.

Access Web site for details and/or send SASE to school for further information.

1171—ROBERT SCHRECK MEMORIAL FUND (Grants)

c/o Texas Commerce Bank—
Trust Dept
P.O. Drawer 140
El Paso TX 79980
915/546-6515

AMOUNT: $500-$1500
DEADLINE(S): JUL 15; NOV 15
FIELD(S): Medicine; Veterinary Medicine; Physics; Chemistry; Architecture; Engineering; Episcopal Clergy

Grants to undergraduate juniors or seniors or graduate students who have been residents of El Paso County for at least two years. Must be U.S. citizen or legal resident and have a high grade point average. Financial need is a consideration.

Write for complete information.

1172—ROSE HILL COLLEGE (Louella Robinson Memorial Scholarship)

P.O. Box 3126
Aiken SC 29802-3126
800/684-3769
FAX: 803/641-0240
E-mail: rosehill@rosehill.edu
Internet: http://www.rosehill.edu

AMOUNT: $10,000/year for four years
DEADLINE(S): Varies
FIELD(S): Liberal arts and humanities curricula

For undergraduate residents of Indian River County, Florida, to attend Rose Hill College in Aiken, South Carolina. The school offers a liberal arts education and follows the Great Books curriculum, a program of reading and seminars.

One annual award. Applicants must meet entry requirements of RHC. Contact above location for details.

1173—ROSE HILL COLLEGE (Scholarships for Children of Eastern Orthodox Priests/Deacons)

P.O. Box 3126
Aiken SC 29802-3126
800/684-3769
FAX: 803/641-0240
E-mail: rosehill@rosehill.edu
Internet: http://www.rosehill.edu

AMOUNT: Full scholarship: $10,000/year for four years
DEADLINE(S): Varies
FIELD(S): Liberal Arts and Humanities Curricula

For undergraduates who are children of Eastern Orthodox Christan priests or deacons to attend Rose Hill College in Aiken, South Carolina. The school offers a liberal arts education and follows the Great Books Curriculum, a program of reading and seminars.

6-10 annual awards. Applicants must meet entry requirements of RHC. Contact above location for details.

1174—ROSE HILL COLLEGE (Scholarships for the Homeschooled)

P.O. Box 3126
Aiken SC 29802-3126
800/684-3769
FAX: 803/641-0240
E-mail: rosehill@rosehill.edu
Internet: http://www.resehill.edu

AMOUNT: Full scholarship: $10,000/year for four years
DEADLINE(S): Varies
FIELD(S): Liberal Arts and Humanities Curricula

For undergraduates who have been homeschooled for three of the last five years of their high school education. For use at Rose Hill College in Aiken, South Carolina. The school offers a liberal arts education and follows the Great Books Curriculum, a program of reading and seminars. Scholarships will be awarded primarily on the basis of an essay which the student will be asked to write.

Four annual awards. Applicants must meet entry requirements of RHC. Contact above location for details.

1175—THE FUND FOR THEOLOGICAL EDUCATION, INC. (North American Doctoral Fellows Program)

825 Houston Mill Road, Suite 250
Atlanta, GA 30329-4211
404/727-1450
E-mail: fte@thefund.org
Internet: http://www.thefund.org

AMOUNT: $1,500
DEADLINE(S): MAR 1
FIELD(S): Religion

Open to talented doctoral students traditionally underrepresented in the fields of religion or theology who already are enrolled in programs leading to the Ph.D. or Th.D. degree and nearing the end of their studies. Fellowships provide assistance to students who otherwise might not have the financial resources to complete their degree programs.

1176—THE HEATH EDUCATION FUND (Scholarships for Ministers, Priests, and Missionaries)

Barnett Bank, N.A.
P.O. Box 40200
Jacksonville FL 32203-0200
904/464-2877

AMOUNT: $750-$1,000
DEADLINE(S): JUL 31
FIELD(S): Ministry, Missionary Work, or Social Work

Scholarships to high school graduates from the southeastern U.S. who wish to study in the above fields. Eligible states of residence: Alabama, Florida, Georgia, Kentucky, Louisiana, Maryland, Mississippi, North and South Carolina, Tennessee, Virginia, and West Virginia.

Write to Barnett Bank's Trust Co., N.A., at above address for details and guidelines. Send SASE and letter with brief background of applicant, field of study, religious denomination and reason for request. Preference to Methodists or Episcopalians.

1177—UNITED METHODIST CHURCH (Youth Ministry-Richard S. Smith Scholarship)

P.O. Box 480
Nashville TN 37202-0840
615/340-7184
FAX: 615/340-1702
E-mail: nymo@aol.com
Internet: http://www.umc.org/nymo/nymohome

AMOUNT: Up to $1,000
DEADLINE(S): JUN 1
FIELD(S): All fields of study

Open to United Methodist church youth from ethnic minority backgrounds who have at least a 2.0 high school GPA, been active in a local church at least 1 year, and are entering college as freshmen.

Must be able to establish need. Obtain application between Nov. 1 and May 15.

1178—UNITED METHODIST CHURCH (Youth Ministry-David W. Self Scholarship)

P.O. Box 840
Nashville TN 37202-0840
615/340-7184
FAX: 615/340-1702
E-mail: nymo@aol.com
Internet: http://www.umc.org/nymo/nymohome

AMOUNT: Up to $1,000
DEADLINE(S): JUN 1
FIELD(S): All fields of study

Open to United Methodist church youth who have at least a 2.0 high school GPA, been active in a local church at least 1 year, and are entering college as freshmen.

Must be able to establish need. Obtain application between November 1 and May 15. Write for complete information.

1179—UNIVERSITY OF OXFORD (Squire and Marriott Bursaries)

University Offices; Wellington Square
Oxford OX1 2JD ENGLAND UK
+44 (0)1865 270000
Internet: http://www.ox.ac.uk/

AMOUNT: Varies
DEADLINE(S): MAR; SEP
FIELD(S): Theology

Applicants must have the intention of offering themselves for ordination in the Church of England or any church in communion therewith and be in need of financial assistance for their university education. Tenable at the University of Oxford.

6 awards annually. Renewable. Contact Mrs. E.A. MacAllister, Assistant to the Secretary, Board of the Faculty of Theology, at Oxford University for an application/enrollment information.

1180—WOMEN OF THE EVANGELICAL LUTHERAN CHURCH IN AMERICA (The Belmer-Flora Prince Scholarships)

8765 West Higgins Road
Chicago IL 60631-4189
800/638-3522 ext. 2736
FAX: 773/380-2419
Internet: http://www.elca.org/wo/scholpro.html
E-mail: fretheim@elca.org

AMOUNT: $2,000 max.
DEADLINE(S): February 15
FIELD(S): Women studying for ELCA service abroad

Assists women who are members of the ELCA studying for ELCA service abroad that does not lead to a church-certified profession. Must be a U.S. citizen at least 21 years of age who has experienced an interruption of two or more years since completion of high school. Academic records of any coursework completed in last five years as well as written confirmation of admission from educational institution are required.

Renewable for an additional year. Contact Faith Fretheim, Program Director, for an application.

SCHOOL OF NATURAL RESOURCES

1181—ALLIANCE FOR YOUNG ARTISTS AND WRITERS, INC./AMERICAN MUSEUM OF NATURAL HISTORY (Young Naturalist Awards)

Scholastic, Inc.
555 Broadway
New York NY 10012-3999
212/343-6582 or 800-SCHOLASTIC
FAX: 212/343-4885
E-mail: A&WGeneralinfo@scholastic.com
Internet: http://www.amnh.org/youngnaturalistawards

AMOUNT: Up to $2,500 + trip to New York to visit AMNH
DEADLINE(S): JAN
FIELD(S): Natural Sciences

For all students in grades 7-12 currently enrolled in a public or nonpublic school in the U.S., Canada, U.S. territories, or U.S.-sponsored schools abroad. Program focuses on finding and rewarding excellence in biology, earth science, astronomy, and cultural studies. Students are encouraged to perform observation-based projects that require creativity, inquiry, and critical analysis. Specific topics vary annually.

48 awards annually. See Web site for application.

1182—ALLIANCE FOR YOUNG ARTISTS AND WRITERS, INC./AMERICAN MUSEUM OF NATURAL HISTORY (Young Naturalist Awards)

Scholastic, Inc.
555 Broadway
New York NY 10012-3999
212/343-6582 or 800-SCHOLASTIC
FAX: 212/343-4885
E-mail: A&WGeneralinfo@scholastic.com
Internet: http://www.amnh.org/youngnaturalistawards

AMOUNT: Up to $2,500 + trip to New York to visit AMNH
DEADLINE(S): JAN
FIELD(S): Natural Sciences

For all students in grades 7-12 currently enrolled in a public or nonpublic school in the U.S., Canada, U.S. territories, or U.S.-sponsored schools abroad. Program focuses on finding and rewarding excellence in biology, earth science, astronomy, and cultural studies. Students are encouraged to perform observation-based projects that require creativity, inquiry, and critical analysis. Specific topics vary annually.

48 awards annually. See Web site for application.

1183—AMERICAN FOUNDATION FOR THE BLIND (Paul W. Ruckes Scholarship)

11 Penn Plaza, Suite 300
New York NY 10001
212/502-7661
FAX: 212/502-7771
E-mail: juliet@afb.org
Internet: http://www.afb.org

AMOUNT: $1,000
DEADLINE(S): APR 30
FIELD(S): Engineering; Computer/Physical/Life Sciences

Open to legally blind and visually impaired undergraduate and graduate students pursuing a degree in one of above fields. Must be U.S. citizen. Must submit written documentation of visual impairment from ophthalmologist or optometrist (need not be legally blind); official transcripts; proof of college/university acceptance; three letters of recommendation; and typewritten statement describing goals, work experience extracurricular activities, and how monies will be used.

1 award annually. See Web site or contact Julie Tucker at AFB for an application.

1184—AMERICAN INDIAN SCIENCE AND ENGINEERING SOCIETY (A.T. Anderson Memorial Scholarship)

P.O. Box 9828
Albuquerque NM 87119-9828
505/765-1052
FAX: 505/765-5608

E-mail: scholarships@aises.org
Internet: http://www.aises.org/scholarships
AMOUNT: $1,000-$2,000
DEADLINE(S): JUN 15
FIELD(S): Medicine; Natural Resources; Science; Engineering

Open to undergraduate and graduate students who are at least 1/4 American Indian or recognized as member of a tribe. Must be member of AISES ($10 fee), enrolled full-time at an accredited institution, and demonstrate financial need.

Renewable. See Web site or contact Patricia Browne for an application and/or membership information.

1185—ASTRONAUT SCHOLARSHIP FOUNDATION (Scholarships)

Exec. Director
6225 Vectorspace Boulevard
Titusville FL 32780
321/269-6119
FAX: 321/267-3970
E-mail: MercurySvn@aol.com;
Internet: http://www.astronautscholarship.org/guidelines.html
AMOUNT: Varies
DEADLINE(S): Varies
FIELD(S): Engineering and Physical Sciences (Medical Research OK, but NOT Professional Medicine)

Open to juniors, seniors, and graduate students at a select group of schools. Must be U.S. citizen with the intention to pursue research or advance field of study upon completion of final degree. Special consideration given to students who have shown initiative, creativity, excellence, and/or resourcefulness in their field. Must be NOMINATED by faculty or staff.

See Web site for list of eligible schools. Contact Howard Benedict, Executive Director, for details.

1186—BARRY GOLDWATER SCHOLARSHIP AND EXCELLENCE IN EDUCATION FOUNDATION (Scholarships)

6225 Brandon Avenue, Suite 315
Springfield VA 22150-2519
703/756-6012
FAX: 703/756-6015
E-mail: GOLDH2o@erols.com
Internet: http://www.act.org/goldwater
AMOUNT: $7,500/year (max.)
DEADLINE(S): FEB 1
FIELD(S): Math; Natural Sciences; Engineering

Open to college sophomores and juniors with a minimum 3.0 GPA. Must be U.S. citizen, resident alien, or American national pursuing a degree at an accredited institution in math, natural sciences, or engineering disciplines that contribute to technological advances.

300 awards annually. See Web site or contact your Goldwater Faculty Representative on campus. Students must be nominated by their institution and cannot apply on their own.

1187—CAREER OPPORTUNITIES FOR YOUTH, INC. (Collegiate Scholarship Program)

P.O. Box 996
Manhattan Beach CA 90266
310/535-4838
AMOUNT: $250-$1,000
DEADLINE(S): SEP 30
FIELD(S): Engineering, Science, Mathematics, Computer Science, Business Administration, Education, Nursing

For students of Latino/Hispanic background residing in the Southern California area who have completed at least one semester/quarter of study at an accredited four-year university. Must have a cumulative GPA of 2.5 or higher.

Priority will be given to students who demonstrate financial need. Send SASE to above location for details.

1188—CHICAGO ROOFING CONTRACTORS ASSOCIATION (Scholarship)

4415 W. Harrison Street, #322
Hillside IL 60162
708/449-3340
FAX: 708/449-0837
E-mail: crcainfo@crca.org
Internet: http://www.crca.org
AMOUNT: $2,000
DEADLINE(S): Varies
FIELD(S): Business; Engineering; Architecture; Liberal Arts; Sciences

Open to high school seniors who reside in one of the eight counties in Northern Illinois: Cook, DuPage, Lake, Kane, Kendall, DeKalb, McHenry, or Will. Must be accepted as a full-time student in a four-year college/university to pursue a degree in one of the above fields. Must be U.S. citizen. Based on academic achievements extracurricular activities, and community involvement.

Renewable. Contact CRCA for an application.

1189—COMMUNITY FOUNDATION SILICON VALLEY (Valley Scholars Program)

111 W. Saint John Street, Suite 230
San Jose CA 95113
408/278-0270
FAX: 408/278-0280
Internet: http://www.cfsv.org
AMOUNT: $20,000 (over 4 years of college)
DEADLINE(S): Varies (early spring)
FIELD(S): Science and/or math

A scholarship program for public high school students in the Silicon Valley (San Mateo and Santa Clara counties and Fremont Union High school District, California) who have demonstrated enthusiasm and aptitude for science and math. Must be U.S. citizen or permanent resident.

Up to 20 students are selected each year. Each Valley Scholar receives financial support, guidance through the college admission process, and a mentor whose interests match their own. Students may apply during their sophomore year of high school and must be academically outstanding.

1190—THE EXPLORERS CLUB (Youth Activity Fund)

46 East 70th Street
New York NY 10021
212/628-8383
FAX: 212/288-4449
E-mail: youth@explorers.org;
Internet: http://www.explorers.org
AMOUNT: $500-$1,500
DEADLINE(S): JAN 31
FIELD(S): Natural Sciences

Open to high school and undergraduate college students to help them participate in field research in the natural sciences anywhere in the world under the supervision of a qualified scientist. Grants are to help with travel costs and expenses. Applicants must provide a brief but knowledgeable explanation of proposed project in own words, as well as two letters of recommendation. Joint funding is encouraged. Must be U.S. citizen or permanent resident.

Write to above address or look on web site for details.

1191—FREEDOM FROM RELIGION FOUNDATION (Student Essay Contest)

P.O. Box 750
Madison WI 53701
608/256-5800
Internet: http://www.infidels.org/org/ffrf
AMOUNT: $1,000; $500; $250
DEADLINE(S): JUL 15
FIELD(S): Humanities; English; Education; Philosophy; Science

Essay contest on topics related to church-state entanglement in public schools or growing up a "freethinker" in religious-oriented society. Topics change yearly, but all are on general theme of maintaining separation of church and state. New topics available in February. For high school seniors and currently enrolled college/technical students. Must be U.S. citizen.

Send SASE to address above for complete information. Please indicate whether wanting information for college competition or high school. Information will be sent when new topics are announced each February. See Web site for details.

1192—GERBER SCIENTIFIC, INC. (H. Joseph Gerber Vision Scholarship Program)

83 Gerber Road West
South Windsor CT 06074
860/648-8027
Internet: http://www.gerberscientific.com
AMOUNT: Varies
DEADLINE(S): MAR 15
FIELD(S): Engineering, Mathematics, Computer Science, Natural Sciences

Scholarship program for high school seniors in Connecticut.

Fifty scholarships to be awarded.

1193—KOREAN-AMERICAN SCIENTISTS AND ENGINEERS ASSOCIATION (KSEA Scholarships)

1952 Gallows Road, Suite 300
Vienna VA 22182
703/748-1221
FAX: 703/748-1331
E-mail: admin@ksea.org
Internet: http://www.ksea.org
AMOUNT: $1,000
DEADLINE(S): FEB 28
FIELD(S): Science, Engineering, or Medicine

Scholarships to encourage Korean-American students to study in a science, engineering, or pre-med discipline and to recognize high-performing students. Must have graduated from a high school in the U.S.

5 to 8 awards yearly. Must be a student member of KSEA or a child of a member.

1194—NATIONAL SCIENCES AND ENGINEERING RESEARCH COUNCIL OF CANADA (Undergraduate Scholarships)

Scholarships/Fellowships Division
350 Albert Street
Ottawa Ontario K1A 1H5 CANADA
613/996-2009
FAX: 613/996-2589
E-mail: schol@nserc.ca
Internet: http://www.nserc.ca
AMOUNT: Up to $3,600
DEADLINE(S): Varies
FIELD(S): Natural Sciences, Engineering, Biology, or Chemistry

Open to Canadian citizens or permanent residents working towards degrees in science or engineering. Academic excellence and research aptitude are considerations.

Write for complete information.

1195—NATURAL SCIENCES AND ENGINEERING RESEARCH COUNCIL OF CANADA (Undergraduate Student Research Awards in Small Universities)

350 Albert Street
Ottawa Ontario K1A 1H5 CANADA
613/995-5992
FAX: 613/992-5337
E-mail: schol@nserc.ca
Internet: http://www.nserc.ca/programs/usrasmen.htm
AMOUNT: $3,600 (max.)
DEADLINE(S): Varies
FIELD(S): Natural Sciences; Engineering

Research awards for Canadian citizens/permanent residents attending eligible institutions, and who have no more than 6 and no fewer than 2 academic terms remaining to complete bachelor's degree. Cumulative GPA of at least second class (B). Must be doing full-time in research and development activities during award tenure.

Students in health sciences not eligible. Students with BAs and who are studying for a second may apply.

1196—PENINSULA COMMUNITY FOUNDATION (Dr. Mary Finegold Scholarship)

1700 S. El Camino Real #300
San Mateo CA 94402
650/358-9369
FAX: 650/358-9817
Internet: http://www.pcf.org/community_grants/scholarships.html
AMOUNT: $1,000
DEADLINE(S): MAR 7 (5 p.m.)
FIELD(S): Sciences

Scholarships for senior girls graduating from high school in Palo Alto, California, who intend to complete a four-year degree in the sciences. Special consideration will be given to girls who have demonstrated a "pioneering" spirit in that they have not been constrained by stereotypical female roles and to those facing financial hardship.

Award was established in the honor of Dr. Mary Finegold who, after completing her medical studies, elected to stay at home until her youngest child was in high school before beginning her medical practice. She was a school physician.

1197—RESOURCES FOR THE FUTURE (RFF Summer Internship Program)

1616 P Street NW
Washington DC 20036-1400
202/328-5000
FAX: 202/939-3460
E-mail: mankin@rff.org or voigt@rff.org
Internet: http://www.rff.org/about_rff/fellowships_internships.htm
AMOUNT: $350-375/week
DEADLINE(S): MAR 14 (5 p.m., eastern time)
FIELD(S): Social Sciences, Natural Resources, Energy, Environment

Resident paid summer internships for undergraduate and graduate students for research in the above fields. Divisions are Risk, Resource and Environmental Management, Energy and Natural Resources, and Quality of the Environment. Candidates should have outstanding policy analysis and writing skills. For both U.S. and non-U.S. citizens.

All information is on Web site. Address inquiries and applications to John Mankin (Energy and Natural Resources and Quality of the Environment) or Marilyn Voigt (Risk, Resource and Environmental Management).

1198—SAN DIEGO AEROSPACE MUSEUM (Bill Gibbs Scholarship)

Education Dept.
2001 Pan American Plaza
San Diego CA 92101
619/234-8291 ext. 19

FAX: 619/233-4526
Internet: http://aerospacemuseum.org/Scholastic.HTML
AMOUNT: Varies
DEADLINE(S): Varies
FIELD(S): Aerospace: Math, Physics, Science, or Engineering

For students who are residents of San Diego County, California, who have an aerospace career interest who have been accepted to a four-year college or university in a degree program relating to math, physics, science, or engineering.

Call or write museum for further information.

1199—SKIDMORE COLLEGE (Porter Presidential Scholarships in Science and Math)

Office of Admissions
815 North Broadway
Saratoga Springs NY 12866-1632
800/867-6007
E-mail: admissions@skidmore.edu
Internet: http://www.skidmore.edu/administration/financial_aid/porter_scholarship.htm
AMOUNT: $10,000/year
DEADLINE(S): JAN 15
FIELD(S): Math, Science, or Computer Science

Scholarships for students excelling in the above fields. Awards are based on talent, not financial need. Recipients are not required to major in a scientific or mathematical discipline, but they will be expected to demonstrate serious research in one or more of these areas.

Five scholarships per year. For more information, visit Web site.

1200—TEXAS SOCIETY OF PROFESSIONAL ENGINEERS (Scholarships)

P.O. Box 2145
Austin TX 78768
512/472-9286 or 800/580-8973
Internet: http://www.tspe.org
AMOUNT: Varies
DEADLINE(S): JAN 30
FIELD(S): Engineering (Math, Sciences)

Scholarships for graduating high school seniors who are Texas residents planning to attend Texas engineering colleges

Contact organization for details. Application is on Web site.

1201—THE BRITISH COUNCIL (Scholarships for Citizens of Mexico)

10 Spring Gardens
London SW1A 2BN ENGLAND UK
+44 (0) 171 930 8466
FAX: +44 (0) 161 957 7188
E-mail: education.enquiries@britcoun.org
Internet: http://www.britcoun.org/mexico/mexschol.htm
AMOUNT: Varies
DEADLINE(S): Varies
FIELD(S): Social Sciences, Applied Sciences, Technology

The British Council in Mexico offers approximately 100 scholarships per year in the above fields for undergraduates and graduates to study in the United Kingdom. Good level of English language retired.

The Web site listed here gives more details. For more information, contact: leticia.magana@bc-mexico.sprint.com. or contact organization in London.

1202—THE DAPHNE JACKSON MEMORIAL FELLOWSHIPS TRUST (Fellowships in Science/Engineering)

School of Physical Sciences,
Dept. of Physics, University of Surrey
Guildford, Surrey GU2 5XH
ENGLAND UK
01483 259166
FAX: 01483 259501
E-mail: J.Woolley@surrey.ac.uk
Internet: http://www.sst.ph.ic.ac.uk/trust/
AMOUNT: Varies
DEADLINE(S): Varies
FIELD(S): Science or Engineering, including Information Sciences

Fellowships to enable well-qualified and highly motivated scientists and engineers to return to appropriate careers following a career break due to family commitments. May be used on a flexible, part-time basis. Tenable at various U.K. universities.

See Web site and/or contact organization for details.

1203—UNITED STATES DEPARTMENT OF AGRICULTURE (1890 National Scholars Program)

14th & Independence Avenue SW;
Room 301-W; Whitten Bldg.
Washington DC 20250-9600
202/720-6905
E-mail: usda-m@fie.com
Internet: http://web.fie.com/htdoc/fed/agr/ars/edu/prog/mti/agrpgaak.htm
AMOUNT: Tuition, employment/benefits, use of pc/software, fees, books, room/board
DEADLINE(S): JAN 15
FIELD(S): Agriculture, Food, or Natural Resource Sciences

For U.S. citizens, high school grad/GED, GPA 3.0+, verbal/math SAT 1000+, composite score 21+ ACT, first-year college student, and attend participating school.

34+ scholarships/year/4 years. Send applications to U.S.D.A. Liaison officer at the 1890 Institution of your choice (see Web page for complete list).

1204—UNIVERSITY OF NEWCASTLE/Australia (R. M. Sheahan Memorial Undergraduate Scholarship)

Student Administration Unit, Student Services Centre, Univ. of Newcastle,
Callaghan NSW
2308 AUSTRALIA
+61-(02)-4921-6539
FAX: +61-(02)-4960-1766
E-mail: scholarships@newcastle.edu.au
Internet: http://www.newcastle.edu.au/services/ousr/stuadmin/schol/index.htm
AMOUNT: $1,000
DEADLINE(S): NOV 1
FIELD(S): Engineering, chemistry, or environmental engineering

Scholarship for undergraduate international as well as Australian students pursuing studies in chemistry, chemical engineering, or environmental engineering. Funded by the Cessnock City Council and Orica (ICI) Explosives, this award is made yearly based on academic merit.

Contact organization for details.

1205—WOODS HOLE OCEANOGRAPHIC INSTITUTION (Traineeships in Oceanography for Minority Group Undergraduates)

360 Woods Hole Road
Woods Hole MA 02543-1541
508/289-2219
FAX: 508/457-2188
E-mail: mgately@whoi.edu
Internet: http://www.whoi.edu
AMOUNT: Varies
DEADLINE(S): FEB 16
FIELD(S): Physical/Natural Sciences, Mathematics, Engineering

For minority undergraduates enrolled in U.S. colleges/universities who have completed at least two semesters. These awards provide training and research experience for students with interests in the above fields. Traineeships may be awarded for a ten- to- twelve-week period in the summer or for a semester during the academic year.

Renewable. For an application/more information, contact the Education Office, Clark Laboratory 223, MS #31, at above address.

AGRICULTURE

1206—ABBIE SARGENT MEMORIAL SCHOLARSHIP INC. (Scholarships)

295 Sheep Davis Road
Concord NH 03301
603/224-1934
FAX: 603/228-8432
AMOUNT: $200-400
DEADLINE(S): MAR 15
FIELD(S): Agriculture; Veterinary Medicine; Home Economics

Open to New Hampshire residents who are high school graduates with good grades and character. For undergraduate or graduate study. Must be legal resident of U.S. and demonstrate financial need.

Renewable with reapplication. Write or call for complete information.

1207—ALLIANCE FOR YOUNG ARTISTS AND WRITERS, INC./AMERICAN MUSEUM OF NATURAL HISTORY (Young Naturalist Awards)

Scholastic, Inc.
555 Broadway
New York NY 10012-3999
212/343-6582 or
800-SCHOLASTIC
FAX: 212/343-4885
E-mail: A&WGeneralinfo @scholastic.com
Internet: http://www.amnh.org/youngnaturalistawards
AMOUNT: Up to $2,500 + trip to New York to visit AMNH
DEADLINE(S): JAN
FIELD(S): Natural Sciences

For all students in grades 7-12 currently enrolled in a public or nonpublic school in the U.S., Canada, U.S. territories, or U.S.-sponsored schools abroad. Program focuses on finding and rewarding excellence in biology, earth science, astronomy, and cultural studies. Students are encouraged to perform observation-based projects that require creativity, inquiry, and critical analysis. Specific topics vary annually.

48 awards annually. See Web site for application.

1208—AMERICAN JUNIOR BRAHMAN ASSOCIATION (Ladies of the ABBA Scholarship)

3003 South Loop West; Suite 140
Houston TX 77054
713/349-0854
FAX: 713/349-9795
E-Mail: cshivers@brahman.org;
Internet: http://www.brahman.org
AMOUNT: $500
DEADLINE(S): MAY 1
FIELD(S): Agriculture

Open to graduating high school seniors who are members of the Junior Brahman Association. For full-time undergraduate study. U.S. citizenship required.

Up to 4 awards per year. Contact the AJBA for complete information.

1209—AMERICAN JUNIOR BRAHMAN ASSOCIATION (AJBA Scholarships)

3003 South Loop West; Suite 140
Houston TX 77054
713/349-0854
FAX: 713/349-9795
E-Mail: cshivers@brahman.org;
Internet: http://www.brahman.org
AMOUNT: $1,000
DEADLINE(S): MAY 1
FIELD(S): Agriculture

Open to graduating high school seniors who are members of the Junior Brahman Association. For full-time undergraduate study. U.S. citizenship required.

Up to 3 awards per year. Contact the AJBA for complete information.

1210—FIRST (Floriculture Industry Research and Scholarship Trust) (Barbara Carlson and Dosatron International, Inc. Scholarships)

P.O. Box 280
East Lansing MI 48826-0280
517/333-4617
FAX: 517/333-4494
E-mail: first@firstinfloriculture.org
Internet: http://www.firstinfloriculture.org
AMOUNT: $1,000
DEADLINE(S): MAY 1
FIELD(S): Horticulture

Open to graduate and undergraduate students already attending a four-year college/university who are majoring in horticulture or related field. For Carlson Scholarship, should intend to intern or work for public gardens. Cash award, with checks issued jointly in name of recipient and college/institution he or she will attend for current year. Must submit references and transcripts.

See Web site or send self-addressed, stamped envelope to FIRST after January 1 for an application. Recipients will be notified.

1211—FIRST (Floriculture Industry Research and Scholarship Trust) (Ball Horticultural Company and Paris Fracasso Scholarships)

P.O. Box 280
East Lansing MI 48826-0280
517/333-4617
FAX: 517/333-4494
E-mail: first@firstinfloriculture.org
Internet: http://www.firstinfloriculture.org
AMOUNT: $1,000-$2,000
DEADLINE(S): MAY 1
FIELD(S): Floriculture

Open to undergraduates entering junior or senior year at a four-year college/university. Ball Scholarship requires pursuit of career in commercial floriculture; Paris Scholarship requires pursuit of career in floriculture production. Cash award, with checks issued jointly in name of recipient and college/institution he or she will attend for current year. Must submit references and transcripts.

See Web site or send self-addressed, stamped envelope to FIRST after January 1 for an application. Recipients will be notified.

1212—FIRST (Floriculture Industry Research and Scholarship Trust) (Carl F. Dietz Memorial Scholarship)

P.O. Box 280
East Lansing MI 48826-0280
517/333-4617
FAX: 517/333-4494
E-mail: first@firstinfloriculture.org
Internet: http://www.firstinfloriculture.org
AMOUNT: $1,000
DEADLINE(S): MAY 1
FIELD(S): Horticulture

Open to undergraduate students already attending a four-year college/university who are majoring in horticulture or related field, with a specific interest in horticultural allied trades such as greenhouse equipment. Cash awards, with checks issued jointly in name of recipient and college or institution he or she will attend for current year. Must submit references and transcripts.

See Web site or send self-addressed, stamped envelope to FIRST after January 1 for an application. Recipient will be notified.

1213—FIRST (Floriculture Industry Research and Scholarship Trust) (Earl J. Small Growers, Inc. Scholarships)

P.O. Box 280
East Lansing MI 48826-0280
517/333-4617
FAX: 517/333-4494
E-mail: first@firstinfloriculture.org
Internet: http://www.firstinfloriculture.org

AMOUNT: $1,000
DEADLINE(S): MAY 1
FIELD(S): Horticulture

Open to undergraduate students already attending a four-year college/university who are majoring in horticulture or related field, with the intention of pursuing a career in greenhouse production. Must be U.S. or Canadian citizen. Cash award, with checks issued jointly in name of recipient and college/institution he or she will attend for current year. Must submit references and transcripts.

See Web site or send self-addressed, stamped envelope to FIRST after January 1 for an application. Recipients will be notified.

1214—BEDDING PLANTS FOUNDATION, INC. (Ed Markham International Scholarship)

P.O. Box 280
East Lansing MI 48826-0280
517/333-4617
FAX: 517/333-4494
E-mail: BPFI@aol.com
Internet: http://www.bpfi.org

AMOUNT: $1,000
DEADLINE(S): MAY 15
FIELD(S): Horticulture AND International Business

Open to graduate and undergraduate students already attending a four-year college/university who are majoring in horticulture or related field. Should wish to further understanding of domestic and international marketing through international horticulturally related study, work, or travel. Cash award, with checks issued jointly in name of recipient and college/institution he or she will attend for current year. Must submit references and transcripts.

1 award annually. See Web site or send printed self-addressed mailing label (or self-addressed, stamped envelope) to BPFI after January 1 for an application. Recipient will be notified.

1215—FIRST (Floriculture Industry Research and Scholarship Trust) (Fran Johnson Scholarship)

P.O. Box 280
East Lansing MI 48826-0280
517/333-4617
FAX: 517/333-4494
E-mail: first@firstinfloriculture.org
Internet: http://www.firstinfloriculture.org

AMOUNT: $500-$1,000
DEADLINE(S): MAY 1
FIELD(S): Horticulture; Floriculture

Open to undergraduate and graduate students at 2- or 4-year college/university in U.S. or Canada. Must be U.S. or Canadian citizen with major in horticulture or related field, specifically bedding plants or other floral crops. Must be reentering an academic program after an absence of at least 5 years. Cash award, with checks issued jointly in name of recipient and college/institution he or she will attend for current year. Must submit references and transcripts.

See Web site or send self-addressed, stamped envelope to FIRST after January 1 for an application. Recipient will be notified.

1216—BEDDING PLANTS FOUNDATION, INC. (Harold Bettinger Memorial Scholarship)

P.O. Box 280
East Lansing MI 48826-0280
517/333-4617
FAX: 517/333-4494
E-mail: BPFI@aol.com
Internet: http://www.bpfi.org

AMOUNT: $1,000
DEADLINE(S): MAY 15
FIELD(S): Horticulture AND Business/Marketing

Open to graduate and undergraduate students already attending a four-year college/university who have either a horticulture major with business/marketing emphasis OR a business/marketing major with horticulture emphasis. Cash award, with checks issued jointly in name of recipient and college/institution he or she will attend for current year. Must submit references and transcripts.

1 award annually. See Web site or send printed self-addressed mailing label (or self-addressed, stamped envelope) to BPFI after January 1 for an application. Recipient will be notified.

1217—FIRST (Floriculture Industry Research and Scholarship Trust) (James Rathmell Memorial Scholarship)

P.O. Box 280
East Lansing MI 48826-0280
517/333-4617
FAX: 517/333-4494
E-mail: first@firstinfloriculture.org
Internet: http://www.firstinfloriculture.org

AMOUNT: $2,500 (max.)
DEADLINE(S): MAY 1
FIELD(S): Horticulture; Floriculture

Open to undergraduates entering junior or senior year at a four-year college/university, and graduate students. Must have plans to work/study outside of U.S. in the field of floriculture or horticulture, with preference to those planning to work/study six months or longer. Cash award, with checks issued jointly in name of recipient and college/institution he or she will attend for current year. Must submit references and transcripts.

See Web site or send self-addressed, stamped envelope to FIRST after January 1 for an application. Recipient will be notified.

1218—FIRST (Floriculture Industry Research and Scholarship Trust) (Jacob Van Namen Scholarship)

P.O. Box 280
East Lansing MI 48826-0280
517/333-4617
FAX: 517/333-4494
E-mail: first@firstinfloriculture.org
Internet: http://www.firstinfloriculture.org

AMOUNT: $1,250
DEADLINE(S): MAY 1
FIELD(S): Agribusiness AND Floriculture

Open to undergraduate students already attending a four-year college/university who wish to be involved in agribusiness marketing and distribution of floral products. Cash award, with checks issued jointly in name of recipient and college/institution he or she will attend for current year. Must submit references and transcripts.

See Web site or send self-addressed, stamped envelope to FIRST after January 1 for an application. Recipients will be notified.

1219—FIRST (Floriculture Industry Research and Scholarship Trust) (Jerry Baker College Freshman Scholarships)

P.O. Box 280
East Lansing MI 48826-0280
517/333-4617
FAX: 517/333-4494
E-mail: first@firstinfloriculture.org
Internet: http://www.firstinfloriculture.org
AMOUNT: $1,000
DEADLINE(S): MAY 1
FIELD(S): Horticulture; Landscaping; Gardening

Open to undergraduates entering freshman year who are interested in careers in horticulture, landscaping, or gardening. Must be enrolled in an accredited four-year college/university program in the U.S. or Canada during next year. Cash awards, with checks issued jointly in name of recipient and college/institution he or she will attend for current year. Must submit references and transcripts.

See Web site or send self-addressed, stamped envelope to FIRST after January 1 for an application. Recipients will be notified.

1220—BEDDING PLANTS FOUNDATION, INC. (Jerry Wilmot Scholarship)

P.O. Box 280
East Lansing MI 48826-0280
517/333-4617
FAX: 517/333-4494
E-mail: BPFI@aol.com
Internet: http://www.bpfi.org
AMOUNT: $2,000
DEADLINE(S): MAY 15
FIELD(S): Horticulture AND Business/Finance; Garden Center Management

Open to undergraduate students already attending a four-year college/university who either have a major in horticulture with business/finance emphasis OR have a major in business/finance with horticulture emphasis. Should wish to pursue a career in garden center management. Cash award, with checks issued jointly in name of recipient and college/institution he or she will attend for current year. Must submit references and transcripts.

1 award annually. See Web site or send printed self-addressed mailing label (or self-addressed, stamped envelope) to BPFI after January 1 for an application. Recipient will be notified.

1221—FIRST (Floriculture Industry Research and Scholarship Trust) (Seed Companies Scholarship)

P.O. Box 280
East Lansing MI 48826-0280
517/333-4617
FAX: 517/333-4494
E-mail: first@firstinfloriculture.org
Internet: http://www.firstinfloriculture.org
AMOUNT: $1,000
DEADLINE(S): MAY 1
FIELD(S): Horticulture

Open to undergraduate students entering junior or senior year at a four-year college/university-and graduate students-who are majoring in horticulture or related field, with the intention of pursuing a career in the seed industry. Cash award, with checks issued jointly in name of recipient and college/institution he or she will attend for current year. Must submit references and transcripts.

See Web site or send self-addressed, stamped envelope to FIRST after January 1 for an application. Recipient will be notified.

1222—FIRST (Floriculture Industry Research and Scholarship Trust) (Perry/Holden/Leonard Bettinger Scholarships)

P.O. Box 280
East Lansing MI 48826-0280
517/333-4617
FAX: 517/333-4494
E-mail: first@firstinfloriculture.org
Internet: http://www.firstinfloriculture.org
AMOUNT: $500-$1,000
DEADLINE(S): MAY 1
FIELD(S): Horticulture; Floriculture

Open to entering freshmen or second year students in a 1- or 2-year program who will be enrolled for entire next year. Must be U.S. or Canadian citizen, have minimum 3.0 GPA, and have major interest in horticulture or related field with intentions of becoming floriculture plant producer and/or greenhouse manager. Cash awards, with checks issued jointly in name of recipient and college/institution he or she will attend for current year. Must submit references and transcripts.

See Web site or send self-addressed, stamped envelope to FIRST after January 1 for an application. Recipients will be notified.

1223—CHS COOPERATIVES FOUNDATION SCHOLARSHIP PROGRAM (Agricultural Studies)

5500 Cenex Drive
Inver Grove Heights MN 55077
651/451-5151; 800/232-3639
E-mail: wnels@CHSco-ops.com
Internet: http://www.CHSco-ops.com
AMOUNT: $600
DEADLINE(S): FEB 15
FIELD(S): Agriculture

For students attending a participating vocational, technical, or community college in the first or second year of their school's two-year program. Participating schools are located in the CHS Cooperatives market area: Colorado, Idaho, Iowa, Kansas, Minnesota, Montana, Nebraska, North Dakota, Oregon, South Dakota, Utah, Washington, Wisconsin, and Wyoming. Selection is based on scholastic achievement rather than need. Schools must submit applications.

81 awards annually. Money is mailed to school at end of term for student's use. Contact CHS Cooperatives Foundation or your participating school for an application.

1224—CHS COOPERATIVES FOUNDATION SCHOLARSHIP PROGRAM (Cooperative Studies)

5500 Cenex Drive
Inver Grove Heights MN 55077
651/451-5151; 800/232/3639
E-mail: wnels@CHSco-ops.com
Internet: http://www.CHSco-ops.com
AMOUNT: $750
DEADLINE(S): Varies
FIELD(S): Agriculture

For students attending agricultural college of participating university enrolled in courses on cooperative principles and cooperative business practices. Must be enrolled in junior or senior year. Selection based on scholastic achievement. Participating universities are within Cenex Harvest States market area: CO State, U ID, IA State, KS State, MN State, U MN, MT State, U NE, ND State, OR State, SD State, UT State, WA State, U WI, and U WY. Universities administer program.

82 awards annually. Renewable if apply in junior year. Contact CHS Cooperatives Foundation or your participating school for an application. Recipients are selected in spring by the university and receive award in fall.

1225—FLORIDA FEDERATION OF GARDEN CLUBS, INC. (FFGC Scholarships for College Students)

6065 21st Street SW
Vero Beach FL 32968-9427
561/778-1023
Internet: http://www.ffgc.org
AMOUNT: $1,500-$3,500
DEADLINE(S): MAY 1
FIELD(S): Ecology; Environmental Issues; Land Management; City Planning; Environmental Control; Horticulture; Landscape Design; Conservation; Botany; Forestry; Marine Biology; Floriculture; Agriculture

Various scholarships for Florida residents with a "B" average or better enrolled full-time as a junior, senior, or graduate student at a Florida college or university.

See Web site or contact Melba Campbell at FFGC for an application.

1226—FLORIDA FEDERATION OF GARDEN CLUBS, INC. (FFGC Scholarships for High School Students)

6065 21st Street SW
Vero Beach FL 32968-9427
561/778-1023
Internet: http://www.ffgc.org
AMOUNT: $1,500
DEADLINE(S): MAY 1
FIELD(S): Ecology; Environmental Issues; Land Management; City Planning; Environmental Control; Horticulture; Landscape Design; Conservation; Botany; Forestry; Marine Biology; Floriculture; Agriculture

Scholarships for Florida residents with a "B" average or better who will be incoming freshmen at a Florida college or university.

See Web site or contact Melba Campbell at FFGC for an application.

1227—GARDEN CLUB OF AMERICA (Katharine M. Grosscup Scholarships)

Cleveland Botanical Garden
11030 East Blvd.
Cleveland OH 44106
No Phone Calls
FAX: 216/721-2056
Internet: http://www.gcamerica.org
AMOUNT: Up to $3,000
DEADLINE(S): FEB 1
FIELD(S): Horticulture and related fields

Financial assistance to college juniors, seniors, or graduate students, preferably from (though not restricted to) Kentucky, Ohio, Pennsylvania, West Virginia, Michigan, and Indiana. Purpose is to encourage the study of horticulture and related fields.

Funds several students annually. See Web site or contact Mrs. Nancy Stevenson at above address for more information/an application.

1228—GOLF COURSE SUPERINTENDENTS ASSOCIATION OF AMERICA (GCSAA Essay Contest)

1421 Research Park Drive
Lawrence KS 66049-3859
785/832-3678
800/472-7878 ext. 678
FAX: 785/832-3665
E-mail: psmith@gcsaa.org
Internet: http://www.gcsaa.org
AMOUNT: $4,500 (total prizes)
DEADLINE(S): MAR 31
FIELD(S): Turfgrass Science; Agronomy; Golf Course Management

Contest open to undergraduate and graduate students pursuing degrees in one of the above fields. Essays should be 7-12 pages long and should focus on the golf course management profession.

See Web site or contact Pam Smith at GCSAA for details.

1229—GOLF COURSE SUPERINTENDENTS ASSOCIATION OF AMERICA (GCSAA Scholars Program)

1421 Research Park Drive
Lawrence KS 66049-3859
785/832-3678
800/472-7878 ext. 678
FAX: 785/832-3665
E-mail: psmith@gcsaa.org
Internet: http://www.gcsaa.org
AMOUNT: $500-$3,500
DEADLINE(S): JUN 1
FIELD(S): Golf/Turf Management

Awards available to outstanding undergraduate students planning careers as golf course superintendents. Must be enrolled in a recognized major field related to golf/turf management. Must successfully have completed at least 24 credit hours or the equivalent of one year of full-time study in an appropriate major. Must be a member of GCSAA.

For membership information or an application, see Web site or contact Pam Smith at GCSAA.

1230—GOLF COURSE SUPERINTENDENTS ASSOCIATION OF AMERICA (The Scotts Company Scholars Program)

1421 Research Park Drive
Lawrence KS 66049-3859
785/832-3678
800/472-7878 ext. 678
FAX: 785/832-3665
E-mail: psmith@gcsaa.org
Internet: http://www.gcsaa.org
AMOUNT: $500 award; $2,500 scholarship + internship
DEADLINE(S): MAR 1
FIELD(S): "Green Industry"

For graduating high school seniors and college freshmen, sophomores, and juniors accepted/currently enrolled in a 2 or more year accredited college. Applicants evaluated on cultural diversity, academic achievement, extracurricular activities, leadership, employment potential, essay responses, and letters of recommendation. Financial need is NOT a factor.

5 finalists receive award; scholarships awarded to 2 of finalists. Scholarship not renewable. Employees of Scotts Company and current members/family members of GCSAA Foundation Board of Trustees not eligible.

1231—GOLF COURSE SUPERINTENDENTS ASSOCIATION OF AMERICA (Valderrama Award)

1421 Research Park Drive
Lawrence KS 66049-3859
785/832-3678
800/472-7878 ext. 678
FAX: 785/832-3665
E-mail: psmith@gcsaa.org
Internet: http://www.gcsaa.org
AMOUNT: $7,000
DEADLINE(S): MAR
FIELD(S): Golf/Turfgrass Management

Awarded to a citizen of Spain who wishes to study golf/turfgrass management in the United States. Selection is based on academic achievement, interest in the profession, and leadership potential.

See Web site or contact Pam Smith at GCSAA for an application.

1232—HOUSTON LIVESTOCK SHOW AND RODEO (4H and FFA Scholarships)

2000 S. Loop West
Houston TX 77054
713/791-9000
FAX: 713-794-9528

E-Mail: info@rodeohouston.com
Internet: http://www.hlsr.com/education/
AMOUNT: $10,000
DEADLINE(S): Varies
FIELD(S): Agriculture; Life Sciences

Open to undergraduate students who are actively involved in the 4-H or FFA programs. Must major in an agricultural or life sciences field of study at a Texas college/university and demonstrate academic potential, citizenship/leadership, and financial need.

140 awards annually. Contact HLSR for an application.

1233—HUBBARD FARMS CHARITABLE FOUNDATION

P.O. Box 505
Walpole NH 03608-0505
603/756-3311
AMOUNT: $1,500-$3,000
DEADLINE(S): APR 1
FIELD(S): Poultry science, genetics, and other life sciences

Scholarships are for financially needy students at universities that the foundation trustees consider to be leaders in the field of progress in technology and efficiency of production of poultry products.

Send SASE to Jane F. Kelly, Clerk, at above address for current application guidelines.

1234—JAPANESE AMERICAN CITIZENS LEAGUE (Kyutaro and Yasuo Abiko Memorial Scholarship)

1765 Sutter Street
San Francisco CA 94115
415/921-5225
FAX: 415/931-4671
E-mail: jacl@jacl.org
Internet: http://www.jacl.org
AMOUNT: $1,000-$5,000
DEADLINE(S): APR 1
FIELD(S): Agriculture; Journalism

Open to JACL members only. For undergraduate students with an interest in either journalism or agriculture and who are planning to attend a college, university, trade school, business school, or any other institution of higher learning. Must submit personal statement, letters of recommendation, and transcripts. Financial need NOT a factor.

For membership information or an application, go to the Web site or send a self-addressed, stamped envelope to above address, stating your level of study. Applications available October 1 through March 20; recipients notified in July.

1235—IRISH ARTS COUNCIL (Awards and Opportunities)

70 Merrion Square
Dublin 2 IRELAND
Tel: +353 1 618 0200
FAX: +353 1 661 0349/676 1302
E-mail: info@artscouncil.ie
Internet: http://www.artscouncil.ie
AMOUNT: Varies (with program)
DEADLINE(S): Varies (with program)
FIELD(S): Creative Arts; Visual Arts; Performing Arts

Numerous programs open to young and established artists who are Irish citizens or legal residents. Purpose is to assist in pursuit of talents and recognize achievements.

See Web site or contact above address for an application.

1236—MIDWAY COLLEGE (Institutional Aid Program)

Financial Aid Office
Midway KY 40347
606/846-4421
AMOUNT: Varies
DEADLINE(S): MAR 1
FIELD(S): Nursing; Paralegal; Education; Psychology; Biology; Equine Studies; Liberal Studies; Business Administration

Scholarships and grants are open to women who are accepted for enrollment at Midway College. Awards support undergraduate study in the above areas.

80 awards annually. Contact Midway College's Financial Aid Office for an application.

1237—NATIONAL COUNCIL OF FARMER COOPERATIVES (Undergraduate Awards and Scholarships)

50 F Street NW; Suite 900
Washington DC 20001
202/626-8700
FAX: 202/626-8722
Internet: http://www.ncfc.org/resources/education/
AMOUNT: $200-$1,000
DEADLINE(S): APR 1 (scholarships)
JUN 1 (awards)
FIELD(S): Agricultural Cooperatives

Awards are open to undergraduate students who are writing term papers on the operations of American cooperatives. Scholarships are open to undergraduates with an expressed interest in agricultural cooperatives who are nominated by the department or instructor at their college/university or by the local cooperative.

7 awards annually. Not renewable. Contact NCFC Education Foundation for registration forms and/or nomination procedures.

1238—NATIONAL GARDEN CLUBS, INC. (Scholarships)

4401 Magnolia Avenue
St. Louis MO 63110-3492
314/776-7574
FAX: 314/776-5108
E-mail: renee_blaschke@juno.com
Internet: http://www.gardenclub.org
AMOUNT: $3,500
DEADLINE(S): MAR 1
FIELD(S): Horticulture, Floriculture, Landscape Design, City Planning, Land Management, and allied subjects.

Open to juniors, seniors, and graduate students who are U.S. citizens and are studying any of the above or related subjects. Student must have the endorsement of the state in which he/she resides permanently. Applications will be forwarded to the National State Chairman and judged on a national level.

30-35 scholarships are awarded. Write to the above address for complete information.

1239—NATIONAL JUNIOR HORTICULTURAL ASSOCIATION (Scottish Gardening Scholarship)

253 Batchelor Street
Grandy MA 01033-9738
413/584-7459
AMOUNT: Varies
DEADLINE(S): DEC
FIELD(S): Horticulture

One-year work/study at Threave School of Gardening in Castle Douglas, Scotland. Students should demonstrate practical work experience in horticulture. Include information on awards and honors received.

1240—NATURAL SCIENCES AND ENGINEERING RESEARCH COUNCIL OF CANADA (Undergraduate Student Research Awards in Small Universities)

350 Albert Street
Ottawa Ontario K1A 1H5 CANADA
613/995-5992

FAX: 613/992-5337
E-mail: schol@nserc.ca
Internet: http://www.nserc.ca/programs/usrasmen.htm
AMOUNT: $3,600 (max.)
DEADLINE(S): Varies
FIELD(S): Natural Sciences; Engineering

Research awards for Canadian citizens/permanent residents attending eligible institutions, and who have no more than 6 and no fewer than 2 academic terms remaining to complete bachelor's degree. Cumulative GPA of at least second class (B). Must be doing full-time in research and development activities during award tenure.

Students in health sciences not eligible. Students with BAs and who are studying for a second may apply.

1241—NORTH CAROLINA STATE UNIVERSITY (Thomas Jefferson Scholarship in Agriculture and Humanities)

115 Patterson Hall, Box 7642
Raleigh NC 27695-7642
Written Inquiry
AMOUNT: $1,000
DEADLINE(S): MAR
FIELD(S): Agriculture AND Humanities

Open to first-year undergraduate students with a double major in agriculture and humanities who attend or plan to attend North Carolina State University.

1242—NORTHERN NEW JERSEY UNIT-HERB SOCIETY OF AMERICA (Scholarship)

2068 Dogwood Drive
Scotch Plains NJ 07076
908/233-2348
AMOUNT: $2,000
DEADLINE(S): FEB 15
FIELD(S): Horticulture; Botany

For New Jersey residents, undergraduate through postgraduate, who will attend colleges/universities east of the Mississippi River. Financial need is considered.

1 award annually. Renewable. Contact Mrs. Charlotte R. Baker at above address for an application.

1243—NORTHERN NEW JERSEY UNIT-HERB SOCIETY OF AMERICA (Scholarship)

2068 Dogwood Drive
Scotch Plains NJ 07076
908/233-2348
AMOUNT: $2,000
DEADLINE(S): FEB 15
FIELD(S): Horticulture; Botany

For New Jersey residents, undergraduate through postgraduate, who will attend colleges/universities east of the Mississippi River. Financial need is considered.

1 award annually. Renewable. Contact Mrs. Charlotte R. Baker at above address for an application.

1244—PENINSULA COMMUNITY FOUNDATION (Dr. Mary Finegold Scholarship)

1700 S. El Camino Real #300
San Mateo CA 94402
650/358-9369
FAX: 650/358-9817
Internet: http://www.pcf.org/community_grants/scholarships.html
AMOUNT: $1,000
DEADLINE(S): MAR 7 (5 p.m.)
FIELD(S): Sciences

Scholarships for senior girls graduating from high school in Palo Alto, California, who intend to complete a four-year degree in the sciences. Special consideration will be given to girls who have demonstrated a "pioneering" spirit in that they have not been constrained by stereotypical female roles and to those facing financial hardship.

Award was established in the honor of Dr. Mary Finegold who, after completing her medical studies, elected to stay at home until her youngest child was in high school before beginning her medical practice. She was a school physician.

1245—RAYMOND J. HARRIS EDUCATION TRUST

P.O. Box 7899
Philadelphia PA 19101-7899
Written Inquiry
AMOUNT: Varies
DEADLINE(S): FEB 1
FIELD(S): Medicine, Law, Engineering, Dentistry, or Agriculture

Scholarships for Christian men to obtain a professional education in medicine, law, engineering, dentistry, or agriculture at nine Philadelphia area colleges.

Contact Mellon Bank, N.A. at above location for details and the names of the nine colleges.

1246—SOCIETY FOR RANGE MANAGEMENT (Masonic-Range Science Scholarship)

445 Union Blvd., Suite#230
Lakewood CO 80228-1259
303/986-3309
FAX: 303/986-3892
E-mail: sglushdo@ix.netcom.com
Internet: http://www.srm.org
AMOUNT: $2,000
DEADLINE(S): JAN 15
FIELD(S): Range Science/Management

Open to high school seniors or college freshmen pursuing a major in range science/management. Must attend a college or university with a range science program.

1 award annually. Applicant must be sponsored by a member of SRM, the National Association of Conservation Districts (NACD), or the Soil and Water Conservation Society (SWCS). Financial need NOT a factor. See Web site or contact the above address for an application/more information.

1247—SOIL AND WATER CONSERVATION SOCIETY (Donald A. Williams Soil Conservation Scholarship)

7515 N.W. Ankeny Road
Ankeny IA 50021-9764
515/289-2331
FAX: 515/289-1227
Internet: http:// http://www.swcs.org/f_aboutSWCS_chrel.htm
AMOUNT: $1,500
DEADLINE(S): FEB 12
FIELD(S): Conservation-related fields (technical or administrative course work)

For SWCS members currently employed in a related field and have completed at least 1 year of natural resource conservation work with a governmental agency or private organization. Need not be working toward a degree. Must show reasonable financial need.

Up to 3 scholarships awarded yearly. Restricted to undergraduates. Write or visit Web site for complete information.

1248—SOIL AND WATER CONSERVATION SOCIETY (Melville H. Cohee Student Leader Conservation Scholarship)

7515 N.E. Ankeny Road
Ankeny IA 50021-9764
515/289-2331
FAX: 515/289-1227
Internet: http://www.swcs.org/f_aboutSWCS_chrel.htm
AMOUNT: $1,000
DEADLINE(S): FEB 12
FIELD(S): Conservation or Natural Resource-Related Field

Open to 1+ year member of SWCS having served as an officer in a student chapter with 15+ members. GPA of 3.0 or better. Final year F/T undergrad or graduate.

Up to 3 awards. Course load must be 50% or more at accredited college or university. Financial need is not a factor. Write or visit Web site for complete information.

1249—SOIL AND WATER CONSERVATION SOCIETY (Kenneth E. Grant Scholarship)

7515 N.E. Ankeny Road
Ankeny IA 50021-9764
515/289-2331; FAX: 515/289-1227
Internet: http:// http://www.swcs.org/f_aboutSWCS_chrel.htm

AMOUNT: $1,300
DEADLINE(S): FEB 12
FIELD(S): Conservation or Natural Resource-Related Field

Open to members of SWCS who are graduate students to conduct interdisciplinary research on an urban conservation topic.

Financial need is a factor. Write or visit Web site for complete information.

1250—SOIL AND WATER CONSERVATION SOCIETY (SWCS Internships)

7515 N.E. Ankeny Road
Ankeny IA 50021-9764
515/289-2331 or 800/THE-SOIL
FAX: 515/289-1227
E-mail: charliep@swcs.org
Internet: http://www.swcs.org

AMOUNT: Varies—most are uncompensated
DEADLINE(S): Varies
FIELD(S): Journalism, Marketing, Database Management, Meeting Planning, Public Policy Research, Environmental Education, Landscape Architecture

Internships for undergraduates and graduates to gain experience in the above fields as they relate to soil and water conservation issues. Internship openings vary through the year in duration, compensation, and objective. SWCS will coordinate particulars with your academic advisor.

Contact SWCS for internship availability at any time during the year or see Web site for jobs page.

1251—SONOMA CHAMBOLLE-MUSIGNY SISTER CITIES, INC. (Henri Cardinaux Memorial Scholarship)

Chamson Scholarship Committee
P.O. Box 1633
Sonoma CA 95476-1633
707/939-1344
FAX: 707/939-1344
E-mail: Baileysci@vom.com

AMOUNT: Up to $1,500 (travel + expenses)
DEADLINE(S): JUL 15
FIELD(S): Culinary Arts; Wine Industry; Art; Architecture; Music; History; Fashion

Hands-on experience working in above or similar fields and living with a family in small French village in Burgundy or other French city. Must be Sonoma County, CA, resident at least 18 years of age and be able to communicate in French. Transcripts, employer recommendation, photograph, and essay (stating why, where, and when) required.

1 award. Nonrenewable. Also offers opportunity for candidate in Chambolle-Musigny to obtain work experience and cultural exposure in Sonoma, CA.

1252—SOUTH CAROLINA FARM BUREAU FOUNDATION (Scholarships)

P.O. Box 754
Columbia SC 29202-0754
803/936-4212
FAX: 800/421-6515
Internet: http://www.scfb.org

AMOUNT: $500-$1,000
DEADLINE(S): APR 30
FIELD(S): Agriculture

Scholarships are awarded to South Carolina residents who are sophomores, juniors, and seniors pursuing a degree in agriculture or an agricultural related major. Based on character, demonstrated leadership abilities, and dedication to agriculture or related fields. Must have minimum 2.3 GPA. Financial need NOT a factor.

1253—STUDENT CONSERVATION ASSOCIATION (SCA Resource Assistant Program)

P.O. Box 550
Charlestown NH 03603
603/543-1700
FAX: 603/543-1828
E-mail: internships@sca-inc.org
Internet: http://www.sca-inc.org

AMOUNT: $1,180-$4,725
DEADLINE(S): Varies
FIELD(S): Environment and related fields

Must be 18 and U.S. citizen; need not be student.

Fields: Agriculture, Archaeology, anthropology, botany, caves, civil/environmental engineering, environmental education, fisheries, forests, herpetology, history, living history/roleplaying, visitor services, landscape architecture/environmental design, paleontology, recreation/resource/range management, trail maintenance/construction, wildlife management, geology, hydrology, library/museums, surveying...

900 positions in U.S. and Canada. Send $1 for postage for application; outside U.S./Canada, send $20.

1254—SUCCESSFUL FARMING-BAYER CORPORATION (Crop Protection Scholarships)

1716 Locust Street, LN 424
Des Moines IA 50309-3023
515/284-2903
E-mail: devans@mdp.com
Internet: http://www.agriculture.com

AMOUNT: $1,000
DEADLINE(S): MAR 15
FIELD(S): Agriculture

For high school seniors entering 2- or 4-year colleges and for college seniors-to-be returning to farm after college. Parents/guardians must derive majority of their income from farming. Must rank in upper 50% of class and in national test scores, demonstrate leadership potential through extracurricular activities/work experience, and have financial need. Scholarships will be granted to the school of your choice in your name in two equal payments (one for each semester).

30 awards annually. Not renewable. Awards announced by May 1. Applications available on Web site or write to above address.

1255—THE DAPHNE JACKSON MEMORIAL FELLOWSHIPS TRUST (Fellowships in Science/Engineering)

School of Physical Sciences,
Dept. of Physics, University of Surrey
Guildford, Surrey GU2 5XH
ENGLAND UK
01483 259166
FAX: 01483 259501
E-mail: J.Woolley@surrey.ac.uk
Internet: http://www.sst.ph.ic.ac.uk/trust/

AMOUNT: Varies
DEADLINE(S): Varies
FIELD(S): Science or Engineering, including Information Sciences

Fellowships to enable well-qualified and highly motivated scientists and engineers to return to appropriate careers following a career break due to family commitments.

May be used on a flexible, part-time basis. Tenable at various U.K. universities.

See Web site and/or contact organization for details.

1256—TYSON FOUNDATION, INC. (Alabama Scholarship Program)

2210 W. Oaklawn
Springdale AR 72762-6999
501/290-4995

AMOUNT: Varies (according to need)
DEADLINE(S): FEB 28
FIELD(S): Business; Agriculture; Engineering; Computer Science; Nursing

Open to residents of the general areas of Albertville, Ashland, Blountsville, Gadsden, Heflin, or Oxford, Alabama, who are U.S. citizens and live in the vicinity of a Tyson facility. Must be pursuing full-time undergraduate study at an accredited U.S. institution and demonstrate financial need. Must also be employed part-time and/or summers to help fund education.

Renewable up to 8 semesters or 12 trimesters as long as student meets criteria. Contact Tyson Foundation for an application no later than last day of February; deadline to return application is April 20.

1257—TYSON FOUNDATION, INC. (Arkansas Scholarship Program)

2210 W. Oaklawn
Springdale AR 72762-6999
501/290-4955

AMOUNT: Varies (according to need)
DEADLINE(S): FEB 28
FIELD(S): Business; Agriculture; Engineering; Computer Science; Nursing

Open to Arkansas residents who are U.S. citizens pursuing full-time undergraduate study at an accredited U.S. institution. Must demonstrate financial need and be employed part-time and/or summers to help fund education.

Renewable up to 8 semesters or 12 trimesters as long as student meets criteria. Contact Tyson Foundation for an application no later than last day of February; deadline to return application is April 20.

1258—TYSON FOUNDATION, INC. (California Scholarship Program)

2210 W. Oaklawn
Springdale AR 72762-6999
501/290-4995
FAX: 501/290-7984
E-mail: coments@tysonfoundation.org
Internet: http://www.tysonfoundation.org

AMOUNT: Varies (according to need)
DEADLINE(S): FEB 28 (to request application); APR 20 (to apply)
FIELD(S): Business; Agriculture; Engineering; Computer Science; Nursing; Biology; Chemistry

Open to residents of Modesto, California, who are U.S. citizens and live in the vicinity of a Tyson facility. Must be pursuing full-time undergraduate study at an accredited U.S. institution and demonstrate financial need. Must also be employed part-time and/or summers to help fund education.

Renewable up to 8 semesters or 12 trimesters as long as student meets criteria. Contact Tyson Foundation to see if area of residence qualifies and for an application.

1259—TYSON FOUNDATION, INC. (Florida Scholarship Program)

2210 Oaklawn
Springdale AR 72762-6999
501/290-4995

AMOUNT: Varies (according to need)
DEADLINE(S): FEB 28
FIELD(S): Business; Agriculture; Engineering; Computer Science; Nursing

Open to residents of the general area of Jacksonville, Florida, who are U.S. citizens and live in the vicinity of a Tyson facility. Must be pursuing full-time undergraduate study in an accredited U.S. institution and demonstrate financial need. Must also be employed part-time and/or summers to help fund education.

Renewable up to 8 semesters or 12 trimesters as long as student meets criteria. Contact Tyson Foundation for an application no later than last day of February; deadline to return application is April 20.

1260—TYSON FOUNDATION, INC. (Georgia Scholarship Program)

2210 Oaklawn
Springdale AR 72762-6999
501/290-4995

AMOUNT: Varies (according to need)
DEADLINE(S): FEB 28
FIELD(S): Business; Agriculture; Engineering; Computer Science; Nursing

Open to residents of the general areas of Cumming, Buena Vista, Dawson, or Vienna, Georgia, who are U.S. citizens and live in the vicinity of a Tyson facility. Must be pursuing full-time undergraduate study in an accredited U.S. institution and demonstrate financial need. Must also be employed part-time and/or summers to help fund education.

Renewable up to 8 semesters or 12 trimesters as long as student meets criteria. Contact Tyson Foundation for an application no later than last day of February; deadline to return application is April 20.

1261—TYSON FOUNDATION, INC. (Illinois Scholarship Program)

2210 Oaklawn
Springdale AR 72762-6999
501/290-4995

AMOUNT: Varies (according to need)
DEADLINE(S): FEB 28
FIELD(S): Business; Agriculture; Engineering; Computer Science; Nursing

Open to residents of the general area of Chicago, Illinois, who are U.S. citizens and live in the vicinity of a Tyson facility. Must be pursuing full-time undergraduate study in an accredited U.S. institution and demonstrate financial need. Must also be employed part-time and/or summers to help fund education.

Renewable up to 8 semesters or 12 trimesters as long as student meets criteria. Contact Tyson Foundation for an application no later than last day of February; deadline to return application is April 20.

1262—TYSON FOUNDATION, INC. (Indiana Scholarship Program)

2210 Oaklawn
Springdale AR 72762-6999
501/290-4995

AMOUNT: Varies (according to need)
DEADLINE(S): FEB 28
FIELD(S): Business; Agriculture; Engineering; Computer Science; Nursing

Open to residents of the general areas of Portland or Corydon, Indiana, who are U.S. citizens and live in the vicinity of a Tyson facility. Must be pursuing full-time undergraduate study at an accredited U.S. institution and demonstrate financial need. Must also be employed part-time and/or summers to help fund education.

Renewable up to 8 semesters or 12 trimesters as long as student meets criteria. Contact Tyson Foundation for an application no later than last day of February; deadline to return application is April 20.

1263—TYSON FOUNDATION, INC. (Mississippi Scholarship Program)

2210 Oaklawn
Springdale AR 72762-6999
501/290-4995

AMOUNT: Varies (according to need)
DEADLINE(S): FEB 28
FIELD(S): Business; Agriculture; Engineering; Computer Science; Nursing

Open to residents of the general areas of Cleveland, Jackson, Forest, or Vicksburg, Mississippi, who are U.S. citizens and live in the vicinity of a Tyson facility. Must be pursuing full-time undergraduate study in an accredited U.S. institution and demonstrate financial need. Must also be employed part-time and/or summers to help fund education.

Renewable up to 8 semesters or 12 trimesters as long as student meets criteria. Contact Tyson Foundation for an application no later than last day of February; deadline to return application is April 20.

1264—TYSON FOUNDATION, INC. (Missouri Scholarship Program)

2210 Oaklawn
Springdale AR 72762-6999
501/290-4995

AMOUNT: Varies (according to need)
DEADLINE(S): FEB 28
FIELD(S): Business; Agriculture; Engineering; Computer Science; Nursing

Open to residents of the general areas of Dexter, Monett, Neosho, Noel, or Sedalia, Missouri, who are U.S. citizens and live in the vicinity of a Tyson facility. Must be pursuing full-time undergraduate study in an accredited U.S. institution and demonstrate financial need. Must also be employed part-time and/or summers to help fund education.

Renewable up to 8 semesters or 12 trimesters as long as student meets criteria. Contact Tyson Foundation for an application no later than last day of February; deadline to return application is April 20.

1265—TYSON FOUNDATION, INC. (North Carolina Scholarship Program)

2210 Oaklawn
Springdale AR 72762-6999
501/290-4995

AMOUNT: Varies (according to need)
DEADLINE(S): FEB 28
FIELD(S): Business; Agriculture; Engineering; Computer Science; Nursing

Open to residents of the general areas of Creswell, Monroe, Sanford, or Wilkesboro, North Carolina, who are U.S. citizens and live in the vicinity of a Tyson facility. Must be pursuing full-time undergraduate study in an accredited U.S. institution and demonstrate financial need. Must also be employed part-time and/or summers to help fund education.

Renewable up to 8 semesters or 12 trimesters as long as student meets criteria. Contact Tyson Foundation for an application no later than the last day of February; deadline to return application is April 20.

1266—TYSON FOUNDATION, INC. (Oklahoma Scholarship Program)

2210 Oaklawn
Springdale AR 72762-6999
501/290-4995

AMOUNT: Varies (according to need)
DEADLINE(S): FEB 28
FIELD(S): Business; Agriculture; Engineering; Computer Science; Nursing

Open to residents of the general areas of Broken Bow or Stillwell, Oklahoma, who are U.S. citizens and live in the vicinity of a Tyson facility. Must be pursuing full-time undergraduate study in an accredited U.S. institution and demonstrate financial need. Must also be employed part-time and/or summers to help fund education.

Renewable up to 8 semesters or 12 trimesters as long as student meets criteria. Contact Tyson Foundation for an application no later than last day of February; deadline to return application is April 20.

1267—TYSON FOUNDATION, INC. (Pennsylvania Scholarship Program)

2210 Oaklawn
Springdale AR 72762-6999
501/290-4995

AMOUNT: Varies (according to need)
DEADLINE(S): FEB 28
FIELD(S): Business; Agriculture; Engineering; Computer Science; Nursing

Open to residents of the general area of New Holland, Pennsylvania, who are U.S. citizens and live in the vicinity of a Tyson facility. Must be pursuing full-time undergraduate study in an accredited U.S. institution and demonstrate financial need. Must also be employed part-time and/or summers to help fund education.

Renewable up to 8 semesters or 12 trimesters as long as student meets criteria. Contact Tyson Foundation for an application no later than last day of February; deadline to return application is April 20.

1268—TYSON FOUNDATION, INC. (Tennessee Scholarship Program)

2210 Oaklawn
Springdale AR 72762-6999
501/290-4995

AMOUNT: Varies (according to need)
DEADLINE(S): FEB 28
FIELD(S): Business; Agriculture; Engineering; Computer Science; Nursing

Open to residents of the general areas of Shelbyville or Union City, Tennessee, who are U.S. citizens and live in the vicinity of a Tyson facility. Must be pursuing full-time undergraduate study in an accredited U.S. institution and demonstrate financial need. Must also be employed part-time and/or summers to help fund education.

Renewable up to 8 semesters or 12 trimesters as long as student meets criteria. Contact Tyson Foundation for an application no later than last day of February; deadline to return application is April 20.

1269—TYSON FOUNDATION, INC. (Texas Scholarship Program)

2210 Oaklawn
Springdale AR 72762-6999
501/290-4995

AMOUNT: Varies (according to need)
DEADLINE(S): FEB 28
FIELD(S): Business; Agriculture; Engineering; Computer Science; Nursing

Open to residents of the general areas of Carthage, Center, or Seguin, Texas, who are U.S. citizens and live in the vicinity of a Tyson facility. Must be pursuing full-time undergraduate study in an accredited U.S. institution and demonstrate financial need. Must also be employed part-time and/or summers to help fund education.

Renewable up to 8 semesters or 12 trimesters as long as student meets criteria. Contact Tyson Foundation for an application no later than last day of February; deadline to return application is April 20.

1270—TYSON FOUNDATION, INC. (Virginia Scholarship Program)

2210 Oaklawn
Springdale AR 72762-6999
501/290-4995

AMOUNT: Varies (according to need)
DEADLINE(S): FEB 28

FIELD(S): Business; Agriculture; Engineering; Computer Science; Nursing

Open to residents of the general areas of Glen Allen, Harrisonburg, or Temperanceville, Virginia, who are U.S. citizens and live in the vicinity of a Tyson facility. Must be pursuing full-time undergraduate study in an accredited U.S. institution and demonstrate financial need. Must also be employed part-time and/or summers to help fund education.

Renewable up to 8 semesters or 12 trimesters as long as student meets criteria. Contact Tyson Foundation for an application no later than last day of February; deadline to return application is April 20.

1271—UNITED AGRIBUSINESS LEAGUE (UAL Scholarship Program)

54 Corporate Park
Irvine CA 92606-5105
800/223-4590 or 949/975-1424
FAX: 949/975-1671
E-mail: info@ual.org
Internet: http://www.ual.org

AMOUNT: Varies
DEADLINE(S): MAR 28
FIELD(S): Agriculture; Agribusiness

Any age student presently enrolled, or who will be enrolled any time during the year of application in any accredited college/university offering a degree in agriculture, may apply. Minimum GPA of 2.5 is required. With application, must submit an essay, resume of education/work/community activities/etc., and three letters of recommendation. Financial need will not be considered unless you specifically request it and provide documentation.

Up to $6,000 available annually. Renewable with new application. Contact Christine M. Steele for more information.

1272—UNITED STATES DEPARTMENT OF AGRICULTURE (1890 National Scholars Program)

14th & Independence Avenue SW; Room 301-W; Whitten Bldg.
Washington, DC 20250-9600
202/720-6905
E-mail: usda-m@fie.com
Internet: http://web.fie.com/htdoc/fed/agr/ars/edu/prog/mti/agrpgaak.htm

AMOUNT: Tuition, employment/benefits, use of pc/software, fees, books, room/board
DEADLINE(S): JAN 15
FIELD(S): Agriculture, Food, or Natural Resource Sciences

For U.S. citizens, high school grad/GED, GPA 3.0+, verbal/math SAT 1000+, composite score 21+ ACT, first-year college student, and attend participating school.

34+ scholarships/year/4 years. Send applications to U.S.D.A. Liaison officer at the 1890 Institution of your choice (see Web page for complete list).

1273—UNIVERSITY OF ILLINOIS COLLEGE OF ACES (Jonathan Baldwin Turner Agricultural Scholarship Program)

115 ACES Library
1101 S. Goodwin Street
Urbana IL 61801
217/244-4540
Internet: http://w3.aces.uiuc.edu/Acad-Prog/

AMOUNT: $4,000 ($1,000/year)
DEADLINE(S): Varies (start of high school senior year)
FIELD(S): Agriculture; Nutritional Science; Natural Resources; Environmental; Social Sciences (agricultural economics, communications, or education)

Scholarships in agricultural, food, and human nutritional sciences for outstanding incoming freshmen at the University of Illinois. Must have minimum ACT composite score of 27, equivalent SAT combined scores, or be in the 10th percentile of high school class rank at the end of junior year. Interview required.

55 awards annually. Contact Charles Olson, Assistant Dean of Academic Programs, College of Agricultural, Consumer and Environmental Sciences, for an application.

1274—UNIVERSITY OF NEWCASTLE/Australia (R. M. Sheahan Memorial Undergraduate Scholarship)

Student Administration Unit, Student Services Centre, Univ. of Newcastle, Callaghan NSW
2308 AUSTRALIA
+61-(02)-4921-6539
FAX: +61-(02)-4960-1766
E-mail: scholarships@newcastle.edu.au
Internet: http://http://www.newcastle.edu.au/services/ousr/stuadmin/schol/index.htm

AMOUNT: $1,000
DEADLINE(S): NOV 1
FIELD(S): Engineering, chemistry, or environmental engineering

Scholarship for undergraduate international as well as Australian students pursuing studies in chemistry, chemical engineering, or environmental engineering. Funded by the Cessnock City Council and Orica (ICI) Explosives, this award is made yearly based on academic merit.

Contact organization for details.

EARTH SCIENCE

1275—AIR FORCE RESERVE OFFICER TRAINING CORPS (AFROTC Scholarships)

551 E. Maxwell Boulevard
Maxwell AFB AL 36112-6106
334/953-7783

AMOUNT: Full tuition, books, and fees for all 4 years of college
DEADLINE(S): DEC 1
FIELD(S): Science; Engineering; Business; Political Science; Psychology; Geography; Foreign Studies; Foreign Language

Competitive scholarships based on individual merit to high school seniors and graduates who have not completed any full-time college work. Must be a U.S. citizen between the ages of 17-27. Must also have GPA of 2.5 or above, be in top 40% of class, and complete Applicant Fitness Test. Cannot be a single parent. Your college/university must offer AFROTC.

2,300 awards annually. Contact above address for application packet.

1276—ALLIANCE FOR YOUNG ARTISTS AND WRITERS, INC./AMERICAN MUSEUM OF NATURAL HISTORY (Young Naturalist Awards)

Scholastic, Inc.; 555 Broadway
New York NY 10012-3999
212/343-6582 or 800-SCHOLASTIC
FAX: 212/343-4885
E-mail: A&WGeneralinfo@scholastic.com
Internet: http://www.amnh.org/youngnaturalistawards

AMOUNT: Up to $2,500 + trip to New York to visit AMNH
DEADLINE(S): JAN
FIELD(S): Natural Sciences

For all students in grades 7-12 currently enrolled in a public or nonpublic school in the U.S., Canada, U.S. territories, or U.S.-sponsored schools abroad. Program focuses on finding and rewarding excellence in biology, earth science, astronomy, and cultural studies. Students are encouraged to perform observation-based projects that require creativity, inquiry, and critical analysis. Specific topics vary annually.

48 awards annually. See Web site for application.

1277—AMERICAN CONGRESS ON SURVEYING AND MAPPING (AAGS Joseph F. Dracup Scholarship Award, Nettie Dracup Memorial Scholarship, and Berntsen International Scholarship in Surveying)

6 Montgomery Village Avenue,
Suite 403
Gaithersburg MD 20879
240/632-9716 ext. 105
FAX: 240/632-1321
E-mail: tmilburn@acsm.net
Internet: http://www.acsm.net/scholar.html

AMOUNT: $2,000 (Joseph and Nettie); $1,500 (Berntsen)
DEADLINE(S): DEC 31
FIELD(S): Geodetic Surveying

Open to students enrolled in four-year degree programs in surveying or closely related degree programs, such as geomatics or surveying engineering. Must submit personal statement (including goals and financial need), letters of recommendation, and transcripts. Nettie Dracup applicants must be U.S. citizens. Must join ACSM.

3 awards annually. Contact ACSM for membership information and/or applications.

1278—AMERICAN CONGRESS ON SURVEYING AND MAPPING (Allen Chelf Scholarship)

6 Montgomery Village Avenue,
Suite 403
Gaithersburg MD 20879
240/632-9716 ext. 105
FAX: 240/632-1321
E-mail: tmilburn@acsm.net
Internet: http://http://www.acsm.net/scholar.html

AMOUNT: $500
DEADLINE(S): DEC 31
FIELD(S): Surveying

Open to students enrolled in a two-year or four-year surveying (or closely related fields) degree program, either full- or part-time, in the U.S.. Must submit personal statement (including goals and financial need), letters of recommendation, and transcripts. Must join ACSM.

1 award annually. Contact ACSM for membership information and/or an application.

1279—AMERICAN CONGRESS ON SURVEYING AND MAPPING (Bernsten International Scholarship in Surveying Technology)

6 Montgomery Village Avenue,
Suite 403
Gaithersburg MD 20879
240/632-9716 ext. 105
FAX: 240/632-1321
E-mail: tmilburn@acsm.net
Internet: http:// www.acsm.net/scholar.html

AMOUNT: $500
DEADLINE(S): DEC 31
FIELD(S): Surveying Technology

Open to students enrolled in two-year degree programs in surveying technology. Must submit personal statement (including goals and financial need), letters of recommendation, and transcripts. Must join ACSM.

1 award annually. Contact ACSM for membership information and/or an application.

1280—AMERICAN CONGRESS ON SURVEYING AND MAPPING (Cady McDonnell Memorial Scholarship)

6 Montgomery Village Avenue,
Suite 403
Gaithersburg MD 20879
240/632-9716 ext. 105
FAX: 240/632-1321
E-mail: tmilburn@acsm.net
Internet: http:// www.acsm.net/scholar.html

AMOUNT: $1,000
DEADLINE(S): DEC 31
FIELD(S): Surveying

Open to women enrolled in a two-year or four-year surveying (or closely related fields) degree program, either full- or part-time. Applicants must be residents of one of the following Western states: MT, ID, WA, OR, WY, CO, UT, NV, CA, AZ, NM, AK, or HI. Must submit personal statement (including goals and financial need), letters of recommendation, and transcripts. Must join ACSM.

1 award annually. Contact ACSM for membership information and/or an application.

1281—AMERICAN CONGRESS ON SURVEYING AND MAPPPING (Cartography and Geographic Information Society Scholarship)

6 Montgomery Village Avenue,
Suite 403
Gaithersburg MD 20879
240/632-9716 ext. 105
FAX: 240/632-1321
E-mail: tmilburn@acsm.net
Internet: http://
http://www.acsm.net/scholar.html

AMOUNT: $1,000
DEADLINE(S): DEC 31
FIELD(S): Cartography; Geographic Information Science

Open to outstanding students enrolled full-time in a four-year or graduate degree program. Preference given to undergraduates with junior or senior standing, the purpose being to encourage completion of undergrad program and/or pursuit of graduate education in above fields. Must submit personal statement (including goals and financial need), letters of recommendation, and transcripts. Must join ACSM.

1 award annually. Contact ACSM for membership information and/or an application.

1282—AMERICAN CONGRESS ON SURVEYING AND MAPPING (National Society of Professional Surveyors Board of Governor's Scholarship)

6 Montgomery Village Avenue
Suite 403
Gaithersburg MD 20879
240/632-9716 ext. 105
FAX: 240/632-1321
E-mail: tmilburn@acsm.net
Internet: http:// www.acsm.net/scholar.html

AMOUNT: $1,000
DEADLINE(S): DEC 31
FIELD(S): Surveying

Open to students enrolled in studies in surveying, entering their junior year of study in a four-year degree program of their choice, and who have maintained a minimum 3.0 GPA. Must submit personal statement (including goals and financial need), letters of recommendation, and transcripts. Must join ACSM.

1 award annually. Contact ACSM for membership information and/or an application.

1283—AMERICAN CONGRESS ON SURVEYING AND MAPPING (National Society of Professional Surveyors Forum for Equal Opportunity/Mary Feindt Scholarship)

6 Montgomery Village Avenue,
Suite 403
Gaithersburg MD 20879
240/632-9716 ext. 105
FAX: 240/632-1321

E-mail: tmilburn@acsm.net
Internet: http://
http://www.acsm.net/scholar.html
AMOUNT: $1,000
DEADLINE(S): DEC 31
FIELD(S): Surveying

Open to women enrolled in a four-year degree program in a surveying and mapping curriculum within the U.S.. Must submit personal statement (including goals and financial need), letters of recommendation, and transcripts. Must join ACSM.

1 award annually. Contact ACSM for membership information and/or an application.

1284—AMERICAN CONGRESS ON SURVEYING AND MAPPING (National Society of Professional Surveyors Scholarships)

6 Montgomery Village Avenue, Suite 403
Gaithersburg MD 20879
240/632-9716 ext. 105
FAX: 240/632-1321
E-mail: tmilburn@acsm.net
Internet: http:// www.acsm.net/scholar.html
AMOUNT: $1,000
DEADLINE(S): DEC 31
FIELD(S): Surveying

Open to students enrolled in four-year degree programs in surveying or closely related degree programs, such as geomatics or surveying engineering. Awards recognize outstanding students enrolled full-time. Must submit personal statement (including goals and financial need), letters of recommendation, and transcripts. Must join ACSM.

2 awards annually. Contact ACSM for membership information and/or an application.

1285—AMERICAN CONGRESS ON SURVEYING AND MAPPING (Schonstedt Scholarships in Surveying)

6 Montgomery Village Avenue, Suite 403
Gaithersburg MD 20879
240/632-9716 ext. 105
FAX: 240/632-1321
E-mail: tmilburn@acsm.net
Internet: http://www.acsm.net/scholar.html
AMOUNT: $1,500
DEADLINE(S): DEC 31
FIELD(S): Surveying

Open to students enrolled in four-year degree programs in surveying or closely related degree programs, such as geomatics or surveying engineering. Preference given to applicants with junior or senior standing. Must submit personal statement (including goals and financial need), letters of recommendation, and transcripts. Must join ACSM.

2 awards annually. Contact ACSM for membership information and/or an application. Schonstedt also donates a magnetic locator to the surveying program at each recipient's school.

1286—AMERICAN FOUNDATION FOR THE BLIND (Paul W. Ruckes Scholarship)

11 Penn Plaza, Suite 300
New York NY 10001
212/502-7661
FAX: 212/502-7771
E-mail: juliet@afb.org
Internet: http://www.afb.org
AMOUNT: $1,000
DEADLINE(S): APR 30
FIELD(S): Engineering; Computer/Physical/Life Sciences

Open to legally blind and visually impaired undergraduate and graduate students pursuing a degree in one of above fields. Must be U.S. citizen. Must submit written documentation of visual impairment from ophthalmologist or optometrist (need not be legally blind); official transcripts; proof of college/university acceptance; three letters of recommendation; and typewritten statement describing goals, work experience extracurricular activities, and how monies will be used.

1 award annually. See Web site or contact Julie Tucker at AFB for an application.

1287—AMERICAN INDIAN SCIENCE AND ENGINEERING SOCIETY (A.T. Anderson Memorial Scholarship)

P.O. Box 9828
Albuquerque NM 87119-9828
505/765-1052
FAX: 505/765-5608
E-mail: scholarships@aises.org
Internet: http://www.aises.org/scholarships
AMOUNT: $1,000-$2,000
DEADLINE(S): JUN 15
FIELD(S): Medicine; Natural Resources; Science; Engineering

Open to undergraduate and graduate students who are at least 1/4 American Indian or recognized as member of a tribe. Must be member of AISES ($10 fee), enrolled full-time at an accredited institution, and demonstrate financial need.

Renewable. See Web site or contact Patricia Browne for an application and/or membership information.

1288—AMERICAN INDIAN SCIENCE AND ENGINEERING SOCIETY (EPA Tribal Lands Environmental Science Scholarship)

P.O. Box 9828
Albuquerque NM 87119-9828
505/765-1052
FAX: 505/765-5608
E-mail: scholarships@aises.org
Internet: http://www.aises.org/scholarships/index.html
AMOUNT: $4,000
DEADLINE(S): JUN 15
FIELD(S): Biochemistry; Biology; Chemical Engineering; Chemistry; Entomology; Environmental Economics/Science; Hydrology; Environmental Studies

Open to American Indian college juniors, seniors, and graduate students enrolled full-time at an accredited institution. Must demonstrate financial need and be a member of AISES ($10 fee). Certificate of Indian blood NOT required.

Not renewable. See Web site for more information and/or an application.

1289—AMERICAN SOCIETY OF ENGINEERS OF INDIAN ORIGIN (Undergraduate Scholarship Programs)

P.O. Box 49494
Atlanta GA 30359-1494
770/451-2299
Internet: http://www.iasf.org/asei.htm
AMOUNT: Up to $1,000
DEADLINE(S): AUG 15
FIELD(S): Engineering Fields: Architecture, Computer Technology, Geotechnical or Geoenvironmental Engineering, and allied sciences

Several scholarships for undergraduate engineering students in the above fields who were born in India or who are Indian by ancestry or relation. For study in the U.S. Some programs have residency requirements in certain states.

Contact Dr. Narsi Narasimhan at above location for applications and details.

1290—AMERICAN WATER RESOURCES ASSOCIATION (Richard A. Herbert Memorial Scholarships)

4 West Federal Street
Middleburg VA 20118-1626

540/687-8390
FAX: 540/687-8395
E-mail: info@awra.org
Internet: http://www.awra.org//student/herbert.html
AMOUNT: $1,000 + complimentary AWRA membership
DEADLINE(S): APR 26
FIELD(S): Water Resources and related fields

For full-time undergraduates working towards first degree and for graduates. Based on academic performance, including cumulative GPA, relevance of curriculum to water resources, and leadership in extracurricular activities related to water resources. Quality and relevance of research is also considered from graduate students. Transcripts, letters of reference, and summary of academic interests/achievements, extracurricular interests, and career goals required (2 page limit).

2 awards annually: 1 undergrad and 1 graduate. Recipients announced in the summer. Contact AWRA Student Activities Committee, for an application.

1291—AMERICAN PLANNING ASSOCIATION (Minority Scholarship and Fellowship Programs)

122 South Michigan Avenue, Suite 1600
Chicago IL 60605
312/431-9100
FAX: 312/431-9985
AMOUNT: $2,000-$5,000 (grads); $2,500 (undergrads)
DEADLINE(S): MAY 14
FIELD(S): Urban Planning, Community Development, Environmental Sciences, Public Administration, Transportation, or Urban Studies

Scholarships for African-Americans, Hispanics, or Native American students pursing undergraduate degrees in the U.S. in the above fields. Must have completed first year. Fellowships for graduate students. Programs must be approved by the Planning Accreditation Board. U.S. citizenship.

Call or write for complete information.

1292—ASTRONAUT SCHOLARSHIP FOUNDATION (Scholarships)

Exec. Director
6225 Vectorspace Boulevard
Titusville FL 32780
321/269-6119
FAX: 321/267-3970
E-mail: MercurySvn@aol.com;
Internet: http://www.astronautscholarship.org/guidelines.html
AMOUNT: Varies
DEADLINE(S): Varies
FIELD(S): Engineering and Physical Sciences (Medical Research ok, but NOT Professional Medicine)

Open to juniors, seniors, and graduate students at a select group of schools. Must be U.S. citizen with the intention to pursue research or advance field of study upon completion of final degree. Special consideration given to students who have shown initiative, creativity, excellence, and/or resourcefulness in their field. Must be NOMINATED by faculty or staff.

See Web site for list of eligible schools. Contact Howard Benedict, Executive Director, for details.

1293—BRITISH INSTITUTE OF ARCHAEOLOGY AT ANKARA (Travel Grants)

10 Carlton House Terrace
London SW1Y 5AH ENGLAND UK
+44-020-7969-5204
FAX: +44-020-7969-5401
E-mail: biaa@britac.ac.uk
Internet: http://www.britac.ac.uk/institutes/ankara/
AMOUNT: 500 pounds sterling (max.)
DEADLINE(S): FEB 1
FIELD(S): Archaeology and Geography of Turkey

Travel grants to enable undergraduate and graduate students to familiarize themselves with the archaeology and geography of Turkey, its museums, and ancient sites. For citizens or residents of the British Commonwealth.

Contact British Institute or check the Web site for an application.

1294—BROOKHAVEN WOMEN IN SCIENCE (Renate W. Chasman Scholarship)

P.O. Box 183
Upton NY 11973-5000
E-mail: pam@bnl.gov
AMOUNT: $2,000
DEADLINE(S): APR 1
FIELD(S): Natural Sciences; Engineering; Mathematics

Open ONLY to women who are residents of the boroughs of Brooklyn or Queens or the counties of Nassau or Suffolk in New York who are reentering school after a period of study. For juniors, seniors, or first-year graduate students.

1 award annually. Not renewable. Contact Pam Mansfield at above location for an application. Phone calls are NOT accepted.

1295—CANADIAN RECREATIONAL CANOEING ASSOCIATION (Bill Mason Memorial Scholarship Fund)

446 Main Street W.
P.O. Box 398
Merrickville Ontario K0G 1N0
CANADA
613/269-2910
FAX: 613/269-2908
Internet: http://www.crca.ca/bill.html
AMOUNT: $1,000
DEADLINE(S): OCT 15
FIELD(S): Outdoor Recreation; Environmental Studies

Scholarship is a tribute to Bill Mason, a Canadian recognized at home and abroad as a canoeist, environmentalist, artist, filmmaker, photographer, and public speaker. Applicant must be a full-time student at a Canadian university or college. Must be planning a career related to the above fields, be a Canadian citizen, maintain a B+ average, and be a second-year student or higher. Financial need must be demonstrated. Background in canoeing/kayaking is an asset.

Scholarship is paid in two installments: $700 by Nov. 10, and $300 after receipt of May 15 progress report.

1296—CANADIAN SOCIETY OF EXPLORATION GEOPHYSICISTS (CSEG Trust Fund)

905, 510-5th Street, SW
Calgary Alberta T2P 3S2 CANADA
403/262-0015
FAX: 403/262-7383
E-mail: info@cseg.org
Internet: http://www.cseg.org
AMOUNT: $2,000 Canadian
DEADLINE(S): JUL 15
FIELD(S): Exploration Geophysics

For undergraduate students whose grades are above average or for graduate students. Must be pursuing a course of studies in Canada directed toward a career in exploration geophysics in industry, teaching, or research. Certain awards impose additional qualifications; completion of questionnaire will aid in determining if applicant meets those qualifications. Letters of recommendation required. Financial need is considered.

Contact CSEG or check the Web site for an application.

1297—COMMUNITY FOUNDATION OF WESTERN MASSACHUSETTS (Nate McKinney Memorial Scholarship)

1500 Main Street
P.O. Box 15769
Springfield MA 01115
413/732-2858
AMOUNT: $1,000
DEADLINE(S): APR 15
FIELD(S): Music; Athletics; Science

Open to graduating seniors of Gateway Regional High School in Huntington, Massachusetts. Recipient must excel academically, demonstrate good citizenship, and have a strong interest in at least two of the following areas: music, science, and athletics. Based on financial need, academic merit, and extracurricular activities. Must submit transcripts and fill out government FAFSA form.

1 award annually. Renewable up to 4 years with reapplication. Contact Community Foundation for an application and your financial aid office for FAFSA. Notification is in June.

1298—CONSULTING ENGINEERS COUNCIL OF NEW JERSEY (Louis Goldberg Scholarship Fund)

66 Morris Avenue
Springfield NJ 07081
973/564-5848
FAX: 973/564-7480
AMOUNT: $1,000
DEADLINE(S): JAN 1
FIELD(S): Engineering or Land Surveying

Open to undergraduate students who have completed at least two years of study (or fifth year in a five-year program) at an ABET-accredited college or university in New Jersey, are in top half of their class, and are considering a career as a consulting engineer or land surveyor. Must be U.S. citizen.

Recipients will be eligible for American Consulting Engineers Council national scholarships of $2,000 to $5,000. Write for complete information.

1299—EDWARD AND ANNA RANGE SCHMIDT CHARITABLE TRUST (Grants and Emergency Financial Assistance)

P.O. Box 770982
Eagle River AK 99577
Written Inquiry
AMOUNT: Varies
DEADLINE(S): None
FIELD(S): Earth and Environmental Sciences

Open to Alaska residents or students in Alaska programs. Grants are awarded for a variety of expenses incurred by students, such as internship support, travel, expenses related to workshops and science fairs, support needed to secure employment in earth science-related fields, or emergency needs. Alaska Natives and other minorities are urged to apply.

Not renewable. Requests are given immediate consideration. Application should be made by letter from a sponsor (teacher, advisor, or other adult familiar with applicant's situation). Both sponsor and applicant should send letter describing applicant, nature of financial need, and amount requested.

1300—FLORIDA FEDERATION OF GARDEN CLUBS, INC. (FFGC Scholarships for College Students)

6065 21st Street SW
Vero Beach FL 32968-9427
561/778-1023
Internet: http://www.ffgc.org
AMOUNT: $1,500-$3,500
DEADLINE(S): MAY 1
FIELD(S): Ecology; Environmental Issues; Land Management; City Planning; Environmental Control; Horticulture; Landscape Design; Conservation; Botany; Forestry; Marine Biology; Floriculture; Agriculture

Various scholarships for Florida residents with a "B" average or better enrolled full-time as a junior, senior, or graduate student at a Florida college or university.

See Web site or contact Melba Campbell at FFGC for an application.

1301—FLORIDA FEDERATION OF GARDEN CLUBS, INC. (FFGC Scholarships for High School Students)

6065 21st Street SW
Vero Beach FL 32968-9427
561/778-1023
Internet: http://www.ffgc.org
AMOUNT: $1,500
DEADLINE(S): MAY 1
FIELD(S): Ecology; Environmental Issues; Land Management; City Planning; Environmental Control; Horticulture; Landscape Design; Conservation; Botany; Forestry; Marine Biology; Floriculture; Agriculture

Scholarships for Florida residents with a "B" average or better who will be incoming freshmen at a Florida college or university.

See Web site or contact Melba Campbell at FFGC for an application.

1302—GAMMA THETA UPSILON INTERNATIONAL GEOGRAPHIC HONOR SOCIETY (Buzzard, Richason, and Maxfield Presidents Scholarships)

1725 State Street
La Crosse WI 54601
608/785-8355
FAX: 608/785-8332
E-mail: holder.virg@uwlax.edu
Internet: http://www.gtuhonors.org
AMOUNT: $500
DEADLINE(S): JUN 1
FIELD(S): Geography

Undergraduate and graduate scholarships are open to Gamma Theta Upsilon members who maintain at least a "B" grade point average in any accredited geography program.

Contact Dr. Virgil Holder, Dept. of Geography, University of Wisconsin, at above address for an application.

1303—INSTITUTE OF INTERNATIONAL EDUCATION (National Security Education Program-Undergraduate Scholarships)

1400 K Street NW, 6th Floor
Washington DC 20005-2403
202/326-7697 or
800/618-NSEP (6737)
E-mail: nsep@iie.org
Internet: http://www.iie.org/nsep/
AMOUNT: Varies: up to $8,000/semester
DEADLINE(S): FEB 8
FIELD(S): Open to all majors; preference to applied sciences, engineering, business, economics, math, computer science, international affairs, political science, history, and the policy sciences.

For study abroad OUTSIDE the U.S., Canada, Australia, New Zealand, and Western Europe. For study in areas deemed critical to U.S. national security. Applications available on U.S. campuses from August through early December. Or contact organization for details.

Inquire at above location for details.

1304—LOUISIANA OFFICE OF STUDENT FINANCIAL ASSISTANCE (Rockefeller State Wildlife Scholarships)

P.O. Box 91202
Baton Rouge LA 70821-9202
800/259-5626 ext. 1012 or
225/922-3258

FAX: 225/922-0790
E-mail: custserv@osfa.state.la.us
Internet: http://www.osfa.state.la.us
AMOUNT: $1,000/year
DEADLINE(S): JUL 1
FIELD(S): Forestry; Wildlife; Marine Science

Open to Louisiana residents pursuing undergraduate or graduate study at a Louisiana public postsecondary institution. Must be U.S. citizen with a minimum 2.5 GPA. Competitive selection. Recipients must obtain a degree in one of the three eligible fields or repay the funds plus interest. Financial need NOT a factor.

60 awards annually. Renewable. Apply by completing the Free Application for Federal Student Aid (FAFSA). Contact Public Information Rep for details.

1305—MICROSOFT CORPORATION (National Minority and/or Women's Scholarships)

One Microsoft Way
Redmond WA 98052-8303
E-mail: scholar@microsoft.com
Internet: http://www.microsoft.com/college/scholarships/
AMOUNT: Tuition for 1 year
DEADLINE(S): JAN 31
FIELD(S): Computer Science, Computer Engineering, or a related technical discipline, such as Math or Physics

Full tuition scholarships awarded for 1 academic year to women and minorities (African-Americans, Hispanics, or Native Americans) enrolled full-time in the above fields with a demonstrated interest in computers and making satisfactory progress towards a degree. Awards are made through designated schools and are not transferable to other institutions.

See Web site above for details.

1306—MICROSOFT CORPORATION (Summer Internships)

One Microsoft Way
Redmond WA 98052-8303
425/882-8080
E-mail: scholar@microsoft.com
Internet: http://www.microsoft.com/college/scholarships/
AMOUNT: Varies
DEADLINE(S): None
FIELD(S): Computer Science, Computer Engineering, or a related technical discipline, such as Math or Physics

Summer internships for individuals with a deep passion for technological advancement. Must commit to a 12-week minimum. Includes transportation, shipping costs, and shared cost of housing. Competitive compensation offered.

Check Web site above for details.

1307—MINERALOGICAL SOCIETY OF AMERICA (MSA Grant for Research in Crystallography)

1015 18th Street NW; Suite 601
Washington DC 20036-5212
202/775-4344
FAX: 202/775-0018
E-mail: j_a_speer@minsocam.org
Internet: http://www.minsocam.org
AMOUNT: $5,000
DEADLINE(S): JUN 1
FIELD(S): Crystallography

Research grant based on qualifications of applicant; quality, innovativeness, and scientific significance of proposed research; and the likelihood of success of the project. Applicant must have reached his or her 25th birthday but not have reached his or her 36th birthday on the date the grant is awarded. There are no restrictions on how the grant funds may be spent, as long as they are used in support of research. MSA Counselors may not apply.

See Web site or contact Dr. J. Alex Speer at the MSA Business Office for an application.

1308—MINERALOGICAL SOCIETY OF AMERICA (MSA Grant for Student Research in Mineralogy and Petrology)

1015 18th Street NW; Suite 601
Washington DC 20036-5274
202/775-4344
FAX: 202/775-0018
E-mail: j_a_speer@minsocam.org
Internet: http://www.minsocam.org
AMOUNT: $5,000
DEADLINE(S): JUN 1
FIELD(S): Mineralogy; Petrology

Research grant for undergraduate or graduate students based on qualifications of applicant; the quality, innovativeness, and scientific significance of the proposed research; and the likelihood of success of the project. There are no restrictions on how the grant funds may be spent, as long as they are used in support of research.

2 awards annually. See Web site or contact Dr. J. Alex Speer at the MSA Business Office for an application.

1309—NATIONAL AERONAUTICS AND SPACE ADMINISTRATION (ACCESS Internships)

Stennis Space Center, Bldg. 1100
Bay Saint Louis MS 39529
228/688-2079
E-mail: covington.pamela@ssc.nasa.gov
AMOUNT: Internship only
DEADLINE(S): None
FIELD(S): Aeronautics/Aerospace; Astronomy; Chemistry; Physics; Engineering; Math; Earth, Life, Materials, Computer, and Physical Sciences

Nine- to ten-week summer internships are open to undergraduates with physical or learning disabilities who maintain a minimum 3.0 GPA and are U.S. citizens. Purpose is to increase the number of students with disabilities pursuing technical degrees related to NASA's mission and to provide on-site experience. Internship takes place at the Stennis Space Center in Mississippi.

Contact Pam Covington for an application.

1310—NATIONAL COUNCIL FOR THE SOCIAL STUDIES (Grant for the Enhancement of Geographic Literacy)

8555 Sixteenth Street, Suite 500
Silver Spring MD 20910
301/588-1800
FAX: 301/588-2049
E-mail: information@ncss.org
Internet: http://www.ncss.org/awards/grants.html
AMOUNT: $2,500
DEADLINE(S): MAR 21
FIELD(S): Social Studies

Grant is co-sponsored by the George F. Cram Company, map publishers. For teachers of any level who present a program to promote and enhance geography education in the schools. Must incorporate the National Geography Standards in "Geography for Life," the "Fundamental Themes in Geography," and appropriate sections of "Expectations of Excellence: Curriculum Standards for Social Studies."

See Web site or contact organization for details.

1311—NATIONAL FEDERATION OF THE BLIND (Howard Brown Rickard Scholarship)

805 Fifth Avenue
Grinnell IA 50112

515/236-3366
AMOUNT: $3,000
DEADLINE(S): MAR 31
FIELD(S): Law; Medicine; Engineering; Architecture; Natural Sciences

For legally blind students pursuing or planning to pursue a full-time postsecondary course of study in the U.S.. Based on academic excellence, service to the community, and financial need. Membership NOT required.

1 award annually. Renewable. Contact Mrs. Peggy Elliot, Scholarship Committee Chairman, for an application.

1312—NATIONAL SCIENCES AND ENGINEERING RESEARCH COUNCIL OF CANADA (Undergraduate Scholarships)

Scholarships/Fellowships Division
350 Albert Street
Ottawa Ontario K1A 1H5 CANADA
613/996-2009
FAX: 613/996-2589
E-mail: schol@nserc.ca
Internet: http://www.nserc.ca
AMOUNT: Up to $3,600
DEADLINE(S): Varies
FIELD(S): Natural Sciences, Engineering, Biology, or Chemistry

Open to Canadian citizens or permanent residents working towards degrees in science or engineering. Academic excellence and research aptitude are considerations.

Write for complete information.

1313—NATURAL SCIENCES AND ENGINEERING RESEARCH COUNCIL OF CANADA (Undergraduate Student Research Awards in Small Universities)

350 Albert Street
Ottawa Ontario K1A 1H5 CANADA
613/995-5992
FAX: 613/992-5337
E-mail: schol@nserc.ca
Internet: http://www.nserc.ca/programs/usrasmen.htm
AMOUNT: $3,600 (max.)
DEADLINE(S): Varies
FIELD(S): Natural Sciences; Engineering

Research awards for Canadian citizens/permanent residents attending eligible institutions, and who have no more than 6 and no fewer than 2 academic terms remaining to complete bachelor's degree. Cumulative GPA of at least second class (B). Must be doing full-time in research and development activities during award tenure.

Students in health sciences not eligible. Students with BAs and who are studying for a second may apply.

1314—OAK RIDGE INSTITUTE FOR SCIENCE AND EDUCATION (ORISE Education and Training Programs)

P.O. Box 117
Oak Ridge TN 37831-0117
Internet: http://www.orau.gov/orise/educ.htm
AMOUNT: Varies
DEADLINE(S): Varies
FIELD(S): Engineering; Aeronautics; Computer Science; Technology; Earth Science; Environmental Studies; Biology; Chemistry; Physics; Medical Research

Numerous programs funded by the U.S. Department of Energy are offered for undergraduate students through postgraduate researchers. Includes fellowship and internship opportunities throughout the U.S.. Some have citizenship restrictions. Travel may be included.

See Web site or write for a catalog of specific programs and requirements.

1315—PENINSULA COMMUNITY FOUNDATION (Dr. Mary Finegold Scholarship)

1700 S. El Camino Real #300
San Mateo CA 94402
650/358-9369
FAX: 650/358-9817
Internet: http://www.pcf.org/community_grants/scholarships.html
AMOUNT: $1,000
DEADLINE(S): MAR 7 (5 p.m.)
FIELD(S): Sciences

Scholarships for senior girls graduating from high school in Palo Alto, California, who intend to complete a four-year degree in the sciences. Special consideration will be given to girls who have demonstrated a "pioneering" spirit in that they have not been constrained by stereotypical female roles and to those facing financial hardship.

Award was established in the honor of Dr. Mary Finegold who, after completing her medical studies, elected to stay at home until her youngest child was in high school before beginning her medical practice. She was a school physician.

1316—PENN STATE UNIVERSITY-COLLEGE OF EARTH AND MINERAL SCIENCES (Scholarships)

Committee on Scholarships and Awards; 116 Deike Bldg.
University Park PA 16802
814/865-7482
FAX: 814/863-7708
Internet: http://www.ems.psu.edu/prospective/financial.html
AMOUNT: $500- $3,500
DEADLINE(S): None
FIELD(S): Geosciences; Meteorology; Energy, Environmental, and Mineral Economics; Materials Science and Engineering; Mineral Engineering; Geography

Scholarship program open to outstanding undergraduate students accepted to or enrolled in Penn State's College of Earth and Mineral Sciences. Minimum GPA of 3.3 or 3.7 (entering student) on 4.0 scale.

Approximately 275 awards per year. Renewable. Contact Dean's office for complete information.

1317—RESOURCES FOR THE FUTURE (RFF Summer Internship Program)

1616 P Street NW
Washington DC 20036-1400
202/328-5000; FAX: 202/939-3460
E-mail: mankin@rff.org or voigt@rff.org
Internet: http://www.rff.org/about_rff/fellowships_internships.htm
AMOUNT: $350-375/week
DEADLINE(S): MAR 14 (5 PM, eastern time)
FIELD(S): Social Sciences, Natural Resources, Energy, Environment

Resident paid summer internships for undergraduate and graduate students for research in the above fields. Divisions are Risk, Resource and Environmental Management, Energy and Natural Resources, and Quality of the Environment. Candidates should have outstanding policy analysis and writing skills. For both U.S. and non-U.S. citizens.

All information is on Web site. Address inquiries and applications to John Mankin (Energy and Natural Resources and Quality of the Environment) or Marilyn Voigt (Risk, Resource and Environmental Management).

1318—SAN DIEGO AEROSPACE MUSEUM (Bill Gibbs Scholarship)

Education Dept.
2001 Pan American Plaza
San Diego CA 92101
619/234-8291 ext. 19
FAX: 619/233-4526
Internet: http://aerospacemuseum.org/Scholastic.HTML

AMOUNT: Varies
DEADLINE(S): Varies
FIELD(S): Aerospace: math, physics, science, or engineering

For students who are residents of San Diego County, California, who have an aerospace career interest who have been accepted to a four-year college or university in a degree program relating to math, physics, science, or engineering.

Call or write museum for further information.

1319—SIEMENS WESTINGHOUSE (Science and Technology Competition)

186 Wood Avenue S.
Iselin NJ 08830
877/822-5233
E-mail: foundation@sc.siemens.com
Internet: http://www.siemens-foundation.org
AMOUNT: $120,000 (max.)
DEADLINE(S): Varies
FIELD(S): Biology; Physical Sciences; Mathematics; Physics; Chemistry; Computer Science; Environmental Science

Open to U.S. high school seniors to pursue independent science research projects, working individually or in teams of 2 or 3 to develop and test their own ideas. May work with one of the universities/laboratories that serve as Siemens' partners. Students from the 50 states, DC, and Territories may compete in one of six geographic areas. Individual and team national prize winners receive a second scholarship award to be applied to undergraduate or graduate education.

See Web site or contact Siemens Foundation for details.

1320—SMITHSONIAN INSTITUTION (Minority Student Internship Program)

Office of Fellowships
750 9th Street NW, Suite 9300
Washington DC 20560-0902
202/275-0655
FAX: 202/275-0489
E-mail: siofg@ofg.si.edu
Internet: http://www.si.edu/research+study
AMOUNT: $350/week + possible travel expenses
DEADLINE(S): Varies
FIELD(S): Humanities; Environmental and Cultural Studies; Natural History; Earth Science; Art History; Biology

Ten-week, full-time internships in residence at the Smithsonian are open to U.S. minority students who wish to participate in research or museum-related activities in above and related fields. Must be undergraduates or beginning graduate students with a minimum 3.0 GPA. Must submit essay, resume, and official transcript.

Contact the Office of Fellowships or see Web site for an application.

1321—SMITHSONIAN INSTITUTION-HARVARD CENTER FOR ASTROPHYSICS (Summer Internships)

Program Director
SAO Summer Intern Program, MS 81
60 Garden Street
Cambridge MA 02138
617/496-7586
E-mail: intern@cfa.harvard.edu
Internet: http://hea-www.harvard.edu/REU/REU.html
AMOUNT: $300/wk. + housing/travel
DEADLINE(S): FEB 1
FIELD(S): Astrophysics; Astronomy

Ten-week summer internships are available to undergraduates who wish to conduct research at the Smithsonian Astrophysical Observatory. Must be currently enrolled in a program leading to a bachelor's degree. Each intern works with a scientist on an individual research project. Also included in the program are weekly lectures, field trips, and workshops specifically designed for the participants. Must be U.S. citizen or hold a valid green card.

See Web site or contact SAO Summer Intern Program Director for an application.

1322—SOCIETY FOR RANGE MANAGEMENT (Masonic-Range Science Scholarship)

445 Union Blvd., Suite #230
Lakewood CO 80228-1259
303/986-3309
FAX: 303/986-3892
E-mail: sglushdo@ix.netcom.com
Internet: http://www.srm.org
AMOUNT: $2,000
DEADLINE(S): JAN 15
FIELD(S): Range Science/Management

Open to high school seniors or college freshmen pursuing a major in range science/management. Must attend a college or university with a range science program.

1 award annually. Applicant must be sponsored by a member of SRM, the National Association of Conservation Districts (NACD), or the Soil and Water Conservation Society (SWCS). Financial need NOT a factor. See Web site or contact the above address for an application/more information.

1323—SOCIETY OF EXPLORATION GEOPHYSICISTS (SEG) FOUNDATION (Scholarships)

P.O. Box 702740
Tulsa OK 74170-2740
918/497-5500
FAX: 918/497-5557
Internet: http://www.seg.org/business/foundation/
AMOUNT: $500-$12,000
DEADLINE(S): MAR 1
FIELD(S): Geophysics

Open to a high school student with above average grades planning to enter college the next fall term or an undergraduate college student whose grades are above average, or a graduate college student whose studies are directed toward a career in exploration geophysics in operations, teaching, or research.

Check the Web site or write to the above address for complete information.

1324—SOCIETY OF SATELLITE PROFESSIONALS INTERNATIONAL (SSPI Scholarships)

225 Reinekers Lane, Suite 600
Alexandria VA 22314
703/857-3717
FAX: 703/857-6335
E-mail: neworbit@aol.com;
Internet: http://www.sspi.org
AMOUNT: $1,500 to $4,000
DEADLINE(S): DEC 1
FIELD(S): Satellites as related to communications, domestic and international telecommunications policy, remote sensing, journalism, law, meteorology, energy, navigation, business, government, and broadcasting services.

Various scholarships for students studying in the above fields.

Access Web site for details and applications or send a self-addressed, stamped envelope (SASE) for a complete listing.

1325—SOIL AND WATER CONSERVATION SOCIETY (Melville H. Cohee Student Leader Conservation Scholarship)

7515 N.E. Ankeny Road
Ankeny IA 50021-9764
515/289-2331

FAX: 515/289-1227
Internet: http://www.swcs.org/f_aboutSWCS_chrel.htm
AMOUNT: $1,000
DEADLINE(S): FEB 12
FIELD(S): Conservation or Natural Resource-Related Field

Open to 1+ year member of SWCS having served as an officer in a student chapter with 15+ members. GPA of 3.0 or better. Final year F/T undergrad or graduate.

Up to 3 awards. Course load must be 50% or more at accredited college or university. Financial need is not a factor. Write or visit Web site for complete information.

1326—STATISTICS NEW ZEALAND (Pacific Islands Scholarship)

EEO Co-ordinator
P.O. Box 2922
Wellington NEW ZEALAND
04/495-4643
FAX: 04/495-4817
E-mail: anisiata_soagia-pritchard@stats.govt.nz
AMOUNT: $3,500/year + travel
DEADLINE(S): OCT 31
FIELD(S): Statistics; Mathematics; Demography; Economics; Geography; Quantitative Social Sciences

Open to all indigenous people of Pacific Islands descent who are resident in New Zealand and who wish to study for an undergraduate tertiary qualification at a New Zealand university. Recipient must spend 6-10 weeks of vacation break in employment with Statistics New Zealand. Based on relevance of course of study; academic ability; language, community involvement, and culture; and personal attributes, including potential leadership qualities. References required.

1 award annually. Renewable up to 3 years. Contact Anisiata Soagia-Pritchard, EEO Coordinator, for an application. Notification in December.

1327—STUDENT CONSERVATION ASSOCIATION (SCA Resource Assistant Program)

P.O. Box 550
Charlestown NH 03603
603/543-1700
FAX: 603/543-1828
E-mail: internships@sca-inc.org
Internet: http://www.sca-inc.org
AMOUNT: $1,180-$4,725
DEADLINE(S): Varies
FIELD(S): Environment and related fields

Must be 18 and U.S. citizen; need not be student. Fields: Agriculture, Archaeology, anthropology, botany, caves, civil/environmental engineering, environmental education, fisheries, forests, herpetology, history, living history/roleplaying, visitor services, landscape architecture/environmental design, paleontology, recreation/resource/range management, trail maintenance/construction, wildlife management, geology, hydrology, library/ museums, surveying...

900 positions in U.S. and Canada. Send $1 for postage for application; outside U.S./Canada, send $20.

1328—THE DAPHNE JACKSON MEMORIAL FELLOWSHIPS TRUST (Fellowships in Science/Engineering)

School of Physical Sciences,
Dept. of Physics, University of Surrey
Guildford, Surrey GU2 5XH
ENGLAND UK
01483 259166
FAX: 01483 259501
E-mail: J.Woolley@surrey.ac.uk
Internet: http://www.sst.ph.ic.ac.uk/trust/
AMOUNT: Varies
DEADLINE(S): Varies
FIELD(S): Science or Engineering, including Information Sciences

Fellowships to enable well-qualified and highly motivated scientists and engineers to return to appropriate careers following a career break due to family commitments. May be used on a flexible, part-time basis. Tenable at various U.K. universities.

See Web site and/or contact organization for details.

1329—UNCF/MERCK SCIENCE INITIATIVE (Undergraduate Science Research Scholarship Awards)

8260 Willow Oaks Corporate Dr.
P.O. Box 10444
FairFAX: VA 22031-4511
703/205-3503
FAX: 703/205-3574
E-mail: uncfmerck@uncf.org
Internet: http://www.uncf.org/merck
AMOUNT: $25,000/year (max.)
DEADLINE(S): DEC 15
FIELD(S): Life and Physical Sciences

Open to African-Americans in their junior year of college who will receive a bachelor's degree in the following academic year. Must be enrolled full-time in any four-year college/university in the U.S. and have a minimum 3.3 GPA. Must be U.S. citizen/permanent resident. Financial need NOT a factor.

15 awards annually. Not renewable. Contact Jerry Bryant, Ph.D., for an application.

1330—UNITED STATES DEPARTMENT OF AGRICULTURE (1890 National Scholars Program)

14th & Independence Avenue SW;
Room 301-W; Whitten Bldg.
Washington, DC 20250-9600
202/720-6905
E-mail: usda-m@fie.com
Internet: http://web.fie.com/htdoc/fed/agr/ars/edu/prog/mti/agrpgaak.htm
AMOUNT: Tuition, employment/benefits, use of pc/software, fees, books, room/board
DEADLINE(S): JAN 15
FIELD(S): Agriculture, Food, or Natural Resource Sciences

For U.S. citizens, high school grad/GED, GPA 3.0+, verbal/math SAT 1000+, composite score 21+ ACT, first-year college student, and attend participating school.

34+ scholarships/year/4 years. Send applications to U.S.D.A. Liaison officer at the 1890 Institution of your choice (see Web page for complete list).

1331—UNIVERSITY OF NEWCASTLE/Australia (R. M. Sheahan Memorial Undergraduate Scholarship)

Student Administration Unit, Student Services Centre, Univ. of Newcastle,
Callaghan NSW
2308 AUSTRALIA
+61-(02)-4921-6539
FAX: +61-(02)-4960-1766
E-mail: scholarships@newcastle.edu.au
Internet: http://www.newcastle.edu.au/services/ousr/stuadmin/schol/index.htm
AMOUNT: $1,000
DEADLINE(S): NOV 1
FIELD(S): Engineering, chemistry, or environmental engineering

Scholarship for undergraduate international as well as Australian students pursuing studies in chemistry, chemical engineering, or environmental engineering. Funded by the Cessnock City Council and Orica (ICI) Explosives, this award is made yearly based on academic merit.

Contact organization for details.

1332—WATER ENVIRONMENT FEDERATION (Canham Graduate Studies Scholarships)

601 Wythe Street
Alexandria VA 22314-1994
703/684-2477 or 800/666-0206
FAX: 703/645-2492
Internet: http://www.wef.org
AMOUNT: $2,000-$2,500
DEADLINE(S): MAR 1
FIELD(S): Water Environment; Water Pollution Control and related fields

Open to graduate students in water environment programs. Must be member of the Water Environment Federation (nominal fee) and commit to working in the environmental field for 2 years following the completion of studies.

2 awards annually. Contact the organization or see Web site for details and application-go to "Membership Benefits" then to "WEF Distinguished Honors and Awards."

1333—WOMEN'S AUXILIARY TO THE AMERICAN INSTITUTE OF MINING, METALLURGICAL, AND PETROLEUM ENGINEERS (WAAIME Scholarship Loan Fund)

Three Park Avenue, Suite 17B
New York NY 10016-5998
212/419-7673
FAX: 212/419-7680
E-mail: waaimeny@juno.com
Internet: http://www.aimeny.org
AMOUNT: Varies
DEADLINE(S): MAR 15
FIELD(S): Earth Sciences, as related to the Minerals Industry

Open to undergraduate juniors and seniors and graduate students, whose majors relate to an interest in the minerals industry. Eligible applicants receive a scholarship loan for all or part of their education. Recipients repay only 50%, with no interest charges. Repayment begins by six months after graduation and should be completed within six years.

See Web site or contact WAAIME at above address for an application.

1334—WOODROW WILSON NATIONAL FELLOWSHIP FOUNDATION (Leadership Program for Teachers)

CN 5281
Princeton NJ 08543-5281
609/452-700
FAX: 609/452-0066
E-mail: marchioni@woodrow.org or irish@woodrow.org
Internet: http://www.woodrow.org
AMOUNT: Varies
DEADLINE(S): Varies
FIELD(S): Science; Mathematics

WWLPT offers summer institutes for middle and high school teachers in science and mathematics. One- and two-week teacher outreach, TORCH Institutes, are held in the summer throughout the U.S.

See Web site or contact WWNFF for an application.

1335—WOODS HOLE OCEANOGRAPHIC INSTITUTION (Traineeships in Oceanography for Minority Group Undergraduates)

360 Woods Hole Road
Woods Hole MA 02543-1541
508/289-2219
FAX: 508/457-2188
E-mail: mgately@whoi.edu
Internet: http://www.whoi.edu
AMOUNT: Varies
DEADLINE(S): FEB 16
FIELD(S): Physical/Natural Sciences, Mathematics, Engineering

For minority undergraduates enrolled in U.S. colleges/universities who have completed at least two semesters. These awards provide training and research experience for students with interests in the above fields. Traineeships may be awarded for a ten- to- twelve-week period in the summer or for a semester during the academic year.

Renewable. For an application/more information, contact the Education Office, Clark Laboratory 223, MS #31, at above address.

ENVIRONMENTAL STUDIES

1336—ALLIANCE FOR YOUNG ARTISTS AND WRITERS, INC./AMERICAN MUSEUM OF NATURAL HISTORY (Young Naturalist Awards)

Scholastic, Inc.; 555 Broadway
New York NY 10012-3999
212/343-6582 or 800-SCHOLASTIC
FAX: 212/343-4885
E-mail: A&WGeneralinfo@scholastic.com
Internet: http://www.amnh.org/youngnaturalistawards
AMOUNT: Up to $2,500 + trip to New York to visit AMNH
DEADLINE(S): JAN
FIELD(S): Natural Sciences

For all students in grades 7-12 currently enrolled in a public or nonpublic school in the U.S., Canada, U.S. territories, or U.S.-sponsored schools abroad. Program focuses on finding and rewarding excellence in biology, earth science, astronomy, and cultural studies. Students are encouraged to perform observation-based projects that require creativity, inquiry, and critical analysis. Specific topics vary annually.

48 awards annually. See Web site for application.

1337—AMERICAN INDIAN SCIENCE AND ENGINEERING SOCIETY (A.T. Anderson Memorial Scholarship)

P.O. Box 9828
Albuquerque NM 87119-9828
505/765-1052
FAX: 505/765-5608
E-mail: scholarships@aises.org
Internet: http://www.aises.org/scholarships
AMOUNT: $1,000-$2,000
DEADLINE(S): JUN 15
FIELD(S): Medicine; Natural Resources; Science; Engineering

Open to undergraduate and graduate students who are at least 1/4 American Indian or recognized as member of a tribe. Must be member of AISES ($10 fee), enrolled full-time at an accredited institution, and demonstrate financial need.

Renewable. See Web site or contact Patricia Browne for an application and/or membership information.

1338—AMERICAN INDIAN SCIENCE AND ENGINEERING SOCIETY (EPA Tribal Lands Environmental Science Scholarship)

P.O. Box 9828
Albuquerque NM 87119-9828
505/765-1052
FAX: 505/765-5608
E-mail: scholarships@aises.org
Internet: http://www.aises.org/scholarships/index.html
AMOUNT: $4,000
DEADLINE(S): JUN 15
FIELD(S): Biochemistry; Biology; Chemical Engineering; Chemistry; Entomology; Environmental Economics/Science; Hydrology; Environmental Studies

Open to American Indian college juniors, seniors, and graduate students enrolled full-time at an accredited institution. Must demonstrate financial need and be a member of AISES ($10 fee). Certificate of Indian blood NOT required.

Not renewable. See Web site for more information and/or an application.

1339—AMERICAN METEOROLOGY SOCIETY INDUSTRY (Undergraduate Scholarships)

45 Beacon Street
Boston MA 02108-3693
617/227-2426
Internet: http://www.ametsoc.org/AMS
AMOUNT: $700-$5,000
DEADLINE(S): multiple
FIELD(S): Meteorology

Ten scholarship opportunities exist for undergraduates pursuing careers in the atmospheric or related sciences. Must attend an accredited university and maintain a 3.0 GPA.

1340—AMERICAN PLANNING ASSOCIATION (Minority Scholarship and Fellowship Programs)

122 South Michigan Avenue, Suite 1600
Chicago IL 60605
312/431-9100
FAX: 312/431-9985
AMOUNT: $2,000-$5,000 (grads); $2,500 (undergrads)
DEADLINE(S): MAY 14
FIELD(S): Urban Planning, Community Development, Environmental Sciences, Public Administration, Transportation, or Urban Studies

Scholarships for African-Americans, Hispanics, or Native American students pursing undergraduate degrees in the U.S. in the above fields. Must have completed first year. Fellowships for graduate students. Programs must be approved by the Planning Accreditation Board. U.S. citizenship.

Call or write for complete information.

1341—AMERICAN SOCIETY OF ENGINEERS OF INDIAN ORIGIN (Undergraduate Scholarship Programs)

P.O. Box 49494
Atlanta GA 30359-1494
770/451-2299
Internet: http://www.iasf.org/asei.htm
AMOUNT: Up to $1,000
DEADLINE(S): AUG 15
FIELD(S): Engineering Fields: Architecture, Computer Technology, Geotechnical or Geoenvironmental Engineering, and allied sciences

Several scholarships for undergraduate engineering students in the above fields who were born in India or who are Indian by ancestry or relation. For study in the U.S. Some programs have residency requirements in certain states.

Contact Dr. Narsi Narasimhan at above location for applications and details.

1342—ARCTIC INSTITUTE OF NORTH AMERICA (Jim Bourque Scholarship)

Univ. of Calgary
2500 University Drive NW
Calgary Alberta T2N 1N4
CANADA
403/220-7515
FAX: 403/282-4609
E-mail: smccaffe@ucalgary.ca
Internet: http://www.ucalgary.ca/UofC/Others/AINA/scholar/scholar.html
AMOUNT: $1,000
DEADLINE(S): JUL 15
FIELD(S): Education; Environmental Studies; Traditional Knowledge; Telecommunications

Open to Canadian Aboriginal students who intend to take, or are enrolled in, postsecondary training in above fields. There is no application; applicants must submit description of program and reasons for choice, transcript, letter of recommendation, statement of financial need, and proof of enrollment or application to a postsecondary institution.

See Web site or contact AINA for details. Award announced on August 1.

1343—CANADIAN RECREATIONAL CANOEING ASSOCIATION (Bill Mason Memorial Scholarship Fund)

446 Main Street W.
P.O. Box 398
Merrickville Ontario K0G 1N0
CANADA
613/269-2910
FAX: 613/269-2908
Internet: http://www.crca.ca/bill.html
AMOUNT: $1,000
DEADLINE(S): OCT 15
FIELD(S): Outdoor Recreation; Environmental Studies

Scholarship is a tribute to Bill Mason, a Canadian recognized at home and abroad as a canoeist, environmentalist, artist, filmmaker, photographer, and public speaker. Applicant must be a full-time student at a Canadian university or college. Must be planning a career related to the above fields, be a Canadian citizen, maintain a B+ average, and be a second-year student or higher. Financial need must be demonstrated. Background in canoeing/kayaking is an asset.

Scholarship is paid in two installments: $700 by Nov. 10, and $300 after receipt of May 15 progress report.

1344—EDWARD AND ANNA RANGE SCHMIDT CHARITABLE TRUST (Grants and Emergency Financial Assistance)

P.O. Box 770982
Eagle River AK 99577
Written Inquiry
AMOUNT: Varies
DEADLINE(S): None
FIELD(S): Earth and Environmental Sciences

Open to Alaska residents or students in Alaska programs. Grants are awarded for a variety of expenses incurred by students, such as internship support, travel, expenses related to workshops and science fairs, support needed to secure employment in earth science-related fields, or emergency needs. Alaska Natives and other minorities are urged to apply.

Not renewable. Requests are given immediate consideration. Application should be made by letter from a sponsor (teacher, advisor, or other adult familiar with applicant's situation). Both sponsor and applicant should send letter describing applicant, nature of financial need, and amount requested.

1345—FIRST UNITED METHODIST CHURCH (Robert Stevenson and Doreene E. Cater Scholarships)

302 5th Avenue, S.
St. Cloud MN 56301
FAX: 320/251-0878
E-mail: fumc@fumc-stcloud.org
AMOUNT: $200-1,500
DEADLINE(S): JUN 1
FIELD(S): Humanitarian and Christian Service: Teaching, Medicine, Social Work, Environmental Studies, etc.

Stevenson Scholarship is open to undergraduate members of the First United Methodist Church of St. Cloud. Cater Scholarship is open to members of the Minnesota United Methodist Conference who are entering the sophomore year or higher of college work. Both require two letters of reference, transcripts, and financial need.

5-6 awards annually. Contact Scholarship Committee for an application.

1346—FLORIDA FEDERATION OF GARDEN CLUBS, INC. (FFGC Scholarships for College Students)

6065 21st Street SW
Vero Beach FL 32968-9427
561/778-1023
Internet: http://www.ffgc.org
AMOUNT: $1,500-$3,500
DEADLINE(S): MAY 1
FIELD(S): Ecology; Environmental Issues; Land Management; City Planning; Environmental Control; Horticulture; Landscape Design; Conservation; Botany; Forestry; Marine Biology; Floriculture; Agriculture

Various scholarships for Florida residents with a "B" average or better enrolled full-time as a junior, senior, or graduate student at a Florida college or university.

See Web site or contact Melba Campbell at FFGC for an application.

1347—FLORIDA FEDERATION OF GARDEN CLUBS, INC. (FFGC Scholarships for High School Students)

6065 21st Street SW
Vero Beach FL 32968-9427
561/778-1023
Internet: http://www.ffgc.org
AMOUNT: $1,500
DEADLINE(S): MAY 1
FIELD(S): Ecology; Environmental Issues; Land Management; City Planning; Environmental Control; Horticulture; Landscape Design; Conservation; Botany; Forestry; Marine Biology; Floriculture; Agriculture

Scholarships for Florida residents with a "B" average or better who will be incoming freshmen at a Florida college or university.

See Web site or contact Melba Campbell at FFGC for an application.

1348—GARDEN CLUB OF AMERICA (GCA Awards for Summer Environmental Studies)

14 East 60th Street
New York NY 10022-1002
212/753-8287; FAX: 212/753-0134
Internet: http://www.gcamerica.org
AMOUNT: $1,500
DEADLINE(S): FEB 10
FIELD(S): Environmental Studies

Financial aid toward a SUMMER studies doing fieldwork or research in above field for college students following their freshman, sophomore, or junior year. Purpose of award is to encourage studies and careers in the environmental field.

Application available on Web site or contact the above address.

1349—GARDEN CLUB OF AMERICA (Frances M. Peacock Scholarship For Native Bird Habitat)

Cornell Lab of Ornithology
Ithaca NY 14850
No Phone Calls
FAX: 607/254-2415
E-mail: 1h17@cornell.edu
Internet: http://www.gcamerica.org
AMOUNT: $4,000
DEADLINE(S): JAN 15
FIELD(S): Habitats of Threatened/Endangered Native Birds

To provide financial aid to an advanced student (college senior or graduate student) to study habitat-related issues that will benefit threatened or endangered bird species and lend useful information for land management decisions.

1 award annually. Contact Scott Sutcliffe, Associate Director, for more information.

1350—HUBBARD FARMS CHARITABLE FOUNDATION

P.O. Box 505
Walpole NH 03608-0505
603/756-3311
AMOUNT: $1,500-$3,000
DEADLINE(S): APR 1
FIELD(S): Poultry science, genetics, and other life sciences

Scholarships are for financially needy students at universities that the foundation trustees consider to be leaders in the field of progress in technology and efficiency of production of poultry products.

Send SASE to Jane F. Kelly, Clerk, at above address for current application guidelines.

1351—INSTITUTE OF INTERNATIONAL EDUCATION (National Security Education Program-Undergraduate Scholarships)

1400 K Street NW, 6th Floor
Washington DC 20005-2403
202/326-7697 or
800/618-NSEP (6737)
E-mail: nsep@iie.org
Internet: http://www.iie.org/nsep/
AMOUNT: Varies: up to $8,000/semester
DEADLINE(S): FEB 8
FIELD(S): Open to all majors; preference to applied sciences, engineering, business, economics, math, computer science, international affairs, political science, history, and the policy sciences.

For study abroad OUTSIDE the U.S., Canada, Australia, New Zealand, and Western Europe. For study in areas deemed critical to U.S. national security. Applications available on U.S. campuses from August through early December. Or contact organization for details.

Inquire at above location for details.

1352—LOUISIANA OFFICE OF STUDENT FINANCIAL ASSISTANCE (Rockefeller State Wildlife Scholarships)

P.O. Box 91202
Baton Rouge LA 70821-9202
800/259-5626 ext. 1012 or
225/922-3258
FAX: 225/922-0790
E-mail: custserv@osfa.state.la.us
Internet: http://www.osfa.state.la.us
AMOUNT: $1,000/year
DEADLINE(S): JUL 1
FIELD(S): Forestry; Wildlife; Marine Science

Open to Louisiana residents pursuing undergraduate or graduate study at a Louisiana public postsecondary institution. Must be U.S. citizen with a minimum 2.5 GPA. Competitive selection. Recipients must obtain a degree in one of the three eligible fields or repay the funds plus interest. Financial need NOT a factor.

60 awards annually. Renewable. Apply by completing the Free Application for Federal Student Aid (FAFSA). Contact Public Information Rep for details.

1353—MICROSOFT CORPORATION (National Minority and/or Women's Scholarships)

One Microsoft Way
Redmond WA 98052-8303
E-mail: scholar@microsoft.com
Internet: http://www.microsoft.com/college/scholarships/
AMOUNT: Tuition for 1 year
DEADLINE(S): JAN 31
FIELD(S): Computer Science, Computer Engineering, or a related technical discipline, such as Math or Physics

Full tuition scholarships awarded for 1 academic year to women and minorities (African-Americans, Hispanics, or Native Americans) enrolled full-time in the above fields with a demonstrated interest in computers and making satisfactory progress towards a degree. Awards are made through designated schools and are not transferable to other institutions.

See Web site above for details.

1354—MICROSOFT CORPORATION (Summer Internships)

One Microsoft Way
Redmond WA 98052-8303
425/882-8080
E-mail: scholar@microsoft.com
Internet: http://www.microsoft.com/college/scholarships/

AMOUNT: Varies
DEADLINE(S): None
FIELD(S): Computer Science, Computer Engineering, or a related technical discipline, such as Math or Physics

Summer internships for individuals with a deep passion for technological advancement. Must commit to a 12-week minimum. Includes transportation, shipping costs, and shared cost of housing. Competitive compensation offered.

Check Web site above for details.

1355—NATIONAL ENVIRONMENTAL HEALTH ASSOCIATION (NEHA/AAS Scholarship)

720 S. Colorado Blvd., Suite 970
South Tower
Denver CO 80246-1925
303/756-9090
E-mail: mthomsen@neha.org
Internet: http://www.neha.org

AMOUNT: Varies
DEADLINE(S): FEB 1
FIELD(S): Environmental Health/Science; Public Health

Undergraduate scholarships to be used for tuition and fees during junior or senior year at an Environmental Health Accreditation Council accredited school or NEHA school. Graduate scholarships are for students or career professionals who are enrolled in a graduate program of studies in environmental health sciences and/or public health. Transcript, letters of recommendation, and financial need considered.

Renewable. Scholarships are paid directly to the college/university for the fall semester of the award.

1356—NATURAL SCIENCES AND ENGINEERING RESEARCH COUNCIL OF CANADA (Undergraduate Student Research Awards in Small Universities)

350 Albert Street
Ottawa Ontario K1A 1H5 CANADA
613/995-5992
FAX: 613/992-5337
E-mail: schol@nserc.ca
Internet: http://www.nserc.ca/programs/usrasmen.htm

AMOUNT: $3,600 (max.)
DEADLINE(S): Varies
FIELD(S): Natural Sciences; Engineering

Research awards for Canadian citizens/permanent residents attending eligible institutions, and who have no more than 6 and no fewer than 2 academic terms remaining to complete bachelor's degree. Cumulative GPA of at least second class (B). Must be doing full-time in research and development activities during award tenure.

Students in health sciences not eligible. Students with BAs and who are studying for a second may apply.

1357—OAK RIDGE INSTITUTE FOR SCIENCE AND EDUCATION (ORISE Education and Training Programs)

P.O. Box 117
Oak Ridge TN 37831-0117
Internet: http://www.orau.gov/orise/educ.htm

AMOUNT: Varies
DEADLINE(S): Varies
FIELD(S): Engineering; Aeronautics; Computer Science; Technology; Earth Science; Environmental Studies; Biology; Chemistry; Physics; Medical Research

Numerous programs funded by the U.S. Department of Energy are offered for undergraduate students through postgraduate researchers. Includes fellowship and internship opportunities throughout the U.S.. Some have citizenship restrictions. Travel may be included.

See Web site or write for a catalog of specific programs and requirements.

1358—PENINSULA COMMUNITY FOUNDATION (Dr. Mary Finegold Scholarship)

1700 S. El Camino Real #300
San Mateo CA 94402
650/358-9369
FAX: 650/358-9817
Internet: http://www.pcf.org/community_grants/scholarships.html

AMOUNT: $1,000
DEADLINE(S): MAR 7 (5 p.m.)
FIELD(S): Sciences

Scholarships for senior girls graduating from high school in Palo Alto, California, who intend to complete a four-year degree in the sciences. Special consideration will be given to girls who have demonstrated a "pioneering" spirit in that they have not been constrained by stereotypical female roles and to those facing financial hardship.

Award was established in the honor of Dr. Mary Finegold who, after completing her medical studies, elected to stay at home until her youngest child was in high school before beginning her medical practice. She was a school physician.

1359—PENN STATE UNIVERSITY-COLLEGE OF EARTH and MINERAL SCIENCES (Scholarships)

Committee on Scholarships and Awards; 116 Deike Bldg.
University Park PA 16802
814/865-7482
FAX: 814/863-7708
Internet: http://www.ems.psu.edu/prospective/financial.html

AMOUNT: $500- $3,500
DEADLINE(S): None
FIELD(S): Geosciences; Meteorology; Energy, Environmental, and Mineral Economics; Materials Science and Engineering; Mineral Engineering; Geography

Scholarship program open to outstanding undergraduate students accepted to or enrolled in Penn State's College of Earth and Mineral Sciences. Minimum GPA of 3.3 or 3.7 (entering student) on 4.0 scale.

Approximately 275 awards per year. Renewable. Contact Dean's office for complete information.

1360—RESOURCES FOR THE FUTURE (RFF Summer Internship Program)

1616 P Street NW
Washington DC 20036-1400
202/328-5000; FAX: 202/939-3460
E-mail: mankin@rff.org or voigt@rff.org
Internet: http://www.rff.org/about_rff/fellowships_internships.htm

AMOUNT: $350-375/week
DEADLINE(S): MAR 14 (5 PM, eastern time)
FIELD(S): Social Sciences, Natural Resources, Energy, Environment

Resident paid summer internships for undergraduate and graduate students for research in the above fields. Divisions are Risk, Resource and Environmental Management, Energy and Natural Resources, and Quality of the Environment.

Candidates should have outstanding policy analysis and writing skills. For both U.S. and non-U.S. citizens.

All information is on Web site. Address inquiries and applications to John Mankin (Energy and Natural Resources and Quality of the Environment) or Marilyn Voigt (Risk, Resource and Environmental Management).

1361—SAN DIEGO AEROSPACE MUSEUM (Bill Gibbs Scholarship)

Education Dept.
2001 Pan American Plaza
San Diego CA 92101
619/234-8291 ext. 19
FAX: 619/233-4526
Internet: http://aerospacemuseum.org/Scholastic.HTML

AMOUNT: Varies
DEADLINE(S): Varies
FIELD(S): Aerospace: math, physics, science, or engineering

For students who are residents of San Diego County, California, who have an aerospace career interest who have been accepted to a four-year college or university in a degree program relating to math, physics, science, or engineering.

Call or write museum for further information.

1362—SIEMENS WESTINGHOUSE (Science and Technology Competition)

186 Wood Avenue S.
Iselin NJ 08830
877/822-5233
E-mail: foundation@sc.siemens.com
Internet: http://www.siemens-foundation.org

AMOUNT: $120,000 (max.)
DEADLINE(S): Varies
FIELD(S): Biology; Physical Sciences; Mathematics; Physics; Chemistry; Computer Science; Environmental Science

Open to U.S. high school seniors to pursue independent science research projects, working individually or in teams of 2 or 3 to develop and test their own ideas. May work with one of the universities/laboratories that serve as Siemens' partners. Students from the 50 states, DC, and Territories may compete in one of six geographic areas. Individual and team national prize winners receive a second scholarship award to be applied to undergraduate or graduate education.

See Web site or contact Siemens Foundation for details.

1363—SMITHSONIAN INSTITUTION (Minority Student Internship Program)

Office of Fellowships
750 9th Street NW, Suite 9300
Washington DC 20560-0902
202/275-0655
FAX: 202/275-0489
E-mail: siofg@ofg.si.edu
Internet: http://www.si.edu/research+study

AMOUNT: $350/week + possible travel expenses
DEADLINE(S): Varies
FIELD(S): Humanities; Environmental and Cultural Studies; Natural History; Earth Science; Art History; Biology

Ten-week, full-time internships in residence at the Smithsonian are open to U.S. minority students who wish to participate in research or museum-related activities in above and related fields. Must be undergraduates or beginning graduate students with a minimum 3.0 GPA. Must submit essay, resume, and official transcript.

Contact the Office of Fellowships or see Web site for an application.

1364—SMITHSONIAN INSTITUTION-ENVIRONMENTAL RESEARCH CENTER (Internship Program)

P.O. Box 28
Edgewater MD 21037-0028
443/482-2217
E-mail: intern@serc.si.edu
Internet: http://www.serc.si.edu/internship/

AMOUNT: $300/week (stipend)
DEADLINE(S): NOV 15 (spring interns); FEB 1 (summer interns)
FIELD(S): Environmental Studies

Ten-to-sixteen-week internships are available to undergraduates and beginning graduate students who wish to conduct individual projects in environmental studies under the supervision of professional staff members at the Center. Projects include terrestrial or estuarine environmental research, resource planning and decision making, and environmental education research and development. Applicants should be currently enrolled or within six months of enrollment.

1365—SOCIETY FOR RANGE MANAGEMENT (Masonic-Range Science Scholarship)

445 Union Blvd., Suite #230
Lakewood CO 80228-1259
303/986-3309
FAX: 303/986-3892
E-mail: sglushdo@ix.netcom.com
Internet: http://www.srm.org

AMOUNT: $2,000
DEADLINE(S): JAN 15
FIELD(S): Range Science/Management

Open to high school seniors or college freshmen pursuing a major in range science/management. Must attend a college or university with a range science program.

1 award annually. Applicant must be sponsored by a member of SRM, the National Association of Conservation Districts (NACD), or the Soil and Water Conservation Society (SWCS). Financial need NOT a factor. See Web site or contact the above address for an application/more information.

1366—SOIL AND WATER CONSERVATION SOCIETY (Donald A. Williams Soil Conservation Scholarship)

7515 N.W. Ankeny Road
Ankeny IA 50021-9764
515/289-2331
FAX: 515/289-1227
Internet: http:// www.swcs.org/f_aboutSWCS_chrel.htm

AMOUNT: $1,500
DEADLINE(S): FEB 12
FIELD(S): Conservation-related fields (technical or administrative course work)

For SWCS members currently employed in a related field and have completed at least 1 year of natural resource conservation work with a governmental agency or private organization. Need not be working toward a degree. Must show reasonable financial need.

Up to 3 scholarships awarded yearly. Restricted to undergraduates. Write or visit Web site for complete information.

1367—SOIL AND WATER CONSERVATION SOCIETY (Melville H. Cohee Student Leader Conservation Scholarship)

7515 N.E. Ankeny Road
Ankeny IA 50021-9764
515/289-2331
FAX: 515/289-1227
Internet: http:// www.swcs.org/f_aboutSWCS_chrel.htm

AMOUNT: $1,000
DEADLINE(S): FEB 12
FIELD(S): Conservation or Natural Resource-Related Field

Open to 1+ year member of SWCS having served as an officer in a student chapter with 15+ members. GPA of 3.0 or better. Final year F/T undergrad or graduate.

Up to 3 awards. Course load must be 50% or more at accredited college or university. Financial need is not a factor. Write or visit Web site for complete information.

1368—SOIL AND WATER CONSERVATION SOCIETY (SWCS Internships)

7515 N.E. Ankeny Road
Ankeny IA 50021-9764
515/289-2331 or 800/THE-SOIL
FAX: 515/289-1227
E-mail: charliep@swcs.org
Internet: http://www.swcs.org

AMOUNT: Varies—most are uncompensated
DEADLINE(S): Varies
FIELD(S): Journalism, marketing, database management, meeting planning, public policy research, environmental education, landscape architecture

Internships for undergraduates and graduates to gain experience in the above fields as they relate to soil and water conservation issues. Internship openings vary through the year in duration, compensation, and objective. SWCS will coordinate particulars with your academic advisor.

Contact SWCS for internship availability at any time during the year or see Web site for jobs page.

1369—SRP/NAVAJO GENERATING STATION (Navajo Scholarship)

P.O. Box 850
Page AZ 86040
520/645-6539
FAX: 520/645-7295
E-mail: ljdawave@srp.gov

AMOUNT: Based on need
DEADLINE(S): APR 30
FIELD(S): Engineering, Environmental Studies, Business, Business Management, Health, Education

Scholarships for full-time students who hold membership in the Navajo Tribe and who are pursuing a degree in a field of study recognized as significant to the Navajo Nation, Salt River Project, or the Navajo Generating Station, such as those listed above. Must be junior or senior, have and maintain a GPA of 3.0

Average of 15 awards per year. Inquire of Linda Dawavendewa at above location.

1370—STUDENT CONSERVATION ASSOCIATION (SCA Resource Assistant Program)

P.O. Box 550
Charlestown NH 03603
603/543-1700
FAX: 603/543-1828
E-mail: internships@sca-inc.org
Internet: http://www.sca-inc.org

AMOUNT: $1,180-$4,725
DEADLINE(S): Varies
FIELD(S): Environment and related fields

Must be 18 and U.S. citizen; need not be student. Fields: Agriculture, Archaeology, anthropology, botany, caves, civil/environmental engineering, environmental education, fisheries, forests, herpetology, history, living history/roleplaying, visitor services, landscape architecture/environmental design, paleontology, recreation/resource/range management, trail maintenance/construction, wildlife management, geology, hydrology, library/museums, surveying.

900 positions in U.S. and Canada. Send $1 for postage for application; outside U.S./Canada, send $20.

1371—THE DAPHNE JACKSON MEMORIAL FELLOWSHIPS TRUST (Fellowships in Science/Engineering)

School of Physical Sciences,
Dept. of Physics, University of Surrey
Guildford, Surrey GU2 5XH
ENGLAND UK
01483 259166
FAX: 01483 259501
E-mail: J.Woolley@surrey.ac.uk
Internet: http://www.sst.ph.ic.ac.uk/trust/

AMOUNT: Varies
DEADLINE(S): Varies
FIELD(S): Science or Engineering, including Information Sciences

Fellowships to enable well-qualified and highly motivated scientists and engineers to return to appropriate careers following a career break due to family commitments. May be used on a flexible, part-time basis. Tenable at various U.K. universities.

See Web site and/or contact organization for details.

1372—THE MORRIS K. UDALL FOUNDATION

Suite 3350, 110 South Church Ave.
Tucson AZ 85701
520/670-5529
FAX: 520/670-5530
Internet: http://www.udall.gov/

AMOUNT: Up to $5,000
DEADLINE(S): FEB 15
FIELD(S): Health Care

Scholarships available to two groups: 1) college sophomores and juniors who have outstanding potential in the study of the environment and related fields and 2) Native American or Alaska Natives in fields related to health care or tribal policy.

1373—UNCF/MERCK SCIENCE INITIATIVE (Undergraduate Science Research Scholarship Awards)

8260 Willow Oaks Corporate Drive
P.O. Box 10444
FairFAX: VA 22031-4511
703/205-3503
FAX: 703/205-3574
E-mail: uncfmerck@uncf.org
Internet: http://www.uncf.org/merck

AMOUNT: $25,000/year (max.)
DEADLINE(S): DEC 15
FIELD(S): Life and Physical Sciences

Open to African-Americans in their junior year of college who will receive a bachelor's degree in the following academic year. Must be enrolled full-time in any four-year college/university in the U.S. and have a minimum 3.3 GPA. Must be U.S. citizen/permanent resident. Financial need NOT a factor.

15 awards annually. Not renewable. Contact Jerry Bryant, Ph.D., for an application.

1374—UNITED STATES DEPARTMENT OF AGRICULTURE (1890 National Scholars Program)

14th & Independence Avenue SW,
Room 301-W; Whitten Bldg.
Washington DC 20250-9600
202/720-6905
E-mail: usda-m@fie.com
Internet: http://web.fie.com/htdoc/fed/agr/ars/edu/prog/mti/agrpgaak.htm

AMOUNT: Tuition, employment/benefits, use of pc/software, fees, books, room/board
DEADLINE(S): JAN 15
FIELD(S): Agriculture, Food, or Natural Resource Sciences

For U.S. citizens, high school grad/GED, GPA 3.0+, verbal/math SAT 1000+, composite score 21+ ACT, first-year college student, and attend participating school.

34+ scholarships/year/4 years. Send applications to U.S.D.A. Liaison officer at the 1890 Institution of your choice (see Web page for complete list).

1375—UNIVERSITY OF NEWCASTLE/ Australia (R. M. Sheahan Memorial Undergraduate Scholarship)

Student Administration Unit, Student Services Centre, Univ. of Newcastle,
Callaghan NSW
2308 AUSTRALIA
+61-(02)-4921-6539
FAX: +61-(02)-4960-1766
E-mail: scholarships@newcastle.edu.au
Internet: http://http://www.newcastle.edu.au/services/ousr/stuadmin/schol/index.htm

AMOUNT: $1,000
DEADLINE(S): NOV 1
FIELD(S): Engineering, chemistry, or environmental engineering

Scholarship for undergraduate international as well as Australian students pursuing studies in chemistry, chemical engineering, or environmental engineering. Funded by the Cessnock City Council and Orica (ICI) Explosives, this award is made yearly based on academic merit.

Contact organization for details.

1376—USA EPA (Star Fellowships for Graduate Environmental Study)

401 M Street SW
Washington DC 20460
800/490-9194
Internet: http://www.epa.gov/ncerqa

AMOUNT: Up to $34,000 annually
DEADLINE(S): NOV
FIELD(S): Environmental Study

Master's level students may receive support for a maximum of two years. Doctoral students may be supported for a maximum of three years. Students do not need to be enrolled in or formally accepted in a full-time graduate program at the time they apply for a fellowship, but proof of enrollment or acceptance must be produced prior to the award of the fellowship.

1377—WATER ENVIRONMENT FEDERATION (Canham Graduate Studies Scholarships)

601 Wythe Street
Alexandria VA 22314-1994
703/684-2477 or 800/666-0206
FAX: 703/645-2492
Internet: http://www.wef.org

AMOUNT: $2,000-$2,500
DEADLINE(S): MAR 1
FIELD(S): Water Environment; Water Pollution Control and related fields

Open to graduate students in water environment programs. Must be member of the Water Environment Federation (nominal fee) and commit to working in the environmental field for 2 years following the completion of studies.

2 awards annually. Contact the organization or see Web site for details and application—go to "Membership Benefits" then to "WEF Distinguished Honors and Awards."

1378—WYOMING TRUCKING ASSOCIATION (Scholarships)

P.O. Box 1909
Casper WY 82602
Written Inquiry

AMOUNT: $250-$300
DEADLINE(S): MAR 1
FIELD(S): Transportation Industry

For Wyoming high school graduates enrolled in a Wyoming college, approved trade school, or the University of Wyoming. Must be pursuing a course of study which will result in a career in the transportation industry in Wyoming, including but not limited to: safety, environmental science, diesel mechanics, truck driving, vocational trades, business management, sales management, computer skills, accounting, office procedures, and management.

1-10 awards annually. Write to WYTA for an application.

MARINE SCIENCE

1379—ALLIANCE FOR YOUNG ARTISTS AND WRITERS, INC./AMERICAN MUSEUM OF NATURAL HISTORY (Young Naturalist Awards)

Scholastic, Inc.; 555 Broadway
New York NY 10012-3999
212/343-6582 or
800-SCHOLASTIC
FAX: 212/343-4885
E-mail: A&WGeneralinfo@scholastic.com
Internet: http://www.amnh.org/youngnaturalistawards

AMOUNT: Up to $2,500 + trip to New York to visit AMNH
DEADLINE(S): JAN
FIELD(S): Natural Sciences

For all students in grades 7-12 currently enrolled in a public or nonpublic school in the U.S., Canada, U.S. territories, or U.S.-sponsored schools abroad. Program focuses on finding and rewarding excellence in biology, earth science, astronomy, and cultural studies. Students are encouraged to perform observation-based projects that require creativity, inquiry, and critical analysis. Specific topics vary annually.

48 awards annually. See Web site for application.

1380—AMERICAN FOUNDATION FOR THE BLIND (Paul W. Ruckes Scholarship)

11 Penn Plaza, Suite 300
New York NY 10001
212/502-7661
FAX: 212/502-7771
E-mail: juliet@afb.org
Internet: http://www.afb.org

AMOUNT: $1,000
DEADLINE(S): APR 30
FIELD(S): Engineering; Computer/Physical/Life Sciences

Open to legally blind and visually impaired undergraduate and graduate students pursuing a degree in one of above fields. Must be U.S. citizen. Must submit written documentation of visual impairment from ophthalmologist or optometrist (need not be legally blind); official transcripts; proof of college/university acceptance; three letters of recommendation; and typewritten statement describing goals, work experience extracurricular activities, and how monies will be used.

1 award annually. See Web site or contact Julie Tucker at AFB for an application.

1381—AMERICAN INDIAN SCIENCE AND ENGINEERING SOCIETY (A.T. Anderson Memorial Scholarship)

P.O. Box 9828
Albuquerque NM 87119-9828
505/765-1052
FAX: 505/765-5608
E-mail: scholarships@aises.org
Internet: http://www.aises.org/scholarships

AMOUNT: $1,000-$2,000
DEADLINE(S): JUN 15
FIELD(S): Medicine; Natural Resources; Science; Engineering

Open to undergraduate and graduate students who are at least 1/4 American Indian or recognized as member of a tribe. Must be member of AISES ($10 fee), enrolled full-time at an accredited institution, and demonstrate financial need.

Renewable. See Web site or contact Patricia Browne for an application and/or membership information.

1382—AMERICAN WATER RESOURCES ASSOCIATION (Richard A. Herbert Memorial Scholarships)

4 West Federal Street
Middleburg VA 20118-1626
540/687-8390
FAX: 540/687-8395
E-mail: info@awra.org
Internet: http://www.awra.org/student/herbert.html

AMOUNT: $1,000 + complimentary AWRA membership
DEADLINE(S): APR 26
FIELD(S): Water Resources and related fields

For full-time undergraduates working towards first degree and for graduates. Based on academic performance, including cumulative GPA, relevance of curriculum to water resources, and leadership in extracurricular activities related to water resources. Quality and relevance of research is also considered from graduate students. Transcripts, letters of reference, and summary of academic interests/achievements, extracurricular interests, and career goals required (2 page limit).

2 awards annually: 1 undergrad and 1 graduate. Recipients announced in the summer. Contact AWRA Student Activities Committee, for an application.

1383—ASTRONAUT SCHOLARSHIP FOUNDATION (Scholarships)

Exec. Director
6225 Vectorspace Boulevard
Titusville FL 32780
321/269-6119
FAX: 321/267-3970
E-mail: MercurySvn@aol.com
Internet: http://www.astronautscholarship.org/guidelines.html

AMOUNT: Varies
DEADLINE(S): Varies
FIELD(S): Engineering and Physical Sciences (Medical Research ok, but NOT Professional Medicine)

Open to juniors, seniors, and graduate students at a select group of schools. Must be U.S. citizen with the intention to pursue research or advance field of study upon completion of final degree. Special consideration given to students who have shown initiative, creativity, excellence, and/or resourcefulness in their field. Must be NOMINATED by faculty or staff.

See Web site for list of eligible schools. Contact Howard Benedict, Executive Director, for details.

1384—BROOKHAVEN WOMEN IN SCIENCE (Renate W. Chasman Scholarship)

P.O. Box 183
Upton NY 11973-5000
E-mail: pam@bnl.gov

AMOUNT: $2,000
DEADLINE(S): APR 1
FIELD(S): Natural Sciences; Engineering; Mathematics

Open ONLY to women who are residents of the boroughs of Brooklyn or Queens or the counties of Nassau or Suffolk in New York who are reentering school after a period of study. For juniors, seniors, or first-year graduate students.

1 award annually. Not renewable. Contact Pam Mansfield at above location for an application. Phone calls are NOT accepted.

1385—CANADIAN RECREATIONAL CANOEING ASSOCIATION (Bill Mason Memorial Scholarship Fund)

446 Main Street W.
P.O. Box 398
Merrickville Ontario K0G 1N0
CANADA
613/269-2910
FAX: 613/269-2908
Internet: http://www.crca.ca/bill.html

AMOUNT: $1,000
DEADLINE(S): OCT 15
FIELD(S): Outdoor Recreation; Environmental Studies

Scholarship is a tribute to Bill Mason, a Canadian recognized at home and abroad as a canoeist, environmentalist, artist, filmmaker, photographer, and public speaker. Applicant must be a full-time student at a Canadian university or college. Must be planning a career related to the above fields, be a Canadian citizen, maintain a B+ average, and be a second-year student or higher. Financial need must be demonstrated. Background in canoeing/kayaking is an asset.

Scholarship is paid in two installments: $700 by Nov. 10, and $300 after receipt of May 15 progress report.

1386—COMMUNITY FOUNDATION OF WESTERN MASSACHUSETTS (Nate McKinney Memorial Scholarship)

1500 Main Street
P.O. Box 15769
Springfield MA 01115
413/732-2858

AMOUNT: $1,000
DEADLINE(S): APR 15
FIELD(S): Music; Athletics; Science

Open to graduating seniors of Gateway Regional High School in Huntington, Massachusetts. Recipient must excel academically, demonstrate good citizenship, and have a strong interest in at least two of the following areas: music, science, and athletics. Based on financial need, academic merit, and extracurricular activities. Must submit transcripts and fill out government FAFSA form.

1 award annually. Renewable up to 4 years with reapplication. Contact Community Foundation for an application and your financial aid office for FAFSA. Notification is in June.

1387—FLORIDA FEDERATION OF GARDEN CLUBS, INC. (FFGC Scholarships for College Students)

6065 21st Street SW
Vero Beach FL 32968-9427
561/778-1023
Internet: http://www.ffgc.org

AMOUNT: $1,500-$3,500
DEADLINE(S): MAY 1
FIELD(S): Ecology; Environmental Issues; Land Management; City Planning; Environmental Control; Horticulture; Landscape Design; Conservation; Botany; Forestry; Marine Biology; Floriculture; Agriculture

Various scholarships for Florida residents with a "B" average or better enrolled full-time as a junior, senior, or graduate student at a Florida college or university.

See Web site or contact Melba Campbell at FFGC for an application.

1388—FLORIDA FEDERATION OF GARDEN CLUBS, INC. (FFGC Scholarships for High School Students)

6065 21st Street SW
Vero Beach FL 32968-9427
561/778-1023
Internet: http://www.ffgc.org

AMOUNT: $1,500
DEADLINE(S): MAY 1
FIELD(S): Ecology; Environmental Issues; Land Management; City Planning; Environmental Control; Horticulture; Landscape Design; Conservation; Botany; Forestry;

Marine Biology; Floriculture; Agriculture

Scholarships for Florida residents with a "B" average or better who will be incoming freshmen at a Florida college or university.

See Web site or contact Melba Campbell at FFGC for an application.

1389—GREAT LAKES COMMISSION (Carol A. Ratza Memorial Scholarship)

400 Fourth Street
Ann Arbor MI 48103-4816
E-mail: mdonahue@glc.org
Internet: http://www.glc.org
AMOUNT: $500
DEADLINE(S): MAR 28
FIELD(S): Electronic Communications Technology

Open to high school seniors and returning students enrolled full-time at a Great Lakes college/university (IL, IN, MI, MN, NY, OH, PA, WI, Ontario, Quebec). Must have a demonstrated interest in the environmental or economic applications of electronic communications technology, exhibit academic excellence, and have a sincere appreciation for the Great Lakes and their protection. Must submit resume, transcripts, recommendations, and essay or Web page on Great Lakes issue.

See Web site or contact Dr. Michael J. Donahue, President/CEO, for an application. Recipient announced by May 1.

1390—LOUISIANA OFFICE OF STUDENT FINANCIAL ASSISTANCE (Rockefeller State Wildlife Scholarships)

P.O. Box 91202
Baton Rouge LA 70821-9202
800/259-5626 ext. 1012 OR 225/922-3258
FAX: 225/922-0790
E-mail: custserv@osfa.state.la.us
Internet: http://www.osfa.state.la.us
AMOUNT: $1,000/year
DEADLINE(S): JUL 1
FIELD(S): Forestry; Wildlife; Marine Science

Open to Louisiana residents pursuing undergraduate or graduate study at a Louisiana public postsecondary institution. Must be U.S. citizen with a minimum 2.5 GPA. Competitive selection. Recipients must obtain a degree in one of the three eligible fields or repay the funds plus interest. Financial need NOT a factor.

60 awards annually. Renewable. Apply by completing the Free Application for Federal Student Aid (FAFSA). Contact Public Information Rep for details.

1391—NATURAL SCIENCES AND ENGINEERING RESEARCH COUNCIL OF CANADA (Undergraduate Scholarships)

Scholarships/Fellowships Division
350 Albert Street
Ottawa Ontario K1A 1H5 CANADA
613/996-2009
FAX: 613/996-2589
E-mail: schol@nserc.ca
Internet: http://www.nserc.ca
AMOUNT: Up to $3,600
DEADLINE(S): Varies
FIELD(S): Natural Sciences, Engineering, Biology, or Chemistry

Open to Canadian citizens or permanent residents working towards degrees in science or engineering. Academic excellence and research aptitude are considerations.

Write for complete information.

1392—NATURAL SCIENCES AND ENGINEERING RESEARCH COUNCIL OF CANADA (Undergraduate Student Research Awards in Small Universities)

350 Albert Street
Ottawa Ontario K1A 1H5 CANADA
613/995-5992
FAX: 613/992-5337
E-mail: schol@nserc.ca
Internet: http://www.nserc.ca/programs/usrasmen.htm
AMOUNT: $3,600 (max.)
DEADLINE(S): Varies
FIELD(S): Natural Sciences; Engineering

Research awards for Canadian citizens/permanent residents attending eligible institutions, and who have no more than 6 and no fewer than 2 academic terms remaining to complete bachelor's degree. Cumulative GPA of at least second class (B). Must be doing full-time in research and development activities during award tenure.

Students in health sciences not eligible. Students with BAs and who are studying for a second may apply.

1393—OUR WORLD-UNDERWATER SCHOLARSHIP SOCIETY (Scholarship and Internships)

200 East Chicago Avenue; Suite 40
Westmont IL 60559-1756
630/986-6990
FAX: 630/986-8098
E-mail: info@owuscholarship.org
Internet: http://www.owuscholarship.org
AMOUNT: $20,000 (experience-based scholarship)
DEADLINE(S): NOV 30
FIELD(S): Marine and Aquatics related disciplines

Must be certified SCUBA divers no younger than 21 and no older than 24 on March 1 of the scholarship year. Cannot have yet received a postgraduate degree. Experiences include active participation in field studies, underwater research, scientific expeditions, laboratory assignments, equipment testing and design, and photographic instruction. Financial need NOT a factor. Funds are used for transportation and minimal living expenses, if necessary.

1 scholarship and several internships annually. Check the Web site for more information or contact the OWU for an application.

1394—PENINSULA COMMUNITY FOUNDATION (Dr. Mary Finegold Scholarship)

1700 S. El Camino Real, #300
San Mateo CA 94402
650/358-9369
FAX: 650/358-9817
Internet: http://www.pcf.org/community_grants/scholarships.html
AMOUNT: $1,000
DEADLINE(S): MAR 7 (5 p.m.)
FIELD(S): Sciences

Scholarships for senior girls graduating from high school in Palo Alto, California, who intend to complete a four-year degree in the sciences. Special consideration will be given to girls who have demonstrated a "pioneering" spirit in that they have not been constrained by stereotypical female roles and to those facing financial hardship.

Award was established in the honor of Dr. Mary Finegold who, after completing her medical studies, elected to stay at home until her youngest child was in high school before beginning her medical practice. She was a school physician.

1395—SAN DIEGO AEROSPACE MUSEUM (Bill Gibbs Scholarship)

Education Dept.
2001 Pan American Plaza
San Diego CA 92101
619/234-8291 ext. 19
FAX: 619/233-4526
Internet: http://aerospacemuseum.org/Scholastic.HTML

AMOUNT: Varies
DEADLINE(S): Varies
FIELD(S): Aerospace: math, physics, science, or engineering

For students who are residents of San Diego County, California, who have an aerospace career interest who have been accepted to a four-year college or university in a degree program relating to math, physics, science, or engineering.

Call or write museum for further information.

1396—SEASPACE (Scholarships)

P.O. Box 3753
Houston TX 77253-3753
E-mail: captx@piovere.com
Internet: http://www.seaspace.org/schship.htm
AMOUNT: $500-$3,000
DEADLINE(S): FEB 1
FIELD(S): Marine/Aquatic Sciences

Open to college juniors, seniors, and graduate students attending school in the U.S. Must have a 3.3/4.0 GPA and demonstrate financial need.

10-15 awards annually. See Web site or contact SEASPACE at above address for an application.

1397—SIEMENS WESTINGHOUSE (Science and Technology Competition)

186 Wood Avenue S.
Iselin NJ 08830
877/822-5233
E-mail: foundation@sc.siemens.com
Internet: http://www.siemens-foundation.org
AMOUNT: $120,000 (max.)
DEADLINE(S): Varies
FIELD(S): Biology; Physical Sciences; Mathematics; Physics; Chemistry; Computer Science; Environmental Science

Open to U.S. high school seniors to pursue independent science research projects, working individually or in teams of 2 or 3 to develop and test their own ideas. May work with one of the universities/laboratories that serve as Siemens' partners. Students from the 50 states, DC, and Territories may compete in one of six geographic areas. Individual and team national prize winners receive a second scholarship award to be applied to undergraduate or graduate education.

See Web site or contact Siemens Foundation for details.

1398—STUDENT CONSERVATION ASSOCIATION (SCA Resource Assistant Program)

P.O. Box 550
Charlestown NH 03603
603/543-1700
FAX: 603/543-1828
E-mail: internships@sca-inc.org
Internet: http://www.sca-inc.org
AMOUNT: $1,180-$4,725
DEADLINE(S): Varies
FIELD(S): Environment and related fields

Must be 18 and U.S. citizen; need not be student. Fields: Agriculture, Archaeology, anthropology, botany, caves, civil/environmental engineering, environmental education, fisheries, forests, herpetology, history, living history/roleplaying, visitor services, landscape architecture/environmental design, paleontology, recreation/ resource/ range management, trail maintenance/construction, wildlife management, geology, hydrology, library/museums, surveying...

900 positions in U.S. and Canada. Send $1 for postage for application; outside U.S./Canada, send $20.

1399—THE DAPHNE JACKSON MEMORIAL FELLOWSHIPS TRUST (Fellowships in Science/Engineering)

School of Physical Sciences,
Dept. of Physics, University of Surrey
Guildford, Surrey GU2 5XH
ENGLAND UK
01483 259166
FAX: 01483 259501
E-mail: J.Woolley@surrey.ac.uk
Internet: http://www.sst.ph.ic.ac.uk/trust/
AMOUNT: Varies
DEADLINE(S): Varies
FIELD(S): Science or Engineering, including Information Sciences

Fellowships to enable well-qualified and highly motivated scientists and engineers to return to appropriate careers following a career break due to family commitments. May be used on a flexible, part-time basis. Tenable at various U.K. universities.

See Web site and/or contact organization for details.

1400—UNCF/MERCK SCIENCE INITIATIVE (Undergraduate Science Research Scholarship Awards)

8260 Willow Oaks Corporate Dr.
P.O. Box 10444
FairFAX: VA 22031-4511
703/205-3503
FAX: 703/205-3574
E-mail: uncfmerck@uncf.org
Internet: http://www.uncf.org/merck
AMOUNT: $25,000/year (max.)
DEADLINE(S): DEC 15
FIELD(S): Life and Physical Sciences

Open to African-Americans in their junior year of college who will receive a bachelor's degree in the following academic year. Must be enrolled full-time in any four-year college/university in the U.S. and have a minimum 3.3 GPA. Must be U.S. citizen/permanent resident. Financial need NOT a factor.

15 awards annually. Not renewable. Contact Jerry Bryant, Ph.D., for an application.

1401—UNITED STATES DEPARTMENT OF AGRICULTURE (1890 National Scholars Program)

14th & Independence Avenue SW;
Room 301-W; Whitten Bldg.
Washington DC 20250-9600
202/720-6905
E-mail: usda-m@fie.com
Internet: http://web.fie.com/htdoc/fed/agr/ars/edu/prog/mti/agrpgaak.htm
AMOUNT: Tuition, employment/benefits, use of pc/software, fees, books, room/board
DEADLINE(S): JAN 15
FIELD(S): Agriculture, Food, or Natural Resource Sciences

For U.S. citizens, high school grad/GED, GPA 3.0+, verbal/math SAT 1000+, composite score 21+ ACT, first-year college student, and attend participating school.

34+ scholarships/year/4 years. Send applications to U.S.D.A. Liaison officer at the 1890 Institution of your choice (see Web page for complete list).

1402—UNIVERSITIES OF GLASGOW AND STRATHCLYDE (Scholarships in Naval Architecture, Ocean Engineering, and Marine Engineering)

Henry Dyer Bldg.
100 Montrose Street
Glasgow G4 0LZ
Scotland UNITED KINGDOM
+44 0141 548 3875
FAX: +44 0141 552 2879
E-mail: s.craufurd@na-me.ac.uk
Internet: http://www.na-me.ac.uk
AMOUNT: 500-1,000 pounds per annum

DEADLINE(S): mid-JAN
FIELD(S): Naval Architecture; Ocean/Offshore Engineering; Marine Engineering

Scholarships for students entering to study in the above fields. Up to 10 bursaries are available, varying in amount. Awards based on merit and performance at an interview. In the second and third years of the course, student may compete for a number of Lloyd's Register Sponsorships, which provide substantial annual bursaries and paid summer employment/training within an organization.

See Web site for further information on the combined programs from these 2 universities. Contact Simon Craufurd, Recruitment Officer, at the above address for information and application forms.

1403—UNIVERSITY OF NEWCASTLE/ Australia (R. M. Sheahan Memorial Undergraduate Scholarship)

Student Administration Unit, Student Services Centre, Univ. of Newcastle, Callaghan NSW
2308 AUSTRALIA
+61-(02)-4921-6539
FAX: +61-(02)-4960-1766
E-mail: scholarships@newcastle.edu.au
Internet: http://www.newcastle.edu.au/services/ousr/stuadmin/schol/index.htm
AMOUNT: $1,000
DEADLINE(S): NOV 1
FIELD(S): Engineering, chemistry, or environmental engineering

Scholarship for undergraduate international as well as Australian students pursuing studies in chemistry, chemical engineering, or environmental engineering. Funded by the Cessnock City Council and Orica (ICI) Explosives, this award is made yearly based on academic merit.

Contact organization for details.

1404—WATER ENVIRONMENT FEDERATION (Canham Graduate Studies Scholarships)

601 Wythe Street
Alexandria VA 22314-1994
703/684-2477 or 800/666-0206
FAX: 703/645-2492
Internet: http://www.wef.org
AMOUNT: $2,000-$2,500
DEADLINE(S): MAR 1
FIELD(S): Water Environment; Water Pollution Control and related fields

Open to graduate students in water environment programs. Must be member of the Water Environment Federation (nominal fee) and commit to working in the environmental field for 2 years following the completion of studies.

2 awards annually. Contact the organization or see Web site for details and application-go to "Membership Benefits" then to "WEF Distinguished Honors and Awards."

1405—WOMAN'S SEAMEN'S FRIEND SOCIETY OF CONNECTICUT, INC. (Scholarships)

291 Whitney Avenue
New Haven CT 06511
203/777-2165
FAX: 203/777-5774
AMOUNT: Varies
DEADLINE(S): MAR 1 (summer); APR 1 (fall/spring)
FIELD(S): Marine Sciences; Merchant Seafarers

Open to Connecticut residents who are merchant seafarers and their dependents attending any institution of higher learning; CT residents studying at state maritime academies; CT residents majoring in marine science in-state or out-of-state; and residents of other states majoring in marine science in CT. Based on financial need, academic achievement, letters of recommendation, and proposed programs of study. Awards also available for graduate work in marine science.

Renewable. Contact Woman's Seamen's Friend Society for applications.

1406—WOODS HOLE OCEANOGRAPHIC INSTITUTION (Summer Student Fellowship)

360 Woods Hole Road
Woods Hole MA 02543-1541
508/289-2219
FAX: 508/457-2188
E-mail: education@whoi.edu
Internet: http://www.whoi.edu
AMOUNT: $355/week stipend for 10-12 weeks, housing, and possible travel allowance
DEADLINE(S): FEB 15
FIELD(S): Science/engineering with interest in ocean sciences

Summer fellowships to study oceanography at the Woods Hole Oceanographic Institution. Open to undergraduates who have completed their junior or senior years. Students with backgrounds in science, math, and engineering with interests in the marine sciences and oceanography are encouraged to apply.

For an application/more information, contact the Education Office, Clark Laboratory 223, MS #31, at above address.

1407—WOODS HOLE OCEANOGRAPHIC INSTITUTION (Traineeships in Oceanography for Minority Group Undergraduates)

360 Woods Hole Road
Woods Hole MA 02543-1541
508/289-2219
FAX: 508/457-2188
E-mail: mgately@whoi.edu
Internet: http://www.whoi.edu
AMOUNT: Varies
DEADLINE(S): FEB 16
FIELD(S): Physical/Natural Sciences, Mathematics, Engineering

For minority undergraduates enrolled in U.S. colleges/universities who have completed at least two semesters. These awards provide training and research experience for students with interests in the above fields. Traineeships may be awarded for a ten- to- twelve-week period in the summer or for a semester during the academic year.

Renewable. For an application/more information, contact the Education Office, Clark Laboratory 223, MS #31, at above address.

NATURAL HISTORY

1408—ALLIANCE FOR YOUNG ARTISTS AND WRITERS, INC./AMERICAN MUSEUM OF NATURAL HISTORY (Young Naturalist Awards)

Scholastic, Inc.
555 Broadway
New York NY 10012-3999
212/343-6582 or 800-SCHOLASTIC
FAX: 212/343-4885
E-mail: A&WGeneralinfo@scholastic.com
Internet: http://www.amnh.org/youngnaturalistawards
AMOUNT: Up to $2,500 + trip to New York to visit AMNH
DEADLINE(S): JAN
FIELD(S): Natural Sciences

For all students in grades 7-12 currently enrolled in a public or nonpublic school in the U.S., Canada, U.S. territories, or U.S.-sponsored schools abroad. Program focuses on finding and rewarding excellence in biology, earth science, astronomy, and cultural studies. Students are encouraged to perform observation-based projects that require creativity, inquiry, and critical analysis. Specific topics vary annually.

48 awards annually. See Web site for application.

1409—AMERICAN CENTER OF ORIENTAL RESEARCH (Jennifer C. Groot Fellowship)

656 Beacon Street, Fifth Floor
Boston MA 02215-2010
617/353-6571
E-mail: acor@bu.edu
Internet: http://www.bu.edu/acor
AMOUNT: $1,500
DEADLINE(S): FEB
FIELD(S): Archaeology

Several awards available for beginners in archaeological fieldwork who have been accepted as staff members on archaeological projects with ASOR/CAP affiliation in Jordan.

Open to undergraduate and graduate students. U.S. or Canadian citizenship required

1410—ASSOCIATION FOR WOMEN IN SCIENCE EDUCATIONAL FOUNDATION (Ruth Satter Memorial Award)

1200 New York Avenue NW, Suite 650
Washington DC 20005
202/326-8940 or 800/886-AWIS
E-mail: awis@awis.org
Internet: http://www.awis.org
AMOUNT: $1,000
DEADLINE(S): JAN 16
FIELD(S): Various Sciences and Social Sciences

Scholarships for female doctoral students who have interrupted their education three years or more to raise a family. Summary page, description of research project, resume, references, transcripts, biographical sketch, and proof of eligibility from department head required. U.S. citizens may attend any graduate institution; noncitizens must be enrolled in U.S. institutions.

See Web site or write to above address for more information or an application.

1411—BRITISH COLUMBIA HERITAGE TRUST (Scholarships)

P.O. Box 9818, Stn Prov Govt.
Victoria BC V8W 9W3 CANADA
250/356-1433
FAX: 250/356-7796
E-mail: heritage@tbc.gov.bc.ca
AMOUNT: $5,000
DEADLINE(S): FEB 1
FIELD(S): British Columbia History; Architecture; Archaeology; Archival Management

Open to graduate students who are Canadian citizens or permanent residents. Criteria are scholarly record and academic performance, educational and career objectives, and proposed program of study.

Write for complete information.

1412—BRITISH INSTITUTE OF ARCHAEOLOGY AT ANKARA (Travel Grants)

10 Carlton House Terrace
London SW1Y 5AH ENGLAND UK
+44-020-7969-5204
FAX: +44-020-7969-5401
E-mail: biaa@britac.ac.uk
Internet: http://www.britac.ac.uk/institutes/ankara/
AMOUNT: 500 pounds sterling (max.)
DEADLINE(S): FEB 1
FIELD(S): Archaeology and Geography of Turkey

Travel grants to enable undergraduate and graduate students to familiarize themselves with the archaeology and geography of Turkey, its museums, and ancient sites. For citizens or residents of the British Commonwealth.

Contact British Institute or check the Web site for an application.

1413—EPILEPSY FOUNDATION OF AMERICA (Behavioral Sciences Student Fellowships)

4351 Garden City Drive
Landover MD 20785-2267
301/459-3700 or 800/EFA-1000
TDD: 800/332-2070
FAX: 301/577-2684
Internet: http://www.epilepsyfoundation.org
AMOUNT: $2,000
DEADLINE(S): FEB 1
FIELD(S): Epilepsy Research/Practice; Sociology; Social Work; Psychology; Anthropology; Nursing; Economics; Vocational Rehabilitation; Counseling; Political Science

Three-month fellowships awarded to undergraduate and graduate students in above fields for work on a project during the summer or other free period. Students propose an epilepsy-related study or training project to be carried out at a U.S. institution of their choice. A preceptor must accept responsibility for supervision of the student and the project.

Contact EFA for an application. Notification by June 1.

1414—FOUNDATION FOR THE ADVANCEMENT OF MESOAMERICAN STUDIES, INC. (Research Grants)

268 S. Suncoast Boulevard
Crystal River FL 34429
352/795-5990
FAX: 352/795-1970
E-mail: famsi@famsi.org
Internet: http://www.famsi.org
AMOUNT: $10,000 (max.)
DEADLINE(S): SEP 30
FIELD(S): Archaeology, Art History, Epigraphy, Linguistics, Ethnography, Sociology

Open to undergraduates, graduates, and postgraduates to pursue research or scholarly works with potential for significant contributions to the understanding of ancient Mesoamerican cultures and continuities thereof among the indigenous cultures in modern Mesoamerica (Mexico, Belize, Guatemala, Honduras, and El Salvador). The foundation encourages interdisciplinary projects.

30-35 awards annually. Renewable. See Web site for an application.

1415—NATURAL SCIENCES AND ENGINEERING RESEARCH COUNCIL OF CANADA (Undergraduate Student Research Awards in Small Universities)

350 Albert Street
Ottawa Ontario K1A 1H5 CANADA
613/995-5992
FAX: 613/992-5337
E-mail: schol@nserc.ca
Internet: http://www.nserc.ca/programs/usrasmen.htm
AMOUNT: $3,600 (max.)
DEADLINE(S): Varies
FIELD(S): Natural Sciences; Engineering

Research awards for Canadian citizens/permanent residents attending eligible institutions, and who have no more than 6 and no fewer than 2 academic terms remaining to complete bachelor's degree. Cumulative GPA of at least second class (B). Must be doing full-time in research and development activities during award tenure.

Students in health sciences not eligible. Students with

B.A. degrees and who are studying for a second may apply.

1416—NAVAL HISTORICAL CENTER (Internship Program)

Washington Navy Yard
901 M Street SE
Washington DC 20374-5060

202/433-6901
FAX: 202/433-8200
E-mail: efurgol@nhc.navy.mil
Internet: http://www.history.navy.mil
AMOUNT: $400 possible honoraria; otherwise, unpaid
DEADLINE(S): None
FIELD(S): Education; History; Public Relations; Design

Registered students of colleges/universities and graduates thereof are eligible for this program, which must be a minimum of 3 weeks, full- or part-time. Four specialties available: Curator, Education, Public Relations, and Design. Interns receive orientation and assist in their departments, and must complete individual project which contributes to Center. Must submit a letter of recommendation, unofficial transcript, and writing sample of not less than 1,000 words.

Contact Dr. Edward M. Furgol, Curator, for an application.

1417—PENINSULA COMMUNITY FOUNDATION (Dr. Mary Finegold Scholarship)

1700 S. El Camino Real, #300
San Mateo CA 94402
650/358-9369
FAX: 650/358-9817
Internet: http://www.pcf.org/community_grants/scholarships.html
AMOUNT: $1,000
DEADLINE(S): MAR 7 (5 p.m.)
FIELD(S): Sciences

Scholarships for senior girls graduating from high school in Palo Alto, California, who intend to complete a four-year degree in the sciences. Special consideration will be given to girls who have demonstrated a "pioneering" spirit in that they have not been constrained by stereotypical female roles and to those facing financial hardship.

Award was established in the honor of Dr. Mary Finegold who, after completing her medical studies, elected to stay at home until her youngest child was in high school before beginning her medical practice. She was a school physician.

1418—ROSE HILL COLLEGE (Louella Robinson Memorial Scholarship)

P.O. Box 3126
Aiken SC 29802-3126
800/684-3769
FAX: 803/641-0240
E-mail: rosehill@rosehill.edu
Internet: http://www.rosehill.edu
AMOUNT: $10,000/year for four years
DEADLINE(S): Varies
FIELD(S): Liberal Arts and Humanities curricula

For undergraduate residents of Indian River County, Florida, to attend Rose Hill College in Aiken, South Carolina. The school offers a liberal arts education and follows the Great Books curriculum, a program of reading and seminars.

One annual award. Applicants must meet entry requirements of RHC. Contact above location for details.

1419—ROSE HILL COLLEGE (Scholarships for Children of Eastern Orthodox Priests/Deacons)

P.O. Box 3126
Aiken SC 29802-3126
800/684-3769
FAX: 803/641-0240
E-mail: rosehill@rosehill.edu
Internet: http://www.rosehill.edu
AMOUNT: Full scholarship: $10,000/year for four years
DEADLINE(S): Varies
FIELD(S): Liberal Arts and Humanities Curricula

For undergraduates who are children of Eastern Orthodox Christian priests or deacons to attend Rose Hill College in Aiken, South Carolina. The school offers a liberal arts education and follows the Great Books Curriculum, a program of reading and seminars.

6-10 annual awards. Applicants must meet entry requirements of RHC. Contact above location for details.

1420—ROSE HILL COLLEGE (Scholarships for the Homeschooled)

P.O. Box 3126
Aiken SC 29802-3126
800/684-3769
FAX: 803/641-0240
E-mail: rosehill@rosehill.edu
Internet: http://www.resehill.edu
AMOUNT: Full scholarship: $10,000/year for four years
DEADLINE(S): Varies
FIELD(S): Liberal Arts and Humanities Curricula

For undergraduates who have been homeschooled for three of the last five years of their high school education. For use at Rose Hill College in Aiken, South Carolina. The school offers a liberal arts education and follows the Great Books Curriculum, a program of reading and seminars. Scholarships will be awarded primarily on the basis of an essay which the student will be asked to write.

Four annual awards. Applicants must meet entry requirements of RHC. Contact above location for details.

1421—SAN DIEGO AEROSPACE MUSEUM (Bill Gibbs Scholarship)

Education Dept.
2001 Pan American Plaza
San Diego CA 92101
619/234-8291 ext. 19
FAX: 619/233-4526
Internet: http://aerospacemuseum.org/Scholastic.html
AMOUNT: Varies
DEADLINE(S): Varies
FIELD(S): Aerospace: math, physics, science, or engineering

For students who are residents of San Diego County, California, who have an aerospace career interest who have been accepted to a four-year college or university in a degree program relating to math, physics, science, or engineering.

Call or write museum for further information.

1422—SMITHSONIAN INSTITUTION (Minority Student Internship Program)

Office of Fellowships
50 9th Street NW, Suite 9300
Washington DC 20560-0902
202/275-0655
FAX: 202/275-0489
E-mail: siofg@ofg.si.edu
Internet: http://www.si.edu/research+study
AMOUNT: $350/week + possible travel expenses
DEADLINE(S): Varies
FIELD(S): Humanities; Environmental and Cultural Studies; Natural History; Earth Science; Art History; Biology

Ten-week, full-time internships in residence at the Smithsonian are open to U.S. minority students who wish to participate in research or museum-related activities in above and related fields. Must be undergraduates or beginning graduate students with a minimum 3.0 GPA. Must submit essay, resume, and official transcript.

Contact the Office of Fellowships or see Web site for an application.

1423—SMITHSONIAN INSTITUTION-COOPER-HEWITT, NATIONAL DESIGN MUSEUM (Peter Krueger Summer Internships)

2 E. 91st Street
New York NY 10128

212/849-8380
FAX: 212/860-6909
E-mail: edu@ch.si.edu
Internet: http://www.si.edu/ndm/
AMOUNT: $2,500 stipend
DEADLINE(S): MAR 15
FIELD(S): Art History; Architectural History; Museum Studies; Museum Education; Design

This ten-week (June-August) internship is open to college students considering a career in one of the above fields as well as graduate students who have not yet completed their M.A. degree. Interns are assigned to specific curatorial, education, or administrative departments where they will assist on special research or exhibition projects, as well as participate in daily museum activities. Housing NOT provided.

To apply, submit resume, transcript, 2 letters of recommendation, and 1-2-page essay on interest. Contact the Intern Coordinator for details. Notification by April 30.

1424—SMITHSONIAN INSTITUTION-FREER/SACKLER GALLERIES (Dick Louie Memorial Internship for Americans of Asian Descent)

Education Dept.
Washington DC 20560-0707
202/357-4880; TTY: 202/786-2374
Internet: http://www.asia.si.edu
AMOUNT: Stipend
DEADLINE(S): Varies
FIELD(S): Asian Art; Art History; Museum Studies

This summer internship is an opportunity for high school students of Asian descent to gain practical experience in a museum setting. Must be entering or completing senior year of high school, and must live and attend high school in the Washington metropolitan area.

Contact the Internship Coordinator for an application.

1425—SOCIETY OF HISPANIC PROFESSIONAL ENGINEERS FOUNDATION (SHPE Scholarships)

5400 E. Olympic Boulevard
Suite 210
Los Angeles CA 90022
323/888-2080
AMOUNT: $500-$3,000
DEADLINE(S): APR 15
FIELD(S): Engineering; Science

Open to deserving students of Hispanic descent who are seeking careers in engineering or science. For full-time undergraduate or graduate study at a college or university. Based on academic achievement and financial need.

Send self-addressed, stamped envelope to above address for an application.

1426—STUDENT CONSERVATION ASSOCIATION (SCA Resource Assistant Program)

P.O. Box 550
Charlestown NH 03603
603/543-1700
FAX: 603/543-1828
E-mail: internships@sca-inc.org
Internet: http://www.sca-inc.org
AMOUNT: $1,180-$4,725
DEADLINE(S): Varies
FIELD(S): Environment and related fields

Must be 18 and U.S. citizen; need not be student. Fields: Agriculture, Archaeology, anthropology, botany, caves, civil/environmental engineering, environmental education, fisheries, forests, herpetology, history, living history/roleplaying, visitor services, landscape architecture/environmental design, paleontology, recreation/ resource/ range management, trail maintenance/construction, wildlife management, geology, hydrology, library/museums, surveying...

900 positions in US & Canada. Send $1 for postage for application; outside U.S./Canada, send $20.

1427—THE LEMMERMANN FOUNDATION (Fondazione Lemmermann Scholarship Awards)

c/o Studio Associato Romanelli
via Cosseria, 5
00192 Roma ITALY
(06) 324.30.23
FAX: (06) 322.17.88
E-mail: lemmermann@mail.nexus.it
Internet: http://www.lemmermann.nexus.it/lemmermann/
AMOUNT: 750 euro per month
DEADLINE(S): MAR 15; SEP 30
FIELD(S): Italian/Roman studies in the subject areas of literature, archaeology, history of art

For university students who need to study in Rome to carry out research and prepare their theses concerning Rome and the Roman culture from the period Pre-Roman to present day time in the subject areas above.

Contact above organization for details. Access Web site for application form.

1428—UNIVERSITY OF NEWCASTLE/Australia (R. M. Sheahan Memorial Undergraduate Scholarship)

Student Administration Unit, Student Services Centre, Univ. of Newcastle, Callaghan NSW
2308 AUSTRALIA
+61-(02)-4921-6539
FAX: +61-(02)-4960-1766
E-mail: scholarships@newcastle.edu.au
Internet: http://www.newcastle.edu.au/services/ousr/stuadmin/schol/index.htm
AMOUNT: $1,000
DEADLINE(S): NOV 1
FIELD(S): Engineering, chemistry, or environmental engineering

Scholarship for undergraduate international as well as Australian students pursuing studies in chemistry, chemical engineering, or environmental engineering. Funded by the Cessnock City Council and Orica (ICI) Explosives, this award is made yearly based on academic merit.

Contact organization for details.

SCHOOL OF SCIENCE

1429—AMERICAN METEOROLOGY SOCIETY INDUSTRY (Undergraduate Scholarships)

45 Beacon Street
Boston MA 02108-3693
617/227-2426
Internet: http://www.ametsoc.org/AMS
AMOUNT: $700-$5,000
DEADLINE(S): Multiple
FIELD(S): Meteorology

Ten scholarship opportunities exist for undergraduates pursuing careers in the atmospheric or related sciences. Must attend an accredited university and maintain a 3.0 GPA.

1430—AIR FORCE RESERVE OFFICER TRAINING CORPS (AFROTC Scholarships)

551 E. Maxwell Boulevard
Maxwell AFB AL 36112-6106
334/953-7783
AMOUNT: Full tuition, books, and fees for all 4 years of college
DEADLINE(S): DEC 1
FIELD(S): Science; Engineering; Business; Political Science; Psychology; Geography; Foreign Studies; Foreign Language

Competitive scholarships based on individual merit to high school seniors and graduates who have not completed any full-time college work. Must be a U.S. citizen between the ages of 17-27. Must also have GPA of 2.5 or above, be in top 40% of class, and complete Applicant Fitness Test. Cannot be a single parent. Your college/university must offer AFROTC.

2,300 awards annually. Contact above address for application packet.

1431—ALPHA KAPPA ALPHA SORORITY INC. (AKA/PIMS Summer Youth Mathematics and Science Camp)

5656 S. Stony Island Avenue
Chicago IL 60637
800/653-6528
Internet: http://www.akaeaf.org

AMOUNT: $1,000 value (for room, board, and travel)
DEADLINE(S): MAY 1
FIELD(S): Mathematics; Science

Open to high school students grades 9-11 who have at least a 'B' average. Essay required for entry. This 2-week camp includes AM classes; PM activities and a minimum of 4 field trips.

30 awards. Write for complete information.

1432—ALVIN M. BENTLEY FOUNDATION (Scholarship Program)

College of Literature, Science, and the Arts
The University of Michigan
500 S. State Street, #2522
Ann Arbor MI 48109
517/729-9040
FAX: 517/723-2454
E-mail: lsascholarship@umich.edu

AMOUNT: $7,500-$10,000 per year
DEADLINE(S): None
FIELD(S): Literature; Science; Arts

Open to Michigan residents applying as freshmen to the University of Michigan's College of Literature, Science, and the Arts. Based on academic excellence and extracurricular activities. Must be nominated; there are no separate applications. Candidates are chosen from U of M applications received from Michigan resident freshmen.

1433—AMERICAN FOUNDATION FOR THE BLIND (Paul W. Ruckes Scholarship)

11 Penn Plaza, Suite 300
New York NY 10001
212/502-7661
FAX: 212/502-7771
E-mail: juliet@afb.org
Internet: http://www.afb.org

AMOUNT: $1,000
DEADLINE(S): APR 30
FIELD(S): Engineering; Computer/Physical/Life Sciences

Open to legally blind and visually impaired undergraduate and graduate students pursuing a degree in one of above fields. Must be U.S. citizen. Must submit written documentation of visual impairment from ophthalmologist or optometrist (need not be legally blind); official transcripts; proof of college/university acceptance; three letters of recommendation; and typewritten statement describing goals, work experience extracurricular activities, and how monies will be used.

1 award annually. See Web site or contact Julie Tucker at AFB for an application.

1434—AMERICAN INDIAN SCIENCE AND ENGINEERING SOCIETY (A.T. Anderson Memorial Scholarship)

P.O. Box 9828
Albuquerque NM 87119-9828
505/765-1052
FAX: 505/765-5608
E-mail: scholarships@aises.org
Internet: http://www.aises.org/scholarships

AMOUNT: $1,000-$2,000
DEADLINE(S): JUN 15
FIELD(S): Medicine; Natural Resources; Science; Engineering

Open to undergraduate and graduate students who are at least 1/4 American Indian or recognized as member of a tribe. Must be member of AISES ($10 fee), enrolled full-time at an accredited institution, and demonstrate financial need.

Renewable. See Web site or contact Patricia Browne for an application and/or membership information.

1435—AMERICAN INDIAN SCIENCE AND ENGINEERING SOCIETY (Burlington Northern Santa Fe Pacific Foundation Scholarships)

P.O. Box 9828
Albuquerque NM 87119-9828
505/765-1052
FAX: 505/765-5608
E-mail: scholarships@aises.org
Internet: http://www.aises.org/scholarships

AMOUNT: $2,500/year
DEADLINE(S): MAR 31
FIELD(S): Business; Education; Science; Engineering; Health Administration

Open to high school seniors who are at least 1/4 American Indian. Must reside in KS, OK, CO, AZ, NM, MN, ND, OR, SD, WA, MT, or San Bernardino County, CA (Burlington Northern and Santa Fe Pacific service areas). Must demonstrate financial need.

5 awards annually. Renewable up to 4 years. See Web site or contact Patricia Browne for an application.

1436—AMERICAN INDIAN SCIENCE AND ENGINEERING SOCIETY (A.T. Anderson Memorial Scholarship)

P.O. Box 9828
Albuquerque NM 87119-9828
505/765-1052
FAX: 505/765-5608
E-mail: scholarships@aises.org
Internet: http://www.aises.org/scholarships

AMOUNT: $1,000-$2,000
DEADLINE(S): JUN 15
FIELD(S): Medicine; Natural Resources; Science; Engineering

Open to undergraduate and graduate students who are at least 1/4 American Indian or recognized as member of a tribe. Must be member of AISES ($10 fee), enrolled full-time at an accredited institution, and demonstrate financial need.

Renewable. See Web site or contact Patricia Browne for an application and/or membership information.

1437—ASSOCIATED WESTERN UNIVERSITIES, INC. (AWU Undergraduate Student Fellowships)

4190 S. Highland Drive, Suite 211
Salt Lake City UT 84124-2600
801/273-8900
FAX: 801/277-5632
E-mail: info@awu.org
Internet: http://www.awu.org

AMOUNT: $300/week stipend + possible travel allowance
DEADLINE(S): FEB 1
FIELD(S): Science; Mathematics; Engineering; Technology

Eight- to sixteen-week fellowships.

1438—ASTRONAUT SCHOLARSHIP FOUNDATION (Scholarships)

Exec. Director
6225 Vectorspace Boulevard
Titusville FL 32780

321/269-6119
FAX: 321/267-3970
E-mail: MercurySvn@aol.com;
Internet: http://www.astronaut scholarship.org/guidelines.html
AMOUNT: Varies
DEADLINE(S): Varies
FIELD(S): Engineering and Physical Sciences (Medical Research ok, but NOT Professional Medicine)

Open to juniors, seniors, and graduate students at a select group of schools. Must be U.S. citizen with the intention to pursue research or advance field of study upon completion of final degree. Special consideration given to students who have shown initiative, creativity, excellence, and/or resourcefulness in their field. Must be NOMINATED by faculty or staff.

See Web site for list of eligible schools. Contact Howard Benedict, Executive Director, for details.

1439—CAREER OPPORTUNITIES FOR YOUTH, INC. (Collegiate Scholarship Program)

P.O. Box 996
Manhattan Beach CA 90266
310/535-4838
AMOUNT: $250 to $1,000
DEADLINE(S): SEP 30
FIELD(S): Engineering, Science, Mathematics, Computer Science, Business Administration, Education, Nursing

For students of Latino/Hispanic background residing in the Southern California area who have completed at least one semester/quarter of study at an accredited four-year university. Must have a cumulative GPA of 2.5 or higher.

Priority will be given to students who demonstrate financial need. Send SASE to above location for details.

1440—CHICAGO ROOFING CONTRACTORS ASSOCIATION (Scholarship)

4415 W. Harrison Street, #322
Hillside IL 60162
708/449-3340
FAX: 708/449-0837
E-mail: crcainfo@crca.org
Internet: http://www.crca.org
AMOUNT: $2,000
DEADLINE(S): Varies
FIELD(S): Business; Engineering; Architecture; Liberal Arts; Sciences

Open to high school seniors who reside in one of the eight counties in Northern Illinois: Cook, DuPage, Lake, Kane, Kendall, DeKalb, McHenry, or Will. Must be accepted as a full-time student in a four-year college/university to pursue a degree in one of the above fields. Must be U.S. citizen. Based on academic achievements extracurricular activites, and community involvement.

Renewable. Contact CRCA for an application.

1441—CIVIL AIR PATROL (CAP Undergraduate Scholarships)

Civil Air Patrol
National Headquarters
Maxwell AFB AL 36112-6332
334/953-5315
AMOUNT: $750
DEADLINE(S): JAN 31
FIELD(S): Humanities; Science; Engineering; Education

Open to CAP members who have received the Billy Mitchell Award or the senior rating in Level II of the senior training program. For undergraduate study in the above areas.

Write for complete information.

1442—COMMUNITY FOUNDATION OF WESTERN MASSACHUSETTS (Nate McKinney Memorial Scholarship)

1500 Main Street
P.O. Box 15769
Springfield MA 01115
413/732-2858
AMOUNT: $1,000
DEADLINE(S): APR 15
FIELD(S): Music; Athletics; Science

Open to graduating seniors of Gateway Regional High School in Huntington, Massachusetts. Recipient must excel academically, demonstrate good citizenship, and have a strong interest in at least two of the following areas: music, science, and athletics. Based on financial need, academic merit, and extracurricular activities. Must submit transcripts and fill out government FAFSA form.

1 award annually. Renewable up to 4 years with reapplication. Contact Community Foundation for an application and your financial aid office for FAFSA. Notification is in June.

1443—COMMUNITY FOUNDATION SILICON VALLEY (Valley Scholars Program)

111 W. Saint John Street, Suite 230
San Jose CA 95113
408/278-0270
FAX: 408/278-0280
Internet: http://www.cfsv.org
AMOUNT: $20,000 (over 4 years of college)
DEADLINE(S): Varies (early spring)
FIELD(S): Science and/or Math

A scholarship program for public high school students in the Silicon Valley (San Mateo and Santa Clara counties and Fremont Union High school District, California) who have demonstrated enthusiasm and aptitude for science and math. Must be U.S. citizen or permanent resident.

Up to 20 students are selected each year. Each Valley Scholar receives financial support, guidance through the college admission process, and a mentor whose interests match their own. Students may apply during their sophomore year of high school and must be academically outstanding.

1444—COUNCIL OF ENERGY RESOURCE TRIBE (CERT)

1999 Broadway, Suite 2600
Denver CO 80202
303/282-7576
AMOUNT: $1,000 per year
DEADLINE(S): JUL 1
FIELD(S): Science, Engineering, or Business

Only for applicants who are members of the T.R.I.B.E.S. program their senior year in high school. TRIBES enrollment is limited to ensure a quality experience for each student. To qualify for TRIBES, students must be graduating seniors, plan to attend a college in the fall, and be interested in business, engineering, science, or related fields. Indian students who wish to attend TRIBES may contact CERT for information and an application.

1445—DAVIDSON INSTITUTE FOR TALENT DEVELOPMENT (Fellows Award)

9665 Gateway Drive, Suite B
Reno NV 89511
775/852-DITD
FAX: 1/775-852-2184
E-mail: mcapurro@ditd.org
Internet: http://www.ditd.org/
AMOUNT: $10,000-$50,000
DEADLINE(S): MAR 29
FIELD(S): Science

Must complete a piece of work that demonstrates the applicant's ability in the field of science. Submissions may include a formal research report and computer models.

1446—FANNIE AND JOHN HERTZ FOUNDATION (Hertz Foundation Graduate Fellowship)

Box 5032
Livermore CA 94551-5032
925/373-1642
Internet: http://www.hertzfoundation.org

AMOUNT: $25,000 annual stipend + tuition and fees
DEADLINE(S): OCT
FIELD(S): Science

Eligible applicants for Hertz Fellowships must be students of the applied physical sciences who are citizens or permanent residents of the United States of America, and who are willing to morally commit to make their skills available to the United States in time of national emergency.

1447—FREEDOM FROM RELIGION FOUNDATION (Student Essay Contest)

P.O. Box 750
Madison WI 53701
608/256-5800
Internet: http://www.infidels.org/org/ffrf

AMOUNT: $1,000; $500; $250
DEADLINE(S): JUL 15
FIELD(S): Humanities; English; Education; Philosophy; Science

Essay contest on topics related to church-state entanglement in public schools or growing up a "freethinker" in religious-oriented society. Topics change yearly, but all are on general theme of maintaining separation of church and state. New topics available in February. For high school seniors and currently enrolled college/technical students. Must be U.S. citizen.

Send SASE to address above for complete information. Please indicate whether wanting information for college competition or high school. Information will be sent when new topics are announced each February. See Web site for details.

1448—GENERAL LEARNING COMMUNICATIONS (DuPont Challenge Science Essay Awards Program)

900 Skokie Boulevard, Suite 200
Northbrook IL 60062-4028
847/205-3000
FAX: 847/564-8197
Internet: http://www.glcomm.com/dupont

AMOUNT: $1,500 (max.)
DEADLINE(S): JAN 28
FIELD(S): Science and Technology

Annual essay competition open to students in grades 7-12 in the U.S. and Canada. Cash awards for first, second, and honorable mention. First-place essayists in each of two divisions, their science teacher, and a parent of each receive a trip to the Space Center Houston/NASA at the end of April.

102 awards annually. See Web site or contact your science teacher or GLC for official entry blank.

1449—GEORGE BIRD GRINNELL AMERICAN INDIAN CHILDREN'S FUND (Al Qoyawayma Award)

11602 Montague Ct.
Potomac MD 20854
301/424-2440
FAX: 301/424-8281
E-mail: Grinnell_Fund@MSN.com

AMOUNT: $1,000
DEADLINE(S): JUN 1
FIELD(S): Science; Engineering

Open to Native American undergraduate and graduate students majoring in science or engineering and who have demonstrated an outstanding interest and skill in any one of the arts. Must be American Indian/Alaska Native (documented with Certified Degree of Indian Blood), be enrolled in college/university, be able to demonstrate commitment to serving community or other tribal nations, and document financial need.

Contact Dr. Paula M. Mintzies, President, for an application after January 1.

1450—GERBER SCIENTIFIC, INC. (H. Joseph Gerber Vision Scholarship Program)

83 Gerber Road West
South Windsor CT 06074
860/648-8027
Internet: http://www.gerberscientific.com

AMOUNT: Varies
DEADLINE(S): MAR 15
FIELD(S): Engineering, Mathematics, Computer Science, Natural Sciences

Scholarship program for high school seniors in Connecticut.

Fifty scholarships to be awarded.

1451—IRON & STEEL SOCIETY FOUNDATION SCHOLARSHIPS

186 Thorn Hill Road
Warrendale PA 15086-7528
724/776-1535

AMOUNT: $2000
DEADLINE(S): APR
FIELD(S): Science

Applicant should have a genuine interest in a career in ferrous-related industries as demonstrated by internship, co-op, or related experiences and/or demonstrable plans to pursue such experience during college.

1452—JEWISH FEDERATION OF METROPOLITAN CHICAGO (Academic Scholarship Program for Studies in the Sciences)

One South Franklin Street
Chicago IL 60606
Written Inquiry

AMOUNT: Varies
DEADLINE(S): MAR 1
FIELD(S): Mathematics, Engineering, or Science

Scholarships for college juniors, seniors, and graduate students who are Jewish and are residents of Chicago, IL and Cook County.

Academic achievement and financial need are considered. Applications accepted after Dec. 1.

1453—JOSEPH BLAZEK FOUNDATION (Scholarships)

8 S. Michigan Avenue
Chicago IL 60603
312/236-3882

AMOUNT: $1,000/year
DEADLINE(S): MAR 15
FIELD(S): Science; Chemistry; Engineering; Mathematics; Physics

Open to residents of Cook County, Illinois, who are high school seniors planning to study at a four-year college/university.

Renewable. Contact Foundation for an application.

1454—JUNIATA COLLEGE (Robert Steele Memorial Scholarship)

Office of Student Financial Planning
Juniata College
1700 Moore Street
Huntingdon PA 16652
814/641-3142
FAX: 814/641-5311
Internet: http://www.juniata.edu/
E-mail: clarkec@juniata.edu

AMOUNT: $4,000 (max.)
DEADLINE(S): APR 1
FIELD(S): Science; Medical Studies

Open to science/medical students applying to Juniata College. Must demonstrate financial need and fill out government FAFSA form.

Contact Randy Rennell, Director of Student Financial Planning, for an application or enrollment information. See your financial aid office for FAFSA.

1455—KOREAN-AMERICAN SCIENTISTS AND ENGINEERS ASSOCIATION (KSEA Scholarships)

1952 Gallows Road, Suite 300
Vienna VA 22182
703/748-1221
FAX: 703/748-1331
E-mail: admin@ksea.org
Internet: http://www.ksea.org

AMOUNT: $1,000
DEADLINE(S): FEB 28
FIELD(S): Science, Engineering, or Medicine

Scholarships to encourage Korean-American students to study in a science, engineering, or pre-med discipline and to recognize high-performing students. Must have graduated from a high school in the U.S.

5 to 8 awards yearly. Must be a student member of KSEA or a child of a member.

1456—MARYLAND HIGHER EDUCATION COMMISSION (Maryland Science and Technology Scholarship Program)

16 Francis Street
Annapolis Park MD 21401
410/974-5370 or 800/974-1024
E-mail: ssamail@mhec.state.md.us
Internet: http://www.mhec.state.md.us/SSA/stech_qa.htm

AMOUNT: $3,000/year (BA); $1,000/year (AA)
DEADLINE(S): None
FIELD(S): Computer Science; Engineering; Technology

Scholarships for college-bound Maryland high school seniors who will major in one of the above fields and who are accepted to an eligible associate or bachelor's degree program in Maryland. The deadline was not known at this writing, so check for deadline date. Must agree to work in the state after graduation in a related field, one year for each year of assistance received.

Must maintain a 3.0 GPA.

1457—NATIONAL AERONAUTICS AND SPACE ADMINISTRATION (ACCESS Internships)

Stennis Space Center, Bldg. 1100
Bay Saint Louis MS 39529
228/688-2079
E-mail: covington.pamela@ssc.nasa.gov

AMOUNT: Internship only
DEADLINE(S): None
FIELD(S): Aeronautics/Aerospace; Astronomy; Chemistry; Physics; Engineering; Math; Earth, Life, Materials, Computer, and Physical Sciences

Nine- to ten-week summer internships are open to undergraduates with physical or learning disabilities who maintain a minimum 3.0 GPA and are U.S. citizens. Purpose is to increase the number of students with disabilities pursuing technical degrees related to NASA's mission and to provide on-site experience. Internship takes place at the Stennis Space Center in Mississippi.

Contact Pam Covington for an application.

1458—NATIONAL SCIENCES AND ENGINEERING RESEARCH COUNCIL OF CANADA (Undergraduate Scholarships)

Scholarships/Fellowships Division
350 Albert Street
Ottawa Ontario K1A 1H5 CANADA
613/996-2009
FAX: 613/996-2589
E-mail: schol@nserc.ca
Internet: http://www.nserc.ca

AMOUNT: Up to $3,600
DEADLINE(S): Varies
FIELD(S): Natural Sciences, Engineering, Biology, or Chemistry

Open to Canadian citizens or permanent residents working towards degrees in science or engineering. Academic excellence and research aptitude are considerations.

Write for complete information.

1459—NATIONAL SPACE CLUB (Dr. Robert H. Goddard Scholarship)

2000 L Street NW, Suite 710
Washington DC 20036-4907
202/973-8661

AMOUNT: $10,000
DEADLINE(S): JAN 8
FIELD(S): Science and Engineering

Open to undergraduate juniors and seniors and graduate students who have scholastic plans leading to future participation in the aerospace sciences and technology. Must be U.S. citizen. Award based on transcript, letters of recommendation, accomplishments, scholastic plans, and proven past research and participation in space-related science and engineering. Personal need is considered, but is not controlling.

Renewable. Send a self-addressed, stamped envelope for more information.

1460—NATIONAL SPACE CLUB (Dr. Robert H. Goddard Historical Essay Award)

2000 L Street NW, Suite 710
Washington DC 20036-4907
202/973-8661

AMOUNT: $1,000 + plaque
DEADLINE(S): DEC 4
FIELD(S): Aerospace History

Essay competition open to any U.S. citizen on a topic dealing with any significant aspect of the historical development of rocketry and astronautics. Essays should not exceed 5,000 words and should be fully documented. Will be judged on originality and scholarship.

Previous winners not eligible. Send self-addressed, stamped envelope for complete information.

1461—NATIONAL TECHNICAL ASSOCIATION, INC. (Scholarship Competitions for Minorities and Women in Science and Engineering)

5810 Kingstowne Ctr., #120221
Alexandria VA 22315-5711
E-mail: ntamfj1@aol.com
Internet: http://www.huenet.com/nta

AMOUNT: $500-$5,000
DEADLINE(S): Varies
FIELD(S): Science; Mathematics; Engineering; Applied Technology

Scholarship competitions for minorities and women pursuing degrees in the above fields. Additional scholarships are available through local chapters of NTA.

See Web site or write to above address for details and for locations of local chapters.

1462—NATIVE AMERICAN SCHOLARSHIP FUND, INC. (Scholarships)

8200 Mountain Road NE, Suite 203
Albuquerque NM 87110
505/262-2351

FAX: 505/262-0543
E-mail: NScholarsh@aol.com
AMOUNT: Varies
DEADLINE(S): MAR 15; APR 15; SEP 15
FIELD(S): Math; Engineering; Science; Business; Education; Computer Science

Open to American Indians or Alaskan Natives (1/4 degree or more) enrolled as members of a federally recognized, state recognized, or terminated tribe. For graduate or undergraduate study at an accredited four-year college or university.

208 awards annually. Contact Lucille Kelley, Director of Recruitment, for an application.

1463—NUCLEAR ENGINEERING EDUCATION FOR THE DISADVANTAGED PROGRAM (NEED)

American Nuclear Society
555 North Kensington Avenue
La Grange Park IL 60526-5592
708/352-6611
E-mail: nucleus@ans.org
Internet: http://www.ans.org
AMOUNT: $3500
DEADLINE(S): MAR
FIELD(S): Science

For disadvantaged students interested in pursuing studies in nuclear science with the intent of developing those studies into a career.

1464—OFFICE OF NAVAL RESEARCH (NSAP-Naval Science Awards Program)

Arlington VA 22217-5660
800/422-6727 or 703/696-5787
E-mail: thurmab@onrhq.onr.navy.mil
Internet: http://www.onr.navy.mil or http://www.jshs.org
AMOUNT: $2,000-$20,000
DEADLINE(S): Varies (established by individual regional, state, and district science fairs)
FIELD(S): Science; Engineering

For high school students (grades 9-12) who participate in a regional/district/state science fair. Winners can participate in Junior Science and Humanities Symposia (JSHS) Program. Awards also offered in each of 14 categories at International Science and Engineering Fair (ISEF), sponsored by Science Service, Inc. Must be U.S. citizen or permanent resident.

24 awards annually. Renewable. See Web site or contact Mrs. Barbara M. Thurman (Project Officer) at address above for complete information on NSAP, ISEF, and JSHS.

1465—OKLAHOMA MEDICAL RESEARCH FOUNDATION (Sir Alexander Fleming Scholar Program)

825 N.E.13th Street
Oklahoma City OK 73104-5046
405/271-8537 or 800/522-0211 (in-state)
Internet: http://www.omrf.ouhsc.edu
AMOUNT: $2,500 salary + housing
DEADLINE(S): Feb 15
FIELD(S): Sciences

Summer scholarship program (June and July) for Oklahoma students who have completed their junior year of high school through those in their junior year of college at time of application. Excellent academic standing and aptitude in science and math are essential. Students will work in the laboratories of the above organization. Research projects will be selected from: alcoholism/liver disease, arthritis/immunology, carcinogenesis, cardiovascular biology, and more.

Named for the scientist who discovered penicillin and dedicated OMRF in 1949. Contact organization for further information and application forms.

1466—SAN DIEGO AEROSPACE MUSEUM (Bill Gibbs Scholarship)

Education Dept.
2001 Pan American Plaza
San Diego CA 92101
619/234-8291 ext. 19
FAX: 619/233-4526
Internet: http://aerospacemuseum.org/Scholastic.HTML
AMOUNT: Varies
DEADLINE(S): Varies
FIELD(S): Aerospace: math, physics, science, or engineering

For students who are residents of San Diego County, California, who have an aerospace career interest who have been accepted to a four-year college or university in a degree program relating to math, physics, science, or engineering.

Call or write museum for further information.

1467—SCIENCE SERVICE (Discovery Young Scientist Challenge)

1719 N Street NW
Washington DC 20036
202/785-2255
FAX: 202/785-1243
E-mail: dkruft@sciserv.org
Internet: http://www.sciserv.org
AMOUNT: Varies
DEADLINE(S): JUN
FIELD(S): Science; Math; Engineering

Open to middle schoolers (5th-8th grades) who win their regional or state science fair. Enables students to participate in a national science competition that emphasizes the student's ability to communicate about science. Must be U.S. citizen and be nominated by the fair director in order to apply.

Contact Danielle Kruft at Science Service for DYSC nomination procedures.

1468—SCIENCE SERVICE (Intel International Science and Engineering Fair)

1719 N Street NW
Washington DC 20036
202/785-2255
FAX: 202/785-1243
E-mail: jkim@sciserv.org
Internet: http://www.sciserv.org
AMOUNT: Varies (totaling $2 million)
DEADLINE(S): DEC 1
FIELD(S): Science; Math; Engineering

Open to high school students (grades 9-12) who participate in this worldwide science competition. Scholarships, internships with noted scientists, and travel and equipment grants are awarded.

Contact Jinny Kim at Science Service for official ISEF entry book. Sponsored by the Intel Corporation.

1469—SCIENCE SERVICE (Intel International Science and Engineering Fair)

1719 N Street NW
Washington DC 20036
202/785-2255
FAX: 202/785-1243
E-mail: jkim@sciserv.org
Internet: http://www.sciserv.org
AMOUNT: Varies (totaling $2 million)
DEADLINE(S): DEC 1
FIELD(S): Science; Math; Engineering

Open to high school students (grades 9-12) who participate in this worldwide science competition. Scholarships, internships with noted scientists, and travel and equipment grants are awarded.

Contact Jinny Kim at Science Service for official ISEF entry book. Sponsored by the Intel Corporation.

1470—SIEMENS WESTINGHOUSE (Science and Technology Competition)

186 Wood Avenue S.
Iselin NJ 08830
877/822-5233
E-mail: foundation@sc.siemens.com
Internet: http://www.siemens-foundation.org

AMOUNT: $120,000 (max.)
DEADLINE(S): Varies
FIELD(S): Biology; Physical Sciences; Mathematics; Physics; Chemistry; Computer Science; Environmental Science

Open to U.S. high school seniors to pursue independent science research projects, working individually or in teams of 2 or 3 to develop and test their own ideas. May work with one of the universities/laboratories that serve as Siemens' partners. Students from the 50 states, DC, and Territories may compete in one of six geographic areas. Individual and team national prize winners receive a second scholarship award to be applied to undergraduate or graduate education.

See Web site or contact Siemens Foundation for details.

1471—SKIDMORE COLLEGE (Porter Presidential Scholarships in Science and Math)

Office of Admissions
815 North Broadway
Saratoga Springs NY 12866-1632
800/867-6007
E-mail: admissions@skidmore.edu
Internet: http://www.skidmore.edu/administration/financial_aid/porter_scholarship.htm

AMOUNT: $10,000/year
DEADLINE(S): JAN 15
FIELD(S): Math, Science, or Computer Science

Scholarships for students excelling in the above fields. Awards are based on talent, not financial need. Recipients are not required to major in a scientific or mathematical discipline, but they will be expected to demonstrate serious research in one or more of these areas.

Five scholarships per year. For more information, visit Web site.

1472—SOCIETY OF HISPANIC PROFESSIONAL ENGINEERS FOUNDATION (SHPE Scholarships)

5400 E. Olympic Boulevard, Suite 210
Los Angeles CA 90022
323/888-2080

AMOUNT: $500-$3,000
DEADLINE(S): APR 15
FIELD(S): Engineering; Science

Open to deserving students of Hispanic descent who are seeking careers in engineering or science. For full-time undergraduate or graduate study at a college or university. Based on academic achievement and financial need.

Send self-addressed, stamped envelope to above address for an application.

1473—SOCIETY OF HISPANIC PROFESSIONAL ENGINEERS FOUNDATION (SHPE Scholarships)

5400 E. Olympic Boulevard, Suite 210
Los Angeles CA 90022
323/888-2080

AMOUNT: $500-$3,000
DEADLINE(S): APR 15
FIELD(S): Engineering; Science

Open to deserving students of Hispanic descent who are seeking careers in engineering or science. For full-time undergraduate or graduate study at a college or university. Based on academic achievement and financial need.

Send self-addressed, stamped envelope to above address for an application.

1474—SPACE COAST CREDIT UNION (Two-Year Scholarships)

Marketing Dept.
P.O. Box 2470
Melbourne FL 32902
Internet: http://www.sccu.com/scholarship/

AMOUNT: $750/year, two years; $1,000 bonus if go on for Bachelor's
DEADLINE(S): APR 15
FIELD(S): Math, Economics, Science, Computer Science, Marketing, Journalism, Political Science

Must be graduating from a high school in Brevard, Volusia, Flagler, or Indian River counties, be a member of SCCU, have a minimum 3.0 GPA, planning to attend a two-year Florida institution of higher education for an associates degree, and be willing to write a 200-word essay on the topic "Why credit unions are valuable to society."

Four annual awards. Students going on to complete a four-year degree could be eligible for a bonus scholarship of $1,000 for the next two years. For membership information or an application, see our Web page or write to the above address.

1475—THE BRITISH COUNCIL (Scholarships for Citizens of Mexico)

10 Spring Gardens
London SW1A 2BN ENGLAND UK
+44 (0) 171 930 8466
FAX: +44 (0) 161 957 7188
E-mail: education.enquiries@britcoun.org
Internet: http://www.britcoun.org/mexico/mexschol.htm

AMOUNT: Varies
DEADLINE(S): Varies
FIELD(S): Social Sciences, Applied Sciences, Technology

The British Council in Mexico offers approximately 100 scholarships per year in the above fields for undergraduates and graduates to study in the United Kingdom. Good level of English language retired.

The Web site listed here gives more details. For more information, contact: leticia.magana@bc-mexico.sprint.com. or contact organization in London.

1476—THE NORWAY-AMERICA ASSOCIATION (The Norwegian Marshall Fund)

Drammensveien 20C
N-0255 Oslo 2 NORWAY
011 47-22-44-76-83

AMOUNT: Up to $5,000
DEADLINE(S): Varies
FIELD(S): All fields of study

The Marshall Fund was established in 1977 as a token of Norway's gratitude to the U.S. for support after World War Two. Objective is to promote research in Norway by Americans in science and humanities. For U.S. citizens.

Contact above location for further information.

1477—THE WALT DISNEY COMPANY (American Teacher Awards)

P.O. Box 9805
Calabasas CA 91372

AMOUNT: $2,500 (36 awards); $25,000 (Outstanding Teacher of the Year)
DEADLINE(S): FEB 15
FIELD(S): Teachers: Athletic Coach, Early Childhood, English, Foreign Language/ESL, General Elementary, Mathematics, Performing Arts, Physical Education/Health, Science, Social Studies, Visual Arts, Voc/Tech Education

Awards for K-12 teachers in the above fields.

Teachers, or anyone who knows a great teacher, can write for applications at the above address.

1478—U.S. DEPARTMENT OF DEFENSE (High School Apprenticeship Program)

U.S. Army Cold Regions Research and Engineering Laboratory
72 Lyme Road
Hanover NH 03755
603/646-4500; DSN: 220-4500;
FAX: 603/646-4693;
Internet: http://www.acq.osd.mil/ddre/edugate/s-aindx.html
AMOUNT: Internship
DEADLINE(S): None specified
FIELD(S): Sciences and Engineering

A teacher must recommend you for these three competitive high school apprenticeships with our Laboratory. High school students from New Hampshire who are at least 16 and who have completed their junior year in high school are eligible. Should have interest and ability in science, engineering, or mathematics.

Applications are available from participating local high school guidance counselors. Contact Susan Koh at the above address for more information.

1479—U.S. DEPARTMENT OF DEFENSE (SEAP Science and Engineering Apprenticeship Program)

707 22nd Street NW
Washington DC 20052
202/994-2234
FAX: 202/994-2459
Internet: http://www.acq.osd.mil/ddre/edugate/ceeindx.htm/#A010
AMOUNT: $1,400 (min.)
DEADLINE(S): JAN 26
FIELD(S): Science; Engineering

Eight-week summer apprenticeships throughout the U.S. are available to high school students who are U.S. citizens planning careers in science or engineering. Based on grades, science/math courses taken, scores on standardized tests, areas of interest, teacher recommendations, and personal student statement. Students responsible for transportation to and from site.

See Web site or contact M. Phillips for an application. Refer to Code #A010.

1480—UNCF/MERCK SCIENCE INITIATIVE (Undergraduate Science Research Scholarship Awards)

8260 Willow Oaks Corporate Drive
P.O. Box 10444
FairFAX: VA 22031-4511
703/205-3503
FAX: 703/205-3574
E-mail: uncfmerck@uncf.org
Internet: http://www.uncf.org/merck
AMOUNT: $25,000/year (max.)
DEADLINE(S): DEC 15
FIELD(S): Life and Physical Sciences

Open to African-Americans in their junior year of college who will receive a bachelor's degree in the following academic year. Must be enrolled full-time in any four-year college/university in the U.S. and have a minimum 3.3 GPA. Must be U.S. citizen/permanent resident. Financial need NOT a factor.

15 awards annually. Not renewable. Contact Jerry Bryant, Ph.D., for an application.

1481—UNIVERSITY OF MARYLAND (John B. and Ida Slaughter Endowed Scholarship in Science, Technology, and the Black Community)

2169 Lefrak Hall
College Park MD 20742-7225
301/405-1158
FAX: 301/314-986
Internet: http://www.bsos.umd.edu/aasp/scholarship.html
AMOUNT: Varies (in-state tuition costs)
DEADLINE(S): MAR
FIELD(S): Science and Technology AND African-American Studies

Open to African-Americans who are U.S. residents with a minimum 2.8 GPA. Must be accepted to or enrolled at UMCP for freshmen year and must submit letter of recommendation from high school counselor or UMCP faculty member. Should have an interest in applying science and technology to the problems of the Black community. Essay required.

Renewable. Contact the Center for Minorities in Science and Engineering at UMCP for an application.

1482—UNIVERSITY OF NEWCASTLE/Australia (R. M. Sheahan Memorial Undergraduate Scholarship)

Student Administration Unit
Student Services Centre
Univ. of Newcastle, Callaghan NSW 2308 AUSTRALIA
+61-(02)-4921-6539
FAX: +61-(02)-4960-1766
E-mail: scholarships@newcastle.edu.au
Internet: http://www.newcastle.edu.au/services/ousr/stuadmin/schol/index.htm
AMOUNT: $1,000
DEADLINE(S): NOV 1
FIELD(S): Engineering, chemistry, or environmental engineering

Scholarship for undergraduate international as well as Australian students pursuing studies in chemistry, chemical engineering, or environmental engineering. Funded by the Cessnock City Council and Orica (ICI) Explosives, this award is made yearly based on academic merit.

Contact organization for details.

1483—WOODROW WILSON NATIONAL FELLOWSHIP FOUNDATION (Leadership Program for Teachers)

CN 5281
Princeton NJ 08543-5281
609/452-700
FAX: 609/452-0066
E-mail: marchioni@woodrow.org or irish@woodrow.org
Internet: http://www.woodrow.org
AMOUNT: Varies
DEADLINE(S): Varies
FIELD(S): Science; Mathematics

WWLPT offers summer institutes for middle and high school teachers in science and mathematics. One- and two-week teacher outreach, TORCH Institutes, are held in the summer throughout the U.S.

See Web site or contact WWNFF for an application.

1484—WOODS HOLE OCEANOGRAPHIC INSTITUTION (Traineeships in Oceanography for Minority Group Undergraduates)

360 Woods Hole Road
Woods Hole MA 02543-1541
508/289-2219
FAX: 508/457-2188
E-mail: mgately@whoi.edu
Internet: http://www.whoi.edu
AMOUNT: Varies
DEADLINE(S): FEB 16
FIELD(S): Physical/Natural Sciences, Mathematics, Engineering

For minority undergraduates enrolled in U.S. colleges/universities who have completed at least two semesters. These awards provide training and research experience for students with interests in the above fields. Traineeships may be awarded for a ten- to- twelve-week period in the summer or for a semester during the academic year.

Renewable. For an application/more information, contact the Education Office, Clark Laboratory 223, MS #31, at above address.

BIOLOGY

1485—ALLIANCE FOR YOUNG ARTISTS AND WRITERS, INC./AMERICAN MUSEUM OF NATURAL HISTORY (Young Naturalist Awards)

Scholastic, Inc.; 555 Broadway
New York NY 10012-3999
212/343-6582 or 800-SCHOLASTIC
FAX: 212/343-4885
E-mail: A&WGeneralinfo@scholastic.com
Internet: http://www.amnh.org/youngnaturalistawards

AMOUNT: Up to $2,500 + trip to New York to visit AMNH
DEADLINE(S): JAN
FIELD(S): Natural Sciences

For all students in grades 7-12 currently enrolled in a public or nonpublic school in the U.S., Canada, U.S. territories, or U.S.-sponsored schools abroad. Program focuses on finding and rewarding excellence in biology, earth science, astronomy, and cultural studies. Students are encouraged to perform observation-based projects that require creativity, inquiry, and critical analysis. Specific topics vary annually.

48 awards annually. See Web site for application.

1486—AMERICAN FOUNDATION FOR THE BLIND (Paul W. Ruckes Scholarship)

11 Penn Plaza, Suite 300
New York NY 10001
212/502-7661
FAX: 212/502-7771
E-mail: juliet@afb.org
Internet: http://www.afb.org

AMOUNT: $1,000
DEADLINE(S): APR 30
FIELD(S): Engineering; Computer/Physical/Life Sciences

Open to legally blind and visually impaired undergraduate and graduate students pursuing a degree in one of above fields. Must be U.S. citizen. Must submit written documentation of visual impairment from ophthalmologist or optometrist (need not be legally blind); official transcripts; proof of college/university acceptance; three letters of recommendation; and typewritten statement describing goals, work experience extracurricular activities, and how monies will be used.

1 award annually. See Web site or contact Julie Tucker at AFB for an application.

1487—AMERICAN INDIAN SCIENCE AND ENGINEERING SOCIETY (EPA Tribal Lands Environmental Science Scholarship)

P.O. Box 9828
Albuquerque NM 87119-9828
505/765-1052
FAX: 505/765-5608
E-mail: scholarships@aises.org
Internet: http://www.aises.org/scholarships/index.html

AMOUNT: $4,000
DEADLINE(S): JUN 15
FIELD(S): Biochemistry; Biology; Chemical Engineering; Chemistry; Entomology; Environmental Economics/Science; Hydrology; Environmental Studies

Open to American Indian college juniors, seniors, and graduate students enrolled full-time at an accredited institution. Must demonstrate financial need and be a member of AISES ($10 fee). Certificate of Indian blood NOT required.

Not renewable. See Web site for more information and/or an application.

1488—AMERICAN MUSEUM OF NATURAL HISTORY (Research Experiences for Undergraduates)

Central Park West at 79th Street
New York NY 10024-5192
FAX: 212/769-5495
E-mail: grants@amnh.org
Internet: http://research.amnh.org

AMOUNT: Stipend, research expenses, and possibly travel
DEADLINE(S): APR
FIELD(S): Evolutionary Biology

Ten-week summer internships for qualified undergraduates to pursue scientific projects in conjunction with Museum scientists. Must be enrolled in a degree program at a college/university, have a high GPA, and a strong science background. Included in program is orientation, biweekly meetings, and seminars. At conclusion, students deliver oral presentations of work and prepare research papers. Must submit list of courses, statement of interest, and recommendations.

See Web site or contact Office of Grants and Fellowships for an application.

1489—AMERICAN ORNITHOLOGISTS' UNION (AOU Student Research Awards)

Nat'l Museum Natural History
MRC-116
McClean VA 22101
202/357-2051
FAX: 202/633-8084
E-mail: AOU@BurkInc.com
Internet: http://www.aou.org

AMOUNT: $500 to $1800
DEADLINE(S): FEB 1
FIELD(S): Ornithology

Student research grants for undergraduates, graduates, and postgraduates; must not have received Ph.D. Must be a member of the American Ornithologists' Union. Financial need NOT a factor.

15-35 awards annually. Not renewable. For membership information or an application, contact check the AOU Web site.

1490—AMERICAN SOCIETY FOR ENOLOGY AND VITICULTURE (Scholarship)

P.O. Box 1855
Davis CA 95617-1855
530/753-3142
Email: society@asev.org
Internet: http://www.asev.com

AMOUNT: Varies (no predetermined amounts)
DEADLINE(S): MAR 1
FIELD(S): Enology (Wine Making); Viticulture (Grape Growing)

For college juniors, seniors, or graduate students enrolled in an accredited North American college or university in a science curriculum basic to the wine and grape industry. Must be resident of North America, have a minimum 3.0 GPA (undergrad) or 3.2 GPA (grad), and demonstrate financial need.

Renewable. Contact ASEV for an application.

1491—AMERICAN WINE SOCIETY EDUCATIONAL FOUNDATION (Scholarships and Grants)

1134 Prospect Avenue
Bethlehem PA 18018-4910
610/865-2401 or 610/758-3845
FAX: 610/758-4344
E-mail: lhs0@lehigh.edu

AMOUNT: $2,500
DEADLINE(S): MAR 31
FIELD(S): Wine industry professional study: enology, viticulture, health aspects of food and wine, and using and appreciating fine wines.

To provide academic scholarships and research grants to students based on academic excellence. Must show financial need and genuine interest in pursuing careers in wine-related fields. For North American citizens, defined as U.S., Canada, Mexico, the Bahamas, and the West Indies at all levels of education.

Contact Les Sperling at above location for application.

1492—ASSOCIATED WESTERN UNIVERSITIES, INC. (AWU Undergraduate Student Fellowships)

4190 S. Highland Drive, Suite 211
Salt Lake City UT 84124-2600
801/273-8900
FAX: 801/277-5632
E-mail: info@awu.org
Internet: http://www.awu.org
AMOUNT: $300/week stipend + possible travel allowance
DEADLINE(S): FEB 1
FIELD(S): Science; Mathematics; Engineering; Technology

Eight- to sixteen-week fellowships.

1493—ASSOCIATION FOR WOMEN IN SCIENCE EDUCATIONAL FOUNDATION (Ruth Satter Memorial Award)

1200 New York Avenue NW, Suite 650
Washington DC 20005
202/326-8940 or 800/886-AWIS
E-mail: awis@awis.org
Internet: http://www.awis.org
AMOUNT: $1,000
DEADLINE(S): JAN 16
FIELD(S): Various Sciences and Social Sciences

Scholarships for female doctoral students who have interrupted their education three years or more to raise a family. Summary page, description of research project, resume, references, transcripts, biographical sketch, and proof of eligibility from department head required. U.S. citizens may attend any graduate institution; noncitizens must be enrolled in U.S. institutions.

See Web site or write to above address for more information or an application.

1494—ASTRONAUT SCHOLARSHIP FOUNDATION (Scholarships)

Exec. Director
6225 Vectorspace Boulevard
Titusville FL 32780
321/269-6119
FAX: 321/267-3970
E-mail: MercurySvn@aol.com;
Internet: http://www.astronaut scholarship.org/guidelines.html
AMOUNT: Varies
DEADLINE(S): Varies
FIELD(S): Engineering and Physical Sciences (Medical Research ok, but NOT Professional Medicine)

Open to juniors, seniors, and graduate students at a select group of schools. Must be U.S. citizen with the intention to pursue research or advance field of study upon completion of final degree. Special consideration given to students who have shown initiative, creativity, excellence, and/or resourcefulness in their field. Must be NOMINATED by faculty or staff.

See Web site for list of eligible schools. Contact Howard Benedict, Executive Director, for details.

1495—BROOKHAVEN WOMEN IN SCIENCE (Renate W. Chasman Scholarship)

P.O. Box 183
Upton NY 11973-5000
E-mail: pam@bnl.gov
AMOUNT: $2,000
DEADLINE(S): APR 1
FIELD(S): Natural Sciences; Engineering; Mathematics

Open ONLY to women who are residents of the boroughs of Brooklyn or Queens or the counties of Nassau or Suffolk in New York who are reentering school after a period of study. For juniors, seniors, or first-year graduate students.

1 award annually. Not renewable. Contact Pam Mansfield at above location for an application. Phone calls are NOT accepted.

1496—ENTOMOLOGICAL SOCIETY OF AMERICA (Stan Beck Fellowship)

9301 Annapolis Road, Suite 300
Lanham MD 20706-3115
301/731-4535 Ext.3029
FAX: 301/731-4538
E-mail: stan.beck.fellowship@entsoc.org
Internet: http://www.entsoc.org
AMOUNT: varies
DEADLINE(S): SEP 1
FIELD(S): Entomology

For undergraduate or graduate study in entomology. Must be enrolled in a recognized college or university in the US. To assist needy students whose need may be based on physical limitations or economic, minority, or environmental condition.

Secure a nomination from an ESA member. Send SASE for complete information.

1497—ENTOMOLOGICAL SOCIETY OF AMERICA (Undergraduate Scholarships)

9301 Annapolis Rd., Suite 300
Lanham MD 20706-3115
301/731-4535 ext. 3029
FAX: 301/731-4538
E-mail: undergrad.scholarship@entsoc.org
Internet: http://www.entsoc.org
AMOUNT: $1,500
DEADLINE(S): MAY 31
FIELD(S): Entomology; Biology; Zoology

For undergraduate study in the above or related fields. Must be enrolled in a recognized college or university in the US, Canada, or Mexico. Applicants must have accumulated at least 30 semester hours by the time award is presented and have completed at least one class or project on entomology. Financial need is NOT a factor.

4 awards annually. Send self-addressed, stamped envelope for an application.

1498—FLORIDA FEDERATION OF GARDEN CLUBS, INC. (FFGC Scholarships for College Students)

6065 21st Street SW
Vero Beach FL 32968-9427
561/778-1023
Internet: http://www.ffgc.org
AMOUNT: $1,500-$3,500
DEADLINE(S): MAY 1
FIELD(S): Ecology; Environmental Issues; Land Management; City Planning; Environmental Control; Horticulture; Landscape Design; Conservation; Botany; Forestry; Marine Biology; Floriculture; Agriculture

Various scholarships for Florida residents with a "B" average or better enrolled full-time as a junior, senior, or graduate student at a Florida college or university.

See Web site or contact Melba Campbell at FFGC for an application.

1499—FLORIDA FEDERATION OF GARDEN CLUBS, INC. (FFGC Scholarships for High School Students)

6065 21st Street SW
Vero Beach FL 32968-9427
561/778-1023
Internet: http://www.ffgc.org
AMOUNT: $1,500
DEADLINE(S): MAY 1
FIELD(S): Ecology; Environmental Issues; Land Management; City

Planning; Environmental Control; Horticulture; Landscape Design; Conservation; Botany; Forestry; Marine Biology; Floriculture; Agriculture

Scholarships for Florida residents with a "B" average or better who will be incoming freshmen at a Florida college or university.

See Web site or contact Melba Campbell at FFGC for an application.

1500—FORD FOUNDATION/NATIONAL RESEARCH COUNCIL (Howard Hughes Medical Institute Predoctoral Fellowships in Biological Sciences)

2101 Constitution Avenue NW
Washington DC 20418
202/334-2872
FAX: 202/334-3419
Internet: nationalacademies.org

AMOUNT: $16,000 stipend + tuition at U.S. institution
DEADLINE(S): NOV 9
FIELD(S): Biochemistry; Biophysics; Epidemiology; Genetics; Immunology; Microbiology; Neuroscience; Pharmacology; Physiology; Virology

Five-year award is open to college seniors and first-year graduate students pursuing a Ph.D. or Sc.D. degree. U.S. citizens/nationals may choose any institution in the U.S. or abroad; foreign students must choose U.S. institution. Based on ability, academic records, proposed study/research, previous experience, reference reports, and GRE scores.

80 awards annually. See Web site or contact NRC for an application.

1501—HOUSTON LIVESTOCK SHOW AND RODEO (4H and FFA Scholarships)

2000 S. Loop West
Houston TX 77054
713/791-9000
FAX: 713-794-9528
E-Mail: info@rodeohouston.com
Internet: http://www.hlsr.com/education/

AMOUNT: $10,000
DEADLINE(S): Varies
FIELD(S): Agriculture; Life Sciences

Open to undergraduate students who are actively involved in the 4-H or FFA programs. Must major in an agricultural or life sciences field of study at a Texas college/university and demonstrate academic potential, citizenship/leadership, and financial need.

140 awards annually. Contact HLSR for an application.

1502—HUBBARD FARMS CHARITABLE FOUNDATION

P.O. Box 505
Walpole NH 03608-0505
603/756-3311

AMOUNT: $1,500-$3,000
DEADLINE(S): APR 1
FIELD(S): Poultry science, genetics, and other life sciences

Scholarships are for financially needy students at universities that the foundation trustees consider to be leaders in the field of progress in technology and efficiency of production of poultry products.

Send SASE to Jane F. Kelly, Clerk, at above address for current application guidelines.

1503—JEWISH VOCATIONAL SERVICE (Academic Scholarship Program)

One S. Franklin Street
Chicago IL 60606
312/357-4500
FAX: 312/855-3282
TTY: 312/855-3282
E-mail: jvschicago@jon.cjfny.org

AMOUNT: $5,000 (max.)
DEADLINE(S): MAR 1
FIELD(S): "Helping" Professions; Mathematics; Engineering; Sciences; Communications (at Univ IL only); Law (certain schools in IL only)

Open to Jewish men and women legally domiciled in the greater Chicago metropolitan area, who are identified as having promise for significant contributions in their chosen careers, and are in need of financial assistance for full-time academic programs in above areas. Must have entered undergraduate junior year in career programs requiring no postgrad education, be in graduate/professional school, or be in a vo-tech training program. Interview required.

Renewable. Contact JVS for an application between December 1 and February 15th.

1504—LOUISIANA OFFICE OF STUDENT FINANCIAL ASSISTANCE (Rockefeller State Wildlife Scholarships)

P.O. Box 91202
Baton Rouge LA 70821-9202
800/259-5626 ext. 1012 or 225/922-3258
FAX: 225/922-0790
E-mail: custserv@osfa.state.la.us
Internet: http://www.osfa.state.la.us

AMOUNT: $1,000/year
DEADLINE(S): JUL 1
FIELD(S): Forestry; Wildlife; Marine Science

Open to Louisiana residents pursuing undergraduate or graduate study at a Louisiana public post-secondary institution. Must be U.S. citizen with a minimum 2.5 GPA. Competitive selection. Recipients must obtain a degree in one of the three eligible fields or repay the funds plus interest. Financial need NOT a factor.

60 awards annually. Renewable. Apply by completing the Free Application for Federal Student Aid (FAFSA). Contact Public Information Rep for details.

1505—MARYLAND HIGHER EDUCATION COMMISSION (Maryland Science and Technology Scholarship Program)

16 Francis Street
Annapolis Park MD 21401
410/974-5370 or 800/974-1024
E-mail: ssamail@mhec.state.md.us
Internet: http://www.mhec.state.md.us/SSA/stech_qa.htm

AMOUNT: $3,000/year (BA); $1,000/year (AA)
DEADLINE(S): None
FIELD(S): Computer Science; Engineering; Technology

Scholarships for college-bound Maryland high school seniors who will major in one of the above fields and who are accepted to an eligible associate or bachelor's degree program in Maryland. The deadline was not known at this writing, so check for deadline date. Must agree to work in the state after graduation in a related field, one year for each year of assistance received.

Must maintain a 3.0 GPA.

1506—MIDWAY COLLEGE (Institutional Aid Program)

Financial Aid Office
Midway KY 40347
606/846-4421

AMOUNT: Varies
DEADLINE(S): MAR 1
FIELD(S): Nursing; Paralegal; Education; Psychology; Biology; Equine Studies; Liberal Studies; Business Administration

Scholarships and grants are open to women who are accepted for enrollment at

Midway College. Awards support undergraduate study in the above areas.

80 awards annually. Contact Midway College's Financial Aid Office for an application.

1507—NATIONAL AERONAUTICS AND SPACE ADMINISTRATION (ACCESS Internships)

Stennis Space Center, Bldg. 1100
Bay Saint Louis MS 39529
228/688-2079
E-mail: covington.pamela@ssc.nasa.gov

AMOUNT: Internship only
DEADLINE(S): None
FIELD(S): Aeronautics/Aerospace; Astronomy; Chemistry; Physics; Engineering; Math; Earth, Life, Materials, Computer, and Physical Sciences

Nine- to ten-week summer internships are open to undergraduates with physical or learning disabilities who maintain a minimum 3.0 GPA and are U.S. citizens. Purpose is to increase the number of students with disabilities pursuing technical degrees related to NASA's mission and to provide on-site experience. Internship takes place at the Stennis Space Center in Mississippi.

Contact Pam Covington for an application.

1508—NATURAL SCIENCES AND ENGINEERING RESEARCH COUNCIL OF CANADA (Undergraduate Scholarships)

Scholarships/Fellowships Division
350 Albert Street
Ottawa Ontario K1A 1H5 CANADA
613/996-2009
FAX: 613/996-2589
E-mail: schol@nserc.ca
Internet: http://www.nserc.ca

AMOUNT: Up to $3,600
DEADLINE(S): Varies
FIELD(S): Natural Sciences, Engineering, Biology, or Chemistry

Open to Canadian citizens or permanent residents working towards degrees in science or engineering. Academic excellence and research aptitude are considerations.

Write for complete information.

1509—NATURAL SCIENCES AND ENGINEERING RESEARCH COUNCIL OF CANADA (Undergraduate Student Research Awards in Small Universities)

350 Albert Street
Ottawa Ontario K1A 1H5 CANADA
613/995-5992
FAX: 613/992-5337
E-mail: schol@nserc.ca
Internet: http://www.nserc.ca/programs/usrasmen.htm

AMOUNT: $3,600 (max.)
DEADLINE(S): Varies
FIELD(S): Natural Sciences; Engineering

Research awards for Canadian citizens/permanent residents attending eligible institutions, and who have no more than 6 and no fewer than 2 academic terms remaining to complete bachelor's degree. Cumulative GPA of at least second class (B). Must be doing full-time in research and development activities during award tenure.

Students in health sciences not eligible. Students with B.A. degrees and who are studying for a second may apply.

1510—NORTHERN NEW JERSEY UNIT-HERB SOCIETY OF AMERICA (Scholarship)

2068 Dogwood Drive
Scotch Plains NJ 07076
908/233-2348

AMOUNT: $2,000
DEADLINE(S): FEB 15
FIELD(S): Horticulture; Botany

For New Jersey residents, undergraduate through postgraduate, who will attend colleges/universities east of the Mississippi River. Financial need is considered.

1 award annually. Renewable. Contact Mrs. Charlotte R. Baker at above address for an application.

1511—OAK RIDGE INSTITUTE FOR SCIENCE AND EDUCATION (ORISE Education and Training Programs)

P.O. Box 117
Oak Ridge TN 37831-0117
Internet: http://www.orau.gov/orise/educ.htm

AMOUNT: Varies
DEADLINE(S): Varies
FIELD(S): Engineering; Aeronautics; Computer Science; Technology; Earth Science; Environmental Studies; Biology; Chemistry; Physics; Medical Research

Numerous programs funded by the U.S. Department of Energy are offered for undergraduate students through postgraduate researchers. Includes fellowship and internship opportunities throughout the U.S.. Some have citizenship restrictions. Travel may be included.

See Web site or write for a catalog of specific programs and requirements.

1512—OKLAHOMA MEDICAL RESEARCH FOUNDATION (Sir Alexander Fleming Scholar Program)

825 N.E.13th Street
Oklahoma City OK 73104-5046
405/271-8537 or
800/522-0211 (in-state)
Internet: http://www.omrf.ouhsc.edu

AMOUNT: $2,500 salary + housing
DEADLINE(S): Feb 15
FIELD(S): Sciences

Summer scholarship program (June and July) for Oklahoma students who have completed their junior year of high school through those in their junior year of college at time of application. Excellent academic standing and aptitude in science and math are essential. Students will work in the laboratories of the above organization. Research projects will be selected from: alcoholism/liver disease, arthritis/immunology, carcinogenesis, cardiovascular biology, and more.

Named for the scientist who discovered penicillin and dedicated OMRF in 1949. Contact organization for further information and application forms.

1513—ORGONE BIOPHYSICAL RESEARCH LABORATORY (Lou Hochberg Awards)

Dr. James DeMeo, Director,
Hochberg Awards
P.O. Box 1148
Ashland, OR 97520
541/552-0118
FAX: 541/552-0118
E-mail: info@orgonelab.org;
Internet: http://www.orgonelab.org

AMOUNT: $200-$1,500
DEADLINE(S): Varies
FIELD(S): Science

Several different award categories available for high school to graduate students. Must be submitted in English. Include written proof of student status, with full address, telephone, E-mail.

1514—PENINSULA COMMUNITY FOUNDATION (Dr. Mary Finegold Scholarship)

1700 S. El Camino Real, #300
San Mateo CA 94402
650/358-9369
FAX: 650/358-9817
Internet: http://www.pcf.org/community_grants/scholarships.html

AMOUNT: $1,000
DEADLINE(S): MAR 7 (5 p.m.)
FIELD(S): Sciences

Scholarships for senior girls graduating from high school in Palo Alto, California, who intend to complete a four-year degree in the sciences. Special consideration will be given to girls who have demonstrated a "pioneering" spirit in that they have not been constrained by stereotypical female roles and to those facing financial hardship.

Award was established in the honor of Dr. Mary Finegold who, after completing her medical studies, elected to stay at home until her youngest child was in high school before beginning her medical practice. She was a school physician.

1515—SAN DIEGO AEROSPACE MUSEUM (Bill Gibbs Scholarship)

Education Dept.,
2001 Pan American Plaza
San Diego CA 92101
619/234-8291 ext. 19
FAX: 619/233-4526
Internet: http://aerospacemuseum.org/Scholastic.html

AMOUNT: Varies
DEADLINE(S): Varies
FIELD(S): Aerospace: math, physics, science, or engineering

For students who are residents of San Diego County, California, who have an aerospace career interest who have been accepted to a four-year college or university in a degree program relating to math, physics, science, or engineering.

Call or write museum for further information.

1516—SIEMENS WESTINGHOUSE (Science and Technology Competition)

186 Wood Avenue S.
Iselin NJ 08830
877/822-5233
E-mail: foundation@sc.siemens.com
Internet: http://www.siemens-foundation.org

AMOUNT: $120,000 (max.)
DEADLINE(S): Varies
FIELD(S): Biology; Physical Sciences; Mathematics; Physics; Chemistry; Computer Science; Environmental Science

Open to U.S. high school seniors to pursue independent science research projects, working individually or in teams of 2 or 3 to develop and test their own ideas. May work with one of the universities/laboratories that serve as Siemens' partners. Students from the 50 states, DC, and Territories may compete in one of six geographic areas. Individual and team national prize winners receive a second scholarship award to be applied to undergraduate or graduate education.

See Web site or contact Siemens Foundation for details.

1517—SMITHSONIAN INSTITUTION (Minority Student Internship Program)

Office of Fellowships
750 9th Street NW, Suite 9300
Washington DC 20560-0902
202/275-0655
FAX: 202/275-0489
E-mail: siofg@ofg.si.edu
Internet: http://www.si.edu/research+study

AMOUNT: $350/week + possible travel expenses
DEADLINE(S): Varies
FIELD(S): Humanities; Environmental and Cultural Studies; Natural History; Earth Science; Art History; Biology

Ten-week, full-time internships in residence at the Smithsonian are open to U.S. minority students who wish to participate in research or museum-related activities in above and related fields. Must be undergraduates or beginning graduate students with a minimum 3.0 GPA. Must submit essay, resume, and official transcript.

Contact the Office of Fellowships or see Web site for an application.

1518—SONOMA CHAMBOLLE-MUSIGNY SISTER CITIES, INC. (Henri Cardinaux Memorial Scholarship)

Chamson Scholarship Committee
P.O. Box 1633
Sonoma CA 95476-1633
707/939-1344
FAX: 707/939-1344
E-mail: Baileysci@vom.com

AMOUNT: Up to $1,500 (travel + expenses)
DEADLINE(S): JUL 15
FIELD(S): Culinary Arts; Wine Industry; Art; Architecture; Music; History; Fashion

Hands-on experience working in above or similar fields and living with a family in small French village in Burgundy or other French city. Must be Sonoma County, CA, resident at least 18 years of age and be able to communicate in French. Transcripts, employer recommendation, photograph, and essay (stating why, where, and when) required.

1 award. Nonrenewable. Also offers opportunity for candidate in Chambolle-Musigny to obtain work experience and cultural exposure in Sonoma, CA.

1519—STUDENT CONSERVATION ASSOCIATION (SCA Resource Assistant Program)

P.O. Box 550
Charlestown NH 03603
603/543-1700
FAX: 603/543-1828
E-mail: internships@sca-inc.org
Internet: http://www.sca-inc.org

AMOUNT: $1,180-$4,725
DEADLINE(S): Varies
FIELD(S): Environment and related fields

Must be 18 and U.S. citizen; need not be student. Fields: Agriculture, Archaeology, anthropology, botany, caves, civil/environmental engineering, environmental education, fisheries, forests, herpetology, history, living history/roleplaying, visitor services, landscape architecture/environmental design, paleontology, recreation/ resource/ range management, trail maintenance/construction, wildlife management, geology, hydrology, library/museums, surveying...

900 positions in US & Canada. Send $1 for postage for application; outside U.S./Canada, send $20.

1520—TYSON FOUNDATION, INC. (Alabama Scholarship Program)

2210 W. Oaklawn
Springdale AR 72762-6999
501/290-4995
FAX: 501/290-7984
E-mail: coments@tysonfoundation.org
Internet: http://www.tysonfoundation.org

AMOUNT: Varies (according to need)
DEADLINE(S): FEB 28 (to request application); APR 20 (to apply)
FIELD(S): Business; Agriculture; Engineering; Computer Science; Nursing; Biology; Chemistry

Open to residents in the general vicinity of a Tyson facility in Alabama, who are U.S. citizens. Must be pursuing full-time undergraduate study at an accredited U.S. institution and demonstrate financial need. Must also be employed part-time and/or summers to help fund education.

Renewable up to 8 semesters or 12 trimesters as long as student meets criteria. Contact Tyson Foundation to see if area of residence qualifies and for an application.

1521—TYSON FOUNDATION, INC. (Arkansas Scholarship Program)

2210 W. Oaklawn
Springdale AR 72762-6999
501/290-4955
FAX: 501/290-7984
E-mail: coments@tysonfoundation.org
Internet: http://www.tysonfoundation.org

AMOUNT: Varies (according to need)
DEADLINE(S): FEB 28(to request application); APR 20 (to apply)
FIELD(S): Business; Agriculture; Engineering; Computer Science; Nursing; Biology; Chemistry

Open to Arkansas residents who are U.S. citizens pursuing full-time undergraduate study at an accredited U.S. institution. Must demonstrate financial need and be employed part-time and/or summers to help fund education.

Renewable up to 8 semesters or 12 trimesters as long as student meets criteria. Contact Tyson Foundation for an application.

1522—TYSON FOUNDATION, INC. (California Scholarship Program)

2210 W. Oaklawn
Springdale AR 72762-6999
501/290-4995
FAX: 501/290-7984
E-mail: coments@tysonfoundation.org
Internet: http://www.tysonfoundation.org

AMOUNT: Varies (according to need)
DEADLINE(S): FEB 28 (to request application); APR 20 (to apply)
FIELD(S): Business; Agriculture; Engineering; Computer Science; Nursing; Biology; Chemistry

Open to residents of Modesto, California, who are U.S. citizens and live in the vicinity of a Tyson facility. Must be pursuing full-time undergraduate study at an accredited U.S. institution and demonstrate financial need. Must also be employed part-time and/or summers to help fund education.

Renewable up to 8 semesters or 12 trimesters as long as student meets criteria. Contact Tyson Foundation to see if area of residence qualifies and for an application.

1523—TYSON FOUNDATION, INC. (Florida Scholarship Program)

2210 Oaklawn
Springdale AR 72762-6999
501/290-4995
FAX: 501/290-7984
E-mail: coments@tysonfoundation.org
Internet: http://www.tysonfoundation.org

AMOUNT: Varies (according to need)
DEADLINE(S): FEB 28 (to request application); APR 20 (to apply)
FIELD(S): Business; Agriculture; Engineering; Computer Science; Nursing; Biology; Chemistry

Open to residents in the general vicinity of a Tyson facility in Florida, who are U.S. citizens. Must be pursuing full-time undergraduate study at an accredited U.S. institution and demonstrate financial need. Must also be employed part-time and/or summers to help fund education.

Renewable up to 8 semesters or 12 trimesters as long as student meets criteria. Contact Tyson Foundation to see if area of residence qualifies and for an application.

1524—TYSON FOUNDATION, INC. (Georgia Scholarship Program)

2210 Oaklawn
Springdale AR 72762-6999
501/290-4995
FAX: 501/290-7984
E-mail: coments@tysonfoundation.org
Internet: http://www.tysonfoundation.org

AMOUNT: Varies (according to need)
DEADLINE(S): FEB 28 (to request application); APR 20 (to apply)
FIELD(S): Business; Agriculture; Engineering; Computer Science; Nursing; Biology; Chemistry

Open to residents in the general vicinity of a Tyson facility in Georgia, who are U.S. citizens. Must be pursuing full-time undergraduate study at an accredited U.S. institution and demonstrate financial need. Must also be employed part-time and/or summers to help fund education.

Renewable up to 8 semesters or 12 trimesters as long as student meets criteria. Contact Tyson Foundation to see if area of residence qualifies and for an application.

1525—TYSON FOUNDATION, INC. (Illinois Scholarship Program)

2210 Oaklawn
Springdale AR 72762-6999
501/290-4995

AMOUNT: Varies (according to need)
DEADLINE(S): FEB 28
FIELD(S): Business; Agriculture; Engineering; Computer Science; Nursing

Open to residents of Chicago, Illinois, who are U.S. citizens and live in the vicinity of a Tyson facility. Must be pursuing full-time undergraduate study in an accredited U.S. institution and demonstrate financial need. Must also be employed part-time and/or summers to help fund education.

Renewable up to 8 semesters or 12 trimesters as long as student meets criteria. Contact Tyson Foundation for an application.

1526—TYSON FOUNDATION, INC. (Indiana Scholarship Program)

2210 Oaklawn
Springdale AR 72762-6999
501/290-4995
FAX: 501/290-7984
E-mail: coments@tysonfoundation.org
Internet: http://www.tysonfoundation.org

AMOUNT: Varies (according to need)
DEADLINE(S): FEB 28 (to request application); APR 20 (to apply)
FIELD(S): Business; Agriculture; Engineering; Computer Science; Nursing; Biology; Chemistry

Open to residents in the general vicinity of a Tyson facility in Indiana, who are U.S. citizens. Must be pursuing full-time undergraduate study at an accredited U.S. institution and demonstrate financial need. Must also be employed part-time and/or summers to help fund education.

Renewable up to 8 semesters or 12 trimesters as long as student meets criteria. Contact Tyson Foundation to see if area of residence qualifies and for an application.

1527—TYSON FOUNDATION, INC. (Mississippi Scholarship Program)

2210 Oaklawn
Springdale AR 72762-6999
501/290-4995
FAX: 501/290-7984
E-mail: coments@tysonfoundation.org
Internet: http://www.tysonfoundation.org

AMOUNT: Varies (according to need)
DEADLINE(S): FEB 28 (to request application); APR 20 (to apply)
FIELD(S): Business; Agriculture; Engineering; Computer Science; Nursing; Biology; Chemistry

Open to residents in the general vicinity of a Tyson facility in Mississippi, who are U.S. citizens. Must be pursuing full-time undergraduate study at an accredited U.S. institution and demonstrate financial need.

Must also be employed part-time and/or summers to help fund education.

Renewable up to 8 semesters or 12 trimesters as long as student meets criteria. Contact Tyson Foundation to see if area of residence qualifies and for an application.

1528—TYSON FOUNDATION, INC. (Missouri Scholarship Program)

2210 Oaklawn
Springdale AR 72762-6999
501/290-4995
FAX: 501/290-7984
E-mail: coments@tysonfoundation.org
Internet: http://www.tysonfoundation.org

AMOUNT: Varies (according to need)
DEADLINE(S): FEB 28 (to request application); APR 20 (to apply)
FIELD(S): Business; Agriculture; Engineering; Computer Science; Nursing; Biology; Chemistry

Open to residents in the general vicinity of a Tyson facility in Missouri, who are U.S. citizens. Must be pursuing full-time undergraduate study at an accredited U.S. institution and demonstrate financial need. Must also be employed part-time and/or summers to help fund education.

Renewable up to 8 semesters or 12 trimesters as long as student meets criteria. Contact Tyson Foundation to see if area of residence qualifies and for an application.

1529—TYSON FOUNDATION, INC. (North Carolina Scholarship Program)

2210 Oaklawn
Springdale AR 72762-6999
501/290-4995
FAX: 501/290-7984
E-mail: coments@tysonfoundation.org
Internet: http://www.tysonfoundation.org

AMOUNT: Varies (according to need)
DEADLINE(S): FEB 28 (to request application); APR 20 (to apply)
FIELD(S): Business; Agriculture; Engineering; Computer Science; Nursing; Biology; Chemistry

Open to residents in the general vicinity of a Tyson facility in North Carolina, who are U.S. citizens. Must be pursuing full-time undergraduate study at an accredited U.S. institution and demonstrate financial need. Must also be employed part-time and/or summers to help fund education.

Renewable up to 8 semesters or 12 trimesters as long as student meets criteria. Contact Tyson Foundation to see if area of residence qualifies and for an application.

1530—TYSON FOUNDATION, INC. (Oklahoma Scholarship Program)

2210 Oaklawn
Springdale AR 72762-6999
501/290-4995
FAX: 501/290-7984
E-mail: coments@tysonfoundation.org
Internet: http://www.tysonfoundation.org

AMOUNT: Varies (according to need)
DEADLINE(S): FEB 28 (to request application); APR 20 (to apply)
FIELD(S): Business; Agriculture; Engineering; Computer Science; Nursing; Biology; Chemistry

Open to residents in the general vicinity of a Tyson facility in Oklahoma, who are U.S. citizens. Must be pursuing full-time undergraduate study at an accredited U.S. institution and demonstrate financial need. Must also be employed part-time and/or summers to help fund education.

Renewable up to 8 semesters or 12 trimesters as long as student meets criteria. Contact Tyson Foundation to see if area of residence qualifies and for an application.

1531—TYSON FOUNDATION, INC. (Pennsylvania Scholarship Program)

2210 Oaklawn
Springdale AR 72762-6999
501/290-4995
FAX: 501/290-7984
E-mail: coments@tysonfoundation.org
Internet: http://www.tysonfoundation.org

AMOUNT: Varies (according to need)
DEADLINE(S): FEB 28 (to request application); APR 20 (to apply)
FIELD(S): Business; Agriculture; Engineering; Computer Science; Nursing; Biology; Chemistry

Open to residents in the general vicinity of a Tyson facility in Pennsylvania, who are U.S. citizens. Must be pursuing full-time undergraduate study at an accredited U.S. institution and demonstrate financial need. Must also be employed part-time and/or summers to help fund education.

Renewable up to 8 semesters or 12 trimesters as long as student meets criteria. Contact Tyson Foundation to see if area of residence qualifies and for an application.

1532—TYSON FOUNDATION, INC. (Tennessee Scholarship Program)

2210 Oaklawn
Springdale AR 72762-6999
501/290-4995
FAX: 501/290-7984
E-mail: coments@tysonfoundation.org
Internet: http://www.tysonfoundation.org

AMOUNT: Varies (according to need)
DEADLINE(S): FEB 28 (to request application); APR 20 (to apply)
FIELD(S): Business; Agriculture; Engineering; Computer Science; Nursing; Biology; Chemistry

Open to residents in the general vicinity of a Tyson facility in Tennessee, who are U.S. citizens. Must be pursuing full-time undergraduate study at an accredited U.S. institution and demonstrate financial need. Must also be employed part-time and/or summers to help fund education.

Renewable up to 8 semesters or 12 trimesters as long as student meets criteria. Contact Tyson Foundation to see if area of residence qualifies and for an application.

1533—TYSON FOUNDATION, INC. (Texas Scholarship Program)

2210 Oaklawn
Springdale AR 72762-6999
501/290-4995
FAX: 501/290-7984
E-mail: coments@tysonfoundation.org
Internet: http://www.tysonfoundation.org

AMOUNT: Varies (according to need)
DEADLINE(S): FEB 28 (to request application); APR 20 (to apply)
FIELD(S): Business; Agriculture; Engineering; Computer Science; Nursing; Biology; Chemistry

Open to residents in the general vicinity of a Tyson facility in Texas, who are U.S. citizens. Must be pursuing full-time undergraduate study at an accredited U.S. institution and demonstrate financial need. Must also be employed part-time and/or summers to help fund education.

Renewable up to 8 semesters or 12 trimesters as long as student meets criteria. Contact Tyson Foundation to see if area of residence qualifies and for an application.

1534—TYSON FOUNDATION, INC. (Virginia Scholarship Program)

2210 Oaklawn
Springdale AR 72762-6999
501/290-4995
FAX: 501/290-7984
E-mail: coments@tysonfoundation.org
Internet: http://www.tysonfoundation.org

AMOUNT: Varies (according to need)

DEADLINE(S): FEB 28 (to request application); APR 20 (to apply)
FIELD(S): Business; Agriculture; Engineering; Computer Science; Nursing; Biology; Chemistry

Open to residents in the general vicinity of a Tyson facility in Virginia, who are U.S. citizens. Must be pursuing full-time undergraduate study at an accredited U.S. institution and demonstrate financial need. Must also be employed part-time and/or summers to help fund education.

Renewable up to 8 semesters or 12 trimesters as long as student meets criteria. Contact Tyson Foundation to see if area of residence qualifies and for an application.

1535—UNCF/MERCK SCIENCE INITIATIVE (Undergraduate Science Research Scholarship Awards)

8260 Willow Oaks Corporate Dr.
P.O. Box 10444
FairFAX: VA 22031-4511
703/205-3503
FAX: 703/205-3574
E-mail: uncfmerck@uncf.org
Internet: http://www.uncf.org/merck

AMOUNT: $25,000/year (max.)
DEADLINE(S): DEC 15
FIELD(S): Life and Physical Sciences

Open to African-Americans in their junior year of college who will receive a bachelor's degree in the following academic year. Must be enrolled full-time in any four-year college/university in the U.S. and have a minimum 3.3 GPA. Must be U.S. citizen/permanent resident. Financial need NOT a factor.

15 awards annually. Not renewable. Contact Jerry Bryant, Ph.D., for an application.

1536—UNITED STATES DEPARTMENT OF AGRICULTURE (1890 National Scholars Program)

14th & Independence Avenue SW
Room 301-W; Whitten Bldg.
Washington, DC 20250-9600
202/720-6905
E-mail: usda-m@fie.com
Internet: http://web.fie.com/htdoc/fed/agr/ars/edu/prog/mti/agrpgaak.htm

AMOUNT: Tuition, employment/benefits, use of pc/software, fees, books, room/board
DEADLINE(S): JAN 15
FIELD(S): Agriculture, Food, or Natural Resource Sciences

For U.S. citizens, high school grad/GED, GPA 3.0+, verbal/math SAT 1000+, composite score 21+ ACT, first-year college student, and attend participating school.

34+ scholarships/yr/4 years. Send applications to U.S.D.A. Liaison officer at the 1890 Institution of your choice (see Web page for complete list).

1537—UNIVERSITY OF CALIFORNIA-DAVIS (Brad Webb Scholarship Fund)

Dept. Enology and Viticulture
One Shields Avenue
Davis CA 95616-8749
530/752-0380
FAX: 530-752-0382
Internet: http://wineserver@ucdavis.edu

AMOUNT: Varies
DEADLINE(S): Varies
FIELD(S): Enology/Viticulture

Open to students attending or planning to attend UC Davis. Award is made in memory of Brad Webb, friend of NSRS President, the late Dan Cassidy.

Contact the Department of Enology and Viticulture for an application.

1538—UNIVERSITY OF NEWCASTLE/Australia (R. M. Sheahan Memorial Undergraduate Scholarship)

Student Administration Unit, Student Services Centre, Univ. of Newcastle, Callaghan NSW
2308 AUSTRALIA
+61-(02)-4921-6539
FAX: +61-(02)-4960-1766
E-mail: scholarships@newcastle.edu.au
Internet: http://http://www.newcastle.edu.au/services/ousr/stuadmin/school/index.htm

AMOUNT: $1,000
DEADLINE(S): NOV 1
FIELD(S): Engineering, chemistry, or environmental engineering

Scholarship for undergraduate international as well as Australian students pursuing studies in chemistry, chemical engineering, or environmental engineering. Funded by the Cessnock City Council and Orica (ICI) Explosives, this award is made yearly based on academic merit.

Contact organization for details.

1539—WILSON ORNITHOLOGICAL SOCIETY (Fuertes, Hall/Mayfield and Stewart Grants)

Midcontinent Ecological Science Center; 4512 McMurray Avenue
Ft. Collins CO 80525-3400
970/226-9466
E-mail: jim_sedgwick@usgs.gov
Internet: http://www.ummz.lsa.umich.edu/birds/wos.html

AMOUNT: $2,500 (Fuertes); $1,000 (Hall/Mayfield); $500 (Stewart)
DEADLINE(S): JAN 15
FIELD(S): Ornithology

Grants to support research on birds only-NOT for general college funding. Open to anyone presenting a suitable research problem in ornithology. Research proposal required.

5-6 awards annually. Not renewable. See Web site for an application.

CHEMISTRY

1540—AIR FORCE RESERVE OFFICER TRAINING CORPS (AFROTC Scholarships)

551 E. Maxwell Boulevard
Maxwell AFB AL 36112-6106
334/953-7783

AMOUNT: Full tuition, books, and fees for all 4 years of college
DEADLINE(S): DEC 1
FIELD(S): Science; Engineering; Business; Political Science; Psychology; Geography; Foreign Studies; Foreign Language

Competitive scholarships based on individual merit to high school seniors and graduates who have not completed any full-time college work. Must be a U.S. citizen between the ages of 17-27. Must also have GPA of 2.5 or above, be in top 40% of class, and complete Applicant Fitness Test. Cannot be a single parent. Your college/university must offer AFROTC.

2,300 awards annually. Contact above address for application packet.

1541—AMERICAN FOUNDATION FOR THE BLIND (Paul W. Ruckes Scholarship)

11 Penn Plaza, Suite 300
New York NY 10001
212/502-7661
FAX: 212/502-7771
E-mail: juliet@afb.org
Internet: http://www.afb.org

AMOUNT: $1,000
DEADLINE(S): APR 30
FIELD(S): Engineering; Computer/Physical/Life Sciences

Open to legally blind and visually impaired undergraduate and graduate students pursuing a degree in one of above fields. Must be U.S. citizen. Must submit written documentation of visual impairment from ophthalmologist or optometrist (need not be legally blind); official transcripts; proof of college/university acceptance; three letters of recommendation; and typewritten statement describing goals, work experience extracurricular activities, and how monies will be used.

1 award annually. See Web site or contact Julie Tucker at AFB for an application.

1542—AMERICAN INDIAN SCIENCE AND ENGINEERING SOCIETY (EPA Tribal Lands Environmental Science Scholarship)

P.O. Box 9828
Albuquerque NM 87119-9828
505/765-1052
FAX: 505/765-5608
E-mail: scholarships@aises.org
Internet: http://www.aises.org/scholarships/index.html

AMOUNT: $4,000
DEADLINE(S): JUN 15
FIELD(S): Biochemistry; Biology; Chemical Engineering; Chemistry; Entomology; Environmental Economics/Science; Hydrology; Environmental Studies

Open to American Indian college juniors, seniors, and graduate students enrolled full-time at an accredited institution. Must demonstrate financial need and be a member of AISES ($10 fee). Certificate of Indian blood NOT required.

Not renewable. See Web site for more information and/or an application.

1543—ASSOCIATED WESTERN UNIVERSITIES, INC. (AWU Undergraduate Student Fellowships)

4190 S. Highland Drive, Suite 211
Salt Lake City UT 84124-2600
801/273-8900
FAX: 801/277-5632
E-mail: info@awu.org
Internet: http://www.awu.org

AMOUNT: $300/week stipend + possible travel allowance
DEADLINE(S): FEB 1
FIELD(S): Science; Mathematics; Engineering; Technology

Eight- to sixteen-week fellowships.

1544—ASSOCIATION FOR WOMEN IN SCIENCE EDUCATIONAL FOUNDATION (Ruth Satter Memorial Award)

1200 New York Avenue NW, Suite 650
Washington DC 20005
202/326-8940 or 800/886-AWIS
E-mail: awis@awis.org
Internet: http://www.awis.org

AMOUNT: $1,000
DEADLINE(S): JAN 16
FIELD(S): Various Sciences and Social Sciences

Scholarships for female doctoral students who have interrupted their education three years or more to raise a family. Summary page, description of research project, resume, references, transcripts, biographical sketch, and proof of eligibility from department head required. U.S. citizens may attend any graduate institution; noncitizens must be enrolled in U.S. institutions.

See Web site or write to above address for more information or an application.

1545—ASTRONAUT SCHOLARSHIP FOUNDATION (Scholarships)

Exec. Director
6225 Vectorspace Boulevard
Titusville FL 32780
321/269-6119
FAX: 321/267-3970
E-mail: MercurySvn@aol.com
Internet: http://www.astronautscholarship.org/guidelines.html

AMOUNT: Varies
DEADLINE(S): Varies
FIELD(S): Engineering and Physical Sciences (Medical Research ok, but NOT Professional Medicine)

Open to juniors, seniors, and graduate students at a select group of schools. Must be U.S. citizen with the intention to pursue research or advance field of study upon completion of final degree. Special consideration given to students who have shown initiative, creativity, excellence, and/or resourcefulness in their field. Must be NOMINATED by faculty or staff.

See Web site for list of eligible schools. Contact Howard Benedict, Executive Director, for details.

1546—BROOKHAVEN WOMEN IN SCIENCE (Renate W. Chasman Scholarship)

P.O. Box 183
Upton NY 11973-5000
E-mail: pam@bnl.gov

AMOUNT: $2,000
DEADLINE(S): APR 1
FIELD(S): Natural Sciences; Engineering; Mathematics

Open ONLY to women who are residents of the boroughs of Brooklyn or Queens or the counties of Nassau or Suffolk in New York who are reentering school after a period of study. For juniors, seniors, or first-year graduate students.

1 award annually. Not renewable. Contact Pam Mansfield at above location for an application. Phone calls are NOT accepted.

1547—CANADIAN SOCIETY FOR CHEMISTRY (Alfred Bader Scholarships)

130 Slater Street, Ste. 550
Ottawa Ontario KIP 6E2 CANADA
613/232-6252 or
Toll free: 888-542-2242
E-mail: info@cheminst.ca
Internet: http://www.cheminst.ca

AMOUNT: $1,000
DEADLINE(S): MAY 15
FIELD(S): Biochemistry; Organic Chemistry

For undergraduate students completing their final year of study in an Honours program. Nominees must be student chapter members of the CSC and be continuing in a graduate program in chemistry or biochemistry at a Canadian university. Nominations must include copy of Honours research project report, statement from supervisor describing student's contribution (academic and extracurricular), second letter of reference, and an official transcript.

3 awards annually. Contact the Program Manager, Awards, for nomination procedures. Award is announced in July.

1548—FORD FOUNDATION/NATIONAL RESEARCH COUNCIL (Howard Hughes Medical Institute Predoctoral Fellowships in Biological Sciences)

2101 Constitution Avenue NW
Washington DC 20418
202/334-2872
FAX: 202/334-3419
Internet: nationalacademies.org

AMOUNT: $16,000 stipend + tuition at U.S. institution
DEADLINE(S): NOV 9
FIELD(S): Biochemistry; Biophysics; Epidemiology; Genetics; Immunology; Microbiology; Neuroscience; Pharmacology; Physiology; Virology

Five-year award is open to college seniors and first-year graduate students pursuing a Ph.D. or Sc.D. degree. U.S. citizens/nationals may choose any institution in the U.S. or abroad; foreign students must choose U.S. institution. Based on ability, academic records, proposed study/research, previous experience, reference reports, and GRE scores.

80 awards annually. See Web site or contact NRC for an application.

1549—H. FLETCHER BROWN FUND (Scholarships)

c/o PNC Bank; Trust Dept.
P.O. Box 791
Wilmington DE 19899
302/429-1186
AMOUNT: Varies
DEADLINE(S): APR 15
FIELD(S): Medicine; Dentistry; Law; Engineering; Chemistry

Open to U.S. citizens born in Delaware and still residing in Delaware. For 4 years of study (undergrad or grad) leading to a degree that enables applicant to practice in chosen field.

Scholarships are based on need, scholastic achievement, and good moral character. Applications available in February. Write for complete information.

1550—INSTITUTION OF ELECTRICAL ENGINEERS (Jubilee Scholarships & Faraday Lecture Scholarship)

Savoy Place
London WC2R 0BL ENGLAND
+44-020-7344-8458
FAX: +44-020-7497-3609
E-mail: scholarships@iee.org.uk
Internet: http://www.iee.org.uk/EduCareers/Awards/
AMOUNT: 750 pounds/year
DEADLINE(S): JUN 30
FIELD(S): Electrical, Electronic, Manufacturing, or Related Engineering

Scholarships for students currently residing in the United Kingdom in the above engineering fields.

12 awards available. Renewable for the entire period of an IEE-accredited course. Check Web site or contact organization for application details.

1551—JEWISH VOCATIONAL SERVICE (Academic Scholarship Program)

One S. Franklin Street
Chicago IL 60606
312/357-4500
FAX: 312/855-3282
TTY: 312/855-3282
E-mail: jvschicago@jon.cjfny.org
AMOUNT: $5,000 (max.)
DEADLINE(S): MAR 1
FIELD(S): "Helping" Professions; Mathematics; Engineering; Sciences; Communications (at Univ IL only); Law (certain schools in IL only)

Open to Jewish men and women legally domiciled in the greater Chicago metropolitan area, who are identified as having promise for significant contributions in their chosen careers, and are in need of financial assistance for full-time academic programs in above areas. Must have entered undergraduate junior year in career programs requiring no postgrad education, be in graduate/professional school, or be in a vo-tech training program. Interview required.

Renewable. Contact JVS for an application between December 1 and February 15th.

1552—JOSEPH BLAZEK FOUNDATION (Scholarships)

8 S. Michigan Avenue
Chicago IL 60603
312/236-3882
AMOUNT: $1,000/year
DEADLINE(S): MAR 15
FIELD(S): Science; Chemistry; Engineering; Mathematics; Physics

Open to residents of Cook County, Illinois, who are high school seniors planning to study at a four-year college/university.

Renewable. Contact Foundation for an application.

1553—LOUISIANA OFFICE OF STUDENT FINANCIAL ASSISTANCE (Tuition Opportunity Program for Students-Teacher Awards)

P.O. Box 91202
Baton Rouge LA 70821-9202
800/259-5626 ext. 1012
FAX: 225/922-0790
E-mail: custserv@osfa.state.la.us;
Internet: http://www.osfa.state.la.us
AMOUNT: $4,000/year (education majors); $6,000/year (math/chemistry majors)
DEADLINE(S): JUL 1
FIELD(S): Education; Math; Chemistry

Open to Louisiana residents pursuing undergraduate or graduate study at a Louisiana public or LAICU private post-secondary institution. Must major in one of above fields leading to teacher certification. Loans are forgiven by working as a certified teacher in Louisiana one year for each year loan is received. Must be U.S. citizen with a minimum 3.0 GPA. Financial need NOT a factor.

90 awards annually. Renewable. Apply by completing Free Application for Federal Student Aid (FAFSA) and Teacher Award application. Contact Public Information Rep.

1554—MARYLAND HIGHER EDUCATION COMMISSION (Maryland Science and Technology Scholarship Program)

16 Francis Street
Annapolis Park MD 21401
410/974-5370 or 800/974-1024
E-mail: ssamail@mhec.state.md.us
Internet: http://www.mhec.state.md.us/SSA/stech_qa.htm
AMOUNT: $3,000/year (BA); $1,000/year (AA)
DEADLINE(S): None
FIELD(S): Computer Science; Engineering; Technology

Scholarships for college-bound Maryland high school seniors who will major in one of the above fields and who are accepted to an eligible associate or bachelor's degree program in Maryland. The deadline was not known at this writing, so check for deadline date. Must agree to work in the state after graduation in a related field, one year for each year of assistance received.

Must maintain a 3.0 GPA.

1555—NAACP NATIONAL OFFICE (NAACP Willems Scholarship)

4805 Mount Hope Drive
Baltimore MD 21215
401/358-8900
AMOUNT: $2,000 undergrads; $3,000 grads
DEADLINE(S): APR 30
FIELD(S): Engineering; Chemistry; Physics; Mathematics

Open to NAACP male members majoring in one of the above areas. Undergrads must have GPA of 2.5+; graduates' GPAs must be 3.0+. Renewable if the required GPA is maintained.

Financial need must be established. Two letters of recommendation typed on letterhead from teachers or professors in the major field of specialization. Write for complete information. Include a legal size, self-addressed, stamped envelope.

1556—NATIONAL AERONAUTICS AND SPACE ADMINISTRATION (ACCESS Internships)

Stennis Space Center, Bldg. 1100
Bay Saint Louis MS 39529
228/688-2079

E-mail: covington.pamela@ssc.nasa.gov
AMOUNT: Internship only
DEADLINE(S): None
FIELD(S): Aeronautics/Aerospace; Astronomy; Chemistry; Physics; Engineering; Math; Earth, Life, Materials, Computer, and Physical Sciences

Nine- to ten-week summer internships are open to undergraduates with physical or learning disabilities who maintain a minimum 3.0 GPA and are U.S. citizens. Purpose is to increase the number of students with disabilities pursuing technical degrees related to NASA's mission and to provide on-site experience. Internship takes place at the Stennis Space Center in Mississippi.

Contact Pam Covington for an application.

1557—NATIONAL ASSOCIATION OF WATER COMPANIES-NEW JERSEY CHAPTER (Scholarship)

Elizabethtown Water Co.
600 South Avenue
Westfield NJ 070
908/654-1234
FAX: 908/232-2719
AMOUNT: $2,500
DEADLINE(S): APR 1
FIELD(S): Business Administration; Biology; Chemistry; Engineering Communications

For U.S. citizens who have lived in NJ at least 5 years and plan a career in the investor-owned water utility industry in disciplines such as those above. Must be undergrad or graduate student in a two- or four-year NJ college or university.

GPA of 3.0 or better required. Contact Gail P. Brady for complete information.

1558—NATURAL SCIENCES AND ENGINEERING RESEARCH COUNCIL OF CANADA (Undergraduate Scholarships)

Scholarships/Fellowships Division
350 Albert Street
Ottawa Ontario K1A 1H5 CANADA
613/996-2009
FAX: 613/996-2589
E-mail: schol@nserc.ca
Internet: http://www.nserc.ca
AMOUNT: Up to $3,600
DEADLINE(S): Varies
FIELD(S): Natural Sciences, Engineering, Biology, or Chemistry

Open to Canadian citizens or permanent residents working towards degrees in science or engineering. Academic excellence and research aptitude are considerations.

Write for complete information.

1559—NATURAL SCIENCES AND ENGINEERING RESEARCH COUNCIL OF CANADA (Undergraduate Student Research Awards in Small Universities)

350 Albert Street
Ottawa Ontario K1A 1H5 CANADA
613/995-5992
FAX: 613/992-5337
E-mail: schol@nserc.ca
Internet: http://www.nserc.ca/programs/usrasmen.htm
AMOUNT: $3,600 (max.)
DEADLINE(S): Varies
FIELD(S): Natural Sciences; Engineering

Research awards for Canadian citizens/permanent residents attending eligible institutions, and who have no more than 6 and no fewer than 2 academic terms remaining to complete bachelor's degree. Cumulative GPA of at least second class (B). Must be doing full-time in research and development activities during award tenure.

Students in health sciences not eligible. Students with B.A. degrees and who are studying for a second may apply.

1560—OAK RIDGE INSTITUTE FOR SCIENCE AND EDUCATION (ORISE Education and Training Programs)

P.O. Box 117
Oak Ridge TN 37831-0117
Internet: http://www.orau.gov/orise/educ.htm
AMOUNT: Varies
DEADLINE(S): Varies
FIELD(S): Engineering; Aeronautics; Computer Science; Technology; Earth Science; Environmental Studies; Biology; Chemistry; Physics; Medical Research

Numerous programs funded by the U.S. Department of Energy are offered for undergraduate students through postgraduate researchers. Includes fellowship and internship opportunities throughout the U.S.. Some have citizenship restrictions. Travel may be included.

See Web site or write for a catalog of specific programs and requirements.

1561—OKLAHOMA MEDICAL RESEARCH FOUNDATION (Sir Alexander Fleming Scholar Program)

825 N.E.13th Street
Oklahoma City OK 73104-5046
405/271-8537 or
800/522-0211 (in-state)
Internet: http://www.omrf.ouhsc.edu
AMOUNT: $2,500 salary + housing
DEADLINE(S): Feb 15
FIELD(S): Sciences

Summer scholarship program (June and July) for Oklahoma students who have completed their junior year of high school through those in their junior year of college at time of application. Excellent academic standing and aptitude in science and math are essential. Students will work in the laboratories of the above organization. Research projects will be selected from: alcoholism/liver disease, arthritis/immunology, carcinogenesis, cardiovascular biology, and more.

Named for the scientist who discovered penicillin and dedicated OMRF in 1949. Contact organization for further information and application forms.

1562—PENINSULA COMMUNITY FOUNDATION (Dr. Mary Finegold Scholarship)

1700 S. El Camino Real, #300
San Mateo CA 94402
650/358-9369
FAX: 650/358-9817
Internet: http://www.pcf.org/community_grants/scholarships.html
AMOUNT: $1,000
DEADLINE(S): MAR 7 (5 p.m.)
FIELD(S): Sciences

Scholarships for senior girls graduating from high school in Palo Alto, California, who intend to complete a four-year degree in the sciences. Special consideration will be given to girls who have demonstrated a "pioneering" spirit in that they have not been constrained by stereotypical female roles and to those facing financial hardship.

Award was established in the honor of Dr. Mary Finegold who, after completing her medical studies, elected to stay at home until her youngest child was in high school before beginning her medical practice. She was a school physician.

1563—ROBERT SCHRECK MEMORIAL FUND (Grants)

c/o Texas Commerce Bank, Trust Dept
P.O. Drawer 140
El Paso TX 79980
915/546-6515
AMOUNT: $500-$1500
DEADLINE(S): JUL 15; NOV 15
FIELD(S): Medicine; Veterinary Medicine; Physics; Chemistry; Architecture; Engineering; Episcopal Clergy

Grants to undergraduate juniors or seniors or graduate students who have been residents of El Paso County for at least two years. Must be U.S. citizen or legal resident and have a high grade point average. Financial need is a consideration.

Write for complete information.

1564—ROYAL SOCIETY OF CHEMISTRY (Corday-Morgan Memorial Fund)

Burlington House; Piccadilly
London W1J 0BA ENGLAND UK
+44 (0) 20 7440 3325
FAX: +44 71 734 1227
Internet: www.rsc.org
E-mail langers@rsc.org
AMOUNT: 500 pounds sterling (max.)
DEADLINE(S): None
FIELD(S): Chemistry

Assists members of any established Chemical Society/Institute in the Commonwealth to visit chemical establishments in another Commonwealth country. The intention is to help applicants make stopovers in or diversions to such countries while travelling elsewhere for other purposes. Visits must clearly benefit the country concerned, and the visitor would be expected to give lectures, etc. Must be citizens of, and domiciled in, any Commonwealth country.

Contact the International Awards Officer at RSC for an application. Applications will normally be considered within one month of receipt.

1565—ROYAL SOCIETY OF CHEMISTRY (Grants to Visit Developing Countries)

Burlington House; Piccadilly
London W1V 0BN ENGLAND UK
+44 71 437 8656
FAX: +44 71 734 1227
AMOUNT: 500 pounds sterling (max.)
DEADLINE(S): None
FIELD(S): Chemistry

Grants for members of the Royal Society of Chemistry to visit chemical establishments in developing countries. The visits must be clearly of benefit to the country concerned, and the visitor would be expected to give lectures, etc. The intention is to help applicants make stopovers in or diversions to a developing country while travelling elsewhere for other purposes. Support for travel within a developing country may be given where appropriate.

Contact the International Affairs Officer at RSC for an application. Applications will normally be considered within one month of receipt.

1566—SAN DIEGO AEROSPACE MUSEUM (Bill Gibbs Scholarship)

Education Dept.
2001 Pan American Plaza
San Diego CA 92101
619/234-8291 ext. 19
FAX: 619/233-4526
Internet: http://aerospacemuseum.org/Scholastic.html
AMOUNT: Varies
DEADLINE(S): Varies
FIELD(S): Aerospace: math, physics, science, or engineering

For students who are residents of San Diego County, California, who have an aerospace career interest who have been accepted to a four-year college or university in a degree program relating to math, physics, science, or engineering.

Call or write museum for further information.

1567—SIEMENS WESTINGHOUSE (Science and Technology Competition)

186 Wood Avenue S.
Iselin NJ 08830
877/822-5233
E-mail: foundation@sc.siemens.com
Internet: http://www.siemens-foundation.org
AMOUNT: $120,000 (max.)
DEADLINE(S): Varies
FIELD(S): Biology; Physical Sciences; Mathematics; Physics; Chemistry; Computer Science; Environmental Science

Open to U.S. high school seniors to pursue independent science research projects, working individually or in teams of 2 or 3 to develop and test their own ideas. May work with one of the universities/laboratories that serve as Siemens' partners. Students from the 50 states, DC, and Territories may compete in one of six geographic areas. Individual and team national prize winners receive a second scholarship award to be applied to undergraduate or graduate education.

See Web site or contact Siemens Foundation for details.

1568—TYSON FOUNDATION, INC. (Alabama Scholarship Program)

2210 W. Oaklawn
Springdale AR 72762-6999
501/290-4995
FAX: 501/290-7984
E-mail: coments@tysonfoundation.org
Internet: http://www.tysonfoundation.org
AMOUNT: Varies (according to need)
DEADLINE(S): FEB 28 (to request application); APR 20 (to apply)
FIELD(S): Business; Agriculture; Engineering; Computer Science; Nursing; Biology; Chemistry

Open to residents in the general vicinity of a Tyson facility in Alabama, who are U.S. citizens. Must be pursuing full-time undergraduate study at an accredited U.S. institution and demonstrate financial need. Must also be employed part-time and/or summers to help fund education.

Renewable up to 8 semesters or 12 trimesters as long as student meets criteria. Contact Tyson Foundation to see if area of residence qualifies and for an application.

1569—TYSON FOUNDATION, INC. (Arkansas Scholarship Program)

2210 W. Oaklawn
Springdale AR 72762-6999
501/290-4955
FAX: 501/290-7984
E-mail: coments@tysonfoundation.org
Internet: http://www.tysonfoundation.org
AMOUNT: Varies (according to need)
DEADLINE(S): FEB 28 (to request application); APR 20 (to apply)
FIELD(S): Business; Agriculture; Engineering; Computer Science; Nursing; Biology; Chemistry

Open to Arkansas residents who are U.S. citizens pursuing full-time undergraduate study at an accredited U.S. institution. Must demonstrate financial need and be employed part-time and/or summers to help fund education.

Renewable up to 8 semesters or 12 trimesters as long as student meets criteria. Contact Tyson Foundation for an application.

1570—TYSON FOUNDATION, INC. (California Scholarship Program)

2210 W. Oaklawn
Springdale AR 72762-6999
501/290-4995
FAX: 501/290-7984
E-mail: coments@tysonfoundation.org
Internet: http://www.tysonfoundation.org
AMOUNT: Varies (according to need)
DEADLINE(S): FEB 28 (to request application); APR 20 (to apply)

FIELD(S): Business; Agriculture; Engineering; Computer Science; Nursing; Biology; Chemistry

Open to residents of Modesto, California, who are U.S. citizens and live in the vicinity of a Tyson facility. Must be pursuing full-time undergraduate study at an accredited U.S. institution and demonstrate financial need. Must also be employed part-time and/or summers to help fund education.

Renewable up to 8 semesters or 12 trimesters as long as student meets criteria. Contact Tyson Foundation to see if area of residence qualifies and for an application.

1571—TYSON FOUNDATION, INC. (Florida Scholarship Program)

2210 Oaklawn
Springdale AR 72762-6999
501/290-4995
FAX: 501/290-7984
E-mail: coments@tysonfoundation.org
Internet: http://www.tysonfoundation.org

AMOUNT: Varies (according to need)
DEADLINE(S): FEB 28 (to request application); APR 20 (to apply)
FIELD(S): Business; Agriculture; Engineering; Computer Science; Nursing; Biology; Chemistry

Open to residents in the general vicinity of a Tyson facility in Florida, who are U.S. citizens. Must be pursuing full-time undergraduate study at an accredited U.S. institution and demonstrate financial need. Must also be employed part-time and/or summers to help fund education.

Renewable up to 8 semesters or 12 trimesters as long as student meets criteria. Contact Tyson Foundation to see if area of residence qualifies and for an application.

1572—TYSON FOUNDATION, INC. (Georgia Scholarship Program)

2210 Oaklawn
Springdale AR 72762-6999
501/290-4995
FAX: 501/290-7984
E-mail: coments@tysonfoundation.org
Internet: http://www.tysonfoundation.org

AMOUNT: Varies (according to need)
DEADLINE(S): FEB 28 (to request application); APR 20 (to apply)
FIELD(S): Business; Agriculture; Engineering; Computer Science; Nursing; Biology; Chemistry

Open to residents in the general vicinity of a Tyson facility in Georgia, who are U.S. citizens. Must be pursuing full-time undergraduate study at an accredited U.S. institution and demonstrate financial need. Must also be employed part-time and/or summers to help fund education.

Renewable up to 8 semesters or 12 trimesters as long as student meets criteria. Contact Tyson Foundation to see if area of residence qualifies and for an application.

1573—TYSON FOUNDATION, INC. (Illinois Scholarship Program)

2210 Oaklawn
Springdale AR 72762-6999
501/290-4995

AMOUNT: Varies (according to need)
DEADLINE(S): FEB 28
FIELD(S): Business; Agriculture; Engineering; Computer Science; Nursing

Open to residents of Chicago, Illinois, who are U.S. citizens and live in the vicinity of a Tyson facility. Must be pursuing full-time undergraduate study in an accredited U.S. institution and demonstrate financial need. Must also be employed part-time and/or summers to help fund education.

Renewable up to 8 semesters or 12 trimesters as long as student meets criteria. Contact Tyson Foundation for an application.

1574—TYSON FOUNDATION, INC. (Indiana Scholarship Program)

2210 Oaklawn
Springdale AR 72762-6999
501/290-4995
FAX: 501/290-7984
E-mail: coments@tysonfoundation.org
Internet: http://www.tysonfoundation.org

AMOUNT: Varies (according to need)
DEADLINE(S): FEB 28 (to request application); APR 20 (to apply)
FIELD(S): Business; Agriculture; Engineering; Computer Science; Nursing; Biology; Chemistry

Open to residents in the general vicinity of a Tyson facility in Indiana, who are U.S. citizens. Must be pursuing full-time undergraduate study at an accredited U.S. institution and demonstrate financial need. Must also be employed part-time and/or summers to help fund education.

Renewable up to 8 semesters or 12 trimesters as long as student meets criteria. Contact Tyson Foundation to see if area of residence qualifies and for an application.

1575—TYSON FOUNDATION, INC. (Mississippi Scholarship Program)

2210 Oaklawn
Springdale AR 72762-6999
501/290-4995
FAX: 501/290-7984
E-mail: coments@tysonfoundation.org
Internet: http://www.tysonfoundation.org

AMOUNT: Varies (according to need)
DEADLINE(S): FEB 28 (to request application); APR 20 (to apply)
FIELD(S): Business; Agriculture; Engineering; Computer Science; Nursing; Biology; Chemistry

Open to residents in the general vicinity of a Tyson facility in Mississippi, who are U.S. citizens. Must be pursuing full-time undergraduate study at an accredited U.S. institution and demonstrate financial need. Must also be employed part-time and/or summers to help fund education.

Renewable up to 8 semesters or 12 trimesters as long as student meets criteria. Contact Tyson Foundation to see if area of residence qualifies and for an application.

1576—TYSON FOUNDATION, INC. (Missouri Scholarship Program)

2210 Oaklawn
Springdale AR 72762-6999
501/290-4995
FAX: 501/290-7984
E-mail: coments@tysonfoundation.org
Internet: http://www.tysonfoundation.org

AMOUNT: Varies (according to need)
DEADLINE(S): FEB 28 (to request application); APR 20 (to apply)
FIELD(S): Business; Agriculture; Engineering; Computer Science; Nursing; Biology; Chemistry

Open to residents in the general vicinity of a Tyson facility in Missouri, who are U.S. citizens. Must be pursuing full-time undergraduate study at an accredited U.S. institution and demonstrate financial need. Must also be employed part-time and/or summers to help fund education.

Renewable up to 8 semesters or 12 trimesters as long as student meets criteria. Contact Tyson Foundation to see if area of residence qualifies and for an application.

1577—TYSON FOUNDATION, INC. (North Carolina Scholarship Program)

2210 Oaklawn
Springdale AR 72762-6999

501/290-4995
FAX: 501/290-7984
E-mail: coments@tysonfoundation.org
Internet: http://www.tysonfoundation.org
AMOUNT: Varies (according to need)
DEADLINE(S): FEB 28 (to request application); APR 20 (to apply)
FIELD(S): Business; Agriculture; Engineering; Computer Science; Nursing; Biology; Chemistry

Open to residents in the general vicinity of a Tyson facility in North Carolina, who are U.S. citizens. Must be pursuing full-time undergraduate study at an accredited U.S. institution and demonstrate financial need. Must also be employed part-time and/or summers to help fund education.

Renewable up to 8 semesters or 12 trimesters as long as student meets criteria. Contact Tyson Foundation to see if area of residence qualifies and for an application.

1578—TYSON FOUNDATION, INC. (Oklahoma Scholarship Program)

2210 Oaklawn
Springdale AR 72762-6999
501/290-4995
FAX: 501/290-7984
E-mail: coments@tysonfoundation.org
Internet: http://www.tysonfoundation.org
AMOUNT: Varies (according to need)
DEADLINE(S): FEB 28 (to request application); APR 20 (to apply)
FIELD(S): Business; Agriculture; Engineering; Computer Science; Nursing; Biology; Chemistry

Open to residents in the general vicinity of a Tyson facility in Oklahoma, who are U.S. citizens. Must be pursuing full-time undergraduate study at an accredited U.S. institution and demonstrate financial need. Must also be employed part-time and/or summers to help fund education.

Renewable up to 8 semesters or 12 trimesters as long as student meets criteria. Contact Tyson Foundation to see if area of residence qualifies and for an application.

1579—TYSON FOUNDATION, INC. (Pennsylvania Scholarship Program)

2210 Oaklawn
Springdale AR 72762-6999
501/290-4995
FAX: 501/290-7984
E-mail: coments@tysonfoundation.org
Internet: http://www.tysonfoundation.org
AMOUNT: Varies (according to need)
DEADLINE(S): FEB 28 (to request application); APR 20 (to apply)
FIELD(S): Business; Agriculture; Engineering; Computer Science; Nursing; Biology; Chemistry

Open to residents in the general vicinity of a Tyson facility in Pennsylvania, who are U.S. citizens. Must be pursuing full-time undergraduate study at an accredited U.S. institution and demonstrate financial need. Must also be employed part-time and/or summers to help fund education.

Renewable up to 8 semesters or 12 trimesters as long as student meets criteria. Contact Tyson Foundation to see if area of residence qualifies and for an application.

1580—TYSON FOUNDATION, INC. (Tennessee Scholarship Program)

2210 Oaklawn
Springdale AR 72762-6999
501/290-4995
FAX: 501/290-7984
E-mail: coments@tysonfoundation.org
Internet: http://www.tysonfoundation.org
AMOUNT: Varies (according to need)
DEADLINE(S): FEB 28 (to request application); APR 20 (to apply)
FIELD(S): Business; Agriculture; Engineering; Computer Science; Nursing; Biology; Chemistry

Open to residents in the general vicinity of a Tyson facility in Tennessee, who are U.S. citizens. Must be pursuing full-time undergraduate study at an accredited U.S. institution and demonstrate financial need. Must also be employed part-time and/or summers to help fund education.

Renewable up to 8 semesters or 12 trimesters as long as student meets criteria. Contact Tyson Foundation to see if area of residence qualifies and for an application.

1581—TYSON FOUNDATION, INC. (Texas Scholarship Program)

2210 Oaklawn
Springdale AR 72762-6999
501/290-4995
FAX: 501/290-7984
E-mail: coments@tysonfoundation.org
Internet: http://www.tysonfoundation.org
AMOUNT: Varies (according to need)
DEADLINE(S): FEB 28 (to request application); APR 20 (to apply)
FIELD(S): Business; Agriculture; Engineering; Computer Science; Nursing; Biology; Chemistry

Open to residents in the general vicinity of a Tyson facility in Texas, who are U.S. citizens. Must be pursuing full-time undergraduate study at an accredited U.S. institution and demonstrate financial need. Must also be employed part-time and/or summers to help fund education.

Renewable up to 8 semesters or 12 trimesters as long as student meets criteria. Contact Tyson Foundation to see if area of residence qualifies and for an application.

1582—TYSON FOUNDATION, INC. (Virginia Scholarship Program)

2210 Oaklawn
Springdale AR 72762-6999
501/290-4995
FAX: 501/290-7984
E-mail: coments@tysonfoundation.org
Internet: http://www.tysonfoundation.org
AMOUNT: Varies (according to need)
DEADLINE(S): FEB 28 (to request application); APR 20 (to apply)
FIELD(S): Business; Agriculture; Engineering; Computer Science; Nursing; Biology; Chemistry

Open to residents in the general vicinity of a Tyson facility in Virginia, who are U.S. citizens. Must be pursuing full-time undergraduate study at an accredited U.S. institution and demonstrate financial need. Must also be employed part-time and/or summers to help fund education.

Renewable up to 8 semesters or 12 trimesters as long as student meets criteria. Contact Tyson Foundation to see if area of residence qualifies and for an application.

1583—UNCF/MERCK SCIENCE INITIATIVE (Undergraduate Science Research Scholarship Awards)

8260 Willow Oaks Corporate Drive
P.O. Box 10444
FairFAX: VA 22031-4511
703/205-3503
FAX: 703/205-3574
E-mail: uncfmerck@uncf.org
Internet: http://www.uncf.org/merck
AMOUNT: $25,000/year (max.)
DEADLINE(S): DEC 15
FIELD(S): Life and Physical Sciences

Open to African-Americans in their junior year of college who will receive a bachelor's degree in the following academic year. Must be enrolled full-time in any four-year college/university in the U.S. and have a minimum 3.3 GPA. Must be U.S. citizen/permanent resident. Financial need NOT a factor.

15 awards annually. Not renewable. Contact Jerry Bryant, Ph.D., for an application.

1584—UNIVERSITY OF NEWCASTLE/ Australia (R. M. Sheahan Memorial Undergraduate Scholarship)

Student Administration Unit, Student Services Centre, Univ. of Newcastle,
Callaghan NSW
2308 AUSTRALIA
+61-(02)-4921-6539
FAX: +61-(02)-4960-1766
E-mail: scholarships@newcastle.edu.au
Internet: http://http://www.newcastle.edu.au/services/ousr/stuadmin/school/index.htm

AMOUNT: $1,000
DEADLINE(S): NOV 1
FIELD(S): Engineering, chemistry, or environmental engineering

Scholarship for undergraduate international as well as Australian students pursuing studies in chemistry, chemical engineering, or environmental engineering. Funded by the Cessnock City Council and Orica (ICI) Explosives, this award is made yearly based on academic merit.

Contact organization for details.

MATHEMATICS

1585—AIR FORCE RESERVE OFFICER TRAINING CORPS (AFROTC Scholarships)

551 E. Maxwell Boulevard
Maxwell AFB AL 36112-6106
334/953-7783

AMOUNT: Full tuition, books, and fees for all 4 years of college
DEADLINE(S): DEC 1
FIELD(S): Science; Engineering; Business; Political Science; Psychology; Geography; Foreign Studies; Foreign Language

Competitive scholarships based on individual merit to high school seniors and graduates who have not completed any full-time college work. Must be a U.S. citizen between the ages of 17-27. Must also have GPA of 2.5 or above, be in top 40% of class, and complete Applicant Fitness Test. Cannot be a single parent. Your college/university must offer AFROTC.

2,300 awards annually. Contact above address for application packet.

1586—ALICE T. SCHAFER MATHEMATICS PRIZE

University of Maryland
4114 Computer & Space Sciences Building
College Park MD 20742-2461
301/405-7892

AMOUNT: $1,000
DEADLINE(S): October
FIELD(S): Mathematics

For female students who excel in mathematics. May be in any year of undergraduate study. Performance in math competitions will be considered for prize.

1587—ALPHA KAPPA ALPHA SORORITY INC. (AKA/PIMS Summer Youth Mathematics and Science Camp)

5656 S. Stony Island Avenue
Chicago IL 60637
800/653-6528
Internet: http://www.akaeaf.org

AMOUNT: $1,000 value (for room, board and travel)
DEADLINE(S): MAY 1
FIELD(S): Mathematics; Science

Open to high school students grades 9-11 who have at least a 'B' average. Essay required for entry. This 2-week camp includes AM classes; PM activities and a minimum of 4 field trips.

30 awards. Write for complete information.

1588—AMERICAN INSTITUTE OF AERONAUTICS AND ASTRONAUTICS (Undergraduate Scholarships)

1801 Alexander Bell Drive, Suite 500
Reston VA 20191-4344
800/639-AIAA; 703/264-7630
FAX: 703/264-7551
E-mail: rayc@aiaa.org
Internet: http://www.aiaa.org

AMOUNT: $2,000
DEADLINE(S): JAN 31
FIELD(S): Science, Engineering, Aeronautics, Astronautics

For students who have completed at least one academic semester or quarter of full-time college work in the area of science or engineering encompassed by the technical activities of the AIAA. Must have GPA of at least 3.0, be currently enrolled in accredited college or university. Membership in AIAA not required to apply but must become one before receiving a scholarship award.

Students who receive these awards are eligible for yearly continuation until completion of senior year upon submission of application, career essay, transcripts and 2 letters of recommendation from college professor.

1589—ARMED FORCES COMMUNICATIONS AND ELECTRONICS ASSOCIATION (AFCEA ROTC Scholarships)

4400 Fair Lakes Court
FairFAX: VA 22033-3899
800/336-4583 ext. 6147 or 703/631-6100
Internet: http://www.afcea.org/awards/scholarships.htm

AMOUNT: $2,000
DEADLINE(S): APR 1
FIELD(S): Electrical Engineering, Electronics, Computer Science, Computer or Aerospace Engineering, Physics, Mathematics

Scholarships in the above fields for ROTC students working toward a degree in an accredited four-year college or university in the U.S.

Must be nominated by Professors of Military Science, Naval Science, or Aerospace Studies. Contact the commander of each ROTC unit at your school.

1590—ARMED FORCES COMMUNICATIONS AND ELECTRONICS ASSOCIATION (AFCEA ROTC Scholarships)

4400 Fair Lakes Court
FairFAX: VA 22033-3899
800/336-4583 ext. 6147 or 703/631-6100
Internet: http://www.afcea.org/awards/scholarships.htm

AMOUNT: $2,000
DEADLINE(S): APR 1
FIELD(S): Electrical Engineering, Electronics, Computer Science, Computer or Aerospace Engineering, Physics, Mathematics

Scholarships in the above fields for ROTC students working toward a degree in an accredited four-year college or university in the U.S.

Must be nominated by Professors of Military Science, Naval Science, or Aerospace Studies. Contact the commander of each ROTC unit at your school.

1591—ARMED FORCES COMMUNICATIONS AND ELECTRONICS ASSOCIATION (General John A. Wickham Scholarships)

4400 Fair Lakes Court
FairFAX: VA 22033-3899
800/336-4583 ext. 6149 or
703/631-6149
Internet: http://www.afcea.org/awards/scholarships.htm

AMOUNT: $2,000
DEADLINE(S): MAY 1
FIELD(S): Electrical Engineering, Electronics, Computer Science, Computer or Aerospace Engineering, Physics, Mathematics

Scholarships in the above fields for persons working toward degrees in accredited four-year colleges or universities in the U.S. Must have GPA of 3.4 or more.

Check Web site or contact AFCEA for information and application.

1592—ASSOCIATED WESTERN UNIVERSITIES, INC. (AWU Undergraduate Student Fellowships)

4190 S. Highland Drive, Suite 211
Salt Lake City UT 84124-2600
801/273-8900
FAX: 801/277-5632
E-mail: info@awu.org
Internet: http://www.awu.org

AMOUNT: $300/week stipend + possible travel allowance
DEADLINE(S): FEB 1
FIELD(S): Science; Mathematics; Engineering; Technology

Eight- to sixteen-week fellowships.

1593—ASSOCIATION FOR WOMEN IN SCIENCE EDUCATIONAL FOUNDATION (Ruth Satter Memorial Award)

1200 New York Avenue NW
Suite 650
Washington DC 20005
202/326-8940 or 800/886-AWIS
E-mail: awis@awis.org
Internet: http://www.awis.org

AMOUNT: $1,000
DEADLINE(S): JAN 16
FIELD(S): Various Sciences and Social Sciences

Scholarships for female doctoral students who have interrupted their education three years or more to raise a family. Summary page, description of research project, resume, references, transcripts, biographical sketch, and proof of eligibility from department head required. U.S. citizens may attend any graduate institution; noncitizens must be enrolled in U.S. institutions.

See Web site or write to above address for more information or an application.

1594—ASTRONAUT SCHOLARSHIP FOUNDATION (Scholarships)

Executive Director
6225 Vectorspace Boulevard
Titusville FL 32780
321/269-6119
FAX: 321/267-3970
E-mail: MercurySvn@aol.com;
Internet: http://www.astronautscholarship.org/guidelines.html

AMOUNT: Varies
DEADLINE(S): Varies
FIELD(S): Engineering and Physical Sciences (Medical Research ok, but NOT Professional Medicine)

Open to juniors, seniors, and graduate students at a select group of schools. Must be U.S. citizen with the intention to pursue research or advance field of study upon completion of final degree. Special consideration given to students who have shown initiative, creativity, excellence, and/or resourcefulness in their field. Must be NOMINATED by faculty or staff.

See Web site for list of eligible schools. Contact Howard Benedict, Executive Director, for details.

1595—AT&T BELL LABORATORIES (Summer Research Program for Minorities and Women)

101 Crawfords Corner Road
Holmdel NJ 07733-3030
Written Inquiry

AMOUNT: Salary + travel and living expenses for summer
DEADLINE(S): DEC 1
FIELD(S): Engineering; Math; Sciences; Computer Science

Program offers minority students and women students technical employment experience at Bell Laboratories. Students should have completed their third year of study at an accredited college or university. U.S. citizen or permanent resident.

Selection is based partially on academic achievement and personal motivation. Write special programs manager-SRP for complete information.

1596—BARRY GOLDWATER SCHOLARSHIP AND EXCELLENCE IN EDUCATION FOUNDATION (Scholarships)

6225 Brandon Avenue, Suite 315
Springfield VA 22150-2519
703/756-6012
FAX: 703/756-6015
E-mail: GOLDH2o@erols.com
Internet: http://www.act.org/goldwater

AMOUNT: $7,500/year (max.)
DEADLINE(S): FEB 1
FIELD(S): Math; Natural Sciences; Engineering

Open to college sophomores and juniors with a minimum 3.0 GPA. Must be U.S. citizen, resident alien, or American national pursuing a degree at an accredited institution in math, natural sciences, or engineering disciplines that contribute to technological advances.

300 awards annually. See Web site or contact your Goldwater Faculty Representative on campus. Students must be nominated by their institution and cannot apply on their own.

1597—BROOKHAVEN WOMEN IN SCIENCE (Renate W. Chasman Scholarship)

P.O. Box 183
Upton NY 11973-5000
E-mail: pam@bnl.gov

AMOUNT: $2,000
DEADLINE(S): APR 1
FIELD(S): Natural Sciences; Engineering; Mathematics

Open ONLY to women who are residents of the boroughs of Brooklyn or Queens or the counties of Nassau or Suffolk in New York who are reentering school after a period of study. For juniors, seniors, or first-year graduate students.

1 award annually. Not renewable. Contact Pam Mansfield at above location for an application. Phone calls are NOT accepted.

1598—COMMUNITY FOUNDATION SILICON VALLEY (Valley Scholars Program)

111 W. Saint John Street, Suite 230
San Jose CA 95113
408/278-0270
FAX: 408/278-0280
Internet: http://www.cfsv.org

AMOUNT: $20,000 (over 4 years of college)
DEADLINE(S): Varies (early spring)

FIELD(S): Science and/or Math

A scholarship program for public high school students in the Silicon Valley (San Mateo and Santa Clara counties and Fremont Union High school District, California) who have demonstrated enthusiasm and aptitude for science and math. Must be U.S. citizen or permanent resident.

Up to 20 students are selected each year. Each Valley Scholar receives financial support, guidance through the college admission process, and a mentor whose interests match their own. Students may apply during their sophomore year of high school and must be academically outstanding.

1599—GERBER SCIENTIFIC, INC. (H. Joseph Gerber Vision Scholarship Program)

83 Gerber Road West
South Windsor CT 06074
860/648-8027
Internet: http://www.gerberscientific.com
AMOUNT: Varies
DEADLINE(S): MAR 15
FIELD(S): Engineering, Mathematics, Computer Science, Natural Sciences

Scholarship program for high school seniors in Connecticut.

Fifty scholarships to be awarded.

1600—INSTITUTE FOR OPERATIONS RESEARCH AND THE MANAGEMENT SCIENCES (INFORMS Summer Internship Directory)

P.O. Box 64794
Baltimore MD 21264-4794
800/4INFORMS
FAX: 410/684-2963
E-mail: jps@informs.org
Internet: http://www.informs.org/INTERN/
AMOUNT: Varies
DEADLINE(S): Varies
FIELD(S): Fields related to information management: business management, engineering, mathematics

A Web site listing of summer internships in the field of operations research and management sciences. Both applicants and employers can register online.

Access Web site for list.

1601—INSTITUTE OF INTERNATIONAL EDUCATION

1400 K Street NW, 6th Floor
Washington DC 20005-2403
202/326-7697 or
800/618-NSEP (6737)
E-mail: nsep@iie.org
Internet: http://www.iie.org/nsep/
AMOUNT: Varies: up to $8,000/semester
DEADLINE(S): FEB 8
FIELD(S): Open to all majors; preference to applied sciences, engineering, business, economics, math, computer science, international affairs, political science, history, and the policy sciences.

For study abroad OUTSIDE the U.S., Canada, Australia, New Zealand, and Western Europe. For study in areas deemed critical to U.S. national security. Applications available on U.S. campuses from August through early December. Or contact organization for details.

Inquire at above location for details.

1602—JEWISH FEDERATION OF METROPOLITAN CHICAGO (Academic Scholarship Program for Studies in the Sciences)

One South Franklin Street
Chicago IL 60606
Written Inquiry
AMOUNT: Varies
DEADLINE(S): MAR 1
FIELD(S): Mathematics, Engineering, or Science

Scholarships for college juniors, seniors, and graduate students who are Jewish and are residents of Chicago, IL and Cook County.

Academic achievement and financial need are considered. Applications accepted after Dec. 1.

1603—JEWISH VOCATIONAL SERVICE (Academic Scholarship Program)

One S. Franklin Street
Chicago IL 60606
312/357-4500
FAX: 312/855-3282
TTY: 312/855-3282
E-mail: jvschicago@jon.cjfny.org
AMOUNT: $5,000 (max.)
DEADLINE(S): MAR 1
FIELD(S): "Helping" Professions; Mathematics; Engineering; Sciences; Communications (at Univ IL only); Law (certain schools in IL only)

Open to Jewish men and women legally domiciled in the greater Chicago metropolitan area, who are identified as having promise for significant contributions in their chosen careers, and are in need of financial assistance for full-time academic programs in above areas. Must have entered undergraduate junior year in career programs requiring no postgrad education, be in graduate/professional school, or be in a vo-tech training program. Interview required.

Renewable. Contact JVS for an application between December 1 and February 15th.

1604—JOSEPH BLAZEK FOUNDATION (Scholarships)

8 S. Michigan Avenue
Chicago IL 60603
312/236-3882
AMOUNT: $1,000/year
DEADLINE(S): MAR 15
FIELD(S): Science; Chemistry; Engineering; Mathematics; Physics

Open to residents of Cook County, Illinois, who are high school seniors planning to study at a four-year college/university.

Renewable. Contact Foundation for an application.

1605—LOS ANGELES COUNCIL OF BLACK PROFESSIONAL ENGINEERS (Al-Ben Scholarship)

P.O. Box 881029
Los Angeles CA 90009
310/635-7734
E-mail: secy1@lablackengineers.org
Internet: http://www.lablackengineers.org/scholarships.html
AMOUNT: Varies
DEADLINE(S): Varies
FIELD(S): Engineering; Mathematics; Computer Studies; Applied Scientific Studies

Open to technically inclined precollege and undergraduate students enrolled in one of the above fields. Must be of African American, Native American, or Hispanic ancestry. Preference given to students attending college in Southern California or who are Southern California residents.

See Web site to download an application.

1606—LOUISIANA OFFICE OF STUDENT FINANCIAL ASSISTANCE (Tuition Opportunity Program for Students-Teacher Awards)

P.O. Box 91202
Baton Rouge LA 70821-9202
800/259-5626 ext. 1012
FAX: 225/922-0790
E-mail: custserv@osfa.state.la.us

Internet: http://www.osfa.state.la.us
AMOUNT: $4,000/year (education majors); $6,000/year (math/chemistry majors)
DEADLINE(S): JUL 1
FIELD(S): Education; Math; Chemistry

Open to Louisiana residents pursuing undergraduate or graduate study at a Louisiana public or LAICU private post-secondary institution. Must major in one of above fields leading to teacher certification. Loans are forgiven by working as a certified teacher in Louisiana one year for each year loan is received. Must be U.S. citizen with a minimum 3.0 GPA. Financial need NOT a factor.

90 awards annually. Renewable. Apply by completing Free Application for Federal Student Aid (FAFSA) and Teacher Award application. Contact Public Information Rep.

1607—MICROSOFT CORPORATION (National Minority and/or Women's Scholarships)

One Microsoft Way
Redmond WA 98052-8303
E-mail: scholar@microsoft.com
Internet: http://www.microsoft.com/college/scholarships/
AMOUNT: Tuition for 1 year
DEADLINE(S): JAN 31
FIELD(S): Computer Science, Computer Engineering, or a related technical discipline, such as Math or Physics

Full tuition scholarships awarded for 1 academic year to women and minorities (African Americans, Hispanics, or Native Americans) enrolled full-time in the above fields with a demonstrated interest in computers and making satisfactory progress towards a degree. Awards are made through designated schools and are not transferable to other institutions.

See Web site above for details.

1608—MICROSOFT CORPORATION (Summer Internships)

One Microsoft Way
Redmond WA 98052-8303
425/882-8080
E-mail: scholar@microsoft.com
Internet: http://www.microsoft.com/college/scholarships/
AMOUNT: Varies
DEADLINE(S): None
FIELD(S): Computer Science, Computer Engineering, or a related technical discipline, such as Math or Physics

Summer internships for individuals with a deep passion for technological advancement. Must commit to a 12-week minimum. Includes transportation, shipping costs, and shared cost of housing. Competitive compensation offered.

Check Web site above for details.

1609—NAACP NATIONAL OFFICE (NAACP Willems Scholarship)

4805 Mount Hope Drive
Baltimore MD 21215
401/358-8900
AMOUNT: $2,000 undergrads; $3,000 grads
DEADLINE(S): APR 30
FIELD(S): Engineering; Chemistry; Physics; Mathematics

Open to NAACP male members majoring in one of the above areas. Undergrads must have GPA of 2.5+; graduates' GPAs must be 3.0+. Renewable if the required GPA is maintained.

Financial need must be established. Two letters of recommendation typed on letterhead from teachers or professors in the major field of specialization. Write for complete information. Include a legal size, self-addressed, stamped envelope.

1610—NATIONAL AERONAUTICS AND SPACE ADMINISTRATION (ACCESS Internships)

Stennis Space Center, Bldg. 1100
Bay Saint Louis MS 39529
228/688-2079
E-mail: covington.pamela@ssc.nasa.gov
AMOUNT: Internship only
DEADLINE(S): None
FIELD(S): Aeronautics/Aerospace; Astronomy; Chemistry; Physics; Engineering; Math; Earth, Life, Materials, Computer, and Physical Sciences

Nine- to ten-week summer internships are open to undergraduates with physical or learning disabilities who maintain a minimum 3.0 GPA and are U.S. citizens. Purpose is to increase the number of students with disabilities pursuing technical degrees related to NASA's mission and to provide on-site experience. Internship takes place at the Stennis Space Center in Mississippi.

Contact Pam Covington for an application.

1611—NATIONAL TECHNICAL ASSOCIATION, INC. (Scholarship Competitions for Minorities and Women in Science and Engineering)

5810 Kingstowne Ctr., #120221
Alexandria VA 22315-5711
E-mail: ntamfj1@aol.com
Internet: http://www.huenet.com/nta
AMOUNT: $500-$5,000
DEADLINE(S): Varies
FIELD(S): Science; Mathematics; Engineering; Applied Technology

Scholarship competitions for minorities and women pursuing degrees in the above fields. Additional scholarships are available through local chapters of NTA.

See Web site or write to above address for details and for locations of local chapters.

1612—NATIVE AMERICAN SCHOLARSHIP FUND, INC. (Scholarships)

8200 Mountain Roa, NE, Suite 203
Albuquerque NM 87110
505/262-2351
FAX: 505/262-0543
E-mail: NScholarsh@aol.com
AMOUNT: Varies
DEADLINE(S): MAR 15; APR 15; SEP 15
FIELD(S): Math; Engineering; Science; Business; Education; Computer Science

Open to American Indians or Alaskan Natives (1/4 degree or more) enrolled as members of a federally recognized, state recognized, or terminated tribe. For graduate or undergraduate study at an accredited four-year college or university.

208 awards annually. Contact Lucille Kelley, Director of Recruitment, for an application.

1613—NATURAL SCIENCES AND ENGINEERING RESEARCH COUNCIL OF CANADA (Undergraduate Student Research Awards in Small Universities)

350 Albert Street
Ottawa Ontario K1A 1H5 CANADA
613/995-599;
FAX: 613/992-5337
E-mail: schol@nserc.ca
Internet: http://www.nserc.ca/programs/usrasmen.htm
AMOUNT: $3,600 (max.)
DEADLINE(S): Varies
FIELD(S): Natural Sciences; Engineering

Research awards for Canadian citizens/permanent residents attending eligible institutions, and who have no more than 6 and no fewer than 2 academic terms remaining to complete bachelor's degree. Cumulative GPA of at least second class (B). Must be doing full-time in research and development activities during award tenure.

Students in health sciences not eligible. Students with B.A. degrees and who are studying for a second may apply.

1614—OAK RIDGE INSTITUTE FOR SCIENCE AND EDUCATION (ORISE Education and Training Programs)

P.O. Box 117
Oak Ridge TN 37831-0117
Internet: http://www.orau.gov/orise/educ.htm
AMOUNT: Varies
DEADLINE(S): Varies
FIELD(S): Engineering; Aeronautics; Computer Science; Technology; Earth Science; Environmental Studies; Biology; Chemistry; Physics; Medical Research

Numerous programs funded by the U.S. Department of Energy are offered for undergraduate students through postgraduate researchers. Includes fellowship and internship opportunities throughout the U.S. Some have citizenship restrictions. Travel may be included.

See Web site or write for a catalog of specific programs and requirements.

1615—OKLAHOMA MEDICAL RESEARCH FOUNDATION (Sir Alexander Fleming Scholar Program)

825 N.E.13th Street
Oklahoma City OK 73104-5046
405/271-8537 or
800/522-0211 (in-state)
Internet: http://www.omrf.ouhsc.edu
AMOUNT: $2,500 salary + housing
DEADLINE(S): Feb 15
FIELD(S): Sciences

Summer scholarship program (June and July) for Oklahoma students who have completed their junior year of high school through those in their junior year of college at time of application. Excellent academic standing and aptitude in science and math are essential. Students will work in the laboratories of the above organization. Research projects will be selected from: alcoholism/liver disease, arthritis/immunology, carcinogenesis, cardiovascular biology, and more.

Named for the scientist who discovered penicillin and dedicated OMRF in 1949. Contact organization for further information and application forms.

1616—PENINSULA COMMUNITY FOUNDATION (Dr. Mary Finegold Scholarship)

1700 S. El Camino Real, #300
San Mateo CA 94402
650/358-9369
FAX: 650/358-9817
Internet: http://www.pcf.org/community_grants/scholarships.html
AMOUNT: $1,000
DEADLINE(S): MAR 7 (5 p.m.)
FIELD(S): Sciences

Scholarships for senior girls graduating from high school in Palo Alto, California, who intend to complete a four-year degree in the sciences. Special consideration will be given to girls who have demonstrated a "pioneering" spirit in that they have not been constrained by stereotypical female roles and to those facing financial hardship.

Award was established in the honor of Dr. Mary Finegold who, after completing her medical studies, elected to stay at home until her youngest child was in high school before beginning her medical practice. She was a school physician.

1617—SAN DIEGO AEROSPACE MUSEUM (Bill Gibbs Scholarship)

Education Dept.
2001 Pan American Plaza
San Diego CA 92101
619/234-8291 ext. 19
FAX: 619/233-4526
Internet: http://aerospacemuseum.org/Scholastic.html
AMOUNT: Varies
DEADLINE(S): Varies
FIELD(S): Aerospace: math, physics, science, or engineering

For students who are residents of San Diego County, California, who have an aerospace career interest who have been accepted to a four-year college or university in a degree program relating to math, physics, science, or engineering.

Call or write museum for further information.

1618—SCIENCE SERVICE (Discovery Young Scientist Challenge)

1719 N Street NW
Washington DC 20036
202/785-2255
FAX: 202/785-1243
E-mail: dkruft@sciserv.org
Internet: http://www.sciserv.org
AMOUNT: Varies
DEADLINE(S): JUN
FIELD(S): Science; Math; Engineering

Open to middle schoolers (5th-8th grades) who win their regional or state science fair. Enables students to participate in a national science competition that emphasizes the student's ability to communicate about science. Must be U.S. citizen and be nominated by the fair director in order to apply.

Contact Danielle Kruft at Science Service for DYSC nomination procedures.

1619—SCIENCE SERVICE (Intel International Science and Engineering Fair)

1719 N Street NW
Washington DC 20036
202/785-2255
FAX: 202/785-1243
E-mail: jkim@sciserv.org
Internet: http://www.sciserv.org
AMOUNT: Varies (totaling $2 million)
DEADLINE(S): DEC 1
FIELD(S): Science; Math; Engineering

Open to high school students (grades 9-12) who participate in this worldwide science competition. Scholarships, internships with noted scientists, and travel and equipment grants are awarded.

Contact Jinny Kim at Science Service for official ISEF entry book. Sponsored by the Intel Corporation.

1620—SIEMENS WESTINGHOUSE (Science and Technology Competition)

186 Wood Avenue S.
Iselin NJ 08830
877/822-5233
E-mail: foundation@sc.siemens.com
Internet: http://www.siemens-foundation.org
AMOUNT: $120,000 (max.)
DEADLINE(S): Varies
FIELD(S): Biology; Physical Sciences; Mathematics; Physics; Chemistry; Computer Science; Environmental Science

Open to U.S. high school seniors to pursue independent science research projects, working individually or in teams of 2 or 3 to develop and test their own ideas. May work with one of the universities/laboratories that serve as Siemens' partners.

Students from the 50 states, DC, and Territories may compete in one of six geographic areas. Individual and team national prize winners receive a second scholarship award to be applied to undergraduate or graduate education.

See Web site or contact Siemens Foundation for details.

1621—SKIDMORE COLLEGE (Porter Presidential Scholarships in Science and Math)

Office of Admissions
815 North Broadway
Saratoga Springs NY 12866-1632
800/867-6007
E-mail: admissions@skidmore.edu
Internet: http://www.skidmore.edu/administration/financial_aid/porter_scholarship.htm

AMOUNT: $10,000/year
DEADLINE(S): JAN 15
FIELD(S): Math, Science, or Computer Science

Scholarships for students excelling in the above fields. Awards are based on talent, not financial need. Recipients are not required to major in a scientific or mathematical discipline, but they will be expected to demonstrate serious research in one or more of these areas.

Five scholarships per year. For more information, visit Web site.

1622—SOCIETY OF HISPANIC PROFESSIONAL ENGINEERS FOUNDATION (SHPE Scholarships)

5400 E. Olympic Boulevard
Suite 210
Los Angeles CA 90022
323/888-2080

AMOUNT: $500-$3,000
DEADLINE(S): APR 15
FIELD(S): Engineering; Science

Open to deserving students of Hispanic descent who are seeking careers in engineering or science. For full-time undergraduate or graduate study at a college or university. Based on academic achievement and financial need.

Send self-addressed, stamped envelope to above address for an application.

1623—SOCIETY OF PHYSICS STUDENTS (SPS Scholarships)

SPS Scholarships Committee
Society of Physics Students
One Physics Ellipse
College Park MD 20740-3843
301/209-3007
Internet: http://www.aip.org/education/sps/

AMOUNT: $4,000 first place; $2,000 second; $1,000 all others
DEADLINE(S): FEB 15
FIELD(S): Physics

SPS members. For final year of full-time study leading to a BS degree in physics. Consideration given to high scholastic performance, potential for continued scholastic development in physics, and active SPS participation.

Nonrenewable. 14 scholarships per year. Write for complete information.

1624—SPACE COAST CREDIT UNION (Two-Year Scholarships)

Marketing Dept.
P.O. Box 2470
Melbourne FL 32902
Internet: http://www.sccu.com/scholarship/

AMOUNT: $750/year, two years; $1,000 bonus if go on for Bachelor's
DEADLINE(S): APR 15
FIELD(S): Math, Economics, Science, Computer Science, Marketing, Journalism, Political Science

Must be graduating from a high school in Brevard, Volusia, Flagler, or Indian River counties, be a member of SCCU, have a minimum 3.0 GPA, planning to attend a two-year Florida institution of higher education for an associates degree, and be willing to write a 200-word essay on the topic "Why credit unions are valuable to society."

Four annual awards. Students going on to complete a four-year degree could be eligible for a bonus scholarship of $1,000 for the next two years. For membership information or an application, see our Web page or write to the above address.

1625—STATE FARM COMPANIES FOUNDATION (Exceptional Student Fellowship)

One State Farm Plaza, SC-3
Bloomington IL 61710-0001
309/766-2039/2161
E-mail: Nancy.Lynn.gr3o@statefarm.com
Internet: http://www.statefarm.com

AMOUNT: $3,000 (nominating institution receives $250)
DEADLINE(S): FEB 15
FIELD(S): Accounting; Business Administration; Actuarial Science; Computer Science; Economics; Finance; Insurance/Risk Management; Investments; Management; Marketing; Mathematics; Statistics

For U.S. citizens who are full-time juniors or seniors when they apply. Must demonstrate significant leadership in extracurricular activities, have minimum 3.6 GPA, and attend accredited U.S. college/university. Must be nominated by dean, department head, professor, or academic advisor.

50 awards annually. Not renewable. See Web site, visit your financial aid office, or write to above address for an application.

1626—STATISTICS NEW ZEALAND (Pacific Islands Scholarship)

EEO Co-ordinator
P.O. Box 2922
Wellington NEW ZEALAND
04/495-4643
FAX: 04/495-4817
E-mail: anisiata_soagia-pritchard@stats.govt.nz

AMOUNT: $3,500/year + travel
DEADLINE(S): OCT 31
FIELD(S): Statistics; Mathematics; Demography; Economics; Geography; Quantitative Social Sciences

Open to all indigenous people of Pacific Islands descent who are resident in New Zealand and who wish to study for an undergraduate tertiary qualification at a New Zealand university. Recipient must spend 6-10 weeks of vacation break in employment with Statistics New Zealand. Based on relevance of course of study; academic ability; language, community involvement, and culture; and personal attributes, including potential leadership qualities. References required.

1 award annually. Renewable up to 3 years. Contact Anisiata Soagia-Pritchard, EEO Coordinator, for an application. Notification in December.

1627—STATISTICS NEW ZEALAND (Te Tari Tatau Scholarship)

EEO Co-ordinator; P.O. Box 2922
Wellington NEW ZEALAND
04/495-4643
FAX: 04/495-4817
Internet: http://www.stats.govt.nz/
E-mail: anisiata_soagia-pritchard@stats.govt.nz

AMOUNT: $3,500/year + travel
DEADLINE(S): OCT 31

FIELD(S): Statistics; Mathematics

Open to all Maori who are resident in New Zealand and who wish to study for a statistics or mathematics undergraduate tertiary qualification at a New Zealand university. Recipient must spend 6-10 weeks of vacation break in employment with Statistics New Zealand. Based on relevance of course of study; academic ability; language, community involvement, and culture; and personal attributes, including potential leadership qualities. References required.

1 award annually. Renewable up to 3 years. Contact Anisiata Soagia-Pritchard, EEO Co-ordinator, for an application. Notification in December.

1628—THE UNIVERSITY OF WALES (Scholarships in Physics With Technical English)

University of Wales
Aberystwyth, Penglais
Cerdigion SY23 2AX WALES UK
+44-(0)1970-622065
FAX: +44-(0)1970-622554
E-mail: kyh@aber.ac.uk
Internet: http://www.aber.ac.uk/~dphwww/tech/tech.html

AMOUNT: Costs of courses

DEADLINE(S): None

FIELD(S): Physics and English

Scholarships for non-English-speaking students who wish to pursue studies in physics at this university in Wales. The scholarship provides an English language course, weekly tutorials in Technical English, and the course work in physics once English in learned to complete the technical work. Student needs IELTS 6.5 or TOFEL 580 or equivalent. Must qualify for British university entrance in physics and mathematics for an Honours Degree Course.

For more information, write, phone, fax, or E-mail Dr. Keith Birkinshaw, Dept. of Physics. Also, see Web site for more details.

1629—THE UNIVERSITY OF WALES (Undergraduate Scholarships in Physics)

University of Wales
Aberystwyth, Penglais
Cerdigion SY23 WALES UK
+44(01970) 622065
E-mail: mqr@aber.ac.uk
Internet: http://www.aber.ac.uk/~dphwww/ugrad/ugscholar.html

AMOUNT: 100-1200 pounds/year

DEADLINE(S): DEC 15

FIELD(S): Physics

Scholarships for students who wish to pursue studies in physics at this university in Wales. Eligibility includes taking a scholarship exam in two subjects, of which physics must be one, in January, which may be taken at the applicant's school.

For exam info., contact Mary Richardson, Marketing and Recruitment Office. For those who do not qualify on the exam, students with 16 points or more in physics and mathematics at A-level will be awarded a 500 point departmental scholarship. See Web site for more details.

1630—THE WALT DISNEY COMPANY (American Teacher Awards)

P.O. Box 9805
Calabasas CA 91372

AMOUNT: $2,500 (36 awards); $25,000 (Outstanding Teacher of the Year)

DEADLINE(S): FEB 15

FIELD(S): Teachers: Athletic Coach, Early Childhood, English, Foreign Language/ESL, General Elementary, Mathematics, Performing Arts, Physical Education/Health, Science, Social Studies, Visual Arts, Vo-Tech Education

Awards for K-12 teachers in the above fields.

Teachers, or anyone who knows a great teacher, can write for applications at the above address.

1631—U.S. DEPARTMENT OF DEFENSE (High School Apprenticeship Program)

U.S. Army Cold Regions Research and Engineering Laboratory
72 Lyme Road
Hanover NH 03755
603/646-4500; DSN: 220-4500
FAX: 603/646-4693
Internet: http://www.acq.osd.mil/ddre/edugate/s-aindx.html

AMOUNT: Internship

DEADLINE(S): None specified

FIELD(S): Sciences and Engineering

A teacher must recommend you for these three competitive high school apprenticeships with our Laboratory. High school students from New Hampshire who are at least 16 and who have completed their junior year in high school are eligible. Should have interest and ability in science, engineering, or mathematics.

Applications are available from participating local high school guidance counselors. Contact Susan Koh at the above address for more information.

1632—U.S. DEPARTMENT OF DEFENSE (SEAP Science and Engineering Apprenticeship Program)

707 22nd Street, NW
Washington DC 20052
202/994-2234
FAX: 202/994-2459
Internet: http://www.acq.osd.mil/ddre/edugate/ceeindx.htm/#A010

AMOUNT: $1,400 (min.)

DEADLINE(S): JAN 26

FIELD(S): Science; Engineering

Eight-week summer apprenticeships throughout the U.S. are available to high school students who are U.S. citizens planning careers in science or engineering. Based on grades, science/math courses taken, scores on standardized tests, areas of interest, teacher recommendations, and personal student statement. Students responsible for transportation to and from site.

See Web site or contact M. Phillips for an application. Refer to Code #A010.

1633—UNCF/MERCK SCIENCE INITIATIVE (Undergraduate Science Research Scholarship Awards)

8260 Willow Oaks Corporate Dr.
P.O. Box 10444
FairFAX: VA 22031-4511
703/205-3503
FAX: 703/205-3574
E-mail: uncfmerck@uncf.org
Internet: http://www.uncf.org/merck

AMOUNT: $25,000/year (max.)

DEADLINE(S): DEC 15

FIELD(S): Life and Physical Sciences

Open to African-Americans in their junior year of college who will receive a bachelor's degree in the following academic year. Must be enrolled full-time in any four-year college/university in the U.S. and have a minimum 3.3 GPA. Must be U.S. citizen/permanent resident. Financial need NOT a factor.

15 awards annually. Not renewable. Contact Jerry Bryant, Ph.D., for an application.

1634—UNIVERSITY OF NEWCASTLE/Australia (R. M. Sheahan Memorial Undergraduate Scholarship)

Student Administration Unit, Student Services Centre, Univ. of Newcastle,
Callaghan NSW
2308 AUSTRALIA
+61-(02)-4921-6539

FAX: +61-(02)-4960-1766
E-mail: scholarships@newcastle.edu.au
Internet: http://http://www.newcastle.edu.au/services/ousr/stuadmin/schol/index.htm
AMOUNT: $1,000
DEADLINE(S): NOV 1
FIELD(S): Engineering, chemistry, or environmental engineering

Scholarship for undergraduate international as well as Australian students pursuing studies in chemistry, chemical engineering, or environmental engineering. Funded by the Cessnock City Council and Orica (ICI) Explosives, this award is made yearly based on academic merit.

Contact organization for details.

1635—WOMEN IN DEFENSE (HORIZONS Scholarship Foundation)

NDIA; 2111 Wilson Boulevard, Suite 400
Arlington VA 22201-3061
703/247-2552
FAX: 703/522-1820
E-mail: cbanks@mciworld.com
Internet: http://www.ndia.org/wid/
AMOUNT: $500+
DEADLINE(S): NOV 1; JUL 1
FIELD(S): Engineering; Computer Science; Physics; Math; Business; Law; International Relations; Political Science; Operations Research; Economics; National Security/Defense

Open to women employed/planning careers in defense/national security areas. Must be currently enrolled full- or part-time at an accredited college/university at the graduate or undergraduate junior/senior level. Must have a minimum 3.25 GPA, demonstrate financial need, and be U.S. citizen. Based on academic achievement, work experience, objectives, and recommendations.

Renewable. See Web site or MUST send self-addressed, stamped envelope to Courtney Banks for application.

1636—WOODROW WILSON NATIONAL FELLOWSHIP FOUNDATION (Leadership Program for Teachers)

CN 5281
Princeton NJ 08543-5281
609/452-700
FAX: 609/452-0066
E-mail: marchioni@woodrow.org or irish@woodrow.org
Internet: http://www.woodrow.org
AMOUNT: Varies
DEADLINE(S): Varies
FIELD(S): Science; Mathematics

WWLPT offers summer institutes for middle and high school teachers in science and mathematics. One- and two-week teacher outreach, TORCH Institutes, are held in the summer throughout the U.S.

See Web site or contact WWNFF for an application.

1637—WOODS HOLE OCEANOGRAPHIC INSTITUTION (Traineeships in Oceanography for Minority Group Undergraduates)

360 Woods Hole Road
Woods Hole MA 02543-1541
508/289-2219
FAX: 508/457-2188
E-mail: mgately@whoi.edu
Internet: http://www.whoi.edu
AMOUNT: Varies
DEADLINE(S): FEB 16
FIELD(S): Physical/Natural Sciences, Mathematics, Engineering

For minority undergraduates enrolled in U.S. colleges/universities who have completed at least two semesters. These awards provide training and research experience for students with interests in the above fields. Traineeships may be awarded for a ten- to- twelve-week period in the summer or for a semester during the academic year.

Renewable. For an application/more information, contact the Education Office, Clark Laboratory 223, MS #31, at above address.

MEDICAL DOCTOR

1638—AMERICAN FOUNDATION FOR THE BLIND (Paul W. Ruckes Scholarship)

11 Penn Plaza, Suite 300
New York NY 10001
212/502-7661
FAX: 212/502-7771
E-mail: juliet@afb.org
Internet: http://www.afb.org
AMOUNT: $1,000
DEADLINE(S): APR 30
FIELD(S): Engineering; Computer/Physical/Life Sciences

Open to legally blind and visually impaired undergraduate and graduate students pursuing a degree in one of above fields. Must be U.S. citizen. Must submit written documentation of visual impairment from ophthalmologist or optometrist (need not be legally blind); official transcripts; proof of college/university acceptance; three letters of recommendation; and typewritten statement describing goals, work experience extracurricular activities, and how monies will be used.

1 award annually. See Web site or contact Julie Tucker at AFB for an application.

1639—AMERICAN HEART ASSOCIATION (Helen N. and Harold B. Shapira Scholarship)

4701 W. 77th Street
Minneapolis MN 55435
952/835-3300
AMOUNT: $1,000
DEADLIN(S): APR 1
FIELD(S): Medicine

For pre-med undergraduate students and medical students who are accepted to or enrolled in an accredited Minnesota college/university. Medical students should be in a curriculum that is related to the heart and circulatory system. Must be U.S. citizen/legal resident.

Renewable an additional year. Contact AHA for an application.

1640—AMERICAN INDIAN SCIENCE AND ENGINEERING SOCIETY (A.T. Anderson Memorial Scholarship)

P.O. Box 9828
Albuquerque NM 87119-9828
505/765-1052
FAX: 505/765-5608
E-mail: scholarships@aises.org
Internet: http://www.aises.org/scholarships
AMOUNT: $1,000-$2,000
DEADLINE(S): JUN 15
FIELD(S): Medicine; Natural Resources; Science; Engineering

Open to undergraduate and graduate students who are at least 1/4 American Indian or recognized as member of a tribe. Must be member of AISES ($10 fee), enrolled full-time at an accredited institution, and demonstrate financial need.

Renewable. See Web site or contact Patricia Browne for an application and/or membership information.

1641—ARTHUR M. MILLER FUND

P.O. Box 1122
Wichita KS 67201-0004
316/261-4609
AMOUNT: Varies
DEADLINE(S): MAR 31

FIELD(S): Medicine or related fields

Scholarships for Kansas residents for the study of medicine or related fields at accredited institutions.

Send SASE for formal application.

1642—ASSOCIATION ON AMERICAN INDIAN AFFAIRS (Emergency Aid and Health Professions Scholarships)

P.O. Box 268
Sisseton SD 57262
605/698-3998
FAX: 605/698-3316
E-mail: aaia@sbtc.net
Internet: http://www.indian-affairs.org

AMOUNT: See Web site for information.
DEADLINE(S): MAY 1
FIELD(S): Health Professions

Open to full-time undergraduate students who are minimally 1/4 degree Indian blood from a federally recognized tribe. Award is based on financial need and is limited to North America/Alaska. Must submit essay on need, certificate of enrollment and quantum from your tribe or BIA, transcript, schedule of classes, and current financial aid award letter.

See Web site for information on requirements or send a self-addressed, stamped envelope to Elena Stops, Scholarship Coordinator, for an application.

1643—BECA FOUNDATION (Alice Newell Joslyn Medical Fund)

830 E. Grand Avenue, Suite B
Escondido CA 92025
760/471-8246
FAX: 760/471-8176

AMOUNT: $500-$1,000
DEADLINE(S): MAR 1
FIELD(S): Medicine; Health Care; Nursing; Dental/Medical Assisting; Physical Therapy

Open to Latino students who live in or attend college in San Diego County, CA, at time of application. For high school seniors and those already in college pursuing undergraduate or graduate education. Based on financial need, scholastic determination, and community/cultural awareness.

Send self-addressed, stamped envelope to BECA for an application.

1644—BOYS AND GIRLS CLUBS OF SAN DIEGO (Spence Reese Scholarship Fund)

1761 Hotel Circle So., Suite 123
San Diego CA 92108
619/298-3520

AMOUNT: $2,000/year
DEADLINE(S): MAY 15
FIELD(S): Medicine; Law; Engineering; Political Science

Open to male high school seniors planning a career in one of the above fields. Must be residents of Imperial, Riverside, Orange, San Diego, or Los Angeles counties in California. Boys and Girls Club affiliation NOT required.

$10 application fee. Renewable up to 4 years. Send a self-addressed, stamped envelope to Boys and Girls Club for an application after January 1.

1645—CLEM JAUNICH EDUCATION TRUST (Scholarships)

7801 E. Bushlake Road, Suite 260
Bloomington MN 55439
612/546-1555

AMOUNT: $750-$3,000
DEADLINE(S): JUL 1
FIELD(S): Theology; Medicine

Open to students who have attended public or parochial school in the Delano (MN) school district or currently reside within 7 miles of the city of Delano MN. Awards support undergraduate or graduate study in theology or medicine.

4-6 awards annually. Contact Joseph Abrahams for an application.

1646—COLUMBIANA COUNTY PUBLIC HEALTH LEAGUE TRUST FUND (Grants)

c/o Mary Kay Withum
P.O. Box 511
Wheeling WV 26003
304/234-4128
FAX: 304/234-4142

AMOUNT: Varies
DEADLINE(S): FEB 28
FIELD(S): Respiratory Illness; Medicine; Medical Research; Pharmacy; Medical Technology; Physical Therapy; Nursing; Dental Hygiene; Occupational Therapy

Open to undergraduate and graduate Columbiana County, Ohio, residents who are pursuing medical education or research in one of the above fields. Preference given to respiratory illness. Students of veterinary medicine NOT eligible.

Contact Sherrill Schmied for an application.

1647—DEMOLAY FOUNDATION INC. (Scholarships)

10200 NW Ambassador Boulevard
Kansas City MO 64153
816/891-8333
FAX: 816/891-9062
Internet: http://www.demolay.org

AMOUNT: $1,500
DEADLINE(S): APR 1
FIELD(S): Dental or medical fields

Open to all active and/or senior DeMolays. Considerations are leadership, academic achievement, and goals.

Four grants per year. Write for complete information.

1648—DEPARTMENT OF THE ARMY (Armed Forces Health Professions Scholarships)

Attn: RC-HS
1307 Third Avenue
Fort Knox KY 40121
502/626-0367
FAX: 502/626-0923

AMOUNT: Tuition + monthly stipend and reimbursement for mandatory books and other specific academic expenses.
DEADLINE(S): None
FIELD(S): Medicine; Osteopathy; Nurse Anesthetist; Veterinary Medicine; Optometry; Psychology; Dentistry

Open to health professionals and students participating in an accredited program of studies in the specialties listed above. Must be U.S. citizen. Award is based on a competitive process, including GPA. Financial need NOT a factor.

400 awards annually. Contact Major Beecher at above address for an application.

1649—EDWARD BANGS KELLEY AND ELZA KELLEY FOUNDATION, INC. (Scholarship Program)

P.O. Drawer M
Hyannis MA 02601-1412
508/775-3117

AMOUNT: $500-$4,000 (max.)
DEADLINE(S): APR 30
FIELD(S): Medicine; Nursing; Education; Health and Social Sciences

Open to residents of Barnstable County, Massachusetts. Scholarships are intended to benefit health and welfare of Barnstable County residents. Awards support study at recognized undergraduate, graduate, and professional institutions. Financial need is considered.

Contact Foundation for an application Scholarship Committee for an application.

1650—FIRST UNITED METHODIST CHURCH (Robert Stevenson and Doreene E. Cater Scholarships)

302 5th Avenue S.
St. Cloud MN 56301
FAX: 320/251-0878
E-mail: fumc@fumc-stcloud.org;
AMOUNT: $200-1,500
DEADLINE(S): JUN 1
FIELD(S): Humanitarian and Christian Service: Teaching, Medicine, Social Work, Environmental Studies, etc.

Stevenson Scholarship is open to undergraduate members of the First United Methodist Church of St. Cloud. Cater Scholarship is open to members of the Minnesota United Methodist Conference who are entering the sophomore year or higher of college work. Both require two letters of reference, transcripts, and financial need.

5-6 awards annually. Contact Scholarship Committee for an application.

1651—FOUNDATION FOR SEACOAST HEALTH (Scholarship Program)

100 Campus Drive, Suite 1
Portsmouth NH 03801
603/422-8200
FAX: 602/422-8207
E-mail: ffsh@communitycampus.org
Internet: http://www.ffsh.org
AMOUNT: $1,000-$10,000
DEADLINE(S): FEB 1
FIELD(S): Health-related fields. For residents of New Hampshire and Maine.

1652—GRACE FOUNDATION (Scholarship Trust Fund)

P.O. Box 924
Menlo Park CA 94026-0924
Written Inquiry
AMOUNT: $1,000-$4,000
DEADLINE(S): JAN 31
FIELD(S): Ministry; Medicine; Teaching; Social Service

Open to students from developing countries in Asia/Southeast Asia to pursue full-time study at an accredited college/university. For training future Christian ministers and professional workers in above fields. Must have completed one or more years of college in or near their native country, be a strong Christian, have a minimum 3.0 GPA, and demonstrate financial need.

Renewable up to 4 years with maintenance of 3.0 GPA. Applications available between September 1 and October 31.

1653—H. FLETCHER BROWN FUND (Scholarships)

c/o PNC Bank; Trust Dept.
P.O. Box 791
Wilmington DE 19899
302/429-1186
AMOUNT: Varies
DEADLINE(S): APR 15
FIELD(S): Medicine; Dentistry; Law; Engineering; Chemistry

Open to U.S. citizens born in Delaware and still residing in Delaware. For 4 years of study (undergrad or grad) leading to a degree that enables applicant to practice in chosen field.

Scholarships are based on need, scholastic achievement, and good moral character. Applications available in February. Write for complete information.

1654—H. FLETCHER BROWN TRUST (Scholarships)

222 Delaware Avenue, 16th Floor
Wilmington DE 19899
302/429-1338
AMOUNT: Varies
DEADLINE(S): APR 9
FIELD(S): Chemistry; Engineering; Law; Medicine; Dentistry

Open to financially needy native-born DELAWARE residents ONLY who are pursuing an undergraduate degree. Must have minimum 1,000 SAT score and rank in upper 20% of class. Interview required.

Send self-addressed, stamped envelope to Donald Drois, Account Administrator, PNC Bank, at above address for an application.

1655—HOUSTON LIVESTOCK SHOW AND RODEO (4H and FFA Scholarships)

2000 S. Loop West
Houston TX 77054
713/791-9000
FAX: 713-794-9528
E-Mail: info@rodeohouston.com
Internet: http://www.hlsr.com/education/
AMOUNT: $10,000
DEADLINE(S): Varies
FIELD(S): Agriculture; Life Sciences

Open to undergraduate students who are actively involved in the 4-H or FFA programs. Must major in an agricultural or life sciences field of study at a Texas college/university and demonstrate academic potential, citizenship/leadership, and financial need.

140 awards annually. Contact HLSR for an application.

1656—INTERNATIONAL ORDER OF THE KING'S DAUGHTERS AND SONS (Health Careers Scholarships)

c/o Mrs. Fred Cannon; Box 1310
Brookhaven MS 39602
Written Inquiry
AMOUNT: $1,000 (max.)
DEADLINE(S): APR 1
FIELD(S): Medicine; Dentistry; Nursing; Physical Therapy; Occupational Therapy; Medical Technologies; Pharmacy

Open to students accepted to/enrolled in an accredited U.S. or Canadian four-year or graduate school. RN candidates must have completed first year of program; MD or DDS candidates must be for at least the second year of medical or dental school; all others must be in at least third year of four-year program. Pre-med students NOT eligible. Must be U.S. or Canadian citizen.

Send self-addressed, stamped envelope, along with a letter stating the field of study and present level, to the Director at above address for an application.

1657—J. HUGH and EARLE W. FELLOWS MEMORIAL FUND (Scholarship Loans)

Pensacola Junior College President
1000 College Boulevard
Pensacola FL 32504-8998
904/484-1700
Internet: http://www.pjc.cc.fl.us/
AMOUNT: Each is negotiated individually
DEADLINE(S): None
FIELD(S): Medicine; Nursing; Medical Technology; Theology (Episcopal)

Open to bona fide residents of the Florida counties of Escambia, Santa Rosa, Okaloosa, or Walton. For undergraduate study in the fields listed above. U.S. citizenship required.

Loans are interest-free until graduation. Write for complete information.

1658—JEWISH VOCATIONAL SERVICE (Academic Scholarship Program)

One S. Franklin Street
Chicago IL 60606
312/357-4500
FAX: 312/855-3282
TTY: 312/855-3282
E-mail: jvschicago@jon.cjfny.org
AMOUNT: $5,000 (max.)

DEADLINE(S): MAR 1
FIELD(S): "Helping" Professions; Mathematics; Engineering; Sciences; Communications (at Univ IL only); Law (certain schools in IL only)

Open to Jewish men and women legally domiciled in the greater Chicago metropolitan area, who are identified as having promise for significant contributions in their chosen careers, and are in need of financial assistance for full-time academic programs in above areas. Must have entered undergraduate junior year in career programs requiring no postgrad education, be in graduate/professional school, or be in a vo-tech training program. Interview required.

Renewable. Contact JVS for an application between December 1 and February 15th.

1659—JUNIATA COLLEGE (Robert Steele Memorial Scholarship)

Office of Student Financial Planning
Juniata College
1700 Moore Street
Huntingdon PA 16652
814/641-3142
FAX: 814/641-5311
Internet: http://www.juniata.edu/
E-mail: clarkec@juniata.edu
AMOUNT: $4,000 (max.)
DEADLINE(S): APR 1
FIELD(S): Science; Medical Studies

Open to science/medical students applying to Juniata College. Must demonstrate financial need and fill out government FAFSA form.

Contact Randy Rennell, Director of Student Financial Planning, for an application or enrollment information. See your financial aid office for FAFSA.

1660—KOREAN-AMERICAN SCIENTISTS AND ENGINEERS ASSOCIATION (KSEA Scholarships)

1952 Gallows Road, Suite 300
Vienna VA 22182
703/748-1221
FAX: 703/748-1331
E-mail: admin@ksea.org
Internet: http://www.ksea.org
AMOUNT: $1,000
DEADLINE(S): FEB 28
FIELD(S): Science, Engineering, or Medicine

Scholarships to encourage Korean-American students to study in a science, engineering, or pre-med discipline and to recognize high-performing students. Must have graduated from a high school in the U.S.

5 to 8 awards yearly. Must be a student member of KSEA or a child of a member.

1661—LADY ALLEN OF HURTWOOD MEMORIAL TRUST (Travel Grants)

21 Aspull Common
Leigh Lancs WN7 3PB ENGLAND
01942-674895
AMOUNT: Up to 1,000 pounds sterling
DEADLINE(S): JAN 15
FIELD(S): Welfare and Education of Children

A travel grant to those whose proposed project will directly benefit their work with children. People working with children and young people may apply, particularly those working with disabled and disadvantaged children. Successful candidates must write up an account of the work which the scholarship has funded. GRANTS ARE NOT FOR ACADEMIC STUDY; ONLY QUALIFIED INDIVIDUALS MAY APPLY.

Contact Dorothy E. Whitaker, Trustee, for application forms-available between May and December each year.

1662—MINNESOTA DEPARTMENT OF HEALTH (Health Professions Grants)

Metro Square Bldg.
121E. 7th Place, Suite 460
St. Paul MN 55101
651/282-3838 or 800/366-5424 (Minnesota only)
AMOUNT: Varies from $3,000 to $25,000 dependent on program
DEADLINE(S): DEC 1
FIELD(S): Health Professions

Five loan repayment programs for health professionals who agree to serve in either federally designated Health Professional Shortage Areas, in designated, underserved urban or rural areas, public program dental recipients, or in licensed nursing homes.

For details contact the Minnesota Department of Health at 651/282-3838 or 800/366-5424 (Minnesota only).

1663—McCORD CAREER CENTER (Level II McCord Medical/Music Scholarship)

Healdsburg High School
1024 Prince Street
Healdsburg CA 95448
707/431-3473
Email: career@husd.com
AMOUNT: Varies
DEADLINE(S): APR 15
FIELD(S): Medicine; Music

For graduates of Healdsburg High School who are planning a career in music or medicine. Must be enrolled full-time at a college/university as an undergraduate junior or senior in the fall, or earning an advanced degree in graduate or medical school, or entering into a vocational/certificate program. Transcripts, proof of attendance, and an essay are required.

Contact the McCord Career Center at Healdsburg High School for an application.

1664—NATIONAL FEDERATION OF THE BLIND (Howard Brown Rickard Scholarship)

805 Fifth Avenue
Grinnell IA 50112
515/236-3366
AMOUNT: $3,000
DEADLINE(S): MAR 31
FIELD(S): Law; Medicine; Engineering; Architecture; Natural Sciences

For legally blind students pursuing or planning to pursue a full-time postsecondary course of study in the U.S.. Based on academic excellence, service to the community, and financial need. Membership NOT required.

1 award annually. Renewable. Contact Mrs. Peggy Elliot, Scholarship Committee Chairman, for an application.

1665—NATIONAL HEALTH SERVICE CORPS (NHSC Scholarship Program)

11300 Rockville Pike, Suite 80
Rockville MD 20852
800/638-0824
Internet: http://www.bhpr.hrsa.dhhs.gov/nhsc
AMOUNT: Full tuition/books/fees/supplies + monthly stipend
DEADLINE(S): MAR
FIELD(S): Family Medicine; General Internal Medicine; General Pediatrics; Obstetrics/Gynecology; Family Nurse Practitioners; Primary Care Physician Assistants; Certified Nurse-Midwives

Must be U.S. citizen attending or enrolled in fully accredited U.S. allopathic/osteopathic medical school, nursing program, or physician assistant program. For each year of support received, you must serve one year in federally designated health professional shortage area of greatest need. Minimum two years service commitment begins upon completion of your residency and/or training.

300 awards annually. Renewable up to 4 years. Contact NHSC for an application.

1666—NATIONAL INSTITUTES OF HEALTH (Minority International Research Training Grant)

Fogarty International Center
Bldg. 31, Room B2C39
Bethesda MD 20892-2220
301/402-9467
FAX: 301/402-0779
E-mail: barbara_sina@cu.nih.gov
Internet: http://www.nih.gov/grants/oer.htm
AMOUNT: Varies
DEADLINE(S): MAR 15
FIELD(S): Biomedical and Behavioral Sciences

Open to minorities that are underrepresented in biomedical research professions (African and Hispanic Americans, Native Americans, Alaskan Natives, and Pacific Islanders). May be undergraduate students pursuing life science curricula (8-12 weeks research/coursework supported), students pursuing doctoral degrees in above fields (3-12 months research training at foreign institution supported), or faculty members in above fields (3-12 months research at foreign institution).

See Web site or contact NIH for an application.

1667—NAVY RECRUITING COMMAND (Armed Forces Health Professions Scholarships)

Chief
5722 Integrity Drive
Millington TN 38054
888/633-9674
Internet: http://www.navy.com
AMOUNT: average of $1,058/month stipend + tuition, fees, books, lab fees, etc.
DEADLINE(S): Applications taken year-around
FIELD(S): Medicine, Dentistry, Optometry, Physical Therapy, Pharmacology, Health Care Administration, Industrial Hygiene, etc.

Open to U.S. citizens enrolled or accepted for enrollment in any of the above fields at an accredited institution in the U.S. or Puerto Rico. Must qualify for appointment as a Navy officer and sign a contractual agreement. Must be between the ages of 18 and 40 for some programs and have a GPA around 3.0.

See Web site, contact local Navy Recruiting Office, or contact the above address.

1668—NEW YORK STATE HIGHER EDUCATION SERVICES CORPORATION (N.Y. State Regents Professional/Health Care Opportunity Scholarships)

Cultural Education Center, Room 5C64
Albany NY 12230
518/486-1319
Internet: http://www.hesc.com
AMOUNT: $1,000-$10,000/year
DEADLINE(S): Varies
FIELD(S): Medicine and Dentistry and Related Fields, Architecture, Nursing, Psychology, Audiology, Landscape Architecture, Social Work, Chiropractic, Law, Pharmacy, Accounting, Speech Language Pathology

For NY state residents who are economically disadvantaged and members of a minority group underrepresented in the chosen profession and attending school in NY state. Some programs carry a service obligation in New York for each year of support. For U.S. citizens or qualifying noncitizens.

Medical/dental scholarships require one year of professional work in NY.

1669—OKLAHOMA MEDICAL RESEARCH FOUNDATION (Sir Alexander Fleming Scholar Program)

825 N.E.13th Street
Oklahoma City OK 73104-5046
405/271-8537 or
800/522-0211 (in-state)
Internet: http://www.omrf.ouhsc.edu
AMOUNT: $2,500 salary + housing
DEADLINE(S): Feb 15
FIELD(S): Sciences

Summer scholarship program (June and July) for Oklahoma students who have completed their junior year of high school through those in their junior year of college at time of application. Excellent academic standing and aptitude in science and math are essential. Students will work in the laboratories of the above organization. Research projects will be selected from: alcoholism/liver disease, arthritis/immunology, carcinogenesis, cardiovascular biology, and more.

Named for the scientist who discovered penicillin and dedicated OMRF in 1949. Contact organization for further information and application forms.

1670—PENINSULA COMMUNITY FOUNDATION (Dr. James L. Hutchinson and Evelyn Ribbs Hutchinson Scholarship Fund)

1700 S. El Camino Real, #300
San Mateo CA 94402
650/358-9369
FAX: 650/358-3950
Internet: http://www.pcs.org
AMOUNT: Up to $2,000
DEADLINE(S): MAY
FIELD(S): Medicine

Scholarships for graduates of a San Mateo County or Santa Clara County, California, high school. Must be U.S. citizen in final year of college and accepted to a medical school or be currently enrolled full-time in an accredited medical school program.

Awards are for one year, but recipients may re-apply.

Contact Wendy Edwards at the Foundation for more information.

1671—PENINSULA COMMUNITY FOUNDATION (Dr. Mary Finegold Scholarship)

1700 S. El Camino Real, #300
San Mateo CA 94402
650/358-9369
FAX: 650/358-9817
Internet: http://www.pcf.org/community_grants/scholarships.html
AMOUNT: $1,000
DEADLINE(S): MAR 7 (5 p.m.)
FIELD(S): Sciences

Scholarships for senior girls graduating from high school in Palo Alto, California, who intend to complete a four-year degree in the sciences. Special consideration will be given to girls who have demonstrated a "pioneering" spirit in that they have not been constrained by stereotypical female roles and to those facing financial hardship.

Award was established in the honor of Dr. Mary Finegold who, after completing her medical studies, elected to stay at home until her youngest child was in high school before beginning her medical practice. She was a school physician.

1672—PILOT INTERNATIONAL FOUNDATION (PIF/Lifeline Scholarship)

P.O. Box 5600
Macon GA 31208-5600
Written Inquiries
AMOUNT: Varies
DEADLINE(S): MAR 1

FIELD(S): Disabilities/Brain-related Disorders

This program assists ADULT students re-entering the job market, preparing for a second career, or improving their professional skills for an established career. Applicants must be preparing for, or already involved in, careers working with people with disabilities/brain-related disorders. GPA of 3.5 or more is required.

Must be sponsored by a Pilot Club in your home town, or in the city in which your college or university is located. Send a self-addressed, stamped envelope for complete information.

1673—PILOT INTERNATIONAL FOUNDATION (Ruby Newhall Memorial Scholarship)

P.O. Box 5600
Macon, GA 31208-5600
Written Inquiries
AMOUNT: Varies
DEADLINE(S): MAR 15
FIELD(S): Disabilities/Brain-related disorders

For international students who have studied in the U.S. for at least one year, and who intend to return to their home country six months after graduation. Applicants must be full-time students majoring in a field related to human health and welfare, and have a GPA of 3.5 or more.

Applicants must be sponsored by a Pilot Club in their home town, or in the city in which their college or university is located. Send a self-addressed, stamped envelope for complete information.

1674—PILOT INTERNATIONAL FOUNDATION (The Pilot International Scholarship Program)

P.O. Box 5600
Macon GA 31208-5600
Written Inquiries
AMOUNT: Varies
DEADLINE(S): MAR 1
FIELD(S): Disabilities/Brain-related disorders

This program provides assistance to undergraduate students preparing for careers working directly with people with disabilities or training those who will. GPA of 3.5 or greater required.

Applicants must be sponsored by a Pilot Club in their home town, or in the city in which their college or university is located. Send a self-addressed, stamped envelope for complete information.

1675—RAYMOND J. HARRIS EDUCATION TRUST

P.O. Box 7899
Philadelphia PA 19101-7899
Written Inquiry
AMOUNT: Varies
DEADLINE(S): FEB 1
FIELD(S): Medicine, Law, Engineering, Dentistry, or Agriculture

Scholarships for Christian men to obtain a professional education in medicine, law, engineering, dentistry, or agriculture at nine Philadelphia area colleges.

Contact Mellon Bank, N.A. at above location for details and the names of the nine colleges.

1676—ROBERT SCHRECK MEMORIAL FUND (Grants)

c/o Texas Commerce Bank, Trust Dept
P.O. Drawer 140
El Paso TX 79980
915/546-6515
AMOUNT: $500-$1500
DEADLINE(S): JUL 15; NOV 15
FIELD(S): Medicine; Veterinary Medicine; Physics; Chemistry; Architecture; Engineering; Episcopal Clergy

Grants to undergraduate juniors or seniors or graduate students who have been residents of El Paso County for at least two years. Must be U.S. citizen or legal resident and have a high grade point average. Financial need is a consideration.

Write for complete information.

1677—SRP/NAVAJO GENERATING STATION (Navajo Scholarship)

P.O. Box 850
Page AZ 86040
520/645-6539
FAX: 520/645-7295
E-mail: ljdawave@srp.gov
AMOUNT: Based on need
DEADLINE(S): APR 30
FIELD(S): Engineering, Environmental Studies, Business, Business Management, Health, Education

Scholarships for full-time students who hold membership in the Navajo Tribe and who are pursuing a degree in a field of study recognized as significant to the Navajo Naiton, Salt River Project, or the Navajo Generating Station, such as those listed above. Must be junior or senior, have and maintain a GPA of 3.0

Average of 15 awards per year. Inquire of Linda Dawavendewa at above location.

1678—U.S. DEPT. OF HEALTH and HUMAN SERVICES (Indian Health Service Health Professions Scholarship Program)

Twinbrook Metro Plaza, Suite 100
12300 Twinbrook Parkway
Rockville MD 20852
301/443-0234
FAX: 301/443-4815
Internet: http://www.ihs.gov/Recruitment/DHPS/SP/SBTOC3.asp
AMOUNT: Tuition + fees and monthly stipend of $938.
DEADLINE(S): APR 1
FIELD(S): Health professions, accounting, social work

Open to Native Americans or Alaska natives who are graduate students or college juniors or seniors in a program leading to a career in a fields listed above. U.S. citizenship required. Renewable annually with reapplication.

Scholarship recipients must intend to serve the Indian people. They incur a one-year service obligation to the IHS for each year of support for a minimum of two years. Write for complete information.

1679—UNIVERSITY OF EDINBURGH (Faculty of Medicine Bursaries and Scholarships)

7-11 Nicolson Street
Edinburgh SCOTLAND EH8 9BE UK
+44 (0) 131 650 1000
Internet: http://www.iprs.ed.ac.uk/progawards/medicine/
AMOUNT: Varies
DEADLINE(S): Varies
FIELD(S): Medicine

Access Web site for more information and/or contact school for details and appropriate application forms.

1680—USAF RESERVE PERSONNEL CENTER (Armed Forces Health Professional Scholarships)

6760 E. Irvington Pl., #7000
Denver CO 80280-7300
Written Inquiry
AMOUNT: Varies
DEADLINE(S): None specified
FIELD(S): Physicans: Anesthesiology, Surgical Specialties; Nursing: Anesthesia, Operating Room, or Medical Surgical Nursing.

For health professionals and students participating in a Reserve Service of the U.S. Armed Forces training in the specialties listed above and for undergraduate nursing students. A monthly stipend is paid, and varying lengths of service are required to pay back the stipend.

Air Force: above address; Army: Headquarters, Dept. of the Army, 5109 Leesburg Pike, Falls Church, VA 22041-3258; Navy: Naval Reserve Recruiting Command, 4400 Dauphine Street, New Orleans, LA 70146.

1681—USAF RESERVE BONUS PROGRAM

6760 East Irvington Place, #7000
Denver CO 80280-7000
800/525-0102 ext 71231 or 71237; DSN 926-6484;
Commercial: 303/676-6484
FAX: 303/676-6164
FAX: DSN: 926-6164
E-mail: Joseph.Andujo@arpc.Denver.af.mil
Internet: http://www.arpc.org
AMOUNT: Varies, see Web site.
DEADLINE(S): Varies, see Web site.
FIELD(S): Various medical fields and specialties.

A bonus pay program to recruit critically needed medical specialties into the Selected Reserve of the U.S. Air Force.

Direct questions to: Medical Readiness and Incentives Division, TSgt. Joseph Andujo at above.

1682—WASHINGTON STATE HIGHER EDUCATION COORDINATING BOARD (Health Professional Loan Repayment and Scholarship Program)

P.O. Box 47834
Olympia WA 98504-3430
360/705-6664
FAX: 360/664-9273
Internet: http://www.hecb.wa.gov
AMOUNT: Varies
DEADLINE(S): APR (scholarship); FEB (loan repayment); JUL (loan repayment)
FIELD(S): Health Care

Scholarships are open to students in accredited undergraduate or graduate health care programs leading to eligibility for licensure in Washington state. Must agree to work in designated shortage area for minimum of three years. Loan repayment recipients receive payment from program for purpose of repaying education loans secured while attending program of health care training leading to licensure in Washington state. Financial need NOT a factor.

Renewable up to 5 years. Contact Program Manager for a loan repayment application after November 15 and for scholarship application after January 15.

1683—WASHINGTON STATE HIGHER EDUCATION COORDINATING BOARD (WICHE Professional Student Exchange)

P.O. Box 43430
Olympia WA 98504-3430
360/753-7850
FAX: 360/753-7808
E-mail: lindala@hecb.wa.gov
AMOUNT: $10,000-$15,000
DEADLINE(S): OCT 15
FIELD(S): Optometry; Osteopathy

Program provides state support to Washington residents pursuing undergraduate or graduate study out-of-state.

12 awards annually (10 renewals, four new). Contact Program Manager for an application.

1684—WOMEN OF THE EVANGELICAL LUTHERAN CHURCH IN AMERICA (The Kahler-Vickers/Raup-Emma Wettstein Scholarships)

8765 West Higgins Road
Chicago IL 60631-4189
800/638-3522 ext. 2736
FAX: 773/380-2419
E-mail: womnelca@elca.org
AMOUNT: $2,000 max.
DEADLINE(S): FEB 15
FIELD(S): Health Professions and Christian Service

Assists women who are members of the ELCA studying for service in health professions associated with ELCA projects abroad that do not lead to church-certified professions. Must be U.S. citizen and have experienced an interruption of two or more years since completion of high school. Academic records of coursework completed in last five years as well as proof of admission from educational institution are required.

Renewable for an additional year. Contact Faith Fretheim, Program Director, for an application.

1685—ZETA PHI BETA SORORITY EDUCATIONAL FOUNDATION (S. Evelyn Lewis Memorial Scholarship in Medical Health Sciences)

1734 New Hampshire Avenue NW
Washington DC 20009
Internet: http://www.zpb1920.org
AMOUNT: $500-$1,000
DEADLINE(S): JAN 1
FIELD(S): Medicine; Health Sciences

Open to graduate and undergraduate young women enrolled in a program leading to a degree in medicine or health sciences. Award is for full-time study for one academic year (Fall-Spring) and is paid directly to college/university. Must submit proof of enrollment.

Send self-addressed, stamped envelope to above address between September 1 and December 15 for an application.

MEDICAL-RELATED DISCIPLINES

1686—ABBIE SARGENT MEMORIAL SCHOLARSHIP INC. (Scholarships)

295 Sheep Davis Road
Concord NH 03301
603/224-1934
FAX: 603/228-8432
AMOUNT: $200-400
DEADLINE(S): MAR 15
FIELD(S): Agriculture; Veterinary Medicine; Home Economics

Open to New Hampshire residents who are high school graduates with good grades and character. For undergraduate or graduate study. Must be legal resident of U.S. and demonstrate financial need.

Renewable with reapplication. Write or call for complete information.

1687—AMERICAN COLLEGE OF MEDICAL PRACTICE EXECUTIVES (ACMPE Scholarships)

104 Inverness Terrace East
Englewood CO 80112-5306
303/643-9573 ext. 206
AMOUNT: $500-$2,000
DEADLINE(S): JUN 1
FIELD(S): Health Care Administration/Medical Practice Management

Open to undergraduate or graduate students who are pursuing a degree relevant to medical practice management at an accredited university or college.

Send #10 SASE to receive application.

1688—AMERICAN DENTAL ASSOCIATION (The ADA Endowment and Assistance Fund, Inc.)

211 East Chicago Avenue
Chicago IL 60611
312/440-2567
AMOUNT: $1,000-$2,500
DEADLINE(S): JUN 15; AUG 15
FIELD(S): Health care

For dental students in their second year of studies currently attending an accredited dental school. Must demonstrate financial need and maintain a 3.0 GPA

1689—AMERICAN FOUNDATION FOR THE BLIND (Paul W. Ruckes Scholarship)

11 Penn Plaza, Suite 300
New York NY 10001
212/502-7661
FAX: 212/502-7771
E-mail: juliet@afb.org
Internet: http://www.afb.org
AMOUNT: $1,000
DEADLINE(S): APR 30
FIELD(S): Engineering; Computer/Physical/Life Sciences

Open to legally blind and visually impaired undergraduate and graduate students pursuing a degree in one of above fields. Must be U.S. citizen. Must submit written documentation of visual impairment from ophthalmologist or optometrist (need not be legally blind); official transcripts; proof of college/university acceptance; three letters of recommendation; and typewritten statement describing goals, work experience extracurricular activities, and how monies will be used.

1 award annually. See Web site or contact Julie Tucker at AFB for an application.

1690—AMERICAN INDIAN SCIENCE AND ENGINEERING SOCIETY (A.T. Anderson Memorial Scholarship)

P.O. Box 9828
Albuquerque NM 87119-9828
505/765-1052
FAX: 505/765-5608
E-mail: scholarships@aises.org
Internet: http://www.aises.org/scholarships
AMOUNT: $1,000-$2,000
DEADLINE(S): JUN 15
FIELD(S): Medicine; Natural Resources; Science; Engineering

Open to undergraduate and graduate students who are at least 1/4 American Indian or recognized as member of a tribe. Must be member of AISES ($10 fee), enrolled full-time at an accredited institution, and demonstrate financial need.

Renewable. See Web site or contact Patricia Browne for an application and/or membership information.

1691—AMERICAN INDIAN SCIENCE AND ENGINEERING SOCIETY (Burlington Northern Santa Fe Pacific Foundation Scholarships)

P.O. Box 9828
Albuquerque NM 87119-9828
505/765-1052
FAX: 505/765-5608
E-mail: scholarships@aises.org
Internet: http://www.aises.org/scholarships
AMOUNT: $2,500/year
DEADLINE(S): MAR 31
FIELD(S): Business; Education; Science; Engineering; Health Administration

Open to high school seniors who are at least 1/4 American Indian. Must reside in KS, OK, CO, AZ, NM, MN, ND, OR, SD, WA, MT, or San Bernardino County, CA (Burlington Northern and Santa Fe Pacific service areas). Must demonstrate financial need.

5 awards annually. Renewable up to 4 years. See Web site or contact Patricia Browne for an application.

1692—AMERICAN MEDICAL WOMEN'S ASSOCIATION FOUNDATION (The Wilhelm-Frankowski Scholarship)

801 North FairFAX: Street, Suite 400
Alexandria VA 22314
703/838-0500
E-mail: mglanz@amwa-doc.org
AMOUNT: $4,000
DEADLINE(S): APR 30
FIELD(S): Medicine

Award selection is based upon community service, activity in women's health issues, and participation in AMWA and other women in medicine groups. Applicants must be an AMWA student member and attending an accredited U.S. medical or

1693—AMERICAN SOCIETY FOR CLINICAL LABORATORY SCIENCE (Ruth M. French Graduate or Undergraduate Scholarship)

7910 Woodmont Avenue, Suite 530
Bethesda MD 20814
301/657-2768
FAX: 301/657-2909
AMOUNT: $1,000
DEADLINE(S): MAR 1
FIELD(S): Clinical Laboratory Science or Medical Technology

Scholarships for students in the above field enrolled in an approved undergraduate or graduate program. Undergrads must be in last year of study. U.S. citizenship or permanent U.S. residency required.

Contact address above for complete information. Enclose self-addressed, stamped business size envelope. Applications available after Nov. 1.

1694—AMERICAN SOCIETY FOR CLINICAL LABORATORY SCIENCE (Alpha Mu Tau Undergraduate Scholarship)

7910 Woodmont Avenue, Suite 530
Bethesda MD 20814
301/657-2768
FAX: 301/657-2909
AMOUNT: Up to $1,000
DEADLINE(S): MAR 15
FIELD(S): Clinical Laboratory Science, Medical Technology, Clinical Laboratory Technician, Cytotechnology, Histotechnology

Scholarships for undergraduate students in their last year of study in the above fields enrolled in an approved NAACLS accredited program. U.S. citizenship or permanent U.S. residency required.

Contact address above for complete information. Enclose self-addressed stamped business size envelope. Applications available after Nov. 1.

1695—AMERICAN SOCIETY FOR CLINICAL LABORATORY SCIENCE (Forum for Concern of Minorities Scholarship)

7910 Woodmont Avenue, Suite 530
Bethesda MD 20814
301/657-2768
FAX: 301/657-2909
AMOUNT: Varies
DEADLINE(S): FEB 15
FIELD(S): Clinical Laboratory Science, Medical Technology, Clinical Laboratory Technology

Scholarships for undergraduate minority students enrolled in an approved NAACLS accredited program in the above fields. Min. 2.5 GPA required. U.S. citizenship or permanent U.S. residency required. Must demonstrate financial need.

Contact address above for complete information. Enclose self-addressed stamped business size envelope. Applications available after Nov. 1.

1696—AMERICAN SPEECH-LANGUAGE HEARING FOUNDATION (Young Scholars Award for Minority Students)

10801 Rockville Pike
Rockville MD 20852
301/897-5700 ext. 4203
FAX: 301/571-0457
Internet: http://www.asha.org
AMOUNT: $2,000
DEADLINE(S): JUN 6
FIELD(S): Speech-Language Pathology; Audiology

Open to racial/ethnic college seniors who are U.S. citizens accepted for graduate study in speech-language pathology or audiology.

Contact Gina Smolka for an application after February 1.

1697—ARTHUR M. MILLER FUND

P.O. Box 1122
Wichita KS 67201-0004
316/261-4609
AMOUNT: Varies
DEADLINE(S): MAR 31
FIELD(S): Medicine or related fields

Scholarships for Kansas residents for the study of medicine or related fields at accredited institutions.

Send SASE for formal application.

1698—ASSOCIATION FOR WOMEN VETERINARIANS (Student Scholarship)

P.O. Box 2039
Starkville MS 39760-2039
Written Inquiry
AMOUNT: $1,500
DEADLINE(S): MAR 2
FIELD(S): Veterinary Medicine

Open to second or third year veterinary medicine students in the U.S. or Canada who are U.S. or Canadian citizens. Both women and men are eligible. Essay is required.

Write for complete information or contact the Dean of your veterinary school.

1699—ASSOCIATION ON AMERICAN INDIAN AFFAIRS (Emergency Aid and Health Professions Scholarships)

P.O. Box 268
Sisseton SD 57262
605/698-3998
FAX: 605/698-3316
E-mail: aaia@sbtc.net
Internet: http://www.indian-affairs.org
AMOUNT: See Web site for information.
DEADLINE(S): MAY 1
FIELD(S): Health Professions

Open to full-time undergraduate students who are minimally 1/4 degree Indian blood from a federally recognized tribe. Award is based on financial need and is limited to North America/Alaska. Must submit essay on need, certificate of enrollment and quantum from your tribe or BIA, transcript, schedule of classes, and current financial aid award letter.

See Web site for information on requirements or send a self-addressed, stamped envelope to Elena Stops, Scholarship Coordinator, for an application.

1700—BECA FOUNDATION (Alice Newell Joslyn Medical Fund)

830 E. Grand Avenue, Suite B
Escondido CA 92025
760/471-8246
FAX: 760/471-8176
AMOUNT: $500-$1,000
DEADLINE(S): MAR 1
FIELD(S): Medicine; Health Care; Nursing; Dental/Medical Assisting; Physical Therapy

Open to Latino students who live in or attend college in San Diego County, CA, at time of application. For high school seniors and those already in college pursuing undergraduate or graduate education. Based on financial need, scholastic determination, and community/cultural awareness.

Send self-addressed, stamped envelope to BECA for an application.

1701—BOYS AND GIRLS CLUBS OF SAN DIEGO (Spence Reese Scholarship Fund)

1761 Hotel Circle So., Suite 123
San Diego CA 92108
619/298-3520
AMOUNT: $2,000/year
DEADLINE(S): MAY 15
FIELD(S): Medicine; Law; Engineering; Political Science

Open to male high school seniors planning a career in one of the above fields. Must be residents of Imperial, Riverside, Orange, San Diego, or Los Angeles counties in California. Boys and Girls Club affiliation NOT required.

$10 application fee. Renewable up to 4 years. Send a self-addressed, stamped envelope to Boys and Girls Club for an application after January 1.

1702—CALIFORNIA ASSOCIATION OF HOSPITALS AND HEALTH SERVICES (CAHHS Health Career Scholarship)

P.O. Box 1442
Sacramento CA 95812-1442
AMOUNT: $1,000
DEADLINE(S): MAY 10
FIELD(S): Health Care

Available to high school seniors who are volunteers in their local hospital and have been accepted into a health-related field at a college or university. Applicant must demonstrate proof of volunteer work.

1703—CALIFORNIA GRANGE FOUNDATION (Deaf Activities Scholarships)

Pat Avila, 2101 Stockton Boulevard
Sacramento CA 95817
Written Inquiry
AMOUNT: Varies
DEADLINE(S): APR 1
FIELD(S): Course work which will be of benefit to the deaf community

Scholarships students entering, continuing, or returning to college to pursue studies that will benefit the deaf community.

Write for information after Feb. 1 of each year.

1704—CALIFORNIA MATHEMATICS COUNCIL (Scholarship)

CMC-SS Scholarship Committee
1500 North Verdugo Road
Glendale CA 91208-2894
E-mail: sjkolpas@sprintmail.com
AMOUNT: $100-$1,000
DEADLINE(S): JAN 31
FIELD(S): Education

Scholarships will be presented for students who are studying elementary education or secondary education. Only applicants who teach, reside, or go to school in Southern California will be considered.

1705—CHARLES E. SAAK TRUST (Educational Grants)

Wells Fargo Bank
8405 N. Fresno Street, Suite 210
Fresno CA 93720
Written Inquiry
AMOUNT: Varies
DEADLINE(S): MAR 31

FIELD(S): Education; Dentistry

Undergraduate grants for residents of the Porterville-Poplar area of Tulare County, California. Must carry a minimum of 12 units, have at least a 2.0 GPA, be under age 21, and demonstrate financial need.

Approximately 100 awards per year. Renewable with reapplication. Write for complete information.

1706—COLUMBIANA COUNTY PUBLIC HEALTH LEAGUE TRUST FUND (Grants)

c/o Mary Kay Withum
P.O. Box 511
Wheeling WV 26003
304/234-4128
FAX: 304/234-4142

AMOUNT: Varies
DEADLINE(S): FEB 28
FIELD(S): Respiratory Illness; Medicine; Medical Research; Pharmacy; Medical Technology; Physical Therapy; Nursing; Dental Hygiene; Occupational Therapy

Open to undergraduate and graduate Columbiana County, Ohio, residents who are pursuing medical education or research in one of the above fields. Preference given to respiratory illness. Students of veterinary medicine NOT eligible.

Contact Sherrill Schmied for an application.

1707—DEMOLAY FOUNDATION INC. (Scholarships)

10200 NW Ambassador Boulevard
Kansas City MO 64153
816/891-8333
FAX: 816/891-9062
Internet: http://www.demolay.org

AMOUNT: $1,500
DEADLINE(S): APR 1
FIELD(S): Dental or medical fields

Open to all active and/or senior DeMolays. Considerations are leadership, academic achievement, and goals.

Four grants per year. Write for complete information.

1708—DEMOLAY FOUNDATION INC. (Scholarships)

10200 NW Ambassador Boulevard
Kansas City MO 64153
816/891-8333
FAX: 816/891-9062
Internet: http://www.demolay.org

AMOUNT: $1,500
DEADLINE(S): APR 1
FIELD(S): Dental or medical fields

Open to all active and/or senior DeMolays. Considerations are leadership, academic achievement, and goals.

Four grants per year. Write for complete information.

1709—EDWARD BANGS KELLEY AND ELZA KELLEY FOUNDATION, INC. (Scholarship Program)

P.O. Drawer M
Hyannis MA 02601-1412
508/775-3117

AMOUNT: $500-$4,000 (max.)
DEADLINE(S): APR 30
FIELD(S): Medicine; Nursing; Education; Health and Social Sciences

Open to residents of Barnstable County, Massachusetts. Scholarships are intended to benefit health and welfare of Barnstable County residents. Awards support study at recognized undergraduate, graduate, and professional institutions. Financial need is considered.

Contact Foundation for an application Scholarship Committee for an application.

1710—FIRST UNITED METHODIST CHURCH (Robert Stevenson and Doreene E. Cater Scholarships)

302 5th Avenue, S.
St. Cloud MN 56301
FAX: 320/251-0878
E-mail: fumc@fumc-stcloud.org

AMOUNT: $200-1,500
DEADLINE(S): JUN 1
FIELD(S): Humanitarian and Christian Service: Teaching, Medicine, Social Work, Environmental Studies, etc.

Stevenson Scholarship is open to undergraduate members of the First United Methodist Church of St. Cloud. Cater Scholarship is open to members of the Minnesota United Methodist Conference who are entering the sophomore year or higher of college work. Both require two letters of reference, transcripts, and financial need.

5-6 awards annually. Contact Scholarship Committee for an application.

1711—FORD FOUNDATION/NATIONAL RESEARCH COUNCIL (Howard Hughes Medical Institute Predoctoral Fellowships in Biological Sciences)

2101 Constitution Avenue NW
Washington DC 20418
202/334-2872
FAX: 202/334-3419
Internet: nationalacademies.org

AMOUNT: $16,000 stipend + tuition at U.S. institution
DEADLINE(S): NOV 9
FIELD(S): Biochemistry; Biophysics; Epidemiology; Genetics; Immunology; Microbiology; Neuroscience; Pharmacology; Physiology; Virology

Five-year award is open to college seniors and first-year graduate students pursuing a Ph.D. or Sc.D. degree. U.S. citizens/nationals may choose any institution in the U.S. or abroad; foreign students must choose U.S. institution. Based on ability, academic records, proposed study/research, previous experience, reference reports, and GRE scores.

80 awards annually. See Web site or contact NRC for an application.

1712—FOUNDATION FOR SEACOAST HEALTH (Scholarship Program)

100 Campus Drive, Suite 1
Portsmouth NH 03801
603/422-8200
FAX: 602/422-8207
E-mail: ffsh@communitycampus.org
Internet: http://www.ffsh.org

AMOUNT: $1,000-$10,000
DEADLINE(S): FEB 1
FIELD(S): Health-related fields. For residents of New Hampshire and Maine.

1713—FOUNDATION OF THE AMERICAN COLLEGE OF HEALTH CARE EXECUTIVES (Albert W. Dent Student Scholarship)

1 North Franklin Street, Suite 1700
Chicago IL 60606-3491

AMOUNT: $3,000
DEADLINE(S): JAN
FIELD(S): Health Care

Available to student associates in good standing of the ACHE. Must be a minority graduate student enrolled in full-time study in a health care management program. Previous recipients may not reapply.

1714—FOUNDATION OF THE AMERICAN COLLEGE OF HEALTH CARE EXECUTIVES (Foster G. McGaw Student Scholarship)

1 North Franklin Street, Suite 1700
Chicago IL 60606-3491
312/424-2800
Internet: http://www.ache.org

AMOUNT: $3,500
DEADLINE(S): MAR 31
FIELD(S): Health Care

Available to student associates in good standing of the ACHE. Must be a graduate student enrolled in full-time study in a health care management program. Previous recipients may not reapply. Must demonstrate financial need.

1715—FOUNDATION OF THE PENNSYLVANIA MEDICAL SOCIETY (Foundation Loans)

777 E. Park Drive
P.O. Box 8820
Harrisburg PA 17105-8820
800/228-7823 (in PA only) or
717/558-7750
FAX: 717/558-7818
E-mail: studentloans-foundation@pamedsoc.org
Internet: http://www.PMSFoundation.org

AMOUNT: $5,000 ($3,000 minimum)
DEADLINE(S): APR 1 (Pennsylvania Medical School Students) Applications submitted to Financial Aid Officers; JUN 1 (Out-of-State Medical School Students) Applications submitted to the Foundation
FIELD(S): Medical

Open to bona fide Pennsylvania residents. Additionally students must be enrolled full-time in an accredited U.S. medical school, have completed a Free Application for Federal Student Aid (FAFSA) form, and are in good standing with other creditors. Loan awards are based upon financial need.

1716—FOUNDATION OF THE PENNSYLVANIA MEDICAL SOCIETY (The Myrtle Siegfried, MD, and Michael Vigilante, MD Scholarship)

The Myrtle Siegfried, MD, and
Michael Vigilante, MD Scholarship
c/o The Foundation
777 E. Park Drive
Harrisburg PA 17105-8820
800/228-7823 (in PA only) or
717/558-7750
FAX: 717/558-7818
E-mail: studentloans-foundation@pamedsoc.org
Internet: http://www.PMSFoundation.org

AMOUNT: $1,000 (one, one-time award)
DEADLINE(S): SEPT 30
FIELD(S): Medical

Open to a qualified medical student who is entering or has entered into his/her first year of medical school. The applicant must be a resident of Lehigh, Berks, or Northampton County in the state of Pennsylvania and be enrolled full-time in an accredited United States medical school.

1717—FOUNDATION OF THE PENNSYLVANIA MEDICAL SOCIETY

The Scott A. Gunder, MD, DCMS
Presidential Scholarship
c/o The Foundation
777 E. Park Drive
P.O. Box 8820
Harrisburg PA 17105-8820
800/228-7823 (in PA only) or
717/558-7750
FAX: 717/558-7818
E-mail: studentloans-foundation@pamedsoc.org
Internet: http://www.PMSFoundation.org

AMOUNT: $1,000 (one, one-time award)
DEADLINE(S): APR 15
FIELD(S): Medical

Open to a second-year medical student enrolled full-time at Penn State University School of Medicine. The applicant must be a bona fide resident of Pennsylvania for at least 12 months before registering as a medical student (not including time spent attending an undergraduate/graduate school in the state of Pennsylvania).

1718—GRACE FOUNDATION (Scholarship Trust Fund)

P.O. Box 924
Menlo Park CA 94026-0924
Written Inquiry

AMOUNT: $1,000-$4,000
DEADLINE(S): JAN 31
FIELD(S): Ministry; Medicine; Teaching; Social Service

Open to students from developing countries in Asia/Southeast Asia to pursue full-time study at an accredited college/university. For training future Christian ministers and professional workers in above fields. Must have completed one or more years of college in or near their native country, be a strong Christian, have a minimum 3.0 GPA, and demonstrate financial need.

Renewable up to 4 years with maintenance of 3.0 GPA. Applications available between September 1 and October 31.

1719—H. FLETCHER BROWN FUND (Scholarships)

c/o PNC Bank; Trust Dept.
P.O. Box 791
Wilmington DE 19899
302/429-1186

AMOUNT: Varies
DEADLINE(S): APR 15
FIELD(S): Medicine; Dentistry; Law; Engineering; Chemistry

Open to U.S. citizens born in Delaware and still residing in Delaware. For 4 years of study (undergrad or grad) leading to a degree that enables applicant to practice in chosen field.

Scholarships are based on need, scholastic achievement, and good moral character. Applications available in February. Write for complete information.

1720—H. FLETCHER BROWN TRUST (Scholarships)

222 Delaware Avenue, 16th Floor
Wilmington DE 19899
302/429-1338

AMOUNT: Varies
DEADLINE(S): APR 9
FIELD(S): Chemistry; Engineering; Law; Medicine; Dentistry

Open to financially needy native-born DELAWARE residents ONLY who are pursuing an undergraduate degree. Must have minimum 1,000 SAT score and rank in upper 20% of class. Interview required.

Send self-addressed, stamped envelope to Donald Drois, Account Administrator, PNC Bank, at above address for an application.

1721—HISPANIC DENTAL ASSOCIATION AND DR. JUAN D. VILLARREAL FOUNDATION (Dental/Dental Hygienist Scholarships)

188 W. Randolph Street, Suite 1811
Chicago IL 60601-3001
800/852-7921 or 312/577-4013
FAX: 312/577-4013
E-mail: hdassoc1@qwest.net
Internet: http://www.hdassoc.org

AMOUNT: $500-$1,000
DEADLINE(S): JUN 15
FIELD(S): Dentistry; Dental Hygiene

Open to Hispanic students pursuing undergraduate study in an accredited Texas dental school.

Contact HDA for an application.

1722—HISPANIC DENTAL ASSOCIATION AND PROCTER AND GAMBLE ORAL CARE (Scholarships)

188 W. Randolph Street, Suite 1811
Chicago IL 60606
800/852-7921 or 312/577-4013

FAX: 312/577-0052
E-mail: hdassoc1@qwest.net
Internet: http://www.hdassoc.org
AMOUNT: $500-$1,000
DEADLINE(S): JUN 15
FIELD(S): Dentistry; Dental Hygiene; Dental Assisting; Dental Technician

Open to Hispanic students for undergraduate study in above programs. Based on scholastic achievement, community service, leadership skills, and commitment to improving health in the Hispanic community.

Contact HDA for an application.

1723—HISPANIC DENTAL ASSOCIATION AND WASHINGTON DENTAL SERVICE FOUNDATION (Dental Assisting/Dental Hygienists Scholarships)

188 W. Randolph Street, Suite 1811
Chicago IL 60606
800/852-7921 or 312/577-4013
FAX: 312/577-0052
E-mail: hdassoc1@qwest.net
Internet: http://www.hdassoc.org
AMOUNT: $250-$500
DEADLINE(S): JUN 15
FIELD(S): Dentistry; Dental Hygiene; Dental Assisting; Dental Technician

Open to Hispanic students for undergraduate study in an accredited state of Washington school.

Contact HDA for an application.

1724—HOUSTON LIVESTOCK SHOW AND RODEO (4H and FFA Scholarships)

2000 S. Loop West
Houston TX 77054
713/791-9000
FAX: 713-794-9528
E-Mail: info@rodeohouston.com
Internet: http://www.hlsr.com/education/
AMOUNT: $10,000
DEADLINE(S): Varies
FIELD(S): Agriculture; Life Sciences

Open to undergraduate students who are actively involved in the 4-H or FFA programs. Must major in an agricultural or life sciences field of study at a Texas college/university and demonstrate academic potential, citizenship/leadership, and financial need.

140 awards annually. Contact HLSR for an application.

1725—INTERNATIONAL ORDER OF THE KING'S DAUGHTERS AND SONS (Health Careers Scholarships)

c/o Mrs. Fred Cannon; Box 1310
Brookhaven MS 39602
Written Inquiry
AMOUNT: $1,000 (max.)
DEADLINE(S): APR 1
FIELD(S): Medicine; Dentistry; Nursing; Physical Therapy; Occupational Therapy; Medical Technologies; Pharmacy

Open to students accepted to/enrolled in an accredited U.S. or Canadian four-year or graduate school. RN candidates must have completed first year of program; MD or DDS candidates must be for at least the second year of medical or dental school; all others must be in at least third year of four-year program. Pre-med students NOT eligible. Must be U.S. or Canadian citizen.

Send self-addressed, stamped envelope, along with a letter stating the field of study and present level, to the Director at above address for an application.

1726—JEWISH FEDERATION OF METROPOLITAN CHICAGO (Academic Scholarship Program/The Marcus and Theresa Levie Educational Fund)

One South Franklin Street
Chicago IL 60606
312/357-4521
FAX: 312/855-3282
E-mail: jvsscholarship@jvschicago.org
Internet http://www.jvschicago.org/scholarship/
AMOUNT: Varies
DEADLINE(S): MAR 1
FIELD(S): Medicine, Dentistry, Dental Hygiene, Emergency Medical Technology, Health Technology, Nursing or Physicians' Assistant, Occupational Therapy, Optometry, Clinical Psychology/Counseling, Education

Scholarships for college juniors, seniors, and graduate students, or students in vocational training programs, who are Jewish and are residents of Chicago, IL, and Cook County. Applicant must have a specific career goal in the "helping professions," such as those above.

Academic achievement and financial need are considered. Applications accepted after December 1. See Web site for more information and applications.

1727—JEWISH VOCATIONAL SERVICE (Academic Scholarship Program)

One S. Franklin Street
Chicago IL 60606
312/357-4500
FAX: 312/855-3282
TTY: 312/855-3282
E-mail: jvschicago@jon.cjfny.org
AMOUNT: $5,000 (max.)
DEADLINE(S): MAR 1
FIELD(S): "Helping" Professions; Mathematics; Engineering; Sciences; Communications (at Univ IL only); Law (certain schools in IL only)

Open to Jewish men and women legally domiciled in the greater Chicago metropolitan area, who are identified as having promise for significant contributions in their chosen careers, and are in need of financial assistance for full-time academic programs in above areas. Must have entered undergraduate junior year in career programs requiring no postgrad education, be in graduate/professional school, or be in a vo-tech training program. Interview required.

Renewable. Contact JVS for an application between December 1 and February 15th.

1728—JUNIATA COLLEGE (Robert Steele Memorial Scholarship)

Office of Student Financial Planning
Juniata College
1700 Moore Street,
Huntingdon PA 16652
814/641-3142
FAX: 814/641-5311
Internet: http://www.juniata.edu/
E-mail: clarkec@juniata.edu
AMOUNT: $4,000 (max.)
DEADLINE(S): APR 1
FIELD(S): Science; Medical Studies

Open to science/medical students applying to Juniata College. Must demonstrate financial need and fill out government FAFSA form.

Contact Randy Rennell, Director of Student Financial Planning, for an application or enrollment information. See your financial aid office for FAFSA.

1729—McCORD CAREER CENTER (Level II McCord Medical/Music Scholarship)

Healdsburg High School
1024 Prince Street
Healdsburg CA 95448
707/431-3473
Email: career@husd.com
AMOUNT: Varies
DEADLINE(S): APR 15
FIELD(S): Medicine; Music

For graduates of Healdsburg High School who are planning a career in music or medicine. Must be enrolled full-time at a college/university as an undergraduate junior or senior in the fall, or earning an advanced degree in graduate or medical school, or entering into a vocational/certificate program. Transcripts, proof of attendance, and an essay are required.

Contact the McCord Career Center at Healdsburg High School for an application.

1730—NATIONAL ENVIRONMENTAL HEALTH ASSOCIATION (NEHA/AAS Scholarship)

720 S. Colorado Blvd., Suite 970
South Tower
Denver CO 80246-1925
303/756-9090
E-mail: mthomsen@neha.org
Internet: http://www.neha.org

AMOUNT: Varies
DEADLINE(S): FEB 1
FIELD(S): Environmental Health/Science; Public Health

Undergraduate scholarships to be used for tuition and fees during junior or senior year at an Environmental Health Accreditation Council accredited school or NEHA school. Graduate scholarships are for students or career professionals who are enrolled in a graduate program of studies in environmental health sciences and/or public health. Transcript, letters of recommendation, and financial need considered.

Renewable. Scholarships are paid directly to the college/university for the fall semester of the award.

1731—NATIONAL FEDERATION OF THE BLIND (Howard Brown Rickard Scholarship)

805 Fifth Avenue
Grinnell IA 50112
515/236-3366

AMOUNT: $3,000
DEADLINE(S): MAR 31
FIELD(S): Law; Medicine; Engineering; Architecture; Natural Sciences

For legally blind students pursuing or planning to pursue a full-time postsecondary course of study in the U.S.. Based on academic excellence, service to the community, and financial need. Membership NOT required.

1 award annually. Renewable. Contact Mrs. Peggy Elliot, Scholarship Committee Chairman, for an application.

1732—NATIONAL FEDERATION OF REPUBLIC WOMEN (National Pathfinders Scholarship)

124 North Alfred Street
Alexandria VA 22314-3011
703/548-9688

AMOUNT: $2,000
DEADLINE(S): FEB 28
FIELD(S): Science

Applicants must be currently enrolled in an undergraduate or graduate program such as chemistry, sociology, psychology, or pharmacology, with intended careers in chemical, biological, or medical research, or counseling of addicts and their families. May not receive more than one scholarship.

1733—NATIONAL INSTITUTES OF HEALTH (Minority International Research Training Grant)

Fogarty International Center, Bldg. 31
Room B2C39
Bethesda MD 20892-2220
301/402-9467
FAX: 301/402-0779
E-mail: barbara_sina@cu.nih.gov
Internet: http://www.nih.gov/grants/oer.htm

AMOUNT: Varies
DEADLINE(S): MAR 15
FIELD(S): Biomedical and Behavioral Sciences

Open to minorities that are underrepresented in biomedical research professions (African and Hispanic Americans, Native Americans, Alaskan Natives, and Pacific Islanders). May be undergraduate students pursuing life science curricula (8-12 weeks research/coursework supported), students pursuing doctoral degrees in above fields (3-12 months research training at foreign institution supported), or faculty members in above fields (3-12 months research at foreign institution).

See Web site or contact NIH for an application.

1734—NATIONAL STRENGTH AND CONDITIONING ASSOCIATION (Challenge Scholarships)

P.O. Box 9908
Colorado Springs CO 80932-0908
719/632-6722
FAX: 719/632-6722
E-mail: nsca@usa.net
Internet: http://www.colosoft.com/nsca

AMOUNT: $1,000
DEADLINE(S): MAR 1
FIELD(S): Body Strength and Conditioning

Open to National Strength and Conditioning Association members to pursue undergraduate or graduate study in fields related to body strength and conditioning.

Contact NSCA for an application or membership information.

1735—NAVY RECRUITING COMMAND (Armed Forces Health Professions Scholarships)

Chief
5722 Integrity Drive
Millington TN 38054
888/633-9674
Internet: http://www.navy.com

AMOUNT: average of $1,058/month stipend + tuition, fees, books, lab fees, etc.
DEADLINE(S): Applications taken year-around
FIELD(S): Medicine, Dentistry, Optometry, Physical Therapy, Pharmacology, Health Care Administration, Industrial Hygiene, etc.

Open to U.S. citizens enrolled or accepted for enrollment in any of the above fields at an accredited institution in the U.S. or Puerto Rico. Must qualify for appointment as a Navy officer and sign a contractual agreement. Must be between the ages of 18 and 40 for some programs and have a GPA around 3.0.

See Web site, contact local Navy Recruiting Office, or contact the above address.

1736—NEW YORK STATE HIGHER EDUCATION SERVICES CORPORATION (N.Y. State Regents Professional/Health Care Opportunity Scholarships)

Cultural Education Center, Room 5C64
Albany NY 12230
518/486-1319
Internet: http://www.hesc.com

AMOUNT: $1,000-$10,000/year
DEADLINE(S): Varies
FIELD(S): Medicine and dentistry and related fields, architecture, nursing, psychology, audiology, landscape architecture, social work, chiropractic, law, pharmacy, accounting, speech language pathology

For NY state residents who are economically disadvantaged and members of a minority group underrepresented in the chosen profession and attending school in NY state. Some programs carry a service obligation in New York for each year of support. For U.S. citizens or qualifying noncitizens.

Medical/dental scholarships require one year of professional work in NY.

1737—NORTH CAROLINA DEPARTMENT OF PUBLIC INSTRUCTION (Scholarship Loan Program for Prospective Teachers)

301 N. Wilmington Street
Raleigh NC 27601-2825
919/715-1120
AMOUNT: Up to $2,500/year
DEADLINE(S): FEB
FIELD(S): Education: Teaching, school psychology and counseling, speech/language impaired, audiology, library/media services

For NC residents planning to teach in NC public schools. At least 3.0 high school GPA required; must maintain 2.5 GPA during freshman year and 3.0 cumulative thereafter. Recipients are obligated to teach one year in an NC public school for each year of assistance. Those who do not fulfill their teaching obligation are required to repay the loan plus interest.

200 awards per year. For full-time students. Applications available in Dec. from high school counselors and college and university departments of education.

1738—NORTH CAROLINA DEPT. OF PUBLIC INSTRUCTION (Teacher Assistant Scholarship Loan)

301 N. Wilmington Street
Raleigh NC 27601-2825
919/715-1120
AMOUNT: Up to $1,200/yr
DEADLINE(S): JAN
FIELD(S): Education: Teaching, school psychology or counseling, speech/language impaired, audiology, library/media services

For NC residents employed as K-12 teaching assistants in public schools who wish to pursue teacher licensure. Must either hold a BA degree or have completed general college courses prerequisite to admission to degree program and be admitted to an approved teacher education program at a four-year institution. Two-year community college early childhood education program is acceptable.

Must remain employed as teaching assistant while pursuing licensure and teach one year in an NC public school for each year of assistance received. Applications available in Sept. from local school superintendent.

1739—OKLAHOMA MEDICAL RESEARCH FOUNDATION (Sir Alexander Fleming Scholar Program)

825 N.E.13th Street
Oklahoma City OK 73104-5046
405/271-8537 or
800/522-0211 (in-state)
Internet: http://www.omrf.ouhsc.edu
AMOUNT: $2,500 salary + housing
DEADLINE(S): Feb 15
FIELD(S): Sciences

Summer scholarship program (June and July) for Oklahoma students who have completed their junior year of high school through those in their junior year of college at time of application. Excellent academic standing and aptitude in science and math are essential. Students will work in the laboratories of the above organization. Research projects will be selected from: alcoholism/liver disease, arthritis/immunology, carcinogenesis, cardiovascular biology, and more.

Named for the scientist who discovered penicillin and dedicated OMRF in 1949. Contact organization for further information and application forms.

1740—PENINSULA COMMUNITY FOUNDATION (Dr. Mary Finegold Scholarship)

1700 S. El Camino Real, #300
San Mateo CA 94402
650/358-9369
FAX: 650/358-9817
Internet: http://www.pcf.org/community_grants/scholarships.html
AMOUNT: $1,000
DEADLINE(S): MAR 7 (5 p.m.)
FIELD(S): Sciences

Scholarships for senior girls graduating from high school in Palo Alto, California, who intend to complete a four-year degree in the sciences. Special consideration will be given to girls who have demonstrated a "pioneering" spirit in that they have not been constrained by stereotypical female roles and to those facing financial hardship.

Award was established in the honor of Dr. Mary Finegold who, after completing her medical studies, elected to stay at home until her youngest child was in high school before beginning her medical practice. She was a school physician.

1741—PHYSICIAN ASSISTANT FOUNDATION (Scholarships, Traineeships, and Grants)

950 N. Washington Street
Alexandria VA 22314-1552
703/519-5686
E-mail: loconnell@aaapa.org
Internet: http://www.aapa.org
AMOUNT: Varies
DEADLINE(S): FEB 1
FIELD(S): Physician Assistant

Must be attending an accredited physician assistant program in order to qualify. Judging is based on financial need, academic standing, community involvement, and knowledge of physician assistant profession.

Contact Edna C. Scott, Administrative Manager, for an application.

1742—RAYMOND J. HARRIS EDUCATION TRUST

P.O. Box 7899
Philadelphia PA 19101-7899
Written Inquiry
AMOUNT: Varies
DEADLINE(S): FEB 1
FIELD(S): Medicine, Law, Engineering, Dentistry, or Agriculture

Scholarships for Christian men to obtain a professional education in medicine, law, engineering, dentistry, or agriculture at nine Philadelphia area colleges.

Contact Mellon Bank, N.A. at above location for details and the names of the nine colleges.

1743—ROBERT SCHRECK MEMORIAL FUND (Grants)

c/o Texas Commerce Bank,
Trust Dept
P.O. Drawer 140
El Paso TX 79980
915/546-6515
AMOUNT: $500-$1500
DEADLINE(S): JUL 15; NOV 15
FIELD(S): Medicine; Veterinary Medicine; Physics; Chemistry; Architecture; Engineering; Episcopal Clergy

Grants to undergraduate juniors or seniors or graduate students who have been residents of El Paso County for at least two years. Must be U.S. citizen or legal resident and have a high grade point average. Financial need is a consideration.

Write for complete information.

1744—SRP/NAVAJO GENERATING STATION (Navajo Scholarship)

P.O. Box 850
Page AZ 86040
520/645-6539
FAX: 520/645-7295
E-mail: ljdawave@srp.gov
AMOUNT: Based on need
DEADLINE(S): APR 30

FIELD(S): Engineering, Environmental Studies, Business, Business Management, Health, Education

Scholarships for full-time students who hold membership in the Navajo Tribe and who are pursuing a degree in a field of study recognized as significant to the Navajo Naiton, Salt River Project, or the Navajo Generating Station, such as those listed above. Must be junior or senior, have and maintain a GPA of 3.0

Average of 15 awards per year. Inquire of Linda Dawavendewa at above location.

1745—U.S. DEPT. OF HEALTH and HUMAN SERVICES (Indian Health Service Health Professions Scholarship Program)

Twinbrook Metro Plaza, Suite 100
12300 Twinbrook Parkway
Rockville MD 20852
301/443-0234
FAX: 301/443-4815
Internet: http://www.ihs.gov/Recruitment/DHPS/SP/SBTOC3.asp

AMOUNT: Tuition + fees and monthly stipend of $938
DEADLINE(S): APR 1
FIELD(S): Health professions, accounting, social work

Open to Native Americans or Alaska natives who are graduate students or college juniors or seniors in a program leading to a career in a fields listed above. U.S. citizenship required. Renewable annually with reapplication.

Scholarship recipients must intend to serve the Indian people. They incur a one-year service obligation to the IHS for each year of support for a minimum of two years. Write for complete information.

1746—UNITED STATES DEPARTMENT OF AGRICULTURE (1890 National Scholars Program)

14th & Independence Avenue SW
Room 301-W; Whitten Bldg.
Washington, DC 20250-9600
202/720-6905
E-mail: usda-m@fie.com
Internet: http://web.fie.com/htdoc/fed/agr/ars/edu/prog/mti/agrpgaak.htm

AMOUNT: Tuition, employment/benefits, use of pc/software, fees, books, room/board
DEADLINE(S): JAN 15
FIELD(S): Agriculture, Food, or Natural Resource Sciences

For U.S. citizens, high school grad/GED, GPA 3.0+, verbal/math SAT 1000+, composite score 21+ ACT, first-year college student, and attend participating school.

34+ scholarships/yr/4 years. Send applications to U.S.D.A. Liaison officer at the 1890 Institution of your choice (see Web page for complete list).

1747—UNIVERSITY OF UTAH COLLEGE OF PHARMACY (Pharmacy Scholarships)

30 So. 2000 E., Room 203
Salt Lake City UT 84112-5820
801/587-7736
E-mail: tricia.lee@deans.pharm.utah.edu

AMOUNT: $500-$4,000
DEADLINE(S): MAR
FIELD(S): Pharmacy

Several scholarship programs for students enrolled in the professional pharmacy program at the University of Utah College of Pharmacy. For second through fourth year students. Some require financial need; others are merit-based.

80+ awards annually. Contact Tricia Lee for an application.

1748—WASHINGTON STATE HIGHER EDUCATION COORDINATING BOARD (Health Professional Loan Repayment and Scholarship Program)

P.O. Box 47834
Olympia WA 98504-3430
360/705-6664
FAX: 360/664-9273
Internet: http://www.hecb.wa.gov

AMOUNT: Varies
DEADLINE(S): APR (scholarship); FEB (loan repayment); JUL (loan repayment)
FIELD(S): Health Care

Scholarships are open to students in accredited undergraduate or graduate health care programs leading to eligibility for licensure in Washington state. Must agree to work in designated shortage area for minimum of three years. Loan repayment recipients receive payment from program for purpose of repaying education loans secured while attending program of health care training leading to licensure in Washington state. Financial need NOT a factor.

Renewable up to 5 years. Contact Program Manager for a loan repayment application after November 15 and for scholarship application after January 15.

1749—WASHINGTON STATE HIGHER EDUCATION COORDINATING BOARD (WICHE Professional Student Exchange)

P.O. Box 43430
Olympia WA 98504-3430
360/753-7850
FAX: 360/753-7808
E-mail: lindala@hecb.wa.gov

AMOUNT: $10,000-$15,000
DEADLINE(S): OCT 15
FIELD(S): Optometry; Osteopathy

Program provides state support to Washington residents pursuing undergraduate or graduate study out-of-state.

12 awards annually (10 renewals, four new). Contact Program Manager for an application.

1750—WOMEN OF THE EVANGELICAL LUTHERAN CHURCH IN AMERICA (The Kahler-Vickers/Raup-Emma Wettstein Scholarships)

8765 West Higgins Road
Chicago IL 60631-4189
800/638-3522 ext. 2736
FAX: 773/380-2419
E-mail: womnelca@elca.org

AMOUNT: $2,000 max.
DEADLINE(S): FEB 15
FIELD(S): Health Professions and Christian Service

Assists women who are members of the ELCA studying for service in health professions associated with ELCA projects abroad that do not lead to church-certified professions. Must be U.S. citizen and have experienced an interruption of two or more years since completion of high school. Academic records of coursework completed in last five years as well as proof of admission from educational institution are required.

Renewable for an additional year. Contact Faith Fretheim, Program Director, for an application.

1751—ZETA PHI BETA SORORITY EDUCATIONAL FOUNDATION (S. Evelyn Lewis Memorial Scholarship in Medical Health Sciences)

1734 New Hampshire Avenue NW
Washington DC 20009
Internet: http://www.zpb1920.org

AMOUNT: $500-$1,000
DEADLINE(S): JAN 1
FIELD(S): Medicine; Health Sciences

Open to graduate and undergraduate young women enrolled in a program leading to a degree in medicine or health sciences. Award is for full-time study for one academic year (Fall-Spring) and is paid directly to college/university. Must submit proof of enrollment.

Send self-addressed, stamped envelope to above address between September 1 and December 15 for an application.

MEDICAL RESEARCH

1752—ARTHRITIS FOUNDATION (Doctoral Dissertation Award for Arthritis Health Professionals)

P.O. Box 7669
Atlanta GA 30357-0669
404/965-7537
Internet: http://www.arthritis.org

AMOUNT: $10,000
DEADLINE(S): SEP 1
FIELD(S): Health

Provide for up to two years of research in investigative or clinical teaching related to the rheumatic diseases. Applicants should be in the research phase of their study.

1753—AMERICAN FOUNDATION FOR THE BLIND (Paul W. Ruckes Scholarship)

11 Penn Plaza, Suite 300
New York NY 10001
212/502-7661
FAX: 212/502-7771
E-mail: juliet@afb.org
Internet: http://www.afb.org

AMOUNT: $1,000
DEADLINE(S): APR 30
FIELD(S): Engineering; Computer/Physical/Life Sciences

Open to legally blind and visually impaired undergraduate and graduate students pursuing a degree in one of above fields. Must be U.S. citizen. Must submit written documentation of visual impairment from ophthalmologist or optometrist (need not be legally blind); official transcripts; proof of college/university acceptance; three letters of recommendation; and typewritten statement describing goals, work experience extracurricular activities, and how monies will be used.

1 award annually. See Web site or contact Julie Tucker at AFB for an application.

1754—AMERICAN INDIAN SCIENCE AND ENGINEERING SOCIETY (A.T. Anderson Memorial Scholarship)

P.O. Box 9828
Albuquerque NM 87119-9828
505/765-1052
FAX: 505/765-5608
E-mail: scholarships@aises.org
Internet: http://www.aises.org/scholarships

AMOUNT: $1,000-$2,000
DEADLINE(S): JUN 15
FIELD(S): Medicine; Natural Resources; Science; Engineering

Open to undergraduate and graduate students who are at least 1/4 American Indian or recognized as member of a tribe. Must be member of AISES ($10 fee), enrolled full-time at an accredited institution, and demonstrate financial need.

Renewable. See Web site or contact Patricia Browne for an application and/or membership information.

1755—AMERICAN SPEECH-LANGUAGE HEARING FOUNDATION (Young Scholars Award for Minority Students)

10801 Rockville Pike
Rockville MD 20852
301/897-5700 ext. 4203
FAX: 301/571-0457
Internet: http://www.asha.org

AMOUNT: $2,000
DEADLINE(S): JUN 6
FIELD(S): Speech-Language Pathology; Audiology

Open to racial/ethnic college seniors who are U.S. citizens accepted for graduate study in speech-language pathology or audiology.

Contact Gina Smolka for an application after February 1.

1756—ARTHUR M. MILLER FUND

P.O. Box 1122
Wichita KS 67201-0004
316/261-4609

AMOUNT: Varies
DEADLINE(S): MAR 31
FIELD(S): Medicine or related fields

Scholarships for Kansas residents for the study of medicine or related fields at accredited institutions.

Send SASE for formal application.

1757—ASSOCIATION ON AMERICAN INDIAN AFFAIRS (Emergency Aid and Health Professions Scholarships)

P.O. Box 268
Sisseton SD 57262
605/698-3998
FAX: 605/698-3316
E-mail: aaia@sbtc.net
Internet: http://www.indian-affairs.org

AMOUNT: See Web site for information
DEADLINE(S): MAY 1
FIELD(S): Health Professions

Open to full-time undergraduate students who are minimally 1/4 degree Indian blood from a federally recognized tribe. Award is based on financial need and is limited to North America/Alaska. Must submit essay on need, certificate of enrollment and quantum from your tribe or BIA, transcript, schedule of classes, and current financial aid award letter.

See Web site for information on requirements or send a self-addressed, stamped envelope to Elena Stops, Scholarship Coordinator, for an application.

1758—ASTRONAUT SCHOLARSHIP FOUNDATION (Scholarships)

Exec. Director
6225 Vectorspace Boulevard
Titusville FL 32780
321/269-6119
FAX: 321/267-3970
E-mail: MercurySvn@aol.com
Internet: http://www.astronaut scholarship.org/guidelines.html

AMOUNT: Varies
DEADLINE(S): Varies
FIELD(S): Engineering and Physical Sciences (Medical Research ok, but NOT Professional Medicine)

Open to juniors, seniors, and graduate students at a select group of schools. Must be U.S. citizen with the intention to pursue research or advance field of study upon completion of final degree. Special consideration given to students who have shown initiative, creativity, excellence, and/or resourcefulness in their field. Must be NOMINATED by faculty or staff.

See Web site for list of eligible schools. Contact Howard Benedict, Executive Director, for details.

1759—BECA FOUNDATION (Alice Newell Joslyn Medical Fund)

830 E. Grand Avenue, Suite B
Escondido CA 92025

760/471-8246
FAX: 760/471-8176
AMOUNT: $500-$1,000
DEADLINE(S): MAR 1
FIELD(S): Medicine; Health Care; Nursing; Dental/Medical Assisting; Physical Therapy

Open to Latino students who live in or attend college in San Diego County, CA, at time of application. For high school seniors and those already in college pursuing undergraduate or graduate education. Based on financial need, scholastic determination, and community/cultural awareness.

Send self-addressed, stamped envelope to BECA for an application.

1760—BOYS AND GIRLS CLUBS OF SAN DIEGO (Spence Reese Scholarship Fund)

1761 Hotel Circle So., Suite 123
San Diego CA 92108
619/298-3520
AMOUNT: $2,000/year
DEADLINE(S): MAY 15
FIELD(S): Medicine; Law; Engineering; Political Science

Open to male high school seniors planning a career in one of the above fields. Must be residents of Imperial, Riverside, Orange, San Diego, or Los Angeles counties in California. Boys and Girls Club affiliation NOT required.

$10 application fee. Renewable up to 4 years. Send a self-addressed, stamped envelope to Boys and Girls Club for an application after January 1.

1761—COLUMBIANA COUNTY PUBLIC HEALTH LEAGUE TRUST FUND (Grants)

c/o Mary Kay Withum
P.O. Box 511
Wheeling WV 26003
304/234-4128
FAX: 304/234-4142
AMOUNT: Varies
DEADLINE(S): FEB 28
FIELD(S): Respiratory Illness; Medicine; Medical Research; Pharmacy; Medical Technology; Physical Therapy; Nursing; Dental Hygiene; Occupational Therapy

Open to undergraduate and graduate Columbiana County, Ohio, residents who are pursuing medical education or research in one of the above fields. Preference given to respiratory illness. Students of veterinary medicine NOT eligible.

Contact Sherrill Schmied for an application.

1762—CYSTIC FIBROSIS FOUNDATION (Student Traineeship Research Grants)

6931 Arlington Road
Bethesda MD 20814
301/951-4422 or 800/FIGHT-CF
Internet: http://www.cff.org
AMOUNT: $1,500
DEADLINE(S): None
FIELD(S): Cystic Fibrosis Research

Doctoral research grants are to introduce students to research related to cystic fibrosis and to maintain an interest in this area of biomedicine. Must be in or about to enter a doctoral program. Senior level undergraduates planning to pursue graduate training may also apply. The project's duration should be 10 weeks or more.

Contact CFF for an application and/or see Web site for listing of programs offered.

1763—EDWARD BANGS KELLEY AND ELZA KELLEY FOUNDATION, INC. (Scholarship Program)

P.O. Drawer M
Hyannis MA 02601-1412
508/775-3117
AMOUNT: $500-$4,000 (max.)
DEADLINE(S): APR 30
FIELD(S): Medicine; Nursing; Education; Health and Social Sciences

Open to residents of Barnstable County, Massachusetts. Scholarships are intended to benefit health and welfare of Barnstable County residents. Awards support study at recognized undergraduate, graduate, and professional institutions. Financial need is considered.

Contact Foundation for an application Scholarship Committee for an application.

1764—EPILEPSY FOUNDATION OF AMERICA (Health Sciences Student Fellowships)

4351 Garden City Drive
Landover MD 20785-2267
301/459-3700 or 800/EFA-1000
FAX: 301/577-2684
TDD: 800/332-2070
E-mail: grants@efa.org
Internet: http://www.epilepsy foundation.org
AMOUNT: $300-$2,000
DEADLINE(S): MAR 1
FIELD(S): Epilepsy Research

Three-month fellowships awarded to medical and health sciences students for work on an epilepsy study project. The project is carried out at a U.S. institution of the student's choice where there are ongoing programs of research, training, or service in epilepsy. A preceptor must accept responsibility for supervision of the student and the project.

Contact EFA for an application.

1765—FIGHT FOR SIGHT RESEARCH DIVISION OF PREVENT BLINDNESS AMERICA (Student Research Fellowship)

500 E. Remington Road
Schaumburg IL 60173
847/843-2020
FAX: 847/843-8458
E-mail: ffs@preventblindness.org
AMOUNT: $700/month ($2,100 max.)
DEADLINE(S): MAR 1
FIELD(S): Ophthalmology; Visual Sciences

Stipend open to undergraduates, medical students, or graduate students for full-time eye-related research, usually during the summer months.

Renewable. Contact Prevent Blindness America for an application.

1766—FIRST UNITED METHODIST CHURCH (Robert Stevenson and Doreene E. Cater Scholarships)

302 5th Avenue, S.
St. Cloud MN 56301
FAX: 320/251-0878
E-mail: fumc@fumc-stcloud.org
AMOUNT: $200-1,500
DEADLINE(S): JUN 1
FIELD(S): Humanitarian and Christian Service: Teaching, Medicine, Social Work, Environmental Studies, etc.

Stevenson Scholarship is open to undergraduate members of the First United Methodist Church of St. Cloud. Cater Scholarship is open to members of the Minnesota United Methodist Conference who are entering the sophomore year or higher of college work. Both require two letters of reference, transcripts, and financial need.

5-6 awards annually. Contact Scholarship Committee for an application.

1767—FORD FOUNDATION/NATIONAL RESEARCH COUNCIL (Howard Hughes Medical Institute Predoctoral Fellowships in Biological Sciences)

2101 Constitution Avenue NW
Washington DC 20418
202/334-2872

FAX: 202/334-3419
Internet: nationalacademies.org
AMOUNT: $16,000 stipend + tuition at U.S. institution
DEADLINE(S): NOV 9
FIELD(S): Biochemistry; Biophysics; Epidemiology; Genetics; Immunology; Microbiology; Neuroscience; Pharmacology; Physiology; Virology

Five-year award is open to college seniors and first-year graduate students pursuing a Ph.D. or Sc.D. degree. U.S. citizens/nationals may choose any institution in the U.S. or abroad; foreign students must choose U.S. institution. Based on ability, academic records, proposed study/research, previous experience, reference reports, and GRE scores.

80 awards annually. See Web site or contact NRC for an application.

1768—FOUNDATION FOR SEACOAST HEALTH (Scholarship Program)

P.O. Box 4606
Portsmouth NH 03802-4606
603/433-3008
FAX: 603/433-2036
E-mail: ffsh@nh.ultranet.com
Internet: http://www.nh.ultranet.com/~ffsh
AMOUNT: $1,000-$10,000
DEADLINE(S): FEB 1
FIELD(S): Health-related fields

Open to undergraduate and graduate students pursuing health-related fields of study who are legal residents of the following cities in New Hampshire: Portsmouth, Newington, New Castle, Rye, Greenland, N. Hampton, or these cities in Maine: Kittery, Eliot, or York, Maine. Must have resided in the area for at least two years.

Write or check Web site for details. $150,000 awarded annually; 35 awards given

1769—GRACE FOUNDATION (Scholarship Trust Fund)

P.O. Box 924
Menlo Park CA 94026-0924
Written Inquiry
AMOUNT: $1,000-$4,000
DEADLINE(S): JAN 31
FIELD(S): Ministry; Medicine; Teaching; Social Service

Open to students from developing countries in Asia/Southeast Asia to pursue full-time study at an accredited college/university. For training future Christian ministers and professional workers in above fields. Must have completed one or more years of college in or near their native country, be a strong Christian, have a minimum 3.0 GPA, and demonstrate financial need.

Renewable up to 4 years with maintenance of 3.0 GPA. Applications available between September 1 and October 31.

1770—HOUSTON LIVESTOCK SHOW AND RODEO (4H and FFA Scholarships)

2000 S. Loop West
Houston TX 77054
713/791-9000
FAX: 713-794-9528
E-mail: info@rodeohouston.com
Internet: http://www.hlsr.com/education/
AMOUNT: $10,000
DEADLINE(S): Varies
FIELD(S): Agriculture; Life Sciences

Open to undergraduate students who are actively involved in the 4-H or FFA programs. Must major in an agricultural or life sciences field of study at a Texas college/university and demonstrate academic potential, citizenship/leadership, and financial need.

140 awards annually. Contact HLSR for an application.

1771—JEWISH VOCATIONAL SERVICE (Academic Scholarship Program)

One S. Franklin Street
Chicago IL 60606
312/357-4500
FAX: 312/855-3282
TTY: 312/855-3282
E-mail: jvschicago@jon.cjfny.org
AMOUNT: $5,000 (max.)
DEADLINE(S): MAR 1
FIELD(S): "Helping" Professions; Mathematics; Engineering; Sciences; Communications (at Univ IL only); Law (certain schools in IL only)

Open to Jewish men and women legally domiciled in the greater Chicago metropolitan area, who are identified as having promise for significant contributions in their chosen careers, and are in need of financial assistance for full-time academic programs in above areas. Must have entered undergraduate junior year in career programs requiring no postgrad education, be in graduate/professional school, or be in a vo-tech training program. Interview required.

Renewable. Contact JVS for an application between December 1 and February 15.

1772—LADY ALLEN OF HURTWOOD MEMORIAL TRUST (Travel Grants)

21 Aspull Common
Leigh Lancs WN7 3PB ENGLAND
01942-674895
AMOUNT: Up to 1,000 pounds sterling
DEADLINE(S): JAN 15
FIELD(S): Welfare and Education of Children

A travel grant to those whose proposed project will directly benefit their work with children. People working with children and young people may apply, particularly those working with disabled and disadvantaged children. Successful candidates must write up an account of the work which the scholarship has funded. GRANTS ARE NOT FOR ACADEMIC STUDY; ONLY QUALIFIED INDIVIDUALS MAY APPLY.

Contact Dorothy E. Whitaker, Trustee, for application forms—available between May and December each year.

1773—LUPUS FOUNDATION OF AMERICA, INC. (Finzi Student Summer Fellowship)

1300 Piccard Drive, Suite 200
Rockville MD 20850-4303
800/558-0121 or 301/670-9292
FAX: 301/670-9486
E-mail: LupusInfo@aol.com
Internet: http://www.lupus.org
AMOUNT: $2,000
DEADLINE(S): FEB 1
FIELD(S): Lupus Erythematosus Research

Open to undergraduates, graduates, and postgraduates, but applicants already having college degree are preferred. Research is conducted under the supervision of an established investigator; student is responsible for locating supervisor and lab (must be in U.S.). Projects may be basic, clinical, or psychosocial research and must be related to the causes, treatments, prevention, or cure of lupus.

See Web site or contact LFA for an application. Notification is in April.

1774—NATIONAL FEDERATION OF THE BLIND (Howard Brown Rickard Scholarship)

805 Fifth Avenue
Grinnell IA 50112
515/236-3366
AMOUNT: $3,000
DEADLINE(S): MAR 31

FIELD(S): Law; Medicine; Engineering; Architecture; Natural Sciences

For legally blind students pursuing or planning to pursue a full-time postsecondary course of study in the U.S.. Based on academic excellence, service to the community, and financial need. Membership NOT required.

1 award annually. Renewable. Contact Mrs. Peggy Elliot, Scholarship Committee Chairman, for an application.

1775—NATIONAL INSTITUTES OF HEALTH (Minority International Research Training Grant)

Fogarty International Center, Bldg. 31
Room B2C39
Bethesda MD 20892-2220
301/402-9467
FAX: 301/402-0779
E-mail: barbara_sina@cu.nih.gov
Internet: http://www.nih.gov/grants/oer.htm

AMOUNT: Varies
DEADLINE(S): MAR 15
FIELD(S): Biomedical and Behavioral Sciences

Open to minorities that are underrepresented in biomedical research professions (African and Hispanic Americans, Native Americans, Alaskan Natives, and Pacific Islanders). May be undergraduate students pursuing life science curricula (8-12 weeks research/coursework supported), students pursuing doctoral degrees in above fields (3-12 months research training at foreign institution supported), or faculty members in above fields (3-12 months research at foreign institution).

See Web site or contact NIH for an application.

1776—OAK RIDGE INSTITUTE FOR SCIENCE AND EDUCATION (ORISE Education and Training Programs)

P.O. Box 117
Oak Ridge TN 37831-0117
Internet: http://www.orau.gov/orise/educ.htm

AMOUNT: Varies
DEADLINE(S): Varies
FIELD(S): Engineering; Aeronautics; Computer Science; Technology; Earth Science; Environmental Studies; Biology; Chemistry; Physics; Medical Research

Numerous programs funded by the U.S. Department of Energy are offered for undergraduate students through postgraduate researchers. Includes fellowship and internship opportunities throughout the U.S. Some have citizenship restrictions. Travel may be included.

See Web site or write for a catalog of specific programs and requirements.

1777—OKLAHOMA MEDICAL RESEARCH FOUNDATION (Sir Alexander Fleming Scholar Program)

825 N.E.13th Street
Oklahoma City OK 73104-5046
405/271-8537 or
800/522-0211 (in-state)
Internet: http://www.omrf.ouhsc.edu

AMOUNT: $2,500 salary + housing
DEADLINE(S): Feb 15
FIELD(S): Sciences

Summer scholarship program (June and July) for Oklahoma students who have completed their junior year of high school through those in their junior year of college at time of application. Excellent academic standing and aptitude in science and math are essential. Students will work in the laboratories of the above organization. Research projects will be selected from: alcoholism/liver disease, arthritis/immunology, carcinogenesis, cardiovascular biology, and more.

Named for the scientist who discovered penicillin and dedicated OMRF in 1949. Contact organization for further information and application forms.

1778—PENINSULA COMMUNITY FOUNDATION (Dr. Mary Finegold Scholarship)

1700 S. El Camino Real, #300
San Mateo CA 94402
650/358-9369
FAX: 650/358-9817
Internet: http://www.pcf.org/community_grants/scholarships.html

AMOUNT: $1,000
DEADLINE(S): MAR 7 (5 p.m.)
FIELD(S): Sciences

Scholarships for senior girls graduating from high school in Palo Alto, California, who intend to complete a four-year degree in the sciences. Special consideration will be given to girls who have demonstrated a "pioneering" spirit in that they have not been constrained by stereotypical female roles and to those facing financial hardship.

Award was established in the honor of Dr. Mary Finegold who, after completing her medical studies, elected to stay at home until her youngest child was in high school before beginning her medical practice. She was a school physician.

1779—PHOENIX INDIAN MEDICAL CENTER AUXILIARY

Indian Health Career Awards
4212 North 16th Street
Phoenix AZ 85016
602/263-1576

AMOUNT: Up to $700
Deadlines: SEP 15, NOV 15
FIELD(S): Human Health

For students majoring in Human Health related fields. Each year, the Foundation awards undergraduate scholarships of up to $5,000 to American juniors and seniors in fields related to the environment, and to Native Americans and Alaska Natives in fields related to health care or tribal policy.

1780—PILOT INTERNATIONAL FOUNDATION (PIF/Lifeline Scholarship)

P.O. Box 5600
Macon GA 31208-5600
Written Inquiries

AMOUNT: Varies
DEADLINE(S): MAR 1
FIELD(S): Disabilities/Brain-related disorders

This program assists ADULT students re-entering the job market, preparing for a second career, or improving their professional skills for an established career. Applicants must be preparing for, or already involved in, careers working with people with disabilities/brain-related disorders. GPA of 3.5 or more is required.

Must be sponsored by a Pilot Club in your home town, or in the city in which your college or university is located. Send a self-addressed, stamped envelope for complete information.

1781—PILOT INTERNATIONAL FOUNDATION (Ruby Newhall Memorial Scholarship)

P.O. Box 5600
Macon, GA 31208-5600
Written Inquiries

AMOUNT: Varies
DEADLINE(S): MAR 15
FIELD(S): Disabilities/Brain-related disorders

For international students who have studied in the U.S. for at least one year, and who intend to return to their home country six months after graduation. Applicants must be full-time students majoring in a field related to human health and welfare, and have a GPA of 3.5 or more.

Applicants must be sponsored by a Pilot Club in their home town, or in the city in which their college or university is located. Send a self-addressed, stamped envelope for complete information.

1782—PILOT INTERNATIONAL FOUNDATION (The Pilot International Scholarship Program)

P.O. Box 5600
Macon GA 31208-5600
Written Inquiries
AMOUNT: Varies
DEADLINE(S): MAR 1
FIELD(S): Disabilities/Brain-related disorders

This program provides assistance to undergraduate students preparing for careers working directly with people with disabilities or training those who will. GPA of 3.5 or greater required.

Applicants must be sponsored by a Pilot Club in their home town, or in the city in which their college or university is located. Send a self-addressed, stamped envelope for complete information.

1783—PINE FAMILY FOUNDATION (Scholarship)

1000 Jo Jo Road
Pensacola FL 32514
AMOUNT: $2,500-$20,000
DEADLINE(S): MAR 15
FIELD(S): Health Care

Applicants must be engaged in active research toward the cure of AIDS or Alzheimer's disease. Must submit a letter from a sponsoring professor and be working toward a graduate degree.

1784—SRP/NAVAJO GENERATING STATION (Navajo Scholarship)

P.O. Box 850
Page AZ 86040
520/645-6539
FAX: 520/645-7295
E-mail: ljdawave@srp.gov
AMOUNT: Based on need
DEADLINE(S): APR 30
FIELD(S): Engineering, Environmental Studies, Business, Business Management, Health, Education

Scholarships for full-time students who hold membership in the Navajo Tribe and who are pursuing a degree in a field of study recognized as significant to the Navajo Naiton, Salt River Project, or the Navajo Generating Station, such as those listed above. Must be junior or senior, have and maintain a GPA of 3.0

Average of 15 awards per year. Inquire of Linda Dawavendewa at above location.

1785—U.S. DEPT. OF HEALTH and HUMAN SERVICES (Indian Health Service Health Professions Scholarship Program)

Twinbrook Metro Plaza, Suite 100
12300 Twinbrook Parkway
Rockville MD 20852
301/443-0234
FAX: 301/443-4815
Internet: http://www.ihs.gov/Recruitment/DHPS/SP/SBTOC3.asp
AMOUNT: Tuition + fees and monthly stipend of $938
DEADLINE(S): APR 1
FIELD(S): Health professions, accounting, social work

Open to Native Americans or Alaska natives who are graduate students or college juniors or seniors in a program leading to a career in a fields listed above. U.S. citizenship required. Renewable annually with reapplication.

Scholarship recipients must intend to serve the Indian people. They incur a one-year service obligation to the IHS for each year of support for a minimum of two years. Write for complete information.

1786—WASHINGTON STATE HIGHER EDUCATION COORDINATING BOARD (Health Professional Loan Repayment and Scholarship Program)

P.O. Box 47834
Olympia WA 98504-3430
360/705-6664
FAX: 360/664-9273
Internet: http://www.hecb.wa.gov
AMOUNT: Varies
DEADLINE(S): APR (scholarship); FEB (loan repayment); JUL (loan repayment)
FIELD(S): Health Care

Scholarships are open to students in accredited undergraduate or graduate health care programs leading to eligibility for licensure in Washington state. Must agree to work in designated shortage area for minimum of three years. Loan repayment recipients receive payment from program for purpose of repaying education loans secured while attending program of health care training leading to licensure in Washington state. Financial need NOT a factor.

Renewable up to 5 years. Contact Program Manager for a loan repayment application after November 15 and for scholarship application after January 15.

1787—WOMEN OF THE EVANGELICAL LUTHERAN CHURCH IN AMERICA (The Kahler-Vickers/Raup-Emma Wettstein Scholarships)

8765 West Higgins Road
Chicago IL 60631-4189
800/638-3522 ext. 2736
FAX: 773/380-2419
E-mail: womnelca@elca.org
AMOUNT: $2,000 max.
DEADLINE(S): FEB 15
FIELD(S): Health Professions and Christian Service

Assists women who are members of the ELCA studying for service in health professions associated with ELCA projects abroad that do not lead to church-certified professions. Must be U.S. citizen and have experienced an interruption of two or more years since completion of high school. Academic records of coursework completed in last five years as well as proof of admission from educational institution are required.

Renewable for an additional year. Contact Faith Fretheim, Program Director, for an application.

1788—ZETA PHI BETA SORORITY EDUCATIONAL FOUNDATION (S. Evelyn Lewis Memorial Scholarship in Medical Health Sciences)

1734 New Hampshire Avenue NW
Washington DC 20009
Internet: http://www.zpb1920.org
AMOUNT: $500-$1,000
DEADLINE(S): JAN 1
FIELD(S): Medicine; Health Sciences

Open to graduate and undergraduate young women enrolled in a program leading to a degree in medicine or health sciences. Award is for full-time study for one academic year (Fall-Spring) and is paid directly to college/university. Must submit proof of enrollment.

Send self-addressed, stamped envelope to above address between September 1 and December 15 for an application.

MEDICAL TECHNOLOGIES

1789—AMERICAN DENTAL HYGIENISTS ASSOCIATION INSTITUTE FOR ORAL HEALTH (William E. Motley Scholarship)

444 N. Michigan Avenue, Suite 3400
Chicago IL 60611
800/735-4916 or 312/440-8900
FAX: 312/440-8929
Internet: http://www.adha.org
AMOUNT: $1,000
DEADLINE(S): JUN 1
FIELD(S): Dental Hygiene

Awarded to applicant who has achieved a 4.0 GPA in dental hygiene. Students must be pursuing a bachelor's degree at a four-year accredited institution in the U.S. Must demonstrate financial need and have completed a minimum one year in a dental hygiene curriculum prior to receiving an award.

1 award annually. Not renewable. Contact Linda Caradine at ADHA for an application.

1790—AMERICAN DENTAL HYGIENISTS ASSOCIATION INSTITUTE FOR ORAL HEALTH (Warner Lambert Joint Oral Hygiene Group Scholarships)

444 N. Michigan Avenue, Suite 3400
Chicago IL 60611
800/735-4916 or 312/440-8900
FAX: 312/440-8929
Internet: http://www.adha.org
AMOUNT: $1,000
DEADLINE(S): JUN 1
FIELD(S): Dental Hygiene

Students must be pursuing a bachelor's degree at a four-year accredited institution in the U.S. Must have a minimum 3.0 GPA, demonstrate financial need, and have completed a minimum one year in a dental hygiene curriculum prior to receiving an award.

5 awards annually. Not renewable. Contact Linda Caradine at ADHA for an application. Sponsored by Warner Lambert Company.

1791—AMERICAN DENTAL HYGIENISTS ASSOCIATION INSTITUTE FOR ORAL HEALTH (Colgate "Bright Smiles, Bright Futures" Minority Scholarships)

444 N. Michigan Avenue, Suite 3400
Chicago IL 60611
800/735-4916 or 312/440-8900
FAX: 312/440-8929
Internet: http://www.adha.org
AMOUNT: $1,250
DEADLINE(S): JUN 1
FIELD(S): Dental Hygiene

Must be enrolled full-time in a Certificate/Associate Degree Program in the U.S. leading to licensure as a dental hygienist. Awarded to members of a minority group currently underrepresented in dental hygiene programs: African-Americans, Hispanics, Asians, Native Americans, and males. Must have a minimum 3.0 GPA, demonstrate financial need, and have completed a minimum one year in a dental hygiene curriculum prior to receiving an award.

2 awards annually. Not renewable. Contact Linda Caradine at ADHA for an application. Sponsored by the Colgate Palmolive Company.

1792—AMERICAN DENTAL HYGIENISTS ASSOCIATION INSTITUTE FOR ORAL HEALTH (Oral-B Laboratories Dental Hygiene Scholarships)

444 N. Michigan Avenue, Suite 3400
Chicago IL 60611
800/735-4916 or 312/440-8900
FAX: 312/440-8929
Internet: http://www.adha.org
AMOUNT: $1,000-$1,500
DEADLINE(S): JUN 1
FIELD(S): Dental Hygiene

Awarded to a full-time student at the baccalaureate degree level who demonstrates an intent to encourage professional, excellence and scholarship, promote quality research, and support dental hygiene through public and private education. Must have a minimum 3.5 GPA, demonstrate financial need, attend an accredited U.S. institution, and have completed a minimum one year in a dental hygiene program in the U.S.

2 awards annually. Not renewable. Contact Linda Caradine at ADHA for an application. Sponsored by Oral-B Laboratories.

1793—AMERICAN DENTAL HYGIENISTS ASSOCIATION INSTITUTE FOR ORAL HEALTH (Dr. Alfred C. Fones Scholarship)

444 N. Michigan Avenue, Suite 3400
Chicago IL 60611
800/735-4916 or 312/440-8900
FAX: 312/440-8929
Internet: http://www.adha.org
AMOUNT: $1,500
DEADLINE(S): JUN 1
FIELD(S): Dental Hygiene Education

Awarded to an applicant in the baccalaureate or graduate degree categories who intends to become a dental hygiene teacher/educator. Must have a minimum 3.0 GPA, demonstrate financial need, attend an accredited four-year U.S. institution, and have completed a minimum one year in a dental hygiene curriculum prior to receiving an award.

1 award annually. Not renewable. Contact Linda Caradine at ADHA for an application.

1794—AMERICAN DENTAL HYGIENISTS ASSOCIATION INSTITUTE FOR ORAL HEALTH (Dr. Harold Hillenbrand Scholarship)

444 N. Michigan Avenue, Suite 3400
Chicago IL 60611
800/735-4916 or 312/440-8900
FAX: 312/440-8929
Internet: http://www.adha.org
AMOUNT: $1,500
DEADLINE(S): JUN 1
FIELD(S): Dental Hygiene

Awarded to an applicant who demonstrates specific academic excellence and outstanding clinical performance. Must have a minimum 3.5 GPA, demonstrate financial need, be working toward a bachelor's degree at an accredited four-year U.S. institution, and have completed a minimum one year in a dental hygiene curriculum prior to receiving an award.

1 award annually. Not renewable. Contact Linda Caradine at ADHA for an application.

1795—AMERICAN DENTAL HYGIENISTS ASSOCIATION INSTITUTE FOR ORAL HEALTH (ADHA Institute Minority Scholarships)

444 N. Michigan Avenue, Suite 3400
Chicago IL 60611
800/735-4916 or 312/440-8900
FAX: 312/440-8929
Internet: http://www.adha.org
AMOUNT: $1,500
DEADLINE(S): JUN 1
FIELD(S): Dental Hygiene

For students enrolled full-time in a Certificate/Associate Degree Program in the U.S. leading to licensure as a dental hygienist. Must be members of a minority group currently underrepresented in dental hygiene programs: African Americans, Hispanics, Asians, Native Americans, and males. Must have a minimum 3.0 GPA, demonstrate financial need, and have completed a minimum one year in a dental hygiene curriculum prior to receiving an award.

2 awards annually. Not renewable. Contact Linda Caradine at ADHA for an application.

1796—AMERICAN DENTAL HYGIENISTS ASSOCIATION INSTITUTE FOR ORAL HEALTH (Irene E. Newman Scholarship)

444 N. Michigan Avenue, Suite 3400
Chicago IL 60611
800/735-4916 or 312/440-8900
FAX: 312/440-8929
Internet: http://www.adha.org
AMOUNT: $1,500
DEADLINE(S): JUN 1
FIELD(S): Dental Hygiene

Awarded to an applicant in the baccalaureate or graduate degree categories who demonstrates strong potential in public health or community dental health. Must have a minimum 3.0 GPA, demonstrate financial need, attend an accredited four-year U.S. institution full-time, and have completed a minimum one year in a dental hygiene curriculum prior to receiving an award.

1 award annually. Not renewable. Contact Linda Caradine at ADHA for an application.

1797—AMERICAN DENTAL HYGIENISTS ASSOCIATION INSTITUTE FOR ORAL HEALTH (ADHA Part-Time Scholarship)

444 N. Michigan Avenue, Suite 3400
Chicago IL 60611
800/735-4916 or 312/440-8900
FAX: 312/440-8929
Internet: http://www.adha.org
AMOUNT: $1,500
DEADLINE(S): JUN 1
FIELD(S): Dental Hygiene

For students enrolled part-time in a Certificate/Associate, Baccalaureate, or Graduate Degree program in the U.S. Must have a minimum 3.0 GPA, demonstrate financial need, and have completed a minimum one year in a dental hygiene program. See application for specific requirements for each degree program.

1 award annually. Not renewable. Contact Linda Caradine at ADHA for an application.

1798—AMERICAN DENTAL HYGIENISTS ASSOCIATION INSTITUTE FOR ORAL HEALTH (Sigma Phi Alpha Undergraduate Scholarship)

444 N. Michigan Avenue, Suite 3400
Chicago IL 60611
800/735-4916 or 312/440-8900
FAX: 312/440-8929
Internet: http://www.adha.org
AMOUNT: $1,000
DEADLINE(S): JUN 1
FIELD(S): Dental Hygiene

For full-time students pursuing a baccalaureate degree or associate degree/certificate in dental hygiene at an accredited U.S. institution. Awarded to an outstanding applicant attending an accredited dental hygiene school with an active chapter of the Sigma Phi Alpha Dental Hygiene Honor Society. Must have a minimum 3.0 GPA, demonstrate financial need, and have completed a minimum one year in a dental hygiene curriculum prior to receiving an award.

1 award annually. Not renewable. Contact Linda Caradine at ADHA for an application.

1799—AMERICAN DENTAL HYGIENISTS ASSOCIATION INSTITUTE FOR ORAL HEALTH (Margaret E. Swanson Scholarship)

444 N. Michigan Avenue, Suite 3400
Chicago IL 60611
800/735-4916 or 312/440-8900
FAX: 312/440-8929
Internet: http://www.adha.org
AMOUNT: $1,500
DEADLINE(S): JUN
FIELD(S): Dental Hygiene

For students enrolled full-time in a Certificate/Associate Degree Program in the U.S. leading to licensure as a dental hygienist. Awarded to an applicant who demonstrates exceptional organizational leadership potential. Must have a minimum 3.0 GPA, demonstrate financial need, and have completed a minimum one year in a dental hygiene curriculum prior to receiving an award.

1 award annually. Not renewable. Contact Linda Caradine at ADHA for an application.

1800—AMERICAN DENTAL HYGIENISTS ASSOCIATION INSTITUTE FOR ORAL HEALTH (Rebecca Fisk Scholarship)

444 N. Michigan Avenue, Suite 3400
Chicago IL 60611
800/735-4916 or 312/440-8900
FAX: 312/440-8929
Internet: http://www.adha.org
AMOUNT: $1,000
DEADLINE(S): JUN 1
FIELD(S): Dental Hygiene

For students enrolled full-time in a Certificate/Associate Degree Program in the U.S. leading to licensure as a dental hygienist. Must have a minimum 3.0 GPA, demonstrate financial need, and have completed a minimum one year in a dental hygiene curriculum prior to receiving an award.

1 award annually. Not renewable. Contact Linda Caradine at ADHA for an application.

1801—AMERICAN FOUNDATION FOR THE BLIND (Paul W. Ruckes Scholarship)

11 Penn Plaza, Suite 300
New York NY 10001
212/502-7661
FAX: 212/502-7771
E-mail: juliet@afb.org
Internet: http://www.afb.org
AMOUNT: $1,000
DEADLINE(S): APR 30
FIELD(S): Engineering; Computer/Physical/Life Sciences

Open to legally blind and visually impaired undergraduate and graduate students pursuing a degree in one of above fields. Must be U.S. citizen. Must submit written documentation of visual impairment from ophthalmologist or optometrist (need not be legally blind); official transcripts; proof of college/university acceptance; three letters of recommendation; and typewritten statement describing goals, work experience extracurricular activities, and how monies will be used.

1 award annually. See Web site or contact Julie Tucker at AFB for an application.

1802—AMERICAN INDIAN SCIENCE AND ENGINEERING SOCIETY (A.T. Anderson Memorial Scholarship)

P.O. Box 9828
Albuquerque NM 87119-9828
505/765-1052
FAX: 505/765-5608
E-mail: scholarships@aises.org
Internet: http://www.aises.org/scholarships
AMOUNT: $1,000-$2,000
DEADLINE(S): JUN 15
FIELD(S): Medicine; Natural Resources; Science; Engineering

Open to undergraduate and graduate students who are at least 1/4 American Indian or recognized as member of a tribe. Must be member of AISES ($10 fee), enrolled full-time at an accredited institution, and demonstrate financial need.

Renewable. See Web site or contact Patricia Browne for an application and/or membership information.

1803—AMERICAN MEDICAL TECHNOLOGISTS (AMT Scholarships)

710 Higgins Road
Park Ridge IL 60068-5765
847/823-5169
AMOUNT: $500
DEADLINE(S): APR 1
FIELD(S): Medical Laboratory Technology; Medical Assisting; Dental Assisting; Phlebotomy; Office Laboratory

Must be a graduate of, or a senior in, an accredited high school (GED okay). Must be enrolled in a school accredited by accrediting agency recognized by U.S. Dept. of Education, or must be enrolled in regionally accredited college/university in the U.S. Applicant MUST be pursuing one of above careers and should provide evidence of career goals, as well as financial need. Must submit transcripts, two letters of personal reference, and statement of why this career chosen.

5 awards annually. Send a self-addressed, stamped, business-sized envelope to AMT for an application. Recipients announced at AMT National Convention held in mid-summer.

1804—AMERICAN SOCIETY FOR CLINICAL LABORATORY SCIENCE (Ruth M. French Graduate or Undergraduate Scholarship)

7910 Woodmont Avenue, Suite 530
Bethesda MD 20814
301/657-2768
FAX: 301/657-2909
AMOUNT: $1,000
DEADLINE(S): MAR 1
FIELD(S): Clinical Laboratory Science or Medical Technology

Scholarships for students in the above field enrolled in an approved undergraduate or graduate program. Undergrads must be in last year of study. U.S. citizenship or permanent U.S. residency required.

Contact address above for complete information. Enclose self-addressed, stamped business size envelope. Applications available after Nov. 1.

1805—AMERICAN SOCIETY FOR CLINICAL LABORATORY SCIENCE (Alpha Mu Tau Undergraduate Scholarship)

7910 Woodmont Avenue, Suite 530
Bethesda MD 20814
301/657-2768
FAX: 301/657-2909
AMOUNT: Up to $1,000
DEADLINE(S): MAR 15
FIELD(S): Clinical Laboratory Science, Medical Technology, Clinical Laboratory Technician, Cytotechnology, Histotechnology

Scholarships for undergraduate students in their last year of study in the above fields enrolled in an approved NAACLS accredited program. U.S. citizenship or permanent U.S. residency required.

Contact address above for complete information. Enclose self-addressed stamped business size envelope. Applications available after Nov. 1.

1806—AMERICAN SOCIETY FOR CLINICAL LABORATORY SCIENCE (Forum for Concern of Minorities Scholarship)

7910 Woodmont Avenue, Suite 530
Bethesda MD 20814
301/657-2768
FAX: 301/657-2909
AMOUNT: Varies
DEADLINE(S): FEB 15
FIELD(S): Clinical Laboratory Science, Medical Technology, Clinical Laboratory Technology

Scholarships for undergraduate minority students enrolled in an approved NAACLS accredited program in the above fields. Min. 2.5 GPA required. U.S. citizenship or permanent U.S. residency required. Must demonstrate financial need.

Contact address above for complete information. Enclose self-addressed stamped business size envelope. Applications available after Nov. 1.

1807—AMERICAN SOCIETY OF RADIOLOGIC TECHNOLOGISTS AND RESEARCH FOUNDATION (Isadore N. Stern Scholarship)

15000 Central Avenue SE
Albuquerque NM 87123-3917
505/298-4500
FAX: 505/298-5063
Internet: http://www.asrt.org
AMOUNT: $1,000
DEADLINE(S): JAN 31
FIELD(S): Radiologic Sciences

Open to ASRT MEMBERS ONLY who are associate, baccalaureate or graduate students with a minimum 3.0 GPA. Must have at least one-year membership with ASRT, ARRT registered/unrestricted state license, and must have worked in the radiologic sciences profession for at least one year in the past five years. Financial need NOT a factor.

4 awards annually. MEMBERS ONLY should contact Phelosha Collaros for an application.

1808—AMERICAN SOCIETY OF RADIOLOGIC TECHNOLOGISTS AND RESEARCH FOUNDATION (Jerman-Cahoon Student Scholarship)

15000 Central Avenue SE
Albuquerque NM 87123-3917
505/298-4500
FAX: 505/298-5063
Internet: http://www.asrt.org
AMOUNT: $2,500
DEADLINE(S): FEB 1
FIELD(S): Radiologic Sciences

Open to academically outstanding students attending an entry level Radiologic Sciences program with a minimum 3.0 GPA. Requirements include a recommendation form and a 250- to 300-word essay. Financial need is a factor.

2 awards annually. MEMBERS ONLY should contact Phelosha Collaros for an application.

1809—AMERICAN SOCIETY OF RADIOLOGIC TECHNOLOGISTS AND RESEARCH FOUNDATION (Royce Osburn Minority Student Scholarship)

15000 Central Avenue SE
Albuquerque NM 87123-3917
505/298-4500
FAX: 505/298-5063
Internet: http://www.asrt.org
AMOUNT: $4,000
DEADLINE(S): FEB 1
FIELD(S): Radiologic Sciences

Open to academically outstanding students attending an entry level Radiologic Sciences program with a minimum 3.0 GPA. Requirements include a recommendation form and a 250- to 300-word essay. Financial need is a factor.

5 awards annually. MEMBERS ONLY should contact Phelosha Collaros for an application.

1810—AMERICAN SOCIETY OF RADIOLOGIC TECHNOLOGISTS AND RESEARCH FOUNDATION (Siemens Scholar Award)

15000 Central Avenue SE
Albuquerque NM 87123-3917
505/298-4500
FAX: 505/298-5063
Internet: http://www.asrt.org
AMOUNT: $3,000
DEADLINE(S): MAR 1
FIELD(S): Radiologic Sciences

Open to ASRT MEMBERS ONLY who are associate, baccalaureate or graduate students in radiation therapy or health sciences with a minimum 3.5 GPA. Must have at least one-year membership with ASRT, ARRT registered/unrestricted state license, and must have worked in the radiologic sciences profession for at least one year in the past five years. Financial need NOT a factor.

1 award annually. MEMBERS ONLY should contact Phelosha Collaros for an application.

1811—AMERICAN SOCIETY OF RADIOLOGIC TECHNOLOGISTS AND RESEARCH FOUNDATION (Varian Radiation Therapy Student Scholarship)

15000 Central Avenue SE
Albuquerque NM 87123-3917
505/298-4500
FAX: 505/298-5063
Internet: http://www.asrt.org
AMOUNT: $5,000
DEADLINE(S): FEB 1
FIELD(S): Radiologic Sciences

Open to academically outstanding students accepted/enrolled in an entry level Radiologic Sciences program with a minimum 3.0 GPA. Requirements include a recommendation form and a 250- to 300-word essay. Financial need is a factor.

2 awards annually. Contact Phelosha Collaros for an application.

1812—AMERICAN SPEECH-LANGUAGE HEARING FOUNDATION (Young Scholars Award for Minority Students)

10801 Rockville Pike
Rockville MD 20852
301/897-5700 ext. 4203
FAX: 301/571-0457
Internet: http://www.asha.org
AMOUNT: $2,000
DEADLINE(S): JUN 6
FIELD(S): Speech-Language Pathology; Audiology

Open to racial/ethnic college seniors who are U.S. citizens accepted for graduate study in speech-language pathology or audiology.

Contact Gina Smolka for an application after February 1.

1813—ARTHUR M. MILLER FUND

P.O. Box 1122
Wichita KS 67201-0004
316/261-4609
AMOUNT: Varies
DEADLINE(S): MAR 31
FIELD(S): Medicine or related fields

Scholarships for Kansas residents for the study of medicine or related fields at accredited institutions.

Send SASE for formal application.

1814—ASSOCIATED WESTERN UNIVERSITIES, INC. (AWU Undergraduate Student Fellowships)

4190 S. Highland Drive, Suite 211
Salt Lake City UT 84124-2600
801/273-8900
FAX: 801/277-5632
E-mail: info@awu.org
Internet: http://www.awu.org
AMOUNT: $300/week stipend + possible travel allowance
DEADLINE(S): FEB 1
FIELD(S): Science; Mathematics; Engineering; Technology

Eight- to sixteen-week fellowships.

1815—ASSOCIATION ON AMERICAN INDIAN AFFAIRS (Emergency Aid and Health Professions Scholarships)

P.O. Box 268
Sisseton SD 57262
605/698-3998
FAX: 605/698-3316
E-mail: aaia@sbtc.net
Internet: http://www.indian-affairs.org
AMOUNT: See Web site for information.
DEADLINE(S): MAY 1
FIELD(S): Health Professions

Open to full-time undergraduate students who are minimally 1/4 degree Indian blood from a federally recognized tribe. Award is based on financial need and is limited to North America/Alaska. Must submit essay on need, certificate of enrollment and quantum from your tribe or BIA, transcript, schedule of classes, and current financial aid award letter.

See Web site for information on requirements or send a self-addressed, stamped envelope to Elena Stops, Scholarship Coordinator, for an application.

1816—BECA FOUNDATION (Alice Newell Joslyn Medical Fund)

830 E. Grand Avenue, Suite B
Escondido CA 92025
760/471-8246
FAX: 760/471-8176
AMOUNT: $500-$1,000
DEADLINE(S): MAR 1
FIELD(S): Medicine; Health Care; Nursing; Dental/Medical Assisting; Physical Therapy

Open to Latino students who live in or attend college in San Diego County, CA, at time of application. For high school seniors and those already in college pursuing undergraduate or graduate education. Based on financial need, scholastic determination, and community/cultural awareness.

Send self-addressed, stamped envelope to BECA for an application.

1817—BOYS AND GIRLS CLUBS OF SAN DIEGO (Spence Reese Scholarship Fund)

1761 Hotel Circle So., Suite 123
San Diego CA 92108
619/298-3520
AMOUNT: $2,000/year
DEADLINE(S): MAY 15
FIELD(S): Medicine; Law; Engineering; Political Science

Open to male high school seniors planning a career in one of the above fields. Must be residents of Imperial, Riverside, Orange, San Diego, or Los Angeles counties in California. Boys and Girls Club affiliation NOT required.

$10 application fee. Renewable up to 4 years. Send a self-addressed, stamped envelope to Boys and Girls Club for an application after January 1.

1818—CALIFORNIA GRANGE FOUNDATION (Deaf Activities Scholarships)

Pat Avila
2101 Stockton Boulevard
Sacramento CA 95817
Written Inquiry
AMOUNT: Varies
DEADLINE(S): APR 1
FIELD(S): Course work which will be of benefit to the deaf community

Scholarships students entering, continuing, or returning to college to pursue studies that will benefit the deaf community.

Write for information after Feb. 1 of each year.

1819—COLUMBIANA COUNTY PUBLIC HEALTH LEAGUE TRUST FUND (Grants)

c/o Mary Kay Withum
P.O. Box 511
Wheeling WV 26003
304/234-4128
FAX: 304/234-4142
AMOUNT: Varies
DEADLINE(S): FEB 28
FIELD(S): Respiratory Illness; Medicine; Medical Research; Pharmacy; Medical Technology; Physical Therapy; Nursing; Dental Hygiene; Occupational Therapy

Open to undergraduate and graduate Columbiana County, Ohio, residents who are pursuing medical education or research in one of the above fields. Preference given to respiratory illness. Students of veterinary medicine NOT eligible.

Contact Sherrill Schmied for an application.

1820—COMMUNITY FOUNDATION OF WESTERN MASSACHUSETTS (James L. Shriver Scholarship)

1500 Main Street
P.O. Box 15769
Springfield MA 01115
413/732-2858
AMOUNT: $750
DEADLINE(S): APR 15
FIELD(S): Technical Fields

Open to residents of Western Massachusetts to pursue technical careers through college, trade, or technical school. Based on financial need, academic merit, and extracurricular activities. Must submit transcripts and fill out government FAFSA form.

1 award annually. Renewable with reapplication. Contact Community Foundation for an application and your financial aid office for FAFSA. Notification is in June.

1821—COMMUNITY FOUNDATION OF WESTERN MASSACHUSETTS (Nate McKinney Memorial Scholarship)

1500 Main Street
P.O. Box 15769
Springfield MA 01115
413/732-2858
AMOUNT: $1,000
DEADLINE(S): APR 15
FIELD(S): Music; Athletics; Science

Open to graduating seniors of Gateway Regional High School in Huntington, Massachusetts. Recipient must excel academically, demonstrate good citizenship, and have a strong interest in at least two of the following areas: music, science, and athletics. Based on financial need, academic merit, and extracurricular activities. Must submit transcripts and fill out government FAFSA form.

1 award annually. Renewable up to 4 years with reapplication. Contact Community Foundation for an application and your financial aid office for FAFSA. Notification is in June.

1822—CYNTHIA E. AND CLARA H. HOLLIS FOUNDATION

100 Summer Street
Boston MA 02110
Written Inquiry
AMOUNT: Varies
DEADLINE(S): APR 1
FIELD(S): Nursing, Social Work, Dental or Medical Technology, and Religion

Scholarships for Massachusetts with preference given to students in the above fields. For undergraduates, graduates, votech, and adult education. Must demonstrate financial need.

Send SASE to Walter E. Palmer, Esq., 35 Harvard Street, Brookline, MA 02146 for application details. Scholarship forms are also available from the rector of All Saints Church, Brookline High School, and St. Mary's High School, all in Brookline, Massachusetts.

1823—EASTER SEAL SOCIETY OF IOWA, INC. (Scholarships and Awards)

P.O. Box 4002
Des Moines IA 50333-4002
515/289-1933
AMOUNT: $400-$600
DEADLINE(S): APR 15
FIELD(S): Physical Rehabilitation, Mental Rehabilitation, and related areas

Open ONLY to Iowa residents who are full-time undergraduate sophomores, juniors, seniors, or graduate students at accredited institutions planning a career in the broad field of rehabilitation. Must indicate financial need and be in top 40% of their class.

6 scholarships per year. Must reapply each year.

1824—EDWARD BANGS KELLEY AND ELZA KELLEY FOUNDATION, INC. (Scholarship Program)

P.O. Drawer M
Hyannis MA 02601-1412
508/775-3117
AMOUNT: $500-$4,000 (max.)
DEADLINE(S): APR 30
FIELD(S): Medicine; Nursing; Education; Health and Social Sciences

Open to residents of Barnstable County, Massachusetts. Scholarships are intended to benefit health and welfare of Barnstable County residents. Awards support study at recognized undergraduate, graduate, and professional institutions. Financial need is considered.

Contact Foundation for an application Scholarship Committee for an application.

1825—EMPIRE COLLEGE (Dean's Scholarship)

3035 Cleveland Avenue
Santa Rosa CA 95403
707/546-4000
FAX: 707/546-4058
AMOUNT: $250-$1,500
DEADLINE(S): APR 15
FIELD(S): Accounting; Secretarial; Legal; Medical (Clinical and Administrative); Travel and Tourism; General Business; Computer Assembly; Network Assembly/Administration

Open to high school seniors who plan to attend Empire College. Must be U.S. citizen.

10 awards annually. Contact Ms. Mary Farha for an application.

1826—FIRST UNITED METHODIST CHURCH (Robert Stevenson and Doreene E. Cater Scholarships)

302 5th Avenue, S.
St. Cloud MN 56301
FAX: 320/251-0878
E-mail: fumc@fumc-stcloud.org
AMOUNT: $200-1,500
DEADLINE(S): JUN 1
FIELD(S): Humanitarian and Christian Service: Teaching, Medicine, Social Work, Environmental Studies, etc.

Stevenson Scholarship is open to undergraduate members of the First United Methodist Church of St. Cloud. Cater Scholarship is open to members of the Minnesota United Methodist Conference who are entering the sophomore year or higher of college work. Both require two letters of reference, transcripts, and financial need.

5-6 awards annually. Contact Scholarship Committee for an application.

1827—FOUNDATION FOR SEACOAST HEALTH (Scholarship Program)

100 Campus Drive, Suite 1
Portsmouth NH 03801
603/422-8200
FAX: 602/422-8207
E-mail: ffsh@communitycampus.org
Internet: http://www.ffsh.org

AMOUNT: $1,000-$10,000
DEADLINE(S): FEB 1
FIELD(S): Health-related fields

Open to undergraduate and graduate students pursuing health-related fields of study who are legal residents of the following cities in New Hampshire: Portsmouth, Newington, New Castle, Rye, Greenland, N. Hampton, or these cities in Maine: Kittery, Eliot, or York, Maine. Must have resided in the area for at least two years.

Write or check Web site for details. $150,000 awarded annually; 35 awards given

1828—GRACE FOUNDATION (Scholarship Trust Fund)

P.O. Box 924
Menlo Park CA 94026-0924
Written Inquiry

AMOUNT: $1,000-$4,000
DEADLINE(S): JAN 31
FIELD(S): Ministry; Medicine; Teaching; Social Service

Open to students from developing countries in Asia/Southeast Asia to pursue full-time study at an accredited college/university. For training future Christian ministers and professional workers in above fields. Must have completed one or more years of college in or near their native country, be a strong Christian, have a minimum 3.0 GPA, and demonstrate financial need.

Renewable up to 4 years with maintenance of 3.0 GPA. Applications available between September 1 and October 31.

1829—HISPANIC DENTAL ASSOCIATION AND DR. JUAN D. VILLARREAL FOUNDATION (Dental/Dental Hygienist Scholarships)

188 W. Randolph Street, Suite 1811
Chicago IL 60601-3001
800/852-7921 or 312/577-4013
FAX: 312/577-4013
E-mail: hdassoc1@qwest.net
Internet: http://www.hdassoc.org

AMOUNT: $500-$1,000
DEADLINE(S): JUN 15
FIELD(S): Dentistry; Dental Hygiene

Open to Hispanic students pursuing undergraduate study in an accredited Texas dental school.

Contact HDA for an application.

1830—INTERNATIONAL ORDER OF THE KING'S DAUGHTERS AND SONS (Health Careers Scholarships)

c/o Mrs. Fred Cannon; Box 1310
Brookhaven MS 39602
Written Inquiry

AMOUNT: $1,000 (max.)
DEADLINE(S): APR 1
FIELD(S): Medicine; Dentistry; Nursing; Physical Therapy; Occupational Therapy; Medical Technologies; Pharmacy

Open to students accepted to/enrolled in an accredited U.S. or Canadian four-year or graduate school. RN candidates must have completed first year of program; MD or DDS candidates must be for at least the second year of medical or dental school; all others must be in at least third year of four-year program. Pre-med students NOT eligible. Must be U.S. or Canadian citizen.

Send self-addressed, stamped envelope, along with a letter stating the field of study and present level, to the Director at above address for an application.

1831—J. HUGH and EARLE W. FELLOWS MEMORIAL FUND (Scholarship Loans)

Pensacola Junior College President
1000 College Boulevard
Pensacola FL 32504-8998
904/484-1700
Internet: http://www.pjc.cc.fl.us/

AMOUNT: Each is negotiated individually
DEADLINE(S): None
FIELD(S): Medicine; Nursing; Medical Technology; Theology (Episcopal)

Open to bona fide residents of the Florida counties of Escambia, Santa Rosa, Okaloosa, or Walton. For undergraduate study in the fields listed above. U.S. citizenship required.

Loans are interest-free until graduation. Write for complete information.

1832—JEWISH FEDERATION OF METROPOLITAN CHICAGO (Academic Scholarship Program/The Marcus and Theresa Levie Educational Fund)

One South Franklin Street
Chicago IL 60606
312/357-4521
FAX: 312/855-3282
E-mail: jvsscholarship@jvschicago.org
Internet: http://www.jvschicago.org/scholarship/

AMOUNT: Varies
DEADLINE(S): MAR 1
FIELD(S): Medicine, Dentistry, Dental Hygiene, Emergency Medical Technology, Health Technology, Nursing or Physicians' Assistant, Occupational Therapy, Optometry, Clinical Psychology/Counseling, Education

Scholarships for college juniors, seniors, and graduate students, or students in vocational training programs, who are Jewish and are residents of Chicago, IL, and Cook County. Applicant must have a specific career goal in the "helping professions," such as those above.

Academic achievement and financial need are considered. Applications accepted after December 1. See Web site for more information and applications.

1833—JEWISH VOCATIONAL SERVICE (Academic Scholarship Program)

One S. Franklin Street
Chicago IL 60606
312/357-4500
FAX: 312/855-3282
TTY: 312/855-3282
E-mail: jvschicago@jon.cjfny.org

AMOUNT: $5,000 (max.)
DEADLINE(S): MAR 1
FIELD(S): "Helping" Professions; Mathematics; Engineering; Sciences; Communications (at Univ IL only); Law (certain schools in IL only)

Open to Jewish men and women legally domiciled in the greater Chicago metropolitan area, who are identified as having promise for significant contributions in their chosen careers, and are in need of financial assistance for full-time academic programs in above areas. Must have entered undergraduate junior year in career programs requiring no postgrad education, be in graduate/professional school, or be in a vo-tech training program. Interview required.

Renewable. Contact JVS for an application between December 1 and February 15.

1834—JUNIATA COLLEGE (Robert Steele Memorial Scholarship)

Office of Student Financial Planning
Juniata College
1700 Moore Street,
Huntingdon PA 16652
814/641-3142
FAX: 814/641-5311
Internet: http://www.juniata.edu/
E-mail: clarkec@juniata.edu
AMOUNT: $4,000 (max.)
DEADLINE(S): APR 1
FIELD(S): Science; Medical Studies

Open to science/medical students applying to Juniata College. Must demonstrate financial need and fill out government FAFSA form.

Contact Randy Rennell, Director of Student Financial Planning, for an application or enrollment information. See your financial aid office for FAFSA.

1835—MARYLAND HIGHER EDUCATION COMMISSION (Maryland Science and Technology Scholarship Program)

16 Francis Street
Annapolis Park MD 21401
410/974-5370 or
800/974-1024
E-mail: ssamail@mhec.state.md.us
Internet: http://www.mhec.state.md.us/SSA/stech_qa.htm
AMOUNT: $3,000/year (BA); $1,000/year (AA)
DEADLINE(S): None
FIELD(S): Computer Science; Engineering; Technology

Scholarships for college-bound Maryland high school seniors who will major in one of the above fields and who are accepted to an eligible associate or bachelor's degree program in Maryland. Students in the class of 1999 will be eligible for the first awards. The deadline was not known at this writing, so check for deadline date. Must agree to work in the state after graduation in a related field, one year for each year of assistance received.

Must maintain a 3.0 GPA.

1836—MARYLAND HIGHER EDUCATION COMMISSION (Tuition Reimbursement of Firefighters and Rescue Squad Members)

State Scholarship Admin.
16 Francis Street
Annapolis MD 21401
410/974-5370
TTY: 800/735-2258
Internet: http://www.ubalt.edu/www.mhec
AMOUNT: Varies (current resident undergraduate tuition rate at Univ. MD-College Park)
DEADLINE(S): JUL 1
FIELD(S): Firefighting; Emergency Medical Technology

Open to firefighters and rescue squad members who successfully complete one year of coursework in a firefighting or EMT program and a two-year service obligation in Maryland.

Contact MHEC for an application.

1837—McCORD CAREER CENTER (Level II McCord Medical/Music Scholarship)

Healdsburg High School
1024 Prince Street
Healdsburg CA 95448
707/431-3473
Email: career@husd.com
AMOUNT: Varies
DEADLINE(S): APR 15
FIELD(S): Medicine; Music

For graduates of Healdsburg High School who are planning a career in music or medicine. Must be enrolled full-time at a college/university as an undergraduate junior or senior in the fall, or earning an advanced degree in graduate or medical school, or entering into a vocational/certificate program. Transcripts, proof of attendance, and an essay are required.

Contact the McCord Career Center at Healdsburg High School for an application.

1838—MICROSCOPY SOCIETY OF AMERICA SCHOLARSHIPS (Undergraduate Research Scholarships)

230 East Ohio Street, Suite 400
Chicago IL 60611-3265
800/538-3672
Internet: http://www.MSA.Microscopy.com
AMOUNT: Up to $3,000
DEADLINE(S): DEC
FIELD(S): Science

Scholarship provides funds to junior or senior undergraduates conducting research involving any area of microscopy. Applicants may not receive more than one scholarship.

1839—NATIONAL ASSOCIATION OF AMERICAN BUSINESS CLUBS (AMBUCS Scholarships for Therapists)

P.O. Box 5127
High Point NC 27262
910/869-2166
FAX: 910/887-8451
E-mail: ambucs@ambucs.com
Internet: http://www.ambucs.com
AMOUNT: $500-$6,000
DEADLINE(S): APR 15
FIELD(S): Physical Therapy, Music Therapy, Occupational Therapy, Speech-Language Pathology, Audiology, Rehabilitation, Recreation Therapy, and related areas

Open to undergraduate juniors and seniors or graduate students who have good scholastic standing and plan to enter the fields listed above. GPA of 3.0 or better (4.0 scale) and U.S. citizenship required. Must demonstrate financial need.

Renewable. Please include a self-addressed stamped envelope (SASE); applications are mailed in December; incomplete applications will not be considered.

1840—NATIONAL ATHLETIC TRAINERS' ASSOCIATION (NATA Scholarship Program)

2952 Stemmons Freeway
Dallas TX 75247
214/637-6282 ext. 121
FAX: 214/637-2206
E-mail: barbara@nata.org
Internet: http://natafoundation.org
AMOUNT: $2,000
DEADLINE(S): FEB 1
FIELD(S): Athletic Training

Open to student members of NATA who have excellent academic records and have excelled as student athletic trainers. Undergraduates may apply after completion of junior year, and graduates may apply after completion of fall semester of their undergraduate senior year. Must have a minimum 3.2 GPA.

Send self-addressed, stamped envelope to Barbara Niland at NATA for membership information or an application.

1841—NATIONAL HEALTH SERVICE CORPS (NHSC Scholarship Program)

11300 Rockville Pike, Suite 80
Rockville MD 20852
800/638-0824
Internet: http://www.bhpr.hrsa.dhhs.gov/nhsc
AMOUNT: Full tuition/books/fees/supplies + monthly stipend
DEADLINE(S): MAR
FIELD(S): Family Medicine; General Internal Medicine; General Pediatrics; Obstetrics/Gynecology; Family Nurse

Practitioners; Primary Care Physician Assistants; Certified Nurse-Midwives

Must be U.S. citizen attending or enrolled in fully accredited U.S. allopathic/osteopathic medical school, nursing program, or physician assistant program. For each year of support received, you must serve one year in federally designated health professional shortage area of greatest need. Minimum two years service commitment begins upon completion of your residency and/or training.

300 awards annually. Renewable up to 4 years. Contact NHSC for an application.

1842—NATIONAL INSTITUTES OF HEALTH (Minority International Research Training Grant)

Fogarty International Center, Bldg. 31
Room B2C39
Bethesda MD 20892-2220
301/402-9467
FAX: 301/402-0779
E-mail: barbara_sina@cu.nih.gov
Internet: http://www.nih.gov/grants/oer.htm

AMOUNT: Varies
DEADLINE(S): MAR 15
FIELD(S): Biomedical and Behavioral Sciences

Open to minorities that are underrepresented in biomedical research professions (African and Hispanic Americans, Native Americans, Alaskan Natives, and Pacific Islanders). May be undergraduate students pursuing life science curricula (8-12 weeks research/coursework supported), students pursuing doctoral degrees in above fields (3-12 months research training at foreign institution supported), or faculty members in above fields (3-12 months research at foreign institution).

See Web site or contact NIH for an application.

1843—NATIONAL STRENGTH AND CONDITIONING ASSOCIATION (Challenge Scholarships)

P.O. Box 9908
Colorado Springs CO 80932-0908
719/632-6722
FAX: 719/632-6722
E-mail: nsca@usa.net
Internet: http://www.colosoft.com/nsca

AMOUNT: $1,000
DEADLINE(S): MAR 1
FIELD(S): Body Strength and Conditioning

Open to National Strength and Conditioning Association members to pursue undergraduate or graduate study in fields related to body strength and conditioning.

Contact NSCA for an application or membership information.

1844—NAVY RECRUITING COMMAND (Armed Forces Health Professions Scholarships)

Chief
5722 Integrity Drive
Millington, TN 38054
888/633-9674
Internet: http://www.navy.com

AMOUNT: Average of $1,058/month stipend + tuition, fees, books, lab fees, etc.
DEADLINE(S): Applications taken year-around
FIELD(S): Medicine, Dentistry, Optometry, Physical Therapy, Pharmacology, Health Care Administration, Industrial Hygiene, etc.

Open to U.S. citizens enrolled or accepted for enrollment in any of the above fields at an accredited institution in the U.S. or Puerto Rico. Must qualify for appointment as a Navy officer and sign a contractual agreement. Must be between the ages of 18 and 40 for some programs and have a GPA around 3.0.

See Web site, contact local Navy Recruiting Office, or contact the above address.

1845—NEW YORK STATE HIGHER EDUCATION SERVICES CORPORATION (N.Y. State Regents Professional/Health Care Opportunity Scholarships)

Cultural Education Center, Room 5C64
Albany NY 12230
518/486-1319
Internet: http://www.hesc.com

AMOUNT: $1,000-$10,000/year
DEADLINE(S): Varies
FIELD(S): Medicine and dentistry and related fields, architecture, nursing, psychology, audiology, landscape architecture, social work, chiropractic, law, pharmacy, accounting, speech language pathology

For NY state residents who are economically disadvantaged and members of a minority group underrepresented in the chosen profession and attending school in NY state. Some programs carry a service obligation in New York for each year of support. For U.S. citizens or qualifying noncitizens.

Medical/dental scholarships require one year of professional work in NY.

1846—NORTH CAROLINA DEPARTMENT OF PUBLIC INSTRUCTION (Scholarship Loan Program for Prospective Teachers)

301 N. Wilmington Street
Raleigh NC 27601-2825
919/715-1120

AMOUNT: Up to $2,500/year
DEADLINE(S): FEB
FIELD(S): Education: Teaching, school psychology and counseling, speech/language impaired, audiology, library/media services

For NC residents planning to teach in NC public schools. At least 3.0 high school GPA required; must maintain 2.5 GPA during freshman year and 3.0 cumulative thereafter. Recipients are obligated to teach one year in an NC public school for each year of assistance. Those who do not fulfill their teaching obligation are required to repay the loan plus interest.

200 awards per year. For full-time students. Applications available in Dec. from high school counselors and college and university departments of education.

1847—NORTH CAROLINA DEPT. OF PUBLIC INSTRUCTION (Teacher Assistant Scholarship Loan)

301 N. Wilmington Street
Raleigh NC 27601-2825
919/715-1120

AMOUNT: Up to $1,200/yr
DEADLINE(S): JAN
FIELD(S): Education: Teaching, school psychology or counseling, speech/language impaired, audiology, library/media services

For NC residents employed as K-12 teaching assistants in public schools who wish to pursue teacher licensure. Must either hold a BA degree or have completed general college courses prerequisite to admission to degree program and be admitted to an approved teacher education program at a four-year institution. Two-year community college early childhood education program is acceptable.

Must remain employed as teaching assistant while pursuing licensure and teach one year in an NC public school for each year of assistance received. Applications available in Sept. from local school superintendent.

1848—OAK RIDGE INSTITUTE FOR SCIENCE AND EDUCATION (ORISE Education and Training Programs)

P.O. Box 117
Oak Ridge TN 37831-0117
Internet: http://www.orau.gov/orise/educ.htm
AMOUNT: Varies
DEADLINE(S): Varies
FIELD(S): Engineering; Aeronautics; Computer Science; Technology; Earth Science; Environmental Studies; Biology; Chemistry; Physics; Medical Research

Numerous programs funded by the U.S. Department of Energy are offered for undergraduate students through postgraduate researchers. Includes fellowship and internship opportunities throughout the U.S. Some have citizenship restrictions. Travel may be included.

See Web site or write for a catalog of specific programs and requirements.

1849—PENINSULA COMMUNITY FOUNDATION (Dr. Mary Finegold Scholarship)

1700 S. El Camino Real, #300
San Mateo CA 94402
650/358-9369
FAX: 650/358-9817
Internet: http://www.pcf.org/community_grants/scholarships.html
AMOUNT: $1,000
DEADLINE(S): MAR 7 (5 p.m.)
FIELD(S): Sciences

Scholarships for senior girls graduating from high school in Palo Alto, California, who intend to complete a four-year degree in the sciences. Special consideration will be given to girls who have demonstrated a "pioneering" spirit in that they have not been constrained by stereotypical female roles and to those facing financial hardship.

Award was established in the honor of Dr. Mary Finegold who, after completing her medical studies, elected to stay at home until her youngest child was in high school before beginning her medical practice. She was a school physician.

1850—PILOT INTERNATIONAL FOUNDATION (PIF/Lifeline Scholarship)

P.O. Box 5600
Macon GA 31208-5600
Written Inquiries
AMOUNT: Varies
DEADLINE(S): MAR 1
FIELD(S): Disabilities/Brain-related Disorders

This program assists ADULT students re-entering the job market, preparing for a second career, or improving their professional skills for an established career. Applicants must be preparing for, or already involved in, careers working with people with disabilities/brain-related disorders. GPA of 3.5 or more is required.

Must be sponsored by a Pilot Club in your home town, or in the city in which your college or university is located. Send a self-addressed, stamped envelope for complete information.

1851—PILOT INTERNATIONAL FOUNDATION (Ruby Newhall Memorial Scholarship)

P.O. Box 5600
Macon, GA 31208-5600
Written Inquiries
AMOUNT: Varies
DEADLINE(S): MAR 15
FIELD(S): Disabilities/Brain-related disorders

For international students who have studied in the U.S. for at least one year, and who intend to return to their home country six months after graduation. Applicants must be full-time students majoring in a field related to human health and welfare, and have a GPA of 3.5 or more.

Applicants must be sponsored by a Pilot Club in their home town, or in the city in which their college or university is located. Send a self-addressed, stamped envelope for complete information.

1852—PILOT INTERNATIONAL FOUNDATION (The Pilot International Scholarship Program)

P.O. Box 5600
Macon GA 31208-5600
Written Inquiries
AMOUNT: Varies
DEADLINE(S): MAR 1
FIELD(S): Disabilities/Brain-related disorders

This program provides assistance to undergraduate students preparing for careers working directly with people with disabilities or training those who will. GPA of 3.5 or greater required.

Applicants must be sponsored by a Pilot Club in their home town, or in the city in which their college or university is located. Send a self-addressed, stamped envelope for complete information.

1853—SRP/NAVAJO GENERATING STATION (Navajo Scholarship)

P.O. Box 850
Page AZ 86040
520/645-6539
FAX: 520/645-7295
E-mail: ljdawave@srp.gov
AMOUNT: Based on need
DEADLINE(S): APR 30
FIELD(S): Engineering, Environmental Studies, Business, Business Management, Health, Education

Scholarships for full-time students who hold membership in the Navajo Tribe and who are pursuing a degree in a field of study recognized as significant to the Navajo Nation, Salt River Project, or the Navajo Generating Station, such as those listed above. Must be junior or senior, have and maintain a GPA of 3.0

Average of 15 awards per year. Inquire of Linda Dawavendewa at above location.

1854—STATE STUDENT ASSISTANCE COMMISSION OF INDIANA (Scholarships for Special Education Teachers and Physical/Occupational Therapists)

150 W. Market Street, 5th Floor
Indianapolis IN 46204
317/232-2350
FAX: 317/232-3260
E-mail: grants@ssaci.in.us
Internet: http://www.ai.org/ssaci/
AMOUNT: $1,000
DEADLINE(S): Varies (with college)
FIELD(S): Special Education; Physical and Occupational Therapy

Open to Indiana residents pursuing full-time undergraduate or graduate study in special education or physical or occupational therapy at an Indiana college/university. Must be U.S. citizen, have a minimum 2.0 GPA, and demonstrate financial need.

See Web site or contact SSACI for an application.

1855—THE AMERICAN COLLEGE OF PREHOSPITAL MEDICINE (Alan R. Klausfelder Memorial Scholarship)

365 Canal Street, Suite 2300
New Orleans LA 70130-1135
800/735-2276
FAX: 800/350-3870
AMOUNT: $500/course
DEADLINE(S): None
FIELD(S): Emergency medical services

Scholarships for students enrolled in bachelor of arts programs in emergency medical services outside the U.S. or Canada.

Send self-addressed, stamped envelope to school for application details.

1856—THE AMERICAN COLLEGE OF PREHOSPITAL MEDICINE (William E. "Bill" Shearer Memorial Scholarship)

365 Canal Street, Suite 2300
New Orleans LA 70130-1135
800/735-2276
FAX: 800/350-3870
AMOUNT: $500/course
DEADLINE(S): None
FIELD(S): Emergency Medical Services

Scholarships for students enrolled in bachelor of arts programs in emergency medical services in Florida.

Send self-addressed, stamped envelope to school for application details.

1857—U.S. DEPT. OF HEALTH and HUMAN SERVICES (Indian Health Service Health Professions Scholarship Program)

Twinbrook Metro Plaza, Suite 100
12300 Twinbrook Parkway
Rockville MD 20852
301/443-0234
FAX: 301/443-4815
Internet: http://www.ihs.gov/Recruitment/DHPS/SP/SBTOC3.asp
AMOUNT: Tuition + fees and monthly stipend of $938.
DEADLINE(S): APR 1
FIELD(S): Health professions, accounting, social work

Open to Native Americans or Alaska natives who are graduate students or college juniors or seniors in a program leading to a career in a fields listed above. U.S. citizenship required. Renewable annually with reapplication.

Scholarship recipients must intend to serve the Indian people. They incur a one-year service obligation to the IHS for each year of support for a minimum of two years. Write for complete information.

1858—WASHINGTON STATE HIGHER EDUCATION COORDINATING BOARD (Health Professional Loan Repayment and Scholarship Program)

P.O. Box 47834
Olympia WA 98504-3430
360/705-6664
FAX: 360/664-9273
Internet: http://www.hecb.wa.gov
AMOUNT: Varies
DEADLINE(S): APR (scholarship); FEB (loan repayment); JUL (loan repayment)
FIELD(S): Health Care

Scholarships are open to students in accredited undergraduate or graduate health care programs leading to eligibility for licensure in Washington state. Must agree to work in designated shortage area for minimum of three years. Loan repayment recipients receive payment from program for purpose of repaying education loans secured while attending program of health care training leading to licensure in Washington state. Financial need NOT a factor.

Renewable up to 5 years. Contact Program Manager for a loan repayment application after November 15 and for scholarship application after January 15.

1859—WOMEN OF THE EVANGELICAL LUTHERAN CHURCH IN AMERICA (The Kahler-Vickers/Raup-Emma Wettstein Scholarships)

8765 West Higgins Road
Chicago IL 60631-4189
800/638-3522 ext. 2736
FAX: 773/380-2419
E-mail: womnelca@elca.org
AMOUNT: $2,000 max.
DEADLINE(S): FEB 15
FIELD(S): Health Professions and Christian Service

Assists women who are members of the ELCA studying for service in health professions associated with ELCA projects abroad that do not lead to church-certified professions. Must be U.S. citizen and have experienced an interruption of two or more years since completion of high school. Academic records of coursework completed in last five years as well as proof of admission from educational institution are required.

Renewable for an additional year. Contact Faith Fretheim, Program Director, for an application.

1860—WOMEN'S SPORTS FOUNDATION (Jackie Joyner-Kersee and Zina Garrison Minority Internships)

Eisenhower Park
East Meadow NY 11554
800/227-3988
FAX: 516/542-4716
E-mail: WoSport@aol.com
Internet: http://www.lifetimetv.com/WoSport
AMOUNT: $4,000-$5,000
DEADLINE(S): Ongoing
FIELD(S): Sports-related fields

Provides women of color an opportunity to gain experience in a sports-related career and interact in the sports community. May be undergraduates, college graduates, graduate students, or women in a career change. Internships are located at the Women's Sports Foundation in East Meadow, New York.

4-6 awards annually. See Web site or write to above address for details.

1861—ZETA PHI BETA SORORITY EDUCATIONAL FOUNDATION (S. Evelyn Lewis Memorial Scholarship in Medical Health Sciences)

1734 New Hampshire Avenue NW
Washington DC 20009
Internet: http://www.zpb1920.org
AMOUNT: $500-$1,000
DEADLINE(S): JAN 1
FIELD(S): Medicine; Health Sciences

Open to graduate and undergraduate young women enrolled in a program leading to a degree in medicine or health sciences. Award is for full-time study for one academic year (Fall-Spring) and is paid directly to college/university. Must submit proof of enrollment.

Send self-addressed, stamped envelope to above address between September 1 and December 15 for an application.

NURSING

1862—AMERICAN COLLEGE OF NURSE-MIDWIVES FOUNDATION (Scholarship Program)

818 Connecticut Avenue NW
Suite 900
Washington DC 20006
202/728-9865
FAX: 202/728-9897
Internet: http://www.midwife.org
AMOUNT: Varies
DEADLINE(S): FEB 15
FIELD(S): Nurse-Midwifery

Open to students currently enrolled in ACNM-accredited certificate or graduate nurse-midwifery programs in the U.S. Student membership in ACNM and completion of one clinical module or semester required.

Contact the directors of nurse-midwifery programs at accredited schools or contact ACNM for membership information and/or an application.

1863—AMERICAN FOUNDATION FOR THE BLIND (Paul W. Ruckes Scholarship)

11 Penn Plaza, Suite 300
New York NY 10001
212/502-7661
FAX: 212/502-7771
E-mail: juliet@afb.org
Internet: http://www.afb.org

AMOUNT: $1,000
DEADLINE(S): APR 30
FIELD(S): Engineering; Computer/Physical/Life Sciences

Open to legally blind and visually impaired undergraduate and graduate students pursuing a degree in one of above fields. Must be U.S. citizen. Must submit written documentation of visual impairment from ophthalmologist or optometrist (need not be legally blind); official transcripts; proof of college/university acceptance; three letters of recommendation; and typewritten statement describing goals, work experience extracurricular activities, and how monies will be used.

1 award annually. See Web site or contact Julie Tucker at AFB for an application.

1864—AMERICAN INDIAN SCIENCE AND ENGINEERING SOCIETY (A.T. Anderson Memorial Scholarship)

P.O. Box 9828
Albuquerque NM 87119-9828
505/765-1052
FAX: 505/765-5608
E-mail: scholarships@aises.org
Internet: http://www.aises.org/scholarships

AMOUNT: $1,000-$2,000
DEADLINE(S): JUN 15
FIELD(S): Medicine; Natural Resources; Science; Engineering

Open to undergraduate and graduate students who are at least 1/4 American Indian or recognized as member of a tribe. Must be member of AISES ($10 fee), enrolled full-time at an accredited institution, and demonstrate financial need.

Renewable. See Web site or contact Patricia Browne for an application and/or membership information.

1865—ARTHUR M. MILLER FUND

P.O. Box 1122
Wichita KS 67201-0004
316/261-4609

AMOUNT: Varies
DEADLINE(S): MAR 31
FIELD(S): Medicine or related fields

Scholarships for Kansas residents for the study of medicine or related fields at accredited institutions.

Send SASE for formal application.

1866—ASSOCIATION ON AMERICAN INDIAN AFFAIRS (Emergency Aid and Health Professions Scholarships)

P.O. Box 268
Sisseton SD 57262
605/698-3998
FAX: 605/698-3316
E-mail: aaia@sbtc.net
Internet: http://www.indian-affairs.org

AMOUNT: See Web site for information.
DEADLINE(S): MAY 1
FIELD(S): Health Professions

Open to full-time undergraduate students who are minimally 1/4 degree Indian blood from a federally recognized tribe. Award is based on financial need and is limited to North America/Alaska. Must submit essay on need, certificate of enrollment and quantum from your tribe or BIA, transcript, schedule of classes, and current financial aid award letter.

See Web site for information on requirements or send a self-addressed, stamped envelope to Elena Stops, Scholarship Coordinator, for an application.

1867—ASSOCIATION OF OPERATING ROOM NURSES (AORN Scholarship Program)

2170 S. Parker Road, Suite 300
Denver CO 80231-5711
303/755-6300 or
800/755-6304 ext. 8366
FAX: 303/755-4219
E-mail: sstokes@aorn.org
Internet: http://www.aorn.org

AMOUNT: Tuition and fees
DEADLINE(S): MAY1
FIELD(S): Nursing

Open to students who have been AORN members for at least 12 consecutive months prior to deadline date. Awards support bachelor's, master's, and doctoral degree programs accredited by the NLN or other acceptable accrediting body. For full- or part-time study of nursing or complementary fields in the U.S. Must have a minimum 3.0 GPA.

Renewable. Contact AORN for an application.

1868—BECA FOUNDATION (Alice Newell Joslyn Medical Fund)

830 E. Grand Avenue, Suite B
Escondido CA 92025
760/471-8246
FAX: 760/471-8176

AMOUNT: $500-$1,000
DEADLINE(S): MAR 1
FIELD(S): Medicine; Health Care; Nursing; Dental/Medical Assisting; Physical Therapy

Open to Latino students who live in or attend college in San Diego County, CA, at time of application. For high school seniors and those already in college pursuing undergraduate or graduate education. Based on financial need, scholastic determination, and community/cultural awareness.

Send self-addressed, stamped envelope to BECA for an application.

1869—CAREER OPPORTUNITIES FOR YOUTH, INC. (Collegiate Scholarship Program)

P.O. Box 996
Manhattan Beach CA 90266
310/535-4838

AMOUNT: $250 to $1,000
DEADLINE(S): SEP 30
FIELD(S): Engineering, Science, Mathematics, Computer Science, Business Administration, Education, Nursing

For students of Latino/Hispanic background residing in the Southern California area who have completed at least one semester/quarter of study at an accredited four-year university. Must have a cumulative GPA of 2.5 or higher.

Priority will be given to students who demonstrate financial need. Send SASE to above location for details.

1870—COLUMBIANA COUNTY PUBLIC HEALTH LEAGUE TRUST FUND (Grants)

c/o Mary Kay Withum, P.O. Box 511
Wheeling WV 26003
304/234-4128
FAX: 304/234-4142

AMOUNT: Varies
DEADLINE(S): FEB 28

FIELD(S): Respiratory Illness; Medicine; Medical Research; Pharmacy; Medical Technology; Physical Therapy; Nursing; Dental Hygiene; Occupational Therapy

Open to undergraduate and graduate Columbiana County, Ohio, residents who are pursuing medical education or research in one of the above fields. Preference given to respiratory illness. Students of veterinary medicine NOT eligible.

Contact Sherrill Schmied for an application.

1871—CYNTHIA E. AND CLARA H. HOLLIS FOUNDATION

100 Summer Street
Boston MA 02110
Written Inquiry

AMOUNT: Varies
DEADLINE(S): APR 1
FIELD(S): Nursing, Social Work, Dental or Medical Technology, and Religion

Scholarships for Massachusetts with preference given to students in the above fields. For undergraduates, graduates, vo-tech, and adult education. Must demonstrate financial need.

Send SASE to Walter E. Palmer, Esq., 35 Harvard Street, Brookline, MA 02146 for application details. Scholarship forms are also available from the rector of All Saints Church, Brookline High School, and St. Mary's High School, all in Brookline, Massachusetts.

1872—DEMOLAY FOUNDATION INC. (Scholarships)

10200 NW. Ambassador Boulevard
Kansas City MO 64153
816/891-8333
FAX: 816/891-9062
Internet: http://www.demolay.org

AMOUNT: $1,500
DEADLINE(S): APR 1
FIELD(S): Dental or medical fields

Open to all active and/or senior DeMolays. Considerations are leadership, academic achievement, and goals.

Four grants per year. Write for complete information.

1873—EDWARD BANGS KELLEY AND ELZA KELLEY FOUNDATION, INC. (Scholarship Program)

P.O. Drawer M
Hyannis MA 02601-1412
508/775-3117

AMOUNT: $500-$4,000 (max.)
DEADLINE(S): APR 30
FIELD(S): Medicine; Nursing; Education; Health and Social Sciences

Open to residents of Barnstable County, Massachusetts. Scholarships are intended to benefit health and welfare of Barnstable County residents. Awards support study at recognized undergraduate, graduate, and professional institutions. Financial need is considered.

Contact Foundation for an application Scholarship Committee for an application.

1874—ENGLISH NATIONAL BOARD FOR NURSING, MIDWIFERY AND HEALTH VISITING (Bursaries and Grants)

NHS Careers, P.O. Box 376
Bristol BS99 3EY ENGLAND UK
0845 606 0655
FAX: 0117 921 9562
E-mail: advice@nhscareers.nhs.uk
Internet: http://www.nhs.uk/careers

AMOUNT: Varies
DEADLINE(S): Varies
FIELD(S): Nursing, Midwifery, Health Visiting Healthcare Science and applied health professions

NHS Careers provides information on the above careers in England. Funding to enter training for different careers varies and may be dependent upon meeting UK residency requirements.

Phone, FAX, or E-mail or mail for information; see Web site.

1875—FOUNDATION FOR NEONATAL RESEARCH AND EDUCATION (FNRE Scholarships and Grants)

East Holly Avenue, Box 56
Pitman NJ 08071-0056
856/256-2343
FAX: 856/589-7463
E-mail: pjjohnson6@aol.com

AMOUNT: Up to $1,500 (scholarship); Up to $10,000 (research grant)
DEADLINE(S): MAY 1
FIELD(S): Neonatal nursing

Scholarships are for neonatal nurses who want to go back and get further education. Research grants are also available to professionally active neonatal nurses.

Contact Patricia Johnson, President, for more information.

1876—FOUNDATION FOR SEACOAST HEALTH (Scholarship Program)

100 Campus Drive, Suite 1
Portsmouth NH 03801
603/422-8200
FAX: 602/422-8207
E-mail: ffsh@communitycampus.org
Internet: http://www.ffsh.org

AMOUNT: $1,000-$10,000
DEADLINE(S): FEB 1
FIELD(S): Health-related fields. For residents of New Hampshire and Maine.

1877—GRACE FOUNDATION (Scholarship Trust Fund)

P.O. Box 924
Menlo Park CA 94026-0924
Written Inquiry

AMOUNT: $1,000-$4,000
DEADLINE(S): JAN 31
FIELD(S): Ministry; Medicine; Teaching; Social Service

Open to students from developing countries in Asia/Southeast Asia to pursue full-time study at an accredited college/university. For training future Christian ministers and professional workers in above fields. Must have completed one or more years of college in or near their native country, be a strong Christian, have a minimum 3.0 GPA, and demonstrate financial need.

Renewable up to 4 years with maintenance of 3.0 GPA. Applications available between September 1 and October 31.

1878—CYNTHIA E. AND CLARA H. HOLLIS FOUNDATION

100 Summer Street
Boston MA 02110
Written Inquiry

AMOUNT: Varies
DEADLINE(S): APR 1
FIELD(S): Nursing, Social Work, Dental or Medical Technology, and Religion

Scholarships for Massachusetts with preference given to students in the above fields. For undergraduates, graduates, vo-tech, and adult education. Must demonstrate financial need.

Send SASE to Walter E. Palmer, Esq., 35 Harvard Street, Brookline, MA 02146 for application details. Scholarship forms are also available from the rector of All Saints Church, Brookline High School, and St. Mary's High School, all in Brookline, Massachusetts.

1879—HOUSTON LIVESTOCK SHOW AND RODEO (4H and FFA Scholarships)

2000 S. Loop West
Houston TX 77054
713/791-9000

FAX: 713-794-9528
E-Mail: info@rodeohouston.com
Internet: http://www.hlsr.com/education/
AMOUNT: $10,000
DEADLINE(S): Varies
FIELD(S): Agriculture; Life Sciences

Open to undergraduate students who are actively involved in the 4-H or FFA programs. Must major in an agricultural or life sciences field of study at a Texas college/university and demonstrate academic potential, citizenship/leadership, and financial need.

140 awards annually. Contact HLSR for an application.

1880—IDAHO STATE BOARD OF EDUCATION (Education Incentive Loan Forgiveness)

P.O. Box 83720
Boise ID 83720-0037
208/334-2270
AMOUNT: Varies
DEADLINE(S): Varies
FIELD(S): Education; Nursing

Open to Idaho residents who have graduated from an Idaho high school within two years, ranking within the top 15% of graduating class or having earned a minimum 3.0 GPA. Must enroll as a full-time student in an Idaho college/university, pursuing a program of study toward an Idaho teaching certificate or licensure by the Board of Nursing as a registered nurse. Must plan to pursue career within Idaho for a minimum of two years.

Renewable. Contact the financial aid office of the Idaho public college/university you plan to attend for an application and deadlines.

1881—INTERNATIONAL ORDER OF THE KING'S DAUGHTERS AND SONS (Health Careers Scholarships)

c/o Mrs. Fred Cannon; Box 1310
Brookhaven MS 39602
Written Inquiry
AMOUNT: $1,000 (max.)
DEADLINE(S): APR 1
FIELD(S): Medicine; Dentistry; Nursing; Physical Therapy; Occupational Therapy; Medical Technologies; Pharmacy

Open to students accepted to/enrolled in an accredited U.S. or Canadian four-year or graduate school. RN candidates must have completed first year of program; MD or DDS candidates must be for at least the second year of medical or dental school; all others must be in at least third year of four-year program. Pre-med students NOT eligible. Must be U.S. or Canadian citizen.

Send self-addressed, stamped envelope, along with a letter stating the field of study and present level, to the Director at above address for an application.

1882—J. HUGH and EARLE W. FELLOWS MEMORIAL FUND (Scholarship Loans)

Pensacola Junior College President
1000 College Boulevard
Pensacola FL 32504-8998
904/484-1700
Internet: http://www.pjc.cc.fl.us/
AMOUNT: Each is negotiated individually
DEADLINE(S): None
FIELD(S): Medicine; Nursing; Medical Technology; Theology (Episcopal)

Open to bona fide residents of the Florida counties of Escambia, Santa Rosa, Okaloosa, or Walton. For undergraduate study in the fields listed above. U.S. citizenship required.

Loans are interest-free until graduation. Write for complete information.

1883—JEWISH VOCATIONAL SERVICE (Academic Scholarship Program)

One S. Franklin Street
Chicago IL 60606
312/357-4500
FAX: 312/855-3282
TTY: 312/855-3282
E-mail: jvschicago@jon.cjfny.org
AMOUNT: $5,000 (max.)
DEADLINE(S): MAR 1
FIELD(S): "Helping" Professions; Mathematics; Engineering; Sciences; Communications (at Univ IL only); Law (certain schools in IL only)

Open to Jewish men and women legally domiciled in the greater Chicago metropolitan area, who are identified as having promise for significant contributions in their chosen careers, and are in need of financial assistance for full-time academic programs in above areas. Must have entered undergraduate junior year in career programs requiring no postgrad education, be in graduate/professional school, or be in a vo-tech training program. Interview required.

Renewable. Contact JVS for an application between December 1 and February 15.

1884—JUNIATA COLLEGE (Robert Steele Memorial Scholarship)

Office of Student Financial Planning
Juniata College
1700 Moore Street,
Huntingdon PA 16652
814/641-3142
FAX: 814/641-5311
Internet: http://www.juniata.edu/
E-mail: clarkec@juniata.edu
AMOUNT: $4,000 (max.)
DEADLINE(S): APR 1
FIELD(S): Science; Medical Studies

Open to science/medical students applying to Juniata College. Must demonstrate financial need and fill out government FAFSA form.

Contact Randy Rennell, Director of Student Financial Planning, for an application or enrollment information. See your financial aid office for FAFSA.

1885—LADY ALLEN OF HURTWOOD MEMORIAL TRUST (Travel Grants)

21 Aspull Common
Leigh Lancs WN7 3PB ENGLAND
01942-674895
AMOUNT: Up to 1,000 pounds sterling
DEADLINE(S): JAN 15
FIELD(S): Welfare and Education of Children

A travel grant to those whose proposed project will directly benefit their work with children. People working with children and young people may apply, particularly those working with disabled and disadvantaged children. Successful candidates must write up an account of the work which the scholarship has funded. GRANTS ARE NOT FOR ACADEMIC STUDY; ONLY QUALIFIED INDIVIDUALS MAY APPLY.

Contact Dorothy E. Whitaker, Trustee, for application forms-available between May and December each year.

1886—MIDWAY COLLEGE (Institutional Aid Program)

Financial Aid Office
Midway KY 40347
606/846-4421
AMOUNT: Varies
DEADLINE(S): MAR 1
FIELD(S): Nursing; Paralegal; Education; Psychology; Biology; Equine Studies; Liberal Studies; Business Administration

Scholarships and grants are open to women who are accepted for enrollment at

Midway College. Awards support undergraduate study in the above areas.

80 awards annually. Contact Midway College's Financial Aid Office for an application.

1887—McCORD CAREER CENTER (Level II McCord Medical/Music Scholarship)

Healdsburg High School
1024 Prince Street
Healdsburg CA 95448
707/431-3473
Email: career@husd.com

AMOUNT: Varies
DEADLINE(S): APR 15
FIELD(S): Medicine; Music

For graduates of Healdsburg High School who are planning a career in music or medicine. Must be enrolled full-time at a college/university as an undergraduate junior or senior in the fall, or earning an advanced degree in graduate or medical school, or entering into a vocational/certificate program. Transcripts, proof of attendance, and an essay are required.

Contact the McCord Career Center at Healdsburg High School for an application.

1888—NATIONAL FEDERATION OF THE BLIND (Howard Brown Rickard Scholarship)

805 Fifth Avenue
Grinnell IA 50112
515/236-3366

AMOUNT: $3,000
DEADLINE(S): MAR 31
FIELD(S): Law; Medicine; Engineering; Architecture; Natural Sciences

For legally blind students pursuing or planning to pursue a full-time postsecondary course of study in the U.S.. Based on academic excellence, service to the community, and financial need. Membership NOT required.

1 award annually. Renewable. Contact Mrs. Peggy Elliot, Scholarship Committee Chairman, for an application.

1889—NATIONAL INSTITUTES OF HEALTH (Minority International Research Training Grant)

Fogarty International Center, Bldg. 31
Room B2C39
31 Center Drive MSC 2220
Bethesda MD 20892-2220
301/402-9467
FAX: 301/402-0779
E-mail: barbara_sina@cu.nih.gov
Internet: http://www.nih.gov/grants/oer.htm

AMOUNT: Varies
DEADLINE(S): MAR 15
FIELD(S): Biomedical and Behavioral Sciences

Open to minorities that are underrepresented in biomedical research professions (African and Hispanic Americans, Native Americans, Alaskan Natives, and Pacific Islanders). May be undergraduate students pursuing life science curricula (8-12 weeks research/coursework supported), students pursuing doctoral degrees in above fields (3-12 months research training at foreign institution supported), or faculty members in above fields (3-12 months research at foreign institution).

See Web site or contact NIH for an application.

1890—NATIONAL STUDENT NURSES' ASSOCIATION FOUNDATION (Scholarship Program)

555 W. 57th Street, Suite 1327
New York NY 10019
212/581-2211
FAX: 212/581-2368
E-mail: nsna@nsna.org
Internet: http://www.nsna.org

AMOUNT: $1,000-$2,000
DEADLINE(S): FEB 1
FIELD(S): Nursing

Open to students currently enrolled in state-approved nursing schools or pre-nursing in associate degree, baccalaureate, diploma, generic doctorate, and generic master's programs. Funds available for graduate study ONLY if first degree in nursing. Based on academic achievement, financial need, and involvement in nursing student organizations and community activities related to health care. Transcripts required.

$10 application fee. See Web site, or, beginning in August, send self-addressed, business-sized envelope with 57 cents postage to NSNA for an application. Winners will be notified in March. GRADUATING HIGH SCHOOL SENIORS NOT ELIGIBLE.

1891—NEW YORK STATE HIGHER EDUCATION SERVICES CORPORATION (N.Y. State Regents Professional/Health Care Opportunity Scholarships)

Cultural Education Center, Room 5C64
Albany NY 12230
518/486-1319
Internet: http://www.hesc.com

AMOUNT: $1,000-$10,000/year
DEADLINE(S): Varies
FIELD(S): Medicine and dentistry and related fields, architecture, nursing, psychology, audiology, landscape architecture, social work, chiropractic, law, pharmacy, accounting, speech language pathology

For NY state residents who are economically disadvantaged and members of a minority group underrepresented in the chosen profession and attending school in NY state. Some programs carry a service obligation in New York for each year of support. For U.S. citizens or qualifying noncitizens.

Medical/dental scholarships require one year of professional work in NY.

1892—ODD FELLOWS AND REBEKAHS (The Ellen F. Washburn Nursing Training Awards)

131 Queens Street Extension
Gorham ME 04038
207/839-4723

AMOUNT: $150-$300
DEADLINE(S): APR 15
FIELD(S): Nursing

For undergraduate students in an RN program enrolled in an accredited Maine school of nursing. Must demonstrate financial need.

20 awards annually. Renewable. Contact Joyce B. Young, chairperson, for more information.

1893—ONCOLOGY NURSING FOUNDATION (Scholarships, Grants, Awards, and Honors)

501 Holiday Drive
Pittsburgh PA 15220-2749
412/921-7373
FAX: 412/921-6565
E-mail: foundation@ons.org

AMOUNT: Varies (with program)
DEADLINE(S): Varies (with program)
FIELD(S): Oncology Nursing

For registered nurses seeking further training or to engage in research in the field of oncology. Various programs range from bachelor's degree level through post-masters and career development. Also honors and awards for oncology nurses who have contributed to professional literature and excellence in their field. Some require ONF membership.

Contact Linda Worrall, Executive Director, for an application. Notification by early April. Awards are offered by Oncology Nursing Society, Oncology Nursing Foundation, Oncology Nursing Certification Corporation, and Oncology Nursing Press, Inc.

1894—PENINSULA COMMUNITY FOUNDATION (Dr. Mary Finegold Scholarship)

1700 S. El Camino Real, #300
San Mateo CA 94402
650/358-9369
FAX: 650/358-9817
Internet: http://www.pcf.org/community_grants/scholarships.html
AMOUNT: $1,000
DEADLINE(S): MAR 7 (5 p.m.)
FIELD(S): Sciences

Scholarships for senior girls graduating from high school in Palo Alto, California, who intend to complete a four-year degree in the sciences. Special consideration will be given to girls who have demonstrated a "pioneering" spirit in that they have not been constrained by stereotypical female roles and to those facing financial hardship.

Award was established in the honor of Dr. Mary Finegold who, after completing her medical studies, elected to stay at home until her youngest child was in high school before beginning her medical practice. She was a school physician.

1895—RED RIVER COLLEGE (Southern Nursing Program)

F210-2055 Notre Dame Avenue
Winnipeg Manitoba R3H OJ9
CANADA
204/632-2180
FAX: 204/633-1437
E-mail: pstevens@rcc.mb.ca
Internet: http://www.rrc.mb.ca
AMOUNT: Varies
DEADLINE(S): APR 1
FIELD(S): Nursing

A joint five-year Baccalaureate Nursing Program is offered by RRC and the University of Manitoba. The Southern Nursing Program provides admission for low income students who have not had the opportunity because of social, economic, cultural factors, residence in remote areas, or lack of formal education. You may be eligible if you are aboriginal, single parents, or immigrants. Must be resident of Manitoba.

15-20 awards annually. Contact RRC for an application.

1896—SRP/NAVAJO GENERATING STATION (Navajo Scholarship)

P.O. Box 850
Page AZ 86040
520/645-6539
FAX: 520/645-7295
E-mail: ljdawave@srp.gov
AMOUNT: Based on need
DEADLINE(S): APR 30
FIELD(S): Engineering, Environmental Studies, Business, Business Management, Health, Education

Scholarships for full-time students who hold membership in the Navajo Tribe and who are pursuing a degree in a field of study recognized as significant to the Navajo Nation, Salt River Project, or the Navajo Generating Station, such as those listed above. Must be junior or senior, have and maintain a GPA of 3.0

Average of 15 awards per year. Inquire of Linda Dawavendewa at above location.

1897—TYSON FOUNDATION, INC. (Alabama Scholarship Program)

2210 W. Oaklawn
Springdale AR 72762-6999
501/290-4995
AMOUNT: Varies (according to need)
DEADLINE(S): FEB 28
FIELD(S): Business; Agriculture; Engineering; Computer Science; Nursing

Open to residents of the general areas of Albertville, Ashland, Blountsville, Gadsden, Heflin, or Oxford, Alabama, who are U.S. citizens and live in the vicinity of a Tyson facility. Must be pursuing full-time undergraduate study at an accredited U.S. institution and demonstrate financial need. Must also be employed part-time and/or summers to help fund education.

Renewable up to 8 semesters or 12 trimesters as long as student meets criteria. Contact Tyson Foundation for an application no later than last day of February; deadline to return application is April 20.

1898—TYSON FOUNDATION, INC. (Arkansas Scholarship Program)

2210 W. Oaklawn
Springdale AR 72762-6999
501/290-4955
AMOUNT: Varies (according to need)
DEADLINE(S): FEB 28
FIELD(S): Business; Agriculture; Engineering; Computer Science; Nursing

Open to Arkansas residents who are U.S. citizens pursuing full-time undergraduate study at an accredited U.S. institution. Must demonstrate financial need and be employed part-time and/or summers to help fund education.

Renewable up to 8 semesters or 12 trimesters as long as student meets criteria. Contact Tyson Foundation for an application no later than last day of February; deadline to return application is April 20.

1899—TYSON FOUNDATION, INC. (California Scholarship Program)

2210 W. Oaklawn
Springdale AR 72762-6999
501/290-4995
FAX: 501/290-7984
E-mail: coments@tysonfoundation.org
AMOUNT: Varies (according to need)
DEADLINE(S): FEB 28 (to request application); APR 20 (to apply)
FIELD(S): Business; Agriculture; Engineering; Computer Science; Nursing; Biology; Chemistry

Open to residents of Modesto, California, who are U.S. citizens and live in the vicinity of a Tyson facility. Must be pursuing full-time undergraduate study at an accredited U.S. institution and demonstrate financial need. Must also be employed part-time and/or summers to help fund education.

Renewable up to 8 semesters or 12 trimesters as long as student meets criteria. Contact Tyson Foundation to see if area of residence qualifies and for an application.

1900—TYSON FOUNDATION, INC. (Florida Scholarship Program)

2210 Oaklawn
Springdale AR 72762-6999
501/290-4995
AMOUNT: Varies (according to need)
DEADLINE(S): FEB 28
FIELD(S): Business; Agriculture; Engineering; Computer Science; Nursing

Open to residents of the general area of Jacksonville, Florida, who are U.S. citizens and live in the vicinity of a Tyson facility. Must be pursuing full-time undergraduate study in an accredited U.S. institution and demonstrate financial need. Must also be employed part-time and/or summers to help fund education.

Renewable up to 8 semesters or 12 trimesters as long as student meets criteria. Contact Tyson Foundation for an application no later than last day of February; deadline to return application is April 20.

1901—TYSON FOUNDATION, INC. (Georgia Scholarship Program)

2210 Oaklawn
Springdale AR 72762-6999
501/290-4995

AMOUNT: Varies (according to need)
DEADLINE(S): FEB 28
FIELD(S): Business; Agriculture; Engineering; Computer Science; Nursing

Open to residents of the general areas of Cumming, Buena Vista, Dawson, or Vienna, Georgia, who are U.S. citizens and live in the vicinity of a Tyson facility. Must be pursuing full-time undergraduate study in an accredited U.S. institution and demonstrate financial need. Must also be employed part-time and/or summers to help fund education.

Renewable up to 8 semesters or 12 trimesters as long as student meets criteria. Contact Tyson Foundation for an application no later than last day of February; deadline to return application is April 20.

1902—TYSON FOUNDATION, INC. (Illinois Scholarship Program)

2210 Oaklawn
Springdale AR 72762-6999
501/290-4995

AMOUNT: Varies (according to need)
DEADLINE(S): FEB 28
FIELD(S): Business; Agriculture; Engineering; Computer Science; Nursing

Open to residents of the general area of Chicago, Illinois, who are U.S. citizens and live in the vicinity of a Tyson facility. Must be pursuing full-time undergraduate study in an accredited U.S. institution and demonstrate financial need. Must also be employed part-time and/or summers to help fund education.

Renewable up to 8 semesters or 12 trimesters as long as student meets criteria. Contact Tyson Foundation for an application no later than last day of February; deadline to return application is April 20.

1903—TYSON FOUNDATION, INC. (Indiana Scholarship Program)

2210 Oaklawn
Springdale AR 72762-6999
501/290-4995

AMOUNT: Varies (according to need)
DEADLINE(S): FEB 28
FIELD(S): Business; Agriculture; Engineering; Computer Science; Nursing

Open to residents of the general areas of Portland or Corydon, Indiana, who are U.S. citizens and live in the vicinity of a Tyson facility. Must be pursuing full-time undergraduate study at an accredited U.S. institution and demonstrate financial need. Must also be employed part-time and/or summers to help fund education.

Renewable up to 8 semesters or 12 trimesters as long as student meets criteria. Contact Tyson Foundation for an application no later than last day of February; deadline to return application is April 20.

1904—TYSON FOUNDATION, INC. (Mississippi Scholarship Program)

2210 Oaklawn
Springdale AR 72762-6999
501/290-4995

AMOUNT: Varies (according to need)
DEADLINE(S): FEB 28
FIELD(S): Business; Agriculture; Engineering; Computer Science; Nursing

Open to residents of the general areas of Cleveland, Jackson, Forest, or Vicksburg, Mississippi, who are U.S. citizens and live in the vicinity of a Tyson facility. Must be pursuing full-time undergraduate study in an accredited U.S. institution and demonstrate financial need. Must also be employed part-time and/or summers to help fund education.

Renewable up to 8 semesters or 12 trimesters as long as student meets criteria. Contact Tyson Foundation for an application no later than last day of February; deadline to return application is April 20.

1905—TYSON FOUNDATION, INC. (Missouri Scholarship Program)

2210 Oaklawn
Springdale AR 72762-6999
501/290-4995

AMOUNT: Varies (according to need)
DEADLINE(S): FEB 28
FIELD(S): Business; Agriculture; Engineering; Computer Science; Nursing

Open to residents of the general areas of Dexter, Monett, Neosho, Noel, or Sedalia, Missouri, who are U.S. citizens and live in the vicinity of a Tyson facility. Must be pursuing full-time undergraduate study in an accredited U.S. institution and demonstrate financial need. Must also be employed part-time and/or summers to help fund education.

Renewable up to 8 semesters or 12 trimesters as long as student meets criteria. Contact Tyson Foundation for an application no later than last day of February; deadline to return application is April 20.

1906—TYSON FOUNDATION, INC. (North Carolina Scholarship Program)

2210 Oaklawn
Springdale AR 72762-6999
501/290-4995

AMOUNT: Varies (according to need)
DEADLINE(S): FEB 28
FIELD(S): Business; Agriculture; Engineering; Computer Science; Nursing

Open to residents of the general areas of Creswell, Monroe, Sanford, or Wilkesboro, North Carolina, who are U.S. citizens and live in the vicinity of a Tyson facility. Must be pursuing full-time undergraduate study in an accredited U.S. institution and demonstrate financial need. Must also be employed part-time and/or summers to help fund education.

Renewable up to 8 semesters or 12 trimesters as long as student meets criteria. Contact Tyson Foundation for an application no later than the last day of February; deadline to return application is April 20.

1907—TYSON FOUNDATION, INC. (Oklahoma Scholarship Program)

2210 Oaklawn
Springdale AR 72762-6999
501/290-4995

AMOUNT: Varies (according to need)
DEADLINE(S): FEB 28
FIELD(S): Business; Agriculture; Engineering; Computer Science; Nursing

Open to residents of the general areas of Broken Bow or Stillwell, Oklahoma, who are U.S. citizens and live in the vicinity of a Tyson facility. Must be pursuing full-time undergraduate study in an accredited U.S. institution and demonstrate financial need. Must also be employed part-time and/or summers to help fund education.

Renewable up to 8 semesters or 12 trimesters as long as student meets criteria. Contact Tyson Foundation for an application no later than last day of February; deadline to return application is April 20.

1908—TYSON FOUNDATION, INC. (Pennsylvania Scholarship Program)

2210 Oaklawn
Springdale AR 72762-6999
501/290-4995

AMOUNT: Varies (according to need)

DEADLINE(S): FEB 28
FIELD(S): Business; Agriculture; Engineering; Computer Science; Nursing

Open to residents of the general area of New Holland, Pennsylvania, who are U.S. citizens and live in the vicinity of a Tyson facility. Must be pursuing full-time undergraduate study in an accredited U.S. institution and demonstrate financial need. Must also be employed part-time and/or summers to help fund education.

Renewable up to 8 semesters or 12 trimesters as long as student meets criteria. Contact Tyson Foundation for an application no later than last day of February; deadline to return application is April 20.

1909—TYSON FOUNDATION, INC. (Tennessee Scholarship Program)

2210 Oaklawn
Springdale AR 72762-6999
501/290-4995
AMOUNT: Varies (according to need)
DEADLINE(S): FEB 28
FIELD(S): Business; Agriculture; Engineering; Computer Science; Nursing

Open to residents of the general areas of Shelbyville or Union City, Tennessee, who are U.S. citizens and live in the vicinity of a Tyson facility. Must be pursuing full-time undergraduate study in an accredited U.S. institution and demonstrate financial need. Must also be employed part-time and/or summers to help fund education.

Renewable up to 8 semesters or 12 trimesters as long as student meets criteria. Contact Tyson Foundation for an application no later than last day of February; deadline to return application is April 20.

1910—TYSON FOUNDATION, INC. (Texas Scholarship Program)

2210 Oaklawn
Springdale AR 72762-6999
501/290-4995
AMOUNT: Varies (according to need)
DEADLINE(S): FEB 28
FIELD(S): Business; Agriculture; Engineering; Computer Science; Nursing

Open to residents of the general areas of Carthage, Center, or Seguin, Texas, who are U.S. citizens and live in the vicinity of a Tyson facility. Must be pursuing full-time undergraduate study in an accredited U.S. institution and demonstrate financial need. Must also be employed part-time and/or summers to help fund education.

Renewable up to 8 semesters or 12 trimesters as long as student meets criteria. Contact Tyson Foundation for an application no later than last day of February; deadline to return application is April 20.

1911—TYSON FOUNDATION, INC. (Virginia Scholarship Program)

2210 Oaklawn
Springdale AR 72762-6999
501/290-4995
AMOUNT: Varies (according to need)
DEADLINE(S): FEB 28
FIELD(S): Business; Agriculture; Engineering; Computer Science; Nursing

Open to residents of the general areas of Glen Allen, Harrisonburg, or Temperanceville, Virginia, who are U.S. citizens and live in the vicinity of a Tyson facility. Must be pursuing full-time undergraduate study in an accredited U.S. institution and demonstrate financial need. Must also be employed part-time and/or summers to help fund education.

Renewable up to 8 semesters or 12 trimesters as long as student meets criteria. Contact Tyson Foundation for an application no later than last day of February; deadline to return application is April 20.

1912—U.S. DEPT. OF HEALTH & HUMAN SERVICES (Indian Health Service Health Professions Scholarship Program)

Twinbrook Metro Plaza, Suite 100
12300 Twinbrook Parkway
Rockville MD 20852
301/443-0234
FAX: 301/443-4815
Internet: http://www:ihs.gov/Recruitment/DHPS/SP/SBTOC3.asp
AMOUNT: Tuition + fees and monthly stipend of $938
DEADLINE(S): APR 1
FIELD(S): Health professions, accounting, social work

Open to Native Americans or Alaska natives who are graduate students or college juniors or seniors in a program leading to a career in a fields listed above. U.S. citizenship required. Renewable annually with reapplication.

Scholarship recipients must intend to serve the Indian people. They incur a one-year service obligation to the IHS for each year of support for a minimum of two years. Write for complete information.

1913—USAF RESERVE PERSONNEL CENTER (Armed Forces Health Professionals Scholarships)

6760 E. Irvington Pl., #7000
Denver CO 80280-7300
Written Inquiry
AMOUNT: Varies
DEADLINE(S): None specified
FIELD(S): Physicans: Anesthesiology, Surgical Specialties; Nursing: Anesthesia, Operating Room, or Medical Surgical Nursing.

For health professionals and students participating in a Reserve Service of the U.S. Armed Forces training in the specialties listed above and for undergraduate nursing students. A monthly stipend is paid, and varying lengths of service are required to pay back the stipend.

Air Force: above address; Army: Headquarters, Dept. of the Army, 5109 Leesburg Pike, Falls Church, VA 22041-3258; Navy: Naval Reserve Recruiting Command, 4400 Dauphine Street, New Orleans, LA 70146.

1914—USAF RESERVE BONUS PROGRAM

6760 East Irvington Place #7000
Denver CO 80280-7000
1/800-525-0102 ext 71231 or 71237; DSN 926-6484;
Commercial: 303/676-6484
FAX: 303/676-6164
FAX: DSN: 926-6164
E-mail: Joseph.Andujo@arpc.Denver.af.mil
Internet: http://www.arpc.org
AMOUNT: Varies, see Web site.
DEADLINE(S): Varies, see Web site.
FIELD(S): Various medical fields and specialties.

A bonus pay program to recruit critically needed medical specialties into the Selected Reserve of the U.S. Air Force.

Direct questions to: Medical Readiness and Incentives Division, TSgt. Joseph Andujo at above.

1915—WASHINGTON STATE HIGHER EDUCATION COORDINATING BOARD (Health Professional Loan Repayment and Scholarship Program)

P.O. Box 47834
Olympia WA 98504-3430
360/705-6664
FAX: 360/664-9273
Internet: http://www.hecb.wa.gov
AMOUNT: Varies

DEADLINE(S): APR (scholarship); FEB (loan repayment); JUL (loan repayment)
FIELD(S): Health Care

Scholarships are open to students in accredited undergraduate or graduate health care programs leading to eligibility for licensure in Washington state. Must agree to work in designated shortage area for minimum of three years. Loan repayment recipients receive payment from program for purpose of repaying education loans secured while attending program of health care training leading to licensure in Washington state. Financial need NOT a factor.

Renewable up to 5 years. Contact Program Manager for a loan repayment application after November 15 and for scholarship application after January 15.

1916—WOMEN OF THE EVANGELICAL LUTHERAN CHURCH IN AMERICA (The Kahler-Vickers/Raup-Emma Wettstein Scholarships)

8765 West Higgins Road
Chicago IL 60631-4189
800/638-3522 ext. 2736
FAX: 773/380-2419
E-mail: womnelca@elca.org
AMOUNT: $2,000 max.
DEADLINE(S): FEB 15
FIELD(S): Health Professions and Christian Service

Assists women who are members of the ELCA studying for service in health professions associated with ELCA projects abroad that do not lead to church-certified professions. Must be U.S. citizen and have experienced an interruption of two or more years since completion of high school. Academic records of coursework completed in last five years as well as proof of admission from educational institution are required.

Renewable for an additional year. Contact Faith Fretheim, Program Director, for an application.

1917—ZETA PHI BETA SORORITY EDUCATIONAL FOUNDATION (S. Evelyn Lewis Memorial Scholarship in Medical Health Sciences)

1734 New Hampshire Avenue NW
Washington DC 20009
Internet: http://www.zpb1920.org
AMOUNT: $500-$1,000
DEADLINE(S): JAN 1
FIELD(S): Medicine; Health Sciences

Open to graduate and undergraduate young women enrolled in a program leading to a degree in medicine or health sciences. Award is for full-time study for one academic year (Fall-Spring) and is paid directly to college/university. Must submit proof of enrollment.

Send self-addressed, stamped envelope to above address between September 1 and December 15 for an application.

NUTRITION

1918—ABBIE SARGENT MEMORIAL SCHOLARSHIP INC. (Scholarships)

295 Sheep Davis Road
Concord NH 03301
603/224-1934
FAX: 603/228-8432
AMOUNT: $200-400
DEADLINE(S): MAR 15
FIELD(S): Agriculture; Veterinary Medicine; Home Economics

Open to New Hampshire residents who are high school graduates with good grades and character. For undergraduate or graduate study. Must be legal resident of U.S. and demonstrate financial need.

Renewable with reapplication. Write or call for complete information.

1919—AMERICAN ASSOCIATION OF CEREAL CHEMISTS (Undergraduate Scholarships and Graduate Fellowships)

3340 Pilot Knob Road
St. Paul MN 55121-2097
651/454-7250
FAX: 651/454-0766
E-mail: aacc@scisoc.org
Internet: http://www.scisoc.org/aacc/ABOUT/foundation/top.html
AMOUNT: $1,000-$2,000 (undergrad); $2,000-$3,000 (graduate)
DEADLINE(S): APR 1
FIELD(S): Grain-Based Food Science and Technology

Open to undergraduate and graduate students majoring or interested in a career in grain-based food science or technology (incl. baking or related areas) as evidenced by coursework or employment. Undergrads must have completed at least one quarter or semester of college/university work. Strong academic record and career interest important; AACC membership helpful but not necessary. Department head endorsement required. Financial need NOT a factor.

Fields such as culinary arts or dietetics NOT eligible. Up to 30 awards annually. Applications are available online or by contacting the Scholarship Coordinator.

1920—AMERICAN SOCIETY FOR HEALTHCARE FOOD SERVICE ADMINISTRATORS (Dorothy Killian Scholarship for Undergraduates)

One North Franklin; 31st Floor
Chicago IL 60606
312/422-3870
AMOUNT: $500 (part-time); $1,000 (full-time)
DEADLINE(S): MAR 1
FIELD(S): Healthcare Food Service Management

Open to undergraduate students at 2- or 4-year colleges.

Contact Avis Gordon at above address for an application.

1921—AMERICAN WINE SOCIETY EDUCATIONAL FOUNDATION (Scholarships and Grants)

1134 Prospect Avenue
Bethlehem PA 18018-4910
610/865-2401 or 610/758-3845
FAX: 610/758-4344
E-mail: lhs0@lehigh.edu
AMOUNT: $2,500
DEADLINE(S): MAR 31
FIELD(S): Wine industry professional study: enology, viticulture, health aspects of food and wine, and using and appreciating fine wines.

To provide academic scholarships and research grants to students based on academic excellence. Must show financial need and genuine interest in pursuing careers in wine-related fields. For North American citizens, defined as U.S., Canada, Mexico, the Bahamas, and the West Indies at all levels of education.

Contact Les Sperling at above location for application.

1922—CANADIAN HOME ECONOMICS ASSOCIATION (Kraft General Foods Undergraduate Scholarship)

Rue Slater Street, Suite 307
Ottawa ON KIP 5H3 CANADA
613/238-8817
FAX: 613/238-1677
E-mail: general@chea-acef.ca
AMOUNT: $1,500
DEADLINE(S): MAR 31 (postmark)
FIELD(S): Home Economics

Open to Canadian citizens or permanent residents who are third or fourth year students enrolled in a home economics/consumer/foods related program at a university offering a home economics perspective approved by CHEA.

Personal qualities and potential contribution to the profession of home economics and scholarship are considerations. Write for complete information.

1923—FOOD INDUSTRY SCHOLARSHIP FUND OF NEW HAMPSHIRE (Scholarships)

110 Stark Street
Manchester NH 03101-1977
Written Inquiry
AMOUNT: $1,000
DEADLINE(S): MAR 15
FIELD(S): Food Industry

Open to students who are residents of New Hampshire and planning to enter a career in the food industry. Ten to 12 awards annually.

Contact Fund for an application.

1924—INSTITUTE OF FOOD TECHNOLOGISTS (Freshman Scholarships)

525 W. Van Buren, Suite 1000
Chicago IL 60607
312/782-8424
FAX: 313/782-8348
E-mail: info@ift.org
AMOUNT: $1,000-$1,500
DEADLINE(S): FEB 15
FIELD(S): Food Science; Food Technology

Open to scholastically outstanding high school graduates and seniors expecting to graduate from high school. Must be entering college for the first time in an approved program in food science/technology.

25 awards annually. Contact IFT for an application. Applicants notified by April 15.

1925—INSTITUTE OF FOOD TECHNOLOGISTS (Junior/Senior Scholarships)

525W. Van Buren, Suite 1000
Chicago IL 60607
312/782-8424
FAX: 312/782-8348
E-mail: info@ift.org
AMOUNT: $1,000-$2,250
DEADLINE(S): FEB 1
FIELD(S): Food Science; Food Technology

Open to scholastically outstanding sophomores and juniors enrolled in an approved food science/technology program.

64 awards annually. Contact IFT for an application. Applicants notified by April 15.

1926—INSTITUTE OF FOOD TECHNOLOGISTS (Sophomore Scholarships)

525 W. Van Buren, Suite 1000
Chicago IL 60607
312/782-8424
FAX: 312/782-8348
E-mail: info@ift.org
AMOUNT: $1,000
DEADLINE(S): MAR 1
FIELD(S): Food Science; Food Technology

Open to scholastically outstanding freshmen with a minimum 2.5 GPA and either pursuing or transferring to an approved program in food science/technology.

23 awards annually. Contact IFT for an application. Applicants notified by April 15.

1927—INTERNATIONAL ASSOCIATION OF CULINARY PROFESSIONALS FOUNDATION (Scholarships)

304 W. Liberty Street, Suite 201
Louisville KY 40202-3068
502/587-7953
FAX: 502/589-3602
E-mail: emcknight@hdqtrs.com
Internet: http://www.iacp.com
AMOUNT: $2,000-$10,000
DEADLINE(S): DEC 15
FIELD(S): Culinary Arts

Culinary scholarships are for basic, continuing, and specialty education courses in the U.S. or abroad. Must have a high school diploma or equivalent by June following deadline. Selection based on merit, foodservice work experience, and financial need. Awards cover partial tuition costs and, occasionally, course-related expenses, such as research, room and board, or travel.

$25 application fee. 16 awards in 2003. Contact Ellen McKnight, Director of Development, at IACP for an application between September 1 and December 1.

1928—JOHNSON AND WALES UNIVERSITY (Annual Johnson and Wales University National High School Recipe Contest)

8 Abbott Place
Providence RI 02903
401/598-2345
AMOUNT: $1,000 to $5,000
DEADLINE(S): JAN 31
FIELD(S): Business, Hospitality, Technology, Culinary Arts

For students planning to attend Johnson & Wales University, Providence, Rhode Island.

Write to above address for detailed description.

1929—JOHNSON AND WALES UNIVERSITY (Gilbane Building Company Eagle Scout Scholarship)

8 Abbott Place
Providence RI 02903
401/598-2345
AMOUNT: $1,200
DEADLINE(S): None
FIELD(S): Business, Hospitality, Technology, Culinary Arts

For students attending Johnson & Wales University, Providence, Rhode Island. Must be Eagle Scouts.

Send letter of recommendation and transcript to above address.

1930—JOHNSON AND WALES UNIVERSITY (National High School Entrepreneur of the Year Contest)

8 Abbott Place
Providence RI 02903
401/598-2345
AMOUNT: $1,000 to $10,000
DEADLINE(S): DEC 27
FIELD(S): Business, Hospitality, Technology, Culinary Arts

For students attending Johnson & Wales University, Providence, Rhode Island.

Renewable for four years. Write for complete information.

1931—JOHNSON AND WALES UNIVERSITY (Scholarships)

8 Abbott Place
Providence RI 02903
401/598-2345
AMOUNT: $200 to $10,000
DEADLINE(S): None
FIELD(S): Business, Hospitality, Technology, Culinary Arts

For students attending Johnson & Wales University, Providence, Rhode Island.

Write for complete information. Renewable for four years.

1932—KAPPA OMICRON NU (Research/Project Grants)

4990 Northwind Drive, Suite 140
East Lansing MI 48823
517/351-8335
AMOUNT: $500 and $3,500
DEADLINE(S): FEB 15
FIELD(S): Home Economics and Related Fields

Open to Kappa Omicron Nu members who have demonstrated scholarship; research; and leadership potential. Awards are for home economics research at institutions having strong research programs.

Two grants. Write for complete information

1933—NATIONAL RESTAURANT ASSOCIATION EDUCATIONAL FOUNDATION (College Undergraduate Scholarships)

250 S. Wacker Drive, Suite 1400
Chicago IL 60606-5834
800/765-2122 ext. 733 or 312/715-1010
FAX: 312/715-1362
E-mail: scholars@foodtrain.org
Internet: http://www.nraef.org
AMOUNT: $2,000
DEADLINE(S): MAY 6 and NOV 30
FIELD(S): Culinary Arts, Restaurant/Hospitality

For college students pursuing a certificate, associate degree, or bachelor's degree in above fields. Must have a minimum 2.75 GPA and be a U.S. citizen/permanent resident or a non-citizen attending school in U.S./territories. Must be enrolled a minimum of nine semester hours, have completed first semester, and have at least 750 hours of work experience in the restaurant/hospitality industry.

Applications available January 1. See Web site for more information.

1934—NATIONAL RESTAURANT ASSOCIATION EDUCATIONAL FOUNDATION (High School Seniors Undergraduate Scholarships)

250 S. Wacker Drive, Suite 1400
Chicago IL 60606-5834
800/765-2122 ext. 733 or 312/715-1010
FAX: 312/715-1362
E-mail: scholars@foodtrain.org
Internet: http://www.nraef.org
AMOUNT: $2,000
DEADLINE(S): APR 19
FIELD(S): Culinary/Restaurant/Hospitality Majors

For high school seniors accepted into an undergraduate program in above fields. Must have a minimum 2.75 GPA and be a U.S. citizen/permanent resident or a non-citizen attending school in U.S./territories. Must have taken a minimum of one food-service-related course and/or have performed a minimum of 250 hours of restaurant/hospitality work experience. For full- or part-time study.

Applications available January 1. See Web site for more information.

1935—PENINSULA COMMUNITY FOUNDATION (Dr. Mary Finegold Scholarship)

1700 S. El Camino Real, #300
San Mateo CA 94402
650/358-9369
FAX: 650/358-9817
Internet: http://www.pcf.org/community_grants/scholarships.html
AMOUNT: $1,000
DEADLINE(S): MAR 7 (5 p.m.)
FIELD(S): Sciences

Scholarships for senior girls graduating from high school in Palo Alto, California, who intend to complete a four-year degree in the sciences. Special consideration will be given to girls who have demonstrated a "pioneering" spirit in that they have not been constrained by stereotypical female roles and to those facing financial hardship.

Award was established in the honor of Dr. Mary Finegold who, after completing her medical studies, elected to stay at home until her youngest child was in high school before beginning her medical practice. She was a school physician.

1936—SCHOOL FOOD SERVICE FOUNDATION (Scholarships)

700 S. Washington Street, Suite 300
Alexandria VA 22314
703/739-3900 ext. 150 or 800/877-8822
FAX: 703/739-3915
E-mail: robrien@asfsa.org
AMOUNT: $1,000 (max.)
DEADLINE(S): APR 15
FIELD(S): Food Science; Nutrition; Food Service Management

Must be an ASFSA member and/or the child of an ASFSA member who plans to study in the above field(s). Must express a desire to make school food service a career, be pursuing an undergraduate degree, and have a satisfactory academic record.

Contact ASFSA for an application.

1937—SONOMA CHAMBOLLE-MUSIGNY SISTER CITIES, INC. (Henri Cardinaux Memorial Scholarship)

Chamson Scholarship Committee
P.O. Box 1633
Sonoma CA 95476-1633
707/939-1344
FAX: 707/939-1344
E-mail: Baileysci@vom.com
AMOUNT: Up to $1,500 (travel + expenses)
DEADLINE(S): JUL 15
FIELD(S): Culinary Arts; Wine Industry; Art; Architecture; Music; History; Fashion

Hands-on experience working in above or similar fields and living with a family in small French village in Burgundy or other French city. Must be Sonoma County, CA, resident at least 18 years of age and be able to communicate in French. Transcripts, employer recommendation, photograph, and essay (stating why, where, and when) required.

1 award. Nonrenewable. Also offers opportunity for candidate in Chambolle-Musigny to obtain work experience and cultural exposure in Sonoma, CA.

1938—STUDENT CONSERVATION ASSOCIATION (SCA Resource Assistant Program)

P.O. Box 550
Charlestown NH 03603
603/543-1700
FAX: 603/543-1828
E-mail: internships@sca-inc.org
Internet: http://www.sca-inc.org
AMOUNT: $1,180-$4,725
DEADLINE(S): Varies
FIELD(S): Environment and related fields

Must be 18 and U.S. citizen; need not be student. Fields: Ag, archaeology, anthropology, botany, caves, civil/environmental engineering, environmental education, fisheries, forests, herpetology, history, living history/roleplaying, visitor services, landscape architecture/environmental design, paleontology, recreation/resource/range management, trail maintenance/construction, wildlife management, geology, hydrology, library/museums, surveying.

900 positions in U.S. and Canada. Send $1 for postage for application; outside U.S./Canada, send $20.

1939—U.S. DEPT. OF HEALTH & HUMAN SERVICES (Indian Health Service Health Professions Scholarship Program)

Twinbrook Metro Plaza, Suite 100
12300 Twinbrook Parkway
Rockville MD 20852
301/443-0234
FAX: 301/443-4815
Internet: http://www:ihs.gov/Recruitment/DHPS/SP/SBTOC3.asp
AMOUNT: Tuition + fees and monthly stipend of $938.
DEADLINE(S): APR 1
FIELD(S): Health professions, accounting, social work

Open to Native Americans or Alaska natives who are graduate students or college juniors or seniors in a program leading to a career in a fields listed above. U.S. citizenship required. Renewable annually with reapplication.

Scholarship recipients must intend to serve the Indian people. They incur a one-year service obligation to the IHS for each year of support for a minimum of two years. Write for complete information.

1940—UNITED STATES DEPARTMENT OF AGRICULTURE (1890 National Scholars Program)

14th & Independence Avenue SW; Room 301-W; Whitten Bldg.
Washington, DC 20250-9600
202/720-6905
E-mail: usda-m@fie.com
Internet: http://web.fie.com/htdoc/fed/agr/ars/edu/prog/mti/agrpgaak.htm
AMOUNT: Tuition, employment/benefits, use of pc/software, fees, books, room/board
DEADLINE(S): JAN 15
FIELD(S): Agriculture, Food, or Natural Resource Sciences

For U.S. citizens, high school grad/GED, GPA 3.0+, verbal/math SAT 1000+, composite score 21+ ACT, first-year college student, and attend participating school.

34+ scholarships/yr/4 years. Send applications to U.S.D.A. Liaison officer at the 1890 Institution of your choice (see Web page for complete list).

1941—UNIVERSITY OF ILLINOIS COLLEGE OF ACES (Jonathan Baldwin Turner Agricultural Scholarship Program)

115 ACES Library
1101 S. Goodwin Street
Urbana IL 61801
217/244-4540
Internet: http://w3.aces.uiuc.edu/Acad-Prog/
AMOUNT: $4,000 ($1,000/year)
DEADLINE(S): Varies (start of high school senior year)
FIELD(S): Agriculture; Nutritional Science; Natural Resources; Environmental; Social Sciences (agricultural economics, communications, or education)

Scholarships in agricultural, food, and human nutritional sciences for outstanding incoming freshmen at the University of Illinois. Must have minimum ACT composite score of 27, equivalent SAT combined scores, or be in the 10th percentile of high school class rank at the end of junior year. Interview required.

55 awards annually. Contact Charles Olson, Assistant Dean of Academic Programs, College of Agricultural, Consumer and Environmental Sciences, for an application.

SCHOOL OF SOCIAL SCIENCE

1942—AMERICAN BAR FOUNDATION (Montgomery Summer Research Fellowships for Minority Undergraduate Students)

750 N. Lake Shore Drive
Chicago IL 60611
312/988-6500
FAX: 312/988-6579
E-mail: fellowships@abfn.org
Internet: http://www.abf-sociolegal.org
AMOUNT: $3,600 stipend
DEADLINE(S): MAR 1
FIELD(S): Social Sciences; Humanities; Law

Summer research opportunity open to sophomore and junior undergraduates who are Native American, African American, Mexican, Puerto Rican, or other minority. Must be U.S. citizen or permanent resident and have at least a 3.0 GPA. Students are assigned a mentor and participate in seminars; must also work at the Foundation's office in Chicago for 35 hours per week for 10 weeks. Essay, transcripts, and letter of recommendation required.

4 awards annually; announced in April. See Web site or contact ABF for an application.

1943—EAST LONGMEADOW SCHOLARSHIP FOUNDATION FUND (Scholarships)

Box 66
East Longmeadow MA 01028
413/525-5462
AMOUNT: Varies
DEADLINE(S): MAR 1
FIELD(S): Science

Open to residents of East Longmeadow, Massachusetts, to pursue undergraduate or graduate study.

Contact Scholarship Fund at the above address for an application or the East Longmeadow High School counselor's office at the above phone number for details.

1944—CHRISTIAN A. JOHNSON ENDEAVOR FOUNDATION (Native American Fellows)

John F. Kennedy School of Government, Harvard University
79 John F. Kennedy Street
Cambridge MA 02138
617/495-1152
FAX: 617/496-3900
Internet: http://www.ksg.harvard.edu/hpaied/index.htm
AMOUNT: Varies
DEADLINE(S): MAY 1
FIELD(S): American Indian Affairs

Fellowships for students of Native American ancestry who attend a John F. Kennedy School of Government degree program. Applicant, parent, or grandparent must hold membership in a federally or state-recognized tribe, band, or other organized group of Native Americans. Must be committed to a career in American Indian affairs. Awards based on merit and need.

Renewable, based on renomination and availability of funds. To apply, contact John F. Kennedy School of Government at above address.

1945—EAST TEXAS HISTORICAL ASSOCIATION (Ottis Lock Endowment Awards)

P.O. Box 6223; SFA Station
Nacogdoches TX 75962
936/468-2407
FAX: 936/468-2190

E-mail: amcdonald@sfasu.edu
Internet: http://leonardo sfasu.edu/etha
AMOUNT: $500
DEADLINE(S): MAY 1
FIELD(S): History; Social Science

Open to residents of East Texas who will be pursuing undergraduate or graduate studies at an East Texas college or university.

Renewable with adequate progress toward degree. See Web site or contact East Texas Historical Association for an application.

1946—EAST TEXAS HISTORICAL ASSOCIATION (Research Grants)

P.O. Box 6223; SFA Station
Nacogdoches TX 75962
936/468-2407
FAX: 936/468-2190
E-mail: amcdonald@sfasu.edu
Internet: http://leonardo.sfasu.edu/etha
AMOUNT: : $500-$1,000
DEADLINE(S): MAY 1
FIELD(S): History; Social Science

See Web site or contact East Texas Historical Association for an application.

1947—EUROPEAN CENTRE OF ANALYSIS IN THE SOCIAL SCIENCES [ECASS] (Bursaries for Research Visits to Essex and for Essex Summer School)

Univ. of Essex, Wivenhoe Park
Colchester, Essex CO4 3SQ
ENGLAND UK
+44 (0) 1206 873087
FAX: +44 (0) 1206 872403
E-mail: ecass@essex.ac.uk
Internet: http://www.iser.essex.ac.uk/ecass
AMOUNT: Accommodation, subsistence, and some travel aid fees for Essex Summer School
DEADLINE(S): Open; FEB 28 for the Summer School Bursaries
FIELD(S): Social Sciences

Bursaries for scientific researchers carrying out non-proprietary research who are nationals of a member state of the European Community or of an Associated State (currently Iceland, Liechtenstein, Norway, and Israel) and who are working in these countries. U.K. researchers or those working inside the U.K. are not eligible for these bursaries. Emphasis is on Data Analysis and Collection in the Social Sciences. Must be computer literate and fluent in English.

Visits are usually 2 weeks to 3 months. Summer bursary recipients are required to spend at least an additional 12 working days at ECASS.

1948—INSTITUTE FOR HUMANE STUDIES (Humane Studies Fellowship)

3301 N. FairFAX: Drive, Suite 440
Arlington VA 22201-4432
703/993-4880 or 800/697-8799
FAX: 703/993-4890
E-mail: ihs@gmu.edu
Internet: http://www.TheIHS.org
AMOUNT: $12,000 (max.)
DEADLINE(S): DEC
FIELD(S): Social Sciences; Liberal Arts; Law; Humanities; Jurisprudence; Journalism

Open to graduate and advanced undergraduate or law students pursuing degrees at any accredited domestic or foreign college/university. Based on academic performance, demonstrated interest in the classical liberal tradition, and potential to contribute to the advancement of a free society.

90 awards annually. Apply online or contact IHS for an application.

1949—KOSCIUSZKO FOUNDATION (Summer Sessions in Poland and Rome)

15 E. 65th Street
New York NY 10021-6595
212/734-2130
FAX: 212/628-4552
E-mail: thekf@pegasusnet.com
Internet: http://www.kosciuszkofoundation.org
AMOUNT: Varies
DEADLINE(S): Varies
FIELD(S): Polish Studies; History; Literature; Art; Economics; Social Studies; Language; Culture

Open to undergraduate and graduate students, graduating high school students who are 18 or older, and persons of any age who are not enrolled in a college/university program. Study programs are offered in Poland and Rome from mid-June through the end of August in above fields. Must be U.S. citizen/permanent resident.

See Web site or send a self-addressed, stamped envelope to Addy Tymczyszyn, Summer Studies Abroad Coordinator, for an application.

1950—MIDWAY COLLEGE (Institutional Aid Program)

Financial Aid Office
Midway KY 40347
606/846-4421
AMOUNT: Varies
DEADLINE(S): MAR 1
FIELD(S): Nursing; Paralegal; Education; Psychology; Biology; Equine Studies; Liberal Studies; Business Administration

Scholarships and grants are open to women who are accepted for enrollment at Midway College. Awards support undergraduate study in the above areas.

80 awards annually. Contact Midway College's Financial Aid Office for an application.

1951—NATIONAL COUNCIL FOR THE SOCIAL STUDIES (Grant for the Enhancement of Geographic Literacy)

8555 Sixteenth Street, Suite 500
Silver Spring MD 20910
301/588-1800
FAX: 301/588-2049
E-mail: information@ncss.org
Internet: http://www.ncss.org/awards/grants.html
AMOUNT: $2,500
DEADLINE(S): MAR 21
FIELD(S): Social Studies

Grant is co-sponsored by the George F. Cram Company, map publishers. For teachers of any level who present a program to promote and enhance geography education in the schools. Must incorporate the National Geography Standards in "Geography for Life," the "Fundamental Themes in Geography," and appropriate sections of "Expectations of Excellence: Curriculum Standards for Social Studies."

See Web site or contact organization for details.

1952—PEW YOUNGER SCHOLARS PROGRAM (Graduate Fellowships)

G-123 Hesburgh Library
University of Notre Dame
Notre Dame IN 46556
219/631-4531
FAX: 219/631-8721
E-mail: Karen.M.Heinig.2@nd.edu
Internet: http://www.nd.edu/~pesp/pew/PYSPHistory.html
AMOUNT: $13,000
DEADLINE(S): NOV 30
FIELD(S): Social Sciences, Humanities, Theology

Program is for use at any Christian undergraduate school and most seminaries. Check with organization to see if your school qualifies. Apply during senior year. Recipients may enter a competition in which ten students will be awarded a $39,000 ($13,000/year) fellowship for three years of dissertation study. For use at top-ranked Ph.D. programs at outstanding universities.

NOT for study in medicine, law business, performing arts, fine arts, or the pastorate. Check Web site and/or organization for details.

1953—RESOURCES FOR THE FUTURE (RFF Summer Internship Program)

1616 P Street NW
Washington DC 20036-1400
202/328-5000; Fax: 202/939-3460
E-mail: mankin@rff.org or voigt@rff.org
Internet: http://www.rff.org/about_rff/fellowships_internships.htm
AMOUNT: $350-375/week
DEADLINE(S): MAR 14 (5 PM, eastern time)
FIELD(S): Social Sciences, Natural Resources, Energy, Environment

Resident paid summer internships for undergraduate and graduate students for research in the above fields. Divisions are Risk, Resource and Environmental Management, Energy and Natural Resources, and Quality of the Environment. Candidates should have outstanding policy analysis and writing skills. For both U.S. and non-U.S. citizens.

All information is on Web site. Address inquiries and applications to John Mankin (Energy and Natural Resources and Quality of the Environment) or Marilyn Voigt (Risk, Resource and Environmental Management).

1954—ROSE HILL COLLEGE (Louella Robinson Memorial Scholarship)

P.O. Box 3126
Aiken SC 29802-3126
800/684-3769
FAX: 803/641-0240
E-mail: rosehill@rosehill.edu
Internet: http://www.rosehill.edu
AMOUNT: $10,000/year for four years
DEADLINE(S): Varies
FIELD(S): Liberal arts and humanities curricula

For undergraduate residents of Indian River County, Florida, to attend Rose Hill College in Aiken, South Carolina. The school offers a liberal arts education and follows the Great Books curriculum, a program of reading and seminars.

One annual award. Applicants must meet entry requirements of RHC. Contact above location for details.

1955—ROSE HILL COLLEGE (Scholarships for Children of Eastern Orthodox Priests/Deacons)

P.O. Box 3126
Aiken SC 29802-3126
800/684-3769
FAX: 803/641-0240
E-mail: rosehill@rosehill.edu
Internet: http://www.rosehill.edu
AMOUNT: Full scholarship: $10,000/year for four years
DEADLINE(S): Varies
FIELD(S): Liberal Arts and Humanities Curricula

For undergraduates who are children of Eastern Orthodox Christian priests or deacons to attend Rose Hill College in Aiken, South Carolina. The school offers a liberal arts education and follows the Great Books Curriculum, a program of reading and seminars.

6-10 annual awards. Applicants must meet entry requirements of RHC. Contact above location for details.

1956—ROSE HILL COLLEGE (Scholarships for the Homeschooled)

P.O. Box 3126
Aiken SC 29802-3126
800/684-3769
FAX: 803/641-0240
E-mail: rosehill@rosehill.edu
Internet: http://www.resehill.edu
AMOUNT: Full scholarship: $10,000/year for four years
DEADLINE(S): Varies
FIELD(S): Liberal Arts and Humanities Curricula

For undergraduates who have been homeschooled for three of the last five years of their high school education. For use at Rose Hill College in Aiken, South Carolina. The school offers a liberal arts education and follows the Great Books Curriculum, a program of reading and seminars. Scholarships will be awarded primarily on the basis of an essay which the student will be asked to write.

Four annual awards. Applicants must meet entry requirements of RHC. Contact above location for details.

1957—THE BRITISH COUNCIL (Scholarships for Citizens of Mexico)

10 Spring Gardens
London SW1A 2BN ENGLAND UK
+44 (0) 171 930 8466
FAX: +44 (0) 161 957 7188
E-mail: education.enquiries@britcoun.org
Internet: http://www.britcoun.org/mexico/mexschol.htm
AMOUNT: Varies
DEADLINE(S): Varies
FIELD(S): Social Sciences, Applied Sciences, Technology

The British Council in Mexico offers approximately 100 scholarships per year in the above fields for undergraduates and graduates to study in the United Kingdom. Good level of English language required.

The Web site listed here gives more details. For more information, contact: leticia.magana@bc-mexico.sprint.com. or contact organization in London.

1958—THE WALT DISNEY COMPANY (American Teacher Awards)

P.O. Box 9805
Calabasas CA 91372
AMOUNT: $2,500 (36 awards); $25,000 (Outstanding Teacher of the Year)
DEADLINE(S): FEB 15
FIELD(S): Teachers: Athletic Coach, Early Childhood, English, Foreign Language/ESL, General Elementary, Mathematics, Performing Arts, Physical Education/Health, Science, Social Studies, Visual Arts, Vo-Tech Education

Awards for K-12 teachers in the above fields.

Teachers, or anyone who knows a great teacher, can write for applications at the above address.

COMMUNICATIONS

1959—ACADEMY OF CANADIAN CINEMA AND TELEVISION (Internship; National Apprenticeship Training Program)

172 King Street East
Toronto Ontario M5A 1J3 CANADA
800/644-5194
FAX: 416/366/8454
E-mail: cmaloney@academy.ca
Internet: http://www.academy.ca/Academy/About/GeneralACCTInfo.html
AMOUNT: $300 per week for 12 weeks
DEADLINE(S): FEB
FIELD(S): Film and Television Production and Management

Program designed to provide hands-on professional training to students in their graduating year from film and/or television diploma/degree programs. Must be Canadian citizen or landed immigrant studying full-time in Canada.

Six awards per year. Contact Christine Maloney for complete information.

1960—AMERICA-ISRAEL CULTURAL FOUNDATION (Sharett Scholarship Program)

51 E. 42nd Street, #400
New York NY 10017
212/557-1600
FAX: 212/557-1611
E-mail: usaaicf@aol.com
Internet: http://www.aicf.webnet.org/involved_overview.html
AMOUNT: Varies
DEADLINE(S): MAR 15
FIELD(S): Music, Dance, Theater, Visual Arts, Film and Television

Scholarships are for one year of study and are renewable.

800 scholarships per year. Write for complete information.

1961—AMERICAN INSTITUTE OF POLISH CULTURE (Scholarships)

1440 79th Street Causeway, Suite 117
Miami FL 33141
305/864-2349
FAX: 305/865-5150
E-mail: info@ampolinstitute.org
Internet: http://www.ampolinstitute.org
AMOUNT: $1,000
DEADLINE(S): FEB 15
FIELD(S): Journalism; Public Relations; Communications

Awards are to encourage young Americans of Polish descent to pursue the above professions. Can be used for full-time study at any accredited American college. Criteria for selection include achievement, talent, and involvement in public life.

$25 processing fee. Renewable. Send self-addressed, stamped envelope to Mrs. Harriet Irsay for an application.

1962—AMERICAN RADIO RELAY LEAGUE FOUNDATION (The PHD ARA Scholarship)

225 Main Street
Newington CT 06111
860/594-0200
FAX: 860/594-0259
Internet: http://www.arrl.org/
AMOUNT: $1,000
DEADLINE(S): FEB 1
FIELD(S): Journalism; Computer Science; Electronic Engineering

For undergraduate or graduate students who are residents of the ARRL Midwest Division (IA, KS, MO, NE) who hold any class of radio amateur license—or student may be the child of a deceased radio amateur.

1 award annually. See Web site or contact ARRL for an application.

1963—AMERICAN WOMEN IN RADIO AND TELEVISION-HOUSTON CHAPTER (Scholarship Program)

Houston TX 77098
713/662-1363
FAX: 713/662-1398
Internet: http://www.awrt.org
AMOUNT: $1,000
DEADLINE(S): MAR
FIELD(S): Broadcasting and allied fields

Scholarships are for Houston area college juniors and seniors who are studying broadcasting or an allied field.

Renewable. Contact Kim Scates, AWRT Houston Chapter President, for an application. Awards are made in May.

1964—ARCTIC INSTITUTE OF NORTH AMERICA (Jim Bourque Scholarship)

Univ. of Calgary
2500 University Drive NW
Calgary Alberta T2N 1N4
CANADA
403/220-7515
FAX: 403/282-4609
E-mail: smccaffe@ucalgary.ca
Internet: http://www.ucalgary.ca/UofC/Others/AINA/scholar/scholar.html
AMOUNT: $1,000
DEADLINE(S): JUL 15
FIELD(S): Education; Environmental Studies; Traditional Knowledge; Telecommunications

Open to Canadian Aboriginal students who intend to take, or are enrolled in, post-secondary training in above fields. There is no application; applicants must submit description of program and reasons for choice, transcript, letter of recommendation, statement of financial need, and proof of enrollment or application to a postsecondary institution.

See Web site or contact AINA for details. Award announced on August 1.

1965—ASSOCIATED PRESS TELEVISION-RADIO ASSOCIATION OF CALIFORNIA/NEVADA (APTRA-Clete Roberts & Kathryn Dettman Memorial Journalism Scholarship Awards)

Rachel Ambrose
221 S. Figueroa Street, #300
Los Angeles CA 90012
213/626-1200
E-mail: rambrose@ap.org
AMOUNT: $1,500
DEADLINE(S): DEC 10
FIELD(S): Broadcast Journalism

Recipients will be students with a broadcast journalism career objective who are enrolled in a California or Nevada college or university. Applicants must complete an entry form and may submit examples of broadcast-related work. Scholarships will be awarded at APTRA's annual awards banquet in March at the Disneyland Hotel in Anaheim, CA.

4 awards annually. Contact Rachel Ambrose at APTRA for an entry form.

1966—ASSOCIATION FOR EDUCATION IN JOURNALISM & MASS COMMUNICATION (Mary A. Gardner Scholarship)

Univ. of S. Carolina
LeConte College, Room 121
Columbia SC 29208-0251
803/777-2005
AMOUNT: $300
DEADLINE(S): MAR 23
FIELD(S): News Reporting and/or Editing

Open to full-time incoming juniors or seniors in a college undergraduate news-editorial program. Must have minimum GPA of 3.0 (on a 4.0 scale). Statement of qualifications/career objectives, biographical narrative (including school/home address/phone), letter of support from professor, official transcript, two letters of recommendation, and copies of clippings/other evidence of journalistic accomplishments required with application.

1 award annually. Send a self-addressed, stamped envelope (SASE) to Jennifer H. McGill, Executive Director, AEJMC, at above address for complete information.

1967—BLUES HEAVEN FOUNDATION, INC. (Muddy Waters Scholarship)

2120 S. Michigan Avenue
Chicago IL 60616

312/808-1286
AMOUNT: $2,000
DEADLINE(S): APR 30
FIELD(S): Music; Music Education; African-American Studies; Folklore; Performing Arts; Arts Management; Journalism; Radio/TV/Film

Scholarship is made on a competitive basis with consideration given to scholastic achievement, concentration of studies, and financial need. Applicant must have full-time enrollment status in a Chicago area college/university in at least their first year of undergraduate studies or a graduate program. Scholastic aptitude extracurricular involvement, grade point average, and financial need are all considered.

Contact Blues Heaven Foundation, Inc. to receive an application between February and April.

1968—BROADCAST EDUCATION ASSOCIATION (Scholarships in Broadcasting)

1771 N Street NW
Washington DC 20036-2891
202/429-5354
E-mail: fweaver@nab.org
Internet: http://www.beaweb.org
AMOUNT: $1,250-$5,000
DEADLINE(S): JAN 14
FIELD(S): Broadcasting; Radio

For full-time juniors, seniors, and graduate students at BEA Member universities. Applicant should show evidence of superior academic performance and potential to become an outstanding electronic media professional. There should be compelling evidence that applicant possesses high integrity and a well-articulated sense of personal and professional responsibility. Awards exclusively for tuition, student fees, textbooks/supplies, and dorm room and board.

15 awards annually. Not renewable. Contact BEA or your campus faculty for an application no later than December 17. See Web site for list of BEA member institutions.

1969—BUCKS COUNTY COURIER TIMES (Summer Internship Program)

8400 Route 13
Levittown PA 19057
215/949-4185; 215/949-4177
E-mail: cper@calkinsnewspapers.com
AMOUNT: $4,380 ($365/wk.)
DEADLINE(S): FEB 1
FIELD(S): News; Business; Feature Reporting

12-week internship for minority students at the Bucks County Courier Times. Must be U.S. resident and have car. Financial need NOT a factor.

5 awards annually. Renewable. Contact Carolyn Per at above address for an application.

1970—BUENA VISTA COLLEGE NETWORK (Internships in Film Marketing)

3900 W. Alameda Avenue
Burbank CA 91505-4316
818/567-5000
E-mail: College_Network@studio.disney.com
AMOUNT: Varies
DEADLINE(S): None
FIELD(S): Fields of study related to the motion picture industry, including marketing and promotion

Internships for full-time college students age 18 and up interested in a career in a facet of the motion picture industry. Must have unlimited access to computer with modem and transportation, be able to work 4-6 hours per week and 2-3 weekends per month. Attend film openings and sneak previews. Evaluate various aspects via an interactive computer system. Compensation ranges from $30 to $60/month. Possible school credit.

Access Web site by writing "Buena Vista College Network" from Yahoo. Available in most states and parts of Canada. Details, an interactive application, and E-mail access are located on Web site.

1971—CANADIAN ASSOCIATION OF BROADCASTERS (Jim Allard Broadcast Journalism; Ruth Hancock Scholarship)

P.O. Box 627; Stn. B
Ottawa Ontario K1P 5S2 CANADA
613/233-4035
AMOUNT: $2,500 (Allard); $1,500 (Hancock)
DEADLINE(S): JUN 30
FIELD(S): Broadcast Communications

Open to Canadian citizens enrolled in Canadian universities. Applicants should have strong character and leadership qualities and a genuine interest in pursuing a broadcasting career.

Write for complete information.

1972—CANADIAN ASSOCIATION OF BROADCASTERS (Raymond Crepault Scholarship)

P.O. Box 627; Stn. B
Ottawa Ontario K1P 5S2 CANADA
613/233-4035
AMOUNT: Up to $5,000
DEADLINE(S): JUN 30
FIELD(S): Communications

Open to French-speaking Canadian citizens enrolled full-time as undergrads or grad students at a Canadian university. Financial need and ability to complete studies must be demonstrated.

Write for complete information.

1973—CENTER FOR ENVIRONMENTAL JOURNALISM/UNIVERSITY OF COLORADO AT BOULDER (Ted Scripps Fellowship)

Univ of Colorado
Macky 201, Campus Box 287
Boulder CO 80309-0287
303/492-0459
FAX: 303/492-0585
E-mail: ackland@spot.colorado.edu
Internet: campuspress.colorado.edu/cej.html or http://www.scripps.com/foundation
AMOUNT: $27,000 for 9 months
DEADLINE(S): MAR 1
FIELD(S): Print or Broadcast Journalism

Five journalists will be selected to spend the academic year at the University of Colorado at Boulder studying environmental science and policy. For print or broadcast journalists with a minimum of five years professional experience. Can be general assignment reporters, editors, and freelancers.

5 awards annually. May also contact the Scripps Howard Foundation for details: P.O. Box 5380, Cincinnati, OH 45202.

1974—CENTRAL NEWSPAPERS, INC. (Pulliam Journalism Fellowships)

Russell B. Pulliam, Director
P.O. Box 145
Indianapolis IN 46206-0145
317/633-9206
FAX: 317/630-9549
AMOUNT: $5,500 stipend
DEADLINE(S): NOV 15 (early admissions); MAR 1 (final)
FIELD(S): Journalism

Open to recent graduates and to undergraduate seniors who will receive their bachelor's degree between August and June preceding fellowship. Award is for a 10-week work and study internship at one of CNI's newspapers in Indianapolis or Phoenix. Includes sessions with a writing coach and seminars with local and national journalists.

20 awards annually. Contact Russ Pulliam at CNI for an application.

1975—CHARLES AND LUCILLE KING FAMILY FOUNDATION (Scholarships)

366 Madison Avenue, 10th Floor
New York NY 10017
212/682-2913
E-mail: info@kingfoundation.org
Internet: http://www.kingfoundation.org
AMOUNT: $2,500 (max.)
DEADLINE(S): APR 15
FIELD(S): Film; Television

Open to juniors, seniors, and graduate students who are majoring in television or film at four-year universities. Must demonstrate academic ability, financial need, and professional potential. Must submit transcripts, three letters of recommendation, and a typed personal statement.

Renewable. See your financial aid office or contact Foundation for an application.

1976—CONCORDIA UNIVERSITY (Susan Carson Memorial Bursary and Gordon Fisher Bursaries)

Journalism Dept.
455 de Maisonneuve Boulevard W.
Loyola BR 305
Montreal Quebec H3G 1M8
CANADA
514/848-3809
FAX: 514/848-2812
E-mail: awardsgs@vax2.concordia.ca
AMOUNT: $1,800; $2,000
DEADLINE(S): SEP 20
FIELD(S): Journalism

Based on academic achievement/performance and financial need. Recipient of Susan Carson award must also demonstrate the highest ideals, concern for humankind, and qualities of citizenship. Selection will be made by the Chair of the Journalism Department in consultation with colleagues and/or relatives of the late Ms. Susan Carson. Preference will be given to students who have custody of one or more dependent children. No preference considered for Gordon Fisher awards.

3 awards annually. Not renewable. Contact the Chair of the Journalism Department at Concordia University for applications.

1977—CUBAN AMERICAN NATIONAL FOUNDATION (The Mas Family Scholarships)

7300 NW 3 Terrace
Miami FL 33122
305/592-7768
FAX: 305/592-7889
E-mail: canfnet.org
Internet: http://www.canfnet.org
AMOUNT: Individually negotiated
DEADLINE(S): MAR 15
FIELD(S): Engineering, Business, International Relations, Economics, Communications, Journalism

For Cuban-Americans students, graduates and undergraduates, born in Cuba or direct descendants of those who left Cuba. Must be in top 10% of high school class or maintain a 3.5 GPA in college.

10,000 awards/year. Recipients may reapply for subsequent years. Financial need considered along with academic success, SAT and GRE scores, and leadership potential. Essays and proof of Cuban descent required.

1978—DOW JONES NEWSPAPER FUND, INC. (Business Reporting Intern Program for Minority Sophomores and Juniors)

Princeton NJ 08543
609/452-2820 or
800/DOWFUND
E-mail: dowfund@wsj.dowjones.com
Internet: http://www.dj.com/dowfund
AMOUNT: $1,000 + paid summer internship
DEADLINE(S): NOV 15
FIELD(S): Journalism; Business Reporting; Editing

Summer internships for college sophomores and juniors whose ethnic backgrounds are African-American, Hispanic, Asian, Native American/Eskimo, or Pacific Islanders who will work at daily newspapers as business reporters. Must demonstrate interest in similar career, though journalism major not required. Interns are paid and will attend a 2-week training program. Students returning to full-time studies will receive $1,000 scholarships.

12 awards annually. Applications available from August 15 to November 1. Contact Dow Jones for an application.

1979—DOW JONES NEWSPAPER FUND, INC. (Newspaper Editing Intern/Scholarship Program)

Princeton NJ 08543-0300
609/452-2820 or
800/DOWFUND
E-mail: dowfund@wsj.dowjones.com
Internet: http://www.dj.com/dowfund
AMOUNT: $1,000 + paid summer internship
DEADLINE(S): NOV 15
FIELD(S): Journalism; Editing

Summer internships for college juniors, seniors, and graduate students to work as copy editors at daily newspapers. Must demonstrate a commitment to a career in journalism, though journalism major not required. Interns are paid by the newspapers for which they work and attend a two-week training program paid for by the Newspaper Fund. Those returning to full-time studies will receive a $1,000 scholarship.

80 awards annually. Applications available from August 15 to November 1. Contact Dow Jones for an application.

1980—DOW JONES NEWSPAPER FUND, INC. (Online Newspaper Editing Intern/Scholarship Program)

Princeton NJ 08543-0300
609/452-2820 or
800/DOWFUND
E-mail: dowfund@wsj.dowjones.com
Internet: http://www.dj.com/dowfund
AMOUNT: $1,000 + paid summer internship
DEADLINE(S): NOV 15
FIELD(S): Journalism; Online Editing

Summer internships for college juniors, seniors, and graduate students to work as editors for online newspapers. Must demonstrate a commitment to a career in journalism, though journalism major not required. Interns are paid by the newspapers for which they work and attend a two-week training program paid for by the Newspaper Fund. Those returning to full-time studies will receive a $1,000 scholarship.

12 awards annually. Applications available from August 15 to November 1. Contact Dow Jones for an application.

1981—DOW JONES NEWSPAPER FUND, INC. (Real-Time Financial News Service Intern/Scholarship Program)

Princeton NJ 08543-0300
609/452-2820 or
800/DOWFUND
E-mail: dowfund@wsj.dowjones.com
Internet: http://www.dj.com/dowfund
AMOUNT: $1,000 + paid summer internship

DEADLINE(S): NOV 15
FIELD(S): Journalism; Financial Journalism; Editing

Summer internship for college juniors, seniors, and graduate students to work as editors and reporters for real-time financial news services. Must demonstrate a commitment to a similar career, though journalism major not required. Interns are paid by the news service for which they work and will attend a two-week training program paid for by the Newspaper Fund. Students returning to full-time studies will receive a $1,000 scholarship.

12 awards annually. Applications available from August 15 to November 1. Contact Dow Jones for an application.

1982—DOW JONES NEWSPAPER FUND, INC. (Summer Workshops in Journalism for Minority High School Students)

Princeton NJ 08543-0300
609/452-2820 or
800/DOWFUND
E-mail: dowfund@wsj.dowjones.com
Internet: http://www.dj.com/dowfund

AMOUNT: $1,000 + paid summer internship
DEADLINE(S): NOV 15
FIELD(S): Journalism

Offered at 35+ colleges around the U.S. for high school students interested in journalism and whose ethnic backgrounds are African-American, Pacific Islander, American Indian/Eskimo, Asian, or Hispanic. Ten days of learning to write, report, design, and lay out a newspaper (free). The eight best writers throughout the U.S. of an article relevant to youth will receive a $1,000 scholarship.

Contact Dow Jones for list of which colleges/states are participating.

1983—DUPONT CHALLENGE (Science Essay Competition)

General Learning Communications
900 Skokie Boulevard, Suite 200
Northbrook IL 60062-4028
Internet: http://www.glcomm.com/dupont/

AMOUNT: $50-$1,500
DEADLINE(S): Varies
FIELD(S): Science

Open to students in grades ten to twelve (Senior Division) and grades seven to nine (Junior Division). All entries become the property of DuPont. Essays should be no shorter than 700 words and no longer than 1,000 words. Include a bibliography of sources on a separate page at the end of your essay.

1984—FUND FOR AMERICAN STUDIES (Institutes on Political Journalism; Business & Government Affairs & Comparative Political & Economic Systems)

1526 18th Street NW
Washington, DC 20036
202/986-0384 800/741-6964
Internet: http://www.dcinternships.com

AMOUNT: Up to $2,975
DEADLINE(S): JAN 31 (early decision); MAR 15 (general application deadline)
FIELD(S): Political Science; Economics; Journalism; Business Administration

The Fund for American Studies, in conjunction with Georgetown University, sponsors summer institutes that include internships, courses for credit, site briefings, and dialogues with policy leaders. Scholarships are available to sophomores and juniors to cover the cost of the program.

Approximately 100 awards per year. For Fund's programs only. Call, check Web site, or write for complete information.

1985—HILLEL: THE FOUNDATION FOR JEWISH CAMPUS LIFE (Steinhardt Jewish Campus Service Corps)

1640 Rhode Island Avenue NW
Washington DC 20036
202/857-6559
FAX:202/857-6626
E-mail: mgruenwald@hillel.org
Internet: http://www.hillel.org

AMOUNT: One-year fellowship
DEADLINE(S): MAR
FIELD(S): Student Leadership

Open to college seniors and recent college graduates with leadership skills and ability to create dynamic and innovative engagement strategies designed to reach Jewish college students. Must possess commitment to service; willingness to use time, abilities, and talents to enhance lives of others; and dedication to strengthening Jewish identity among students with whom they work. Corps fellows get to know interests and concerns of students and build programs and activities to match.

See Web site or contact Melanie Sasson Gruenwald or Rachel Gurshman for an application.

1986—HISPANIC COLLEGE FUND (Scholarships for Hispanic Students)

One Thomas Circle NW, Suite 375
Washington DC 20005
202/296-5400
FAX: 202/296-3774
E-mail: Hispanic.Fund@InternetMCI.com
Internet: http://hispanicfund.org

AMOUNT: Varies
DEADLINE(S): APR 15
FIELD(S): Most college majors leading to a career in business

Scholarships for deserving Hispanic college students pursuing a higher education in a major leading to a business career and who are full-time students at accredited institutions. U.S. citizenship. Must demonstrate financial need.

Contact above organization for details or visit Web site for application.

1987—INSTITUTE FOR HUMANE STUDIES (Felix Morley Journalism Competition)

3401 N. FairFAX: Dr., Suite 440
Arlington VA 22201-4432
703/993-4880 or 800/697-8799
FAX: 703/993-4890
E-mail: ihs@gmu.edu
Internet: http://www.TheIHS.org

AMOUNT: $2,500 (1st prize)
DEADLINE(S): DEC 1
FIELD(S): Journalism

This competition awards cash prizes to outstanding young writers whose work demonstrates an appreciation of classical liberal principles (i.e., individual rights; their protection through private property, contract, and law; voluntarism in human relations; and the self-ordering market, free trade, free migration, and peace). Must be a full-time student aged 25 or younger.

Must submit 3-5 articles, editorials, opinion pieces, essays, and reviews published in student newspapers or other periodicals between July 1 and December 1. See Web site for complete rules or contact IHS for an entry form.

1988—INSTITUTE FOR HUMANE STUDIES (Humane Studies Fellowship)

3301 N. FairFAX: Drive, Suite 440
Arlington VA 22201-4432
703/993-4880 or 800/697-8799
FAX: 703/993-4890
E-mail: ihs@gmu.edu
Internet: http://www.TheIHS.org

AMOUNT: $12,000 (max.)

DEADLINE(S): DEC
FIELD(S): Social Sciences; Liberal Arts; Law; Humanities; Jurisprudence; Journalism

Open to graduate and advanced undergraduate or law students pursuing degrees at any accredited domestic or foreign college/university. Based on academic performance, demonstrated interest in the classical liberal tradition, and potential to contribute to the advancement of a free society.

90 awards annually. Apply online or contact IHS for an application.

1989—INSTITUTE FOR HUMANE STUDIES (Summer Seminars Program)

3401 N. FairFAX: Drive, Suite 440
Arlington VA 22201-4432
703/993-4880 or 800/697-8799
FAX: 703/993-4890
E-mail: ihs@gmu.edu
Internet: http://www.TheIHS.org
AMOUNT: Free summer seminars, including room/board, lectures, seminar materials, and books
DEADLINE(S): MAR
FIELD(S): Social Sciences; Humanities; Law; Journalism; Public Policy; Education; Film; Writing; Economics; Philosophy

Open to college students, recent graduates, and graduate students who share an interest in learning and exchanging ideas about the scope of individual rights, free markets, the rule of law, peace, and tolerance.

See Web site for seminar information or to apply online or contact IHS for an application.

1990—INTERNATIONAL DEVELOPMENT RESEARCH CENTRE (Fellowship in Journalism—Internship with L'Agence Periscoop Multimedia)

Ottawa Ontario K1G 3H9
CANADA
613/236-6163 ext.2098
FAX: 613/563-0815
Internet: http://www.idrc.ca/awards
AMOUNT: $30,000 Canadian
DEADLINE(S): MAY 1
FIELD(S): Journalism

Open to Canadian citizens or permanent residents employed by a Canadian newspaper, news agency, radio, or television station with at least three years experience. Guaranteed leave of absence and reemployment by employer is required. Recipient will be a member of the Agence Periscoop Multimedia team in France and must be fluent in spoken and written French.

Contact IDRC for an application.

1991—INTERNATIONAL DEVELOPMENT RESEARCH CENTRE (Fellowship in Journalism—Internship with Gemini News Service)

Ottawa Ontario K1G 3H9
CANADA
613/236-6163 ext.2098
FAX: 613/563-0815
Internet: http://www.idrc.ca/awards
AMOUNT: $30,000 Canadian
DEADLINE(S): MAY 1
FIELD(S): Journalism

Open to Canadian citizens or permanent residents employed by a Canadian newspaper, news agency, radio, or television station with at least three years of experience. Guaranteed leave of absence and reemployment by employer is required. Recipient will be a member of the Gemini News Service in London and will be assigned to a developing country for a few months.

Contact IDRC for an application.

1992—INTERNATIONAL RADIO AND TELEVISION SOCIETY FOUNDATION (Summer Fellowship Program)

420 Lexington Avenue, Suite 1714
New York NY 10170
212/867-6650
FAX: 212/867-6653
Internet: http://www.irts.org
AMOUNT: Housing, stipend, and travel
DEADLINE(S): NOV 12
FIELD(S): Broadcasting; Communications; Sales; Marketing

Nine-week summer fellowship program in New York City is open to outstanding full-time undergraduate juniors and seniors with a demonstrated interest in a career in communications. Financial need NOT a factor.

20-25 awards annually. Not renewable. See Web site or contact Maria DeLeon-Fisher at IRTS for an application.

1993—INVESTIGATIVE REPORTERS AND EDITORS (Minority Fellowships)

138 Neff Annex
Missouri School of Journalism
Columbia MO 65211
573/882-2042
FAX: 573/882-5431
E-mail: jourire@muccmail.missouri.edu
Internet: http://www.ire.org/resources/scholarship/fellowship
AMOUNT: Costs to attend various conferences
DEADLINE(S): NOV 1; DEC 15 (depending on which event)
FIELD(S): Journalism: Investigative

Fellowships for minorities who are either journalism students or employed in the field of journalism various conference of the above organization. Must send clips or audio or visual tape showing your talent as a potential journalist, reference letters, resume, and a goals essay.

Twenty-five fellowships. Application and details are on Web site and/or contact organization.

1994—INVESTIGATIVE REPORTERS AND EDITORS (Small News Organization Fellowships)

138 Neff Annex
Missouri School of Journalism
Columbia MO 65211
573/882-2042
FAX: 573/882-5431
E-mail: jourire@muccmail.missouri.edu
Internet: http://www.ire.org/resources/scholarship/smallnews/
AMOUNT: Costs to attend various conferences
DEADLINE(S): NOV 1; DEC 15 (depending on which event)
FIELD(S): Journalism: Investigative

Fellowships for reporters producing solid investigative projects in small news organizations to receive financial assistance to attend any of the various conferences of the above organization.

See Web site and/or contact organization for further information.

1995—JAPANESE AMERICAN CITIZENS LEAGUE

1765 Sutter Street
San Francisco CA 94115
415/921-5225
FAX: 415/931-4671
E-mail: jacl@jacl.org
Internet: http://www.jacl.org
AMOUNT: $1,000-$5,000
DEADLINE(S): APR 1
FIELD(S): Agriculture; Journalism

Open to JACL members only. For undergraduate students with an interest in either journalism or agriculture and who are planning to attend a college, university, trade school, business school, or any other institution of higher learning. Must submit personal statement, letters of recommendation, and transcripts. Financial need NOT a factor.

For membership information or an application, go to the Web site or send a self-addressed, stamped envelope to above address, stating your level of study. Applications available October 1 through March 20; recipients notified in July.

1996—JEWISH VOCATIONAL SERVICE (Academic Scholarship Program)

One S. Franklin Street
Chicago IL 60606
312/357-4500
FAX: 312/855-3282
TTY: 312/855-3282
E-mail: jvschicago@jon.cjfny.org
AMOUNT: $5,000 (max.)
DEADLINE(S): MAR 1
FIELD(S): "Helping" Professions; Mathematics; Engineering; Sciences; Communications (at Univ IL only); Law (certain schools in IL only)

Open to Jewish men and women legally domiciled in the greater Chicago metropolitan area, who are identified as having promise for significant contributions in their chosen careers, and are in need of financial assistance for full-time academic programs in above areas. Must have entered undergraduate junior year in career programs requiring no postgrad education, be in graduate/professional school, or be in a vo-tech training program. Interview required.

Renewable. Contact JVS for an application between December 1 and February 15th.

1997—LOS ANGELES PROFESSIONAL CHAPTER OF SOCIETY OF PROFESSIONAL JOURNALISTS (Bill Farr Scholarship)

SPJ/LA Scholarships
9951 Barcelona Lane
Cypress CA 90630-3759
Written Inquiry
AMOUNT: Up to $1,000
DEADLINE(S): MAR 1
FIELD(S): Journalism

Open to college juniors, seniors, or graduate students who attend school in Los Angeles, Orange, or Ventura counties in California and are preparing for a career in journalism.

Contact SPJ/LA at above address for an application. Applications available year-round.

1998—LOS ANGELES PROFESSIONAL CHAPTER OF SOCIETY OF PROFESSIONAL JOURNALISTS (Carl Greenberg Prize)

SPJ/LA Scholarships
9951 Barcelona Lane
Cypress CA 90630-3759
Written Inquiry
AMOUNT: Up to $1,000
DEADLINE(S): MAR 1
FIELD(S): Journalism: Political or Investigative Reporting

Open to college juniors, seniors, or graduate students who reside or attend school in Lost Angeles, Orange, or Ventura counties in California and are preparing for a career in journalism. Award based on the best published political or investigative report.

Contact SPJ/LA at above address for an application. Applications available year-round.

1999—LOS ANGELES PROFESSIONAL CHAPTER OF SOCIETY OF PROFESSIONAL JOURNALISTS (Helen Johnson Scholarship)

SPJ/LA Scholarships
9951 Barcelona Lane
Cypress CA 90630-3759
Written Inquiry
AMOUNT: Up to $1,000
DEADLINE(S): MAR 1
FIELD(S): Broadcast Journalism

Open to college juniors, seniors, or graduate students who reside or attend school in Los Angeles, Ventura, or Orange counties in California and are preparing for a career in broadcast journalism.

Contact SPJ/LA at above address for an application. Applications available year-round.

2000—LOS ANGELES PROFESSIONAL CHAPTER OF SOCIETY OF PROFESSIONAL JOURNALISTS (Ken Inouye Scholarship)

SPJ/LA Scholarships
9951 Barcelona Lane
Cypress CA 90630-3759
Written Inquiry
AMOUNT: Up to $1,000
DEADLINE(S): MAR 1
FIELD(S): Journalism

Open to ethnic minority students who will be juniors, seniors, or graduate students the following year. Must reside or attend school in Los Angeles, Orange, or Ventura counties in California and be preparing for a career in journalism.

Contact SPJ/LA at above address for an application. Applications available year-round.

2001—MEXICAN AMERICAN WOMEN'S NATIONAL ASSOCIATION (MANA) (Rita DiMartino Scholarship in Communication)

1725 K Street NW, Suite 105
Washington DC 20006
202/833-0060
FAX: 202/496-0588
E-mail: HerMANA2@aol.com
AMOUNT: Varies
DEADLINE(S): APR 1
FIELD(S): Communications

For Hispanic female students enrolled in undergraduate or graduate programs in communication at accredited colleges or universities. Must demonstrate financial need and academic achievement. Must be MANA member. There is a $10 application fee.

Send self-addressed, stamped envelope for application for membership and scholarship.

2002—MICROSOFT CORPORATION (National Minority and/or Women's Scholarships)

One Microsoft Way
Redmond WA 98052-8303
E-mail: scholar@microsoft.com
Internet: http://www.microsoft.com/college/scholarships/
AMOUNT: Tuition for 1 year
DEADLINE(S): JAN 31
FIELD(S): Computer Science, Computer Engineering, or a related technical discipline, such as Math or Physics

Full tuition scholarships awarded for 1 academic year to women and minorities (African-Americans, Hispanics, or Native Americans) enrolled full-time in the above fields with a demonstrated interest in computers and making satisfactory progress towards a degree. Awards are made through designated schools and are not transferable to other institutions.

See Web site above for details.

2003—MICROSOFT CORPORATION (Summer Internships)

One Microsoft Way
Redmond WA 98052-8303
425/882-8080
E-mail: scholar@microsoft.com
Internet: http://www.microsoft.com/college/scholarships/

AMOUNT: Varies
DEADLINE(S): None
FIELD(S): Computer Science, Computer Engineering, or a related technical discipline, such as Math or Physics

Summer internships for individuals with a deep passion for technological advancement. Must commit to a 12-week minimum. Includes transportation, shipping costs, and shared cost of housing. Competitive compensation offered.

Check Web site above for details.

2004—NATION INSTITUTE (I.F. Stone Award for Student Journalism)

33 Irving Pl., 8th Floor
New York NY 10003
212/209-5400
E-mail: instinfo@nationinstitute.org
Internet: http://www.thenation.com/institute/masur.htm
AMOUNT: $1,000 cash
DEADLINE(S): SEP 30
FIELD(S): Journalism

Contest is open to all undergraduate students enrolled in a U.S. college. Articles may be submitted by writers themselves or nominated by editors of student publications or faculty members. While entries published in student publications are preferred, all will be considered provided they weren't written as part of regular coursework. Winning article will represent the most outstanding example of student journalism in the tradition of I.F. Stone. May submit 3 entries.

Contact Nation Institute for entry rules.

2005—NATION INSTITUTE (Nation Internship Program)

33 Irving Pl., 8th Floor
New York NY 10003
212/209-5400
E-mail: instinfo@nationinstitute.org
Internet: http://www.thenation.com/institute/masur.htm
AMOUNT: $150/week stipend
DEADLINE(S): NOV 12; MAR 17
FIELD(S): Journalism; Publishing

Full-time internships for college students and recent graduates interested in magazine journalism and publishing. Each applicant evaluated on basis of his/her resume, recommendations, and writing samples. All ages are welcome, though most interns have completed junior year of college. Possible housing and travel grants based on financial need. Internships take place in New York and Washington, DC. Must submit career goals, resume, recommendations, and writing samples.

16 awards annually. Contact Nation Institute for an application.

2006—NATIONAL ASSOCIATION OF BLACK JOURNALISTS (NABJ Scholarship Program)

University of Maryland
3100 Taliaferro Hall
College Park MD 20742-7717
301/405-8500
FAX: 301/405-8555
E-mail: nabj@jmail.umd.edu or nabj@nabj.org
Internet: nabj.org
AMOUNT: $2,500
DEADLINE(S): MAR 20
FIELD(S): Journalism: print, photography, radio, television OR planning a career in one of those fields

Minimum of 10 scholarships for African-American undergraduate or graduate students who are accepted to or enrolled in an accredited, four-year journalism program majoring in print, photo, radio, or television journalism OR planning a career in one of those fields. GPA of 2.5 or better (4.0 scale) is required. Also, 2 four-year scholarships are for African-American high school seniors planning to pursue education for a journalism career.

Access Web site for application forms or contact above location. Write for complete information.

2007—NATIONAL ASSOCIATION OF BLACK JOURNALISTS (NABJ Summer Internships)

University of Maryland
3100 Taliaferro Hall
College Park MD 20742-7717
301/405-8500
FAX: 301/405-8555
E-mail: nabj@jmail.umd.edu OR nabj@nabj.org
Internet: nabj.org
AMOUNT: Varies
DEADLINE(S): DEC 15
FIELD(S): Journalism: print, photography, radio, television OR planning a career in one of those fields

Internships for African-American sophomores, juniors, seniors, and graduate students committed to careers in journalism. Programs are throughout the U.S. Minimum 2.5 GPA required.

Access Web site for application forms or contact above location for further information. For foreign or U.S. students. Write for complete information.

2008—NATIONAL ASSOCIATION OF HISPANIC JOURNALISTS (NAHJ Scholarship Program)

1193 National Press Bldg.
Washington DC 20045-2100
202/662-7483
FAX: 202/662-7144
Internet: http://www.nahj.org
AMOUNT: $1,000-$2,000
DEADLINE(S): FEB 25
FIELD(S): Print/Broadcast Journalism; Photojournalism

Open to high school seniors, undergraduates, and graduate students who are committed to a career in print or broadcast journalism or photojournalism. Tenable at two- or four-year schools in the U.S. and its territories. Hispanic ancestry NOT required.

See Web site or send a self-addressed, stamped envelope to Ana Carrion at NAHJ for an application.

2009—NATIONAL ASSOCIATION OF HISPANIC JOURNALISTS (Newhouse Scholarship Program)

1193 National Press Bldg.
Washington DC 20045-2100
202/662-7483
FAX: 202/662-7144
Internet: http://www.nahj.org
AMOUNT: $5,000
DEADLINE(S): FEB 25
FIELD(S): Print/Broadcast Journalism; Photojournalism

Open to undergraduate juniors and seniors and graduate students who are committed to pursuing a career in print or broadcast journalism or photojournalism. Awards tenable at accredited institutions in the U.S. and its territories. It is not necessary to be a journalism or broadcast major, and Hispanic ancestry is NOT required.

See Web site or send a self-addressed, stamped envelope to Ana Carrion at NAHJ for an application.

2010—NATIONAL ASSOCIATION OF WATER COMPANIES-NEW JERSEY CHAPTER (Scholarship)

Elizabethtown Water Co.
600 South Avenue
Westfield NJ 070

908/654-1234
FAX: 908/232-2719
AMOUNT: $2,500
DEADLINE(S): APR 1
FIELD(S): Business Administration; Biology; Chemistry; Engineering Communications

For U.S. citizens who have lived in NJ at least 5 years and plan a career in the investor-owned water utility industry in disciplines such as those above. Must be undergrad or graduate student in a two- or four-year NJ college or university.

GPA of 3.0 or better required. Contact Gail P. Brady for complete information.

2011—NATIONAL BROADCASTING SOCIETY (Alpha Epsilon Rho Scholarships)

P.O. Box 1058
Street Charles MO 63302-1058
888/NBS-1-COM ext. 2000
AMOUNT: $500-$1,000
DEADLINE(S): JAN 1
FIELD(S): Broadcasting

Open ONLY to active student members of NBS-AERho as nominated by local chapters.

Awards are renewable. Contact local NBS-AERho chapter for complete information.

2012—NATIONAL FEDERATION OF PRESS WOMEN (Communications Contest)

P.O. Box 5556
Arlington VA 22205
800/780-2715
Fax: 703/534-5751
E-mail : Presswomen@aol.com
Internet: http://www.nfpw.org
AMOUNT: $100 + plaque
DEADLINE(S): FEB 10
FIELD(S): Communications

Students may enter work in editorial, feature, review, news, sports, column, feature photo, cartooning, single-page layout, or graphics categories to earn awards in each category. The contest is managed through the state affiliates. Please contact state contest directors about state contests early in the school year, because state deadlines usually are in early February, to allow time for judging and processing for the national contest by mid-March.

Entries must be the work of students enrolled in grades 9-12 during the current school year or the last semester of the senior year for students' work published after the current deadline. Submit two tear sheets (the entire page on which the article or graphic appears) for each entry.

2013—NATIONAL PRESS CLUB (Ellen Masin Persina Scholarship for Minorities in Journalism)

529 14th Street NW, 13th Floor
Washington DC 20045
Internet: http://npc.press.org
AMOUNT: $2,500/yr. for 4 years
DEADLINE(S): FEB 1
FIELD(S): Journalism (newspapers, radio, TV, magazine, trade paper)

Scholarships for talented minorities planning to pursue a career in journalism (see above fields). Must provide work samples, an essay, letters of recommendation, etc. Minimum 2.75 GPA required.

Access application from Web site or address above.

2014—NATIONAL PRESS PHOTOGRAPHERS FOUNDATION (Bob East Scholarship)

3200 Croasdaile Drive, Suite 306
Durham NC 27705
919/383-7246 or 800/289-6772
FAX: 919/383-7261
E-mail: nppa@mindspring.com
Internet: sunsite.unc.edu/nppa/scholarships
AMOUNT: $1,000
DEADLINE(S): MAR 1
FIELD(S): Photojournalism

Must be an undergraduate in the first three and one-half years of college or be planning to pursue graduate work (with proof of acceptance). Academic ability and financial need considered, but primary consideration is portfolio (6+ photos, photo-story counts as one; video journalists should submit a tape with 3 stories). Applicant's school must be in the U.S. or Canada.

1 award annually. See Web site or contact NPPF for an application/specific details.

2015—NATIONAL PRESS PHOTOGRAPHERS FOUNDATION (Joseph Ehrenreich Scholarships)

3200 Croasdaile Drive, Suite 306
Durham NC 27705
919/383-7246 or 800/289-6772
FAX: 919/383-7261
E-mail: nppa@mindspring.com
Internet: sunsite.unc.edu/nppa/scholarships
AMOUNT: $1,000
DEADLINE(S): MAR 1
FIELD(S): Photojournalism

Must have completed one year at a recognized four-year college/university having courses in photojournalism leading to a bachelor's degree. Must also have at least one-half year of undergraduate schooling remaining at time of award. Aimed at those with journalism potential with little opportunity and great need. Must include portfolio (6+ photos, photo-story counts as one; video journalists must submit tape with 3 stories). Applicant's school must be in U.S. or Canada.

5 awards annually. See Web site or contact NPPF for an application/specific details.

2016—NATIONAL PRESS PHOTOGRAPHERS FOUNDATION (NPPF Still Scholarship)

3200 Croasdaile Drive, Suite 306
Durham NC 27705
919/383-7246 or 800/289-6772
FAX: 919/383-7261
E-mail: nppa@mindspring.com
Internet: sunsite.unc.edu/nppa/scholarships
AMOUNT: $1,000
DEADLINE(S): MAR 1
FIELD(S): Photojournalism

Must have completed one year at a recognized four-year college/university having courses in photojournalism leading to a bachelor's degree. Must also have at least one-half year of undergraduate schooling remaining at time of award. Aimed at those with journalism potential but with little opportunity and great need. Must submit portfolio of 6+ photos (picture-story counts as one) or for video journalists, tape with 3 stories. Applicant's school must be in U.S. or Canada.

See Web site or contact NPPF for an application/specific details.

2017—NATIONAL PRESS PHOTOGRAPHERS FOUNDATION (NPPF Television News Scholarship)

3200 Croasdaile Drive, Suite 306
Durham NC 27705
919/383-7246 or 800/289-6772
FAX: 919/383-7261
E-mail: nppa@mindspring.com
Internet: sunsite.unc.edu/nppa/scholarships
AMOUNT: $1,000
DEADLINE(S): MAR 1
FIELD(S): TV News Photojournalism

For students with potential but little opportunity and great need. Must be enrolled in recognized 4-year college/university in U.S. or Canada w/ courses in TV News Photojournalism leading to bachelor's degree. Must be junior or senior at time award is given. Entry should include video tape with examples of work-no more than 3 complete stories (6 minutes total) with voice narration and natural sound. Letter from professor/advisor and biographical sketch w/ goals required.

1 award annually. See Web site or contact NPPF for an application/more information.

2018—NATIONAL PRESS PHOTOGRAPHERS FOUNDATION (Reid Blackburn Scholarship)

3200 Croasdaile Drive, Suite 306
Durham NC 27705
919/383-7246 or 800/289-6772
FAX: 919/383-7261
E-mail: nppa@mindspring.com
Internet: sunsite.unc.edu/nppa/scholarships

AMOUNT: $1,000
DEADLINE(S): MAR 1
FIELD(S): Photojournalism

Must have completed one year at a recognized four-year college/university having courses in photojournalism leading towards a bachelor's degree. Must also have at least one-half year of undergraduate schooling remaining at time of award. Academic ability, aptitude, and financial need are considered. Applicant's school must be in the U.S. or Canada. Portfolio required with entry (6+ photos, picture-story counts as one; video journalists should send a tape of 3 stories).

1 award annually. See Web site or contact NPPF for an application/specific details.

2019—NATIONAL PRESS PHOTOGRAPHERS FOUNDATION, KAPPA ALPHA MU (College Photographer of the Year Competition)

University of Missouri
School of Journalism
105 Lee Hills Hall
Columbia MO 65211
573/882-4442
E-mail: info@cpoy.org
Internet: http://www.cpoy.org

AMOUNT: $250-$1,000 + plaque/certificate and film
DEADLINE(S): MAR 31
FIELD(S): Photojournalism

Undergraduate or graduate students who have NOT worked two years or more as full-time professional photographers may enter. All entries must have been taken or published for the first time between March 1 and Feb 28 of the current year. First prize includes a 3-month paid internship at the Dallas Morning News and a camera as well as above-mentioned prizes. You may enter as many pictures as you like, and there is no entry fee.

See Web site or contact CPOY Coordinator Catherine Mohesky or CPOY Director David Rees for rules and entry form.

2020—NATIONAL URBAN LEAGUE (Reginald K. Brack, Jr. NULITES Scholarship)

120 Wall Street
New York NY 10005
212/558-5373
Internet: http://www.nul.org

AMOUNT: Varies
DEADLINE(S): Varies
FIELD(S): Communications; Journalism; Publishing; Public Relations; Broadcasting

For NULITERS graduating from high school with an interest in communications and former NULITES currently in their freshman or sophomore year of college majoring in communications, journalism, or publishing. Must maintain a minimum 3.0 GPA. Scholarships are based on need, merit, community service, and academic achievement. Letter of recommendation from an Urban League affiliate CEO and/or a NULITES Advisor/Youth Development Director/Education Director is required.

Contact your local Urban League or the National Urban League for an application.

2021—NATIVE AMERICAN JOURNALISTS ASSOCIATION (NAJA Scholarships and Internships)

1433 East Franklin Avenue, Suite 11
Minneapolis MN 55404
612/874-8833
FAX: 612/874-9007
E-mail: najaut@aol.com
Internet: http://www.medill.nwu.edu/naja/

AMOUNT: Varies
DEADLINE(S): MAR 31
FIELD(S): Journalism/Communication

Various scholarships and internships in journalism for Native American journalists and students.

Access Web site or send self-addressed, stamped envelope (SASE) for details.

2022—NATURAL SCIENCES AND ENGINEERING RESEARCH COUNCIL OF CANADA (Undergraduate Student Research Awards in Small Universities)

350 Albert Street
Ottawa Ontario K1A 1H5 CANADA
613/995-5992
FAX: 613/992-533
E-mail: schol@nserc.ca
Internet: http://www.nserc.ca/programs/usrasmen.htm

AMOUNT: $3,600 (max.)
DEADLINE(S): Varies
FIELD(S): Natural Sciences; Engineering

Research awards for Canadian citizens/permanent residents attending eligible institutions, and who have no more than 6 and no fewer than 2 academic terms remaining to complete bachelor's degree. Cumulative GPA of at least 2nd class (B). Must be doing full-time in research and development activities during award tenure.

Students in health sciences not eligible. Students with BAs and who are studying for a second may apply.

2023—NEW YORK FINANCIAL WRITERS' ASSOCIATION (Scholarship Program)

New York NY 10001-0003
800/533-7551

AMOUNT: $3,000
DEADLINE(S): MAR
FIELD(S): Financial Journalism

Open to undergraduate and graduate students enrolled in an accredited college or university in metropolitan New York City and are pursuing a course of study leading to a financial or business journalism career.

Contact NYFWA for an application.

2024—NEW YORK STATE SENATE (Legislative Fellows Program; R. J. Roth Journalism Fellowship; R. A. Wiebe Public Service Fellowship)

NYS Senate Student Programs Office
90 South Swan Street, Rm. 401
Albany NY 12247
518/455-2611
FAX: 518/432-5470

E-mail: students@senate.state.ny.us
AMOUNT: $25,000 stipend (not a scholarship)
DEADLINE(S): MAY (first Friday)
FIELD(S): Political Science; Government; Public Service; Journalism; Public Relations

One year programs for U.S. citizens who are grad students and residents of New York state or enrolled in accredited programs in New York state. Fellows work as regular legislative staff members of the office to which they are assigned. The Roth Fellowship is for communications/journalism majors, and undergrads may be considered for this program.

14 fellowships per year. Fellowships take place at the New York State Legislative Office. Write for complete information.

2025—NEW YORK STATE THEATRE INSTITUTE (Internships in Theatrical Production)

155 River Street
Troy NY 12180
518/274-3573; nysti@crisny.org
Internet: http://www.crisny.org/not-for-profit/nysti/int.htm
AMOUNT: None
DEADLINE(S): None
FIELD(S): Fields of study related to theatrical production, including box office and PR

Internships for college students, high school seniors, and educators-in-residence interested in developing skills in above fields. Unpaid, but college credit is earned. Located at Russell Sage College in Troy, NY. Gain experience in box office, costumes, education, electrics, music, stage management, scenery, properties, performance, and public relations. Interns come from all over the world.

Must be associated with an accredited institution. See Web site for more information. Call Ms. Arlene Leff, Intern Director at above location. Include your postal mailing address.

2026—ORGANIZATION OF CHINESE AMERICANS (Journalist Award)

1001 Connecticut Avenue NW
Suite 601
Washington DC 20036
202/223-5500
FAX: 202/296-0540
E-mail: oca@ocanatl.org
Internet: http://www.ocanatl.org
AMOUNT: $500 (1st prize); $300 (2nd); $200 (3rd)
DEADLINE(S): MAY 1
FIELD(S): Journalism

Open to Chinese American journalists who submit an article from a publication printed since January of current year with national circulation. Purpose of this award is to recognize the best newspaper, magazine, or published piece on social, political, economic, or cultural issues facing Chinese Americans and/or Asian Americans. Submission may be in English or Chinese. Based on completeness, accuracy, readability, and importance to understanding issues.

See Web site or send a self-addressed, stamped envelope to OCA for details.

2027—OUTDOOR WRITERS ASSOCIATION OF AMERICA (Bodie McDowell Scholarship Program)

27 Fort Missoula Road; Suite 1
Missoula MT 59804
406/728-7434
AMOUNT: $2,000-$3,000
DEADLINE(S): FEB
FIELD(S): Outdoor Communications/Journalism

This scholarship is open to undergraduate and graduate students interested in writing about outdoor activities, not including organized sports. Acceptable topics include hiking, backpacking, climbing, etc. Availability varies with school participation.

Send self-addressed, stamped envelope to OWAA for an application.

2028—OUTDOOR WRITERS ASSOCIATION OF AMERICA (OWAA Scholarship Awards)

121 Hickory Street
Missoula MT 59801
406/728-7434
FAX: 406/728-7445
E-mail: owaaa@montana.com
Internet: http://www.owaa.org
AMOUNT: $2,500-$3,500
DEADLINE(S): MAR 1
FIELD(S): Outdoor Communications: Print, Film, Art, Broadcasting, etc.

Open to junior and senior undergraduates and graduate students in above fields. Must attend an accredited school of journalism or mass communications that has registered with OWAA as a scholarship program participant. Based on career goals in outdoor communications, examples of work, letters of recommendation, and academic achievement. Must be U.S. or Canadian citizen/permanent resident.

3+ awards annually. Contact your school or send a self-addressed, stamped envelope to Steve Wagner, Executive Director, for guidelines.

2029—PENNSYLVANIA WOMEN'S PRESS ASSOCIATION (Scholarship)

P.O. Box 152
Sharpsville PA 16150
Written Inquiry
Internet: http://www.regiononline.com/~pwpa/
AMOUNT: At least $750
DEADLINE(S): APR 20
FIELD(S): Print journalism

Scholarship for Pennsylvania residents majoring in print journalism in a four-year or graduate-level program in a Pennsylvania college or university. Must be a junior, senior, or graduate. Selection based on proven journalistic ability, dedication to journalism, and general merit.

Write a 500-word essay summarizing your interest in journalism, your career plans, and any other information on why you should receive this scholarship. You may include a statement of financial need. Send transcript copy, clippings of published work (photocopies OK), and list of your brothers and sisters, their ages and educational status. Send to Teresa Spatara at above address.

2030—PHILADELPHIA COLLEGE OF BIBLE (Scholarships, Grants, and Loans)

Financial Aid Dept
200 Manor Avenue
Langhorne PA 19047
800/366-0049
Internet: http://www.pcb.edu
AMOUNT: Varies
DEADLINE(S): Varies
FIELD(S): Fields of study relating to Christian education

Various scholarships, loans, and grants are available to students attending this undergraduate Bible college in Philadelphia, PA. High school seniors, transfer students, and others may apply. Some programs are for students with outstanding academic achievement, musical talent, or leaderships skills. Some are for dependents of Christian workers, missionaries, or alumni. Some are based on financial need.

Access Web site for details and/or send SASE to school for further information.

2031—PHILLIPS FOUNDATION (Journalism Fellowship Program)

7811 Montrose Road; Suite 100
Potomac MD 20854
301/340-2100
FAX: 301/424-0245
Internet: http://www.phillips.com
AMOUNT: $50,000 (full-time); $25,000 (part-time)
DEADLINE(S): MAR 1
FIELD(S): Journalism

For working print journalists with less than five years of professional experience to complete a one-year writing project supportive of American culture and a free society. Subject matter changes each year.

1 full-time and 2 part-time awards annually. Contact Phillips Foundation for an application.

2032—PRESS CLUB OF DALLAS FOUNDATION (Scholarship)

400 N. Olive
Dallas TX 75201
214/740-9988
AMOUNT: $1,000-$3,000
DEADLINE(S): APR 15
FIELD(S): Journalism and Public Relations

Open to students who are at least sophomore level in undergraduate studies or working toward a masters degree in the above fields in a Texas college or university. This scholarship is renewable by reapplication.

Write to Carol Wortham at the above address for complete information.

2033—PUBLIC RELATIONS STUDENT SOCIETY OF AMERICA (Gary Yoshimura Scholarship)

Director
33 Irving Place
New York NY 10003-2376
Internet: http://www.prssa.org
AMOUNT: $2,400
DEADLINE(S): JAN 15
FIELD(S): Public Relations

Must be a PRSSA member with a minimum 3.0 GPA required. Submit an Official Transcript and Letter of Recommendation from an internship supervisor/employer or faculty advisor. In a 1,000-word essay describe a challenge you have faced, either personally or professionally, and how you have overcome it. Must not exceed two typed pages.

2034—QUILL & SCROLL (Edward J. Nell Memorial Scholarship)

Univ Iowa School of Journalism & Mass Communications
Iowa City IA 52242-1528
319/335-5795
AMOUNT: $500
DEADLINE(S): MAY 10
FIELD(S): Journalism

Open to high school seniors who are winners in the National Writing/Photo Contest (deadline FEB 5th) or Yearbook Excellence Contest (deadline NOV 1st) sponsored by Quill & Scroll and who plan to enroll in an accredited journalism program. Must be U.S. citizen or legal resident.

Contact your journalism teacher or Quill & Scroll for contest information.

2035—RADIO AND TELEVISION NEWS DIRECTORS FOUNDATION (George Foreman Tribute To Lyndon B. Johnson Scholarship)

1000 Connecticut Avenue NW
Suite 615
Washington DC 20036-5302
202/467-5218
FAX: 202/223-4007
E-mail: danib@rtndf.org
Internet: http://www.rtndf.org
AMOUNT: $6,000
DEADLINE(S): MAY 3
FIELD(S): Broadcast/Cable Journalism

Any full-time graduate or undergraduate w/ at least one full year of college remaining may apply. Must be officially enrolled in University of Texas in Austin, be in good standing, and be U.S. citizen. Entry must include 1-3 examples (less than 15 minutes) showing skills on audio/VHS tape, accompanied by scripts and brief statement describing your role in stories, who worked on each one, and what they did. Letter of endorsement and statement explaining career goals required.

1 award annually. See Web site or contact Dani Browne at RTNDF for an application.

2036—RADIO AND TELEVISION NEWS DIRECTORS FOUNDATION (RTNDF Fellowships)

1000 Connecticut Avenue NW
Suite 615
Washington DC 20036-5302
202/467-5218
FAX: 202/223-4007
E-mail: danib@rtndf.org
Internet: http://www.rtndf.org
AMOUNT: $1,000-$2,000
DEADLINE(S): APR 1
FIELD(S): Electronic Journalism

Awards for young journalists in radio or television with 10 years or less experience. Cover letter describing reasons for seeking fellowship and how you intend to use award, letter of recommendation from your news director or general manager, and a script and standard audio cassette/video tape (VHS) of your best work (relevant to fellowship to which you are applying) that is less than 15 minutes are required. Must be U.S. citizen.

6 awards annually. See Web site or contact Dani Browne at RTNDF for an application.

2037—ROSE HILL COLLEGE (Louella Robinson Memorial Scholarship)

P.O. Box 3126
Aiken SC 29802-3126
800/684-3769
FAX: 803/641-0240
E-mail: rosehill@rosehill.edu
Internet: http://www.rosehill.edu
AMOUNT: $10,000/year for four years
DEADLINE(S): Varies
FIELD(S): Liberal arts and humanities curricula

For undergraduate residents of Indian River County, Florida, to attend Rose Hill College in Aiken, South Carolina. The school offers a liberal arts education and follows the Great Books curriculum, a program of reading and seminars.

One annual award. Applicants must meet entry requirements of RHC. Contact above location for details.

2038—ROSE HILL COLLEGE (Scholarships for Children of Eastern Orthodox Priests/Deacons)

P.O. Box 3126
Aiken SC 29802-3126
800/684-3769
FAX: 803/641-0240
E-mail: rosehill@rosehill.edu
Internet: http://www.rosehill.edu
AMOUNT: Full scholarship: $10,000/year for four years
DEADLINE(S): Varies
FIELD(S): Liberal Arts and Humanities Curricula

For undergraduates who are children of Eastern Orthodox Christian priests or deacons to attend Rose Hill College in Aiken, South Carolina. The school offers a liberal arts education and follows the Great Books Curriculum, a program of reading and seminars.

6-10 annual awards. Applicants must meet entry requirements of RHC. Contact above location for details.

2039—ROSE HILL COLLEGE (Scholarships for the Homeschooled)

P.O. Box 3126
Aiken SC 29802-3126
800/684-3769
FAX: 803/641-0240
E-mail: rosehill@rosehill.edu
Internet: http://www.resehill.edu

AMOUNT: Full scholarship: $10,000/year for four years
DEADLINE(S): Varies
FIELD(S): Liberal Arts and Humanities Curricula

For undergraduates who have been homeschooled for three of the last five years of their high school education. For use at Rose Hill College in Aiken, South Carolina. The school offers a liberal arts education and follows the Great Books Curriculum, a program of reading and seminars. Scholarships will be awarded primarily on the basis of an essay which the student will be asked to write.

Four annual awards. Applicants must meet entry requirements of RHC. Contact above location for details.

2040—SAN FRANCISCO CHRONICLE (Chronicle Publishing Company Scholarship)

901 Mission Street
San Francisco CA 94103-2988
415/777-7180
FAX: 415/495-3843
E-mail: logansa@sfgate.com
Internet: http://www.sfgate.com

AMOUNT: $1,500 + summer job
DEADLINE(S): FEB 28
FIELD(S): Print or Broadcast Journalism

Must be a Bay Area high school senior. Two programs: KRON-TV 4 scholarship and summer entry-level job, and SF Chronicle scholarship and summer copy clerk job. Official transcripts and letters of recommendation required; samples of work optional. Must answer essay question (up to 500 words, typed, double-spaced), "If you were given the opportunity to cover a story for NewsCenter 4 or for the SF Chronicle, what would it be and why?" Financial need NOT a factor.

2 awards annually. Contact Sandy Logan at the *SF Chronicle* for an application.

2041—SCRIPPS HOWARD FOUNDATION (Robert P. Scripps Graphic Arts Scholarships)

312 Walnut Street
P.O. Box 5380
Cincinnati OH 45201-5380
513/977-3847
FAX: 513/977-3800
E-mail: cottingham@scripps.com
Internet: http://www.scripps.com/foundation

AMOUNT: Varies
DEADLINE(S): Varies
FIELD(S): Newspaper Operations Management

Students must be attending the University of Rochester (NY) and majoring in newspaper operations management.

5 awards annually. Applications are available at the university.

2042—SCRIPPS HOWARD FOUNDATION (Ted Scripps Scholarships & Lecture)

312 Walnut Street
P.O. Box 5380
Cincinnati OH 45201-5380
513/977-3847
FAX: 513/977-3800
E-mail: cottingham@scripps.com
Internet: http://www.scripps.com/foundation

AMOUNT: $3,000 + medal
DEADLINE(S): Varies
FIELD(S): Journalism

Students must be attending the University of Nevada at Reno and majoring in journalism.

4 awards annually. Applications are available at the university.

2043—SOCIETY FOR TECHNICAL COMMUNICATION (Undergraduate Scholarships)

901 N. Stuart Street, Suite 904
Arlington VA 22203
703/522-4114
FAX: 703/522-2075
E-mail: stc@stcva.org
Internet: http://www.stcva.org/scholarships.html

AMOUNT: $2,000
DEADLINE(S): FEB 15
FIELD(S): Technical Communication

Open to full-time undergraduate students who have completed at least one year of study and are enrolled in an accredited 2- or 4-year degree program for career in any area of technical communication: technical writing, editing, graphic design, multimedia art, etc.

Awards tenable at recognized colleges and universities in U.S. and Canada. Fourteen awards per year—seven undergraduate and seven graduate. See Web site and/or write for complete information.

2044—SOCIETY OF PROFESSIONAL JOURNALISTS (Mark of Excellence Awards Competition)

16 South Jackson Street
Greencastle IN 46135-1514
765/653-3333
FAX: 765/653-4631
E-mail: spj@link2000.net
Internet: http://spj.org/prodevelopment/MOE97/moe97/rules.htm

AMOUNT: Varies
DEADLINE(S): JAN 31
FIELD(S): All fields of study

A competition for professional journalists, though journalists may be studying in any field. Awards are for print or broadcast journalism.

See Web site for details.

2045—SOCIETY OF SATELLITE PROFESSIONALS INTERNATIONAL

225 Reinekers Lane, Suite 600
Alexandria VA 22314
703/857-3717
FAX: 703/857-6335
E-mail: neworbit@aol.com;
Internet: http://www.sspi.org

AMOUNT: $1,500 to $4,000
DEADLINE(S): DEC 1
FIELD(S): Satellites as related to communications, domestic and international telecommunications policy, remote sensing, journalism, law, meteorology, energy, navigation, business, government, and broadcasting services

Various scholarships for students studying in the above fields.

Access Web site for details and applications or send a self-addressed, stamped envelope (SASE) for a complete listing.

2046—SOIL AND WATER CONSERVATION SOCIETY (SWCS Internships)

7515 N.E. Ankeny Road
Ankeny IA 50021-9764

515/289-2331 or 800/THE-SOIL
FAX: 515/289-1227
E-mail: charliep@swcs.org
Internet: http://www.swcs.org
AMOUNT: Varies—most are uncompensated
DEADLINE(S): Varies
FIELD(S): Journalism, marketing, database management, meeting planning, public policy research, environmental education, landscape architecture

Internships for undergraduates and graduates to gain experience in the above fields as they relate to soil and water conservation issues. Internship openings vary through the year in duration, compensation, and objective. SWCS will coordinate particulars with your academic advisor.

Contact SWCS for internship availability at any time during the year or see Web site for jobs page.

2047—SPACE COAST CREDIT UNION (Two-Year Scholarships)

Marketing Dept.
P.O. Box 2470
Melbourne FL 32902
Internet: http://www.sccu.com/scholarship/
AMOUNT: $750/year, two years; $1,000 bonus if go on for Bachelors
DEADLINE(S): APR 15
FIELD(S): Math, Economics, Science, Computer Science, Marketing, Journalism, Political Science

Must be graduating from a high school in Brevard, Volusia, Flagler, or Indian River counties, be a member of SCCU, have a minimum 3.0 GPA, planning to attend a two-year Florida institution of higher education for an associates degree, and be willing to write a 200-word essay on the topic "Why credit unions are valuable to society."

Four annual awards. Students going on to complete a four-year degree could be eligible for a bonus scholarship of $1,000 for the next two years. For membership information or an application, see our Web page or write to the above address.

2048—SPORTS JOURNALISM INSTITUTE (Scholarships/Internships)

Sports Illustrated
1271 Avenue of the Americas
New York NY 10020-1393
212/522-6407
FAX: 212/522-4543
E-mail: sandrite@aol.com
AMOUNT: $500 for 6-week internship
DEADLINE(S): JAN (date varies yearly)
FIELD(S): Print journalism with sports emphasis

Ten six-week scholarships for college juniors to support internships in sports journalism. Women and minorities are especially encouraged to apply.

Contact Sandy Baily at above location for details.

2049—STATE NEWS (Scholarships)

Michigan State University
343 Student Services
E. Lansing MI 48824-1113
E-mail: recruiter@statenews.com
Internet: http://statenews.com/scholarship/
AMOUNT: $2,000/year for 4 years + job
DEADLINE(S): FEB 5
FIELD(S): Journalism; Advertising

Open to high school seniors who will start at MSU in the fall. Must have an above-average GPA and have demonstrated a strong interest in high school journalism or advertising through their newspapers and yearbooks. Recipients work in paying positions at *The State News* after the first semester of their freshman year, either in the newsroom or in the advertising department. *State News* pay will be in addition to the scholarship. May major in any academic program.

2 awards annually. See Web site or contact Ben Schwartz, *State News* General Manager, for an application.

2050—STUDENT CONSERVATION ASSOCIATION (SCA Resource Assistant Program)

P.O. Box 550
Charlestown NH 03603
603/543-1700
FAX: 603/543-1828
E-mail: internships@sca-inc.org
Internet: http://www.sca-inc.org
AMOUNT: $1,180-$4,725
DEADLINE(S): Varies
FIELD(S): Environment and related fields

Must be 18 and U.S. citizen; need not be student. Fields: Agriculture, archaeology, anthropology, botany, caves, civil/environmental engineering, environmental education, fisheries, forests, herpetology, history, living history/roleplaying, visitor services, landscape architecture/environmental design, paleontology, recreation/resource/range management, trail maintenance/construction, wildlife management, geology, hydrology, library/museums, surveying...

900 positions in U.S. and Canada. Send $1 for postage for application; outside U.S./Canada, send $20.

2051—THE CARTER CENTER MENTAL HEALTH PROGRAM (Rosalynn Carter Fellowships for Mental Health Journalism)

One Copenhill
453 Freedom Parkway
Atlanta GA 30307
404/420-5165
FAX: 404/420-5158
E-mail: jgates@emory.edu
Internet: http://www.emory.edu/CARTER_CENTER
AMOUNT: $10,000 + 2 trips to Center
DEADLINE(S): MAY 1
FIELD(S): Print or Broadcast Journalism

Five one-year fellowships for journalists to pursue an individual project related to mental health or mental illness. Must have at least two years of experience in print or broadcast journalism. Fellows are matched with a member of the Advisory Board for mentoring during their fellowship year.

Call or write for application information.

2052—THE CONCLAVE (Talent-Based Scholarships)

4517 Minnetonka Boulevard, #104
Minneapolis MN 55416
612/927-4487
FAX: 612/927-6427
E-mail: info@theconclave.com
Internet: http://www.theconclave.com
AMOUNT: Tuition
DEADLINE(S): APR 14
FIELD(S): Broadcasting

Open to U.S. citizens/permanent residents who have received a high school diploma and wish to attend a nine-month program at either the Brown Institute in Minneapolis or Specs-Howard in Detroit, Michigan. Financial need NOT a factor.

2 awards annually. Not renewable. Contact John Sweeney at the Conclave for an application.

2053—THE FUND FOR INVESTIGATIVE JOURNALISM, INC. (Grants for Journalists)

5120 Kenwood Drive
Annandale VA 22003
703/750-3849

E-mail: fundfij@aol.com
Internet: http://fij.org
AMOUNT: $500 and up
DEADLINE(S): JUN 1; NOV 1
FIELD(S): Journalism

Grants for journalists working outside the protection and backing of major news organizations. Limited to journalists seeking help for investigative pieces involving corruption, malfeasance, incompetence, and societal ills in general as well as for media criticism. No application form. Write a letter outlining the story, what he or she expects to prove, how this will be done, and the sources for the proof.

Include a letter of commitment from an editor or publisher to consider publishing or broadcasting the final product. Check Web site for details.

2054—THE NATIONAL ITALIAN AMERICAN FOUNDATION (Communications Scholarship)

1860 19th Street NW
Washington DC 20009
202/530-5315
AMOUNT: $2,500
DEADLINE(S): MAY 31
FIELD(S): Journalism or communications majors

For students of Italian family heritage majoring in journalism or communications. Write a 2-3 page typed essay on a family member or a personality you consider: "An Italian American Hero." Also, please submit an essay of your best work. Also please submit an example of your best work.

Two awards given. Also considered are academic merit, financial need, and community service. Write for application and details.

2055—THE PUBLIC RELATIONS SOCIETY OF AMERICA (Multicultural Affairs Scholarship)

33 Irving Place
New York NY 10003-2376
212/995-2230
FAX: 212/995-0757
TDD: 212/254-3464
AMOUNT: $1,500
DEADLINE(S): APR 11
FIELD(S): Communications studies/public relations

For students whose ethnic backgrounds are African-American, Hispanic, Asian, Native American, Alaskan Native, or Pacific Islander interested in practicing in the career of public relations. Must be a full-time undergraduate student at an accredited four-year college or university, at least a junior, and have a GPA of 3.0 or better.

Two awards given.

2056—THE REUTER FOUNDATION (Fellowships at Oxford for Journalists)

The Director, 85 Fleet Street
London EC4P 4AJ ENGLAND
(+44) 171 542 2913
E-mail: rtrfoundation@easynet.co.uk
Internet: http://www.foundation.reuters.com/usjourn.html
AMOUNT: Travel, tuition, and living allowance
DEADLINE(S): OCT 31
FIELD(S): Journalism—print and broadcast

Fellowships for working journalists at Green College, Oxford University, in London for working journalists with at least five years experience. (Program is for three months.) Subjects include news writing, TV news production, and reporting on the environment, and medical, international, and business news.

Access Web site or write for application details. Application form is on Web site.

2057—THE REUTER FOUNDATION (Fellowships for Journalists)

13 Norham Gardens
Oxford OX2 6PS ENGLAND
01865 513576
FAX: 01865 513576
Internet: http://www.green.ox.ac.uk/rfp
AMOUNT: Travel, tuition, and living allowance
DEADLINE(S): Varies
FIELD(S): Journalism—all areas

Fellowships for working journalists at Green College, Oxford University, in London. Programs vary in length (three to nine months), and deadline dates vary for application. Subjects include news writing, TV news production, and reporting on the environment, and medical, international, and business news.

Access Web site or write for application details.

2058—THE REUTER FOUNDATION (Fellowships for Journalists: Oxford, Stanford, & Bordeaux)

The Director, 85 Fleet Street
London EC4P 4AJ ENGLAND
(+44) 171 542 2913
E-mail: rtrfoundation@easynet.co.uk
Internet: http://www.foundation.reuters.com/unijour.html
AMOUNT: Travel, tuition, and living allowance
DEADLINE(S): DEC 31
FIELD(S): Journalism

Fellowships at Green College (Oxford University), in London; Stanford University in Calif., U.S.; or L'Universite de Bordeaux III, France for journalists with at least five years experience. Must be fluent in the language of the school attended. Open to journalists of all media and to specialist writers in economic, environmental, medical and scientific subjects. Three, six, or nine months.

Fully funded fellowships are for journalists from the developing world and central/eastern Europe. English-speaking journalists from other parts of the world may apply for self-funded fellowships. Application form and details are on Web site.

2059—THE REUTER FOUNDATION (Fellowships in Medical Journalism)

The Director, 85 Fleet Street
London EC4P 4AJ ENGLAND
(+44) 171 542 2913
E-mail: rtrfoundation@easynet.co.uk
Internet: http://www.foundation.reuters.com/medic.html
AMOUNT: Travel, tuition, and living allowance
DEADLINE(S): SEP 15 (Columbia); OCT 31 (Oxford)
FIELD(S): Medical Journalism

Fellowships for English-speaking journalists, world-wide, for research and study relating to medical issues. Tenable at the Universities of Oxford, England, and Columbia, New York, U.S. The Oxford award is for one term within the Reuter Foundation Programme for international journalists at Green College at Oxford. Terms start in October, January, and April. The Columbia award is for one semester starting in January. Must be between ages of 28 and 45.

Access application form and information are on Web site or write for application details.

2060—THE REUTER FOUNDATION (The Alva Clarke Memorial Fellowship for Journalists From the Caribbean)

The Director, 85 Fleet Street
London EC4P 4AJ ENGLAND

(+44) 171 542 2913
E-mail: rtrfoundation@easynet.co.uk
Internet: http://www.foundation.reuters.com/alva.html
AMOUNT: Travel, tuition, and living allowance
DEADLINE(S): DEC 31
FIELD(S): Journalism

Fellowships at Green College (Oxford University) in London for full-time journalists from a country in the Caribbean. Must be fluent in English. For three months, starting in October, January, or April.

Application form and details are on Web site.

2061—THE REUTER FOUNDATION (The Mogadishu Fellowship for Photojournalists)

The Director, 85 Fleet Street
London EC4P 4AJ ENGLAND
(+44) 171 542 2913
E-mail: rtrfoundation@easynet.co.uk
Internet: http://www.foundation.reuters.com/photo.html
AMOUNT: Travel, tuition, and living allowance
DEADLINE(S): DEC 31
FIELD(S): Photojournalism

A one-semester practical study opportunity for full-time photojournalists from Africa. Tenable at the School of Journalism at the University of Missouri-Columbia, U.S. from January to May. Fellows may also spend one or two weeks with the Reuters News Pictures Desk in Washington DC or London. Must be under age 35 and have at least three years professional experience.

Access Web site or write for application details.

2062—THE REUTER FOUNDATION (The Peter Sullivan Memorial Fellowships for News Graphics Journalists)

The Director, 85 Fleet Street
London EC4P 4AJ ENGLAND
(+44) 20 7542 7015
E-mail: rtrfoundation@easynet.co.uk
AMOUNT: Travel, tuition, and living allowance
DEADLINE(S): SEP 30
FIELD(S): Journalism-news graphics

Fellowships for working, full-time news graphics journalists with at least five years experience. The three-month program offers an opportunity for talented news graphic journalists and designers to create a university study plan suited to their individual needs. Must be fluent in either Spanish or English.

Access Web site or write for application details. Application form is on Web site.

2063—THE REUTER FOUNDATION (The Willie Vicoy Fellowship for Photojournalists)

The Director, 85 Fleet Street
London EC4P 4AJ ENGLAND
(+44) 171 542 2913
E-mail: rtrfoundation@easynet.co.uk
Internet: http://www.foundation.reuters.com/photo.html
AMOUNT: Travel, tuition, and living allowance
DEADLINE(S): DEC 31
FIELD(S): Photojournalism

A one-semester practical study opportunity for full-time photojournalists from the developing world and countries in transition. Tenable at the School of Journalism at the University of Missouri-Columbia, U.S. from August to December. Fellows may also spend one or two weeks with the Reuters News Pictures Desk in Washington DC or London. Must be under age 35 and have at least three years professional experience.

Access Web site or write for application details.

2064—THE SOUTHERN CALIFORNIA CHAPTER OF WOMEN IN CABLE AND TELECOMMUNICATIONS (The Jeanne Cardinal Grant)

c/o Pamela Drake
Avenue TV Cable Service
P.O. Box 1458
Ventura CA 93002
AMOUNT: $1,000
DEADLINE(S): JAN 31
FIELD(S): Telecommunications

Grants are available to junior and senior class women who are pursuing a degree in the telecommunications industry. A minimum GPA of 3.0 is required. Applicants must be involved in at least one school-related organization or participate in community service.

2065—THE UNIVERSITY OF NEW MEXICO FOUNDATION (The Kelly Richmond Memorial Fund)

Univ. of New Mexico
Hodgin Hall, 2nd Floor
Albuquerque NM 87131
Internet: http://www.ire.org/resources/scholarship
AMOUNT: Varies
DEADLINE(S): None
FIELD(S): Journalism: Investigative reporting

Scholarship for journalism students at the University of New Mexico to honor Kelly Richmond, an award-winning journalist who died of lung cancer at age 33.

Write for details.

2066—UNITED METHODIST COMMUNICATIONS (Leonard Perryman Communications Scholarships)

Nashville TN 37202-0320
615/742-5140
FAX: 615/742-5404
E-mail: scholarships@umcom.umc.org
Internet: http://www.umcom.org/scholarships
AMOUNT: $2,500
DEADLINE(S): MAR 15
FIELD(S): Religious Journalism/Communications

Open to students of Christian faith who are ethnic minority undergraduate juniors and seniors enrolled in accredited U.S. schools of communication or journalism (print, electronic, or audiovisual). Candidates should be pursuing career in religious communication.

2 awards annually. Not renewable. See Web site or contact Jackie Vaughan at UMC for an application.

2067—UNIVERSITY OF MARYLAND (College of Journalism Scholarships)

Journalism Building, Room 1117
College Park MD 20742-7111
301/405-2399
Internet: http://www.inform.umd.edu/jour
AMOUNT: $250-$1,500
DEADLINE(S): FEB 15
FIELD(S): Journalism

Variety of journalism scholarships, prizes, and awards tenable at the University of Maryland. Application forms for all scholarships are available at the address above.

Access Web site or write for complete information.

2068—UNIVERSITY OF OKLAHOMA—H.H. HERBERT SCHOOL OF JOURNALISM AND MASS COMMUNICATION (Undergraduate Scholarships)

860 Van Vleet Oval, Room 101
Norman OK 73019

405/325-2721
AMOUNT: $5,000/year
DEADLINE(S): FEB
FIELD(S): Journalism: Print or Broadcast, Advertising, Electronic Media, News Communication, Professional Writing, Public Relations

For undergraduate students studying in the above fields who plan to attend the University of Oklahoma. Interview is part of acceptance process.

Contact David Dary at above location for details.

2069—UTA ALUMNI ASSOCIATION (Karin McCallum Scholarship)

University of Texas at Arlington
Box 19457
Arlington TX 76019
Internet: http://www.uta.edu/alumni/scholar.htm
AMOUNT: $250
DEADLINE(S): Varies
FIELD(S): Speech-Communications

Must be a full-time junior or senior at the University of Texas at Arlington. Must submit transcript, professional resume, and letter of recommendation from a Communications professor.

1 award annually. Contact UTA Alumni Association for an application.

2070—UTA ALUMNI ASSOCIATION (Lloyd Clark Scholarship Journalism)

University of Texas at Arlington
Box 19457
Arlington TX 76019
Internet: http://www.uta.edu/alumni/scholar.htm
AMOUNT: $250
DEADLINE(S): Varies
FIELD(S): Journalism

Must be a full-time junior or higher with at least 15 hours completed at the University of Texas at Arlington and have a commitment to a career in journalism. Must show noticeable academic achievement and evidence of success in journalism. Financial need may be considered. Writing sample required.

1 award annually. Contact UTA Alumni Association for an application.

2071—W. EUGENE SMITH MEMORIAL FUND, INC. (Grants)

c/o ICP
1130 Fifth Avenue
New York NY 10128
212/860-1777
FAX: 212/860-1482
AMOUNT: $20,000; $5,000
DEADLINE(S): JUL 15
FIELD(S): Photojournalism

Career support for photojournalists of any nationality. Must submit a photographic project with a written proposal, illustrated in the humanistic manner of W. Eugene Smith. Financial need NOT a factor.

2 awards annually. Not renewable. Contact Ms. Anna Winand for an application.

2072—WILLIAM RANDOLPH HEARST FOUNDATION (Journalism Awards Program)

90 New Montgomery Street
Suite 1212
San Francisco CA 94105
415/543-6033
FAX: 415/243-0760
AMOUNT: $500-$3,000
DEADLINE(S): Varies (OCT-APR)
FIELD(S): Print/Photojournalism; Broadcast News

Journalism awards program offers monthly competitions open to undergraduate college journalism majors who are currently enrolled in one of the 107 participating journalism schools.

6 print journalism, 3 photojournalism, and 4 broadcast news competitions annually. Entry forms and details on monthly contests are available ONLY through the journalism department of participating schools.

2073—WOMEN'S SPORTS FOUNDATION (Jackie Joyner-Kersee and Zina Garrison Minority Internships)

Eisenhower Park
East Meadow NY 11554
800/227-3988
FAX: 516/542-4716
E-mail: WoSport@aol.com
Internet: http://www.lifetimetv.com/WoSport
AMOUNT: $4,000-$5,000
DEADLINE(S): Ongoing
FIELD(S): Sports-related fields

Provides women of color an opportunity to gain experience in a sports-related career and interact in the sports community. May be undergraduates, college graduates, graduate students, or women in a career change. Internships are located at the Women's Sports Foundation in East Meadow, New York.

4-6 awards annually. See Web site or write to above address for details.

HISTORY

2074—AMERICAN HISTORICAL ASSOCIATION (Michael Kraus Research Award Grant)

400 A Street SE
Washington DC 20003
202/544-2422
FAX: 202/544-8307
E-mail: aha@theaha.org
Internet: http://www.theaha.org
AMOUNT: $800
DEADLINE(S): FEB 1
FIELD(S): American Colonial History

For research in American colonial history with particular reference to intercultural aspects of American and European relations. Must be AHA member.

See Web site or contact AHA for details.

2075—ASSOCIATION FOR WOMEN IN SCIENCE EDUCATIONAL FOUNDATION (Ruth Satter Memorial Award)

1200 New York Avenue NW
Suite 650
Washington DC 20005
202/326-8940 or 800/886-AWIS
E-mail: awis@awis.org
Internet: http://www.awis.org
AMOUNT: $1,000
DEADLINE(S): JAN 16
FIELD(S): Various Sciences and Social Sciences

Scholarships for female doctoral students who have interrupted their education three years or more to raise a family. Summary page, description of research project, resume, references, transcripts, biographical sketch, and proof of eligibility from department head required. U.S. citizens may attend any graduate institution; noncitizens must be enrolled in U.S. institutions.

See Web site or write to above address for more information or an application.

2076—AUSTRALIAN WAR MEMORIAL (John Treloar Grants-In-Aid & AWM Research Fellowship)

GPO Box 345
Canberra ACT 2601 AUSTRALIA
02/6243 4210

FAX: 02/6243 4325
E-mail: ian.hodges@awm.gov.au
Internet: http://www.awm.gov.au
AMOUNT: $A6,000 (max. grant); $A12,000 (max. fellowship)
DEADLINE(S): Varies
FIELD(S): Australian Military History

Grants and fellowships for students at any level in any country to study Australian Military History. Financial need NOT a factor.

Not renewable. Contact Ian Hodges at AWM for an application.

2077—BRITISH COLUMBIA HERITAGE TRUST (Scholarships)

P.O. Box 9818, Stn Prov Govt.
Victoria BC V8W 9W3 CANADA
250/356-1433
FAX: 250/356-7796
E-mail: heritage@tbc.gov.bc.ca
AMOUNT: $5,000
DEADLINE(S): FEB 1
FIELD(S): British Columbia History; Architecture; Archaeology; Archival Management

Open to graduate students who are Canadian citizens or permanent residents. Criteria are scholarly record and academic performance, educational and career objectives, and proposed program of study.

Write for complete information.

2078—CHINESE HISTORICAL SOCIETY OF SOUTHERN CALIFORNIA (CHHSC Scholarships)

P.O. Box 862647
Los Angeles CA 90086-2647
E-mail: chssc@chssc@org
Internet: http://www.chssc.org
AMOUNT: $1,000
DEADLINE(S): MAR 10
FIELD(S): History

Scholarship for sophomores and juniors currently enrolled at a college or University in Southern California. Must be studying Chinese-American Studies in the humanities or social sciences.

2079—CHRISTIAN A. JOHNSON ENDEAVOR FOUNDATION (Native American Fellows)

John F. Kennedy School of Government, Harvard University
79 John F. Kennedy Street
Cambridge MA 02138
617/495-1152
FAX: 617/496-3900
Internet: http://www.ksg.harvard.edu/hpaied/index.htm
AMOUNT: Varies
DEADLINE(S): MAY 1
FIELD(S): American Indian Affairs

Fellowships for students of Native American ancestry who attend a John F. Kennedy School of Government degree program. Applicant, parent, or grandparent must hold membership in a federally or state-recognized tribe, band, or other organized group of Native Americans. Must be committed to a career in American Indian affairs. Awards based on merit and need.

Renewable, based on renomination and availability of funds. To apply, contact John F. Kennedy School of Government at above address.

2080—EAST TEXAS HISTORICAL ASSOCIATION (Ottis Lock Endowment Awards)

P.O. Box 6223; SFA Station
Nacogdoches TX 75962
936/468-2407
FAX: 936/468-2190
E-mail: amcdonald@sfasu.edu
Internet: http://leonardo sfasu.edu/etha
AMOUNT: $500
DEADLINE(S): MAY 1
FIELD(S): History; Social Science

Open to residents of East Texas who will be pursuing undergraduate or graduate studies at an East Texas college or university.

Renewable with adequate progress toward degree. See Web site or contact East Texas Historical Association for an application.

2081—HARRY S. TRUMAN LIBRARY INSTITUTE (Harry S. Truman Book Award)

500 W. U.S. Highway 24
Independence MO 64050-1798
816/833-0425
FAX: 816/833-2715
E-mail: library@truman.nara.gov
Internet: http://www.trumanlibrary.org/institut/scholars.htm
AMOUNT: $1,000
DEADLINE(S): JAN 20
FIELD(S): American History: Harry S. Truman or His Era

Award is for the best book written within a two-year period dealing primarily and substantially with some aspect of U.S. history between April 12, 1945 and January 20, 1953, or with the public career of Harry S. Truman. Three copies of each book entered must be submitted.

Awarded only in even-numbered years. See Web site or contact Book Awards Administrator for guidelines.

2082—HARRY S. TRUMAN LIBRARY INSTITUTE (Undergraduate Student Grant)

500 W. U.S. Highway 24
Independence MO 64050-1798
816/833-0425
FAX: 816/833-2715
E-mail: library@truman.nara.gov
Internet: http://www.trumanlibrary.org/institut/scholars.htm
AMOUNT: $1,000 (max.)
DEADLINE(S): DEC 1
FIELD(S): American History: Harry S. Truman or His Era

For undergraduate students writing a senior thesis on some aspect of life and career of Harry S. Truman or public and foreign policy issues which were prominent during the Truman years. Award is intended to offset expenses for research conducted at Truman Library. Applicants must describe in writing the proposed project and its rationale, and indicate how a research experience at the Truman Library will contribute to applicant's future development.

1 award annually. See Web site or contact Grants Administrator for an application. Applicants notified of decision within six weeks after deadline.

2083—HILLSDALE COLLEGE (Freedom as Vocation Scholarship)

33 E. College Street
Hillsdale MI 49242-1298
517/437-7341
Internet: http://www.hillsdale.edu
AMOUNT: Varies
DEADLINE(S): None
FIELD(S): Business; History; Political Science; Economics

Open to Hillsdale College undergraduates who maintain a minimum 3.0 GPA and commit to a series of courses in the above fields. Student must rank in top 20% of class and top 10% of test scores. Must possess excellent communications, public speaking, and leadership skills and demonstrate outstanding character and citizenship. Financial need NOT a factor.

Renewable. No application process; students are selected. See Web site for details.

2084—INSTITUTE FOR HUMANE STUDIES (Humane Studies Fellowship)

3301 N. FairFAX: Drive, Suite 440
Arlington VA 22201-4432
703/993-4880 or 800/697-8799
FAX: 703/993-4890
E-mail: ihs@gmu.edu
Internet: http://www.TheIHS.org

AMOUNT: $12,000 (max.)
DEADLINE(S): DEC
FIELD(S): Social Sciences; Liberal Arts; Law; Humanities; Jurisprudence; Journalism

Open to graduate and advanced undergraduate or law students pursuing degrees at any accredited domestic or foreign college/university. Based on academic performance, demonstrated interest in the classical liberal tradition, and potential to contribute to the advancement of a free society.

90 awards annually. Apply online or contact IHS for an application.s

2085—INSTITUTE OF INTERNATIONAL EDUCATION (National Security Education Program-Undergraduate Scholarships)

1400 K Street NW, 6th Floor
Washington DC 20005-2403
202/326-7697 or
800/618-NSEP (6737)
E-mail: nsep@iie.org
Internet: http://www.iie.org/nsep/

AMOUNT: Varies: up to $8,000/semester
DEADLINE(S): FEB 8
FIELD(S): Open to all majors; preference to applied sciences, engineering, business, economics, math, computer science, international affairs, political science, history, and the policy sciences.

For study abroad OUTSIDE the U.S., Canada, Australia, New Zealand, and Western Europe. For study in areas deemed critical to U.S. national security. Applications available on U.S. campuses from August through early December. Or contact organization for details.

Inquire at above location for details.

2086—INTERNATIONAL MEDIEVAL NSTITUTE (K.H. Wick Bursary Fund for Attending Meetings)

University of Leeds
Parkinson Bldg., Room 1.03
Leeds LSs2 9JT ENGLAND UK
+44 (113) 233-3614
FAX: +44 (113) 233-3616
E-mail: imc@leeds.ac.uk
Internet: http://www.leeds.ac.uk/imi/imc/khwick.htm

AMOUNT: Varies
DEADLINE(S): Varies
FIELD(S): Medieval history

This fund is to help pay for attendance at the International Medieval Congress held at Leeds University in England each July. Open to students and independent and retired scholars. Preference is given to scholars from Central and Eastern Europe.

Contact listed office for details.

2087—JAMES MADISON MEMORIAL FELLOWSHIP FOUNDATION (Fellowships)

2000 K Street NW, Suite 303
Washington DC 20006
202/653-870
FAX: 202/653-6045
Internet: http://www.jamesmadison.com

AMOUNT: Tuition, fees, books, and room/board
DEADLINE(S): MAR 1
FIELD(S): Education: American History, American Government, Social Studies

Open to U.S. citizens/nationals who are teachers, or planning to become teachers, in above fields at the secondary school level. Must currently possess a bachelor's degree, or plan to receive one no later than August 31. Fellows must teach above subjects in grades 7-12 for no less than one year for each full year of study under the fellowship. Proposed graduate study should contain substantial constitutional coursework.

See Web site or contact Foundation for an application.

2088—KOSCIUSZKO FOUNDATION (Summer Sessions in Poland and Rome)

15 E. 65th Street
New York NY 10021-6595
212/734-2130
FAX: 212/628-4552
E-mail: thekf@pegasusnet.com
Internet: http://www.kosciuszkofoundation.org

AMOUNT: Varies
DEADLINE(S): Varies
FIELD(S): Polish Studies; History; Literature; Art; Economics; Social Studies; Language; Culture

Open to undergraduate and graduate students, graduating high school students who are 18 or older, and persons of any age who are not enrolled in a college/university program. Study programs are offered in Poland and Rome from mid-June through the end of August in above fields. Must be U.S. citizen/permanent resident.

See Web site or send a self-addressed, stamped envelope to Addy Tymczyszyn, Summer Studies Abroad Coordinator, for an application.

2089—LOUISIANA STATE UNIVERSITY AT SHREVEPORT (Walter O. Bigby Scholarship)

Bronson Hall
Shreveport LA 71115-2399
318/797-5371
Internet: http://www.lsus.edu

AMOUNT: Up to $500/semester
DEADLINE(S): Varies
FIELD(S): Political Science; English; History; Law

Recipient must be entering the junior or senior year at LSUS with a major in political science, English, or history; may also be enrolled in some other Liberal Arts degree program if preparing to enter law school.

Contact the Dean's Office in the College of Liberal Arts at LSU.S.for an application.

2090—DAUGHTERS OF AMERICAN REVOLUTION

1776 D Street NW
Washington DC 20006-5392
202/628-1776
Internet: http://www.dar.org

AMOUNT: $1,000
DEADLINE(S): FEB 15
FIELD(S): History; Political Science; Government; Economics

Open to undergraduate juniors and seniors (US citizens) attending an accredited U.S. college or university. Awards are placed on deposit with school. Awards are judged on academic excellence, commitment to field of study, and need. Affiliation with DAR not required.

Not renewable. See Web site or send a self-addressed, stamped envelope for an application or more information.

2091—NATIONAL SPACE CLUB (Dr. Robert H. Goddard Historical Essay Award)

2000 L Street NW, Suite 710
Washington DC 20036-4907
202/973-8661

AMOUNT: $1,000 + plaque
DEADLINE(S): DEC 4

FIELD(S): Aerospace History

Essay competition open to any U.S. citizen on a topic dealing with any significant aspect of the historical development of rocketry and astronautics. Essays should not exceed 5,000 words and should be fully documented. Will be judged on originality and scholarship.

Previous winners not eligible. Send self-addressed, stamped envelope for complete information.

2092—NATURAL SCIENCES AND ENGINEERING RESEARCH COUNCIL OF CANADA (Undergraduate Student Research Awards in Small Universities)

350 Albert Street
Ottawa Ontario K1A 1H5 CANADA
613/995-5992
FAX: 613/992-533
E-mail: schol@nserc.ca
Internet: http://www.nserc.ca/programs/usrasmen.htm
AMOUNT: $3,600 (max.)
DEADLINE(S): Varies
FIELD(S): Natural Sciences; Engineering

Research awards for Canadian citizens/permanent residents attending eligible institutions, and who have no more than 6 and no fewer than 2 academic terms remaining to complete bachelor's degree. Cumulative GPA of at least 2nd class (B). Must be doing full-time in research and development activities during award tenure.

Students in health sciences not eligible. Students with BAs and who are studying for a second may apply.

2093—NAVAL HISTORICAL CENTER (Internship Program)

Washington Navy Yard
901 M Street SE
Washington DC 20374-5060
202/433-6901
FAX: 202/433-8200
E-mail: efurgol@nhc.navy.mil
Internet: http://www.history.navy.mil
AMOUNT: $400 possible honoraria; otherwise, unpaid
DEADLINE(S): None
FIELD(S): Education; History; Public Relations; Design

Registered students of colleges/universities and graduates thereof are eligible for this program, which must be a minimum of 3 weeks, full- or part-time. Four specialties available: Curator, Education, Public Relations, and Design. Interns receive orientation and assist in their departments, and must complete individual project which contributes to Center. Must submit a letter of recommendation, unofficial transcript, and writing sample of not less than 1,000 words.

Contact Dr. Edward M. Furgol, Curator, for an application.

2094—PHI ALPHA THETA HISTORY HONOR SOCIETY (Nels Andrew N. Cleven Founder's Paper Prize Awards)

6201 Hamilton Boulevard, Suite 116
Allentown PA 18106-9691
800/394-8195
FAX: 610/336-4929
E-mail: phialpha@ptd.net
AMOUNT: $150-$250
DEADLINE(S): JUL 1
FIELD(S): History

Open to undergraduate and graduate Phi Alpha Theta members who submit essays on a historical topic. Should combine original historical research on a significant subject, based on source material and manuscripts, if possible, with good English composition and superior style. Must include bibliography. Papers should not exceed 25 typewritten pages in length. Dr. George P. Hammond Prize and Dr. Lynn W. Turner Prize included in this category.

3 awards annually. Contact PAT National Headquarters for guidelines.

2095—PHI ALPHA THETA HISTORY HONOR SOCIETY/WORLD HISTORY ASSOCIATION (World History Paper Prize)

6201 Hamilton Boulevard, Suite 116
Allentown PA 18106-9691
800/394-8195
FAX: 610/336-4929
E-mail: phialpha@ptd.net
AMOUNT: $200
DEADLINE(S): JUL 1
FIELD(S): World History

Open to undergraduate and graduate students who submit an essay on world history, which is one that examines any historical issue with global implications. Must be member of either Phi Alpha Theta or the World History Association, and must have composed the paper while enrolled at an accredited college/university during previous academic year (proven by letter from faculty). Bibliography must be included. Papers must be no longer than 25 typewritten pages.

2 awards annually. Contact PAT National Headquarters for guidelines.

2096—ROCK ISLAND ARSENAL MUSEUM (Richard C. Maguire Scholarship)

Rock Island IL 61299-5000
309/782-5021
AMOUNT: $1,000
DEADLINE(S): MAR
FIELD(S): History

For students who intend to complete a master's degree or higher in history or a related field. Interested applicants should submit a self-addressed stamped envelope for full information and requirements.

2097—ROSE HILL COLLEGE (Louella Robinson Memorial Scholarship)

P.O. Box 3126
Aiken SC 29802-3126
800/684-3769
FAX: 803/641-0240
E-mail: rosehill@rosehill.edu
Internet: http://www.rosehill.edu
AMOUNT: $10,000/year for four years
DEADLINE(S): Varies
FIELD(S): Liberal arts and humanities curricula

For undergraduate residents of Indian River County, Florida, to attend Rose Hill College in Aiken, South Carolina. The school offers a liberal arts education and follows the Great Books curriculum, a program of reading and seminars.

One annual award. Applicants must meet entry requirements of RHC. Contact above location for details.

2098—ROSE HILL COLLEGE (Scholarships for Children of Eastern Orthodox Priests/Deacons)

P.O. Box 3126
Aiken SC 29802-3126
800/684-3769
FAX: 803/641-0240
E-mail: rosehill@rosehill.edu
Internet: http://www.rosehill.edu
AMOUNT: Full scholarship: $10,000/year for four years
DEADLINE(S): Varies
FIELD(S): Liberal Arts and Humanities Curricula

For undergraduates who are children of Eastern Orthodox Christian priests or deacons to attend Rose Hill College in Aiken, South Carolina. The school offers a liberal arts education and follows the Great Books Curriculum, a program of reading and seminars.

6-10 annual awards. Applicants must meet entry requirements of RHC. Contact above location for details.

2099—ROSE HILL COLLEGE (Scholarships for the Homeschooled)

P.O. Box 3126
Aiken SC 29802-3126
800/684-3769
FAX: 803/641-0240
E-mail: rosehill@rosehill.edu
Internet: http://www.resehill.edu
AMOUNT: Full scholarship: $10,000/year for four years
DEADLINE(S): Varies
FIELD(S): Liberal Arts and Humanities Curricula

For undergraduates who have been homeschooled for three of the last five years of their high school education. For use at Rose Hill College in Aiken, South Carolina. The school offers a liberal arts education and follows the Great Books Curriculum, a program of reading and seminars. Scholarships will be awarded primarily on the basis of an essay which the student will be asked to write.

Four annual awards. Applicants must meet entry requirements of RHC. Contact above location for details.

2100—SMITHSONIAN INSTITUTION (Minority Student Internship Program)

Office of Fellowships
750 9th Street NW, Suite 9300
Washington DC 20560-0902
202/275-0655
FAX: 202/275-0489
E-mail: siofg@ofg.si.edu
Internet: http://www.si.edu/research+study
AMOUNT: $350/week + possible travel expenses
DEADLINE(S): Varies
FIELD(S): Humanities; Environmental and Cultural Studies; Natural History; Earth Science; Art History; Biology

Ten-week, full-time internships in residence at the Smithsonian are open to U.S. minority students who wish to participate in research or museum-related activities in above and related fields. Must be undergraduates or beginning graduate students with a minimum 3.0 GPA. Must submit essay, resume, and official transcript.

Contact the Office of Fellowships or see Web site for an application.

2101—SONOMA CHAMBOLLE-MUSIGNY SISTER CITIES, INC. (Henri Cardinaux Memorial Scholarship)

Chamson Scholarship Committee
P.O. Box 1633
Sonoma CA 95476-1633
707/939-1344
FAX: 707/939-1344
E-mail: Baileysci@vom.com
AMOUNT: Up to $1,500 (travel + expenses)
DEADLINE(S): JUL 15
FIELD(S): Culinary Arts; Wine Industry; Art; Architecture; Music; History; Fashion

Hands-on experience working in above or similar fields and living with a family in small French village in Burgundy or other French city. Must be Sonoma County, CA, resident at least 18 years of age and be able to communicate in French. Transcripts, employer recommendation, photograph, and essay (stating why, where, and when) required.

1 award. Nonrenewable. Also offers opportunity for candidate in Chambolle-Musigny to obtain work experience and cultural exposure in Sonoma, CA.

2102—SONS OF THE REPUBLIC OF TEXAS (Presidio La Bahia Award)

1717 8th Street
Bay City TX 77414
409/245-6644
E-mail: srttexas@srttexas.org
Internet: http://www.srttexas.org
AMOUNT: $1,200+
DEADLINE(S): SEP 30
FIELD(S): Texas History: Spanish Colonial Period

A competition on the best book, paper, or article which promotes suitable preservation of relics, appropriate dissemination of data, and research into Texas heritage with particular attention to the Spanish Colonial period. Research writings have proved in the past to be the most successful type of entry, however, careful consideration will be given to other literary forms, as well as art, architecture, and archaeological discovery. Entries accepted June-September.

Contact Melinda Williams, SRT Executive Secretary, for a brochure.

2103—STUDENT CONSERVATION ASSOCIATION (SCA Resource Assistant Program)

P.O. Box 550
Charlestown NH 03603
603/543-1700
FAX: 603/543-1828
E-mail: internships@sca-inc.org
Internet: http://www.sca-inc.org
AMOUNT: $1,180-$4,725
DEADLINE(S): Varies
FIELD(S): Environment and related fields

Must be 18 and U.S. citizen; need not be student. Fields: Agriculture, archaeology, anthropology, botany, caves, civil/environmental engineering, environmental education, fisheries, forests, herpetology, history, living history/roleplaying, visitor services, landscape architecture/environmental design, paleontology, recreation/resource/range management, trail maintenance/construction, wildlife management, geology, hydrology, library/museums, surveying...

900 positions in U.S. and Canada. Send $1 for postage for application; outside U.S./Canada, send $20.

2104—THE J. EDGAR HOOVER FOUNDATION

50 Gull Point Road
Hilton Head Island SC 29928
803/671-5020
AMOUNT: $500
DEADLINE(S): Ongoing
FIELD(S): Government, law enforcement

Scholarships for the study of government, the promotion of good citizenship, and law enforcement. The foundation strives to safeguard the heritage and freedom of the U.S., to promote good citizenship through an appreciation of the American form of government, and to combat communism or any other ideology or doctrine opposed to the principles set forth in the U.S. Constitution.

Send letter to Cartha D. De Loach, Chair, at above address.

2105—U.S. INSTITUTE OF PEACE (National Peace Essay Contest)

1200 17th Street NW; Suite 200
Washington DC 20036
202/457-1700
FAX: 202/429-6063
E-mail: essay_contest@usip.org
Internet: http://www.usip.org
AMOUNT: $1,000-$10,000
DEADLINE(S): JAN
FIELD(S): Political Science; U.S. History

1,500-word essay contest for high school students on the U.S. response to international conflict. No restrictions as to citizenship/residency.

Not renewable. See Web site or contact USIP for specific guidelines.

2106—UCLA CENTER FOR 17TH- AND 18TH-CENTURY STUDIES (Fellowships)

UCLA
310 Royce Hall
Los Angeles CA 90095-1404
310/206-8552
FAX: 310/206-8577
E-mail: c1718cs@humnet.ucla.edu
Internet : http://www.humnet.ucla.edu/humnet/C1718CS/Postd.htm#AhmGet

AMOUNT: $1,000-$18,400
DEADLINE(S): Varies
FIELD(S): British Literature/History (17th and 18th Centuries)

Undergraduate stipends, graduate assistantships, and postdoctoral fellowships are for advanced study and research regarding British literature and history of the 17th and 18th centuries.

Contact the Center for current year's theme and an application.

LAW

2107—AMERICAN BAR FOUNDATION (Montgomery Summer Research Fellowships for Minority Undergraduate Students)

750 N. Lake Shore Drive
Chicago IL 60611
312/988-6500
FAX: 312/988-6579
E-mail: fellowships@abfn.org
Internet: http://www.abf-sociolegal.org

AMOUNT: $3,600 stipend
DEADLINE(S): MAR 1
FIELD(S): Social Sciences; Humanities; Law

Summer research opportunity open to sophomore and junior undergraduates who are Native American, African American, Mexican, Puerto Rican, or other minority. Must be U.S. citizen or permanent resident and have at least a 3.0 GPA. Students are assigned a mentor and participate in seminars; must also work at the Foundation's office in Chicago for 35 hours per week for 10 weeks. Essay, transcripts, and letter of recommendation required.

4 awards annually; announced in April. See Web site or contact ABF for an application.

2108—ASSOCIATION OF CERTIFIED FRAUD EXAMINERS (Scholarships)

The Gregor Building
716 West Avenue
Austin TX 78701
800/245-3321 or 512/478-9070
FAX: 512/478-9297
E-mail: acfe@tpoint.net
Internet: http://www.cfenet.com

AMOUNT: $500
DEADLINE(S): MAY 15
FIELD(S): Accounting and/or criminal justice

Scholarships for full-time graduate or undergraduate students majoring in accounting or criminal justice degree programs. Awards are based on overall academic achievement, three letters of recommendation, and an original 250-word essay explaining why the applicant deserves the award and how fraud awareness will affect his or her professional career development. Also required is a letter of recommendation from a Certified Fraud Examiner or a local CFE Chapter.

Contact organization for applications and further details.

2109—BOYS AND GIRLS CLUBS OF SAN DIEGO

1761 Hotel Circle So., Suite 123
San Diego CA 92108
619/298-3520

AMOUNT: $2,000/year
DEADLINE(S): MAY 15
FIELD(S): Medicine; Law; Engineering; Political Science

Open to male high school seniors planning a career in one of the above fields. Must be residents of Imperial, Riverside, Orange, San Diego, or Los Angeles counties in California. Boys and Girls Club affiliation NOT required.

$10 application fee. Renewable up to 4 years. Send a self-addressed, stamped envelope to Boys and Girls Club for an application after January 1.

2110—COLLEGE MISERICORDIA (Presidential Scholarships)

301 Lake Street
Dallas PA 18612-1098
800/852-7675
Internet: http://www.miseri.edu

AMOUNT: Full or part tuition
DEADLINE(S): MAR 1
FIELD(S): Prelaw or the humanities

Scholarships for incoming freshmen to this coeducational Catholic college in Pennsylvania. High school senior applicants must rank in the upper 20% of their classes and have achieved SAT or ACT scores in the 8th percentile or better.

Obtain applications from the Admissions Office.

2111—DEPARTMENT OF JUSTICE (Graduate Research Fellowships: Tomorrow's Research Community)

810 7th Street NW
Washington DC 20531
202/514-5981
E-mail: mamalian@ojp.usdoj.gov

AMOUNT: $15,000
DEADLINE(S): SEP 14; JAN 15
FIELD(S): Law

Applicants should submit a proposal about their graduate project, including information on research strategy and a timeline. Proposal should demonstrate how the project will contribute to crime and justice policy.

2112—DEPARTMENT OF JUSTICE CANADA (Legal Studies for Aboriginal People Program)

284 Wellington Street
EMB Suite 6206
Ottawa Ontario K1A 0H8 CANADA
613/941-0388 or 888/606-5111
FAX: 613/941-2269
E-mail: LSAP@justice.gc.ca
Internet: canada.justice.gc.ca/Recrutement/bourse/intermediaire_en.html

AMOUNT: Varies
DEADLINE(S): MAR 31 (pre-law); JUN 1 (law school)
FIELD(S): Law

Must be non-status Indian or Metis of Canadian citizenship, living in Canada, who has received acceptance to or is registered in pre-law orientation or law school. Purpose of program is to promote equitable representation of Aboriginal people in the legal profession.

See Web site or contact Mireille Provost, Program Administrator, for an application.

2113—H. FLETCHER BROWN FUND (Scholarships)

c/o PNC Bank; Trust Dept.
P.O. Box 791
Wilmington DE 19899

302/429-1186
AMOUNT: Varies
DEADLINE(S): APR 15
FIELD(S): Medicine; Dentistry; Law; Engineering; Chemistry

Open to U.S. citizens born in Delaware and still residing in Delaware. For 4 years of study (undergrad or grad) leading to a degree that enables applicant to practice in chosen field.

Scholarships are based on need, scholastic achievement, and good moral character. Applications available in February. Write for complete information.

2114—H. FLETCHER BROWN TRUST (Scholarships)

222 Delaware Avenue, 16th Floor
Wilmington DE 19899
302/429-1338
AMOUNT: Varies
DEADLINE(S): APR 9
FIELD(S): Chemistry; Engineering; Law; Medicine; Dentistry

Open to financially needy native-born DELAWARE residents ONLY who are pursuing an undergraduate degree. Must have minimum 1,000 SAT score and rank in upper 20% of class. Interview required.

Send self-addressed, stamped envelope to Donald Drois, Account Administrator, PNC Bank, at above address for an application.

2115—INSTITUTE FOR HUMANE STUDIES (Humane Studies Fellowship)

3301 N. FairFAX: Drive, Suite 440
Arlington VA 22201-4432
703/993-4880 or 800/697-8799
FAX: 703/993-4890
E-mail: ihs@gmu.edu
Internet: http://www.TheIHS.org
AMOUNT: $12,000 (max.)
DEADLINE(S): DEC
FIELD(S): Social Sciences; Liberal Arts; Law; Humanities; Jurisprudence; Journalism

Open to graduate and advanced undergraduate or law students pursuing degrees at any accredited domestic or foreign college/university. Based on academic performance, demonstrated interest in the classical liberal tradition, and potential to contribute to the advancement of a free society.

90 awards annually. Apply online or contact IHS for an application.

2116—INSTITUTE FOR HUMANE STUDIES (Koch Summer Fellow Program)

3401 N. FairFAX: Drive, Suite 440
Arlington VA 22201-4432
703/993-4880 or 800/697-8799
FAX: 703/993-4890;
E-mail: ihs@gmu.edu
Internet: http://www.TheIHS.org
AMOUNT: $1,500 + airfare and housing
DEADLINE(S): FEB 15
FIELD(S): Economics; Public Policy; Law; Government; Politics

Open to undergraduates and graduates to build skills and gain experience by participating in an 8-week summer internship program. Includes two week-long seminars, the internship, and research and writing projects with professionals. Must submit college transcripts, essays, and application. Financial need NOT a factor.

32 awards annually. Not renewable. Apply online or contact IHS for an application.

2117—INSTITUTE FOR HUMANE STUDIES (Summer Seminars Program)

3401 N. FairFAX: Drive, Suite 440
Arlington VA 22201-4432
703/993-4880 or 800/697-8799
FAX: 703/993-4890
E-mail: ihs@gmu.edu
Internet: http://www.TheIHS.org
AMOUNT: Free summer seminars, including room/board, lectures, seminar materials, and books
DEADLINE(S): MAR
FIELD(S): Social Sciences; Humanities; Law; Journalism; Public Policy; Education; Film; Writing; Economics; Philosophy

Open to college students, recent graduates, and graduate students who share an interest in learning and exchanging ideas about the scope of individual rights, free markets, the rule of law, peace, and tolerance.

See Web site for seminar information or to apply online or contact IHS for an application.

2118—INTER-AMERICAN BAR ASSOCIATION (Writing Competition)

1211 Connecticut Avenue NW
Suite 202
Washington DC 20036
202/393-1217
FAX: 202/393-1241
E-mail: iaba@iaba.org
http://www.iaba.org
AMOUNT: $400-$800
DEADLINE(S): FEB 15
FIELD(S): Law

Writing competition for law students on one of the Association's themes. Papers may be prepared in English, Spanish, Portuguese, or French.

Contact organization for details.

2119—INTERNATIONAL ASSOCIATION OF ARSON INVESTIGATORS (John Charles Wilson Scholarship)

12770 Boenker Road
St. Louis MO 63044
314/739-4224
FAX: 314/739-4219
Internet: http://www.fire-investigators.org
AMOUNT: Varies
DEADLINE(S): FEB 15
FIELD(S): Police or Fire Sciences, including Fire Investigation and related subjects

Open to IAAI members, their immediate families, and non-members who are recommended and sponsored by members in good standing. Awards are for undergraduate study in above areas at accredited two and four year institutions.

3 awards annually. Transcripts and 500-word essay describing background and goals required. Write to the Executive Director at above address for more information.

2120—JEWISH VOCATIONAL SERVICE (Academic Scholarship Program)

One S. Franklin Street
Chicago IL 60606
312/357-4500
FAX: 312/855-3282
TTY: 312/855-3282
E-mail: jvschicago@jon.cjfny.org
AMOUNT: $5,000 (max.)
DEADLINE(S): MAR 1
FIELD(S): "Helping" Professions; Mathematics; Engineering; Sciences; Communications (at Univ IL only); Law (certain schools in IL only)

Open to Jewish men and women legally domiciled in the greater Chicago metropolitan area, who are identified as having promise for significant contributions in their chosen careers, and are in need of financial assistance for full-time academic programs in above areas. Must have entered undergraduate junior year in career programs requiring no postgrad education, be in graduate/professional school, or be in a vo-tech training program. Interview required.

Renewable. Contact JVS for an application between December 1 and February 15.

2121—JOHN RANKIN FUND (Travel Scholarships in Accounting or Law)

Trustees of the John Rankin Fund,
c/o Jonathan Stone Esq., The Hall
East Ilsley, Newbury RG20 7LW
ENGLAND
Written Inquiry

AMOUNT: 5,000 pounds
DEADLINE(S): MAR 31
FIELD(S): Accounting, Law

A biannual award for either a law or accounting student, barrister, solicitor, or qualified accountant to study abroad. Applicant must be under 26 on Oct. 1 of the year of application.

Write to organization for information

2122—LOUISIANA STATE UNIVERSITY AT SHREVEPORT (Walter O. Bigby Scholarship)

Bronson Hall
Shreveport LA 71115-2399
318/797-5371
Internet: http://www.lsus.edu

AMOUNT: Up to $500/semester
DEADLINE(S): Varies
FIELD(S): Political Science; English; History; Law

Recipient must be entering the junior or senior year at LSUS with a major in political science, English, or history; may also be enrolled in some other Liberal Arts degree program if preparing to enter law school.

Contact the Dean's Office in the College of Liberal Arts at LSUS for an application.

2123—NATIONAL SCIENCES AND ENGINEERING RESEARCH COUNCIL OF CANADA (Undergraduate Scholarships)

Scholarships/Fellowships Division
350 Albert Street
Ottawa Ontario K1A 1H5 CANADA
613/996-2009
FAX: 613/996-2589
E-mail: schol@nserc.ca
Internet: http://www.nserc.ca

AMOUNT: Up to $3,600
DEADLINE(S): Varies
FIELD(S): Natural Sciences, Engineering, Biology, or Chemistry

Open to Canadian citizens or permanent residents working towards degrees in science or engineering. Academic excellence and research aptitude are considerations.

Write for complete information.

2124—NATIONAL FEDERATION OF THE BLIND (Howard Brown Rickard Scholarship)

805 Fifth Avenue
Grinnell IA 50112
515/236-3366

AMOUNT: $3,000
DEADLINE(S): MAR 31
FIELD(S): Law; Medicine; Engineering; Architecture; Natural Sciences

For legally blind students pursuing or planning to pursue a full-time postsecondary course of study in the U.S. Based on academic excellence, service to the community, and financial need. Membership NOT required.

1 award annually. Renewable. Contact Mrs. Peggy Elliot, Scholarship Committee Chairman, for an application.

2125—NATIONAL ITALIAN AMERICAN FOUNDATION (Assunta Luchetti Martino Scholarship for International Studies)

1860 19th Street NW
Washington DC 20009-5599
202/530-5315

AMOUNT: $1,000
DEADLINE(S): MAY 31
FIELD(S): International studies

For undergraduates of Italian ancestry who are pursuing degrees in international studies.

Considerations are academic merit, financial need, and commmunity service. Write for application and further information.

2126—NATURAL SCIENCES AND ENGINEERING RESEARCH COUNCIL OF CANADA (Undergraduate Student Research Awards in Small Universities)

350 Albert Street
Ottawa Ontario K1A 1H5 CANADA
613/995-5992
FAX: 613/992-533
E-mail: schol@nserc.ca
Internet: http://www.nserc.ca/programs/usrasmen.htm

AMOUNT: $3,600 (max.)
DEADLINE(S): Varies
FIELD(S): Natural Sciences; Engineering

Research awards for Canadian citizens/permanent residents attending eligible institutions, and who have no more than 6 and no fewer than 2 academic terms remaining to complete bachelor's degree. Cumulative GPA of at least 2nd class (B). Must be doing full-time in research and development activities during award tenure.

Students in health sciences not eligible. Students with BAs and who are studying for a second may apply.

2127—NEW YORK STATE HIGHER EDUCATION SERVICES CORPORATION (N.Y. State Regents Professional/Health Care Opportunity Scholarships)

Cultural Education Center
Room 5C64
Albany NY 12230
518/486-1319
Internet: http://www.hesc.com

AMOUNT: $1,000-$10,000/year
DEADLINE(S): Varies
FIELD(S): Medicine and dentistry and related fields, architecture, nursing, psychology, audiology, landscape architecture, social work, chiropractic, law, pharmacy, accounting, speech language pathology

For NY state residents who are economically disadvantaged and members of a minority group underrepresented in the chosen profession and attending school in NY state. Some programs carry a service obligation in New York for each year of support. For U.S. citizens or qualifying noncitizens.

Medical/dental scholarships require one year of professional work in NY.

2128—PRESIDENT'S COMMISSION ON WHITE HOUSE FELLOWSHIPS

712 Jackson Place NW
Washington DC 20503
202/395-4522
FAX: 202/395-6179
E-mail: almanac@ace.esusda.gov

AMOUNT: Wage (up to GS-14 Step 3)
DEADLINE(S): DEC 1
FIELD(S): Public Service; Government; Community Involvement; Leadership

Mid-career professionals spend one year as special assistants to senior executive branch officials in Washington. Highly competitive. Nonpartisan; no age or educational requirements. Fellowship year runs September 1 through August 31.

1,200 candidates applying for 11 to 19 fellowships each year. Write for complete information.

2129—RAYMOND J. HARRIS EDUCATION TRUST

P.O. Box 7899
Philadelphia PA 19101-7899
Written Inquiry
AMOUNT: Varies
DEADLINE(S): FEB 1
FIELD(S): Medicine, Law, Engineering, Dentistry, or Agriculture

Scholarships for Christian men to obtain a professional education in medicine, law, engineering, dentistry, or agriculture at nine Philadelphia area colleges.

Contact Mellon Bank, N.A. at above location for details and the names of the nine colleges.

2130—ROYAL THAI EMBASSY, OFFICE OF EDUCATIONAL AFFAIRS (Revenue Dept. Scholarships for Thai Students)

1906 23rd Street NW
Washington DC 20008
202/667-9111 or 202/667-8010
FAX: 202/265-7239
AMOUNT: Varies
DEADLINE(S): APR
FIELD(S): Computer Science (Telecommunications), Law, Economics, Finance, Business Administration

Scholarships for students under age 35 from Thailand who have been accepted to study in the U.S or U.K. for the needs of the Revenue Dept., Ministry of Finance. Must pursue any level degree in one of the above fields.

Selections are based on academic records, employment history, and advisor recommendations.

2131—SOCIETY OF SATELLITE PROFESSIONALS INTERNATIONAL (SSPI Scholarships)

225 Reinekers Lane, Suite 600
Alexandria VA 22314
703/857-3717
FAX: 703/857-6335
E-mail: neworbit@aol.com
Internet: http://www.sspi.org
AMOUNT: $1,500 to $4,000
DEADLINE(S): DEC 1
FIELD(S): Satellites as related to communications, domestic and international telecommunications policy, remote sensing, journalism, law, meteorology, energy, navigation, business, government, and broadcasting services.

Various scholarships for students studying in the above fields.

Access Web site for details and applications or send a self-addressed, stamped envelope (SASE) for a complete listing.

2132—STUDENT CONSERVATION ASSOCIATION (SCA Resource Assistant Program)

P.O. Box 550
Charlestown NH 03603
603/543-1700
FAX: 603/543-1828
E-mail: internships@sca-inc.org
Internet: http://www.sca-inc.org
AMOUNT: $1,180-$4,725
DEADLINE(S): Varies
FIELD(S): Environment and related fields

Must be 18 and U.S. citizen; need not be student. Fields: Agriculture, archaeology, anthropology, botany, caves, civil/environmental engineering, environmental education, fisheries, forests, herpetology, history, living history/roleplaying, visitor services, landscape architecture/environmental design, paleontology, recreation/resource/range management, trail maintenance/construction, wildlife management, geology, hydrology, library/museums, surveying...

900 positions in U.S. and Canada. Send $1 for postage for application; outside U.S./Canada, send $20.

2133—UNITARIAN UNIVERSALIST ASSN. (Otto M. Stanfield Legal Scholarship)

25 Beacon Street
Boston MA 02144
617/742-2100
AMOUNT: Varies
DEADLINE(S): FEB 15
FIELD(S): Law

Scholarships for law students. Applicants must be Unitarian Universalists.

No phone calls please.

2134—UNIVERSITY OF SOUTH DAKOTA (Criminal Justice Dept. Scholarships)

414 East Clark Street
Vermillion SD 57069-2390
605/677-5446
E-mail: admiss@usd.edu
Internet: http://www.usd.edu/cjus/scholarships.htm#orderofpolice
AMOUNT: Varies
DEADLINE(S): Varies
FIELD(S): Criminal Justice; Political Science; Public Service

The University of South Dakota's Department of Crimal Justice administers 17 different award programs in the above fields. Some require a high GPA and/or financial need, others require an essay or research project.

See Web site or contact USD for specific details of each award. The Criminal Justice Department gives out an average of $77,000/year to USD students.

2135—WESTERN SOCIETY OF CRIMINOLOGY (Student Paper Competition)

Criminal Justice Division
Cal State Univ; 6000 J Street
Sacramento CA 95819-6085
Internet: http://www.sonoma.edu/CJA/WSC/WSCstu00.html
AMOUNT: $125 (1st prize); $75 (2nd) + certificates
DEADLINE(S): DEC 15
FIELD(S): Criminology

Any student currently enrolled full- or part-time in an academic program at either the undergraduate or graduate level may enter. All entries must be papers relating to criminology. Papers must be 10 to 20 pages, typewritten, double-spaced on 8 1/2 x 11 white paper, using a standard format for the organization of papers and citations. Two copies must be submitted.

Send your entries to the attention of Dr. Miki Vohryzek-Bolden in the Criminal Justice Division at California State University. Winners will be notified in writing by February 7.

2136—WOMEN IN DEFENSE (HORIZONS Scholarship Foundation)

NDIA
2111 Wilson Boulevard, Suite 400
Arlington VA 22201-3061
703/247-2552
FAX: 703/522-1820
E-mail: cbanks@mciworld.com
Internet: http://www.ndia.org/wid/
AMOUNT: $500+
DEADLINE(S): NOV 1; JUL 1
FIELD(S): Engineering; Computer Science; Physics; Math; Business; Law; International Relations; Political Science; Operations Research; Economics; National Security/Defense

Open to women employed/planning careers in defense/national security areas. Must be currently enrolled full- or part-time at an accredited college/university at the graduate or undergraduate junior/senior level. Must have a minimum 3.25 GPA, demonstrate financial need, and be

U.S. citizen. Based on academic achievement, work experience, objectives, and recommendations.

Renewable. See Web site or MUST send self-addressed, stamped envelope to Courtney Banks for application.

2137—WYOMING PEACE OFFICERS ASSOCIATION (WPOA Scholarships)

1556 Riverbend Dr.
Douglas WY 82633
307/358-3617
FAX: 307/358-9603
AMOUNT: $500/semester
DEADLINE(S): JUL 31
FIELD(S): All fields of study; Law Enforcement

Available to dependents of active (dues current), lifetime, or deceased WPOA members regardless of field of study or college attended, or students planning to enroll in a law enforcement program at a Wyoming college or university. Applicants must complete 12 semester credit hours and maintain at least a "C" average. Scholarship is awarded upon completion of each semester.

4 awards annually. Renewable up to four semesters. Contact Lucille Taylor at WPOA for an application.

POLITICAL SCIENCE

2138—AIR FORCE RESERVE OFFICER TRAINING CORPS (AFROTC Scholarships)

551 E. Maxwell Boulevard
Maxwell AFB AL 36112-6106
334/953-7783
AMOUNT: Full tuition, books, and fees for all 4 years of college
DEADLINE(S): DEC 1
FIELD(S): Science; Engineering; Business; Political Science; Psychology; Geography; Foreign Studies; Foreign Language

Competitive scholarships based on individual merit to high school seniors and graduates who have not completed any full-time college work. Must be a U.S. citizen between the ages of 17-27. Must also have GPA of 2.5 or above, be in top 40% of class, and complete Applicant Fitness Test. Cannot be a single parent. Your college/university must offer AFROTC.

2,300 awards annually. Contact above address for application packet.

2139—AMERICA ISRAEL PUBLIC AFFAIRS COMMITTEE (Internships)

440 First Street NW; Suite 600
Washington DC 20001
202/639-5327
Internet: http://www.aipac.org
AMOUNT: Internship
DEADLINE(S): SEP 15; DEC 1; JAN 15; APR 1
FIELD(S): U.S.-Israel Issues

For highly qualified pro-Israel students for internships in national and regional offices working to strengthen the U.S.-Israel relationship. Interns are expected to return to campus to promote pro-Israel political activity. Cover letter stating interest, resume indicating political experience (student government, etc.) and involvement, one-page typewritten essay about involvement in pro-Israel work on campus, and letter of recommendation from AIPAC campus liaison required.

Contact Steve Bocknek at AIPAC for an application.

2140—AMERICAN BAR FOUNDATION (Montgomery Summer Research Fellowships for Minority Undergraduate Students)

750 N. Lake Shore Drive
Chicago IL 60611
312/988-6500
FAX: 312/988-6579
E-mail: fellowships@abfn.org
Internet: http://www.abf-sociolegal.org
AMOUNT: $3,600 stipend
DEADLINE(S): MAR 1
FIELD(S): Social Sciences; Humanities; Law

Summer research opportunity open to sophomore and junior undergraduates who are Native American, African American, Mexican, Puerto Rican, or other minority. Must be U.S. citizen or permanent resident and have at least a 3.0 GPA. Students are assigned a mentor and participate in seminars; must also work at the Foundation's office in Chicago for 35 hours per week for 10 weeks. Essay, transcripts, and letter of recommendation required.

4 awards annually; announced in April. See Web site or contact ABF for an application.

2141—ASSOCIATION FOR WOMEN IN SCIENCE EDUCATIONAL FOUNDATION (Ruth Satter Memorial Award)

1200 New York Avenue NW
Suite 650
Washington DC 20005
202/326-8940 or 800/886-AWIS
E-mail: awis@awis.org
Internet: http://www.awis.org
AMOUNT: $1,000
DEADLINE(S): JAN 16
FIELD(S): Various Sciences and Social Sciences

Scholarships for female doctoral students who have interrupted their education three years or more to raise a family. Summary page, description of research project, resume, references, transcripts, biographical sketch, and proof of eligibility from department head required. U.S. citizens may attend any graduate institution; noncitizens must be enrolled in U.S. institutions.

See Web site or write to above address for more information or an application.

2142—BOYS AND GIRLS CLUBS OF SAN DIEGO (Spence Reese Scholarship Fund)

1761 Hotel Circle So., Suite 123
San Diego CA 92108
619/298-3520
AMOUNT: $2,000/year
DEADLINE(S): MAY 15
FIELD(S): Medicine; Law; Engineering; Political Science

Open to male high school seniors planning a career in one of the above fields. Must be residents of Imperial, Riverside, Orange, San Diego, or Los Angeles counties in California. Boys and Girls Club affiliation NOT required.

$10 application fee. Renewable up to 4 years. Send a self-addressed, stamped envelope to Boys and Girls Club for an application after January 1.

2143—CANADIAN BUREAU FOR INTERNATIONAL EDUCATION (Celanese Canada Internationalist Council Fellowships)

220 Laurier Avenue W., Suite 1100
Ottawa Ontario K1P 5Z9 CANADA
613/237-4820
FAX: 613/237-1073
E-mail: smelanson@cbie.ca
Internet: http://www.cbie.ca
AMOUNT: $10,000 Canadian
DEADLINE(S): MAR 1
FIELD(S): International Relations

Open to university graduates from all disciplines of study. For Canadians who hold at least one university degree or are in the final year of a degree program. The latest degree must normally have been awarded no longer than five years from the date of application. For study, research, and/or work outside Canada. May include more than one location.

125-150 awards annually. Contact CBIE for an application.

2144—CHRISTIAN A. JOHNSON ENDEAVOR FOUNDATION (Native American Fellows)

John F. Kennedy School of Government, Harvard University
79 John F. Kennedy Street
Cambridge MA 02138
617/495-1152
FAX: 617/496-3900
Internet: http://www.ksg.harvard.edu/hpaied/index.htm

AMOUNT: Varies
DEADLINE(S): MAY 1
FIELD(S): American Indian Affairs

Fellowships for students of Native American ancestry who attend a John F. Kennedy School of Government degree program. Applicant, parent, or grandparent must hold membership in a federally or state-recognized tribe, band, or other organized group of Native Americans. Must be committed to a career in American Indian affairs. Awards based on merit and need.

Renewable, based on renomination and availability of funds. To apply, contact John F. Kennedy School of Government at above address.

2145—CONFERENCE OF MINORITY PUBLIC ADMINISTRATORS (Scholarships and Travel Grants)

P.O. Box 3010
Fort Worth TX 76113
817/871-8325
Internet: http://www.compa.org

AMOUNT: $400 (travel grants); up to $1,500 (academic year)
DEADLINE(S): Varies
FIELD(S): Public administration/public affairs

COMPA offers two academic scholarships, at least five travel grants, and a $1,000 gift to the college that has the largest number of student registrants at its annual conference. Travel grants are for attending the conference. For minorities and women pursuing full-time education in the above fields and committed to excellence in public service and administration in city, county, state, and federal governments.

Contact Edwin Cook at above location for details.

2146—CUBAN AMERICAN NATIONAL FOUNDATION (The Mas Family Scholarships)

7300 NW 3 Terrace
Miami FL 33122
305/592-7768
FAX: 305/592-7889
E-mail: canfnet.org
Internet: http://www.canfnet.org

AMOUNT: Individually negotiated
DEADLINE(S): MAR 15
FIELD(S): Engineering, Business, International Relations, Economics, Communications, Journalism

For Cuban-Americans students, graduates and undergraduates, born in Cuba or direct descendants of those who left Cuba. Must be in top 10% of high school class or maintain a 3.5 GPA in college.

10,000 awards/year. Recipients may reapply for subsequent years. Financial need considered along with academic success, SAT and GRE scores, and leadership potential. Essays and proof of Cuban descent required.

2147—EAST TEXAS HISTORICAL ASSOCIATION (Ottis Lock Endowment Awards)

P.O. Box 6223; SFA Station
Nacogdoches TX 75962
936/468-2407
FAX: 936/468-2190
E-mail: amcdonald@sfasu.edu
Internet: http://leonardosfasu.edu/etha

AMOUNT: $500
DEADLINE(S): MAY 1
FIELD(S): History; Social Science

Open to residents of East Texas who will be pursuing undergraduate or graduate studies at an East Texas college or university.

Renewable with adequate progress toward degree. See Web site or contact East Texas Historical Association for an application.

2148—EISENHOWER TRANSPORTATION (Fellowship Program)

National Highway Institute, HH1-20
Federal Highway Administration
Arlington VA 22203
703/235-0538
Internet: http://www.nhi.fhwa.dot.gov

AMOUNT: Varies
DEADLINE(S): MAR
FIELD(S): Transportation

For full-time students enrolled in a transportation-related discipline who plan to enter the transportation profession.

2149—EPILEPSY FOUNDATION OF AMERICA (Behavioral Sciences Student Fellowships)

4351 Garden City Drive
Landover MD 20785-2267
301/459-3700 or 800/EFA-1000
TDD: 800/332-2070
FAX: 301/577-2684
Internet: http://www.epilepsyfoundation.org

AMOUNT: $2,000
DEADLINE(S): FEB 1
FIELD(S): Epilepsy Research/Practice; Sociology; Social Work; Psychology; Anthropology; Nursing; Economics; Vocational Rehabilitation; Counseling; Political Science

Three-month fellowships awarded to undergraduate and graduate students in above fields for work on a project during the summer or other free period. Students propose an epilepsy-related study or training project to be carried out at a U.S. institution of their choice. A preceptor must accept responsibility for supervision of the student and the project.

Contact EFA for an application. Notification by June 1.

2150—FUND FOR AMERICAN STUDIES (Institutes on Political Journalism; Business & Government Affairs & Comparative Political & Economic Systems)

1526 18th Street NW
Washington, DC 20036
202/986-0384 800/741-6964
Internet: http://www.dcinternships.com

AMOUNT: Up to $2,975
DEADLINE(S): JAN 31 (early decision); MAR 15 (general application deadline)
FIELD(S): Political Science; Economics; Journalism; Business Administration

The Fund for American Studies, in conjunction with Georgetown University, sponsors summer institutes that include internships, courses for credit, site briefings, and dialogues with policy leaders. Scholarships are available to sophomores and juniors to cover the cost of the program.

Approximately 100 awards per year. For Fund's programs only. Call, check Web site, or write for complete information.

2151—GENERAL FEDERATION OF WOMEN'S CLUBS OF MASSACHUSETTS (International Affairs Scholarships)

245 Dutton Road, Box 679
Sudbury MA 01776-0679
508/481-3354
AMOUNT: $500
DEADLINE(S): MAR 1
FIELD(S): International affairs; International relations

For undergraduate and/or graduate study abroad for legal residents of Massachusetts. Letter of endorsement from sponsoring GFWC of MA club, personal statement of "what I hope to gain from this experience," letter of reference from department head of your major, transcripts, and personal interview required with application.

For further information or an application, send self-addressed, stamped envelope to Sheila E. Shea, Counselor, International Affairs Department, at above address.

2152—HARRY S. TRUMAN SCHOLARSHIP FOUNDATION (Scholarships)

712 Jackson Pl. NW
Washington DC 20006-4901
202/395-4831
Internet: http://www.truman.gov
AMOUNT: $30,000 ($3,000 for senior year + $27,000 for grad studies)
DEADLINE(S): FEB 1
FIELD(S): Public Service; Government

Merit-based awards for those who pursue careers in government or public service and wish to attend graduate/professional school in U.S. or foreign country. Must be full-time junior at four-year institution pursuing bachelor's degree, in upper quarter of class, and U.S. citizen/national. State scholarships available to nominees from each of 50 states, DC, Puerto Rico, and Guam/Virgin Islands/American Samoa/Northern Mariana Islands. Must show community service and leadership.

75-80 awards annually. Applicants must be nominated by their institution. See Web site or contact Foundation for more information.

2153—HILLSDALE COLLEGE (Freedom as Vocation Scholarship)

33 E. College Street
Hillsdale MI 49242-1298
517/437-7341
Internet: http://www.hillsdale.edu
AMOUNT: Varies
DEADLINE(S): None
FIELD(S): Business; History; Political Science; Economics

Open to Hillsdale College undergraduates who maintain a minimum 3.0 GPA and commit to a series of courses in the above fields. Student must rank in top 20% of class and top 10% of test scores. Must possess excellent communications, public speaking, and leadership skills and demonstrate outstanding character and citizenship. Financial need NOT a factor.

Renewable. No application process; students are selected. See Web site for details.

2154—INSTITUT D'ETUDES POLITIQUES DE PARIS (US Sciences Po Alumni Association Scholarships)

27, rue Saint Guillaume
75337 Paris Cedex 07 FRANCE
331/4549-5047
FAX: 331/4544-1252
Internet: http://sciencespo.org/bourses.htm
AMOUNT: $5,000 (max.)
DEADLINE(S): Varies
FIELD(S): European Studies; Political Science; Economics; Finance

Open to U.S. citizens who will pursue undergraduate, graduate, or postgraduate studies at IEP Paris, either through admission to the school or through an exchange program with an accredited U.S. school. Must have sufficient fluency in French to meet instructional requirements. Must submit cover letter, resume, and brief essay. Award may be used to cover educational costs and related expenses, including fees, round-trip airfare to Paris, textbooks, and school supplies.

See Web site or contact Mr. P. Cauchy, Director of International Student Services, for an application.

2155—INSTITUTE FOR HUMANE STUDIES (Humane Studies Fellowship)

3301 N. FairFAX: Drive, Suite 440
Arlington VA 22201-4432
703/993-4880 or 800/697-8799
FAX: 703/993-4890
E-mail: ihs@gmu.edu
Internet: http://www.TheIHS.org
AMOUNT: $12,000 (max.)
DEADLINE(S): DEC
FIELD(S): Social Sciences; Liberal Arts; Law; Humanities; Jurisprudence; Journalism

Open to graduate and advanced undergraduate or law students pursuing degrees at any accredited domestic or foreign college/university. Based on academic performance, demonstrated interest in the classical liberal tradition, and potential to contribute to the advancement of a free society.

90 awards annually. Apply online or contact IHS for an application.

2156—INSTITUTE FOR HUMANE STUDIES (Koch Summer Fellow Program)

3401 N. FairFAX: Drive, Suite 440
Arlington VA 22201-4432
703/993-4880 or 800/697-8799
FAX: 703/993-4890
E-mail: ihs@gmu.edu
Internet: http://www.TheIHS.org
AMOUNT: $1,500 + airfare and housing
DEADLINE(S): FEB 15
FIELD(S): Economics; Public Policy; Law; Government; Politics

Open to undergraduates and graduates to build skills and gain experience by participating in an 8-week summer internship program. Includes two week-long seminars, the internship, and research and writing projects with professionals. Must submit college transcripts, essays, and application. Financial need NOT a factor.

32 awards annually. Not renewable. Apply online or contact IHS for an application.

2157—INSTITUTE FOR HUMANE STUDIES (Summer Seminars Program)

3401 N. FairFAX: Drive, Suite 440
Arlington VA 22201-4432
703/993-4880 or 800/697-8799
FAX: 703/993-4890
E-mail: ihs@gmu.edu
Internet: http://www.TheIHS.org
AMOUNT: Free summer seminars, including room/board, lectures, seminar materials, and books
DEADLINE(S): MAR
FIELD(S): Social Sciences; Humanities; Law; Journalism; Public Policy; Education; Film; Writing; Economics; Philosophy

Open to college students, recent graduates, and graduate students who share an interest in learning and exchanging ideas about the scope of individual rights, free markets, the rule of law, peace, and tolerance.

See Web site for seminar information or to apply online or contact IHS for an application.

2158—INSTITUTE OF INTERNATIONAL EDUCATION (National Security Education Program-Undergraduate Scholarships)

1400 K Street NW, 6th Floor
Washington DC 20005-2403
202/326-7697 or
800/618-NSEP (6737)
E-mail: nsep@iie.org
Internet: http://www.iie.org/nsep/
AMOUNT: Varies: up to $8,000/semester
DEADLINE(S): FEB 8
FIELD(S): Open to all majors; preference to applied sciences, engineering, business, economics, math, computer science, international affairs, political science, history, and the policy sciences.

For study abroad OUTSIDE the U.S., Canada, Australia, New Zealand, and Western Europe. For study in areas deemed critical to U.S. national security. Applications available on U.S. campuses from August through early December. Or contact organization for details.

Inquire at above location for details.

2159—JAMES FORD BELL FOUNDATION (Summer Internship Program)

2925 Dean Parkway, Suite 811
Minneapolis MN 55416
612/285-5435
FAX: 612/285-5437
E-mail: famphiladv@uswest.net
AMOUNT: $4,000 for 3 months
DEADLINE(S): APR 30
FIELD(S): Business/Public Administration; Public Policy; Organization Leadership; Nonprofit Management

Interns spend the summer with organizations selected by the Foundation; the organizations select interns from master's degree programs in above or related fields and college seniors with strong interest in nonprofit work. Internships normally in the Twin Cities area.

Contact Foundation for a list of internship opportunities in February and March ONLY; students should request position list, not an application for the program itself (only organizations apply for the program).

2160—JAMES MADISON MEMORIAL FELLOWSHIP FOUNDATION (Fellowships)

2000 K Street NW, Suite 303
Washington DC 20006
202/653-8700;
FAX: 202/653-6045
Internet: http://www.jamesmadison.com
AMOUNT: Tuition, fees, books, and room/board
DEADLINE(S): MAR 1
FIELD(S): Education: American History, American Government, Social Studies

Open to U.S. citizens/nationals who are teachers, or planning to become teachers, in above fields at the secondary school level. Must currently possess a bachelor's degree, or plan to receive one no later than August 31. Fellows must teach above subjects in grades 7-12 for no less than one year for each full year of study under the fellowship. Proposed graduate study should contain substantial constitutional coursework.

See Web site or contact Foundation for an application.

2161—JAPANESE AMERICAN CITIZENS LEAGUE (Alice Yuriko Endo Memorial Scholarship)

1765 Sutter Street
San Francisco CA 94115
415/921-5225
FAX: 415/931-4671
E-mail: jacl@jacl.org
Internet: http://www.jacl.org
AMOUNT: $1,000-$5,000
DEADLINE(S): APR 1
FIELD(S): Public and Social Service

Open to JACL members and their children only. For undergraduate students with an interest in public or social service who are planning to attend a college, university, trade school, business school, or any other institution of higher learning. Preference given to students residing in the Eastern District Council and/or those studying in above fields. Financial need NOT a factor.

For membership information or an application, send a self-addressed, stamped envelope to above address, stating your level of study. Applications available October 1 through March 20; recipients notified in July.

2162—JAPANESE AMERICAN CITIZENS LEAGUE (Yoshiko Tanaka Memorial Scholarship)

1765 Sutter Street
San Francisco CA 94115
415/921-5225
FAX: 415/931-4671
E-mail: jacl@jacl.org
Internet: http://www.jacl.org
AMOUNT: $1,000-$5,000
DEADLINE(S): APR 1
FIELD(S): Japanese Language/Culture; U.S.-Japan Relations

Open to JACL members and their children only. For undergraduate students with an interest in Japanese language, culture, or the enhancement of U.S.-Japan relations and who are planning to attend a college, university, trade school, business school, or any other institution of higher learning. Must submit personal statement, letters of recommendation, and transcripts. Financial need NOT a factor.

For membership information or an application, send a self-addressed, stamped envelope to above address, stating your level of study. Applications available October 1 through March 20; recipients notified in July.

2163—LONDON SCHOOL OF ECONOMICS AND POLITICAL SCIENCE (Scholarships)

Scholarships Office; Houghton Street
London WC2A 2AE ENGLAND UK
+44 (0) 171 955 7162/7155
FAX: +44 (0) 171 831 1684
E-mail: scholarships@lse.ac.uk
Internet: http://www.lse.ac.uk/index/EDUCATE/CONTACTS.HTM
or http://www.lse.ac.uk/index/restore/GRADUATE/Financial/text/funding.htm or
http://www.britcoun.org/eis/profiles/lse/lseschp.htm
AMOUNT: Varies with award
DEADLINE(S): Varies
FIELD(S): Economics; Accounting; Finance; Political Science; International Relations

Various scholarships, awards, and prizes are available to international students. Several are for students from specific countries, and some are limited to certain fields of study. Some include all expenses, and others pay partial expenses. For undergraduates and graduate students.

Accessing LSE's Web site and using their "search" option, write in "scholarships," and a vast array of programs will appear.

2164—LOUISIANA STATE UNIVERSITY AT SHREVEPORT (Walter O. Bigby Scholarship)

Bronson Hall
Shreveport LA 71115-2399
318/797-5371

Internet: http://www.lsus.edu
AMOUNT: Up to $500/semester
DEADLINE(S): Varies
FIELD(S): Political Science; English; History; Law

Recipient must be entering the junior or senior year at LSUS with a major in political science, English, or history; may also be enrolled in some other Liberal Arts degree program if preparing to enter law school.

Contact the Dean's Office in the College of Liberal Arts at LSUS for an application.

2165—NATIONAL ITALIAN AMERICAN FOUNDATION (Assunta Luchetti Martino Scholarship for International Studies)

1860 19th Street NW
Washington DC 20009-5599
202/530-5315
AMOUNT: $1,000
DEADLINE(S): MAY 31
FIELD(S): International studies

For undergraduates of Italian ancestry who are pursuing degrees in international studies.

Considerations are academic merit, financial need, and commmunity service. Write for application and further information.

2166—DAUGHTERS OF AMERICAN REVOLUTION

1776 D Street NW
Washington DC 20006-5392
202/628-1776
Internet: http://www.dar.org
AMOUNT: $1,000
DEADLINE(S): FEB 15
FIELD(S): History; Political Science; Government; Economics

Open to undergraduate juniors and seniors (US citizens) attending an accredited U.S. college or university. Awards are placed on deposit with school. Awards are judged on academic excellence, commitment to field of study, and need. Affiliation with DAR not required.

Not renewable. See Web site or send a self-addressed, stamped envelope for an application or more information.

2167—NATURAL SCIENCES AND ENGINEERING RESEARCH COUNCIL OF CANADA (Undergraduate Student Research Awards in Small Universities)

350 Albert Street
Ottawa Ontario K1A 1H5 CANADA
613/995-5992
FAX: 613/992-533
E-mail: schol@nserc.ca
Internet: http://www.nserc.ca/programs/usrasmen.htm
AMOUNT: $3,600 (max.)
DEADLINE(S): Varies
FIELD(S): Natural Sciences; Engineering

Research awards for Canadian citizens/permanent residents attending eligible institutions, and who have no more than 6 and no fewer than 2 academic terms remaining to complete bachelor's degree. Cumulative GPA of at least 2nd class (B). Must be doing full-time in research and development activities during award tenure.

Students in health sciences not eligible. Students with BAs and who are studying for a second may apply.

2168—NATIONAL SOCIETY OF ACCOUNTANTS SCHOLARSHIP FOUNDATION (Stanley H. Stearman Scholarship Award)

1010 North FairFAX: Street
Alexandria VA 22314-1574
703/549-6400
FAX: 703/549-2984
E-mail: snoell@mindspring.com
Internet: http://www.nsacct.org
AMOUNT: $2,000/year
DEADLINE(S): MAR 10
FIELD(S): Accounting

For U.S. or Canadian citizens in undergraduate or graduate programs in the U.S. who have a minimum 3.0 GPA. Must be the spouse, child, grandchild, niece, nephew, or son/daughter-in-law of an active or deceased NSA member who have held membership for at least one year. Must include letter of intent, outlining reasons for seeking award, intended career objective, and how this award would be used to accomplish that objective.

1 award annually. Renewable up to 3 years. See Web site or contact Susan Noell, Foundation Director, for an application.

2169—NEW YORK CITY DEPT. OF CITYWIDE ADMINISTRATIVE SERVICES (Government Scholars Internship Program)

1 Centre Street, 24th Floor
New York NY 10007
212/487-5600
FAX: 212/487-5720
AMOUNT: $3,000 stipend
DEADLINE(S): JAN 13
FIELD(S): Public Administration; Urban Planning; Government; Public Service; Urban Affairs

10-week summer intern program open to undergraduate sophomores, juniors, and seniors. Program provides students with unique opportunity to learn about NY City government. Internships available in virtually every city agency and mayoral office.

Write to New York City Fellowship Programs at above address for complete information.

2170—NEW YORK STATE SENATE (Legislative Fellows Program; R. J. Roth Journalism Fellowship; R. A. Wiebe Public Service Fellowship)

NYS Senate Student Programs Office, 90 South Swan Street, Room 401
Albany NY 12247
518/455-2611
FAX: 518/432-5470
E-mail: students@senate.state.ny.us
AMOUNT: $25,000 stipend (not a scholarship)
DEADLINE(S): MAY (first Friday)
FIELD(S): Political Science; Government; Public Service; Journalism; Public Relations

One year programs for U.S. citizens who are grad students and residents of New York state or enrolled in accredited programs in New York state. Fellows work as regular legislative staff members of the office to which they are assigned. The Roth Fellowship is for communications/journalism majors, and undergrads may be considered for this program.

14 fellowships per year. Fellowships take place at the New York State Legislative Office. Write for complete information.

2171—PRESIDENT'S COMMISSION ON WHITE HOUSE FELLOWSHIPS

712 Jackson Place NW
Washington DC 20503
202/395-4522
FAX: 202/395-6179
E-mail: almanac@ace.esusda.gov
AMOUNT: Wage (up to GS-14 Step 3)
DEADLINE(S): DEC 1
FIELD(S): Public Service; Government; Community Involvement; Leadership

Mid-career professionals spend one year as special assistants to senior executive branch officials in Washington. Highly competitive. Nonpartisan; no age or educational requirements. Fellowship year runs September 1 through August 31.

1,200 candidates applying for 11 to 19 fellowships each year. Write for complete information.

2172—ROSE HILL COLLEGE (Louella Robinson Memorial Scholarship)

P.O. Box 3126
Aiken SC 29802-3126
800/684-3769
FAX: 803/641-0240
E-mail: rosehill@rosehill.edu
Internet: http://www.rosehill.edu
AMOUNT: $10,000/year for four years
DEADLINE(S): Varies
FIELD(S): Liberal Arts and Humanities Curricula

For undergraduate residents of Indian River County, Florida, to attend Rose Hill College in Aiken, South Carolina. The school offers a liberal arts education and follows the Great Books curriculum, a program of reading and seminars.

One annual award. Applicants must meet entry requirements of RHC. Contact above location for details.

2173—ROSE HILL COLLEGE (Scholarships for Children of Eastern Orthodox Priests/Deacons)

P.O. Box 3126
Aiken SC 29802-3126
800/684-3769
FAX: 803/641-0240
E-mail: rosehill@rosehill.edu
Internet: http://www.rosehill.edu
AMOUNT: Full scholarship: $10,000/year for four years
DEADLINE(S): Varies
FIELD(S): Liberal Arts and Humanities Curricula

For undergraduates who are children of Eastern Orthodox Christian priests or deacons to attend Rose Hill College in Aiken, South Carolina. The school offers a liberal arts education and follows the Great Books Curriculum, a program of reading and seminars.

6-10 annual awards. Applicants must meet entry requirements of RHC. Contact above location for details.

2174—ROSE HILL COLLEGE (Scholarships for the Homeschooled)

P.O. Box 3126
Aiken SC 29802-3126
800/684-3769
FAX: 803/641-0240
E-mail: rosehill@rosehill.edu
Internet: http://www.resehill.edu
AMOUNT: Full scholarship: $10,000/year for four years
DEADLINE(S): Varies
FIELD(S): Liberal Arts and Humanities Curricula

For undergraduates who have been homeschooled for three of the last five years of their high school education. For use at Rose Hill College in Aiken, South Carolina. The school offers a liberal arts education and follows the Great Books Curriculum, a program of reading and seminars. Scholarships will be awarded primarily on the basis of an essay which the student will be asked to write.

Four annual awards. Applicants must meet entry requirements of RHC. Contact above location for details.

2175—SOCIETY OF SATELLITE PROFESSIONALS INTERNATIONAL (SSPI Scholarships)

225 Reinekers Lane, Suite 600
Alexandria VA 22314
703/857-3717
FAX: 703/857-6335
E-mail: neworbit@aol.com
Internet: http://www.sspi.org
AMOUNT: $1,500 to $4,000
DEADLINE(S): DEC 1
FIELD(S): Satellites as related to communications, domestic and international telecommunications policy, remote sensing, journalism, law, meteorology, energy, navigation, business, government, and broadcasting services

Various scholarships for students studying in the above fields.

Access Web site for details and applications or send a self-addressed, stamped envelope (SASE) for a complete listing.

2176—SOIL AND WATER CONSERVATION SOCIETY (SWCS Internships)

7515 N.E. Ankeny Road
Ankeny IA 50021-9764
515/289-2331 or 800/THE-SOIL
FAX: 515/289-1227
E-mail: charliep@swcs.org
Internet: http://www.swcs.org
AMOUNT: Varies—most are uncompensated
DEADLINE(S): Varies
FIELD(S): Journalism, marketing, database management, meeting planning, public policy research, environmental education, landscape architecture

Internships for undergraduates and graduates to gain experience in the above fields as they relate to soil and water conservation issues. Internship openings vary through the year in duration, compensation, and objective. SWCS will coordinate particulars with your academic advisor.

Contact SWCS for internship availability at any time during the year or see Web site for jobs page.

2177—SOUTHEAST MISSOURI STATE UNIVERSITY (Constance Rowe French Scholarship)

One University Plaza
Cape Girardeau MO 63701
573/651-2476
Internet: http://www.2.semo.edu/foreignlang/SCH-FR.HTML
AMOUNT: Up to full tuition and fees
DEADLINE(S): Varies
FIELD(S): French or Education with a French minor

Scholarships for French majors or Education majors with a French minor at Southeast Missouri State University. Awarded for study in a French-speaking country for the summer after the sophomore year, either semester of the junior year, or for the summer after the junior year. Financial need may be considered.

Contact Dr. Daniel A. MacLeay at the University for more information. His E-mail contact point is accessible at the Web site listed.

2178—SPACE COAST CREDIT UNION (Two-Year Scholarships)

Marketing Dept.
P.O. Box 2470
Melbourne FL 32902
Internet: http://www.sccu.com/scholarship/
AMOUNT: $750/year, two years; $1,000 bonus if go on for Bachelor's
DEADLINE(S): APR 15
FIELD(S): Math, Economics, Science, Computer Science, Marketing, Journalism, Political Science

Must be graduating from a high school in Brevard, Volusia, Flagler, or Indian River counties, be a member of SCCU, have a minimum 3.0 GPA, planning to attend a two-year Florida institution of higher education for an associates degree, and be willing to write a 200-word essay on the topic "Why credit unions are valuable to society."

Four annual awards. Students going on to complete a four-year degree could be eligible for a bonus scholarship of $1,000 for the next two years. For membership information or an application, see our Web page or write to the above address.

2179—TRUMAN SCHOLARSHIP FOUNDATION

712 Jackson Place NW
Washington DC 20006
202/395-4831
FAX: 202/395-6995
Recorded Information Line:
202/395-7429
E-mail: office@truman.gov
Internet: http://www.truman.gov/

AMOUNT: $30,000
DEADLINE(S): JAN 28
FIELD(S): Government

The Truman Scholarship is a merit-based grant awarded to undergraduate students who wish financial support to attend graduate or professional school in preparation for careers in government, the non-profit sector, or elsewhere in public service.

2180—U.S. INSTITUTE OF PEACE (National Peace Essay Contest)

1200 17th Street NW, Suite 200
Washington DC 20036
202/457-1700
FAX: 202/429-6063
E-mail: essay_contest@usip.org
Internet: http://www.usip.org

AMOUNT: $1,000-$10,000
DEADLINE(S): JAN
FIELD(S): Political Science; U.S. History

1,500-word essay contest for high school students on the U.S. response to international conflict. No restrictions as to citizenship/residency.

Not renewable. See Web site or contact USIP for specific guidelines.

2181—UNIVERSITY OF SOUTH DAKOTA (Criminal Justice Dept. Scholarships)

414 East Clark Street
Vermillion SD 57069-2390
605/677-5446
E-mail: admiss@usd.edu
Internet: http://www.usd.edu/cjus/scholarships.htm#orderofpolice

AMOUNT: Varies
DEADLINE(S): Varies
FIELD(S): Criminal Justice; Political Science; Public Service

The University of South Dakota's Department of Criminal Justice administers 17 different award programs in the above fields. Some require a high GPA and/or financial need, others require an essay or research project.

See Web site or contact USD for specific details of each award. The Criminal Justice Department gives out an average of $77,000/year to USD students.

2182—WOMEN IN DEFENSE (HORIZONS Scholarship Foundation)

NDIA
2111 Wilson Boulevard, Suite 400
Arlington VA 22201-3061
703/247-2552
FAX: 703/522-1820
E-mail: cbanks@mciworld.com
Internet: http://www.ndia.org/wid/

AMOUNT: $500+
DEADLINE(S): NOV 1; JUL 1
FIELD(S): Engineering; Computer Science; Physics; Math; Business; Law; International Relations; Political Science; Operations Research; Economics; National Security/Defense

Open to women employed/planning careers in defense/national security areas. Must be currently enrolled full- or part-time at an accredited college/university at the graduate or undergraduate junior/senior level. Must have a minimum 3.25 GPA, demonstrate financial need, and be U.S. citizen. Based on academic achievement, work experience, objectives, and recommendations.

Renewable. See Web site or MUST send self-addressed, stamped envelope to Courtney Banks for application.

2183—WOODROW WILSON NATIONAL FELLOWSHIP FOUNDATION/INSTITUTE FOR INTERNATIONAL PUBLIC POLICY (IIPP Fellowships)

CN 5281
Princeton NJ 08543-5281
609/452-7007
FAX: 609/452-0066
E-mail: richard@woodrow.org
Internet: http://www.woodrow.org

AMOUNT: Varies
DEADLINE(S): Varies
FIELD(S): International Affairs; Foreign Policy

Open to minorities preparing for careers in international affairs at U.S. colleges/universities. Must apply during sophomore year of college. Program draws from Historically Black Colleges and Universities, the Hispanic Association of Colleges and Universities, and the American Indian Higher Education Consortium.

See Web site or contact WWNFF for an application.

2184—ZONTA INTERNATIONAL FOUNDATION (YOUNG WOMEN IN PUBLIC AFFAIRS AWARD)

557 West Randolph Street
Chicago IL 60661-2206
312/930-5848
FAX: 312/930-0951
E-mail: zontafdtn@zonta.org
Internet: http://www.zonta.org

AMOUNT: $1,000
DEADLINE(S): Varies
FIELD(S): Public Affairs

Zonta International YWPA Program (Young Women in Public Affairs) was established in 1990 to encourage secondary-school women, 21 years of age or younger, to pursue careers and leadership positions in social policy-making, government, and volunteer organizations. The Zonta International Foundation awards $500 U.S. to each district winner and $1,000 U.S. to the international winner.

PSYCHOLOGY

2185—AIR FORCE RESERVE OFFICER TRAINING CORPS (AFROTC Scholarships)

551 E. Maxwell Boulevard
Maxwell AFB AL 36112-6106
334/953-7783

AMOUNT: Full tuition, books, and fees for all 4 years of college
DEADLINE(S): DEC 1
FIELD(S): Science; Engineering; Business; Political Science; Psychology; Geography; Foreign Studies; Foreign Language

Competitive scholarships based on individual merit to high school seniors and graduates who have not completed any full-time college work. Must be a U.S. citizen between the ages of 17-27. Must also have GPA of 2.5 or above, be in top 40% of class, and complete Applicant Fitness Test. Cannot be a single parent. Your college/university must offer AFROTC.

2,300 awards annually. Contact above address for application packet.

2186—AMERICAN BAR FOUNDATION (Montgomery Summer Research Fellowships for Minority Undergraduate Students)

750 N. Lake Shore Drive
Chicago IL 60611
312/988-6500
FAX: 312/988-6579
E-mail: fellowships@abfn.org
Internet: http://www.abf-sociolegal.org

AMOUNT: $3,600 stipend
DEADLINE(S): MAR 1
FIELD(S): Social Sciences; Humanities; Law

Summer research opportunity open to sophomore and junior undergraduates who are Native American, African American, Mexican, Puerto Rican, or other minority. Must be U.S. citizen or permanent resident and have at least a 3.0 GPA. Students are assigned a mentor and participate in seminars; must also work at the Foundation's office in Chicago for 35 hours per week for 10 weeks. Essay, transcripts, and letter of recommendation required.

4 awards annually; announced in April. See Web site or contact ABF for an application.

2187—ASSOCIATION FOR WOMEN IN SCIENCE EDUCATIONAL FOUNDATION (Ruth Satter Memorial Award)

1200 New York Avenue NW, Suite 650
Washington DC 20005
202/326-8940 or 800/886-AWIS
E-mail: awis@awis.org
Internet: http://www.awis.org

AMOUNT: $1,000
DEADLINE(S): JAN 16
FIELD(S): Various Sciences and Social Sciences

Scholarships for female doctoral students who have interrupted their education three years or more to raise a family. Summary page, description of research project, resume, references, transcripts, biographical sketch, and proof of eligibility from department head required. U.S. citizens may attend any graduate institution; noncitizens must be enrolled in U.S. institutions.

See Web site or write to above address for more information or an application.

2188—BRITISH COLUMBIA PARAPLEGIC FOUNDATION (Douglas John Wilson Scholarship)

780 SW Marine Dr.
Vancouver BC V6P 5Y7 CANADA
604/324-3611
FAX: 604/324-3671

AMOUNT: Varies
DEADLINE(S): JUL 31
FIELD(S): Rehabilitation Counseling

For a person with a disability studying for a degree in rehabilitation counseling at a university in British Columbia. Must be a Canadian citizen or landed immigrant or a resident of British Columbia.

To assist with tuition, books, transportation, or other educational expenses.

2189—DEMOLAY FOUNDATION INC. (Scholarships)

10200 NW. Ambassador Boulevard
Kansas City MO 64153
816/891-8333
FAX: 816/891-9062
Internet: http://www.demolay.org

AMOUNT: $1,500
DEADLINE(S): APR 1
FIELD(S): Dental or medical fields

Open to all active and/or senior DeMolays. Considerations are leadership, academic achievement, and goals.

Four grants per year. Write for complete information.

2190—EASTER SEAL SOCIETY OF IOWA, INC. (Scholarships and Awards)

P.O. Box 4002
Des Moines IA 50333-4002
515/289-1933

AMOUNT: $400-$600
DEADLINE(S): APR 15
FIELD(S): Physical Rehabilitation, Mental Rehabilitation, and related areas

Open ONLY to Iowa residents who are full-time undergraduate sophomores, juniors, seniors, or graduate students at accredited institutions planning a career in the broad field of rehabilitation. Must indicate financial need and be in top 40% of their class.

6 scholarships per year. Must reapply each year.

2191—EPILEPSY FOUNDATION OF AMERICA (Behavioral Sciences Student Fellowships)

4351 Garden City Drive
Landover MD 20785-2267
301/459-3700 or 800/EFA-1000
TDD: 800/332-2070
FAX: 301/577-2684
Internet: http://www.epilepsyfoundation.org

AMOUNT: $2,000
DEADLINE(S): FEB 1
FIELD(S): Epilepsy Research/Practice; Sociology; Social Work; Psychology; Anthropology; Nursing; Economics; Vocational Rehabilitation; Counseling; Political Science

Three-month fellowships awarded to undergraduate and graduate students in above fields for work on a project during the summer or other free period. Students propose an epilepsy-related study or training project to be carried out at a U.S. institution of their choice. A preceptor must accept responsibility for supervision of the student and the project.

Contact EFA for an application. Notification by June 1.

2192—HISPANIC COLLEGE FUND (Scholarships for Hispanic Students)

One Thomas Circle NW, Suite 375
Washington DC 20005
202/296-5400
FAX: 202/296-3774
E-mail: Hispanic.Fund@InternetMCI.com
Internet: http://hispanicfund.org

AMOUNT: Varies
DEADLINE(S): APR 15
FIELD(S): Most college majors leading to a career in business

Scholarships for deserving Hispanic college students pursuing a higher education in a major leading to a business career and who are full-time students at accredited institutions. U.S. citizenship. Must demonstrate financial need.

Contact above organization for details or visit Web site for application.

2193—INSTITUTE FOR HUMANE STUDIES (Humane Studies Fellowship)

3301 N. FairFAX: Drive, Suite 440
Arlington VA 22201-4432
703/993-4880 or 800/697-8799
FAX: 703/993-4890
E-mail: ihs@gmu.edu
Internet: http://www.TheIHS.org

AMOUNT: $12,000 (max.)
DEADLINE(S): DEC

FIELD(S): Social Sciences; Liberal Arts; Law; Humanities; Jurisprudence; Journalism

Open to graduate and advanced undergraduate or law students pursuing degrees at any accredited domestic or foreign college/university. Based on academic performance, demonstrated interest in the classical liberal tradition, and potential to contribute to the advancement of a free society.

90 awards annually. Apply online or contact IHS for an application.

2194—LADY ALLEN OF HURTWOOD MEMORIAL TRUST (Travel Grants)

21 Aspull Common
Leigh Lancs WN7 3PB ENGLAND
01942-674895

AMOUNT: Up to 1,000 pounds sterling
DEADLINE(S): JAN 15
FIELD(S): Welfare and Education of Children

A travel grant to those whose proposed project will directly benefit their work with children. People working with children and young people may apply, particularly those working with disabled and disadvantaged children. Successful candidates must write up an account of the work which the scholarship has funded. GRANTS ARE NOT FOR ACADEMIC STUDY; ONLY QUALIFIED INDIVIDUALS MAY APPLY.

Contact Dorothy E. Whitaker, Trustee, for application forms-available between May and December each year.

2195—MIDWAY COLLEGE (Institutional Aid Program)

Financial Aid Office
Midway KY 40347
606/846-4421

AMOUNT: Varies
DEADLINE(S): MAR 1
FIELD(S): Nursing; Paralegal; Education; Psychology; Biology; Equine Studies; Liberal Studies; Business Administration

Scholarships and grants are open to women who are accepted for enrollment at Midway College. Awards support undergraduate study in the above areas.

80 awards annually. Contact Midway College's Financial Aid Office for an application.

2196—NATIONAL INSTITUTES OF HEALTH (Minority International Research Training Grant)

Fogarty International Center, Bldg. 31
Room B2C39
Bethesda MD 20892-2220
301/402-9467
FAX: 301/402-0779
E-mail: barbara_sina@cu.nih.gov
Internet: http://www.nih.gov/grants/oer.htm

AMOUNT: Varies
DEADLINE(S): MAR 15
FIELD(S): Biomedical and Behavioral Sciences

Open to minorities that are underrepresented in biomedical research professions (African and Hispanic Americans, Native Americans, Alaskan Natives, and Pacific Islanders). May be undergraduate students pursuing life science curricula (8-12 weeks research/coursework supported), students pursuing doctoral degrees in above fields (3-12 months research training at foreign institution supported), or faculty members in above fields (3-12 months research at foreign institution).

See Web site or contact NIH for an application.

2197—NATURAL SCIENCES AND ENGINEERING RESEARCH COUNCIL OF CANADA (Undergraduate Student Research Awards in Small Universities)

350 Albert Street
Ottawa Ontario K1A 1H5 CANADA
613/995-5992
FAX: 613/992-533
E-mail: schol@nserc.ca
Internet: http://www.nserc.ca/programs/usrasmen.htm

AMOUNT: $3,600 (max.)
DEADLINE(S): Varies
FIELD(S): Natural Sciences; Engineering

Research awards for Canadian citizens/permanent residents attending eligible institutions, and who have no more than 6 and no fewer than 2 academic terms remaining to complete bachelor's degree. Cumulative GPA of at least 2nd class (B). Must be doing full-time in research and development activities during award tenure.

Students in health sciences not eligible. Students with BAs and who are studying for a second may apply.

2198—NEW YORK STATE HIGHER EDUCATION SERVICES CORPORATION (N.Y. State Regents Professional/Health Care Opportunity Scholarships)

Cultural Education Center, Room 5C64
Albany NY 12230
518/486-1319
Internet: http://www.hesc.com

AMOUNT: $1,000-$10,000/year
DEADLINE(S): Varies
FIELD(S): Medicine and dentistry and related fields, architecture, nursing, psychology, audiology, landscape architecture, social work, chiropractic, law, pharmacy, accounting, speech language pathology

For NY state residents who are economically disadvantaged and members of a minority group underrepresented in the chosen profession and attending school in NY state. Some programs carry a service obligation in New York for each year of support. For U.S. citizens or qualifying noncitizens.

Medical/dental scholarships require one year of professional work in NY.

2199—PARAPSYCHOLOGY FOUNDATION (D. Scott Rogo Award for Parapsychological Award)

228 E. 71st Street
New York NY 10021
212/628-1550
FAX: 212/628-1559

AMOUNT: $3,000
DEADLINE(S): APR 15
FIELD(S): Parapsychology

Annual award given to an author working on a manuscript pertaining to the science of parapsychology. A brief synopsis of the proposed contents of the manuscript should be included in the initial application.

Contact Parapsychology Foundation for more information. Recipient notified around May 1st.

2200—PARAPSYCHOLOGY FOUNDATION (Eileen J. Garrett Scholarship)

228 E. 71st Street
New York NY 10021
212/628-1550
FAX: 212/628-1559

AMOUNT: $3,000
DEADLINE(S): JUL 15
FIELD(S): Parapsychology

Open to any undergraduate or graduate student wishing to pursue the academic study of the science of parapsychology. Funding is for study, research, and experimentation only. Applicants must demonstrate previous academic interest in parapsycholgy. Letters of reference are required from three individuals who are familiar with the applicant's work and/or studies in parapsychology.

Contact Parapsychology Foundation for an application.

2201—PILOT INTERNATIONAL FOUNDATION (PIF/Lifeline Scholarship)

P.O. Box 5600
Macon GA 31208-5600
Written Inquiries
AMOUNT: Varies
DEADLINE(S): MAR 1
FIELD(S): Disabilities/Brain-related disorders

This program assists ADULT students reentering the job market, preparing for a second career, or improving their professional skills for an established career. Applicants must be preparing for, or already involved in, careers working with people with disabilities/brain-related disorders. GPA of 3.5 or more is required.

Must be sponsored by a Pilot Club in your home town, or in the city in which your college or university is located. Send a self-addressed, stamped envelope for complete information.

2202—PILOT INTERNATIONAL FOUNDATION (Ruby Newhall Memorial Scholarship)

P.O. Box 5600
Macon, GA 31208-5600
Written Inquiries
AMOUNT: Varies
DEADLINE(S): MAR 15
FIELD(S): Disabilities/Brain-related disorders

For international students who have studied in the U.S. for at least one year, and who intend to return to their home country six months after graduation. Applicants must be full-time students majoring in a field related to human health and welfare, and have a GPA of 3.5 or more.

Applicants must be sponsored by a Pilot Club in their home town, or in the city in which their college or university is located. Send a self-addressed, stamped envelope for complete information.

2203—PILOT INTERNATIONAL FOUNDATION (The Pilot International Scholarship Program)

P.O. Box 5600
Macon GA 31208-5600
Written Inquiries
AMOUNT: Varies
DEADLINE(S): MAR 1
FIELD(S): Disabilities/Brain-related disorders

This program provides assistance to undergraduate students preparing for careers working directly with people with disabilities or training those who will. GPA of 3.5 or greater required.

Applicants must be sponsored by a Pilot Club in their home town, or in the city in which their college or university is located. Send a self-addressed, stamped envelope for complete information.

2204—ROSE HILL COLLEGE (Louella Robinson Memorial Scholarship)

P.O. Box 3126
Aiken SC 29802-3126
800/684-3769
FAX: 803/641-0240
E-mail: rosehill@rosehill.edu
Internet: http://www.rosehill.edu
AMOUNT: $10,000/year for four years
DEADLINE(S): Varies
FIELD(S): Liberal arts and humanities curricula

For undergraduate residents of Indian River County, Florida, to attend Rose Hill College in Aiken, South Carolina. The school offers a liberal arts education and follows the Great Books Curriculum, a program of reading and seminars.

One annual award. Applicants must meet entry requirements of RHC. Contact above location for details.

2205—ROSE HILL COLLEGE (Scholarships for Children of Eastern Orthodox Priests/Deacons)

P.O. Box 3126
Aiken SC 29802-3126
800/684-3769
FAX: 803/641-0240
E-mail: rosehill@rosehill.edu
Internet: http://www.rosehill.edu
AMOUNT: Full scholarship: $10,000/year for four years
DEADLINE(S): Varies
FIELD(S): Liberal Arts and Humanities Curricula

For undergraduates who are children of Eastern Orthodox Christian priests or deacons to attend Rose Hill College in Aiken, South Carolina. The school offers a liberal arts education and follows the Great Books Curriculum, a program of reading and seminars.

6-10 annual awards. Applicants must meet entry requirements of RHC. Contact above location for details.

2206—ROSE HILL COLLEGE (Scholarships for the Homeschooled)

P.O. Box 3126
Aiken SC 29802-3126
800/684-3769
FAX: 803/641-0240
E-mail: rosehill@rosehill.edu
Internet: http://www.resehill.edu
AMOUNT: Full scholarship: $10,000/year for four years
DEADLINE(S): Varies
FIELD(S): Liberal Arts and Humanities Curricula

For undergraduates who have been homeschooled for three of the last five years of their high school education. For use at Rose Hill College in Aiken, South Carolina. The school offers a liberal arts education and follows the Great Books Curriculum, a program of reading and seminars. Scholarships will be awarded primarily on the basis of an essay which the student will be asked to write.

Four annual awards. Applicants must meet entry requirements of RHC. Contact above location for details.

2207—SCOTTISH RITE CHARITABLE FOUNDATION (Bursaries for College Students)

Roeher Institute, Kinsmen Bldg.
4700 Keele Street
North York Ontario M3J 1P3
CANADA
416/661-9611; TDD: 416/661-2023
FAX: 416/661-5701
E-mail: mail@aacl.org
Internet: http://www.aacl.org
AMOUNT: $2,000 (max.)
DEADLINE(S): JUL 1
FIELD(S): Human Services; Intellectual Disability; Special Education; DSW

Open to Canadian citizens/landed immigrants accepted into a full-time undergraduate college program in a Canadian college/university. Must submit outline of intended study, transcripts, community involvement, and letters of reference from supervisors. Financial need NOT a factor.

3 awards annually. Must be recommended by a Provincial Association of the Canadian Association for Community Living. Contact your provincial association for details.

2208—SOCIETY FOR THE SCIENTIFIC STUDY OF SEXUALITY (Student Research Grant)

P.O. Box 208
Mount Vernon IA 52314-0208
319/895-8407
FAX: 319/895-6203
E-mail: TheSociety@worldnet.att.net
Internet: http://www.ssc.wisc.edu/ssss
AMOUNT: $750
DEADLINE(S): FEB 1; SEP 1
FIELD(S): Human Sexuality

Open to students doing research in the area of human sexuality. Must be enrolled in a degree-granting program at an accredited institution; can be master's thesis or doctoral dissertation, but this is not a requirement. With application, must submit letter from Department Chairperson stating your status and educational purpose of research, 150-word abstract of proposed research, short biographical sketch, and proposed budget.

3 awards annually. Contact Ilsa Lottes, Ph.D., at SSSS for an application. Recipients announced in November at SSSS annual meeting.

2209—WOMEN'S SPORTS FOUNDATION (Jackie Joyner-Kersee and Zina Garrison Minority Internships)

Eisenhower Park
East Meadow NY 11554
800/227-3988
FAX: 516/542-4716
E-mail: WoSport@aol.com
Internet: http://www.lifetimetv.com/WoSport
AMOUNT: $4,000-$5,000
DEADLINE(S): Ongoing
FIELD(S): Sports-related fields

Provides women of color an opportunity to gain experience in a sports-related career and interact in the sports community. May be undergraduates, college graduates, graduate students, or women in a career change. Internships are located at the Women's Sports Foundation in East Meadow, New York.

4-6 awards annually. See Web site or write to above address for details.

2210—ZETA PHI BETA SORORITY EDUCATIONAL FOUNDATION (Lullelia W. Harrison Scholarship in Counseling)

1734 New Hampshire Avenue NW
Washington DC 20009
Internet: http://www.zpb1920.org/nefforms.htm
AMOUNT: $500-$1,000
DEADLINE(S): FEB 1
FIELD(S): Counseling

Open to graduate and undergraduate level students enrolled in a degree program in counseling. Award is for full-time study for one academic year (Fall-Spring). Must submit proof of enrollment.

Send self-addressed, stamped envelope to above address between September 1 and December 15 for an application.

SOCIOLOGY

2211—AMERICAN BAR FOUNDATION (Montgomery Summer Research Fellowships for Minority Undergraduate Students)

750 N. Lake Shore Drive
Chicago IL 60611
312/988-6500
FAX: 312/988-6579
E-mail: fellowships@abfn.org
Internet: http://www.abf-sociolegal.org
AMOUNT: $3,600 stipend
DEADLINE(S): MAR 1
FIELD(S): Social Sciences; Humanities; Law

Summer research opportunity open to sophomore and junior undergraduates who are Native American, African American, Mexican, Puerto Rican, or other minority. Must be U.S. citizen or permanent resident and have at least a 3.0 GPA. Students are assigned a mentor and participate in seminars; must also work at the Foundation's office in Chicago for 35 hours per week for 10 weeks. Essay, transcripts, and letter of recommendation required.

4 awards annually; announced in April. See Web site or contact ABF for an application.

2212—ASSOCIATION FOR WOMEN IN SCIENCE EDUCATIONAL FOUNDATION (Ruth Satter Memorial Award)

1200 New York Avenue NW
Suite 650
Washington DC 20005
202/326-8940 or 800/886-AWIS
E-mail: awis@awis.org
Internet: http://www.awis.org
AMOUNT: $1,000
DEADLINE(S): JAN 16
FIELD(S): Various Sciences and Social Sciences

Scholarships for female doctoral students who have interrupted their education three years or more to raise a family. Summary page, description of research project, resume, references, transcripts, biographical sketch, and proof of eligibility from department head required. U.S. citizens may attend any graduate institution; noncitizens must be enrolled in U.S. institutions.

See Web site or write to above address for more information or an application.

2213—B'NAI B'RITH YOUTH ORGANIZATION (Scholarship Program)

1640 Rhode Island Avenue NW
Washington DC 20036
202/857-6633
AMOUNT: $2,500 per year
DEADLINE(S): Varies (spring)
FIELD(S): Social Work

Open to U.S. citizens of Jewish faith who are first- or second-year grad students attending accredited graduate schools of social work or who are college seniors planning to attend a graduate school of social work.

Must show evidence of good scholarship, interest in working for Jewish agencies, and have knowledge of Jewish communal structure and institutions. Renewable. Write for complete information.

2214—CHRISTIAN A. JOHNSON ENDEAVOR FOUNDATION (Native American Fellows)

John F. Kennedy School of Government, Harvard University
79 John F. Kennedy Street
Cambridge MA 02138
617/495-1152
FAX: 617/496-3900
Internet: http://www.ksg.harvard.edu/hpaied/index.htm
AMOUNT: Varies
DEADLINE(S): MAY 1
FIELD(S): American Indian Affairs

Fellowships for students of Native American ancestry who attend a John F. Kennedy School of Government degree program. Applicant, parent, or grandparent must hold membership in a federally or state-recognized tribe, band, or other organized group of Native Americans. Must be committed to a career in American Indian affairs. Awards based on merit and need.

Renewable, based on renomination and availability of funds. To apply, contact John F. Kennedy School of Government at above address.

2215—CONTINENTAL SOCIETY DAUGHTERS OF INDIAN WARS (Scholarship)

Route 2; Box 184
Locust Grove OK 74352
918/479-5670
AMOUNT: $1,000
DEADLINE(S): JUN 15
FIELD(S): Education; Social Work; Social Service

Open to Native American, certified tribal members with plans to work on a reservation. Must be an undergraduate junior or senior accepted to or already attending an accredited college/university, be carrying at least eight semester hours, and have a minimum 3.0 GPA. Must be U.S. citizen and demonstrate financial need.

1 award annually. Renewable. Contact Mrs. Ronald Jacobs for an application.

2216—CYNTHIA E. AND CLARA H. HOLLIS FOUNDATION

100 Summer Street
Boston MA 02110
Written Inquiry
AMOUNT: Varies
DEADLINE(S): APR 1
FIELD(S): Nursing, Social Work, Dental or Medical Technology, and Religion

Scholarships for Massachusetts with preference given to students in the above fields. For undergraduates, graduates, votech, and adult education. Must demonstrate financial need.

Send SASE to Walter E. Palmer, Esq., 35 Harvard Street, Brookline, MA 02146 for application details. Scholarship forms are also available from the rector of All Saints Church, Brookline High School, and St. Mary's High School, all in Brookline, Massachusetts.

2117—EAST TEXAS HISTORICAL ASSOCIATION (Ottis Lock Endowment Awards)

P.O. Box 6223; SFA Station
Nacogdoches TX 75962
936/468-2407
FAX: 936/468-2190
E-mail: amcdonald@sfasu.edu
Internet: http://leonardo sfasu.edu/etha
AMOUNT: $500
DEADLINE(S): MAY 1
FIELD(S): History; Social Science

Open to residents of East Texas who will be pursuing undergraduate or graduate studies at an East Texas college or university.

Renewable with adequate progress toward degree. See Web site or contact East Texas Historical Association for an application.

2218—EASTER SEAL SOCIETY OF IOWA, INC. (Scholarships and Awards)

P.O. Box 4002
Des Moines IA 50333-4002
515/289-1933
AMOUNT: $400-$600
DEADLINE(S): APR 15
FIELD(S): Physical Rehabilitation, Mental Rehabilitation, and related areas

Open ONLY to Iowa residents who are full-time undergraduate sophomores, juniors, seniors, or graduate students at accredited institutions planning a career in the broad field of rehabilitation. Must indicate financial need and be in top 40% of their class.

6 scholarships per year. Must reapply each year.

2219—EPILEPSY FOUNDATION OF AMERICA (Behavioral Sciences Student Fellowships)

4351 Garden City Drive
Landover MD 20785-2267
301/459-3700 or 800/EFA-1000
TDD: 800/332-2070
FAX: 301/577-2684
Internet: http://www.epilepsy foundation.org
AMOUNT: $2,000
DEADLINE(S): FEB 1
FIELD(S): Epilepsy Research/Practice; Sociology; Social Work; Psychology; Anthropology; Nursing; Economics; Vocational Rehabilitation; Counseling; Political Science

Three-month fellowships awarded to undergraduate and graduate students in above fields for work on a project during the summer or other free period. Students propose an epilepsy-related study or training project to be carried out at a U.S. institution of their choice. A preceptor must accept responsibility for supervision of the student and the project.

Contact EFA for an application. Notification by June 1.

2220—FOUNDATION FOR SEACOAST HEALTH (Scholarship Program)

100 Campus Drive, Suite 1
Portsmouth NH 03801
603/422-8200
FAX: 602/422-8207
E-mail: ffsh@communitycampus.org
Internet: http://www.ffsh.org
AMOUNT: $1,000-$10,000
DEADLINE(S): FEB 1
FIELD(S): Health-related fields. For residents of New Hampshire and Maine.

2221—HIGHER EDUCATION PROGRAMS (Javits Fellowship Board)

U.S. Department of Education
1990 K Street NW, 6th Floor
Washington DC 20006-8521
202/502-7700
E-mail: OPE_Javits_Program@ed.gov
Internet: http://www.ed.gov/offices/OPE/HEP/iegps/javits.html
AMOUNT: $10,000-$18,000
DEADLINE(S): NOV 30
FIELD(S): Arts, Humanities, and Social Sciences

Fellowships can be offered to individuals who at the time of application have not yet completed their first full year of doctoral or MFA study or are entering graduate school for the first time in the next academic year. Students who have already received a Ph.D. or M.F.A., or received a Javits fellowship in previous years, are not eligible.

2222—INSTITUTE FOR HUMANE STUDIES (Humane Studies Fellowship)

3301 N. FairFAX: Drive, Suite 440
Arlington VA 22201-4432
703/993-4880 or 800/697-8799
FAX: 703/993-4890
E-mail: ihs@gmu.edu
Internet: http://www.TheIHS.org
AMOUNT: $12,000 (max.)
DEADLINE(S): DEC
FIELD(S): Social Sciences; Liberal Arts; Law; Humanities; Jurisprudence; Journalism

Open to graduate and advanced undergraduate or law students pursuing degrees at any accredited domestic or foreign college/university. Based on academic performance, demonstrated interest in the classical liberal tradition, and potential to contribute to the advancement of a free society.

90 awards annually. Apply online or contact IHS for an application.

2223—INTERNATIONAL ASSOCIATION OF FIRE CHIEFS FOUNDATION (Scholarship Program)

1257 Wiltshire Road
York PA 17403
717/854-9083
AMOUNT: $250-$4,000
DEADLINE(S): AUG 15
FIELD(S): Business and Urban Administration, Fire Science

Open to members of a fire service of a state, county, provincial, municipal, community, industrial, or federal fire department.

Renewable. Write for complete information.

2224—JAMES FORD BELL FOUNDATION (Summer Internship Program)

2925 Dean Parkway, Suite 811
Minneapolis MN 55416
612/285-5435
FAX: 612/285-5437
E-mail: famphiladv@uswest.net
AMOUNT: $4,000 for 3 months
DEADLINE(S): APR 30
FIELD(S): Business/Public Administration; Public Policy; Organization Leadership; Nonprofit Management

Interns spend the summer with organizations selected by the Foundation; the organizations select interns from master's degree programs in above or related fields and college seniors with strong interest in nonprofit work. Internships normally in the Twin Cities area.

Contact Foundation for a list of internship opportunities in February and March ONLY; students should request position list, not an application for the program itself (only organizations apply for the program).

2225—JEWISH VOCATIONAL SERVICE (Academic Scholarship Program)

One S. Franklin Street
Chicago IL 60606
312/357-4500
FAX: 312/855-3282
TTY: 312/855-3282
E-mail: jvschicago@jon.cjfny.org
AMOUNT: $5,000 (max.)
DEADLINE(S): MAR 1
FIELD(S): "Helping" Professions; Mathematics; Engineering; Sciences; Communications (at Univ IL only); Law (certain schools in IL only)

Open to Jewish men and women legally domiciled in the greater Chicago metropolitan area, who are identified as having promise for significant contributions in their chosen careers, and are in need of financial assistance for full-time academic programs in above areas. Must have entered undergraduate junior year in career programs requiring no postgrad education, be in graduate/professional school, or be in a vo-tech training program. Interview required.

Renewable. Contact JVS for an application between December 1 and February 15th.

2226—JEWISH WELFARE BOARD (Scholarships)

15 E. 26th Street
New York NY 10010
212/532-4949
AMOUNT: $1,000-$4,000
DEADLINE(S): FEB 1
FIELD(S): Social work, adult education, early childhood education, health education, physical education, cultural studies, Jewish education

Scholarships for Jewish college juniors or seniors pursuing careers in the above fields. Must be committed to the work of the YMHA, YWHA, or Jewish community centers. Must do a year of field work in a Jewish community center.

Renewable. Contact organization for details.

2227—LADY ALLEN OF HURTWOOD MEMORIAL TRUST (Travel Grants)

21 Aspull Common
Leigh Lancs WN7 3PB ENGLAND
01942-674895
AMOUNT: Up to 1,000 pounds sterling
DEADLINE(S): JAN 15
FIELD(S): Welfare and Education of Children

A travel grant to those whose proposed project will directly benefit their work with children. People working with children and young people may apply, particularly those working with disabled and disadvantaged children. Successful candidates must write up an account of the work which the scholarship has funded. GRANTS ARE NOT FOR ACADEMIC STUDY; ONLY QUALIFIED INDIVIDUALS MAY APPLY.

Contact Dorothy E. Whitaker, Trustee, for application forms—available between May and December each year.

2228—NATURAL SCIENCES AND ENGINEERING RESEARCH COUNCIL OF CANADA (Undergraduate Student Research Awards in Small Universities)

350 Albert Street
Ottawa Ontario K1A 1H5 CANADA
613/995-5992
FAX: 613/992-533
E-mail: schol@nserc.ca
Internet: http://www.nserc.ca/programs/usrasmen.htm
AMOUNT: $3,600 (max.)
DEADLINE(S): Varies
FIELD(S): Natural Sciences; Engineering

Research awards for Canadian citizens/permanent residents attending eligible institutions, and who have no more than 6 and no fewer than 2 academic terms remaining to complete bachelor's degree. Cumulative GPA of at least 2nd class (B). Must be doing full-time in research and development activities during award tenure.

Students in health sciences not eligible. Students with BAs and who are studying for a second may apply.

2229—NATIONAL SOCIETY OF ACCOUNTANTS SCHOLARSHIP FOUNDATION (Stanley H. Stearman Scholarship Award)

1010 North FairFAX: Street
Alexandria VA 22314-1574
703/549-6400
FAX: 703/549-2984
E-mail: snoell@mindspring.com
Internet: http://www.nsacct.org
AMOUNT: $2,000/year
DEADLINE(S): MAR 10
FIELD(S): Accounting

For U.S. or Canadian citizens in undergraduate or graduate programs in the U.S. who have a minimum 3.0 GPA. Must be the spouse, child, grandchild, niece, nephew, or son/daughter-in-law of an active or deceased NSA member who have held membership for at least one year. Must include letter of intent, outlining reasons for seeking award, intended career objective, and how this award would be used to accomplish that objective.

1 award annually. Renewable up to 3 years. See Web site or contact Susan Noell, Foundation Director, for an application.

2230—NEW YORK CITY DEPT. OF CITY-WIDE ADMINISTRATIVE SERVICES (Government Scholars Internship Program)

1 Centre Street, 24th Floor
New York NY 10007
212/487-5600
FAX: 212/487-5720
AMOUNT: $3,000 stipend
DEADLINE(S): JAN 13
FIELD(S): Public Administration; Urban Planning; Government; Public Service; Urban Affairs

10-week summer intern program open to undergraduate sophomores, juniors, and seniors. Program provides students with unique opportunity to learn about NY City government. Internships available in virtually every city agency and mayoral office.

Write to New York City Fellowship Programs at above address for complete information.

2231—NEW YORK STATE HIGHER EDUCATION SERVICES CORPORATION (N.Y. State Regents Professional/Health Care Opportunity Scholarships)

Cultural Education Center, Room 5C64
Albany NY 12230
518/486-1319
Internet: http://www.hesc.com
AMOUNT: $1,000-$10,000/year
DEADLINE(S): Varies
FIELD(S): Medicine and dentistry and related fields, architecture, nursing, psychology, audiology, landscape architecture, social work, chiropractic, law, pharmacy, accounting, speech language pathology

For NY state residents who are economically disadvantaged and members of a minority group underrepresented in the chosen profession and attending school in NY state. Some programs carry a service obligation in New York for each year of support. For U.S. citizens or qualifying noncitizens.

Medical/dental scholarships require one year of professional work in NY.

2232—PHILADELPHIA COLLEGE OF BIBLE (Scholarships, Grants, and Loans)

Financial Aid Dept
200 Manor Avenue
Langhorne PA 19047
800/366-0049
Internet: http://www.pcb.edu
AMOUNT: Varies
DEADLINE(S): Varies
FIELD(S): Fields of study relating to Christian education

Various scholarships, loans, and grants are available to students attending this undergraduate Bible college in Philadelphia, PA. High school seniors, transfer students, and others may apply. Some programs are for students with outstanding academic achievement, musical talent, or leaderships skills. Some are for dependents of Christian workers, missionaries, or alumni. Some are based on financial need.

Access Web site for details and/or send SASE to school for further information.

2233—PRESIDENT'S COMMISSION ON WHITE HOUSE FELLOWSHIPS

712 Jackson Place NW
Washington DC 20503
202/395-4522
FAX: 202/395-6179
E-mail: almanac@ace.esusda.gov
AMOUNT: Wage (up to GS-14 Step 3)
DEADLINE(S): DEC 1
FIELD(S): Public Service; Government; Community Involvement; Leadership

Mid-career professionals spend one year as special assistants to senior executive branch officials in Washington. Highly competitive. Nonpartisan; no age or educational requirements. Fellowship year runs September 1 through August 31.

1,200 candidates applying for 11 to 19 fellowships each year. Write for complete information.

2234—ROSE HILL COLLEGE (Louella Robinson Memorial Scholarship)

P.O. Box 3126
Aiken SC 29802-3126
800/684-3769
FAX: 803/641-0240
E-mail: rosehill@rosehill.edu
Internet: http://www.rosehill.edu
AMOUNT: $10,000/year for four years
DEADLINE(S): Varies
FIELD(S): Liberal arts and humanities curricula

For undergraduate residents of Indian River County, Florida, to attend Rose Hill College in Aiken, South Carolina. The school offers a liberal arts education and follows the Great Books curriculum, a program of reading and seminars.

One annual award. Applicants must meet entry requirements of RHC. Contact above location for details.

2235—ROSE HILL COLLEGE (Scholarships for Children of Eastern Orthodox Priests/Deacons)

P.O. Box 3126
Aiken SC 29802-3126
800/684-3769
FAX: 803/641-0240
E-mail: rosehill@rosehill.edu
Internet: http://www.rosehill.edu
AMOUNT: Full scholarship: $10,000/year for four years
DEADLINE(S): Varies
FIELD(S): Liberal Arts and Humanities Curricula

For undergraduates who are children of Eastern Orthodox Christian priests or deacons to attend Rose Hill College in Aiken, South Carolina. The school offers a liberal arts education and follows the Great Books Curriculum, a program of reading and seminars.

6-10 annual awards. Applicants must meet entry requirements of RHC. Contact above location for details.

2236—ROSE HILL COLLEGE (Scholarships for the Homeschooled)

P.O. Box 3126
Aiken SC 29802-3126
800/684-3769
FAX: 803/641-0240
E-mail: rosehill@rosehill.edu
Internet: http://www.resehill.edu
AMOUNT: Full scholarship: $10,000/year for four years
DEADLINE(S): Varies
FIELD(S): Liberal Arts and Humanities Curricula

For undergraduates who have been homeschooled for three of the last five years of their high school education. For use at Rose Hill College in Aiken, South Carolina. The school offers a liberal arts education and follows the Great Books Curriculum, a program of reading and seminars. Scholarships will be awarded primarily on the basis of an essay which the student will be asked to write.

Four annual awards. Applicants must meet entry requirements of RHC. Contact above location for details.

2237—SCOTTISH RITE CHARITABLE FOUNDATION (Bursaries for College Students)

Roeher Institute, Kinsmen Bldg.
4700 Keele Street
North York Ontario M3J 1P3
CANADA

416/661-961; TDD: 416/661-2023
FAX: 416/661-5701
E-mail: mail@aacl.org
Internet: http://www.aacl.org
AMOUNT: $2,000 (max.)
DEADLINE(S): JUL 1
FIELD(S): Human Services; Intellectual Disability; Special Education; DSW

Open to Canadian citizens/landed immigrants accepted into a full-time undergraduate college program in a Canadian college/university. Must submit outline of intended study, transcripts, community involvement, and letters of reference from supervisors. Financial need NOT a factor.

3 awards annually. Must be recommended by a Provincial Association of the Canadian Association for Community Living. Contact your provincial association for details.

2238—THE HEATH EDUCATION FUND (Scholarships for Ministers, Priests, and Missionaries)

Barnett Bank, N.A.
P.O. Box 40200
Jacksonville FL 32203-0200
904/464-2877
AMOUNT: $750-$1,000
DEADLINE(S): JUL 31
FIELD(S): Ministry, Missionary Work, or Social Work

Scholarships to high school graduates from the southeastern U.S. who wish to study in the above fields. Eligible states of residence: Alabama, Florida, Georgia, Kentucky, Louisiana, Maryland, Mississippi, North and South Carolina, Tennessee, Virginia, and West Virginia.

Write to Barnett Bank's Trust Co., N.A., at above address for details and guidelines. Send SASE and letter with brief background of applicant, field of study, religious denomination and reason for request. Preference to Methodists or Episcopalians.

2239—U.S. DEPT. OF HEALTH & HUMAN SERVICES (Indian Health Service Health Professions Scholarship Program)

Twinbrook Metro Plaza, Suite 100
12300 Twinbrook Parkway
Rockville MD 20852
301/443-0234
FAX: 301/443-4815
Internet: http://www:ihs.gov/Recruitment/DHPS/SP/SBTOC3.asp
AMOUNT: Tuition + fees and monthly stipend of $938.
DEADLINE(S): APR 1
FIELD(S): Health professions, accounting, social work

Open to Native Americans or Alaska natives who are graduate students or college juniors or seniors in a program leading to a career in a fields listed above. U.S. citizenship required. Renewable annually with reapplication.

Scholarship recipients must intend to serve the Indian people. They incur a one-year service obligation to the IHS for each year of support for a minimum of two years. Write for complete information.

2240—UNIVERSITY OF SOUTH DAKOTA (Criminal Justice Dept. Scholarships)

414 East Clark Street
Vermillion SD 57069-2390
605/677-5446
E-mail: admiss@usd.edu
Internet: http://www.usd.edu/cjus/scholarships.htm#orderofpolice
AMOUNT: Varies
DEADLINE(S): Varies
FIELD(S): Criminal Justice; Political Science; Public Service

The University of South Dakota's Department of Criminal Justice administers 17 different award programs in the above fields. Some require a high GPA and/or financial need, others require an essay or research project.

See Web site or contact USD for specific details of each award. The Criminal Justice Department gives out an average of $77,000/year to USD students.

2241—WOMEN'S SPORTS FOUNDATION (Jackie Joyner-Kersee and Zina Garrison Minority Internships)

Eisenhower Park
East Meadow NY 11554
800/227-3988
FAX: 516/542-4716
E-mail: WoSport@aol.com
Internet: http://www.lifetimetv.com/WoSport
AMOUNT: $4,000-$5,000
DEADLINE(S): Ongoing
FIELD(S): Sports-related fields

Provides women of color an opportunity to gain experience in a sports-related career and interact in the sports community. May be undergraduates, college graduates, graduate students, or women in a career change. Internships are located at the Women's Sports Foundation in East Meadow, New York.

4-6 awards annually. See Web site or write to above address for details.

SCHOOL OF VOCATIONAL EDUCATION

2242—AERO CLUB OF NEW ENGLAND (Aviation Scholarships)

ACONE Education Committee
4 Thomas Road
Danvers MA 01923
978/263-7793
E-mail: jbuckaroo@mindspring.com
Internet: http://www.acone.org
AMOUNT: $500-$2,500
DEADLINE(S): MAR 30
FIELD(S): Aviation and Related Fields

Several scholarships with varying specifications for eligibility for New England residents to be used at FAA-approved flight schools in New England states.

Information and applications are on Web site above.

2243—AIRCRAFT ELECTRONICS ASSOCIATION EDUCATIONAL FOUNDATION (Scholarships)

P.O. Box 1963
Independence MO 64055
816/373-6565
FAX: 816/478-3100
Internet: http://aeaavnews.org
AMOUNT: $1,000-$16,000
DEADLINE(S): Varies
FIELD(S): Avionics; Aircraft Repair

Various scholarships for high school and college students attending postsecondary institutions, including technical schools. Some are for study in Canada or Europe as well as the U.S.

25 programs. See Web site or contact AEA for specific details and applications.

2244—AMERICAN ASSOCIATION OF COSMETOLOGY SCHOOLS (ACE Grants)

11811 N. Tatum Boulevard, Suite 1085
Phoenix AZ 85028
602/788-1170
FAX: 602/404-8900
E-mail: jim@beautyschools.org
Internet: http://www.beautyschools.org
AMOUNT: $1,000 (average)
DEADLINE(S): None
FIELD(S): Cosmetology

Grants for U.S. citizens/permanent residents who are accepted to a participating ACE grant school. Must be high school graduate or equivalent. Financial need is NOT a factor.

500+ awards annually. Not renewable. Contact Jim Cox at the American Association of Cosmetology Schools for an application.

2245—AMERICAN FOUNDATION FOR THE BLIND (Paul W. Ruckes Scholarship)

11 Penn Plaza, Suite 300
New York NY 10001
212/502-7661
FAX: 212/502-7771
E-mail: juliet@afb.org
Internet: http://www.afb.org
AMOUNT: $1,000
DEADLINE(S): APR 30
FIELD(S): Engineering; Computer/Physical/Life Sciences

Open to legally blind and visually impaired undergraduate and graduate students pursuing a degree in one of above fields. Must be U.S. citizen. Must submit written documentation of visual impairment from ophthalmologist or optometrist (need not be legally blind); official transcripts; proof of college/university acceptance; three letters of recommendation; and typewritten statement describing goals, work experience extracurricular activities, and how monies will be used.

1 award annually. See Web site or contact Julie Tucker at AFB for an application.

2246—AMERICAN FOUNDATION FOR THE BLIND (R. L. Gillette Scholarships)

11 Penn Plaza, Suite 300
New York NY 10001
212/502-7661
FAX: 212/502-7771
E-mail: afbinfo@afb.org
Internet: http://www.afb.org
AMOUNT: $1,000
DEADLINE(S): APR
FIELD(S): Literature; Music

Open to legally blind women enrolled in a four-year undergraduate degree program in literature or music. Must be U.S. citizen. Must submit evidence of legal blindness; official transcripts; proof of college/university acceptance; three letters of recommendation; performance tape (30 minutes max.) or creative writing sample; and typewritten statement describing educational and personal goals, work experience, extracurricular activities, and how monies will be used.

2 awards annually. See Web site or contact Julie Tucker at AFB for an application.

2247—AMERICAN INSTITUTE OF AERONAUTICS AND ASTRONAUTICS (Undergraduate Scholarships)

1801 Alexander Bell Drive, Suite 500
Reston VA 20191-4344
800/639-AIAA; 703/264-7630
FAX: 703/264-7551
E-mail: rayc@aiaa.org
Internet: http://www.aiaa.org
AMOUNT: $2,000
DEADLINE(S): JAN 31
FIELD(S): Science, Engineering, Aeronautics, Astronautics

For students who have completed at least one academic semester or quarter of full-time college work in the area of science or engineering encompassed by the technical activities of the AIAA. Must have GPA of at least 3.0, be currently enrolled in accredited college or university. Membership in AIAA not required to apply but must become one before receiving a scholarship award.

Students who receive these awards are eligible for yearly continuation until completion of senior year upon submission of application, career essay, transcripts and 2 letters of recommendation from college professor.

2248—AMERICAN INSTITUTE OF BAKING (Scholarships)

1213 Bakers Way
Manhattan KS 66502
800/633-5737
FAX: 785/537-1493
E-mail: kembers@aibonline.org
Internet: http://www.aibonline.org
AMOUNT: $500-$4,000
DEADLINE(S): None
FIELD(S): Baking Industry; Electrical/Electronic Maintenance

Award is to be used towards tuition for a 16- or 10-week course in baking science and technology or maintenance engineering at the Institute. Experience in baking, mechanics, or an approved alternative is required. Awards are intended for people who plan to seek new positions in the baking and maintenance engineering fields.

45 awards annually. Contact AIB for an application.

2249—AMERICAN WELDING SOCIETY (Scholarships)

550 NW LeJeune Road
Miami FL 33126
800/443-9353 ext. 461 or 305/445-6628
FAX: 305/443-7559
Internet: http://www.aws.org
AMOUNT: $2,500-$3,000
DEADLINE(S): JAN 15
FIELD(S): Welding Engineering and Technology

AWS has nine different scholarship programs for U.S. citizens pursuing undergraduate study at an accredited U.S. institution. Two programs are also for Canadian citizens studying at Canadian institutions. Must be at least 18 years of age with a high school diploma or equivalent and a minimum 2.0 GPA. Some programs require financial need. Must submit two letters of reference, brief biography, transcript, proposed curriculum, and verification of enrollment/employment.

Renewable up to 4 years. Contact AWS for details on specific scholarships. Awards announced in February.

2250—AMERICAN WINE SOCIETY EDUCATIONAL FOUNDATION (Scholarships and Grants)

1134 Prospect Avenue
Bethlehem PA 18018-4910
610/865-2401 or 610/758-3845
FAX: 610/758-4344
E-mail: lhs0@lehigh.edu
AMOUNT: $2,500
DEADLINE(S): MAR 31
FIELD(S): Wine industry professional study: enology, viticulture, health aspects of food and wine, and using and appreciating fine wines

To provide academic scholarships and research grants to students based on academic excellence. Must show financial need and genuine interest in pursuing careers in wine-related fields. For North American citizens, defined as U.S., Canada, Mexico, the Bahamas, and the West Indies at all levels of education.

Contact Les Sperling at above location for application.

2251—AUTOMOTIVE HALL OF FAME (Educational Fund)

21400 Oakwood Boulevard
Dearborn MI 48124-4078

313/240-4000
FAX: 313/240-8641
Internet: http://www.automotive halloffame.org
AMOUNT: $250-$2,000
DEADLINE(S): MAY 30
FIELD(S): Automotive-Related Careers

Open to full-time undergraduate and graduate students who have a sincere interest in pursuing an automotive career upon graduation from college. Must be at least a college freshman at a 4-year institution or a high school senior for an 18-month or 2-year program. Must be attending or accepted into an accredited college, university, or trade school in the U.S. Transcripts and letters of recommendation required. Financial need considered but not necessary.

12+ awards annually. Renewable. See Web site or send self-addressed, stamped envelope for an application. Recipients notified mid-September.

2252—ASSOCIATED WESTERN UNIVERSITIES, INC. (AWU Undergraduate Student Fellowships)

4190 S. Highland Drive, Suite 211
Salt Lake City UT 84124-2600
801/273-8900
FAX: 801/277-5632
E-mail: info@awu.org
Internet: http://www.awu.org
AMOUNT: $300/week stipend + possible travel allowance
DEADLINE(S): FEB 1
FIELD(S): Science; Mathematics; Engineering; Technology

Eight- to sixteen-week fellowships.

2253—AVIATION DISTRIBUTORS AND MANUFACTURERS ASSOCIATION INTERNATIONAL (ADMA International Scholarship Fund)

1900 Arch Street
Philadelphia PA 19103-1498
215/564-3484
FAX: 215/564-2175
E-mail: assnhqt@netaxs.com
AMOUNT: Varies
DEADLINE(S): MAR 15
FIELD(S): Aviation Management; Professional Pilot

Open to students seeking a career in aviation management or as a professional pilot. Emphasis may be in general aviation, airway science management, aviation maintenance, flight engineering, or airway a/c systems management.

Applicants must be studying in the aviation field in a four-year school having an aviation program. Write for complete information.

2254—AVIATION INSURANCE ASSOCIATION (Scholarship)

Aviation Technology Department
1 Purdue Airport
West Lafayette, IN 47906-3398
765/494-5782
AMOUNT: $1,000
DEADLINE(S): FEB 28
FIELD(S): Aviation

Scholarships for aviation students who have completed at least 30 college credits, 15 of which are in aviation. Must have GPA of at least 2.5 and be a U.S. citizen.

Write to Professor Bernard Wulle at Purdue University at above address for application and details.

2255—AVIATION MAINTENANCE EDUCATION FUND (AMEF Scholarship Program)

P.O. Box 2826
Redmond WA 98073
206/827-2295
AMOUNT: $250-$1000
DEADLINE(S): None
FIELD(S): Aviation Maintenance Technology

AMEF scholarship program open to any worthy applicant who is enrolled in a federal aviation administration (FAA) certified aviation maintenance technology program.

Write for complete information.

2256—COLORADO RESTAURANT ASSOCIATION (Scholarship Education Fund)

430 E. 7th Avenue
Denver CO 80203
800/522-2972 or 303/830-2972
FAX: 303/830-2973
E-mail: info@coloradorestaurant.com
Internet: http://www.colorado restaurant.com
AMOUNT: $500-$2,500
DEADLINE(S): MAR 20
FIELD(S): Foodservice; Hospitality

Open to junior and senior level college students enrolled in a two- or four-year degree program in foodservice and hospitality related fields at a Colorado college/university.

Contact CRA for an application.

2257—COMMUNITY FOUNDATION OF WESTERN MASSACHUSETTS (James L. Shriver Scholarship)

1500 Main Street
P.O. Box 15769
Springfield MA 01115
413/732-2858
AMOUNT: $750
DEADLINE(S): APR 15
FIELD(S): Technical Fields

Open to residents of Western Massachusetts to pursue technical careers through college, trade, or technical school. Based on financial need, academic merit, and extracurricular activities. Must submit transcripts and fill out government FAFSA form.

1 award annually. Renewable with reapplication. Contact Community Foundation for an application and your financial aid office for FAFSA. Notification is in June.

2258—COOPERATIVE ASSOCIATION OF STATES FOR SCHOLARSHIPS (CASS) (Scholarships)

c/o Commonwealth Liaison
Unit 310 The Garrison
St. Michael BARBADOS
809/436-8754
AMOUNT: Varies
DEADLINE(S): None
FIELD(S): Business application/computer science

Scholarships for economically disadvantaged deaf youth, ages 17-25, with strong leadership potential and an interest in computer science/business applications. Must be from Barbados, St. Kitts/Nevis, Grenada, St. Vincent, Antigua/Barbuda, St. Lucia, Dominica, or Jamaica.

Write to E. Caribbean Reg. Coordinator (CASS) at above address.

2259—EAA AVIATION FOUNDATION (Scholarship Program)

P.O. Box 3065
Oshkosh WI 54903-3065
920/426-6815 or 888/EAA-EAA9 or 888/322-3229
E-mail: education@eaa.org
Internet: http://www.eaa.org
AMOUNT: $500-$5,000
DEADLINE(S): MAY 1
FIELD(S): Aviation

Six different scholarship programs open to well-rounded individuals involved in school and community activities as well as aviation. Applicant's academic records should verify his/her ability to complete educational activity for which scholarship is requested. For all but one scholarship, students must major in aviation. Financial need considered in some programs. One scholarship includes tuition, books, fees, etc. at the Fox Valley Technical College in Wisconsin.

Renewable. $5 application fee. Contact EAA for an application (one application covers all of the scholarship programs).

2260—EMPIRE COLLEGE (Dean's Scholarship)

3035 Cleveland Avenue
Santa Rosa CA 95403
707/546-4000
FAX: 707/546-4058

AMOUNT: $250-$1,500
DEADLINE(S): APR 15
FIELD(S): Accounting; Secretarial; Legal; Medical (Clinical and Administrative); Travel and Tourism; General Business; Computer Assembly; Network Assembly/Administration

Open to high school seniors who plan to attend Empire College. Must be U.S. citizen.

10 awards annually. Contact Ms. Mary Farha for an application.

2261—FOOD INDUSTRY SCHOLARSHIP FUND OF NEW HAMPSHIRE (Scholarships)

110 Stark Street
Manchester NH 03101-1977
Written Inquiry

AMOUNT: $1,000
DEADLINE(S): MAR 15
FIELD(S): Food Industry

Open to students who are residents of New Hampshire and planning to enter a career in the food industry. Ten to 12 awards annually.

Contact Fund for an application.

2262—GOLDEN GATE RESTAURANT ASSOCIATION (Scholarship Foundation Awards)

720 Market Street, Suite 200
San Francisco CA 94102
415/781-5348
FAX: 415/781-3925
E-mail: AdministrationCoordinator@ggra.org

AMOUNT: $500-$2,500
DEADLINE(S): MAR 31
FIELD(S): Foodservice Industry

Open to California residents who are undergrads majoring in foodservice at a college/university. Category I awards require students to be full-time and have graduated from high school in the San Francisco Bay Area; Category II requires students to be full-time, have completed at least one semester, and have a minimum 2.75 GPA; and Category III requires students to be part-time, working in the foodservice/hospitality industry 20 hours/week, and have a minimum 2.75 GPA.

Contact Matthew Bass, GGRASF Administration Coordinator, for an application.

2263—HAYSTACK MOUNTAIN SCHOOL OF CRAFTS (Scholarship Program)

Admissions Office
P.O. Box 518
Deer Isle ME 04627
207/348-2306
FAX: 207/348-2307
E-mail: haystack@haystack-mtn.org
Internet: http://www.haystack-mtn.org

AMOUNT: $500-$1,000
DEADLINE(S): MAR 25
FIELD(S): Crafts

Open to technical assistants and work-study students in graphics, ceramics, weaving, jewelry, glass, blacksmithing, fabric, or wood. Tenable for one of the six two- to three-week summer sessions at Haystack Mountain School. One year of graduate study or equivalent experience is required for TA applicants.

100 scholarships awarded annually. Must be 18 years of age or older.

2264—HOBART INSTITUTE OF WELDING TECHNOLOGY (Scholarships)

400 Trade Square East
Troy OH 45373
800/332-9448 or 937/332-5090
FAX: 937/332-5200
E-mail: hiwt@welding.org
Internet: http://www.welding.org

AMOUNT: $6,725
DEADLINE(S): APR 1; AUG 1; DEC 1
FIELD(S): Structural Welding

Open to undergraduates and technical school students in a structural welding program at the Hobart Institute of Welding Technology. Must have graduated from high school within the past seven years, or have obtained a GED equivalent during that time. Based on an essay, grades, and references; financial need NOT a factor.

3 awards annually. See Web site or send self-addressed, stamped envelope to above address for an application.

2265—ILLINOIS PILOTS ASSOCIATION (IPA Memorial Scholarship)

40 West Apache Lane
Huntley IL 60142
Internet: http://www.illinoispilots.com/

AMOUNT: $500
DEADLINE(S): APR 1
FIELD(S): Aviation

Scholarships for individuals majoring in an aviation-oriented curriculum who are residents of Illinois and attending a college or university in Illinois.

Check Web site or write for details.

2266—INTERNATIONAL ASSOCIATION OF ARSON INVESTIGATORS (John Charles Wilson Scholarship)

12770 Boenker Road
St. Louis MO 63044
314/739-4224
FAX: 314/739-4219
Internet: http://www.fire-investigators.org

AMOUNT: Varies
DEADLINE(S): FEB 15
FIELD(S): Police or Fire Sciences, including Fire Investigation and related subjects

Open to IAAI members, their immediate families, and non-members who are recommended and sponsored by members in good standing. Awards are for undergraduate study in above areas at accredited two and four year institutions.

3 awards annually. Transcripts and 500-word essay describing background and goals required. Write to the Executive Director at above address for more information.

2267—INTERNATIONAL ASSOCIATION OF FIRE CHIEFS FOUNDATION (Scholarship Program)

1257 Wiltshire Road
York PA 17403
717/854-9083

AMOUNT: $250-$4,000
DEADLINE(S): AUG 15
FIELD(S): Business and Urban Administration, Fire Science

Open to members of a fire service of a state, county, provincial, municipal, community, industrial, or federal fire department.

Renewable. Write for complete information.

2268—INTERNATIONAL FOOD SERVICE EXECUTIVES ASSOCIATION (Worthy Goal Scholarship)

3739 Mykonos Ct.
Boca Raton FL 33487-1282
561/998-7758
FAX: 561/998-3878
FAX-On-Demand: 954/977-0767
E-mail: hq@ifsea.org
Internet: http://www.ifsea.org
AMOUNT: $500
DEADLINE(S): FEB 1
FIELD(S): Food Service Management

Undergraduate scholarship for deserving individuals to receive training in food service management. Additional scholarships are available through IFSEA branches.

Renewable by reapplication. Use Fax-On-Demand service or send a self-addressed, stamped envelope to IFSEA for an application.

2269—JAMES F. LINCOLN ARC WELDING FOUNDATION (Award Program)

P.O. Box 17188
Cleveland OH 44117
216/481-4300
Internet: http://www.jflf.org
AMOUNT: Varies
DEADLINE(S): MAY 1
FIELD(S): Arc Welding and Engineering Design

Open to high school students, college undergraduates, and graduate students, and to professionals working in the fields of arc welding and engineering design. Various programs are available.

See Web site or send self-addressed, stamped envelope to Roy Morrow, President, at above address.

2270—JOHN K. and THIRZA F. DAVENPORT FOUNDATION (Scholarships in the Arts)

20 North Main Street
South Yarmouth MA 02664-3143
508/398-2293
FAX: 508/394-6765
Internet: http://www.davenportrealty.com/pdf/foundationapplication.pdf
AMOUNT: Varies
DEADLINE(S): JUL 15
FIELD(S): Theatre, Music, Art

For Barnstable County, Massachusetts residents in their last two years of undergraduate or graduate (preferred) study in visual or performing arts. Must demonstrate financial need.

6-8 awards annually. Renewable. Contact Mrs. Chris M. Walsh for more information.

2271—JOHNSON AND WALES UNIVERSITY (Annual Johnson and Wales University National High School Recipe Contest)

8 Abbott Place
Providence RI 02903
401/598-2345
AMOUNT: $1,000 to $5,000
DEADLINE(S): JAN 31
FIELD(S): Business, Hospitality, Technology, Culinary Arts

For students planning to attend Johnson & Wales University, Providence, Rhode Island.

Write to above address for detailed description.

2272—JOHNSON AND WALES UNIVERSITY (Gilbane Building Company Eagle Scout Scholarship)

8 Abbott Place
Providence RI 02903
401/598-2345
AMOUNT: $1,200
DEADLINE(S): None
FIELD(S): Business, Hospitality, Technology, Culinary Arts

For students attending Johnson & Wales University, Providence, Rhode Island. Must be Eagle Scouts.

Send letter of recommendation and transcript to above address.

2273—JOHNSON AND WALES UNIVERSITY (National High School Entrepreneur of the Year Contest)

8 Abbott Place
Providence RI 02903
401/598-2345
AMOUNT: $1,000 to $10,000
DEADLINE(S): DEC 27
FIELD(S): Business, Hospitality, Technology, Culinary Arts

For students attending Johnson & Wales University, Providence, Rhode Island.

Send for detailed description to above address.

2274—JOHNSON AND WALES UNIVERSITY (Scholarships)

8 Abbott Place
Providence RI 02903
401/598-2345
AMOUNT: $200 to $10,000
DEADLINE(S): None
FIELD(S): Business, Hospitality, Technology, Culinary Arts

For students attending Johnson & Wales University, Providence, Rhode Island.

Renewable for four years. Write for complete information.

2275—MARYLAND HIGHER EDUCATION COMMISSION (Tuition Reimbursement of Firefighters and Rescue Squad Members)

State Scholarship Admin.
16 Francis Street
Annapolis MD 21401
410/974-5370
TTY: 800/735-2258
Internet: http://www.ubalt.edu/www.mhec
AMOUNT: Varies (current resident undergraduate tuition rate at Univ. MD-College Park)
DEADLINE(S): JUL 1
FIELD(S): Firefighting; Emergency Medical Technology

Open to firefighters and rescue squad members who successfully complete one year of coursework in a firefighting or EMT program and a two-year service obligation in Maryland.

Contact MHEC for an application.

2276—MIDWAY COLLEGE (Institutional Aid Program)

Financial Aid Office
Midway KY 40347
606/846-4421
AMOUNT: Varies
DEADLINE(S): MAR 1
FIELD(S): Nursing; Paralegal; Education; Psychology; Biology; Equine Studies; Liberal Studies; Business Administration

Scholarships and grants are open to women who are accepted for enrollment at Midway College. Awards support undergraduate study in the above areas.

80 awards annually. Contact Midway College's Financial Aid Office for an application.

2277—McCORD CAREER CENTER (Level II McCord Medical/Music Scholarship)

Healdsburg High School
1024 Prince Street
Healdsburg CA 95448
707/431-3473
Email: career@husd.com
AMOUNT: Varies
DEADLINE(S): APR 15
FIELD(S): Medicine; Music

For graduates of Healdsburg High School who are planning a career in music or medicine. Must be enrolled full-time at a college/university as an undergraduate junior or senior in the fall, or earning an advanced degree in graduate or medical school, or entering into a vocational/certificate program. Transcripts, proof of attendance, and an essay are required.

Contact the McCord Career Center at Healdsburg High School for an application.

2278—NATIONAL AIR TRANSPORTATION ASSOCIATION FOUNDATION (John W. Godwin, Jr., Memorial Scholarship Fund)

4226 King Street
Alexandria VA 22302
808/808-NATA or 703/845-9000
FAX: 703/845-8176
AMOUNT: $2,500
DEADLINE(S): None
FIELD(S): Flight training

Scholarship for flight training for any certificate and/or flight rating issued by the FAA, at any NATA-Member company offering flight training. Must accumulate a minimum of 15 dual or solo flight hours each calendar month.

Contact organization for details.

2279—NATIONAL AIR TRANSPORTATION ASSOCIATION FOUNDATION (The Pioneers of Flight Scholarship)

4226 King Street
Alexandria VA 22302
703/845-9000
FAX: 703/845-8176
AMOUNT: $2,500
DEADLINE(S): None
FIELD(S): General aviation

Scholarship for college students who are in the sophomore or junior year at the time of application intending to pursue full-time study at an accredited four-year college or university and can demonstrate an interest in pursuing a career in general aviation.

Must be nominated by an NATA Regular or Associate Member company.

2280—NATIONAL ASSN OF EXECUTIVE SECRETARIES AND ADMINISTRATIVE ASSISTANTS (Scholarship Award Program)

900 S. Washington Street, Suite G-13
Falls Church VA 22046
Written Inquiry
AMOUNT: $250
DEADLINE(S): MAY 31
FIELD(S): Secretarial

Open to post secondary students working toward a college degree (Associates; Bachelors; Masters) who are NAESAA members or the spouse, child, or grandchild of a member.

Scholarship may be used for Certified Professional Secretary Exam or to buy required books. Write for complete information.

2281—NATIONAL BUSINESS AVIATION ASSOCIATION (Indiana Business Aviation Association PDP Scholarships)

1200 Eighteenth Street NW
Suite 400
Washington DC 20036-2527
202/783-9353
FAX: 202/331-8364
E-mail: jevans@nbaa.org
Internet: http://www.nbaa.org/scholarships/
AMOUNT: $1,150
DEADLINE(S): AUG 31
FIELD(S): Aviation-related curricula

Valid only for students enrolled at institutions that are NBAA and University Aviation Association (UAA) members. Open to college sophomores, juniors, or seniors who will be continuing in school the following academic year in an aviation-related baccalaureate or graduate program at these specific member institutions. Must be U.S. citizen and have 3.0 or better GPA.

Four awards per year. Check Web site or contact NBAA for complete information and application.

2282—NATIONAL FOUNDATION FOR ADVANCEMENT IN THE ARTS (Arts Recognition and Talent Search)

800 Brickell Avenue
Miami FL 33131
800/970-ARTS or 305/377-1140
FAX: 305/377-1149
E-mail: info@nfaa.org
Internet: http://www.ARTSawards.org
AMOUNT: $100-$3,000
DEADLINE(S): OCT 1
FIELD(S): Creative and Performing Arts

Talent contest for high school seniors and 17-18 year olds in dance, jazz, music, photography, theatre, visual arts, voice, and writing. Except for those applying in Music/Jazz, applicants must be U.S. citizens or permanent residents. May apply in more than one category, but only one financial award will be given to any individual, and a fee is required for each category in which student applies.

$35 application fee ($25 if apply by June 1); fee may be waived if you are unable to meet this requirement). 400 awards annually. Not renewable. Contact NFAA for an application packet.

2283—NATIONAL GARDEN CLUBS, INC. (Scholarships)

4401 Magnolia Avenue
St. Louis MO 63110-3492
314/776-7574
FAX: 314/776-5108
E-mail: renee_blaschke@juno.com
Internet: http://www.gardenclub.org
AMOUNT: $3,500
DEADLINE(S): MAR 1
FIELD(S): Horticulture, Floriculture, Landscape Design, City Planning, Land Management, and allied subjects.

Open to juniors, seniors, and graduate students who are U.S. citizens and are studying any of the above or related subjects. Student must have the endorsement of the state in which he/she resides permanently. Applications will be forwarded to the National State Chairman and judged on a national level.

30-35 scholarships are awarded. Write to the above address for complete information.

2284—NATIONAL GAY PILOTS ASSOCIATION (Pilot Scholarships)

13140 Coit Road
Suite 320, LB 120
Dallas, TX 75240
972/233-9107, ext. 203
FAX: 972/490-4219
E-mail: ngpa@ngpa.org
Internet: http://www.ngpa.org
AMOUNT: $2,000
DEADLINE(S): APR 30
FIELD(S): Pilot Training and Related Fields in Aerospace, Aerodynamics, Engineering, Airport Management, etc.

Scholarships for tuition or flight training costs for student pilots enrolled at a college or university offering an accredited aviation curriculum in the above fields. Also for flight training costs in a professional pilot training program at any training facility certified by the FAA. Not for training for a Private Pilot license. Send SASE for application or visit Web site for further instructions.

For applicants who can provide evidence of volunteering in any group that supports the gay/lesbian community and their rights.

2285—NATIONAL SPACE CLUB (Dr. Robert H. Goddard Historical Essay Award)

2000 L Street NW, Suite 710
Washington DC 20036-4907
202/973-8661

AMOUNT: $1,000 + plaque
DEADLINE(S): DEC 4
FIELD(S): Aerospace History

Essay competition open to any U.S. citizen on a topic dealing with any significant aspect of the historical development of rocketry and astronautics. Essays should not exceed 5,000 words and should be fully documented. Will be judged on originality and scholarship.

Previous winners not eligible. Send self-addressed, stamped envelope for complete information.

2286—NINETY-NINES, INC. (Amelia Earhart Memorial Scholarships)

Box 965, 7100 Terminal Drive
Oklahoma City OK 73159-0965
800/994-1929 or 405/685-7969
FAX: 405/685-7985
E-mail: 99s@ninety-nines.org
Internet: http://www.ninety-nines.org

AMOUNT: Varies
DEADLINE(S): DEC 31
FIELD(S): Advanced Aviation Ratings

Scholarships for female licensed pilots who are members of the 99s, Inc.

15-20 awards annually. Financial need considered. Contact Liz Rousch at above address for application and/or membership information.

2287—NINETY-NINES, SAN FERNANDO VALLEY CHAPTER/VAN NUYS AIRPORT (Aviation Career Scholarships)

P.O. Box 8160
Van Nuys CA 91409
818/989-0081

AMOUNT: $3,000
DEADLINE(S): MAY 1
FIELD(S): Aviation Careers

For men and women of the greater Los Angeles area pursuing careers as professional pilots, flight instructors, mechanics, or other aviation career specialists. Applicants must be at least 21 years of age and U.S. citizens.

3 awards annually. Send self-addressed, stamped, business-sized envelope to above address for application after January 1.

2288—PROFESSIONAL AVIATION MAINTENANCE ASSOCIATION (PAMA Scholarship Fund)

636 Eye Street NW, Suite 300
Washington DC 20001-3736
202/216-9220
FAX: 202/216-9224

AMOUNT: $1,000
DEADLINE(S): OCT 31
FIELD(S): Aviation Maintenance

Open to students enrolled in an institution to obtain an airframe and powerplant (A&P) license who have completed 25% of the required curriculum. Must have 3.0 or better GPA, demonstrate financial need, and be recommended by instructor.

Applications to be submitted through student's school. Write for complete information. The application period runs from July 1 through October 31.

2289—PROFESSIONAL AVIATION MAINTENANCE ASSOCIATION (Scholarships)

636 Eye Street NW, Suite 300
Washington DC 20001-3736
202/216-9220
FAX: 202/216-9224
E-mail: hq@pama.org
Internet: http://www.pama.org

AMOUNT: $1,000 per year
DEADLINE(S): OCT 31
FIELD(S): Aviation Maintenance

For students pursuing airframe and powerplant (A&P) technician certification through an FAA Part 147 aviation maintenance technician school. Must have completed 25% of required curriculum and have a 3.0 or better GPA.

Access Web site or contact above location for more details and application forms, which are accepted between July 1 and Oct. 31.

2290—SOCIETY FOR TECHNICAL COMMUNICATION (Undergraduate Scholarships)

901 N. Stuart Street, Suite 904
Arlington VA 22203
703/522-4114
FAX: 703/522-2075
E-mail: stc@stcva.org
Internet: http://www.stcva.org/scholarships.html

AMOUNT: $2,000
DEADLINE(S): FEB 15
FIELD(S): Technical Communication

Open to full-time undergraduate students who have completed at least one year of study and are enrolled in an accredited 2- or 4-year degree program for career in any area of technical communication: technical writing, editing, graphic design, multimedia art, etc.

Awards tenable at recognized colleges and universities in U.S. and Canada. Fourteen awards per year-seven undergraduate and seven graduate. See Web site and/or write for complete information.

2291—STUDENT CONSERVATION ASSOCIATION (SCA Resource Assistant Program)

P.O. Box 550
Charlestown NH 03603
603/543-1700
FAX: 603/543-1828
E-mail: internships@sca-inc.org
Internet: http://www.sca-inc.org

AMOUNT: $1,180-$4,725
DEADLINE(S): Varies
FIELD(S): Environment and related fields

Must be 18 and U.S. citizen; need not be student. Fields: Agriculture, archaeology, anthropology, botany, caves, civil/environmental engineering, environmental education, fisheries, forests, herpetology, history, living history/roleplaying, visitor services, landscape architecture/environmental design, paleontology, recreation/resource/range management, trail maintenance/construction, wildlife management, geology, hydrology, library/museums, surveying...

900 positions in U.S. and Canada. Send $1 for postage for application; outside U.S./Canada, send $20.

2292—THE FRASCA FAMILY/UNIVERSITY AVIATION ASSOCIATION (The Joseph Frasca Excellence in Aviation Scholarship)

c/o College of Applied Sciences and Art
Southern Illinois University
Carbondale IL 62901-6623
618/453-8898

AMOUNT: $1,000

DEADLINE(S): JUN 3
FIELD(S): Aviation Maintenance or Flight Training

Scholarships for college juniors or seniors currently enrolled in a University Aviation Association (UAA)-affiliated institution and pursuing a career in one of the above fields. Minimum GPA of 3.0. Must show membership in a flight-related organization.

Two awards yearly.

2293—THE WALT DISNEY COMPANY (American Teacher Awards)

P.O. Box 9805
Calabasas CA 91372
AMOUNT: $2,500 (36 awards); $25,000 (Outstanding Teacher of the Year)
DEADLINE(S): FEB 15
FIELD(S): Teachers: Athletic Coach, Early Childhood, English, Foreign Language/ESL, General Elementary, Mathematics, Performing Arts, Physical Education/Health, Science, Social Studies, Visual Arts, Voc/Tech Education

Awards for K-12 teachers in the above fields.

Teachers, or anyone who knows a great teacher, can write for applications at the above address.

2294—U.S. DEPARTMENT OF TRANSPORTATION (Dwight D. Eisenhower Transportation Fellowship Program)

4600 N. FairFAX: Drive, Suite 800
Arlington VA 22203
703/235-0538
FAX: 703/235-0593
Internet: http://www.nhi.fhwa.dot.gov
AMOUNT: Varies
DEADLINE(S): FEB 15
FIELD(S): Transportation

Open to graduate students and undergraduate juniors and seniors to pursue studies or research in any area of the U.S. transportation industry. Must be U.S. citizen. Objectives of program are to attract the nation's brightest minds to the field of transportation, to enhance the careers of transportation professionals by encouraging them to seek advanced degrees, and to retain top talent in the U.S. transportation industry.

See Web site or contact Universities and Grants Programs at the Dept. of Transportation for an application and specific details on each of the six award programs.

2295—UNIVERSAL TECHNICAL INSTITUTE (Joe Gibbs National High School Competition)

3121 W. Weldon Avenue
Phoenix AZ 85017
800/859-1202 or 888/884-3678 or 602/264-4164
Internet: http://www.uticorp.com/utiedu/national.html
AMOUNT: $5,000 (max.)
DEADLINE(S): Varies
FIELD(S): Technical (Auto/Truck Mechanics or HVAC)

Competition for high school seniors pursuing careers as technicians in the above areas. Winners will receive scholarships valued from $500 to $5,000 for use at UTI, which has campuses in Arizona, Illinois, and Texas. Awards are based on a written test of technical skills to be taken at various sites in the U.S. Awards also are given to schools by students finishing in the top 10%.

Nearly $400,000 will be awarded in the Auto/Truck competition, and over $100,000 in the HVAC/R competition. Call, check Web site, or write for details.

2296—VIRGINIA AVIATION AND SPACE EDUCATION FORUM (Aviation Scholarship)

c/o Virginia Department of Aviation
5702 Gulfstream Road
Richmond VA 23250-2422
804/236-3624
FAX: 804/236-3625
E-mail: director@doav.state.va.us
Internet: www.doav.state.va.us/
AMOUNT: $1,000
DEADLINE(S): FEB 14
FIELD(S): Aviation-related programs

Scholarships for high school seniors planning a career in aviation who are residents of Virginia who have been accepted and are enrolled in an accredited college. Must have at least a 3.5 GPA.

Contact above location or access Web site for application and details of eligibility requirements.

2297—WHIRLY-GIRLS INC. (International Women Helicopter Pilots Scholarships)

Executive Towers 10-D
207 West Clarendon Avenue
Phoenix AZ 85013
602/263-0190
FAX: 602/264-5812
AMOUNT: $4,500
DEADLINE(S): NOV 15
FIELD(S): Helicopter Flight Training

Three scholarships available to licensed women pilots for flight training. Two are awarded to Whirly-Girls who are helicopter pilots; one is awarded to a licensed woman pilot holding a private license (airplane, balloon, or glider).

Applications are available April 15. Write, call, or FAX: for complete information.

2298—WYOMING TRUCKING ASSOCIATION (Scholarships)

P.O. Box 1909
Casper WY 82602
Written Inquiry
AMOUNT: $250-$300
DEADLINE(S): MAR 1
FIELD(S): Transportation Industry

For Wyoming high school graduates enrolled in a Wyoming college, approved trade school, or the University of Wyoming. Must be pursuing a course of study which will result in a career in the transportation industry in Wyoming, including but not limited to: safety, environmental science, diesel mechanics, truck driving, vocational trades, business management, sales management, computer skills, accounting, office procedures, and management.

1-10 awards annually. Write to WYTA for an application.

GENERAL

2299—SOCIETY OF THE FIRST INFANTRY DIVISION FOUNDATION (Lt. Gen. C.R. Huebner Scholarship Program)

1933 Morris Road
Blue Bell PA 19422-1422
888/324-4733
FAX: 215/661-1934
E-mail: Soc1ID@aol.com
Internet: http://wwwbigredone.org
AMOUNT: $3,000/year (max.)
DEADLINE(S): JUN 1
FIELD(S): All fields of study

Open to high school seniors who are the children or grandchildren of soldiers who have served in the 1st Infantry Division of the U.S. Army. Based on scholastic achievements, career objectives, 200-word essay (analyzing problem facing our country and recommendations for solution), and letters of recommendation. Financial need NOT a factor.

3 awards annually. Renewable. Send a self-addressed, stamped envelope to Rosemary Wirs, Secretary-Treasurer, for an application.

2300—1ST MARINE DIVISION ASSN. (Scholarship Program)

14325 Willard Road, Suite 107
Chantilly VA 20151-2110
Phone: 703/803-3195
FAX: 703/803-7114
E-mail oldbreed@aol.com
Internet: http://1stmarine.anthill.com/
AMOUNT: Up to $1,500
DEADLINE(S): Varies
FIELD(S): All fields of study

For dependents of persons who served in the First Marine Division or in a unit attached to or in support of the Division and are deceased from any cause or permanently 100% disabled.

For undergraduate study only. Write for complete information.

2301—37th DIVISION VETERANS ASSOCIATION (Scholarship/Grant)

65 South Front Street, Room 432
Columbus OH 43215
614/228-3788
AMOUNT: $1,000
DEADLINE(S): APR 1
FIELD(S): All fields of study

Scholarship/grant open to high school seniors or college students who are direct descendants 37th Infantry Division veterans who served in World War I, II, or the Korean conflict.

Financial need is a consideration particularly if the father is deceased. Two scholarships per year. Write for complete information.

2302—A. MARLYN MOYER, JR. SCHOLARSHIP FOUNDATION (Scholarships)

409 Hood Boulevard
Fairless Hills PA 19030
215/943-7400
AMOUNT: Varies
DEADLINE(S): APR 20
FIELD(S): All fields of study

Scholarships for partial support for graduating high school seniors who are enrolling for the first time in colleges, universities, technical schools, nursing schools, and other accredited postsecondary institutions. Must be U.S. citizen and resident of Bucks County, Pennsylvania. Considerations are financial need, academic achievement, activities in school, community, or church.

Contact organization for details.

2303—A.H. BEAN FOUNDATION

c/o First Alabama Bank
2222 Ninth Street
Tuscaloosa AL 35401
Written Inquiry
AMOUNT: $200-$600
DEADLINE(S): None given
FIELD(S): All fields of study

Scholarships for Alabama residents who are Christian individuals who are active members of a church, enrolled in a postsecondary educational institution, and recommended for aid by a minister.

Write to Trust Dept. at above location for details. Transcript and minister's recommendation required.

2304—ABBIE M. GRIFFIN EDUCATIONAL FUND (Scholarships)

c/o Winer & Bennett
111 Concord Street
Nashua NH 03060
603/882-5157
AMOUNT: $300-$2,000
DEADLINE(S): MAY 1
FIELD(S): All areas of study

Open ONLY to residents of Merrimack, NH. Awards ONLY to entering freshmen for full-time undergraduate study at an accredited college or university. Based on economic need.

10-15 awards per year. Write for complete information.

2305—ABE AND ANNIE SEIBEL FOUNDATION (Interest-free Educational Loan Fund)

P.O. Box 8210
Galveston TX 77553-8210
409/770-5665 or 409/770-5666
Internet: http://www.window.state.tx.us/scholars/aid/scholarship/scaasf.html
AMOUNT: Up to $3,000 a year
DEADLINE(S): Feb 28
FIELD(S): All fields of study

Open to Texas residents who are U.S. citizens and will be or are enrolled (for at least 12 credit hours per semester) as undergraduate students at a Texas college or university accredited by the Southern Association of Colleges and Schools. Must maintain 3.0 or better GPA. For study leading to first 4-year degree.

Applications available after Dec. 25. Apply Dec. 1 through Feb. 28. Write for complete information.

2306—ABRAHAM BURTMAN CHARITY TRUST

Burns Bldg.
P.O. Box 608
Dover NH 03820-0608
603/742-2332
AMOUNT: $1,000
DEADLINE(S): MAY 1
FIELD(S): All areas of study

Scholarships for financially needy residents of New Hampshire.

Send SASE to David A. Goodwin at above address for application guidelines.

2307—ACACIA COMMUNITY SCHOOL (Scholarships)

P.O. Box 492
El Prado NM 87529
505/751-7780
E-mail: angroach@laplaza.org
AMOUNT: Varies
DEADLINE(S): Varies
FIELD(S): All fields of study

A few scholarships are available to attend this independent, coeducational school which includes grades six through eight.

Contact school for details.

2308—ACADEMIC STUDY GROUP (Travel Bursaries to Israel)

John D. A. Levy, ASG
25 Lyndale Avenue
London NW2 2QB ENGLAND UK
0171 435 6803
AMOUNT: Varies
DEADLINE(S): MAR; NOV
FIELD(S): All fields of study

Travel opportunities to Israel are offered by this charitable foundation, which promotes collaboration between British scholars and their Israeli counterparts.

To apply, send a detailed curriculum vitae, summary of the reason to visit Israel, plus names of academic counterparts in Israel.

2309—ACADEMY HILL SCHOOL (Scholarships)

1190 Liberty Street
Springfield MA 01104
413/788-0300
FAX: 413/781-4806
E-mail: academy@vgernet.net
AMOUNT: Varies
DEADLINE(S): Varies

FIELD(S): All fields of study

Scholarships for gifted children with financial need at this independent elementary school in Springfield, Massachusetts. Canadian citizens or landed immigrants.

6-8 awards yearly. Contact school for details.

2310—ADDISON H. GIBSON FOUNDATION (Low-Interest Loans)

One PPG Place, Suite 2230
Pittsburgh PA 15222
412/261-1611
FAX: 412/261-5733
Internet: http://www.gibson-fnd.org/Docs/Education_Loan.htm

AMOUNT: Varies
DEADLINE(S): None
FIELD(S): Most fields of study

Recipients must have completed at least one full-time year at the college or university from which a B.A. degree will be earned. Student's family home must be in western Pennsylvania, which is determined by an imaginary north-south line drawn through the state at Johnstown, PA. Must be in good academic standing and must demonstrate financial need. Other restrictions may apply.

Do NOT write! Interested/eligible students should telephone the Foundation for more information and to establish residence eligibility.

2311—ADELPHI UNIVERSITY (Various Scholarships)

1 South Avenue
Garden City NY 11530
516/877-3080
FAX: 516/877-3380
Internet: http://www.adelphi.edu/finaid/awards.html

AMOUNT: Up to $13,500
DEADLINE(S): FEB 15
FIELD(S): All fields of study

Various scholarships for full-time and part-time students at Adelphi University. Must document financial need—fill out a FAFSA form. Must have a 3.0 GPA after freshman year; some require 3.3 GPA in subsequent years to maintain scholarship.

See Web site for further information; contact school to apply.

2312—AEROSPACE EDUCATION FOUNDATION (Eagle Plan Grant)

1501 Lee Highway
Arlington VA 22209-1198
800/291-8480 ext. 4869 or
703/247-5800 ext. 4869
FAX: 703/247-5853
E-mail: AEFStaff@aef.org

AMOUNT: $400
DEADLINE(S): Varies
FIELD(S): All fields of study

Open to graduates of the Community College of the Air Force who are pursuing a baccalaureate degree. Must be enlisted personnel—E-4, E-5, E-6, or E-7. Based on academic achievement, educational goals, leadership, and extracurricular activities.

Not renewable. Contact Harriet McCollum for an application.

2313—AFS INTERCULTURAL PROGRAMS (International Exchange Student Program)

198 Madison Avenue, 8th Floor
New York NY 10016
212/299-9000 or 800/AFS-INFO
FAX: 212/299-9090
Internet: http://www.afs.org

AMOUNT: Varies
DEADLINE(S): Varies
FIELD(S): Study abroad—all high school subjects

International exchange of high school students for semester or school year. Students live with host families and attend local secondary schools. Students go to and from 50 countries. Scholarship assistance for summer, school year, and semester.

Deadlines are in the fall and spring. 10,000 participants world wide. Call 800/876-2377; access Web site or write for complete information.

2314—AGNES T. MAGUIRE TRUST

P.O. Box 91210
Baton Rouge LA 70821-9210
504/332-4011

AMOUNT: Varies
DEADLINE(S): JUL 1
FIELD(S): All fields of study

Student loans for college-bound young women who are residents of Louisiana.

Send letter requesting detailed information after May 1 to Premier Bank, N.A., Trust Dept., at above address.

2315—AID ASSOCIATION FOR LUTHERANS(All-College, Vocational/Technical, and Lutheran Campus Scholarships)

4321 N. Ballard Road
Appleton, WI 54919-0001
800/225-5225 (800/CALL-AAL)
E-mail: lutheransonline@aal.org
Internet: http://www.aal.org

AMOUNT: $1,000/year-$10,000/4 years (All-College); $500 (Vo-Tech); $200-$1,000 (Lutheran Campus)
DEADLINE(S): NOV
FIELD(S): All fields of study

For AAL members seeking post-high school education. An applying student must have an AAL insurance policy or an AAL annuity in his or her name.

For membership information, contact the above address or your local AAL district representative. In 1996, 2,800 AAL members received a total of $4.5 million in scholarships.

2316—AIR FORCE ACADEMY

USAF Academy
CO 80840-4480
719/333-4096

AMOUNT: $3,000
DEADLINE(S): APR 30
FIELD(S): All areas of study

Scholarships to attend private preparatory schools for students who plan to seek admission to the U.S. Air Force Academy. Open to single students age 17-21 in excellent health and highly motivated to attend the Academy. Must be a U.S. citizen.

100 awards per year. Send a self-addressed stamped envelope for application.

2317—AIR FORCE AID SOCIETY (General Henry H. Arnold Education Grant Program)

1745 Jefferson Davis Highway, #202
Arlington VA 22202
800/429-9475

AMOUNT: $1,500/year
DEADLINE(S): MAR
FIELD(S): All fields of study

Open to undergraduates who are dependent children of active duty, retired, or deceased members of the U.S. Air Force, and spouses of active duty members or members who died on active duty or in retired status residing in continental U.S. (lower 48 states) only. Applicants should be full-time students with a minimum 2.0 GPA at accredited institutions. Must be U.S. citizen/legal resident and demonstrate financial need.

Renewable. Contact Aid Society for an application.

2318—AIR FORCE AID SOCIETY (Vo-Tech Loan Program)

1745 Jefferson Davis Highway, #202
Arlington VA 22202

800/429-9475
AMOUNT: $1,000 maximum
DEADLINE(S): None specified
FIELD(S): All fields of study in vocational/technical areas.

For spouses and children of active duty members at all stateside bases enrolled vocational/technical programs that increase employment opportunities.

One-time basis only. To be repaid in two years. Upon verification of student's program completion, 25% of the balance will be converted to a grant.

2319—AIR FORCE SERGEANTS' ASSOCIATION (Scholarship Awards Program)

5211 Auth Road
Suitland MD 20746
Internet: http://www.avscholars.com/militarylist.phtml
AMOUNT: Varies
DEADLINE(S): APR 1
FIELD(S): All fields of study

Open to single dependent children (under 23) of AFSA members or its auxiliary. For undergraduate study at accredited institutions only. Awards are based on academic excellence.

For application and complete information send self-addressed, stamped ($1.47), 7x10 envelope to AFSA/AMF Scholarship Administrator at above address.

2320—AIR LINE PILOTS ASSOCIATION (Scholarship Program)

1625 Massachusetts Avenue NW
Washington DC 20036
202/797-4050
Internet: http://www.free-4u.com/airline1.htm
AMOUNT: $12,000/year
DEADLINE(S): APR 1
FIELD(S): All fields of study

Four-year award is open to undergraduate sons and daughters of medically retired, long-term disabled, or deceased pilot members of the Air Line Pilots Association. Must be pursuing bachelor's degree and should not apply before senior year of high school. Based on academic capability and financial need.

Renewable each year with minimum 3.0 GPA. Contact Jan Redden for an application ONLY if above qualifications are met. Selections made by July 1st.

2321—AIR TRAFFIC CONTROL ASSOCIATION INC (Scholarships for Children of Air Traffic Specialists)

2300 Clarendon Boulevard, #711
Arlington VA 22201
703/522-5717
FAX: 703/527-7251
E-mail: atca@worldnit.att.net
AMOUNT: Varies
DEADLINE(S): MAY 1
FIELD(S): All fields of study

For children of persons serving or having served as air traffic control specialists (either natural or adopted) with either government, U.S. military, or in a private facility in the U.S. Must be enrolled in an accredited college or university and planning to continue the following year in bachelor's program or higher. Attendance must be equal to at least half-time (6 hours).

Write for complete information.

2322—AIRMEN MEMORIAL FOUNDATION (AFSA/AMF Scholarship Awards Program)

5211 Auth Road
Suitland, MD 20746
800/638-0594
Internet: http://www.avscholars.com/militarylist.phtml
AMOUNT: Varies
DEADLINE(S): APR 1
FIELD(S): All fields of study

Open to unmarried dependent children (under 25) of Air Force enlisted personnel (active or retired) of all components, including Air National Guard and Reserves. For undergraduate study at any accredited academic or trade/technical school.

See Web site for more information. Send self-addressed, stamped ($1.47) 9x12 envelope to above address for application details. Applications available November 1 thru March 31.

2323—ALABAMA COMMISSION ON HIGHER EDUCATION (Scholarships, Grants, & Loans)

Montgomery AL 36130-2000
334/242-1998
E-mail: hhector@ache.state.al.us
Internet: http://www.ache.state.al.us/
AMOUNT: Varies
DEADLINE(S): Varies
FIELD(S): All fields of study

The Commission administers a number of financial aid programs tenable at post-secondary institutions in Alabama. Some awards are need-based.

Contact your financial aid office or the Commission for "Financial Aid Sources in Alabama" brochure.

2324—ALBANY ACADEMY FOR GIRLS (Scholarships)

140 Academy Road
Albany NY 12208
518/463-2201
FAX: 518/463-5096
E-mail: lewisj@albanyacademy for girls.org
AMOUNT: $3,000/year for 4 years + $12,000
DEADLINE(S): DEC 1
FIELD(S): All fields of secondary school study

Scholarship for the school listed above. Based on grades, testing, and recommendations to be admitted; must score well on scholarship exam and essays.

Write for details.

2325—ALBERT BAKER FUND (Student Loans)

5 Third Street, #717
San Francisco CA 94103
415/543-7028
AMOUNT: $1800-$2500 per academic year
DEADLINE(S): July 1
FIELD(S): All fields of study

Open to students who are members of the First Church of Christ Scientist in Boston, MA. Students' residency can be anywhere in the world. For study in the U.S. Student must have other primary lender and be enrolled in an accredited college or university. Interest rate is 3% below prime.

All students must have cosigner who is a U.S. citizen. Average of 160 awards per year. Write or call for complete information. Applicant must be the one who calls.

2326—ALBERT O.J. LANDUCCI, DDS (Scholarships)

2720 Edison Street
San Mateo CA 94403-2495
650/574-4444
FAX: 650/574-4441
E-mail: e@DrLanducci.com
Internet: http://www.drlanducci.com/scholarships.htm
AMOUNT: Varies
DEADLINE(S): Varies
FIELD(S): All fields of study

Awards and scholarships for elementary and high school students who reside in San Mateo County, California, or for those who attend or plan to attend College of San Mateo. Annual scholarships are in four areas: academic excellence, outstanding community and school volunteerism, science and math achievement, and dental assisting.

For more information, contact your school's scholarship representative.

2327—ALBERTA HERITAGE SCHOLARSHIP FUND

Box 28000 STN MAIN
Edmonton Alberta T5J 4R4 CANADA
780/427-8640
FAX: 780/427-1288
E-mail: heritage@gov.ab.ca
Internet: http://www.alis.gov.ab.ca/scholarships/main.asp

AMOUNT: Varies
DEADLINE(S): Varies
FIELD(S): All

Provides funding for over 40 scholarships to outstanding achievers in intellectual, cultural, social, or physical pursuits. Also establishes and administers scholarships for other individuals and organizations.

2328—ALBUQUERQUE COMMUNITY FOUNDATION (Financial Aid Program)

Albuquerque NM 87176-6960
505/883-6240
E-mail: acf@albuquerquefoundation.org
Internet: http://www.albuquerquefoundation.org/scholar/scholar.htm

AMOUNT: Varies
DEADLINE(S): Varies
FIELD(S): All fields of study

Open to New Mexico residents who are pursuing undergraduate study at a four-year college/university. Must be a federal financial aid recipient.

Renewable. See Web site for an application.

2329—ALCOA FOUNDATION (Sons and Daughters Scholarship Program)

Carol Greco, Program Assistant
201 Isabella Street
Pittsburgh PA 15212-5858
412/553-4786
FAX: 412/553-4532
E-mail: carol.greco@alcoa.com

AMOUNT: $1,500
DEADLINE(S): FEB 28
FIELD(S): All

Open to dependents of Alcoa Inc. employees. Should apply during senior year of high school through the employment location of parents. Merit is considered. Must be enrolled full- or part-time at a two-year, four-year, or technical institution or university. 2.5 GPA or higher.

2330—ALEXANDER GRAHAM BELL ASSOCIATION FOR THE DEAF (School Age Financial Aid Awards)

3417 Volta Place NW
Washington DC 20007-2778
202/337-5220 (voice/TTY)
E-mail: agbell2@aol.com
Internet: http://www.agbell.org financialaid.cfm

AMOUNT: Varies
DEADLINE(S): APR 1 (Request application by mail or e-mail between January 1 and April 1)
FIELD(S): All fields of study

For aural/oral students (aged 6-21) with moderate to profound hearing losses that they acquired before they developed language. Must be registered full-time in an elementary, middle, or high school that enrolls primarily students with normal hearing. Must use speech, residual hearing, and/or speechreading as their primary form of communication.

Request application IN WRITING to the Bell Association's Financial Aid Coordinator; make sure you indicate which program you would like to apply for, and include your name and address on the letter.

2331—ALEXANDER GRAHAM BELL ASSOCIATION FOR THE DEAF (College Scholarship Awards)

3417 Volta Place NW
Washington DC 20007-2778
202/337-5220 (voice/TTY)
E-mail: agbell2@aol.com
Internet: http://www.agbell.org financialaid.cfm

AMOUNT: Varies
DEADLINE(S): DEC 1 (Request application by then. Deadline is MAR 15 postmark)
FIELD(S): All fields of study

For prelingually deaf or hard-of-hearing students who use speech and speechreading to communicate and who are attending or have been admitted to a college or university that primarily enrolls students with normal hearing.

Must have a 60dB or greater hearing loss in the better ear in the speech frequencies of 500, 1000, and 2000 Hz. Application requests must be made IN WRITING to the Bell Association's Financial Aid Coordinator; make sure you indicate which program you would like to apply for, and include your name and address on your letter.

2332—ALEXANDER GRAHAM BELL ASSOCIATION FOR THE DEAF (Parent Infant Preschool Awards)

3417 Volta Place NW
Washington DC 20007-2778
202/337-5220 (voice/TTY)
E-mail: agbell2@aol.com
Internet: http://www.agbell.org financialaid.cfm

AMOUNT: Varies
DEADLINE(S): Candidates must request an application by mail or e-mail June 1 to September 1.
FIELD(S): All fields of study

Stipends are awarded to parents of infants (younger than 6 years old) who have been diagnosed with moderate to profound hearing losses. May be used to cover expenses associated with early intervention educational and rehabilitative services. The parent or guardian must be committed to an auditory-oral philosophy of education. Family must demonstrate financial need.

Must request application IN WRITING to the Bell Association's Financial Aid Coordinator; make sure you indicate which program you would like to apply for, and include your name and address on the letter.

2333—ALEXANDER SCHOLARSHIP FUND

P.O. Box 719
Evansville IN 47115
812/464-3215

AMOUNT: $2,000
DEADLINE(S): Varies (Set by high school)
FIELD(S): All areas of study

For college-bound high school seniors attending one of three high school in Posey County, Indiana and who reside in that county.

Ten awards. Renewable for three years at $750. Obtain application from high school counselor.

2334—ALL SAINTS' ACADEMY (Financial Aid Awards)

5000 State Road 540 W.
Winter Haven FL 33880
941/293-5980
FAX: 941/294-2819

AMOUNT: $200-$5,000
DEADLINE(S): MAR 1
FIELD(S): All fields of K-12 study

Scholarships for financially needy students in good academic standing at the above K-12 private school.

Contact Debbie Ford at school for details.

2335—ALLIED JEWISH FEDERATION (Charles and Louise Rosenbaum Scholarship Fund)

300 Dahlia Street
Denver CO 80222
Written Inquiry
Internet: http://www.free-4u.com/charles_and_louise_rosenbaum_scholarship_loan_fund.htm
AMOUNT: Varies
DEADLINE(S): MAR 15
FIELD(S): All fields of study

Scholarships for Jewish high school seniors who are residents of Colorado.

Contact above location for details.

2336—AMARILLO AREA FOUNDATION (Scholarship Program)

801 S. Fillmore, Suite 700
Amarillo TX 79101
806/376-4521
FAX: 806/373-3656
E-mail: laquita@aaf-hf.org
Internet: http://www.aaf-hf.org/scholarships.html
AMOUNT: Varies
DEADLINE(S): March 1 by 5 p.m.
FIELD(S): All fields of study

Open to residents and/or graduating high school seniors of the 26 northern most counties of the Texas Panhandle: Armstrong, Briscoe, Carson, Castro, Childress, Collingsworth, Dallam, Deaf Smith, Donley, Gray, Hall, Hansford, Hartley, Hemphill, Hutchison, Lipscomb, Moore, Ochiltree, Oldham, Parmer, Potter, Randall, Roberts, Sherman, Swisher, or Wheeler.

Renewable. Contact Sylvia Artho, Scholarship Coordinator, for an application.

2337—AMAZON FOUNDATION (Scholarships and Grants)

3610 North Prince Village Place, Suite 100
Tucson AZ 85719
520/795-5288
Internet: http://www.amazonfound.org
AMOUNT: $500-$1,500 per semester
DEADLINE(S): MAY 31
FIELD(S): All

This scholarship program funds several areas including undergraduate and graduate education, career development, non-traditional education, and professional learning opportunities to residents of Southeast Arizona. Preference is given to women of color; women with disabilities; lesbians, bisexual women, and transgender people; and women facing economic challenges.

2338—AMERICA'S JUNIOR MISS (Scholarship Competition)

Powell, Administrator
Mobile AL 36652-2786
334/438-3621
FAX: 334/431-0063
E-mail: leslie@ajm.org ; Leslie
AMOUNT: up to $30,000
DEADLINE(S): Varies (from state to state)
FIELD(S): All fields of study.

For college-bound high school senior girls who are U.S. citizens, legal residents of the county and state in which they seek to compete, and have never been married. Must apply your sophomore or junior year. Competition based on judge's interview, creative and performing arts, scholastic achievement, presence and composure, and fitness.

Several scholarships are awarded annually at the local, state, and national levels, totaling approximately $5 million. The 50 winners, one from each state, compete at the Junior Miss pageant in Mobile, Alabama.

2339—AMERICAL DIVISION VETERANS ASSOCIATION (ADVA Scholarships)

1085 Bunkerhill Drive
Kalamazoo, MI 49009
616/372-2192
E-mail: C146thinf@aol.com
AMOUNT: $1,000-$3,000
DEADLINE(S): MAY 1
FIELD(S): All fields of study

Open to children and grandchildren of current ADVA members or members who were killed in action or died in active duty with Americal Division. May be high school seniors or undergraduates pursuing college/vocational studies. Must submit letter from ADVA member attesting to eligibility, letter of admission from school of choice, letters of recommendation from teachers, 200-300 word essay on subject pertaining to patriotism/loyalty to nation, and parents' income.

3+ awards annually. Renewable. Contact Robert G. Short, Chairman, for an application.

2340—AMERICAN ASSOCIATION OF BIOANALYSTS (David Birenbaum Scholarship Fund)

917 Locust Street, Suite 1100
Saint Louis MO 63101-1419
314/241-1445
FAX: 314/241-1449
E-mail: aab@aab.org
Internet: http://www.aab.org
AMOUNT: Varies
DEADLINE(S): APR 15
FIELD(S): All fields of study

Open to AAB regular and associate members, their spouses, and dependent children. Must have graduated from an accredited high school or equivalent. Based on several factors, such as need, goals, achievements, community involvement, etc.

Contact AAB for an application.

2341—AMERICAN ASSOCIATION OF UNIVERSITY WOMEN-HARRISBURG BRANCH (Beverly J. Smith Memorial Scholarship)

P.O. Box 1625
Harrisburg PA 17105-1625
E-mail: scholarship@aauwharrisburg.org
Internet: http://www.aauwharrisburg.org
AMOUNT: Up to $2,500
DEADLINE(S): MAY 3
FIELD(S): All

Available to any woman who is enrolled full-time with least 60 credits toward a baccalaureate degree. Must be a resident of Dauphin, Cumberland, or Perry County, Pennsylvania, attending an accredited college or university in Pennsylvania.

2342—AMERICAN ASSOCIATION OF UNIVERSITY WOMEN-STATE COLLEGE BRANCH (Scholarship Grant)

P.O. Box 185
Pine Grove Mills PA 16868
814/237-9233
E-mail: mopeek@juno.com
AMOUNT: $3,000
DEADLINE(S): FEB 28
FIELD(S): All

Must be a female resident of Centre County with at least one quarter (or 30 credit hours) of course work required for a baccalaureate degree. Candidate must have interrupted her studies, at some point, for a period of at least two years or delayed her higher education for at least two years after graduating from high school.

2343—AMERICAN ASSOCIATION OF UNIVERSITY WOMEN (Foundation for Education—Livermore, Pleasanton, Dublin, Sunol CA)

Scholarship Coordinator
P.O. Box 661
Livermore CA 94551
Written Inquiry

AMOUNT: Varies
DEADLINE(S): MAR 1
FIELD(S): All fields of study

For female residents of Livermore, Pleasanton, Dublin, or Sunol, CA or graduates of a high school in those cities.

Three scholarships to be awarded to juniors or seniors at an accredited 4-year college or university.

2344—AMERICAN ASSOCIATION OF UNIVERSITY WOMEN-HONOLULU BRANCH (Ruth E. Black Scholarship)

1802 Keeaumoku Street
Honolulu HI 96822
808/537-4702

AMOUNT: Varies
DEADLINE(S): MAR 1
FIELD(S): All fields of study

Open to women who are legal residents of Hawaii. For undergraduate study at an accredited college or university in Hawaii. Must demonstrate financial need.

Applications become available October 1st of each year. Contact above address for an application or more information.

2345—AMERICAN BAPTIST CHURCH (Award)

10th and Cedar Streets
Ottawa KS 66067
785/242-5200
E-mail: admiss@ottawa.edu
Internet: http://www.ottawa.edu

AMOUNT: $500
DEADLINE(S): Varies
FIELD(S): All

Applicant must be a member of an American Baptist Church and recommended by their pastor. Available to students at Ottawa University.

2346—AMERICAN/BAPTIST FINANCIAL AID PROGRAM (Marion Burr Scholarship)

Lynne Eckman
Director of Financial Aid
American Baptist
Financial Aid Program
PO Box 851
Valley Forge PA 19482-0851

AMOUNT: $1,000-$2,000
DEADLINE(S): MAY 31
FIELD(S): All

Renewable award for Native Americans who are members of an American Baptist Church/U.S.A. congregation. Applicant must be enrolled full-time at a four-year institution or university and pursuing a career in human services.

2347—AMERICAN BUSINESS WOMEN'S ASSOCIATION (Stephen Bufton Memorial Scholarship)

118 Concord Lane
Osterville MA 02655
Written Inquiries

AMOUNT: $2,100
DEADLINE(S): MAY 31
FIELD(S): All

Open to junior, senior, or graduate-level women who are citizens of Cape Cod, Martha's Vineyard, or Nantucket Island MA. Must have at least a 2.5 GPA on a scale of 4.0.

2348—AMERICAN CANCER SOCIETY (College Scholarship Program)

1205 E. Saginaw Street
Lansing MI 48906
800/723-0360
Internet: http://www.dcl.edu/finaid/fswc/scholarships/Cancer_Society.htm

AMOUNT: $1,000
DEADLINE(S): APR 14 by 5 p.m.
FIELD(S): All fields of study

For Michigan and Indiana residents who are U.S. citizens and have had a diagnosis of cancer before age 21. Must be an undergraduate under age 21 attending an accredited college/university within Michigan or Indiana. Based on financial need, scholarship, community service, and leadership.

Renewable. phone the American Cancer Society's Great Lakes Division (800-723-0360) for application packet

2349—AMERICAN COUNCIL OF THE BLIND (ACB Scholarship Program)

1155 15th Street NW, Suite 1004
Washington DC 20005
202/467-5081
FAX: 202-467-5085
Internet: http://www.ischool.washington.edu/services/finaiddisab.htm

AMOUNT: $500-$3,000
DEADLINE(S): MAR 1
FIELD(S): All fields of study

Open to legally blind students who have been accepted to or are enrolled in an accredited institution for vocational, technical, undergraduate, graduate, or professional studies. Must be U.S. citizen/legal resident.

25 awards annually. Contact Terry Pacheco for an application.

2350—AMERICAN FEDERATION OF STATE, COUNTY & MUNICIPAL EMPLOYEES, AFL-CIO (AFSCME Family Scholarship)

1625 L Street NW
Washington DC 20036
202/429-1250; FAX: 202/659-0446
E-mail: education@afscme.org
Internet: http://www.afscme.org/about/scholarf.htm

AMOUNT: $2,000 per year for 4 years
DEADLINE(S): DEC 31
FIELD(S): All areas of study

Open to high school seniors who are dependent children of active AFSCME members. Awards for full-time undergraduate study.

Renewable for 4 years.

2351—AMERICAN FEDERATION OF STATE, COUNTY, AND MUNICIPAL EMPLOYEES-AFL-CIO (MasterCard Scholarship Award Program)

1625 L Street NW
Washington DC 20036
800/238-2539

AMOUNT: $500-$4,000
DEADLINE(S): MAY 31
FIELD(S): All fields of study

Open to AFSCME members and their spouses and children. Member must have at least one year of continuous membership in good-standing. Applicant must be accepted for undergraduate study into an accredited college, community college, or recognized technical/trade school by June 30th. Need not be MasterCard holders.

For application, send a postcard with name, local union number, social security number, and address to: Union Plus Scholarship, P.O. Box 34800, Washington, DC 20043-4800.

2352—AMERICAN FEDERATION OF TEACHERS (Robert G. Porter Scholars Program)

555 New Jersey Avenue NW
Washington DC 20001-2079
202/879-4400
E-mail: porterscholars@aft.org
Internet: http://www.aft.org/scholarships/index.html
AMOUNT: $1,000 (AFT members); $8,000 (dependents)
DEADLINE(S): MAR 31
FIELD(S): All fields of study

Open to members of the American Federation of Teachers seeking continuing education in their fields of study. Also open to high school seniors who are dependents of AFT members. Preferably, applicants should be pursuing a career in labor, education, health care, or government service.

20 awards annually for AFT members and 4 for dependents. Contact AFT for an application.

2353—AMERICAN FIRE SPRINKLER ASSOCIATION (Scholarship Contest)

12959 Jupiter Road, Suite 142
Dallas TX 75238
214/349-5965
FAX: 343-8898
Internet:http://www.firesprinkler.org
E-mail: afsainfo@firesprinkler.org
AMOUNT: Up to $3,000
DEADLINE(S): DEC 7
FIELD(S): Fire safety

A nationwide essay contest for high school seniors. Topic: "How fire sprinklers affect your community." 700-1,000 typed words, double-spaces, 1" margins. Regional and nationwide scholarship prizes. Not open to AFSA staff relatives or board members.

Send to "Scholarship Contest" at above location for application.

2354—AMERICAN FOREIGN SERVICE ASSOCIATION (Financial Aid Awards)

2101 E Street NW
Washington DC 20037
202/944-5504
800-704-AFSA (within the US)
FAX: 202-338-6820
E-mail: scholar@afsa.org
AMOUNT: $500-$2,500
DEADLINE(S): FEB 6
FIELD(S): All fields of study

The American Foreign Service Association offers financial aid scholarships to dependents of U.S. Government Foreign Service employees. Students must be enrolled in undergraduate study at a U.S. college or university.

Write to the above address for complete information.

2355—AMERICAN FOREIGN SERVICE ASSOCIATION (Merit Awards)

2101 E. Street NW
Washington DC 20037
202/944-5504;800-704-AFSA (within the US)
FAX: 202-338-6820
E-mail: scholar@afsa.org
AMOUNT: $1,000
DEADLINE(S): FEB 6
FIELD(S): All fields of study

Open to dependents of U.S. Government Foreign Service employees. Students must be high school seniors.

Write to the above address for complete information.

2356—AMERICAN FOUNDATION FOR THE BLIND (Ferdinand Torres Scholarship)

11 Penn Plaza, Suite 300
New York NY 10001
212/502-7661
FAX: 212/502-7771
E-mail: juliet@afb.org
Internet: http://www.afb.org
AMOUNT: $1,000
DEADLINE(S): APR 30
FIELD(S): All fields of study

Open to legally blind full-time postsecondary students who present evidence of economic need. Must reside in the US. Preference given to applicants residing in New York City metropolitan area and new immigrants to the US. Must submit evidence of legal blindness; official transcripts; proof of college/university acceptance; evidence of need; three letters of recommendation; proof of residence; and statement of goals, work experience, activities, and how money will be used.

New immigrants should also include country of origin and reason for coming to US. 1 award annually. See Web site or contact Julie Tucker at AFB for an application.

2357—AMERICAN GI FORUM OF THE U.S. HISPANIC EDUCATION FOUNDATION (Chapter Scholarships)

3301 Mountain Road NW
Albuquerque NM 87104
505/243-7551 or 505/843-8224
FAX: 505/247-2993
Internet: http://www.incacorp.com/agifhef
AMOUNT: Varies
DEADLINE(S): Varies
FIELD(S): All fields of study

Open to Hispanic undergraduate students residing in certain states that have chapters of the above organization. Students must obtain applications from nearest awarding chapter.

Send self-addressed, stamped envelope (SASE) to the above address for complete information.

2358—AMERICAN HEALTH AND BEAUTY AIDS INSTITUTE (Entrepreneurial Leadership Conference)

401 North Michigan Avenue
Chicago IL 60611-4267
312/644-6610
Internet: http://www.ahbai.org/scholar/
AMOUNT: $100 travel allowance plus conference registration.
DEADLINE(S): None specified
FIELD(S): All fields of study.

The American Health and Beauty Aids Institute Entrepreneurial Leadership Conference is held each November. Two winners are chosen from each of the 117 Historically Black Colleges and Universities. Winners receive registration plus a $100 travel allowance. Program includes leadership workshops with presidents and key executives from multimillion dollar African-American-owned hair care corporations.

Eleven students will be selected for additional scholarships totaling over $30,000 in scholarship prizes. Submit an essay on entrepreneurship in the Black community.

2359—AMERICAN INDIAN HERITAGE FOUNDATION

6051 Arlington Boulevard
Falls Church VA 22044-2788
703/538-1585
FAX: 703-532-1921
http://www.indian.org
E-mail PaleMoom@indian.org or CindyRose@indian.org

AMOUNT: over $30,000
DEADLINE(S): April 1
FIELD(S): All fields of study

9th Miss Indian USA Scholarship Program in Washington DC. Crowning Ceremony in May. Prizes for academic achievement, Miss Walk in Beauty, Miss Photogenic, Miss Congeniality, talent traditional dress, and evening gown sections. Must be of American Indian descent.

Must be a high school graduate between 18-26. Can never have cohabitated, been pregnant, or married.

2360—AMERICAN INSTITUTE FOR FOREIGN STUDY (AIFS) (International Scholarships)

River Plaza, 9 West Broad Street
Stamford CT 06902-3788
800/727-2437
Internet: http://www.aifs.com/college/scholar.htm
AMOUNT: $1,000/semester; $750/summer
DEADLINE(S): MAR 15 (summer); APR 15 (fall); OCT 15 (spring)
FIELD(S): All fields of study

Scholarship program for undergraduates with at least a 3.0 GPA desiring to spend a semester or summer studying in a participating foreign universities. Criteria include leadership potential and extra-curricular involvement in multicultural or international issues.

100 semester scholarships and 10 for summer study. Visit Web site and/or contact above address for details.

2361—AMERICAN INSTITUTE FOR FOREIGN STUDY (AIFS) (International Scholarships for Minorities)

River Plaza, 9 West Broad Street
Stamford CT 06902-3788
800/727-2437
Internet: http://www.aifs.com/college/scholar.htm
AMOUNT: Two Minority Scholarships for full tuition, room, board and transportation are awarded one per semester. Three runner-up Minority Scholarships each worth $2,000 are awarded per semester.
DEADLINE(S): APR 15 (fall); OCT 15 (spring)
FIELD(S): All fields of study

Scholarship program for minority undergraduates with at least a 3.0 GPA desiring to spend a semester or summer studying in a participating foreign universities. Criteria include leadership potential and extra-curricular involvement in multicultural or international issues. Must be African-American, Asian-American, Native American, Hispanic-American, or Pacific Islander currently enrolled at a U.S. institution.

One full scholarship, and 5 semester scholarships. Visit Web site and/or contact above address for details.

2362—AMERICAN JEWISH LEAGUE FOR ISRAEL (University Scholarship Fund)

130 E. 59th Street,12th Fl.
New York NY 10022
212/371-1583
FAX: 212/371-3265
E-mail: ajlimlk@aol.com
AMOUNT: $2,000
DEADLINE(S): MAY 1
FIELD(S): All fields of study

Open to U.S. citizens of Jewish faith who have been accepted for a year of undergraduate or graduate study in Israel at Bar Ilan Univ., Ben Gurion Univ., Haifa Univ., Hebrew Univ.-Jerusalem, Technion, Tel Aviv Univ., or Weizmann Institute of Science. Financial need NOT a factor.

15-20 awards annually. Not renewable. Contact should be addressed to Dr. Martin L. Kalmanson, National President.

2363—AMERICAN JUNIOR BRAHMAN ASSOCIATION (Scholarships)

1313 La Concha Lane
Houston TX 77054-1890
Written Inquiry
AMOUNT: Varies
DEADLINE(S): APR 30
FIELD(S): All fields of study

Open to graduating high school seniors who are members of the American Junior Brahman Association who have made outstanding contributions to agriculture and the Brahman industry. For full-time undergraduate study.

Applicants must submit an essay stating why they believe they are deserving of this scholarship. Write for complete information.

2364—AMERICAN LEGION-KANSAS (Dr. "Click" Cowger Scholarship)

1314 SW Topeka Boulevard
Topeka, KS 66612-1886
785/232-9315
FAX: 785/232-1399
Internet: http://www.ksamlegion.org/Default.htm
AMOUNT: $500
DEADLINE(S): JUL 15
FIELD(S): Any field of study

This scholarship is offered to players who have played Kansas American Legion Baseball. It is open to high school seniors, college freshman, and sophomores. Scholarships must be used at an approved Kansas college, university, or trade school.

Write to above address for complete information.

2365—AMERICAN LEGION (Eagle Scout of the Year Scholarship)

P.O. Box 1055
Indianapolis IN 46206
317/630-1200
FAX: 317/630-1223
Internet: http://www.legion.org/get_involved/gi_edaid_scholarships.htm#eagle
AMOUNT: $10,000 to winner; $2,500 to three 2nd place winners
DEADLINE(S): MAR 1 (to state or dept.); APR 1 (national)
FIELD(S): All fields of study

Scholarship for an Eagle Scout chosen as "The American Legion Eagle Scout of the Year." Recipient will receive scholarship immediately upon high school graduation. Must be an active member of a duly chartered Boy Scout Troop, Varsity Scout Team, or Explorer Post, and the son or grandson of Legionnaire or Auxiliary member. Must have received a Boy Scout religious emblem, demonstrated practical citizenship in church, school, Scouting, and community, and be 15-18.

Apply through American Legion State Headquarters. Contact above location for address list.

2366—AMERICAN LEGION-KANSAS (Legion Oratorical Contest)

1314 SW Topeka Boulevard
Topeka KS 66612-1886
785/232-9315
Internet: http://www.legion.org/events/evt_oratorical.htm
AMOUNT: $1,500(1st); $500(2nd); $250(3rd); $150(4th)
DEADLINE(S): Varies
FIELD(S): Any field of study

This oratory contest is for boys or girls attending a Kansas high school.

For complete information write to the above address.

2367—AMERICAN LEGION-KANSAS (Paul Flaherty Athletic Scholarship)

1314 SW Topeka Boulevard
Topeka KS 66612-1886
785/232-9315
E-mail: margiet@ksamiegion.org
Internet: http://www.ksamlegion.org
AMOUNT: $250
DEADLINE(S): JUL 15
FIELD(S): Any field of study

This scholarship is open to any Kansas boy or girl who has participated in any form of Kansas high school athletics. Scholarship must be used at an approved Kansas college, university, or trade school.

Write to above address for complete information.

2368—AMERICAN LEGION-KANSAS (Ted and Nora Anderson Scholarship Fund; Albert M. Lappin Scholarship; Hugh A. Smith Scholarship)

1314 SW Topeka Boulevard
Topeka KS 66612-1886
785/232-9315
Internet: http://www.jeffw340.k12.ks.us/HS_Counselor/pages_here/Deborah%20Schmidt%20schol.htm#February
AMOUNT: $500-$1,000
DEADLINE(S): FEB 15
FIELD(S): Any field of study

These scholarships are offered to sons or daughters of Kansas Legion and Auxiliary members. Students must be high school seniors, college freshman, or sophomores. Scholarships must be at an approved Kansas college, university or trade school.

Write to the above address for complete information.

2369—AMERICAN LEGION AUXILIARY (Dept. of Minnesota Scholarships)

Dept. of Minnesota
State Veterans Service Building
St. Paul MN 55155
612/224-7634
Internet: http://www.free-4u.com/american_legion_auxiliary_department_of_minnesota.htm
AMOUNT: $500
DEADLINE(S): MAR 15
FIELD(S): All fields of study

Open to Minnesota residents who are children or grandchildren of U.S. veterans of armed conflicts. Must be high school senior or grad with GPA of 'C' or better, attend Minnesota vocational/business school, college, or university, and demonstrate financial need. 7 scholarships are awarded.

Write for complete information.

2370—AMERICAN LEGION AUXILIARY-KANSAS (Scholarship)

1314 SW Topeka Boulevard
Topeka KS 66612-1886
785/232-1396
Internet: http://www.jeffw340.k12.ks.us/HS_Counselor/pages_here/Deborah%20Schmidt%20schol.htm#April
AMOUNT: (2-3) $250 Scholarships
DEADLINE(S): May 1
FIELD(S): Any field of study

This scholarship is open to children, spouses, or unremarried widows of veterans. Applicants must be entering college for the first time. This scholarship can be used only at Kansas schools.

Write to the above address for complete information.

2371—AMERICAN LEGION AUXILIARY-DEPARTMENT OF ALABAMA (Scholarships)

120 N. Jackson Street
Montgomery AL 36104
334/262-1176
FAX: (334) 262-9694
E-mail: americanlegionaux1@juno.com
Written Inquiry
AMOUNT: Varies
DEADLINE(S): APR 1
FIELD(S): All fields of study (esp. nursing)

Open to descendants of veterans serving during a war from WWI to current. Veteran and applicant must be residents of Alabama. Credit given for books, tuition, and board. Submit in handwriting a letter stating qualifications, age, need, etc., with a complete transcript of high school and/or college record. Offered at 13 colleges/universities in Alabama for undergraduate/vo-tech study.

40 awards annually. Send a self-addressed, stamped envelope for details.

2372—AMERICAN MENSA EDUCATION & RESEARCH FOUNDATION (Scholarships)

3437 West 7th Street, Suite 264
Fort Worth TX 76107
817/332-2600; 800/666-3672
Internet: http://merf.us.mensa.org/scholarships/index.php3
AMOUNT: $200 to $1,000
DEADLINE(S): JAN 31
FIELD(S): All fields of study

Open to students enrolled for the academic year following the award in a degree program in an accredited American institution of postsecondary education. Applicants must submit an essay describing career, vocational, and academic goals.

Essay should be fewer than 550 words and must be specific rather than general. It MUST be on an official application. Send self-addressed, stamped envelope no later than January 1 for application. Between October 1 and December 31 of each year applications are available ONLY through the advertising efforts of participating Mensa local groups.

2373—AMERICAN MORGAN HORSE INSTITUTE (Scholarship Program)

122 Bostwick Road, P.O. Box 960
Shelburne VT 05482
802/985-4944
FAX: 802/985-8897
E-mail: info@morganhorse.com
AMOUNT: 3,000
DEADLINE(S): MAR 1
FIELD(S): All fields of study

Scholarships for students 21 years or younger who are or will be high school graduates or who hold a GED. Selection based on need, community service, and achievement with horses. Requests for applications MUST include a stamped, self-addressed envelope (SASE).

Five scholarships yearly.

2374—AMERICAN NATIONAL CAN COMPANY (Scholarship Program)

8770 W. Brynmawr Avenue, #11-Q
Chicago IL 60631
773/399-3000 or 507/931-1682
FAX: 773/399-8090
AMOUNT: $500-$4,000
DEADLINE(S): MAR 1
FIELD(S): All fields of study

Open to children of employees of at least three years and retirees of American National Can Company. Must be high school seniors and students who have never enrolled in college and who plan to enroll full time in an accredited two- or four-year college/university in the U.S. or Canada that grants a Bachelor's or Associate degree. Based on academic record, demonstrated leadership, work experience, goals, unusual personal circumstances, and applicant appraisal.

Renewable. Contact American National Can Company or write to CSFA, 1505 Riverview Road, P.O. Box 297, Street Peter, MN 56082, for an application.

2375—AMERICAN RADIO RELAY LEAGUE FOUNDATION ("You've Got A Friend in Pennsylvania" Scholarship)

225 Main Street
Newington CT 06111
860-594-0230
FAX:860-594-0259

AMOUNT: $1,000
DEADLINE(S): FEB 1
FIELD(S): All fields of study

For AARL members who hold a general radio license and are residents of Pennsylvania.

1 award annually. Contact ARRL for an application.

2376—AMERICAN RADIO RELAY LEAGUE FOUNDATION (ARRL Scholarship Honoring Senator Barry Goldwater, K7UGA)

225 Main Street
Newington Ct 06111
860/594-0200
FAX: 860/594-0259
Internet: http://www.arrl.org/

AMOUNT: $5,000
DEADLINE(S): FEB 1
FIELD(S): All fields of study

Open to students who are licensed radio amateurs (at least novice level) and enrolled full-time as a bachelor's or graduate student at a regionally accredited institution.

1 award annually. Contact ARRL for an application.

2377—AMERICAN RADIO RELAY LEAGUE FOUNDATION (Albuquerque Amateur Radio Club Scholarship)

225 Main Street
Newington CT 06111
860/594-0200
FAX: 860/594-0259
Internet: http://www.arrl.org/

AMOUNT: $500
DEADLINE(S): FEB 1
FIELD(S): All fields of study

Open to radio amateurs holding any class of license and who are residents of New Mexico. For undergraduate study at any institution. Must supply a one-page essay on the role Amateur Radio has played in your life.

1 award annually. Contact ARRL for an application.

2378—AMERICAN RADIO RELAY LEAGUE FOUNDATION (Charles Clarke Cordle Memorial Scholarship)

225 Main Street
Newington CT 06111
860/594-0200
FAX: 860/594-0259
Internet: http://www.arrl.org/

AMOUNT: $1,000
DEADLINE(S): FEB 1
FIELD(S): All fields of study

For undergraduate or graduate residents of Georgia or Alabama who hold any class of amateur radio license. Must attend school in Georgia or Alabama and have a minimum 2.5 GPA.

1 award annually. Contact ARRL for an application.

2379—AMERICAN RADIO RELAY LEAGUE FOUNDATION (Mary Lou Brown Scholarship)

225 Main Street
Newington CT 06111
860/594-0200
FAX: 860/594-0259
Internet: http://www.arrl.org/

AMOUNT: $2,500
DEADLINE(S): FEB 1
FIELD(S): All fields of study

Open to residents of the ARRL Northwest Division (AK, ID, MT, OR, WA) who are radio amateurs holding at least a general license. For study leading to a bachelor's degree or higher course of study. Must have GPA of at least 3.0 and a demonstrated interest in promoting the Amateur Radio Service.

Multiple scholarships annually, as income allows. Contact ARRL for an application.

2380—AMERICAN RADIO RELAY LEAGUE FOUNDATION (The New England FEMARA Scholarships)

225 Main Street
Newington CT 06111
860/594-0200
FAX: 860/594-0259
Internet: http://www.arrl.org/

AMOUNT: $600
DEADLINE(S): FEB 1
FIELD(S): All fields of study

Open to residents of the New England states (ME, NH, VT, MA, CT, RI) who are radio amateurs with a technician license.

Multiple awards annually. Contact ARRL for an application.

2381—AMERICAN RADIO RELAY LEAGUE FOUNDATION (The General Fund Scholarships)

225 Main Street
Newington CT 06111
860/594-0200
FAX: 860/594-0259
Internet: http://www.arrl.org/

AMOUNT: $1,000
DEADLINE(S): FEB 1
FIELD(S): All fields of study

Open to undergraduate or graduate students holding any level amateur radio license.

Multiple awards annually. Contact ARRL for an application.

2382—AMERICAN RADIO RELAY LEAGUE FOUNDATION (The K2TEO Martin J. Green, Sr. Memorial Scholarship)

225 Main Street
Newington CT 06111
860/594-0200
FAX: 860/594-0259
Internet: http://www.arrl.org/

AMOUNT: $1,000
DEADLINE(S): FEB 1
FIELD(S): All fields of study

Open to undergraduate or graduate students holding any level amateur radio license. Preference is given to a student ham from a ham family.

1 award annually. Contact ARRL for an application.

2383—AMERICAN RADIO RELAY LEAGUE FOUNDATION (The North Texas Section-Bob Nelson KB5BNU Memorial Scholarship)

225 Main Street
Newington CT 06111
860/594-0200
FAX: 860/594-0259
Internet: http://www.arrl.org/

AMOUNT: $750

DEADLINE(S): FEB 1
FIELD(S): All fields of study

For radio amateurs with any class of license who are residents of Texas or Oklahoma. Must be enrolled in a full-time degree program, with a minimum 12 credit hours per semester. Character, humanitarianism, and active amateur radio participation are highly important.

Multiple awards annually, when funds support it. Contact ARRL for an application.

2384—AMERICAN RADIO RELAY LEAGUE FOUNDATION (Tom and Judith Comstock Scholarship)

225 Main Street
Newington CT 06111
860/594-0200
FAX: 860/594-0259
Internet: http://www.arrl.org/
AMOUNT: $1,000
DEADLINE(S): FEB 1
FIELD(S): All fields of study

For a high school senior who holds any class amateur radio license and is accepted at a two- or four-year college. Must be a resident of Texas or Oklahoma.

1 award annually. Contact ARRL for an application.

2385—AMERICAN RADIO RELAY LEAGUE FOUNDATION (The Six Meter Club of Chicago Scholarship)

225 Main Street
Newington CT 06111
860/594-0200
FAX: 860/594-0259
Internet: http://www.arrl.org/
AMOUNT: $500
DEADLINE(S): FEB 1
FIELD(S): All fields of study

Open to radio amateurs holding any class of license who are students in a postsecondary course of study leading to an undergraduate degree. Must be a resident of Illinois attending any institution in Illinois (technical school, community college, university). If no qualified Illinois student is found, award is open to remaining ARRL Central Division (Indiana and Wisconsin).

1 award annually. Contact ARRL for an application.

2386—AMERICAN RADIO RELAY LEAGUE FOUNDATION (The Chicago FM Club Scholarships)

225 Main Street
Newington CT 06111
860/594-0200
FAX: 860/594-0259
Internet: http://www.arrl.org/
AMOUNT: $500
DEADLINE(S): FEB 1
FIELD(S): All fields of study

Open to radio amateurs holding a technician license and who are residents of the FCC Ninth Call District (IN, IL, WI). Students must be in a postsecondary course of study at an accredited 2- or 4-year college or trade school. Must be U.S. citizen or within three months of citizenship.

Multiple awards annually. Contact ARRL for an application.

2387—AMERICAN RADIO RELAY LEAGUE FOUNDATION (The Michael J. Flosi Memorial Scholarship)

225 Main Street
Newington CT 06111
860/594-0200
FAX: 860/594-0259
Internet: http://www.arrl.org/
AMOUNT: $500
DEADLINE(S): FEB 1
FIELD(S): All fields of study

Open to radio amateurs holding a technician license and who are residents of the FCC Ninth Call District (IN, IL, WI). Must be a high school senior or graduate and be a U.S. citizen or within three months of citizenship.

Multiple awards annually. Contact ARRL for an application.

2388—AMERICAN RADIO RELAY LEAGUE FOUNDATION (The Eugene "Gene" Sallee, W4YFR Memorial Scholarship)

225 Main Street
Newington CT 06111
860/594-0200
FAX: 860/594-0259
Internet: http://www.arrl.org/
AMOUNT: $500
DEADLINE(S): FEB 1
FIELD(S): All fields of study

Open to radio amateurs holding a technician plus license and who are residents of Georgia. Must have a minimum 3.0 GPA.

1 award annually. Contact ARRL for an application.

2389—AMERICAN SAMOA GOVERNMENT (Financial Aid Program)

Dept. of Education
Office of Student Financial Program
Pago Pago AMERICAN SAMOA 96799
684/633-5237
Internet: http://www.free-4u.com/american_samoan_government_financial_aid_program.htm
AMOUNT: $5,000
DEADLINE(S): APR 30
FIELD(S): All fields of study

Scholarships open to residents of American Samoa. Awards support undergraduate and graduate study at all accredited colleges and universities. Applicants from off islands may be eligible if their parents are citizens of American Samoa.

Approximately 50 awards per year. Renewable. Write for complete information.

2390—AMERICAN SAVINGS BANK FOUNDATION, INC. (Scholarships)

New Britain CT 06050
860/827-2556
E-mail: foundation@americansb.com
Internet:http://www.americansavingsfoundation.org
AMOUNT: $500-$3,000
DEADLINE(S): MAR 31
FIELD(S): All fields of study

Open to college-bound high school seniors and those currently enrolled in 2- or 4-year undergraduate programs. Must be Connecticut residents and reside in the Bank's 45-town service area (these towns are in the counties of New Haven, Windham, Tolland, Middlesex, and Hartford). Based on academic standing, extracurricular activities, community service, and financial need.

See Web site or contact Bank for an application after January 15.

2391—AMERICAN SCANDINAVIAN FOUNDATION OF LOS ANGELES (Scholarship Program)

3445 Winslow Drive
Los Angeles CA 90026
213/661-4273
AMOUNT: $1,000
DEADLINE(S): MAR
FIELD(S): All fields of study

Open to full-time upper level and graduate students at Los Angeles area colleges/universities who exhibit a connection to Scandinavia via life experience, field of study, or heritage.

5 to be awarded. Not renewable.

2392—AMERICAN WATER WORKS ASSOCIATION (Holly A. Cornell Scholarship)

6666 West Quincy Avenue
Denver CO 80235
303/794-7711
FAX: 303/794-8915
E-mail: vbaca@awwa.org;
Internet: http://www.awwu.org

AMOUNT: $5,000
DEADLINE(S): JAN 15
FIELD(S): All

Successful scholarship applicants will be women or minority students seeking a master's degree. Selection is based upon academic record and leadership potential.

2393—AMERICAN YOUNG WOMAN OF THE PROGRAM (Scholarship)

P.O. Box 2786
Mobile, AL 36652

AMOUNT: Varies
DEADLINE(S): Early autumn
FIELD(S): All

Available for women who are seniors in high school. Awards are based on SAT or ACT scores, GPA, transcript, interview, physical fitness, talent, poise, and appearance.

2394—AMVETS (National Four-Year Undergraduate Scholarship)

4647 Forbes Boulevard
Lanham MD 20706-4380
301/459-9600
FAX: 301/459-7924

AMOUNT: $1,000 each year for 4 years
DEADLINE(S): APR 15
FIELD(S): All fields of study

Four-year scholarship for graduating high school seniors who are dependents of an American veteran. Must demonstrate academic achievement, show financial need, and demonstrate involvement in extracurricular activities.

Must provide an acceptance letter from a four-year college or university.

2395—AMVETS (National Four-Year Undergraduate Scholarship for Vets)

4647 Forbes Boulevard
Lanham, MD 20706-4380
301/459-9600
FAX: 301/459-7924

AMOUNT: $1,000 each year for 4 years
DEADLINE(S): APR 15
FIELD(S): All fields of study

Four-year scholarship for former members of the U.S. Armed Forces who have exhausted all government financial aid. Must demonstrate academic achievement, show financial need, and demonstrate involvement in extracurricular activities.

Must provide an acceptance letter from a four-year college or university. Write for details.

2396—AN UNCOMMON LEGACY FOUNDATION, INC. (Scholarships)

150 West 26th Street, Suite 602
New York NY 10001
212/366-6507
FAX: 212/366-4425
Internet: http://www.uncommonlegacy.org/scholguidelines.html

AMOUNT: $1,000
DEADLINE(S): MAY 1
FIELD(S): All fields of study

Scholarships for outstanding lesbian undergraduate and graduate full-time students enrolled at accredited colleges or universities in the U.S. Min. GPA 3.0. Must demonstrate commitment or contribution to the lesbian community, demonstrate financial need, and follow required application procedures.

Application is available on Web site and at the organization. Notification dates occur at different times, according to state of residence.

2397—ANNA AND CHARLES STOCKWITZ FUND FOR EDUCATION OF JEWISH CHILDREN (Scholarships)

1600 Scott Street
San Francisco CA 94115
415/561-1226

AMOUNT: $400-$750
DEADLINE(S): Varies
FIELD(S): All fields of study

Scholarships for Jewish undergrads who reside in San Francisco, CA. High school seniors may apply.

Contact above location for complete information.

2398—ANTWERP INTERNATIONAL SCHOOL (Tuition Reduction Grants)

Veltwijcklaan 180
2180 Ekeren BELGIUM
323/543-9300
FAX: 323/541-8201
E-mail: ais@ais-antwerp.be
Internet: http://ais-antwerp.be

AMOUNT: Varies
DEADLINE(S): Varies
FIELD(S): All fields of study

Grants are open to elementary and secondary students at this private day school. Recipients must demonstrate financial need, and grants may not exceed 50 percent of the tuition fee.

50 awards annually. Contact Robert F. Schaecher for an application.

2399—APPALOOSA YOUTH FOUNDATION (Scholarships)

5070 Highway 8 West
Moscow ID 83843
208/882-5578

AMOUNT: $1,000-$2,000
DEADLINE(S): JUN 10
FIELD(S): All fields of study

Open to members of the Appaloosa Youth Association or the Appaloosa Horse Club, children of Appaloosa Horse Club members, and individuals sponsored by a regional club or racing association.

Nine scholarships per year—1 equine related, 8 all areas of study. Renewable. Must demonstrate financial need, number of children, and number of children in college. Contact the Youth Coordinator at address above for complete information.

2400—APPLEBY COLLEGE (Edgecombe Family Scholars [Gr. 7]; Appleby College Foundation [Gr. 9])

540 Lakeshore Road W.
Oakville Ontario L6K 3P1 CANADA
905/845-4681
FAX: 905/845-9505
E-mail: enrol@appleby.on.ca
Internet: http://www.appleby.on.ca/

AMOUNT: $500 each
DEADLINE(S): None
FIELD(S): All fields of study

Two scholarships for this independent school, grades 7-12 and OAC, for students entering grades 7 and 9. Criteria based on entrance examinations and candidate's file.

Renewable for two years, provided that academic excellence is maintained as well as citizenship in the school community.

2401—APPLEBY SPURLING AND KEMPE (Nicholl Scholarships)

Hamilton HM EX BERMUDA
+441/295-2244

FAX: +441/292-8666
E-mail: Tnusum@ASK.BM
Internet: http://www.ask.bm
AMOUNT: BD$18,000
DEADLINE(S): JUN 15
FIELD(S): All fields of study

Open to Bermuda residents with at least five years of schooling in Bermuda who are at least 18 and not more than 24 years old as of September 1st of application year. For undergraduate or graduate study at accredited universities in British Commonwealth countries or the US.

4 awards annually. Renewable up to 4 years. Contact Kristina M. Nusum, Secretary of the Nicholl Scholarships, for an application.

2402—ARCTIC EDUCATION FOUNDATION (Shareholder Scholarships)

Box 129+
Barrow AK 99723
907/852-8633
AMOUNT: Varies according to need
DEADLINE(S): None specified
FIELD(S): All areas of study

Open to Arctic Slope Regional Corporation shareholders and their children. For full time undergraduate or graduate study at any accredited institution of higher education. Must maintain 2.0 or better GPA and demonstrate financial need.

Available for studies leading to certificates in any type of vocational training. Write for complete information.

2403—ARIZONA SCHOOL CHOICE TRUST (Tuition Grants)

3737 E. Broadway Road
Phoenix AZ 85040
602/454-1360
FAX: 602/454-1362
E-mail: info@asct.org
Internet: http://www.asct.org
AMOUNT: Partial Tuition
DEADLINE(S): None
FIELD(S): All fields of study

Open to Arizona residents in grades K-12 who demonstrate financial need. Grants pay 25%, 50%, or 75% of private school tuition, based on parents' income. Must be U.S. citizen.

100 awards annually. Renewable. Contact Lynn Short for an application.

2404—ARKANSAS DEPARTMENT OF HIGHER EDUCATION (Arkansas Academic Challenge Scholarship)

114 East Capitol
Little Rock AR 72201-3818
501/371-2000 or 800/54-STUDY
FAX: 501/371-2001
E-mail: finaid@adhe.arknet.edu
Internet: http://www.arscholarships.com
AMOUNT: $2,500
DEADLINE(S): JUL 1
FIELD(S): All fields of study

For high school seniors who are Arkansas residents planning to attend approved Arkansas public or private colleges/universities. Requires financial need and academic achievement on ACT and in precollegiate or tech preparation core curricula.

See Web site or contact ADHE for an application. Submit program application no later than October 1st, BUT to ensure payment before the fall term starts, submit application no later than July 1st.

2405—ARKANSAS DEPARTMENT OF HIGHER EDUCATION (Governor's Scholars)

114 East Capitol
Little Rock AR 72201-3818
501/371-2000 or 800/54-STUDY
FAX: 501/371-2001
E-mail: finaid@adhe.arknet.edu
Internet: http://www.arscholarships.com
AMOUNT: $4,000 for Scholars; Tuition, fees, + room and board for Distinguished Scholars
DEADLINE(S): MAR 1
FIELD(S): All fields of study

For high school seniors who are Arkansas residents attending approved Arkansas public or private colleges/universities. Two kinds of awards: 1) must have at least 27 ACT, 1100 SAT, or 3.60 GPA; and 2) Governor's Distinguished Scholars must have 32 ACT, 1410 SAT, or be a National Merit Finalist. Based on academic excellence and leadership, NOT financial need.

Up to 100 Scholar awards annually; ALL Distinguished Scholars will receive awards. See Web site or contact ADHE for an application.

2406—ARKANSAS DEPARTMENT OF HIGHER EDUCATION (Law Enforcement Officers Dependents' Scholarship)

114 East Capitol
Little Rock AR 72201-3818
501/371-2000 or 800/54-STUDY
FAX: 501/371-2001
E-mail: finaid@adhe.arknet.edu
Internet: http://www.arscholarships.com
AMOUNT: Waiver for in-state tuition/on-campus room/fees
DEADLINE(S): AUG 1; DEC 1; MAY 1; JUL 1
FIELD(S): All fields of study

For Arkansas residents who are undergraduate dependent children or spouses of persons killed or permanently disabled in the line of duty as a law enforcement officer, fireman, forester, correctional officer, and certain Highway and Transportation Dept. employees. For study at an approved Arkansas public college/university. Limited to 8 semesters or until dependent child becomes 23 years of age, whichever occurs first. Spouses lose eligibility if remarried.

See Web site or contact ADHE for an application.

2407—ARKANSAS DEPARTMENT OF HIGHER EDUCATION (MIA/KIA Dependents' Scholarship)

114 East Capitol
Little Rock AR 72201-3818
501/371-2000 or 800/54-STUDY
FAX: 501/371-2001
E-mail: finaid@adhe.arknet.edu
Internet: http://www.arscholarships.com
AMOUNT: Waiver of in-state tuition/on-campus room/fees
DEADLINE(S): AUG 1; DEC 1; MAY 1; JUL 1
FIELD(S): All fields of study

For full-time undergrad/graduate students who are dependent children/spouses of persons who were declared Killed in Action/Missing in Action/Prisoners of War 1960 or after. Must attend approved Arkansas public college/university or technical school. Arkansas residency not required, but parent/spouse must have been resident. Aid to receive bachelor's degree or certification of completion; student may pursue professional degree if undergrad education was not in Arkansas.

See Web site or contact ADHE for an application.

2408—ARKANSAS DEPARTMENT OF HIGHER EDUCATION (Second Effort Scholarship)

114 East Capitol
Little Rock AR 72201-3818
501/371-2000 or 800/54-STUDY
FAX: 501/371-2001
E-mail: finaid@adhe.arknet.edu
Internet: http://www.arscholarships.com

AMOUNT: $1,000
DEADLINE(S): None
FIELD(S): All fields of study

For Arkansas residents who haven't graduated from high school but who have taken the GED and plan to enroll in an Arkansas post-secondary institution. Must have achieved one of the ten highest scores on the Arkansas High School Diploma test during the previous calendar year. *You do not need to apply for this award; ADHE will contact you directly if you have one of the high test scores.

10 awards annually. Renewable up to 4 years (or equivalent if part-time). See Web site or contact ADHE for more information.

2409—ARKANSAS SINGLE PARENT SCHOLARSHIP FUND (Scholarships)

614 E. Emma, Suite 119
Springdale AR 72764
501/927-1402
FAX: 501/751-1110
E-mail: jwobser@jtlshop.jonesnet.org
Internet: http://www.aspsf.org/

AMOUNT: up to $600/semester
DEADLINE(S): Varies
FIELD(S): All fields of study

Scholarships are for Arkansas single parents to assist with expenses that would, otherwise, keep them from attending school—childcare, transportation, books, tuition, etc.

Each of the 51 county affiliates has its own set of guidelines; please contact your county's office for details and/or an application. Contact information can be found on the ASPSF Web site.

2410—ARKANSAS TECH UNIVERSITY (Scholarships)

Russellville AR 72801-2222
501/968-0400 or 888-275-8321
FAX: 501-964-0839
E-mail: foundation@mail.atu.edu
Internet: http://foundation.atu.edu/availablescholarships.htm

AMOUNT: Varies
DEADLINE(S): March 15
FIELD(S): All fields of study

Scholarships are available to students planning to attend Arkansas Tech University. Must have a minimum 3.25 GPA. Recipients will have opportunity to participate in early registration.

See Web site or contact Arkansas Tech for an application.

2411—ARLINE P. PADELFORD SCHOLARSHIP TRUST (Scholarships)

c/o State Street Bank & Trust Co.
P.O. Box 351
Boston MA 02101
617/786-3000

AMOUNT: $600
DEADLINE(S): None specified
FIELD(S): All areas of study

Scholarships for worthy and deserving students at Taunton (MA) High School to pursue college or technical education.

12 scholarships per year. Contact Taunton High guidance counselor for complete information.

2412—ARMENIAN RELIEF SOCIETY OF EASTERN USA, INC. (Grants)

80 Bigelow Avenue, Suite 200
Watertown MA 02472
617/926-3801
FAX: 617/924-7238
E-mail: ARSEastUS@aol.com

AMOUNT: $400-$1,000 Undergrad; $1,000-4,000 Graduate
DEADLINE(S): APR 1
FIELD(S): All fields of study

Open to undergrad and grad students of Armenian ancestry who are attending an accredited 4-year college or university in the U.S. and have completed at least one semester. Awards based on need, merit, and involvement in Armenian community.

Write to scholarship committee at address above for complete information. Enclose self-addressed stamped envelope and indicate whether undergrad or grad student.

2413—ARMENIAN STUDENTS' ASSOCIATION OF AMERICA, INC. (Scholarships)

Attention: Christine Williamson, Scholarship Administrator
395 Concord Avenue
Belmont MA 02178
617/484-9548
E-mail: asa@asainc.org
Internet: http://www.asainc.org

AMOUNT: $500-$5,000
DEADLINE(S): JAN 15
FIELD(S): All fields of study

Applicants must be of Armenian ancestry and be full-time students who plan to attend a four-year, accredited college/university in the U.S. full-time during the next academic year (must have completed or be in the process of completing first year of college or higher). Must demonstrate financial need, have good academic performance, show self help, and participate in extracurricular activities.

30 awards annually. $15 application fee. Contact ASA Scholarship Committee in the fall to request application forms. Deadline for requests is January 15th; completed application package must be returned by March 15th.

2414—ARMONA UNION ACADEMY (Booster Club Tuition Assistance)

Armona CA 93202
559/582-4468
FAX: 559/582-6609
E-mail: aua@cnetech.com
Internet: http://members.cnetech.com/aua/

AMOUNT: Varies
DEADLINE(S): Varies
FIELD(S): All fields of study

Open to K-12th grade students planning to attend this private Seventh-Day Adventist day school. Award is based on financial need. Students should apply for the award before they are admitted to the school.

20+ awards annually. Contact Marianne Brock for an application.

2415—ARMY EMERGENCY RELIEF (MG James Ursano Scholarship)

200 Stovall Street, Room 5N13
Alexandria VA 22332-0600
703/428-0000
FAX: 703/325-7183
Internet: http://www.aerhq.org/

AMOUNT: $700-$1,800
DEADLINE(S): MAR 1
FIELD(S): All

The MG James Ursano Scholarship Fund, as administered by Army Emergency Relief, is a secondary mission to help Army families with the costs of higher education. The fund's purpose is to assist students in need with tuition, fees, books, and room and board.

Awards are based primarily on financial need, as evidenced by income, assets, family size, special financial obligations, and circumstances

2416—ARMY ROTC (Scholarships)

Army ROTC Scholarships
Ft. Monroe VA 23651-5238
800/USA-ROTC
Internet: http://www.usarotc.com/four.htm

AMOUNT: Tiered tuition scholarships up to $16,000.
DEADLINE(S): JUL 15 (early cycle); NOV 15 (regular cycle)
FIELD(S): All fields of study

Open to U.S. citizens between the ages of 17 and 27. For undergraduate study at colleges having Army ROTC programs. Must have minimum of 2.5 GPA and SAT score of 920 or ACT score of 19 and meet minimum physical standards.

Renewable yearly. Must be high school graduate. Must have minimum of 920 on SAT or 19 on composite ACT. Must attend an institution with Army ROTC program (more than 600 across the nation). Must meet minimum physical standards. Direct questions to Headquarters, Cadet Command, at above address.

2417—ARROWSMITH ACADEMY (Tuition Assistance)

2300 Bancroft Way
Berkeley CA 94704-1604
510/540-0440
FAX: 510 540 054
E-mail mail@arrowsmith.org
Internet: http://www.arrowsmith.org/profile.html

AMOUNT: 10%-90% tuition reduction
DEADLINE(S): MAR 1
FIELD(S): All fields of study

Open to U.S. citizens/permanent residents who wish to attend this college preparatory day school. Must be at the appropriate level of studies to enter high school and show proof of good behavior and a commitment to learning. Must demonstrate financial need; school looks at the family situation of each applicant.

32-35 awards annually. Renewable. See Web site or contact William Fletcher, Director, for an application.

2418—ARTS & ENTERTAINMENT NETWORK (A&E Teacher Grant Competition)

235 East 45th Street
New York NY 10017
212/661-4500
Internet: http://www.doe.mass.edu/tgfa/tgfas3.html

AMOUNT: $1,000 Savings Bond (12); $2,500 Savings Bond (Grand Prize + prizes for the school
DEADLINE(S): MAR 1
FIELD(S): All fields of study

Awards for teachers of grades 6-12 who have demonstrated how imaginative use of A&E programming results in innovative approaches to classroom instruction. Applicants are to write above a unique classroom project based on an A&E program. Also, a teacher's project can be submitted by a principal, school librarian, or peer teacher.

Three winners in each of four regions: Eastern, Central, Western, and Southern. Contact organization for details.

2419—ASIAN PACIFIC AMERICAN SUPPORT GROUP (Scholarship)

USC, Student Union 410
Los Angeles CA 90089-4851
213/740-4999
FAX: 213/740-5284
E-mail: apass@usc.edu
Internet: http://www.usc.edu/dept/apass

AMOUNT: $1,000-$2,500
DEADLINE(S): MAR 22
FIELD(S): All fields of study.

Scholarships for full-time students who have close ties with the Asian Pacific Community. GPA of 3.0 or above required.

15-20 awards per year. Recipients may reapply for second year. Applications available Dec. 2.

2420—ASSOCIATION FOR COMPUTING MACHINERY-WASHINGTON, DC CHAPTER (Undergraduate Scholarship)

1444 Eye Street NW, Suite 700
Washington DC 20005-2210 (202) 216-9623
FAX: 202/216-9646

DEADLINE(S): MAY 12
FIELD(S): Any field of study involving computer applications

Grant for a candidate enrolled in an undergraduate program at a college or university in Maryland, Virginia, or the District of Columbia in a field involving computers. Must of at least sophomore standing. Applications from students in any academic dept. will be considered.

Access Web site for details and application.

2421—ASSOCIATION OF THE SONS OF POLAND (Scholarship)

333 Hackensack Street
Carlstadt NJ 07072
201/935-2807
FAX: 201/935-2752
E-mail: sonsofpoland@yahoo.com
Internet: http://www.sonsofpoland.com

AMOUNT: $1,000 scholarship; $100 Achievement Award
DEADLINE(S): May 14
FIELD(S): All

Open to high school students who have been members of the association for at least 2 years and are insured by the association. Must be entering an accredited college in September of the year of high school graduation.

2422—ASSOCIATION ON AMERICAN INDIAN AFFAIRS (Adolph Van Pelt Special Fund for Indian Scholarships)

Sisseton SD 57262
605/698-3998
FAX: 605/698-3316
E-mail: aaia@tnics.com
Internet: http://www.indian-affairs.org

AMOUNT: $500-$800
DEADLINE(S): AUG 15
FIELD(S): All fields of study

Open to undergraduates who are minimally 1/4 degree Indian blood from a federally recognized tribe. Awards are based on financial need and merit, and are limited to North America/Alaska. Must submit essay on goals, two letters of recommendation, certificate of enrollment and blood quantum of tribe or BIA, transcript, schedule of classes, and current financial aid award letter. Grants are paid directly to the school.

Renewable up to 4 years. Send a self-addressed, stamped envelope to Elena Stops, Scholarship Coordinator, for an application. Recipients notified by September 25.

2423—ASSOCIATION ON AMERICAN INDIAN AFFAIRS (Displaced Homemaker Scholarships)

Sisseton SD 57262
605/698-3998
FAX: 605/698-3316
E-mail: aaia@tnics.com
Internet: http://www.indian-affairs.org

AMOUNT: Varies
DEADLINE(S): SEP 10
FIELD(S): All fields of study

Open to mid-life homemakers (female and male) who are minimally 1/4 degree Indian blood from federally recognized tribes and unable to fill their educational goals. Augments expected financial sources of educational money to assist those students with child care, transportation, and some living expenses. Must demonstrate special financial needs as heads of households, single parents, or as displaced homemakers. Limited to North America/Alaska. Essay and blood proof required.

Renewable up to 3 years. Send a self-addressed, stamped envelope to Elena Stops, Scholarship Coordinator, for an application. Recipients notified by October 20.

2424—ASSOCIATION OF INTERNATIONAL EDUCATION, JAPAN (Honors Scholarships for Private International Students)

4-5-29 Komaba, Meguro-KU
Tokyo 153 JAPAN
03-5454-5213
FAX: 03-4343-5233
Internet: http://www.kyoto-u.ac.jp/kokuryu/kyotouniv/info04.htm

AMOUNT: 52,000-73,000 yen
DEADLINE(S): Middle of April
FIELD(S): All fields of study

Scholarships for study in Japan. For undergraduate and graduate students of all nationalities enrolled at junior colleges, technological or vocational schools, colleges, or universities. Grantees are selected on the basis of recommendations from the scholarship committee at their college or university in Japan.

4,540 awards per year. Apply through the school attended. Write for complete information.

2425—ASSOCIATION OF INTERNATIONAL EDUCATION, JAPAN (Peace and Friendship Scholarship for Private International Students)

4-5-29 Komaba, Meguro-KU
Tokyo 153 JAPAN
03-5454-5213
FAX: 03-4343-5233
Internet: http://www.kyoto-u.ac.jp/kokuryu/kyotouniv/info04.htm

AMOUNT: 61,000-81,000 yen per month
DEADLINE(S): Varies (Closing date is designated by the university.)
FIELD(S): All fields of study

For privately financed international students from Asian countries and areas who play a central role in friendship and exchange activities between Japan and their countries. Must be enrolled at a junior college, technological or vocational school, college, or university.

Must demonstrate financial need. Apply through the school attended.

2426—ASSOCIATION OF INTERNATIONAL EDUCATION, JAPAN (Short-term Student Exchange Scholarships for International Students)

4-5-29 Komaba, Meguro-ku
Tokyo 153-8503 JAPAN
03-5454-5214
FAX: 03-4343-5234
Internet: http://www.kyoto-u.ac.jp/kokuryu/kyotouniv/info04.htm

AMOUNT: 80,000 yen (up to 12 months); Travel expenses: Economy class round-trip air ticket; Settling in allowance: 25,000 yen
DEADLINE(S): May 10
FIELD(S): All fields of study

Open to international students planning to study in Japan. Must be enrolled in an undergraduate or graduate program and plan to continue with that program after the stay in Japan. Can be any nationality except Japanese. Must demonstrate financial need. Programs are from more than 3 months to one year.

1,700 scholarships. Must demonstrate financial need. Write to above address or check with your university for details. Information also at above Web site.

2427—ASSOCIATION OF UNIVERSITIES AND COLLEGES OF CANADA (CAP Canadian Awards Program)

Int'l & Canadian Programs Branch
350 Albert Street, Suite 600
Ottawa Ontario K1R 1B1 CANADA
613/563-1236
FAX: 613/563-9745
Internet: http://www.aucc.ca

AMOUNT: $1,000-$27,000 (depending on program)
DEADLINE(S): Varies (with program)
FIELD(S): All fields of study

AUCC administers numerous scholarships and fellowships to Canadian citizens/permanent residents for undergraduate or graduate study at eligible Canadian postsecondary institutions. Specific sections include awards for high school seniors, undergraduates, graduates, and disabled students. Some require certain fields of study, nomination by university, or high academic achievement.

Renewable. See Web site or contact AUCC for booklet detailing specific programs.

2428—ASTHMA AND ALLERGY FOUNDATION OF AMERICA (Scholarship)

220 Boylston Street
Chestnut Hill MA 02467
617/965-7771
FAX: 617/965-8886
Internet: http://www.asthmaandallergies.org

AMOUNT: $500
DEADLINE(S): FEB 1
FIELD(S): All

Open to all high school juniors and seniors planning to attend college who suffer from asthma or significant allergies. Selection is based on academic achievement, activities, and a one-page essay.

2429—ASTRAEA LESBIAN ACTION FOUNDATION (Margot Karle Scholarship)

116 E. 16th Street, 7th Floor
New York NY 1000388
212/529-8021
FAX: 212/982-3321
E-mail: grants@astraea.org
Internet: http://www.astraea.org

AMOUNT: $300-$500
DEADLINE(S): AUG 15; DEC 15
FIELD(S): All fields of study

Open ONLY to female undergraduates enrolled full-time in the City University of New York system. Must demonstrate financial need and a high degree of community involvement. Two essays and transcript required.

2 awards annually. Not renewable. Contact Astraea Foundation for an application.

2430—ATHEISTS OF FLORIDA, INC. (Mark Twain Scholarship Fund)

Ft. Pierce FL 34948-3893
FAX: 561/465-6402
E-mail: AthALFLE@aol.com

AMOUNT: $500 (1st and 2nd place); $300 (3rd and 4th)
DEADLINE(S): DEC 31
FIELD(S): Most fields of study

Promotes and assists the postsecondary education of qualified young Americans in their chosen discipline within the fields of the Arts and Humanities, Applied Arts, Education, Science, Social Sciences, Mathematics, Engineering, or Law. Applicants must be of a Freethinking persuasion, against all efforts to impose superstitious relgious teachings and interpretations on society and anything that inhibits freedom. Must be full-time bachelors degree students. Essay required.

Contact the Mark Twain Scholarship Fund for an application and yearly essay topic. Recipients notified by February 28th.

2431—ATHENIAN SCHOOL (Financial Aid)

2100 Mt. Diablo Scenic Boulevard
Danville CA 94506
925/362-7223
FAX: 925/855-9342
E-mail: chris_beeson@athenian.org
Internet:http://www.athenian.org

AMOUNT: Full tuition (max.)
DEADLINE(S): FEB 1
FIELD(S): All fields of study

Grants are open to 6th-12th grade students planning to attend this day/boarding school. Must have a strong academic record and the ability to take a positive contributory role in the school community and programs.

Renewable. See Web site or Contact: Director of Admission Christopher Beeson

2432—AURORA FOUNDATION (Scholarships)

111 W. Downer Place, Suite 312
Aurora IL 60506
630/896-7800
Internet: http://www.aurorafdn.org scholarships.html

AMOUNT: $1,000
DEADLINE(S): Varies
FIELD(S): All fields of study

Scholarships are administered by this Foundation for residents of the Greater Aurora Area, including the Tri-Cities and Kendall County, Illinois.

Write or call for details. Scholarship applications are available only during the month of
January and early February.

2433—AUSTIN CHILDREN'S EDUCATIONAL OPPORTUNITY FOUNDATION (Scholarships)

111 Congress, Suite 3000
Austin TX 78701
512/472-0153
FAX: 512/310-1688
E-mail: austinceo@aol.com
Internet: http://ceoaustin.org/about.html

AMOUNT: $1,000/year (max. = half tuition)
DEADLINE(S): None
FIELD(S): All fields of study

Open to children who are residents of Travis County, Texas, aged 6-14 (as of Sept. 1st of the school year) attending any school. Family must qualify for the federal school lunch program guidelines.

Awards are first come, first served. Renewable up to 3 years. Contact Jane Kilgore for an application.

2434—AUSTRALIA FEDERATION SCHOLARSHIP PROGRAM

Australian Education Office
1601 Massachusetts Avenue NW
Washington DC 20036
800/245-2575
E-mail: grad@austudies.org
Internet: http://www.austudies.org/aeo

AMOUNT: Varies by university
DEADLINE(S): Multiple
FIELD(S): All

Funding for U.S. and Canadian students toward graduate study in Australia. This aid is available through foundations, fellowships, and scholarships.

2435—AUSTRIAN FEDERAL MINISTRY OF SCIENCE AND TRANSPORT (Exchange Scholarships)

Minoritenplatz 5
A-1014 Wien 1 AUSTRIA
+43/1/53 120-0
FAX: +43/1/53 120-3099
E-mail: ministerium@bmbwk.gv.at
Internet:http://www.bmbwk.gv.at

AMOUNT: Varies
DEADLINE(S): Varies
FIELD(S): All areas of study

Awards open to undergraduate and graduate students who wish to study in Austria.

Write or visit Web site for details.

2436—AVON LATINA MODEL OF THE YEAR (Competition)

Rules Requests, 1251 Sixth Avenue
New York NY 10020-1196
800/FOR-AVON
E-mail: infobrokr1@aol.com

AMOUNT: Up to $15,000 in educational awards and modeling fees and gifts
DEADLINE(S): FEB 15
FIELD(S): All fields of study

For Hispanic females between the ages of 17 and 25 who are "intelligent, poised, and beautiful."

Send self-addressed, stamped envelope for application and official rules.

2437—AYN RAND INSTITUTE (Anthem Essay Contest)

Inglewood CA 90312
E-mail: anthemessay@aynrand.org
Internet: http://www.aynrand.org/contests/

AMOUNT: $2,000 (1 1st prize); $500 (10 2nd); $200 (20 3rd)
DEADLINE(S): March 18
FIELD(S): All fields of study

Open to 9th and 10th graders who write a 600-1,200-word essay on Ayn Rand's novelette *Anthem.* Purpose is to encourage analytical thinking and excellence in writing, and to expose students to the philosophic ideas of Ayn Rand. Essays judged on style and content.

See Web site or contact your English teacher or guidance counselor for guidelines—submit your essay via e-mail. Winners announced June 4th.

2438—AYN RAND INSTITUTE (Fountainhead Essay Contest)

Inglewood CA 90312
E-mail: tf-essay@aynrand.org
Internet: http://www.aynrand.org/contests/

AMOUNT: $10,000 (1 1st prize); $2,000 (5 2nd); $1,000 (10 3rd)
DEADLINE(S): APR 15
FIELD(S): All fields of study

Open to 11th and 12th graders who write a 800-1,600-word essay on Ayn Rand's *The Fountainhead.* Purpose is to encourage analytical thinking and excellence in writing, and to expose students to the philosophic ideas of Ayn Rand. Essays judged on style and content.

See Web site or contact your English teacher or guidance counselor for guidelines—do NOT write to above address. Winners announced June 4th.

2439—BACKPACKER (Outdoor Scholarship)

33 East Minor Street
Emmaus PA 18098-0099

610/967-5171
FAX: 610/967-8181
AMOUNT: Varies
DEADLINE(S): MAR 31
FIELD(S): All

Must be enrolled as a full-time student in a four-year college or university and maintain a 3.0 GPA or better. Also, applicants must be entering junior or senior year in the fall semester. Open to all majors.

2440—BAKER BOYER BANK (George T. Welch Scholarships)

Trust Dept.; P.O. Box 1796
Walla Walla WA 99362-0353
509/522-3136
Internet: http://www.washington.edu/students/ugrad/scholar/special/welch.html
AMOUNT: $2,500 (max.) for 4 years; $1,000 (max.) for 2 years
DEADLINE(S): April 1
FIELD(S): All fields of study

Open to residents of Walla Walla County, Washington, who have graduated from a Walla Walla high school and are pursuing undergraduate or graduate study. Must be U.S. citizen.

45 awards annually. Contact Holly T. Howard for an application.

2441—BAKERY, CONFECTIONERY, TOBACCO WORKERS AND GRAIN MILLERS INTERNATIONAL UNION (BCTGM Scholarship Program)

10401 Connecticut Avenue
Kensington MD 20895-3961
301/933-8600
FAX: 301/946-8452
Internet: http://www.bctgmlocal19.com/members/index3.html
AMOUNT: $1,000
DEADLINE(S): JAN 31
FIELD(S): All fields of study

Open to BCTGM members, their children, and children of deceased members. BCTGM members may be at any level of study; children may NOT previously have attended college or vo-tech school. Must submit SAT/ACT scores and essay.

20 awards annually. Not renewable. Contact BCTGM for an application.

2442—BAPTIST GENERAL CONVENTION OF TEXAS (Scholarships)

333 N. Washington Street, Suite 371
Dallas TX 75246-1798
214/828-5131
Internet: http://www.nbcusa.org
AMOUNT: Varies
DEADLINE(S): Varies
FIELD(S): All fields of study

Scholarships for college-bound high school seniors and undergraduates who are members of the Baptist Church and also an ethnic minority. Must attend or plan to attend a Baptist college.

Send SASE for details.

2443—BARKER FOUNDATION INC. (Scholarship Grants)

Nashua NH 03061-0328
603-889-1763
Internet: http://www.free-4u.com/barker_foundation,_inc_.htm
Written Inquiry
AMOUNT: Varies
DEADLINE(S): None
FIELD(S): All fields of study

Open to New Hampshire residents who are pursuing undergraduate studies. Based primarily on financial need. Grants are paid directly to students' institutions.

6-12 awards annually. To apply, submit letter outlining proposed institution, annual tuition cost, expected family contribution, personal information, and photocopy of financial aid award letter from school. Requests without this information will not be considered.

2444—BARNABAS MINISTRIES OF SHREVEPORT

4451 Charter Point Boulevard
Jacksonville FL 32211-1027
318/227-1313
AMOUNT: Varies
DEADLINE(S): Ongoing
FIELD(S): All fields of study

Scholarships and assistance to financially needy residents of the state of Louisiana.

Send letter to Dr. John Sullivan, Trustee, at above address.

2445—BARNARD COLLEGE PRE-COLLEGE PROGRAMS (Grants for Summer in New York)

Columbia University
3009 Broadway
New York NY 10027-6598
212/854-8866
FAX: 212/854-8867
E-mail: pcp@barnard.edu
Internet: http://www.barnard.edu/pcp/index.html
AMOUNT: $200-$800 towards program cost
DEADLINE(S): APR 19
FIELD(S): All fields of study

A summer pre-college program at Barnard College in New York City (June 27-July 31) for high school students who are intellectually prepared for college-level work and will have completed the 10th or 11th grade by start of program. Grants are offered only on the basis of financial need. Selection based on strong high school records, recommendations, and involvement in extra-curricular activities.

Cost is $3,295 for residential students and $2,150 for commuters. The grant would offset part of this. Write to above address for booklet describing program which also contains application forms.

2446—BASIN ELECTRIC POWER COOPERATIVE (Scholarship Program)

1717 E. Interstate Avenue
Bismark ND 58503-0564
701/223-0441
FAX: 701/224-5336
E-mail: info@bepc.com
AMOUNT: $1,000
DEADLINE(S): MAR 14
FIELD(S): All fields of study

Available to children of full-time employees of Basin Electric Power Cooperative and its subsidiaries, and the children of member-system employees and consumers. Must be a student who is enrolled or planning to enroll in a full-time graduate or undergraduate course of study at an accredited two-year or four-year college, university, or vocational/technical school.

20 awards annually. Contact Mike LaLonde or Deb Meyhoff in human resources for an application at headquarters. The phone number is 701-223-0441.

2447—BEAVER LUMBER, INC. (Scholarships)

7303 Warden Avenue
Markham Ontario L3R 5Y6
CANADA
800/387-0460
FAX: 905/479-6997
E-mail: awards@aucc.ca
AMOUNT: $1,200-$2,400
DEADLINE(S): JUN 1
FIELD(S): All fields of study

Open to children of full-time Beaver Lumber associates. Applicants must be Canadian citizens/permanent residents accepted at a Canadian college/university to pursue full-time undergraduate studies.

Based on scholastic achievements and extracurricular activities. Financial need NOT a factor.

6 awards annually. Renewable. Contact Crystal Greenough for an application. Awards are decided by the Association of Universities and Colleges of Canada (AUCC). Notification by August 31st.

2448—BECA FOUNDATION (Daniel Gutierrez Memorial General Scholarship Fund)

1070 South Commerce Street
Suite B
San Marcos CA 92069
Internet: http://www.iit.edu/~cmp/opportunity.html#scholarships
AMOUNT: $1,000
DEADLINE(S): MAR 1
FIELD(S): All fields of study

Open to Latino students who are residents of San Diego County. Must be high school graduates or graduating seniors entering college in the fall. Award may be used for any field of study anywhere in the US. BECA also provides role models for Latino students by assigning a mentor to each scholarship recipient.

Not renewable. Send a self-addressed, stamped envelope to Ana Garcia for an application.

2449—BECA FOUNDATION (General Scholarship Fund)

1070 South Commerce Street
Suite B
San Marcos CA 92069
619/489-6978
Internet: http://www.iit.edu/~cmp/opportunity.html#scholarships
AMOUNT: $500-$1,000
DEADLINE(S): Varies
FIELD(S): All fields of study

Open to Latino high school seniors attending a North San Diego County high school who plan to attend a U.S. college/university in the fall. BECA also provides role models for Latino students by assigning a mentor to each scholarship recipient.

Send a self-addressed, stamped envelope for an application or call for deadline.

2450—BEDDING PLANTS FOUNDATION, INC. (BPI Family Member Scholarship)

East Lansing MI 48826-0280
517/333-4617
FAX: 517/333-4494
E-mail: BPFI@aol.com
Internet: http://www.bpfi.org
AMOUNT: $1,000
DEADLINE(S): MAY 15
FIELD(S): All fields of study

Open to graduate and undergraduate students at an accredited university in the U.S. or Canada who are majoring in any field. Must be a child, parent, or spouse of a current member of Bedding Plants International. Cash award, with checks issued jointly in name of recipient and college/institution he or she will attend for current year. Must submit references and transcripts.

1 award annually. See Web site or send printed self-addressed mailing label (or self-addressed, stamped envelope) to BPFI after January 1st for an application. Recipient will be notified.

2451—BEINECKE SCHOLARSHIP

1200 Main Street
Bethlehem PA 18018
610/625-7830
FAX: 610/625-7919
E-mail: BeineckeScholarship@moravian.edu
Internet: http://www.beineckescholarship.org/
AMOUNT: $32,000
DEADLINE(S): MAR 15
FIELD(S): ALL

To be eligible for a Beinecke Scholarship, a student must demonstrate superior standards of intellectual ability, scholastic achievement, and personal promise during his or her undergraduate career.

2452—BETTY HANSEN NATIONAL SCHOLARSHIP

7326 Lehigh Ct.
Zephyrhills FL 33540
813/715-0642
AMOUNT: $1,000
DEADLINE(S): FEB 28
FIELD(S): All

Must be the son or daughter of a member of the Danish Sisterhood of America. Also available to members of the Sisterhood who are in good standing for at least one year.

2453—BIA HIGHER EDUCATION/ HOPI SUPPLEMENTAL GRANT

P.O. Box 123
Kykotsmovi AZ 86039
520/734-3533; 800/762-9630
E-mail: IPolingyumptewa@hopi.nsn.us or FLomakema@hopi.nsn.us
Internet: http://www.nau.edu/~hcpop/ current/student/grant.htm
AMOUNT: BIA Higher Education Grant: $2500 per semester/ Hopi Supplemental Grant: $1500 per semester
DEADLINE(S): JUL 31 (fall); NOV 30 (spring); APR 30 (summer)
FIELD(S): All fields of study

For enrolled members of the Hopi Tribe pursuing associate, baccalaureate, graduate, or post-graduate degrees. Minimum 2.0 GPA required. Grant is a supplemental source of financial aid the eligible students.

Financial need is primary consideration.

2454—BILLY BARTY FOUNDATION (Evelyn Barty Scholarship Awards Programs)

929 W. Olive Avenue; Suite C
Burbank CA 91506
818/953-5410
E-mail: billybarty@myself.com
Internet: http://www.rth.org/bbf/
AMOUNT: $2,000 per applicant
DEADLINE(S): JUL 15
FIELD(S): All fields of study

Open to undergraduates who are 4 feet 10 inches and under (or who are related to someone of this stature). Must be a U.S. citizen studying in the continental US. Financial need; leadership and scholarship are award criteria.

8-15 awards per year. Renewable. Write for complete information.

2455A—BIG 33 SCHOLARSHIP FOUNDATION (Scholarships)

Mickey Minnich, Executive Director
511 Bridge Street
P.O. Box 213
New Cumberland PA 17070
717/774-3303
FAX: 717/774-1749
E-mail: info@big33.org
Internet: http://www.big33.org
AMOUNT: $500-$2,000
DEADLINE(S): FEB 12
FIELD(S): All

Open to all high school seniors in PA and OH. Quantity of scholarships awarded, dollar amount of each, and type of scholarships vary each year. This is a one-time award only. Available to applicants who have attained a 2.0 cumulative GPA (GPA on a 4.0 scale) for the previous two academic years (grades 10 and 11).

2455B—BIG 33 SCHOLARSHIP FOUNDATION, INC. (Scholarships)

Mickey Minnich, Executive Director
511 Bridge Street
PO Box 213
New Cumberland PA 17070
717/774-3303
FAX: 717/774-1749
E-mail: info@big33.org
Internet: http://www.big33.org

AMOUNT: $500-$2000
DEADLINE(S): FEB 12
FIELD(S): All

Open to all high school seniors in PA and OH currently enrolled in a public or accredited private school who have attained a 2.0 cumulative GPA (GPA on a 4.0 scale) for the previous two academic years (grades 10 and 11) planning to continue their education beyond high school in an accredited institution of higher education or technical school.

2456—BLACKFEET HIGHER EDUCATION PROGRAM (BIA Grant)

P.O. Box 850
Browning MT 59417
406/338-7539
FAX: 406-338-7530
E-mail: bhep@3rivers.net
http://www.3rivers.net

AMOUNT: $3,200-$3,800
DEADLINE(S): MAR 1
FIELD(S): All fields of study

Open to enrolled members of the Blackfeet Tribe for undergraduate or vocational education.

Write to the above address for complete information.

2457—BLACK PAGES USA (Scholarship)

P.O. Box 5012
1400 Barnwell Street
Columbia SC 29250
803/799-8150

AMOUNT: $1,500
DEADLINE(S): JAN 1
FIELD(S): All

Awarded to an African-American graduating high school senior, male or female, who plans to become an entrepreneur after graduating from college. This scholarship is offered through the Columbia Urban League.

2458—BLINDED VETERANS ASSOCIATION (Kathern F. Gruber Scholarship Program)

477 H Street NW
Washington DC 20001-2694
800/669-7079 or 202/371-8880
FAX: 202/371-8258
E-mail: bjones@bva.org.
Internet: http://www.bva.org/around2.html

AMOUNT: $1,000-$2,000
DEADLINE(S): APR 12
FIELD(S): All fields of study

Open to children and spouses of blinded veterans. The vet must be legally blind, either service or non-service connected. Student must be accepted or already enrolled full-time in a college or vocational school and be a U.S. citizen.

8 awards of $2,000 and 8 of $1,000 annually. Contact BVA for an application.

2459—BOB JONES UNIVERSITY (Rebate Program)

1700 Wade Hampton Boulevard
Greenville SC 29614-0001
800-BJ-AND-ME
Internet: http//:www.bju.edu/academic/academics.asp

AMOUNT: $1,000-$2,000
DEADLINE(S): Varies (beginning of semester)
FIELD(S): All fields of study

Bob Jones University is a private, Christian-oriented college which offers vocational, technical, and academic programs. The financial aid program requires that the student participate in a work program for at least seven hours per week. Must be U.S. citizen.

Renewable. Contact the Financial Aid Office for details.

2460—BOETTCHER FOUNDATION (Scholarships)

600 17th Street, 22nd Floor
Suite 221
Denver CO 80202-5422
303-534-1927
E-mail: scholarships@boettcherfoundation.org
Internet: http//:www.boettcherfoundation.org

AMOUNT: $2,800 stipend (total amount of scholarship could amount to between $35,000-$100,000)
DEADLINE(S): Nov 1
FIELD(S): All fields of study

Open to Colorado high school seniors presently in the top 5% of their class who have been accepted as an incoming freshman at any Colorado college/university. Must have minimim 27 ACT or 1200 SAT score, demonstrate high school leadership and service, and be a U.S. citizen. Financial need NOT a factor.

40 awards annually. Renewable up to 4 years. Application available every September from Colorado High counselors.

2461—BONNEVILLE TRANSLOADERS, INC. (Scholarship)

642 South Federal
Riverton WY 82501
Written Inquiry
Internet: http://siswww.uwyo.edu

AMOUNT: $1,000
DEADLINE(S): MAY 1
FIELD(S): All fields of study

Available to high school graduates of Fremont or Sweetwater Counties in Wyoming.

Write to above address for an application.

2462—BOSWELL SCHOLARSHIP

1809 East 71st Street, Suite 205
Chicago IL 60649
773/667-7061
FAX: 773/667-7064

AMOUNT: $1,000
DEADLINE(S): MAR 1
FIELD(S): All

Available to African-American students who graduate from high school and submit a written essay and transcripts. Five scholarships awarded per year. Organized by the National Hook-Up of Black Women, Inc.

2463—BOWLING GREEN UNIVERSITY (Scholarships for Study Abroad Program)

1106 Offenhauer West
Bowling Green OH 43403
419/372-0309 or 419/372-0479
E-mail: sallyr@bgnet.bgsu.edu
Internet: http://conted.bgsu.edu

AMOUNT: Varies
DEADLINE(S): SEPT 30 (for spring semester)
FIELD(S): All fields of study

The International Education Committee offers travel grants for study abroad and other credit-bearing overseas programs. For undergraduate students at Bowling Green University who are U.S. citizens or permanent residents.

Contact school for deadline date for summer or fall semesters.

2464—BOY SCOUTS OF AMERICA (National Eagle Scout Scholarships)

1325 West Walnut Hill Lane
P.O. Box 152079
Irving TX 75015-2079
972/580-2431
Internet: http://www.bsa.scouting.org/nesa/scholar/

AMOUNT: Varies
DEADLINE(S): FEB 28
FIELD(S): All fields of study

For college-bound high school seniors currently registered in the Boy Scouts of American who have been granted the Eagle Scout Award. Must document leadership ability in Scouting and a strong record of participation of activities outside of scouting.

Not for two-year or technical schools. Send SASE to above location for application.

2465—BOY SCOUTS OF AMERICA-DR. HARRY BRITENSTOOL SCHOLARSHIP COMMITTEE (Greater New York City Councils Scholarship Fund)

345 Hudson Street
New York NY 10014-4588
212/242-1100 ext. 271
Internet: http://www.free-4u.com/dr__harry_britenstool_scholarship_fund.htm

AMOUNT: Varies
DEADLINE(S): JUN 1
FIELD(S): All fields of study

Undergraduate scholarships for students who have been at one time registered with the Greater New York councils, Boy Scouts of America or employed by that organization. Must show academic excellence, financial need, and study at least 24 credit hours during the school year. U.S. citizens only.

Must submit essay on "What Scouting has meant to me."

2466—BOYS AND GIRLS CLUB OF VENTURA (Emma Nylen Scholarship)

2021 Sperry Drive, #5
Ventura CA 93003
805/641-5585
FAX: 805/639-0180
E-mail: wendy@www.bgclubventura.org
Internet: http://www.bgclubventura.org

AMOUNT: $200-$1,000
DEADLINE(S): March (early)
FIELD(S): All fields of study

Scholarships for residents of Ventura County who are full-time students and who have at least a "C" average. U.S. citizenship. Under age of 30.

Money divided among several awards. Must reapply to renew. Contact is Wendy Ropes.

2467—BREAD AND ROSES COMMUNITY FUND (Jonathan R. Lax Scholarship Fund)

Michelle Jackson
Administrative Director
1500 Walnut Street, Suite 1305
Philadelphia PA 19102
215/731-1107
FAX: 215/731-0453
E-mail: info@breadrosesfnd.org
Internet: http://www.breadrosesfund.org/grants/lax.html

AMOUNT: $5,000-$20,000
DEADLINE(S): JAN 2
FIELD(S): All

This scholarship fund was established to encourage gay men to obtain additional education, aspire to positions in which they contribute to society, be open about their sexual preference, and act as role models for other gay men with similar potential. Tuition awards are available with at least one graduate and one undergraduate award of $20,000 each year. Awards are restricted to men from Philadelphia studying elsewhere or men from anywhere studying in Philadelphia.

2468—BREWER FOUNDATION, INC.

Rocky Mount NC 27804
252-446-5334
FAX: 252-446-4823

AMOUNT: Varies
DEADLINE(S): None specified
FIELD(S): All fields of study

Scholarships for higher education to residents of North Carolina.

Contact Joseph B. Brewer, Jr., President, at foundation listed above for current application deadline and procedures.

2469—BRITISH AMERICAN EDUCATIONAL FOUNDATION (Scholars' Program)

Larchmont, NY 10538
914/834-2064
FAX: 914/833-3718
E-mail: scholars@baef.org
Internet: http://www.baef.org

AMOUNT: up to $5,000
DEADLINE(S): MAY 1
FIELD(S): Wide variety limited by British 'A' level offerings at each school

Open to American high school seniors who are 18 or younger and want to spend a year at an independent boarding school in the United Kingdom prior to entering college in either the UK or US. Must have financial need.

See Web site or contact Stephen Bauer for complete information.

2470—BRITISH COLUMBIA MINISTRY OF ADVANCED EDUCATION TRAINING AND TECHNOLOGY (Student Assistance Program)

2nd Floor, 1106 Cook Street
Victoria BC V8V 3Z9 CANADA
250/387-6100
FAX: 250/387-4858
Internet: http://www.aett.gov.bc.ca/studentservices

AMOUNT: Varies
DEADLINE(S): Varies (6 weeks before end of study period)
FIELD(S): All fields of study

Federal and provincial student loans and grants are open to residents of British Columbia who are enrolled full time for credit at a designated college, institute, or university. Must be "legal" resident of British Columbia or a Canadian citizen.

See Web site or contact the Student Services Branch for an application.

2471—BRITISH COLUMBIA PARAPLEGIC ASSOCIATION (Canadian Paraplegic Association Women's Auxiliary Bursaries)

780 SW Marine Dr.
Vancouver BC V6P 5Y7 CANADA
604/324-3611
FAX: 604/326-1229
E-mail: vancouver@canparaplegic.org
http://www.canparaplegic.org

AMOUNT: Varies
DEADLINE(S): JUL 31
FIELD(S): All fields of study

Open to spinal cord injured students for beginning or continuing undergraduate or graduate studies in a university in British Columbia. Must be Canadian citizen, landed immigrant, or British Columbia resident. Based on academic standing and financial need. Must be members of the BC Paraplegic Assn.

Contact BCPA for membership information or an application.

2472—BRITISH COLUMBIA PARAPLEGIC ASSOCIATION (IODE Bursary for Physically Disabled Persons)

780 SW Marine Dr.
Vancouver BC V6P 5Y7 CANADA
604/324-3611
FAX: 604/324-3671
E-mail: vancouver@canparaplegic.org
Internet: http://www.canparaplegic.org

AMOUNT: Varies
DEADLINE(S): JUL 31
FIELD(S): All fields of study

Establised by the Independent Order of the Daughters of the Empire, Provincial Chapter of British Columbia. For physically disabled postsecondary students who are Canadian citizens in financial need.

Funds are to be used to assist with expenses for tuition, books, transportation, or teaching assistance.

2473—BRITISH COLUMBIA PARAPLEGIC FOUNDATION (Barbara E. Adams Scholarship)

780 SW Marine Dr.
Vancouver BC V6P 5Y7 CANADA
604/324-3611
FAX: 604/324-3671
E-mail: vancouver@canparaplegic.org
Internet: http://www.canparaplegic.org

AMOUNT: Varies
DEADLINE(S): JUL 31
FIELD(S): All fields of study

Open to British Columbia residents who are mobility-impaired with a significant degree of disability. Applicants should be promising students pursuing a vocational or academic education.

Must be a Canadian citizen, legal resident, or a resident of British Columbia and a member of the BC Paraplegic Assn. Write for complete information. Funds may be used for tuition, books and supplies, help or equipment for study purposes, and/or finance of transportation.

2474—BRITISH COLUMBIA PARAPLEGIC FOUNDATION (Joseph David Hall/Don Vaux/John MacNeal Memorial Scholarships & BC IYDP Bursaries)

780 SW Marine Drive
Vancouver BC V6P 5Y7 CANADA
604/324-3611
FAX: 604/324-3671
E-mail: vancouver@canparaplegic.org
Internet: http://www.canparaplegic.org

AMOUNT: Varies
DEADLINE(S): JUL 31
FIELD(S): All fields of study

Scholarships are awarded to physically disabled persons to further their vocational or academic training. Recipients must be Canadian citizens or legal residents and are expected to attend institutions in British Columbia.

Must be member of the British Columbia Paraplegic Assn. (except IYDP). Write for complete information.

2475—BRITISH INFORMATION SERVICES (British Marshall Scholarships)

845 Third Avenue
New York NY 10022-6691
212/745-0277
FAX: 212/745-0359
Internet: http://www.marshallscholarship.org

AMOUNT: 16,500 pounds sterling (average—includes allowance, tuition fees, books, travel, cost of thesis preparation, and possible dependent spouse support)
DEADLINE(S): mid-October of year preceding tenure.
FIELD(S): All fields of study

Open to U.S. citizens who have graduated from an accredited four-year U.S. college/university with a minimum 3.7 (A-) GPA. Tenable for two years at any British university at the undergraduate or graduate level leading to British university degree. Must submit letter of endorsement (from school or employer), outline of proposed studies (500 words), and personal essay (1,000 words).

Up to 40 awards annually. Renewable. See Web site for complete information and an application.

2476—BUCK INSTITUTE FOR EDUCATION (American Revolution Bicentennial Scholarships)

18 Commercial Boulevard
Novato CA 94949
415/883-0122
Internet: http://www.bie.org/bicentennial

AMOUNT: $500-$2,000
DEADLINE(S): MAR 31
FIELD(S): All fields of study

For Marin County students who have been county residents since Sept. 1 of the year prior to submitting an application. Scholarships tenable at accredited colleges, universities, and vocational or trade programs.

Contact high school or college counselor or send self-addressed, stamped envelope with inquiry to Marie Kanarr, Buck Institute for Education.

2477—BUDDHIST COMPASSION RELIEF TZU-CHI FOUNDATION, U.S.A. (Scholarships)

206 East Palm Avenue
Monrovia CA 91016
626/305-1188
FAX: 626/305-1185
Internet: http://www.tzuchi.org/usa/english

AMOUNT: $1,000
DEADLINE(S): MAY 31
FIELD(S): All fields of study

Scholarships for college-bound high school seniors (at least 3.8 GPA) and college students (at least 3.5 GPA). Must demonstrate financial need. Application process includes submitting a 500-word essay on why you think you should receive this scholarship and a description of your family background.

For more details on application requirements, contact organization or access Web site.

2478—BUFFALO AFL-CIO COUNCIL

295 Main Street, Room 532
Buffalo NY 14203
716/852-0375
FAX: 716/855-1802

AMOUNT: $500-$1,000
DEADLINE(S): MAR 1
FIELD(S): All

Awarded to high school seniors who are sons or daughters of the Buffalo AFL-CIO Council affiliated members. Decisions are based on academic achievement, extracurricular activities, guidance counselor recommendation, student essay, and financial need.

2479—BUREAU OF MAINE VETERANS SERVICES (Veterans Dependents Educational Benefits)

117 State House Station
Augusta ME 04333-0117
207/626-4464 or 800/345-0116
FAX: 207/626-4471
E-mail: mvs@me.ngb.army.mil
Internet: http://www.state.me.us/va/defense/vdeb.htm

AMOUNT: Tuition Waiver

DEADLINE(S): None
FIELD(S): All fields of study

For undergraduates, aged 16-21, to attend any state of Maine supported university or technical college. Must be a dependent (child or spouse) of 100% permanently disabled or deceased veteran. Veteran must have entered service from Maine or have lived in Maine at least five years preceding application. Financial need NOT a factor.

Renewable. Contact Leslie Breton at above address for an application.

2480—BURSARY FOR PEOPLE WITH SPINA BIFIDA

780 SW Marine Drive
Vancouver BC V6P5Y7 CANADA
604/326-1241
FAX: 604/326-1229
E-mail: aingram@bcpara.org
AMOUNT: $1,500
DEADLINE(S): JAN 1
FIELD(S): All

Designed for students attending an institution of higher organization who have Spina Bifida. Candidates must be residents of British Columbia and enrolled in an accredited facility in Canada. This award may be use in conjunction with other financial aid awards.

2481—BUTLER MANUFACTURING COMPANY FOUNDATION (Scholarship Program)

P.O. Box 419917
BMA Tower, Penn Valley Park
Kansas City MO 64141
816/968-3208
FAX: 816/968-3211
E-mail: blfay@butlermfg.org
Internet: http://www.butlermfg.com
AMOUNT: $2,500
DEADLINE(S): FEB 18
FIELD(S): All

Awarded to the children of full-time employees of Butler Manufacturing Company and its subsidiaries, including international locations. Must be high school seniors. Award is renewable for up to four years. Recipients must maintain academic standing in the top half of their class.

2482—BUTTE CREEK FOUNDATION (Scholarships)

1350 E. Lassen Avenue, #2
Chico CA 95926
530/895-1512
FAX: 530/895-0844
AMOUNT: Varies
DEADLINE(S): None
FIELD(S): All fields of study

Open to residents of Butte County, California, who wish to pursue undergraduate or graduate study.

Apply by letter to John Burghardt, President & Secretary, at above address.

2483—C. BASCOM SLEMP FOUNDATION (Scholarships)

Star Bank NA
P.O. Box 5208
Cincinnati OH 45201
513/762-8878
AMOUNT: $2,000
DEADLINE(S): OCT 1
FIELD(S): All fields of study

Open ONLY to residents of Lee or Wise counties in Virginia. For undergraduate study.

30 awards per year. Write for complete information.

2484—C.G. FULLER FOUNDATION (Scholarships)

Personal Trust Division
Nations Bank of South Carolina
Columbia SC 29202-0448
(864) 379-8832
http://www.erskine.edu/admissions/finaid.scholarships.html
Written Inquiry
AMOUNT: up to $2,000/year
DEADLINE(S): MAR 15
FIELD(S): All fields of study

Open to South Carolina residents who are high school seniors and will enroll in an accredited undergraduate college/university in South Carolina. Must have a minimum 3.0 GPA and be a U.S. citizen. Family income must be less than $60,000 per year.

Approximately 10 awards annually.

2485—CABRILLO CIVIC CLUBS OF CALIFORNIA (Scholarships)

1455 Willow Street
San Diego CA 92106
619/223-7026
Internet: http://www.collegeview.com/financial_aid
AMOUNT: $400
DEADLINE(S): May 1
FIELD(S): All fields of study

Open to California high school seniors of Portuguese descent who have a minimum 3.5 GPA. Tenable for undergraduate study at two- or four-year colleges. Must be U.S. citizen/permanent resident.

2486—CALIFORNIA COLLEGE DEMOCRATS (Internships)

See Web site
Internet: http://www.collegedems.org
E-mail: office@collegedems.com
AMOUNT: Varies
DEADLINE(S): None
FIELD(S): All fields of study

Internships available for various California Democratic office holders, candidates for office, and for several organizations, especially those working on environmental issues.

See Web site for list of statewide openings, which constantly changes. Some offer pay. Possible credit through your university.

2487—CALIFORNIA CORRECTIONAL PEACE OFFICERS ASSOCIATION (Joe Harper Scholarship Foundation)

755 Riverpoint Drive, Suite 200
West Sacramento CA 95605-1634
Written Inquiry
AMOUNT: Varies
DEADLINE(S): APR 30
FIELD(S): All fields of study, scholastic or vocational

For active members, retired members, or immediate family members of current or deceased members the California Correctional Peace Officers Association. Applicants will be judge on academic achievement, school activities, financial need, and community service.

Renewable if college GPA is maintained at 3.5. For scholastic or vocational field. Contact location above for complete information.

2488—CALIFORNIA GOVERNOR'S COMMITTEE FOR EMPLOYMENT OF DISABLED PERSONS (Hal Connolly Scholar-Athlete Award)

P.O. Box 826880, MIC 41
Sacramento CA 94280-0001
916/654-8055
TDD: 916/654-9820
Internet: http://www.disabilityemployment.org.
AMOUNT: $1,000
DEADLINE(S): FEB 2

FIELD(S): All fields of study

Must have competed during high school in varsity level or equivalent athletics and have a disability. Academic and athletic histories must demonstrate the qualities of leadership and accomplishment. Minimum 2.8 GPA. Age 19 or under.

Six awards—3 to females and 3 to males. Must be a California resident; write for more information.

2489—CALIFORNIA GRANGE FOUNDATION (Scholarships)

Pat Avila
2101 Stockton Boulevard
Sacramento CA 95817
Written Inquiry
Internet: http://www.calpoly.edu/~cagr/scholarships.html

AMOUNT: $250 (2 awards)
DEADLINE(S): March 2
FIELD(S): All fields of study

Four scholarship programs for members of the California Grange or their dependents. Some are for high school seniors, and others are for students already enrolled in college.

Write for information after Feb. 1 of each year.

2490—CALIFORNIA JUNIOR MISS PROGRAM (Scholarships and Awards)

Windsor CA 95492
707/837-1900
FAX: 707/837-9410
Internet: http://www.ajm.org/california
E-mail: cjm@saber.net

AMOUNT: Up to $15,000
DEADLINE(S): Varies
FIELD(S): All fields of study

Competition open to girls in their junior year of high school who are U.S. citizens and California residents. Winner receives a $15,000 college scholarship; runners-up share up to $30,000 in awards. For undergraduate or graduate study.

Apply before or early in junior year of high school. Award can be used for books, fees, and tuition at any college in the world. Write to Ms. Katy Gillwood at above address for complete information, or visit Web site.

2491—CALIFORNIA MASONIC FOUNDATION (Scholarship Program)

1111 California Street
San Francisco CA 94108-2284
415/776-7000
FAX: 415/776-7170
Email: foundation@mhcsf.org
Internet: http://californiamason.org;

AMOUNT: $40,000 ($10,000 per year for four years) or $10,000 ($2,500 per year for four years)
DEADLINE(S): March 15
FIELD(S): All fields of study

Open to high school seniors who are California residents with a minimum 3.0 GPA. Must be U.S. citizens planning to attend an accredited 2- or 4-year institution of higher learning as a full-time undergraduate. Must demonstrate financial need.

2492—CALIFORNIA STUDENT AID COMMISSION (Law Enforcement Dependents Scholarships-LEPD)

Rancho Cordova CA 95741-9026
916/526-7590
TDD: 916/526-7542
FAX: 916/526-8002
E-mail: custsvcs@csac.ca.gov
Internet: http://www.csac.ca.gov

AMOUNT: $100-$9,036/year
DEADLINE(S): None given
FIELD(S): All fields of study

Need-based grant to dependents/spouses of California peace officers (Hwy Patrol/marshalls/sheriffs/police), specified CA Dept of Corrections and CA Youth Authority employees, and firefighters employed by public entities who have been killed or totally disabled in the line of duty. If you receive a Cal Grant, your LEPD will match your Cal Grant award. Receiving LEPD will not prevent you from receiving Cal Grant or any other grant/fee waiver.

Renewable up to four years. For more information, contact the California Student Aid Commission.

2493—CALIFORNIA STUDENT AID COMMISSION (Robert C. Byrd Honors Scholarships)

Rancho Cordova CA 95741-9029
916/526-8250
TDD: 916/526-7542
FAX: 916/526-8002
E-mail: custsvcs@csac.ca.gov
Internet:http://www.csac.ca.gov

AMOUNT: up to $1,500/year
DEADLINE(S): APR 30
FIELD(S): All fields of study

A federally funded program administered by the California Student Aid Commission designed to recognize exceptionally able students who show promise of continued academic excellence. Scholarships are awarded solely on the basis of merit; GPA, SAT, and ACT scores considered.

Renewable up to four years. Each California public and private secondary school may nominate up to 2 applicants. Contact your high school scholarship coordinator to apply.

2494—CALIFORNIA TABLE GRAPE COMMISSION (California Table Grape Field Worker Scholarship Program)

392 W. Fallbrook, Suite 101
Fresno CA 93711-6150
559/447-8350
FAX: 559/447-9184
E-mail: info@tablegrape.com
Internet: http://www.tablegrape.com

AMOUNT: $12,000 (3 awards)
DEADLINE(S): APR 1
FIELD(S): All fields of study

Scholarships for undergraduates in a four-year college program who worked in the California table grape fields, or whose families did so, during the previous year. U.S. citizenship required.

2495—CALIFORNIA TEACHERS ASSOCIATION (CTA Scholarships for Dependent Children)

Burlingame CA 94011-0921
650/697-1400
E-mail: scholarships@cta.org
Internet: http://www.cta.org

AMOUNT: $2,000
DEADLINE(S): FEB 15
FIELD(S): All fields of study

For undergraduate students who are dependents of an active, retired-life, or deceased California Teachers Association member. Financial need is NOT considered.

25 awards annually. Contact the Human Rights Department at above address in October for application.

2496—CALIFORNIA-HAWAII ELKS ASSOCIATION (Undergraduate Scholarship Program for Students with Disabilities)

5450 E. Lamona Avenue
Fresno CA 93727-2224
559/255-4531
FAX: 559/456-2659
E-mail: chea@chea-elks.org
Internet: http://www.chea-elks.org

AMOUNT: $1,000 to $2,000
DEADLINE(S): MAR 15
FIELD(S): All fields of study

Open to residents of California and Hawaii who have a physical impairment, neurological impairment, visual impairment, hearing impairment, and/or speech/language disorder. Must be a senior in high school, a high school graduate, or have passed the GED. Must be U.S. citizen and demonstrate financial need. Award may be used at accredited community colleges, vocational schools, and four-year colleges/universities. Based on GPA, severity of disability, and depth of character.

20-30 awards annually. Renewable. Contact your local Elks Lodge for an application after November 15th. Notification by June 1st.

2497—CALLEJO-BOTELLO FOUNDATION CHARITABLE TRUST

4314 North Central Expressway
Dallas TX 75206
214/741-6710
AMOUNT: Varies
DEADLINE(S): APR 23
FIELD(S): All areas of study

Scholarships for students planning to attend educational institutions in Texas.

Send SASE to William F. Callejo, Trustee, at above address

2498—CAMBRIDGE MONTESSORI SCHOOL (Financial Aid)

161 Garden Street
Cambridge MA 02138
617/492-3410
FAX: 617/576-5154
AMOUNT: $1,000-$6,000
DEADLINE(S): JAN 15
FIELD(S): All fields of study

Financial aid for students accepted at this independent day school in Cambridge, MA. Must demonstrate financial need. School program includes primary and elementary school programs. Must be a Massachusetts resident.

15-20 awards yearly. Renewable. Contact school for details.

2499—CAMP FOUNDATION (Scholarship Grants)

Franklin VA 23851
757/562-3439
AMOUNT: $3,000-$4,500
DEADLINE(S): MAR 1
FIELD(S): All fields of study

Open to graduating high school seniors in the city of Franklin and the counties of Isle of Wight and Southampton, Virginia, or to residents of these areas who graduated from high school elsewhere and are pursuing undergraduate study.

7 awards annually. Contact Camp Foundation for an application ONLY if you meet residency requirements.

2500—CAMPBELL HALL SCHOOL (Scholarships)

4533 Laurel Canyon Boulevard
North Hollywood CA 91607
818/980-7280
FAX: 818/505-5319
E-mail: powerse@campbellhall.org
Internet: http://www.campbellhall.org
AMOUNT: Up to full tuition
DEADLINE(S): FEB 1
FIELD(S): All fields of study

Financial aid for students who meet admissions criteria to this Episcopalian day school serving grades K-12 in California. Must demonstrate financial need.

30 awards yearly. Contact school for details.

2501—CANADA HUMAN RESOURCES DEVELOPMENT (Canada Student Loans Program)

P.O. Box 2090, Station "D"
Ottawa Ontario K1P 6C6 CANADA
819/994-1844
E-mail: pcpe-cslp-response@hrdcdrhc.gc.ca
Internet: http://wwwcanlearn.ca
AMOUNT: Maximum of $165 per week of study
DEADLINE(S): None
FIELD(S): All fields of study

Program provides loan assistance toward meeting the costs of full-time post-secondary study as a supplement to other resources available to the student. Canadian citizen or permanent resident.

Write for complete information.

2502—CANADIAN FEDERATION OF UNIVERSITY WOMEN (Margaret Dale Philp Award)

251 Bank Street, Suite 600
Ottawa Ontario K2P 1X3 CANADA
613/234-8252
Internet: http://www.cfuw.ca
AMOUNT: $1,000
DEADLINE(S): NOV 15
FIELD(S): All

Award is available to female Canadian citizens currently residing in Canada who are working toward a postgraduate degree in social sciences, the humanities, or Canadian history. Application forms are available at the CFUS Web site.

2503—CANADIAN NATIONAL INSTITUTE FOR THE BLIND (Various Scholarships and Grants)

100-5055 Joyce Street
Vancouver BC V5R 6B2 CANADA
604/431-2020
FAX: 604/431-2099
E-mail: hirjif@bc.cnib.ca
Internet: http://www.cnib.ca
AMOUNT: Varies
DEADLINE(S): Varies
FIELD(S): All fields of study

Scholarships open to legally blind residents of British Columbia and the Yukon who are college or university students registered with CNIB. Awards tenable at recognized 2-year and 4-year undergraduate institutions. Canadian citizen.

Write for complete information.

2504—CANNON SCHOOL (Scholarships)

5801 Poplar Tent Road
Concord NC 28027
704/786-8171
FAX: 704/788-7779
E-mail: info@cannonschool.org
Internet: http://www.cannonschool.org
AMOUNT: Varies (three scholarship programs)
DEADLINE(S): None
FIELD(S): All fields of secondary school study

Financial aid to attend this private K-12 school in North Carolina.

20 annual awards. Renewable. Must demonstrate financial need. Admission is competitive.

2505—CAPE CANAVERAL CHAPTER RETIRED OFFICERS ASSOCIATION (Scholarships)

Patrick AFB FL 32925-4708
Written Inquiry
AMOUNT: $2,000/year
DEADLINE(S): MAY 31
FIELD(S): All fields of study

Open ONLY to Brevard County, Florida, residents who have completed at least three semesters at any accredited four-year college in the US. Must be descendants or dependents of active duty or retired military personnel. U.S. citizenship required.

Renewable an additional year. Send self-addressed, stamped envelope to the Scholarship Committee at above address for an application.

2506—CAPE FEAR ACADEMY (CFA Academic Fellowships)

3900 S. College Road
Wilmington NC 28412
910/791-0287
FAX: 910/791-0290
E-mail: cfa@isaac.net
Internet: http://www.capefear academy.org
AMOUNT: 1/2 tuition
DEADLINE(S): None
FIELD(S): All fields of study

Scholarships are available to 6th-12th grade students at this private day school. Must have a minimum 3.0 GPA and other talents, such as music, drama, sports, etc. Financial need NOT a factor.

Renewable. Contact Susan Harrell for an application.

2507—CAREER COLLEGE ASSOCIATION/ CAREER TRAINING FOUNDATION (Imagine America Scholarship)

Bob Martin
Executive Director/Vice President
10 G Street NE, Suite 750
Washington DC 20002-4213
202/336-6800
FAX: 202/408-8102
E-mail: scholarships@career.org
Internet: http://www.petersons.com/cca/
AMOUNT: $1,000
DEADLINE(S): Varies
FIELD(S): All

Must apply only to career colleges participating in the program, as listed on http://www.petersons.com/cca. Must meet that career college's normal entrance requirements for the requested program of study. Must be nominated by school counselor or principal.

Applicant must have 2.5 GPA or higher. Financial need must be demonstrated.

2508—CAREER COLLEGE ASSOCIATION/CAREER TRAINING FOUNDATION (Imagine America Scholarship)

Bob Martin
Executive Director/Vice President
10 G Street NE, Suite 750
Washington DC 20002-4213
202/336-6800
FAX: 202/408-8102
E-mail: scholarships@career.org
Internet: http://www.petersons.com/cca/
AMOUNT: $1,000
DEADLINE(S): OCT 31
FIELD(S): All

One time award available to any graduating high school senior. Must be accepted and planning to attend one of the 892 accredited private postsecondary institutions. Ask your high school guidance counselor or principal for nomination information.

2509—CARGILL (Scholarship Program for Rural America)

Minneapolis MN 55440-5650
952/742-6247
E-mail: bonnie_blue@cargill.com;
Internet: http://www.cargill.com
AMOUNT: $500-$3,000
DEADLINE(S): Jan 1-Feb 15 (2 different scholarships)
FIELD(S): All fields of study

Open to high school seniors who are from a family whose livelihood is at least 50 percent derived from farming. Applicant must be a U.S. citizen planning to attend a U.S. school of higher education, either a 2- or 4-year college/university or a vocational-technical school.

50 awards annually. Contact Bonnie Blue for an application.

2510—CARIBBEAN PREPARATORY SCHOOL (Admissions Scholarship for Talented Students)

San Juan PR 00936
787/765-4411
FAX: 787/764-3809
E-mail: rmarracino@cpspr.coqui.net
Internet: http://www.cpspr.org/
AMOUNT: Half tuition (approx. $3,000)
DEADLINE(S): APR 1
FIELD(S): All fields of study

Open to 7th- to 11th-grade residents of the San Juan metro area who would like to attend this day school. Must be a talented student in any area and demonstrate financial need.

1 award annually. Renewable. Contact Ebelmar Concepcion for an application.

2511—CASCADE POLICY INSTITUTE (Independence Essay Competition)

813 SW Alder, Suite 450
Portland OR 97205
503/242-0900
FAX: 503/242-3822
E-mail: angela@cascadepolicy.org
Internet: http://www.Cascade Policy.org
AMOUNT: Varies, up to $5,000
DEADLINE(S): MAR 15
FIELD(S): All fields of study

Essay competition open to Oregon high school age students attending a private, public, or homeschool. Subject is "Exploring the Foundations of Freedom."

Up to 5 awards annually. Contact Angela Eckhardt for details.

2512—CATHOLIC AID ASSOCIATION (College Tuition Scholarship Program)

3499 N. Lexington Avenue
St. Paul MN 55126
651/490-0170
E-mail: agoserud@catholicaid.com
http://www.catholicaid.com
AMOUNT: $500 for those attending a Catholic college or university and $300 for attending a state state college, university, community college or technical school
DEADLINE(S): FEB 1
FIELD(S): All fields of study

Open to Catholic Aid Association members (insurance or annuity) of at least two years. Must be entering freshman or sophomore year in an accredited college, university, or tech school.

Contact Catholic Aid Assn. for an application.

2513—CATHOLIC DIOCESE OF KANSAS CITY-ST. JOSEPH—CENTRAL CITY SCHOOL FUND (Scholarships)

P.O. Box 419037
Kansas City MO 64141-6037
816/756-1850
FAX: 816/756-1571
Internet: http://www.diocese-kcsj.org
E-mail: catholicschools@ diocesekcsj.org
AMOUNT: Tuition
DEADLINE(S): None
FIELD(S): All fields of study

Provides educational support in the Central City Schools for the children of the urban core of Kansas City. Grades K-12.

Applicants need not be Catholic. Contact above location for details.

2514—CENTRAL CATHOLIC HIGH SCHOOL (Scholarships)

200 S. Carpenter Road
Modesto Ca 95351
209/524-6822
FAX: 209/524-5646
Internet: http://www.cchsca.org

AMOUNT: $500-$2,500
DEADLINE(S): Varies
FIELD(S): All fields of study

Open to high school students at this private Catholic college-prep day school. There are several different scholarships available as well as tuition assistance and work-study; some require financial need, others are based on merit.

90 awards annually. Renewable. Contact Mrs. Patricia Crist for an application.

2515—CENTRAL SCHOLARSHIP BUREAU (Interest-Free Loans)

1700 Reisterstown Road, Suite 220
Baltimore MD 21208-2903
410/415-5558
FAX: 410/415-5501
E-mail: info@centralsb.org
Internet: http://www.centralsb.org

AMOUNT: $2,500-$15,000 (max. thru grad school)
DEADLINE(S): Varies
FIELD(S): All fields of study

Open to permanent residents of Baltimore City or Anne Arundel, Baltimore, Carroll, Harford, or Howard Counties, MD. Must have exhausted all other available avenues of funding. Awards are for study at any accredited undergraduate or graduate institution and are made on a non-competitive basis to anyone with a sound educational plan.

125 awards annually. Must apply first through government and school. See Web site or contact Central Scholarship Bureau for details.

2516—CEO AMERICA (School Choice Scholarships)

P O Box 330
Bentonville AR 72712
501/273-6957
FAX: 501/273-9362
E-mail: ceoamerica@ceoamerica.org
Internet: http://www.ceoamerica.org

AMOUNT: Varies
DEADLINE(S): Varies
FIELD(S): All fields of study

Tuition assistance for K-12 students to attend private schools. Typically for low-income families meeting federal free/reduced lunch guidelines. Residence and eligibility requirements vary from program to program.

Contact Fritz Steiger, President, for details.

2517—CHAIRSCHOLARS FOUNDATION, INC. (Scholarships)

16101 Carancia Lane
Odessa FL 33556-3278
813/920-2737
E-mail: hugokeim@earthlink.net
Internet: http://www.chairscholars.org

AMOUNT: $5,000
DEADLINE(S): None
FIELD(S): All fields of study

Scholarships for high school seniors of college freshmen confined to wheelchairs or who are otherwise physically challenged. Must demonstrate financial need, satisfactory academic past performance, and some degree of past community service. Must sign contract to remain drug-free and crime-free.

Three annual awards. Send name, address, age, and sex to the above address to begin application process.

2518—CHAROTAR PATIDAR SAMAJ (Sardar Patel Scholarships)

4767 Dunbarton Drive
Orlando FL 32817
407/671-2447
E-mail: rahil@erols.com
Internet: http://www.patidar.net

AMOUNT: $1,000 (4); $201 (5)
DEADLINE(S): OCT 20 (of sr. year in h.s.)
FIELD(S): All fields of study

This organization is a private group of people from the State of Gujarat, India, who are U.S. residents. The group strives to unite all Patel familes in the U.S. and assist with educational expenses. Applicants must apply during senior year in high school, have a minimum GPA of 3.5, Min. SAT score of 1100 or ACT of 25. An essay is required.

Print application from Web site and/or contact Mrs. Meena Patel at above address for details.

2519—CHARTER FUND (Scholarships)

370 17th Street, Suite 5300
Denver CO 80202
303/572-1727
FAX: 303/628-3839
Internet: http://www.piton.org

AMOUNT: $100-$2,500
DEADLINE(S): May 1
FIELD(S): All fields of study

Open ONLY to Colorado residents who are currently high school seniors applying for freshman year of college.

Contact Jeanette Montoya for an application after February 1st.

2520—CHATTANOOGA CHRISTIAN SCHOOL (CCS Scholarship Fund)

3354 Broad Street
Chattanooga TN 37409
423/265-6411
FAX: 423/756-4044
E-mail: sdonalds@ccsk12.com

AMOUNT: Varies
DEADLINE(S): APR
FIELD(S): All fields of study

Open to K-12th grade students attending this Christian day school. Awards are based on financial need.

100 awards annually. Renewable. Contact Sarah Donaldson for an application.

2521—CHAUTAUQUA REGION COMMUNITY FOUNDATION, INC. (Scholarships)

418 Spring Street
Jamestown NY 14701
716/661-3390
FAX: 716/488-0387
E-mail: crcf@crcfonline.org
Internet: http://www.crcfonline.org

AMOUNT: $100-$3,000
DEADLINE(S): JUN 1 (high school applications); JUL 15 (college students)
FIELD(S): All fields of study

Numerous scholarships with varying requirements are open ONLY to full-time students living in the vicinity of Jamestown, New York. Preference given to students in 12 school districts in Southern Chautauqua County. Financial need NOT a factor.

Contact JoAnn Carlson for an application.

2522—CHEROKEE NATION (Higher Education Need-based Grant Program)

P.O. Box 948
Tahlequah OK 74465
918/456-0671
Internet: http://www.devry-phx.edu/finaid/scholshp1.htm
AMOUNT: up to $1,500
DEADLINE(S): APR 1
FIELD(S): All areas of study

Grants available to members of the Cherokee Nation of Oklahoma. Awards are tenable at accredited undergraduate 2-year and 4-year colleges and universities in the U.S. U.S. citizenship required. Students must be eligible for Pell grants.

500 awards per year. Write for complete information.

2523—CHESTNUT HILL ACADEMY (Scholarships and Financial Aid)

500 W. Willow Grove Avenue
Philadelphia PA 19118-4198
215/247-4700
FAX: 215/242-4055
Internet: http://www.chestnuthill academy.org
AMOUNT: Varies (up to 100% of demonstrated need)
DEADLINE(S): DEC (early)
FIELD(S): All fields of K-12 study

Varying degrees of financial aid available at this independent day school for boys in Philadelphia, PA. Specific programs are available for students of color entering grades 4-7 or 9-11 as well as for all students for grades K-12 (up to 100% for grades 6-12).

Criteria relate to group exam, interview, and recommendations.

2524—CHEYENNE AND ARAPAHO TRIBES OF OKLAHOMA (Scholarships)

P.O. Box 38
Concho OK 73022
405/262-0345 or 800/247-4612
FAX: 405/262-0745
Internet: http://www.devryphx.edu/finaid/scholshp1.asp
AMOUNT: $1,000
DEADLINE(S): JUN 1-Nov 1
FIELD(S): All fields of study

For enrolled members of the Cheyenne-Arapaho Tribes of Oklahoma enrolled at the Concho agency. Must be certified to be at least 1/4 or more degree Cheyenne-Arapaho Indian, be a high school graduate or GED recipient, and in need of financial aid. For grads and undergrads. Summer and part-time students may be considered.

Write to Cheyenne-Arapaho Education Department at above address for details.

2525—CHICKASAW NATION EDUCATION FOUNDATION (Higher Education Grant)

Andy Kirkpatrick, Director of Education
224 Rosedale Road
Ada OK 74820
580/421-7711
FAX: 580/436-3733
Internet: http://www.cflink.org/scholars.htm#General
AMOUNT: $500
DEADLINE(S): JUN 1; DEC 1
FIELD(S): All

This scholarship is available for high school Chickasaw Citizens who requiring financial aid.

Scholarship applications must contain a one page essay describing the applicant's long-term goals. A minimum GPA of 2.0 is required.

2526—CHILDREN OF AIR TRAFFIC CONTROL SPECIALIST (Scholarships)

2300 Clarendon Boulevard
Suite 711
Arlington VA 22201
703/522-5717
FAX: 703/527-7251
E-mail: atca@worldnet.att.net
Internet: http://www.atca.org/scholars.htm
AMOUNT: $1,500-$2,500
DEADLINE(S): MAY 15
FIELD(S): ALL

Scholarships will be awarded to students enrolled in programs leading to a bachelor's degree in an aviation-related major. Must be either a child of an air traffic control specialist or a full-time aviation employee looking to advance their skills for employment.

2527—CHILDREN OF DEAF ADULTS ORGANIZATION (The Millie Brother Annual Scholarship)

Dr. Robert Hoffmeister
Director, Program in Deaf Studies
CODA International
605 Commonwealth Avenue
Boston MA 02215
617/353-3205
FAX: 617/353-3292
E-mail: deafstudy@bu.edu
Internet: http://www.coda-international.org/scholarship.htm
AMOUNT: $1,500
DEADLINE(S): MAY 4
FIELD(S): All

Available to a hearing child of deaf parents who is seeking higher education. One-time award based on transcripts, letters of reference, and essay. Essay should include a description of the applicant's future career aspirations as well as a description of their experience with CODA.

Two scholarships are awarded each year, but separate essays should be submitted to be considered for both. Applicant must be enrolled full-time at a two-year, four-year, or technical institution or university. Available to U.S. and non-U.S. citizens.

2528—CHILDREN'S EDUCATIONAL OPPORTUNITY FOUNDATION OF MICHIGAN (K-8 Scholarships)

126 Ottawa NW, Suite 401
Grand Rapids MI 49503
616/459-2222
FAX: 616/459-2198
E-mail: ceomich@iserv.net;Internet http://www.educationfreedom fund.org
AMOUNT: $1,000/year up to 3 years
DEADLINE(S): APR 30
FIELD(S): All fields of study, grades K-8

Scholarships for students in grades K-8 for use in Michigan private schools. Family income must fall within guidelines established for the federal school lunch program. U.S. citizenship and Michigan residency required.

Contact Linda Ploeg, Executive Director, or Pamela Pettibone, Program Administrator, at above location for application and details.

2529—CHINESE AMERICAN CITIZENS ALLIANCE FOUNDATION

415 Bamboo Lane
Los Angeles CA 90012
213/250-5515
Internet: http://www.cacanational.org
AMOUNT: $1,000
DEADLINE(S): JUL 31
FIELD(S): All fields of study

Scholarships for students of Chinese ancestry who are entering their junior year at colleges and universities in the Southern California area.

Awards based primarily on scholastic achievement, but consideration is also given to community and extracurricular activities.

2530—AMERICAN INDIAN GRADUATE CENTER (American Indian Graduate Center Fellowships)

4520 Montgomery Boulevard NE, Suite 1B
Albuquerque NM 87109-1291
505/881-4584
E-mail: marvelinevallo@marveline@aigc
Internet: http://www.aigc.com

AMOUNT: $250-$5,500
DEADLINE(S): Varies
FIELD(S): All

Application deadline: Should contact center, as deadline varies each year. For graduate and professional study in any field. Must be a U.S. citizen and member of a federally recognized tribe. Student must first apply for other aid through university financial aid office. Call or write for application and to confirm that funding is available. Contact person is Marveline Vallo. Need-based.

2531—AMERICAN INDIAN HERITAGE FOUNDATION (National Miss Indian U.S. Scholarship)

Pageant Director
6051 Arlington Boulevard
Falls Church VA 22044
703/237-7500

AMOUNT: Up to $10,000
DEADLINE(S): SEP 15
FIELD(S): All

Available to female Native American high school graduates between the ages of 18 and 26, who were never married or pregnant, and who never cohabited. Applicants must have a Native American sponsor.

2532—CHINESE CHRISTIAN HERALD CRUSADES (Chinese Collegiate Merit Scholarship for New York Schools)

Dr. Timothy Kok C. Tam
48 Allen Street
New York NY 10002
212/334-2033

AMOUNT: Up to $1,500
DEADLINE(S): JUL 31
FIELD(S): All fields of study

Open to Chinese students who are NOT U.S. citizens and who are attending a school within a 100-mile radius of New York City.

Two undergraduate and two graduate awards each year. Write for complete information.

2533—CHOATE ROSEMARY HALL (Need-Based Financial Aid)

333 Christian Street
Wallingford CT 06492
203/697-2239
FAX: 203/697-2629
E-mail: admissions@choate.edu
Internet: www.choate.edu

AMOUNT: Varies
DEADLINE(S): JAN 15
FIELD(S): All fields of study

Open to financially needy students in grades 9-12 at this private preparatory day/boarding school. Must first be deemed admissible by the Choate Rosemary Hall Admission Committee. Preference given to U.S. citizens.

Contact Ray Diffley III for an application.

2534—CHOCTAW NATION OF OKLAHOMA HIGHER EDUCATION PROGRAM (Grants)

Drawer 1210
Durant OK 74702-1210
580/924-8280 or 800/522-6170
FAX: 580/924-1267

AMOUNT: Up to $1,600/year
DEADLINE(S): MAR 15
FIELD(S): All fields of study leading to a degree

For enrolled members of the Choctaw Nation of Oklahoma who are undergraduates or graduates. Must be seeking at least an Associate of Arts degree. Priority is given undergrads depending on availability of funds. For use at accredited colleges or universities.

Must submit copies of Certificate of Degree of Indian Blood and Tribal Membership cards showing Choctaw descent, photo, and transcripts. Apply between Jan. 1 and March 15. For renewal must reapply each year.

2535—CHRIST SCHOOL (Headmaster's Scholarship Program)

500 Christ School Road
Arden NC 28704
828/684-6232 ext. 106 or
800-422-3212
FAX: 828/684-2745
E-mail: admission@christschool.org
Internet: www.christschool.org

AMOUNT: $2,500-$12,000
DEADLINE(S): JAN 31
FIELD(S): All fields of study

Open to 8th- to 12th-grade students attending this private Episcopal boarding/day school for males. Must have a minimum 3.5 GPA over most recent three semesters, 75th percentile or better on SSAT or ISEE, 85th percentile on other nationally standardized tests, or state finalist in Duke TIP or John Hopkins Program. Must be U.S. citizen/permanent resident. Financial need NOT a factor.

8-12 awards annually. Renewable. Contact Colin Dunnigan for an application.

2536—CHRISTIAN RECORD SERVICES, INC. (Scholarships)

4444 S. 52nd Street
Lincoln NE 68516-1302
402/488-0981 (U.S.) or
905/436-6938 (Canada)
FAX: 402/488-7582
E-mail: info@christianrecord.org
Internet: http://www.christian record.org

AMOUNT: Varies
DEADLINE(S): APR 1
FIELD(S): All fields of study

Open to legally blind undergraduate students to help them secure training that will enable independence and self-support.

Visit Web site or contact Christian Record Services for an application. Alternate address: 1300 King Street East, Suite 119, Oshawa, Ontario L1H 8N9 Canada.

2537—CHUNG KUN AI FOUNDATION

P.O. Box 1559
Honolulu HI 96806
Written Inquiry

AMOUNT: $2,000
DEADLINE(S): Ongoing
FIELD(S): All areas of study

Scholarships to financially needy residents of Hawaii with a GPA of at least 2.8.

Contact Samuel S. Chung, Trustee, at above address for application procedures.

2538—CIRI FOUNDATION (CIRI Achievement Scholarships)

2600 Cordova Street, Suite 206
Anchorage AK 99503
907/263-5582
FAX: 907/263-5588
E-mail: tcf@ciri.com
Internet: http://www.ciri.com/tcf

AMOUNT: $7,000
DEADLINE(S): JUN 1

FIELD(S): All

Merit scholarships are awarded annually to applicants with at least a 3.0 GPA who are enrolled in a two- or four- year program. Can be used for either undergraduate or graduate work. Applicants must be Native American.

2539—CIRIUS (Government Scholarships for Foreign Nationals)

Fiolstraede 44
DK-1171 Copenhagen K DENMARK
+45/3395-7000
FAX: +45/3395-7001
E-mail: lh@ciriusmail.dk
Internet: www.ciriusonline.dk
AMOUNT: Tuition + 5,000 DKK/month
DEADLINE(S): MAR 1
FIELD(S): All fields of study

Open to nationals of 28 foreign countries (NOT including the US). Awards are to enable advanced students, graduates, and specialists to carry out 2-9 months of research at a Danish university. Instruction language is normally Danish, but English or other language often used. Not for elementary study of Danish language and not for an academic degree. Must be nominated.

Summer Language Courses also available. Contact Lis Hauschultz for list of eligible countries and other details.

2540—CITIZENS' SCHOLARSHIP FOUNDATION OF AMERICA (Dollars for Scholars Scholarship)

1505 Riverview Road
St. Peter MN 56082
800/248-8080
Internet: http://www.csfa.org
AMOUNT: $500
DEADLINE(S): Varies
FIELD(S): All

Community-based organizations that award a total of $15 million through their local chapters. Web site gives full contact information. Applicant must be enrolled full-time at a two-year, four-year, or technical institution. Restricted to U.S. and Canadian citizens.

2541—CITIZENS SCHOLARSHIP FOUNDATION OF GUERNSEY COUNTY (Dollars For Scholars)

Cambridge OH 43725
740/439-3558
FAX: 740/439-0012
AMOUNT: Varies
DEADLINE(S): JUN 1
FIELD(S): All fields of study

For residents of Guernsey County, Ohio who are pursuing undergraduate studies. Must have graduated from one of the following high schools: Cambridge, Meadowbrook, Buckeye Trail, Newcomerstown, John Glenn, Bishop Rosecrans, Guernsey-Noble Career Center, Muskingum-Perry Career Center, or Guernsey County ABLE/GED Center. U.S. citizenship NOT required.

Approx. 280 awards annually. Renewable up to four years. Financial need must be demonstrated. Contact Melody Greathouse at above address for an application/more information.

2542—CITIZENS' SCHOLARSHIP FOUNDATION OF WAKEFIELD, INC. (Scholarships)

Wakefield MA 01880
781/245-4890
FAX: 781/245-6761
E-mail: csfofwakefield@earthlink.net
Internet: http://www.wakefield.org/csf
AMOUNT: $300-$2,000
DEADLINE(S): MAR 15
FIELD(S): All fields of study

For full-time students (undergrads, graduates, vo-tech, continuing ed, etc.) who are residents of Wakefield, Massachusetts. Must demonstrate financial need.

300+ awards annually. Renewable with reapplication. Contact Yvonne Raia at above address or visit Wakefield High School's Guidance Office for an application.

2543—CITY AND COUNTRY SCHOOL (Financial Aid)

146 West 13th Street
New York NY 10011
212/242-7802
FAX: 212/242-7996
E-mail: LisaH@cityandcountry.org
Internet: http//www.cityandcountry.org
AMOUNT: Varies
DEADLINE(S): Dec 15
FIELD(S): All fields of study

Scholarships available to attend this independent, coeducational school which includes Pre-K through eighth grade. Awards based on family's financial need.

Contact school for details.

2544—CITY UNIVERSITY (Cyprus Scholarships)

International Office, City University,
Northampton Square
London EC1V 0HB ENGLAND UK
+44 (0) 20 7040 8019
FAX: +44 (0) 20 7040 8322
E-mail: international@city.ac.uk
Internet: www.city.ac.uk
AMOUNT: 2,500 pounds/year
DEADLINE(S): None
FIELD(S): Engineering

Scholarships for undergraduate students from Cyprus for use at City University in London.

Selection based on academic merit. Renewable for term of course. Program is through the British Council.

2545—CLAN MacBEAN FOUNDATION (Grant Program)

Raymond Heckethorn, Treasurer
441 Wadsworth Boulevard,
Suite 213
Denver CO 80226
303/233-6002
FAX: 303/233-6002
E-mail: macbean@ecentral.com
AMOUNT: up to $5,000
DEADLINE(S): MAY 31
FIELD(S): All

This grant provides students of any race, color, creed, or nationality the opportunity to study or create a project which demonstrates involvement in the enhancement of Scottish culture. Applications may be obtained directly from the foundation. Limited to U.S. and non-U.S. citizen applicants who are enrolled full-time at a two-year or four-year institution or university.

2546—COCA-COLA SCHOLARS FOUNDATION (Scholarship)

P.O. Box 442
Atlanta GA 30301-0442
800/306-COKE
AMOUNT: $1,000-$5,000 (per year for 4 years)
DEADLINE(S): OCT 31
FIELD(S): All areas of study

Open to college-bound H.S. seniors who are involved in school leadership, civic, and other extracurricular activities. Award is based on merit, academic achievement, and motivation to succeed. Students must live in a participating area.

Call or write to the above address for complete information.

2547—COLEGIO SAN JOSE (Student Aid Program)

San Juan PR 00928-1300
787/751-8177

FAX: 787/767-1746
E-mail: alumni@csj-pr.org
Internet: www.csj-pr.org
AMOUNT: $3,700 (max.)
DEADLINE(S): APR 15
FIELD(S): All fields of study

Open to 7th- to 12th-grade male students who wish to attend this Roman Catholic day school. Must be U.S. citizen, have a 75% GPA, and demonstrate good conduct and financial need.

55 awards annually. Renewable. Contact the Alumni and Development Office for an application.

2548—COLLEGE BOUND STUDENT OF THE YEAR (Contest)

1200 South Avenue, Suite 202
Staten Island NY 10314
718/761-4800
FAX: 718/761-3300
E-mail: information@collegebound.net
Internet: www.collegebound.net/soy/soy.html
AMOUNT: $1,000 + various prizes, including personal computer
DEADLINE(S): MAY 15
FIELD(S): All fields of study

For outstanding high school students planning to attend college. Write a typed, 300-500 word essay about the event or experience that motivated you to pursue a college education.

2 winners annually; 25 runners-up also receive prizes. Send a self-addressed, stamped envelope to above address for an application. Or complete the application and essay online, and mail a copy of your most recent transcript to the above address. Winners announced June 15th.

2549—COLLEGE FOUNDATION INC. (Federal Plus Loans Under NC Federal Family Education Loan Program)

2100 Yonkers Road
P.O. Box 12100
Raleigh NC 27605
888/234-6400
FAX: 919/821-3139
E-mail: info@cfi-nc.org
Internet: www.cfnc.org
AMOUNT: Difference between cost of attending and other financial aid received
DEADLINE(S): Varies
FIELD(S): All fields of study

For parent of student who is dependent (by Federal definition) and enrolled in eligible U.S. college. If the student is at a college not in NC, borrower must be legal NC resident. Parent does not have to demonstrate need but must NOT have "adverse credit history." Must meet nationwide Federal Plus Loans requirements.

Approximately 2,600 loans per year. Must reapply each year. Write for complete information and an application.

2550—COLLEGE FOUNDATION INC. (North Carolina Federal Family Education Loan Program; Stafford Loans-Subsidized and Unsubsidized-and PLUS loans)

P.O. Box 12100
Raleigh NC 27605
888/234-6400
FAX: 919/821-3139
E-mail: info@cfi-nc.org
Internet: www.cfnc.org
AMOUNT: $2,625 and up
DEADLINE(S): Varies
FIELD(S): All fields of study

Open to U.S. citizens who are legal residents of NC enrolled in an eligible in-state or out-of-state college or an out-of-state student attending an eligible NC college. Must meet nationwide eligibility requirements of Stafford loans. Must complete and file the Free Application for Federal Student Aid (FAFSA).

Approximately 56,000 loans per year. Financial need must be established for subsidized loan. New loan application is required yearly. Write for complete information.

2551—COLLEGE FOUNDATION INC. (North Carolina's Federal Family Education Loan Program)

P.O. Box 12100
Raleigh NC 27605
888/234-6400
FAX: 919/821-3139
E-mail: info@cfi-nc.org
Internet: www.cfnc.org
AMOUNT: Varies
DEADLINE(S): Varies
FIELD(S): All fields of study

For North Carolina students attending eligible institutions of higher education and vocational schools in state or out of state, and for out-of-state students attending eligible institutions of higher education and vocational schools in North Carolina.

Write for complete information and application.

2552—COLLEGE FOUNDATION INC. (North Carolina Student Incentive Grant)

P.O. Box 12100
Raleigh NC 27605
888/234-6400
FAX: 919/821-3139
E-mail: info@cfi-nc.org
Internet: www.cfnc.org
AMOUNT: Up to $1,500
DEADLINE(S): MAR 15
FIELD(S): All fields of study

Undergraduate grants to students who are U.S. citizens, North Carolina residents, and attending or planning to attend college in North Carolina. Must demonstrate substantial financial need and maintain satisfactory academic progress. Must complete and file the Free Application for Federal Student Aid (FAFSA).

Approximately 4,300 grants per year. Renewable to a maximum of 5 years of undergraduate study.

2553—COLLEGE MISERICORDIA (Honor Scholarships)

301 Lake Street
Dallas PA 18612
866/262-6363
E-mail: admiss@misericordia.edu
Internet: http://www.misericordia.edu
AMOUNT: $1,000-$10,000/year
DEADLINE(S): Varies
FIELD(S): All fields of study

Scholarships for incoming freshmen and transfer students to this co-educational Catholic college in Pennsylvania. Must have attained outstanding academic records. For undergraduates and graduate students.

Renewable until graduation provided minimum GPAs are maintained. GPA requirements are outlined in the scholarship notification letter. Obtain applications from the Admissions Office.

2554—COLLEGE MISERICORDIA (McAuley Awards)

301 Lake Street
Dallas PA 18612
866/262-6363
E-mail: admiss@misericordia.edu
Internet: http://www.misericordia.edu
AMOUNT: $1,000-$5,000/year
DEADLINE(S): Varies
FIELD(S):

Scholarships for incoming freshmen and transfer students to this co-educational Catholic college in Pennsylvania. Must have attained outstanding academic records. For undergraduates and graduate students.

Renewable annually based on leadership, school and community involvement

Obtain applications from the Admissions Office.

2555—COLLEGE MISERICORDIA (Partner Scholarships)

301 Lake Street
Dallas PA 18612
866/262-6363
E-mail: admiss@misericordia.edu
Internet: http://www.misericordia.edu

AMOUNT: $2,500/yr
DEADLINE(S): Varies
FIELD(S): Various fields of study

Scholarships for incoming freshmen and transfer students to this co-educational Catholic college in Pennsylvania. Must have attained outstanding academic records. For undergraduates and graduate students.

Renewable annually in the following majors: School Partnership: Education; Partners in Service: Psychology, Social Work; Partners in Medical Imaging: Medical Imaging; Partners in Business: Business Administration, Marketing, Management, Computer Science and Accounting; Partners in Nursing: Nursing. Obtain applications from the Admissions Office.

2556—COLLEGE OF MARIN FOUNDATION (Disabled Students Program)

Kentfield CA 94914
415/485-9382
FAX: 415/485-1379
E-mail: comf@marine.cc.ca.us
Internet: http://www.comf.org

AMOUNT: $100-$1,200
DEADLINE(S): MAR 3
FIELD(S): All fields of study

Open to undergraduate students enrolled in or planning to enroll in the disabled students program at the College of Marin. Must be a U.S. citizen and demonstrate financial need.

Contact Marie McCarthy at the C.O.M. Foundation for an application.

2557—COLLEGE OF SAINT ELIZABETH (Scholarships)

2 Convent Road
Morristown NJ 07960
973/290-4000
E-mail: webadmin@liza.st-elizabeth.edu
Internet: www.st-elizabeth.edu

AMOUNT: Varies
DEADLINE(S): Varies
FIELD(S): All fields of study

Various scholarships available for use at this private Catholic college for females in New Jersey.

Check Web site and/or write for details.

2558—COLLEGE OF ST. FRANCIS (Various Scholarship/Grant Programs)

500 Wilcox Street
Joliet IL 60435
815/740-3360
E-mail: webmaster@stfrancis.edu
Internet: www.stfrancis.edu

AMOUNT: Varies
DEADLINE(S): Varies
FIELD(S): All fields of study

Scholarships and grants for students at St. Francis College at all levels—incoming freshmen and transfers, undergraduates and graduates. Some are tied to certain requirements, such as athletics, biology, academic achievement , financial need, minority group, leadership, choir participation, and community activities.

See Web site and/or contact college for details on financial aid.

2559—COLLEGE PREPARATORY SCHOOL (Financial Aid Program)

6100 Broadway
Oakland CA 94618-1824
510/652-0111
FAX: 510/652-7467
E-mail: Lucia_Heldt@college-prep.org
Internet: www.college-prep.org

AMOUNT: Varies (with need)
DEADLINE(S): Early JAN (for following Fall)
FIELD(S): All fields of study

Open to financially needy 9th-12th grade students accepted to this private day school. Additional aid may be available for minority students through the newly established Minority Students Fund.

75 awards annually. Renewable. Contact Lucia H. Heldt, Dean of Admissions, for an application.

2560—COLLEGE STEPS (Scholarships)

Megan Reidy, Product Manager
Wells Fargo Education
Financial Services
301 East 58th Street N.
Sioux Falls SD 57104
605/575-4906
FAX: 605/575-4550
E-mail: megan.reidy@wellsfargoefs.com
Internet: http://www.wellsfargo.com/student

AMOUNT: $1000
DEADLINE(S): Varies
FIELD(S): All

High school students can sign up for information and advice on college applications, scholarships, and standardized tests, and also enter to win one of 250 $1,000 scholarships.

2561—COLLEGENET (Scholarship)

Ms. Dawna Allison
Marketing Manager
805 SW Broadway, Suite 1600
Portland OR 97205
503/973-5200
FAX: 503/973-5252
E-mail: dallison@collegenet.com
Internet: http://www.collegenet.com

AMOUNT: $10,000
DEADLINE(S): FEB 23
FIELD(S): All

Scholarship available for students who use the CollegeNET application process. A complete program description is available at the Web site. After applying to a member school, students must be nominated by the university based on their own criteria. Must enroll in classes by fall term.

2562—COLORADO ACADEMY (Financial Aid)

3800 S. Pierce Street
Denver CO 80235
303/914-2513
FAX: 303/914-2589
E-mail: claskey@mail.coloacad.org
Internet: www.coloacad.org

AMOUNT: Varies
DEADLINE(S): Varies
FIELD(S): All fields of study

Open to pre-K to 12th grade students who have been admitted to this private day school. Must demonstrate financial need and be U.S. citizen/permanent resident.

100+ awards annually. Renewable. Contact Catherine Laskey for an application.

2563—COLORADO COMMISSION ON HIGHER EDUCATION (Law Enforcement/POW/MIA Dependents Scholarship-Colorado)

Rita Beachem
1380 Lawrence Street, Suite 1200
Denver CO 80204

303/866-2723
FAX: 303/866-4266
Internet: http://www.state.co.us/cche
AMOUNT: Tuition, room, and board
DEADLINE(S): Varies
FIELD(S): All

Pays tuition, room, and board for dependents of Colorado law enforcement officers, fire or national guard personnel killed or disabled in the line of duty, and for dependents of prisoners of war or service personnel listed as missing in action. Applications are available at the Colorado Commission on Higher Education.

2564—COLORADO MASONS BENEVOLENT FUND ASSOCIATION (Scholarship Program)

1130 Panorama Drive
Colorado Springs CO 80904
719/471-9587 or
800/482-4441 ext. 19
E-mail: Rkadera@aol.com
AMOUNT: Up to $5,000/year renewable for four years
DEADLINE(S): MAR 15
FIELD(S): All fields of study (including trades)

Open to seniors in Colorado public high schools who plan to attend a Colorado college or university. Must be Colorado resident but Masonic affiliation is not required. Need is considered but is not paramount.

Applications are mailed early in November to all Colorado public schools. Contact Colorado schools. DO NOT write address above.

2565—COLORADO ROCKY MOUNTAIN SCHOOL (Scholarships)

1493 County Road 106
Carbondale CO 81623
970/963-2562
FAX: 970/963-9865
E-mail: Kscott@crms.ort
Internet: www.crms.org
AMOUNT: Varies
DEADLINE(S): Mar 1
FIELD(S): All areas

Scholarship for tuition at this private secondary school in Colorado, grades 9-12. Awards based on financial need. Contact Greg Williams.

45 awards yearly.

2566—COLORADO STATE UNIVERSITY (First Generation Award)

Student Financial Services
Administration Annex
Fort Collins CO 80523
970/491-6321
FAX: 970/491-5010
Internet: http://www.colstate.edu
AMOUNT: Tuition and fees
DEADLINE(S): APR 1
FIELD(S): All fields of study

Open ONLY to Colorado residents whose parents have never received a bachelor's degree. Students must be accepted for full-time study at CSU in a program leading to a bachelor's degree. Must demonstrate financial need.

Contact CSU for an application. Renewable for 6 additional semesters, providing requirements are met.

2567—COLUMBUS SCHOOL FOR GIRLS (Financial Aid)

56 S. Columbia Avenue
Columbus OH 43209
614/252-0781
FAX: 614/252-0571
E-mail: atimm@columbusschool forgirls.org (grades 6-12) or dlindberg@columbusschoolforgirls.org (Infants-Grade 5)
Internet: www.columbusschool forgirls.org
AMOUNT: $1,000-$13,200 (Avg. Grant $3,000-$6,000)
DEADLINE(S): APR 1
FIELD(S): All fields of study

Open to female secondary school students who are current or entering students to this private day school. Must demonstrate financial need, and must submit parent financial statement and tax form 1040.

120 awards annually. Renewable. Contact Ann Boston Timm, Director of Admissions and Financial Aid, Grades 6 - 12 or Donna Lindberg, Director of Admissions and Financial Aid, Infants-Grade 5.

2568—CDR. WILLIAM S. STUHR SCHOLARSHIP FUND FOR MILITARY SONS AND DAUGHTERS(Scholarships)

1200 Fifth Avenue, Apt. 9-D
New York NY 10029
E-mail: stuhrstudents@earthlink.net
Written Inquiry
AMOUNT: $1,125/year for 4 years
DEADLINE(S): FEB 28
FIELD(S): All fields of study

Open to high school seniors who are dependents of active duty or retired career members of one of five branches of the U.S. armed services. For study at an accredited 4-year college only. Applicants should be in the top 10 percent of their class and demonstrate leadership ability and financial need.

Send a self-addressed, stamped, business-sized envelope to above address for an application.

2569—COMMITTEE ON INSTITUTIONAL COOPERATION (SROP Summer Research Opportunities Program)

302 E. John Street, Suite 1705
Champaign IL 61820-5698
800/457-4420 or 217/333-8475
FAX: 217/244-7127
E-mail: aeprice@uiuc.edu
Internet: www.cic.uiuc.edu
AMOUNT: $4,000 max. stipend (varies per campus) + $1,100 towards room, board, and travel
DEADLINE(S): FEB 1
FIELD(S): All fields of study

To interest talented undergrad minorities in academic careers and enhance preparation for grad study through research with faculty mentors. African Americans, Mexican Americans, Puerto Ricans, and other Latinos who are sophomores or juniors are eligible. Must devote full-time to program during 8- to 10-week summer session. Need transcripts and recommendations.

See Web site or contact Anne Price, CIC Secretary, for application. Sessions at CIC campus (U Chicago, U IL, IN U, U IA, U MI, MI State, U MN, Northwestern, OH State, PA State, Purdue, or U WI).

2570—COMMONWEAL FOUNDATION (Pathways to Success Scholarship Program)

10770 Columbia Pike, Suite 100
Silver Spring MD 20901
301/592-1313
FAX: 301/592-1307
E-mail: sharonrubin@commonweal-foundation.org
Internet: http://www.commonweal-foundation.org
AMOUNT: $4,000/year (max.)
DEADLINE(S): None
FIELD(S): All fields of study

Open to junior high and high school students who live in the Baltimore-

Washington area and wish to attend accredited boarding schools with diverse programs, primarily in surrounding states. Must be new to the boarding school experience, who a need and strong desire to change school situation, have potential to be successful, demonstrate financial need, and be willing to participate in work and community service opportunities.

Contact Sharon Rubin for details.

2571—COMMONWEALTH OF VIRGINIA DEPARTMENT OF VETERANS' AFFAIRS (War Orphans Education Program)

270 Franklin Road SW, Room 503
Poff Federal Bldg.
Roanoke VA 24011-2215
540/857-7104
FAX: 540/857-6437
Internet: http://VDVA.VIPNEG.org

AMOUNT: Tuition and required fees
DEADLINE(S): None
FIELD(S): All fields of study

Open to surviving/dependent children (aged 16-25) of U.S. military personnel who were/are Virginia residents and as a result of war/armed conflict are deceased, disabled, prisoners of war, or missing in action. Must attend a state-supported secondary/postsecondary educational institution to pursue any vocational, technical, undergraduate, or graduate program.

Contact Dept. of Veterans' Affairs for an application.

2572—COMMUNITY FOUNDATION OF GREATER LORAIN COUNTY (Various Scholarship Programs)

1865 N. Ridge Road E, Suite A
Lorain OH 44055
440/277-0142 or 888-695-7645
FAX: 440/277-6955
E-mail: foundation@CFGLC.org
Internet: http://www.CFGLC.org

AMOUNT: Varies
DEADLINE(S): Apr 20
FIELD(S): All fields of study

For residents of Lorain County, Ohio. Various programs, ranging from opportunities for high school seniors through doctoral programs. Dollar amounts vary as do deadlines.

Contact the organization above for details.

2573—COMMUNITY FOUNDATION OF SIDNEY AND SHELBY COUNTY (Scholarship Program)

Sidney OH 45365-4186
937/497-7800
FAX: 937/497-7799
E-mail: info@commfoun.com
Internet: www.commfoun.com

AMOUNT: $500-$2,500
DEADLINE(S): APR 10 (most); MAY 31
FIELD(S): All fields of study

Various scholarship programs are open to residents of Sidney County, Ohio, to pursue any level of study. Some require attendance/graduation from certain high schools, parent employed at certain company, or student studying certain field (specifically, nursing).

See Web site or contact Marian Spicer for details.

2574—COMMUNITY FOUNDATION OF WESTERN MASSACHUSETTS (Albert Steiger Memorial Scholarships)

1500 Main Street
P.O. Box 15769, Suite 622
Springfield MA 01115
413/732-2858
FAX: 413/733/8565
E-mail: wmass@community foundation.org

AMOUNT: $2,500
DEADLINE(S): APR 16
FIELD(S): All fields of study

Open to graduating seniors of Central High School in Springfield, Massachusetts. Based on financial need, academic merit, and extracurricular activities. Must submit transcripts and fill out government FAFSA form.

2-4 awards annually. Renewable with reapplication. Contact Community Foundation for an application and your financial aid office for FAFSA. Notification is in June.

2575—COMMUNITY FOUNDATION OF WESTERN MASSACHUSETTS (Arrighi Memorial Scholarship)

1500 Main Street
P.O. Box 15769
Springfield MA 01115
413/732-2858
FAX: 413/733/8565
E-mail: wmass@community foundation.org

AMOUNT: $2,500
DEADLINE(S): APR 16
FIELD(S): All fields of study

Open to residents of Greenfield, Massachusetts, for full-time undergraduate, graduate, trade, or professional school. Based on financial need, academic merit, and extracurricular activities. Must submit transcripts and fill out government FAFSA form.

1-2 awards annually. Renewable with reapplication. Contact Community Foundation for an application and your financial aid office for FAFSA. Notification is in June.

2576—COMMUNITY FOUNDATION OF WESTERN MASSACHUSETTS (African-American Achievement Scholarships)

1500 Main Street
P.O. Box 15769
Springfield MA 01115
413/732-2858
FAX: 413/733/8565
E-mail: wmass@community foundation.org

AMOUNT: $2,500-$3,000
DEADLINE(S): APR 16
FIELD(S): All fields of study

Open to African-American residents of Hampden, Hampshire, and Franklin Counties, Massachusetts, who attend or plan to attend a four-year college full-time. These are loans which can be repaid by demonstrating community service. Based on financial need, academic merit, and extracurricular activities. Must submit transcripts and fill out government FAFSA form.

5 awards annually. Renewable with reapplication. Contact Community Foundation for an application and your financial aid office for FAFSA. Notification is in June.

2577—COMMUNITY FOUNDATION OF WESTERN MASSACHUSETTS (Anthony and Madeline Sampson Kapinos Scholarships)

1500 Main Street
P.O. Box 15769
Springfield MA 01115
413/732-2858
FAX: 413/733/8565
E-mail: wmass@community foundation.org

AMOUNT: $1,300
DEADLINE(S): APR 16
FIELD(S): All fields of study

Open to graduates of Chicopee High School in Massachusetts to assist with continuing their education. Based on financial need. Must submit transcripts and fill out government FAFSA form.

2 awards annually. Renewable with reapplication. Contact Community Foundation for an application and your financial aid office for FAFSA. Notification is in June.

2578—COMMUNITY FOUNDATION OF WESTERN MASSACHUSETTS (Charles F. Warner Loans)

1500 Main Street
Box 15769
Springfield MA 01115
413/732-2858
FAX: 413/733/8565
E-mail: wmass@community foundation.org

AMOUNT: $250
DEADLINE(S): APR 16
FIELD(S): All fields of study

Interest-free loans are open to residents of Springfield, Massachusetts, to pursue full-time undergraduate or graduate study. Based on financial need, academic merit, and extracurricular activities. Must submit transcripts and fill out government FAFSA form.

4-5 awards annually. Renewable with reapplication. Contact Community Foundation for an application and your financial aid office for FAFSA. Notification is in June.

2579—COMMUNITY FOUNDATION OF WESTERN MASSACHUSETTS (Carlos B. Ellis Scholarships)

1500 Main Street
Box 15769
Springfield MA 01115
413/732-2858
FAX: 413/733/8565
E-mail: wmass@community foundation.org

AMOUNT: $300-$1,000
DEADLINE(S): APR 16
FIELD(S): All fields of study

Open to members and graduates of Commerce High School in Massachusetts to continue their education. Based on financial need, academic merit, and extracurricular activities. Must submit transcripts and fill out government FAFSA form.

14 awards annually. Renewable with reapplication. Contact Community Foundation for an application and your financial aid office for FAFSA. Notification is in June.

2580—COMMUNITY FOUNDATION OF WESTERN MASSACHUSETTS (Clarence H. Matteson Scholarships)

1500 Main Street
Box 15769
Springfield MA 01115
413/732-2858
FAX: 413/733/8565
E-mail: wmass@community oundation.org

AMOUNT: $1,850
DEADLINE(S): APR 16
FIELD(S): All fields of study

Open to residents of Greenfield, Massachusetts, with a high scholastic ability to pursue full-time education beyond high school (college, graduate, or postgraduate studies). Based on financial need, academic merit, and extracurricular activities. Must submit transcripts and fill out government FAFSA form.

6 awards annually. Renewable with reapplication. Contact Community Foundation for an application and your financial aid office for FAFSA. Notification is in June.

2581—COMMUNITY FOUNDATION OF WESTERN MASSACHUSETTS (C. Kenneth Sanderson Scholarship)

1500 Main Street
Box 15769
Springfield MA 01115
413/732-2858
FAX: 413/733/8565
E-mail: wmass@community foundation.org

AMOUNT: $5,000
DEADLINE(S): APR 16
FIELD(S): All fields of study

Open to top graduates of Monson High School in Massachusetts to assist with college tuition. Based on financial need, academic merit, and extracurricular activities. Must submit transcripts and fill out government FAFSA form.

1 award annually. Renewable with reapplication. Contact Community Foundation for an application and your financial aid office for FAFSA. Notification is in June.

2582—COMMUNITY FOUNDATION OF WESTERN MASSACHUSETTS (Deerfield Plastics/Barker Family Fund)

1500 Main Street
Box 15769
Springfield MA 01115
413/732-2858
FAX: 413/733/8565
E-mail: wmass@community foundation.org

AMOUNT: $1,000-$2,500
DEADLINE(S): APR 16
FIELD(S): All fields of study

Open to children of Deerfield Plastics employees who wish to pursue full-time undergraduate or graduate study. Based on financial need, academic merit, and extracurricular activities. Must submit transcripts and fill out government FAFSA form.

12 awards annually. Renewable with reapplication. Contact Community Foundation for an application and your financial aid office for FAFSA. Notification is in June.

2583—COMMUNITY FOUNDATION OF WESTERN MASSACHUSETTS (Dr. Jeffrey A. Ferst Valedictorian Memorial Scholarship)

1500 Main Street
Box 15769
Springfield MA 01115
413/732-2858
FAX: 413/733/8565
E-mail: wmass@community foundation.org

AMOUNT: $2,000-$3,500
DEADLINE(S): APR 16
FIELD(S): All fields of study

Awarded annually to the valedictorian of Westfield High School in Massachusetts.

1 award annually. Contact Community Foundation for details.

2584—COMMUNITY FOUNDATION OF WESTERN MASSACHUSETTS (Donald A. and Dorothy F. Axtell Grant Scholarships)

1500 Main Street
Box 15769
Springfield MA 01115
413/732-2858
FAX: 413/733/8565
E-mail: wmass@community foundation.org

AMOUNT: $500-$1,000
DEADLINE(S): APR 16
FIELD(S): All fields of study

Open to Protestant residents of Hampshire County, Massachusetts, for full-time undergraduate or graduate study. Based on financial need, academic merit, and extracurricular activities. Must submit transcripts and fill out government FAFSA form.

2-4 awards annually. Renewable with reapplication. Contact Community Foundation for an application and your financial aid office for FAFSA. Notification is in June.

2585—COMMUNITY FOUNDATION OF WESTERN MASSACHUSETTS (First National Bank of Amherst Centennial Educational Scholarships)

1500 Main Street
P.O. Box 15769
Springfield MA 01115
413/732-2858
FAX: 413/733/8565
E-mail: wmass@community foundation.org

AMOUNT: $450
DEADLINE(S): APR 16
FIELD(S): All fields of study

Open to students from Northampton, Hadley, Amherst, UMass, Amherst College, and Hampshire College in Massachusetts to pursue full-time undergraduate or graduate study. Based on financial need, academic merit, and extracurricular activities. Must submit transcripts and fill out government FAFSA form.

6 awards annually. Renewable with reapplication. Contact Community Foundation for an application and your financial aid office for FAFSA. Notification is in June.

2586—COMMUNITY FOUNDATION OF WESTERN MASSACHUSETTS (Frank W. Jendrysik, Jr. Memorial Scholarship)

1500 Main Street
P.O. Box 15769
Springfield MA 01115
413/732-2858
FAX: 413/733/8565
E-mail: wmass@community foundation.org

AMOUNT: $1,000
DEADLINE(S): APR 16
FIELD(S): All fields of study

Open to residents of Chicopee, Holyoke, and Springfield, Massachusetts, to pursue full-time undergraduate or graduate study. Based on financial need, academic merit, and extracurricular activities. Must submit transcripts and fill out government FAFSA form.

1 award annually. Renewable with reapplication. Contact Community Foundation for an application and your financial aid office for FAFSA. Notification is in June.

2587—COMMUNITY FOUNDATION OF WESTERN MASSACHUSETTS (Frederick W. Porter Scholarships)

1500 Main Street
Box 15769
Springfield MA 01115
413/732-2858
FAX: 413/733/8565
E-mail: wmass@community foundation.org

AMOUNT: $1,000
DEADLINE(S): APR 16
FIELD(S): All fields of study

Open to graduates of Greenfield High School in Massachusetts to pursue full-time undergraduate or graduate study. Based on financial need, academic merit, and extracurricular activities. Must submit transcripts and fill out government FAFSA form.

2 awards annually. Renewable with reapplication. Contact Community Foundation for an application and your financial aid office for FAFSA. Notification is in June.

2588—COMMUNITY FOUNDATION OF WESTERN MASSACHUSETTS (Gertrude and William C. Hill Scholarships)

1500 Main Street
Box 15769
Springfield MA 01115
413/732-2858
FAX: 413/733/8565
E-mail: wmass@community foundation.org

AMOUNT: $3,000
DEADLINE(S): APR 16
FIELD(S): All fields of study

Open to graduates of Central High School in Springfield, Massachusetts, to obtain a college education. Preference given to those majoring in liberal arts. Based on financial need, academic merit, and extracurricular activities. Must submit transcripts and fill out government FAFSA form.

5 awards annually. Renewable with reapplication. Contact Community Foundation for an application and your financial aid office for FAFSA. Notification is in June.

2589—COMMUNITY FOUNDATION OF WESTERN MASSACHUSETTS (Horace Hill Scholarships)

1500 Main Street
Box 15769
Springfield MA 01115
413/732-2858
FAX: 413/733/8565
E-mail: wmass@community oundation.org

AMOUNT: $750
DEADLINE(S): APR 16
FIELD(S): All fields of study

Open to children and grandchildren of the members of the Springfield Newspapers' 25 Year Club to pursue full-time undergraduate or graduate study. Based on financial need, academic merit, and extracurricular activities. Must submit transcripts and fill out government FAFSA form.

4 awards annually. Renewable with reapplication. Contact Community Foundation for an application and your financial aid office for FAFSA. Notification is in June.

2590—COMMUNITY FOUNDATION OF WESTERN MASSACHUSETTS (James W. Colgan Loan Fund)

1500 Main Street
Box 15769
Springfield MA 01115
413/732-2858
FAX: 413/733/8565
E-mail: wmass@community foundation.org

AMOUNT: $2,000-$4,000
DEADLINE(S): APR 16
FIELD(S): All fields of study

Interest-free loans are open to residents of Massachusetts for the past five years to pursue full-time undergraduate study. Based on financial need, academic merit, and extracurricular activities. Must submit transcripts, copy of parents' and applicant's Federal Income Tax Return and W-2 form, and three letters of reference for first-time applicants. Must fill out government FAFSA form.

170 loans annually. Renewable with reapplication. Send self-addressed, stamped envelope to Community Foundation for an application and contact your financial aid office for FAFSA. Notification is in June.

2591—COMMUNITY FOUNDATION OF WESTERN MASSACHUSETTS (Jeffrey I. Glaser, M.D. Memorial Scholarship)

1500 Main Street
Box 15769
Springfield MA 01115
413/732-2858
FAX: 413/733/8565
E-mail: wmass@community foundation.org

AMOUNT: $500
DEADLINE(S): APR 16
FIELD(S): All fields of study

Open to a graduating Longmeadow High School (Longmeadow, MA) senior who has distinguished himself or herself on the swim team and academically. Based on financial need, academic merit, and extracurricular activities. Must be nominated by your school and fill out government FAFSA form.

1-2 awards annually. Contact Community Foundation for details and your financial aid office for FAFSA. Notification is in June.

2592—COMMUNITY FOUNDATION OF WESTERN MASSACHUSETTS (Jane A. Korzeniowski Memorial Scholarship)

1500 Main Street
Box 15769
Springfield MA 01115
413/732-2858
FAX: 413/733/8565
E-mail: wmass@community foundation.org
AMOUNT: $600
DEADLINE(S): APR 16
FIELD(S): All fields of study

Open to Chicopee, Massachusetts, residents who attend or plan to attend college for full-time graduate or undergraduate study. Based on financial need, academic merit, and extracurricular activities. Must submit transcripts and fill out government FAFSA form.

1 award annually. Renewable with reapplication. Contact Community Foundation for an application and your financial aid office for FAFSA. Notification is in June.

2593—COMMUNITY FOUNDATION OF WESTERN MASSACHUSETTS (James Z. Naurison Scholarships)

1500 Main Street
Box 15769
Springfield MA 01115
413/732-2858
FAX: 413/733/8565
E-mail: wmass@community foundation.org
AMOUNT: $1,000
DEADLINE(S): APR 16
FIELD(S): All fields of study

Open to residents of Hampden, Hampshire, Franklin, and Berkshire Counties, Massachusetts, and Enfield and Suffield, Connecticut. For graduates and undergraduates to pursue full-time study. Based on financial need, academic merit, and extracurricular activities. Must submit transcripts and fill out government FAFSA form.

655 awards annually. Renewable up to 4 years with reapplication. Contact Community Foundation for an application and your financial aid office for FAFSA. Notification is in June.

2594—COMMUNITY FOUNDATION OF WESTERN MASSACHUSETTS (Jessie M. Law Scholarships)

1500 Main Street
Box 15769
Springfield MA 01115
413/732-2858
FAX: 413/733/8565
E-mail: wmass@community foundation.org
AMOUNT: $500-$2,000
DEADLINE(S): APR 16
FIELD(S): All fields of study

Open to residents of Hamden County, Massachusetts, to pursue full-time undergraduate or graduate study. Based on financial need, academic merit, and extracurricular activities. Must submit transcripts and fill out government FAFSA form.

9 awards annually. Renewable with reapplication. Contact Community Foundation for an application and your financial aid office for FAFSA. Notification is in June.

2595—COMMUNITY FOUNDATION OF WESTERN MASSACHUSETTS (John P. and James F. Mahoney Memorial Scholarships)

1500 Main Street
Box 15769
Springfield MA 01115
413/732-2858
FAX: 413/733/8565
E-mail: wmass@community foundation.org
AMOUNT: $2,000
DEADLINE(S): APR 16
FIELD(S): All fields of study

Open to residents of Hampshire County, Massachusetts, who will be attending college or vocational school full-time at the graduate or undergraduate level. Based on financial need, academic merit, and extracurricular activities. Must submit transcripts, two letters of reference from teachers, and fill out government FAFSA form. One-page essay on personal ambition, future plans, and why you would be an appropriate recipient required.

15 awards annually. Renewable with reapplication. Contact Community Foundation for an application and your financial aid office for FAFSA. Notification is in June.

2596—COMMUNITY FOUNDATION OF WESTERN MASSACHUSETTS (Kimber Richter Family Scholarship)

1500 Main Street
Box 15769
Springfield MA 01115
413/732-2858
FAX: 413/733/8565
E-mail: wmass@community foundation.org
AMOUNT: $700
DEADLINE(S): APR 16
FIELD(S): All fields of study

Open to students of the Baha'i faith who attend or plan to attend college full-time at the undergraduate or graduate level. Must be resident of Western Massachusetts. Based on financial need, academic merit, and extracurricular activities. Must submit transcripts and fill out government FAFSA form.

1 award annually. Renewable with reapplication. Contact Community Foundation for an application and your financial aid office for FAFSA. Notification is in June.

2597—COMMUNITY FOUNDATION OF WESTERN MASSACHUSETTS (Kenneth B. and Adeline J. Graves Scholarships)

1500 Main Street
Box 15769
Springfield MA 01115
413/732-2858
FAX: 413/733/8565
E-mail: wmass@community foundation.org
AMOUNT: $2,500
DEADLINE(S): APR 16
FIELD(S): All fields of study

Open to residents of Granby, Massachusetts, to pursue full-time undergraduate or graduate study. Based on financial need, academic merit, and extracurricular activities. Must submit transcripts and fill out government FAFSA form.

13 awards annually. Renewable with reapplication. Contact Community Foundation for an application and your financial aid office for FAFSA. Notification is in June.

2598—COMMUNITY FOUNDATION OF WESTERN MASSACHUSETTS (Louis W. and Mary S. Doherty Scholarships)

1500 Main Street
Box 15769
Springfield MA 01115
413/732-2858
FAX: 413/733/8565
E-mail: wmass@community foundation.org

AMOUNT: $4,000
DEADLINE(S): APR 16
FIELD(S): All fields of study

Open to students from Hampden, Hampshire, and Franklin Counties in Massachusetts who attend or plan to attend college full-time. Based on financial need, academic merit, and extracurricular activities. Must submit transcripts and fill out government FAFSA form.

12 awards annually. Renewable with reapplication. Contact Community Foundation for an appliccation and your financial aid office for FAFSA. Notification is in June.

2599—COMMUNITY FOUNDATION OF WESTERN MASSACHUSETTS (Latino Scholarships)

1500 Main Street
Box 15769
Springfield MA 01115
413/732-2858
FAX: 413/733/8565
E-mail: wmass@community foundation.org

AMOUNT: $500
DEADLINE(S): APR 16
FIELD(S): All fields of study

Open to Latino residents of Holyoke, Massachusetts, who are graduating high school seniors who demonstrate academic promise and are community service oriented. Based on financial need, academic merit, and extracurricular activities. Must submit transcripts and fill out government FAFSA form.

10 awards annually. Renewable with reapplication. Contact Community Foundation for an application and your financial aid office for FAFSA. Notification is in June.

2600—COMMUNITY FOUNDATION OF WESTERN MASSACHUSETTS (Lucius H. Tarbell and Dorothy J. Tarbell Scholarships)

1500 Main Street
Box 15769
Springfield MA 01115
413/732-2858
FAX: 413/733/8565
E-mail: wmass@community foundation.org

AMOUNT: $2,700
DEADLINE(S): APR 16
FIELD(S): All fields of study

Open to students of Western New England College in Massachusetts to pursue full-time undergraduate or graduate study. Based on financial need, academic merit, and extracurricular activities. Must submit transcripts and fill out government FAFSA form.

2 awards annually. Renewable with reapplication. Contact Community Foundation for an application and your financial aid office for FAFSA. Notification is in June.

2601—COMMUNITY FOUNDATION OF WESTERN MASSACHUSETTS (Lena A. Tucker Scholarships)

1500 Main Street
Box 15769
Springfield MA 01115
413/732-2858
FAX: 413/733/8565
E-mail: wmass@community foundation.org

AMOUNT: $250-$1,000
DEADLINE(S): APR 16
FIELD(S): All fields of study

Open to Springfield students from the High School of Commerce and Putnam Vocational-Technical High School in Massachusetts to pursue college education. Based on financial need, academic merit, and extracurricular activities. Must submit transcripts and fill out government FAFSA form.

20 awards annually. Renewable with reapplication. Contact Community Foundation for an application and your financial aid office for FAFSA. Notification is in June.

2602—COMMUNITY FOUNDATION OF WESTERN MASSACHUSETTS (Maury Ferriter Memorial Scholarship)

1500 Main Street
Box 15769
Springfield MA 01115
413/732-2858
FAX: 413/733/8565
E-mail: wmass@community foundation.org

AMOUNT: $500
DEADLINE(S): APR 16
FIELD(S): All fields of study

Open to full-time undergraduate or graduate students from Holyoke Catholic High School, Amherst College, or Georgetown Law School. Based on financial need, academic merit, and extracurricular activities. Must submit transcripts and fill out government FAFSA form.

1 award annually. Renewable with reapplication. Contact Community Foundation for an application and your financial aid office for FAFSA. Notification is in June.

2603—COMMUNITY FOUNDATION OF WESTERN MASSACHUSETTS (Margaret J. Hyland Scholarships)

1500 Main Street
Box 15769
Springfield MA 01115
413/732-2858
FAX: 413/733/8565
E-mail: wmass@community foundation.org

AMOUNT: $1,800
DEADLINE(S): APR 16
FIELD(S): All fields of study

Open to undergraduates and graduates pursuing full-time study at the University of Massachusetts who have been Holyoke residents for ten years or longer. Preference given to financially needy students of the Roman Catholic faith. Based on financial need, academic merit, and extracurricular activities. Must submit transcripts and fill out government FAFSA form.

50 awards annually. Renewable with reapplication. Contact Community Foundation for an application and your financial aid office for FAFSA. Notification is in June.

2604—COMMUNITY FOUNDATION OF WESTERN MASSACHUSETTS (Mt. Sugarloaf Lodge Memorial Scholarships)

1500 Main Street
Box 15769
Springfield MA 01115
413/732-2858
FAX: 413/733/8565
E-mail: wmass@community foundation.org

AMOUNT: $375
DEADLINE(S): APR 16
FIELD(S): All fields of study

Open to students from Frontier Regional High School in Massachusetts to pursue full-time undergraduate or graduate study. Based on financial need, academic merit, and extracurricular activities. Must submit transcripts and fill out government FAFSA form.

4 awards annually. Renewable with reapplication. Contact Community Foundation for an application and your financial aid office for FAFSA. Notification is in June.

2605—COMMUNITY FOUNDATION OF WESTERN MASSACHUSETTS (Permelia A. Butterfield Scholarship)

1500 Main Street
Box 15769
Springfield MA 01115
413/732-2858
FAX: 413/733/8565
E-mail: wmass@community foundation.org

AMOUNT: $3,700
DEADLINE(S): APR 16
FIELD(S): All fields of study

Open to residents of Athol, Erving, New Salem, Wendell, Orange, Shutesbury, and Franklin Counties, Massachusetts to pursue full-time undergraduate or graduate study. Preference goes to the support and education of orphan children (students with one or no living parent or those deprived of parental care). Based on financial need, academic merit, and extracurricular activities. Must submit transcripts and fill out government FAFSA form.

2 awards annually. Renewable with reapplication. Contact Community Foundation for an application and your financial aid office for FAFSA. Notification is in June.

2606—COMMUNITY FOUNDATION OF WESTERN MASSACHUSETTS (Ruth L. Brocklebank Memorial Scholarships)

1500 Main Street
Box 15769
Springfield MA 01115
413/732-2858
FAX: 413/733/8565
E-mail: wmass@community foundation.org

AMOUNT: $2,200
DEADLINE(S): APR 16
FIELD(S): All fields of study

Open to African-American students from the Springfield Public School System high schools to attend college. Based on financial need, academic merit, and extracurricular activities. Must submit transcripts and fill out government FAFSA form.

7 awards annually. Renewable with reapplication. Contact Community Foundation for an application and your financial aid office for FAFSA. Notification is in June.

2607—COMMUNITY FOUNDATION OF WESTERN MASSACHUSETTS (Sarah and Abraham Milstein Scholarships)

1500 Main Street
Box 15769
Springfield MA 01115
413/732-2858
FAX: 413/733/8565
E-mail: wmass@community foundation.org

AMOUNT: $150
DEADLINE(S): APR 16
FIELD(S): All fields of study

Awarded annually to the valedictorian and salutatorian of Westfield High School in Massachusetts.

2 awards annually. Contact Community Foundation for details.

2608—COMMUNITY FOUNDATION OF WESTERN MASSACHUSETTS (Stanley Ciejek, Sr. Scholarships)

1500 Main Street
Box 15769
Springfield MA 01115
413/732-2858
FAX: 413/733/8565
E-mail: wmass@community foundation.org

AMOUNT: $1,000
DEADLINE(S): APR 16
FIELD(S): All fields of study

Open to residents of Hampden, Hampshire, and Franklin Counties, Massachusetts to pursue full-time undergraduate or graduate study at a Massachusetts institute of higher education. Based on financial need, academic merit, and extracurricular activities. Must submit transcripts and fill out government FAFSA form.

11 awards annually. Renewable with reapplication. Contact Community Foundation for an application and your financial aid office for FAFSA. Notification is in June.

2609—COMMUNITY FOUNDATION OF WESTERN MASSACHUSETTS (Stuart D. Mackey Scholarship)

1500 Main Street
Box 15769
Springfield MA 01115
413/732-2858
FAX: 413/733/8565
E-mail: wmass@communityf oundation.org

AMOUNT: $750
DEADLINE(S): APR 16
FIELD(S): All fields of study

Open to graduates of East Longmeadow High School in Massachusetts who have strong academic records to pursue full-time undergraduate or graduate study. Based on financial need, academic merit, and extracurricular activities. Must submit transcripts and fill out government FAFSA form.

1-2 awards annually. Renewable with reapplication. Contact Community Foundation for an application and your financial aid office for FAFSA. Notification is in June.

2610—COMMUNITY FOUNDATION OF WESTERN MASSACHUSETTS (Springfield Teachers' Club Scholarships)

1500 Main Street
Box 15769
Springfield MA 01115
413/732-2858
FAX: 413/733/8565
E-mail: wmass@community foundation.org

AMOUNT: Varies
DEADLINE(S): APR 16
FIELD(S): All fields of study

Open to graduates of Springfield high schools to obtain further education. Based on financial need, academic merit, and extracurricular activities. Must submit transcripts and fill out government FAFSA form.

Renewable with reapplication. Contact Community Foundation for an application and your financial aid office for FAFSA. Notification is in June.

2611—COMMUNITY FOUNDATION OF WESTERN MASSACHUSETTS (Wilcox-Ware Scholarships)

1500 Main Street
Box 15769
Springfield MA 01115
413/732-2858
FAX: 413/733/8565
E-mail: wmass@community foundation.org

AMOUNT: $1,500
DEADLINE(S): APR 16
FIELD(S): All fields of study

Open to graduates of Mohawk Regional High School in Massachusetts who reside in Buckland, Shelburne, Colrain, or contiguous towns to pursue undergraduate or graduate study. Based on financial need, academic merit, and extracurricular activities. Must submit transcripts and fill out government FAFSA form.

18 awards annually. Renewable with reapplication. Contact Community Foundation for an application and your financial aid office for FAFSA. Notification is in June.

2612—COMMUNITY SCHOOL (Financial Aid Program)

Sun Valley ID 83353
208/622-3955
FAX: 208/622-3962
E-mail: abaker@community school.org
Internet: www.communityschool.org

AMOUNT: Varies
DEADLINE(S): APR 15
FIELD(S): All fields of study

Open to PK-12th grade students at this private day school. Must be local residents and demonstrate financial need.

67 awards annually. Contact Andrea Baker for an application.

2613—CONCORD ACADEMY (Grants and Loans)

166 Main Street
Concord MA 01742
978/369-6080
FAX: 978/369-3452
E-mail: admissions@concord academy.org
Internet: www.concordacademy.org

AMOUNT: $1,000 up to full tuition less $200
DEADLINE(S): JAN 31
FIELD(S): All fields of study

Open to 9th-12th grade students at this private day/boarding school. Must demonstrate financial need and be a U.S. citizen.

65 awards annually. Renewable. Contact the Financial Aid Office for an application.

2614—CONCORDIA ACADEMY (Tuition Assistance)

2400 N. Dale Street
Roseville MN 55113
651/484-8429
FAX: 651/484-0594
E-mail: lhenry@mail.concordia-academy.pvt.k12.mn.us
Internet: http://www.concordia-academy.pvt.k12.mn.us

AMOUNT: Varies
DEADLINE(S): MAR 1, MAY 1, JUL 1
FIELD(S): All fields of study

Open to 9th-12th grade students at this private Lutheran college prep day school. Must demonstrate financial need and be U.S. citizen/permanent resident.

40 awards annually. Renewable. Contact L. Henry for an application.

2615—CONCORDIA UNIVERSITY (Loyola Alumni Association Inc. Educational Grant)

Financial Aid and Awards Office
1455 de Maisonneuve Boulevard W.
LB-085
Montreal Quebec H3G 1M8
CANADA
514/848-3507
FAX: 514/848-3508
E-mail: gardd@vax2.concordia.ca
Internet: http://www.financialaid.concordia.ca or http://www.concordia.ca

AMOUNT: $1,500
DEADLINE(S): APR 1
FIELD(S): All fields of study

Full-time Concordia students at any level may apply for this entrance or in-course award. Any Concordia applicant is eligible, however, preference will be given to children and grandchildren of active Loyola Alumni Association members. Grant is awarded on the basis of scholastic achievement, the applicant's statement, and letters of reference.

5 awards annually. Contact the Graduate Awards Office in the School of Graduate Studies at Concordia University for an application.

2616—CONCORDIA UNIVERSITY (Senior Scholarships)

Financial Aid and Awards Office
1455 de Maisonneuve Boulevard W.
LB 085
Montreal Quebec H3G 1M8
CANADA
514/848-3507
FAX: 514/848-3508
E-mail: admreg@alcor.concordia.ca
Internet: http://www.financialaid.concordia.ca or http://www.concordia.ca

AMOUNT: $500
DEADLINE(S): AUG 1
FIELD(S): All fields of study

Candidates must be Canadian citizens/permanent residents, intending to study full-time and aged 60 years or more in the year of application. Awards are made on the basis of the academic record and an interview.

1 award annually. Renewable up to four years. Contact the Financial Aid and Awards Office at Concordia University for an application.

2617—CONCORDIA UNIVERSITY (Entrance Scholarships)

Financial Aid Office
1455 de Maisonneuve Boulevard W.
LB 085
Montreal Quebec H3G 1M8
CANADA
514/848-3507
FAX: 514/848-3508
E-mail: awardsgs@vax2.concordia.ca

AMOUNT: $1,000-$2,000
DEADLINE(S): MAR 1 (Fall Term) and NOV 1 (Winter Term)
FIELD(S): All fields of study

A number of scholarships are available to students entering their first year of full-time study. These non-renewable scholarships are awarded by the Undergraduate Scholarships and Awards Committee on the basis of academic achievement during the first three semesters of CEGEP or equivalent. Some Fine Arts Departments may select Entrance Scholarships on the basis of portfolios, auditions or interviews. Please be advised that all Entrance Scholars must be enrolled in a full-course load (30 credits) for the academic year. Please contact our office before any changes in course load are implemented in order to ensure the receipt of your scholarship. All students who submit an application for admission to Concordia University by March 1 for the Fall Term and November 1 for the Winter Term will be considered automatically for an Entrance Scholarship. Only those students offered an Entrance Scholarship will be notified.

2618—CONCORDIA UNIVERSITY (The Rona and Irving Levitt Family Foundation Entrance Scholarships)

Financial Aid Office
1455 de Maisonneuve Boulevard W.
LB 085
Montreal Quebec H3G 1M8
CANADA
514/848-3507
FAX: 514/848-3508
E-mail: awardsgs@vax2.concordia.ca

AMOUNT: $1,000
DEADLINE(S): Apr 1
FIELD(S): All fields of study

Intended to assist students attending Concordia University, a number of scholarships are available to students entering their first year of full-time study. These scholarships are non-renewable. They are awarded by the Undergraduate Scholarships and Awards Committee on the basis of academic achievement during the first three semesters of CEGEP or equivalent, and a personal statement provided by the applicant. Application forms are available from the Financial Aid and Awards Office.

2619—CONCORDIA UNIVERSITY (Mature Entrance Scholarships)

Financial Aid Office
1455 de Maisonneuve Boulevard W.
LB 085
Montreal Quebec H3G 1M8
CANADA
514/848-3507
FAX: 514/848-3508
E-mail: awardsgs@vax2.concordia.ca
AMOUNT: $2,000
DEADLINE(S): Apr 1
FIELD(S): All fields of study

This program is intended for students admitted to the University as Mature students. Mature student candidates will be considered upon successful completion of their first 18 credits at Concordia University. Non-renewable.

2620—CONCORDIA UNIVERSITY (Loyola Foundation Inc. Entrance Scholarships)

Financial Aid Office
1455 de Maisonneuve Boulevard W.
LB 085
Montreal Quebec H3G 1M8
CANADA
514/848-3507
FAX: 514/848-3508
E-mail: awardsgs@vax2.concordia.ca
AMOUNT: $2,000
DEADLINE(S): Aug 1
FIELD(S): All fields of study

The Loyola Foundation offers two renewable entrance scholarships to students entering their first year of full-time study who are graduates of Loyola High School. They are required to present a letter of recommendation from Loyola High School, following the completion of cégep or equivalent. The awards will be made on the basis of academic ranking as assigned by the University in the course of admission file processing, and on the strength of the recommendation by Loyola High School. Renewability is subject to continuing full-time enrollment and maintenance of a GPA of 3.00 or better. Application and recommendation forms are available from the Financial Aid and Awards Office of Concordia University and the Admissions Office of Loyola High School.

2621—CONGRESS OF MINNESOTA RESORTS (Scholarships)

Secretary
5280 132nd Avenue NE
Spicer MN 56288
888/761-4245
E-mail: CMR@Minnesota-Resorts.com
AMOUNT: $500
DEADLINE(S): MAR 15
FIELD(S): All fields of study

Open to members of the Congress of Minnesota Resorts with three consecutive years membership, and their children/grandchildren. Must be pursuing undergraduate study. Financial need NOT a factor.

3 awards annually. Not renewable. Contact Vicky Krattenmaker for an application.

2622—CONGRESSIONAL HISPANIC CAUCUS INSTITUTE (Summer Internship Program)

504 C Street NE
Washington DC 20002
800/EXCEL-DC or 202/543-1771
E-mail: comments@chci.org
Internet: www.chci.org
AMOUNT: Stipend, round-trip transportation, and housing
DEADLINE(S): JAN 31
FIELD(S): All fields of study

Two-month stay in D.C. (June-Aug) to gain first-hand knowledge of how government works. College-bound high school seniors and currently enrolled undergraduates (except college seniors) are eligible. Must be Hispanic and have a minimum 3.0 GPA, excellent written and oral communication skills, active interest/participation in community affairs, a solid work ethic, and leadership potential. Must be U.S. citizen/permanent resident or have student work visa.

30 students reflecting the diversity of the Hispanic community are selected each summer. See Web site or contact CHCI for an application.

2623—CONNECTICUT DEPARTMENT OF HIGHER EDUCATION (Capitol Scholarship Program)

61 Woodland Street
Hartford CT 06015-2326
860/947-1855
FAX: 860/947-1311
E-mail: SFA@ctdhe.org
Internet: www.ctdhe.org
AMOUNT: $2,000 (max.)
DEADLINE(S): FEB 15
FIELD(S): All fields of study

Open to Connecticut high school seniors and graduates who ranked in top 20% of their high school class or scored above 1200 on SAT. For undergraduate study at a Connecticut college or at colleges in states which have reciprocity agreements with Connecticut. U.S. citizenship or legal residency required.

3,000 awards annually. Write for complete information.

2624—CONNECTICUT DEPARTMENT OF HIGHER EDUCATION (Student Financial Aid Programs)

61 Woodland Street
Hartford CT 06105-2326
860/947-1855
FAX: 860/947-1311
E-mail: SFA@ctdhe.org
Internet: www.ctdhe.org
AMOUNT: Varies (programs differ)
DEADLINE(S): Varies (programs differ)
FIELD(S): All fields of study

Various state and federal programs providing financial aid to Connecticut students. Programs include tuition waivers for veterans and senior citizens, work study programs, loans, scholarships, and grants.

Most programs emphasize financial need. Write for brochure listing programs and application information.

2625—CONVERSE COUNTY 4-H FOUNDATION (Scholarships)

Extension Office
107 N. 5th
Douglas WY 82633
307/358-2417
Written Request for application
AMOUNT: Varies
DEADLINE(S): JAN
FIELD(S): All fields of study

Available to former Converse County 4-H program members who have completed at least three years of active 4-H club work and are currently enrolled in an institution of higher education. Eligible students may apply as often as they wish. Priority consideration is given to first-time applicants. Scholarships are for use during the Spring semester.

Write to the Converse County Extension Office for an application.

2626—COOPER WOOD PRODUCTS FOUNDATION, INC. (Scholarships and Loans)

Executive Secretary
P.O. Box 489
Rocky Mount VA 24151
800/262-34453
Written request for application
AMOUNT: Varies
DEADLINE(S): APR 1
FIELD(S): All fields of study

Open to Virginia residents who intend to remain in Virginia after completion of education.

Write to Sue Chitwood, Executive Secretary, for an application.

2627—COUNCIL FOR INTERNATIONAL EDUCATIONAL EXCHANGE (Bowman Travel Grant)

Rosemary Clarke, Executive Assistant
633 Third Avenue, 20th Floor
New York NY 10017
212/822-2695
FAX: 212/822-2779
Internet: http://www.ciee.org/study
AMOUNT: $500-$1700
DEADLINE(S): APR 1; OCT 26
FIELD(S): All

Applicants must be high school or undergraduate students (U.S. citizens or permanent residents only) participating in a study, work, or volunteer program in one of the designated countries. Applications must include a personal statement, a typed statement explaining your financial need, transcripts, and references.

2628—COUNCIL OF CITIZENS WITH LOW VISION INTERNATIONAL (CCLVI Telesensory Scholarship)

1400 N. Drake Road, No. 218
Kalamazoo MI 49006
616/381-9566
AMOUNT: $1,000
DEADLINE(S): APR 15
FIELD(S): All fields of study

Open to an undergraduate or graduate students who are vision impaired but NOT legally blind and who have a GPA of 3.0 or better.

Four awards per year. Write for complete information.

2629—COUNCIL ON INTERNATIONAL EDUCATIONAL EXCHANGE (Bailey Minority Student Scholarships)

633 Third Avenue, 20th Fl.
New York NY 10017-6706
800-40-STUDY
FAX: 212/822-2779
E-mail: scholarships@ciee.org
Internet: www.ciee.org
AMOUNT: $500
DEADLINE(S): MAR 15; OCT 15
FIELD(S): All fields of study

International exchange program for study, work, volunteer, and homestay programs anywhere in the world except: Australia, Canada, Europe, Israel, Japan, Korea, New Zealand, Russia, Singapore, or the United States. Must be a minority who is a U.S. citizen/permanent resident at any level of study. Can apply for study-abroad program and scholarship at the same time.

Send self-addressed, stamped envelope for details.

2630—CRAFTSMAN/NATIONAL SCIENCE TEACHERS ASSOCIATION (Young Inventors Awards Program)

1840 Wilson Boulevard
Arlington VA 22201-3000
888/494-4994
E-mail: younginventors@nsta.org
Internet: http://www.nsta.org/programs/craftsman
AMOUNT: $10,000 U.S. Savings Bond for two national winner; $5,000 savings bond for 10 national finalists; $500 Savings Bonds for 12 Regional winners; $250 Savings Bonds for 12 Regional winners
DEADLINE(S): Mid March
FIELD(S): Invention of a tool

For students in grades 4-6 who, with guidance from a teacher and an adult, create, design, and build a tool that performs a function. Plan could be a modification of an existing tool.

Every entrant receives a gift. Teacher/advisors and schools of the 12 finalists will each receive products from Sears, Roebuck and Co. Top winners will attend an awards banquet hosted by Bob Vila, Craftsman's spokesperson.

2631—CRANBROOK SCHOOLS (Financial Aid)

39221 N. Woodward Avenue
P.O. Box 801
Bloomfield Hills MI 48303-0801
248/645-3463
FAX: 248/645-3025
E-mail: KMurdock@cranbrook.edu
Internet: www.cranbrookschools.org
AMOUNT: Varies (need-based)
DEADLINE(S): FEB
FIELD(S): All fields of study

Open to pre-K through 12th grade students at this private day/boarding school. Must demonstrate financial need and have strong academic and leadership skills.

500 awards annually. Renewable. Contact Kate Murdock for an application. Robert J. Hill Memorial Scholarship for full tuition is also available to residents of Midland, Michigan in grades 9-12.

2632—CROATION SCHOLARSHIP FUND (CSF)

31 Mesa Vista Court
San Ramon CA 94583
925/867-3768
FAX: 925/355-9040
E-mail: brankobarbir@home.com
Internet: htp://www.croatian scholarship.org
AMOUNT: $1,200/year (rural residents); $600/year (urban)
DEADLINE(S): Varies
FIELD(S): All fields of study

Open to high school seniors from Croatia and Bosnia-Herzegovina who plan to attend a college/university in Croatia. Based on GPA, courses completed, name of selected college/university, major, ages of siblings, vocation of parents, location of home, and recommendations from school, church, and/or civic representatives. Recipients are assigned specific responsibilities.

Renewable up to 4 years. Contact CSF for an application and list of terms and conditions.

2633—CRYSTAL SPRINGS UPLANDS SCHOOL (Financial Aid)

400 Uplands Drive
Hillsborough CA 94010
650/342-4175
Internet: www.csus.com
AMOUNT: Varies
DEADLINE(S): Varies
FIELD(S): All fields of study

This independent school in San Mateo County, California, offers eduational programs for grades 6-12. The school seeks students who are athletes, artists, performers, activists, thinkers, and comedians. Financial aid is available.

Contact school for details.

2634—CUBAN AMERICAN TEACHERS' ASSOCIATION (CATA Scholarship Program)

Dr. A.C. del Calvo
12037 Peoria Street
Sun Valley CA 91352
818/768-2669
AMOUNT: $300-$500
DEADLINE(S): March
FIELD(S): All fields of study

Open to high school seniors of Cuban descent who live in Los Angeles County, CA, and plan to continue their education at the college level. Applicants must have a minimum "B" average, speak acceptable Spanish, be active in school and community affairs, and demonstrate an interest in their cultural heritage. Financial need NOT a factor.

30 awards annually. Not renewable. Contact Dr. Alberto C. del Calvo for an application.

2635—CULVER ACADEMIES (Financial Aid Programs)

1300 Academy Road
Culver IN 46511-1291
219/842-7100 or 800/5 CULVER
FAX: 219/842-8066
E-mail: joyners@culver.org
Internet: www.culver.org
AMOUNT: Varies
DEADLINE(S): Varies
FIELD(S): All fields of study

Open to 9th-12th grade students at this private boarding/day school. Must be admitted to Culver Academies and be U.S. citizens to apply for awards. Grants, available to all students, are based on financial need. Full-tuition scholarships for incoming freshmen and sophomores are based on merit.

Renewable. Contact Scott Joyner, Director of Financial Aid, for an application.

2636—CULVER ACADEMIES (Batten Scholars Programs)

1300 Academy Road
Culver IN 46511-1291
219/842-7100 or 800/5Culver
FAX: 219/842-8066
E-mail: joyners@culver.org
Internet: www.culver.org
AMOUNT: 4-year full-ride scholarship
DEADLINE(S): Feb 1
FIELD(S): All fields of study

Open to 9th-12th grade students at this private boarding/day school. Must be admitted to Culver Academies and be U.S. citizens to apply for awards.

Full-tuition scholarships for incoming freshmen and sophomores are based on merit.

Renewable. Contact Scott Joyner, Director of Financial Aid, for an application.

2637—D. D. HACHAR CHARITABLE TRUST FUND (Undergraduate Scholarships)

Laredo National Bank; Trustee
P.O. Box 59
Laredo TX 78042-0059
956/723-1151 ext. 2670
AMOUNT: Varies
DEADLINE(S): APR (last Friday)
FIELD(S): All areas of study

Open to residents of Laredo (Webb County), Texas. Scholarships available for undergraduate study. College freshmen and sophomores must maintain minimum 2.0 GPA; juniors and seniors at least 2.5 GPA. Must be enrolled full-time.

Annual family income cannot exceed $60,000. U.S. citizenship or legal residency required. Write for complete information.

2638—DANISH SISTERHOOD OF AMERICA (Scholarships and Grants)

7326 Lehigh Court
Zephyrhills FL 33540-1014
Internet: www.danishsisterhood.org
Written Inquiry
AMOUNT: Up to $1,000
DEADLINE(S): Varies
FIELD(S): All fields study

Open to members and children of members of the Danish Sisterhood of America who are in good standing. Must have been members for at least one year. Students must be attending approved schools. Based on academic achievement; financial need NOT a factor. 25 available.

Renewable. Write to Joyce G. Houck, National Vice President/Scholarship Chairman, for an application.

2639—DATATEL SCHOLARS FOUNDATION (Angelfire Scholarships)

4375 Fair Lakes Court
FairFAX: VA 22033
703/968-9000 or 800/486-4332
E-mail: scholars@datatel.com
Internet: www.datatel.com
AMOUNT: $700-$2,000—based on tuition costs
DEADLINE(S): FEB 15
FIELD(S): All fields of study

Scholarships for part- or full-time students, both undergraduates and graduates. Must be: a military veteran of the Vietnam War; or a child or spouse of a military veteran of the Vietnam War; or a Vietnamese, Cambodian, or Laotian refugee who entered the United States between 1964 and 1975. Nationalization is not a requirement. For use at a higher learning institution selected from one of Datatel's more than 400 client sites.

Apply through the institution's Financial Aid or Scholarship office, which may nominate up to 2 students. Or contact Aimee Allenback, Director, for details.

2640—DATATEL SCHOLARS FOUNDATION (Datatel Scholarships)

4375 Fair Lakes Court
FairFAX: VA 22033
703/968-9000 or 800/486-4332
E-mail: scholars@datatel.com
Internet: www.datatel.com
AMOUNT: $700-$2,000—based on tuition costs
DEADLINE(S): FEB 15
FIELD(S): All fields of study

Scholarships for part- or full-time students, both undergraduates and graduates. For use at a higher learning institution selected from one of Datatel's more than 400 client sites.

Apply through the institution's Financial Aid or Scholarship office, which may nominate up to 2 students. Or contact organization for details.

2641—DATATEL SCHOLARS FOUNDATION (Returning Student Scholarship)

4375 Fair Lakes Court
FairFAX: VA 22033
800/486-4332
E-mail: scholars@datatel.com
Internet: http://www.datatel.com
AMOUNT: $1,000
DEADLINE(S): FEB 15
FIELD(S): All

For any student returning to school in the upcoming year after a five-year absence or more. Transcripts from those earlier years are required.

The Returning Student scholarship personal statement essay should discuss the impact of being a returning student, the challenges of combining life interests, such as work and family, along with school, and the importance of receiving a Returning Student scholarship to help achieve a dream.

2642—DAUGHTERS OF PENELOPE (Undergraduate Scholarships)

1909 Q Street NW, Suite 500
Washington D.C. 20009
202/234-9741
FAX: 202/483-6983
E-mail: daughters@ahepa.org
AMOUNT: 2 at $1,500; 8 at $1,000
DEADLINE(S): JUN 20
FIELD(S): All fields of study

Open to female undergraduates of Greek descent who are members of Daughters of Penelope or Maids of Athena or the daughter of a member of Daughters of Penelope or Order of AHEPA. Academic performance and need are main considerations.

8 scholarships available, 2 based on financial need/academic merit and 8 are based on academic merit. Renewable. For membership information or an application, write to the above address.

2643—DAUGHTERS OF THE AMERICAN REVOLUTION (American Indians Scholarship)

Office of Committees, NSDAR
1776 D Street NW
Washington DC 20006-5303
Written Inquiry
AMOUNT: $500
DEADLINE(S): JUL 1; NOV 1
FIELD(S): All fields of study

Open to American Indians, both youth and adults, striving to get an education. Funds help students of any tribe in any state based on need, academic achievement, and ambition.

Send SASE to above address for complete information.

2644—DAUGHTERS OF THE AMERICAN REVOLUTION (DAR Schools' Scholarships)

Office of Committees, NSDAR
1776 D Street NW
Washington DC 20006-5303
Written Inquiries
202/628-1776
Internet: www.dar.org
AMOUNT: $1,000-$2,000
DEADLINE(S): Varies
FIELD(S): All fields of study

For graduates of Kate Duncan Smith (in AL) or Tamassee (in SC) DAR Schools. Applications are through the respective school scholarship committees; awards are made in June. Includes Idamae Cox Otis Scholarship, Longman-Harris Scholarship, and Mildred Louise Brackney Scholarship.

Renewable. Contact individual schools for more information. Send self-addressed, stamped envelope to DAR for info about their other scholarships (DAR affiliation not required).

2645—DAUGHTERS OF THE CINCINNATI (Scholarship Program)

122 East 58th Street
New York NY 10022
212/319-6915
AMOUNT: Varies
DEADLINE(S): MAR 15
FIELD(S): All fields of study

Open to high school seniors who are daughters of commissioned officers (active, retired, or deceased) in the U.S. Army, Navy, Air Force, Marine Corps, or Coast Guard. For undergraduate study at any accredited four-year institution.

Awards based on need and merit. Include parent's rank and branch of service when writing for application or further information.

2646—DAUGHTERS OF UNION VETERANS OF THE CIVIL WAR (Grand Army of the Republic Living Memorial Scholarships)

503 S. Walnut Street
Springfield IL 62704-1932
217/544-0616
Written Inquiry (no later than FEB 1 postmark for an application)
AMOUNT: $200
DEADLINE(S): APR 30
FIELD(S): All fields of study

Open to LINEAL descendants of a union veteran of the Civil War. Must be a junior or senior in college, in good scholastic standing, of good moral character, and have a firm belief in the U.S. form of government.

3-4 awards annually. Send a self-addressed, stamped envelope and PROOF of direct lineage to Civil War union veteran (military record), for an application no later than February 1st.

2647—DAVID W. SELF SCHOLARSHIP

P.O. Box 340003
Nashville TN 37203-0003
615/340-7181
FAX: 615/340-1764
E-mail: umyouthorg@gbod.org
AMOUNT: $1,000
DEADLINE(S): JUN 1
FIELD(S): All

Available to students who have been active in a United Methodist church. Open to graduating high school seniors. Must be a U.S. citizen or permanent resident who will be pursuing a "church-related" career. Financial need must be established.

2648—DAVID WASSERMAN SCHOLARSHIP FUND, INC. (Award Program)

Adirondack Center
4722 State Hwy. 30
Amsterdam NY 12010
518/843-2800
FAX: 518/843-2801
E-mail: sherbunt@superior.net
Written Request for application (APR 15)
AMOUNT: $300/year
DEADLINE(S): JUN 15
FIELD(S): All fields of study

Open to bona fide residents of Montgomery County, New York, who are U.S. citizens pursuing an undergraduate degree.

25-30 awards annually. Renewable. Write to above address for an application.

2649—DAVIES'S INDEPENDENT 6TH FORM COLLEGE (Scholarships for International Students)

25 Old Gloucester Street
London ENGLAND UK
+44 171 430 1622
FAX: +44 171 430 9212
E-mail: enquiry@daviesscoll.u-net.com
Internet: www.daviesscoll.u-net.com/
AMOUNT: Varies
DEADLINE(S): Varies
FIELD(S): All fields of study

Davies's Independent 6th Form College (equivalent to grade 12 in the U.S.) is similar to a college prep school. It prepares students for entrance to Oxford, Cambridge, the Armed Services, and the Civil Service. A number of scholarships are offered to international students that cover full or partial tuition fees.

Contact school for details.

2650—DAVIS-ROBERTS SCHOLARSHIP FUND INC. (Scholarships to DeMolays and Job's Daughters)

Cheyenne WY 82003
307/632-0491
AMOUNT: $350
DEADLINE(S): JUN 15
FIELD(S): All fields of study

Open to Wyoming residents who are or have been a DeMolay or a Job's Daughter in the state of Wyoming. Scholarships for full-time undergraduate study. Financial need is a consideration. U.S. citizenship required.

12 awards annually. Renewable. Write for complete information.

2651—DAYTON-MONTGOMERY COUNTY SCHOLARSHIP PROGRAM

348 West First Street
Dayton OH 45402
937/542-3398
FAX: 937/542-3213
E-mail: dmcsp@earthlink.com
Internet: http://www.dmscp.org

AMOUNT: $300-$2,000
DEADLINE(S): APR 15
FIELD(S): All fields of study

Open to students who are residents of Dayton or Montgomery County, OH, and graduating from a participating high school. Must demonstrate financial need.

Contact Program for an application.

2652—DEAKIN UNIVERSITY (Scholarships for International Students)

Deakin University
336 Glenferrie Road
Malvern Victoria 3144 AUSTRALIA
(61-3) 9244 5100
FAX: (61-3) 9244 5478
E-mail: du.info@deakin.edu.au
Internet: http://www.deakin.edu.au

AMOUNT: Varies
DEADLINE(S): Varies
FIELD(S): All fields of study

Awards for international students include: Faculty of Business and Law Undergraduate Scholarships for Best International Students; Deakin University Research Scholarships for International Students (DURSIS); Deakin University Faculty of Science and Technology's Doctoral Scholarships; OPRS at Deakin University

Contact university for specifics on above scholarships. Some include full tuition and living stipend.

2653—DEAKIN UNIVERSITY (Deakin Exchange Scholarships)

Deakin University
336 Glenferrie Road
Malvern Victoria 3144 AUSTRALIA
(61-3)9244 5095
FAX: (61-3)9244 5094
E-mail: du.info@deakin.edu.au

AMOUNT: $1,500
DEADLINE(S): Varies
FIELD(S): All fields of study

Scholarships of $1500 each are available for currently enrolled undergraduate students who have been accepted in one of Deakin University's approved overseas exchange programs and have completed at least one full year of degree studies.

Applications are invited from both Australian residents and international students. It should be noted that scholarships will not be awarded for international students to go on exchange to their home country. Award of the Deakin Exchange scholarships is competitive and based on judgments of merit and benefit of the exchange to the student and the University by a committee made up of representatives of Deakin International, returned exchange students and the Faculties.

2654—DEAKIN UNIVERSITY (Gordon Council Scholarships)

Deakin University
336 Glenferrie Road
Malvern Victoria 3144 AUSTRALIA
(61-3)9244 5095
FAX: (61-3)9244 5094
E-mail: du.info@deakin.edu.au

AMOUNT: $200
DEADLINE(S): MAR 7
FIELD(S): All fields of study

The scholarships are awarded on academic merit based upon academic achievement at the University and will continue subject to satisfactory academic achievement. Submissions must be made using the proforma available on this Web site. Completed application forms must be forwarded to the Secretary, Vice-Chancellor's Prizes Committee.

2655—DEAKIN UNIVERSITY (Spotless Scholarships)

Deakin University
336 Glenferrie Road
Malvern Victoria 3144 AUSTRALIA
(61-3)9244 5095
FAX: (61-3)9244 5094
E-mail: du.info@deakin.edu.au

AMOUNT: $10,000; $4,000 in the first year, $3,000 in the second year and $3,000 in the third year, based on satisfactory academic progress.
DEADLINE(S): DEC 19
FIELD(S): All fields of study

The Spotless Scholarship is an annual scholarship awarded on a rotational basis to a commencing student at the Warrnambool/Geelong/metropolitan campuses. Awarded to a commencing undergraduate student (school leaver) and based on academic merit and need. (Youth Allowance/Austudy recipient). Submissions must be made using the proforma available on this Web site. Completed application forms must be forwarded to the Secretary, Vice-Chancellor's Prizes Committee.

2656—DEBRA LEVY NEIMARK SCHOLARSHIP

800 Corporate Drive, Suite 420
Fort Lauderdale FL 33334
954/493-8000
FAX: 954/493-6505

AMOUNT: $1,500
DEADLINE(S): APR 1
FIELD(S): All

Available to female residents of Broward County, Florida. To be considered for this nonrenewable award, applicants are required to submit resume, last two years tax returns, official transcript of grades, and three letters of recommendation along with application.

2657—DELAWARE STATE COMMUNITY ACTION PROGRAM UAW REGION 8 (UAW Labor Essay Contest)

Terry Connor, Vice President
698 Old Baltimore Pike
Newark DE 19702
302/738-9046
FAX: 302/738-9040

AMOUNT: $400-$1,200
DEADLINE(S): FEB 28
FIELD(S): All

Available to all students graduating from a Delaware High School regardless of parental membership. Essay topics may include: biography of any great labor leaders; history of international unions; women's role in labor's past; labor history specific era; labor's role in education or politics. Four prizes are awarded each year.

2658—DELTA GAMMA FOUNDATION

3250 Riverside Drive,
Box 21397
Columbus OH 43221-0397
614/481-8169

AMOUNT: $1,000-$2,500
DEADLINE(S): FEB 1; APR 1
FIELD(S): All fields of study

Scholarships and fellowships open to Delta Gamma members. Loans open to Delta Gamma members and their dependents. Awards may be used for undergraduate or graduate study.

Approx 200 awards per year. Contact the Grants and Loans chairman, address above, for complete information.

2659—DELTA PHI EPSILON EDUCATIONAL FOUNDATION

16A Worthington Drive
Maryland Heights MO 63043
314/275-2626
FAX: 314/275-2655
E-mail: ealper@dphie.org
Internet: www.dphie.org
AMOUNT: Varies
DEADLINE(S): APR 1 (undergrads); APR 15 (grads)
FIELD(S): All fields of study

Scholarships for women students who are members or daughters or granddaughters of members of Delta Phi Epsilon sorority.

Applications available in January. Write or E-mail Ellen Alper, Executive Director, at above address.

2660—DELTA SIGMA THETA SORORITY (Scholarship)

Century City Alumnae Chapter
P.O. Box 90956
Los Angeles CA 90009
213/243-0594
AMOUNT: Varies
DEADLINE(S): APR 15
FIELD(S): All

Scholarships are available to women who have a good personal character, a commitment to serving others, and an outstanding potential for success. Requires a minimum 3.0 GPA.

2661—DENISON UNIVERSITY (Financial Aid)

Financial Aid and Student Employment
Nancy Hoover, Director
100 South Road
Granville OH 43023
800/DENISON
E-mail: finaid@denison.edu
Internet: www.denison.edu
AMOUNT: Varies
DEADLINE(S): Varies
FIELD(S): All fields of study

Denison University offers opportunities for students to receive financial assistance, including grants and loans, from various sources in addition to merit-based scholarships.

Renewable for four years after reevaluation. See Web site and/or contact Financial Aid Office for further information.

2662—DENISON UNIVERSITY (Honors Program)

Prof. Anthony J. Lisska
Granville OH 43023
740/587-6573 or 800/DENISON
E-mail: mcintyre@denison.edu or sunkle@denison.edu
Internet: www.denison.edu
AMOUNT: Varies
DEADLINE(S): Varies: Denison College application due by JAN 1, 2003
FIELD(S): All fields of study

Denison University offers an Honors Program for high-performing incoming freshmen and transfer students. Applicants will be most competitive if they are in the top 10 of graduating class, have an ACT of 28 or higher and a combined SAT of 1230. After their first year, students with a 3.4 GPA not already enrolled in the program will receive invitations to participate. Certain scholarships are available only to students in the Honors Program.

See Web site for details or send letter of inquiry to Prof. Lisska or Ms. Ann Marie McIntyre (Admissions Office) for further information.

2663—DENISON UNIVERSITY (Merit-Based Scholarships)

Admissions Office
100 South Road
Granville OH 43023
800/DENISON or 740/587-6276
E-mail: admissions@denison.edu
Internet: www.denison.edu
AMOUNT: Varies
DEADLINE(S): JAN 1 (of senior year)
FIELD(S): All fields of study

Denison University offers more than 200 academic scholarships for first-year students. Some are related to specific fields of study, some are for National Merit Scholars, some are tied to certain high schools, and some are for minority students. All require excellence in academic achievement, and some are based on personal merit combined with financial need. See web page under "Scholarships" for list.

Renewable for four years if stipulated GPA is maintained. Contact Admissions Office for information on merit-based scholarships.

2664—DENNIS W. CABARET FEDERATION (Scholarship)

76 Agostino
Irvine CA 92614-8416
Written Inquiries
AMOUNT: Varies
DEADLINE(S): MAY 26
FIELD(S): All

Applicants must have a permanent address in Orange County, regardless of the location of the post high school institution they are attending. Must have visible involvement and activism in the Orange County lesbian, gay, and HIV/AIDS community and completion of at least one full year of post high school education in an institution of higher education such as a community college, junior college, or four-year college or university.

2665—DEPARTMENT OF VETERANS AFFAIRS (Survivors and Dependents Educational Assistance Program)

810 Vermont Avenue NW
Washington DC 20420
800/827-1000
AMOUNT: $670/mo. for full-time study; $503/mo. for 3/4-time study; and $335/mo. for half-time study
DEADLINE(S): Varies
FIELD(S): All fields of study

Educational support for children (aged 18-26) and spouses/widows of veterans who are 100% disabled or deceased due to military service or are classified currently as prisoner of war or missing in action. Training in approved institution.

Spouses are eligible up to 10 years after determination of eligibility. Contact the nearest VA office for complete information.

2666—DESCENDANTS OF THE SIGNERS OF THE DECLARATION OF INDEPENDENCE (Scholarship Grant)

Scholarship Chairman
Box 146
Deale MD 20751
Internet: http://www.dsdi1776.org
Written Inquiry only
AMOUNT: Average $1,100
DEADLINE(S): MAR 15
FIELD(S): All areas of study

Undergrad and grad awards for students who are DSDI members (proof of direct descent of signer of Declaration of Independence necessary, STUDENT MUST BE A MEMBER OF D.S.D.I before he/she can apply). Write to Scholarhip Chairmanat the above address for membership. Must be full-time student accepted or enrolled in a recognized U.S. four-year college or university.

Applicants for membership must provide proof of direct, lineal descendancy from a Signer. Enclose stamped, self-addressed envelope.

2667—DISABLED AMERICAN VETERANS AUXILIARY (DAVA Student Loans)

3725 Alexandria Pike
Cold Spring KY 41076
859/441-7300

AMOUNT: $1,500/year (max.)
DEADLINE(S): APR 25
FIELD(S): All fields of study

Open to children whose living mother is a life member of DAV Auxiliary or (if mother is deceased) whose father is a life member of at least one year. Must be a full-time student at a U.S. institution of higher education with a minimum of 12 credit hours. Must maintain a minimum 2.0 GPA and be a U.S. citizen.

40-42 awards annually. Renewable up to 4 years. Contact DAVA for an application.

2668—DISCOVER CARD TRIBUTE AWARD (Scholarship)

American Association of School Administrators,
Box 9338
Arlington VA 22219
703/875-0708
E-mail: tributeaward@aasa.org
Internet: http://www.asa.org/discover.htm or http://www.discovercard.com/tribute.htm

AMOUNT: $2,500-$25,000
DEADLINE(S): JAN
FIELD(S): Any field of study

Open to high school juniors whose cumulative GPA for the 9th and 10th grades was at least 2.75 (on a 4.0 scale). This scholarship can be used for any type of accredited training, licensing, or certification program or for any accredited degree program. Applicants must have achievement in 3 of these 4 areas: Special talent, leadership, obstacles overcome, community service

Total of up to 9 scholarships available in each of the 50 states and DC. The top State Tribute Award recipients are automatically entered to compete for 9 national scholarships. Application materials sent in September of each year to guidance offices of all U.S. high schools. Application materials also available on the Web sites listed above beginning October 1 of each year.

2669—DISTRICT OF COLUMBIA (LEAP Program)

State Education Office
441 Fourth Street NW
Suite 350 North
Washington DC 20001
202/727-6436
FAX: 202/727-2834
Internet: http://www.seo.dc.gov

AMOUNT: $1,000/yr for full-time study
DEADLINE(S): JUN 27
FIELD(S): All undergrad majors and 1st year of M.A. program. NOT for Law and Medicine

Open to U.S. citizens or legal residents who have lived in DC for at least 15 consecutive months, have at least a 2.0 GPA, can demonstrate financial need, and are enrolled in an eligible U.S. institution.

Renewable scholarships for undergraduate study. Must have high school diploma or equivalent. Write for complete information.

2670—DISTRICT OF COLUMBIA (Tuition Assistance Grant)

State Education Office
441 Fourth Street NW
Suite 350 North
Washington DC 20001
202/727-2824 or 877-485-6751
TTY: 202/727-1675
Internet: http://www.tuitiongrant.washingtondc.gov

AMOUNT: Up to $10,000/yr
DEADLINE(S): JUN 27
FIELD(S): All fields of study

Students must currently be DC residents and have lived in the District of Columbia for at least 12 months prior to the beginning of their freshman year of college. Students must have graduated from high school or received the equivalent of a secondary school diploma (G.E.D.) on or after January 1, 1998 and have begun their freshman year of college within three years of graduating. Students must be enrolled at least half-time in an undergraduate degree or certificate program. Students must not have already completed an undergraduate degree. The DC College Access Act of 1999 provides up to $10,000 per year to DC residents to pay the difference between in-state and out-of-state tuition at any public college or university in the United States. The Program also provides grants of up to $2,500 per year to DC students attending private colleges in the DC metropolitan area and private Historically Black Colleges and Universities in the state of Virginia. Funding is for tuition only. Payments are made directly to the participating college or university

2671—THE DIXIE GROUP FOUNDATION, INC. (George West Scholarship Fund)

Chattanooga TN 37422-5107
423/510-7005

AMOUNT: Varies
DEADLINE(S): FEB 1
FIELD(S): All fields of study

Open ONLY to children of employees of Dixie Group, Inc. for undergraduate study.

Contact Dixie Group for an application.

2672—DODD AND DOROTHY L. BRYAN FOUNDATION (Interest-Free Loans)

2 N. Main, Suite 401
Sheridan WY 82801
307/672-3535

AMOUNT: $4,000/yr
DEADLINE(S): JUN 15
FIELD(S): All fields of study

Open to undergraduate, graduate, and postgraduate students who live in one of these six counties: Sheridan WY, Johnson WY, Campbell WY, Rosebud MT, Big Horn MT, or Powder River MT. Must demonstrate financial need.

Contact Foundation for an application.

2673—DOG WRITERS' EDUCATIONAL TRUST (Scholarships)

Ms. Allene McKewen, DWET
Executive Secretary
St. Petersburg FL 33742-2322
Internet: www.dwet.org
Written Inquiries only

AMOUNT: Varies
DEADLINE(S): JAN 31
FIELD(S): All fields of study

For college students who have participaed in organized activities with dogs or whose parents or other close relatives have done so.

Scholarships support undergraduate or graduate study. Send SASE to above location for complete information.

2674—DOLPHIN SCHOLARSHIP FOUNDATION (Scholarships)

5040 Virginia Beach Boulevard
Suite 104-A
Virginia Beach VA 23462
757/671-3200
FAX: 757/671-3330
Internet: www.dolphinscholarship.org

AMOUNT: $3,000/year
DEADLINE(S): MAR 15
FIELD(S): All fields of study

Open to high school seniors and undergraduate college students who are children or stepchildren of current or former members of the U.S. Navy Submarine Force. Members must have qualified in submarines and served in the force for at least 8 years, have served at least 10 years in direct support of the Submarine Force, or died in active duty of Submarine Force. Financial need is considered.

25-30 awards annually. Renewable yearly up to 4 years. See Web site or send a self-addressed, stamped, business-sized envelope to above address for an application.

2675—DRY CREEK NEIGHBORS CLUB (Scholarships)

Contact Scholarship Coordinator at
Your High School
707/431-3473

AMOUNT: Varies
DEADLINE(S): FEB 15
FIELD(S): All fields of study

Scholarships are awarded to graduating seniors from Healdsburg and Geyserville High Schools in California.

2 awards annually. Contact your high school for an application.

2676—EAR FOUNDATION (Minnie Pearl Scholarship Program)

1817 Patterson Street
Nashville TN 37203
Voice/TDD: 800/545-HEAR
FAX: 615/329-7935
E-mail: earfound@earfoundation.org
Internet: http://www.earfoundation.org

AMOUNT: $2,000
DEADLINE(S): FEB 15
FIELD(S): All fields of study

Open to mainstreamed high school seniors with a severe to profound bilateral hearing loss who are U.S. citizens. Must have a minimum 3.0 GPA and be accepted but not yet in attendance at a full-time university, college, junior college, or technical school. Recipients are exceptional students who have achieved academic excellence, are class leaders, and are aspiring to even higher levels.

Renewable with minimum 3.0 GPA. Contact EAR Foundation for an application.

2677—EARTHWATCH STUDENT CHALLENGE AWARDS (High School Student Research Expeditions)

3 Clock Tower Place, Suite 100
Box 75
Maynard MA 01754
800/776-0188 or
978/461-0081 ext. 118
FAX: 6978/461-2332
E-mail: scap@earthwatch.org
Internet: www.earthwatch.org/

AMOUNT: Travel/Living expenses
DEADLINE(S): NOV 12
FIELD(S): Field-based sciences

Awards for high school sophomores, juniors, and seniors, especially those gifted in the arts and humanities. Awardees will have an intimate look at the world of science and state-of-the-art technology. Teams of 6 to 8 students from across the U.S. will spend 2 to 3 weeks at sites in North or Central America. Must be at least age 16 by June 15 during year of program.

Students must be nominated by a teacher in their school. Write or visit Web site for further information. Interested students may submit the name and school address of a high school teacher whom they would like to receive a brochure.

2678—EARTHWATCH INSTITUTE'S STUDENT CHALLENGE AWARD PROGRAM (SCAP)

3 Clock Tower Place, Suite 100
Box 75
Maynard MA 01754
800/776-0188 or
978/461-0081 ext. 118
FAX: 6978/461-2332
E-mail: scap@earthwatch.org
Internet: www.earthwatch.org/

AMOUNT: Full Fellowship for ~2 week research expedition and travel (~$1,000-$1,500)
DEADLINE(S): NOV 8
FIELD(S): Field-based sciences

The SCAP program encourages gifted students talented in the arts and humanities to explore the world of science. Each year small teams of 6-8 students join field research for a couple weeks over the summer. The expeditions all take place in North America and work with professional scientists. Project topics include astrophysics, biology, geophysics, genetics, etc. Students must be nominated by a teacher. For more information please call 800-776-0188 ext. 109 or visit our website.

2679—EAST LONGMEADOW SCHOLARSHIP FOUNDATION FUND (Scholarships)

Box 66
East Longmeadow MA 01028
413/525-5462

AMOUNT: Varies
DEADLINE(S): MAR 1
FIELD(S): All fields of study

Open to residents of East Longmeadow, Massachusetts, to pursue undergraduate or graduate study.

Contact Scholarship Fund at above address for an application or the East Longmeadow High School counselor's office at above phone number for details.

2680—EAST-WEST CENTER (Undergraduate Scholarships for Pacific Islanders)

Award Service Office
1601 East-West Road
Honolulu HI 96848-1601
808/944-7735
FAX: 808/944-7730
E-mail: pidpusia@eastwestcenter.org
Internet: www.EastWestCenter.org

AMOUNT: Varies
DEADLINE(S): FEB 1
FIELD(S): All fields of study except medicine, law and engineering.

Undergraduate scholarships are available for study at the East-West Center to citizens from a select group of countries, which include: Cook Islands, Fiji, Kiribati, Niue, Papua New Guinea, Samoa, Solomon Islands, Tonga, Tuvalu, and Vanuatu. Must meet admission criteria for the University of Hawaii if not currently enrolled.

Contact EWC for an application. Funds provided by the U.S. Government.

2681—EAST-WEST CENTER (The Asian Development Bank-Government of Japan Scholarship Program)

ADB Scholarship Education Program
Honolulu HI 96848-1601
808/944-7597

FAX: 808/944-7730
E-mail: adbjsp@ewc.hawaii.edu
Internet: www.EastWestCenter.org
AMOUNT: Full tuition and fees at UHM, residence in a EWC dormitory, monthly stipend for food and incidental expenses, allowance for books, round trip airfare to Hawaii, and health insurance.
DEADLINE(S): NOV 1
FIELD(S): Various fields of study

The Asian Development Bank-Japan Scholarship Program (ADB Scholarship) provides support for graduate (post-baccalaureate) degree studies in approved fields of study at the University of Hawai'i at Manoa (UHM) and for participation in educational activities at the East-West Center (EWC).

These approved fields of study at UHM are: Agricultural and Resource Economics (MS, PhD), Business Administration (MBA, Japan-focused MBA [JEMBA]), Economics (MA, PhD), Geography (MA, PhD), Horticulture (MS, PhD), Ocean Engineering (MS, PhD), Oceanography (MS, PhD), Pacific Islands Studies (MA), Public Administration (MPA), Sociology (MA, PhD), and Urban and Regional Planning (MURP). The application deadline each year for commencement of study in August of the following year is November 1 (postmarked). All application forms (including UHM and JEMBA) and supporting documents must be mailed to the ADB Scholarship Coordinator at the East-West Center by this date. Required tests (TOEFL and GRE or GMAT) should be taken by the end of October.

Eligibility requirements for the ADB Scholarship at the East-West Center include having citizenship in a developing member country of the Asian Development Bank, a minimum of the equivalent of a four-year bachelor's degree, a minimum of two years' work experience, and a minimum score of 550 on the TOEFL exam.

The East-West Center requires three (3) letters of reference completed by persons who have played a significant role in the education or work experience of the applicant. Letters from senior professors in the major field are very helpful.

2682—EAST-WEST CENTER (French Pacific Scholarship Program)

Ms Linda Moriarty
Scholarship Coordinator
1601 East-West Road
Honolulu HI 96848-1601
808/944-7597
FAX: 808/944-7730
E-mail: EWCUHM@eastwestcenter.org
Internet: www.EastWestCenter.org
AMOUNT: Full tuition and fees at UHM, residence in a EWC dormitory, monthly stipend for food and incidental expenses, allowance for books, round trip airfare to Hawaii, and health insurance.
DEADLINE(S): FEB 1
FIELD(S): Various fields of study

The Program, funded by the Government of France and East-West Center, is a competitive, merit-based scholarship program open to citizens of French Polynesia and New Caledonia who meet specific selection criteria.

Eligible fields of study emphasize areas of critical development needs in French Polynesia and New Caledonia. Students admitted to the master's degree program will have access to fields related to agriculture, business administration, economics, environmental sciences, communication, political science, public administration, community/public health, tourism management, and urban and regional planning. Study for a professional degree in fields such as engineering, law or medicine is not within the scope of this fellowship.

2683—EASTER SEAL SOCIETY OF IOWA, INC. (James L. and Lavon Madden Mallory Annual Disability Scholarship Program)

Des Moines IA 50333-4002
515/289-1933
AMOUNT: $1,000
DEADLINE(S): MAR 1
FIELD(S): All fields of study

Open ONLY to Iowa residents with a permanent disability who are graduating high school seniors. Award supports undergraduate study at a recognized college or university.

Contact Easter Seal Society of Iowa for an application after December 1st.

2684—EASTERN ORTHODOX COMMITTEE ON SCOUTING (Scholarships)

862 Guy Lombardo Avenue
Freeport NY 11520
516/868-4050
FAX: 516/868-4052
E-mail: Gboulukos@eocs.org
Internet: www.eocs.org
AMOUNT: $1,000; $500
DEADLINE(S): APR 15
FIELD(S): All fields of study

Open to Boy Scouts and Girl Scouts who have received an Eagle or Gold Award and are seniors in high school. Students MUST be of the Eastern Orthodox religion and be U.S. citizens studying in the US. Financial need NOT a factor.

2 awards annually. Not renewable. Contact George N. Boulukos for an application ONLY if you meet requirements.

2685—EATON CORPORATION (Minority Engineering Scholars Program)

1111 Superior Avenue
Cleveland OH 44114
216/523-4354
FAX: 216/479-7354
Internet: http://www.eaton.com
AMOUNT: Varies
DEADLINE(S): Varies
FIELD(S): All

Scholarships are paid directly to the university and can be used to defray the cost of tuition, books, supplies, equipment, and course-related fees. Scholarships are intended to fill a financial need that has not been met from other sources.

2686—EBELL OF LOS ANGELES SCHOLARSHIP PROGRAM

743 S. Lucerne Boulevard
Los Angeles CA 90005-3707
323/931-1277
Internet: http://www.ebellla.com
AMOUNT: $2,500 (4-year college); $,500 (Junior college)
DEADLINE(S): MAR 31
FIELD(S): All fields of study

For Los Angeles County residents who are undergraduate sophomores, juniors, or seniors enrolled in a Los Angeles County college or university. Must be a U.S. citizen. GPA of 3.25 must be maintained for renewal.

50-60 awards per year. Financial need is a consideration. Paid quarterly. Students must contact Ebell of Los Angeles for an application.

2687—EDMUND F. MAXWELL FOUNDATION (Scholarships)

Seattle WA 98122-0537
E-mail: admin@maxwell.org
Internet: www.maxwell.org
AMOUNT: $3,500
DEADLINE(S): APR 30
FIELD(S): All fields of study

Open to entering college freshmen who are bona fide residents of Western Washington (particularly in or around Seattle). May be entering any accredited institution of higher learning which receives its fundamental support from sources other than taxes. Must have financial need, outstanding academic records, and combined SAT scores over 1200.

Renewable. See Web site or contact Foundation in the fall for an application.

2688—EDUCAID (Gimme Five Scholarship Sweepstakes)

Educaid, A First Union Company
5970 Six Forks Road, Suite C
Raleigh NC 27609
919/847-2832
FAX: 919/847-7303
Internet: http://www.educaid.com
AMOUNT: $5,000
DEADLINE(S): Continuous
FIELD(S): All

Educaid will hold monthly drawings from August to December. Each scholarship will be made payable to the school of attendance. Scholarships are not based on grades or financial need, so every eligible high school senior who enters has an equal chance of winning. Winners of monthly prizes will be determined by random drawings. Winners will be notified by mail.

2689—EDUCATION ASSISTANCE CORPORATION (Federal Family Education Loan Program)

115 First Avenue SW
Aberdeen SD 57401
800/592-1802
E-mail: Eac@eac-easci.org
Internet: http://www.eac-easci.org
AMOUNT: Varies
DEADLINE(S): None
FIELD(S): All fields of study

Loans for South Dakota residents enrolled in eligible schools on at least a half-time basis. Must be a U.S. citizen or national or eligible non-resident (see federal guidelines).

Renewable. Write for an application and complete information.

2690—EDUCATIONAL CREDIT MANAGEMENT CORPORATION (Loan Programs for Virginia Students)

Boulders Building VII
7325 Beaufont Springs Drive
Richmond VA 23225
804/267-7100 or 888/775-ECMC
FAX: 804/344-6743
E-mail: mellyson@ecmc.org
Internet: http://www.ecmc.org
AMOUNT: Varies
DEADLINE(S): None
FIELD(S): All fields of study

Various loan programs open to students enrolled in approved institutions. Eligibility governed by ECMC and federal regulations.

Contact college financial aid office or write to address above for complete information.

2691—EDUCATIONAL COMMUNICATIONS SCHOLARSHIP FOUNDATION (Scholarships)

721 N. McKinley Road
Lake Forest IL 60045
847/295-6650
FAX: 847/295-3972
E-mail: school@ecsf.org
AMOUNT: $1,000
DEADLINE(S): MAY 15
FIELD(S): All fields of study

Open to current high school students who are legal residents of the U.S. and have taken the SAT or ACT examination. Based on GPA, achievement test scores, leadership, work experience, essay, and financial need.

200 awards annually. Send name, home address, current year in high school, and approximate grade point average to ECSF for an application no later than March 15th; deadline to return application is May 15th.

2692—EDUCATIONAL COMMUNICATIONS SCHOLARSHIP FOUNDATION (Scholarship Award Program)

721 N. McKinley Road
Lake Forest IL 60045
847/295-6650
FAX: 847/295-3972
E-mail: school@ecsf.org
AMOUNT: $1,000
DEADLINE(S): MAY 15
FIELD(S): All fields of study

Open to undergraduate and graduate students with a minimum B+ GPA. Must be U.S. citizen and attending an accredited college/university. Based on GPA, achievement test scores, leadership qualifications, work experience, essay, and some consideration for financial need. Payments are issued directly to institution.

50 awards annually. Contact ECSF with your name, home address, college name, GPA, and year in school for an application no later than March 15th. Winners are notified by August 5th.

2693—EDWARDS SCHOLARSHIP FUND (Undergraduate and Graduate Scholarships)

10 Post Office Square So.
12th Floor
Boston MA 02109
617/426-4434
AMOUNT: $250 to $5,000
DEADLINE(S): MAR 1
FIELD(S): All fields of study

Open ONLY to city of Boston residents under age 25 who can demonstrate financial need, scholastic ability, and good character. For undergraduate or graduate study but undergrads receive preference. Family home must be within Boston city limits.

Applicants must have lived in Boston from at least the beginning of their junior year in high school. Metropolitan Boston is NOT included.

2694—EL PASO COMMUNITY FOUNDATION (Scholarships)

Cortez Building
310 N. Mesa, Tenth Floor
El Paso TX 79901
915/533-4020
FAX: 915/532-0716
E-mail: info@epcf.org
Internet: http://www.epcf.org
AMOUNT: Varies
DEADLINE(S): Varies
FIELD(S): All fields of study

Various scholarships for residents of El Paso County, Texas.

Contact organization for details.

2695—ELI LILLY AND COMPANY (Lilly for Learning Diabetes Scholarships)

Lilly Corporate Center
Indianapolis IN 46285
317/276-2000
Internet: http://www.lilly.com/diabetes
AMOUNT: $2,500
DEADLINE(S): APR 15
FIELD(S): All

Available to seniors and full-time undergraduates who have been diagnosed with Type 1 (insulin-dependent) diabetes. Applicants must demonstrate involvement in the diabetes community which advances diabetes awareness.

2696—ELIE WIESEL FOUNDATION FOR HUMANITY (Prize in Ethics Essay Contest)

529 Fifth Avenue, Suite 1802
New York NY 10017
212/490-7777
FAX: 212/490-6006
E-mail: info@eliewieselfoundation.org
Internet: www.eliewiesel foundation.org

AMOUNT: $5,000 (1st prize); $2,500 (2nd); $1,500 (3rd); $500 (2 honorable mentions)
DEADLINE(S): DEC (exact date will be posted on Web site in late spring)
FIELD(S): All fields of study

Open to undergraduate juniors and seniors at accredited four-year colleges/universities in the US. Entries must be personal essays that: explore how a moral society's perception of the "other" may result in social separation, prejudice, discrimination, hate crimes and violence; examine ethical aspects/implications of a major literary work, a film, or a significant piece of art; or reflect on the most profound moral dilemma you have personally experienced and learned from.

See Web site or send self-addressed, stamped envelope for guidelines.

2697—ELLA LYMAN CABOT TRUST GRANTS

The Ella Lyman Cabot Trust
98 River Street
Dedham MA 02026

DEADLINE(S): Multiple
AMOUNT: Varies
FIELD(S): All

Provides support for individuals to embark on a project that is unique and meaningful to the individual and will benefit others.

May not be a part of general course work.

2698—ELLIE BEARDEN SCHOLARSHIP

Shirley Dempel, Chapter LZ
4570 Brighton Drive
Santa Rosa CA 95403

AMOUNT: Varies
DEADLINE(S): APR 20
FIELD(S): All

This scholarship is available to any student, male or female, who is currently enrolled at an accredited four-year institution or graduate school with a minimum 3.0 GPA or admission to Graduate School.

2699—ELMER O. AND IDA PRESTON EDUCATIONAL TRUST (Scholarships)

801 Grand Avenue, Suite 3700
Des Moines IA 50309
515/243-4191
FAX: 515/246-5808

AMOUNT: $500-$5,000
DEADLINE(S): JUN 30
FIELD(S): All fields of study

Scholarships for students, undergraduates and graduates, who are members of a Protestant church, are residents of Iowa, and attending any college in the state of Iowa.

Renewable. 70 awards. Contact organization for details.

2700—EMANUEL STERNBERGER EDUCATIONAL FUND (Interest-Free Loan Program)

Greensboro NC 27402
336/275-6316 or 336/379-0479
E-mail: bhenley369@aol.com

AMOUNT: $1,000 (1st year) and $2,000 (subsequent years if funds are available); maximum $5,000
DEADLINE(S): MAR 31
FIELD(S): All fields of study

Open to North Carolina residents who are entering their junior or senior year of college or are graduate students. Considerations include grades, economic situation, references, and credit rating.

Personal interview is required. Can be used at any college or university. Write for complete information.

2701—EMBASSY OF JAPAN (Monbukagakusho Scholarship for Undergraduates)

255 Sussex Drive
Ottawa Ontario K1N 9E6 CANADA
613/241-8541
FAX: 613/241-4261
E-mail: infocul@embassyjapan canada.org
Internet: www.embassyjapan canada.org

AMOUNT: 142,500 yen per month
DEADLINE(S): Middle to late JUN
FIELD(S): All areas of study

Five-year scholarship open to Canadian citizens between 17 and 22 who wish to study at Japanese universities as undergraduate students. Must have high school diploma, be in good health, and be willing to study the Japanese language. First year is spent in Japanese language studies. Also provides transportation to/from Japan, arrival allowance of 25,000 yen, school fees and accommodations.

Apply through the most convenient Japanese diplomatic mission in Canada or write for complete information.

2702—EMBASSY OF JAPAN (Research Studies Scholarship for Graduate students)

255 Sussex Drive
Ottawa Ontario K1N 9E6 CANADA
613/241-8541
FAX: 613/241-4261
E-mail: infocul@embassyjapan canada.org
Internet: www.embassyjapan canada.org

AMOUNT: 185,500 yen per month
DEADLINE(S): Middle to late JUN
FIELD(S): All areas of study

Applicants must be under 35 years. The term of this scholarship is 18 months to two years (including 6 months of Japanese language studies). Applicants must be university graduates. The study area should be the same field that the applicant has studied or a related field. Also provides transportation to/from Japan, arrival allowance of 25,000 yen, school fees and accommodations.

Applicants should contact a Japanese professor at the university they wish to study at and obtain a letter of acceptance.

Apply through the most convenient Japanese diplomatic mission in Canada or write for complete information.

2703—ENGLISH-SPEAKING UNION (Lucy Dalbiac Luard Scholarships)

144 E. 39th Street
New York NY 10016
212/818-1200
FAX: 212/867-4177
E-mail: info@english-speakingunion.org
Internet: http://www.english-speakingunion.org

AMOUNT: Full tuition and expenses
DEADLINE(S): NOV
FIELD(S): All fields of study

Open to students attending a United Negro College or Howard or Hampton University. Full scholarship to spend undergraduate junior year at a university in England. Must be U.S. citizen.

Application must be made through student's college or university. Information and applications are sent each fall to the Academic Dean/VP for Academic Affairs at participating schools.

2704—ETHEL AND EMERY FAST SCHOLARSHIP FOUNDATION, INC.

12620 Rolling Road
Potomac MD 20854
301/762-1102
FAX: 301/279-0201
AMOUNT: Varies
DEADLINE(S): Ongoing
FIELD(S): All fields of study

Scholarships for graduate and undergraduate Native Americans who have successfully completed one year of postsecondary studies and are full-time students.

Write or phone above location for application procedures.

2705—ETHEL LOUISE ARMSTRONG FOUNDATION, INC. (Scholarship)

ELA Foundation Scholarship
2460 North Lake Avenue, PMB #128
Altadena CA 91001
E-mail: info@ela.org
Internet: http://www.ela.org
AMOUNT: $2,000
DEADLINE(S): JUN 25
FIELD(S): All

Be a female with a physical disability currently enrolled or actively applying to a graduate program in an accredited college or university in the United States. Must be willing to partner with the ELA Foundation within her chosen field of study, to "Change the Face of Disability on the Planet."

2706—ETHEL N. BOWEN FOUNDATION (Scholarships)

P.O. Box 1559
Bluefield WV 24701-1559
304/325-8181
AMOUNT: Varies
DEADLINE(S): APR 30
FIELD(S): All fields of study

Undergraduate and occasional graduate scholarships open to residents of southern West Virginia and southwest Virginia.

20-25 awards per year. Send self-addressed, stamped envelope for complete information.

2707—ETHICAL CULTURE FIELDSTON SCHOOL (Financial Aid and Loans)

33 Central Park West
New York NY 10023
212/712-6220
FAX: 212/712-8444
Internet: www.ECFS.ORG
AMOUNT: Varies
DEADLINE(S): Varies
FIELD(S): All fields of study

Need-based scholarships and low-interest loans available to attend this independent, coeducational school which includes preschool through high school. Must submit documentation indicating financial need.

Must apply at time of admission. Contact school for details.

2708—EVANGELICAL CHRISTIAN SCHOOL (Financial Aid Program)

7600 Macon Road
P.O. Box 1030
Cordova TN 38018-1030
901/754-7217 ext. 1101
FAX: 901/754-8123
E-mail: Adurham@ecseagles.com
Internet: www.ecseagles.com
AMOUNT: 55% tuition (max.)
DEADLINE(S): None
FIELD(S): All fields of study

Open to K-12 students at this private Christian day school. Must demonstrate financial need.

185 awards annually. Renewable. Contact Alan Durham or Patti Danner for an application.

2709—EVEREG-FENESSE MESROBIAN-ROUPINIAN EDUCATIONAL SOCIETY, INC.

4140 Tanglewood Court
Bloomfield Hills MI 48301
Written Inquiry
AMOUNT: Varies
DEADLINE(S): DEC 15
FIELD(S): All fields of study

Scholarships for students attending Armenian day schools, and for full-time undergraduate or graduate students of Armenian descent attending colleges and universities. Participating chapters of the society are New York/New Jersey, California, and Detroit, Michigan.

Applications available from designated local chapter representatives.

2710—EVERGREEN STATE COLLEGE (Scholarships)

Dean of Enrollment Services
2700 Evergreen Parkway NW
Olympia WA 98505
360/866-6310
FAX: 360/867-6576
E-mail: elhardtm@evergreen.edu
Internet: http://www.evergreen.edu
AMOUNT: Varies
DEADLINE(S): Varies
FIELD(S): All fields of study

Variety of scholarships open to new or currently enrolled students at Evergreen State College, Olympia, Washington. Some awards are limited to specific ethnic groups; others require demonstration of financial need. All require enrollment at Evergreen.

Write to Evergreen College to request a scholarship brochure.

2711—FALMOUTH ACADEMY (Tuition Scholarships)

7 Highfield Drive
Falmouth MA 02540
508/457-9696
FAX: 508/457-4112
Internet: http://www.falmouth academy.org
AMOUNT: Varies
DEADLINE(S): Varies
FIELD(S): All fields of study

Scholarships are available for students in grades 7-12 to attend this academic country day school. Must demonstrate financial need.

70 awards annually. Contact Elen Itamuniz for an application.

2712—FAR BROOK SCHOOL (Financial Aid)

52 Great Hills Road
Short Hills NJ 07078
973/379-3442
FAX: 973/379-6740
E-mail: farbrook@farbrook.com
Internet: www.farbrook.org
AMOUNT: Varies
DEADLINE(S): Varies
FIELD(S): All fields of study

A private school for students in grades nursery through 8 in New Jersey. Financial aid is awarded on the basis of need as well as the academic or social contribution a student makes to his or her class. Special programs exist for ability in the arts and in math/science.

Contact school for details.

2713—FEDERAL EMPLOYEE EDUCATION AND ASSISTANCE FUND (OK Scholarship Fund)

8441 W. Bowles Avenue, Suite 200
Littleton CO 80123-9501

303/933-7580 or 800/323-4140
FAX: 303/933-7587
E-mail: feeahq@aol.com
Internet: www.feea.org
AMOUNT: Full tuition
DEADLINE(S): None
FIELD(S): All fields of study

FEEA will provide a full college education to all the children who lost a parent in the Oklahoma City Bombing. By the time the program ends in 2018, over 200 children will have received a complete college education, including the six pre-schoolers from the daycare center who survived the bombing.

Contact FEEA for details.

2714—FEDERAL EMPLOYEE EDUCATION AND ASSISTANCE FUND (FEEA Scholarship Program)

8441 W. Bowles Avenue, Suite 200
Littleton CO 80123-9501
303/933-7580 or 800/323-4140
FAX: 303/933-7587
E-mail: feeahq@aol.com
Internet: www.feea.org
AMOUNT: $300-$1,500
DEADLINE(S): MAR 31
FIELD(S): All fields of study

Open to current civilian federal and postal employees (w/ at least 3 years service) and dependent family members enrolled or planning to enroll in a 2-year, 4-year, graduate, or postgraduate degree program. Must have minimum 3.0 GPA, and an essay is required. Involvement in extracurricular/community activities is considered.

See Web site or send a business-sized, self-addressed, stamped envelope for an application after January 1st. Notification by August 31st.

2715—FEDERAL EMPLOYEE EDUCATION AND ASSISTANCE FUND (NARFE Scholarship Program)

8441 W. Bowles Avenue, Suite 200
Littleton CO 80123-9501
800/323-4140 or 303/933-7580
FAX: 303/933-7587
E-mail: feeahq@aol.com
Internet: www.feea.org
AMOUNT: Varies
DEADLINE(S): Early MAY
FIELD(S): All fields of study

FEEA, along with the National Association of the Retired Federal Employees (NARFE), offers scholarships to the children and grandchildren of federal retirees who are NARFE members.

Send a self-addressed, stamped envelope to FEEA for an application, or contact NARFE at above 800 number.

2716—FEDERATION OF AMERICAN CONSUMERS AND TRAVELERS (Continuing Education Scholarship Program)

Vicki Rolens, Managing Director
318 Hillsboro Avenue
P.O. Box 104
Edwardsville IL 62025
800/872-3228
FAX: 618/656-5369
E-mail: gmsfact@aol.com
Internet: http://www.fact-org.org
AMOUNT: $2,500-$10,000
DEADLINE(S): JAN 2
FIELD(S): All

Each year, scholarships are offered in three categories: 1) for present high school seniors; 2) for people who graduated from high school four or more years ago but missed the chance at that time to go on to college; and 3) for students currently enrolled in a college or university or trade school. There are six scholarships: one for $10,000 and one for $2,500 in each category. Must be either a member of FACT or the immediate family of a member.

2717—FEILD CO-OPERATIVE ASSOCIATION, INC. (Permanent Student Loan Fund)

Jackson MS 39296-5054
601/713-2312
AMOUNT: $5,000/calendar year (12 months)
DEADLINE(S): None
FIELD(S): All fields of study

Open ONLY to Mississippi residents of good character who have satisfactorily completed two years of college work (juniors), are graduate students, or are in special fields. Must show evidence of need, and promise of social and financial responsibility. Must be U.S. citizen/legal resident. First payment on account is due not later than three months from date of graduation.

Renewable. Contact Feild Co-Operative Assn. for an application. Student is notified as soon as application is processed.

2718—FERN BROWN MEMORIAL FUND

P.O. Box 1
Tulsa OK 74102
918/586-5594
AMOUNT: Varies
DEADLINE(S): Jun 30
FIELD(S): All fields of study

Scholarships for residents of Oklahoma. Send SASE to Paula Etter, Trust Advisor.

2719—FINANCIAL MARKETS CENTER (Henry B. Gonzalez Award)

Award Information
PO Box 334
Philomont VA 20131
540/338-7754
FAX: 540-338-7757
E-mail: info@fmcenter.org
Internet: http://www.fmcenter.org
AMOUNT: $2,500
DEADLINE(S): APR 28
FIELD(S): All

The Financial Markets Center sponsors an annual contest for papers on the subject of central bank reform. The contest is open to all entrants, including students enrolled in graduate and undergraduate programs. Entries should be no longer than 15,000 words, not including footnotes, endnotes, and references. Preference will be given to clearly written entries accessible to a broad audience.

2720—FINANCIAL SERVICE CENTERS OF AMERICA (Scholarship Fund)

Henry Shyne, Executive Director
Financial Service Centers of America, Inc.
25 Main Street
P.O. Box 647
Hackensack NJ 07602
201/487-0412
FAX: 201/487-3954
E-mail: fiscahfs@aol.com
Internet: http://www.fisca.org
AMOUNT: $2,500
DEADLINE(S): JUN 1
FIELD(S): All

The FISCA Scholarship Program will award a minimum cash grant of $2,500 for the freshman year of study to at least two high school seniors from each of the 5 geographic regions across the country. Criteria are based upon several factors, including: academic achievement, financial need, leadership skills, and an essay written expressly for the competition. Applicant must be single. Minimum 3.0 GPA required.

2721—FINTONA GIRLS' SCHOOL (Scholarships)

79 Balwyn Road
Balwyn AUSTRALIA 3103

(03) 9830 1388
E-mail: registrar@fintona.vic.edu.au
Internet: http://www.fintona.vic.edu.au
AMOUNT: Partial tuition
DEADLINE(S): MAY 11
FIELD(S): All fields of study

Scholarships for this private girls' school in Melbourne, Australia. The fields are academic, music, art, and math/science. Scholarship tests are given.

Contact school for details.

2722—FIRST CATHOLIC SLOVAK LADIES ASSOCIATION (College Scholarships)

National Headquarters
24950 Chagrin Boulevard
Beachwood OH 44122-5634
800/464-4642 ext. 128 or
216/464-8015
FAX: 216/464-9260
E-mail: info@fcsla.com
Internet: http://www.fcsla.com
AMOUNT: $1,250-$1,750
DEADLINE(S): MAR 1
FIELD(S): All fields of study

For full-time undergraduate or graduate students who have been members of FCSLA for at least three years and who will attend an accredited institution in the U.S. or Canada. Must submit transcripts, autobiographical statement, and wallet-size photo with application. Award must be used for tuition. Financial need is NOT a factor.

80 awards annually. Not renewable, though undergraduate recipients may reapply as graduate students. Contact the Receptionist at above address for an application.

2723—FIRST CATHOLIC SLOVAK LADIES ASSOCIATION (Elementary School Grades 1-2-3-4 Scholarships)

24950 Chagrin Boulevard
Beachwood OH 44122-5634
800/464-4642 ext. 128 or
216/464-8015
FAX: 216/464-9260
E-mail: info@fcsla.com
Internet: http://www.fcsla.com
AMOUNT: $500
DEADLINE(S): MAR 1
FIELD(S): All fields of study

Must have been a member of FCSLA for at least three years and be planning on attending a private or Catholic accredited elementary school in the U.S. or Canada. With application, must submit transcripts, wallet-sized photo, and a written report (100 words) on "What I like best about my school." Award must be used for tuition. Financial need is NOT a factor.

16 awards annually. Not renewable, though recipients may reapply as high school, undergraduate, and graduate students. Contact the Receptionist at above address for an application.

2724—FIRST CATHOLIC SLOVAK LADIES ASSOCIATION (Elementary School Grades 5-6-7-8 Scholarships)

24950 Chagrin Boulevard
Beachwood OH 44122-5634
800/464-4642 ext. 128 or
216/464-8015
FAX: 216/464-9260
E-mail: info@fcsla.com
Internet: http://www.fcsla.com
AMOUNT: $500
DEADLINE(S): MAR 1
FIELD(S): All fields of study

Must have been a member of FCSLA for at least three years and be planning on attending a private or Catholic accredited elementary school in the U.S. or Canada. With application, must submit transcripts, wallet-sized photo, and a written report (100 words) on "What I like best about my school." Award must be used for tuition. Financial need is NOT a factor.

16 awards annually. Not renewable, though recipients may reapply as high school, undergraduate, and graduate students. Contact the Receptionist at above address for an application.

2725—FIRST CATHOLIC SLOVAK LADIES ASSOCIATION (High School Scholarships)

24950 Chagrin Boulevard
Beachwood OH 44122-5634
800/464-4642 ext. 128 or
216/464-8015
FAX: 216/464-9260
E-mail: info@fcsla.com
Internet: http://www.fcsla.com
AMOUNT: $750
DEADLINE(S): MAR 1
FIELD(S): All fields of study

Must have been a member of FCSLA for at least three years and be planning on attending a private or Catholic accredited high school in the U.S. or Canada. With application, must submit transcripts, wallet-sized photo, and a written report (250 words) on "What this high school scholarship will do for me." Award must be used for tuition. Financial need is NOT a factor.

20 awards annually. Not renewable, though recipients may reapply as undergradute and graduate students. Contact the Receptionist at above address for an application.

2726—FIRST CAVALRY DIVISION ASSOCIATION (Scholarships)

Director of Scholarships
302 N. Main
Copperas Cove TX 76522-1799
254/547-6537
E-mail: firstcav@vvm.com
AMOUNT: $800/year
DEADLINE(S): None
FIELD(S): All fields of study

Open to children of those soldiers of 1st Cavalry Division of the U.S. Army who died or were totally and permanently disabled, to the extent of preventing performance of any work for substantial compensation or profit, as a result of wounds received or disease contracted while serving with said 1st Cavalry Division in any armed conflict. Also open to children of members of 1st Cavalry Division Association who died while serving with the 1st Cavalry Division in peacetime. And open to children and/or grandchildren of soldiers of 1st Cavalry Division, USAF Forward Air Controllers, and A1E pilots and War Correspondents who served in designated qualifying units which were involved in battles of Ia Drang valley during the period 3-19 November 1965.

Renewable up to 4 years. Send a self-addressed, stamped envelope to Arthur J. Junot, Secretary, for an application for registration as an eligible recipient.

2727—FIRST CITIZENS FOUNDATION, INC.

P.O. Box 1377
Smithfield NC 27577-1377
Written Inquiry
AMOUNT: Varies
DEADLINE(S): Varies
FIELD(S): All fields of study

Scholarships to students in North Carolina in financial distress for educational purposes in accredited trade schools, colleges, and universities.

Contact above location for deadline information and application.

2728—FIRST UNITED METHODIST CHURCH STUDENT LOAN PROGRAM (Stephen McCready Fund)

1126 E. Silver Springs Boulevard
Ocala FL 34470
352/622-3244

FAX: 352/732-9701
E-mail: fumcross@fumcocala.org
Internet: http://www.fumcocala.org
Written Inquiry
AMOUNT: Varies
DEADLINE(S): MAY 1
FIELD(S): All fields of study

College loans available to undergraduate students. Preference given to theological students or those who intend to enter into full-time religious work. Preference also given to residents of Mairon County, Florida.

20-25 annual loans. Must reapply each year. Contact Sue Ross for an application.

2729—FLEET RESERVE ASSOCIATION (Scholarships and Awards)

FRA Scholarship Administrator
125 N. West Street
Alexandria VA 22314
800/FRA-1924
E-mail: news-fra@fra.org
Internet: http://www.fra.org
AMOUNT: Approximately $500
DEADLINE(S): APR 15
FIELD(S): All areas of study

Open to children/spouses of Fleet Reserve Association members. Dependents of retired or deceased members also may apply. For undergraduate study. Awards based on financial need, scholastic standing, character, and leadership qualities.

'Dependent child' is defined as unmarried, under 21, or under 23 if currently enrolled in college. Write for complete information.

2730—FLORIDA DEPT. OF EDUCATION (Florida Student Assistance Grants)

Student Financial Assist.
1940 North Monroe Street, Suite 70
Tallahassee FL 32302-4759
888/827-2004
E-mail: OSFABF@mail.doe.state.fl.us
Internet: www.firn.edu/doe/offa
AMOUNT: $200-$1,300
DEADLINE(S): Varies (Spring)
FIELD(S): All fields of study

Need-based grant program for full-time undergraduate students attending eligible public or private Florida institutions. Must be U.S. citizens, Florida residents, and be enrolled in eligible academic degree programs. Must also submit the FAFSA form (available online at www.fafsa.ed.gov).

40,000+ awards annually. Renewable. Forms (including FAFSA) available from your school's financial aid office, or contact Florida Department of Education. Actual deadline varies with each participating institution.

2731—FLORIDA DEPT. OF EDUCATION (Florida Work Experience Program)

Student Financial Assist.
1940 North Monroe Street, Suite 70
Tallahassee FL 32302-4759
888/827-2004
E-mail: OSFABF@mail.doe.state.fl.us
Internet: www.firn.edu/doe
AMOUNT: Varies
DEADLINE(S): Varies (established by each institution)
FIELD(S): All fields of study

Employment program to introduce undergraduate students who demonstrate financial need to work experiences that will complement and reinforce their educational and career goals. Must be enrolled at least half-time, be in good standing at an eligible Florida institution, and meet residency requirements for state student aid. Must submit the FAFSA (available online at www.fafsa.ed.gov).

458 awards annually. Applications (as well as the FAFSA) are available from the financial aid office at participating institutions.

2732—FLORIDA DEPT. OF EDUCATION (Jose Marti Scholarship Challenge Grant Fund)

Student Financial Assist.
1940 North Monroe Street, Suite 70
Tallahassee FL 32302-4759
888/827-2004
E-mail: OSFABF@mail.doe.state.fl.us
Internet: www.firn.edu/doe
AMOUNT: $2,000
DEADLINE(S): APR 1
FIELD(S): All fields of study

A need-based scholarship for students of Hispanic culture who were born in, or who have a natural parent who was born in Mexico, Spain, South America, Central America, or the Caribbean. Must apply as a high school senior or as a graduate student and have a minimum unweighted GPA of 3.0. Must enroll full-time, be a U.S. citizen or eligible non-citizen, and be a Florida resident. Must also submit the FAFSA (available online at www.fafsa.ed.gov).

98 awards annually. Renewable. Forms (including FAFSA) available from your school's financial aid office or contact Florida Department of Education.

2733—FLORIDA DEPT. OF EDUCATION (Mary McLeod Bethune Scholarship)

Student Financial Assist.
1940 North Monroe Street, Suite 70
Tallahassee FL 32302-4759
888/827-2004
E-mail: OSFABF@mail.doe.state.fl.us
Internet: www.firn.edu/doe
AMOUNT: $3,000/academic year
DEADLINE(S): Varies (established by each institution)
FIELD(S): All fields of study

A need-based scholarship for high school seniors who have at least a 3.0 GPA, who will attend Florida A&M University, Bethune-Cookman College, Edward Walters College, or Florida Memorial College, and who meet residency requirements for receipt of state student aid.

180 awards annually. Applications are available from the financial aid offices at the four participating institutions.

2734—FLORIDA DEPT. OF EDUCATION (Rosewood Family Scholarship Fund)

Student Financial Assist.
1940 North Monroe Street, Suite 70
Tallahassee FL 32302-4759
888/827-2004
E-mail: OSFABF@mail.doe.state.fl.us
Internet: www.firn.edu/doe
AMOUNT: Up to $4,000
DEADLINE(S): APR 1
FIELD(S): All fields of study

Need-based scholarship for undergraduate students who are descendants of affected African-American Rosewood families and who are enrolled full-time in eligible programs at state universities, public community colleges, or public postsecondary vocational-technical schools in Florida. Other minority undergraduate students will be considered for awards if funds remain available after awarding Rosewood descendants. Must fill out FAFSA (available online www.fafsa.ed.gov).

25 awards annually. Award is amount of tuition and fees for up to 15 semester hours or 450 clock hours per term of undergrad study, not to exceed $4,000. For an application, contact Florida Department of Education.

2735—FLORIDA DEPT. OF EDUCATION (Scholarships for Children of Deceased or Disabled Veterans)

Student Financial Assist.
1940 North Monroe Street, Suite 70
Tallahassee FL 32302-4759
888/827-2004
E-mail: OSFABF@mail.doe.state.fl.us
Internet: www.firn.edu/doe

AMOUNT: Tuition + fees for the academic year
DEADLINE(S): APR 1
FIELD(S): All fields of study

For dependent children of deceased or 100% disabled veterans, or for children of servicemen classified as POW or MIA for attendance at eligible public or private institutions. Residency requirements vary.

200 awards annually. Applications are available from Florida Department of Education or from Florida Department of Veterans' Affairs, P.O. Box 31003, Street Petersburg, FL 33731-8903.

2736—FLORIDA DEPT. OF EDUCATION (William L. Boyd, IV, Florida Resident Access Grant)

Student Financial Assist.
1940 North Monroe Street, Suite 70
Tallahassee FL 32302-4759
888/827-2004
E-mail: OSFABF@mail.doe.state.fl.us
Internet: www.firn.edu/doe

AMOUNT: Varies
DEADLINE(S): Varies (established by each institution)
FIELD(S): All fields of study

Provides tuition assistance for Florida residents who are full-time undergraduate students attending eligible private non-profit Florida colleges or universities. Financial need is NOT considered.

23,000+ awards annually. Applications available from the financial aid office at the private institution you plan to attend.

2737—FLORIDA STATE DEPT. OF EDUCATION (Seminole/Miccosukee Indian Scholarships)

Student Financial Assist.
1940 North Monroe Street, Suite 70
Tallahassee FL 32302-4759
888/827-2004
E-mail: OSFABF@mail.doe.state.fl.us
Internet: www.firn.edu/doe

AMOUNT: Varies (determined by respective tribe)
DEADLINE(S): Varies (established by tribe)
FIELD(S): All fields of study

For Seminole and Miccosukee Indians of Florida who arc enrolled as full-time or part-time undergraduate or graduate students at eligible Florida institutions.

23 awards annually. Applications available from each tribe's Higher Education Committee or contact Florida Department of Education.

2738—FOND DU LAC RESERVATION (Scholarship/Grants Program)

1720 Big Lake Road
Cloquet MN 55720
218/879-4593 or 800/365-1613
FAX: 218/878-7529
Internet: http://www.fdlrez.com

AMOUNT: Varies
DEADLINE(S): Varies
FIELD(S): All fields of study

For tribally enrolled members of the Fond du Lac Reservation who plan to pursue postsecondary education, including vocational schools in accredited higher education institutions. Must apply for all financial aid available and submit an education plan. Will assist out-of-state education for those attending colleges but not vocational schools.

Contact Bonnie Wallace, Scholarship Director, at above address.

2739—FOUNDATION FOR AMATEUR RADIO (Scholarships)

Riverdale MD 20738
Written Inquiry

AMOUNT: $500-$2,500
DEADLINE(S): JUN 1
FIELD(S): All fields of study

Program open to active, licensed, radio amateurs ONLY. Since this specialized program changes so much each year, the Foundation annually places announcements with complete eligibility requirements in the amateur radio magazines.

To determine your eligibility look for announcements in magazines such as *QST, CQ, 73, Worldradio,* etc. Write for complete information. Request an application before APR 30.

2740—FOUNDATION FOR EXCEPTIONAL CHILDREN (Infinitec Scholarship Award)

1110 N. Glebe Road, Suite 300
Arlington VA 22201
703/264-3507
FAX: 703/620-4334
E-mail: fec@cec.sped.org
Internet: www.cec.sped.org/fd/scholapp.htm

AMOUNT: $500
DEADLINE(S): FEB 1
FIELD(S): All fields of study

Undergraduate awards for students with disabilities who use augmentative communication devices or other technology-based alternative to oral communication.

Financial need considered. Must be entering freshman. Application and further information are at above Web site or write for complete information.

2741—FOUNDATION FOR EXCEPTIONAL CHILDREN (Stanley E. Jackson Scholarship Awards)

1110 N. Glebe Road, Suite 300
Arlington VA 22201
703/264-3507
FAX: 703/620-4334
E-mail: fec@cec.sped.org
Internet: www.cec.sped.org/fd/scholapp.htm

AMOUNT: $500
DEADLINE(S): FEB 1
FIELD(S): All fields of study

Open to entering freshmen in four categories: 1. Students with disabilities; 2. Ethnic minority students with disabilities; 3. Gifted/talented students with disabilities; 4. Ethnic minority gifted/talented students with disabilities. Students may apply in only one category. Must be U.S. citizen/permanent resident and demonstrate financial need.

See Web site or contact Foundation for Exceptional Children for an application.

2742—FOURTH TUESDAY (Pat Hoban Memorial Scholarship)

235 Ponce de Leon Place, Suite H
Decatur GA 30030
770/662-4353
E-mail: chair@fouthtuesday.org
Internet: www.fourthtuesday.org/scholarship.html

AMOUNT: $1,000
DEADLINE(S): Varies
FIELD(S): All fields of study

Scholarship for an Atlanta area lesbian attending an institution of higher education. Fourth Tuesday is a nonprofit professional social networking organization for lesbians.

Contact organization for details.

2743—FRANCIS A. WINCH FUND (Scholarships)

3538 Central Avenue
Suite 2-A
Riverside CA 92506-2700
909/684-6778
E-mail: scholars@urs2.net
Internet: www.scholarshipsite.org
AMOUNT: $100-$7,500
DEADLINE(S): None
FIELD(S): All fields of study

Open to college sophomores, juniors, seniors, and graduate students who demonstrate financial need (income less than $10,000). There are no citizenship/residency restrictions. Award is based on achievement, need, purpose, and recommendations of college/university personnel.

$15 processing fee. Applications are reviewed on a monthly basis for one year, and each one is presented to scholarship committee three times each year for consideration. 50 awards annually. Renewable. See Web site or contact the Executive Director for an application.

2744—FRANCIS OUIMET SCHOLARSHIP FUND

Golf House, 190 Park Road
Weston MA 02493-2256
781/891-6400
FAX: 781/891-9471
E-mail: bobd@ouimet.org
Internet: http://www.ouimet.org
AMOUNT: $1,000-$5,000
DEADLINE(S): DEC 1
FIELD(S): All fields of study

Undergraduate needs-based scholarships for residents of Massachusetts who have worked as golf caddies, in pro shops, or as course superintendents of operations in Massachusetts for three years. Must work at a golf course.

263 awards. Renewable. Contact Bob Donovan at above address.

2745—FRANK H. AND EVA BUCK FOUNDATION (Frank H. Buck Scholarships)

Vacaville CA 95696-5610
707/446-7700
FAX: 707/446-7766
E-mail: febaunt@aol.com
AMOUNT: Tuition, books, and room/board
DEADLINE(S): JAN 1
FIELD(S): All fields of study

Open to unique students in colleges/universities or private high schools who have an overwhelming motivation to succeed in all endeavors. Preference given to residents of Solano, Napa, Yolo, Sacramento, San Joaquin, and Contra Costa Counties in California.

Renewable annually. Contact Gloria J. Brown, Student Liaison, from September 1 to mid-November for an application.

2746—FRANKLIN LINDSAY STUDENT AID FUND

Bank One, Private Client Services
Franklin TX1-1315, Box 901057
Fort Worth TX 76101-2057
512/479-2634
AMOUNT: Up to $5,000 per year ($20,000 max. total)
DEADLINE(S): Varies
FIELD(S): All fields of study

Loans for undergraduate and graduate students who have completed at least one year of college attending Texas colleges or universities.

Send SASE for brochure to Bank One, Private Client Services, at above address. May reapply in subsequent years for up to $9,000 per student provided the recipient maintains at least a C average.

2747—FRED B. and RUTH B. ZIGLER FOUNDATION (Scholarships)

P.O. Box 986
324 Broadway
Jennings LA 70546
337/824-2413
FAX: 337/824-2414
E-mail: ziglerfoundation@centurytel.net
Internet: http://www.zigler foundation.org
AMOUNT: $1,250 per semester
DEADLINE(S): MAR 10
FIELD(S): All areas of study

Scholarships open to graduating seniors at Jefferson Davis Parish (LA) high schools. Awards are tenable at recognized colleges and universities.

10-18 scholarships per year. Renewable for up to 4 years. Write for complete information.

2748—FREDERICA ACADEMY (Tuition Assistance)

200 Hamilton Road
St. Simons Island GA 31522
912/638-9981
FAX: 912/638-1442
E-mail: admission@frederica academy.org
Internet: fredericaacademy.org
AMOUNT: Varies
DEADLINE(S): Varies
FIELD(S): All fields of study

Open to PK-12th grade students at this private day school. Must demonstrate financial need and be qualified for placement in Frederica.

20 awards annually. Renewable. Contact Mrs. Jeris M. Wright, Director of Admissions, for an application.

2749—FRIEDRICH-NAUMANN FOUNDATION (Educational Scholarships)

Wissenschaftliche Dienste and
Begabtenforderung
Alt-Nowawes 67
14482 Potsdam-Babelsberg
GERMANY
+49(0)331-7019-349
FAX: +49(0)331-7019-222
E-mail: fnst@fnst.org
Internet: www.fnst.org
AMOUNT: Varies
DEADLINE(S): MAY 31; NOV 30
FIELD(S): All fields of study

Open to German and foreign students and postgraduates at German universities. Must have exceptional academic ability, an outstanding personality, and liberal political and social activities. Scholarships are offered to undergraduates, postgraduates, and Ph.D. work. Apart from political dialogue, civic education and political consultancy, supporting the development of liberal-minded young academics is one of the central tasks of the Foundation.

See Web site for further requirements and contact Foundation for an application.

2750—FRIENDS SCHOOL HAVERFORD (Community Scholarship Program and Financial Aid)

851 Buck Lane
Haverford PA 19041-1228
610/642-2334
FAX: 610/642-0870
E-mail: fsh@friendshaverford.org
AMOUNT: $500-$9,000
DEADLINE(S): MAR 1
FIELD(S): All fields of K-6 study

Scholarships and other forms of financial aid for students in grades K-6 in this Quaker-based independent school. Scholarship recipients must live within a two-mile radius of the school. All applicants for financial aid must demonstrate need and must be accepted for admission.

Contact school for details.

2751—FRIENDS SCHOOL OF BALTIMORE (Scholarships)

5114 N. Charles Street
Baltimore MD 21210
410/649-3200
FAX: 410/649-3213
E-mail: TJacks@mail.friendsbalt.org
Internet: www.friendsbalt.org

AMOUNT: Varies
DEADLINE(S): Varies
FIELD(S): All fields of study

Open to K-12th grade students at this private Quaker day school. Must demonstrate financial need.

240 awards annually. Contact Tad Jacks for an application.

2752—FRYEBURG ACADEMY (Financial Aid Program)

152 Main Street
Fryeburg ME 04037
207/935-2013 or 877/935-2013
FAX: 207/935-4292
E-mail: admissions@fryeburg academy.org
Internet: www.fryeburgacademy.org

AMOUNT: Varies
DEADLINE(S): None (first come, first served)
FIELD(S): All fields of study

Open to college-prep high school students at this private day/boarding school. Awards go to worthy candidates who demonstrate financial need.

35-40 awards annually. Renewable. Contact Alan D. Whittemore for an application.

2753—FUND FOR EDUCATION AND TRAINING (FEAT Loans)

1830 Connecticut Avenue NW
Washington DC 20009
202/483-2220
FAX: 202/483-1246
E-mail: nisbco@nisbco.org
Internet: http://www.nisbco.org

AMOUNT: $2,500
DEADLINE(S): None
FIELD(S): All fields of study

For male non-registrants of the Selective Service for undergraduate or graduate study, as well as career support. Financial need is NOT a factor.

Renewable. Contact Rachel Zuses at above address for an application.

2754—GABRIEL J. BROWN TRUST (Loan Fund)

112 Avenue E. West
Bismarck ND 58501
701/223-5916

AMOUNT: $1,000-$5,000
DEADLINE(S): JUN 15
FIELD(S): All fields of study

Special low-interest loans (6%) are open to residents of North Dakota who have completed at least two years of undergraduate study at a recognized college/university and have a minimum 2.5 GPA. Must be U.S. citizen and demonstrate financial need.

75 awards annually. Renewable. Contact Trust for an application.

2755—GATES MILLENIUM SCHOLARS PROGRAM (Scholarships for High School Seniors)

FairFAX: VA 22031-4511
877/690-4677
Internet: www.gmsp.org

AMOUNT: Varies
DEADLINE(S): FEB 1
FIELD(S): All fields of study

High school principals, teachers, and counselors may nominate high school seniors who are African-Americans, Native Americans, Hispanic Americans, or Asian Americans planning to enter college. Based on academic performance in math and science, commitment to academic study, involvement in community service and school activities, potential for leadership, and financial need. Must submit transcripts and letters of recommendation. Must be U.S. citizen with a minimum 3.3 GPA.

Application materials available November 1st; scholars will be notified in May. Funded by the Bill and Melinda Gates Foundation, and administered by the United Negro College Fund.

2756—GATES MILLENIUM SCHOLARS PROGRAM (Scholarships for College Students)

FairFAX: VA 22031-4511
877/690-4677
Internet: www.gmsp.org

AMOUNT: Varies
DEADLINE(S): FEB 1
FIELD(S): All fields of study

College presidents, professors, and deans may nominate undergraduates who are African-Americans, Native Americans, Hispanic Americans, or Asian Americans enrolled in college. Based on academic performance in math, science, and education; commitment to academic study; involvement in community service and school activities; potential for leadership; career goals; and financial need. Must submit transcripts and letters of recommendation. Must be U.S. citizen with a minimum 3.3 GPA.

Application materials available November 1st; scholars will be notified in May. Funded by the Bill and Melinda Gates Foundation, and administered by the United Negro College Fund.

2757—GEORGE ABRAHAMIAN FOUNDATION (Scholarships for Rhode Island Armenians)

945 Admiral Street
Providence RI 02904
401/831-2887

AMOUNT: $600-$900
DEADLINE(S): SEP 1
FIELD(S): All areas of study

Open to undergraduate and graduate students who are U.S. citizens of Armenian ancestry and live in Rhode Island, are of good character, have the ability to learn, and can demonstrate financial need. Must be affiliated with an Armenian Church and attend or plan to attend college in Rhode Island. Min. GPA of 3.0 required.

Renewable. Write for complete information.

2758—GEORGE BIRD GRINNELL AMERICAN INDIAN CHILDREN'S FUND (Schulyer M. Meyer, Jr. Scholarship Award)

11602 Montague Court
Potomac MD 20854
301/424-2440
FAX: 301/424-8281

AMOUNT: $1,000/year (max.)
DEADLINE(S): JUN 1
FIELD(S): All fields of study

Opent to Native American students enrolled in undergraduate or graduate programs at two- or four-year institutions. Must be American Indian/Alaska Native (documented with Certified Degree of Indian Blood), be enrolled in college/university, be able to demonstrate commitment to serving community or other tribal nations, and document financial need.

Renewable. Contact Dr. Paula M. Mintzies, President, for an application after January 1.

2759—GEORGE E. ANDREWS TRUST (George E. Andrews Scholarship)

Trust Dept., Blackhawk State Bank
P.O. Box 719
Beloit WI 53512-0179
608/364-8914

AMOUNT: $2,500 or more
DEADLINE(S): FEB 15
FIELD(S): All fields of study

Open to seniors at high schools in the City of Beloit, Town of Beloit, Wisconsin. Awards based on scholastic standing, financial need, moral character, industriousness, and other factors.

To assist and encourage a worthy, needy, and industrious student by defraying the student's expense for the first year of college.

2760—THE GATES CAMBRIDGE TRUST

P.O. Box 252
Cambridge CB2 1TZ
Internet: http://www.gates.scholarships.cam.ac.uk/

AMOUNT: Tuition
DEADLINE(S): MAR 31
FIELD(S): All

For applicants who wish to study at the University of Cambridge, candidates will be expected to have excellent transcripts with high GPA scores showing evidence of sustained academic achievement in study, and a strong performance in GRE scores, together with references able to speak knowledgeably about the candidate's actual academic performance and his or her potential for scholarly growth.

2761—GEORGE GROTEFEND SCHOLARSHIP FUND (Grotefend Scholarship)

1644 Magnolia Avenue
Redding CA 96001
916/225-0227

AMOUNT: $150-$400
DEADLINE(S): APR 20
FIELD(S): All fields of study

Scholarships open to applicants who completed all 4 years of high school in Shasta County California. Awards support all levels of study at recognized colleges and universities.

300 awards per year. Write for complete information.

2762—GEORGE SCHOOL (Grants, Loans, and Anderson Scholarships)

P.O. Box 4000
Newtown PA 18940-0962
215/579-6547
FAX: 215/579-6549
E-mail: admission@georgeschool.org
Internet: http://www.georgeschool.org

AMOUNT: $10,000 (scholarship); $500 (loan); grant varies
DEADLINE(S): MAR 1
FIELD(S): All fields of study

Anderson Scholarship is open to boarding students at this private Quaker high school. Based on academic achievement (minimum B+ GPA), community involvement, and potential for leadership. Essays required. Grants and loans are based on financial need and merit. Preference given to those with strong academic records and those who are either children of Quaker or alumni families.

4 scholarships annually. Contact Barbara McLean for a scholarship application; grant and loan applicants should check off appropriate box on admissions application.

2763—GEORGE W. AND ANNE A. HOOVER SCHOLARSHIP FUND (Student Loans)

2-16 South Market Street
P.O. Box 57
Selinsgrave PA 17870
717/374-4252

AMOUNT: $2,500/year for two-year schools; $5,000/year for four-year schools
DEADLINE(S): None specified
FIELD(S): All fields of study

Student loans to individuals to attend colleges or universities.

Send self-addressed, stamped envelope to above address for details.

2764—GEORGIA BOARD OF REGENTS (Scholarships)

244 Washington Street SW
Atlanta GA 30334
404/656-2272

AMOUNT: $500 for junior college; $750 for 4-year college; $1000 for grad school students
DEADLINE(S): Varies
FIELD(S): All areas of study

Must be legal Georgia resident enrolled or accepted in an institution of the university system of GA. Must be in upper 25% of class (based on high school and SAT scores) and demonstrate financial need.

DO NOT contact the GA Board of Regents above; contact the appropriate school for complete information.

2765—GEORGIA STUDENT FINANCE COMMISSION (HOPE Scholarships)

2082 East Exchange Place
Tucker GA 30084
770/724-9000 (metro Atlanta) or 800/546-HOPE (toll-free in Georgia)
Internet: http://www.gsfc.org/gsfc/apphope.htm

AMOUNT: Varies
DEADLINE(S): Varies (end of spring term)
FIELD(S): All fields of study

The HOPE Scholarship Program (Helping Outstanding Pupils Educationally) is funded by the Georgia Lottery for Education. Program details are subject to change. For use at all Georgia colleges, universities, and technical institutes.

Applicants must complete the Free Application for Federal Student Aid (FAFSA) form. Contact the financial aid office at the public or private institution you plan to attend. High school students should check with counselor for eligibility requirements.

2766—GERBER REWARDS (Scholarship Drawings)

P.O. Box 651
St. Petersburg FL 33731-0651
800/376-BABY
Internet: http://www.gerber.com

AMOUNT: Up to $250,000
DEADLINE(S): JUL; DEC
FIELD(S): All fields of study

Drawing for parents of a child up to 24 months. Purchase at least 16 Gerber food products, remove and save the UPC labels, and receive a game piece with a toll-free number.

Check the Web site or 800 number above for details.

2767—GERONIMO CORPORATION, INC. (William B. Klusty Memorial Scholarship Fund for Native Americans)

206 Zion Road
Salisbury MD 21804
Internet: http://www.geronimo.org/scholarship

AMOUNT: $1,000

DEADLINE(S): Varies (second Friday of the fall quarter)
FIELD(S): All fields of study

Scholarships for Native American students, both undergraduate and graduate. Criteria are previous academic work, community involvement, career goals, leadership ability, financial need, and an explanation as to why the students should receive a scholarship (as explained in a 250-word, typed essay). Submit proof of Native American heritage. Must have 3.5 GPA.

Access Web site or contact organization for application.

2768—GETCOLLEGE.COM, INC. (The Strivers Scholarship)

Vincent Waterhouse, President
725 Buoy Road
North Palm Beach FL 33408
561/848-7402
FAX: 561/848-5047
E-mail: vwaterhouse@getcollege.com
Internet: http://www.getcollege.com/scholarship-strivers.html
AMOUNT: $2,000-$10,000
DEADLINE(S): APR
FIELD(S): All

Available to a high school senior who will be enrolling in a full-time undergraduate course of study year at an accredited two- or four-year college/university in the U.S. Must provide an academic transcript. Must have completed the following courses: Math 3-4 units, English 4 units, Science 2-4 units (preferable with 2 lab courses), Social Studies 3-4 units, and 2-4 units in Foreign Language. Student should have a combined SAT Score of 950 to 1100 points with a GPA of 2.7 to 3.3.

2769—GHIDOTTI FOUNDATION (Scholarships)

Wells Fargo Private Banking Group
P.O. Box 2511
Sacramento CA 95812
916/440-4433
AMOUNT: Not specified
DEADLINE(S): None given
FIELD(S): All areas of study

Open to graduates of public or private high schools located within the boundaries of Nevada County California.

Write for complete information.

2770—GILL ST. BERNARD'S SCHOOL (Financial Aid)

P.O. Box 604
Gladstone NJ 07934
908/234-1611
FAX: 908/719-8865
AMOUNT: Varies
DEADLINE(S): Varies
FIELD(S): All fields of study

A need-based merit scholarship for students in grades 7-12 at this private secondary, college preparatory school in New Jersey.

Renewable.

2771—GLAMOUR MAGAZINE (Top Ten College Women Competition)

Conde Nast Pub.
4 Times Square
New York NY 10036-6593
800/244-GLAM or 212/286-6667
FAX: 212/286-6922
E-mail: ttcw@Glamour.com
AMOUNT: $1,000 + trip to New York City
DEADLINE(S): JAN 31
FIELD(S): All fields of study

Open to any woman who is currently a full-time undergraduate junior at an accredited U.S. college/university. Based on leadership experience, personal involvement in community/campus affairs, and academic excellence. Must submit official college transcript, list of activities, photograph, letter(s) of recommendation, and essay describing meaningful achievements and how they relate to your field of study and future goals. Must be U.S. resident.

Notification by June 1. Contact *Glamour* for an application and specific details.

2772—GLENDALE COMMUNITY FOUNDATION (Scholarships)

P.O. Box 313
Glendale CA 91209-0313
818/241-8040
AMOUNT: Varies
DEADLINE(S): Feb. 15
FIELD(S): All fields of study

Scholarships through this Foundation for needy students who are residents of Glendale, La Canada Flintridge, La Crescenta, Montrose, or Verdugo City, California.

Contact organization for details.

2773—GLENLYON-NORFOLK SCHOOL (Entrance Scholarships)

801 Bank Street
Victoria BC CANADA V85 4A8
250/370-6801
FAX: 250/370-6838
E-mail: gns@islandnet.com
Internet: http://www.islandnet.com~gns/
AMOUNT: $1,000 max.
DEADLINE(S): FEB 1
FIELD(S): All fields of study

For students applying to this university preparatory private school in grades 8-12 with a high academic standing (86%), and a demonstrated interest in co-curricular activities. If not a Canadian student, student authorization is required. Financial need NOT a factor.

8-10 awards annually. Renewable. See Web site or write to above address for more information.

2774—GLORIA FECHT MEMORIAL SCHOLARSHIP FUND (Scholarships)

402 W. Arrow Highway, #10
San Dimas CA 91773
619/562-0304
FAX: 619/562-4116
E-mail: rlmfswingle@home.com
AMOUNT: $2,000-$3,000
DEADLINE(S): MAR 1
FIELD(S): All fields of study

Open to undergraduate and graduate females who are residents of Southern California. Must have a minimum 3.0 GPA, an interest in golf, and demonstrate financial need.

30 awards annually. Renewable. Contact Fund for an application.

2775—GOLDEN KEY NATIONAL HONOR SOCIETY (Graduate Scholar Award)

1189 Ponce de Leon Avenue
Atlanta GA 30306-4624
800/377-2401 or 404/377-2400
E-mail: lgailey@gknhs.gsu.edu
AMOUNT: $10,000
DEADLINE(S): FEB 15
FIELD(S): All fields of study

Open to Golden Key lifetime members in good standing who are undergraduates or recent alumni who will hold a baccalaureate degree by the time they receive scholarship. Must enroll full-time in a post-baccalaureate program of study at an accredited institution of higher education. Based on scholastic achievement, leadership, and service; significant involvement in Golden Key NHS chapter; and demonstrated commitment to campus and community service.

10 awards annually. Contact Laurie Gailey for an application. Notification by May 15.

2776—GOLDIE GIBSON SCHOLARSHIP FUND (Student Loans)

1601 S.E. Harned Drive
Bartlesville OK 74006
918/333-5268
AMOUNT: Varies
DEADLINE(S): Ongoing
FIELD(S): All fields of study

Student loans for residents of Oklahoma.

Renewable. Write to Ruth Andrews, Secretary-Treasurer, for application information.

2777—GOLF COURSE SUPERINTENDENTS ASSOCIATION OF AMERICA (Legacy Awards)

1421 Research Park Drive
Lawrence KS 66049-3859
785/832-3678
FAX: 785/832-3665
E-mail: psmith@gcsaa.org
Internet: http://www.gcsaa.org
AMOUNT: $1,500
DEADLINE(S): APR 15
FIELD(S): All fields of study (except golf course management)

Available to the children and grandchildren of GCSAA members who have been an active member for five or more consecutive years. The student must be studying a field UNRELATED to golf course management. Must be enrolled full-time at an accredited institution of higher learning, or in the case of high school seniors, must be accepted at such institution for the next academic year.

See Web site or contact Pam Smith at GCSAA for an application.

2778—GORE FAMILY MEMORIAL (Foundation Trust)

4747 North Ocean Drive, Suite 204
Ft. Lauderdale FL 33308
954/781-8634
AMOUNT: up to $2,000
DEADLINE(S): multiple
FIELD(S): All

Several awards are available for severely handicapped students with demonstrated financial need. These funds are for educational purposes only and are available to undergraduate students in Broward County, FL

2779—GOUGH SCHOLARSHIP FUND

J. David Gough
Scholarship Coordinator
CMR 443, Box 655
APO, AE 09096
E-mail: dgough@wiesbaden.vistec.net
AMOUNT: $1,000
DEADLINE(S): Continuous
FIELD(S): All

The Gough Family will award two to four $1,000 scholarships each year. These scholarships are non-income based and require transcripts and an essay to be considered. Please request more information via E-mail address. If inquiring by mail, include an SASE. An application fee may be required.

2780—GOVERNMENT OF GIBRALTER (Scholarships)

Dept. of Education and Training
40 Town Range
GIBRALTER
350/45973
AMOUNT: Varies
DEADLINE(S): Varies
FIELD(S): All fields of study

Open to students who are residents in Gibralter ONLY. For study in the United Kingdom, Spain, or America.

Contact Paul Lyon, Education Adviser, for details.

2781—GRACE EDWARDS SCHOLARSHIP FUND (Scholarships)

10 Post Office Square, Suite 1230
Boston MA 02109
Written Inquiry
AMOUNT: Varies
DEADLINE(S): MAR 1
FIELD(S): All fields of study

Scholarships for legal residents of Boston, Massachusetts. Must be under age 25 and demonstrate academic excellence and need.

Renewable for up to six years.

2782—GRAHAM-FANCHER SCHOLARSHIP TRUST

149 Josephine Street, Suite A
Santa Cruz CA 95060-2798
408/423-3640
AMOUNT: Varies
DEADLINE(S): MAY 1
FIELD(S): All fields of study

Open to graduating seniors from high schools in Northern Santa Cruz County, California. School and community activities and financial need are considerations.

10 awards annually. Applications accepted only through school scholarship committee at school attended by applicant.

2783—GRAND LODGE OF ILLINOIS (Illinois Odd Fellow-Rebekah Scholarship Award)

P.O. Box 248
305 North Kickapoo Street
Lincoln IL 62656
217/735-2561
AMOUNT: Varies
DEADLINE(S): DEC 1 (application request); MAR 1 (completed application)
FIELD(S): All fields of study

Illinois residents. Scholarships for undergraduate study. Applicants must use the official Odd Fellow-Rebekah scholarship form, submit official transcript of latest grades, and demonstrate need. U.S. citizenship required.

Write to address above for complete information and application forms.

2784—GRAND LODGE OF MASONS OF WYOMING (Scholarships)

Grand Secretary
P.O. Box 459
Casper WY 82602
Written Inquiry
AMOUNT: Varies
DEADLINE(S): MAY 1
FIELD(S): All fields of study

Available to undergraduate students who are residents of Wyoming. Must submit an original application form; copies are not acceptable.

30 awards annually. Write to above address for an application.

2785—GRAPHIC COMMUNICATIONS INTERNATIONAL UNION (GCIU-A.J. DeAndrade Scholarship Awards Program)

1900 L Street NW
Washington DC 20036-5080
202/462-1400
FAX: 331-9516
AMOUNT: $2,000 (payable $500 per year)
DEADLINE(S): FEB 15
FIELD(S): All areas of study

Open to citizens of the U.S. or Canada who are graduating high school seniors to be graduated in January or June of the current school year and recent high school graduates who, by September 1, will not have completed more than a half-year of college. Must be dependents of Graphic Communications International Union members.

10 awards per year. Write for complete information.

2786—GRAY FOUNDATION (Scholarship Program)

1712 Corby Ave
Santa Rosa CA 95407
707/544-7409

AMOUNT: $2,000
DEADLINE(S): MAR 31
FIELD(S): Any field of study

The Gray Foundation offers scholarships for undergraduate study to Sonoma County high school graduates, or those from Middletown HS in Lake County, or GED certificate receivers of Sonoma County, California. Applicants must complete the FAF form.

Write to the above address for complete information.

2787—GREATER KANAWHA VALLEY FOUNDATION (Scholarships

Susan Hoover,
Scholarship Coordinator
P.O. Box 3041
Charleston WV 25331
304/346-3620
FAX:304/346-3640
Internet: http://www.tgkvf.com

AMOUNT: $1,000
DEADLINE(S): FEB 15
FIELD(S): All

Applicants must be a resident of West Virginia resident and a full-time student. Must demonstrate academic achievement of at least 2.5 GPA, minimum score of 20 on ACT, and demonstrate good moral character. Applications are available on the Web site.

2788—GREATER SPRINGFIELD CHAMBER OF COMMERCE (Women's Partnership Scholarship Fund)

1350 Main Street, 3rd Floor
Springfield MA 01103
413/732-2858

AMOUNT: Varies
DEADLINE(S): APR 15
FIELD(S): All fields of study

Open to women 25 years or older in the greater Springfield area attending any accredited college for an associate or baccalaureate degree.

Contact Chamber of Commerce at above address for an application or the Community Foundation of Western Massachusetts at above phone number for details.

2789—GREENPOINT FOUNDATION (Achievers Scholarship)

1505 Riverview Road
P.O. Box 297
St. Peter MN 56082
507/931-1682
FAX: 507/931-9278;
E-mail: gmiller@csfa.org
Internet: http://www.greenpoint.com

AMOUNT: $2,500
DEADLINE(S): MAR 1
FIELD(S): All

Applicants must have a cumulative 3.0 GPA (on a 4.0 scale) or its equivalent and a minimum combined SAT score of 1000. Applicants must reside in the boroughs of Brooklyn, Queens, Manhattan, the Bronx, or Staten Island, or Westchester, Nassau, or Suffolk Counties.

Employees and dependents of employees of GreenPoint Financial Corp and its subsidiaries are not eligible to participate in this program.

2790—GUIDEPOSTS MAGAZINE (Young Writers' Contest)

16 E. 34th Street
New York NY 10016
212/251-8100
FAX: 212/684-0679

AMOUNT: Varies
DEADLINE(S): DEC 1
FIELD(S): All fields of study

Open to high school juniors and seniors (U.S. and foreign citizens) who write an original 1,200-word personal experience story (in English) in which the writer's faith in God played a role. Stories should be true and written in the first person.

Prizes are not redeemable in cash, not transferable, and must be used within five years after high school graduation. Send a self-addressed, stamped envelope to above address for guidelines.

2791—GUNNERY (Financial Aid)

99 Green Hill Road
Washington CT 06793
860/868-7334
FAX: 860/868-1614
E-mail: admissions@gunnery.org
Internet: http://www.gunnery.org

AMOUNT: Varies
DEADLINE(S): FEB 10
FIELD(S): All fields of study

Open to 9th-12th grade students at this independent college prep day/boarding school. Based on financial need, academic excellence, good citizenship, and athletic and other extracurricular involvement. Must be U.S. citizen.

50 awards annually. Renewable annually upon review of student's record. Contact Admissions Office for an application.

2792—GUSTAVUS ADOLPHUS COLLEGE (Andrew Thorson Scholarships)

Office of Admission
800 West College Avenue
St. Peter MN 56082
507/933-7676 or 800/GUSTAVUS
E-mail: admission@gustavus.edu
Internet: http://www.gustavus.edu/

AMOUNT: Up to $3,000
DEADLINE(S): MAR 1
FIELD(S): All fields of study

Scholarships tenable at Gustavus Adolphus College, St. Peter, Minnesota, for students who come from a farm family or rural area or in a town of fewer that 2,000 people, or who attend a school with a graduating class of fewer than 100 students. Financial need considered.

Contact college for details.

2793—GUSTAVUS ADOLPHUS COLLEGE (Congregational Scholarship Matching Program)

Office of Admission
800 West College Avenue
St. Peter MN 56082
507/933-7676 or 800/GUSTAVUS
E-mail: admission@gustavus.edu
Internet: http://www.gustavus.edu/

AMOUNT: Up to $1,000
DEADLINE(S): MAR 1
FIELD(S): All fields of study

Scholarships tenable at Gustavus Adolphus College, St. Peter, Minnesota, for students whose home church congregation has provided scholarship funding in amounts of up to $1,000. This program will match this at a rate of 1.5 times each scholarship dollar. Congregational scholarships from any denomination will be matched.

Contact college for details.

2794—GUSTAVUS ADOLPHUS COLLEGE (National Merit College-Sponsored Scholarships)

Office of Admission
800 West College Avenue
St. Peter MN 56082
507/933-7676 or 800/GUSTAVUS
E-mail: admission@gustavus.edu
Internet: http://www.gustavus.edu/
AMOUNT: $750-$2,000
DEADLINE(S): None
FIELD(S): All fields of study

Scholarships tenable at Gustavus Adolphus College, St. Peter, Minnesota, for students selected as finalists in the National Merit Scholarship competition and who designate Gustavus as their first-choice college.

Renewable. Amount of award is based on need. Contact college for details.

2795—GUSTAVUS ADOLPHUS COLLEGE (Partners in Scholarship)

Office of Admission
800 West College Avenue
St. Peter MN 56082
507/933-7676 or 800/GUSTAVUS
E-mail: admission@gustavus.edu
Internet: http://www.gustavus.edu/
AMOUNT: $7,500/year
DEADLINE(S): APR 15
FIELD(S): All fields of study

Scholarships tenable at Gustavus Adolphus College, St. Peter, Minnesota, for students who rank at or near the top of their high school graduating class, have composite test scores of at least 32 on the ACT or 1400 on the SAT and intend to pursue a graduate degree after Gustavus.

Renewable yearly if GPA of 3.25 is maintained. Contact college for details.

2796—GUSTAVUS ADOLPHUS COLLEGE (Trustee Scholarships)

Office of Admission
800 West College Avenue
St. Peter MN 56082
507/933-7676 or 800/GUSTAVUS
E-mail: admission@gustavus.edu
Internet: http://www.gustavus.edu/
AMOUNT: $1,000-$5,000/year
DEADLINE(S): APR 15
FIELD(S): All fields of study

Scholarships tenable at Gustavus Adolphus College, St. Peter, Minnesota, for students who have shown academic achievement in high school as measured by the difficulty of courses taken, grades earned, and standardized test scores.

Renewable yearly if GPA of 3.0 is maintained. Contact college for details.

2797—H.G. AND A.G. KEASBEY MEMORIAL FOUNDATION

One Logan Square, Suite 2000
Philadelphia PA 19103-6993
Written Inquiry
AMOUNT: Varies
DEADLINE(S): Varies
FIELD(S): All areas of study

Scholarships to individuals primarily for study in the United Kingdom.

Contact Geraldine J. O'Neill, Executive Secretary, at above address for application guidelines.

2798—HAGGAR CLOTHING COMPANY (Haggar Foundation Scholarship Program)

P.O. Box 311370
Denton TX 76203-1370
940/565-2302
FAX: 940/565-2738
E-mail: jonnie@dsa.admin.unt.edu
AMOUNT: $4,000/year
DEADLINE(S): APR 30
FIELD(S): All fields of study

Open to immediate relatives of employees of the Haggar Clothing Company. Applicants must be pursuing undergraduate or graduate study in the U.S.

Renewable up to 4 years. Contact Haggar for an application.

2799—HARNESS HORSEMEN INTERNATIONAL FOUNDATION (J. L. Hauck Memorial Scholarship Fund)

14 Main Street
Robbinsville NJ 08691
609/259-3717
AMOUNT: $4,000
DEADLINE(S): JUN 1
FIELD(S): All fields of study

Open to sons and daughters of Harness Horseman International Association members. Supports undergraduate study at any recognized college or university.

Renewable. Contact Foundation for an application.

2800—HARNESS TRACKS OF AMERICA (Scholarships)

4640 E. Sunrise, Suite 200
Tucson AZ 85718
520/529-2525; FAX: 520/529-3235
AMOUNT: $5,000
DEADLINE(S): JUN 15
FIELD(S): All fields of study

Open ONLY to children of licensed harness racing drivers, trainers, breeders, or caretakers (including retired or deceased) and young people actively engaged in harness racing. For study beyond the high school level. Based on academic merit, financial need, and harness racing involvement.

6 awards annually. Contact Harness Tracks for an application.

2801—HARRY E. AND FLORENCE W. SNAYBERGER MEMORIAL FOUNDATION (Grant Award)

Keystone Financial Bank N.A.
Trust Dept., Center and Norwegian
Pottsville PA 17901-7150
570/622-4200
AMOUNT: Varies
DEADLINE(S): FEB (last business day)
FIELD(S): All fields of study

Open to residents of Schuylkill County, PA, who are pursuing undergraduate or graduate study. Based on college expense need.

Contact trust clerk Carolyn Bernatonis for an application.

2802—HARVARD COLLEGE-OFFICE OF ADMISSIONS AND FINANCIAL AID (Scholarships, Grants, Loans, and Work-Study Programs)

3rd Floor, Byerly Hall
8 Garden Street
Cambridge MA 02138
617/495-1581
FAX: 617/496-0256
AMOUNT: Varies
DEADLINE(S): None
FIELD(S): All fields of study

Open to students accepted for admission to Harvard College. Many factors, including need, are considered.

Contact Amy C. Morse for an application.

2803—HARVARD TRAVELLERS CLUB

P.O. Box H
Canton MA 02021
781/821-0400
FAX: 781-828-4254
AMOUNT: $500-$1,000
DEADLINE(S): MAR 31

FIELD(S): All

Several small grants are awarded each year to students whose study involves travel and exploration. The travel must be closely related to the subject being studied. Students working on advanced degrees are encouraged to apply.

2804—HARVARD UNIVERSITY-NIEMAN FOUNDATION (Fellowships for Journalists)

Walter Lippmann House
One Francis Avenue
Cambridge MA 02138
617/495-2237; FAX: 617/495-8976
E-mail: nieman@harvard.edu
Internet: http://www.Nieman.harvard.edu/nieman.html

AMOUNT: $25,000 stipend + tuition
DEADLINE(S): JAN 31 (American journalists); MAR 1 (foreign journalists)
FIELD(S): All fields of study

Must be full-time staff or freelance journalist working for the news or editorial dept. of newspaper, news service, radio, TV, or magazine of broad public interest and must have at least 3 years of professional experience in the media and must be fluent in English.

Consists of an academic year of non-credit study. Approximately 24 fellowships awarded annually. Fellows design their own course of study. Write for complete information.

2805—HATTIE M. STRONG FOUNDATION (No-interest Loans)

1620 Eye Street NW, Room 700
Washington DC 20006
202/331-1619
FAX: 202/466-2894

AMOUNT: Up to $3,000
DEADLINE(S): MAR 31 (Applications available JAN 1)
FIELD(S): All fields of study

Open to U.S. undergraduate and graduate students in their last year of study in the U.S. or abroad. Loans are made solely on the basis of individual merit. There is no interest and no collateral requirement. U.S. citizen or permanent resident. Repayment terms are based upon monthly income after graduation and arranged individually.

Financial need is a consideration. Approximately 240 awards per year. For complete information send SASE and include personal history, school attended, subject studied, date expected to complete studies, and amount of funds needed.

2806—HAUSS-HELMS FOUNDATION, INC. (Grants and Scholarships)

P.O. Box 25
Wapakoneta OH 45895
419/738-4911
FAX: 419/738-3403

AMOUNT: Varies
DEADLINE(S): APR 15
FIELD(S): All fields of study

Open to graduating seniors who are residents of Auglaize or Allen County, Ohio, and are recommended by their high school principal, responsible faculty member, or guidance counselor. Must be full-time student in upper 50% of high school graduating class, maintain a minimum 2.0 GPA during grant academic year, and be a U.S. citizen.

195 awards annually. Renewable with reapplication. Send a self-addressed, stamped envelope to above address for an application.

2807—HAVENS FOUNDATION, INC.

25132 Oakhurst, Suite 210
Spring TX 77386
Written Inquiry

AMOUNT: Varies
DEADLINE(S): Ongoing
FIELD(S): All fields of study

Undergraduate scholarhips primarily for residents of Texas.

Write to Joe Havens, President, at above location for detail.

2808—HEAVENLY MOUNTAIN IDEAL GIRLS' SCHOOL (Scholarship Program)

3555 Heavenly Mountain Drive, Suite 3
Boone NC 28607
828/268-1424
FAX: 828/264-0727
E-mail: IGS@heavenly-mountain.com
Internet: http://www.ideal-girlsschools.org

AMOUNT: $5,750 (average)
DEADLINE(S): AUG 1
FIELD(S): All fields of study

Open to female 6th-12th grade students at this private day/boarding school. Must demonstrate financial need and be U.S. citizen/permanent resident. Satisfactory completion of previous grade and recommendation of previous school required.

4-5 awards annually. Renewable. Contact Susan Fox for an application.

2809—HEBREW IMMIGRANT SOCIETY (HIAS Scholarship Program)

333 Seventh Avenue
New York NY 10001-5004
212/613-1358
FAX: 212/629-0921
Internet: http://www.hias.org

AMOUNT: $1,500
DEADLINE(S): MAR 15
FIELD(S): All fields of study

Open to refugees and asylees who were assisted by HIAS to come to the U.S. For high school seniors planning to pursue postsecondary education or students already enrolled in undergraduate or graduate study who will continue the following year. Must provide transcripts for one full year (two semesters) of study at any combination of accredited U.S. schools, a personal essay, and demonstrate financial need and Jewish communal involvement.

100+ awards annually. Not renewable. See Web site or send a self-addressed, stamped, business-sized envelope to HIAS Scholarship Department for an application.

2810—HEBRON ACADEMY (Scholarships)

P.O. Box 309
Hebron ME 04238
207/966-2100
FAX: 207/966-1111
E-mail: admissions@hebronacademy.org

AMOUNT: $500 to $14,000
DEADLINE(S): None
FIELD(S): All fields of secondary school study

Scholarships for students admitted to Hebron Academy in Hebron, Maine, a private college prep. secondary school.

Send SASE for details. Financial need must be demonstrated.

2811—HELLENIC TIMES (Scholarship Fund)

823 Eleventh Avenue, 5th Floor
New York NY 10019-3535
212/986-6881
Fax: 212/977-3662
E-mail: htsfund@aol.com
Internet: http://www.htsfund.org

AMOUNT: $1,000-$10,000
DEADLINE(S): FEB 15
FIELD(S): All

Applicants must be of Greek descent and between the ages of 17 and 30. Students receiving a full scholarship from any other source, or a partial scholarship exceeding 50% of their annual tuition, are ineligible. Scholarships will be awarded on the basis of necessity and merit.

2812—HELPING HANDS FOUNDATION (Book Scholarship Program)

P.O. Box 720379
Atlanta GA 30358
Written Inquiries
AMOUNT: Varies
DEADLINE(S): JUL 15 for Fall semester; DEC 15 for spring
FIELD(S): All

The Helping Hands stipend is in one-time amounts of $100-$1000. Awards may be used in any year but are nonrenewable. Awards are paid in one installment and mailed to the student's home address at least two weeks prior to the upcoming semester. Checks are made payable to recipient.

2813—HERBERT HOOVER PRESIDENTIAL LIBRARY ASSOCIATION (Uncommon Student Award)

P.O. Box 696
West Branch IA 52245
319/643-5327
FAX: 319/643-2391
E-mail: scholarship@hooverassoc.org
Internet: http://www.hoover association.org
AMOUNT: $500; $5,000
DEADLINE(S): MAR 31
FIELD(S): All fields of study

For Iowa high school or home-schooled program juniors to use for their undergraduate college studies. Grades, test scores and financial need are NOT evaluated. Applicants propose a project in March. Notifications are made by the end of April. Approximately 15 uncommon students are chose each year. In October of their senior year, they make presentations about their projects.

15 $750 awards and 3 students given $5,000 awards annually, payable to any two-year or four-year college/university in the U.S. Not renewable. Contact Patricia Hand at above address for an application.

2814—HERBERT LEHMAN EDUCATION FUND (Scholarships)

99 Hudson Street, Suite 1600
New York NY 10013-2897
Written Inquiry
AMOUNT: $2,000
DEADLINE(S): APR 30
FIELD(S): All fields of study

Open to African-American high school graduates planning to begin undergraduate study at a four-year institution having a below-average enrollment of African-Americans. Must be U.S. citizen and have outstanding potential, as evidenced by high school academic records, test scores, personal essays, community/school involvement, and educational goals. Must demonstrate financial need.

25-40 awards annually. Renewable. Requests for application forms must be in writing and requested by the applicant-include education to date, educational and career goals, planned college, and why assistance is being requested. Applications available November 30-February 15.

2815—HERITAGE ACADEMY (Scholarships)

594 Converse Street
Longmeadow MA 01106
413/567-1517
FAX: 413/567-2167
E-mail: haoffice@javanet.com
Internet: http://www.heritage academy.org
AMOUNT: Up to $4,000/year
DEADLINE(S): APR 1
FIELD(S): All fields of study

Heritage Academy is a Hebrew day school for grades K-8. Scholarships are based on financial need.

U.S. citizenship or legal residency required.

2816—HERMAN O. WEST FOUNDATION (Scholarships)

101 Gordon Drive
Lionville PA 19341-0645
610/594-2945
AMOUNT: $2,500/year (max.)
DEADLINE(S): FEB 28
FIELD(S): All fields of study

Open to high school seniors entering college in the fall of the same year who are dependents of full-time employees of West Pharmaceutical Services, Inc. Based on academic achievement, extracurricular activities, and/or community service.

7 awards annually. Renewable. Contact Foundation for an application.

2817—HISPANIC ALLIANCE FOR CAREER ENHANCEMENT (National Scholarship Program)

Anabel Ruiz-Morales
Student Development Coordinator
14 East Jackson Avenue, Suite 1310
Chicago IL 60604
312/435-0498 ext. 21
FAX: 312/435-1494
E-mail: amorales@hace-usa.org
Internet: http://www.hace-usa.org
AMOUNT: $500-$1,000
DEADLINE(S): AUG 1
FIELD(S): All

Undergraduates must carry at least 12 hours of college course work for each term. Graduate students must carry at least 6 credit hours each term. Applicants must have completed a minimum of 12 credit hours of college coursework from an accredited college or university prior to submitting the application. Applicants must have a GPA of at least 2.50/4.0 or 3.50/5.0 scale.

2818—HISPANIC SCHOLARSHIP FUND (Scholarships)

One Sansome Street, Suite 1000
San Francisco CA 94104
415/445-9930 or
877-HSF-INFO ext. 33
FAX: 415/445-9942
E-mail: info@hsf.net
Internet: http://www.hsf.net
AMOUNT: $500-$2,500
DEADLINE(S): OCT 15
FIELD(S): All fields of study

HSF scholarships are available to students who are of Hispanic background (at least half), are U.S. citizens/permanent residents, have earned at least 15 undergraduate credits from an accredited college, have a minimum GPA of 2.5, and are enrolled in and attending college full-time (undergraduates min. 12 credits/term; graduate students min. 6 credits/term).

See Web site or send business-sized, self-addressed stamped envelope to HSF for an application.

2819—THE HITACHI FOUNDATION (The Yoshiyama Award for Exemplary Service to the Community)

P.O. Box 19247
Washington, DC 20036
202/457-0588
AMOUNT: Varies
DEADLINE(S): APR 1
FIELD(S): All

Provides a $5,000 gift to be dispensed over two years. Recipients may use the award at their discretion. This Award recognizes exemplary service and community involvement rather than academic achievement. Grade point or SAT scores are not considered.

2820—HOLY CROSS HIGH SCHOOL (Scholarships/Financial Aid)

587 Oronoke Road
Waterbury CT 06708
203/757-9248
FAX: 203/757-3423
E-mail: info@holycrosshs-ct.com

AMOUNT: Up to $2,500
DEADLINE(S): Varies
FIELD(S): All fields of study

A private, Catholic high school in Connecticut. The two students who score the highest on the Entrance Exam receive renewable $2,500 scholarships. Financial aid grants available based strictly on need. Students can also work part-time. Eight-graders can apply for local sources of financial aid.

Contact school for details.

2821—HOPI PRIVATE HIGH SCHOOL SCHOLARSHIP

P.O. Box 123
Kykotsmovi AZ 86039-0123
520/734-2441 ext. 520
800/762-9630
FAX: 520/734-2435

AMOUNT: Varies
DEADLINE(S): JUL 31
FIELD(S): All fields of study

For enrolled members of the Hopi Tribe to encourage achievement of a high level of academic excellence in accredited private high schools. Entering freshmen must have a GPA of 3.5; continuing students must have GPA of 3.2.

Two awards. Academic merit is primary consideration.

2822—HOPI SCHOLARSHIP

P.O. Box 123
Kykotsmovi AZ 8603-0123
520/734-2441 ext. 520
800/762-9630
FAX: 520/734-2435

AMOUNT: Varies
DEADLINE(S): JUL 31
FIELD(S): All fields of study

For enrolled members of the Hopi Tribe pursuing associate, baccalaureate, graduate, or post-graduate degrees. Minimum 3.0 GPA (3.2 for graduates). Entering freshmen must be in the top 10% of graduating class or score min. of 21 on ACT or 930 on SAT; undergrads must have and maintain 3.0 GPA.

Academic merit is primary consideration.

2823—HOPI TRIBE (Peabody Scholarship)

P.O. Box 123
Kykotsmovi AZ 86039-0123

AMOUNT: $50-$1,000
DEADLINE(S): APR 30; JUL 31; NOV 30
FIELD(S): All

Winning applicant will be a Native American or Eskimo who is enrolled at a two- or four-year institution. Applicants must have a minimum GPA of 3.0. Available to U.S. citizens only.

2824—HORACE MANN COMPANIES (Scholarship Program)

1 Horace Mann Plaza
Springfield IL 62715-0001
217/789-2500
Internet: http://www.horacemann.com

AMOUNT: $20,000 (1); $4,000 (5); $1,000 (10)
DEADLINE(S): FEB 28
FIELD(S): All fields of study

Open to college-bound high school seniors whose parent or legal guardian is a U.S. public education employee. Must have a minimum 3.0 GPA and score at least 23 on the ACT or 1,100 on the SAT. Essay, transcript, list of activities/honors, and two letters of recommendation are required. Financial need NOT a factor. Scholarships are awarded directly to the college/university of each recipient's choice for tuition, fees, and other educational expenses.

16 awards annually. Renewable each year of college provided a GPA of at least 2.0 is maintained. See Web site or contact your local Horace Mann representative for an application.

2825—HORACE MANN SCHOOL (Scholarships)

231 W. 246th Street
Riverdale NY 10471
718/432-4100
FAX: 718/432-3610
E-mail: admission@horacemann.org
Internet: http://www.horacemann.org

AMOUNT: Varies
DEADLINE(S): JAN 15 for new applicants, FEB 1 for returning recipients
FIELD(S): All fields of study

Scholarships available to attend this independent, coeducational school which includes nursery through twelfth grade. Students must qualify by submitting a form from School and Student Service for Financial Aid (SSS) and other documentation indicating financial need.

315 annual awards. Renewable, but must reapply. Contact school for details.

2826—HORACE SMITH FUND (Loans)

1441 Main Street
Springfield MA 01102
413/739-4222

AMOUNT: Varies
DEADLINE(S): JUN 15 (college students); JUL 1 (high school seniors)
FIELD(S): All fields of study

Open to graduates of secondary schools in Hampden County, MA, who are pursuing full-time undergraduate study. Must demonstrate financial need. If repayment is made within one year after student completes formal education, no interest is charged.

Renewable. Contact the Executive Secretary for an application after April 1.

2827—HORACE SMITH FUND (Walter S. Barr Scholarships)

1441 Main Street
Springfield MA 01102
413/739-4222

AMOUNT: Varies
DEADLINE(S): DEC 31
FIELD(S): All fields of study

Open to high school seniors who are class members of Hampden County, MA, private or public secondary schools. Based on school records, college entrance examinations, general attainments, and financial need.

Renewable. Contact the Executive Secretary for an application after September 1.

2828—HORATIO ALGER ASSOCIATION (Scholarships)

99 Canal Center Plaza
Alexandria VA 22314
703/684-9444
FAX: 703/684-9445
E-mail: programs@horatioalger.com
Internet: http://www.horatioalger.com

AMOUNT: Tuition, room and board, textbooks
DEADLINE(S): Varies
FIELD(S): All fields of study involving service to others

A scholarship program for college-bound high school seniors combined with leadership and civic education training through participation in the National Scholars Conference. Must be committed to use their college degrees in service to others.

The organization focuses on young people who have faced and triumphed over exceptional hardships. Send SASE to above address for details. Visit Web site for more information on scholarships.

2829—HORIZONS FOUNDATION (George Choy Memorial/Gay Asian Pacific Alliance Scholarships)

870 Market Street, Suite 728
San Francisco CA 94102
415/398-2333
FAX: 415/398-4733
E-mail: info@horizonsfoundation.org
Internet: http://www.horizons foundation.org
AMOUNT: $500/year (max.)
DEADLINE(S): JUN 30
FIELD(S): All fields of study

Open to lesbian/gay/bisexual/transgender Asian/Pacific Islanders entering their first or second year at an accredited postsecondary institution. Must live in one of the nine Bay Area counties: Alameda, Contra Costa, Marin, San Francisco, San Mateo, Santa Clara, Napa, Sonoma, and Solano. Must have a minimum 2.5 GPA and submit transcript, letter of recommendation, and essay on how to contribute to understanding LGBT community. Awards granted directly to recipients.

Contact Sergio Sandoval for an application.

2830—HORIZONS FOUNDATION (Joseph Towner Scholarship Fund for Gay and Lesbian Families)

870 Market Street, Suite 728
San Francisco CA 94102
415/398-2333
FAX: 415/398-4733
E-mail: info@horizonsfoundation.org
Internet: http://www.horizons foundation.org
AMOUNT: $1,000/year (max.)
DEADLINE(S): JUN 30
FIELD(S): All fields of study

Open to postsecondary students who have at least one gay or lesbian parent residing in one of the nine Bay Area counties: Alameda, Contra Costa, Marin, San Francisco, San Mateo, Santa Clara, Napa, Sonoma, and Solano. Must be 25 years of age or younger, be enrolled full-time in an accredited postsecondary institution, and have a minimum 2.5 GPA (or GED). Must submit transcripts and essay on goals. Financial need NOT a factor. Awards granted directly to recipients.

Contact Sergio Sandoval for an application.

2831—HOUSTON CEO FOUNDATION (Scholarships)

952 Echo Lane, Suite 350
Houston TX 77024
713/722-8555
FAX: 713/722-7442
Internet: http://www.hern.org/ceo
AMOUNT: $1,450 max.
DEADLINE(S): None
FIELD(S): All fields of study

For residents of Harris County, Texas to attend K-8 private schools. Must demonstrate financial need.

500 awards annually. Contact Stacy Bandfield, Administrator, for an application.

2832—HOWARD AND MAMIE NICHOLS SCHOLARSHIP TRUST (Scholarships)

Wells Fargo Bank, Trust Dept.
5262 N. Blackstone
Fresno CA 93710
Written Inquiries only
AMOUNT: Varies
DEADLINE(S): FEB 28
FIELD(S): All fields of study

Open to graduates of Kern County, California high schools for full-time undergraduate or graduate study at a postsecondary institution. Must demonstrate financial need and have a 2.0 or better GPA.

Approximately 100 awards per year. Renewable with reapplication. Write for complete information.

2833—HOYT FOUNDATION (May Emma Hoyt Scholarship)

P.O. Box 788
New Castle PA 16103
724/652-5511
FAX: 724/654-8413
AMOUNT: Varies
DEADLINE(S): JUN 15
FIELD(S): All fields of study

Open to residents of Lawrence County, PA for undergraduate study. There are no restrictions on the choice of a college.

Renewable. $150,000 given annually, number of awards varies. Contact Jaimie L. Kopp, Secretary, at above address for an application.

2834—HUALAPAI TRIBAL COUNCIL (Scholarship Program)

P.O. Box 179
Peach Springs AZ 86434
520/769-2200
FAX: 520/769-2250
AMOUNT: $2,500/semester (max.)
DEADLINE(S): JUL 1; NOV 1; APR 1
FIELD(S): All fields of study

Open only to American Indians who are full-time undergraduate or graduate students maintaining passing grades. Priority given to members of the Hualapai Tribe. Must be U.S. citizen.

Apply four weeks before each semester. Contact Sheri K. Yellowhawk for an application.

2835—HUMANITARIAN TRUST (Grants)

36-38 Westbourne Grove
London W2 5SH ENGLAND UK
Written Inquiry
AMOUNT: 200 pounds sterling
DEADLINE(S): None
FIELD(S): All fields of study (except arts)

Grants for undergraduate, graduate, and postgraduate students to take courses in the UK.

15 awards annually. Not renewable. Contact Mrs. M. Meyers, Secretary, for an application.

2836—HUMBOLDT AREA FOUNDATION (Scholarships)

P.O. Box 99
Bayside CA 95524
707/442-2993
FAX: 707/442/3811
E-mail: hafound@northcoast.com
Internet: http://www.northcoast. com/~hafound
AMOUNT: Varies
DEADLINE(S): Varies
FIELD(S): All fields of study

Scholarships through this Foundation for needy students who are residents of Humboldt County, California.

Contact organization for details.

2837—HYMAN BRAND HEBREW ACADEMY (Scholarships)

5801 W. 115th Street
Overland Park KS 66211
913/327-8154
FAX: 913/327-8180
E-mail: info@hbha.edu

Internet: http://www.hbha.edu
AMOUNT: $1,000-$20,000
DEADLINE(S): MAR 17; MAY 17
FIELD(S): All fields of study

Open to K-12 students at this Jewish day school. Must demonstrate financial need.

95-100 awards annually. Renewable. Contact Nola Kroner at 913/327-8153, for an application.

2838—IDAHO STATE BOARD OF EDUCATION (Idaho Governor's Challenge Scholarship)

P.O. Box 83720
Boise ID 83720-0037
208/334-2270
AMOUNT: $3,000/year
DEADLINE(S): DEC 15
FIELD(S): All fields of study (50% academic, 50% prof/tech)

Open to Idaho residents who are current graduating seniors of an Idaho high school. Must be U.S. citizen and plan to enroll as a full-time student in an academic or professional-technical program at an Idaho college/university. Must have minimum 2.8 GPA and have a demonstrated commitment to public service. Academic applicants must take the ACT or SAT test.

Renewable up to 4 years. Contact Caryl Smith at the State Board of Education or your high school counselor for an application.

2839—IDAHO STATE BOARD OF EDUCATION (Idaho Minority and "At-Risk" Student Scholarship)

P.O. Box 83720
Boise ID 83720-0037
208/334-2270
AMOUNT: $3,000/year
DEADLINE(S): Varies
FIELD(S): All fields of study

Open to Idaho residents who have graduated from an Idaho high school and are U.S. citizens. Must meet 3 of the following 5 criteria: 1) be first-generation college student, 2) be disabled, 3) be a migrant farmworker or dependent, 4) have substandard financial need, 5) be a member of an ethnic minority historically under-represented in higher education. Recipients must be, or plan to be, full-time undergraduate students of BSU, ISU, LCSC, UI, NIC, CSI, EITC, or ACI.

Renewable up to 4 years. Contact your high school counselor or the financial aid office of the college/university you plan to attend for an application and deadlines.

2840—IDAHO STATE BOARD OF EDUCATION (LEAP Leveraging Educational Assistance State Partnership Program)

P.O. Box 83720
Boise ID 83720-0037
208/334-2270
AMOUNT: $5,000/year (max.)
DEADLINE(S): Varies
FIELD(S): All fields of study

Open to part-time and full-time undergraduate and graduate students attending a public or private college/university within the state of Idaho, regardless of their state of residence. Must demonstrate financial need.

Renewable. Contact the financial aid office of the Idaho college/university you plan to attend for an application and deadlines.

2841—IDAHO STATE BOARD OF EDUCATION (State of Idaho Scholarship Program)

P.O. Box 83720
Boise ID 83720-0037
208/334-2270
AMOUNT: $2,750/year
DEADLINE(S): DEC 15
FIELD(S): All fields of study (75% academic; 25% prof/tech)

Open to Idaho residents who are current graduating seniors from an Idaho high school. Must be U.S. citizen and plan to enroll as a full-time student in an academic or professional-technical program at an Idaho college/university. Academic applicants must be in top 10% of graduating class with minimum 3.5 GPA and minimum 28 ACT score. Professional-technical applicants must have minimum 2.8 GPA and must take COMPASS test.

20 new awards annually. Renewable up to 4 years. Contact Caryl Smith at the State Board of Education or your high school counselor for an application.

2842—IDAHO STATE BOARD OF EDUCATION (Tschudy Family Scholarship)

P.O. Box 83720
Boise ID 83720-0037
208/334-2270
AMOUNT: $2,000/year
DEADLINE(S): DEC 15
FIELD(S): All fields of study

Open to Idaho residents who are current graduating seniors from Emmett High School or have graduated from Emmett High School within seven years. Must be U.S. citizen and planning to enroll as a full-time student (at least 14 credit hours) at BSU, ISU, LCSCC, or UI. Based on academic merit and financial need.

Renewable up to 5 years. Contact Caryl Smith at the State Board of Education or your high school counselor for an application.

2843—IFDA EDUCATIONAL FOUNDATION (Charles E. Mayo Scholarship)

Ria Oliva, Executive Director
12133 Pawnee Drive
Gaithersburg MD 20878
AMOUNT: $1,000
DEADLINE(S): OCT 1
FIELD(S): All

Scholarship applicant does not need to be an IFDA student member. Must be enrolled as a full-time student. Include: a certified transcript of course work that verifies full-time status with your GPA, a 200- to 300-word essay explaining your future plans and goals, why you believe you are deserving of this scholarship award, and a letter of recommendation from a professor or instructor on official school stationery.

2844—IFDA EDUCATIONAL FOUNDATION (Vercille Voss Scholarship)

Ria Oliva, Executive Director
12133 Pawnee Drive
Gaithersburg MD 20878
AMOUNT: $1,500
DEADLINE(S): OCT 1
FIELD(S): All

Applicant does not need to be a member of IFDA. Must be enrolled full time and include transcript, essay, and letter of recommendation with application.

2845—ILLINOIS AMVETS (Scholarships)

2200 South Sixth Street
Springfield IL 62703-3496
217/528-4713
FAX: 217/528-9896
E-mail: amvets@warpnet.net
Internet: http://www.amvets.com
AMOUNT: $500-$1,000
DEADLINE(S): MAR 1
FIELD(S): All fields of study

Various scholarships for Illinois residents who are unmarried high school seniors and are children of a veteran. Must have taken the A.C.T. at time of application and must demonstrate financial need.

40 awards annually. Renewable. See Web site or contact Len Baumgartner, Executive Director, at above address for more information.

2846—ILLINOIS DEPARTMENT OF THE AMERICAN LEGION (Scholarships)

P.O. Box 2910
Bloomington IL 61702-2910
309/663-0361
AMOUNT: $1,000
DEADLINE(S): MAR 15
FIELD(S): All fields of study

Open to high school seniors who are children of Illinois American Legion members. Tenable at recognized undergraduate colleges, universities, and vocational or nursing schools. Academic achievement and financial need are considered. Must be U.S. citizen.

20 awards annually. Contact IL Dept. of the American Legion for an application.

2847—ILLINOIS DEPARTMENT OF THE AMERICAN LEGION (Boy Scout Scholarships)

P.O. Box 2910
Bloomington IL 61702-2910
309/663-0361
AMOUNT: $1,000 and four $200 runner-up awards
DEADLINE(S): APR 15
FIELD(S): All fields of study

Scholarships for high school seniors who are Boy Scouts or Explorer Scouts and are Illinois residents. Must write a 500-word essay on Legion's Americanism and Boy Scout programs. U.S. citizenship required. Academic achievement and financial need considered.

Contact local Boy Scout Office or Legion Boy Scout Chairman at the above address for complete application information.

2848—ILLINOIS DEPARTMENT OF THE AMERICAN LEGION (Essay Contest)

P.O. Box 2910
Bloomington IL 61702-2910
309/663-0361
AMOUNT: $50 to $75
DEADLINE(S): FEB 12
FIELD(S): All fields of study

Scholarship awards for high school students, grades 9-12, who are winners in the American Legion's Americanism Essay Contest for Illinois residents. Must write a 500-word essay on a selected topic.

Contact local American Legion Post or Legion Headquarters, Bloomington, IL 61702, for details.

2849—ILLINOIS DEPARTMENT OF THE AMERICAN LEGION (Oratorical Contest)

P.O. Box 2910
Bloomington IL 61702-2910
309/663-0361
AMOUNT: Prizes range from $1,600 to $75
DEADLINE(S): JAN (Contest begins)
FIELD(S): All fields of study

Scholarships for high school students, grades 9-12, who are state and regional winners in the American Legion's speech contests for Illinois residents. Winners can go on to national level.

Contact local American Legion Post or Headquarters listed above for details.

2850—ILLINOIS STUDENT ASSISTANCE COMMISSION (Grants for Descendents of Police, Fire, or Correctional Officers)

1755 Lake Cook Road
Deerfield IL 60015-5209
800/899-ISAC
Internet: http://www.isac1.org
AMOUNT: Tuition and fees
DEADLINE(S): None
FIELD(S): All fields of study

Grants Illinois post-secondary students who are descendants of police, fire, and correctional personnel killed or disabled in the line of duty.

Thirty annual awards. Apply at end of academic year. Illinois residency and U.S. citizenship required. Access Web site or write for complete information.

2851—ILLINOIS STUDENT ASSISTANCE COMMISSION (Illinois Incentive for Access)

1755 Lake Cook Road
Deerfield IL 60015-5209
800/899-ISAC
Internet: http://www.isac1.org
AMOUNT: Up to $500
DEADLINE(S): JUN
FIELD(S): All fields of study

This program provides eligible Illinois first-time freshmen a one-time grant for use at approved Illinois institutions. Applicants must fill out FAFSA.

19,000 annual awards. Illinois residency and U.S. citizenship required. Write for complete information.

2852—ILLINOIS STUDENT ASSISTANCE COMMISSION (Illinois National Guard Grant)

1755 Lake Cook Road
Deerfield IL 60015-5209
800/899-ISAC
Internet: http://www.isac1.org
AMOUNT: Tuition and fees-average $1,350
DEADLINE(S): SEP 15
FIELD(S): All fields of study

Grants for qualified personnel of the Illinois National Guard attending public universities and community colleges.

2,500 annual awards. Illinois residency and U.S. citizenship required. Access Web site or write for complete information.

2853—ILLINOIS STUDENT ASSISTANCE COMMISSION (Illinois Veterans' Grant)

1755 Lake Cook Road
Deerfield IL 60015-5209
800/899-ISAC
Internet: http://www.isac1.org
AMOUNT: Tuition and fees—average $1,350
DEADLINE(S): Varies
FIELD(S): All fields of study

Grants for veterans of the U.S. Armed Forces attending public universities and community colleges.

150,000 annual awards. Illinois residency and U.S. citizenship required. Apply three months after end of term. Write for complete information.

2854—ILLINOIS STUDENT ASSISTANCE COMMISSION (Merit Recognition Scholarship)

1755 Lake Cook Road
Deerfield IL 60015-5209
800/899-ISAC
Internet: http://www.isac1.org
AMOUNT: $1,000
DEADLINE(S): JUN 15
FIELD(S): All fields of study

Scholarships to recognize Illinois high school seniors who are in the top 2.5% of their high school class and who will attend approved Illinois institutions or a U.S. service academy. Illinois residency and U.S. citizenship required.

Access Web site or write for complete information.

2855—ILLINOIS STUDENT ASSISTANCE COMMISSION (Monetary Award Program)

1755 Lake Cook Road
Deerfield IL 60015-5209
800/899-ISAC
Internet: http://www.isac1.org
AMOUNT: Tuition and fees up to $4,320
DEADLINE(S): JUN 1 (continuing students); OCT 1 (new students)

FIELD(S): All fields of study

This program is Illinois' primary need-based grant program. Awards are provided for tuition and fees for eligible students at approved Illinois institutions. Applicants must fill out FAFSA.

130,000 annual awards. Illinois residency and U.S. citizenship required. Write for complete information.

2856—IMATION COMPUTER ARTS (Scholarship)

1 Imation Place
Oakdale MN 55128-3414
FAX: 651/704-3892
E-mail: cas@imation.com
AMOUNT: $1,000
DEADLINE(S): Varies
FIELD(S): All

Open to United State high school students. Need not be enrolled in art classes. Must be nominated by their school through a competition.

2857—INDEPENDENCE FEDERAL SAVINGS BANK (Federal Family Education Loans)

1900 L Street NW; Suite 700
Washington DC 20036-5001
800/733-0473 or 202/626-0473
FAX: 202/775-4533
E-mail: ifsb@aol.com
Internet: http://www.ifsb.com
AMOUNT: up to $8,500
DEADLINE(S): None
FIELD(S): All fields of study

Loans are open to U.S. citizens or legal residents who are undergraduate or graduate students accepted to or enrolled in a school approved by the U.S. Department of Education. Includes Federal Subsidized/Unsubsidized Stafford Loans and Federal Parent Loans (Plus). Financial need considered for some loans. Repayment begins six months after graduation or when student withdraws/stops attending school at least half time.

Contact IFSB for an application.

2858—INSTITUTE FOR THE INTERNATIONAL EDUCATION OF STUDENTS (Scholarships)

223 West Ohio Street
Chicago IL 60610-4196
800/995-2300 or 312/944-1750
FAX: 312/944-1448
E-mail: info@iesa.broad.org
Internet: http://www.iesabroad.org
AMOUNT: Varies
DEADLINE(S): APR 1 (fall semester and full-year students); OCT 1 (spring semester students)
FIELD(S): All fields of study

IES offers many scholarships for studying abroad in various countries; some are based on academic merit, and some are based on financial need. The organization wants to encourage students with a variety of interests and abilities and who represent a wide range of social and economic backgrounds to study abroad.

The Web site is quite comprehensive and includes application forms, scholarship lists, and descriptions of what is available country-by-country. If you do not have Web access, contact IES for the necessary materials.

2859—INSTITUTE FOR WOMEN'S POLICY RESEARCH (IWPR Fellowship)

1400 20th Street, NW, Suite 104
Washington DC 20036
202/785-5100
AMOUNT: $1,200/month
DEADLINE(S): APR 1
FIELD(S): All

Applicants should have at least a bachelor's degree in a social science discipline, statistics, or women's studies. Graduate work is desirable but not required. Applicants should have basic quantitative and library research skills and knowledge of women's issues; familiarity with spreadsheets and graphics software a plus.

2860—INSTITUTE OF INTERNATIONAL EDUCATION (National Security Education Program)

809 United Nations Plaza
New York NY 10017
Internet: http://www.iie.org/nsep
AMOUNT: Varies
DEADLINE(S): JAN
FIELD(S): All

Financial assistance for students to spend a semester in underrepresented countries to study language and culture that is critical to U.S. security.

2861—INTERNATIONAL ALLIANCE OF THEATRICAL STAGE EMPLOYEES AND MOVING PICTURE MACHINE OPERATORS (Richard F. Walsh Foundation)

1515 Broadway, Suite 601
New York NY 10036
212/730-1770
AMOUNT: $1,750
DEADLINE(S): DEC 31
FIELD(S): All fields of study

Scholarship is offered to high school seniors who are children of members in good standing. Awards are based on transcripts, SAT scores, and letter(s) of recommendation from clergy or teacher.

Award renewable for 4 years. Write for complete information.

2862—INTERNATIONAL ASSOCIATION OF BRIDGE STRUCTURAL, ORNAMENTAL, AND REINFORCING IRON WORKERS (John H. Lyons Scholarship Program)

1750 New York Avenue NW
Suite 400
Washington DC 20006
202/383-4800
AMOUNT: $2,500/year (max.)
DEADLINE(S): MAR 31
FIELD(S): All fields of study

Open to children of current or deceased Association members in good standing. Applicants must be high school seniors who rank in the upper half of their graduating class and be pursuing undergraduate study in the U.S. or Canada. Financial need NOT a factor.

2 awards annually. Renewable. Contact Association for an application.

2863—INTERNATIONAL ASSOCIATION OF FIRE FIGHTERS (W.H. "Howie" McClennan Scholarship)

1750 New York Avenue NW
Washington DC 20006
202/737-8484
FAX: 202/737-8418
Internet: http://www.iaff.org
AMOUNT: $2,500
DEADLINE(S): FEB 1
FIELD(S): All

Provides financial assistance for sons, daughters, or legally adopted children of fire fighters killed in the line of duty planning to attend a university, accredited college, or other institution of higher learning. Applicants must submit a brief statement (about 200 words) prepared by the applicant that indicates their reasons for wanting to continue their education. Two letters of recommendation from a teacher, school administrator, counselor, clergy, work supervisor, or military supervisor (active, reserve, or National Guard) who can address the qualifications and academic aptitude of the scholarship applicant. The required letters of recommendation may not be from immediate family members, close family friends, blood relatives, or relationships by marriage

2864—INTERNATIONAL BILL ONEXIOCA II (Founders Memorial Award)

911 Bartlett Place
Windsor CA 95492
Written Inquiry only
AMOUNT: $2,500
DEADLINE(S): JAN 31
FIELD(S): All fields of study

Annual award in memory of Hernesto K. Onexioca/founder. Anyone with the legal surname of Onexioca who is not a relative of Onexioca by blood or marriage and was born on Jan. 1 is eligible to apply.

All inquiries MUST include proof of name and birth date. Those without such proof will NOT be acknowledged.

2865—INTERNATIONAL BROTHERHOOD OF TEAMSTERS (Scholarship Fund)

25 Louisiana Avenue NW
Washington DC 20001
202/624-8735
AMOUNT: $1,000-$1,500/year
DEADLINE(S): DEC 15
FIELD(S): All fields of study

Open to high school seniors who are dependent children of Teamster members. For students in top 20% of their class with excellent SAT/ACT scores. Must be U.S. or Canadian citizen and demonstrate financial need.

25 awards annually. Renewable. Contact the Teamsters for an application.

2866—INTERNATIONAL CHRISTIAN SCHOOL (Ameri-Asian Scholarship Fund)

P.O. Box 23
Uijongbu 480-600 SOUTH KOREA
0351 879-8573
FAX: 0351 872-1458
AMOUNT: Varies
DEADLINE(S): AUG
FIELD(S): All fields of study

Financial aid for students demonstrating financial need who wish to attend this elementary and secondary school in South Korea (for ages 5-18). For non-Koreans or for Korean citizens who have lived out of Korea and in a foreign school for more than one year.

Contact school for details.

2867—INTERNATIONAL LADIES GARMENT WORKERS UNION (National College Award Program)

1710 Broadway
New York NY 10019
212/265-7000
AMOUNT: $350 annually; renewable for up to four years
DEADLINE(S): JAN 31
FIELD(S): All fields of study

Open to sons or daughters of union members who have been members in good standing for at least 2 years. Applications accepted only from high school seniors.

10 scholarships per year. Write for complete information.

2868—INTERNATIONAL READING ASSOCIATION (Dina Feitelson Research Award)

Marcella Moore, Senior Secretary
800 Barksdale Road
P.O. Box 8139
Newark DE 19714-8139
302-731-1600 ext. 423
FAX: 302-731-1057
E-mail: mmoore@reading.org
Internet: http://www.reading.org
AMOUNT: $500
DEADLINE(S): SEP 15
FIELD(S): All

Prize awarded for an article published in a refereed journal. May be submitted by the author or anyone else. Work should report on one or more aspects of literary acquisition. Applicant must be enrolled at an accredited university.

2869—INTERNATIONAL SCHOOL OF KARACHI (ISK Scholarships)

Amir Khusro Road
KDA Scheme 1
Karachi 75350 PAKISTAN
9221/453-9096
FAX: 9221/454-7305
E-mail: ameschi@khi.fascom.com OR guidance@www.fascom.com
AMOUNT: Varies
DEADLINE(S): Varies
FIELD(S): All fields of study

Need-based and merit-based awards are for middle school and high school students at the International School of Karachi.

Contact Carol Kiper, Director of Admissions/Guidance for an application; use e-mail for quickest reply.

2870—INTERNATIONAL UNION OF BRICKLAYERS AND ALLIED CRAFTSMEN (Harry C. Bates Merit Scholarship Program)

815 Fifteenth Street NW
Washington, DC 20005
202/783-3788
AMOUNT: $500 to $2,000 per year up to 4 years
DEADLINE(S): OCT (PSAT tests)
FIELD(S): All areas of study

Open to natural or legally adopted children of current; retired or deceased BAC members. Competition is administered by National Merit Scholarship Corp. which conducts PSAT/NMSQT during October of student's junior year of high school.

Applicants must be national merit semifinalists. Award tenable at any accredited university or community college the student attends full-time. Write for complete information.

2871—INTERNATIONAL UNION OF ELECTRONIC, ELECTRICAL, SALARIES, MACHINE, & FURNITURE WORKERS-IEU (J. B. Carey, D. J. Fitzmaurice, and W. H. Bywater Scholarships)

1126 Sixteenth Street NW
Washington DC 20036-4866
202/296-1200
AMOUNT: $1,000-JBC (9 awards); $2,000-DJF (1); $3,000-WHB (1)
DEADLINE(S): APR 15
FIELD(S): All fields of study

Programs open to undergraduate dependents of union members. JBC scholarships support undergraduate study for one year in all fields of study. DJF scholarship supports undergraduate study for one year in engineering only. WHB Scholarship available only to children of elected union officials.

Contact local union representative for complete information.

2872—IOWA AMERICAN LEGION (Boy Scout of the Year Contest Scholarship)

720 Lyon Street
Des Moines IA 50309
515/282-5068
AMOUNT: $2,000
DEADLINE(S): FEB 1
FIELD(S): All fields of study

Open to Iowa Boy Scouts who have received the Eagle Scout award. Scholarship is given based on scout's outstanding service to his religious institution, school, and community. For undergraduate study at an Iowa college or university.

Write for complete information.

2873—IOWA AMERICAN LEGION (Oratorical Contest Scholarship)

720 Lyon Stret
Des Moines IA 50309
515/282-5068

AMOUNT: $2000 (first prize); $600 (second); $400 (third)
DEADLINE(S): DEC 1
FIELD(S): All fields of study

Speech Contest based on the U.S. Constitution open to Iowa high school students in the ninth through twelfth grades. Prizes are in the form of scholarships to attend a college or university in Iowa.

Write for complete information.

2874—IOWA COLLEGE STUDENT AID COMMISSION (Federal Stafford and PLUS Loan Programs)

200 Tenth Street, 4th Floor
Des Moines IA 50309-3609
515/242-3344

AMOUNT: $2,625-$5,500 (undergrad); $18,500 (graduate)
DEADLINE(S): None
FIELD(S): All fields of study

Open to Iowa residents enrolled in or attending approved institutions to pursue undergraduate or graduate study. Must be U.S. citizen/legal resident and demonstrate financial need.

Contact Student Aid Commission for an application.

2875—IOWA COLLEGE STUDENT AID COMMISSION (Iowa Tuition Grant Program)

200 Tenth Street, 4th Floor
Des Moines IA 50309-3609
515/242-3344

AMOUNT: $4,000
DEADLINE(S): JULY 1
FIELD(S): All fields of study

Open to Iowa residents enrolled or planning to enroll as undergraduates at eligible privately supported colleges/universities, business schools, or hospital nursing programs in Iowa. Must be U.S. citizen/legal resident and demonstrate financial need.

10,140 awards annually. Renewable. Awards based on FAFSA results. Contact Student Aid Commission for an application.

2876—IOWA COLLEGE STUDENT AID COMMISSION (State of Iowa Scholarships)

200 Tenth Street, 4th Floor
Des Moines IA 50309-3609
515/242-3344

AMOUNT: $400
DEADLINE(S): NOV 1
FIELD(S): All fields of study

Open to Iowa high school seniors who are in the top 15% of their class and plan to attend an eligible Iowa college/university. Based on ACT/SAT composite test scores, GPA, and class rank. Must be U.S. citizen.

3,000 awards annually. Contact your school counselor or Student Aid Commission for an application.

2877—IOWA COMMISSION OF VETERANS AFFAIRS (War Orphans Educational Scholarship Aid)

7700 NW Beaver Drive
Camp Dodge #A6A
Johnston IA 50131
800/VET-IOWA or 515/242-5331
FAX: 515/242-5659

AMOUNT: $600/year ($3,000 lifetime max.)
DEADLINE(S): None
FIELD(S): All fields of study

Open to Iowa residents of at least two years prior to application. Must be child of parent who died in or as a result of military service during wartime. Also eligible are orphans of National Guardsmen and other members of Reserve Components who died performing duties ordered by appropriate Federal or State authorities. Tenable for undergraduate or graduate study at an Iowa postsecondary institution.

Renewable. Contact Iowa Commission of Veterans Affairs for an application.

2878—ISRAEL AMATEUR RADIO CLUB (Holyland Award)

Mark Stern, 4Z4KX
P.O. Box 3033
Rishon 75130 ISRAEL
Internet: http://hamradio.iarc.org/contests/contests.html

AMOUNT: Trophies, plaques, and certificates
DEADLINE(S): MAY 31
FIELD(S): All fields of study

Worldwide contest to promote contacts between Radio Amateurs around the globe and Israelli Hams. For all licensed amateurs and SWL's worldwide. Object is to contact as many different Israeli amateur radio stations on as many bands, and from as many Areas, as possible in both modes, CW and SSB.

Contact the Contest Manager at IARC for details.

2879—ITALIAN AMERICAN CHAMBER OF COMMERCE OF CHICAGO (Scholarships)

30 S. Michigan Avenue; Suite 504
Chicago IL 60603
312/553-9137
FAX: 312/553-9142
E-mail: chicago@italchambers.net
Internet: http://www.italchambers.net/chicago

AMOUNT: $1,000
DEADLINE(S): MAY 31
FIELD(S): All fields of study

For students of Italian ancestry who are residents of one of the following Illinois counties: Cook, DuPage, Kane, Lake, Will, or McHenry. Must be a full-time student between last year in high school and last year of a fully accredited four-year college/university. Must have a minimum GPA of 3.5. Good moral character and scholastic achievement are the basic criteria for the award.

Not renewable. Applicants will be notified by November 1. Contact Leonora or Frank at above address for an application.

2880—ITALIAN CATHOLIC FEDERATION, INC. (Scholarships)

675 Hegenberger Road #230
Oakland CA 94621
888/ICF-1924
FAX: 510/633-9758

AMOUNT: $400-$1,000
DEADLINE(S): MAR 15
FIELD(S): All fields of study

Open to graduating high school seniors of Italian ancestry and Catholic faith. Non-Italian graduating high school seniors may qualify if their Catholic parents or grandparents are members of the Italian Catholic Federation. Must live in states where the federation is located (California, Nevada, and Illinois (primarily the Chicago area and nearby cities) and Arizona (Green Valley, AZ)), have a minimum 3.2 GPA, and be U.S. citizens.

Approximately 200 awards annually. Send a self-addressed, stamped envelope to ICF for an application.

2881—J. WOOD PLATT CADDIE SCHOLARSHIP TRUST (Grants)

P.O. Box 808
Southeastern PA 19399-0808
610/687-2340
FAX: 610/687-2082
E-mail: gapl@bellatlantic.net
AMOUNT: $12,000 (max.)
DEADLINE(S): APR 25; SEP 1
FIELD(S): All fields of study

Open to high school seniors and undergraduate students who have served as a caddie at a Golf Association of Philadelphia member club. Must demonstrate financial need and have the capability to successfully complete undergraduate degree.

Approx. 180 awards annually. Renewable. Contact John A. Pergolin for an application.

2882—J.H. BAKER SCHOLARSHIP FUND (Student Loans)

c/o Tom Dechant CPA
P.O. Box 280
La Crosse KS 67548
913/222-2537
AMOUNT: $2,000 per year
DEADLINE(S): JUL 15
FIELD(S): All undergrad fields of study

For graduates of high schools in the Kansas counties of Rush, Barton, Ellis, Ness, and Pawnee. Must be under 25 years of age. Selection is based on academic performance, character, ability, and need.

Contact address above for complete information.

2883—J. W. SAXE MEMORIAL PRIZE

1524 31st Street NW
Washington DC 20007-3074
DEADLINE(S): MAR
AMOUNT: $1,500
FIELD(S): All

An award that allows students to gain public service experience while supplementing a low-paying job, internship, or volunteer service.

2884—JACK KENT COOKE FOUNDATION (Graduate Scholarship Program)

44115 Woodridge Parkway
Suite 200
Lansdowne VA 20176
703/723-8000
E-mail: jkc@jackkentcooke foundation.org
Internet: http://www.jackkentcooke foundation.org/
AMOUNT: Up to $50,000
DEADLINE(S): FEB 1
FIELD(S): All

Must be a college senior and a resident of Maryland, Virginia, or the District of Columbia

2885—JACKSONVILLE STATE UNIVERSITY

Financial Aid Office
Jacksonville AL 36265
Written Inquiry
AMOUNT: Varies
DEADLINE(S): MAR 15
FIELD(S): All fields of study

Numerous scholarship programs tenable at Jacksonville State University, Alabama, in all subject areas and with various restrictions concerning residency, year in school, major, etc.

Write to above address for complete listing and application.

2886—JACKSONVILLE UNIVERSITY (Scholarship and Grant Programs)

Director of Student Financial Assistance
Jacksonville FL 32211
904/745-7060
AMOUNT: Varies
DEADLINE(S): JAN 1
FIELD(S): All fields of study

Open to undergraduate and graduate students accepted to or enrolled at Jacksonville University. Programs include scholarships, grants-in-aid, service awards, and campus employment. Financial need is not necessarily a consideration. Early applications are advised.

100 awards annually. Contact the financial aid office for an application.

2887—JACQUELINE ELVIRA HODGES JOHNSON FUND, INC. (Scholarships)

P.O. Box 12393
St. Petersburg FL 33733-2393
727/867-9567
AMOUNT: Varies
DEADLINE(S): APR 1; OCT 1
FIELD(S): All fields of study

Open to students who have experienced cancer; also open to needy students with a minimum 2.5 GPA. Must be a high school senior or undergraduate and be a U.S. citizen/permanent resident.

3-6 awards annually. Contact Georgia Johnson for an application.

2888—JACQUELINE ELVIRA HODGES JOHNSON FUND, INC. (Scholarship)

P.O. Box 1442
Walterboro SC 29488
803/538-8640
AMOUNT: Varies
DEADLINE(S): APR 1
FIELD(S): All fields of study

This scholarship is for cancer survivors and residents of South Carolina who are college-bound high school seniors or students enrolled in postsecondary study. Must demonstrate financial need and have at least a 3.0 GPA

Write to the above address for complete information.

2889—JAMES F. BYRNES FOUNDATION

P.O. Box 9596
Columbia SC 29290
803/254-9325
AMOUNT: $2,500
DEADLINE(S): FEB 15
FIELD(S): All fields of study

Undergraduate scholarships for young South Carolina residents who are high school seniors, college freshmen of sophomores, and whose parent or parents are deceased. Must be seeking B.S. or B.A. degree-not for technical education or associate degrees. GPA 2.5 or above. Must indicate qualities of character, ability, and enterprise.

Renewable for four years. Program also provides counseling, social events, a retreat, and awards luncheon. Involvement in the Byrnes Scholarship Program is expected. Phone or write to Jean P. Elton, Executive Secretary, at above address for details.

2890—JAMES G. K. MCCLURE EDUCATIONAL AND DEVELOPMENT FUND (Western North Carolina Scholarships)

11 Sugar Hollow Road
Fairview NC 28730
828/628-2114
E-mail: jager@ioa.com
AMOUNT: $300-$2,000
DEADLINE(S): MAY 15
FIELD(S): All fields of study

Open to students residing in western North Carolina who are entering the freshman class of a North Carolina college/university. Must demonstrate financial need.

100 awards annually. Not renewable. Contact John Ager for an application.

2891—JAMES M. HOFFMAN SCHOLARSHIP (Undergraduate Scholarship)

Southtrust Bank Asset Mngmt. Co.
P.O. Box 1000
Anniston AL 36202
205/238-1000 ext. 338

AMOUNT: Varies
DEADLINE(S): MAR 1
FIELD(S): All fields of study

For high school seniors attending schools in Calhoun County, Alabama. For undergraduate study at accredited colleges and universities. Must submit copies of parents' W-2 forms.

Write to attention of William K. Priddy for complete information.

2892—JAMES P. AND RUTH C. GILLROY FOUNDATION, INC. (Grants)

President
125 Park Avenue, 3rd Floor
New York NY 10017
Written Inquiry

AMOUNT: $1,250/semester
DEADLINE(S): Varies (two months prior to date payment is due to college)
FIELD(S): All fields of study

Open to undergraduates who are residents of the five boroughs of the City of New York and, in some cases, to non-residents who will attend institutions within the five boroughs. Must be U.S. citizen with an outstanding academic record, community service, and financial need.

20+ awards annually. Renewable. Contact Edmund C. Grainger, Jr., President, for application guidelines.

2893—JAPANESE AMERICAN CITIZENS LEAGUE (Abe and Esther Hagiwara Student Aid Award)

1765 Sutter Street
San Francisco CA 94115
415/921-5225
FAX: 415/931-4671
E-mail: jacl@jacl.org
Internet: http://www.jacl.org

AMOUNT: $1,000-$5,000
DEADLINE(S): APR 1
FIELD(S): All fields of study

Open to JACL members and their children only who demonstrate severe financial need. For undergraduate and graduate students planning to attend a college, university, trade school, business school, or any other institution of higher learning. Purpose is to provide financial assistance to a student who otherwise would have to delay or terminate his/her education due to lack of financing. Must submit personal statement, letters of recommendation, and transcripts.

For membership information or an application, send a self-addressed, stamped envelope to above address, stating your level of study. Applications available October 1 through March 20; recipient notified in July.

2894—JAPANESE AMERICAN CITIZENS LEAGUE (Entering Freshmen Awards)

1765 Sutter Street
San Francisco CA 94115
415/921-5225
FAX: 415/931-4671
E-mail: jacl@jacl.org
Internet: http://www.jacl.org

AMOUNT: $1,000-$5,000
DEADLINE(S): MAR 1
FIELD(S): All fields of study

Open to JACL members and their children only. For entering freshmen planning to attend a college, university, trade school, business school, or any other institution of higher learning. Must submit personal statement, letters of recommendation, and transcript.

For membership information or an application, send a self-addressed, stamped envelope to above address, stating your level of study. Applications available October 1 through February 20; recipients notified in July.

2895—JAPANESE AMERICAN CITIZENS LEAGUE (Undergraduate Awards)

1765 Sutter Street
San Francisco CA 94115
415/921-5225
FAX: 415/931-4671
E-mail: jacl@jacl.org
Internet: http://www.jacl.org

AMOUNT: $1,000-$5,000
DEADLINE(S): APR 1
FIELD(S): All fields of study

Open to JACL members and their children only. For undergraduate students planning to attend a college, university, trade school, business school, or any other institution of higher learning. Must submit personal statement, letters of recommendation, and transcripts.

For membership information or an application, send a self-addressed, stamped envelope to above address, stating your level of study. Applications available October 1 through March 20; recipients notified in July.

2896—JAPANESE GOVERNMENT (Monbusho Vocational School Student Scholarships)

350 S. Grand Avenue, Suite 1700
Los Angeles CA 90071
213/617-6700 ext. 338
FAX: 213/617-6728
Internet: http://embjapan.org/la

AMOUNT: Tuition + $1,400-$1,800/month
DEADLINE(S): AUG
FIELD(S): Vocational Skills

For high school graduates, between the ages of 18-22, who wish to study at a vocational school in Japan. Includes one-year Japanese language course, roundtrip airfare, one-time arrival allowance, partly subsidized housing expenses, and partly subsidized medical expenses.

Term of study is for three years. For more information or an application, contact Mr. Cory Crocker, Consulate General of Japan, Information and Culture Center, at above address.

2897—JAYCEE WAR MEMORIAL (Scholarship Program)

Department 94922
Tulsa OK 74114-1116
800/JAYCEES
Internet: http://www.usjaycees.org/education/scholarships.htmx

AMOUNT: $1,000-$3,000
DEADLINE(S): MAR 1
FIELD(S): All fields of study

Open to undergraduate and graduate students who are enrolled in or accepted for admission to a college or university. Must possess academic potential, leadership traits, demonstrate financial need, and be a U.S. citizen.

$5 application fee. Send self-addressed, stamped, business-sized envelope and application fee to JWMF between July 1 and February 1 for an application. Alternate address: Dept. 94922, Tulsa, OK 74194-0001.

2898—JEANNETTE RANKIN FOUNDATION AWARDS (Scholarships)

Kristina White, Administrator
Jeannette Rankin Foundation, Inc.
P.O. Box 6653
Athens GA 30604

706/208-1211
FAX: 706/208-1211
E-mail: info@rankinfoundation.org
Internet: http://www.rankin
foundation.org
AMOUNT: $1,500
DEADLINE(S): MAR 1
FIELD(S): All

Must be a female U.S. citizen, at least 35 years old.

Must be pursuing a technical/vocational award or her first degree at the undergraduate level. Download application from Web site during November, December, and January.

2899—JEWISH FAMILY AND CHILDREN'S SERVICES (Anna and Charles Stockwitz Children and Youth Fund)

2150 Post Street
San Francisco CA 94115
415/449-1226
E-mail: erics@JFCS.org
AMOUNT: $6,000 (max.)
DEADLINE(S): None
FIELD(S): All fields of study

Open to Jewish children and teens to assist with a valuable educational, social, or psychological experience, or to assist them in attending undergraduate school. Must reside in San Francisco, San Mateo, northern Santa Clara, Marin, or Sonoma County for grants; Alameda or Contra Costa County for loans. Grant applicants must demonstrate financial need. Loan applicants must be able to provide qualified guarantors (co-signers) that reside in the Bay Area.

Contact Eric Singer at JFCS Loans and Grants for an application package.

2900—JEWISH FAMILY AND CHILDREN'S SERVICES (David, Nancy, and Liza Cherney Scholarship Fund)

2150 Post Street
San Francisco CA 94115
415/449-1226
E-mail: erics@JFCS.org
AMOUNT: $100 (max.)
DEADLINE(S): None
FIELD(S): All fields of study

Open to Jewish women who demonstrate financial need and wish to pursue undergraduate study. Must reside in San Francisco, San Mateo, northern Santa Clara, Marin, or Sonoma County.

Contact Eric Singer at JFCS Loans and Grants for an application package.

2901—JEWISH FAMILY AND CHILDREN'S SERVICES (DeHovitz-Senturia Campership Fund)

2150 Post Street
San Francisco CA 94115
415/449-1226
E-mail: erics@JFCS.org
AMOUNT: $600 (max.)
DEADLINE(S): None
FIELD(S): All fields of study

Open to Jewish children aged 26 or younger who wish to attend summer camp. Must reside in San Francisco, San Mateo, northern Santa Clara, Marin, or Sonoma County. Must demonstrate financial need and be referred by an agency caseworker.

Contact Eric Singer at JFCS Loans and Grants for an application package.

2902—JEWISH FAMILY AND CHILDREN'S SERVICES (Esther Shiller Memorial Endowment Loan Fund)

2150 Post Street
San Francisco CA 94115
415/449-1226
E-mail: erics@JFCS.org
AMOUNT: $6,000 (max.)
DEADLINE(S): None
FIELD(S): All fields of study

Open to Jewish undergraduate and graduate students who demonstrate academic promise and ability to repay the loans. Must reside in San Francisco, San Mateo, northern Santa Clara, Marin, Sonoma, Alameda, or Contra Costa County. Must be able to provide qualified guarantors (co-signers) that reside in the Bay Area.

Contact Eric Singer at JFCS Loans and Grants for an application package.

2903—JEWISH FAMILY AND CHILDREN'S SERVICES (Fogel Loan Fund)

2150 Post Street
San Francisco CA 94115
415/449-1226
E-mail: erics@JFCS.org
AMOUNT: $6,000 (max.)
DEADLINE(S): None
FIELD(S): All fields of study

Open to Jewish students of all ages who are pursuing college, university, or vocational studies. Must reside in San Francisco, San Mateo, northern Santa Clara, Marin, Sonoma, Alameda, or Contra Costa County. Must be able to provide qualified guarantors (co-signers) that reside in the Bay Area.

Contact Eric Singer at JFCS Loans and Grants for an application package.

2904—JEWISH FAMILY AND CHILDREN'S SERVICES (Harry and Florence Wornick Endowment Fund)

2150 Post Street
San Francisco CA 94115
415/449-1226
E-mail: erics@JFCS.org
AMOUNT: $5,800 (max.)
DEADLINE(S): None
FIELD(S): All fields of study

Open to Jewish students of all ages who are pursuing college, university, or vocational studies. Special consideration given to students seeking careers in the use of wood or careers in music. Must reside in San Francisco, San Mateo, northern Santa Clara, Marin, Sonoma, Alameda, or Contra Costa County. Must be able to provide qualified guarantors (co-signers) that reside in the Bay Area.

Contact Eric Singer at JFCS Loans and Grants for an application package.

2905—JEWISH FAMILY AND CHILDREN'S SERVICES (Henry and Tilda Shuler Scholarship Fund for Young People)

2150 Post Street
San Francisco CA 94115
415/449-1226
E-mail: erics@JFCS.org
AMOUNT: $950 (max.)
DEADLINE(S): None
FIELD(S): All fields of study

Open to Jewish youths aged 26 or younger to pursue vocational training, college education, or other studies. Must reside in San Francisco, San Mateo, northern Santa Clara, Marin, or Sonoma County. Must demonstrate financial need.

Contact Eric Singer at JFCS Loans and Grants for an application package.

2906—JEWISH FAMILY AND CHILDREN'S SERVICES (Jacob Rassen Memorial Scholarships)

2150 Post Street
San Francisco CA 94115
415/449-1226
E-mail: erics@JFCS.org
AMOUNT: $1,900 (max.)
DEADLINE(S): None
FIELD(S): All fields of study

Open to Jewish boys and girls under age 22 to go on a study trip to Israel. Must reside in San Francisco, San Mateo, northern Santa Clara, Marin, or Sonoma County. Must demonstrate financial need.

Contact Eric Singer at JFCS Loans and Grants for an application package.

2907—JEWISH FAMILY AND CHILDREN'S SERVICES (Kaminer Family Fund)

2150 Post Street
San Francisco CA 94115
415/449-1226
E-mail: erics@JFCS.org
AMOUNT: $475 (max.)
DEADLINE(S): None
FIELD(S): All fields of study

Open to Jewish children aged 26 or younger who wish to attend summer camp. Must reside in San Francisco, San Mateo, northern Santa Clara, Marin, or Sonoma County. Must demonstrate financial need. Grants may be made for such general and specific purposes as camperships, counseling, and supportive services.

Contact Eric Singer at JFCS Loans and Grants for an application package.

2908—JEWISH FAMILY AND CHILDREN'S SERVICES (Lillian Fried Scholarship Fund)

2150 Post Street
San Francisco CA 94115
415/449-1226
E-mail: erics@JFCS.org
AMOUNT: $130 (max.)
DEADLINE(S): None
FIELD(S): All fields of study

Open to deserving Jewish women who wish to pursue collegiate or graduate studies. Must reside in San Francisco, San Mateo, northern Santa Clara, Marin, or Sonoma County. Must demonstrate financial need.

Contact Eric Singer at JFCS Loans and Grants for an application package.

2909—JEWISH FAMILY AND CHILDREN'S SERVICES (Miriam S. Grunfeld Scholarship Fund)

2150 Post Street
San Francisco CA 94115
415/449-1226
E-mail: erics@JFCS.org
AMOUNT: $950 (max.)
DEADLINE(S): None
FIELD(S): All fields of study

Open to Jewish students aged 26 or younger who wish to pursue undergraduate or graduate studies, and who, without financial assistance, would not be able to fulfill their educational aspirations. Must reside in San Francisco, San Mateo, northern Santa Clara, Marin, or Sonoma County. Must demonstrate financial need.

Contact Eric Singer at JFCS Loans and Grants for an application package.

2910—JEWISH FAMILY AND CHILDREN'S SERVICES (Selig Fund)

2150 Post Street
San Francisco CA 94115
415/449-1226
E-mail: erics@JFCS.org
AMOUNT: $6,000 (max.)
DEADLINE(S): None
FIELD(S): All fields of study

Open to Jewish undergraduate students who reside in San Francisco, San Mateo, northern Santa Clara, Marin, Sonoma, Alameda, or Contra Costa County. Must be able to provide qualified guarantors (co-signers) that reside in the Bay Area.

Contact Eric Singer at JFCS Loans and Grants for an application package.

2911—JEWISH FAMILY AND CHILDREN'S SERVICES (Stanley Olson Youth Scholarships)

2150 Post Street
San Francisco CA 94115
415/449-1226
E-mail: erics@JFCS.org
AMOUNT: $2,500 (max.)
DEADLINE(S): None
FIELD(S): All fields of study

Open to Jewish youth aged 26 or younger who plan to pursue undergraduate or graduate study. Must reside in San Francisco, San Mateo, northern Santa Clara, Marin, or Sonoma County. Preference given to studies in liberal arts. Must demonstrate financial need.

Contact Eric Singer at JFCS Loans and Grants for an application package.

2912—JEWISH FAMILY AND CHILDREN'S SERVICES (Vivienne Camp College Scholarship Fund)

2150 Post Street
San Francisco CA 94115
415/449-1226
E-mail: erics@JFCS.org
AMOUNT: $4,350 (max.)
DEADLINE(S): None
FIELD(S): All fields of study

Open to young Jewish men and women pursuing undergraduate college or vocational study at a California institution. Must reside in San Francisco, San Mateo, northern Santa Clara, Marin, or Sonoma County. Must demonstrate academic achievement, promise, and financial need.

4 awards annually. Contact Eric Singer at JFCS Loans and Grants for an application package.

2913—JEWISH SOCIAL SERVICE AGENCY OF METROPOLITAN WASHINGTON (Jewish Educational Loan Fund)

6123 Montrose Road
Rockville MD 20852
301/881-3700
TTY: 301/984-5662
FAX: 301/770-8741
AMOUNT: $2,000 (max.)
DEADLINE(S): MAY 15
FIELD(S): All fields of study

No-interest loans are available to Jewish undergraduate and graduate students from the Metropolitan Washington area who are U.S. citizens/permanent residents. Must be within 18 months of completing degree or vocational training in the U.S. Based primarily on financial need, this loan is for students with few other resources available. Awardees must repay $50/month beginning three months after completing degree.

Not renewable and may apply only once. Contact the Scholarship and Loan Coordinator for an application.

2914—JEWISH SOCIAL SERVICE AGENCY OF METROPOLITAN WASHINGTON (Max and Emmy Dreyfuss Jewish Undergraduate Scholarship Fund)

6123 Montrose Road
Rockville MD 20852
301/881-3700
TTY: 301/984-5662
FAX: 301/770-8741
AMOUNT: $1,500-$3,500
DEADLINE(S): MAY 15
FIELD(S): All fields of study

Open to Jewish undergraduates from the Metropolitan Washington area who are U.S. citizens/permanent residents. Must be under the age of 30 and be accepted into an accredited four-year program on a full-time basis in the U.S. Based primarily on financial need. This award may not be used for attending a community college or any study abroad program. Any awardee who doesn't complete a full year of school must pay back the grant.

8-10 awards annually. Renewable. Contact the Scholarship and Loan Coordinator for an application. Notification in July.

2915—JEWISH SOCIAL SERVICE AGENCY OF METROPOLITAN WASHINGTON (Jeanette Siegel Memorial Scholarships)

6123 Montrose Road
Rockville MD 20852
301/881-3700
TTY: 301/984-5662
FAX: 301/770-8741

AMOUNT: Varies
DEADLINE(S): MAY 15
FIELD(S): All fields of study

Open to Jewish students in grades 4-12 to attend a private primary or secondary school in the U.S. Must be from the Metropolitan Washington area and be U.S. citizens/permanent residents. Based primarily on financial need.

Contact the Scholarship and Loan Coordinator for an application.

2916—JEWISH VOCATIONAL SERVICE (JVS) (Community Scholarship Fund)

5700 Wilshire Boulevard, Suite 2303
Los Angeles CA 90036
213/761-8888 ext. 122
FAX: 213/761-8850

AMOUNT: Up to $2,000
DEADLINE(S): APR 15 (March 1 for application requests)
FIELD(S): All fields of study

For undergraduate students who are sophomores or higher, graduate or professional students, or students pursuing vocational training. Must be Jewish permanent residents of Los Angeles County, California with financial need, U.S. citizens or permanent residents, and are in a full-time course of study in an accredited institution.

Renewable annually. Preference given to students in California schools. Call or write for application.

2917—JOHN C. CHAFFIN EDUCATIONAL FUND (Scholarships and Loans Programs)

100 Walnut Street
Newtonville MA 02160
617/552-7652

AMOUNT: Scholarships: $500/semester; Loans: $600/semester
DEADLINE(S): None given
FIELD(S): All fields of study

Open only to graduates of Newton North and Newton South High Schools in Newton, Massachusetts. Preference to students enrolling in four-year accredited undergraduate programs; trustees may also support those attending less than four-year degree and non-degree granting school provided they are accredited schools.

Approximately 30 awards per year. Renewable to a maximum of $2000 for scholarships and $4,800 for loans. Loans begin to accrue 6% interest rate six months after graduation. Write for complete information.

2918—JOHN EDGAR THOMSON FOUNDATION (Grants)

201 South 18th Street, Suite 318
Philadelphia PA 19103
Phone/FAX: 215/545-6083

AMOUNT: Monthly Stipend
DEADLINE(S): None
FIELD(S): All fields of study

Financial assistance for females from infancy through age 22 whose deceased parent was a railroad worker. Support ends at age 18 if daughter does not seek higher education. The cause of death need not be work-related. The daughter must live in the home of the surviving parent, except while living at a college campus. Eligibility is dependent upon the daughter and parent remaining unmarried. Financial need considered.

The Foundation also provides special health care benefits to the daughter. Contact Sheila Cohen, Director, for more information.

2919—JOHN G. WILLIAMS SCHOLARSHIP FOUNDATION

P.O. Box 1229
Camp Hill PA 17001-1229
717/763-1333
FAX: 717/763-1336
E-mail: amgrpmld@aol.com
Internet: http://www.jgwfoundation.org

AMOUNT: Varies
DEADLINE(S): MAR 15; JUN 15; NOV 15
FIELD(S): All

The John G. Williams Scholarship Foundation was founded to provide financial assistance to deserving Pennsylvania residents for their pursuit of college, postgraduate, and/or professional educational opportunities, in courses and at educational institutions that they select and that are acceptable to the Board of Trustees. The Foundation and its financial assistance shall be administered and provided without regard to race, religion, age, creed, or ancestry. Neither the Foundation nor any member of the Board of Trustees, nor their respective spouses, lineal descendants, or spouses of lineal descendants, shall be eligible to receive and financial assistance.

2920—JOHN GYLES EDUCATION FUND (Scholarship)

The John Gyles Education Fund
Attention: The Secretary
712 Riverside Drive
P.O. Box 4808
Fredericton, New Brunswick,
CANADA E3B 5G4

AMOUNT: Varies
DEADLINE(S): NOV 15; APR 1; JUN 1
FIELD(S): All

Available to a full-time student in Canada or the United States with a minimum GPA of 2.7. Financial need and academic ability taken into consideration. Send a self-addressed stamped envelope to the above address for more information.

2921—JOHN T. HALL TRUST

P.O. Box 4655
Atlanta GA 30302-4655
Written Inquiry

AMOUNT: Varies
DEADLINE(S): Ongoing
FIELD(S): All areas of study

Student loans to residents of Georgia for undergraduate and graduate education.

Write to Miss Dale Welch, c/o SunTrust Bank, Atlanta, at above address for application details.

2922—JOHN WOOLMAN SCHOOL (Native American Scholarship Program)

13075 Woolman Lane
Nevada City CA 95959
530/273-3183
FAX: 530/273-9028
E-mail: jwsadmit@nccn.net
Internet: http://www.pacificnet.
~woolman/

AMOUNT: $500-$5,000
DEADLINE(S): JUN 1
FIELD(S): All fields of study

Needs-based scholarships for Native American students accepted at this co-ed, college preparatory boarding school in Nevada City, CA. Must demonstrate financial need. The school is associated with the Friends, or Quaker, religion.

1-2 awards yearly. Renewable. Contact school for details.

2923—JOHNS HOPKINS UNIVERSITY (Citizenship Essay Contest)

Wyman Park Bldg., 5th Floor
3400 North Charles Street
Baltimore MD 21218-2692

Internet: http://www.jhu.edu/ips/
maps/essay.html
AMOUNT: Up to $2,000
DEADLINE(S): MAY
FIELD(S): All

A national essay contest about citizenship. Students are encouraged to draw upon their own experiences. Available to full-time juniors and seniors.

2924—JOHNSON AND WALES UNIVERSITY (Gaebe Eagle Scout Scholarships)

8 Abbott Place
Providence RI 02903
401/598-1000
AMOUNT: $300
DEADLINE(S): APR 30
FIELD(S): All fields of study

Open to undergraduate freshmen who have been accepted at Johnson and Wales University. Must be Eagle Scout who has received a religious award of his faith.

All eligible freshmen receive award of $300. Write for complete information.

2925—JOHNSON CONTROLS FOUNDATION (Scholarship Program)

5757 N. Green Bay Avenue X-34
Milwaukee WI 53201
414/228-2296
AMOUNT: $2,000/year
DEADLINE(S): FEB 1
FIELD(S): All fields of study

Open only to children of Johnson Controls, Inc. employees. Students must be high school seniors or full-time undergraduate students and in the upper 30% of high school graduating class. Must be U.S. citizen.

Renewable. Contact Foundation for an application.

2926—JOHNSTON COUNTY EDUCATION FOUNDATION (SCHOLARSHIPS)

P.O. Box 1075
Smithfield NC 27577
919/934-7977
AMOUNT: Up to $1,000
DEADLINE(S): Varies
FIELD(S): All fields of study

The Johnston County Education Foundation administers scholarship funds for a number of scholarships. Criteria and applications are available through the guidance departments at local high schools. For more information, please contact the guidance counselor at your local high school.

2927—JULIA HENRY FUND (Fellowships at Harvard and Yale Universities)

The Old Schools
Cambridge CB2 ENGLAND UK
Written Request
AMOUNT: $15,535 + travel grant, tuition, health insurance
DEADLINE(S): DEC 5
FIELD(S): All fields of study

Scholarships for unmarried citizens under age 26 of the U.K./British Commonwealth to study at Harvard or Yale in the U.S. (One at each.) Undergraduates must have completed at least six terms in a U.K. university; graduates must be in their first year of study in a U.K. university. Recipients are expected to return to the British Isles or some part of the Commonwealth at the expiration of their term of tenure.

Request details and application forms from Dr. A. Clark, Secretary of the Trustees, University Registry, at above address.

2928—JUNIATA COLLEGE (Church of the Brethren Scholarships)

Financial Aid Office
Huntingdon PA 16652
814/641-3603
FAX: 814/641-3355
AMOUNT: up to $5,000 (max.)
DEADLINE(S): APR 1
FIELD(S): All fields of study

Open to Church of the Brethren members in various geographic areas who are applying to Juniata College. Must fill out government FAFSA form.

Contact Randy Rennell, Office of Student Financial Planning, Juniata College, for an application or enrollment information. See your financial aid office for FAFSA.

2929—JUNIATA COLLEGE (Frederick and Mary F. Beckley Scholarship Fund)

Financial Aid Office
Huntingdon PA 16652
814/641-3603
FAX: 814/641-3355
AMOUNT: Varies
DEADLINE(S): None
FIELD(S): All fields of study

Open to needy left-handed students who have junior or senior standing at Juniata College.

Contact Randy Rennell, Office of Student Financial Planning, for an application or enrollment information.

2930—JUNIATA COLLEGE (Friendship Scholarships)

Financial Aid Office
Huntingdon PA 16652
814/641-3603
FAX: 814/641-3355
AMOUNT: $2,000
DEADLINE(S): MAR 15
FIELD(S): All fields of study

Open to international students applying to Juniata College.

Contact Randy Rennell, Office of Studwnt Financial Planning, for an application or enrollment information.

2931—JUNIATA COLLEGE (Sam Hayes, Jr. Scholarship)

Financial Aid Office
Huntingdon PA 16652
814/641-3603
FAX: 814/641-3355
AMOUNT: up to $1,500 (max.)
DEADLINE(S): APR 1
FIELD(S): All fields of study

Open to Pennsylvania 4H and FFA members who are applying to Juniata College. Must demonstrate financial need and fill out government FAFSA form.

Contact Randy Rennell, Office of Student Financial Planning, for an application or enrollment information. See your financial aid office for FAFSA.

2932—JUNIOR LEAGUE OF NORTHERN VIRGINIA (Scholarships)

7921 Jones Branch Drive, #320
McLean VA 22102
703/893-0258
AMOUNT: $500 to $2,000
DEADLINE(S): DEC 15
FIELD(S): All fields of study

Open to women who are 23 years old or more and accepted to or enrolled in an accredited college or university as an undergraduate student in northern Virginia unless the course is not offered at a northern Virginia school. Must be resident of Northern Virginia, a U.S. citizen, and demonstrate financial need.

8-10 awards per year. Write for complete information.

2933—JUNIPERO SERRA HIGH SCHOOL (Tuition Assistance)

451 W. 20th Avenue
San Mateo CA 94403

650/345-8207
FAX: 650/573-6638
E-mail: Josullivan@serrahs.com
Internet: http://serrahs.com
AMOUNT: $500-$4,000
DEADLINE(S): APR 10
FIELD(S): All fields of study

Open to male 9th-12th grade students at this private Catholic day school. Must demonstrate financial need and be U.S. citizen/permanent resident.

170 awards annually. Renewable. Contact John O'Sullivan for an application.

2934—KAISER FOUNDATION, INC.

90 13th Street
Wheatland WY 82201
307/322-2026
AMOUNT: $1,000
DEADLINE(S): MAY 1
FIELD(S): All fields of study

Scholarships for high school students who are residents in Wyoming.

Write to Edward W. Hunter, Executive Director, at above address.

2935—KANSAS AMERICAN LEGION (Scholarships)

1314 SW Topeka Boulevard
Topeka KS 66612
Written Inquiry
AMOUNT: $150-$1,000
DEADLINE(S): FEB 15; JUL 15
FIELD(S): All fields of study

Variety of scholarships and awards for Kansas residents to attend Kansas colleges, universities, or trade schools. Some are limited to Legion members and/or designated fields of study.

Write for complete information.

2936—KANSAS BOARD OF REGENTS (Ethnic Minority Scholarship)

700 SW Harrison Street, Suite 1410
Topeka KS 66603-3760
785/296-3518
AMOUNT: up to $1,500/year
DEADLINE(S): APR 1
FIELD(S): All fields of study

For financially needy, academically competitive students who Kansas residents and are American Indian/Alaskan Native, Asian/Pacific Islander, Black, or Hispanic. Priority given to high school seniors. Must have one of the following: ACT 21/SAT 816, GPA 3.0, high school rank of upper 33%, completion of Regents Recommended Curriculum, selection by National Merit Corporation in any category, or selection by College Board as a Hispanic Scholar. Must complete the FAFSA.

$10 application fee. Renewable for 4 years (5 years if a 5-year program). Contact Kansas Board of Regents for an application. See your financial aid office for the FAFSA.

2937—KANSAS BOARD OF REGENTS (Kansas Comprehensive Grants)

700 SW Harrison Street, Suite 1410
Topeka KS 66603-3760
785/296-3518
FAFSA: 800/433-3243
Internet: http://www.fafsa.ed.gov
AMOUNT: $200-$2,500 (private); $100-$1,100 (public)
DEADLINE(S): APR 1
FIELD(S): All fields of study

Available to needy Kansas residents enrolled full-time at the seventeen private colleges/universities located in Kansas, the six public universities, and Washburn University. The Kansas Legislature provides limited assistance to financially needy students. To be considered, you must complete and submit the FAFSA, listing one or more eligible colleges in Step 5.

1 in 5 eligible students are funded annually. See Web site or contact your financial aid office for a copy of the FAFSA.

2938—KANSAS BOARD OF REGENTS (Kansas State Scholarship)

700 SW Harrison Street, Suite 1410
Topeka KS 66603-3760
785/296-3518
AMOUNT: up to $1,000
DEADLINE(S): MAY 15
FIELD(S): All fields of study

Assists financially needy students in top 20-40% of Kansas high school graduates who are designated as Kansas Scholars. Applicants must have received a letter of designation in their senior year of high school. Must have taken ACT Assessment between April of sophomore year and December of senior year, AND complete Regents Recommended Curriculum. The seventh semester GPA and curriculum data will be provided by high school official by March. Must complete the FAFSA.

Renewable. Contact Kansas Board of Regents for an application. See your financial aid office for the FAFSA.

2939—KANSAS COMMISSION ON VETERANS' AFFAIRS (Scholarships)

700 SW Jackson Street #701
Topeka KS 66603
913/296-3976
AMOUNT: Free tuition and fees in state supported institutions
DEADLINE(S): Varies
FIELD(S): All areas of study

Open to dependent child of person who entered U.S. military service as a resident of Kansas and was prisoner of war, missing, or killed in action or died as a result of service-connected disabilities incurred during service in Vietnam.

Application must be made prior to enrollment. Renewable to maximum of 12 semesters. Write for complete information.

2940—KANSAS STATE UNIVERSITY FOUNDATION (Various Scholarships)

Office of Student Financial Assistance, 104 Fairchild Hall
Manhattan KS 66506-1104
785/532-6420
FAX: 785/532-7628
E-mail: ksusfa@ksu.edu
Internet: http://www.found.ksu.edu/Schshps/Sch-txt.htm
AMOUNT: Varies
DEADLINE(S): Varies
FIELD(S): All fields of study

More than 1,300 scholarships are administered by the KSU Foundation for students attending KSU at either the Manhattan or Salina campus.

Salina campus address: Office of Student Financial Assistance, 223 College Center, Salina, KS 67401; Phone: 785/826-2638; FAX: 785/826-2936; E-mail: Hheter@mail.sal.ksu.edu. Web site above is the same for Salina.

2941—KAPPA SIGMA ENDOWMENT FUND (Scholarship/Leadership Awards Program)

P.O. Box 5643
Charlottesville VA 22905
804/295-3193
FAX: 804/296-5733
E-mail: ksef@imh.kappasigma.org
AMOUNT: $500-$2,500
DEADLINE(S): OCT 10
FIELD(S): All fields of study

Undergraduate awards are for members of Kappa Sigma Fraternity. Based on scholarship, leadership, and campus involvement. This is a merit-based program; financial need is NOT considered.

Awards not automatically renewable. Contact David M. Coyne, Chief Development Officer, for information, but access http://www.ksefnet.org (under "Educational Programs") for an application.

2942—KENNEDY FOUNDATION (Scholarships)

P.O. Box 27296
Denver CO 80227
303/933-2435
AMOUNT: Approx. $1,000
DEADLINE(S): JUN 30
FIELD(S): All fields of study

Scholarships for Colorado residents attending colleges or universities.

Send SASE to Jacqueline Kennedy, Vice President, at above location for application information.

2943—KENNEDY MEMORIAL TRUST (Kennedy Scholarships)

16 Great College Street
London SW1P 3RX ENGLAND
0171 222 1151
AMOUNT: Tuition; travel expenses; health insurance; stipend
DEADLINE(S): NOV 1
FIELD(S): Political Science; Public Service; Government; Arts and Sciences

Scholarships tenable in U.S. at Harvard or MIT. Open to United Kingdom citizens who are recent graduates or are currently studying for a first or higher degree and have spent 2 of the last five years at their university in Britain.

In awarding scholarships the trustees will take into consideration qualities of personal character as well as intellectual attainment and promise. Write for complete information.

2944—KENNEDY MEMORIAL TRUST (Scholarships at Harvard and the Massachusetts Institute of Technology)

16 Great College Street
London SW1P ENGLAND UK
0171 222 1151
Internet: http://www.admin.cam.ac.uk/reporter/1997-8/special/07/94.html
AMOUNT: $15,000 stipend + travel and tuition
DEADLINE(S): OCT 24
FIELD(S): All fields of study

Scholarships in honor of John F. Kennedy for U.K. citizens, normally residents of the U.K., tenable in the U.S. at Harvard or MIT. The disciplines of humane studies, economics, and modern technology are favored. Business administration students must have completed two years' full-time employment in business or public service. Those studying for a first degree must be in final year during application year.

Up to 12 annual awards. A one-year program; however, M.A. and Ph.D. candidates may apply for various positions, such as research or teaching assistants. See Web site for details.

2945—KENTUCKY CENTER FOR VETERANS AFFAIRS (Benefits for Veterans' Dependents, Spouses, and Widows)

545 S. 3rd Street, Room 123
Louisville KY 40202
502/595-4447
FAX: 502/595-4448
AMOUNT: Varies
DEADLINE(S): None
FIELD(S): All fields of study

Kentucky residents. Open to dependent children, spouses, and non-remarried widows of permanently and totally disabled war veterans who served during periods of federally recognized hostilities or who were MIA or a POW.

Veteran must be a resident of KY or, if deceased, a resident at time of death.

2946—KENTUCKY HIGHER EDUCATION ASSISTANCE AUTHORITY (Education Loans)

1050 U.S. Highway 127 S.
Frankfort KY 40601-4323
800/928-8926
FAX: 502/696-7373
Internet: http://www.kheaa.com
AMOUNT: $2,625-$18,500
DEADLINE(S): Varies
FIELD(S): All fields of study

Federal Stafford, PLUS, and Consolidation Loans are open to undergraduates, graduates, professional students, and parents of dependent students. Must fill out government FAFSA form, fill out loan applications, and sign promissory notes.

Contact KHEAA or your school's financial aid office for FAFSA and loan applications.

2947—KENTUCKY HIGHER EDUCATION ASSISTANCE AUTHORITY (Scholarships, Grants, and Work-Study Programs)

1050 U.S. Highway 127 S.
Frankfort KY 40601-4323
800/928-8926
FAX: 502/696-7373
Internet: http://www.kheaa.com
AMOUNT: Varies by program
DEADLINE(S): None
FIELD(S): All fields of study

Open to Kentucky residents pursuing undergraduate study. College Access Program (CAP) Grant recipients must plan to attend a Kentucky college, technical school, or proprietary school. Kentucky Tuition Grant recipients must plan to attend a private Kentucky college. Apply by filling out the government FAFSA form. Kentucky Educational Excellence Scholarship (KEES) recipients must have a minimum 2.5 GPA and be high school students or GED recipients.

Renewable. Contact KHEAA or your school's financial aid office for FAFSA as soon as possible after January 1. For information on work-study programs, see your school's KWSP Coordinator.

2948—KEY BANK OF CENTRAL MAINE FOUNDATION

P.O. Box 1054
Augusta ME 04330
Written Inquiry
AMOUNT: Varies
DEADLINE(S): Ongoing
FIELD(S): All fields of study

Scholarships for individuals to attend Main colleges and universities.

Send SASE to Key Bank of Maine at above address.

2949—KIDSFIRST SCHOLARSHIP FUND OF MINNESOTA (Scholarships)

800 Nicollet Mall, Suite 2680
Minneapolis MN 55402
612/573-2020
FAX: 612/573-2021
Internet: http://www.kidsfirstmn.org
AMOUNT: $1,200 max.
DEADLINE(S): APR 1
FIELD(S): All fields of study

Partial tuition scholarships for low-income children to attend private and parochial schools in the Twin Cities seven-county metro area.

Usually 200 awards are granted annually. Renewable every four years if guidelines are met. Visit Web site or contact Margie Lauer for details.

2950—KITTIE M. FAIREY EDUCATIONAL FUND

P.O. Box 1465
Taylors SC 29687-1465
803/765-3677
AMOUNT: Varies
DEADLINE(S): MAR 15
FIELD(S): All fields of study

Scholarships for residents of South Carolina attending four-year colleges or universities in SC.

Write to Sandra Lee, Director, at above address.

2951—KNIGHTS OF COLUMBUS (Fourth Degree Pro Deo and Pro Patria Scholarships)

P.O. Box 1670
New Haven CT 06507-0901
203/772-2130 ext. 332
FAX: 203/772-2696
AMOUNT: $1,500
DEADLINE(S): MAR 1
FIELD(S): All fields of study

Open to entering freshmen at a Catholic college who can show evidence of satisfactory academic performance. Must be a member in good standing of the Knights of Columbus, the child of such a member or deceased member, or a member in good standing of the Columbian Squires.

62 awards annually; 50 at any Catholic college and 12 at The Catholic University of America in Washington DC. Renewable up to 4 years. Contact the Director of Scholarship Aid for an application.

2952—KNIGHTS OF COLUMBUS (Francis P. Matthews and John E. Swift Educational Trust Scholarship)

P.O. Box 1670
New Haven CT 06507-0901
203/772-2130 ext. 332
FAX: 203/772-2696
AMOUNT: Varies
DEADLINE(S): None
FIELD(S): All fields of study

Open to children of Knights of Columbus members in good standing who died or became permanently and totally disabled while 1) serving in the military from a cause connected directly with military service during a period of conflict, or 2) as a result of criminal violence while in the lawful performance of their duties as full-time law enforcement officers or full-time firemen. Tenable for undergraduate study leading to a bachelor's degree at a Catholic college.

Contact the Director of Scholarship Aid for an application.

2953—KNIGHTS OF COLUMBUS (Pro Deo and Pro Patria Scholarships)

P.O. Box 1670
New Haven CT 06507-0901
203/772-2130 ext. 332
FAX: 203/772-2696
AMOUNT: $1,500
DEADLINE(S): MAR 1
FIELD(S): All fields of study

Open to entering freshmen pursuing bachelor's degrees at U.S. Catholic colleges. Must be a member in good standing of the Knights of Columbus, the son or daughter of such a member or deceased member, or a member in good standing of the Columbian Squires. Based on academic excellence.

62 awards annually. Renewable up to 4 years. Contact the Director of Scholarship Aid for an application.

2954—KNIGHTS OF COLUMBUS (Pro Deo and Pro Patria [Canada] Scholarships)

P.O. Box 1670
New Haven CT 06507-0901
203/772-2130 ext. 224
FAX: 203/772-2696
AMOUNT: $1,500
DEADLINE(S): MAY 1
FIELD(S): All fields of study

Open to students entering the first year of university study leading to a baccalaureate degree at colleges/universities in Canada. Must be a member in good standing in a Canadian council of the Knights of Columbus or the son or daughter of such a member or deceased member. Based on academic excellence.

12 awards annually. Renewable up to 4 years. Contact the Director of Scholarship Aid for an application.

2955—KNIGHTS TEMPLAR EDUCATIONAL FOUNDATION (Special Low-Interest Loans)

5097 N. Elston; Suite 101
Chicago IL 60630-2460
312/777-3300
AMOUNT: $6,000 maximum per student
DEADLINE(S): Varies
FIELD(S): All fields of study

Special low-interest loans (5% fixed rate). No payments while in school. Interest and repayments start after graduation or when you leave school. Open to voc-tech students or junior/senior undergraduate students or graduate students.

U.S. citizen or legal resident. Request information from Charles R. Neumann (Grand Recorder-Secretary). Call or write to your state's grand commandery for proper application.

2956—KODAIKANAL INTERNATIONAL SCHOOL (Fee Waiver)

P.O. Box 25
Kodaikanal Tamil Nadu 624 101
INDIA
91/4542-41104
FAX: 91/4542-41109
E-mail: principal@kis.ernet.in
Internet: http://www.kis.ernet.in
AMOUNT: $4,000 (max.)
DEADLINE(S): APR 1
FIELD(S): All fields of study

Open to Indian citizens in grades 4 through 12 who wish to attend this private Christian boarding school. Must also be an Indian resident and demonstrate financial need.

130 awards annually. Renewable. Contact Julie Stengele for an application.

2957—KOOMRUIAN EDUCATION FUND

3333 South Beaudry Avenue, Box 16
Los Angeles, CA 90017-1466
Written Inquiry
AMOUNT: Varies
DEADLINE(S): None specified
FIELD(S): All fields of study

Scholarships to students of Armenian descent residing in California.

Send SASE to Bank of America at above location.

2958—KOREAN AMERICAN SCHOLARSHIP FOUNDATION (Scholarships)

P.O. Box 486
Pacific Palisades CA 90272
310/459-4080
Internet: http://www.kasf.org
AMOUNT: Up to $1,000
DEADLINE(S): JAN 31
FIELD(S): All fields of study

Scholarships for students of Korean descent who are U.S. citizens or permanent residents.

Send SASE to Scholarship Committee at above address or visit Web site.

2959—KOSCIUSZKO FOUNDATION (Tuition Scholarships)

15 E. 65th Street
New York NY 10021-6595
212/734-2130
FAX: 212/628-4552
E-mail: thekf@pegasusnet.com
Internet: http://www.kosciuszko foundation.org
AMOUNT: $1,000-$5,000
DEADLINE(S): JAN 16
FIELD(S): All fields of study

Open to full-time undergraduate juniors and seniors and graduate students of Polish descent. Must be U.S. citizens/permanent residents attending a U.S. institution. Must have a minimum 3.0 GPA. Other criteria include special achievements and extracurricular activities, academic interest in Polish subjects and/or involvement in Polish American community, educational/professional goals, and financial need.

$25 application fee (1 application is valid for 2 years). Renewable. See Web site or send a self-addressed, stamped envelope to Addy Tymczyszyn for an application from September to December. Notification in May.

2960—LaFETRA OPERATING FOUNDATION (Fellowships for Training of Volunteers Abroad)

1221 Preservation Park Way; #100
Oakland CA 94612-1216
510/763-9206
FAX: 510/763-9290
E-mail: fellowship@lafetra.org
Internet: http://www.lafetra.org
AMOUNT: Stipend for internship + travel and program costs
DEADLINE(S): DEC 18
FIELD(S): All fields of study

An internship in SF Bay Area, CA, to learn skills in volunteering, and a fellowship for living and working in another country. Open to persons of color, individuals who demonstrate financial need, and adult professionals in various fields. Applicants from the Bay Area are preferred because housing/transportation for SF training cannot be provided for persons outside that area, but those who can provide their own housing/transportation in SF are welcome to apply.

See Web site or contact above address for an application/more information.

2961—LAMBDA ALUMNI PROGRAM (Scholarship)

P.O. Box 24C48
Los Angeles CA 90024
Written Inquiries
AMOUNT: $1,000
DEADLINE(S): MAR 15
FIELD(S): All

Available to any gay or lesbian undergraduate or graduate student. May be used for any field of study. Write to the above address for more information.

2962—LANCASTER COUNTRY DAY SCHOOL (Financial Aid)

725 Hamilton Road
Lancaster PA 17603
717/397-6399
FAX: 717/392-0425
E-mail: http://thiryj@e-lcds.org
AMOUNT: Varies
DEADLINE(S): MAR 1
FIELD(S): All fields of study

Open to K-12th grade students admitted to this private day school. Must demonstrate financial need.

100 awards annually. Renewable. Contact J.K. Thiry for an application.

2963—LARAMIE COUNTY FARM BUREAU (Scholarships)

206 Main Street, Box 858
Pine Bluffs WY 82082-0858
Written Inquiry
AMOUNT: $300
DEADLINE(S): MAY 1
FIELD(S): All fields of study

Available to needy high school seniors and college students whose parents have been members of Laramie County Farm Bureau for more than one year and who are current members. Award may be used at any institution of postsecondary education. Interviews will be done by appointment.

3 awards annually. Write to above address for an application.

2964—LEADERS IN FURTHERING EDUCATION (LIFE Unsung Hero Program Scholarships)

252 Ocean Boulevard
Manalapan FL 33462
561/547-9307
FAX: 561/585-3235
E-mail: life@life-edu.org
Internet: http://www.life-edu.org
AMOUNT: $10,000 for recipient's college tuition, books, housing; $2,500 to the charity with which they are involved; $2,500 to their high school
DEADLINE(S): DEC 15
FIELD(S): All fields of study

Scholarships for high school students (grades 9-12) who are residents of Palm Beach County, Florida, who engage in volunteer community service. Service must have been carried out for at least the past two years. GPA of 2.5 must be maintained.

Contact organization or access Web site for details.

2965—LEAGUE OF UNITED LATIN AMERICAN CITIZENS (LULAC National Scholarship Fund)

2000 L Street NW; #610
Washington DC 20036
202/835-9646
FAX: 202/835-9685
Internet: http://www.lulac.org/
AMOUNT: Varies
DEADLINE(S): Varies
FIELD(S): All fields of study

Open to high school seniors, undergraduates, and graduate students of Hispanic origin. Some awards are for specific fields of study, such as business or engineering, and some have certain GPA requirements.

Send self-addressed, stamped envelope for an application.

2966—LEE-JACKSON FOUNDATION (Scholarship Program)

P.O. Box 8121
Charlottesville VA 22906
Written Inquiry
AMOUNT: $3,000 (grand prize); $1,000 (each region)
DEADLINE(S): Varies
FIELD(S): All fields of study

Open to juniors and seniors in Virginia public high schools who plan to attend an accredited U.S. four-year college/university (community college okay if plan to transfer). Awards are for outstanding essays which demonstrate an appreciation of the exemplary character and soldierly virtues of Generals Lee and Jackson. Essays judged on accuracy, research, and ability to express one's thoughts. Length not as important as topic, idea, and points developed.

33 awards annually. Contact your school principal/guidance counselor or the Foundation for an application.

2967—LEGACY SOCCER FOUNDATION, INC./UNILEVER (Endowed Scholarships)

P.O. Box 3481
Winter Park FL 32790
407/263-8285
FAX: 407/740-8406
Internet: http://www.legacysoc.org
AMOUNT: Varies
DEADLINE(S): Varies
FIELD(S): All fields of study

Scholarships for Florida residents of either Brevard, Orange, Osceola, Seminole, or Volusa counties. Must be a U.S. citizen with a high school GPA of at least 2.5. Must graduate in top 1/3 of class and have played organized soccer for two out of past five years. Must meet financial aid requirements of the institution. Tenable at institutions in those same five counties.

Contact financial aid offices for Brevard, Valencia, and Seminole Community Colleges; contact athletic departments for University of Central Florida (Florida Institute of Technology) for more information.

2968—LEON L. GRANOFF FOUNDATION

P.O. Box 2148
Gardena CA 90247-0148
Written Inquiry
AMOUNT: Varies
DEADLINE(S): Varies
FIELD(S): All fields of study

Undergraduate scholarships for California residents to attend California colleges and universities.

Renewable provided recipients maintain at least a 3.25 GPA. Contact foundation for current application deadline and procedures.

2969—LEON M. JORDAN SCHOLARSHIP AND MONUMENT FUND

Box 15544
Kansas City MO 64106
Written Inquiry
AMOUNT: Varies
DEADLINE(S): Varies
FIELD(S): All fields of study

Scholarships to residents of Missouri.

Write to Alexander Ellison, Treasurer, Advisory Committee, at above address for application details.

2970—LEONARD H. BULKELEY SCHOLARSHIP FUND (Scholarship Grants)

c/o R. N. Woodworth, Treasurer
17 Crocker Street
New London CT 06320
860/447-1461
AMOUNT: $1,000 (approximately)
DEADLINE(S): APR 1
FIELD(S): All fields of study

Open ONLY to residents of New London, CT, for undergraduate study in an accredited college or university. Must demonstrate financial need.

Write for complete information.

2971—LEOPOLD SCHEPP FOUNDATION (Undergraduate Awards)

551 Fifth Avenue, Suite 3000
New York NY 10176-2597
212/986-3078
AMOUNT: Up to $7,500
DEADLINE(S): Not given
FIELD(S): All fields of study

Undergraduates should write detailing their education to date, year in school, length of course of study, vocational goal, financial need, age, citizenship, and availability for interview in New York City.

Approximately 200 new awards per year. Recipients may reapply for subsequent years. Applicants should already be in college and not older than 30. High school seniors may NOT apply. Print or type name and address. Send SASE with above information for application.

2972—LHU Foundation (Clara M. Clendenen Memorial Scholarship)

Ackley Hall
Lock Haven PA 17745
570/893-2293
Internet: http://www.lhup.edu/foundation/index.htm
AMOUNT: $12,000
DEADLINE(S): Varies
FIELD(S): All

For rising sophomore, junior, or senior students from western Clinton County, especially from Noyes Towhship, with first preference to English majors from western Clinton County, second preference to English majors from Clinton County, and third preference to any major from western Clinton County with demonstrated financial need.

2973—LHU Foundation (Hall & Elizabeth Achenbach Fund)

Ackley Hall
Lock Haven PA 17745
570/893-2293
Internet: http://www.lhup.edu/foundation/index.htm
AMOUNT: $400
DEADLINE(S): Varies
FIELD(S): All

For research expenses and learned conference travel for students in the social studies area of history, economics and political science, and for students in the ROTC program at LHU.

2974—LHU FOUNDATION (Sue Hall Memorial Scholarship)

Ackley Hall
Lock Haven PA 17745
570/893-2293
Internet: http://www.lhup.edu/foundation/index.htm
AMOUNT: $500
DEADLINE(S): Varies
FIELD(S): All

For a full-time female student who entered college at least one year after high school graduation. Priority shall be given to those who must be employed in order to be enrolled. Please include year of high school graduation and specifics of present employment on application form.

2975—LHU FOUNDATION (Vivienne Potter Elby Scholarship)

Ackley Hall
Lock Haven PA 17745
570/893-2293
Internet: http://www.lhup.edu/foundation/index.htm
AMOUNT: $650
DEADLINE(S): Varies
FIELD(S): All

For a full-time African-American student, who has achieved at least sophomore status, with a minimum GPA of 2.5 and who has demonstrated financial need. Preference to be given to graduates of Harrisburg High School, second to York High School.

2976—LILLY REINTEGRATION PROGRAMS

Lilly Secretariat
PMB 1167
734 North LaSalle Street
Chicago IL 60610
800/809-8202
FAX: 312/664-5454
E-mail: lillyscholarships@ims-chi.com
Internet: http://www.zyprexa.com/scholar.htm
AMOUNT: Up to $20,000
DEADLINE(S): JAN 31
FIELD(S): All

To be considered for a scholarship, applicants must be diagnosed with schizophrenia, schizophreniform or a schizoaffective disorder; be currently receiving medical treatment for the disease, including medications and psychiatric follow-up. Be actively involved in rehabilitative or reintegrative efforts, such as clubhouse membership, part-time work, volunteer efforts, or school enrollment.

2977—LINCOLN UNIVERSITY (Scholarships and Prizes)

P.O. Box 94
Canterbury NEW ZEALAND
(64) (3) 325 2811
FAX: (64) (3) 325 3850
AMOUNT: Varies
DEADLINE(S): Varies
FIELD(S): All fields of study

Hundreds of scholarships, bursaries, and prizes listed in the handbook published by Lincoln University, New Zealand. All fields of study, many for exchange students and travel, as well as for studying abroad.

Write to The Registrar, Lincoln University, at above address for booklet, "Scholarships and Prizes."

2978—LLOYD D. SWEET SCHOLARSHIP FOUNDATION (Scholarships)

Box 638 (Attn: Academic year)
Chinook MT 59523
406/357-2236
AMOUNT: Varies
DEADLINE(S): MAR 2
FIELD(S): All fields of study

Scholarships open to graduates of Chinook (MT) High School. Awards are for full-time undergraduate or graduate study at accredited colleges and universities in the U.S.

Approximately 75 awards per year. Write for complete information.

2979—LONE STAR INDUSTRIES (John H. Mathis Scholarship)

Deborah Bahnick, Director of Employee Relations
10401 North Meridian Street, Suite 400
Indianapolis IN 46290
317/706-3357
FAX: 317/805-3357
E-mail: dbahnick@lonestarind.com
Internet: http://www.lonestarind.com
AMOUNT: $2,500
DEADLINE(S): APR 9
FIELD(S): All

Eligible applicants will be unmarried children of Lone Star Industries employees. Employees must have been employed at Lone Star for at least one year full time. Renewable for four years of undergraduate study. Academic merit and extracurricular activities taken into consideration.

2980—LONG & FOSTER REAL ESTATE, INC. (Scholarship Program)

Melissa Lenard
Public Relations Coordinator
11351 Random Hills Road
FairFAX: VA 22030-6082
703/359-1757
FAX: 703/591-5493
E-mail: melissa.lenard@longandfoster.com
Internet: http://www.longandfoster.com
AMOUNT: $1,000
DEADLINE(S): MAR 1
FIELD(S): All

Scholarship selection will be based on financial need and a cumulative ranking of the following criteria: Academic Performance-SAT I and II test scores; High School GPA; Leadership Extracurricular Activities-Arts, Athletics, Community Service, etc.; Work Experience. This one-time award is only for residents of MD, PA, DC, VA, and DE.

2981—LOS MOLINOS UNIFIED SCHOOL DISTRICT (S. R. Pritchett Scholarship Fund)

District Superintendent
P.O. Box 609
Los Molinos CA 96055
916/384-7900
FAX: 916/384-1534
AMOUNT: Not specified
DEADLINE(S): APR 15
FIELD(S): All fields of study

Undergraduate scholarships open only to current year graduates of high school in the Vina area of Tehama County, CA.

Write for complete information.

2982—LOU AND LUCIENNE BRIGHTMAN SCHOLARSHIP

94 Pleasant Street
Malden MA 02148
Written Inquiry
AMOUNT: Varies
DEADLINE(S): JUN 1
FIELD(S): All areas of study

Scholarships for college-bound high school seniors who are residents of Maine.

Renewable. Send SASE to Robert M. Wallask, V.P. Eastern Bank and Trust Co. at above address.

2983—LOUISIANA DEPARTMENT OF VETERANS AFFAIRS (Awards Program)

P.O. Box 94095; Capitol Station
Baton Rouge LA 70804
504/922-0500
FAX: 504/922-0511
AMOUNT: Varies
DEADLINE(S): Varies
FIELD(S): All fields of study

Open to Louisiana residents who are children (aged 16-25) or widows/spouses of deceased/100% disabled war veterans who were Louisiana residents for at least one year prior to service. For undergraduate study at state supported schools in Louisiana.

200 awards annually. Renewable up to 4 years. Contact Dept. of Veterans Affairs for an application.

2984—LOUISIANA OFFICE OF STUDENT FINANCIAL ASSISTANCE (Tuition Opportunity Program for Students-Opportunity, Performance, Honors)

P.O. Box 91202
Baton Rouge LA 70821-9202
800/259-5626 ext. 1012
FAX: 225/922-0790
E-mail: custserv@osfa.state.la.us
Internet: http://www.osfa.state.la.us
AMOUNT: Equal to tuition at public institution (or weighted average tuition at LAICU member institution)
DEADLINE(S): JUL 1
FIELD(S): All fields of study

Open to Louisiana residents who will be first-time, full-time freshmen no later than fall following first anniversary of high school graduation. Must have minimum 2.5 GPA, minimum ACT score based on state's prior year average, and completion of 16.5 units college-prep core curriculum. Must be U.S. citizen planning to attend a Louisiana public or LAICU private post-secondary institution. Must not have any criminal convictions. Merit-based award.

Renewable. Apply by completing the Free Application for Federal Student Aid (FAFSA). Contact Public Information Rep for details.

2985—LOUISIANA OFFICE OF STUDENT FINANCIAL ASSISTANCE (Tuition Opportunity Program for Students-Performance Awards)

P.O. Box 91202
Baton Rouge LA 70821-9202
800/259-5626 ext. 1012
FAX: 225/922-0790
E-mail: custserv@osfa.state.la.us
Internet: http://www.osfa.state.la.us
AMOUNT: Equal to tuition at public institution + $400
DEADLINE(S): JUL 1
FIELD(S): All fields of study

Open to Louisiana residents who will be first-time, full-time freshmen by fall following first anniversary of high school graduation. Must have a minimum 3.5 GPA, minimum ACT score of 23, and completion of 16.5 units college-prep core curriculum. Must be U.S. citizen planning to attend a Louisiana public or LAICU private post-secondary institution. Must be registered with selective service (if necessary) and not have any criminal convictions. Financial need NOT a factor.

Renewable. Apply by completing the Free Application for Federal Student Aid (FAFSA). Contact Public Information Rep for details.

2986—LOUISIANA OFFICE OF STUDENT FINANCIAL ASSISTANCE (Tuition Opportunity Program for Students-Honors Awards)

P.O. Box 91202
Baton Rouge LA 70821-9202
800/259-5626 ext. 1012
FAX: 225/922-0790
E-mail: custserv@osfa.state.la.us
Internet: http://www.osfa.state.la.us
AMOUNT: Equal to tuition at public institution
DEADLINE(S): JUL 1
FIELD(S): All fields of study

Open to Louisiana residents who will be first-time, full-time freshmen by fall following first anniversary of high school graduation. Must have a minimum 2.5 GPA, minimum ACT score of 19, and completion of 16.5 units college-prep core curriculum. Must be U.S. citizen planning to attend a Louisiana public or LAICU private post-secondary institution. Must be registered with selective service (if necessary) and not have any criminal convictions. Financial need NOT a factor.

Renewable. Apply by completing the Free Application for Federal Student Aid (FAFSA). Contact Public Information Rep for details.

2987—LOUISIANA OFFICE OF STUDENT FINANCIAL ASSISTANCE (LEAP-Leveraging Educational Assistance Partnership)

P.O. Box 91202
Baton Rouge LA 70821-9202
800/259-5626 ext. 1012
FAX: 225/922-0790
E-mail: custserv@osfa.state.la.us
Internet: http://www.osfa.state.la.us
AMOUNT: $200-$2,000
DEADLINE(S): JUL 1
FIELD(S): All fields of study

Open to Louisiana residents planning to pursue undergraduate study at eligible Louisiana institutions. Must have minimum high school or college GPA of 2.0, 45 on GED, or ACT score of at least 20. Selection by post-secondary institution; institution may have additional requirements. Must be U.S. citizen and demonstrate financial need.

2,800 awards annually. Renewable. Apply by completing the Free Application for Federal Student Aid (FAFSA). Contact Public Information Rep for details.

2988—LOUISIANA STATE UNIVERSITY AT SHREVEPORT (LSUS Academic Scholarship)

Financial Aid Office
One University Place
Shreveport LA 71115-2399
318/797-5363
FAX: 318/797-5366
E-mail: finaid@pilot.lsus.edu
Internet: http://www.lsus.edu
AMOUNT: Tuition and fees +$400 for books and supplies
DEADLINE(S): DEC 1
FIELD(S): All fields of study

This may be a one-year or a four-year award. Student must be a Louisiana resident, a high school graduate/equivalent (or a senior in high school), have at least a 28 composite score on the ACT (which must be taken in October to have the results on file with LSUS by December 1 deadline), and must have a minimum 3.5 GPA.

Contact your high school counselor or the Student Financial Aid Office at LSUS for an application. Awards are made by the end of February.

2989—LOUISIANA STATE UNIVERSITY AT SHREVEPORT (LSUS Foundation Scholarship)

Financial Aid Office
One University Place
Shreveport LA 71115-2399
318/797-5363
FAX: 318/797-5366
E-mail: finaid@pilot.lsus.edu
Internet: http://www.lsus.edu
AMOUNT: $300-$750/semester
DEADLINE(S): DEC 1; MAR
FIELD(S): All fields of study

Student must be an entering freshman with at least a 20 ACT composite score and minimum 3.0 cumulative GPA or be a transfer student with at least 48 credit hours and a 3.5 or higher college GPA. Entering freshmen awards are for up to eight semesters, and transfer student awards range from two to four semesters.

High school students should submit the LSUS scholarship application by December 1 of senior year. Transfer students should send a letter of application to the Financial Aid Office with an official college transcript of all coursework by the March prior to the fall semester they are entering.

2990—LOUISIANA STATE UNIVERSITY AT SHREVEPORT (LSUS Alumni Association Scholarship)

Financial Aid Office
One University Place
Shreveport LA 71115-2399
318/797-5363
FAX: 318/797-5366
E-mail: finaid@pilot.lsus.edu
Internet: http://www.lsus.edu
AMOUNT: $1,000/year
DEADLINE(S): FEB 1
FIELD(S): All fields of study

This four-year award is for entering freshmen with at least a 3.2 cumulative high school GPA (grades 9-11) and a 25 or higher composite score on the ACT. To retain scholarship, the recipient must complete at least 12 hours credit and make at least a 3.0 GPA average each semester. Must apply during senior year of high school.

Contact your high school counselor or the Student Financial Aid Office at LSUS for an application.

2991—LUBBOCK AREA FOUNDATION, INC. (Scholarships)

1655 Main Street, #209
Lubbock TX 79401
806/762-8061
FAX: 806/762-8551
E-mail: lubaf@worldnet.att.net

AMOUNT: Varies
DEADLINE(S): Varies
FIELD(S): All fields of study

Several scholarships are administered by this Foundation for residents of the Lubbock, Texas, area. There are no scholarships available for applicants not connected with these institutions.

Contact organization for specifics.

2992—LUCY E. MEILLER EDUCATIONAL TRUST

P.O. Box 13888
Roanoke VA 24038
Written Inquiry

AMOUNT: $3,000
DEADLINE(S): Ongoing
FIELD(S): All fields of study

Scholarships for financially needy residents of Virginia to attend colleges and universities.

Apply through the financial aid office the the Virginia college or university or contact Perry Gorham, Crestar Bank, at above address for details.

2993—LYONS CLUB OF RAWLINS (K. Craig Williams Memorial Scholarship)

Rawlins High School Guidance Office
Rawlins WY 82301
307/328-9288

AMOUNT: $250-$600
DEADLINE(S): APR 15
FIELD(S): All fields of study

Available to current year Rawlins High School graduates. Award may be used at any accredited postsecondary institution.

1 award annually. Applications are available from the Rawlins High School Guidance Office.

2994—M.O.S.T., INC. (Memphis Opportunity Scholarship Trust)

850 Ridge Lake Boulevard; Suite 220
Memphis TN 38120
901/767-7005
FAX: 901/818-5260
E-mail: trentwilliamson@rfshotel.com

AMOUNT: $1,500 max.
DEADLINE(S): MAR 31
FIELD(S): All fields of study

Need-based scholarship/tuition assistance for residents of Shelby County, Tennessee in grades K-5 to attend private school.

600-700 awards annually. Renewable. Contact Trent Williamson, Executive Director, for an application and/or income guidelines.

2995—MACDUFFIE SCHOOL (Financial Aid)

One Ames Hill Drive
Springfield MA 01105
413/734-4971
FAX: 413/734-6693
E-mail: admissions@macduffie.com

AMOUNT: Varies
DEADLINE(S): Varies
FIELD(S): All fields of study

Open to 6th-12th grade students at this private day/boarding school. Must demonstrate financial need.

Contact the Admissions Office for an application.

2996—MADDEN BROTHERS (Goshen County Community Scholarships)

Route 1; Box 360
Torrington WY 82240
307/532-7079

AMOUNT: $300
DEADLINE(S): Varies
FIELD(S): All fields of study

Available to recent graduates of a Goshen County high school who will be attending any college, university, or trade school, and entering as freshmen. Participation in 4-H or FFA activities will be considered but is not mandatory.

3 awards annually. Contact Madden Brothers for an application.

2997—MAGNA FOR CANADA SCHOLARSHIP FUND (As Prime Minister Awards Program)

337 Magna Drive
Aurora Ontario L4G 7K1 CANADA
800/97-MAGNA
Internet: http://www.asprime minister.com

AMOUNT: $10,000 + 1-year internship (national winner); $10,000 + 4-month internship (10 finalists); $500 (semi-finalists)
DEADLINE(S): JUN 5
FIELD(S): All fields of study

Open to full-time undergraduate and graduate students currently enrolled in an accredited Canadian college/university or CEGEP. Must submit a maximum 2,500-word essay in either official language, responding to the question, "If you were the Prime Minister of Canada, what political vision would you offer to improve our living standards?" Essays judged primarily on merit, but consideration will also be given to extracurricular activities, grades, and essay composition.

See Web site or contact Magna for Canada for guidelines.

2998—MAINE AMERICAN LEGION, PAST COMMANDERS CLUB (James V. Day Scholarship)

P.O. Box 545
Union, ME 04862

AMOUNT: Not specified
DEADLINE(S): MAY 1
FIELD(S): All fields of study in accredited college or vocational or technical school

Open to students in the graduating class of their high schools. Parent must be a current member of an American Legion Post in the Department of Maine. Must be of good character and have demonstrated that he/she believes in the American way of life.

Application requires 300-word essay describing student's objectives for furthering education.

2999—MAINE COMMUNITY FOUNDATION (Scholarship Program)

245 Main Street
Ellsworth ME 04605
207/667-9735
Internet: http://www.mainecf.org

AMOUNT: Varies
DEADLINE(S): Varies
FIELD(S): Varied fields of study

All scholarships are available to Maine residents only. The Maine Community Foundation offers over 170 scholarships, covering a wide range of fields of study.

Eligible applicants should visit the MCF Web site for a complete listing of its scholarships.

3000—MAINE STATE GRANT PROGRAM

5 Community Drive
P.O. Box 969
Augusta ME 04330
800/228-3734
Internet: http://www.famemaine.com

AMOUNT: $1,000 for in-state public schools; $1,250 for in-state private schools; $500 out-of-state public schools; $1,000 out-of-state private schools
DEADLINE(S): MAY 1 (receipt date of FAFSA)
FIELD(S): All fields of study

Open to Maine residents attending regional accredited colleges in PA, and New England states. Awards are for full-time undergraduate study.

10,000 awards per year. Application is the Free Application for Federal Student Aid (FAFSA) available in your college financial aid office.

3001—MAINE VETERANS' SERVICES (Grants for Dependents)

State House Station 117
Augusta ME 04333-0117
207/626-4464 or 800/345-0116 (in ME only)

AMOUNT: Tuition at state-supported Maine schools
DEADLINE(S): None
FIELD(S): All fields of study

Open to Maine residents who are children/step-children (high school graduates, ages 16-21) and spouses/widows of military veterans who are totally disabled due to service or who died in service or as a result of service. Tenable for undergraduate study at all branches of University of Maine system, all State of Maine vo-tech colleges, and Maine Maritime Academy at Castine. Veteran must have lived in Maine at time of entering service or for 5 years prior to application.

Contact Maine Veterans' Services for an application.

3002—MAKARIOS SCHOLARSHIP FUND, INC. (Scholarships)

13 East 40th Street
New York NY 10016
212/696-4590 or 800/775-7217

AMOUNT: Varies
DEADLINE(S): MAY 5
FIELD(S): All fields of study

For students from Cyprus with valid student visas who are pursuing studies in an accredited United States college or university on a full-time basis. Includes Theodore and Wally Lappas Award and Thomas and Elaine Kyrus Endowment.

Financial need determines award. Applications must be typewritten and include various documents-please write or call for complete information.

3003—MAMIE ADAMS MEMORIAL AWARD

4126 Pocahontas Drive
Baytown TX 77521
713/421-2915
FAX: 713/421-2915

AMOUNT: $1,000/year
DEADLINE(S): APR 30
FIELD(S): All fields of study

A scholarship for a high school senior planning to attend college in the fall or for undergraduate college students enrolled at a 2- or 4-year institution. Min. 2.5 GPA required. Preference give to students who have demonstrated consistency and improvement in their scholastic records.

1 award. Can apply between Feb. 1 and April 30. Write or call for detailed eligibility requirements. Key qualification is to show improvement in academic standing.

3004—MANITOBA STUDENT FINANCIAL ASSISTANCE PROGRAM

409-1181 Portage Avenue
Winnipeg Manitoba R3G OT3
CANADA
800/204-1685

AMOUNT: Varies
DEADLINE(S): Varies
FIELD(S): All fields of study

For Manitoba residents taking 60% + of full-course load (college/university) or 100% for private vocational schools. Must be Canadian citizen/permanent resident. May apply for assistance to attend out-of-country provided meet eligibility criteria. Funds include loans and other federal/provincial assistance, some of which is non-repayable. Assistance is also provided for Canadian aboriginal students, students w/ dependents, part-time stuents, and students w/ disabilities.

12,500 awards annually. Write for an application.

3005—THE MARGARET MCNAMARA MEMORIAL FUND

1818 H Street NW, Room H2-204
Washington DC 20433
202/473-8751
FAX: 202/522-3142
E-mail: MMMF@worldbank.org

AMOUNT: $11,000
DEADLINE(S): FEB 8
FIELD(S): All

This grant was established to aid women from developing countries reach their higher education goals. Applicants must demonstrate financial need and use grant money toward their degree. Must not be related to a member of the World Bank Group.

3006—MARIE L. ROSE HUGUENOT SOCIETY OF AMERICA (Scholarships)

122 East 58th Street
New York NY 10022
212/755-0592
FAX: 212/317-0676

AMOUNT: $1,800/year
DEADLINE(S): JUN 1
FIELD(S): All fields of study

For American undergraduates who submit proof of descent from a Huguenot who emigrated from France and either settled in what is now the U.S. or left France for countries other than America before 1787. Only students approved by one of the participating colleges may apply; no application sent directly to the Huguenot Society will be considered. Financial need is NOT a factor.

25 awards annually. Renewable. Contact your school's financial aid office for an application or contact Dorothy Kimball at above address for a list of participating colleges/universities.

3007—MARIN EDUCATION FUND (Asian Scholarship Fund)

1010 B Street, Suite 300
San Rafael CA 94901
415/459-4240
FAX: 415/459-0527

AMOUNT: $500 to $2,500
DEADLINE(S): MAR 31
FIELD(S): All fields of study

For students who have been residents of Marin or Sonoma counties in California, for at least one year. Must have one biological parent of Asian ancestry; proof may be requested. Scholarships based on outstanding achievement, demonstrated community responsibility and service, leadership, and financial need. Must be attending an accredited or state-approved high school and will be enrolling in a full-time, undergraduate academic program leading to a degree.

10 awards annually. May be attending an educational institution outside of Marin or Sonoma counties provided applicant has satisfied the one-year residency requirement.

3008—MARIN EDUCATIONAL FUND (Undergraduate Scholarship Program)

1010 'B' Street, Suite 300
San Rafael CA 94901
415/459-4240

AMOUNT: $800-$2,000
DEADLINE(S): MAR 2
FIELD(S): All fields of study

Open to Marin County (CA) residents only for undergraduate study in 2- or 4-year colleges and for fifth-year teaching credentials. Must be enrolled at least half-time and demonstrate financial need.

Write for complete information.

3009—MARINE CORPS TANKERS ASSOCIATION (John Cornelius Memorial Scholarship)

1112 Alpine Heights Road
Alpine CA 91901-2814
619/445-8423

AMOUNT: $1,500+
DEADLINE(S): MAR 15
FIELD(S): All fields of study

Must be a survivor, a dependent, or under legal guardianship of a Marine Tanker-active duty, reserve, retired, or honorably discharged-who served in a Marine Tank unit OR be a Marine or Navy Corpsman who *personally* qualifies in the foregoing. Must be a member of MCTA, or will join. May apply as a high school senior, undergraduate, or graduate student. Letters of recommendation, transcripts, and personal narrative required with application.

12 awards annually. Renewable with reapplication. Notification by the end of April. Contact Phil Morell, Scholarship Chairman, for an application.

3010—MARINE CORPS SCHOLARSHIP FOUNDATION (Scholarships to Sons and Daughters of Marines)

P.O. Box 3008
Princeton NJ 08543-3008
800/292-7777 or 609/921-3534
FAX: 609/452-2259
E-mail: mcsf@marine-scholars.org
Internet: http://www.marinescholars.org

AMOUNT: $500-$2,500
DEADLINE(S): APR 1
FIELD(S): Any field of study

The Marine Corps Scholarship Foundation offers scholarships to undergraduates who are sons and daughters of current or former Marines. Special consideration is given to an applicant whose parent was killed or wounded in action. Applicants must be seniors or high school graduates or be enrolled in an accredited college or vocational school. Parents combined income cannot exceed $42,000.

Financial need considered. Application requests are available at the above Web site or by mail. No phone requests.

3011—MARION BRILL SCHOLARSHIP FOUNDATION, INC. (Undergraduate Scholarships)

97 West Street
P.O. Box 420
Ilion NY 13357
315/895-7771

AMOUNT: $100-$500
DEADLINE(S): JAN 15
FIELD(S): All fields of study

Undergraduate scholarships open to residents of Ilion (Herkimer County) NY who graduated from Ilion Central School District. Must demonstrate financial need to satisfaction of screening committee. FAF form required.

Write for complete information.

3012—MARK R. FUSCO FOUNDATION

Attn: Lauren Fusco Baumann
555 Long Wharf Drive
New Haven CT 06511
203/777-7451

AMOUNT: Varies
DEADLINE(S): Ongoing
FIELD(S): All fields of study

Scholarships for students who are residents of Connecticut for all academic fields (solely for educational expenses incurred). Applicants must write a detailed letter including career goals and financial and academic history. Community involvement and extracurricular activity will be considered.

Non-renewable. Contact the Foundation.

3013—MARY E. HODGES FUND

222 Tauton Avenue
East Providence RI 02914-4556
401/435-4650

AMOUNT: Varies
DEADLINE(S): MAY 1
FIELD(S): All fields of study

Scholarships for students who have a Rhode Island Masonic affiliation or who have been residents of Rhode Island for at least five years.

Send SASE to John M. Faulhaber, Secretary, at above address for details.

3014—MARY INSTITUTE AND SAINT LOUIS COUNTRY DAY SCHOOL (Financial Aid)

101 North Warson Road
Saint Louis MO 63124
314/995-7367
FAX: 314/872-3257
E-mail: jhall@micds.pvt.k12.mo.us
Internet: http://micds.pvt.k12.mo.us

AMOUNT: Tuition
DEADLINE(S): None
FIELD(S): All fields of secondary school study

Financial aid for this co-ed private school, grades K-12, in St. Louis, MO. The aid is for the secondary level.

Access Web site for information about the school. Renewable yearly. Must demonstrate financial need.

3015—MARY LOUIS ACADEMY (Scholarships and CSJ Scholar Incentive Awards)

176-21 Wexford Terrace
Jamaica Estates NY 11432-2926
718/297-2120
FAX: 718/739-0037
Internet: http://www.tmla.org

AMOUNT: $2,450-$4,900 (scholarships); $1,000 (awards)
DEADLINE(S): SEP 30
FIELD(S): All fields of study

Open to female 9th-12th grade students at this private Roman Catholic day school. Apply through the co-operative entrance examination administered in the fall (usually November). Financial need NOT a factor.

50 scholarships and 28 awards annually. Renewable. Contact Sister Filippa Luciano for an application.

3016—MARY M. AARON MEMORIAL TRUST (Scholarships)

1190 Civic Center Boulevard
Yuba City CA 95997
Written Inquiry

AMOUNT: $500 to $1,000
DEADLINE(S): MAR 15
FIELD(S): All areas of study

Open to any needy student from Sutter County, California, attending an accredited 2-year (approx. $500) or 4-year (approx. $1,000) California college or university. Grants based mainly on financial need. Grades and activities are not considered as significant.

Write for complete information.

3017—MARYLAND HIGHER EDUCATION COMMISSION (Delegate Scholarships)

State Scholarship Admin.
16 Francis Street
Annapolis MD 21401-1781
410/974-5370
TTY: 800/735-2258

AMOUNT: Varies: $200 minimum
DEADLINE(S): Varies
FIELD(S): All fields of study

For Maryland residents who are undergraduate or graduate students in Maryland (or out-of-state with a unique major).

Duration is up to 4 years; 2 to 4 scholarships per district. Also for full- or part-time study at certain private career schools and diploma schools of nursing. Write to your delegate for complete information.

3018—MARYLAND HIGHER EDUCATION COMMISSION (Educational Assistance Grant)

State Scholarship Admin.
16 Francis Street
Annapolis MD 21401-1781
410/974-5370
TTY: 800/735-2258

AMOUNT: $400-$3,000
DEADLINE(S): MAR 1 (via FAFSA)
FIELD(S): All areas of study

Open to Maryland residents for full-time undergraduate study at a Maryland degree-granting institution or hospital school of nursing. Financial need must be demonstrated.

Renewable with reapplication for up to 3 years. Write for complete information.

3019—MARYLAND HIGHER EDUCATION COMMISSION (Edward T. Conroy Memorial Scholarships)

State Scholarship Admin.
16 Francis Street
Annapolis MD 21401-1781
410/974-5370
TTY: 800/735-2258

AMOUNT: Up to $4,699 for tuition and mandatory fees
DEADLINE(S): JUL 15
FIELD(S): All fields of study

For sons and daughters of persons 100% disabled or killed in the line of military duty who were Maryland residents at the time of disability or death, to sons and daughters of MIAs or POWs, and to sons, daughters, and un-remarried spouses of public safety employees disabled or killed in the line of duty. Also for 100%-disabled public safety employees.

For undergraduate or graduate study, full- or part-time, in an MD institution. Write for complete information.

3020—MARYLAND HIGHER EDUCATION COMMISSION (Guaranteed Access Grant)

State Scholarship Admin.
16 Francis Street
Annapolis MD 21401-1781
410/974-5370
TTY: 800/735-2258
Internet: http://www.ubalt.edu/www.mhec

AMOUNT: $8,700
DEADLINE(S): MAR 1
FIELD(S): All fields of study

For Maryland high school seniors who have completed high school in Maryland with a GPA of at least 2.5. Must have completed a college preparatory or an articulated tech prep program. Family income may not exceed 130% of the federal poverty level.

Must demonstrate financial need. Write for complete information.

3021—MARYLAND HIGHER EDUCATION COMMISSION (Senatorial Scholarship Program)

State Scholarship Admin.
16 Francis Street
Annapolis MD 21401-1781
410/974-5370
TTY: 800/735-2258

AMOUNT: $400-$2,000
DEADLINE(S): MAR 1 (via FAFSA)
FIELD(S): All fields of study

Open to Maryland residents for undergrad or grad study at MD degree-granting institutions, certain private career schools, nursing diploma schools in Maryland. For full- or part-time study. SAT or ACT required for some applicants.

Students with unique majors or with impaired hearing may attend out of state. Duration is 1 to 4 years with automatic renewal until degree is granted. Senator selects recipients. Write for complete information.

3022—MASSACHUSETTS BOARD OF HIGHER EDUCATION (Public Service Grant)

Office of Student Financial Assistance
330 Stuart Street, 3rd Floor
Boston MA 02116
617/727-9420

AMOUNT: Varies with school (covers tuition; not fees)
DEADLINE(S): MAY 1
FIELD(S): All fields of study

Open to permanent Massachusetts residents who are the child or deceased police/fire/corrections officer killed in line of duty or child of deceased veteran whose death was service-related.

Write for complete information.

3023—MASSACHUSETTS BOARD OF HIGHER EDUCATION (Veterans Tuition Exemption Program)

330 Stuart Street, 3rd Floor
Boston MA 02116
617/727-9420

AMOUNT: Tuition exemption
DEADLINE(S): None
FIELD(S): All areas of study

Open to military veterans who are permanent residents of Massachusetts. Awards are tenable at Massachusetts post-secondary institutions.

Contact veterans agent at college or address above for complete information.

3024—MASSACHUSETTS COMPANY (The M. Geneva Gray Scholarship Fund)

Trust Dept.; 125 High Street
Boston MA 02110
617/556-2335

AMOUNT: Up to $1,000
DEADLINE(S): MAR 1
FIELD(S): All fields of study

Open to undergraduate students who are Mass. residents and are unable to qualify for financial aid due to high parental income. Family must have more than one child to educate. Income between $25,000 and $50,000.

There are no academic requirements other than enrollment and good standing. Send a self-addressed stamped envelope for an application and list of instructions.

3025—MASSACHUSETTS OFFICE OF STUDENT FINANCIAL ASSISTANCE (National Guard Tuition Waiver)

454 Broadway, Suite 200
Revere MA 02151

617/727-9420
AMOUNT: Tuition waiver
DEADLINE(S): None
FIELD(S): All areas of study

Program open to undergraduate students who are enrolled at a Massachusetts public college or university and are active members of the Massachusetts National Guard or the Massachusetts Air National Guard.

Contact the veterans office at your college or address above for complete information.

3026—MASSACHUSETTS OFFICE OF STUDENT FINANCIAL ASSISTANCE (General Scholarship Program)

454 Broadway, Suite 200
Revere MA 02151
617/727-9420
AMOUNT: $300-$2,900
DEADLINE(S): MAY 1
FIELD(S): All fields of study

Open to permanent residents of Massachusetts. Awards are for undergraduate study at accredited colleges and universities in Massachusetts. Must complete FAFSA by May 1.

40,000-50,000 awards per year. Write for complete information.

3027—MAUD GLOVER FOLSOM FOUNDATION, INC. (Scholarships and Grants)

21 Deepwood Lane
Norwalk CT 06854-3903
Written Inquiry
AMOUNT: $5,000/year (max.)
DEADLINE(S): None
FIELD(S): All fields of study

Scholarships are open to men of Anglo-Saxon or German descent to the age of 35 who are U.S. citizens. Initial Grants are given only to males between the ages of 14 and 20. For use in preparatory school, high school, college, professional/graduate school, or any advanced school of the individual's choice.

Write to Leon A. Francisco, President, at above address for an application.

3028—MAY THOMPSON HENRY TRUST (Scholarships)

Central National Bank and Trust Co.
P.O. Box 3448
Enid OK 73702
405/233-3535
AMOUNT: Varies
DEADLINE(S): None
FIELD(S): All fields of study

Open to Oklahoma students attending state-supported Oklahoma colleges/universities.

Contact Trust Department for an application.

3029—McCURDY MEMORIAL SCHOLARSHIP FOUNDATION (Emily Scofield Scholarship Fund)

134 West Van Buren Street
Battle Creek MI 49017
616/962-9591
AMOUNT: $100-$1,000
DEADLINE(S): MAR 31
FIELD(S): All areas of study

Scholarships for residents of Calhoun County, Michigan. Must be undergraduate.

4-5 scholarships per year. Renewable with reapplication and satisfactory grades. Write for complete information.

3030—McCURDY MEMORIAL SCHOLARSHIP FOUNDATION (McCurdy Scholarship)

134 West Van Buren Street
Battle Creek MI 49017
616/962-9591
AMOUNT: $1,000
DEADLINE(S): MAR 31
FIELD(S): All fields of study

Must be a resident of Calhoun County, Michigan. Program is for undergraduate students.

Seven scholarships per year. Renewable with reapplication and satisfactory grades. Write for complete information.

3031—McDONALD'S HISPANIC AMERICAN COMMITMENT TO EDUCATIONAL RESOURCES PROGRAM (Scholarships For High School Seniors)

One Sansome Street, Suite 1000
San Francisco CA 94104
800/736-5219; 415/445-9930
FAX: 415/445-9942
E-mail: info@nhsf.org
Internet: http://www.nhsf.org
AMOUNT: $1,000 (more in certain areas)
DEADLINE(S): MAR 1
FIELD(S): All fields of study

For college-bound Hispanic high school seniors who are U.S. citizens or permanent residents. Available in certain counties in 21 states throughout the U.S. Designated counties are at above Internet site.

Inquire of high school counselor, local McDonald's manager, the above 800 number, or the National Hispanic Scholarship Fund at above location. Not renewable. Refer to RMHC/HACER program (Ronald McDonald House Charities/Hispanic American Commitment to Educational Resources).

3032—McDONALD'S RESTAURANTS OF WEST NEW YORK (BOMAC Scholarship Award)

c/o Stern Advertising, 6265 Sheridan Drive, Bldg. A, Suite 216
Amherst NY 14221
716/631-2476
FAX: 716/631-5317
AMOUNT: $500
DEADLINE(S): Varies
FIELD(S): All fields of study

Open to employees of McDonald's who are high school seniors living in West New York-the McDonald's you are employed at must belong to the co-op of 66 restaurants that oversees this award. This scholarship is to be used for postsecondary study.

20 awards annually. Contact your store manager to see if your McDonald's belongs to this co-op.

3033—McDONALD'S (RMHC/HACER Scholarship Program)

Kroc Drive
Oak Brook IL 60523
800/736-5219
Internet: http://www.mcdonalds.com/community/education/scholarships/hacer/index.html
AMOUNT: $1,000+
DEADLINE(S): FEB 1
FIELD(S): All fields of study

For college-bound Hispanic students who have a demonstrated record of academic achievement, financial need, and community involvement. Must be U.S. citizen or permanent resident and live in District of Columbia, Puerto Rico, or one of the following states: AZ, CA, CO, CT, DE, FL, IL, IN, MD, MA, NJ, NM, NY, OK, PA, RI, TX, VA, WV, WI, or WY. Essay, transcripts, SAT/ACT scores, and letters of recommendation required with application.

Not renewable. Applications are available from your local participating McDonald's restaurant or high school counselor, or call the RMHC/HACER hotline above.

3034—McDONALD'S (UNCF New York Tri-State Scholarships)

See your local McDonald's
Tri-State restaurant
Internet: http://www.archinginto education.com/
AMOUNT: $1,000; $10,000
DEADLINE(S): MAR 31
FIELD(S): All fields of study

New York Tri-State residents (NYC, Long Island and specific counties in CT and NJ) who are planning to attend a United Negro College Fund institution are eligible.

50 $1,000 awards annually; 1 $10,000 award for a student demonstrating outstanding academic merit. Pick up an application in your local New York, New Jersey, or Connecticut McDonald's.

3035—McDONOGH SCHOOL (Scholarships)

P.O. Box 380
Owings Mills MD 21117-0380
410/581-4719
FAX: 410/581-4777
Internet: http://www.mcdonogh.org
AMOUNT: Partial tuition
DEADLINE(S): DEC 15
FIELD(S): All fields of study

Need-based scholarships with a merit component for students admitted to this co-educational, college preparatory independent school in Maryland. Grades K-12. For U.S. citizens.

Renewable if need is determined.

3036—MEETING SCHOOL (Tuition Assistance)

56 Thomas Road
Rindge NH 03461
603/899-3366
FAX: 603/899-6216
E-mail: office@meetingschool.org
Internet: http://meetingschool.org
AMOUNT: Varies
DEADLINE(S): MAY
FIELD(S): All fields of study

Open to 9th-12th grade students accepted to this private Society of Friends (Quaker) day/boarding school (mostly boarding). Must be in good standing, demonstrate financial need, and be U.S. citizen/permanent resident. Priority given to children of alums and Quakers.

30 awards annually. Renewable. Contact the Admissions Office for an application.

3037—MENOMINEE INDIAN TRIBE OF WISCONSIN (Grants)

Virginia Nuske, Education Director
P.O. Box 910
Keshena WI 54135
715-799-5110
FAX: 715-799-1364
E-mail: vnuske@itol.com
Internet: http://www.menominee.nsn.us/educationoffice/eduagencies educationofc.htm
AMOUNT: $100-$1,100
DEADLINE(S): Varies
FIELD(S): All

Grant available to Menominee tribal member currently enrolled at a two- or four-year institution of higher learning. Must be able to show proof of Indian blood. Must demonstrate need for financial aid. This award is renewable.

3038—MERCANTILE BANK OF TOPEKA (Claude and Ina Brey Memorial Endowment Fund)

c/o Trust Dept.
P.O. Box 192
Topeka KS 66601
913/291-1118
AMOUNT: $500
DEADLINE(S): APR 15
FIELD(S): All fields of study

Scholarships open to fourth degree Kansas Grange members. Awards tenable at recognized undergraduate colleges and universities. U.S. citizen.

8 awards per year. Renewable. For complete information write to Marlene Bush, P.O. Box 186; Melvern KS 66510.

3039—MERCHISTON CASTLE SCHOOL (Scholarships)

294 Colinton Road
Edinburgh EH13 OPU SCOTLAND UK
0131/312-2200
FAX: 0131/441-6060
E-mail: admissions@merchiston.co.uk
Internet: http://www.merchiston.co.uk
AMOUNT: From 5% up to a maximum 50% full fees
DEADLINE(S): Varies
FIELD(S): All fields of study

Open to boys aged 8-18 who wish to attend this private day/boarding school. Usually awarded to boys aged 13+, who demonstrate strong academic performance and that they will contribute to the school community. Various different awards are available and are based on such factors as merit, financial need, and activities (sports, music, drama, art, etc.). If parents not resident in the UK, a UK guardian must be appointed.

See Web site or contact Mrs. Anne Rickard, Admissions Coordinator, for an information packet.

3040—MERVYN'S (Kilmartin Educational Scholarship Program)

Mervyn's store
Apply in person
AMOUNT: Ask store manager
DEADLINE(S): Varies
FIELD(S): All fields of study

Scholarships for employees of Mervyn's stores who have accumulated at least 1,000 hours of employment with Mervyn's and have graduated from high school or an equivalent. Available nationwide.

Recipients are eligible to reapply.

3041—METHODIST LADIES' COLLEGE (Scholarships)

207 Barkers Road Kew
Melbourne Victoria 3101
AUSTRALIA
+61 (3) 9274 6333
FAX: +61 (3) 9819 2345
E-mail: college@mlc.vic.edu.au
Internet: http://www.mic.vic.edu.au
AMOUNT: Varies
DEADLINE(S): Varies, usually end of March in the preceding year
FIELD(S): All fields of study

Various scholarships at this pre-kindergarten-grade 12 boarding school for girls in Melbourne, Australia. Scholarships are for students in grades 7-12. Some are for music students. Selection is based on scholarship test results, school grade results, and interview. Some are based on financial need. Although the school is rooted in the Methodist church, girls from all religious and ethnic backgrounds are welcome. For citizens or permanent residents of Australia.

Approximately 33 awards yearly, full- or half-scholarships. Contact school for details.

3042—METROPOLITAN MILWAUKEE ASSOCIATION OF COMMERCE (Scholarships)

756 N. Milwaukee Street
Milwaukee WI 53202
AMOUNT: Up to $3,500/year

DEADLINE(S): MAY 1
FIELD(S): All fields of study

Must be a graduate of a Milwaukee Public High School with a 90% cumulative attendance rate. Must have a cumulative GPA of 2.5 or better, demonstrate financial need, and attend the University of Wisconsin at Milwaukee full-time.

Apply through your high school guidance counselor or by contacting MMAC, Education and Scholarship Programs, at above address.

3043—MEXICAN AMERICAN BUSINESS AND PROFESSIONAL SCHOLARSHIP ASSOCIATION (Scholarship Program)

P.O. Box 22292
Los Angeles CA 90022
Written Inquiry only
AMOUNT: $100-$1,000
DEADLINE(S): MAY 1 (postmark)
FIELD(S): All fields of study

Open to Los Angeles County residents who are of Mexican-American descent and are enrolled full-time in an undergraduate program. Awards are based on financial need and past academic performance.

Send self-addressed, stamped envelope (SASE) with request for complete information.

3044—MICHIGAN COMMISSION ON INDIAN AFFAIRS; MICHIGAN DEPT OF CIVIL RIGHTS (Tuition Waiver Program)

201 N. Washington Square,
Suite 700
Lansing MI 48933
517/373-0654
AMOUNT: Tuition (only) waiver
DEADLINE(S): Varies (8 weeks prior to class registration)
FIELD(S): All areas

Open to any Michigan resident who is at least 1/4 North American Indian (certified by their tribal nation) and willing to attend any public Michigan community college, college, or university.

Award is for all levels of study and is renewable. Must be Michigan resident for at least 12 months before class registration. Write for complete information.

3045—MICHIGAN ELKS ASSOCIATION CHARITABLE GRANT FUND

43904 Lee Ann Lane
Canton MI 48187
Written Inquiry
AMOUNT: Varies
DEADLINE(S): JAN 20
FIELD(S): All fields of study

Scholarships to physically disabled students who are residents of Michigan.

Contact local Elks Lodge for application information.

3046—MICHIGAN GUARANTY AGENCY (Stafford and PLUS Loans)

P.O. Box 30047
Lansing MI 48909
800/642-5626
FAX: 517/335-6703
AMOUNT: Varies
DEADLINE(S): None
FIELD(S): All fields of study

Guaranteed student loans are available to students or parents of students who are Michigan residents enrolled in an eligible institution. Must be U.S. citizen/permanent resident.

Contact Agency for an application.

3047—MICHIGAN HIGHER EDUCATION ASSISTANCE AUTHORITY (Michigan Competitive Scholarships)

Office of Scholarships and Grants
P.O. Box 30462
Lansing MI 48909
888/447-2687
AMOUNT: $100-$1,200
DEADLINE(S): FEB 21
FIELD(S): All fields of study (except BRE degree)

Open to Michigan residents who are undergraduates enrolled at least half time in an eligible Michigan college/university. Must demonstrate financial need, submit ACT scores, and file government FAFSA form.

Renewable. Contact your school counselor for an application and/or the FAFSA form.

3048—MICHIGAN HIGHER EDUCATION ASSISTANCE AUTHORITY (Michigan Tuition Grants)

Office of Scholarships and Grants
P.O. Box 30462
Lansing MI 48909
888/447-2687
AMOUNT: $100-$2,650
DEADLINE(S): Varies
FIELD(S): All fields of study (except BRE degree)

Open to Michigan residents enrolled at least half time at independent non-profit Michigan institutions (list available from above address). Both undergraduate and graduate students who can demonstrate financial need are eligible. Must file government FAFSA form.

Renewable. Contact MHEAA for an application.

3049—MICHIGAN VETERANS TRUST FUND (Tuition Grant Program)

611 West Ottawa, 3rd Floor
Lansing MI 48913
517/373-3130
AMOUNT: Up to $2,500/year
DEADLINE(S): None
FIELD(S): All areas of study

Open to Michigan residents of at least 12 months preceding enrollment who are aged 16-26 and are children of Michigan veterans killed in action or who later died or were totally disabled due to a service-connected cause.

Renewable for 36 months. Grants are for undergraduate study at Michigan post-secondary schools. Write for complete information.

3050—MIDWEST STUDENT EXCHANGE PROGRAM (Tuition Reduction)

Midwestern Higher Education Commission
Attn: Jennifer Wright
Program Officer
1300 South Second Street,
Suite 130
Minneapolis MN 55454-1079
612/626-1602
FAX: 612/626-8290
AMOUNT: Usually between $500 and $3,000
DEADLINE(S): FEB 1
FIELD(S): All fields of study

At least 10% off the tuition at designated private colleges and universities participating in the out-of-state program for residents of Kansas, Michigan, Minnesota, Missouri, and Nebraska who attend participating institutions in those same states.

Contact your high school counselor or the Office of Admissions at the college you plan to attend for further requirements. When applying to a college, mark prominently on the form that you seek admission as a MSEP student.

3051—MILITARY ORDER OF THE PURPLE HEART (Sons, Daughters, and Grandchildren Scholarship Program)

Nat'l Headquarters
5413-B Backlick Road
Springfield VA 22151
703/642-5360
FAX: 703/642-2054
AMOUNT: $1,750/year
DEADLINE(S): MAR 15
FIELD(S): All fields of study

Open to children and grandchildren of Military Order of the Purple Heart Members/Recipients. Applicants must be U.S. citizens/permanent residents and pursuing undergraduate or graduate study. Must demonstrate academic achievement and financial need.

$5 application fee. 4-8 awards annually. Renewable up to 4 years with minimum 3.5 GPA. Contact National Headquarters for an application.

3052—MINISTRY OF EDUCATION AND TRAINING; ONTARIO STUDENT ASSISTANCE PROGRAM (OSAP)

P.O. Box 4500
189 Red River Road, 4th Floor
Thunder Bay, Ontario P7B 6G9
CANADA
807/343-7260
TDD: 800/465-3958
AMOUNT: Varies
DEADLINE(S): Varies
FIELD(S): All areas of study

OSAP offers Federal and provincial loans to Canadian citizens or residents who live in Ontario and are enrolled in an approved Ontario college, university, or private postsecondary institution.

Bursaries are available to students with disabilities/children. Write for information.

3053—MINISTRY OF SMALL BUSINESS, TOURISM and CULTURE, RECREATION AND SPORT BRANCH (B.C. Athlete Assistance Program)

P.O. Box 9820
Victoria BC V8W 1X4 9W3
CANADA
604/356-1180
AMOUNT: $500-$3,500
DEADLINE(S): Varies (Specific to each sport)
FIELD(S): All areas of study

Open to student athletes who are Canadian citizens or have landed immigrant status and have resided in BC for at least one year (academic year for students). Must participate in a sport included in the Olympic Games, Commonwealth Games, Pan-American Games, Canada Games, and Olympic-level competition for the disabled.

Contact AAP (above) for complete information.

3054—MINNESOTA GAY/LESBIAN/BISEXUAL/TRANSGENDER EDUCATIONAL FUND (Grants)

P.O. Box 7275
Minneapolis MN 55407-0275
612/220-4888
AMOUNT: Varies
DEADLINE(S): APR 1
FIELD(S): All fields of study

Open to GLBT postsecondary students. Purpose is to recognize outstanding GLBT students and activities, to support the continuing education for self-identified GLBT persons, and to foster a positive public image of GLBT people in society.

Contact Minnesota GLBT Educational Fund for an application.

3055—MINNESOTA HIGHER EDUCATION SERVICES OFFICE (Financial Aid Programs)

1450 Energy Park Drive, #350
St. Paul MN 55108-5265
651/642-0567
FAX: 651/642-0675
E-mail: info@heso.state.mn.us
Internet: http://www.mheso.state.mn.us/
AMOUNT: Varies
DEADLINE(S): Varies
FIELD(S): All fields of study

Grants, scholarships, loans, and work-study programs are open to Minnesota residents to attend colleges and universities. Also offers summer programs at college campuses for students in grades 7-12. Most programs require attendance at Minnesota institutions. Tuition reciprocity (waiver of non-resident tuition charges) for out-of-state tuition is available in certain other states.

See Web site or send for booklet "Focus on Financial Aid" for details.

3056—MINNESOTA HIGHER EDUCATION SERVICES OFFICE (Minnesota Indian Scholarship Program)

Indian Education
1819 Bemidji Avenue
Bemidji MN 56601
218/755-2926
AMOUNT: Average $1,450/year
DEADLINE(S): None
FIELD(S): All fields of study

For Minnesota residents who are one-fourth or more Indian ancestry and members of or elgible for membership in a tribe. Must be high school graduates or GED recipients and be accepted by an approved college, university, or vocational school in Minnesota, and approved by the Minnesota Indian Scholarship Committee. Apply as early as possible before starting your post-high school program.

Indian students also must apply to federally funded grant programs, including the Pell Grant Program, their respective tribal anency, and the Minnesota Grant Program. Contact Joe Aitken at the above location.

3057—MINNESOTA HIGHER EDUCATION SERVICES OFFICE (Summer Scholarships for Academic Enrichment)

1450 Energy Park Drive, #350
St. Paul MN 55108-5265
612/296-3974
FAX: 612/297-8880
E-mail: info@heso.state.mn.us
Internet: http://www.heso.state.mn.us/
AMOUNT: Up to $1,000
DEADLINE(S): Varies
FIELD(S): All academic subjects

For Minnesota students in grades 7-12 to attend eligible summer academic programs sponsored by Minnesota postsecondary schools-University of Minnesota campuses, state universities, community colleges, private colleges, and technical colleges. Must be U.S. citizen or permanent resident, hold at least a B average for the most recent term, or have a B average in the subject area of the enrichment course, and demonstrate financial need (based on parents' income).

Deadline dates vary depending on the program. Contact above address for list of participating postsecondary institutions.

3058—MINNESOTA STATE DEPARTMENT OF VETERANS AFFAIRS (Deceased Veterans' Dependents Scholarships)

Veterans Service Bldg.
20 W. 12th, 2nd Floor
St. Paul MN 55155-2079
612/296-2562
AMOUNT: Tuition + $350
DEADLINE(S): None
FIELD(S): All fields of study

Open to 2-year (or more) residents of Minnesota who are sons/daughters of veterans killed in service or who died as a result of a service-caused condition. Parent must have been a resident of Minnesota at time of entry into service. Must be U.S. citizen/legal resident and an undergraduate planning to attend a Minnesota college/university.

Renewable. Contact the Minnesota State Department of Veterans Affairs for an application.

3059—MINNESOTA STATE DEPARTMENT OF VETERANS AFFAIRS (Veterans Grants)

Veterans Service Bldg.
20 W. 12th, 2nd Floor
St. Paul MN 55155-2079
612/296-2562

AMOUNT: $350
DEADLINE(S): None
FIELD(S): All fields of study

Open to veterans who were residents of Minnesota at the time of their entry into the armed forces of the U.S. and were honorably discharged after having served on active duty for at least 181 consecutive days. Must be U.S. citizen/legal resident and planning to attend an accredited institution in Minnesota. Must also have time remaining on federal education period and have exhausted through use any federal educational entitlement. Must demonstrate financial need.

Contact the Minnesota State Department of Veterans Affairs for an application.

3060—MISS HALL'S SCHOOL (Berkshire County Scholarships)

492 Holmes Road
Pittsfield MA 01201
413/499-1300
FAX: 413/448-2994
E-mail: info@misshalls.com
Internet: http://www.misshalls.com

AMOUNT: $7,000
DEADLINE(S): MAR 2
FIELD(S): All fields of study

Miss Hall's is a private girls' prep high school (grades 9-12) in Massachusetts. It is both a boarding and day school. Scholarship applicants must be entering 9th or 10th grade and be residents of Bershire County, Massachusetts. U.S. citizenship.

Contact Elaine Cooper at above location for further information. Applicants considered on academic record, interview, and essays.

3061—MISSISSIPPI OFFICE OF STATE STUDENT FINANCIAL AID (Law Enforcement Officers and Firemen Scholarship Program)

3825 Ridgewood Road
Jackson MS 39211-6453
601/982-6663 or 800/327-2980 (MS only)
FAX: 601/982-6527

AMOUNT: Tuition, room, and required fees
DEADLINE(S): None
FIELD(S): All fields of study

Open to children, step-children, and spouses of Mississippi law enforcement officers or full-time firemen who were fatally injured or were totally disabled while on duty. Children must be under age 23. Tenable for eight semesters of undergraduate study at any state-supported college/university in Mississippi.

Contact Susan Eckels, Program Administrator, for an application.

3062—MISSISSIPPI OFFICE OF STATE STUDENT FINANCIAL AID (Southeast Asia POW/MIA Scholarship Program)

3825 Ridgewood Road
Jackson MS 39211-6453
601/982-6663 or 800/327-2980 (MS only)
FAX: 601/982-6527

AMOUNT: Tuition, room, and required fees
DEADLINE(S): None
FIELD(S): All fields of study

Open to Mississippi residents under age 23 who are dependent children of military veterans formerly or currently listed as missing in action in Southeast Asia or as prisoners of war as a result of military action against the U.S. Naval Vessel Pueblo. Tenable for eight semesters of undergraduate study at any state-supported Mississippi college/university.

Contact Susan Eckels, Program Administrator, for an application.

3063—MOBIL CORPORATION (Desert Storm Scholarship Program)

3225 Gallows Road
Fairfax, VA 22037-0001
Written Inquiry only

AMOUNT: Varies
DEADLINE(S): Varies (with institution)
FIELD(S): All fields of study

Open to veterans of Operation Desert Shield/Desert Storm, their spouses, and their children. The spouses and children of those who died in the operations receive highest priority. For full-time undergraduate study leading to a bachelor's degree.

Scholarships are renewable and available at 20 U.S. colleges and universities. Financial need is a consideration. Write for list of participating schools and complete information.

3064—MODERN WOODMEN OF AMERICA (Fraternal College Scholarship Program)

1701 First Avenue
Rock Island IL 61201
Written Inquiry

AMOUNT: $1,000-$3,000
DEADLINE(S): JAN 1
FIELD(S): All fields of study

Open to high school seniors who have been beneficial members of Modern Woodmen for at least two years. Must be in the upper half of graduating class and planning to attend an accredited four-year college/university in the U.S. Based on qualities of character/leadership, scholastic records, and aptitude for college work.

39 renewable awards and 24 one-time awards annually. Contact the Scholarship Administrator for an application.

3065—MONGOLIA SOCIETY (Dr. Gombojab Hangin Memorial Scholarship)

322 Goodbody Hall; Indiana Univ.
Bloomington IN 47405
812/855-4078
FAX: 812/855-7500
E-mail: MONSOC@Indiana.edu

AMOUNT: $2,500
DEADLINE(S): JAN 1
FIELD(S): All fields of study

Open to students of Mongolian heritage (defined as an individual of Mongolian ethnic orgins who is a citizen of Mongolia, the People's Republic of China, or the former Soviet Union) to pursue studies in the U.S. Award does not include transportation from recipient's country to U.S. nor does it include room and board at university. Upon conclusion of the award year, recipient must write a report of his/her activities which resulted from receipt of the scholarship.

Recipient will receive scholarship monies in one lump sum after enrollment in the scholarship holder's institution in the U.S. Write for complete information.

3066—MONGOLIA SOCIETY (Dr. Gombojab Hangin Memorial Scholarship)

322 Goodbody Hall; Indiana Univ.
Bloomington IN 47405-7005
E-mail: monsoc@indiana.edu
AMOUNT: up to $2,400
DEADLINE(S): JAN 1
FIELD(S): All fields of study

The scholarship is given to a student of Mongolian heritage (defined as an individual of Mongolian ethnic origins who has permanent residency in Mongolia, China, or the Former Soviet Union) to pursue studies in the U.S. Award will be made in competitive application. Does NOT include transportation, board, or lodging. Recipient will receive scholarship in one lump sum after enrollment, and must write report of activities which resulted from scholarship.

1 award annually. Each applicant must individually request the application in English, and the application must be returned written in English. Write to the Scholarship Committee at above address.

3067—MONTANA UNIVERSITY SYSTEM (Montana State Student Incentive Grants)

2500 Broadway
P.O. Box 203101
Helena MT 59620
406/444-6594
AMOUNT: Up to $600
DEADLINE(S): None
FIELD(S): All fields of study

Open to Montana residents who are full-time undergraduate students attending accredited schools in Montana. Must demonstrate need.

1,150 awards per year. Contact financial aid office of the school you plan to attend as these grants are decentralized.

3068—MORRIS SCHOLARSHIP FUND (Scholarships for Minorities in Iowa)

525 SW 5th Street, Suite A
Des Moines IA 50309-4501
515/282-8192
FAX: 515/282-9117
E-mail: morris@assoc-mgmt.com
Internet: http://www.morris scholarship.org
AMOUNT: Varies
DEADLINE(S): MAR 1
FIELD(S): All fields of study

Program to provide fiancial assistance, motivation, and counseling for minority students pursuing higher education. Awards are based on academic achievement, community service, and financial need. Preference is given to Iowa residents attending an Iowa-based college or university.

Contact organization or check Web site for details.

3069—MORRISON ACADEMY (Tuition Assistance)

136 Shui-Nan Road
Taichung 406 TAIWAN
886/4-292-1171
FAX: 886/4-292-1174
E-mail: mcgillt@mca.tc.edu.tw
Internet: http://www.morrison.mknet.org
AMOUNT: Varies
DEADLINE(S): AUG 1
FIELD(S): All fields of study

Open to K-12 students at this private Protestant/Christian day/boarding school. Students must either demonstrate financial need or be affiliated with religious missionary sending agencies.

Renewable. Contact Tim McGill, Director of Operations, for an application.

3070—MOSTARS/MISSOURI DEPARTMENT OF HIGHER EDUCATION (Charles Gallagher Student Financial Assistance Program)

3515 Amazonas Drive
Jefferson City MO 65018
800/473-6757 or 573/751-3940
FAX: 573/751-6635
Internet: http://www.mocbhe.gov
AMOUNT: $100-$1,500
DEADLINE(S): APR 1
FIELD(S): All fields of study (except Theology and Divinity)

Grants are open to Missouri residents who are U.S. citizens pursuing undergraduate studies full-time at eligible Missouri institutions. Must fill out the government FAFSA form and check that you want information released to the state. Must demonstrate financial need.

Renewable with reapplication. See Web site or contact MOSTARS Information Center for details.

3071—MOSTARS/MISSOURI DEPARTMENT OF HIGHER EDUCATION ("Bright Flight" Academic Scholarship Program)

3515 Amazonas Drive
Jefferson City MO 65018
800/473-6757 or 573/751-3940
FAX: 573/751-6635
Internet: http://www.mocbhe.gov
AMOUNT: $2,000
DEADLINE(S): JUL 31
FIELD(S): All fields of study (except Theology and Divinity)

Scholarships are for Missouri residents who are U.S. citizens accepted to or enrolled at eligible Missouri institutions. Must be pursuing undergraduate studies and have a composite ACT or SAT score in top 3 percent. Apply for fall term immediately following graduation from high school or obtaining GED.

Renewable yearly as an undergraduate. See Web site or contact MOSTARS Information Center for an application.

3072—MOSTARS/MISSOURI DEPARTMENT OF HIGHER EDUCATION (Marguerite Ross Barnett Memorial Scholarship)

3515 Amazonas Drive
Jefferson City MO 65018
800/473-6757 or 573/751-3940
FAX: 573/751-6635
Internet: http://www.mocbhe.gov
AMOUNT: Varies
DEADLINE(S): JUL 31
FIELD(S): All fields of study (except Theology and Divinity)

Scholarship is open to Missouri residents who are pursuing undergraduate studies at eligible Missouri institutions. Must be attending school at least half-time but less than full-time. Compensated for employment at least 20 hours per week. Must demonstrate financial need.

Renewable with reapplication. See Web site or contact MOSTARS Information Center for details.

3073—MOTHER JOSEPH ROGAN MARYMOUNT FOUNDATION (Grant and Loan Programs)

c/o Nations Bank
P.O. Box 14737
St. Louis MO 63101
314/391-6248
AMOUNT: $400 to $750
DEADLINE(S): MAY 1
FIELD(S): All fields of study

Grants and loans for students who are U.S. citizens, live in the metropolitan St. Louis area, and are entering or enrolled in a high school, vocational/technical school, college, or university.

Applications are NOT accepted. Grants and loans are awarded by the administration and faculty of various St.

Louis schools. Please do not send inquiries to this address. Contact your school for more information.

3074—MOUNT DE CHANTAL ACADEMY (Scholarships)

410 Washington Avenue
Wheeling WV 26003
304/233-3771
FAX: 304/233-8598
E-mail: mountdec@ovnet.com
AMOUNT: $1,500-$3,500
DEADLINE(S): AUG 1
FIELD(S): All fields of study

Open to female pre-K to 12th grade students at this private Catholic day/boarding school. Must be a minority with a minimum 3.0 GPA and demonstrate financial need. Secondary awards limited primarily to exceptional students.

10 awards annually. Renewable. Contact Sandra L. Clerici for an application.

3075—MOUNT SAINT JOSEPH ACADEMY (Partial Scholarships)

120 West Wissahickon Avenue
Flourtown PA 19031
215/233-3177
Internet: mciunix.mciu.k12.pa.us/~msjaweb/Mount_web_page.html
AMOUNT: Partial tuition-varies
DEADLINE(S): OCT 31
FIELD(S): All fields of study

A private Catholic high school (grades 9-12) for girls in Pennsylvania. Partial scholarships available for academic ability, musical ability, and art talent. Also, one is for a high-ranking African American student and one for a daughter, granddaughter, or niece of an alumna.

3076—NAACP NATIONAL OFFICE (Agnes Jones Jackson Scholarship)

4805 Mt. Hope Drive
Baltimore MD 21215
401/358-8900
AMOUNT: $1,500 undergrads; $2,500 grads
DEADLINE(S): APR 30
FIELD(S): All areas of study

Undergraduates must have GPA of 2.5+; graduates must possess 3.0 GPApplicants must be NAACP members and must be under the age of 25 by April 30.

Send legal-size, self-addressed, stamped envelope to address above for application and complete information.

3077—NAACP NATIONAL OFFICE (Roy Wilkins Scholarship)

4805 Mount Hope Drive
Baltimore MD 21215
401/358-8900
AMOUNT: $1,000
DEADLINE(S): APR 30
FIELD(S): All fields of study

Open to graduating high school seniors who are members of the NAACP. Applicants must have at least a 2.5 (C+) grade point average.

Write for complete information. Include a legal size self-addressed stamped envelope.

3078—NATIONAL 4TH INFANTRY (IVY) DIVISION ASSOCIATION (Scholarship Program)

Alexander Cooker, 4 IDA
Scholarship Fund Treasurer
80 North Dupont
Carney's Point NJ 08069
609/299-4406
E-mail: al4thinf@gateway.net
Internet: http://www.4thinfantry.org
AMOUNT: $500-$1,000
DEADLINE(S): Varies
FIELD(S): All

Available to U.S. and non-U.S. citizens. Applicant must be a blood relative of current Association member. Applicant must be enrolled full- or part-time at a two-year, four-year, or technical institution or university. Raffle-type drawing each year during annual banquet.

3079—NATIONAL ACADEMY OF AMERICAN SCHOLARS (Easley National Scholarships)

Merit Committee
1249 South Diamond Bar Boulevard, #325
Diamond Bar CA 91765-4122
E-mail: staff@naas.org
Internet: http://www.naas.org
AMOUNT: $200-$10,000
DEADLINE(S): FEB 1
FIELD(S): All

Applicant must be enrolled in either a public, private, charter, Magnet, or parochial, or Bureau of Indian Affairs School, or Department of Defense Dependents School, as a high school senior and plan to attend a four-year college or university. Must possess a cumulative GPA of at least a C or higher at time of application.

3080—NATIONAL ACADEMY OF AMERICAN SCHOLARS (Easley National Scholarships)

1249 South Diamond Bar Boulevard #325
Diamond Bar CA 91765-4122
E-mail: staff@naas.org
Internet: http://www.naas.org
AMOUNT: $200-$10,000
DEADLINE(S): Varies
FIELD(S): All

Applicant must be enrolled in either a public, private, charter, Magnet, or parochial, or Bureau of Indian Affairs School, or Department of Defense Dependents School, as a high school senior and plan to attend a four-year college or university. Must have a GPA of 2.0 or higher.

3081—NATIONAL ACADEMY OF AMERICAN SCHOLARS (NAAS II National Scholarship)

Dr. H. Borgstedt
Scholarship Chairperson
1249 South Diamond Bar Boulevard, #325
Diamond Bar CA 91765-4122
909/621-6856
E-mail: staff@naas.org
Internet: http://www.naas.org
AMOUNT: $1,000-$3,000
DEADLINE(S): MAR 1
FIELD(S): All

Applicant must be enrolled in a two- or four-year American college/university as a college freshman or sophomore pursuing a four-year bachelor's degree. Applicant need not be a U.S. citizen but must have at least a 2.0 GPA. Must be younger than 25 at time of application.

3082—NATIONAL ALLIANCE FOR EXCELLENCE, INC. (National Scholarship Competition)

63 Riverside Avenue
Red Bank NJ 07701
732/747-0028
E-mail: info@excellence.org
Internet: http://www.excellence.org
AMOUNT: $1,000-$5,000
DEADLINE(S): None
FIELD(S): All fields of study

Students must be planning to attend college full-time.

Send SASE for application or download from Web site.

3083—NATIONAL ART MATERIALS TRADE ASSOCIATION (NAMTA Scholarships)

10115 Kincey Avenue; Suite 260
Huntersville NC 28078
704/948-5554
E-mail: scholarships@namta.org

AMOUNT: $1,000
DEADLINE(S): MAR 1
FIELD(S): All fields of study

Open to undergraduate and graduate students who are employees or relatives of employees of a NAMTA member firm. Based on financial need, grades, activities, interests, and career goals.

Contact NAMTA for an application.

3084—NATIONAL ASSOCIATION OF NEGRO BUSINESS AND PROFESSIONAL WOMENS CLUB (Scholarships)

1806 New Hampshire Avenue NW
Washington DC 20009-3208
202/483-4206
FAX: 462-7253
Internet: http://www.afrika.com

AMOUNT: $1,000
DEADLINE(S): MAR 31 (request applications Sept. 1-Dec. 31)
FIELD(S): All fields of study

Scholarships for college-bound graduating high school seniors and first-year college students. U.S. citizenship or permanent residency required. For males or females of any ethnic background.

10 national awards and 750 awards by local clubs. Send self-addressed, stamped envelope with request application (if not, requests will not be answered!).

3085—NATIONAL ASSOCIATION OF SECONDARY SCHOOL PRINCIPALS (National Honor Society Scholarships)

1904 Association Dr
Reston VA 22091
800/253-7746

AMOUNT: $1,000
DEADLINE(S): FEB 1
FIELD(S): All fields of study

Open to National Honor Society Members. Each chapter nominates two seniors to compete for scholarships at the national level.

250 scholarships per year. Contact your NHS chapter; high school principal or guidance counselor for complete information.

3086—NATIONAL ASSOCIATION OF SECONDARY SCHOOL PRINCIPALS (Wendy's High School Heisman Award)

1904 Association Drive
Reston VA 22091
800/253-7746

AMOUNT: Trip to New York City for December Heisman awards ceremony plus grants for schools of winners
DEADLINE(S): SEP (early)
FIELD(S): All fields of study

For high school juniors. Award recognizes scholarship, citizenship, and athletic ability. Twelve national finalists will visit New York City and two finalists will be named the Wendy's High School Heisman Award winners. Winners' schools will receive grants of up to $3,000.

Contact Association for details.

3087—NATIONAL ASSOCIATION OF SECONDARY SCHOOL PRINCIPALS (Century III Leaders Program)

1904 Association Drive
Reston VA 22091
800/253-7746

AMOUNT: Not specified
DEADLINE(S): NOV
FIELD(S): All fields of study

Program recognizes outstanding high school seniors who have a good academic record, are involved in school and community activities, and have an awareness of world events. Application process includes a two-page projection written by school winners concerning a problem America will face in its third century as a nation. A current events exam is also given.

Funds total $142,000 for awards. Funded by Sylvan Learning Centers. Ask your high school principal for application materials or contact above location.

3088—NATIONAL ASSOCIATION TO ADVANCE FAT ACCEPTANCE-THE NEW ENGLAND CHAPTER (NAAFA Scholarship Program)

P.O. Box 1820
Boston MA 02205
781/986-2232

AMOUNT: $500
DEADLINE(S): MAY 1
FIELD(S): All fields of study

This scholarship is offered to any fat or large-sized college-bound high school senior student in the New England states. Students will be required to complete an application.

Send SASE to Sharon Irinms at the above address for complete information.

3089—NATIONAL BAPTIST CONVENTION USA, INC. (Scholarships)

356 E. Boulevard
Baton Rouge LA 70802
Written Inquiry

AMOUNT: $1,000
DEADLINE(S): Varies
FIELD(S): All fields of study

Scholarships for college-bound high school seniors and undergraduates who are active members of the a church of the National Baptist Convention.

Send SASE for details.

3090—NATIONAL BETA CLUB (Scholarship)

151 West Lee Street
Spartanburg SC 29306-3012
Internet: http://www.betaclub.org

AMOUNT: $1,000-$3,750
DEADLINE(S): DEC 10
FIELD(S): All

Available to senior high school students who are active National Beta Club members and are registered with the national headquarters. May be nominated by their Beta Club chapters to participate. Each chapter may nominate two senior members who exemplify the club's goals of academic excellence, leadership, and school/ community service

Application fee: $10.

3091—NATIONAL BURGLAR & FIRE ALARM ASSOCIATION (NBFAA/Security Dealer Youth Scholarship Program)

7101 Wisconsin Avenue, #901
Bethesda MD 20814
301/907-3202
FAX: 301/907-7897
E-mail: staff@alarm.org
Internet: http://www.alarm.org

AMOUNT: $6,500 (National first prize), $3,500 (second); $1,000 (State first prize), $500 (second)
DEADLINE(S): JUN 1
FIELD(S): All fields of study

Must be the child of active-duty police or fire personnel and living in a state that has NBFAA chartered state association. Award is for high school seniors and is based on academic achievement, community and extracurricular activities, and an essay describing "How (their) Father, Mother, or Guardian Helps Us Secure Our

Community." Each state chapter has own contest, and winners are automatically entered in national competition.

Contact local NBFAA chapter, or write to above address for application. Participating states include WA, NC, CA, GA, IN, PA, NJ, CT, and VA.

3092—NATIONAL CENTER FOR LEARNING DISABILITIES (Anne Ford Scholarship for College-Bound Students With Learning Disabilities)

381 Park Avenue South, Suite 1401
New York NY 10016
800/575-7373
FAX: 212/545-9665
Internet: http://www.ld.org

AMOUNT: $10,000
DEADLINE(S): Varies
FIELD(S): All

Open to a promising high school senior with learning disabilities who plans to pursue a university degree. The ideal candidate is a person who has faced the challenges of having a learning disability and who, through perseverance and academic endeavor, has created a life of purpose and achievement. The candidate embraces new opportunities and ventures, and has a well-rounded perspective shaped by experiences in school, with family and friends, and through community involvement. The candidate understands how LD affects his/her life and knows the importance of self-advocacy. Available in any field of study.

3093—NATIONAL CHAMBER OF COMMERCE FOR WOMEN (Millie Belafonte Wright Scholarship and Grant Evaluation)

Ms. Caroline Westbrook, Coordinator
10 Waterside Plaza, Suite 6H
New York NY 10010
212/685-3454
FAX: 212/685-4547
E-mail: commerce-for-women@juno.com

AMOUNT: $1,000-$2,500
DEADLINE(S): Continuous
FIELD(S): All

Interested applicants may submit a researched paper relating to workplace behavioral psychology. This paper should give women insight into how to reach their business goal.

Applicant must be currently enrolled at a two- or four-year institution or university.

3094—NATIONAL COLLEGIATE ATHLETIC ASSOCIATION (Degree Completion Awards)

P.O. Box 6222
317/917-6222
FAX: 317/917-6336
E-mail: kcooper@ncaa.org
Internet: http://www.ncaa.org

AMOUNT: Tuition/fees, room/board, and books
DEADLINE(S): MAY 1; OCT 1
FIELD(S): All fields of study

Open to NCAA Division I student-athletes who have received but exhausted institutional eligibility for athletics-related financial aid and are within 30 semester hours (45 quarter hours) of graduation. Financial information will be required.

175 awards annually. Not renewable. Application and documentation must be submitted by student's director of athletics. Contact Karen Cooper for details.

3095—NATIONAL COLLEGIATE ATHLETIC ASSOCIATION (Walter Byers Postgraduate Scholarships)

P.O. Box 6222
Indianapolis IN 46206-6222
317/917-6222
FAX: 317/917-6336
E-mail: kcooper@ncaa.org
Internet: http://www.ncaa.org

AMOUNT: $12,500
DEADLINE(S): JAN
FIELD(S): All fields of study

Open to NCAA student-athletes who have a minimum 3.5 GPA and are committed to graduate study on a full-time basis. Must have evidenced superior character and leadership. Must be in final year of athletics eligibility per NCAA law 14.2. Must be nominated by faculty athletics representative.

Award goes to one male and one female annually. Contact Karen Cooper for nomination procedures.

3096—NATIONAL COUNCIL OF JEWISH WOMEN-GREATER BOSTON SECTION (Amelia Greenbaum/Rabbi Marshall Lipson Scholarships)

831 Beacon Street, PMB 138
Newton Centre MA 02459-9100
617/825-9191

AMOUNT: $500 (max.)
DEADLINE(S): JUN 30
FIELD(S): Fields of Study Related to NCJW Objectives

Open to Jewish women who are Boston area residents and attending a Massachusetts college/university as an undergraduate in a degree-granting program. Priority is given to those returning to school after at least a five-year absence. Must demonstrate financial need.

2-5 awards annually. Contact Laurie Ansorge Ball for an application.

3097—NATIONAL FALLEN FIREFIGHTERS FOUNDATION (Scholarship Program)

P.O. Drawer 498
Emmitsburg MD 21727
301/447-1365
FAX: 301/447-1645
E-mail: firehero@erols.com
Internet: http://www.firehero.org

AMOUNT: Varies
DEADLINE(S): APR 1
FIELD(S): All fields of study

For spouse or child of fallen firefighter who met criteria for inclusion on National Fallen Firefighters Memorial in MD. Children must be under age 30. Applicant must have high school diploma/equivalency and be pursuing undergraduate, graduate, or job skills training at an accredited university, college, or community college, either full- or part-time. Minimum 2.0 GPA and 2 letters of recommendation required; extracurricular activities and special circumstances considered.

Contact NFFF for an application.

3098—NATIONAL FEDERATION OF THE BLIND (American Action Fund Scholarship)

805 Fifth Avenue
Grinnell IA 50112
515/236-3366

AMOUNT: $10,000
DEADLINE(S): MAR 31
FIELD(S): All fields of study

Applicants must be legally blind and pursuing or planning to pursue a full-time postsecondary course of study in the U.S. Based on academic excellence, service to the community, and financial need. Membership NOT required. Given by the American Action Fund for Blind Children and Adults.

1 award annually. Renewable. Contact Mrs. Peggy Elliot, Scholarship Committee Chairman, for an application.

3099—NATIONAL FEDERATION OF THE BLIND (E.U. Parker Scholarship)

805 Fifth Avenue
Grinnell IA 50112

515/236-3366
AMOUNT: $3,000
DEADLINE(S): MAR 31
FIELD(S): All fields of study

For legally blind students pursuing or planning to pursue a full-time postsecondary course of study in the U.S. Based on academic excellence, service to the community, and financial need. Membership NOT required.

1 award annually. Renewable. Contact Mrs. Peggy Elliot, Scholarship Committee Chairman, for an application.

3100—NATIONAL FEDERATION OF THE BLIND (Hermione Grant Calhoun Scholarship)

805 Fifth Avenue
Grinnell IA 50112
515/236-3366
AMOUNT: $3,000
DEADLINE(S): MAR 31
FIELD(S): All fields of study

Open to legally blind female undergraduate or graduate students pursuing or planning to pursue a full-time postsecondary course of study in the U.S. Based on academic excellence, service to the community, and financial need. Membership NOT required.

1 award annually. Renewable. Contact Mrs. Peggy Elliot, Scholarship Committee Chairman, for an application.

3101—NATIONAL FEDERATION OF THE BLIND (Kuchler-Killian Memorial Scholarship)

805 Fifth Avenue
Grinnell IA 50112
515/236-3366
AMOUNT: $3,000
DEADLINE(S): MAR 31
FIELD(S): All fields of study

Open to legally blind students pursuing or planning to pursue a full-time postsecondary course of study in the U.S. Based on academic excellence, service to the community, and financial need. Membership NOT required.

1 award annually. Renewable. Contact Mrs. Peggy Elliot, Scholarship Committee Chairman, for an application.

3102—NATIONAL FEDERATION OF THE BLIND (Melva T. Owen Memorial Scholarship)

805 Fifth Avenue
Grinnell IA 50112
515/236-3366
AMOUNT: $4,000
DEADLINE(S): MAR 31
FIELD(S): All fields of study

Open to legally blind students for all postsecondary areas of study directed towards attaining financial independence. Excludes religion and those seeking only to further their general and cultural education. For full-time study in the U.S. Based on academic excellence, service to the community, and financial need. Membership NOT required.

1 awards annually. Renewable. Contact Mrs. Peggy Elliot, Scholarship Committee Chairman, for an application.

3103—NATIONAL FEDERATION OF THE BLIND (Mozelle and Willard Gold Memorial Scholarship)

805 Fifth Avenue
Grinnell IA 50112
515/236-3366
AMOUNT: $3,000
DEADLINE(S): MAR 31
FIELD(S): All fields of study

Open to legally blind students pursuing or planning to pursue a full-time postsecondary course of study in the U.S. Based on academic excellence, service to the community, and financial need. Membership NOT required.

1 award annually. Renewable. Contact Mrs. Peggy Elliot, Scholarship Committee Chairman, for an application.

3104—NATIONAL FEDERATION OF THE BLIND (NFB General Scholarships)

805 Fifth Avenue
Grinnell IA 50112
515/236-3366
AMOUNT: $3,000-$4,000
DEADLINE(S): MAR 31
FIELD(S): All fields of study

Open to legally blind students pursuing or planning to pursue a full-time postsecondary course of study in the U.S. Based on academic excellence, service to the community, and financial need. Membership NOT required. One of the awards will be given to a person working full-time who is attending or planning to attend a part-time course of study which will result in a new degree and broader opportunities in present or future work.

15 awards annually (2 for $4,000, 13 for $3,000). Renewable. Contact Mrs. Peggy Elliot, Scholarship Committee Chairman, for an application.

3105—NATIONAL FOREST FOUNDATION (Firefighters' Scholarship Fund)

1099 14th Street NW; Suite 5600W
Washington DC 20005
202/501-2473
FAX: 202/219-6585
Internet: http://www.nffweb.org/
AMOUNT: $500-$3,000
DEADLINE(S): MAY 15
FIELD(S): All fields of study

This fund provides for the continued education of firefighters or the dependants of firefighters who have been significantly disabled or killed in the line of duty fighting forest fires after January 1, 1980. These individuals must be employed by the Forest Service, Department of Interior, or state firefighting agencies. The scholarships go to those seeking admission to a college, university, or trade/technical school.

Contact NFF for an application. Award announcements made by June 30th.

3106—NATIONAL HORSESHOE PITCHERS ASSOCIATION (Junior Scholar Pitcher Program)

3085 76th Street
Franksville WI 53124
414/835-9108
AMOUNT: $250
DEADLINE(S): None
FIELD(S): All fields of study

Open to students who compete in a horseshoe pitching league and are 18 or younger.

Write to the above address for complete information.

3107—NATIONAL ITALIAN AMERICAN FOUNDATION (Scholarship Program)

1860 19th Street NW
Washington DC 20009
202/387-0600
FAX: 202/387-0800
E-mail: scholarships@niaf.org
Internet: http://www.niaf.org/scholarships
AMOUNT: $2,000
DEADLINE(S): MAY 31
FIELD(S): All fields of study

140 scholarships awarded annually to undergraduate, graduate, and doctoral students of Italian-American descent in any field of study, or to students from any ehtnic background majoring or minoring in Italian language, Italian studies, Italian-American studies, or a related field. Selection based on academic merit, finan-

cial need, and community service. Applications can only be submitted online. See Web site for application and more information on requirements.

Financial need, scholastic merit, and community service are considered.

3108—NATIONAL MAKE IT YOURSELF WITH WOOL COMPETITION (Scholarship/Awards)

P.O. Box 175
Lavina MT 59046
406/636-2731

AMOUNT: Various awards including $2,000 scholarship
DEADLINE(S): Varies (with state)
FIELD(S): All fields of study

Sewing, knitting, and crocheting competition open to students who make a wool garment from a current pattern. Fabric must contain at least 60% wool. Awards tenable at any recognized college or university.

Teenagers and older pay an entry fee of $10/; preteens pay $5. State winners advance to national competition. Write for complete information.

3109—NATIONAL MERIT SCHOLARSHIP CORPORATION (National Achievement Scholarship Program)

1560 Sherman Avenue, Suite 200
Evanston IL 60201
847/866-5100

AMOUNT: Varies
DEADLINE(S): Varies
FIELD(S): All fields of study

For Black American high school students to use for undergraduate studies. Must take the PSAT/NMSQT in the proper high school year (usually junior year). Financial need NOT required.

700 awards annually. Renewable. See school counselor for a PSAT/NMSQT Student Bulletin. The Achievement Program will contact students to be recognized through their schools.

3110—NATIONAL ROOFING FOUNDATION (Scholarship Program)

Scholarship Coordinator
National Roofing Foundation
10255 W. Higgins Road, Suite 600
Rosemont IL
847-299-9070
FAX: 847/299-1183
E-mail: NRCA@nrca.net
Internet: http://www.nrca.net

AMOUNT: $1,000/year
DEADLINE(S): JAN 31
FIELD(S): All fields of study

Open to employees, immediate family members of employees, or immediate family members of NRCA contractor members. Must be high school seniors/graduates who plan to enroll or are already enrolled in full-time undergraduate course of study at accredited two- or four-year college, university, or vo-tech school. Based on academic record, potential to succeed, leadership, school/community activities, honors, work experience, goals, and references. Financial need NOT a factor.

Renewable up to 4 years with minimum C+ GPA. Contact NRF for an application.

3111—NATIONAL RURAL EDUCATION ASSOCIATION (Essay Contest)

Rm. 10, School of Education,
Colorado State Univ.
Ft. Collins CO 80523-1588
970/491-7022 or 308/432-9156
FAX: 970/491-1317
Internet: http://www.nrea.colostate.edu

AMOUNT: $300 (Elementary, grades 3-5); $500 (Middle School, grades 6-9); $500 (High School, grades 10-12)
DEADLINE(S): APR 15
FIELD(S): All fields of study

Open to 3rd-12th graders who attend a rural school. Topic announced in January on NREA Web site. Essays must be supervised and prescreened by teacher so no more than 5 entries/category are submitted. Must be in ink on 1 side of paper or typed and double-spaced. Elementary essays should be 250 words; others should be 500. No names on essays-must include cover sheet with name, school info, and teacher.

For details, contact NREA headquarters.

3112—NATIONAL SCIENCE TEACHERS ASSOCIATION (Toshiba/NSTA ExploraVision Awards)

1840 Wilson Boulevard
Arlington VA 22201-3000
703/243-7100 or 800/EXPLOR-9
E-mail: exploravision@nsta.org
Internet: http://www.toshiba.com/tai/exploravision

AMOUNT: Up to $10,000 in U.S. Savings Bonds, plus gifts all participants, plus electronic gifts for schools and teachers.
DEADLINE(S): FEB 3
FIELD(S): Students working in teams of two to four students consider the impact that science and technology have on society and how innovative thinking can change the future, then use the tools of science to envision new technologies that might exist in twenty years.

Write to above location for details.

3113—NATIONAL SLOVAK SOCIETY (Peter V. Rovnianek Scholarship Fund)

333 Technology Drive, Suite 112
Canonsburg PA 15317-9513
412/488-1890

AMOUNT: Varies
DEADLINE(S): MAY 1
FIELD(S): All fields of study

Open to deserving and needy high school seniors enrolling in a 2- or 4-year colleges, universities, or trade schools. Applicants must have been a beneficial member of the society for at least two years before applying.

Contact National Slovak Society for an application.

3114—NATIONAL SOCIETY DAUGHTERS OF THE AMERICAN REVOLUTION (Margaret Howard Hamilton Scholarship)

1776 D Street NW
Washington DC 20006-5392
202/628-1776
Internet: http://www.dar.org

AMOUNT: $1,000
DEADLINE(S): FEB 15
FIELD(S): All fields of study

For a graduating high school senior who has been accepted into the Jones Learning Center, University of the Ozarks. Applications must be requested directly from the Learning Center upon acceptance into this program for learning disabled students. Awards are placed on deposit with the school and are based on academic excellence and need. No affiliation with DAR required.

Renewable up to four years, with annual transcript review. For information on DAR's other scholarships, see Web site or send a self-addressed, stamped envelope.

3115—NATIONAL SOCIETY OF THE SONS OF THE AMERICAN REVOLUTION (Eagle Scout Scholarships)

1000 S. Fourth Street
Louisville KY 40203

502/589-1776
Internet: http://www.sar.org
AMOUNT: $8,000 (first); $4,000 (second); $2,000 (third)
DEADLINE(S): Varies
FIELD(S): All fields of study

Open to any Eagle Scout currently registered in an active unit, who is under the age of 19 during the year of his application. College plans do not need to be completed in order to win the cash scholarships. Must complete an application form (includes Scout history, activities, etc.), a four-generation ancestor chart, and a patriotic theme of 500 words or less with bibliography. Three merit badges are required: American Heritage, Genealogy, and Law.

See Web site or contact your local SAR Eagle Scout Chairman for an application.

3116—NATIONAL TWENTY AND FOUR (Memorial Scholarships)

6000 Lucerne Court #2
Mequon WI 53092
Written Inquiry
AMOUNT: Up to $500/year
DEADLINE(S): MAY 1
FIELD(S): All areas of study

Open to members and children, grandchildren, or great-grandchildren of women who are members of the Twenty and Four, Honor Society of Women Legionnaires. Also for descendents of deceased former members. Must be between the ages of 16 and 25. For use at a school, college, university, or vocational institution beyond high school. Selection is based on financial need, scholastic standing, and school activities.

Write to "National Aide" for complete information ONLY if above qualifications are met.

3117—NATIONAL WELSH-AMERICAN FOUNDATION (Exchange Scholarship Program)

P.O. Box 1827
Shavertown PA 18708
570/696-1525
FAX: 570/696-1808
AMOUNT: $5,000 (max.)
DEADLINE(S): MAR 1
FIELD(S): All fields of study

Open to U.S. citizens of Welsh descent who are enrolled in undergraduate or graduate degree programs at recognized U.S. institutions. For study of Welsh-oriented subjects at a college in Wales. Welsh family ties are required.

Contact NWAF for an application.

3118—NATIONS BANK TRUST DEPT (Minne L. Maffett Scholarship Trust)

P.O. Box 831515
Dallas TX 75283
214/559-6476
AMOUNT: $50-$1,000
DEADLINE(S): APR 1
FIELD(S): All fields of study

Open to U.S. citizens who graduated from Limestone County. Texas high schools. Scholarships for full-time study at an accredited Texas institution.

30 scholarships per year. Write to Debra Hitzelberger, vice president and trust officer, at address above for complete information.

3119—NATIVE SONS OF THE GOLDEN WEST (Annual High School Public Speaking Contest)

414 Mason Street, Rm. 300
San Francisco CA 94102
415/566-4117
AMOUNT: $600-$2,000
DEADLINE(S): DEC 1
FIELD(S): California History

Public speaking competition open to California high school students under age 20. Speeches should be 7-9 minutes in length and may be on any subject related to California's past or present.

District eliminations take place in February and March; finals are in May. Write for complete information.

3120—NATRONA COUNTY EDUCATION ASSOCIATION (Scholarships)

851 Werner Court; Suite 105
Casper WY 82601
Written Inquiry
AMOUNT: $500
DEADLINE(S): MAR 1
FIELD(S): All fields of study

Available to graduating high school seniors from Natrona County, Wyoming, high schools. Parents must be NCEA members or retired NCEA members who are currently WEA members.

Write to the NCEA Scholarship Committee for an application.

3121—NAVY SUPPLY CORPS FOUNDATION (Scholarships)

1425 Prince Avenue
Athens GA 30606-2205
706/354-4111
FAX: 706/354-0334
Internet: http://www.usnscf.com
AMOUNT: $1,000-$4,000
DEADLINE(S): APR 10
FIELD(S): All fields of study

Open to dependent sons/daughters of Navy Supply Corps Officers (including Warrant and Supply Corps associated enlisted ratings) on active duty, in reserve status, retired-with-pay, or deceased. For undergraduate study at accredited two- or four-year colleges/universities. Must have minimum 3.0 GPA.

90 awards annually. Renewable up to 4 years. See Web site after January 10 for an application; NSCF no longer mails out hard copies.

3122—NAVY WIVES CLUBS OF AMERICA (Scholarship Foundation)

Barbara Stead, NWCA Director
3848 Old Colony Circle
Virginia Beach VA 23452
757/340-2088
AMOUNT: $1,000
DEADLINE(S): MAR 15
FIELD(S): All fields of study

Open to dependents of enlisted members of the U.S. Navy, Marine Corps, or Coast Guard who are on active duty, retired with pay, or deceased. For undergraduate study. Must demonstrate financial need.

Applicants must be previously approved for admission to an accredited school. 29 awards per year. Send self-addressed, stamped business-size envelope for complete information.

3123—NAVY-MARINE CORPS RELIEF SOCIETY (USS STARK Memorial Fund)

801 N. Randolph Street, Suite 1228
Arlington VA 22203-1978
703/696-4960
AMOUNT: Varies
DEADLINE(S): JUN 30
FIELD(S): All fields of study

Limited to children and widows of deceased crewmembers of the USS IOWA who perished as a result of the 19 April 1989 turret explosion and the USS STARK crewmembers who perished as a result of the Persian Gulf missile attack 17 May 1987. Students must be pursuing undergraduate studies.

Contact NMCRF for an application.

3124—NAVY-MARINE CORPS RELIEF SOCIETY (Grants for Children of Deceased Servicemembers)

801 N. Randolph Street, Suite 1228
Arlington VA 22203-1978
703/696-4960

AMOUNT: Up to $2,000
DEADLINE(S): JUN 30
FIELD(S): All fields of study

Open to children of servicemembers who died in retired status or on active duty. Must be pursuing undergraduate studies.

Contact NMCRF for an application.

3125—NAVY-MARINE CORPS RELIEF SOCIETY (Spouse Tuition Aid Program)

801 N. Randolph Street, Suite 1228
Arlington VA 22203-1978
703/696-4960

AMOUNT: Up to 50% tuition for on-base education programs, up to a maximum of $300/undergraduate term ($1,500/academic year), or $350/graduate term ($1,750/academic year)
DEADLINE(S): Varies according to term schedule for overseas locations
FIELD(S): All fields of study

Open to spouses of active U.S. Navy or Marine personnel who reside overseas with the active dutry servicemember. Students may be pursuing undergraduate or graduate studies, full- or part-time.

Administered overseas by an NMCRS office.

3126—NAVY-MARINE CORPS RELIEF SOCIETY (USS TENNESSEE Scholarship Fund)

801 N. Randolph Street, Suite 1228
Arlington VA 22203-1978
703/696-4960

AMOUNT: $1,000/year
DEADLINE(S): MAR 1
FIELD(S): All fields of study

Open to dependent children of active duty and retired personnel assigned to or previously assigned to duty aboard the USS TENNESSEE. Students must be pursuing undergraduate studies.

Contact NMCRF for an application.

3127—NAVY-MARINE CORPS RELIEF SOCIETY (VADM E.P. Travers Scholarship and Loan Program)

801 N. Randolph Street, Suite 1228
Arlington VA 22203-1978
703/696-4960

AMOUNT: Up to $2,000 (scholarship); $500-$3,000 (loan)
DEADLINE(S): MAR 1
FIELD(S): All fields of study

Open to undergraduate students who are dependents of an active duty or retired member of the U.S. Marines or U.S. Navy. Also open to spouses of active members. Must have a minimum 2.0 GPA. Loans must be repaid by the active duty/retired service member in 24 months by allotment of pay.

Contact NMCRF for an application.

3128—NELLIE MAE (Student Loans)

50 Braintree Hill Park, Suite 300
Braintree MA 02184-1763
617/849-1325 or 800/634-9308

AMOUNT: Up to cost of education less financial aid
DEADLINE(S): None specified
FIELD(S): All fields of study

Variety of loans available for undergraduate and graduate study at accredited degree-granting colleges or universities. Varied repayment and interest rate options. Savings programs for on-time repayments.

Write for complete information.

3129—NELLIE YEOH WHETTEN AWARD (Grant)

American Vacuum Society
120 Wall Street, 32nd Floor
New York NY 10005
212/248-0200
Internet: http://www.vacuum.org

AMOUNT: $1,500
DEADLINE(S): MAR 31
FIELD(S): All

Applicants must be women studying in North America. Selection is based upon academic and research excellence. This award is designed to recognize a woman doing excellent graduate work in vacuum science

3130—NETHERLANDS ORGANIZATION FOR INTERNATIONAL COOPERATION IN HIGHER EDUCATION (Grants from Dutch Government and European Union)

Kortenaerkade 11, Postbus 29777
2502 LT Den Haag
THE NETHERLANDS
+31 070 426 02 00
FAX: +31 070 426 03 99
E-mail: nuffic@nuffic.nl
Internet: http://www.nuffic.nl

AMOUNT: Varies
DEADLINE(S): Varies
FIELD(S): All fields of study

The Dutch Government and European Union offer grants under several programmes for students who wish to study in The Netherlands. To be eligible, student must be from one of the following countries: Austria, Belgium, Denmark, Finland, France, Germany, Greece, Iceland, Ireland, Italy, Luxembourg, Norway, Portugal, Spain, Sweden, or the United Kingdom.

Contact the Netherlands Embassy in your country or NUFFIC at above address for details. Also ask about Cultural Agreements.

3131—NETHERLANDS ORGANIZATION FOR INTERNATIONAL COOPERATION IN HIGHER EDUCATION (Cultural Agreements)

Kortenaerkade 11, Postbus 29777
2502 LT Den Haag
THE NETHERLANDS
+31 070 426 02 00
FAX: +31 070 426 03 99
E-mail: nuffic@nuffic.nl
Internet: http://www.nuffic.nl

AMOUNT: Varies
DEADLINE(S): Varies
FIELD(S): All fields of study

The Dutch government offers grants for periods of study/research in the Netherlands. Must be from Europe, China, India, Indonesia, Japan, Australia, Belarus, Egypt, Estonia, Georgia, Israel, Jordan, Latvia, Lithuania, Mexico, Morocco, Russia, Turkey, or Ukraine.

Contact the Netherlands Embassy in your country or NUFFIC at above address for details.

3132—NETHERLANDS ORGANIZATION FOR INTERNATIONAL COOPERATION IN HIGHER EDUCATION (NFP-Netherlands Fellowships Programme)

Kortenaerkade 11, Postbus 29777
2502 LT Den Haag
THE NETHERLANDS
+31 070 426 02 00
FAX: +31 070 426 03 99
E-mail: nuffic@nuffic.nl
Internet: http://www.nuffic.nl

AMOUNT: Varies
DEADLINE(S): Varies
FIELD(S): All fields of study

The Dutch government offers grants for students and staff from developing countries who have already started a career in specialized field. Offers possibilities for taking part in certain international courses and training programmes given in the Netherlands. Candidates must be nominated by their employers. The NFP also provides funds for training and courses that are tailor-made to meet specific needs. University Fellowships Programme also available for bachelor's students.

Contact the Netherlands Embassy in your country or NUFFIC at above address for details.

3133—NETTIE MILLHOLLON EDUCATIONAL TRUST ESTATE (Student Loans)

309 West Saint Anna Street
P.O. Box 643
Stanton TX 79782
915/756-2261
E-mail: millhollon@earthlink.net
Internet: http://www.millhollon.com

AMOUNT: Up to $2000 per semester (not to exceed $16,000 total)
DEADLINE(S): JUL 1 (for Fall); JAN 2 (for Spring)
FIELD(S): All fields of study

Students loans for financially needy Texas residents under 25 years of age. Rinancial need, character, evidence of ability, and desire to learn and further one's education, and unavailability of other financial resources are all considered. At least 2.5 GPA required.

Send SASE to above address for details.

3134—NEVADA DEPARTMENT OF EDUCATION (Nevada High School Scholars Program and Robert C. Byrd Honors Scholarship Program)

700 E. Fifth Street
Carson City NV 89701
775/687-9228
FAX: 775/687-9101

AMOUNT: $1,500 (max.)
DEADLINE(S): JAN 1 (SAT/ACT must be taken by then)
FIELD(S): All fields of study

Nevada High School Scholars Program is open to Nevada high school seniors with a minimum 3.50 GPA and a score of at least 25 on the ACT or 1100 on the SAT. Recipients are eligible for the Robert C. Byrd Honors Scholarship Program. Eligible ACT scores are automatically submitted by ACT to the Dept. of Education; SAT scores must be requested by student to be submitted to Dept. of Education by designating code 2707 on SAT registration form.

Renewable. Contact your school counselor or the NV Dept. of Education for details. Scholars are announced annually in May.

3135—NEVADA DEPARTMENT OF EDUCATION (Student Incentive Grant Program)

700 E. Fifth Street
Carson City NV 89701
775/687-9228
FAX: 775/687-9101

AMOUNT: Varies
DEADLINE(S): Varies
FIELD(S): All fields of study

Open to Nevada residents pursuing undergraduate or graduate study in eligible Nevada institutions.

Application must be made through the financial aid office of eligible participating institutions.

3136—NEVADA OFFICE OF THE STATE TREASURER (Millennium Scholarship)

555 East Washington Avenue
Suite 4600
Las Vegas NV 89101
888/477-2667
E-mail: millennium@Nevade Treasurer.com
Internet: http://nevadatreasurer.com/millennium/

AMOUNT: Approximately $1,200
DEADLINE(S): Varies
FIELD(S): All

For Nevada high school graduates with at least a 3.0 GPA and a passing score on all Nevada High School Proficiency Examinations. The GPA may be weighted or unweighted.

Must maintain a 2.0 GPA each semester to remain eligible.

3137—NEW BEDFORD PORT SOCIETY-LADIES BRANCH (Limited Scholarship Grant)

15 Johnny Cake Hill
New Bedford MA 02740
Written Inquiry only

AMOUNT: $300-$400
DEADLINE(S): MAY 1
FIELD(S): All areas of study

Open to residents of greater New Bedford, MA, who are descended from seafarers such as whaling masters and other fishermen. For undergrad and marine biology studies.

Renewable. Write for complete information.

3138—NEW ENGLAND BOARD OF HIGHER EDUCATION (New England Regional Student Program)

45 Temple Pl.
Boston MA 02111
617/357-9620
FAX: 617/338-1577
E-mail: rsp@nebhe.org
Internet: http://www.nebhe.org

AMOUNT: Varies; out-of-state tuition break at public campuses in New England
DEADLINE(S): Varies
FIELD(S): Many fields of study

Open to New England residents who wish to pursue undergraduate, graduate, or professional degrees at public colleges/universities in other New England states. Recipients receive a reduced out-of-state tuition rate when enrolled in certain majors which are not available in their own state's public institutions. Financial need NOT a factor.

Contact Wendy Lindsay or Sondra Lage (at rsp@nebhe.org) for information regarding eligible majors and campuses.

3139—NEW HAMPSHIRE HIGHER EDUCATION ASSISTANCE FOUNDATION (Federal Family Education Loan Program)

4 Barrell Court
P.O. Box 877
Concord NH 03302-0877
800/525-2577 ext. 119 or 603/225-6612

AMOUNT: Varies
DEADLINE(S): None
FIELD(S): All fields of study

Open to New Hampshire residents pursuing a college education in or out of state and to non-residents who attend a New Hampshire college or university. U.S. citizenship required.

Also provides scholarship searches, career searches, college searches, and individual counseling to parents and prospective college students (all free of charge). Interested students/parents may call or write to above address.

3140—NEW JERSEY DEPT. OF HIGHER EDUCATION (Educational Opportunity Fund Grants)

Office of Student Assistance
CN 540
Trenton NJ 08625
609/588-3230
800/792-8670 in NJ
TDD: 609/588-2526

AMOUNT: $200-$2,100 undergrads; $200-$4,150 graduate students
DEADLINE(S): Varies
FIELD(S): All areas of study

Must be New Jersey resident for at least 12 months prior to application. Grants for economically and educationally disadvantaged students. For undergraduate or graduate study in New Jersey. Must demonstrate need and be U.S. citizen or legal resident.

Grants renewable. Write for complete information.

3141—NEW JERSEY DEPT. OF HIGHER EDUCATION (Public Tuition Benefits Program)

Office of Student Assistance
CN 540
Trenton NJ 08625
609/588-3230
800/792-8670 in NJ

AMOUNT: Actual cost of tuition
DEADLINE(S): OCT 1; MAR 1
FIELD(S): All areas of study

Open to New Jersey residents who are dependents of emergency service personnel and law officers killed in the line of duty in N.J. For undergraduate study in N.J. U.S. citizenship or legal residency required.

Renewable. Write for complete information.

3142—NEW JERSEY DEPARTMENT OF MILITARY AND VETERANS AFFAIRS (Veterans Tuition Credit Program)

P.O. Box 340
Attn: DCVA-FO
Trenton NJ 08625-0340
609/530-6961
800/624-0508 (NJ only)

AMOUNT: $400 (full-time); $200 (half-time)
DEADLINE(S): OCT 1; MAR 1
FIELD(S): All fields of study

Open to U.S. military veterans who served between Dec. 31, 1960 and May 7, 1975 and were residents of New Jersey for one year prior to application or were New Jersey residents at time of induction or discharge. Proof of residency is required. For undergraduate or graduate study.

Contact NJ Dept. of Military and Veterans Affairs for an application.

3143—NEW JERSEY DEPARTMENT OF MILITARY AND VETERANS AFFAIRS (POW/MIA Dependents Grants)

P.O. Box 340, Attn: DCVA-FO
Trenton NJ 08625-0340
609/530-6961 or
800/624-0508 (NJ only)

AMOUNT: Tuition
DEADLINE(S): OCT 1; MAR 1
FIELD(S): All fields of study

Open to New Jersey residents who are dependent children of U.S. military personnel who were officially declared POW or MIA after January 1, 1960. Grants will pay undergraduate tuition at any accredited public or independent college/university in New Jersey.

Contact NJ Dept. of Military and Veterans Affairs for an application.

3144—NEW JERSEY STATE GOLF ASSOCIATION (Caddie Scholarships)

P.O. Box 6947
Freehold NJ 07728
201/338-8334
E-mail: njsga@usga.org

AMOUNT: $800-$2,500
DEADLINE(S): MAY 1
FIELD(S): All fields of study

Open to students who have served as a caddie at a New Jersey golf club which is a member of the NJ State Golf Association. Must be pursuing full-time undergraduate study at an accredited college/university. Based on scholastic achievement, financial need, SAT scores, character, and length of service as a caddie.

40-50 new awards annually. Renewable for 3 years. Contact J.O. Petersen, Educ. Dir., for an application.

3145—NEW JERSEY TESOL/BE (Scholarships)

Amy Kargauer
620 Red Oak Drive
Riverdale NJ 07675
800/95E-BESL

AMOUNT: $1,000
DEADLINE(S): APR 1
FIELD(S): All fields of study

Open to New Jersey high school seniors and undergraduates planning to attend college in New Jersey. Must be current ESL/bilingual students.

Call the 800 number and leave a clearly stated message of interest in the scholarship.

3146—NEW MEXICO COMMISSION ON HIGHER EDUCATION (Student Incentive Grant)

P.O. Box 15910
Santa Fe NM 87506-5910
505/827-7383
FAX: 505/827-7393
E-mail: highered@che.state.nm.us
Internet: http://www.nmche.org

AMOUNT: $200-$2500 per year
DEADLINE(S): Varies
FIELD(S): All fields of study

Open to New Mexico residents who are undergraduates attending public or selected private/nonprofit postsecondary institutions in New Mexico. Must be enrolled at least half-time and demonstrate financial need.

Renewable. Contact your school's financial aid office for deadlines and an application.

3147—NEW MEXICO FARM AND LIVESTOCK BUREAU (Memorial Scholarships)

P.O. Box 20004
Las Cruces NM 88004-9004
505/532-4702
FAX: 505/532-4710
E-mail: nmflb@zianet.com

AMOUNT: Varies
DEADLINE(S): MAY 1
FIELD(S): All fields of study

Available to members of New Mexico Farm and Livestock Bureau families for one year of continuing education at an institution of their choice. Must be a resident of New Mexico and have a minimum 2.5 GPA. Transcripts, two letters of recommendation, and a recent photograph for publicity purposes are required. Financial need NOT a factor.

5 awards annually. Renewable through reapplication. Contact Missy Aguayo at NMFLB for an application.

3148—NEW MEXICO TECH (Freshmen and Transfer Student Scholarships)

CS Box M-801 Leroy Place
Socorro NM 87801

505/835-5333
AMOUNT: $1,750-$5,000
DEADLINE(S): MAR 1
FIELD(S): All fields of study

Various scholarship programs for entering freshmen and transfer students to New Mexico Tech. Also for gradutating high school seniors who are winners at the NM Science and Engineering Fair or at NM Science Olympiad.

Write to above address for details.

3149—NEW MEXICO TECH (Scholarships for Non-resident Students)

CS Box M-801 Leroy Place
Socorro NM 87801
505/835-5333
AMOUNT: $700
DEADLINE(S): MAR 1
FIELD(S): All fields of study

Scholarship for non-residents of New Mexico planning to attend New Mexio Tech. Priority given to transfer students. Non-resident part of tuition is waived. GPA required: 3.0 freshmen; 3.5 college transfers.

Renewable up to four years. Contact above location for details.

3150—NEW MEXICO TECH (Transfer Student Scholarship)

CS Box M-801 Leroy Place
Socorro NM 87801
505/835-5333
AMOUNT: $3,500/year
DEADLINE(S): MAR 1
FIELD(S): All fields of study

Scholarships for transfer students to New Mexico Tech with GPA of 3.5 or better.

Renewable for up to three years.

3151—NEW MEXICO VETERANS' SERVICE COMMISSION (Scholarship Program)

P.O. Box 2324
Santa Fe NM 87503
505/827-6300
AMOUNT: Full Tuition + $300
DEADLINE(S): None
FIELD(S): All fields of study

Open to New Mexico residents (aged 16-26) who are son or daughter of person who was killed in action or died as a result of military service in the U.S. Armed Forces during a period of armed conflict.

Veteran must have been NM resident at time of entry into service and must have served during a period of armed conflict. Approx 13 full tuition scholarships for undergrads per year. Write for complete information.

3152—NEW YORK STATE EDUCATION DEPARTMENT (Awards, Scholarships, and Fellowships)

Scholarship Processing Unit
Rm. 1078 EBA
Albany NY 12234
518/486-1319
FAX: 518/486-5346
AMOUNT: Varies
DEADLINE(S): Varies
FIELD(S): All fields of study

Various state and federal programs are open to residents of New York state. One year's NY residency immediately preceding effective date of award is required.

Contact NY State Education Dept. for details.

3153—NEW YORK STATE HIGHER EDUCATION SERVICES CORPORATION (Robert C. Byrd Honors Scholarship)

Student Information
Albany NY 12255
518/486-1319
Internet: http://www.hesc.com
AMOUNT: $1,500/year
DEADLINE(S): None
FIELD(S): All fields of study

Open to New York state academically talented high school seniors who plan to attend any approved institution of higher education in the United States.

Contact HESC for an application.

3154—NEW YORK STATE HIGHER EDUCATION SERVICES CORPORATION (Memorial Scholarships for Families of Deceased Police Officers and Firefighters)

HESC, 99 Washington Avenue
Albany NY 12255
518/486-1319
Internet: http://www.hesc.com
AMOUNT: Varies
DEADLINE(S): None
FIELD(S): All fields of study

Scholarships for NY state children and spouses of deceased police officers, firefighters, and volunteer firefighters who died as the result of injuries sustained in the line of duty.

Complete a Free Application for Federal Student Aid (FAFSA) and the New York State Tuition Assistance Program (TAP) application to apply.

3155—NEW YORK STATE HIGHER EDUCATION SERVICES CORPORATION (Vietnam Veterans and Persian Gulf Veterans Tuition Awards)

HESC, Student Information
Albany NY 12255
518/486-1319
Internet: http://www.hesc.com
AMOUNT: $500 (part-time); $1,000 (full-time). Total awards cannot exceed $10,000.
DEADLINE(S): MAY 1
FIELD(S): All fields of study

Scholarships for NY residents who are veterans of either the Vietnam War or the Persian Gulf War (Desert Storm/Desert Shield). For vocational/tech. training, undergraduate, and graduate study.Contact a local County Veterans' Service Agency or the N.Y. State Division of Veterans' Affairs for details.

Complete a Free Application for Federal Student Aid (FAFSA) and the New York State Tuition Assistance Program (TAP) application to apply.

3156—NEW YORK STATE HIGHER EDUCATION SERVICES CORPORATION (Tuition Assistance Program (TAP) and Aid for Part-Time Study (APTS))

HESC, Student Information
Albany NY 12255
518/486-1319
Internet: http://www.hesc.com
AMOUNT: Varies
DEADLINE(S): MAY 1 (TAP)
FIELD(S): All fields of study

Grants for students at all levels, including some for part-time study.

Contact above location for details of these and other New York state programs.

3157—NEW YORK STATE SENATE (Undergraduate Session Assistants Program)

NYS Student Programs Office
90 South Swan Street, Rm. 416
Albany NY 12247
518/455-2611
FAX: 518-426-6827
E-mail: students@senate.state.ny.us
AMOUNT: $3,500 stipend
DEADLINE(S): OCT (last Friday)
FIELD(S): All fields of study

Open to talented undergraduates (except freshmen) who want first-hand experience at the New York state legislature. Need a good academic record. All majors may apply. Must be enrolled in a college or university in New York state. U.S. citizenship. Must demonstrate keen writing skills and have the recommendation and support of on-campus faculty.

Contact Dr. Russell J. Williams at above location for complete information.

3158—NON-COMMISSIONED OFFICERS ASSOCIATION (Scholarships)

P.O. Box 33610
San Antonio TX 78265-3610
210/653-6161
AMOUNT: $900-$1,000
DEADLINE(S): MAR 31
FIELD(S): All fields of study

Open to spouses and children of members of the Non-Commissioned Officers Association. Children must be under age 25 to receive initial scholarship; there are no age restrictions for spouses. Students must attend a four-year undergraduate college or an accredited vocational institution. Based on academic achievements and a sense of patriotism. Student applications require an essay on Americanism.

16 awards annually. Renewable if student remains full-time, carries 15 credit hours, maintains minimum "B" average, and remains spouse/child of current NCOA member. Contact NCOA for an application.

3159—NORRIS BURSARY SCHOLARSHIP FUND

431 Alhambra Circle
Miami FL 33134-4901
305/266-3333
AMOUNT: $1,000
DEADLINE(S): Ongoing
FIELD(S): All fields of study

Scholarships for residents of Florida for undergraduate study at an accredited college or trade school.

Send SASE to Matthew Slepin, Trustee, at above address.

3160—NORTH CAROLINA ASSOCIATION OF EDUCATORS (Martin Luther King, Jr., Scholarship)

P.O. Box 27347
Raleigh NC 27611-7347
Written Inquiry
AMOUNT: Varies
DEADLINE(S): FEB 1
FIELD(S): All fields of study

Open to college-bound North Carolina high school seniors. Children of NCAE members will be considered first. Other selection criteria are character, personality, and scholastic achievement.

Number and amount of scholarships annually are determined by the funds received from fund-raising efforts of the organization. Send self-addressed, stamped envelope to Scholarship Committee for application.

3161—NORTH CAROLINA DEPARTMENT OF PUBLIC INSTRUCTION (Scholarship Loan Program for Prospective Teachers)

301 N. Wilmington Street
Raleigh NC 27601-2825
919/715-1120
AMOUNT: $1,110/year
DEADLINE(S): FEB
FIELD(S): All fields of study

For North Carolina high school senior with GPAs of at least 3.0 and SATs of 900+. For use at four-year institutions.

160 awards. Renewable up to four year.

3162—NORTH CAROLINA DIVISION OF SERVICES FOR THE BLIND (Rehabilitation Assistance for Visually Impaired)

309 Ashe Avenue
Raleigh NC 27606
919/733-9700 or 919/733-9822
FAX: 919/733-9769
AMOUNT: Tuition, fees, books and supplies
DEADLINE(S): None
FIELD(S): All fields of study

Open to North Carolina residents who are legally blind or have a progressive eye condition which may result in blindness (thereby creating an impediment for the individual) and who are undergraduate or graduate students at a North Carolina school.

Contact NCDSB for an application.

3163—NORTH CAROLINA DIVISION OF VETERANS AFFAIRS (Dependents Scholarship Program)

325 N. Salisbury Street, Suite 1065
Raleigh NC 27603
919/733-3851
AMOUNT: $1,500 to $3,000 (private college); tuition and fees + room and board (public college)
DEADLINE(S): MAY 31
FIELD(S): All fields of study

Undergraduate scholarships open to children of veterans who died as a result of wartime service or were disabled; POW; MIA or received pension from the VA Veteran Entered Service as NC resident or applicant NC resident since birth.

Awards tenable at private and public colleges in North Carolina. 350-400 awards per year. Renewable up to 4 years. Write for complete information.

3164—NORTH CAROLINA STATE EDUCATION ASSISTANCE AUTHORITY (Student Financial Aid for North Carolinians)

P.O. Box 13663
Research Triangle Park NC 27709
919/549-8614
FAX: 919/248-4687
Internet: http://www.cfnc.org
AMOUNT: Varies
DEADLINE(S): Varies
FIELD(S): All fields of study

The state of North Carolina, private NC organizations, and the federal government fund numerous scholarships, grants, work-study, and loan programs for North Carolina residents at all levels of study.

See Web site or contact NCSEAA for program details.

3165—NORTH CAROLINA STATE UNIVERSITY (John Gatling Scholarship Program)

2119 Pullen Hall, Box 7342
Raleigh NC 27695
919/515-3671
FAX: 919/515-6021
E-mail: PAT_LEE@NCSU.EDU
AMOUNT: $8,000 per year
DEADLINE(S): FEB 1
FIELD(S): All fields of study

If you were born with surname of "Gatlin" or "Gatling" this program will provide $8,000 toward the cost of attending NC State Univ. as an undergraduate provided you meet NC State Univ. entrance and transfer requirements. U.S. citizenship.

Award is renewable each year if you study full time (24 or more credits per year) and maintain at least 2.0 GPA. Contact the NCSU merit awards program coordinator at address above for complete information.

3166—NORTH CROSS SCHOOL (Scholarships)

4254 Colonial Avenue
Roanoke VA 24018
540/989-6641

FAX: 540/989-7299
Internet: http://www.NorthCross.org
AMOUNT: $1,500-$3,000
DEADLINE(S): JUN 1 (merit)
FIELD(S): All fields of study

Grants for students attending this independent, nonprofit, nonsectarian K-12 college preparatory school Roanoke, Virginia. Two programs: merit scholarships (2) are based on academics and testing; need-based scholarships (50) are for students demonstrating financial need.

No deadline for scholarships based on need. Contact school for details.

3167—NORTH DAKOTA STUDENT FINANCIAL ASSISTANCE AGENCY (Grants)

State Capitol, 10th Floor
600 East Boulevard
Bismarck ND 58505
701/328-4114
AMOUNT: Up to $600
DEADLINE(S): APR 15
FIELD(S): All fields of study

Open to residents of North Dakota for undergraduate study at colleges and universities in North Dakota. Must be citizen or legal U.S. resident.

2,400 awards per year. Renewable. Write for complete information.

3168—NORTH DAKOTA INDIAN SCHOLARSHIP PROGRAM (Scholarships)

State Capitol Building, 10th Floor
Bismarck ND 58505
701/328-2960
AMOUNT: $700-$2,000
DEADLINE(S): JUL 15
FIELD(S): All fields of study

Open to North Dakota residents who have at least 1/4 Indian blood or are enrolled members of a North Dakota tribe. Awards are tenable at recognized undergraduate colleges and universities in North Dakota. U.S. citizenship required.

100-150 scholarships per year. Renewable. Write for complete information.

3169—NORTHEASTERN LOGGERS ASSOCIATION, INC. (Scholarship Contest)

P.O. Box 69
Old Forge NY 13420-0069
315/369-3078
FAX: 315/369-3736
E-mail: nela@telenet.net
AMOUNT: $500
DEADLINE(S): APR 1
FIELD(S): All fields of study

Scholarships awards for families of individual members or employees of Industrial and Associate Members of the Northeastern Loggers' Association. Open to high school seniors, students in two-year associate degree of technical school programs, or juniors or seniors in four-year B.A. programs. Must prepare a 1,000-word essay on "What it means to grow up in the forest industry." Essay must be typed and will be about four pages double-spaced.

Send for official application form and return in withessay and grade transcript/ report card data before April 1.

3170—NORTHWEST DANISH FOUNDATION (Scholarships)

Scandinavian Dept.
Univ. of Washington, 318 Raitt Hall
Box 353420
Seattle WA 98195-3420
206/543-0645 or 206/543-6084
AMOUNT: $250
DEADLINE(S): MAR 15
FIELD(S): All fields of study

Scholarship for students of Danish descent or married to someone of Danish descent. Must be residents of Washington or Oregon. May be used for study in the U.S. or in Denmark.

Contact Professor Marianne Stecher-Hanson at above address or phone numbers or the Foundation at 206/523-3263.

3171—NORTHWEST SCHOOL (Financial Aid)

1415 Summit Avenue
Seattle WA 98122
206/328-1129
FAX: 206/328-1776
Internet: http://www.northwest school.org
AMOUNT: $1,000-full tuition
DEADLINE(S): MAR
FIELD(S): All fields of study

Tuition assistance is available to 6th-12th grade students at this private day/boarding school. Must live in the Seattle area (King County), be a U.S. citizen, and demonstrate financial need in accordance with established policies of the Northwest School.

Over 50 awards annually. Renewable. Contact Jonathan Hochberg for an application.

3172—OAKWOOD FRIENDS SCHOOL (Scholarships)

22 Spackenkill Road
Poughkeepsie NY 12601
845/462-4200
FAX: 845/843-3341
E-mail: admissions@oakwood friends.org
Internet: http://www.oakwood friends.org
AMOUNT: Varies
DEADLINE(S): Varies
FIELD(S): Varies

Need-based financial need only.

Contact Robert J. Suphan, Director of Admissions, for more information.

3173—OCA AVON (SCHOLARSHIP)

1001 Connecticut Avenue NW, #601
Washington DC
202/223-5500
FAX: 202/296-0540
E-mail: oac@ocanatl.org
AMOUNT: $2,000
DEADLINE(S): APR 15
FIELD(S): All

Funding available to Asian Pacific American women in financial need entering first year of college. Must be Permanent Resident or U.S. Citizen. Cumulative GPA 3.00 or above on a 4.0 scale. For a weighted GPA, please ask your counselor to convert it to a 4.0 scale.

3174—OHEF SHOLOM TEMPLE (Sarah Cohen Scholarship Fund)

530 Raleigh Avenue
Norfolk VA 23507
757/625-4295
FAX: 757/625-3762
AMOUNT: Varies
DEADLINE(S): MAR
FIELD(S): All areas of study

Open to residents of Norfolk VA who have high academic standing and a marked potential for service to the community.

Apply before the end of the spring semester. For undergraduate study at a recognized college or university which grants a degree. Must show financial need. Write for complete information.

3175—OHIO AMERICAN LEGION (Scholarships)

P.O. Box 8007
Delaware OH 43015

740/362-1429
FAX: 740/362-1429
E-mail: ohlegion@iwaynet.net
AMOUNT: $2,000
DEADLINE(S): APR 15
FIELD(S): All fields of study

Open to undergraduate students with a minimum 3.5 GPA or composite ACT score of 25 if high school senior. Must be direct descendants of Legionnaires, direct descendants of deceased Legionnaires, and/or surviving spouses or children of deceased or disabled U.S. military persons.

Renewable. Contact Ohio American Legion for an application.

3176—OHIO ASSOCIATION OF CAREER COLLEGES AND SCHOOLS (Legislative Scholarship)

Max Lerner, Executive Director
1857 Northwest Boulevard
The Annex
Columbus OH 43212
614/487-8180
FAX: 614/487-8190
AMOUNT: $2,500-$13,534
DEADLINE(S): JAN 31
FIELD(S): All

Renewable award to full-time students attending a trade/technical institution or a two-year college who have been nominated by an Ohio State Senator or Representative. A minimum GPA of 2.5 is required.

3177—OHIO BOARD OF REGENTS (Ohio Academic Scholarship Program)

State Grants and Scholarships Dept.
P.O. Box 182452
Columbus OH 43218-2452
888/833-1133 or 614/752-9528
FAX: 614/752-5903
AMOUNT: $2,000/year
DEADLINE(S): FEB 23
FIELD(S): All fields of study

Open to Ohio residents who are seniors at chartered Ohio high schools and intend to enroll full-time in eligible Ohio institutions of higher education.

1,000 awards annually. Renewable up to 4 years. Contact your high school guidance office for an application.

3178—OHIO BOARD OF REGENTS (Ohio Instructional Grant Program)

State Grants and Scholarships Dept.
P.O. Box 182452
Columbus OH 43218-2452
888/833-1133 or 614/466-7420
FAX: 614/752-5903
AMOUNT: $288-$4,296
DEADLINE(S): OCT 1
FIELD(S): All fields of study (except Theology)

Open to Ohio residents enrolled full-time in an eligible Ohio or Pennsylvania institution of higher education. Must be in good academic standing and demonstrate financial need. Based on family income and number of dependents in family. Benefits are restricted to student's instructional and general fee charges.

90,000 awards annually. Renewable. Apply by completing the government FAFSA form, available from your school's financial aid office or above address.

3179—OHIO BOARD OF REGENTS (Ohio Student Choice Grants)

State Grants and Scholarships Dept.
P.O. Box 182452
Columbus OH 43218-2452
888/833-1133 or 614/752-9535
FAX: 614/752-5903
AMOUNT: $1,062
DEADLINE(S): Varies
FIELD(S): All fields of study

Open to Ohio residents enrolled as full-time undergraduate students at eligible private non-profit Ohio colleges/universities. Assists in narrowing the tuition gap between the state's public and private non-profit colleges and universities.

Renewable up to 5 years. Contact Board of Regents for an application.

3180—OHIO BOARD OF REGENTS (Regents Graduate/Professional Fellowship Program)

State Grants and Scholarships Dept.
P.O. Box 182452
Columbus OH 43218-2452
888/833-1133 or 614/752-9535
FAX: 614/752-5903
AMOUNT: $3,500/year
DEADLINE(S): None
FIELD(S): All fields of study

Open to students receiving their bachelor's degrees from an Ohio institution and beginning graduate school in Ohio in the same year.

Renewable up to 2 years. Contact a college financial aid administrator, the university's graduate school, for an application.

3181—OHIO BOARD OF REGENTS (Robert C. Byrd Honors Scholarship Program)

State Grants and Scholarships Dept.
P.O. Box 182452
Columbus OH 43218-2452
888/833-1133 or 614/644-7420
FAX: 614/752-5903
AMOUNT: Varies
DEADLINE(S): MAR
FIELD(S): All fields of study

Open to seniors who demonstrate outstanding academic achievement in high school. Based on class rank, grades, test scores, and participation in leadership activities. At least one scholarship is awarded in each congressional district.

Renewable up to 4 years provided satisfactory progress is made. Apply through high school guidance office.

3182—OHIO BOARD OF REGENTS (War Orphans Scholarship Program)

State Grants and Scholarships Dept.
P.O. Box 182452
Columbus OH 43218-2452
888/833-1133 or 614/752-9528
FAX: 614/752-5903
AMOUNT: Full tuition at public schools (equivalent amount at private schools)
DEADLINE(S): JUL 1
FIELD(S): All fields of study

Open to Ohio residents who are dependents of veterans who served during war and are now severely disabled or deceased. Students must be full-time undergraduates at Ohio institutions.

Contact your financial aid office, veterans service offices, or the Board of Regents for an application.

3183—OHIO NATIONAL GUARD ADJUTANT GENERAL'S DEPARTMENT (Scholarship Program)

Attn: AGOH-JO-SP
2825 W. Granville Road
Columbus OH 43235
614/336-7032; 888-400-6484
FAX: 614/336-7318
AMOUNT: Tuition (100% at public schools; average of state school fees at private schools)
DEADLINE(S): NOV 1; FEB 1; APR 1; JUL 1
FIELD(S): All fields of study

Open to students who are members of the Ohio National Guard and enroll in a school of higher education in an associate or baccalaureate degree program.

Contact nearest Ohio National Guard Recruiting Office for an application.

3184—OHIO UNIVERSITY (Charles Kilburger Scholarship)

Asst. Dir. Student Services
1570 Granville Pike
Lancaster OH 43130
614/654-6711
AMOUNT: Tuition
DEADLINE(S): FEB 1
FIELD(S): All fields of study

Scholarship open to seniors graduating from a Fairfield County (Ohio) high school who will enroll at Ohio University Lancaster for at least two years. For undergraduate study only. U.S. citizenship required.

Applications available ONLY from Fairfield County, OH high school counselors. Must demonstrate financial need.

3185—OLDFIELDS SCHOOL (Grants and Loans)

P.O. Box 697
Glencoe MD 21152-0697
410/472-4800
FAX: 410/472-6839
E-mail: admissions@Oldfields.pvt.k12.md.us
Internet: http://www.oldfieldsschool.com
AMOUNT: Varies
DEADLINE(S): FEB 15
FIELD(S): All fields of study, grades 8-12

Grants and loans for needy students enrolled in the private 8-12 school in Maryland listed above.

Contact school for details.

3186—OLIN L. LIVESEY SCHOLARSHIP FUND (OLLSF Awards)

3538 Central Avenue; Suite 2A
Riverside CA 92506-2700
909/684-6778
E-mail: ollsf@scholarshipsite.org
Internet: http://www.scholarshipsite.org
AMOUNT: $250-$10,000
DEADLINE(S): JUN 1
FIELD(S): All fields of study

Open to high school seniors with a minimum 2.5 GPA and 850 SAT score. Financial need NOT a factor, and there are no citizenship/residence restrictions. There is no fee for preliminary application; however, finalists must submit $15 processing fee.

200+ awards annually. Not renewable. See Web site or contact the Executive Director for preliminary application.

3187—ONEIDA HIGHER EDUCATION (Various Fellowships, Internships, and Scholarships)

P.O. Box 365
Oneida WI 54155
920/869-4333 or
800/236-2214 ext. 4333
Internet: http://highered.oneidanation.org
AMOUNT: Varies with program
DEADLINE(S): APR 15 (fall term); OCT 1 (spring term); MAY 1 (summer term)
FIELD(S): All fields of study

For enrolled members of the Oneida Tribe of Indians of Wisconsin. Several programs are offered for all levels of study in various fields, including internships, emergency funding, and special scholarships for economics and business majors and those in the hotel/restaurant management field.

Some programs list deadlines dates different from those above. Send for descriptive brochure.

3188—ONTARIO MINISTRY OF EDUCATION AND TRAINING (The Aird Scholarship)

189 Red River Road, 4th Floor
Box 4500
Thunder Bay Ontario P7B 6G9
CANADA
800/465-3957
TDD: 800/465-3958
Internet: osap.gov.on.ca
AMOUNT: $2,500
DEADLINE(S): Varies
FIELD(S): All fields of study

Scholarships are intended to help Canadian citizens/permanent residents with physical disabilities study in the first year of a full-time program at a recognized Ontario postsecondary institution. Awards go to those who best demonstrate outstanding achievement, motivation, and initiative.

2 awards annually. Contact the Ministry of Education & Training for an application.

3189—ONTARIO MINISTRY OF EDUCATION AND TRAINING (Summer Language Bursary Program)

189 Red River Road, 4th Floor
Box 4500
Thunder Bay Ontario P7B 6G9
CANADA
800/465-3957
TDD: 800/465-3958
Internet: osap.gov.on.ca OR http://cmec.ca
AMOUNT: Tuition, room and board
DEADLINE(S): Varies
FIELD(S): All fields of study

Canadian citizens are awarded bursaries for spring or summer immersion courses in their second official language, English or French. Paid directly to designated Ontario institution.

Contact secondary school guidance offices, university or college French departments, student affairs, financial aid departments, or Ministry of Education & Training for an application.

3190—OPEN SOCIETY INSTITUTE (Network Scholarship Programs)

400 West 59th Street
New York NY 10019
212/548-0175
FAX: 212/548-4652
E-mail: scholar@sorosny.org
Internet: http://www.soros.org
AMOUNT: Varies
DEADLINE(S): Varies
FIELD(S): All fields of study

Various financial aid programs for students, faculty, and professionals from Eastern and Central Europe, the former Soviet Union, Mongolia, Myanmar, and the former Yugoslavia.

See Web site for details of requirements for each program. To apply, contact your local Soros Foundation/Open Society Institute.

3191—OPERATING ENGINEERS LOCAL UNION NO. 3 (IUOE Scholarship Program)

1620 South Loop Road
Alameda CA 94502
510/748-7400
Internet: http://www.oe3.com
AMOUNT: Up to $3,000
DEADLINE(S): MAR 1
FIELD(S): All areas of study

Open to dependent children of members of IUOE Local No. 3 who are high school seniors with at least a 3.0 GPA. Awards tenable at recognized undergraduate colleges and universities. U.S. citizenship required.

Write for complete information.

3192—OPTIMIST INTERNATIONAL FOUNDATION (Essay Contest)

Dana Seipp, Programs Manager
4494 Lindell Boulevard
St. Louis MO 63108

800/300-8130 ext. 224
FAX: 314/371-6006
E-mail: programs@optimist.org
Internet: http://www.optimist.org/index=ns-prog.html
AMOUNT: $650; $2,000-$5,000
DEADLINE(S): Varies
FIELD(S): All
FIELD(S): All fields of study

$650 college scholarship is offered at the district level; $2000-$5000 scholarships are offered at the international level. Eligible students are under age 19 as of December 31 of the current school year. Open to residents of the U.S., Canada and the Caribbean. Must be conducted through a local Optimist Club.

3193—ORDER OF THE EASTERN STAR (Grand Chapter of California Scholarships)

870 Market Street, Suite 722
San Francisco CA 94102-2996
Written Inquiry
Internet: http://www.oescal.org
AMOUNT: $250-$500 (2-year college); $500-$1,000 (4-year college)
DEADLINE(S): MAR 15
FIELD(S): All fields of study, including vocational/technical/special religious

Open to all California residents who are accepted to or enrolled in California colleges, universities, or trade schools and have at least a 3.5 GPA (4.0 scale). Must demonstrate financial need and be U.S. citizen.

Access Web site for application or send SASE to Mrs. Shirley Orth, Grand Secretary, address above, for complete information.

3194—OREGON CREDIT UNION LEAGUE EDUCATIONAL FOUNDATION (Lois M. Hartley Benefit Scholarship)

P.O. Box 1900
Beaverton OR 97075
800/688-6098
AMOUNT: $4,000
DEADLINE(S): MAR 31
FIELD(S): All fields of study

Open to any member of an Oregon credit union who is currently enrolled in an undergraduate program at an accredited institution and has some form of hearing impairment.

1 award annually. Award announced in May. Contact your credit union.

3195—OREGON DEPARTMENT OF VETERANS' AFFAIRS (Educational Aid for Oregon Veterans)

700 Summer Street NE, Suite 150
Salem OR 97310-1289
800/692-9666 or 503/373-2085
AMOUNT: $200 a semester
DEADLINE(S): None
FIELD(S): All fields of study

For veterans on active duty during the Korean War or post-Korean War veterans who received a campaign or expeditionary medal or ribbon. Must be resident of Oregon and U.S. citizen with a qualifying military service record at time of application. For study in an accredited Oregon school.

Write for complete information.

3196—OREGON STATE SCHOLARSHIP COMMISSION (Federal Family Education Loan Program)

1500 Valley River Drive, #100
Eugene OR 97401
800/452-8807; 503/687-7400
Internet: http://www.teleport.com~ossc
AMOUNT: $2,625-$6,635 undergrad; $8,500-$18,500 graduate (annual maximum)
DEADLINE(S): None specified
FIELD(S): All fields of study

Open to U.S. citizens or permanent residents who are attending an eligible Oregon institution and to Oregon residents attending any eligible institution outside of Oregon at least half-time.

Write or visit Web site for complete information.

3197—OREGON STATE SCHOLARSHIP COMMISSION (Oregon Need Grants)

1500 Valley River Drive, #100
Eugene OR 97401
503/687-7400
AMOUNT: $906-$1,584
DEADLINE(S): APR 1
FIELD(S): All areas of study

Open to Oregon residents enrolled full-time in any 2- or 4-year nonprofit college or university in Oregon. Must be U.S. citizen or legal resident and demonstrate financial need.

It is not necessary to take SAT/ACT for need grants. 22,000 awards and grants per year. Renewable. Write for complete information.

3198—OREGON STATE SCHOLARSHIP COMMISSION (Private Scholarship Programs Administered by the Commission)

1500 Valley River Drive, Suite 100
Eugene OR 97401
503/687-7395
AMOUNT: $250-$3,000
DEADLINE(S): MAR 1
FIELD(S): All fields of study

100 different private scholarship programs are administered by the Commission and are for Oregon residents only. Some are tied to a specific field and/or level of study but in general they are available to all levels and fields of study.

Dependent students must have parents residing in Oregon. Independent students must live in Oregon for 12 months prior to Sept. 1 of the academic year for which the application is made. For complete information send a 55-cent, stamped, self-addressed #10 business-sized envelope to the above address.

3199—ORGANIZATION OF AMERICAN STATES (Leo S. Rowe Pan American Fund)

1889 F Street NW
Washington DC 20006
202/458-6208
FAX: 202/458-3878
E-mail: rowefund@oas.org
Internet: http://www.oas.org
AMOUNT: $7,500/year
DEADLINE(S): None
FIELD(S): All fields of study

No-interest loans are open to undergraduate and graduate students who are nationals of Latin American and Caribbean OAS member states who wish to study in the US. Undergrads must be within two years of completing degree/research, and graduates must be within three years. Based on meritorious personal/academic record and proof of financial need. Loan repayable within fifty months of completion of studies.

100 awards annually. Renewable. See Web site for an application.

3200 —ORGANIZATION OF CHINESE AMERICANS (Avon College Scholarships)

1001 Connecticut Avenue NW, Suite 601
Washington DC 20036
202/223-5500
FAX: 202/296-0540

E-mail: oca@ocanatl.org
Internet: http://www.ocanatl.org
AMOUNT: $1,500
DEADLINE(S): MAY 1
FIELD(S): All fields of study

Open to Asian Pacific American women who will be entering their first year of college and have *significant* financial need. Must have a minimum 3.0 GPA and be a U.S. citizen/permanent resident. High school transcript, essay on importance of higher education, list of activities/work experience, letter of acceptance, and Student Aid Report required. Must fill out government FAFSA form.

See Web site or send a self-addressed, stamped envelope to OCA for an application and contact your school for FAFSA.

3201—ORGANIZATION OF CHINESE AMERICANS (National Essay Contest)

1001 Connecticut Avenue NW, Suite 601
Washington DC 20036
202/223-5500
FAX: 202/296-0540
E-mail: oca@ocanatl.org
Internet: http://www.ocanatl.org
AMOUNT: $400 (1st place); $200 (2nd); $100 (3rd)
DEADLINE(S): MAY 1
FIELD(S): All fields of study

Open to Asian Pacific American high school students. Essay topic changes yearly, but essay should be 800-1,000 words, typed, double-spaced, and on 8 1/2" x 11" white bond paper. Judged on theme and content (50%), organization and development (20%), grammer and mechanics (20%), and style (10%). Five copies of essay required. Students must be U.S. citizens/permanent residents.

See Web site or contact OCA for an application. Winners announced at OCA National Convention in July.

3202—ORGANIZATION OF CHINESE AMERICANS (UPS Gold Mountain Scholarships)

1001 Connecticut Avenue NW, Suite 601
Washington DC 20036
202/223-5500
FAX: 202/296-0540
E-mail: oca@ocanatl.org
Internet: http://www.ocanatl.org
AMOUNT: $2,000 + attendance at OCA National Convention
DEADLINE(S): MAY 1
FIELD(S): All fields of study

Open to Asian Pacific Americans who are the first person in their immediate family to attend college. Must be entering first year of college, have a minimum 3.0 GPA, demonstrate financial need, and be a U.S. citizen/permanent resident. High school transcript, essay on what it means to be first in family to go to college, list of activities/work experience, letter of acceptance, and Student Aid Report required. Must fill out government FAFSA form.

10 awards annually. See Web site or send a self-addressed, stamped envelope to OCA for an application and contact school for FAFSA.

3203—ORIEL COLLEGE DEVELOPMENT TRUST (Fellowships, Scholarships)

Mrs. Helen Kingsley
Trust Development Officer
Oxford OX1 4EW ENGLAND
01865 276599
FAX: 01865 276532
E-mail: helen.kingsley@oriel.ox.ac.uk
Internet: http://www.oriel.ox.ac.uk/development
AMOUNT: 500-1,200 pounds/year
DEADLINE(S): None
FIELD(S): All fields of study

Scholarships and fellowships for able students who may need financial help. Preference to students who come from the West Country (Somerset, Wiltshire, and former Avon areas) who obtain admission to Oriel whose circumstances, in the opinion of the head teachers, would warrant such an award.

Renewable provided academic performance is satisfactory. Contact college for details at address given.

3204—ORPHAN FOUNDATION OF AMERICA (Scholarship Program)

12020-D North Shore Drive
Reston VA 20190-4977
571/203-0270
FAX: 571/203-0273
Internet: http://www.orphan.org
AMOUNT: $800-$2,500
DEADLINE(S): April 15
FIELD(S): All areas of study

Program open to orphans or youth in foster care at the age of 18. who have not been adopted. Awards tenable at any recognized undergraduate or vocational school in the U.S. Must be U.S. citizens or legal resident.

50+ Scholarships per year. Renewable with reapplication. Send self-addressed stamped envelope for application and information.

3205—OTTO A. HUTH SCHOLARSHIP FUND

P.O. Box 40908
Reno NV 89504
800-879-9175
AMOUNT: Varies
DEADLINE(S): March 15
FIELD(S): All areas of study

Scholarships to financially needy high school seniors who are orphans and who are residents of Nevada.

3206—P.L.A.T.O. JUNIOR EDUCATION LOAN

205 Van Buren Street, Suite 200
Herndon VA 20170
888/PLATO-JR or 703/709-8100
FAX: 703/904-1541
E-mail: info@platojr.com
Internet: http://www.platojr.com
AMOUNT: $1,000-$20,000 per year
DEADLINE(S): None
FIELD(S): All fields of study

Education loans for parents of students in kindergarten-12th grade private schools. Must be U.S. citizen or permanent resident, earn minimum of $15,000 annually, and have a good credit history. Co-applicants allowed.

Renewable. Unlimited funding available. Financial need is NOT a factor.

3207—PADGETT BUSINESS SERVICES FOUNDATION (Scholarship Program)

160 Hawthorne Park
Athens GA 30606
800/723-4388
E-mail: scholarship@smallbizpros.com
AMOUNT: $500 (regional); $4,000 (international)
DEADLINE(S): MAR 1
FIELD(S): All fields of study

Open to dependents of small business owners who employ fewer than 20 individuals, own at least 10 percent of the stock or capital of the business, and are active in the day-to-day operations of the organization. Students must be graduating high school seniors planning to attend an accredited postsecondary institution and be U.S. or Canadian citizens/permanent residents. Essay describing education and career plans is required.

Contact Padgett Business Services in your community for an application. Local winners announced in May; all regional winners are eligible for one international scholarship announced in June. Separate scholarship is available to dependents of FTD Association member florists.

3208—PAPER, ALLIED-INDUSTRIAL, CHEMICAL, AND ENERGY WORKERS INTERNATIONAL UNION (PACE Scholarship Program)

P.O. Box 1475
Nashville TN 37202
AMOUNT: $1,000
DEADLINE(S): MAR 15
FIELD(S): All fields of study

Open to high school seniors who are sons or daughters of paid-up union members of at least one year. Must be U.S. or Canadian citizen planning to pursue undergraduate study at an accredited college/university. Financial need is considered. Recipients are asked to take at least one labor course during their college career.

22 awards annually. Contact PACE for an application.

3209—PARENTS AND FRIENDS OF LESBIANS AND GAYS—PFLAG CINCINNATI (Scholarships)

P.O. Box 19634
Cincinnati OH 45219
513/721-7900
AMOUNT: $500
DEADLINE(S): APR 15
FIELD(S): All fields of study

Scholarships for students who are gay, lesbian, bisexual, and transgender. Can be high school senior, undergraduate, or graduate student. Applications from students in the Cincinnati area will have preference.

Contact organization for details.

3210—PARENTS WITHOUT PARTNERS (International Scholarship)

401 N. Michigan Avenue
Chicago IL 60611-4267
312/644-6610
AMOUNT: Varies
DEADLINE(S): MAR 15
FIELD(S): All fields of study

Open to dependent children (up to 25 years of age) of Parents Without Partners members. Can be a graduating high school senior or college student. For undergraduate study at trade or vocational school, college, or university.

Write for complete information (send postage paid envelope).

3211—PARENTS, FAMILIES, AND FRIENDS OF LESBIANS AND GAYS-NEW ORLEANS CHAPTER (Scholarships)

P.O. Box 15515
New Orleans LA 70175
504/895-3936
E-mail: lhpeebles@aol.com
Internet: http://www.gaynew orleans.org/pflag/
AMOUNT: Varies
DEADLINE(S): FEB 17
FIELD(S): All fields of study

Scholarships for self-identified gay and lesbian students pursuing college degrees. For residents of Louisiana.

Application materials are at Web site (which also features great music!). Contact organization for details.

3212—PARENTS, FAMILIES, AND FRIENDS OF LESBIANS AND GAYS-SAN JOSE/PENINSULA CHAPTER (Scholarships)

690-57 Persian Drive
Sunnyvale CA 94089
408/745-1736 or 408/269-8418
FAX: 408/745-6063
E-mail: BobPhoto@webtv.net
Internet: http://www.pflag.org (follow links to San Jose/Peninsula Chapter)
AMOUNT: $1,000
DEADLINE(S): APR 10
FIELD(S): All fields of study

Scholarships for college-bound gay and lesbian high school seniors in public, private, or parochial high schools. For residents of San Mateo or Santa Clara counties in California. Also for students who have demonstrated support for justice and equality for gay, lesbian, and bisexual persons in their community.

For use at two- or four-year college, university, or business/technical school, full- or part-time. Contact organization for details.

3213—PARENTS, FAMILIES, AND FRIENDS OF LESBIANS AND GAYS-ATLANTA (Scholarships)

P.O. Box 8482
Atlanta GA 31106
770/662-6475
FAX: 404/864-3639
E-mail: mcjcatl@mindspring.com
AMOUNT: Varies
DEADLINE(S): APR 1
FIELD(S): All fields of study

Scholarships for college-bound gay, lesbian, or bisexual high school seniors, undergraduates, graduates, or postgraduates who are either George residents or attend or will attend a college or university in Georgia. Part-time students considered for reduced awards.

Renewable. Contact organization for details.

3214—PARENTS, FAMILIES AND FRIENDS OF LESBIANS AND GAYS (PFLAG)-NORTH BAY CHAPTER (Scholarships)

P.O. Box 2626
Petaluma CA 94953-2626
707/762-0107
Internet: http://www.pflag-nb.org/scholarship/app-schol.html
AMOUNT: Varies
DEADLINE(S): APR 12
FIELD(S): All fields of study

Scholarships for college-bound high school seniors in some way involved in the struggle against prejudice and discrimination against lesbian, gay, bisexual, and transgendered people. Must be graduating from a high school in Marin, Napa, or Sonoma counties in California between Jan. and June. Amounts vary according to donations to organization.

A typewritten essay, not to exceed 500 words, is required. Topic: Describe the way(s) in which you have been involved in the struggle against prejudice and homophobia. Why is discrimination against lesbian, gay, bisuxual, and transgendered people a concern of all citizens? For more instructions and application form, access Web site. Use of official form is required.

3215—PARTNERS ADVANCING VALUES IN EDUCATION (PAVE) (Scholarships for K-12 Private/Parochial School Students in Milwaukee, WI)

1434 W. State Street
Milwaukee WI 53233
414/342-1505
FAX: 414/342-1513
Internet: http://www.pave.org
AMOUNT: Half of tuition
DEADLINE(S): None
FIELD(S): All fields of study in K-12 schools

Scholarships for students from kindergarten through high school for use at any of 112 private or parochial schools in Milwaukee, WI. Pays half the tuition for needy families who meet the criteria established for the federal school lunch program. Must be residents of Milwaukee, WI.

School may require service work by families to assist with tuition program. Apply through your school of choice.

3216—PAUL AND MARY HAAS FOUNDATION (Scholarship Grants)

P.O. Box 2928
Corpus Christi TX 78403
512/887-6955

AMOUNT: $1,000 per semester
DEADLINE(S): Varies (initially fall of high school senior year)
FIELD(S): All fields of study

Program open to high school seniors who are Corpus Christi, Texas, residents. Awards support full-time pursuit of first undergraduate degree.

Approximately 50 awards per year. Must prove financial need. Write for complete information.

3217—PAUL O. AND MARY BOGHOSSIAN FOUNDATION

One Hospital Trust Plaza
Providence RI 02903
401/278-8752

AMOUNT: $500-$2,500
DEADLINE(S): MAY 1
FIELD(S): All fields of study

Scholarships for residents of Rhode Island.

Write c/o The Rhode Island Hospital Trust National Bank at above address for details and application.

3218—PENINSULA COMMUNITY FOUNDATION (African-American Scholarship Fund)

1700 S. El Camino Real, #300
San Mateo CA 94402
650/358-9369
FAX: 650/358-3950
Internet: http://www.pcf.org

AMOUNT: $5,000
DEADLINE(S): Varies
FIELD(S): All fields of study

Scholarship for African-American graduating high school seniors of a high school in San Mateo County or Northern Santa Clara County (Daly City to Mountain View), California. Must have GPA of at least 2.5. Award contingent upon acceptance at a California community college, state university, or branch of the University of California.

Program was designed to assist a motivated African-American student who otherwise would be unable to attend college.

3219—PENINSULA COMMUNITY FOUNDATION (Crain Educational Grants Program)

1700 S. El Camino Real, #300
San Mateo CA 94402
650/358-9369
FAX: 650/358-3950
Internet: http://www.pcf.org

AMOUNT: Up to $5,000
DEADLINE(S): Varies
FIELD(S): All fields of study

Scholarships for students who have graduated from or are current high school seniors of a public or private high school in San Mateo County or Santa Clara County, California. Must be U.S. citizen have financial need, have demonstrated community involvement over a period of years, and maintain a GPA of at least 3.0. For full-time enrollment in an accredited two- or four-year college, university, or vocational school in the U.S.

Program was established to enable worthy high school graduates to pursue courses of study that they would otherwise by unable to follow due to limited financial means.

3220—PENINSULA COMMUNITY FOUNDATION (Curry Award for Girls and Young Women)

1700 S. El Camino Real, #300
San Mateo CA 94402
650/358-9369
FAX: 650/358-3950
Internet: http://www.pcf.org

AMOUNT: $1,000
DEADLINE(S): Varies
FIELD(S): All fields of study

Awards for young women, age 16 to 26, who have attended a high school in San Mateo County, California. Must need financial support to reenter a post-secondary school, community college, university, or vocational school. Award is to help women who have dropped out of school for reasons beyond their control or have undergone unusual hardships to remain in school.

Awards are for one year, but recipients may reapply.

3221—PENINSULA COMMUNITY FOUNDATION (Ruppert Educational Grant Program)

1700 S. El Camino Real, #300
San Mateo CA 94402
650/358-9369
FAX: 650/358-3950
Internet: http://www.pcf.org

AMOUNT: Up to $1,000
DEADLINE(S): Varies
FIELD(S): All fields of study

Grants for current graduating seniors of a high school in San Mateo County, California. Must be U.S. citizen, have financial need. Grants are awarded for an accredited two- or four-year college, university, or trade school.

Program is designed for students who show academic promise but who are not likely to receive other scholarships because of lower GPAs. Awards are for one time only. "Late bloomers" are encouraged to apply.

3222—PENINSULA COMMUNITY FOUNDATION (Scholarship Fund for Gay/Lesbian Asian Students)

1700 S. El Camino Real, #300
San Mateo CA 94402
650/358-9369
FAX: 650/358-9817

AMOUNT: $2,000-$12,000
DEADLINE(S): MAR 27 (5 p.m.)
FIELD(S): All fields of study

Scholarships for gay/lesbian high school seniors graduating from San Mateo County, California, public or private high schools. Applicants must be U.S. citizens of Asian descent. Financial need and academic promise are considered. For use at accredited colleges and universities or vo-tech schools.

The Fund's donor understands the abandonment, alienation, and loneliness a gay or lesbian person may experience in today's social, economic, and political environment.

3223—PENNSYLVANIA HIGHER EDUCATION ASSISTANCE AGENCY (Robert C. Byrd Honors Scholarship Program)

P.O. Box 8114
Harrisburg PA 17105-8114
717/720-2850

AMOUNT: Determined yearly by the federal government
DEADLINE(S): MAY 1
FIELD(S): All fields of study

Open to Penn. high school seniors in the top 5 percent of their graduating class with a 3.5 or better GPA and an SAT score of 1200 or higher. Must be U.S. citizen and have been accepted for enrollment in an institution of higher education.

Renewable to a maximum of four years. Write for complete information.

3224—PENNSYLVANIA DEPARTMENT OF MILITARY AFFAIRS—BUREAU OF VETERANS AFFAIRS (Scholarships)

Fort Indiantown Gap
Annville PA 17003-5002
717/861-8904 or 717/861-8910
FAX: 717/861-8589
AMOUNT: Up to $500/term ($4,000 for 4 years)
DEADLINE(S): None
FIELD(S): All areas of study

Open to children of military veterans who died or were totally disabled as a result of war, armed conflict, or terrorist attack. Must have lived in Pennsylvania for 5 years prior to application, be age 16-23, and demonstrate financial need.

70 awards per year. Renewable. For study at Pennsylvania schools. Must be U.S. citizen. Write for complete information.

3225—PENNSYLVANIA YOUTH FOUNDATION (Leon M. Abbott Scholarship)

Executive Director
1244 Bainbridge Road
Elizabethtown PA 17022-9423
E-mail: pyf@pagrandlodge.org
Internet: http://www.pagrandlodge.org/pyf
AMOUNT: $2,500
DEADLINE(S): MAR 15
FIELD: All
FIELD(S): All fields of study

Annual awards for children of grandchildren of Scottish Rite Masons, and/or Pennsylvania DeMolays, Rainbow Girls, and Jobs Daughters. Applicant must be a graduate of a public or private secondary/preparatory school. Contact the Secretary of the local Scottish Rite Valley.

3226—PERKIOMEN SCHOOL (Grants)

200 Seminary Avenue
Pennsburg PA 18073
215/679-9511
FAX: 215/679-1146
E-mail: cdougherty@perkiomen.org
Internet: http://www.perkiomen.org
AMOUNT: Varies
DEADLINE(S): MAR 1
FIELD(S): All fields of study

Open to 5th-12th grade students at this private college prep Christian day/boarding school. Must have a minimum 3.0 GPA, demonstrate financial need, and be a U.S. citizen. This school is affiliated with the Schwenkfelder religion.

80 awards annually. Renewable. Contact Carol Dougherty for an application.

3227—PERRY & STELLA TRACY SCHOLARSHIP FUND (Scholarships)

Wells Fargo Private Banking Group
P.O. Box 2511
Sacramento CA 95812
916/440-4449
AMOUNT: Varies $350-$750
DEADLINE(S): None given
FIELD(S): All areas of study

Open to applicants who are graduates of El Dorado County high schools and have resided in El Dorado County CA for at least 2 years. Awards are tenable at recognized undergraduate colleges and universities.

Approximately 125 awards per year. Renewable. Contact high school counselor for complete information. DO NOT contact Wells Fargo.

3228—PETALUMA AND CASA GRANDE HIGH SCHOOLS (Carmen Scott Fry and Niels & Amalia Scott Scholarship Fund)

201 Fair Street
Petaluma CA 94952
707/778-4651
AMOUNT: $21,000
DEADLINE(S): Varies
FIELD(S): All fields of study

Open to high school seniors graduating from Petaluma High or Casa Grande High in Petaluma, CA. Must demonstrate financial need.

See your school's financial aid office for details. Awards began in 2001 and are provided by the late Arnold C. Scott of Petaluma.

3229—PETER BLOSSER STUDENT LOAN FUND

P.O. Box 6160
Chilliclothe OH 45601-6160
740/773-0043
E-mail: blosser@bright.net
Internet: http://www.bright.net/~blosser
AMOUNT: $5,000 max/year
DEADLINE(S): None
FIELD(S): All areas of study

A student loan for students who have been residents of Ross County, Ohio, for at least three years, have a minimum GPA of 2.0, graduated from a Ross County high school, or received a GED in the state of Ohio. To be used at an institution in Ross County.

Renewable up to $8,000. 15-40 annual loans.

3230—PFLAG/H.A.T.C.H. (Scholarship Fund)

P.O. Box 667010
Houston TX 77266
713/467-3524
Internet: http://www.pflaghouston.org
AMOUNT: $500-$10,000
DEADLINE(S): Varies
FIELD(S): All fields of study

For undergraduate/voc-tech students from the Greater Houston Metropolitan Area. Students must be gay or lesbian and be between the ages of 17-26. Financial need is NOT a factor.

10-15 awards annually. Renewable for four years with at least a "C" average.

3231—PHI KAPPA THETA NATIONAL FOUNDATION (Scholarship Program)

c/o Maria Mandel
3901 W. 86th Street, Suite 125
Indianapolis IN 46268
317/872-9934
AMOUNT: $1,500 (max.)
DEADLINE(S): APR 30
FIELD(S): All fields of study

Open to undergraduate students who are members of Phi Kappa Theta, a men's social fraternity. Not available to high school or graduate students. Financial need is considered but is relative to other applicants.

Renewable. Contact your local chapter or the national office for an application.

3232—PHI THETA KAPPA INTERNATIONAL HONOR SOCIETY (Guistwhite Scholar Program)

P.O. Box 13729
Jackson, MS 39236
601/957-2241
E-mail: scholarship.programs@ptk.org
Internet: http://www.ptk.org
AMOUNT: Varies
DEADLINE(S): Varies
FIELD(S): All fields of study

For active members of Phi Theta Kappa who are pursuing an associates degree and who plan on continuing their education at an accredited senior institution. Minimum GPA of 3.5 is required, and student must be at junior level at time of transfer. Letters of recommendation, typed application, official transcript, college registrar's certification form, and student essay required.

3233—PHILLIPS EXETER ACADEMY (Financial Aid)

20 Main Street
Exeter NH 03833
603/777-3637
FAX: 603/777-4384
E-mail: pmahoney@exeter.edu
Internet: http://www.exeter.edu
AMOUNT: $1,000-$25,000
DEADLINE(S): Varies
FIELD(S): All fields of study

Grants and loans are available to 9th-12th grade students who have been accepted for admission to this highly competitive private boarding/day school. Must demonstrate financial need.

150 awards annually. Renewable.

3234—PHILIPS NORTH AMERICA CORPORATION (Scholarship Program)

1251 Avenue of the Americas
New York NY 10017
212/536-0500
AMOUNT: 2,500; $500-$1,500
DEADLINE(S): DEC 1
FIELD(S): All

Open to dependent children of Philips North America employees. Applicants must be high school seniors who expect to graduate during the current year. Considerations include academic record, SAT or ACT scores, and biographical questionnaire.

3235—PICKETT AND HATCHER EDUCATIONAL FUND, INC. (Loans)

P.O. Box 8169
Columbus GA 31908-8169
706/327-6586
Internet: http://www.phef.org
AMOUNT: $5,500/year
DEADLINE(S): Varies
FIELD(S): All fields of study (except Law, Medicine, or Ministry)

Open to U.S. citizens who are legal residents of and attend schools located in AL, FL, GA, KY, MS, NC, SC, TN, or VA. Must be incoming freshman enrolling in four-year program of study in four-year college/university. Must have minimum 950 SAT/20 ACT score, demonstrate financial need, and have credit worthy endorser. Loans are not for graduate or vo-tech studies, and applicants may not have other educational loans.

500-600 awards annually. Renewable. Contact Pickett & Hatcher after January 1 preceding academic year for which loan is needed.

3236—PINE BLUFFS AREA CHAMBER OF COMMERCE (Scholarship)

P.O. Box 486
Pine Bluffs WY 82082-0486
Written Inquiry
AMOUNT: $300
DEADLINE(S): Varies
FIELD(S): All fields of study

Available to a graduate of Pine Bluffs High School to attend any accredited college, trade, or technical school in the US. Award is based on need, aptitude, academic, and overall performance. Must submit an essay on plans to help community in which student will live.

1 award annually. Not renewable. Write to above address for an application.

3237—PNG DEPARTMENT OF EDUCATION (Sponsorship Program)

PSA Haus
P.O. Box 446
Waigani 131
PAPUA NEW GUINEA
675/301-3555
FAX: 675/325-4648
AMOUNT: $365-$21,900/year
DEADLINE(S): None
FIELD(S): All fields of study

Open to PNG citizen employees of the Education Department to pursue studies in various fields, depending on which sector of the education system an applicant works in. Awards cover in-country as well as overseas sponsorships and may include travel. Financial need NOT a factor.

200-300 awards annually. Not renewable. Contact PNG Department of Education for an application.

3238—PORTSMOUTH HIGH SCHOOL (George C. Cogan Scholarship)

50 Alumni Circle
Portsmouth NH 03801
603/436-7100
FAX: 603/427-2320
AMOUNT: Varies
DEADLINE(S): APR 15
FIELD(S): All fields of study

For male graduates of Portsmouth (New Hampshire) High School or Street Thomas Aquinas High School (in Dover, NH) who were residents in Portsmouth, NH for at least four years prior to graduation. For undergraduate study. Financial need is NOT a factor.

15 awards annually. Renewable for three more years of undergraduate work. Send proof of residency and high school transcripts (including date of graduation) to Sonya Desjardins at above address.

3239—PORTUGUESE CONTINENTAL UNION OF THE USA (Scholarships)

30 Cummings Park
Woburn MA 01801
781/376-0271
FAX: 781/376-2033
E-mail: upceua@aol.com
Internet: members.aol.com/upceua/
AMOUNT: Varies
DEADLINE(S): MAR 31
FIELD(S): All fields of study

Open to members of the Portuguese Continental Union with at least one year membership in good standing and who plan to enroll or are already enrolled in any accredited college/university. Must demonstrate financial need, be of good character, and have grades which meet entrance standards at the college/university of your choice. Awards are paid directly to the school.

Contact Scholarship Committee for an application. Applicants notified of results in April.

3240—POWER STUDENTS NETWORK (Scholarship)

c/o Imagine Media
150 North Hill Drive, Suite 40
Brisbane CA 94005
Internet: http://www.powerstudents.com
AMOUNT: $1,000
DEADLINE(S): MAR 15
FIELD(S): All fields of study

High school students and undergraduates may apply. Awards may only be used to finance your education at an accredited college, junior college, community college, technical school, or university.

See Web site to request application or send a self-addressed, stamped envelope to above address. If you sign up online you will receive a free Power Students Network Survival Kit and access to exclusive admissions, financial aid, and college success articles. With your application you must submit your transcript and an essay on a topic of your choice (less than four pages).

3241—PRESBYTERIAN CHURCH (U.S.A.) (Appalachian Scholarship)

1000 Witherspoon Street
Louisville KY 40202-1396
888/728-7228 ext. 5745
E-mail: KSmith@ctr.pcusa.org
Internet: http://www.pcusa.org/highered

AMOUNT: $200-$1,000
DEADLINE(S): JUL 1
FIELD(S): All fields of study

For undergraduate residents of the Appalachian areas of Kentucky, North Carolina, Tennessee, Virginia, and West Virginia. Must be U.S. citizens or permanent residents, demonstrate financial need, and be members of the Presbyterian Church. Nontraditional age students with no previous college experience are encouraged to apply.

Renewable. Contact Kathy Smith at above address for more information.

3242—PRESBYTERIAN CHURCH (U.S.A.) (Native American Education Grant)

100 Witherspoon Street
Louisville KY 40202-1396
888/728-7228 ext. 5760
E-mail: MariaA@ctr.pcusa.org
Internet: http://www.pcusa.org/highered

AMOUNT: $200-$2,500
DEADLINE(S): JUN 1
FIELD(S): All fields of study

For Native Americans and Alaska Natives pursuing full-time post-secondary education. Must be members of the Presbyterian Church (U.S.A.), be U.S. citizens or permanent residents, and demonstrate financial need.

Renewable. Contact Maria Alvarez at above address for more information.

3243—PRESBYTERIAN CHURCH (U.S.A.) (National Presbyterian College Scholarship)

100 Witherspoon Street
Louisville KY 40202-1396
888/728-7228 ext. 8235
E-mail: Megan_Willman@ctr.pcusa.org
Internet: http://www.pcusa.org/highered

AMOUNT: $500-$1,400
DEADLINE(S): DEC 1
FIELD(S): All fields of study

Scholarships for full-time incoming freshmen at one of the participating colleges related to the Presbyterian Church (U.S.A.). Applicants must be superior high school seniors and members of the Presbyterian Church. Must be US citizen or permanent resident and demonstrate financial need. Must take the SAT/ACT exam no later than December 15th of senior year.

Renewable. Application and brochure available after September 1st. Contact Megan Willman at above address for more information.

3244—PRESBYTERIAN CHURCH (U.S.A.) (Samuel Robinson Award)

100 Witherspoon Street
Louisville KY 40202-1396
502/569-5745
E-mail: KSmith@ctr.pcusa.org
Internet: http://www.pcusa.org/highered

AMOUNT: $200-$1,000
DEADLINE(S): APR 1
FIELD(S): All fields of study

For undergraduate juniors and seniors enrolled full-time in one of the colleges related to the Presbyterian Church. Applicants must successfully recite the answers to the Westminster Shorter Catechism and write a 2,000-word original essay on a related assigned topic.

20-30 awards per year. Not renewable. Contact Kathy Smith at above address for more information.

3245—PRESBYTERIAN CHURCH (U.S.A.) (Service Program)

100 Witherspoon Street
Louisville KY 40202-1396
888/728-7228 ext. 5735
E-mail: LBryan@ctr.pcusa.org
Internet: http://www.pcusa.org/highered

AMOUNT: $1,500
DEADLINE(S): APR 1
FIELD(S): All fields of study

Provides undergraduate students with an opportunity to pay a portion of their educational expenses through service in various school, church, or community projects. Applicants must be in 2nd or 3rd year of full-time study, be recommended by campus pastor or chaplain of college/university, and complete 250 hours of community service. Money must be repaid if service project is not completed by graduation or discontinuation of studies.

Not renewable. Contact Laura Bryan at above address for more information.

3246—PRESBYTERIAN CHURCH (U.S.A.) (Student Opportunity Scholarship)

100 Witherspoon Street
Louisville KY 40202-1396
888/728-7228 ext. 5760
E-mail: MariaA@ctr.pcusa.org
Internet: http://www.pcusa.org/highered

AMOUNT: $100-$1,400
DEADLINE(S): APR 1
FIELD(S): All fields of study

Designed to assist racial ethnic undergraduate students (African American, Alaska Native, Asian American, Hispanic American, Native American) finance their undergraduate education. Applicants must be US citizens/permanent residents who are high school seniors and members of the Presbyterian Church (U.S.A.). Must demonstrate financial need.

Renewable. Applications available after February 1st. Contact Maria Alvarez at above address for more information.

3247—PRESBYTERIAN CHURCH (U.S.A.) (Undergraduate/Graduate Loan Programs)

100 Witherspoon Street
Louisville KY 40202-1396
888/728-7228 ext.5735
E-mail: LBryan@ctr.pcusa.org
Internet: http://www.pcusa.org/highered

AMOUNT: $200-$7,000/year
DEADLINE(S): None
FIELD(S): All fields of study

Loans open to members of the Presbyterian Church (U.S.A.) who are US citizens or permanent residents. For full-time undergraduate or graduate study at an accredited college/university. No interest while in school; repayment begins six months after graduation or discontinuation of studies. Must demonstrate financial need, be in good academic standing, and give evidence of financial reliability.

Renewable. May apply for maximum amount in final year of study if have not previously borrowed. Contact Laura Bryan at above address for more information.

3248—PRIDE FOUNDATION & GREATER SEATTLE BUSINESS ASSOCIATION (Scholarships for Gays & Lesbians)

1122 E. Pike Street, Suite 1001
Seattle WA 98122-3934
206/323-3318 or
800/735-7287-outside Seattle area
FAX: 206/323-1017
E-mail: scholarshipsd@pride foundation.org
Internet: http://www.pride foundation.org

AMOUNT: Up to $5,000
DEADLINE(S): Varies
FIELD(S): All fields of study

A variety of scholarships for gay, lesbian, bisexual, and transgender youth and adults who reside in Washington, Oregon, Idaho, Montana, or Alaska. For all levels of postsecondary education—community college, four-year college, or vocational training. Some require financial need.

Check Web site and/or write to organization for details. Applications available Nov. 1.

3249—PRINCE GEORGE'S CHAMBER OF COMMERCE FOUNDATION (Scholarship)

4601 Presidents Drive, Suite 150
Lanham MD 20706
301/731-5000
FAX: 301/731-5013

AMOUNT: Full tuition at Maryland schools; partial tuition at out-of-state schools
DEADLINE(S): MAY 15
FIELD(S): All fields of study

Open to residents of Prince George's County, MD, for undergraduate study. Must be U.S. citizen. Financial need is a consideration.

Write for complete information.

3250—PROFESSIONAL BOWLERS ASSOCIATION (Billy Welu Memorial Scholarship)

Young American Bowling Alliance
5301 S. 76th Street
Greendale WI 53129-1139
Written Inquiry

AMOUNT: $1,000
DEADLINE(S): MAY 15
FIELD(S): All fields of study

Open to undergraduate students who are enrolled in college and are current members of a college ABC, WIBC, or YABA league. Aim of the PBA is to support and promote the sport of bowling.

Send self-addressed, stamped, #10 envelope to above address for an application.

3251—PROFESSIONAL HORSEMEN'S SCHOLARSHIP FUND, INC. (Scholarships)

c/o Mrs. Ann Grenci
204 Old Sleepy Hollow Road
Pleasantville NY 10570
561/694-6893 (Nov.-Apr.)
914/769-1493 (May-Oct.)

AMOUNT: $1,000 (max.)
DEADLINE(S): MAY 1
FIELD(S): All fields of study

Open to members and dependents of members of the Professional Horsemen's Association. Awards can be used for college or trade school.

Up to 10 awards annually. Contact Mrs. Ann Grenci for an application.

3252—PUBLIC EMPLOYEES ROUNDTABLE (Public Service Scholarships)

P.O. Box 75248
Washington DC 20013
202/927-4923
Internet: http://www.theround table.org

AMOUNT: $500 (part-time); $1,000 (full-time)
DEADLINE(S): MAY
FIELD(S): All fields of study

Open to graduate students and undergraduate sophomores, juniors, and seniors who are planning a career in government service at the local, state, or federal level. Minimum of 3.5 cumulative GPA. Preference to applicants with some public service work experience (paid or unpaid).

3253—PUEBLO OF ZUNI HIGHER EDUCATION (Scholarships)

Scholarship Officer
P.O. Box 339
Zuni NM 87327
505-782-2191
FAX: 505-782-2921
E-mail: zunihe@unm.edu

AMOUNT: Varies
DEADLINE(S): Varies
FIELD(S): All

Various scholarships are available to Zuni Tribe members who are pursuing higher education. Must show proof of tribal enrollment. 2.5 GPA required.

3254—QUEEN'S UNIVERSITY OF BELFAST (Entrance Scholarships)

Academic Council Office
Belfast BT7 1NN
NORTHERN IRELAND UK
+44 (0) 28 9024 5133
Internet: http://www.qub.ac.uk

AMOUNT: Varies
DEADLINE(S): Varies
FIELD(S): All fields of study

Scholarships based on entrance qualifications. Approximately 15 are available to the best A-level entrants each year, and all entrants with at least three grade "A"s will automatically be considered for the awards. Two further entrance scholarships are available to entrants with non-A-Level qualifications, e.g., Irish Leaving Certificate, and other awards based on first semester Level 1 examinations.

Contact the University's Academic Couoncil Office at the address above for complete information.

3255—QUEEN'S UNIVERSITY OF BELFAST (Guiness Sports Bursary Awards)

Guiness Sports Bursary Awards
The Physical Education Centre
Botanic Park, Belfast BT9 5EX
NORTHERN IRELAND UK
+44 (0) 28 9024 5133
Internet: http://www.qub.ac.uk

AMOUNT: Varies
DEADLINE(S): Varies
FIELD(S): All fields of study

Sport has played an integral role in university life at Queen's. Thus, financial assistance is available for current and potential students who have participated in sports and are gifted athletes of good academic standing. Bursaries are open to full-time students.

Approximately 15 annual awards. Contact the University at the address above for complete information.

3256—REALTY FOUNDATION OF NEW YORK (Scholarship Program)

551 Fifth Avenue, Suite 1105
New York NY 10176-0166
212/697-25103943

AMOUNT: Varies
DEADLINE(S): Varies
FIELD(S): All fields of study

Open to Realtors and their children or employees of real estate firms and their children. The student or his parent are required to be employed in the real estate industry in Metropolitan New York.

Write to the above address for complete information.

3257—RECORDING FOR THE BLIND AND DYSLEXIC (Marion Huber Learning Through Listening Awards)

20 Roszel Road
Princeton NJ 08540
609/452-0606
FAX: 609/520-7990
Internet: http://www.rfbd.org

AMOUNT: $2,000 and $6,000
DEADLINE(S): FEB 1
FIELD(S): Any field of study

Awards for college-bound high school seniors with specific learning disabilities registered with RFB&D for at least one year prior to the filing deadline, who have an overall GPA of B or above, based on grades 10-12, and plan to continue formal education beyond high school at either a two- or four-year college or a vocational school.

Academic achievement and service to others through extracurricular activities considered. Contact above address for details.

3258—RECORDING FOR THE BLIND AND DYSLEXIC (Mary P. Oenslager Scholastic Achievement Awards)

20 Roszel Road
Princeton NJ 08540
800/221-4792 or 609/452-0606
FAX: 609/520-7990
Internet: http://www.rfbd.org

AMOUNT: $1,000-$6,000
DEADLINE(S): FEB 21
FIELD(S): All fields of study

Open to legally blind college seniors who are registered with RFB&D for at least one year prior to deadline (individually or through a school). Must have received or will receive a bachelor's degree from a four-year college/university in the United States or its territories between July 1 and June 30 (of year applying). Must have a minimum 3.0 GPA and provide evidence of leadership, enterprise, and service to others. Need not plan to continue education further.

9 awards annually. Contact RFB&D for an application.

3259—RED RIVER COLLEGE (Access Program)

F210-2055 Notre Dame Avenue
Winnipeg Manitoba R3H OJ9
CANADA
204/632-2180 or 800-903-7707
FAX: 204/633-1437
Internet: http://www.rrcc.mb.ca

AMOUNT: Varies
DEADLINE(S): MAR 1
FIELD(S): All fields of study

The Community College Access Program provides admission to Red River College. You may be eligible if you have not had the opportunity because of social, economic, cultural factors, residence in remote areas, or lack of formal education. Must be resident of Manitoba. Priority will be given to Status Indian, Non-Status Indian, and Metis people.

10-15 awards annually. Renewable. Contact RRC for an application.

3260—RED RIVER VALLEY FIGHTER PILOTS ASSOCIATION (River Rats Scholarship Grant Programs)

P.O. Box 1551
North Fork CA 93643
559/877-5000
FAX: 559/877-5001
E-mail: AFBridger@aol.com
Internet: http://www.eos.net/rrva

AMOUNT: $500-$3,500
DEADLINE(S): MAY 15
FIELD(S): All fields of study

For a) immediate dependents (spouse/children) of any member of US Armed Forces who is listed in KIA/MIA status from any combat situation involving our military since 8/64; b) immediate dependents of military aircrew members killed as result of performing aircrew duties during non-combat mission; c) immediate dependents of current/deceased RRVA-members in good standing; and d) grandchildren of qualifying military relative. Must be US citizen/permanent resident.

15-40 awards annually. Renewable. Based on need, achievement, and activities. See Web site or contact Al Bache, Executive Director, for an application.

3261—RESERVE OFFICERS ASSOCIATION OF THE UNITED STATES (Henry J. Reilly Memorial Scholarships for Undergraduates)

One Constitution Avenue NE
Washington DC 20002-5655
202/479-2200 or 800/809-9448
FAX: 202/479-0416
E-mail: 71154.1267@compserve.com

AMOUNT: $500
DEADLINE(S): Varies (applications available in FEB)
FIELD(S): All fields of study

Must be active or associate members of ROA or ROAL, or be children or grandchildren, aged 26 or younger, of members. Children of deceased members eligible if under age 21. For full-time study at a four-year college/university. Must have minimum 3.3 high school GPA and 3.0 college GPA. 500-word (handwritten) essay on career goals, leadership qualities, and SAT/ACT scores required. Spouses not eligible unless they are members.

75 awards annually. Contact Ms. Mickey Hagen for an application—please specify your grade level.

3262—RESERVE OFFICERS ASSOCIATION OF THE UNITED STATES (Henry J. Reilly Memorial Scholarships for Graduates)

One Constitution Avenue NE
Washington DC 20002-5655
202/479-2200 or 800/809-9448
FAX: 202/479-0416
E-mail: 71154.1267@compserve.com

AMOUNT: $500
DEADLINE(S): Varies (applications available in FEB)
FIELD(S): All fields of study

Must be active or associate members of ROA who are graduate students at a regionally accredited US college/university. Must be enrolled in at least two courses (if you are employed full-time, you may be eligible if enrolled in only one course) and have a minimum 3.2 GPA. Must demonstrate leadership qualities—letter of recommendation from military or civilian "reporting senior" is required, as well as two letters in regards to academic ability and curriculum vitae.

35 awards annually. Contact Ms. Mickey Hagen for an application—please specify your grade level. Undergrad program for ROA/ROAL members also available.

3263—RHODE ISLAND HIGHER EDUCATION ASSISTANCE AUTHORITY (Loan Program; Plus Loans)

560 Jefferson Boulevard
Warwick RI 02886
401/736-1160

AMOUNT: Up to $5,500 for undergrads and up to $8,500 for graduates (subsidized); up to $5,000 for undergrads and up to $10,000 for graduates (unsubsidized)
DEADLINE(S): None specified
FIELD(S): All fields of study

Open to Rhode Island residents or non-residents attending an eligible school. Must be U.S. citizen or legal resident and be enrolled at least half-time. Rhode Island residents may attend schools outside the state.

Must demonstrate financial need. Write for current interest rates and complete information.

3264—RHODE ISLAND HIGHER EDUCATION ASSISTANCE AUTHORITY (Undergraduate Grant & Scholarship Program)

560 Jefferson Boulevard
Warwick RI 02886
407/736-1100
AMOUNT: $250-$2,000
DEADLINE(S): MAR 1
FIELD(S): All fields of study

Open to Rhode Island residents who are US citizens or eligible non-citizens and are enrolled or planning to enroll at least 1/2 time in a program that leads to a degree or certificate at the undergraduate level. Grant is limited to eligible schools in the US, Canada, and Mexico. Must demonstrate financial need: Cost of education minus estimated Pell Grant minus expected family contribution equal need (must have at least $1,000 in need).

Contact RIHEAA for an application.

3265—RICHARD E. MERWIN SCHOLARSHIP

1730 Massachusetts Avenue NW
Washington DC 20036
202/371-1013
FAX: 202/728-0884
AMOUNT: $3,000
DEADLINE(S): MAY 31
FIELD(S): Computers and Engineering

Full-time graduate students, Juniors and Seniors in electrical engineering, computer engineering, computer science, or well-defined computer related field who are active members of the Computer Society Student Branch Chapter at their institution. Minimum overall grade point average should be 2.5. Funded by the IEEE Computer Society

3266—RIDLEY COLLEGE PREPARATORY SCHOOL (Scholarships & Bursaries)

P.O. Box 3013
2 Ridley Road
Street Catharines Ontario L2R 7C3
CANADA
905/684-1889
FAX: 905/684-8875
E-mail: admission@ridley.on.ca
Internet: http://www.ridley.on.ca
AMOUNT: Varies
DEADLINE(S): Varies
FIELD(S): All fields of study

Merit scholarships and need-based bursaries/loans are available to students in grades 5-12 at this private boarding/day school. Based on SSAT scores, GPA, an interview, and letters of commendation.

160 awards annually. Renewable. Contact Don Riekers, Director of Admission, for an application.

3267—RIPON COLLEGE (Academic Tuition Scholarships)

Admissions Office
300 Seward Street
P.O. Box 248
Ripon WI 54971
800/94-RIPON
E-mail: adminfo@ripon.edu
Internet: http://www.ripon.edu
AMOUNT: $2,500-$15,000/year
DEADLINE(S): MAR 1
FIELD(S): All fields of study

Open to entering first-year students at Ripon College. Must have minimum 3.2 GPA and ACT score of at least 24 or SAT score of at least 1110. Interview may be required.

Renewable. Contact Office of Admission for an application.

3268—RISING STAR INTERNSHIPS (Internships and Part-Time Employment for Students)

1904 Hidden Point Road
Annapolis MD 21401
410/974-4783
E-mail: info@rsinternships.com
Internet: http://www.rsinternships.com
AMOUNT: Varies
DEADLINE(S): None
FIELD(S): All fields

A Web site containing opportunities for internships and part-time student employment nationwide. The search is free, but there is a charge for students to post a resume. Organizations offering opportunities can do so for free for one month, but must pay $10 per month thereafter. Many vocational areas are available.

Most internships are unpaid.

3269—ROCKY MOUNT ACADEMY (Scholarships)

1313 Avondale Avenue
Rocky Mount NC 27803
252/443-4126
FAX: 252/937-7922
E-mail: bdavis@rmacademy.com;
Internet: http://rmacademy.com
AMOUNT: Full tuition (max.)
DEADLINE(S): APR 1
FIELD(S): All fields of study

Open to 6th-12th grade students at this private day school. Awards are based on merit. Financial need NOT a factor.

8 awards annually. Renewable. Contact Thomas Stevens, Headmaster, for an application.

3270—RON BROWN SCHOLAR PROGRAM

1160 Pepsi Place, Suite 306B
Charlottesville VA 22901
814/964-1588
FAX: 804/964-1589
E-mail: franh@ronbrown.org
Internet: http://www.ronbrown.org
Amount: $2,500
DEADLINE(S): JAN 9
FIELD(S): All
FIELD(S): All fields of study

Renewable awards for African-American high school seniors who intend to pursue full-time undergraduate study at a four-year college or university. Must excel academically, demonstrate leadership ability, participate in community service activities. Must be a US citizen or hold permanent resident visa and demonstrate financial need.

3271—ROSE AND JOSEPH SOKOL SCHOLARSHIP

c/o Dorothy S. Kipnis
118 Chadwick Dr.
Charleston SC
843/766-4766
Amount: $500
DEADLINE(S): NOV 15
FIELD(S): All
FIELD(S): All fields of study

Applicant must be a Jewish resident of South Carolina who demonstrates financial need. Application should consist of information about applicant and his/her family and copy of family's most recent tax return.

Renewable if recipient maintains good grades and continues to demonstrate financial need.

3272—ROTARY FOUNDATION OF ROTARY INTERNATIONAL (Ambassadorial Scholarships)

1 Rotary Center
1560 Sherman Avenue
Evanston IL 60201-3698
847/866-3000
FAX: 847/328-8554
Internet: http://www.rotary.org
AMOUNT: Travel, language training, fees, room/board, and educational supplies
DEADLINE(S): Varies (MAR-JUL)
FIELD(S): All fields of study

Open to those who have completed at least two years of university/college coursework and to those with a secondary school education who have been employed in a recognized vocation for at least two years. Must be citizen of a country in which there is a Rotary club. Scholars are expected to be outstanding ambassadors of goodwill to the people of the host country.

1,300 awards annually. See Web site or contact your local Rotary club for specific details and an application.

3273—ROTARY FOUNDATION OF ROTARY INTERNATIONAL (Grants for University Teachers)

1 Rotary Center
1560 Sherman Avenue
Evanston IL 60201-3698
847/866-3000
FAX: 847/328-8554
Internet: http://www.rotary.org
AMOUNT: $22,500 (max.)
DEADLINE(S): Varies (with local Rotary Club)
FIELD(S): All fields of study

An opportunity for university teachers to teach at a university in a low-income country. Grants are for either three to five months (US$12,500) or six to ten months (US$22,500). Must be as a citizen of a country where there is a Rotary club. Rotarians and their relatives are eligible as well as non-Rotarians.

See Web site or contact local Rotary club for deadlines and an application.

3274—ROOTHBERT FUND, INC. (Scholarships)

475 Riverside Drive, Room 252
New York NY 10115
212/870-3116
AMOUNT: Up to $2,000
DEADLINE(S): FEB
FIELD(S): All

Scholarships are open to all students regardless of sex, age, color, nationality, or religious background. The fund seeks to provide support to persons motivated by spiritual values. Preference will be given to those who can satisfy high scholastic requirements and are considering careers in education.

3275—ROYAL A. & MILDRED D. EDDY STUDENT LOAN TRUST FUND; LOUISE I. LATSHAW STUDENT LOAN TRUST FUND (Student Loans)

NBD Bank Trust Dept.
8585 Broadway, Suite 396
Merriville IN 46410
Written Inquiry
AMOUNT: $4,000/year
DEADLINE(S): Ongoing
FIELD(S): All fields of study

Loan fund available to undergraduate juniors and seniors who are U.S. citizens. Two credit-worthy co-signers are required. Interest rate is 10%, and payments must begin five months after graduation. For study in the U.S. only.

Write to above address for complete information.

3276—ROYAL NEIGHBORS OF AMERICA (Fraternal Scholarships)

230 16th Street
Rock Island IL 61201
309/788-4561
AMOUNT: $100 to $2,500
DEADLINE(S): DEC 1
FIELD(S): All areas of study

Open to high school seniors who are RNA members of at least 2 years and in the upper quarter of their class. Awards tenable by U.S. citizens at recognized undergrad colleges and universities.

3277—ROYAL NEIGHBORS OF AMERICA (Non-traditional Scholarship)

230 16th Street
Rock Island IL 61201
309/788-4561
AMOUNT: $500-$1,000
DEADLINE(S): Varies
FIELD(S): All areas of study

For those who have been RNA members for at least two years and are 25 years of age or older.

15 awards per year.

3278—ROYAL NORWEGIAN EMBASSY (May 8th Memorial Fund)

2720 34th Street NW
Washington DC 20008
202/333-6000
FAX: 202/337-0870
AMOUNT: Tuition and food/lodging
DEADLINE(S): MAR 15
FIELD(S): None specified

Scholarship commemorating 25th anniversary of Liberation of Norway for one year's residence at a Norwegian Folk High School. No formal credits, not college; objective is to prepare young people for everyday life in the community.

Must be between 18 and 22 years of age; your country must be among those selected for this year's bursaries. Other restrictions apply. Write for complete information.

3279—RURITAN NATIONAL FOUNDATION (Grant and Loan Program)

P.O. Box 487
Dublin VA 24084
540/674-9441
AMOUNT: Varies—minimum grant $200; minimum loan $500
DEADLINE(S): Varies
FIELD(S): All fields of study

Grants and loans for postsecondary education. Applicant must be recommended by two active Ruritans. Clubs are located in 25 states.

Financial need, character, scholarship, and academic promise, and desire for further education are considered.

3280—SACHS FOUNDATION (Scholarship Program)

90 S. Cascade Avenue, Suite 1410
Colorado Springs CO 80903
719/633-2353
E-mail: sachs@frii.com
AMOUNT: $4,000
DEADLINE(S): MAR 1
FIELD(S): All fields of study

Open to African-American undergraduates who have been residents of Colorado for at least five years. Must have a minimum 3.5 GPA, be a US citizen, and demonstrate financial need. Tenable at any accredited college/university.

50 awards annually. Renewable up to 4 years with minimum 2.5 GPA. Contact Sachs Foundation for an application. Graduate awards of $5,000 are available to current Sachs undergraduates.

3281—SACRAMENTO SCOTTISH RITE OF FREEMASONRY (Charles M. Goethe Memorial Scholarship)

P.O. Box 19497
Sacramento CA 95819-0497
916/452-5881
AMOUNT: $350-$1,700
DEADLINE(S): JUN 10
FIELD(S): All fields of study

For any field of study but preference is to students majoring in eugenics or biological sciences. Grants are limited to students who are members or senior members of the Order of Demolay.

Also open to children of members or deceased members of a California Masonic Lodge. Write for complete information.

3282—SACRED HEART ACADEMY OF STAMFORD (Merit Scholarships)

200 Strawberry Hill Avenue
Stamford CT 06902-2519
203/323-3173
FAX: 203/975-7804
E-mail: sha200adm@aol.com
Internet: shastamford.org
AMOUNT: $1,500
DEADLINE(S): DEC
FIELD(S): All fields of study

Open to students entering this private secondary school. Must take December or March exam the year before entering the 9th grade. Top scorers are awarded scholarships, and must maintain a minimum 3.2 GPA to continue receiving scholarship. Financial aid is also available based on need, determined by application with W-2 forms.

3 merit scholarships and variable financial aid awards annually. Renewable up to 4 years. Contact Academy for an application.

3283—SAINT ANTHONY OF PADUA SCHOOL (Tuition Assistance)

906 Jenkins Street
Endicott NY 13760
607/754-0875
Internet: http://home.stny.rr.com/stanthonys
AMOUNT: Varies
DEADLINE(S): Varies
FIELD(S): All fields of study

Tuition assistance for this private Catholic school for children in grades K-4 in Endicott, NY.

Check Web site or write for details.

3284—SAINT GEORGE'S SCHOOL (Scholarships)

4175 W. 29th Avenue
Vancouver BC V6S 1V6 CANADA
604/222-5810
FAX: 604/224-7066
E-mail: info@stgeorges.bc.ca
Internet: http://www.stgeorges.bc.ca
AMOUNT: $500-$10,000
DEADLINE(S): Varies
FIELD(S): All fields of study

Open to students in 8th through 12th grade at Street George's School. This K-12 boarding/day school is for males only, and bursaries are awarded to academically strong students. Must be U.S. or Canadian citizens/permanent residents.

50 awards annually. Renewable yearly. Contact Bill McCracken for an application.

3285—SAINT GEORGE'S SCHOOL OF MONTREAL (Financial Assistance)

3100 The Boulevard
Montreal Quebec H3Y 1R9
CANADA
514/937-9289
FAX: 514/933-3621
AMOUNT: 50% tuition (max.)
DEADLINE(S): APR 15
FIELD(S): General Arts and Sciences

Open to pre-K through high school students who are successfully admitted to this private school. Must demonstrate financial need.

55 awards annually. Renewable. Contact James Officer for an application.

3286—SAINT JAMES LUTHERAN CHURCH (Generations for Peace Scholarship)

1315 Southwest Park Avenue
Portland, OR 97201
AMOUNT: $750-$1,500
DEADLINE(S): APR 1
FIELD: All
FIELD(S): All fields of study

First ($1500) and second place ($750) scholarships awarded to winners of an essay contest. For guidelines and essay topic send self-addressed stamped envelope and one dollar to Generations for Peace. Open to high school students.

3287—ST. JAMES LUTHERAN CHURCH (Generations for Peace Scholarship)

1315 Southwest Park Avenue
Portland OR 97201
AMOUNT: $750-$1,500
DEADLINE(S): APR 1
FIELD(S): All

Guidelines and essay topics vary by year. Please request more information by sending a self-addressed stamped envelope and one dollar to "Generations for Peace." Scholarships are available to United States high school students.

3288—SAINT JOHN'S SCHOOL OF ALBERTA (Bursary Trust)

RR #5
Stony Plain Alberta T7Z 1X5
CANADA
780/848-2881 or 800/563-6456
FAX: 780/848-2395
E-mail: pjackson@sjsa.ab.ca
Internet: http://www.sjsa.ab.ca
AMOUNT: $500-$10,000
DEADLINE(S): JUN 1
FIELD(S): All fields of study

Scholarships are open to 7th-12th grade students accepted to this private day/boarding school for males. Must demonstrate financial need.

28 awards annually. Renewable.

3289—SAINT JOHN'S PREPARATORY SCHOOL (President's Scholarship)

P.O. Box 4000
Collegeville MN 56321-4000
320/363-3315 or 800/525-7737
FAX: 320/363-3513
E-mail: admitprep@csbsju.edu
Internet: http://www.sjprep.net
AMOUNT: $800/year
DEADLINE(S): Varies
FIELD(S): All fields of study

Academic scholarship for a student at this independent high school who has demonstrated an interest in academics, athletics, and community service. Must be U.S. citizen or permanent resident.

Renewable for 4 years. Contact school for details.

3290—SAINT JOSEPH'S UNIVERSITY (Presidential Scholarship)

5600 City Avenue
Philadelphia PA 19131-1395
610/660-1555 or 610/660-1556
FAX: 610/660-1342
E-mail: finaid@sju.edu
Internet: http://www.sju.edu/admissions/
AMOUNT: $36,000-$56,000 (over four years)

DEADLINE(S): Varies
FIELD(S): All
FIELD(S): All fields of study

Presidential Scholarships are available to students with an SAT score of 1300-1390 and a GPA of 3.0.

3291—SAINT MARK'S SCHOOL (Financial Aid)

25 Marlbourough Road
Southboro MA 01772
508/786-6114
FAX: 508/786-6120
E-mail: davidlubick@stmarksschool.org
Internet: stmarksschool.org
AMOUNT: Varies
DEADLINE(S): JAN
FIELD(S): All fields of study

Grants and loans are available to 9th-12th grade students at this private boarding school. Must demonstrate financial need and be a US citizen.

Contact David Lubick for an application.

3292—SAINT MARK'S SCHOOL (Financial Aid)

39 Trellis Drive
San Rafael CA 94903
415/472-8007
FAX: 415/472-0722
E-mail: mwilliams@saintmarksschool.org
Internet: http://www.saintmarks school.org
AMOUNT: $3,000-$11,450
DEADLINE(S): JAN 29
FIELD(S): All fields of study

Financial aid programs based on need are available at this independent K-8 elementary school in San Rafael, California.

Contact school for details.

3293—SAINT MARY'S UNIVERSITY (Entrance Scholarships)

Financial Services
923 Robie Street
HaliFAX: Nova Scotta B3H 3C3
CANADA
902/420-5468
FAX: 902/496-8184
AMOUNT: $500-$5,000
DEADLINE(S): MAR 15
FIELD(S): All areas of study

Renewable for up to 3 years, providing high academic standards are maintained.

3294—SAINT MARY'S EPISCOPAL SCHOOL (Financial Aid)

60 Perkins
Memphis TN 38117
901/537-1405
E-mail: myandell@stmarysschool.org
Internet: http://www.stmarysschool.org
AMOUNT: Varies
DEADLINE(S): FEB 10
FIELD(S): All fields of study

Financial aid programs based on need are available at this K-12 Episcopalian girls' day school in Memphis, Tennessee.

Contact school for details.

3295—SAMUEL HUNTINGTON PUBLIC SERVICE AWARD

The Samuel Huntington Fund
25 Research Drive
Westborough MA 01582
508/389-2877
AMOUNT: $10,000
DEADLINE(S): FEB
FIELD(S): All

Provides assistance to seniors graduating from college who wish to spend a year performing public service activities. Students may travel anywhere in the world for up to one year with award.

3296—SAMUEL LEMBERG SCHOLARSHIP-LOAN FUND, INC. (Scholarships-Loans)

60 E. 42nd Street, Suite 1814
New York NY 10165
Written Inquiry
AMOUNT: $5,000/year (max.)
DEADLINE(S): APR 1
FIELD(S): All fields of study

Special no-interest scholarship-loans are open to Jewish men and women pursuing any undergraduate, graduate, or professional degree. Recipients assume an obligation to repay their loans within ten years after the completion of their studies.

Send a self-addressed, stamped envelope to above address for an application.

3297—SAN DIEGO AEROSPACE MUSEUM (Convair Alumni Association Scholarship)

Education Dept.
2001 Pan American Plaza
San Diego CA 92101
619/234-8291 ext. 19
AMOUNT: $3,000-$4,000
DEADLINE(S): MAR 1
FIELD(S): All

For graduating seniors of San Diego County, California, who are direct descendants of persons employed by divisions of the General Dynamics Corporation that existed on or before January 1, 1998. Selection based on merit, community service, and leadership potential.

Call or write museum for further information.

3298—SAN FRANCISCO INDEPENDENT SCHOLARS

755 Sansome Street, Suite 450
San Francisco CA 94111
415/989-0833 ext. 114
FAX: 415/561-4606
E-mail: csparks@pacificresearch.org
Internet: http://www.pacificre search.org
AMOUNT: $2,000
DEADLINE(S): MID JAN
FIELD(S): All fields of study

Step scholarships are for 8th graders in public schools in San Francisco who wish to apply to a private or parochial high school. Star scholarships are for middle school and high school students who are homeschooled and who wish to design or enroll in an independent study program within state laws. Must be resident of San Francisco. Essays, transcripts, etc. are considered.

3299—SAN FRANCISCO STATE UNIVERSITY (Over-60 Program)

Admissions Office
3150 20th Avenue
San Francisco CA 94132
415/566-9347
AMOUNT: Admissions and registration fees waiver
DEADLINE(S): None
FIELD(S): All fields of study

Open to California residents over 60 years of age. Must meet the university's regular admissions standards. Total cost for student is $3.00 per semester.

Contact the Admissions Office for an application.

3300—SAN FRANCISCO UNIVERSITY HIGH SCHOOL (Financial Aid Grants)

3065 Jackson Street
San Francisco CA 94115
415/447-3100
FAX: 415/447-5801
Internet: http://www.sfuhs.pvt. k12.ca.us

AMOUNT: $100 to full tuition
DEADLINE(S): MID JAN
FIELD(S): All fields of study

Financial aid for students admitted to this independent, co-ed high school (9-12) in San Francisco, California. Must demonstrate financial need.

90 awards yearly. Contact Web site and/or school for more information.

3301—SAN JOSE STATE UNIVERSITY (Scholarships)

Financial Aid Office, SJSU
One Washington Square
San Jose CA 95192-0036
408/924-7500
FAX: 408/924-6065
E-mail: fao@sjsu.edu
Internet: http://www.sjsu.edu
AMOUNT: $100 to $1,000 (based on GPA)
DEADLINE(S): MAR 15
FIELD(S): All fields of study

Students must have established a GPA at SJSU based on the successful completion of at least 8 graduate or 12 undergraduate units prior to filing an application. Incoming freshmen/transfer students not eligible. Must attend full-time and have filled out the FAFSA (however, foreign nationals are eligible to apply). Financial need considered.

300-500 awards annually. Note: Students should contact their department majors for information on any departmental scholarships that may be available.

3302—SAN MATEO COUNTY FARM BUREAU (Scholarship)

765 Main Street
Half Moon Bay CA 94019
650/726-4485
FAX: 650/724-4488
AMOUNT: Varies
DEADLINE(S): APR 1
FIELD(S): All areas of study

Open to entering college freshman and continuing students who are members of the San Mateo County Farm Bureau or the dependent child of a member.

Write for complete information.

3303—SANTA ROSA JUNIOR COLLEGE (Business and Community Scholarships)

Barnett Hall, #1284
1501 Mendocino Avenue
Santa Rosa CA 95401-4395
707/527-4740
E-mail: merle_martin@garfield.santarosa.edu
Internet: http://www.santarosa.edu/scholarship
AMOUNT: Varies
DEADLINE(S): MAR 1
FIELD(S): Varies

For students attending Santa Rosa Junior College, Santa Rosa, CA. Applications are at SRJC Scholarship Office, Barnett Hall, Room 1284. The Resource Center works with more than 175 different businesses and community organization. Awards are based on various criteria. For high school seniors, students already attending SRJC pursuing A.A. degree or units necessary to transfer to a four-year institution, and for vo-tech students. Amounts and deadlines vary.

Contact SRJC scholarship office for details.

3304—SANTA ROSA JUNIOR COLLEGE (Doyle Scholarship Program)

Barnett Hall, #1284
1501 Mendocino Avenue
Santa Rosa CA 95401-4395
707/527-4740
E-mail: merle_martin@garfield.santarosa.edu
Internet: http://www.santarosa.edu/scholarship
AMOUNT: $800-$1,400
DEADLINE(S): MAR 1
FIELD(S): All fields of study

For students attending Santa Rosa Junior College, Santa Rosa, CA. Applications through the SRJC scholarship office, Barnett Hall, Room 1284. Awards are based on scholastic achievement. For high school seniors, students already attending SRJC pursuing A.A. degree or units necessary to transfer to a four-year institution, and for students planning to complete one of the Occupational Certificate programs. U.S. citizenship or permanent residency.

Financial need may determine award amount but is not required to receive a Doyle Scholarship. See Web site for details and/or contact SRJC scholarship office. Applications available from Jan. 4 through March 1.

3305—SANTA ROSA JUNIOR COLLEGE (SRJC Foundation Scholarships)

Barnett Hall, #1284
1501 Mendocino Avenue
Santa Rosa CA 95401-4395
707/527-4740
E-mail: merle_martin@garfield.santarosa.edu
Internet: http://www.santarosa.edu/scholarship
AMOUNT: Varies
DEADLINE(S): MAR 1
FIELD(S): All fields of study

For continuing students at Santa Rosa Junior College, Santa Rosa, CA, who have completed at least 12 units at SRJC (GPA 2.5 or +) and for students with at least 56 transferable units transferring to a four-year institution during the upcoming academic year (GPA 3.0 or +). Applications through the SRJC scholarship office, Barnett Hall, Room 1284. Various awards—completing one application will put you in the running for more than 200 different scholarships.

See Web site for details and/or contact SRJC scholarship office.

3306—SARA LEE CORPORATION (Nathan Cummings Scholarship Program)

Three First National Plaza
Chicago IL 60602-4260
312/558-8448
AMOUNT: $500-$2,000/year
DEADLINE(S): JAN 1
FIELD(S): All fields of study

Open to high school juniors who are the natural or legally adopted children of regular full-time employees of a Sara Lee Corporation. Children of retired and deceased employees are also eligible. Must take SAT/National Merit Scholarship Qualifying Test in October of junior year. Scholarship continues as long as students remain in good scholastic and disciplinary standing. Must be US citizen/permanent resident.

See guidance counselor for SAT/National Merit testing information. Contact Sara Lee Corp. for scholarship application.

3307—SARA LEE CORPORATION (Nathan Cummings Scholarship Program)

350 Albert Street, Suite 600
Ottawa Ontario K1R 1B1 CANADA
613/563-1236
FAX: 613/563-9745
AMOUNT: $1,500
DEADLINE(S): JUNE 1
FIELD(S): All fields of study

Scholarships for dependent children, including adopted children, step-children, and wards in legal guardianship of regular active full-time employees of Sara Lee

Corporation and its Canadian divisions. Children of deceased and retired employees also are eligible. For use at recognized Canadian university-transfer colleges. For study in a full-time program leading to a degree.

Write to Awards Division, Association of Universities and Colleges of Canada at above address.

3308—SARA'S WISH FOUNDATION (Scholarships)

23 Ash Lane
Amherst MA 01002
413/256-0914
FAX: 413/253-3338
E-mail: info@saraswish.org
Internet: saraswish.org
AMOUNT: Varies
DEADLINE(S): None
FIELD(S): All fields of study

Scholarships for individuals who share Sara Schewe's zest for life, love of adventure, and zeal to excel. Sara was killed in a bus accident in India while on a student tour. The scholarship is for students dedicated to community service, who actively participate in creative pursuits, and who will be advocates for safe travel conditions.

3309—SCHERING/KEY PHARMACEUTICALS ("Will to Win" Asthma Athlete Scholarships)

2000 Galloping Hill Road
Kenilworth NJ 07033
800/558-7305
AMOUNT: $1,000-$10,000
DEADLINE(S): APR 30
FIELD(S): All fields of study

Open to high school seniors and undergraduates who suffer from asthma yet are outstanding athletes and students. Must be a U.S. citizen/permanent resident attending an accredited U.S. college. Financial need NOT a factor.

10 awards annually. Not renewable. Contact Cheryl Johnson for an application. In some years, deadline may be extended to May.

3310—SCHOLARSHIP FOUNDATION OF SAINT LOUIS (Interest-free Loan Program)

8215 Clayton Road
St. Louis MO 63117
314/725-7990
Internet: http://www.sfsl.org
AMOUNT: Up to $4,500
DEADLINE(S): APR 15; NOV 15
FIELD(S): All areas except ministry

Residents of the St. Louis area who are high school graduates and who can demonstrate financial need. Loans are interest-free. Six years to repay following graduation.

Loans are renewable up to a maximum of $4,500 per person provided student is in good academic standing and continues to show need. Write for complete information.

3311—SCHOOL CHOICE SCHOLARSHIPS, INC. (Scholarships)

P.O. Box 221546
Louisville KY 40252-1546
502/254-7274
FAX: 502/245-4792
E-mail: SCSIKY@aol.com
AMOUNT: 60%, up to $1,000
DEADLINE(S): APR 20
FIELD(S): All fields of study

SCSI provides scholarships for low-income families who are residents of Jefferson County, Kentucky, to send their K-6th grade children to private school. Your child must qualify for the "free" or "reduced-price" Federal lunch program. Preference is given to children attending public schools. A lottery is held in May to determine recipients. If one child in a family is selected, all eligible children in the family automatically receive scholarships.

425 awards annually. Renewable for three years. Contact the principal of the private school of your choice or Diane Crowne at above address for more information.

3312—SCHOOL FOR INTERNATIONAL TRAINING (College Semester Abroad and Other Scholarships Related to International Education)

Kipling Road
P.O. Box 676
Brattleboro VT 05302-0676
888/272-7881
FAX: 802/258-3296
E-mail: info@sit.edu
Internet: http://www.sit.edu
AMOUNT: $500-$4,000
DEADLINE(S): Varies
FIELD(S): All fields of study

Several scholarships are available through this organization for studying abroad or for training others in international relations areas. Some are for teachers, some are for undergraduates, some are for former Peace Corps volunteers and other similar organizations, and some are for majors in fields such as international business management, foreign language and ESL teachers, etc.

Contact organization for detailed information concerning all of their programs.

3313—SCOTTISH RITE FOUNDATION OF WYOMING (Scholarships)

Masonic Temple
1820 Capitol Avenue
Cheyenne WY 82001
smasom@juno.com
Written Inquiry
AMOUNT: $1,000
DEADLINE(S): JUN 1
FIELD(S): All fields of study

Available to full-time college sophomores of Scottish ancestry who have completed at least 30 credit hours with a minimum 2.0 GPA. Applicants must be graduates of a Wyoming high school or hold a GED certificate obtained through a Wyoming community college or the University of Wyoming.

3 awards annually. Write to above address for an application.

3314—SCREEN ACTORS GUILD FOUNDATION (John L. Dales Scholarship Fund)

5757 Wilshire Boulevard
Los Angeles CA 90036-3600
323/549-6708
FAX: 323-549-6710
Internet: http://www.sagfoundation.org
AMOUNT: Varies-Determined annually
DEADLINE(S): SPR
FIELD(S): All areas of study

Scholarships open to SAG members with at least five years' membership or dependent children of members with at least eight years' membership. Awards are for any level of undergraduate, graduate, or post-graduate study at an accredited institution.

Financial need is a consideration. Renewable yearly with reapplication. Write for complete information.

3315—SEABEE MEMORIAL SCHOLARSHIP ASSOCIATION, INC. (Scholarships)

P.O. Box 6574
Silver Spring MD 20916
301/570-2850
E-mail: smsa@erols.com
Internet: http://www.seabee.org
AMOUNT: Varies

DEADLINE(S): APR 15
FIELD(S): All fields of study

Undergraduate scholarships open to children and grandchildren (NOT great grandchildren) of regular, reserve, retired, or deceased officers or enlisted members who have served or who are now serving with the Seabees or the Naval Civil Engineer Corps. US citizenship required.

70 awards per year. Renewable up to 4 years. See Web site or write to above address for complete information.

3316—SEAFARERS' WELFARE PLAN (Charlie Logan Scholarship Program for Seamen)

5201 Auth Way
Camp Springs MD 20746
301/899-0675
AMOUNT: $6,000-$20,000
DEADLINE(S): APR 15
FIELD(S): All fields of study

Contact Plan for an application.

3317—SEAFARERS' WELFARE PLAN (Charlie Logan Scholarship Program for Dependents)

5201 Auth Way
Camp Springs MD 20746
301/899-0675
AMOUNT: $20,000
DEADLINE(S): APR 15
FIELD(S): All fields of study

Contact Plan for an application.

3318—SELBY FOUNDATION (Direct Scholarship Program)

1800 Second Street, Suite 750
Sarasota FL 34236
941/957-0442
FAX: 941/957-3135
AMOUNT: $1,000-$5,000
DEADLINE(S): VARIES
FIELD(S): All fields of study (preference for Technology, Science, and Math majors)

For undergraduate study by residents of Charlotte, DeSoto, Sarasota, or Manatee County, Florida, who are attending an accredited college full-time and have a GPA of 3.0 or better. Must demonstrate financial need and be a US citizen.

Write for complete information.

3319—SEMINOLE TRIBE OF FLORIDA (Higher Education Awards)

6300 Stirling Road
Hollywood FL 33024
800/683-7800
AMOUNT: None specified
DEADLINE(S): APR 15; JUL 15; NOV 15
FIELD(S): All areas of study

Open to enrolled members of the Seminole Tribe of Florida or to those eligible to become a member. For undergraduate or graduate study at an accredited college or university.

Awards renewable. Write for complete information.

3320—SERB NATIONAL FOUNDATION (Scholarships)

One Fifth Avenue
Pittsburgh PA 152222
800/538-SERB or 412/642-SERB
FAX: 642-1372
E-mail: snf@serbnatlfed.org
Internet: http://serbnatlfed.org/membership.htm
AMOUNT: Varies
DEADLINE(S): Varies (spring)
FIELD(S): All fields of study

Scholarships for students of Serbian ancestry attending postsecondary institutions in the U.S. Must have been members of the organization for at least two years.

Contact above organization for details.

3321—SERTOMA FOUNDATION INTERNATIONAL (Scholarships for Students With Hearing Loss)

1912 East Meyer Boulevard
Kansas City MO 64132-1174
Phone and TTY: 816/333/8300
FAX: 816/333-4320
Internet: http://www.sertom.org
AMOUNT: $1,000
DEADLINE(S): MAY 1
FIELD(S): All fields of study

For students with a documented hearing loss who are entering or continuing students are universities or colleges in the U.S. or Canada pursuing four-year bachelor's degrees. Must have at least 3.2 GPA or at least 85% in all high school and college classes.

Renewable up to four times; however, student must submit a new application and compete with other students each year. To apply, starting in October send #10 SASE to "$1,000 Scholarships" at above address.

3322—SERVICE EMPLOYEES INTERNATIONAL UNION (Scholarship Program)

1313 'L' Street NW
Washington DC 20005
800/448-7348
Internet: http://seiu.org
AMOUNT: $500 and $3,000
DEADLINE(S): MAR (mid-month)
FIELD(S): All fields of study

Scholarships open to Service Employees International Union members (in good standing) and their dependent children. Awards can be used at a community college or trade/tech school or to continue education at a 4-year college or university.

48 awards per year. Write for complete information.

3323—SHOSHONE HIGHER EDUCATION PROGRAM (Shoshone Tribal Scholarship)

P.O. Box 538
Fort Washakie WY 82514
Written Inquiry
AMOUNT: Varies
DEADLINE(S): Varies
FIELD(S): All fields of study

Available to high school graduates who are enrolled members of the Wind River Shoshone Tribe and may be used at any public institution in Wyoming. Applicants must have a financial need analysis completed by the college financial aid office. New applicants should forward to the agency a letter of acceptance from a postsecondary institution, a transcript or GED certificate, and a letter stating a proposed course of full-time study and plans upon receiving a degree.

Renewable. Write to above address for an application at least six weeks prior to beginning of school year.

3324—SICO FOUNDATION (Scholarships)

Scholarships Coordinator
150 Mount Joy Street
Mount Joy PA 17552
Internet: http://www.sicoco.com
AMOUNT: $1,000 per year
DEADLINE(S): VARIES
FIELD(S): All fields of study

Open to high school seniors residing in the state of Delaware or the Pennsylvania counties of Adams, Berks, Chester, Cumberland, Dauphin, Delaware, Lancaster, Lebanon, or York.

Also available to residents of New Jersey counties of Atlantic, Cape May,

Cumberland, Gloucester, and Salem and to residents of Cecil County, Maryland. Write for complete information.

3325—SIDNEY-SHELBY COUNTY YMCA (Lee E. Schauer Memorial Scholarship)

300 E. Parkwood
Sidney OH 45365
937/492-9134
FAX: 937/492-4705
E-mail: info@sidney-ymca.org
Internet: http://www.sidney-ymca.org
AMOUNT: $5,000
DEADLINE(S): Varies
FIELD(S): All fields of study

Scholarship is for a college-bound high school senior who is a member of the Sidney-Shelby County YMCA for at least three years prior to application. Must have a minimum 2.5 GPA, demonstrate Christian values and leadership, be involved in sports or fitness activities, and volunteer at the Y or in the community. Scholarship must "make a significant difference" to recipient. Financial need NOT a factor.

1 award annually. Renewable for four years. Contact Barbara Sperl at YMCA for an application.

3326—SIGMA PHI EPSILON FRATERNITY (National Balanced Man Scholarship)

John Paul Adams, Director of
Education and Communications
310 South Boulevard
Richmond VA 23220
804/353-1901
FAX: 804/359-8160
E-mail: john.adams@sigep.net
Internet: http://www.sigep.org
AMOUNT: $2,500
DEADLINE(S): APR 30
FIELD: All
FIELD(S): All fields of study

The Balanced Man Scholarship is awarded to four, single males who will be entering a four-year college or university as full-time freshmen. The one-time award is given to those who excel in athletics, scholarship, and leadership. Minimum GPA of 3.0 required.

3327—SIGNET CLASSIC SCHOLARSHIP ESSAY COMPETITION

Penguin USA
375 Hudson Street
New York NY 10014
AMOUNT: $1,000
DEADLINE(S): APR 15
FIELD(S): For all fields of study

Essay contest for high school juniors and seniors on a work of classic literature chosen by Signet Classic, publisher of literary works. Contact company or check Web site for next year's subject and deadline. Must be submitted by a high school English teacher on behalf of the student. Each teacher may submit one junior and one senior essay.

For U.S. citizens or permanent residents. Five winners. Winning students' schools will also receive a signet Classic library for their school valued at $1,700.

3328—SISTER TO SISTER (Scholarship)

1809 E. 71st Street, Suite 205
Chicago IL 60649
773/667-7061
FAX: 773/667-7064
AMOUNT: $500
DEADLINE(S): MAR 3
FIELD(S): All

Available to an African-American woman returning to school who demonstrates financial need.

3329—SKY PEOPLE HIGHER EDUCATION (Northern Arapaho Tribal Scholarship)

P.O. Box 8480
Ethete WY 82520
Written Inquiry
AMOUNT: Varies
DEADLINE(S): Varies
FIELD(S): All fields of study

Scholarships are available to high school graduates who are enrolled members of the Northern Arapaho Tribe and may be used at any public institution in Wyoming. New applicants should forward to the agency a letter of acceptance from a postsecondary institution, a high school transcript or GED certificate, and a letter stating a proposed course of full-time study and plans upon receiving a degree. Applications should be made a least six weeks prior to school year.

Renewable. Contact above address for an application.

3330—SMART MONEY MAGAZINE (Girls Going Places Scholarship)

1755 Broadway, 2nd Floor
New York, NY 10019
AMOUNT: $3,000-$15,000
DEADLINE(S): AUG 27
FIELD(S): ALL

Nominee must be female between 12 and 16 and a U.S. resident. Must be nominated by a legal U.S. resident. Nominator must also write an essay of 1.000 words or less explaining why the nominee deserves the award.

3331—SOCIETY OF DAUGHTERS OF THE U.S. ARMY (Scholarships)

7717 Rock Ledge Ct.
Springfield VA 22152
Written Inquiry
AMOUNT: $1,000
DEADLINE(S): MAR 1 (to receive application); MAR 31 (completed application)
FIELD(S): All fields of study

Open to daughters, step-, and granddaughters of commissioned officers of the U.S. Army who are on active duty, are retired, or who died on active duty, or after eligible retirement. Must demonstrate financial need and merit.

Approximately 8 scholarships per year. Renewable. Include qualifying parent's name, rank, Social Security number, and dates of service. Send self-addressed stamped envelope and a pre-paid postal card between November 1 and March 1.

3332—SONOMA STATE UNIVERSITY (Scholarship Program)

Scholarship Office
1801 E. Cotati Avenue
Rohnert Park CA 94928
707/664-2261
FAX: 707/664-4242
Internet: http://www.sonoma.edu/scholarships
AMOUNT: $250-$2,500
DEADLINE(S): FEB 15
FIELD(S): All fields of study

Open to applicants and full-time students at Sonoma State University who have a minimum 3.0 GPA. Financial need NOT a factor.

300 awards annually. See Web site or contact SSU Scholarship Coordinator for an application.

3333—SONS OF ITALY FOUNDATION (National Leadership Grants)

219 'E' Street NE
Washington DC 20002
202/547-2900 or 202/547-5106
FAX: 202-546-8168
Internet: http://www.osia.org
AMOUNT: Up to $5,000
DEADLINE(S): Varies
FIELD(S): All fields of study

Open to full-time undergraduate and graduate students of Italian heritage studying at accredited colleges/universities. Financial need NOT a factor.

10-12 awards annually. Contact Foundation for an application, and also see local and state lodges for information regarding scholarships offered to members and their children.

3334—SONS OF NORWAY FOUNDATION (Scholarship Fund)

1455 W. Lake Street
Minneapolis MN 55408
Internet: http//www.sofn.com
AMOUNT: $250-$750; $3,000
DEADLINE(S): MAR 1
FIELD(S): All fields of study

Open to CURRENT members of Sons of Norway and children or grandchildren of current Sons of Norway members. Must be enrolled in postsecondary training or education (college or vo-tech/trade). Based on financial need, clarity of study plan, career goals, GPA, letter of recommendation, and extracurricular involvements. Awards are jointly payable to student and institution.

1 award ($250-$750) annually in each of 6 districts; most qualified receives additional $3,000 award. Contact Sons of Norway for an application.

3335—SONS OF THE AMERICAN REVOLUTION (Joseph S. Rumbaugh Historical Oration Contest)

1000 South 4th Street
Louisville KY 40203
Internet: http://www.sar.org/youth/rumbaugh.htm
AMOUNT: $200-$3,000
DEADLINE(S): VARIES
FIELD(S): All fields of study

Oratory competition for high school sophomores, juniors, and seniors who submit an original 5- to 6-minute oration on a personality, event, or document of the American Revolutionary War and how it relates to the U.S. today.

Oration must be delivered from memory without props or charts. Applicants must be U.S. citizens. Write for complete information.

3336—SONS OF THE REPUBLIC OF TEXAS (Texas History Essay Contest)

1717 8th Street
Bay City TX 77414
409/245-6644
Internet: http://www.srttexas.org
AMOUNT: $3,000; $2,000; $1,000
DEADLINE(S): EARLY FEB
FIELD(S): All fields of study

An essay contest for high school seniors on the historical period of the Republic of Texas (1836-1846). Authors of the three essays judged to be the winners will receive the above prizes. Check with organization for current year's topic. Only one essay judged best in each high school may be submitted.

Contact Janet Hickl, SRT Executive Secretary, for guidelines.

3337—SOROPTIMIST FOUNDATIONS (Soroptimist International of the Americas—Youth Citizenship Award)

Two Penn Center Plaza, Suite 1000
Philadelphia PA 19102-1883
215/557-9300
FAX: 215/568-5200
E-mail: siahq@soroptimist.org
Internet: http://www.soroptimist.org
AMOUNT: $1,250 (54 awards); $2000 (1)
DEADLINE(S): DEC 15 (of senior year)
FIELD(S): All fields of study

Award of merit open to outstanding high school seniors who have demonstrated service in the home, school, and community. Applications available from participating Soroptimist clubs.

54 regional U.S. awards and 17 in other countries/territories within the limits of Soroptimist International of the Americas. Applications available from participating Soroptimist clubs. Contact local club or send SASE to SIA at above address for complete information.

3338—SOROPTIMIST FOUNDATIONS (Soroptimist International of the Americas-Women's Opportunity Awards)

Two Penn Center Plaza, Suite 1000
Philadelphia PA 19102-1883
215/557-9300
FAX: 568-5200
E-mail: siahq@soroptimist.org
Internet: http://www.soroptimist.org
AMOUNT: $3,000-$10,000 (54 awards); $10,000 (1 award)
DEADLINE(S): DEC 15
FIELD(S): All fields of study

Open to mature women heads of households furthering their skills/training to upgrade employment status. Preference to vo- tech training or undergrad degree completion. Not available for grad work. Must document financial need.

54 regional U.S. awards; 17 in other countries/territories within the territorial limits of Soroptimist International of the Americas. Contact local club or send SASE to SIA (Attn: Women's Opportunity Award) at above address for complete information.

3339—SOROPTIMIST INTERNATIONAL OF GREAT BRITAIN AND IRELAND (Golden Jubilee Fellowships)

127 Wellington Road, S
Stockport Cheshire SK1 3TS
ENGLAND UK
0161/480-7686
FAX: 0161/477-6152
AMOUNT: 100-500 pounds sterling/year
DEADLINE(S): APR 30
FIELD(S): All fields of study

Open to women residing within the boundaries of Soroptimist International GBI, who NEED NOT be Soroptimists, to attend any agreed institution. Preference given to mature women seeking to train or retrain for a business/profession. Must demonstrate financial need.

3340—SOUTH AFRICAN ASSOCIATION OF WOMEN GRADUATES (Students' Aid Grant)

Suite 329, Private Bag X18
Rondebosch 7701 SOUTH AFRICA
+27 021/477-8989
AMOUNT: R600-00/year
DEADLINE(S): NOV 30
FIELD(S): All fields of study

For South African citizens who are females entering their second year of a bachelor's degree program at a South African university (Cape Town, Western Cape, Stellenbosch, Medunsa). This grant is given on the recommendation of the bursaries officer of the university, who has noted a deserving student who has worked well in her first year at the university. Financial need is considered.

4 awards annually.

3341—SOUTH CAROLINA GOVERNOR'S OFFICE, DIVISION OF VETERANS AFFAIRS (Free Tuition for Certain War Veterans' Children)

VA Regional Office, Room 141
1801 Assembly Street
Columbia SC 29201
803/255-4255
FAX: 803/255-4257
AMOUNT: Tuition
DEADLINE(S): None
FIELD(S): All fields of study

Open to children of South Carolina war veterans who were legal residents of South Carolina at time of entry into service and who (during service) were MIA, POW, KIA, totally disabled, or died of disease as rated by VA, and/or who is recipient of Medal of Honor. Students must be South Carolina residents planning to pursue undergraduate study at South Carolina state-supported schools. Financial need NOT a factor.

3342—SOUTH CAROLINA HIGHER EDUCATION TUITION GRANTS COMMISSION (Tuition Grants Program)

101 Business Park Boulevard
Suite 2100
Columbia SC 29203-9498
803/896-1120
FAX: 803/896-1126
E-mail: earl@sctuitiongrants.com
Internet: http://www.sctuitiongrants.com

AMOUNT: Approx. $2,400
DEADLINE(S): JUN 30
FIELD(S): All fields of study

Open to South Carolina residents who are either entering freshmen that rank in upper 75% of high school class or score 900 on SAT, or those who are upperclassmen that pass 24 credit hours annually. Must demonstrate financial need and be pursuing their first bachelor's degree at independent, South Carolina-based, accredited colleges. Must be US citizen/permanent resident.

10,000 awards annually. Renewable. Contact your school's financial aid office or Earl Mayo, Deputy Director, at Commission for an application.

3343—SOUTH CAROLINA STUDENT LOAN CORPORATION

P.O. Box 21487
Columbia SC 29221
803/798-0916
Internet: http://www.slc.sc.edu

AMOUNT: Varies
DEADLINE(S): Varies
FIELD(S): All areas of study

Open to South Carolina residents who are U.S. citizens or eligible non-citizens. Must be enrolled or accepted for enrollment at an eligible postsecondary school. Amount of loan determined by cost of school and financial need.

Interest is variable not to exceed at 8.25%. Loan must be renewed annually. Write or visit Web site for complete information.

3344—SOUTH DAKOTA DEPARTMENT OF EDUCATION AND CULTURAL AFFAIRS (Robert Byrd Honors Scholarship)

700 Governors Drive
Pierre SD 57501-2291
605/773-5669
FAX: 605/773-6139

AMOUNT: $1,500
DEADLINE(S): MAY 1
FIELD(S): All fields of study

Open to high school seniors who are South Dakota residents with a minimum 24 ACT score and minimum 3.5 GPA. Must not have had a final grade below a "C" in four years of English, math, science, three years of social studies, two years of foreign language, or two years of computer science.

Renewable up to 4 years.

3345—SOUTH DAKOTA DIVISION OF VETERANS AFFAIRS (Aid to Veterans)

500 E. Capitol Avenue
Pierre SD 57501-5070
605/773-3269
FAX: 605/773-5380

AMOUNT: Free tuition in state-supported schools
DEADLINE(S): None
FIELD(S): All fields of study

Open to veterans (as defined by SDCL) who are residents of South Dakota, were honorably discharged (as defined by SDCL), have exhausted their GI Bill, and have no other federal educational benefits available. One month of free tuition is available for each month of qualified service. Benefits must be used within 20 years of cessation of hostilities or 6 years from discharge, whichever is later.

Contact Veterans Affairs for an application.

3346—SOUTH DAKOTA DIVISION OF VETERANS AFFAIRS (Aid to Dependents of Deceased Veterans)

500 E. Capitol Avenue
Pierre SD 57501-5070
605/773-3269
FAX: 605/773-5380

AMOUNT: Free tuition in state-supported schools
DEADLINE(S): None
FIELD(S): All fields of study

Open to residents of South Dakota under 25 years of age who are children of veterans who were residents of South Dakota at least 6 months immediately prior to entry into active service and who died from any cause while in the service of the US Armed Forces. Must attend a state-supported college/university in South Dakota.

Contact Veterans Affairs for an application.

3347—SOUTH DAKOTA DIVISION OF VETERANS AFFAIRS (Aid to Dependents of Prisoners of War or Missing in Action)

500 E. Capitol Avenue
Pierre SD 57501-5070
605/773-3269
FAX: 605/773-5380

AMOUNT: 8 semesters or 12 quarters of free tuition and mandatory fees, other than subsistence expenses, in a state-supported institution.
DEADLINE(S): None specified
FIELD(S): All fields of study, including technical or vocational

Open to children born before or during the period of time a parent served as a prisoner of war or was declared missing in action OR legally adopted OR in the legal custody of the parent prior to and during the time the parent served as a POW or was MIA OR the spouse of a POW or MIA. Once qualified, the return of the qualifying veteran will not remove any provisions or benefits.

No state benefits are available if equal or greater federal benefits are available; state benefits can supplement any lesser benefits from federal sources.

3348—SOUTHERN ORANGE COUNTY ALUMNAE (Panhellenic Awards)

SOCAP
2709 Muirfield
Mission Viejo CA 92692-1576

AMOUNT: $1,000
DEADLINE(S): MID FEB
FIELD(S): All

Successful scholarship recipients will be college women who are members of a National Panhellenic Sorority in the Southern Orange County Panhellenic (California) areas. Must have a minimum 3.0 GPA.

3349—SOUTHERN SCHOLARSHIP FOUNDATION (Housing scholarship)

322 Stadium Drive
Tallahassee FL 32304
850/222-3832 or 800/253-2769
Internet: http://www.scholarships.org/ssf/

AMOUNT: Housing expenses
DEADLINE(S): Varies
FIELD(S): All
FIELD(S): All fields of study

Provide a rent-free room in a completely furnished home. The Florida-based program serves the University of Florida, Florida State University, Florida A&M University, and Bethune-Cookman College.

3350—SOUTHWESTERN UNIVERSITY (Scholarships and Grants)

1001 E. University Avenue
Georgetown TX 78626
512/863-6511 (main) or
512/863-1200 or
800/252-3166 (admissions)
Internet: http://www.southwestern.edu
AMOUNT: Varies
DEADLINE(S): JAN 15
FIELD(S): All fields of study

Both merit-based and need-based scholarships and awards are available through this undergraduate, United Methodist-related, liberal arts college in Georgetown, TX. Some are subject-related, i.e. awards in vocal and instrumental music, theatre, and art. Funds are also available for students planning careers within the church and for dependents of United Methodist clergy. SAT, ACT, and GPAs, and need are all considered.

See Web site for further details; contact university for latest and complete information.

3351—SPINSTERS INK (Young Feminist Scholarship)

32 East First Street, #330
Duluth MN 55802-2002
218/727-3222
FAX: 218/727-3119
E-mail: claire@spinsters-ink.com
Internet: http://www.spinsters-ink.com
AMOUNT: $1,000
DEADLINE(S): DEC 31
FIELD(S): All
FIELD(S): All fields of study

Applicant must be a woman. Selection is based upon an essay about feminism. Visit Web site for more information.

3352—SPRINGSIDE SCHOOL (Grants)

8000 Cherokee Street
Philadelphia PA 19118
215/247-7007
FAX: 215/247-7308
AMOUNT: Varies
DEADLINE(S): MAR 1
FIELD(S): All fields of study

Grants for students attending this independent K-12 college preparatory school for girls in Philadelphia, Pennsylvania.

3353—DAVID'S SOCIETY (Scholarship)

47 5th Avenue
New York NY 10003
212/397-1346
AMOUNT: Varies
DEADLINE(S): SPR
FIELD(S): All fields of study

Scholarships for college students who are either of Welsh heritage, attending a Welsh school, or studying Welsh culture and/or language. For graduates or undergraduates.

Approximately 12 awards per year. Renewable.

3354—STANFORD UNIVERSITY (Dofflemyer Honors Eagle Scout Scholarship)

Financial Aid Office
520 Lasuen Mall
Stanford University
Stanford CA 94305-3021
650/723-3058 or 888-FAO-3773
E-mail: financialaid@stanford.edu
AMOUNT: Varies
DEADLINE(S): MAY 31
FIELD(S): All areas of study

Open to Eagle Scouts who have been admitted to and plan to attend, or currently attend, Stanford. Financial need considered.

Write for complete information.

3355—STATE COLLEGE AND UNIVERSITY SYSTEMS OF WEST VIRGINIA—CENTRAL OFFICE (WV Higher Education Grant Program)

1018 Kanawha Boulevard E.,
Suite 700
Charleston WV 25301-2827
304/558-4614
E-mail: long@hepc.wvnet.edu
Internet: http://www.hepc.wvnet.edu
AMOUNT: $350 to $2,532
DEADLINE(S): JAN 1; MAR 1
FIELD(S): All areas of study

Open to high school grads who have lived in WV for one year prior to application and are enrolled full-time as an undergrad in an approved WV or PA educational institution. Must be U.S. citizen and demonstrate financial need.

Approximately 12,000 grants per year. Renewable up to 8 semesters. Write for complete information.

3356—STATE FARM COMPANIES FOUNDATION (Scholarships for Dependents)

One State Farm Plaza, B-4
Bloomington IL 61710-0001
309/766-2161
Internet: http://www.statefarm.com
AMOUNT: Varies
DEADLINE(S): Varies
FIELD(S): All fields of study

Scholarships are for high school seniors who are legal dependents of full-time State Farm agents, employees, or retirees. Winners are selected by the National Merit Scholarship Corporation on the basis of test scores, academic record, extracurricular activities, personal essay, and counselor recommendation.

100 awards annually. Contact Jill Jones at above address for more information.

3357—STATE OF NEW JERSEY OFFICE OF STUDENT ASSISTANCE (Edward J. Bloustein Distinguished Scholars Program)

P.O. Box 540
Trenton NJ 08625
800/792-8670
AMOUNT: $1,000 per year for 4 years
DEADLINE(S): OCT 1
FIELD(S): All areas of study

Open to New Jersey residents who are academically outstanding high school students planning to attend an N.J. college or university. U.S. citizenship or legal residency required.

Students may not apply directly to the program. Applications must be made through the high school. Contact guidance counselor or address above for complete scholarship information.

3358—STATE OF NEW JERSEY OFFICE OF STUDENT ASSISTANCE (Tuition Aid Grants)

P.O. Box 540
Trenton NJ 08625
800/792-8670
AMOUNT: Up to $7,272
DEADLINE(S): Varies
FIELD(S): All areas of study

For students who have been New Jersey residents for at least 12 months and who are or intend to be enrolled as full-time undergraduate in any college; university or degree-granting postsecondary institution in N.J. U.S. citizen or legal resident.

Grants renewable. Write to Office of Student Assistance for complete information.

3359—STATE OF NEW JERSEY OFFICE OF STUDENT ASSISTANCE (Garden State Scholarships)

P.O. Box 540
Trenton NJ 08625
800/792-8670

AMOUNT: $500 per year for 4 years
DEADLINE(S): Varies
FIELD(S): All areas of study

Must be a resident of New Jersey for at least 12 months prior to receiving award. For undergraduate study in N.J. Demonstrate scholastic achievement and need. U.S. citizen or legal resident.

Renewable. Students may not apply directly to the program. Contact high school guidance counselor or address above for complete information.

3360—STATE OF NEW JERSEY OFFICE OF STUDENT ASSISTANCE (NJClass Loan Program)

P.O. Box 540
Trenton NJ 08625
800/792-8670

AMOUNT: May not exceed cost of attendance minus other financial assistance
DEADLINE(S): None specified
FIELD(S): All areas of study

For U.S. citizens or legal residents who are N.J. residents. Must be enrolled at least half-time at an approved school making satisfactory academic progress towards a degree. Repayment is 23 years from date of first disbursement. Various options available.

Apply at least two months prior to need. Write for complete information.

3361—STATE STUDENT ASSISTANCE COMMISSION OF INDIANA (Higher Education & Freedom of Choice Grants)

150 W. Market Street, Suite 500
Indianapolis IN 46204
317/232-2350
E-mail: em-grants@ssaci.state.in.us;
Internet: http://www.ai.org/ssaci

AMOUNT: $500-$7,412
DEADLINE(S): MAR 1
FIELD(S): All fields of study

Open to Indiana residents who are accepted to or enrolled in eligible Indiana institutions as full-time undergraduate students. U.S. citizen or legal resident.

Approx 56,000 grants per year. Grants are based on financial need. Students must complete the Free Application for Federal Student Aid (FAFSA). No other application is required. Write for complete information.

3362—STATE STUDENT ASSISTANCE COMMISSION OF INDIANA (Robert C. Byrd Honors Scholarships)

150 W. Market Street, Suite 500
Indianapolis IN 46204-2811
317/232-2350
FAX: 317/232-3260
E-mail: special@ssaci.state.in.us
Internet: http://www.ai.org/ssaci/

AMOUNT: $1,500
DEADLINE(S): APR 24
FIELD(S): All areas of study

For Indiana high school seniors for use at a not-for-profit private or public institution in the U.S. U.S. citizenship required.

Score of 1300 on SAT or 65 on ACT required.

3363—STEPHEN M. PRICE FOUNDATION (Aviation Training Scholarships for Youth)

6910 Atlantic Boulevard, Suite B
Jacksonville FL 32211
904/724-6885
FAX: 904/725-4371
Internet: http://www.smpf.org

AMOUNT: Tuition and training
DEADLINE(S): Varies
FIELD(S): Pilot training and airplane maintenance and repair

"Young Aviators" program for boys and girls, age 14-16, who reside in the area of Jacksonville, Florida. Two years of ground school classroom and flight training. Students must maintain 2.5 GPA in school subjects, observe certain dress codes, abstain from all illegal substances, and perform community service projects. Training will lead to a private pilot's license.

Contact organization for details.

3364—STEPHEN T. MARCHELLO SCHOLARSHIP FOUNDATION (Scholarships)

1170 E. Long Pl.
Littleton CO 80122
303/886-5018
E-mail: FMarchello@ntr.net
Internet: http://www.stmfoundation.org

AMOUNT: $2,500
DEADLINE(S): MAR 15
FIELD(S): All fields of study

Undergraduate scholarships are available to survivors of childhood cancer. Must be resident of Colorado or Arizona, but will open to other states as funding permits. Applicants must have a minimum 2.7 GPA. Letter from doctor or place of treatment is required. Financial need NOT a factor.

Renewable. Send a self-addressed, stamped envelope to Franci Marchello for an application or visit Web site.

3365—STEPHEN KNEZEVICH TRUST (Grants)

161 W. Wisconsin Avenue
Milwaukee WI 53202
414/271-6364

AMOUNT: $100 to $800
DEADLINE(S): NOV 1
FIELD(S): All areas of study

Undergraduate and graduate grants for students of Serbian descent. Must establish evidence of ancestral heritage. It is common practice for students to be interviewed in Milwaukee prior to granting the award.

Address inquiries to Stanley Hack. Include self-addressed stamped envelope.

3366—STUDENT AID FOUNDATION, INC. (Loans)

2520 E. Piedmont Road, Suite F-180
Marietta GA 30062
770/973-7077
FAX: 770/973-2220

AMOUNT: $3,500/year (undergrad); $5,000/year (graduate)
DEADLINE(S): APR 15
FIELD(S): All fields of study

Low-interest loans for women who are residents of Georgia or out-of-state women attending a Georgia school. Grades, financial need, personal integrity, and sense of responsibility are considerations.

70 loans annually. Renewable with reapplication. Send a self-addressed, stamped envelope for an application.

3367—COMCAST FOUNDATION

1500 Market Street, East Tower
35th Floor
Philadelphia PA 19102
Internet: http://www.comcast.com

AMOUNT: $1,000
DEADLINE(S): MAR 1

FIELD(S): All fields of study

Scholarships for high school seniors within a community served by Comcast Cable's Eastern Division.

3368—SUDBURY FOUNDATION ATKINSON SCHOLARSHIP PROGRAM

278 Old Sudbury Road
Sudbury MA 01776
978/443-0849
FAX: 978/443-3767
AMOUNT: Up to $5,000 per year
DEADLINE(S): NOV 1
FIELD(S): All fields of study

Open to Lincoln-Sudbury High School (Mass.) graduating seniors or dependents of Sudbury residents for postsecondary studies, including vocational training.

Must demonstrate financial need. Academic and non-academic factors are considered in evaluating candidates.

3369—SUMMIT COUNTRY DAY SCHOOL (Scholarships & Grants)

2161 Grandin Road
Cincinnati OH 45208
513/533-5349
FAX: 513/533-5373
E-mail: Geppert_M@SCDS.org
Internet: http://www.summitcds.org
AMOUNT: Varies
DEADLINE(S): FEB 20
FIELD(S): All fields of study

Open to 7th-12th grade students at this private college preparatory Roman Catholic day school. Scholarships are for academic achievements; grants are for those with financial need. Must be U.S. citizen/permanent resident.

120 awards annually. Renewable. Contact Mary Lisa Geppert for an application.

3370—SUNKIST GROWERS, INC. (A.W. Bodine-Sunkist Memorial Scholarship)

P.O. Box 7888
Van Nuys CA 91409-7888
818/986-4800
AMOUNT: $2,000-$3,000
DEADLINE(S): APR 30
FIELD(S): All fields of study

Open to California and Arizona undergraduates who come from an agricultural background and are in need of financial assistance. Must have a minimum 3.0 GPA.

Contact Sunkist Growers for an application.

3371—SUNSHINE COAST BURSARY AND LOAN SOCIETY (Scholarships & Loans)

c/o Mrs. M. Mackenzie
Box 44
Sechelt BC VON 3AO CANADA
604/885-9436
AMOUNT: $500 (loans); Varies (bursaries)
DEADLINE(S): JUN 15
FIELD(S): All fields of study

Open to graduates of one of the high schools of the Sunshine Coast School District #46 in Gibsons, Sechelt, or Pender Harbour, BC, Canada. Bursaries and loans can be used at any postsecondary institution.

Contact your high school or the Society for an application.

3372—SUPERCOLLEGE.COM (Scholarship)

Scholarship Coordinator
4546 B10 El Camino Real, #281
Los Altos CA 94022
FAX: 650-618-2221
E-mail: scholarships@supercollege.com
Internet: http://www.supercollege.com
AMOUNT: $500-$2,500
DEADLINE(S): Varies
FIELD: All
FIELD(S): All fields of study

An award for outstanding high school students or college undergraduates. Based on academic and extracurricular achievement, leadership, and integrity. May study any major and attend or plan to attend any accredited college or university in the U.S.

3373—SWEDISH INSTITUTE/SVENSKA INSTITUTET (Fellowships for Study/Research in Sweden)

Dept. for Educational and Research Exchange
Box 7434
SE-103 91 Stockholm SWEDEN
Written Inquiry
AMOUNT: Varies
DEADLINE(S): Vaires
FIELD(S): All fields of study

Program to encourage study or research in Sweden. For persons from any country except Nordic countries (Finland, Sweden, Norway, Denmark, or Iceland).

Contact above organization for details.

3374—SWISS BENEVOLENT SOCIETY OF CHICAGO (Scholarship Fund)

P.O. Box 2137
Chicago IL 60690
Internet: http://sbschicago.org
AMOUNT: Varies
DEADLINE(S): Varies
FIELD(S): All areas of study

Undergraduate scholarships open to Swiss nationals or those of proven Swiss descent who are permanent residents of Illinois or Southern Wisconsin and accepted to or enrolled in accredited colleges or universities. Minimum 3.3 GPA required.

Swiss students studying in the USA on a student or visitors visa are NOT eligible. Write for complete information.

3375—SWISS BENEVOLENT SOCIETY IN SAN FRANCISCO (Clement & Frieda Amstutz Fund Scholarship)

c/o Swiss Consulate General
456 Montgomery Street, Suite 1500
San Francisco CA 94104-1233
415/456-1597
E-mail: lutzky@aol.com
AMOUNT: Varies
DEADLINE(S): MAY 15
FIELD(S): All fields of study

Undergrad scholarships at U.S. colleges open to Swiss nationals who have lived within a 150-mile radius of the San Francisco City Hall for 3 years prior to application date. Applicant must have applied for admission to any institution of higher learning in the U.S. (community colleges and trade schools excluded).

Number of awards varies each year. Write for complete information.

3376—SYD VERNON FOUNDATION (Scholarship)

6608 Adera Street
Vancouver BC V6P5C1 CANADA
Written request only
Amount: $2,500
DEADLINE(S): OCT 2
FIELD(S): All
FIELD(S): All fields of study

Available to Canadian Students who show need for financial assistance and have demonstrated their commitment to working with people with mental and physical disabilities.

3377—SYNOD OF THE NORTHEAST (Wurffel/Sills Student Loan Program)

5811 Heritage Landing Drive
E. Syracuse NY 13057-9360
800/585-5881
FAX: 315/446-3708
AMOUNT: $500-$8,000
DEADLINE(S): APR 1
FIELD(S): All fields of study

Interest-free loans are open to Presbyterians who are undergraduates or seminary students. Must show need for funds by completing application and required worksheet/forms.

Renewable. Contact Synod of the Northeast for an application.

3378—TAILHOOK FOUNDATION (Scholarship Fund)

P.O. Box 26626
San Diego CA 92196
800/269-8267
Internet: http://www.tailhook.org/foundation.htm
AMOUNT: $1,000
DEADLINE(S): Varies
FIELD(S): All fields of study

Scholarships for students at all levels whose parent was or is serving in any branch of military service on an aircraft carrier. Must be U.S. citizen and enrolled in or attending a four-year college or university.

5 awards per year. May reapply for renewal.

3379—TALBOTS (Women's Scholarship Fund)

1505 Riverview Road
P.O. Box 297
St. Peter MN 56082
507/931-1682
Internet: http://www.talbots.com
AMOUNT: $1,000-$10,000
DEADLINE(S): EARLY MAR
FIELD(S): All fields of study

Open to women returning to college to complete their undergraduate degrees. Must be U.S. citizen/permanent resident.

55 awards annually. Applications available November 15th through March 3rd at all U.S. Talbots stores. Recipients announced by July.

3380—TALL CLUBS INTERNATIONAL (Kae Sumner Einfeldt Scholarship Award)

Box 60074
Palatine, IL 90074
888/I-M-TALL-2
E-mail: tci-tallteen@tall.org; Internet: http://www.tall.org
AMOUNT: $1,000
DEADLINE(S): Varies
FIELD(S): All fields of study

Scholarships for unusually tall college-bound high school seniors (girls-5'10", boys-6'2"). Must apply through regional clubs or members-at-large. Tall Clubs also has a group for teens called "Skywriters"-a way to meet pen pals who are also tall.

Several scholarships available. Contact organization for location of your nearest Tall Club. Send self-addressed, stamped envelope (SASE) for information.

3381—TARGET STORES (Target All-Around Scholarships)

Citizen's Scholarship Fdn.
1505 Riverview Road
St. Peter MN 56082-0480
800/316-6142
Internet: http://www.target.com
AMOUNT: $1,000-$10,000
DEADLINE(S): NOV 1
FIELD(S): All fields of study

Open to well-rounded high school graduates and current college students who volunteer in their communities. Must be U.S. resident under the age of 24.

2,100 awards annually. See Web site or contact your local Target store for an application.

3382—TARGET STORES (Target Teachers Scholarships)

Citizen's Scholarship Fdn.
1505 Riverview Road
St. Peter MN 56082-0480
800/316-6142
Internet: http://www.target.com
AMOUNT: $1,000-$5,000
DEADLINE(S): NOV 1
FIELD(S): All fields of study

Open to teachers and school administrators to further their education through classes, seminars, and other staff development opportunites.

1,800 awards annually (2 per store) + 96 District Teacher Scholarships annually. See Web site or contact your local Target store for an application.

3383—TEEN MAGAZINE (Miss Teenage America Program)

6420 Wilshire Boulevard,
15th Floor
Los Angeles CA 90048
323/782-2950
Internet: http://www.missteenamerica.com
AMOUNT: $10,000
DEADLINE(S): SEP 15
FIELD(S): All fields of study

Open to young women between the ages of 12 and 18. Candidates are judged on scholastic achievement, individual accomplishment, community service, poise, appearance, and personality. Competition is held in Los Angeles, CA.

Write for complete information.

3384—TEMPLE UNIVERSITY (Philadelphia Outstanding Achievement Scholarships)

1801 N. Broad St.
Ground Floor, Conwell Hall
Philadelphia, PA 19122
215/204-2244
FAX: 215/204-5897
E-mail: finaid@blue.temple.edu
Internet: http://www.temple.edu/sfs
AMOUNT: Half or full tuition
DEADLINE(S): MAR 1
FIELD(S): All
FIELD(S): All fields of study

Entering freshmen living and attending high school in Philadelphia. Recipients are generally in the top 10% of their high school graduating classes. Scholarships are renewable for four years with the provision they maintain a 3.0 GPA.

3385—TENACRE COUNTRY DAY SCHOOL (Financial Aid)

78 Benvenue Street
Wellesley MA 02482
781/235-2282
AMOUNT: Varies
DEADLINE(S): FEB 1
FIELD(S): All fields of study

Financial aid to attend this coeducational independent school which encompasses preschool through grade 6. Award is based on family's financial need.

Contact school for details.

3386—TENNESSEE STUDENT ASSISTANCE CORPORATION (Ned McWherter Scholars Program)

Suite 1950,
Parkway Towers
404 James Robertson Parkway
Nashville, TN 37243-0820
615/741-1346; 800/342-1663
AMOUNT: $6,000 for max. of 4 yrs.
DEADLINE(S): FEB 15
FIELD(S): Any field of study

Scholarships for entering freshman with at least a 3.5 high school GPA and an ACT of 29 or SAT in the top 5% nationally. Must be a resident of Tennessee AND must attend an eligible Tennessee institution.

Renewable for 4 years. Contact your high school guidance office or the address above in December for an application.

3387—TENNESSEE STUDENT ASSISTANCE CORPORATION (Robert C. Byrd Honors Scholarship Program)

Suite 1950, Parkway Towers
404 James Robertson Parkway
Nashville TN 37243-0820
615/741-1346
AMOUNT: Varies
DEADLINE(S): APR 1
FIELD(S): Any field of study at an accredited postsecondary institution

For Tennessee high school seniors or GED students, the award must be utilized in the same year of graduation. Students must have achieved a 3.5 GPA or have an average GED score of 57. Students with at least a 3.0 GPA and an ACT or SAT in the top quartile nationally may also apply.

Contact the high school guidance office or the above address for more information.

3388—TERRY FOX HUMANITARIAN AWARD PROGRAM (Scholarships)

Simon Fraser University
8888 University Drive
Burnaby BC V5A 1S6 CANADA
604/291-3057
FAX: 604/291-3311
E-mail: terryfox@sfu.ca
Internet: http://www.terryfox.org
AMOUNT: $4,000 ($2,500 for students attending institutions having no tuition fees)
DEADLINE(S): FEB 1
FIELD(S): All fields of study

Open to Canadian citizens 25 years old or under who are high school seniors or undergraduates at Canadian colleges/universities. Based on community service, sports/fitness, courage in overcoming obstacles, and academics.

20 awards annually. Renewable. Contact Sabrine Barakat, Administrative Assistant, for an application.

3389—TEXAS A&M UNIVERSITY (Academic Excellence Awards)

Student Financial Aid Dept.
College Station TX 77843
409/845-3236/3987
AMOUNT: $500-$1,500
DEADLINE(S): MAR
FIELD(S): All fields of study

Open to full-time undergraduate and graduate students at Texas A&M University. Awards are intended to recognize and assist students who are making excellent scholastic progress, campus and community activities, leadership positions, and work experience.

Approximately 800 awards per year. Awards granted for one year. Applications are available at the student financial aid office during January and February.

3390—TEXAS A&M UNIVERSITY (Opportunity Award Scholarship)

Student Financial Aid Office
Texas A&M University
College Station TX 77843
409/845-3236
AMOUNT: $500- $2,500
DEADLINE(S): JAN
FIELD(S): All fields of study

Scholarships to Texas A&M University for college freshmen with outstanding high school records. Selection based on leadership ability, character, SAT scores, activities, and high school record. U.S. citizen or permanent resident.

Recipients from outside Texas receive a waiver on no-resident tuition. Contact financial aid office for complete information.

3391—TEXAS A&M UNIVERSITY (President's Achievement Award Scholarship and Aggie Spirit Award Scholarship)

Office of Honors Programs &
Academic Scholarships
College Station TX 77843
979/458-1572
AMOUNT: President's: $3,000/year; Aggies: $1,000/year
DEADLINE(S): JAN 8
FIELD(S): All fields of study

This competitive academic scholarship program provides 4-year scholarships for high school seniors who will be attending Texas A&M University. For U.S. citizens or permanent residents. Must maintain 2.5 GPA to remain in good scholarship standing.

Recipients from outside Texas receive a waiver of non-resident tuition.

3392—TEXAS A&M UNIVERSITY (President's Endowed Scholarship; Lechner Scholarship; McFadden Scholarship)

Office of Honors Programs &
Academic Scholarships
College Station TX 77843
979/458-1572
AMOUNT: $2,500-$3,000 per year over 4 years
DEADLINE(S): JAN
FIELD(S): All fields of study

For high school seniors who will be attending Texas A&M. Must score 1300 or higher on SAT (or equivalent of 30 on ACT) and rank in the top 10% of high school graduating class or are National Merit Scholarship semi-finalists.

U.S. citizenship or legal residency required. Non-Texans qualify for a waiver on non-resident tuition.

3393—TEXAS A&M UNIVERSITY (Scholarships, Grants, and Loans)

Division of Student Affairs
College Station TX 77843-1252
409/845-3236
AMOUNT: Varies
DEADLINE(S): Varies
FIELD(S): All fields of study

Texas A&M University offers several scholarship and loan programs. They are awarded on the basis of academic criteria and/or combinations of financial need, campus/community activities, leadership positions, and work experience. Some are for minorities, teacher candidates, cadets, and Texas high school class valedictorians. Applicants do not have to be prior Texas residents and should begin inquiries as high school seniors.

Send to above location for comprehensive information.

3394—TEXAS HIGHER EDUCATION COORDINATING BOARD (Scholarships, Grants, & Loans)

Student Services
P.O. Box 12788
Austin TX 78711-2788
512/427-6101 or 800/242-3062
FAX: 512/427-6420
E-mail: grantinfo@thecb.state.tx.us
Internet: http://www.thecb.state.tx.us
AMOUNT: Varies (with program)
DEADLINE(S): Varies (with program)
FIELD(S): All fields of study

Open to high school seniors, undergraduates, and graduate students who are pursuing full- or part-time studies at 2- or

4-year Texas public/private institutions. Some awards require Texas residency, financial need, specific field of study, disability, academic excellence, or other qualification.

Some awards renewable. See Web site or contact your school's financial aid office or the Student Services Division for details on specific awards.

3395—THE ADVENT SCHOOL (Grants)

17 Brimmer Street
Boston MA 02108
617/742-0520
FAX: 617/723-2207
Internet: http://www.adventschool.org
AMOUNT: Varies
DEADLINE(S): None
FIELD(S): Varies

Need-based grants for students accepted to this private, co-educational, elementary (K-6) school in Boston, Massachusetts.

Contact school for details.

3396—THE ALBERTA HERITAGE SCHOLARSHIP FUND

9940 106 Street, 6th Floor
Edmonton Alberta T5K 2V1
CANADA
780/427-8640
E-mail: heritage@gov.ab.ca
AMOUNT: Varies
DEADLINE(S): Varies
FIELD(S): All fields of study

Several scholarships and fellowships for all fields of study. For high school seniors, undergraduates, and graduates. Some are for specialized fields of study, and some are general. Includes opportunities to study abroad.

Send for pamphlet at above address for complete listing.

3397—THE ALBERTA HERITAGE SCHOLARSHIP FUND ("Persons Case" Scholarship)

9940 106 Street, 6th Floor
Edmonton Alberta T5K 2V1
CANADA
780/427-8640
AMOUNT: $1,000-$5,000
DEADLINE(S): SEP 30
FIELD(S): All fields of study where women are under-represented

Awards for women whose studies will contribute to the advancement of women or who are studying in fields where women are traditionally few in number. Selection is based on program of studies, academic achievement, and financial need.

A maximum of $20,000 is available each year.

3398—THE ALBERTA HERITAGE SCHOLARSHIP FUND (Charles S. Noble Scholarships for Study at Harvard)

9940 106 Street, 6th Floor
Edmonton Alberta T5K 2V1
CANADA
780/427-8640
AMOUNT: $10,000
DEADLINE(S): MAY 15
FIELD(S): All fields of study

Awards for Alberta undergraduates for study at Harvard University in Massachusetts, U.S.

Two awards.

3399—THE ALBERTA HERITAGE SCHOLARSHIP FUND (Charles S. Noble Scholarships for Student Leadership)

9940 106th Street, 6th Floor
Edmonton Alberta T5K 2V1
CANADA
780/427-8640
AMOUNT: $300
DEADLINE(S): MAR 1
FIELD(S): All fields of study

Awards to recognize outstanding leadership in the areas of student government, student societies, clubs, or organizations at the postsecondary level.

Contact above location for details.

3400—THE ALBERTA HERITAGE SCHOLARSHIP FUND (Louise McKinney Postsecondary Scholarships)

9940 106 Street, 6th Floor
Edmonton Alberta T5K 2V1
CANADA
780/427-8640
AMOUNT: $1,500
DEADLINE(S): JUN 1
FIELD(S): All fields of study

For undergraduate students with a 8.0 GPA to reward them for academic achievements and to encourage continued undergraduate study.

930 awards. Contact above location for details.

3401—THE AMERICAN LEGION, DEPARTMENT OF MAINE (Daniel E. Lambert Memorial Scholarship)

21 College Avenue
Waterville ME 04901
207/873-3229
Internet: http://www.me.legion.org
AMOUNT: $500
DEADLINE(S): MAY 1
FIELD(S): All fields of study in an accredited college or vocational technical school.

Open to students showing evidence of being enrolled in or attendingan accredited school. Must be of good character and have demonstrated that he/she believes in the American way of life.

Parent must be a veteran.

3402—THE AMERICAN LEGION, DEPT. OF SOUTH CAROLINA (Robert E. David Children's Scholarship Fund)

P.O. Box 11355
Columbia SC 29211
803/799-1992
FAX: 803/771-9831
AMOUNT: $500
DEADLINE(S): MAY 1
FIELD(S): All fields of study

Open to undergraduates in any area of study who are residents of South Carolina. Must have a relative who is a member of the American Legion in South Carolina. Financial statement and copies of state and federal tax returns must be submitted with application.

5-10 awards annually. Renewable—must reapply each year. Write to above address for complete information.

3403—THE ANGLO-DANISH SOCIETY (The Hambros Bank Scholarships for U.K. Citizens to Study in Denmark)

Secretary, Danewood
4 Daleside
Gerrards Cross, Bucks SL9 7JF
ENGLAND UK
01753 884846
AMOUNT: 175 pounds/month
DEADLINE(S): JAN 12
FIELD(S): All fields of study

Scholarships for U.K. citizens to study in Denmark. Can be used at a Danish university. Scholarships run for up to six months.

Applications available between October 1 and December 31. Write to Secretary of the Anglo-Danish Society; please enclose a stamped, self-addressed envelope or International Reply Coupon.

3404—THE ANGLO-DANISH SOCIETY (The Hambros Bank Scholarships for Danish Citizens to Study in the U.K.)

Secretary
Danewood 4 Daleside
Gerrards Cross, Bucks SL9 7JF
ENGLAND UK
01753 884846

AMOUNT: 175 pounds/month
DEADLINE(S): JAN 12
FIELD(S): All fields of study

Scholarships for Danish citizens to study in the United Kingdom. Scholarships run for up to six months.

Applications available between October 1 and December 31. Write to Secretary of the Anglo-Danish Society; please enclose a stamped, self-addressed envelope or International Reply Coupon.

3405—THE AUGUSTUS SOCIETY (Scholarships)

3910 Pecos-McLeod C-100
Las Vegas NV 89121
Internet: http://www.augustus.org

AMOUNT: $1,500
DEADLINE(S): FEB
FIELD(S): All fields of study

College scholarships for students of Italian-American ancestry who are residents of Clark County, Nevada. Considerations are need and ability.

Contact organization for details.

3406—THE BRITISH COUNCIL (Scholarships for English Language Assistants to Mexico)

10 Spring Gardens
London SW1A 2BN ENGLAND UK
+44 (0) 161 957 7755
FAX: +44 (0) 161 957 7762
E-mail: education.enquiries@britcoun.org
Internet: http://www.languageassistant.co.uk

AMOUNT: Varies
DEADLINE(S): Varies
FIELD(S): Teaching English

The British Council in Mexico offers the opportunity, funded by the Mexican Ministries of Education and Foreign Affairs, to British citizens to teach English in Mexico.

3407—THE BRITISH COUNCIL (Scholarships for Residents of Myanmar [Burma])

78 Kanna Road/P.O. Box 638
Yangon MYANMAR (BURMA)
(00 95 1) 254 658
FAX: (00 95 1) 245 345
Internet: http://www.britcoun.org/burma

AMOUNT: Varies
DEADLINE(S): Varies
FIELD(S): All fields of study

The British Council lists several scholarship programs for residents of Myanmar (Burma). Some are for specific fields of study (computing, management, science), and some are general.

The Web site listed here gives more details; the British council lists hundreds of educational programs world wide on its Web site. Enter "scholarship" as the search word. Another contact is the Education Advisory Service. The E-mail is: enquires@britishcouncil.org.mm. The Education Officer can provide further advice for anyone hoping to study in Britain.

3408—THE BRITISH WOMEN PILOT'S ASSOCIATION (The Diana Britten Aerobatic Scholarship)

Brooklands Museum
Brooklands Road
Weybridge KT13 0QN Surrey
ENGLAND UK
Written Inquiry
Internet: http://www.aerobatics.org.uk

AMOUNT: Cost of training
DEADLINE(S): Varies
FIELD(S): Aviation

A scholarship for a licensed female British pilot to receive 10 hours of comprehensive instruction in aerobatics. Must hold a current PPL and medical clearance and have no previous aerobatic experience or training.

Visit Web site for more information. Write to organization for detailed application information and next deadline date.

3409—THE BRYN MAWR SCHOOL (Grants)

109 West Melrose Avenue
Baltimore MD 21210
410/323-8800
FAX: 410/435-4678
E-mail: admissions@brynmawrschool.org
Internet: http://www.brynmawr.pvt.k12.md.us

AMOUNT: Varies
DEADLINE(S): JAN
FIELD(S): All fields of study

Grants for girls in a private school in Baltimore, MD, in grades K-12. Must be U.S. citizen or permanent resident. Must demonstrate financial need.

Renewable, but must reapply each year.

3410—THE BUFFETT FOUNDATION

P.O. Box 4508
Decatur IL 62525
402/451-6011
E-mail: buffettfound@aol.com

AMOUNT: Tuition and fees for Nebraska state colleges and universities; $500 per semester at other institutions
DEADLINE(S): APR 10; OCT 15
FIELD(S): All areas of study

Scholarships for financially needy residents of Nebraska.

Must demonstrate financial need. Send SASE to Devon Buffett, P.O. Box 4508, Decatur, IL 62525; 402/451-6011.

3411—THE CAMBRIDGE SCHOOL OF WESTON (Scholarships)

Georgian Road
Weston MA 02493
781/642-8650
E-mail: admissions@csw.org
Internet: http://www.csw.org

AMOUNT: Up to full tuition
DEADLINE(S): FEB 1
FIELD(S): All fields of study

Need-based, work-study tuition scholarships for this private high school in Massachusetts. For U.S. citizens.

Sixty annual awards. Renewable. Contact Arnold J. Klingenberg at above location.

3412—THE CANADIAN-SCANDINAVIAN FOUNDATION (Scholarships and Grants for Studies and Research in Scandinavia)

McGill University Libraries
3459 McTavish Street
Montreal Quebec H3A 1Y1
CANADA

514/398-4740
Internet: http://www.canada-scandinavia.ca
AMOUNT: Varies
DEADLINE(S): JAN 31
FIELD(S): All fields of study

Scholarships and grants open to Canadian citizens for study and research in Scandinavian countries: Denmark, Sweden, Norway, Finland, and Iceland. Also a European travel study tour for a deserving young Canadian artist. No particular form is needed for application.

4-5 grants per year. Write for complete information. Contact Dr. Jan O.J. Lundgren, CSF Secretary, at above location.

3413—THE COLORADO SPRINGS SCHOOL (K-12 Scholarships)

21 Broadmoor Avenue
Colorado Springs CO 80906
719/475-9747
FAX: 719/475-9864
Internet: http://www.css.org
AMOUNT: Up to $2,500
DEADLINE(S): Varies
FIELD(S): All fields of study

Scholarships and other financial aid available for students at this independent, private school in Colorado Springs. A day school for all grades K-12 as well as a boarding school for grades 9-12.

Contact above location for details.

3414—THE CULTURAL SOCIETY, INC.

200 West 19th Street
Panama City FL 32045
Written Inquiry
AMOUNT: Varies
DEADLINE(S): Ongoing
FIELD(S): All areas of study

Scholarship for Muslim students.

3415—THE CYPRUS CHILDREN'S FUND, INC. (Scholarship Endowment)

13 East 40th Street
New York NY 10016
212/696-4590 or 800/775-7217
AMOUNT: Varies
DEADLINE(S): MAY 5
FIELD(S): All fields of study

To students of Greek or Greek Cypriot origin. Applicants can be U.S. residents, U.S. citizens, or citizens of Greece or Cyprus. May be pursuing studies in accredited college or university in the U.S., Greece, or Cyprus.

Financial need determines award. Applications must be typewritten and include various documents—please write or call for complete information.

3416—THE DAVID AND DOVETTA WILSON SCHOLARSHIP FUND (Scholarships)

115-67 237th Street
Elmont NY 11003-3926
800/759-7512
FAX: 212/669-2961
E-mail: info@wilsonfund.org
Internet: http://www.wilsonfund.org
AMOUNT: $1,000
DEADLINE(S): MAR 1
FIELD(S): All fields of study

Scholarships for college-bound high school seniors who are U.S. citizens and selected for their academic achievement and involvement in community and religious activities.

$20 application fee. To receive a list of the last 9 winners, send SASE to above address. Nine annual awards. Financial need a consideration.

3417—THE EDDIE G. ROBINSON FOUNDATION (Scholarships)

5 Concourse Parkway, Suite 3100
Atlanta GA 30328
Phone 770/481-1943
E-mail: erob@txdirect.net
Internet: http://www.eddierobinson.com
AMOUNT: Up to $5,000
DEADLINE(S): VARIES
FIELD(S): All fields of study

Scholarships for Louisiana college-bound 8th graders and high school seniors who demonstrate leadership, academic, and/or athletic skills. Additionally, one scholarship is for students with demonstrated financial need. The awards for 8th graders will be held in an account for later use in college. Recipients must attend accredited institutions.

Contact organization for details.

3418—THE EDUCATION RESOURCES INSTITUTE (Parent Loans for Elementary and Secondary Education-PLEASE)

P.O. BOX 312
Boston MA 02117-0312
800/255-8374
FAX: 888/329-8374
E-mail: custserv@teri.org
Internet: teri.org
AMOUNT: $1,000-$20,000/year ($80,000 max. total)
DEADLINE(S): None
FIELD(S): All fields of study

Elementary and secondary students enrolled at TERI-approved, private institutions are eligible for a PLEASE loan. To qualify, parents or other creditworthy individuals must have established, satisfactory credit history; sufficient current income of at least $1,500/month to meet current liabilities; and stable residence and employment history. At least one applicant must be U.S. citizen or permanent resident, and have been residing in the U.S. for the previous two years.

Low interest rates. Allows up to 10 years for repayment, depending on amount borrowed. Repayment begins within 45 days after funds are dispersed (at least $50/month). No prepayment penalty. Contact Customer Service for more information.

3419—THE FLINN FOUNDATION (Flinn Scholarships)

1802 N. Central Avenue
Phoenix AZ 85004-1506
602/744-6800
FAX: 602/744-6815
E-mail: fscholars@flinn.org
Internet: http://www.flinnscholars.org
AMOUNT: $40,000 value (total for four years)
DEADLINE(S): NOV 1
FIELD(S): All fields of study

A full scholarship for students who have been accepted at Arizona State University, Northern Arizona University, or the University of Arizona. Highly competitive. For U.S. citizens and legal residents of Arizona for two years prior to the application deadline. Must have at least a 3.5 GPA and rank in the top 5 percent of high school class. Merit is the only factor considered, which includes academic assessment and personal achievement.

20 awards yearly. Includes two travel-study experiences abroad. Must submit progress reports and evidence of participation in campus activities for renewals.

3420—THE FOUNDATION OF THE SAINT ANDREW'S SOCIETY OF PHILADELPHIA (Study-Abroad Scholarships)

1104 Kresson Road
Cherry Hill NJ 08003-2727

E-mail: ecattelljr@msn.com
AMOUNT: Varies
DEADLINE(S): Varies
FIELD(S): All areas of study

Scholarships for U.S. citizens of Scottish descent who are from the Philadelphia, Pennsylvania, area who wish to spend their junior year abroad.

Write to organization for details in care of Edward V. Cattell Jr.

3421—THE GERBER FOUNDATION (Scholarship Program)

4747 W. 48th Street, Suite 153
Fremont MI 49412
213/924-3175
FAX: 213-924-7906
E-mail: tgf@ncisd.net
Internet: http://www.gerber foundation.org
AMOUNT: $1,500/year
DEADLINE(S): MAR 31
FIELD(S): All areas of study

Undergraduate scholarship for dependents of a Gerber Products Company associate. Must have GPA of 2.0 or above.

Renewable for three years. Contact above location for details.

3422—THE GRAND RAPIDS FOUNDATION (Edwin F. Doyle Scholarship)

209-C Waters Bldg.
161 Ottawa Avenue NW
Grand Rapids MI 49503-2703
616/454-1751
FAX: 616/454-6455
E-mail: grfound@grfoundation.org
Internet: http://www.grfoundation.org
AMOUNT: Varies
DEADLINE(S): APR
FIELD(S): All fields of study

Grants are available for seniors graduating in Kent County, Michigan.

3423—THE GRAND RAPIDS FOUNDATION (Lavina Laible Scholarship)

209-C Waters Bldg.
161 Ottawa Avenue NW
Grand Rapids MI 49503-2703
616/454-1751
FAX: 616/454-6455
E-mail: grfound@grfoundation.org
Internet: http://www.grfoundation.org
AMOUNT: Varies
DEADLINE(S): APR
FIELD(S): All fields of study

Grants are available to women students at the University of Michigan for their junior year.

3424—THE GRAND RAPIDS FOUNDATION (Harry J. and Lucille B. Brown Scholarships)

209-C Waters Bldg.
161 Ottawa Avenue NW
Grand Rapids MI 49503-2703
616/454-1751
FAX: 616/454-6455
AMOUNT: Varies
DEADLINE(S): APR
FIELD(S): All fields of study

Must be Kent County resident for at least 3 yrs. and have 3.0 or better GPA.

Send SASE to above address for complete information.

3425—THE HARLEY SCHOOL (Grants)

1981 Clover Street
Rochester NY 14618
716/442-1770
FAX: 716/442-5758
http://www.harleyschool.org
AMOUNT: Varies
DEADLINE(S): MAR 15
FIELD(S): All fields of study

Need-based grants available to attend this independent, coeducational school which includes kindergarten through twelfth grade. Must submit documentation indicating financial need.

125-130 annual grants. Renewable. Must maintain an overall "C" average. Contact school for details.

3426—THE HUDSON SCHOOL (Scholarships)

506 Park Avenue
Hoboken NJ 07030
201/659-8335
FAX: 201/222-3669
E-mail: Hudson@Hudsonet.com
Internet: http://www.hudsonet.com
AMOUNT: $500-$5,000
DEADLINE(S): APR
FIELD(S): All fields of study

Scholarships available to attend this independent, coeducational school which includes grades five through twelve. Students must qualify by scoring at or above 90th percentile on admission test, present a school transcript and letters or recommendation which indicate their ability to handle a vigorous program of studies, a passion for the arts and sciences, and good character. Financial need considered.

50-60 annual awards. Renewable depending on performance. Contact school for details.

3427—THE JACKIE ROBINSON FOUNDATION (Scholarships)

3 West 35th Street
New York NY 10001-2204
212/290-8600
Internet: http://www.jackie robinson.org
AMOUNT: $6,000/year for 4 years
DEADLINE(S): APR 1
FIELD(S): All fields of study

Scholarships for college-bound high school seniors who are members of a minority group. Program also includes personal and career counseling on a year-round basis, assistance obtaining summer jobs, and permanent employment after graduation. Financial need, leadership potential, high academic achievement, and satisfactory SAT or ACT scores required.

Contact organizations for details and/or check Web site.

3428—THE JERUSALEM FELLOWSHIPS (Internships in Israel for Leaders)

2124 Broadway, Suite 244
New York NY 10023
800/ FELLOWS
E-mail: jf@aish.edu
Internet: http://www.jerusalem fellowships.org
AMOUNT: $4,000 and up
DEADLINE(S): Varies
FIELD(S): All fields of study

Program for young Jewish student leaders to deepen their understanding of the people of and explore the land of Israel. Open to all Jewish students; however, additional and more valuable scholarships are available in Alabama and the Southeastern United States through the Ruttenberg Foundation of Birmingham, AL. Additional programs available at Rutgers, Cornell, Penn State, U. of Georgia, emory, Tulane, and U of Alabama.

Check Web site for details. Applications available online or at above location; $25 application fee.

3429—THE KIMBO FOUNDATION

685 Harrington Street
San Francisco CA 94107
415/522-5100
AMOUNT: $1,000

DEADLINE(S): JUN 1
FIELD(S): All fields of study

Scholarships for financially needy students of Korean descent residing in California. For use at four-year colleges and university. High school senious and current undergraduates may apply.

Application process includes essay in English or Korean. Program is announced in the Korea Central daily paper in March or April every years. Send SASE to Mr. Yeon Taek, Korea Central Daily, at above address for details.

3430—THE KISKI SCHOOL (Financial Aid)

1888 Brett Lane
Saltsburg PA 15681
724/639-3586
FAX: 724/639-8596
Internet: http://www.kiski.org
AMOUNT: Up to $23,500
DEADLINE(S): APR 1
FIELD(S): All fields of study

Financial aid to attend this private college preparatory secondary school, grades 9-12. Award is based on family's financial need. U.S. citizenship required.

Renewable. Contact school for details.

3431—THE KNOTT SCHOLARSHIP FUNDS (Scholarships)

P.O. Box 9589
Silver Springs MD 20916
877/603-9980
E-mail: info@knottscholar.org
Internet: http://www.knottscholar.org
AMOUNT: Full tuition
DEADLINE(S): None specified
FIELD(S): All fields of study

Open to Catholic students to attend Catholic parish elementary or Catholic secondary school in the archdiocese of Baltimore (city) or attend one of the 3 Catholic colleges in Maryland. Residency in the Archdiocese of Baltimore is required. Scholarships based primarily on outstanding academic achievement.

Student involvement in church, school and community taken into account. Send business-sized self-addressed stamped envelope for information, stating level of education.

3432—THE MADEIRA SCHOOL (Scholarships)

8328 Georgetown Road
McLean VA 22102
703/556-8200
E-mail: admissions@madeira.org
Internet: http://www.madeira.org
AMOUNT: Varies
DEADLINE(S): FEB 15
FIELD(S): All fields of study

Need-based and merit scholarships available to freshman and sophomore girls attending this independent girls college preparatory school which encompasses grades 9-12. Although scholarships are for boarding students, the institution also operates as a day school.

Renewable. Contact school for details.

3433—THE MILLER SCHOOL OF ALBEMARLE (Grants)

1000 Samuel Miller Loop
Charlottesville VA 22903
804/823-4805
FAX: 804/823-6617
E-mail: jim@millerschool.org
Internet: http://www.millerschool.org
AMOUNT: Average $4,500
DEADLINE(S): Varies
FIELD(S): All fields of study

Financial aid is available for needy students attending this independent school in Virginia which includes 5-12. The school has both boarding and day students.

35-45 annual awards. Student population is approximately 110.

3434—THE NATIONAL ITALIAN AMERICAN FOUNDATION (Capital Area Regional Scholarship)

1860 19th Street NW
Washington DC 20009
202/387-0600
E-mail: scholarships@niaf.org
Internet: http://www.niaf.org
AMOUNT: $1,000
DEADLINE(S): SPRING
FIELD(S): For all areas of study.

For students of Italian family heritage residing in Maryland, Virginia, West Virginia, or Washington DC. Write a 2-3 page typed essay on a family member or a personality you consider: "An Italian American Hero." For undergraduates.

Write for application and details. Four awards given. Also considered are academic merit, financial need, and community service.

3435—THE NATIONAL ITALIAN AMERICAN FOUNDATION (Italian Regional Scholarship)

1860 19th Street NW
Washington DC 20009
202/387-0600
E-mail: scholarships@niaf.org
Internet: http://www.niaf.org
AMOUNT: $1,000
DEADLINE(S): MAY 31
FIELD(S): For all areas of study

For undergraduate students of Italian family heritage accepted at Italian universities for courses offering credits toward their undergraduate degrees. Write a 2-3 page typed essay on a family member or a personality you consider: "An Italian American Hero."

Academic merit, financial need, and community service. Contact organization for application details.

3436—THE NATIONAL ITALIAN AMERICAN FOUNDATION (Lower Mid-Atlantic Regional Scholarship)

1860 19th Street NW
Washington DC 20009
202/387-0600
E-mail: scholarships@niaf.org
Internet: http://www.niaf.org
AMOUNT: $1,000
DEADLINE(S): MAY 31
FIELD(S): For all areas of study.

For students of Italian family heritage residing in Pennsylvania, Southern New Jersey (including Trenton), and Delaware.

Considered are academic merit, financial need, and community service.

3437—THE NATIONAL ITALIAN AMERICAN FOUNDATION (Mid-America Regional Scholarship)

1860 19th Street NW
Washington DC 20009
202/387-0600
E-mail: scholarships@niaf.org
Internet: http://www.niaf.org
AMOUNT: $1,000
DEADLINE(S): MAY 31
FIELD(S): For all areas of study

For students of Italian family heritage residing in Iowa, Missouri, Arkansas, Oklahoma, Kansas, Nebraska, or Colorado. Write a 2-3 page typed essay on a family member or a personality you consider: "An Italian American Hero." For undergraduates.

Considered are academic merit, financial need, and community service.

3438—THE NATIONAL ITALIAN AMERICAN FOUNDATION (Mid-Pacific Regional Scholarship)

1860 19th Street
Washington DC 20009
202/387-0600
E-mail: scholarships@niaf.org
Internet: http://www.niaf.org
AMOUNT: $1,000
DEADLINE(S): MAY 31
FIELD(S): For all areas of study

For students of Italian family heritage residing in Northern California, Northern Nevada (Reno), Utah, Guam, and Hawaii. Write a 2-3 page typed essay on a family member or a personality you consider: "An Italian American Hero." For undergraduates.

Considered are academic merit, financial need, and community service.

3439—THE NATIONAL ITALIAN AMERICAN FOUNDATION (New England Regional Scholarship)

1860 19th Street NW
Washington DC 20009
202/387-0600
E-mail: scholarships@niaf.org
Internet: http://www.niaf.org
AMOUNT: $1,000
DEADLINE(S): MAY 31
FIELD(S): All areas of study

For undergraduate students of Italian heritage residing in Maine, Vermont, New Hampshire, Massachusetts, Rhode Island, or Connecticut. Write a 2-3 page typed essay on a family member or a personality you consider: "An Italian American Hero."

Considered are academic merit, financial need, and community service.

3440—THE NATIONAL ITALIAN AMERICAN FOUNDATION (North Central Regional Scholarship)

1860 19th Street NW
Washington DC 20009
202/387-0600
E-mail: scholarships@niaf.org
Internet: http://www.niaf.org
AMOUNT: $1,000
DEADLINE(S): MAY 31
FIELD(S): All areas of study

For undergraduate students of Italian family heritage residing in Ohio, Kentucky, Indiana, Illinois, Wisconsin, Michigan, Minnesota, South Dakota, and North Dakota. Write a 2-3 page typed essay on a family member or a personality you consider: "An Italian American Hero."

Considered are academic merit, financial need, and community service.

3441—THE NATIONAL ITALIAN AMERICAN FOUNDATION (North Regional Scholarship)

1860 19th Street
Washington DC 20009
202/387-0600
E-mail: scholarships@niaf.org
Internet: http://www.niaf.org
AMOUNT: $1,000
DEADLINE(S): MAY 31
FIELD(S): For all areas of study

For students of Italian family heritage residing in Washington state, Oregon, Idaho, Montana, Wyoming, and Alaska. Write a 2-3 page typed essay on a family member or a personality you consider: "An Italian American Hero." For undergraduates.

Considered are academic merit, financial need, and community service.

3442—THE NATIONAL ITALIAN AMERICAN FOUNDATION (South Central Regional Scholarship)

1860 19th Street NW
Washington DC 20009
202/387-0600
E-mail: scholarships@niaf.org
Internet: http://www.niaf.org
AMOUNT: $1,000
DEADLINE(S): MAY 31
FIELD(S): All areas of study

For students of Italian family heritage residing in Alabama, Mississippi, Tennessee, Louisiana, and Texas. Write a 2-3 page typed essay on a family member or a personality you consider: "An Italian American Hero." For undergraduates.

Four awards given. Also considered are academic merit, financial need, and community service.

3443—THE NATIONAL ITALIAN AMERICAN FOUNDATION (Southeast Regional Scholarship)

1860 19th Street NW
Washington DC 20009
202/387-0600
E-mail: scholarships@niaf.org
Internet: http://www.niaf.org
AMOUNT: $1,000
DEADLINE(S): MAY 31
FIELD(S): For all areas of study

For students of Italian family heritage residing in North Carolina, South Carolina, Georgia, and Florida. Write a 2-3 page typed essay on a family member or a personality you consider: "An Italian American Hero." For undergraduates.

Four awards given. Also considered are academic merit, financial need, and community service.

3444—THE NATIONAL ITALIAN AMERICAN FOUNDATION (Southwest Regional Scholarship)

1860 19th Street
Washington DC 20009
202/387-0600
E-mail: scholarships@niaf.org
Internet: http://www.niaf.org
AMOUNT: $1,000
DEADLINE(S): MAY 31
FIELD(S): For all areas of study

For undergraduate of Italian family heritage residing in Southern California, Southern Nevada (Las Vegas), Arizona, and New Mexico. Write a 2-3 page typed essay on a family member or a personality you consider: "An Italian American Hero." For undergraduates.

Four awards given. Also considered are academic merit, financial need, and community service.

3445—THE NATIONAL ITALIAN AMERICAN FOUNDATION (St. Anselm's College Scholarship)

1860 19th Street NW
Washington DC 20009
202/387-0600
E-mail: scholarships@niaf.org
Internet: http://www.niaf.org
AMOUNT: $5,000
DEADLINE(S): MAY 31
FIELD(S): All areas of study

For undergraduate students of Italian heritage entering Street Anselm's College, New Hampshire. For students who are NOT residents of New England, Maine, Vermont, New Hampshire, Massachusetts, Rhode Island, or Connecticut.

Considered are academic merit, financial need, and commmunity service. Tenable ONLY at Street Anselm's College.

3446—THE NATIONAL ITALIAN AMERICAN FOUNDATION (Upper Mid-Atlantic Regional Scholarship)

1860 19th Street NW
Washington DC 20009
202/387-0600
E-mail: scholarships@niaf.org
Internet: http://www.niaf.org

AMOUNT: $1,000
DEADLINE(S): MAY 31
FIELD(S): All areas of study

For students of Italian family heritage residing in New York or Northern New Jersey (north of Trenton). Write a 2-3 page typed essay on a family member or a personality you consider: "An Italian American Hero." For undergraduates.

Four awards given. Also considered are academic merit, financial need, and community service.

3447—THE NATIONAL HEMOPHILIA FOUNDATION (Kevin Child Scholarship)

116 W. 32nd Street, 11th Floor
New York NY 10001
212/328-3700 or 800/42-HANDI
FAX: 212/328-3777
E-mail: info@hemophilia.org
Internet: http://www.hemophilia.org

AMOUNT: $500-$1,000
DEADLINE(S): VARIES
FIELD(S): All fields of study

Scholarships for college students with a bleeding disorder—hemophilia, etc. through HANDI (Hemophilia and AIDS/HIV Network for the Dissemination of Information).

Contact HANDI at above location for applications.

3448—THE NUFFIELD FOUNDATION (Education for Women)

28 Bedford Square
London WC1B 3J5 ENGLAND UK
020 7631 0566
FAX: 020 7323 4877
Internet: http://www.nuffield.org

AMOUNT: 500-1,800 pounds
DEADLINE(S): None
FIELD(S): All fields of study

Scholarships for childcare provided for women ages 25-50 to help them in their employment prospects.

3449—THE OVERLAKE SCHOOL (Scholarships)

20301 NE 108th
Redmond WA 98053-7499
425/868-6194 ext 613
FAX: 425/868-5771
E-mail: bdraper@overlade.org
Internet: http://www.overlake.org

AMOUNT: Varies
DEADLINE(S): FEB
FIELD(S): All fields of study

Financial aid for students already accepted and enrolled at this independent, nondenominational 5-12 college preparatory school in the state of Washington. Must demonstrate financial need.

65 awards yearly. Contact school for details.

3450—THE PARKERSBURG AREA COMMUNITY FOUNDATION (Scholarships)

501 Avery Street
Parkersburg WV 26102
304/428-4438
FAX: 304/428-1200
E-mail: moriha@wirefire.com
Internet: http://pacf.wirefire.com

AMOUNT: Varies
DEADLINE(S): Varies
FIELD(S): All fields of study

This Foundation administers more than 70 different scholarship funds. Many are for high school seniors at specific area high schools in West Virginia, Ohio, and Pennsylvania; others are for dependents of employees of certain companies or are for specific subject areas.

Contact organization for details.

3451—THE PAUL & DAISY SOROS FELLOWSHIPS FOR NEW AMERICANS (Graduate Fellowships)

400 West 59th Street
New York NY 10019
212/547-6926
FAX: 212/548-4623
E-mail: pdsoros_fellows@sorosny.org
Internet: http://www.pdsoros.org

AMOUNT: $20,000/year + 1/2 tuition
DEADLINE(S): NOV 30
FIELD(S): All fields of study leading to a graduate degree

Two-year graduate level fellowships for "New Americans"—1) holds a Green Card, or 2) is a naturalized U.S. citizen, or 3) is the child of two naturalized citizens. Must hold a B.A. degree or be in final year of undergraduate study and be at least 20 but not older than 30 years of age. Must be pursuing a graduate degree in any professional or scholarly discipline, including the Fine and Performing Arts. For use only in the U.S.

Thirty awards per year. Applications and details are available from college academic advisors, the Internet, or the organization (see location/Web site).

3452—THE RENTOKIL FOUNDATION (Scholarships for U.K. Citizens to Study in Denmark)

Sophus Berendsen A/S
1 Klausdalbrovej
DK-2860 Soborg DENMARK
Written Inquiry

AMOUNT: Varies
DEADLINE(S): DEC 31
FIELD(S): All fields of study

Scholarships for U.K. citizens to study in Denmark. For use anywhere in Denmark. Scholarships run for up to twelve months.

Applications available after October 1. Send a stamped, self-addressed envelope or International Reply Coupon for detailed information.

3453—THE RETIRED OFFICERS ASSOCIATION (TROA Scholarship Fund)

201 North Washington Street
Alexandria VA 22314-2539
800/245-8762
E-mail: edassist@troa.org
Internet: http://www.troa.org

AMOUNT: $3,500
DEADLINE(S): MAR 1
FIELD(S): All fields of study

Interest-free loans for full-time undergraduate study. Students must be under age 24, never-married dependent sons and daughters of TROA members, or unmarried dependent sons and daughters of active-duty, reserve, National Guard, and retired enlisted personnel. Students must have a minimum 3.0 GPA. Awards are based on scholastic ability, potential, character, leadership, and financial need. To be used for educational (including living) expenses only.

Renewable for five years. Loan recipients may also be considered for grants. See Web site or contact TROA for an application.

3454—THE RUMSON COUNTRY DAY SCHOOL (Financial Aid)

35 Bellevue Avenue
Rumson NJ 07760
732/842-0527
FAX: 732/758-6528
E-mail: spost@rcds.com
Internet: http://www.rcds.com

AMOUNT: Varies
DEADLINE(S): MAR 1
FIELD(S): All fields of study

Financial aid for students who plan to attend this independent, coeducational school which includes grades kindergarten through eight.

Renewable. Contact school for details.

3455—THE SAGE SCHOOL (Grants)

171 Mechanic Street
Foxboro MA 02035-1542
508/543-9619
FAX: 508/543-1152

AMOUNT: Varies
DEADLINE(S): Varies
FIELD(S): All fields of study

Need-based scholarships available to attend this independent, coeducational school which includes preschool through eighth grade. Must submit documentation indicating financial need.

Must go through application process. Profile of students is high ability/academically gifted. Contact school for details.

3456—THE SCHOOL CHOICE SCHOLARSHIPS FOUNDATION (Scholarships for Elementary Students in Private Schools in New York City)

730 Fifth Avenue, 9th Floor
New York NY 10019
212/333-8711
FAX: 212/307-3230
E-mail: scsf@worldnet.att.net
Internet: http://www.nygroup.com/scs

AMOUNT: Tuition up to $1,400
DEADLINE(S): None
FIELD(S): All subjects in elementary school

Scholarships for students in grades 1-6 in certain school districts in New York City, specifically in Manhattan, the Bronx, and Brooklyn. For use only in private or parochial schools recognized by New York State.

1,000 awards yearly. Parents must be financially eligible for the federal free lunch program. Scholarships are guaranteed for three years.

3457—THE SUSQUEHANNA SCHOOL AT SOUTH BRIDGE (Scholarship)

75 Pennsylvania Avenue
Binghamton NY 13903
607/723-5797
Internet: http://www.tier.net/TSS

AMOUNT: Varies
DEADLINE(S): APR 15
FIELD(S): All fields of study

Tuition assistance available to attend this independent, coeducational elementary school.

Must be enrolled to apply for aid. Contact school for details.

3458—THE THAI NATIONAL COMMISSION FOR UNESCO (Sponsored Fellowships Programme)

Ext Rel Div, Ministry of Ed.
Rajdamneonnok Avenue
Dusit District Bangkek 10300
THAILAND
662/281-6370
FAX: 662/281-0953
E-mail: duangtip@winning.com

AMOUNT: Varies
DEADLINE(S): MAR 15
FIELD(S): All fields of study

Fellowships, scholarships, and junior scholarships open to students who wish to study in Thailand. Must be a citizen of UNESCO member country. Postgraduates must be no more than than 45 years of age, undergrads no more than 30, and junior undergrads no more than 25.

3459—THE THANKS BE TO GRANDMOTHER WINIFRED FOUNDATION (Scholarship)

P.O. Box 15910
Santa Fe NM 87506-5910
505/827-7383 or 800/279-9777
FAX: 505/827-7392
E-mail: highered@che.state.nm.us
Internet: http://www.nmche.org
Amount: Varies

DEADLINE(S): JAN 1
FIELD(S): All
FIELD(S): All fields of study

This scholarship is for applicants who are women. To apply for any financial need based program, you must first complete the Free Application for Federal Student Aid (FAFASA) Must be a female 54 years of age or over; encourages women to have confidence in their knowledge and wisdom.

3460—UNIVERSITY OF HULL (International Scholarships)

Dr. Xiao Fang, Ass't. Registrar
International Services Division
Univ. of Hull
Hull HU6 7RX ENGLAND UK
0044 1482 465359
FAX: 0044 1482 466554
E-mail: x.fang@admin.hull.ac.uk
Internet: http://www.hull.ac.uk/international/int_office/

AMOUNT: Up to 1,000 pounds
DEADLINE(S): Varies
FIELD(S): All fields of study

The University of Hull offers scholarships to students from mainland China. The programs are a partial tuition fee waiver. For undergraduates and graduates.

Application forms and more data are on Web site. Please write clearly in block capitals. Awards are based on academic achievement and potential.

3461—UNIVERSITY OF NEWCASTLE/AUSTRALIA (International Postgraduate Research Scholarships)

Student Administration Unit
Student Services Centre
Univ. of Newcastle
Callaghan NSW 2308
AUSTRALIA
+61-(02)-4921-6541
FAX: +61-(02)-4960-1766
E-mail: scholarships@newcastle.edu.au
Internet: http://www.newcastle.edu.au/services/ousr/stuadmin/schol/index.htm

AMOUNT: Full tuition and medical insurance for 2-3 years + living allowance
DEADLINE(S): SEP 30
FIELD(S): All

Funded by the Australian government, this scholarship is open to new international graduate students to conduct high-quality research in Australia. A base living allowance of 17,000 pounds Australian is included.

See Web site or contact the University or the Australian Diplomatic Post in your country for application details.

3462—THE UPS FOUNDATION (The George D. Smith Scholarship Program)

55 Glenlake Parkway NE
Atlanta GA 30328
404/828-6374

AMOUNT: $500-$2,000

DEADLINE(S): VARIES
FIELD(S): All fields of study

For high school seniors planning to attend business schools, vocational-technical schools, associate degree programs, or 4-year colleges. Students must be children of United Parcel Service employees.

Contact local human resources department at UPS for an application and additional information.

3463—THE UPS FOUNDATION (The James E. Casey Scholarship Program)

55 Glenlake Parkway NE
Atlanta GA 30328
404/828-6374
AMOUNT: $2,000-$6,000
DEADLINE(S): VARIES
FIELD(S): All fields of study

Open to children of United Parcel Service employees. Students must be attending a four-year degree program. Applicants must provide PSAT scores.

Contact local UPS human resources department for application and complete information.

3464—THE WASIE FOUNDATION (Scholarship Program)

U.S. Bank Place, Suite 4700
601 2nd Avenue So.
Minneapolis MN 55402
612/332-3883
AMOUNT: $1,000-$23,000
DEADLINE(S): MAR
FIELD(S): All fields of study

Scholarships for high school students, college undergraduates, and graduate students of Polish descent who are enrolled in specified private high schools and colleges in Minnesota. Approx. 87 awards per year.

Applicants must be full-time students who can demonstrate financial need. Applications available Sept. 1 in financial aid offices of the institutions. Contact organization for list of schools.

3465—THE WILLIAM LOEB MEMORIAL FUND

P.O. Box 9555
Manchester NH 03108
603/668-4321
800/562-8218 ext. 506
AMOUNT: Varies
DEADLINE(S): MAR 15
FIELD(S): All fields of study

Scholarships for high school seniors who have been New Hampshire residents for at least two years for attendance at colleges, universities, and vo-tech schools. Prime consideration is given to those who demonstrate initiative, involvment, and a high degree of volunteerism in community and school activities.

3466—THIRD MARINE DIVISION ASSOCIATION (Scholarships)

P.O. Box 634
Inverness FL 34451
Written Inquiry
AMOUNT: $500-$2,400
DEADLINE(S): SPRING
FIELD(S): All fields of study

Undergrad scholarships for dependent children of U.S. MC and USN personnel who died as a result of service in Vietnam or the Southeast Asia Operations, OR Desert Shield and Desert Storm as a result of service with the 3rd Marine Division.

Also open to children of Association members (living or dead) who held membership 2 years or more. Must demonstrate financial need. Awards renewable. Write for complete information.

3467—THOMAS J. WATSON FOUNDATION (Fellowship Program)

293 S. Main Street
Providence RI 02903
401/274-1952
FAX: 401/274-1954
Internet: http://www.watson fellowship.org
AMOUNT: $22,000 (single); $31,000 (with accompanying financial and legal dependent)
DEADLINE(S): NOV 7
FIELD(S): All fields of study

Open to graduating seniors at the 50 U.S. colleges on the Foundation's roster. Fellowship provides for one year of independent study and travel abroad immediately following graduation. Candidates must be nominated by their college and should demonstrate integrity, imagination, strong ethical character, intelligence, capacity for vision and leadership, promise of creative achievement/excellence within chosen field, and potential for humane and effective participation in world.

60 awards annually. Not renewable.

3468—THURGOOD MARSHALL SCHOLARSHIP FUND

120 Wall Street
New York NY 10005
212/558-5300 or 888/839-0467
FAX: 212/344-5332
Internet: http://www.nul.org
Amount: Varies
DEADLINE(S): JAN 1
FIELD(S): Varies
FIELD(S): All fields of study

U.S. citizen pursuing a bachelor's degree in any discipline at a historically black public or private college/university. Must have SAT score or 1100 or ACT score of 25 or higher and a high school GPA of not less than 3.0. Must be an African-American entering freshman and apply directly to the Thurgood Marshall Coordinator at each of the 38 participating institutions.

3469—TOPS HONORS AWARD

Box 91202
Baton Rouge LA 70821
225/922-1012
800/259-5626 ext. 1012
FAX: 225/922-0790
E-mail: custserv@osfa.state.la.us
AMOUNT: $1,110-$3,002
DEADLINE(S): April 16
FIELD(S): All
FIELD(S): All fields of study

Applicant must have at least a 3.5 high school GPA, a 27 on the ACT, 16.5 core curriculum units, no criminal convictions and graduate from a Louisiana public or state approved private high school. Student must be independent student or at least one parent must be a resident of LA 24 months prior to high school graduation.

3470—TOWSON STATE UNIVERSITY (Scholarship & Award Programs)

Enrollment Services
Towson MD 21252
410/704-4236
AMOUNT: Varies
DEADLINE(S): Varies
FIELD(S): All fields of study

Numerous scholarship and award programs are available to entering freshmen, graduate, and transfer students attending or planning to attend Towson State University.

Contact Towson State's Scholarship Office for a booklet describing each program in detail.

3471—TOZER FOUNDATION (Scholarships)

104 N. Main Street
Stillwater MN 55082

Written Inquiry
AMOUNT: Varies
DEADLINE(S): Varies
FIELD(S): All fields of study

Available to students from Pine, Kanabec, and Washington Counties in Minnesota for four years of undergraduate studies.

Write to above address for an application.

3472—TRANSPORT WORKERS UNION OF AMERICA (Michael J. Quill Scholarship Fund)

80 West End Avenue
New York NY 10023
212/873-6000
Internet: http://www.twu.com
AMOUNT: $1200
DEADLINE(S): MAY 1
FIELD(S): All fields of study

Open to high school seniors (under 21) who are dependents of TWU members in good standing or of a deceased member who was in good standing at time of death. Dependent brothers or sisters of members in good standing also may apply.

15 scholarships per year. Renewable up to 4 years. Write for complete information.

3473—TREACY COMPANY (Scholarship)

P.O. Box 1700
Helena MT 59624
406/442-3632
AMOUNT: $400/year
DEADLINE(S): JUN 15
FIELD(S): All areas of study

For college freshmen and sophomores who reside in Montana, North or South Dakota, or Idaho.

3474—TRI-STATE GENERATION AND TRANSMISSION ASSOCIATION (Scholarships)

1100 W. 116th Ave
Westminister CO 80234
303/452-6111
Internet: http://www.tristategf.org
AMOUNT: $500
DEADLINE(S): Varies
FIELD(S): All fields of study

Available to children of Tri-State Generation and Transmission member-system employees or consumers.

2 awards annually. Write to above address for an application.

3475—TRIDENT ACADEMY (Scholarships)

1455 Wakendaw Road
Mt. Pleasant SC 29464
843/884-3494
FAX: 843/884-1483
E-mail: admissions@trident academy.com
Internet: http://www.trident academy.com
AMOUNT: $1,000-$3,000
DEADLINE(S): MAY
FIELD(S): All fields of study

Need-based scholarships for students attending this independent K-12 school in South Carolina for students with diagnosed learning disabilities.

Contact school for details.

3476—TRINITY EPISCOPAL CHURCH (Shannon Scholarship)

200 South Second St.
Pottsville PA 17901
717/622-8720
AMOUNT: $2,500
DEADLINE(S): Varies
FIELD(S): All
FIELD(S): All fields of study

Applicant must be the daughter of an Episcopal priest and reside in one of the five dioceses of Pennsylvania.

3477—TRINITY UNIVERSITY (Various Scholarships)

Financial Aid Office
715 Stadium Drive
San Antonio TX 78212-7200
210/999-8315
Internet: http://www.trinity.edu
AMOUNT: Up to $10,000
DEADLINE(S): Varies
FIELD(S): All fields of study

Various scholarships and other forms of financial aid based on merit, need, or a combination of these, for students at this private college in San Antonio, TX, which has Presbyterian roots. SAT, ACT, and GPA scores are all considered. Some are specifically for certain subject area, such as music. Music scholarships are based on an audition in person or by tape—for majors or non-majors (up to $2,000/year).

See Web site for scholarship list and how to apply for financial aid and when. Contact the Office of Admissions for application details.

3478—TRINITY-PAWLING SCHOOL (Scholarships/Grants)

300 Route 22
Pawling NY 12564
914/855-4825
FAX: 914/855-3816
E-mail: grobinson@trinitypawling.org
Internet: http://www.trinitypawling.org
AMOUNT: Varies
DEADLINE(S): Varies
FIELD(S): All fields of study

Scholarships and grants are available at this independent, college preparatory school for boys, grades 7-12, in Pawling, New York. Must demonstrate financial need.

35 annual awards. Send for information.

3479—TRUCKLOAD CARRIERS ASSOCIATION (Scholarship)

Attn: Scholarship Applications
2200 Mill Road
Alexandria VA 22314
Internet: http://www.truckload.org
AMOUNT: $1,500-$2,500
DEADLINE(S): MAY
FIELD(S): All

The recipient of the award must show financial need, excellent scholastic achievement in the freshman and sophomore years, maintain full-time student status, and be an individual of high character and integrity. Those students pursuing transportation and business degrees will be given special consideration. Awarded without regard to sex, race, color, national origin, or religion. Applicants must be the child, grandchild, or spouse of an employee or an employee of a trucking company.

3480—TULANE UNIVERSITY (Scholarships & Fellowships)

205 Mechanical Engineering Bldg.
New Orleans LA 70118
504/865-5723
Internet: http://www.tulane.edu/~finaid
AMOUNT: Varies
DEADLINE(S): Varies
FIELD(S): All areas of study

Numerous need-based and merit-based scholarship and fellowship programs for undergraduate and graduate study at Tulane University. There is also an honors program for outstanding students accepted for enrollment at Tulane.

Write for complete information.

3481—TWO/TEN INTERNATIONAL FOOTWEAR FOUNDATION (Scholarship Program)

1466 Main Street
Waltham MA 02451
781/736-1500 or 800/346-3210
FAX: 781/736-1555
E-mail: scholarship@twoten foundation.org
Internet: http://www.twoten foundation.org

AMOUNT: $210-$3,000
DEADLINE(S): DEC 15
FIELD(S): All fields of study

Open to dependent children of footwear, leather, and allied industry workers (employed a minimum of one year) and to students employed a minimum of 500 hours in one of the above industries. Must be U.S. citizen/permanent resident pursuing full-time undergraduate study in the U.S. Must demonstrate superlative academic achievement and financial need.

200 new and 400 renewal awards annually. Contact the Scholarship Director for an application.

3482—TY COBB EDUCATIONAL FOUNDATION (Undergraduate Scholarship Program)

P.O. Box 725
Forest Park GA 30051
E-mail: tycobb@mindspring.com

AMOUNT: $400-$1,000
DEADLINE(S): JUN 15
FIELD(S): All fields of study

Open to Georgia residents who have completed at least 45 quarter or 30 semester hours of academic credits in an accredited college with a minimum "B" average. Priority given to students with higher academic averages and greatest need.

Renewable. Write to Foundation for an application.

3483—TYLENOL (Scholarship Fund)

1505 Riverview Road
St. Peter MN 56082
800/676-8437

AMOUNT: $10,000; $1,000
DEADLINE(S): Varies
FIELD(S): All fields of study

Open to U.S. residents who will be attending an undergraduate course of study in the fall at an accredited two- or four-year college, university, or vo-tech school. This includes students currently enrolled in an undergraduate course of study and have one or more years of school remaining. Must demonstrate leadership in community and school activities.

510 awards annually (10 $10,000 and 500 $1,000). See local drug store or contact Citizen's Scholarship Foundation at above address for an application.

3484—U.N.I.T.E. (Philadelphia-South Jersey District Council Scholarship Awards)

Education Director
35 S. 4th Street
Philadelphia PA 19106
215/351-0750

AMOUNT: $1,000 per year
DEADLINE(S): APR 15 (to return application)
FIELD(S): All fields of study

Contact organization for full information and application.

3485—UNCOMMON LEGACY FOUNDATION (Lesbian Leadership Scholarship)

150 West 26th Street, Suite 602
New York NY 10001
212/366-6507
FAX: 212/366-4425
E-mail: uncmlegacy@aol.com
Internet: http://www.uncommon legacy.org

AMOUNT: $1,000
DEADLINE(S): MAY 1
FIELD(S): All
FIELD(S): All fields of study

Must be a female with a minimum 30. GPA, demonstrate financial aid, and show a commitment or contribution to the lesbian/gay/bisexual/transgendered community.

3486—UNION PACIFIC SCHOLARSHIP PROGRAM (Scholarships)

1700 Farnam Street,
10th Floor North
Omaha, NE 68102.

AMOUNT: $1,000
DEADLINE(S): JAN 1
FIELD(S): All
FIELD(S): All fields of study

Graduating high school seniors who are sons or daughters of active Union Pacific Railroad employees; dependents of retired or deceased employees are also eligible. Applicants must take PSAT/NMSQT and finalize application in junior year.

3487—U.S. AIR FORCE ACADEMY (Academy Appointment)

HQ USAFA/RRS
(Admissions Office)
2304 Cadet Drive, Suite 200
USAF Academy CO 80840-5025
800/443-9226
Internet: http://www.usafa.edu/rr/

AMOUNT: Full tuition and all costs + salary
DEADLINE(S): JAN 31
FIELD(S): All fields of study

Appointment is for a 4-year undergraduate degree followed by a commission as a second lieutenant in the USAF. Recipients are obligated to five years of active duty. Must be U.S. citizen between the ages of 17 and 23, unmarried, and with no dependents.

Nomination is required for appointment. Essay, interview, and SAT/ACT scores required. Write for information on obtaining nomination and for detailed admission requirements.

3488—U.S. DEPARTMENT OF STATE (Internships)

2401 E. Street NW Room 518
Washington DC 20522
Written Inquiry

AMOUNT: Varies—unpaid and paid internships
DEADLINE(S): Varies
FIELD(S): All fields of study

Internships during summer, fall, or spring through the U.S. Department of State. Some assignments are in the U.S.; some are abroad. Most are unpaid.

Write to organization for application and other details.

3489—U.S. DEPARTMENT OF THE INTERIOR-BUREAU OF INDIAN AFFAIRS (Higher Education Grant Programs)

1849 C Street NW
Washington DC 20240
202/208-3478

AMOUNT: Varies (with need)
DEADLINE(S): Varies
FIELD(S): All fields of study

Open to enrolled members of American Indian tribes and Alaskan native descendants eligible to receive services from the Secretary of the Interior.

For study leading to an undergraduate or graduate degree. Must demonstrate financial need.

Contact home agency, area office, tribe, BIA office, or financial aid office at chosen college/university for an application.

3490—U.S. DEPT OF INTERIOR-BUREAU OF INDIAN AFFAIRS (Higher Education Grant Programs-Northern Calif. and Nevada)

Western Nevada Agency
1677 Hot Springs Road
Carson City NV 89707
702/887-3515
FAX: 702/887-0496

AMOUNT: $500-$4,000
DEADLINE(S): JUL 15; DEC 15
FIELD(S): All areas of study

Open to enrolled members of Indian tribes or Alaskan native descendants eligible to receive services from the Secretary of the Interior who reside in Northern California or Nevada. For study leading to associate's, bachelor's, graduate degrees, or adult education.

Must demonstrate financial need. Contact home agency, area office, tribe, or BIA office. Check Web site for details, including address and phone numbers of area offices nationwide.

3491—U.S. DEPT. OF EDUCATION (Robert C. Byrd Honors Scholarship Program)

1900 K Street NW, 6th Floor
Washington DC 20006-8511
202/502-7657
FAX: 202/502-7861

AMOUNT: Up to $1,500/year
DEADLINE(S): Varies (by state)
FIELD(S): All fields of study

Open to outstanding high school seniors who graduate in the same academic year the award is being made or who have a GED and who have applied to or been accepted by an institution of higher education. Must be U.S. citizen or permanent resident.

Available for up to four years of study. State educational agencies receive funding from the U.S. Dept. of Education. Apply through your state board of education or contact school counselor for complete information.

3492—U.S. MARINE CORPS (Naval Reserve Officer Training Corps-NROTC)

College Scholarship Program
801 N. Randolph Street
Arlington VA 22203-9933
800/MARINES
Internet: http://www.usmc.mil

AMOUNT: Full scholarship + $150/mo.
DEADLINE(S): DEC 1
FIELD(S): All fields of study

Open to U.S. citizens who are high school seniors or graduates. Requires a four- or eight-year enlistment, qualifying scores on SAT or ACT, and physical qualification by Marine Corps standards.

Renewable yearly.

3493—U.S. SPACE CAMP FOUNDATION (Space Camp, Space Academy, Advanced Space Academy)

P.O. Box 070015
Huntsville AL 35807-7015
800/63-SPACE
Internet: http://www.spacecamp.com

AMOUNT: Full- or part-tuition
DEADLINE(S): DEC 1; JUN 1 (essays due)
FIELD(S): For all fields of study

Full- or partial-tuition scholarships to Space Camp and related events for deserving students currently attending fourth through twelfth grades. Based on essay competition. The five-day camps are located in California, Florida, and Alabama. For students in grades 4-12. An opportunity to learn about and participate in experiences related to our space program and aeronautics.

Call phone number above for scholarship applications, which are available from Oct. 1 to May 1.

3494—UNITE (Duchessi-Sallee Scholarship)

1710 Broadway
New York NY 10019
212/265-7000

AMOUNT: $1,000
DEADLINE(S): MAR 15
FIELD(S): All fields of study

Three winners are selected each year for scholarships to any 2-year or 4-year degree granting college. Awards are made ONLY to incoming freshmen who are the daughter or son of a union member in good standing for 2 years or more.

Scholarship is renewable for one additional year. Write for complete information.

3495—UNITED CHURCH OF CHRIST—SPECIAL HIGHER EDUCATION PROGRAM (Commission for Racial Justice)

700 Prospect Avenue
Cleveland OH 44115-1100
216/736-3839

AMOUNT: Varies
DEADLINE(S): Varies
FIELD(S): All fields of study

Scholarships for undergraduates who are members of the United Church of Christ and who are members of a minority ethnic group. Considered are essay, extracurricular activities, personal and career goals.

Renewable. Contact organization for details.

3496—UNITED DAUGHTERS OF THE CONFEDERACY (Scholarships)

Business Office, Memorial Bldg.
328 North Boulevard
Richmond VA 23220-4057
804/355-1636
FAX: 804/353-1396
Internet: http://www.hqudc.orgi

AMOUNT: $800 to $1,000
DEADLINE(S): FEB 15
FIELD(S): All fields of study

Various programs for descendants of worthy Confederate veterans. Applicants who are collateral descendants must be active members of the United Daughters of the Confederacy or of the Children of the Confederacy and MUST be sponsored by a UDC chapter.

Most awards for undergraduate study. For complete information send self-addressed, stamped #10 envelope (SASE) to address above or contact the education director in the division where you reside. Division addresses are on Internet site.

3497—UNITED FEDERATION OF TEACHERS (Albert Shanker College Scholarship Fund)

260 Park Avenue South
New York NY 10010
212/598-6800
Internet: http://www.uft.org

AMOUNT: $1,000/year
DEADLINE(S): DEC 15
FIELD(S): All fields of study

Open to New York City residents who attend New York City public high schools. Scholarships support undergraduate study at recognized colleges and universities. Financial need and academic standing are considerations.

Students are eligible in the year they graduate. Approximately 250 awards per year. Renewable. Write for complete information.

3498—UNITED FOOD & COMMERCIAL WORKERS INTERNATIONAL UNION (UFCW Scholarship Program)

1775 'K' Street NW
Washington DC 20006
201/223-3111
Internet: http://www.ufcw.org
AMOUNT: $1,000 per year for 4 years
DEADLINE(S): DEC 31
FIELD(S): All fields of study

Open to UFCW members or high school seniors who are children of members. Applicants must meet certain eligibility requirements. Awards for full-time study only.

3499—UNITED FOOD & COMMERCIAL WORKERS UNION—UFCW LOCAL 555 (L. Walter Derry Scholarship Fund)

P.O. Box 235 55
Tigard OR 92781
503/684-2822
Internet: http://www.ufcw555.com
AMOUNT: $1,900 (any field) + up to $2,500 (labor relations)
DEADLINE(S): MAY
FIELD(S): All fields of study

Members of Local 555 in good standing for at least 1 year prior to application deadline are eligible to apply, or sponsor their child or spouse. Confidential questionnaire, high school and college transcripts, and 3 personal references required. May be used at any accredited college/university, technical/vocational, or junior/community college for any course of study. Additional award in field of labor relations available; submit 500-word essay on plans, with application.

3500—UNITED JEWISH FOUNDATION OF GREATER PITTSBURGH (Central Scholarship)

5743 Bartlett Street
Pittsburgh, PA 15217
412/422-7200
Internet: http://trfn.clpgh.org/jfcs/
AMOUNT: Varies
DEADLINE(S): FEB 12
FIELD(S): All fields of study

Must be a Pennsylvania resident of Allegheny, Beaver, Washington, or Westmoreland counties for at least two years and a high school senior or college undergraduate or graduate of Jewish faith. Must demonstrate financial need.

3501—UNITED METHODIST CHURCH (Scholarship and Loan Program)

P.O. Box 340007
Nashville TN 37203-0007
615/340-7346
FAX: 615/340-7367
Internet: http://www.gbhem.org
AMOUNT: Varies
DEADLINE(S): JUN 1
FIELD(S): All fields of study

Scholarships and loans for undergraduates and graduate students. Most graduate scholarships are limited to theology, higher education administration, or older adults changing careers. Must have been a full and active member of a United Methodist church for at least one year. U.S. citizenship/permanent residency required. Minimum GPA of 2.5 required.

Check with financial aid dept. at your United Methodist college, the chairperson of your annual conference board of Higher Education and campus Ministry, or the address above for application details.

3502—UNITED NEGRO COLLEGE FUND (Scholarships)

8260 Willow Oaks Corporate Drive
FairFAX: VA 22031
703/205-3400 or 800/331-2244
Internet: http://www.uncf.org
AMOUNT: Varies
DEADLINE(S): Varies
FIELD(S): All areas of study

Scholarships available to students who enroll in one of the 39 United Negro College Fund member institutions. Financial need must be established through the financial aid office at a UNCF college.

For information and a list of the UNCF campuses write to the address above.

3503—UNITED SOUTH AND EASTERN TRIBES (Scholarship Fund)

Wanda Janes, Tribal Liaison Officer
United South and Eastern Tribes, Inc.
711 Stewarts Ferry Pike, Suite 100
Nashville TN 37214-2634
615/872-7900
FAX: 615/872-7417
E-mail: uset@bellsouth.net
Internet: http://www.oneida-nation.net/uset
AMOUNT: $500
DEADLINE(S): APR 30
FIELD: All
FIELD(S): All fields of study

One-time award for American Indian students who are members of a United South and Eastern Tribes member tribe. Submit college acceptance letter per proof of enrollment, certificate of tribal affiliation, letter stating intended use of award, application, transcript if available, financial need analysis, and essay.

3504—UNITED STATES INSTITUTE OF PEACE (National Peace Essay Contest)

Contest Coordinator
Education Program
1200 17th Street NW
Washington DC 20036-3011
202/457-3854
FAX: 202/429-6063
E-mail: essay_contest@usip.org
Internet: http://www.usip.org
AMOUNT: $1000-$10,000
DEADLINE(S): Varies
FIELD: All
FIELD(S): All fields of study

Essay contest designed to have students research and write about international peace and conflict resolution. Topic changes yearly. State winners are invited to Washington, DC for the awards program. Deadline varies. Must be a high school student or a U.S. citizen.

3505—UNITED STUDENT AID FUNDS INC. (Guaranteed Student Loan Program; Plus Loans)

1912 Capital Avenue, #320
Cheyenne WY 82001
307/635-3259
AMOUNT: Varies
DEADLINE(S): None
FIELD(S): All fields of study

Low-interest loans are available to Wyoming residents who are citizens or permanent residents of the U.S. and enrolled at least 1/2-time in school. Must demonstrate financial need.

Write for complete information.

3506—UNIVERSITY COLLEGE LONDON (International Scholarships)

Registrar's Division
University College London
Gower Street
London WC1E 6BT ENGLAND UK
+44 (0) 207 679 7765
FAX: +44 (0) 207 679 3001
E-mail: international@ucl.ac.uk
Internet: http://www.ucl.ac.uk

AMOUNT: Varies
DEADLINE(S): Varies
FIELD(S): All fields of study

Scholarships for undergraduate, graduate, and postgraduate international students pursuing degrees in most fields of study. For use at University College London.

At Web site, specific details are listed. Contact Mark Pickerill for details.

3507—UNIVERSITY OF BIRMINGHAM (International Scholarships)

International Office
Univ. of Birmingham
Edgebaston Birmingham B15 2TT
ENGLAND UK
+44 (0) 121 414 71673886
FAX: +44 (0) 121 414 3850
E-mail: international@bham.ac.uk
Internet: http://www.bham.ac.uk

AMOUNT: Varies
DEADLINE(S): Varies
FIELD(S): All fields of study

Scholarships for undergraduate, graduate, and postgraduate international students pursuing degrees in most fields of study. For use at Birmingham University in Central England.

3508—UNIVERSITY OF BRIDGEPORT (Undergraduate Scholarships & Grants)

126 Park Avenue
Bridgeport CT 06601
203/576-4567 or 800/EXCEL-UB
FAX: 203/576-4941
E-mail: jstoltz@bridgeport.edu
Internet: http://www.bridgeport.edu

AMOUNT: Varies
DEADLINE(S): Varies
FIELD(S): All fields of study, especially Religion

Undergraduate grants and other award programs are available to both U.S. and international students. Some are merit-based; others are need-based. All majors are considered; however, World Religions applicants stand a very good chance, as it's a relatively new program.

100 full tuition awards + several other awards annually. Renewable for four years with satisfactory academic progress.

3509—UNIVERSITY OF CALIFORNIA AT BERKELEY (Undergraduate Scholarships)

Room 210, Sproul Hall
Berkeley CA 94720
510/642-6363
Internet: http://www.berkeley.edu

AMOUNT: Varies
DEADLINE(S): Varies
FIELD(S): All fields of study

Various scholarships are available to students at UC Berkeley on the basis of academic achievement and financial need. To be considered for scholarships that require financial need, student must have filled out the government FAFSA form.

2,500 awards annually. Entering students should fill out the UC Application for Undergraduate Admissions & Scholarships, and continuing UCB students should complete a UC Berkeley Scholarship Data Sheet (SDS). See your financial aid office for the FAFSA form.

3510—UNIVERSITY OF HULL (Lord Wilberforce Scholarship)

Cecilia Yates
Hull HU6 7RX ENGLAND UK
0044 1482 466884
E-mail: r.a.lee@admin.hull.ac.uk
Internet: http://www.hull.ac.uk

AMOUNT: Full tuition
DEADLINE(S): Varies
FIELD(S): All fields of study

The University of Hull offers up to 5 Lord Wilberforce scholarships to students. The program is a full tuition fee waiver.

3511—UNIVERSITY OF HULL (Undergraduate & Postgraduate Scholarships)

Joanne Clarke, Secretary
Scholarships Committee
Hull HU6 7RX ENGLAND UK
01482 466577
FAX: 01482 466554
Internet: http://www.hull.ac.uk

AMOUNT: Varies
DEADLINE(S): Varies
FIELD(S): All fields of study

The University of Hull claims to operate on the most extensive scholarship plans in the United Kingdom—almost 1 million pounds per year. There is a large assortment of programs for many different types of students. Some are shared arrangements with private sources.

Check Web site and contact the university for application forms and details of available funding programs.

3512—UNIVERSITY OF LEEDS (Scholarships for International Students)

Research Degrees &
Scholarships Office
Univ. of Leeds; Stoner Building
Leeds LS2 9JT ENGLAND UK
+44 (0) 113 233 4007
E-mail: scholarships@leeds.ac.uk
Internet: http://www.leeds.ac.uk/students/schol.htm

AMOUNT: Varies
DEADLINE(S): Varies
FIELD(S): All fields of study

Various scholarships for international students. Several of them are for students from specific countries, and some or limited to certain areas of study. All levels of study—undergraduate through doctoral.

Contact university or access Web site for complete information.

3513—UNIVERSITY OF LEEDS (Tetley and Lupton Scholarships for Overseas Students)

Research Degrees &
Scholarships Office
Leeds LS2 9JT ENGLAND UK
+44 (0) 113 233 4007
E-mail: c.edwards@leeds.ac.uk
Internet: http://www.leeds.ac.uk/students/schol.htm

AMOUNT: 1,800 pounds sterling (undergrads, postgrads in taught courses); $2,490 (postgrad research)
DEADLINE(S): MAR 1 (undergraduates and taught postgraduates); APR 30 (research postgraduates)
FIELD(S): All fields of study

Scholarships open to overseas students of high academic standards who are accepted for admission by the university as a full-time undergraduate or graduate student.

70 awards per year. Awards renewable. Contact address above for complete information.

3514—UNIVERSITY OF MICHIGAN (Scholarships and Merit Programs for Undergraduates)

2011 Student Activities Building
Ann Arbor MI 48109-1316
734/763-6600
FAX: 734/647-3081
E-mail: Financial.aid@umich.edu
Internet: http://www.finaid.umich.edu
AMOUNT: Varies
DEADLINE(S): MAR 1
FIELD(S): All fields of study

A wide variety of scholarships and merit programs for undergraduates. Michigan residency NOT required. Send for brochure: "A Guide to scholarships and Merit Programs for Undergraduates" at the Office of Financial Aid at above address. Requirements vary. Entering freshmen will be automatically considered for most programs. Some scholarships are for out-of-state students.

Equal consideration is given to students admitted to the University before February 1 and apply for financial aid by March 1.

3515—UNIVERSITY OF MISSOURI, ROLLA (Program for Non-Missouri Residents)

G-1 Parker Hall
1870 Miner Circle
Rolla MO 65409-1060
573/341-4282 or 800/522-0938
FAX: 573/341-4274
E-mail: umroll@umr.edu
Internet: http://www.umr.edu/admissions/scholarnonmo.html
AMOUNT: $1,000-$5,000 reduced non-resident fees
DEADLINE(S): FEB 1
FIELD(S): All fields of study

Tuition reduction for out-of-state students at the University of Missouri, Rolla. Top students are automatically considered when they submit the Undergraduate Application for Admission, Financial Aid & Scholarships.

Renewable provided student completes 24 credit hours/year and maintains a 3.0 cumulative GPA.

3516—UNIVERSITY OF NEBRASKA AT LINCOLN (Regents, David, Davis, National Merit, and Departmental Scholarships)

16 Canfield Administration Bldg.
P.O. Box 880411
Lincoln NE 68588-0411
401/472-2030
FAX: 402/472-4826
AMOUNT: Varies
DEADLINE(S): JAN 15 (preceding fall semester)
FIELD(S): All fields of study

Open to Nebraska high school graduates who have taken the ACT or SAT and sent scores to University of Nebraska, Lincoln. Variety of scholarships available—some for minorities, some based on financial need, and various other requirements.

By applying for admission by Jan 15 of the preceding fall semester, submitting the need supplement (optional) and the activities resume (optional), the student is competing for approximately 1,500 other individual scholarship programs at UNL. Write for complete information.

3517—UNIVERSITY OF NEW MEXICO (Amigo/Amigo Transfer Scholarships)

Mesa Hall, Room 3019
Albuquerque NM 87131-2001
505/277-6090
FAX: 505/277-5325
E-mail: finaid@unm.edu
Internet: http://www.unm.edu/~schol/apps/amigo.pdf
AMOUNT: Waiver of out-of-state tuition + $250/semester
DEADLINE(S): JAN 10; AUG 15
FIELD(S): All fields of study

The University of New Mexico offers awards non-New Mexico residents who are new freshmen or transfer students. Must be U.S. citizen or permanent resident.

Contact Scholarships Office (address above) for complete information.

3518—UNIVERSITY OF NEW MEXICO (Scholarships)

Mesa Hall, Room 3019
Albuquerque NM 87131-2081
505/277-6090
FAX: 505/277-5325
E-mail: finaid@unm.edu
Internet: http://www.unm.edu//~schol/schol.html
AMOUNT: Varying amounts to $8,800
DEADLINE(S): DEC (Regents & Presidential); FEB 1 (UNM Scholars)
FIELD(S): All fields of study

The University of New Mexico awards to eligible first-time freshmen more than 1,000 scholarships from six major scholarship programs. Considerations include extra-curricular activities and personal statement. Must be U.S. citizen or permanent resident.

Contact Scholarships Office (address above) for complete information.

3519—UNIVERSITY OF OXFORD—ST. HILDA'S COLLEGE (New Zealand Bursaries)

College Secretary
St. Hilda's College
Oxford OX4 1DY ENGLAND UK
44 1865 276884
FAX: 44 1865 276816
AMOUNT: Up to 1,700 pounds sterling
DEADLINE(S): AUG 1
FIELD(S): All fields of study

Open to women from New Zealand for undergraduate or graduate study at Street Hilda's college. Preference to descendants of the late Francis Bateman Raymond of Timaru New Zealand.

Bursaries renewable for a 2nd and 3rd year subject to satisfactory progress. Write for complete information and application form.

3520—UNIVERSITY OF SASKATCHEWAN (Awards for Undergraduate Students)

Awards Office
105 Administration Pl.
Saskatoon SK S7N 5A2 CANADA
306/966-6748
FAX: 306/966-6730
E-mail: awards@usask.ca
Internet: http://www.usask.ca/students/acholarships
AMOUNT: Varies
DEADLINE(S): FEB 15
FIELD(S): All fields of study

Open to full-time undergraduates who have successfully completed at least one year of study at the University. Cash value of awards is applied toward payment of fees; any balance is paid out to the recipient.

Approximately $1.4 million paid out in awards each year. Student may not hold a number of awards administered by the University whose aggregate sum equals more than two times that student's tuition.

3521—UNIVERSITY OF WINDSOR (John B. Kennedy Memorial Entrance Award)

401 Sunset Avenue
Windsor Ontario N9B 3P4
CANADA
519/253-3000
FAX: 519/973-7087

Internet: http://www.uwindsor.ca
AMOUNT: $600/year
DEADLINE(S): MAY 31
FIELD(S): All fields of study

Open to undergraduate students registering in Year 1 at the University of Windsor. Must have superior grades.

Renewable up to 4 years. Contact AASE Cuthbert for an application.

3522—UPPER CANADA COLLEGE (National Scholarship Program)

200 Lonsdale Road
Toronto Ontario M4V 1W6
CANADA
416/488-1125
FAX: 416/484-8611
E-mail: administration@ucc.on.ca
Internet: http://www.ucc.on.ca
AMOUNT: Varies
DEADLINE(S): APR 1
FIELD(S): All fields of study

Open to males in grades 7-12 to attend this day/boarding school. Must have first class standing, SSAT scores with an average 90th percentile, and involvement in extracurricular activities. Must be Canadian citizen and demonstrate financial need.

3523—U.S. COAST GUARD MUTUAL ASSISTANCE (Adm. Roland Student Loan Program)

2100 2nd Street SW
Washington DC 20593-0001
202/267-1683
AMOUNT: Up to full tuition
DEADLINE(S): None specified
FIELD(S): All areas of study

For members and dependents of Coast Guard Mutual Assistance members who are enrolled at least half-time in an approved postsecondary school.

Loans renewable for up to four years. Must reapply annually. Write for complete information.

3524—U.S. DEPARTMENT OF DEFENSE (Student Educational Employment Program)

Defense Employment Information Ctr
Washington Headquarters
1155 Defense Pentagon
Washington DC 203011-1155
703/617-0652
Internet: http://www.hrsc.osd.mil
AMOUNT: Paid employment while in school
DEADLINE(S): None specified
FIELD(S): All fields of study

U.S. citizens. Student Career Experience assigns work to students that relates to their career goals or interests. Includes benefits and can't interfere with academic studies. Non-competitive conversion to permanent position if requirements met. Student Temporary Employment is yearly, and the nature of the student's duties doesn't have to be related to academic/career goals. No opportunity for conversion.

3525—U.S. DEPT OF VETERANS AFFAIRS (Vocational Rehabilitation)

1120 Vermont Avenue NW (28)
Washington DC 20420
VA regional office in each state or 800-827-1000
AMOUNT: Tuition; books; fees; equipment; subsistence allowance
DEADLINE(S): Varies (Within 12 years from date of notification of entitlement to VA comp)
FIELD(S): All fields of study

Open to U.S. military veterans disabled during active duty, honorably discharged and in need of rehab services to overcome an employment handicap.

Program will provide college, trade, technical, on-job or on-farm training (at home or in a special rehab facility if vet's disability requires). Contact nearest VA office for complete information.

3526—U.S. EDUCATIONAL FOUNDATION IN INDIA (AT&T Leadership Award)

Fulbright House
12 Hailey Road
New Delhi 110 001 INDIA
011-3328944
FAX: 011-3329718
E-mail: vijaya@usefid.ernet.in
AMOUNT: $5,000
DEADLINE(S): SEP 15
FIELD(S): All fields of study

For first year undergraduate and graduate students who are citizens/permanent residents of Asian Pacific countries (Australia, China, Hong Kong, India, Indonesia, Japan, Korea, Malaysia, Philippines, Singapore, Taiwan, and Tailand). Must plan to attend accredited U.S. college/university.

36 awards annually. Contact Vijaya Rao, Educational Advisor & AT&T Chair, at above address for an application.

3527—U.S. SUBMARINE VETERANS OF WWII (Scholarship Program)

5040 Virginia Beach Boulevard, Suite 104-A
Virginia Beach VA 23462
757/671-3200
FAX: 757/671-3330
AMOUNT: $3,000/year
DEADLINE(S): MAR 15
FIELD(S): All fields of study

Open to children and step-children of paid-up regular members of U.S. submarine veterans of WWII. Applicant must be an unmarried high school senior or have graduated from high school no more than four years prior to applying and be under the age of 24. Grandchildren NOT eligible.

List those submarines in which your sponsor served during WWII and include sponsor's membership card number when requesting application. Contact Tomi Roeske, Scholarship Administrator, for details.

3528—USA TODAY (All-USA Academic Team Awards)

1000 Wilson Boulevard, 10th Floor
Arlington VA 22229
703/276-5890
AMOUNT: $2,500 + 2-page newspaper article
DEADLINE(S): FEB 25
FIELD(S): All fields of study

Open to high school seniors or juniors who plan to graduate from high school sometime in current year. Must be enrolled in U.S. high school, be U.S. home-school student, or be U.S. citizen enrolled in high school outside U.S. . Based on grades, honors, leadership, and how nominees apply intellectual skills beyond the classroom. Key element is essay describing nominee's most outstanding endeavor in scholarly research, the arts, journalism, public affairs, or community service.

20 awards annually. Students must be nominated by educator. Contact your high school's financial aid office for details.

3529—UTA ALUMNI ASSOCIATION (African-American Endowed Scholarship)

University of Texas at Arlington
Box 19457
Arlington TX 76019
817/272-2594
E-mail: alumni@uta.edu
Internet: http://www.uta.edu/alumni/scholar.htm
AMOUNT: $350
DEADLINE(S): Varies
FIELD(S): All fields of study

Must be a full-time sophomore or higher in good standing at the University of Texas at Arlington. Must have demonstrated financial need and success and be of African-American descent.

1 award annually. Contact UTA Alumni Association for an application.

3530—UTA ALUMNI ASSOCIATION (Frankie S. Hansell Endowed Scholarship)

University of Texas at Arlington
Box 19457
Arlington TX 76019
817/272-2594
E-mail: alumni@uta.edu
Internet: http://www.uta.edu/alumni/scholar.htm

AMOUNT: $1,000
DEADLINE(S): Varies
FIELD(S): All fields of study

For undergraduate or graduate students at the University of Texas at Arlington. Must be U.S. citizen and demonstrate financial need. Preference is given to females.

9 awards annually. Contact UTA Alumni Association for an application.

3531—UTA ALUMNI ASSOCIATION (Hispanic Scholarship)

University of Texas at Arlington
Box 19457
Arlington TX 76019
817/272-2594
E-mail: alumni@uta.edu
Internet: http://www.uta.edu/alumni/scholar.htm

AMOUNT: $300
DEADLINE(S): Varies
FIELD(S): All fields of study

For students of Hispanic origin who attend full-time with at least 15 hours completed at the University of Texas at Arlington. Must have a minimum 2.5 GPA, be in good standing, and demonstrate financial need, leadership ability, and potential for success. Transcripts and letter stating financial need are required.

1 award annually. Contact UTA Alumni Association for an application.

3532—UTA ALUMNI ASSOCIATION (Simmons-Blackwell Endowed Scholarship)

University of Texas at Arlington
Box 19457
Arlington TX 76019
817/272-2594
E-mail: alumni@uta.edu
Internet: http://www.uta.edu/alumni/scholar.htm

AMOUNT: $250
DEADLINE(S): Varies
FIELD(S): All fields of study

Must be a first-generation college student with less than 90 hours and attend the University of Texas at Arlington. Must have demonstrated financial need and a minimum 2.5 GPA. Letter outlining career goals is required.

1 award annually. Contact UTA Alumni Association for an application.

3533—UTA ALUMNI ASSOCIATION (Student Foundation Sophomore Scholarship)

University of Texas at Arlington
Box 19457
Arlington TX 76019
817/272-2594
E-mail: alumni@uta.edu
Internet: http://www.uta.edu/alumni/scholar.htm

AMOUNT: $250
DEADLINE(S): Varies
FIELD(S): All fields of study

Must be a sophomore enrolled in at least nine hours at the University of Texas at Arlington. Must demonstrate financial need and have a minimum 2.75 GPA.

1 award annually. Contact UTA Alumni Association for an application.

3534—UTAH HIGHER EDUCATION ASSISTANCE AUTHORITY (Centennial Opportunity Program for Education)

355 W. North Temple
3 Triad, Suite 550
Salt Lake City UT 84180
801/321-7200 or 800/418-8757
FAX: 801/321-7299
E-mail: uheaa@utahsbr.edu
Internet: http://www.uheaa.org

AMOUNT: Up to $5,000
DEADLINE(S): Varies
FIELD(S): All fields of study

Open to Utah residents with substantial financial need who are pursuing undergraduate studies at an eligible Utah institution.

Renewable with reapplication. Contact your school for details.

3535—UTAH HIGHER EDUCATION ASSISTANCE AUTHORITY (State Student Incentive Grants)

355 W. North Temple
3 Triad, Suite 550
Salt Lake City UT 84180
801/321-7200 or 800/418-8757
FAX: 801/321-7299
E-mail: uheaa@utahsbr.edu
Internet: http://www.uheaa.org

AMOUNT: Up to $2,500
DEADLINE(S): Varies
FIELD(S): All fields of study

Open to Utah residents with substantial financial need who are attending eligible Utah schools. Grants are intended to enable such students to continue their studies. Must be U.S. citizen/legal resident.

Awards are made through the financial aid office at each eligible institution.

3536—UTILITY WORKERS UNION OF AMERICA (Scholarship Awards)

815 16th Street NW
Washington DC 20006
202/347-8105
Internet: http://www.uwua.org

AMOUNT: $500-$2,000/year
DEADLINE(S): DEC 31
FIELD(S): All fields of study

Open to sons and daughters of active Utility Workers Union members in good standing. Winners are selected from the group of high school juniors who take the national merit scholarship exams.

2 awards annually. Contact UWUA for details.

3537—VALENCIA COMMUNITY COLLEGE FOUNDATION (Scholarships)

P.O. Box 3028
Orlando FL 32802-3028
407/317-7950
FAX: 407/317-7956
Internet: http://www.valencia.org/scholar.html

AMOUNT: Varies
DEADLINE(S): Varies
FIELD(S): All fields of study

The Valencia Community College Foundation lists numerous financial aid programs. The listed Web site is comprehensive.

Access Web site or write to foundation for list of financial aid programs.

3538—VENTURE CLUBS OF THE AMERICAS (Student Aid Awards)

Two Penn Center Plaza, Suite 1000
Philadelphia PA 19102-1883
215/557-9300
FAX: 215/568-5200
E-mail: siahq@voicenet.com

AMOUNT: $2,500 and $5,000
DEADLINE(S): DEC 31
FIELD(S): All fields of study

Awards for young, physically disabled individuals in need of further education who are between 15 and 40 years old. A Venture Club is an organization for young business and professional women sponsored by Soroptimist International of the Americas. The major selection criteria are financial need and the capacity to profit from further education.

Applicants should contact the nearest Venture Club or Soroptimist Club for application or send self-addressed, stamped envelope (SASE) to above address. Allow plenty of time before deadline date for application to be returned to the nearest local club.

3539—VERMONT STUDENT ASSISTANCE CORPORATION (Incentive Grants for Undergraduates)

P.O. Box 2000
Winooski VT 05404-2601
802/655-9602 or 800/642-3177
TDD: 800/281-3341
FAX: 802/654-3765
Internet: http://www.vsac.org

AMOUNT: $500-$8,650
DEADLINE(S): None
FIELD(S): All fields of study

Open to Vermont residents enrolled full-time at approved postsecondary institutions. Must meet need test. Award amounts depend on expected family contribution, Pell Grant eligibility, and institution attended.

Contact VSAC for an application.

3540—VERMONT STUDENT ASSISTANCE CORPORATION (Non-Degree Grant)

P.O. Box 2000
Winooski VT 05404-2601
802/655-9602 or 800/642-3177
TDD: 800/281-3341
FAX: 802/654-3765
Internet: http://www.vsac.org

AMOUNT: $650 (max.) for one course/semester
DEADLINE(S): None
FIELD(S): All fields of study

Open to Vermont residents enrolled in a non-degree course that will improve employability or encourage further study. Must meet need test.

1,000+ awards annually. Contact VSAC for an application.

3541—VERMONT STUDENT ASSISTANCE CORPORATION (Part-Time Grant)

P.O. Box 2000
Winooski VT 05404-2601
802/655-9602 or 800/642-3177
TDD: 800/281-3341
FAX: 802/654-3765
Internet: http://www.vsac.org

AMOUNT: Varies
DEADLINE(S): None
FIELD(S): All fields of study

Open to Vermont residents pursuing part-time undergraduate study in a degree, diploma, or certificate program. Must be taking fewer than 12 credit hours, have not received a bachelor's degree, and meet need test. Award amounts depend on number of credit hours taken.

2,600 awards annually. Contact VSAC for an application.

3542—VETERANS OF FOREIGN WARS/V.F.W. LADIES AUXILIARY (M.J. "Mel" Ornelas Memorial Scholarships)

4432 E. 7th
Cheyenne WY 82001
Written Inquiry

AMOUNT: $100
DEADLINE(S): Varies
FIELD(S): All fields of study

Available to graduating high school seniors who are children or grandchildren of members of the Veterans of Foreign Wars or the V.F.W. Ladies Auxiliary. Applicants must have a minimum 2.5 GPA, write a letter of application, and a 200-word essay on: "Serving the Dead While Helping the Living What the V.F.W. Motto Means to Me." Certification of GPA as well as of V.F.W. membership from Post commander or Auxiliary president required.

2 awards annually (one to a man and one to a woman). To apply, send above materials to Sandy Ross.

3543—VETERANS OF FOREIGN WARS OF THE UNITED STATES (Voice of Democracy Audio-Essay Scholarship Contest)

VFW Bldg.
406 W. 34th Street
Kansas City MO 64111
816/756-3390
FAX: 816/968-1149
E-mail: harmer@vfw.org
Internet: http://www.vfw.org

AMOUNT: $1,000-$25,000
DEADLINE(S): NOV 1
FIELD(S): All fields of study

Open to students in public, private, and parochial high schools in the U.S. Contestants will be judged on their treatment of an annual theme. Essay may not refer to themselves, their schools, states, cities, etc. as a means of identification. Foreign exchange students NOT eligible.

56 national awards annually. Contact local VFW post or high school for current theme and guidelines.

3544—VIETNOW (National Scholarship)

Carol Knudsen
Committee Chairperson
VietNow National Headquarters
1835 Broadway
Rockford IL 61104-5409
815/227-5100
FAX: 815-227-5127
E-mail: vnnatl@inwave.com
Internet: http://www.vietnow.com

AMOUNT: $1,000-$3,000
DEADLINE(S): APR 1
FIELD(S): All

Available to U.S. citizens under 35 years old who are dependents of members of VietNow. Academic accomplishments and activities will be considered for the award.

3545—VICE ADMIRAL E.P. TRAVERS SCHOLARSHIP PROGRAM

801 North Randolph Street
Suite 1228
Arlington VA 22203
703/696-4960
FAX: 703/696-0144
E-mail: laesuema@mncrs.org

AMOUNT: $2,000-$3,000
DEADLINE(S): MAR 1
FIELD(S): All
FIELD(S): All fields of study

Provides a qualified student with a $2,000 grant as well as a $3,000 loan. Based on need. GPA 2.0 or higher. Student must have a current military dependent ID card.

3546—VIKKI CARR SCHOLARSHIP FOUNDATION (Scholarships)

P.O. Box 57756
Sherman Oak CA 91413
Written Inquiry

AMOUNT: Up to $3,000
DEADLINE(S): APR 15
FIELD(S): All fields of study

Open to Latino residents of California and Texas between the ages of 17 and 22. Awards are for undergrad study at accredited colleges and universities. No U.S. citizenship requirement.

3547—VINCENT L. HAWKINSON FOUNDATION FOR PEACE AND JUSTICE (Scholarship Award)

Grace University Lutheran Church
324 Harvard Street SE
Minneapolis MN 55414
612/331-8125

AMOUNT: Approx. $1,500 (varies)
DEADLINE(S): APR 30
FIELD(S): All fields of study

Scholarships for students who either reside in or attend college in one of the following states: Minnesota, Iowa, Wisconsin, North Dakota or South Dakota. Must have demonstrated a commitment to peace and justice through study, internships, or projects that illustrate their commitment. For undergraduates, graduates, or M.A. candidates.

Two awards. Contact organization for details.

3548—VIRGIN ISLANDS BOARD OF EDUCATION (Exceptional Children Scholarship)

P.O. Box 11900
Saint Thomas VI 00801
809/774-4546

AMOUNT: $2,000
DEADLINE(S): MAR 31
FIELD(S): All fields of study

Open to bona fide residents of the Virgin Islands who suffer from physical, mental, or emotional impairment and have demonstrated exceptional abilities and the need of educational training not available in Virgin Islands schools.

NOT for study at the college level. Write for complete information.

3549—VIRGIN ISLANDS BOARD OF EDUCATION (Territorial Scholarship Grants)

P.O. Box 11900
Saint Thomas VI 00801
809/774-4546

AMOUNT: $1,000-$3,000
DEADLINE(S): MAR 31
FIELD(S): All fields of study

Grants open to bona fide residents of the Virgin Islands who have a cumulative GPA of at least 'C' and are enrolled in an accredited institution of higher learning.

300-400 loans and grants per year. Renewable provided recipient maintains an average of 'C' or better. Loans are also available. Write for complete information.

3550—VIRGINIA MILITARY INSTITUTE (Scholarships)

Financial Aid Office
Lexington VA 24450-0304
540/464-7208
FAX: 540/464-7629
Internet: http://www.web.vmi.edu

AMOUNT: Varies
DEADLINE(S): Varies
FIELD(S): All fields of study

Scholarships are available to attend this four-year, coeducational, undergraduate university in Lexington, Virginia. Awards include ROTC Scholarships, State Cadetships, and the Institute Scholars Program. Must complete government FAFSA form as well as the VMI financial aid form found in the admissions packet.

Contact VMI for descriptions of programs and details of the school.

3551—VIRGINIA SMITH SCHOLARSHIP TRUST (Scholarships)

632 West 13th Street
Merced CA 95340
209/381-6604

AMOUNT: Varies
DEADLINE(S): MAY 1
FIELD(S): All fields of study

Scholarships for students who attended a public high school in the City of Merced, California, for at least three years. Must have 60 units and/or junior status, and must have applied for admission to a public or private institution of higher learning, excluding community colleges, in the State of California. GPA of at least 2.8 required. Financial need considered.

3552—VIRGINIA STATE COUNCIL OF HIGHER EDUCATION (Tuition Assistance Grant Program)

101 N. 14th Street
James Monroe Bldg.
Richmond VA 23219
804/224-2614
E-mail: andeso@schev.edu
Internet: http://www.schev.edu

AMOUNT: $3,000 (max.)
DEADLINE(S): JUL 31
FIELD(S): All fields of study (except Theology)

Open to Virginia residents who are full-time undergraduate, graduate, or professional students at eligible private colleges/universities in Virginia. Financial need NOT a factor. Late applications may be considered if funds are available.

15,000+ awards annually. Contact your financial aid office or the State Council of Higher Education for an application.

3553—VIRGINIA STATE COUNCIL OF HIGHER EDUCATION (Virginia Transfer Grant Program)

101 N.14th Street
James Monroe Bldg
Richmond VA 23219
804/225-2604
E-mail: andes@schev.edu
Internet: http://www.schev.edu

AMOUNT: Up to full tuition and fees
DEADLINE(S): Varies (check with financial aid office)
FIELD(S): All fields of study

For minority students who enroll in one of the Commonwealth's 13 historically white college or universities and all transfer students at Norfolk State and Virginia State Universities. Applicants must qualify for entry as first-time transfer students.

Contact college financial aid office for complete information.

3554—VMFA/VMF/VMF(N)-531 (Gray Ghost Scholarship Program)

Col. Robert H. Schultz
105 Lakeside Drive
Havelock NC 28532
252/447-2555

AMOUNT: $1,000
DEADLINE(S): MAR 15
FIELD(S): All fields of study

Open to undergraduate students who are children of former members of the Marine Corps Squadron VMF/VMF(N) or VMFA-531. The living or deceased parent must have received an honorable discharge from the USMC. Gross family income should not exceed $45,000 per year.

1-2 awards annually. Contact Colonel Robert H. Schultz for nomination procedures.

3555—W. ROSS MACDONALD SCHOOL (Rixon Rafter Scholarships)

350 Brant Ave
Brantford Ontario N3T 3J9
CANADA
519/759-0730

AMOUNT: $300-$500
DEADLINE(S): SEP 30
FIELD(S): All fields of study

Open to legally blind Canadians pursuing postsecondary studies at accredited

Canadian institutions. Must have strong career aspirations.

3556—WAL-MART FOUNDATION (Sam Walton Scholarship)

702 SW 8th Street
Bentonville AR 72716-8071
501/277-1905
FAX: 501/273-6850
Internet: http://www.walmart foundation.org
AMOUNT: $1,000
DEADLINE(S): None
FIELD(S): All fields of study

For a college-bound high school senior in each community where a Wal-Mart store is operating. An informational packet and scholarship applications will be available through your local Wal-Mart.

3557—WAL-MART FOUNDATION SCHOLARSHIPS (Distribution Center Scholarships)

702 SW 8th Street
Bentonville AR 72716-8071
501/277-1905
FAX: 501/273-6850
http://www.walmartfoundation.org
AMOUNT: $2,500 payable over 4 years
DEADLINE(S): MAY 1
FIELD(S): All fields of study

Open to Wal-Mart associates who work for a Distribution Center. ACT, SAT, counselor recommendations, transcripts, class rank, community activities, leadership, and financial need will be considered.

Two scholarships will be awarded in each unit that has been operating for at least one year. Contact the distribution Personnel Manager for complete information.

3558—WAL-MART FOUNDATION SCHOLARSHIPS (Wal-Mart Associate Scholarship)

702 SW 8th Street
Bentonville AR 72716-8071
501/273-1905
FAX: 501/273-6850
http://www.walmartfoundation.org
AMOUNT: $1,000
DEADLINE(S): MAR 1
FIELD(S): All fields of study

Open to high school seniors who work for Wal-Mart and to those associates' children ineligible for the Walton Foundation Scholarship due to length of employment or not working full-time. Applications available at local store in January or call or write above location.

ACT, SAT, transcripts, class rank, community activities, leadership, and financial need are considered.

3559—WAL-MART FOUNDATION SCHOLARSHIPS (Walton Foundation Scholarship)

702 SW 8th Street
Bentonville, AR 72716-8071
501/273-1905
FAX: 501/273-6850
http://www.walmartfoundation.org
AMOUNT: $6,000 over 4 years
DEADLINE(S): MAR 1
FIELD(S): All fields of study

Open to college-bound high school seniors who are dependents of Wal-Mart associates who are employed full-time (28 hours/week or more) for one year as of March 1. Applications are available in January at local store or you can call the Wal-Mart Foundation.

100 awards. Write to the above address for complete information.

3560—WALDEN SCHOOL (Scholarships)

74 S. San Gabriel Boulevard
Pasadena CA 91107
626/792-6166 ext. 12
FAX: 626/792-1335
Internet: http://www.waldenschool.net
AMOUNT: Varies
DEADLINE(S): FEB 1
FIELD(S): All fields of study

Financial aid for students already accepted and enrolled at this school in California which serves children from age 3 through 6th grade. Must demonstrate financial need.

20 awards yearly. Contact school for details.

3561—WAR ORPHANS SCHOLARSHIP

Box 340
Trenton NJ 08625-0340
609/530-6961 or 800/624-0508
FAX: 609/530-6970
AMOUNT: $250-$500
DEADLINE(S): March; October
FIELD(S): All
FIELD(S): All fields of study

Available to any child between the ages of 16 and 21 years of age domiciled in New Jersey for at least 12 years prior to the time of application who is a child of veteran resident who died or shall die of disease or disability resulting from such war or emergency.

3562—WASHINGTON CROSSING FOUNDATION

Box 503
Levittown PA 19058-0503
215/949-8841
Internet: http:www.gwcf.org
AMOUNT: $1,000-$20,000
DEADLINE(S): JAN 15
FIELD(S): All
FIELD(S): All fields of study

Available to high school senior, U.S. citizen, planning a career in government service. Essay, recommendation, transcript, test scores, resume. Scholarships of more than $1,000 paid over a four-year period. 8 awards per year.

3563—WASHINGTON HIGHER EDUCATION COORDINATING BOARD (American Indian Endowed Scholarship)

P.O. Box 43430
Olympia WA 98504-3430
360/753-7843
Internet: http://www.hecb.wa.gov/
AMOUNT: $1,000
DEADLINE(S): Varies
FIELD(S): All fields of study

For undergraduate and graduate American Indian students who are residents of Washington state. The purpose is to create an educational opportunity for American Indians to attend and graduate from higher education institutions in the state of Washington. Interest earned from the endowment is used each year to award scholarships to financially needy, resident, American Indian students.

Awards are renewable. Amounts dependent upon endowment earnings. Applications are available in the spring from above address.

3564—WASHINGTON HIGHER EDUCATION COORDINATING BOARD (Washington State Educational Opportunity Grant)

P.O. Box 43430
917 Lakeridge Way
Olympia WA 98504-3430
360/753-7846
Internet: http://www.hecb.wa.gov/
AMOUNT: $2,500
DEADLINE(S): MAR 31
FIELD(S): All fields of study

Open to financially needy, placebound residents of Washington state residing in one of 14 certain counties. Must be upper division students (juniors or seniors) planning to attend eligible Washington colleges/universities.

3565—WASHINGTON HIGHER EDUCATION COORDINATING BOARD (Washington State Need Grant)

P.O. Box 43430
Olympia WA 98504-3430
360/753-7800
Internet: http://www.hecb.wa.gov/
AMOUNT: Varies
DEADLINE(S): None specified
FIELD(S): All fields of study

Open to financially needy residents of Washington state who attend participating institutions.

For details, write to above address.

3566—WASHINGTON HIGHER EDUCATION COORDINATING BOARD (Washington Scholars)

P.O. Box 43430
Olympia WA 98504-3430
360/753-7800
Internet: http://www.hecb.wa.gov/
AMOUNT: Varies
DEADLINE(S): None specified
FIELD(S): All fields of study

For three high school seniors in each legislative district in Washington state. High school principals nominate the top one percent of the graduating senior class based upon academic accomplishments, leadership, and community service.

To encourage outstanding students to attend Washington public and independent colleges and universities. For details, write to above address.

3567—WASHINGTON INTERNATIONAL SCHOOL (Scholarships)

3100 Macomb Street NW
Washington DC 20008-3324
202/243-1815
FAX: 202/243-1807
E-mail: admiss@wis.edu
Internet: http://www.wis.edu
AMOUNT: Tuition assistance
DEADLINE(S): JAN 15 (admission); FEB 15 (financial aid)
FIELD(S): All fields of study (K-12)

Financial assistance towards tuition for this independent, coed day school which enrolls 685 students, nursery-12, in Washington DC. The students represent 90 different countries; faculty and staff come from 25 countries. Multi-lingual opportunities. Applicants must be currently enrolled or newly admitted.

Renewable. No merit-based or athletic scholarships—financial need must be documented. 10-12% of the student body receives financial assistance; all families must pay some portion of tuition and fees.

3568—WASHINGTON SCHOLARSHIP FUND (K-8 Scholarships)

1010 16th Street NW, Suite 500
Washington DC 20036
202/293-5560
FAX: 202/293-7893
Internet: http://www.wsf-dc.org
AMOUNT: Varies
DEADLINE(S): None
FIELD(S): All fields of study

Scholarships for needy students in grades K-8 who reside in Washington, DC, and who wish to attend private schools.

Contact Patrick Purtill, Executive Director, for an application.

3569—WASHINGTON HIGHER EDUCATION COORDINATING BOARD (Aid to Blind Students)

P.O. Box 43430
Olympia WA 98504-3430
360/753-7846
Internet: http://www.hecb.wa.gov/
AMOUNT: $800
DEADLINE(S): Varies
FIELD(S): All fields of study

Small grant is available to needy blind students who are Washington state residents. Recipients are reimbursed for special equipment, services, and books and supplies required because of their visual impairment.

Contact Program Manager for an application.

3570—WASHINGTON STATE PTA (Financial Grant Foundation)

2003 65th Avenue West
Tacoma WA 98466-6215
253/565-2153
FAX: 253/565-7753
E-mail: wapta@wastatepta.org
Internet: http://www.wastatepta.org
AMOUNT: $2,000 (4-year schools); $1,000 (2-year schools)
DEADLINE(S): MAR 1
FIELD(S): All fields of study

Open to Washington state residents. Grant program is designed to assist Washington state high school seniors and graduates who will be entering freshmen at an accredited college or university, community college, vo-tech school, or other accredited. Applicants need not be current graduates. Financial need is primary consideration.

Check with high school counselor or contact above location for complete information.

3571—WASHINGTON TRUST BANK (Herman Oscar Schumacher Scholarship Fund)

Trust Dept.
P.O. Box 2127
Spokane WA 99210-2127
509/353-4180
AMOUNT: $500
DEADLINE(S): OCT 1
FIELD(S): All fields of study

Open to male residents of Spokane County, Washington. Preference given to orphans. Must have completed at least one full year at an accredited school of higher education as a full-time student. Must demonstrate financial need.

50-55 awards annually. Renewable. Contact Trust Dept. for an application.

3572—AVISTA CORPORATION

1411 E. Mission MS18
P.O. Box 3727
Spokane WA 99220
509/495-3727
Internet: http://www.avistacorp.com
AMOUNT: Varies
DEADLINE(S): Varies
FIELD(S): All fields of study

Various scholarships offered to seniors graduating from high schools in Avista's service area.

3573—WELLESLEY COLLEGE (Fellowships for Wellesley Graduates & Graduating Seniors)

Center for Work & Service
106 Central Street
Wellesley MA 02481-8203
781/283-2352
FAX: 781/283-3674
E-mail: cws@wellesley.edu
Internet: http://www. wellesley.edu/CWS
AMOUNT: $1,200-$60,000
DEADLINE(S): JAN 3

FIELD(S): All fields of study

Numerous fellowship programs open to Wellesley College graduating seniors and Wellesley College graduates. For graduate study or research at institutions in the U.S. or abroad. Awards are based on merit and need.

3574—WEST VIRGINIA DIVISION OF VETERANS' AFFAIRS (War Orphans Education Program)

1321 Plaza East; Suite 101
Charleston WV 25301-1400
304/558-3661
FAX: 304/558-3662
E-mail: wvvetaff@aol.com

AMOUNT: $400-$500/year; Tuition waiver
DEADLINE(S): JUL 15; DEC 1
FIELD(S): All fields of study

Open to surviving children (aged 16-23) of deceased veterans whose active duty service in the U.S. armed forces involved hostile action. Student must have been a resident of West Virginia for one year prior to initial application. Death of parent must have occurred in active duty or (if subsequent to discharge) must have been a result of a disability incurred during such wartime service. Awards tenable for undergraduate study at any state-supported college/university.

Contact WV Veterans' Affairs for an application.

3575—WESTERN GOLF ASSOCIATION/ EVANS SCHOLARS FOUNDATION (Caddie Scholarships)

1 Briar Road
Golf IL 60029
847/724-4600

AMOUNT: Full tuition and housing
DEADLINE(S): NOV 1
FIELD(S): All fields of study

Open to U.S. high school seniors in the top 25% of their class who have served as a caddie at a WGA member club for at least 2 years. Outstanding personal character and financial need are considerations.

Applications are accepted after completion of junior year in high school (between July 1 and November 1) 200 awards per year; renewable for 4 years. Contact your local country club or write to address above for complete information.

3576—WESTERN INTERSTATE COMMISSION FOR HIGHER EDUCATION (WICHE Exchange Programs)

P.O. Box 9752
Boulder CO 80301-9752
303/541-0210
E-mail: info-sep@wiche.edu
Internet: http://www.wiche.edu

AMOUNT: Varies (out-of-state tuition waiver)
DEADLINE(S): Varies (according to school)
FIELD(S): All fields of study

Tuition assistance program allows undergraduate and graduate students in the following states to attend school in a different state from this list: AK, AR, CA, CO, HI, ID, MT, NV, NM, ND, OR, SD, UT, WA, WY. Eligibility requirements vary from school to school. Financial need NOT a factor.

3577—WESTOVER SCHOOL (Scholarships)

1237 Whittemore Road
P.O. Box 847
Middlebury CT 06762-0847
203/758-2423
FAX: 203/577-4588
E-mail: admission@westoverschool.org
Internet: http://www.westover school.org

AMOUNT: Tuition
DEADLINE(S): FEB 1
FIELD(S): All fields of study

Three awards are open to female high school students who wish to attend this private boarding/day school and meet all criteria for admission. One award is limited to residents of Maine who demonstrate financial need; another is for daughters of a teacher who is the primary family provider; the third is for students who wish to attend the Manhattan School of Music.

5-6 awards annually. Renewable.

3578—WESTRIDGE SCHOOL (Financial Aid)

324 Madeline Drive
Pasadena CA 91105-3309
626/799-1153
FAX: 626/799-9236
E-mail: HHopper@westridge.org
Internet: http://www.westridge.org

AMOUNT: Varies
DEADLINE(S): FEB 6
FIELD(S): All fields of study

Financial aid for students already accepted and enrolled at this independent school for girls, grades 4-12 in Pasadena, California. Must demonstrate financial need.

3579—WHEATLAND COMMUNITY SCHOLASTIC FUND, INC. (Scholarships)

1250 Oak Street
Wheatland WY 82001
Written Inquiry

AMOUNT: Varies
DEADLINE(S): Varies
FIELD(S): All fields of study

Available to graduates of Wheatland High School in Wyoming.

Write to Mr. Marvin L. Dunham at above address for an application.

3580—WHEATLAND R.E.A. (Scholarships)

P.O. Box 1209
2154 South Road
Wheatland WY 82201
Written Inquiry

AMOUNT: $200
DEADLINE(S): MAR 1
FIELD(S): All fields of study

Available to undergraduate students in any major, whose parents reside within the Wheatland REA service area and who plan to attend the University of Wyoming or a Wyoming community college.

2 awards annually. Write to above address for an application.

3581—WHITTIER COLLEGE (John Greenleaf Whittier Scholars Program)

P.O. Box 634
Whittier CA 90608
562/907-4238
FAX: 562/907-4870
E-mail: admission@whittier.edu
Internet: http://www.whittier.edu

AMOUNT: $6,000
DEADLINE(S): FEB 1
FIELD(S): All fields of study

GPA, SAT or ACT, and class rank are all considered in determining award eligibility and amount. Available for transfer admission only.

Write above address for complete information.

3582—WILDSHAW FOUNDATION (Scholarships/Tuition Assistance)

1555 Irving Street
San Francisco CA 94122-1908

PHONE/FAX: 415/546-1063
AMOUNT: $500-$3,000
DEADLINE(S): MAR 15
FIELD(S): All fields of study

Open to 6th-12th grade students to pursue college prep studies at Woodside International School. Must have minimum 3.3 GPA, good citizenship, financial need, and two letters of recommendation (unless student is already in attendance).

3583—WILLIAM COOPER FUND (Scholarships)

First Union National Bank-PCM
P.O. Box 9947
Savannah GA 31412
Written Inquiries only.
AMOUNT: $1,000-$1,500/year
DEADLINE(S): MAY 15
FIELD(S): All fields of study (except Law, Theology, and Medicine; Nursing acceptable)

Open to female residents of Georgia who are pursuing undergraduate study. Based on financial need and GPA. First preference is for women who live in Chatham County.

3584—WILLIAM LOEB MEMORIAL FUND (Educational Grants)

P.O. Box 9555
Manchester NH 03108-9555
603/668-4321 ext 506 or 800/562-8218
FAX: 603/668-8920
AMOUNT: $1,000
DEADLINE(S): MAR 15
FIELD(S): All
FIELD(S): All fields of study

Resident of NH for a minimum of 2 years; plan to attend a structural post-secondary program; demonstrate community involvement, independence and leadership potential.

3585—WILLIAM RANDOLPH HEARST FOUNDATION (U.S. Senate Youth Program)

90 New Montgomery Street, Suite 1212
San Francisco CA 94105-4504
415/543-4057 or 800/841-7048
FAX: 415/243-0760
E-mail: ussyp@hearstfdn.org
Internet: http://hearstfdn.org
AMOUNT: $2,000 + all-expenses-paid week in Washington
DEADLINE(S): Varies
FIELD(S): All fields of study

Open to any high school junior or senior who is serving as an elected student body officer at a U.S. high school. Student receives a week's stay in Washington as guest of the Senate, and the scholarship is presented during the visit. Student must become a candidate for a degree at an accredited U.S. college/university within two years of high school graduation, pledging to include courses in government or related subjects to his or her undergraduate program.

Two students are selected from each state and the District of Columbia. Contact your high school principal or the William Randolph Hearst Foundation for an application.

3586—WINDHAM FOUNDATION, INC. (Scholarships)

P.O. Box 70
Grafton VT 05146
802/843-2211
FAX: 802/843-2205
Internet: http://www.windham-foundation.org
AMOUNT: Varies
DEADLINE(S): APR 1
FIELD(S): All fields of study

Open ONLY to students who are RESIDENTS OF WINDHAM COUNTY, VERMONT. Tenable at recognized undergraduate colleges and universities.

Renewable up to 4 years. Contact Windham Foundation for an application.

3587—WINONA PUBLIC SCHOOLS (Community Education Scholarships)

1570 Homer Road
Winona MN 55987
507/454-1004
Internet: http://www.winonaschoolfoundation.com
AMOUNT: Varies
DEADLINE(S): None
FIELD(S): All fields of study

Scholarships for all ages in the community education section of this school district. Includes programs for pre-school, K-12, and adult education in a variety of fields (computers, languages, arts, etc.). Also parent training.

Write or call for complete information.

3588—WINSTON CHURCHILL MEMORIAL TRUST (Churchill Fellowships)

30 Balmain Crescent
Braddon Acton 2601 AUSTRALIA
02/6247-8333
Internet: http://www.churchilltrust.org/au
AMOUNT: A$15,000 (average)
DEADLINE(S): FEB 28
FIELD(S): All fields of study

Open to Australian residents over age 18 at any level of study who can demonstrate merit in a particular field and show the benefit to Australian society that would result from the proposed overseas study.

130 awards annually. Contact Trust for an application.

3589—WINSTON SCHOOL (Financial Aid)

5707 Royal Ln.
Dallas TX 75229
214/691-6950
FAX: 214/691-1509
E-mail: amy_smith@winston-school.org
Internet: http://www.winston-school.org
AMOUNT: Varies
DEADLINE(S): APR 20
FIELD(S): All fields of study

Grants are available to elementary and secondary students at this private day school. Must have a diagnosed learning disability and be of mid-range average to superior intelligence. Must be U.S. citizen and demonstrate financial need.

40 awards annually. Renewable. Contact Amy C. Smith for an application.

3590—WISCONSIN DEPARTMENT OF VETERANS AFFAIRS (Deceased Veterans' Survivors Economic Assistance Loan/Education Grants)

30 W. Mifflin Street
P.O. Box 7843
Madison WI 53703-7843
608/266-1311 or 800/947-8387
Internet: http://dva.state.wi.us/Ben_education.asp
AMOUNT: Varies
DEADLINE(S): None specified
FIELD(S): All areas of study

Open to surviving spouses (who have not remarried) of deceased eligible veterans and to the minor dependent children of the deceased veterans. Must be residents of Wisconsin at the time of application.

Approximately 5,700 grants and loans per year. Contact a Wisconsin veterans' service officer in your county of residence for complete information.

3591—WISCONSIN DEPARTMENT OF VETERANS AFFAIRS (Veterans Personal Loan/Education Grants)

30 W. Mifflin Street
P.O. Box 7843
Madison WI 53703-7843
608/266-1311 or 800/947-8387
Internet: http://dva.state.wi.us/Ben_education.asp

AMOUNT: $10,000 maximum
DEADLINE(S): None specified
FIELD(S): All areas of study

For veterans (as defined in Wisconsin Statute 45.35.5) who are living in Wisconsin at the time of application. There are limitations on income.

Approximately 5,700 grants and loans per year. Write for complete information.

3592—WISCONSIN HIGHER EDUCATION AIDS BOARD (Student Financial Aid Program)

30 W. Mifflin Street
P.O. Box 7885
Madison WI 53707
608/267-2206
FAX: 608/267-2808
Internet: http://dva.state.wi.us/

AMOUNT: Varies
DEADLINE(S): VAries
FIELD(S): All fields of study

Board administers a variety of state and federal programs available to Wisconsin residents enrolled at least half-time and who maintain satisfactory academic record. Most require demonstration of financial need.

Write for complete information.

3593—WOMEN OF THE EVANGELICAL LUTHERAN CHURCH IN AMERICA (The Amelia Kemp Scholarship)

8765 West Higgins Road
Chicago IL 60631-4189
800/638-3522 ext. 2730
FAX: 773/380-2419
E-mail: womnelca@elca.org
Internet: http://www.elca.org/wo/

AMOUNT: $5,000 max.
DEADLINE(S): MAR 1
FIELD(S): All fields of study

Assists women of color who are members of the ELCA studying in undergraduate, graduate, professional, or vocational courses of study leading to a career other than a church-certified profession.

3594—WOMEN OF THE EVANGELICAL LUTHERN CHURCH IN AMERICA (Arne Administrative Leadership Scholarship)

8765 West Higgins Road
Chicago IL 60631-4189
800/638-3552
Internet: http://www.elca.org/wo/index.html

AMOUNT: Varies
DEADLINE(S): FEB 15
FIELD(S): All
FIELD(S): All fields of study

Applicant must be a U.S. citizen, be a woman, hold membership in the Evangelical Lutheran Church of America, have completed a B.A. or B.S. degree or its equivalent, and submit academic records.

3595—WOMEN OF THE EVANGELICAL LUTHERAN CHURCH IN AMERICA (The Cronk Memorial-First Triennium Board-General-Mehring-Paepke-Piero/Wade/Wade-Edwin/Edna Robeck Scholarships)

8765 West Higgins Road
Chicago IL 60631-4189
800/638-3522 ext. 2730
FAX: 773/380-2419
E-mail: womnelca@elca.org
Internet: http://www.elca.org/wo/

AMOUNT: $2,000 max.
DEADLINE(S): MAR 1
FIELD(S): All fields of study

Assists women who are members of ELCA in undergraduate, graduate, professional, and vocational courses of study not leading to a church-certified profession.

3596—WOMEN'S OPPORTUNITY (Scholarship Fund)

418 East Rosser Avenue, #320
Bismarck, ND 58501
701/255-6240 or 800/255-6240
FAX: 701/255-1904
E-mail: ndcaws@btigate.com

AMOUNT: $200-$1,200
DEADLINE(S): MAY 15
FIELD(S): All fields of study

Applicant must be a woman, a resident of North Dakota and enrolled in a North Dakota college. Application accepted between March 28 and June 15 of each year. This scholarship requires an essay describing the applicants reasons for pursuing higher education. It also allows a "special circumstances" essay in which the applicant may detail special needs for assistance. This essay is optional.

3597—WOMEN'S OVERSEAS SERVICE LEAGUE (Scholarships)

P.O. Box 7124
Washington DC 20044-7124

AMOUNT: $500-$1,000
DEADLINE(S): MAR 1
FIELD(S): All

Financial assistance is available to women who have served overseas and are committed to a career in the military or public service. Must have completed 18 units with a GPA of 2.5.

3598—WOMEN'S SPORTS FOUNDATION (AQHA Female Equestrian Award)

Eisenhower Park
East Meadow NY 11554
800/227-3988
FAX: 516/542-4716

AMOUNT: $2,000
DEADLINE(S): SPRING
FIELD(S): All fields of study

Honors an outstanding female equestrian and rewards her for her accomplishments as a horsewoman and as an athlete. For female equestrians with national ranking and competition who exhibit leadership, sportsmanship, and commitment to the sport and its athletes.

1 award annually. Awarded in March. See Web site or write to above address for details.

3599—WOMEN'S SPORTS FOUNDATION (Linda Riddle/SMGA Endowed, Gart Sports Sportmart, & Mervyn's WSF College Scholarships)

Eisenhower Park
East Meadow NY 11554
800/227-3988
FAX: 516/542-4716
E-mail: WoSport@aol.com
Internet: http://www.lifetimetv.com/WoSport

AMOUNT: $1,500 (Linda); $5,000 (Gart); $1,000 (Mervyn's)
DEADLINE(S): Varies
FIELD(S): All fields of study

These scholarships provide female high school student-athletes with a means to continue their athletic participation as well as their college education. For Linda Riddle award, must be high school senior (athlete) who will be pursuing full-time course of study at 2- or 4-year accredited school in the Fall. For Gart Sports & Mervyn's awards, must be high school senior who has participated in one or more interscholastic sports and is attending college in the Fall.

3-5 Linda Riddle, 8 Gart Sports, & 100 Mervyn's awards annually. See Web site or write to above address for details.

3600—WOMEN'S SPORTS FOUNDATION (Ocean Spray Travel & Training Grants)

Eisenhower Park
East Meadow NY 11554
800/227-3988
FAX: 516/542-4716
E-mail: WoSport@aol.com
Internet: http://www.lifetimetv.com/WoSport

AMOUNT: Up to $1,500 (individual); up to $3,000 (team)
DEADLINE(S): NOV 15
FIELD(S): All fields of study

Provides financial assistance to aspiring female athletes and teams for coaching, specialized training, equipment, and/or travel. Must have regional and/or national ranking or successful competitive records, and have the potential to achieve higher performance levels and rankings. High school and college/university varsity and/or rec. teams are NOT eligible.

20 individual grants and 8 team grants annually. Awards made in February. See Web site or write to above address for details.

3601—WOMEN'S WESTERN GOLF FOUNDATION (Grants)

393 Ramsay Road
Deerfield IL 60015
Internet: http://www.wwga.org

AMOUNT: $2,000/year
DEADLINE(S): MAR 1
FIELD(S): All fields of study

Open to female high school seniors with academic excellence, financial need, involvement in golf (skill not criterion), and excellence of character. Must be U.S. citizen planning to attend a four-year accredited college/university.

15-20 four-year awards annually.

3602—WORLD BANK GROUP (Margaret McNamara Memorial Fund)

Room G-1000
1818 H. Street NW
Washington, DC 20433
202/473-8751
Amount: $6,000

DEADLINE(S): FEB 1
FIELD(S): All
FIELD(S): All fields of study

This fund is for women from developing countries during their studies in the U.S.. Must be planning to return to your native country within 2 years of receiving the grant.

3603—WORLD OF KNOWLEDGE (International Programs)

4037 Metric Drive #120
Winter Park FL 32793
888/953-7737
E-mail: knowledgetoall@aol.com
Internet: http://www.worldofknowledge.org

AMOUNT: Varies
DEADLINE(S): Varies
FIELD(S): All fields of study

Open to undergraduate and graduate international students who will be attending college in the United States. Programs vary from year to year; scholarships sometimes available.

See Web site for "News You Can Use" and current programs.

3604—WYOMING ASSOCIATION OF FUTURE HOMEMAKERS OF AMERICA (FHA/HERO Scholarship)

LCCC-B105
1400 E. College Drive
Cheyenne WY 82007
307/778-4312

AMOUNT: $400
DEADLINE(S): Varies
FIELD(S): All fields of study

Available to high school seniors, college freshmen, and college sophomores who are/were members of FHA/HERO in Wyoming or who completed one Family and Consumer Sciences course at a Wyoming high school. Applicants must submit a 100-word essay relating their FHA/HERO membership to their declared college major. May be used at any Wyoming institution of postsecondary education.

3605—WYOMING DEPARTMENT OF CORRECTIONS (Wayne Martinez Memorial Scholarships)

P.O. Box 393
Rawlins WY 82301
307/324-2622

AMOUNT: Varies
DEADLINE(S): Varies
FIELD(S): All fields of study

Available to employees and children of employees of the Wyoming Department of Corrections.

Write to above address, attention: application request, or call above number for an application.

3606—WYOMING DEPARTMENT OF EDUCATION (Douvas Memorial Scholarship)

2300 Capitol Avenue
Hathaway Building
Cheyenne WY 82002
Internet: http://www.k12.wy.us/awards/index.html

AMOUNT: $500
DEADLINE(S): Varies
FIELD(S): All fields of study

Available to high school seniors or others between the ages of 18 and 22 who are first-generation Americans and Wyoming residents. May be used at any Wyoming public institution of higher education.

1 award annually. Write to Jim Lendino at above address for an application.

3607—WYOMING DEPARTMENT OF VETERANS AFFAIRS (War Orphans Scholarships)

2360 E. Pershing Boulevard
Cheyenne WY 82001
Written Inquiry

AMOUNT: Tuition and mandatory fees
DEADLINE(S): Varies
FIELD(S): All fields of study

Available to a limited number of orphans of Wyoming war veterans and children of Wyoming service people who are listed officially in the military records of the U.S. as being a prisoner of war or missing in action as a result of the Korean or Vietnam conflicts. Eligibility will be verified by the Department of Veterans Affairs.

Write to above address for an application.

3608—WYOMING FARM BUREAU FEDERATION (Dodge Merit Award)

Box 1348
Laramie WY 82073
Written Inquiry
AMOUNT: $500
DEADLINE(S): MAR 1
FIELD(S): All fields of study

Available to a student from a Wyoming Farm Bureau family. May be used at any public institution of postsecondary education in Wyoming.

2 awards annually. Applications are available from each county Farm Bureau or from the above address.

3609—WYOMING FEDERATION OF WOMEN'S CLUBS (Mary N. Brooks Education Fund-Men)

316 Hwy. 14A East
Lovell WY 82431
307/548-2860
AMOUNT: $500
DEADLINE(S): MAR 1
FIELD(S): All fields of study

Available to a boy who is a recent graduate of a Wyoming high school. Award may be used at any Wyoming institution of postsecondary education.

3610—WYOMING FEDERATION OF WOMEN'S CLUBS (Mary N. Brooks Education Fund-Daughters & Granddaughters)

316 Hwy. 14A East
Lovell WY 82431
307/548-2860
AMOUNT: $500
DEADLINE(S): MAR 1
FIELD(S): All fields of study

Available to a daughter or granddaughter of WFWC member in good standing attending any Wyoming institution of higher education.

Contact Mrs. Delsa H. Asay at above address for an application.

3611—WYOMING STUDENT LOAN CORPORATION (Leadership Scholarship)

P.O. Box 209
Cheyenne WY 82003-0209
Written Inquiry
AMOUNT: $500/semester
DEADLINE(S): MAR 15
FIELD(S): All fields of study

For Wyoming residents who are first-year, first-time students attending Wyoming postsecondary institutions. Applicants must submit a letter of recommendation, an official transcript, and a typed, 500-word autobiographical essay. Must also submit a resume or a list of activity information. Minimum 2.5 GPA required for renewal.

6 awards annually. Renewable up to eight semesters of undergraduate work. Write to the WSLC Scholarship Committee for an application.

3612—XEROX CANADA SCHOLARSHIP

5163 Duke Street
Halifax NS B3J3J6 CANADA
902/494-8130
FAX: 902/425-2987
E-mail: ann@nscad@ns.ca
Amount: $800
DEADLINE(S): JAN 1
FIELD(S): All
FIELD(S): All fields of study

Fall only; A $800 scholarship is awarded each Fall semester from a fund established by Xerox Canada. Eligibility is restricted to senior level students (60+ credits) who have completed two full time semesters at NSCAD and worked with electronic technology in their program of studies.

3613—YORK HOUSE SCHOOL (Scholarships)

4176 Alexandra Street
Vancouver BC V6J 2V6 CANADA
604/736-6551
FAX: 604/736-6530
E-mail: admissions@yorkhouse.bc.ca
Internet: http://www.yorkhouse.bc.ca
AMOUNT: Full tuition
DEADLINE(S): Varies
FIELD(S): All fields of study

Financial aid for students accepted at this independent girls' day school in Vancouver, British Columbia, Canada. Must demonstrate financial need. School program is for K-12; scholarships are for students in 8th grade through high school. For Canadian citizens or landed immigrants.

20 awards yearly. Renewable. Contact school for details.

3614—YOUNG AMERICAN BOWLING ALLIANCE (Alberta E. Crowe Star of Tomorrow Scholarship)

5301 S. 76th Street
Greendale WI 53129
Written Inquiry
AMOUNT: $1,000 per year
DEADLINE(S): Varies
FIELD(S): Any field of study

Open to women who are amateur bowlers and members in good standing with WIBC or YABA. Must be at most age 22 or younger preceding Jan. 15. Must be a senior in high school or attending college.

Send #10 SASE to above address for complete information.

3615—YOUNG AMERICAN BOWLING ALLIANCE (Al Thompson Junior Bowler Scholarship)

P.O. Box 5118
Akron OH 44334
Written Inquiry
AMOUNT: $1,500/$1,000
DEADLINE(S): JUN 15
FIELD(S): All fields of study

Open to high school seniors who are good standing members with ABC, YABA or WIBC. Students must carry at least a 2.5 GPA. Applicant must also carry a current season average of 170 (females) and 190 (Males).

Write to the above address for complete information.

3616—YOUNG AMERICAN BOWLING ALLIANCE (Chuck Hall Star of Tomorrow Scholarship)

5301 S. 76th Street
Greendale WI 53129
Written Inquiry
AMOUNT: $1,000
DEADLINE(S): JAN 15
FIELD(S): Any field of study

Open to male students who are amateur bowlers and members in good standing with ABC or YABA. Students must be age 21 or younger before deadline. Must be a senior in high school or attending college with at least a 2.5 GPA.

Send #10 SASE to above address for complete information.

3617—YOUTH FOR UNDERSTANDING INTERNATIONAL EXCHANGE (Congress Bundestag Youth Exchange Program)

3501 Newark Street NW
Washington DC 20016-3199
800/TEENAGE
Internet: http://www.usagermany scholarship.org
AMOUNT: Partial program expenses
DEADLINE(S): DEC 1
FIELD(S): All fields of study

This full-year scholarship to study in Germany is open to high school sophomores and juniors with a minimum 3.0 GPA. Students attend a German high school and live with a host family. There is no language requirement. Must be U.S. citizen.

300 awards annually. See Web site or contact YFU for an application.

3618—CDS INTERNATIONAL (Congress-Bundestag Senior Program)

871 United Nations Plaza
New York NY 10017-1814
212/497-3500
FAX: 212/497-3535
Internet: http://www.cdsintl.org/cbyxintro.html
AMOUNT: Program expenses
DEADLINE(S): DEC 15
FIELD(S): All fields of study

This program is intended primarily for young adults in business, technical, vocational, and agricultural fields. 60 Americans participated in program year 2000-2001. The 12-month program begins in late July, 2000 and consists of 2 months intensive German, 4 months classroom instruction at a German University of Applied Sciences, 5 months internship in career field.

3619—YOUTH FOR UNDERSTANDING INTERNATIONAL EXCHANGE (Face of America)

3501 Newark St NW
Washington DC 20016-3199
800/TEENAGE
Internet: http://www.yfu.org
AMOUNT: Domestic and international travel, insurance, + $150 spending money
DEADLINE(S): Varies
FIELD(S): All fields of study

A nationwide competition for 40 minority high school students to spend the summer in select countries living with a host family. Students must have a minimum 2.0 GPA, and family income must not exceed $55,000. Recipients must pay $650 program contribution.

See Web site or contact YFU for an application.

3620—YOUTH FOR UNDERSTANDING INTERNATIONAL EXCHANGE (Finland-U.S. Senate Youth Exchange)

3501 Newark Street NW
Washington DC 20016-3199
800/TEENAGE
Internet: http://www.yfu.org
AMOUNT: Partial program expenses
DEADLINE(S): OCT
FIELD(S): All fields of study

Merit scholarships are open to high school juniors for study in Finland during the summer months. Must have a minimum 3.2 GPA and be a U.S. citizen. Must pay $500 toward program.

3621—YOUTH FOR UNDERSTANDING INTERNATIONAL EXCHANGE (Future Homemakers of America/Kikkoman Corporation Scholarships)

3501 Newark Street NW
Washington DC 20016-3199
800/TEENAGE
Internet: http://www.yfu.org
AMOUNT: Partial program expenses
DEADLINE(S): DEC
FIELD(S): All fields of study

Merit scholarships are open to members of Future Homemakers of America (in partnership with Kikkoman Corporation) who are high school students wishing to go to Japan for a summer (6 weeks).

20 awards annually. See Web site or contact YFU for an application.

3622—YOUTH FOR UNDERSTANDING INTERNATIONAL EXCHANGE (Mazda National Scholarships)

3501 Newark Street NW
Washington DC 20016-3199
800/TEENAGE
Internet: http://www.yfu.org
AMOUNT: Partial program expenses
DEADLINE(S): NOV
FIELD(S): All fields of study

Merit scholarships are open to U.S. high school students for summer program in Japan living with a host family. Must have a minimum 2.0 GPA.

See Web site or contact YFU for an application.

3623—YOUTH FOR UNDERSTANDING INTERNATIONAL EXCHANGE (Scholarship Programs)

3501 Newark Street NW
Washington DC 20016-3199
800/TEENAGE
Internet: http://www.yfu.org
AMOUNT: Program expenses
DEADLINE(S): OCT (Applications available then. Deadline is JAN.)
FIELD(S): All fields of study

Scholarships for high school students who wish to go overseas for a summer or for a school year. Some are corporate-sponsored and for dependents of employees of 60+ corporations, some are for specific countries only, and some are for students from specific states or cities/counties.

Parents of interested students should check with their personnel office at work to see if their firm is a participant. Call above number for brochure.

3624—YOUTH FOUNDATION, INC. (Study-Abroad Scholarships)

36 West 44th Street
New York NY 10036
Written Inquiry
AMOUNT: Varies
DEADLINE(S): Varies
FIELD(S): All areas of study

This organization offers scholarships for an undergraduate's Junior Year Abroad. Selection is based on character, need, scholastic achievement, objective, motivation, potential for leaderships, and good citizenship.

Write for details.

3625—ZETA PHI BETA SORORITY EDUCATIONAL FOUNDATION (Deborah Partridge Wolfe International Fellowship for U.S. Students)

1734 New Hampshire Avenue NW
Washington DC 20009
Internet: www.zpb1920.org
AMOUNT: $500-$1,000
DEADLINE(S): FEB 1
FIELD(S): All fields of study

Open to graduate and undergraduate U.S. students planning to study abroad. Award is for full-time study for one academic year (Fall-Spring) and is paid directly to recipient. Must submit documented proof of academic study and plan of program with signature of school administrator or Program Director.

3626—ZETA PHI BETA SORORITY EDUCATIONAL FOUNDATION (Deborah Partridge Wolfe International Fellowship for Non-U.S. Students)

1734 New Hampshire Avenue NW
Washington DC 20009
Internet: http://www.zpb1920.org
AMOUNT: $500-$1,000
DEADLINE(S): FEB 1
FIELD(S): All fields of study

Open to graduate and undergraduate foreign students planning to study in the U.S. Award is for full-time study for one academic year (Fall-Spring) and is paid directly to recipient. Must submit documented proof of academic study and plan of program with signature of school administrator or Program Director.

Send self-addressed, stamped envelope (or self-addressed envelope with international reply coupons) to above address between September 1 and December 15 for an application.

3627—ZETA PHI BETA SORORITY EDUCATIONAL FOUNDATION (General Undergraduate Scholarships)

1734 New Hampshire Avenue NW
Washington DC 20009
Internet: http://www.zpb1920.org/
AMOUNT: $500-$1,000
DEADLINE(S): FEB 1
FIELD(S): All fields of study

Open to undergraduate college students and graduating high school seniors planning to enter college in the Fall. Award is for full-time study for one academic year (Fall-Spring) and is paid directly to college/university to be applied for tuition or appropriate fees. Must submit proof of enrollment/university acceptance.

Send self-addressed, stamped envelope to above address between September 1 and December 15 for an application.

LAST-MINUTE ADDITIONS

3627A—AMERICAN INDIAN COMMITTEE (American Indian Scholarship)

Mary-Mac Bernett,
National Vice Chairman
Route 3 Box 530,
Cynthiana, KY 41031
AMOUNT: Varies
DEADLINE: NOV 1; JUL 1
FIELDS: All

Must be Native American/American Indian in need of financial assistance for higher education. A minimum grade point average of at least 2.75 is required of candidates.

3627B—ATTACHÉ OF THE FLEMISH COMMUNITY (Flemish Community Fellowships)

c/o Embassy of Belgium
3330 Garfield Street, NW
Washington, DC 20008
202/625-5850
AMOUNT: Monthly stipend of 26.200 Belgian Franks + tuition fees
DEADLINE: JAN
FIELDS: Art, music, humanities, social and political sciences, law, economics, sciences and medicine.

Study abroad opportunity for U.S. citizen who has graduated college. This fellowship is based upon the applicant's record of academic excellence for study or research in Flanders, Belgium.

3627C—BECA FOUNDATION (Pepperdine University Scholarships)

830 E. Grand Avenue, Suite B
Escondido CA 92025
760/471-8246
FAX: 760/471-8176
AMOUNT: Up to $5,000 each academic year
DEADLINE(S): MAR 1
FIELD(S): General (any academic major)

Open to spring San Diego high school students who plan to attend Pepperdine University in the fall. Renewable each academic year and contigent upon full-time enrollment at Pepperdine University and satisfactory academic progress.

Send self-addressed, stamped envelope to BECA for an application.

3627D—DAVID BIRENBAUM SCHOLARSHIP FUND

International Society for Clinical Laboratory Technology (Scholarship)
917 Locust Street, Suite 1100
St. Louis, MO 63101-1419
314/241-1445
FAX: 314/241-1449
Internet: http://www.aab.org/scholarship.htm
AMOUNT: Varies
DEADLINE: APR 1
FIELDS: Science

One-time award for students who have graduated from an accredited high school or equivalent. Applicant eligibility is limited to AAB regular members and associate members in good standing, their spouses and their children. Apply online.

3627E—IRON & STEEL SOCIETY FOUNDATION SCHOLARSHIPS

186 Thorn Hill Road
Warrendale, PA 15086-7528
724/776-1535
AMOUNT: $2000
DEADLINE: APR
FIELDS: Science

Applicant should have a genuine interest in a career in ferrous-related industries as demonstrated by internship, co-op or related experiences and/or demonstrable plans to pursue such experience during college.

3627F—UNITED STATES NAVAL SEA CADET CORPS (Stockholm Scholarship Program)

2300 Wilson Boulevard
Arlington, VA 22201-3308
703-243-6910
FAX: 703-243-3985; E-mail: mford@navyleague.org
Internet: http://resources.seacadets.org
AMOUNT: Varies
DEADLINE: MAY 15
FIELDS: All

Cadets, and former cadets, applying for scholarships must have been a member of NSCC for at least two years; have attained, at a minimum, the rate of NSCC E-3; be recommended by his/her unit commanding officer, the President/NSCC Committee Chairman of the sponsoring organization, and by the appropriate school authority (principal/counselor, etc.); present evidence of academic excellence ("B" average or better, SAT/ACT scores, class standing).

3627G—WOMEN'S OVERSEAS SERVICE LEAGUE (Scholarships)

P.O. Box 7124
Washington, DC 20044-7124
AMOUNT: $500-$1,000
DEADLINE: MAR 1
FIELDS: All

Financial assistance is available to women who have served overseas and are committed to a career in the military or public service. Must have completed 18 units with a GPA of 2.5.

3627H—ZONTA INTERNATIONAL FOUNDATION (Amelia Earhart Fellowship Award)

557 W. Randolph Street
Chicago, IL 60661-2206
312/930-5848
FAX: 312/930-0951
E-mail: zontafdtn@zonta.org
Internet: www.zonta.org
AMOUNT: $6,000
DEADLINE: NOV 15
FIELDS: Science

Awards grants to women who are pursuing advanced degrees in aerospace-related sciences and engineering. The Foundation board determines the number of grants awarded each year based on contributions received.

Helpful Publications

3628—"ACE" ANY TEST

AUTHOR-Ron Fry; ISBN 1-56414-460-7
Career Press/New Page Books
3 Tice Road
P.O. Box 687
Franklin Lakes NJ 07417
800/227-3371
FAX: 201/848-1727
Internet: http://www.careerpress.com
COST-$8.99

Walks test-takers through successful test preparation, including reading for maximum retention, researching the teacher's test-giving history, and "psyching up" for test day. 128 pages.

3629—101 GREAT ANSWERS TO THE TOUGHEST INTERVIEW QUESTIONS

AUTHOR-Ron Fry; ISBN 1-56414-464-X
Career Press/New Page Books
3 Tice Road
P.O. Box 687
Franklin Lakes NJ 07417
800/227-3371
FAX: 201/848-1727
Internet: http://www.careerpress.com
COST-$11.99

For part-time job seekers or those seeking permanent careers, this guide includes overview of the interviewing process and covers the full range of possible interview topics-everything from "Why are you thinking of leaving your current job?" to "When can you start?" 224 pages.

3630—101 GREAT RESUMES

AUTHOR-Editors; ISBN 1-56414-201-9
Career Press/New Page Books
3 Tice Road
P.O. Box 687
Franklin Lakes NJ 07417
800/227-3371
FAX: 201/848-1727
Internet: http://www.careerpress.com
COST-$9.99

Covers the greatest range of formats, personal situations, and careers. 216 pages.

3631—270 WAYS TO PUT YOUR TALENT TO WORK IN THE HEALTH FIELD

AUTHOR-
National Health Council
1730 M Street, Suite 500
Washington DC 20036
202/785-3910
FAX: 202/785-5923
E-mail: info@nationalhealthcouncil.org
Internet: http://www.nationalhealth council.org
COST-$15.00

A resource book containing career information on various health fields.

3632—A CAREER GUIDE TO MUSIC EDUCATION

AUTHOR-Barbara Payne
The National Association for Music Education
1806 Robert Fulton Drive
Reston VA 20191
800/336-3768 or 703/860-4000
Internet: http://www.menc.org
COST-Free (available only on Internet at above Web site)

A comprehensive guide to careers in music, how to find a job, prepare a resume, etc.

3633—A TEACHER'S GUIDE TO FELLOWSHIPS AND AWARDS

AUTHOR-
Massachusetts Dept. of Education
350 Main Street
Malden MA 02148-5123
781/388-3000
Internet: http://www.doe.mass.edu
COST-Free

Lists financial aid sources for teachers in many fields. Available on Web site: www.doe. mass. edu.

3634—ACADEMIC YEAR ABROAD

AUTHOR-ISBN 0-87206-247-3
Institute of International Education
IIE Books
P.O. Box 371
Annapolis Junction MD 20701-0371
800/445-0443 or 301/617-7804
FAX: 301/206-9789
E-mail: iiebooks@pmds.com
Internet: http://www.iie.org
COST-$44.95

Provides information on nearly 2,700 academic-year and semester-length programs offered by U.S. and foreign universities and private organizations. 728 pages.

3635—ADVENTURE CAREERS

AUTHOR-Alex Hiam & Susan Angle; ISBN 1-56414-175-6
Career Press/New Page Books
3 Tice Road
P.O. Box 687
Franklin Lakes NJ 07417
800/227-3371
FAX: 201/848-1727
Internet: http://www.careerpress.com
COST-$11.99

This comprehensive source for information about completely different and decidedly unroutine career paths is packed with practical how-to's, lists of contacts, and first-hand experiences. 288 pages.

3636—AFL-CIO UNION-SPONSORED SCHOLARSHIPS AND AID

AUTHOR-AFL-CIO Department of Education
AFL-CIO
815 16th Street NW
Washington DC 20006
202/637-5058
Internet: http://www.aflcio.org/scholarships/scholar
COST-Free on the Web site

Comprehensive guide for union members and their dependent children. Describes local, national, and international union-sponsored scholarship programs. Includes a bibliography of other financial aid sources.

3637—ANIMATION SCHOOL DIRECTORY

AUTHOR-AWN
Animation World Network, Inc.
6525 Sunset Boulevard
Garden Suite 10
Hollywood CA 90028
323/606-4200
FAX: 323/466-6619
E-mail: sales@awn.com
Internet: http://www.awn.com
COST-$24.99

Reference guide to over 400 animation-related schools and educational institutions from 34 different countries. Free version is available online; however, the deluxe edition contains special information, such as interviews, articles, links, and recommendations. May order online.

3638—ANNUAL REGISTER OF GRANT SUPPORT

AUTHOR-Reed Reference Publishing
Information Today, Inc.
143 Old Marlton Pike
Medford NJ 08055
800/300-9868
Internet: http://www.infotoday.com
COST-$299.00

Annual reference book found in most major libraries. Details thousands of grants for research that are available to individuals and organizations.

3639—ART CALENDAR

AUTHOR-Art Calendar
Art Calendar
P.O. Box 2675
Salisbury MD 21802
FAX: 410/749-9626
E-mail:info@artcalendar.com
Internet: http://www.artcalendar.com
COST-$33.00/one year

Monthly publication contains articles of interest to artists including listings of grants, fellowships, exhibits, etc. Annual edition lists opportunities without deadlines. Access Web site for more information.

3640—INTERNATIONAL AWARDS

AUTHOR-ACU; ISBN 0-85143-176-3
Association of Commonwealth Universities
36 Gordon Sq.
London WC1H OPF United Kingdom
(0) 20 7380 6700
E-mail:info@acu.ac.uk
Internet: http://www.acu.ac.uk
COST-40 pounds sterling (43 by airmail)

An annual with 950 detailed entries of scholarships, grants, loans, etc. for Commonwealth students wishing to study for a first degree at a Commonwealth university outside their own country. 396 pages.

3641—BARRON'S GUIDE TO LAW SCHOOLS

AUTHOR-Barron's Educational Series, Inc.; ISBN 0-8120-9558-8
Barron's Educational Series Inc.
250 Wireless Boulevard
Hauppauge NY 11788
800/645-3476
Internet: http://www.barronseduc.com
COST-$15.26

Comprehensive guide covering more than 200 ABA-approved American law schools. Advice on attending law school.

3642—BETTER GRAMMAR IN 30 MINUTES A DAY

AUTHOR-Constance Immel & Florence Sacks; ISBN 1-56414-204-3
Career Press/New Page Books
3 Tice Road
P.O. Box 687
Franklin Lakes NJ 07417
800/227-3371
FAX: 201/848-1727
Internet: http://www.careerpress.com
COST-$10.99

Here's help for anyone who has something to say or write but has difficulty doing so in standard English. It features thorough coverage of key areas of grammar, clear explanations with a minimum of grammatical terms, and in an abundant variety of exercises. 252 pages.

3643—BETTER SENTENCE WRITING IN 30 MINUTES A DAY

AUTHOR-Dianna Campbell; ISBN 1-56414-203-5
Career Press/New Page Books
3 Tice Road
P.O. Box 687
Franklin Lakes NJ 07417
800/227-3371
FAX: 201/848-1727
Internet: http://www.careerpress.com
COST-$10.99

Features clear discussions of rules and strategies for good writing, concise explanations with a minimum of grammatical terms, and an abundant variety of exercises, from filling-in-the-blanks to joining short sentences into longer and more graceful combinations. 224 pages.

3644—BETTER SPELLING IN 30 MINUTES A DAY

AUTHOR-Harry H. Crosby & Robert W. Emery; ISBN 1-56414-202-7
Career Press/New Page Books
3 Tice Road
P.O. Box 687
Franklin Lakes NJ 07417
800/227-3371
FAX: 201/848-1727
Internet: http://www.careerpress.com
COST-$10.99

Features diagnostic exercises that allow readers to identify their weak spelling areas, thorough coverage of key areas of phonics, a focus on the most commonly misspelled words, ample opportunity for proofreading practice, and clear explanations with a minimum of difficult terms. 224 pages.

3645—BETTER VOCABULARY IN 30 MINUTES A DAY

AUTHOR-Edie Schwager; ISBN 1-56414-247-7
Career Press/New Page Books
3 Tice Road
P.O. Box 687
Franklin Lakes NJ 07417
800/227-3371
FAX: 201/848-1727
Internet: http://www.careerpress.com
COST-$10.99

Offers a comprehensive method for adding a more impressive list of words to your everyday speech and learning how to use them effortlessly and accurately. 192 pages.

3646—BUILDING A GREAT RESUME

AUTHOR-Kate Wendleton; ISBN 1-56414-433-X
Career Press/New Page Books
3 Tice Road
P.O. Box 687
Franklin Lakes NJ 07417
800/227-3371
FAX: 201/848-1727
Internet: http://www.careerpress.com
COST-$12.99

Learn how to turn your resume into a marketing piece that presents you just the way you want a prospective employer to see you. Includes scores of sample resumes and case studies as it takes you through the entire process of developing a resume that's right for you. 192 pages.

3647—CARE AND FEEDING OF YOUR BRAIN

AUTHOR-Kenneth Giuffre, MD; ISBN 1-56414-380-5
Career Press/New Page Books
3 Tice Road
P.O. Box 687
Franklin Lakes NJ 07417
800/227-3371
FAX: 201/848-1727
Internet: http://www.newpagebooks.com
COST-$16.99

Explains why many functions of the brain that are seemingly uncontrollable and unpredictable are in fact readily affected by the things we eat, drink, smoke, and swallow. Describes how brain and body work together on a physical level and how our diet and environment can be altered to improve how we think and what we feel. 224 pages.

3648—CAREER GUIDE FOR SINGERS

AUTHOR-Mary McDonald
OPERA America
1156 15th Street NW, Suite 810
Washington DC 20005-1704
202/293-4466
FAX: 202/393-0735
E-mail: Frontdesk@operaam.org
Internet: http://www.operaam.org
COST-$70.00 non-members; $40.00 members

Directory of producing organizations, institutes, and workshops for advanced training, degree-granting educational institutions with opera/performance degrees, and major opera workshops, competitions, and grants. A resource for aspiring artists seeking opportunities in the opera field. Entries include casting policies, repertoire, and auditiion/application procedures, along with other pertinent information.

3649—CAREERS WITHOUT COLLEGE: CARS

AUTHOR-ISBN: 0-7689-0265-7
Peterson's, Inc.
Princeton Pike Corporate Center
200 Lenox Drive
Lawrenceville NJ 08648
609/896-1800
Internet: http://www.petersons.com
COST-$9.95

Helps you gear up for your career in the auto industry. Find out about skills and training, salary, benefits, promotions, and more. Features interviews with experts in the field. Learn how to make it as a CAD Specialist, Car Salesperson, Service Technician, Claims Representative, or Electronics Specialist. 142 pages.

3650—CATALOG OF MATERIALS FOR EARLY EDUCATION

AUTHOR-David S. Ward, Publisher
Early Advantage
270 Monroe Turnpike
P.O. Box 4063
Monroe CT 06468
888/248-0480
FAX: 800/301-9268
Internet: http://www.early-advantage.com
COST-Free

Various books, videos, and software are available for parents of young children.

3651—CFKR CAREER MATERIALS CATALOG

AUTHOR-CFKR
CFKR Career Materials
11860 Kemper Road, #7
Auburn CA 95603
800/525-5626 or 530/889-2357
FAX: 800/770-0433
E-mail:info@cfkr.com
Internet: http://www.cfkr.com
COST-Free

A catalog of printed materials, software, and videotapes covering career planning, college financing, and college test preparation. Includes materials applicable to all ages-from the primary grades through graduate school.

3652—CHRONICLE FINANCIAL AID GUIDE

AUTHOR-CGP; ISBN 1-55631-298-9
Chronicle Guidance Publications, Inc.
66 Aurora Street
Moravia NY 13118-3576
800/899-0454
FAX: 315/497-3359
E-mail: customerservice@ChronicleGuidance.com
Internet: http://www.ChronicleGuidance.com
COST-$24.98 + shipping/handling

Contains information about all kinds of financial aid programs. 424 pages.

3653—CHRONICLE FOUR-YEAR COLLEGE DATABOOK

AUTHOR-CGP; ISBN 1-55631-297-0
Chronicle Guidance Publications, Inc.
66 Aurora Street
Moravia NY 13118-3576
800/899-0454
FAX: 315/497-3359
E-mail: customerservice@ChronicleGuidance.com
Internet: http://www.ChronicleGuidance.com
COST-$24.99 + shipping/handling

Includes 2,235 colleges/universities and over 790 undergraduate, graduate, and professional school majors classified by CIP majors. Chart format gives data on institutions, and one section guides users through college decision process. 522 pages.

3654—CHRONICLE TWO-YEAR COLLEGE DATABOOK

AUTHOR-CGP; ISBN 1-55631-296-2
Chronicle Guidance Publications, Inc.
66 Aurora Street
Moravia NY 13118-3576
800/899-0454
FAX: 315/497-3359
E-mail: customerservice@ChronicleGuidance.com
Internet: http://www.ChronicleGuidance.com
COST-$24.97 + shipping/handling

Includes 2,335 colleges and over 760 certificate/diploma, associate, and transfer programs classified by CIP majors. Chart format gives data on institutions, and one section guides users through college decision process. 404 pages.

3655—CHRONICLE VOCATIONAL SCHOOL MANUAL

AUTHOR-CGP; ISBN 1-55631-295-4
Chronicle Guidance Publications, Inc.
66 Aurora Street
Moravia NY 13118-3576
800/899-0454
FAX: 315/497-3359
E-mail: customerservice@ChronicleGuidance.com
Internet: http://www.ChronicleGuidance.com
COST-$24.96 + shipping/handling

Includes 3,055 accredited vocational and technical schools and over 930 programs of study. Chart format gives data on institutions, and there are extensive cross-references. 243 pages.

3656—COLLEGE DEGREES BY MAIL & INTERNET

AUTHOR-John Bear, Ph.D. & Mariah Bear, M.A.; ISBN: 1-58008-217-3
Ten Speed Press
P.O. Box 7123
Berkeley CA 94707
800/841-BOOK or 510/559-1600
FAX: 510/559-1629
E-mail: order@tenspeed.com
Internet: http://www.tenspeed.com
COST-$14.95

With the rise of Internet-based education, distance learning has never been hotter. You really can earn a fully accredited degree (undergraduate or graduate) in a wide range of fields without ever leaving your home. This guide is updated every year and provides full information on the top 100 distance-learning schools worldwide, including chapters on getting credit from life experience and how to tell the good schools from the bad. 216 pages.

3657—COLLEGE FINANCIAL AID FOR DUMMIES

AUTHOR-Joyce Lain Kennedy and Dr. Herm Davis. ISBN: 0-7645-5049-7. Also in bookstores.
COLLEGE FINANCIAL AID
FOR DUMMIES
IDG Books Worldwide, Inc.
919 E. Hillsdale Boulevard, Suite 400
Foster City, Ca 94404
800/762-2974
Internet: http://www.dummies.com
COST-$19.99

This book is a major new guide to understanding the financial aid maze. Useful for high school and college students and also for adults returning to school.

3658—COLLEGE IS POSSIBLE

AUTHOR-
Coalition of America's Colleges and Universities
Internet: http://www.collegeis possible.org
COST-Free on the Internet

An online resource guide for parents, students, and education professionals, containing information on preparing for college, choosing the right college, and paying for college.

3659—COLLEGE READY REPORT: THE FIRST STEP TO COLLEGE

AUTHOR-Student Resources, Inc.
Student Resources, Inc.
260 Maple Avenue
Barrington RI 02806
800/676-2900
COST-$45

Students and parents fill out a questionnaire to receive an individualized report with valuable college information. This includes a quick reference to the twelve colleges which most closely match the student's profile, along with admissions selections guides, detailed summaries of the schools, and estimated costs and financial aid planning.

3660—COLLEGE SMARTS—THE OFFICIAL FRESHMAN HANDBOOK

AUTHOR-Joyce Slayton Mitchell; ISBN 0-912048-92-1
Garrett Park Press
P.O. Box 190
Garrett Park MD 20896
301/946-2553
FAX:301/949-3955
COST-$9.95

Cogent advice for the college freshman. Covers such practical subjects as what things to take, coping with dorm life/your roommate, registration, fraternity/sorority rush, and even your laundry. Advice is practical and to the point.

3661—COLLEGE SURVIVAL INSTRUCTION BOOK

AUTHOR-Steve Mott & Susan Lutz; ISBN 1-56414-248-5
Career Press/New Page Books
3 Tice Road
P.O. Box 687
Franklin Lakes NJ 07417
800/227-3371
FAX: 201/848-1727
Internet: http://www.careerpress.com
COST-$6.99

Filled with tips, advice, suggestions, and secrets for making your college life more interesting and rewarding. 128 pages.

3662—COLLEGES WITH PROGRAMS FOR STUDENTS WITH LEARNING DISABILITIES OR ATTENTION DEFICIT DISORDER

AUTHOR-ISBN: 1-7689-0455-2
Peterson's, Inc.
Princeton Pike Corporate Center
2000 Lenox Drive
Lawrenceville NJ 08648
609/896-1800
Internet: http://www.petersons.com
COST-$20.97

A bonus CD-ROM guides you to find the assistance and accomodations for your specific requirements at more than 1,000 two- and four-year colleges in the U.S. and Canada. Students with learning disabilities or Attention Deficit Disorder can find out what's available for them with full descriptions of special services and programs on campus.

3663—CREATIVE GUIDE TO RESEARCH

AUTHOR-Robin Rowland; ISBN 1-56414-442-9
Career Press/New Page Books
3 Tice Road
P.O. Box 687
Franklin Lakes NJ 07417
800/227-3371
FAX: 201/848-1727
Internet: http://www.careerpress.com
COST-$16.99

Guide for students, professionals, and others pursuing research, describing how to find what you need, online or offline.

3664—CULINARY SCHOOLS

AUTHOR-ISBN: 0-7689-0563-X
Peterson's, Inc.
Princeton Pike Corporate Center
2000 Lenox Drive
Lawrenceville NJ 08648
609/896-1800
Internet: http://www.petersons.com
COST-$17.47

Leading chefs and cooking school directors stir up the pot to guide you through this unique guide of complete listings of professional culinary programs at two- and four-year colleges and culinary institutes. Easy-to-use profiles and additional resources add the right spice.

3665—DEBT-FREE GRADUATE: HOW TO SURVIVE COLLEGE WITHOUT GOING BROKE

AUTHOR-Murray Baker; ISBN 1-56414-472-0
Career Press/New Page Books
3 Tice Road
P.O. Box 687
Franklin Lakes NJ 07417
800/227-3371
FAX: 201/848-1727
Internet: http://www.careerpress.com
COST-$13.99

Tells students how they can stay out of debt by taking simple and easy measures, while still having the time of their lives at college. Includes how to get a great summer job and make it pay; how to negotiate with a bank-and win; how to find affordable student housing; how to eat, drink, and be merry on a budget; how to graduate without a huge student debt; and how to cut costs with bills. 320 pages.

3666—DIRECTORY FOR EXCEPTIONAL CHILDREN

AUTHOR-ISBN 0-87558-131-5
Porter Sargent Publishers, Inc.
11 Beacon Street, Suite 1400
Boston MA 02108-3099
617/523-1670
FAX: 617/523-1021

E-mail: info@portersargent.com
Internet: http://www.portersargent.com
COST-$75.00

This reference book, now in its 14th edition, can be found in most libraries. It is a comprehensive survey of 2,500 schools, facilities, and organizations across the U.S. serving children and young adults with developmental, emotional, physical, and medical disabilities. 1056 pages. Cloth.

3667—DIRECTORY OF FINANCIAL AID FOR STUDENTS OF ARMENIAN DESCENT

AUTHOR-Armenian Assembly of America
Armenian Assembly of America
122 'C' Street NW; Suite 350
Washington DC 20001
201/393-3434
Internet: http://www.aaainc.org/intern/financialaiddirectory.htm
COST-Free

The Armenian Assembly prepares this annual booklet that describes numerous scholarship, loan, and grant programs available from sources in the Armenian community. Available online.

3668—DIRECTORY OF FINANCIAL AIDS FOR WOMEN

AUTHOR-Gail Ann Schlachter; ISBN 1-58841-000-5
Reference Service Press
5000 Windplay Drive, Suite 4
El Dorado Hills CA 95762
916/939-9620
FAX: 916/939-9626
Internet: http://www.rspfunding.com
COST-$45

Comprehensive and current source of information on 1,600 scholarships, fellowships, loans, grants, internships, and awards designed primarily or exclusively for women. 552 pages.

3669—DIRECTORY OF POSTSECONDARY EDUCATIONAL RESOURCES IN ALASKA

AUTHOR-ACPE
Alaska Commission on Postsecondary Education
3030 Vintage Boulevard
Juneau AK 99801
907/465-2962 or 800/441-2962
Internet: http://www.state.ak.us/acpe/
COST-Free

Comprehensive directory of postsecondary institutions and programs in Alaska plus information on state and federal grants, loans, and scholarships for Alaska residents (those who have lived in Alaska for two years).

3670—DIRECTORY OF RESEARCH GRANTS

AUTHOR-Oryx. ISBN: 1-57356-269-6.
Greenwood Publishing Group, Inc.
88 Post Road West
West Point, CT 06881
800/225-5800 or 203/226-3571
Internet: http://www.oryxpress.com
COST-$135.00

Annual reference book found in most major libraries. Provides current data on funds available from foundations, corporations, and state/local organizations, as well as from federal sources, for research projects in medicine, physical/social sciences, arts, humanities, and education. More than 5,900 sources. 1,448 pages.

3671—DIRECTORY OF ACCREDITED INSTITUTIONS

AUTHOR-ACICS
Accrediting Council for Independent Colleges and Schools
750 1st Street NE, Suite 980
Washington DC 20002
202/336-6780
Internet: http://www.acics.org
COST-Free (and is also on Web site)

Annual directory containing information on more than 650 institutions offering business or business-related career programs and accredited by ACICS.

3672—DIRECTORY OF UNDERGRADUATE POLITICAL SCIENCE FACULTY

AUTHOR-Patricia Spellman
American Political Science Association
1527 New Hampshire Ave. NW
Washington DC 20036-1206
202/483-2512
FAX: 202/483-2657
E-mail: apsa@apsanet.org
Internet: http://www.apsanet.org
COST-$10 (APSA members); $16 (non-members)

Directory listing nearly 600 separate political science departments in the U.S. and Canada. Includes department names, addresses, telephone numbers, names, and specializations of faculty members.

3673—DIRECTORY OF MEMBER SCHOOLS

AUTHOR-
Association of Independent Schools in New England
600 Longwater Drive
Norwell, MA 02061
781/982-8600
Internet: http://www.aisne.org
COST-Free

A directory of independent schools in five New England states; includes preschool through postgraduate schools and both day and boarding programs. Some are coed, and others are for a single sex. Some are religious, and some are for students with learning disabilities. Access Internet for a list and/or call for more information.

3674—PRINT AND GRAPHICS SCHOLARSHIP FOUNDATION DIRECTORY OF SCHOOLS

AUTHOR-PGSF
Print and Graphics Scholarship Foundation
200 Deer Run Road
Sewickley PA 15153-2600
412/741-6860
FAX: 412/741-2311
E-mail:pgsf@gatf.org
Internet: http://www.gatf.org
COST-Free on the Internet

A listing of accredited institutions which offer degrees in graphic arts and related fields.

3675—DOLLARS FOR COLLEGE: THE QUICK GUIDE TO SCHOLARSHIPS, FELLOWSHIPS, LOANS, AND OTHER FINANCIAL AID PROGRAMS FOR...

AUTHOR-
Garrett Park Press
P.O. Box 190
Garrett Park MD 20896
301/946-2553
FAX: 301/949-3955
COST-$7.95 each or $60 for set of all ten booklets

User-friendly series of 12 booklets pinpoints awards in areas of particular concern to students: Art, Music, Drama; Business and Related Fields; The Disabled; Education; Engineering; Journalism and Mass Communications; Law; Liberal Arts-Humanities and Social Science; Medicine, Dentistry, and Related Fields; Nursing and Other Health Fields; Science; and Women In All Fields. Booklets are revised every 18 months, and each cites from 300 to 400 programs. 70-90 pages each.

3676—EDITOR & PUBLISHER JOURNALISM AWARDS AND FELLOWSHIPS DIRECTORY

AUTHOR-
Editor & Publisher
770 Broadway
New York NY 10003-9595
888/612-7095
E-mail:bpi@realtimepub.com
Internet: http://www.editorandpublisher.com/editorandpublisher/business_resources/index
COST-$15.00

A source of information for awards, fellowships, grants, and scholarships for journalism students and professionals. Also available as a pullout section of the December issues of *Editor & Publisher* magazine. Both national and international awards.

3677—EDUCATION AND TRAINING PROGRAMS IN OCEANOGRAPHY AND RELATED FIELDS

AUTHOR-Marine Technology Society
Marine Technology Society
5565 Sterrett Place, Suite 108
Columbia MD 21044
410/884-5330
E-mail:mtspubs@aol.com
Internet: http://www.mtsociety.org
COST-$6 shipping/handling

A guide to current marine degree programs and vocational instruction available in the marine field. Consolidates and highlights data needed by high school students as well as college students seeking advanced degrees.

3678—EDUCATIONAL LEADERSHIP, EDUCATION UPDATE, & CURRICULUM UPDATE

AUTHOR-ASCD
Association for Supervision and Curriculum Development
1703 N. Beauregard Street
Alexandria VA 22311-1714
800/933-2723 or 703/578-9600
Internet: http://www.ascd.org
COST-$49 for basic membership

Membership includes issues of Educational Leadership Journal, giving you case studies of successful programs, interviews with experts, and features by educators and administrators in the field. Also included are issues of Education Update, advising you of significant trends affecting education, networking opportunities, and the newest resources and ASCD services. The quarterly newsletter, Curriculum Update, also included, examines current, major issues in education.

3679—EDUCATIONAL REGISTER

AUTHOR-
Vincent/Curtis
224 Clarendon Street, Suite 40
Boston MA 02116
617/536-0100
FAX: 617/536-8098
Internet: http://www.vincentcurtis.com
COST-Free

This guide to independent schools and summer camps helps families with children ages 8-18 with their educational plans. An expanded version of more than 1,200 schools/camps is available online.

3680—ENCYCLOPEDIA OF ASSOCIATIONS-Vol. 1

AUTHOR-ISBN #0-8103-7945-7
Gale
P.O. Box 9187
Farmington Hills, MI 48333-9187
800/877-GALE or 313/961-2242
Internet: http://www.gale.com
COST-$415.00

An outstanding research tool. 3-part set of reference books found in most major libraries. Contains detailed information on over 22,000 associations; organizations; unions; etc. Includes name and key word index.

3681—EVERYDAY MATH FOR THE NUMERICALLY CHALLENGED

AUTHOR-Audrey Carlan; ISBN 1-56414-355-4
Career Press/New Page Books
3 Tice Road
P.O. Box 687
Franklin Lakes NJ 07417
800/227-3371
FAX: 201/848-1727
Internet: http://www.careerpress.com
COST-$11.99

Presents real-life math in an understandable format that actually makes math enjoyable, practical, and useful. Written for everyone-even if you'd just love to balance your checkbook the first time through. 160 pages.

3682—FINANCIAL AID FOR AFRICAN AMERICANS

AUTHOR-Gail Ann Schlachter and R. David Weber; ISBN 0-918276-76-4
Reference Service Press
5000 Windplay Drive, Suite 4
El Dorado Hills CA 95762
916/939-9620
FAX: 916/939-9626
Internet: http://www.rspfunding.com
COST-$37.50 + $5 shipping

This directory describes 1,500 scholarships, fellowships, loans, grants, awards, and internships for African-Americans. 500 pages.

3683—FINANCIAL AID FOR ASIAN AMERICANS

AUTHOR-Gail Ann Schlachter and R. David Weber; ISBN 1-58841-002-1
Reference Service Press
5000 Windplay Drive, Suite 4
El Dorado Hills CA 95762
916/939-9620
FAX: 916/939-9626
Internet: http://www.rspfunding.com
COST-$35.00

This directory describes nearly 1,400 funding opportunities for Americans of Chinese, Japanese, Korean, Vietnamese, Filipino, or other Asian origins. 336 pages.

3684—FINANCIAL AID FOR HISPANIC AMERICANS

AUTHOR-Gail Ann Schlachter and R. David Weber; ISBN 1-58841-003-X
Reference Service Press
5000 Windplay Drive, Suite 4
El Dorado Hills CA 95762
916/939-9620
FAX: 916/939-9626
Internet: http://www.rspfunding.com
COST-$37.50

This directory describes 1,300 funding opportunities open to Americans of Mexican, Puerto Rican, or other Latin American heritage. 472 pages.

3685—FINANCIAL AID FOR MINORITIES

AUTHOR-
Garrett Park Press
P.O. Box 190
Garrett Park MD 20896
301/946-2553
COST-$5.95 each

Several booklets with hundreds of sources of financial aid for minorities.

When ordering, please specify which of the following you are interested in: Students Of Any Major; Business and Law; Education; Journalism and Mass Communications; Health Fields; or Engineering and Science. Booklets average 80 pages in length, and each lists between 300 and 400 different sources of aid.

3686—FINANCIAL AID FOR NATIVE AMERICANS

AUTHOR-Gail Ann Schlachter and R. David Weber; ISBN 1-58841-004-8
Reference Service Press
5000 Windplay Drive, Suite 4
El Dorado Hills CA 95762
916/939-9620
FAX: 916/939-9626
Internet: http://www.rspfunding.com
COST-$37.50

This directory describes nearly 1,500 funding opportunities set aside just for American Indians, Native Alaskans, and Native Pacific Islanders. 546 pages.

3687—FINANCIAL AID FOR STUDY AND TRAINING ABROAD

AUTHOR-Gail Ann Schlachter and R. David Weber; ISBN 1-58841-031-5
Reference Service Press
5000 Windplay Drive, Suite 4
El Dorado Hills CA 95762
916/939-9620
FAX: 916/939-9626
Internet: http://www.rspfunding.com
COST-$39.50

This directory describes 1,000 financial aid opportunities open to Americans at any level (high school through postdoctorate and professional) who are interested in studying abroad. 398 pages. Another book, *Financial Aid for Research and Creative Activities Abroad,* is also available to students interested in research, professional, and creative activities abroad.

3688—FINANCIAL AID FOR THE DISABLED AND THEIR FAMILIES

AUTHOR-Gail Ann Schlachter & R. David Weber; ISBN 0-918276-94-2
Reference Service Press
5000 Windplay Drive, Suite 4
El Dorado Hills CA 95762
916/939-9620
FAX: 916/939-9626
Internet: http://www.rspfunding.com
COST-$40

This comprehensive directory identifies nearly 1,000 scholarships, fellowships, loans, internships, awards, and grants for the disabled and their families. 490 pages.

3689—FINANCIAL AID FOR VETERANS, MILITARY PERSONNEL, & THEIR DEPENDENTS

AUTHOR-Gail Ann Schlachter & R. David Weber; ISBN 0-918276-95-0
Reference Service Press
5000 Windplay Drive, Suite 4
El Dorado Hills CA 95762
916/939-9620
FAX: 916/939-9626
Internet: http://www.rspfunding.com
COST-$40

This directory identifies nearly 1,100 scholarships, fellowships, loans, awards, grants, and internships established just for veterans, military personnel, and their families. 350 pages.

3690—FINANCIAL AID INFORMATION FOR PHYSICIAN ASSISTANT STUDENTS

AUTHOR-
American Academy of Physician Assistants
950 North Washington Street
Alexandria VA 22314-1552
703/836-2272
E-mail:aapa@aapa.org
Internet: http://www.aapa.org
COST-Free

A comprehensive listing of scholarships, traineeships, grants, loans, and related publications relation to the physician assistant field of study.

3691—FINANCIAL AID RESOURCE GUIDE-#17.97

AUTHOR-
National Clearinghouse for Professions in Special Education
The Council for Exceptional Children
1110 North Glebe Road, Suite 300
Arlington, VA 22201-5704
888/CEC-SPED or 703/620-3660
FAX: 703/264-9494; E-mail:cecpubs@cec.sped.org
Internet: http://www.cec.sped.org
COST-Free

General information on finding financial assistance for students preparing for careers in special education and related services.

3692—FISKE GUIDE TO COLLEGES

AUTHOR-Edward B. Fiske; ISBN 812-92534-1
Source Books, Inc.
1934 Brookdale Road, Suite 139
Naperville, IL 60563
COST-$22.95

Describes the top-rated 265 out of 2,000 possible four-year schools in the U.S. They are rated for academics, social life, and quality of life.

3693—FUNDING FOR PERSONS WITH VISUAL IMPAIRMENTS

AUTHOR-Gail Ann Schlachter; ISBN 1-58841-025-0 (Large Print Edition), ISBN 1-58841-026-9 (PLUS Edition)
Reference Service Press
5000 Windplay Drive, Suite 4
El Dorado Hills CA 95762
916/939-9620
FAX: 916/939-9626
Internet: http://www.rspfunding.com
COST-$30 (Large Print Edition) or $50 (PLUS Edition)

Available in two versions: a Large Print Edition, describing 250 financial aid opportunities just for persons with visual impairments; and the PLUS Edition on disk, either IBM or Mac compatible, which includes an additional 300 funding opportunities open to persons with any disability.

3694—GET ORGANIZED

AUTHOR-Ron Fry; ISBN 1-56414-461-5
Career Press/New Page Books
3 Tice Road
P.O. Box 687
Franklin Lakes NJ 07417
800/227-3371
FAX: 201/848-1727
Internet: http://www.careerpress.com
COST-$8.99

Teaches you how to create your "ideal study environment" by using simple time-management tips to develop to-do lists, daily schedules, monthly calendars, and project boards. Includes electronic and online planning tools. 128 pages.

3695—GETTING INTERVIEWS

AUTHOR-Kate Wendleton; ISBN 1-56414-448-8
Career Press/New Page Books
3 Tice Road
P.O. Box 687
Franklin Lakes NJ 07417

800/227-3371
FAX: 201/848-1727
Internet: http://www.careerpress.com
COST-$12.99

Guide for job hunters, career changers, consultants, and freelancers that tells you how to find out whom you should be talking to and how to get those people to meet with you. 192 pages.

3696—GETTING STARTED IN THE MUSIC BUSINESS

AUTHOR-
Texas Music Office
P.O. Box 13246
Austin TX 78711
512/463-6666
FAX: 512/463-4114
E-mail: music@governor.state.tx.us
Internet: http://www.governor.state.tx.us/music/tmlp_intro.htm
COST-Free Online Information

This online guide for musicians in Texas provides short-answer reference to the basic legal and business practices associated with the music industry. Links to many informative sites.

3697—GIFTED & TALENTED EDUCATION CATALOG

AUTHOR-
Prufrock Press
P.O. Box 8813
Waco TX 76714-8813
800/998-2208
FAX: 800/240-0333
Internet: http://www.prufrock.com
COST-Free

This catalog is filled with books for teachers and parents of gifted and talented children.

3698—GIFTED CHILD QUARTERLY

AUTHOR-
National Association for Gifted Children
1707 L Street NW; Suite 550
Washington DC 20036
202/785-4268
Internet: http://www.nagc.org
COST-Associate Membership is $25; Full Membership (including newsletter) is $50; Various publications also available

See Web site or contact NAGC for information on specific helpful publications for parents of gifted children.

An organization of parents, educators, other professionals, and community leaders who unite to address the unique needs of all children and youth with demonstrated gifts and talents as well as those who may be able to develop their talent potential with appropriate educational experiences.

3699—GOVERNMENT ASSISTANCE ALMANAC (9th edition)

AUTHOR-J. Robert Dumouchel; ISBN 0-7808-0580-1
OmniGraphics Inc.
Order Department
P.O. Box 625
Holmes, PA 19043
800/234-1340 or 313/961-1340
Fax: 800/875-1340
E-mail: info@omnigraphics.com;
Internest: http://www.omnigraphics.com
COST-$225.00

Comprehensive guide to more than $1.5 trillion worth of federal programs available to the American public. Contains 1,000 pages and 1370 entries detailing programs of benefit to students; educators; researchers and consumers.

3700—GRANTS AND AWARDS AVAILABLE TO AMERICAN WRITERS

AUTHOR-ISBN: 0-934638-16-0
Pen American Center
568 Broadway
New York NY 10012-3225
212/334-1660; FAX: 212/334-2181
E-mail: pen@pen.org
Internet: http://www.pen.orgg
COST-$18

More than 1,000 awards listed for poets, journalists, playwrights, etc., including American as well as international grants (including residencies at writers' colonies). Order by mail or FAX: only. 328 pages.

3701—GRANTS, FELLOWSHIPS, AND PRIZES OF INTEREST TO HISTORIANS

AUTHOR-AHA
American Historical Association
400 A Street, SE
Washington DC 20003
202/544-2422
FAX: 202/544-8307
E-mail: aha@theaha.org
Internet: http://www.theaha.org
COST-Free to members on the Internet

Offering information on more than 450 funding sources-from undergraduate scholarships to postdoctoral fellowships and awards for written work and publications-the AHA's annual guide can help individuals find funding to begin or continue a research project or degree program. Includes suggestions for writing successful grant proposals and a bibliography of other sources for grant, fellowship and prize information.

3702—GREAT BIG BOOK OF HOW TO STUDY

AUTHOR-Ron Fry; ISBN 1-56414-423-2
Career Press/New Page Books
3 Tice Road
P.O. Box 687
Franklin Lakes NJ 07417
800/227-3371
FAX: 201/848-1727
Internet: http://www.careerpress.com
COST-$15.95

More than 400 pages of useful information and advice, written in a direct, motivational style that will help students regain the confidence they need to succeed in school. 448 pages.

3703—GREAT LITTLE BOOK ON PERSONAL ACHIEVEMENT

AUTHOR-Brian Tracy; ISBN 1-56414-283-3
Career Press/New Page Books
3 Tice Road
P.O. Box 687
Franklin Lakes NJ 07417
800/227-3371
FAX: 201/848-1727
Internet: http://www.careerpress.com
COST-$6.99

Inspiration for anyone who wants to build wealth into the 21st century, attain a fulfilling personal life, and meet high career goals. 128 pages. Other "Great Little Books" include Mastering Your Time, Motivational Minutes, Peak Performance Woman, and Wisdom.

3704—GUIDANCE MANUAL FOR THE CHRISTIAN HOME SCHOOL

AUTHOR-David & Laurie Callihan; ISBN 1-56414-452-6
Career Press/New Page Books
3 Tice Road
P.O. Box 687
Franklin Lakes NJ 07417
800/227-3371
FAX: 201/848-1727
Internet: http://www.careerpress.com
COST-$22.99

Guide to preparing home school students for college or career, giving parents information they need to successfully mentor their children in grades 7 through 12 toward adulthood. 264 pages.

3705—GUIDE TO MERIT AND OTHER NO-NEED FUNDING

AUTHOR-Gail Ann Schlachter and R. David Weber; ISBN 0-918276-87-X (high school), ISBN 0-918276-88-8 (college)
Reference Service Press
5000 Windplay Drive, Suite 4
El Dorado Hills CA 95762
916/939-9620
FAX: 916/939-9626
Internet: http://www.rspfunding.com
COST-$27.95 (high school) or $32 (college)

Two guides are available-one for high school seniors (400 pages) and one for college students (450 pages). Detailed are merit awards and other no-need funding programs that never look at income when awarding money.

3706—GUIDE TO SOURCES OF INFORMATION ON PARAPSYCHOLOGY

AUTHOR-Eileen J. Garrett Library; ISBN 0-912328-87-8
Parapsychology Foundation, Inc.
228 E. 71st Street
New York NY 10021
212/628-1550
FAX: 212/628-1559
E-mail: info@parapsychology.org
Internet: http://www.parapsychology.org
COST-$3.00

An annual listing of sources of information on major parapsychology organizations, journals, books, and research.

3707—GUIDE TO SUMMER CAMPS AND SUMMER SCHOOLS

AUTHOR-ISBN 0-87558-133-1 (cloth); ISBN 0-87558-134-X (paper)
Porter Sargent Publishers, Inc.
11 Beacon Street, Suite 1400
Boston MA 02108-3099
617/523-1670
FAX: 617/523-1021
E-mail: info@portersargent.com
Internet: http://www.portersargent.com
COST-$35 (cloth) or $25 (paper)

This reference book, now in its 27th edition, can be found in most libraries. It covers the broad spectrum of recreational and educational summer opportunities. Current facts from 1,300 camps and schools, as well as programs for those with special needs or learning disabilities, make the Guide a comprehensive and convenient resource. 560 pages. Cloth or paper.

3708—HANDBOOK OF PRIVATE SCHOOLS

AUTHOR-ISBN 0-87558-140-4
Porter Sargent Publishers, Inc.
11 Beacon Street, Suite 1400
Boston MA 02108-3099
617/523-1670
FAX: 617/523-1021
E-mail: info@portersargent.com
Internet: http://www.portersargent.com
COST-$93 + $5 shipping

This annual reference book, now in its 80th edition, can be found in most libraries. It offers objective, detailed listings of the top private elementary and secondary schools in the U.S. Tuition, endowment, curriculum, faculty, and college placement records are among the topics that parents, educators, librarians, and consultants will need in helping place the right child in the right school. 1336 pages. Cloth.

3709—HOMESCHOOLING ALMANAC

AUTHOR-Mary & Michael Leppert; ISBN 0-7615-2856-3
Prima Publishing
P.O. Box 1260
Rocklin CA 95677
800/632-8676 or 916/787-7000
Internet: http://www.primalifestyles.com
COST-$24.95

This all-encompassing guide includes more than 900 educational products, such as books/magazines, software, videos, games, crafts, science kits, prepackaged curricula, cybersources, methods, etc. Provides state-by-state breakdown of legal requirements, support groups, and organizations. 688 pages.

3710—HOW TO STUDY

AUTHOR-Ron Fry; ISBN 1-56414-456-9
Career Press/New Page Books
3 Tice Road
P.O. Box 687
Franklin Lakes NJ 07417
800/227-3371
FAX: 201/848-1727
Internet: http://www.careerpress.com
COST-$12.99

Includes how to create a work environment, excel in class, use the library, do research online, and more. 224 pages.

3711—IMPROVE YOUR MEMORY

AUTHOR-Ron Fry; ISBN 1-56414-459-3
Career Press/New Page Books
3 Tice Road
P.O. Box 687
Franklin Lakes NJ 07417
800/227-3371
FAX: 201/848-1727
Internet: http://www.careerpress.com
COST-$8.99

For high school students, college students, and anyone seeking to improve his or her memory power. Learn the essential principles of memory to help you increase your ability to retain what you read, perform better on tests, or just remember where you last put your car keys. 128 pages.

3712—IMPROVE YOUR READING

AUTHOR-Ron Fry; ISBN 1-56414-458-5
Career Press/New Page Books
3 Tice Road
P.O. Box 687
Franklin Lakes NJ 07417
800/227-3371
FAX: 201/848-1727
Internet: http://www.careerpress.com
COST-$8.99

Presents a practical way to increase what you learn from texts, notes, and resources. Whether reading texts or your own notes, you'll learn effective reading comprehension skills required for success in high school, college, and throughout life. 128 pages.

3713—IMPROVE YOUR WRITING

AUTHOR-Ron Fry; ISBN 1-56414-457-7
Career Press, Inc.
3 Tice Road
P.O. Box 687
Franklin Lakes NJ 07417
800/227-3371
FAX: 201/848-1727
Internet: http://www.careerpress.com
COST-$8.99

Presents all the elements important to turning in an excellent research paper. This step-by-step walk-through includes selecting a topic, library research, developing an outline, writing from the first to final draft, proofreading, online research, and more. 128 pages.

3714—INDEX OF MAJORS & GRADUATE DEGREES

AUTHOR-CBP; ISBN #0-87447-666-6
The College Board Publications
Department CBO
P.O. Box 869010
Plano, TX 75074
800/323-7155
FAX: 888/321-7183
Internet: http://www.collegeboard.org
COST-$22.95

Describes over 600 major programs of study at 3,200 undergraduate and graduate schools. Also lists schools that have religious affiliations, special academic programs, and special admissions procedures. 695 pages.

3715—INTERNATIONAL JOBS

AUTHOR-Eric Kocher;
ISBN 7382-0039-5
Perseus Books Group
Customer Service Department
5500 Central Avenue
Boulder CO 80301
800/386-5656
E-mail: info@perseuspublishing.com
Internet: http://www.perseus publishing.com
COST-$18.00

The 5th edition provides everything you need to navigate complex international job market (including Web sites).

3716—INTERNATIONAL SCHOOL DIRECTORY

AUTHOR-ECIS; ISBN #0-901577-61-8
John Catt Educational
Great Glemham
Sulfolk IP17 2DH ENGLAND
E-mail: enquiries@johncatt.co.uk
Internet: http://www.johncatt.com
COST-$35.00

Compendium of international schools at all levels of study. Provides detailed information on over 800 elementary, secondary and postsecondary schools. Organized by country. 580 pages.

3717—CHOOSING A GIRLS SCHOOL

AUTHOR-
THE NATIONAL COALITION OF GIRLS SCHOOLS (Informational Brochure)
228 Main Street
Concord MA 01742
508/287-4485
FAX: 508/287-6014
E-mail: ncgs@ncgs.org
Internet: http://www.ncgs.org
COST-Free

A valuable, free resource for parents of elementary and secondary school-aged girls whether in private or public schools.

A free brochure listing member schools in 23 states, Washington DC, New Zealand, Canada, and Australia, of the Coalition. 28 pages.

3718—A GUIDE TO GRANTS, FELLOWSHIPS, AND SCHOLARSHIPS IN INTERNATIONAL FORESTRY AND NATURAL RESOURCES

AUTHOR-Damon A. Job
United States Department of Agriculture
P.O. Box 96090
Washington DC 20090-6090
http://www.fs.fed.us/people/gf/gf 00.htm
COST-

An online guide to grants, fellowships, and scholarships in international forestry and natural resources.

3719—LANGUAGE LIAISON PROGRAM DIRECTORY

AUTHOR-
Language Liaison
1610 Woodstead Court, Suite 130
The Woodlands TX 77380
973/898-1416 or 800/284-4448
FAX: 973/898-1710
E-mail: learn@launguageliaison.com
Internet: http://www.language liaison.com
COST-Free

Want to learn another language? Learn it like a native in the country where it is spoken. New programs start every week year-round from two weeks to a year long. Programs are open to students, teachers, executives, teens, seniors, families, and leisure travelers. Includes activities, excursions, and homestays. See Web site for details on this program as well as various language tools.

3720—LAST MINUTE COLLEGE FINANCING

AUTHOR-Daniel J. Cassidy;
ISBN 1-56414-468-2
National Scholarship Research Service
5577 Skylane Boulevard, Suite 6A
Santa Rosa CA 95403
707/546-6777
Internet: http://www.1800headstart.com
COST-$10.99 + $5 shipping (CA residents add $1.09 tax)

Whether your child starts college in 15 years or next semester, this helpful guide answers such questions as, "How do I get the money together in time?" "How do I locate quality low-cost colleges?" and "How do I find sources of financial aid that I may have overlooked?" 128 pages.

3721—LAST MINUTE INTERVIEW TIPS

AUTHOR-Brandon Toropov;
ISBN 1-56414-240-X
Career Press/New Page Books
3 Tice Road
P.O. Box 687
Franklin Lakes NJ 07417
800/227-3371
FAX: 201/848-1727
Internet: http://www.careerpress.com
COST-$7.99

Gives you all the tips, tricks, and techniques you need to ace an interview with little preparation and win the job. 128 pages.

3722—LAST MINUTE RESUMES

AUTHOR-Brandon Toropov;
ISBN 1-56414-354-6
Career Press/New Page Books
3 Tice Road
P.O. Box 687
Franklin Lakes NJ 07417
800/227-3371
FAX: 201/848-1727
Internet: http://www.careerpress.com
COST-$9.99

Quickly takes you step by step through the whole resume-preparation process, from self-evaluation to powerful resume models to add drama and excitement to your application. 160 pages.

3723—LAST MINUTE STUDY TIPS

AUTHOR-Ron Fry; ISBN 1-56414-238-8
Career Press/New Page Books
3 Tice Road
P.O. Box 687
Franklin Lakes NJ 07417
800/227-3371
FAX: 201/848-1727
Internet: http://www.careerpress.com
COST-$7.99

Guide to help students with study habits. 128 pages.

3724—LESKO'S SELF-HELP BOOKS

AUTHOR-Matthew Lesko
Information USA
P.O. Box E
Kensington MD 20895
800/955-7693
E-mail: infojoeusa@aol.com
Internet: http://www.lesko.com
COST-Varies

A variety of self-help books on "free stuff." Author gives information on free government information, expert advice, and money. See Web site or contact publisher for a list of titles.

3725—LIFE AFTER DEBT

AUTHOR-Bob Hammond; ISBN 1-56414-421-6
Career Press/New Page Books
3 Tice Road
P.O. Box 687
Franklin Lakes NJ 07417
800/227-3371
FAX: 201/848-1727
Internet: http://www.careerpress.com
COST-$14.99

Attacks the causes of debt and how to solve credit problems. Also provides addresses/phone numbers of consumer credit services, state banking authorities, and other resources to get you on your way to financial stability, regardless of income. 256 pages.

3726—LINK HOMESCHOOL NEWSPAPER

AUTHOR-
The Link
587 No. Ventu Park Road, Suite F-911
Newbury Park CA 91320
888/470-4513 or 805/492-1373
FAX: 805/493-9216
E-mail: the.link@verizon.net
Internet: http://www.homeschoolnewslink.com
COST-Free

Bimonthly newspaper for parents whose children are homeschooled.

3727—LIST OF SCHOLARSHIPS AND AWARDS IN ELECTRICAL, ELECTRONICS, AND COMPUTER ENGINEERING

AUTHOR-
IEEE-USA Computer Society
1730 Massachusetts Avenue, N.W.
Washington DC 20036-1992
202/371-0101
FAX: 202/778-9614
Internet: http://www.ieeeusa.org
COST-Free on the Internet

A source of information containing a multitude of scholarships in the above fields, including application information.

3728—MAKING THE MOST OF YOUR COLLEGE EDUCATION

AUTHOR-Marianne Ragins; Order Code: MMC-999dsc
The Scholarship Workshop
P.O. Box 176
Centreville VA 20122
478/755-8428
Internet: http://www.scholarshipworkshop.com
COST-$10.67

This book shows you how to pack your college years with career-building experiences that can lead to graduate and professional schools clamoring to admit you; how to write an impressive professional resume; and how to gain keen entrepreneurial skills, an investment portfolio, and multiple job offers. Offers information on securing internships, travel opportunities, managing your money, using the Internet to your advantage, and other helpful advice.

3729—MASTER MATH

AUTHOR-Debra Anne Ross
Career Press/New Page Books
3 Tice Road
P.O. Box 687
Franklin Lakes NJ 07417
800/227-3371
FAX: 201/848-1727
Internet: http://www.careerpress.com
COST-From $10.99 to 11.99

Four books focusing on mathematical principles that establish a solid foundation and help students move on to more advanced topics. Specify which book when ordering: Algebra, Basic Math and Pre-Algebra, Calculus, or Pre-Calculus and Geometry.

3730—MEDICAL SCHOOL ADMISSION REQUIREMENTS

AUTHOR-Cynthia T. Bennett
Association of American Medical Colleges
2450 N Street NW
Washington DC 20037-1126
202/828-0400
FAX: 202/828-1125
Internet: http://www.aamc.org
COST-$25 + $5 shipping

Contains admission requirements of accredited medical schools in the U.S. and Canada.

3731—MITCHELL EXPRESS—THE FAST TRACK TO THE TOP COLLEGES

AUTHOR-Joyce Slayton Mitchell; ISBN 1-880774-03-8
Garrett Park Press
P.O. Box 190
Garrett Park MD 20896
301/946-2553
FAX: 301/949-3955
COST-$15.00

A college catalog-sized directory describing 270 of America's most popular colleges. It profiles the colleges and provides information on admissions, financial aid, and campus life. 269 pages.

3732—NATIONAL DIRECTORY OF COLLEGE ATHLETICS (Men's and Women's Editions)

AUTHOR-Kevin Cleary, Editor/Publisher
Collegiate Directories Inc.
P.O. Box 450640
Cleveland OH 44145
800/426-2232
FAX: 440/835-8835
E-mail: info@collegiatedirectories.com
Internet: http://www.collegiatedirectories.com
COST-$39.95 (both men's and women's edition

Comprehensive directory of college athletic programs in the U.S. and Canada. Revised for each new school year.

3733—NATIONAL DIRECTORY OF CORPORATE GIVING

AUTHOR-TFC; ISBN 0-87954-400-7
Foundation Center (The)
79 Fifth Ave.
New York NY 10003
800/478-4661 or 212/620-4230
E-mail: fdonline@fdncenter.org
Internet: http://fdncenter.org
COST-$195.00

Book profiles 2000 programs making contributions to nonprofit organizations. A valuable tool to assist grant seekers in finding potential support.

3734—NEED A LIFT? (49th edition-2000 Issue)

AUTHOR-
The American Legion
Attn: National Emblem Sales
P.O. Box 1050
Indianapolis IN 46206
888/453-4466 or 317/630-1200
FAX: 317/630-1223
Internet: http://www.legion.org
COST-$3.95 (pre-paid only)

Outstanding guide to federal and state government-related financial aid as well as private sector programs. Contains information on the financial aid process (how, when, and where to start) and addresses for scholarship, loan, and career information. 152 pages.

3735—OCCUPATIONAL OUTLOOK HANDBOOK

AUTHOR-U.S. Dept. of Labor Bureau of Statistics; 1998-99
CFKR Career Materials
11860 Kemper Road, #7
Auburn CA 95603
800/525-5626 or 916/889-2357
FAX: 800/770-0433
E-mail: info@cfkr.com
Internet: http://www.cfkr.com
COST-$10.00 (soft cover); $20.95 (hard cover)

Annual publication designed to assist individuals in selecting appropriate careers. Describes approximately 250 occupations in great detail and includes current and projected job prospects for each. A great resource for teachers and counselors. Versions for grades 5-12 and related activity books also available. 508 pages.

3736—CLEP OFFICIAL STUDY GUIDE

AUTHOR-CBP; ISBN #0-87447-661-5
The College Board Publications
Department CBO
P.O. Box 869010
Plano TX 75074
800/323-7155
FAX: 888/321-7183
Internet: http://www.college board.org
COST-$22.00

Official guide to College Level Examination Program (CLEP) tests from the actual sponsors of the tests. Contains sample questions and answers, advice on how to prepare for tests, which colleges grant credit for CLEP, and more. 448 pages.

3737—ONLINE STUDY ABROAD DIRECTORY

AUTHOR-Web site is associated with the University of Minnesota.
International Study and Travel Center
94 Blegen Hall
269 19th Avenue South
Minneapolis MN 55455
800/770-ISTC or 612/626-ISTC
FAX: 612/626-0979
E-mail: istc@umn.edu
Internet: http://www.istc.umn.edu
COST-Free

An easy-to-access database of opportunities for studying abroad. Click on "scholarships and funding" on the opening page for a list of study opportunities all over the world for which there is financial aid available.

3738—PERSPECTIVES: AUDITION ADVICE FOR SINGERS

AUTHOR-Various leaders in the opera field.
OPERA America
1156 15th Street NW, Suite 810
Washington DC 20005-1704
202/293-4466
FAX: 393-0735
E-mail: Frontdesk@operaam.org
Internet: http://www.operaam.org
COST-$15/non-members; $10/members

A collection of personal observations from professionals who want to help singers perpare for and perform winning auditions. Features 27 valuable essays from general directors, artistic administrators, training program directors, artist managers, stage directors, teachers, established singers, and university and conservatory directors.

3739—PERSPECTIVES: THE SINGER/MANAGER RELATIONSHIP

AUTHOR-Various leaders in the opera field
OPERA America
1156 15th Street NW, Suite 810
Washington DC 20005-1704
202/293-4466; FAX: 393-0735
E-mail: Frontdesk@operaam.org
Internet: http://www.operaam.org
COST-$17/nonmembers; $12/members

Features essays by leaders in the field about artist managers and their roles and responsibilities in identifying and advancing the careers of aspiring singers. Opera professionals, including artist managers, singers, and opera company casting representatives share experiences and give insights to the most frequently asked questions.

3740—FOUR YEAR COLLEGES

AUTHOR-ISBN: 0-7689-0534-6
Peterson's
Princeton Pike Corporate Center
2000 Lenox Drive
Lawrenceville NJ 08648
609/896-1800
Internet: http://www.petersons.com
COST-$18.87

Begin your college search by exploring accurate, current, and impartial profiles of over 2,000 accredited colleges and universities. Find out about specific academic programs, campus life, and athletics. QuickFind college search indexes and charts speed your search. The bonus CD-ROM provides in-depth college descriptions. Get a head start with SAT and ACT practice tests. 3,176 pages.

3741—PRIVATE SECONDARY SCHOOLS

AUTHOR-ISBN: 0-7689-0531-1
Peterson's
Princeton Pike Corporate Center
2000 Lenox Drive
Lawrenceville NJ 08648
609/896-1800
Internet: http://www.petersons.com
COST-$20.97

Explore 1,500 accredited day, boarding, religious, military, junior boarding, and special needs schools worldwide. School profiles cover programs, cost and financial aid, facilities, and student life. 1,451 pages.

3742—SPORTS SCHOLARSHIPS AND COLLEGE ATHLETIC PROGRAMS

AUTHOR-ISBN: 0-7689-0273-8
Peterson's
Princeton Pike Corporate Center
2000 Lenox Drive
Lawrenceville NJ 08648
609/896-1800
Internet: http://www.petersons.com
COST-$18.87

This is a college-by-college, sport-by-sport guide that covers 32 men's and women's sports. 872 pages.

3743—TWO YEAR COLLEGES

AUTHOR-ISBN: 0-7689-0535-4
Peterson's
Princeton Pike Corporate Center
2000 Lenox Drive
Lawrenceville NJ 08648
609/896-1800
Internet: http://www.petersons.com
COST-$18.87

Get all the details on 1,600 junior and community colleges in the U.S. and Canada, including programs offered, tuition, and financial aid. 811 pages.

3744—PING AMERICAN COLLEGE GOLF GUIDE

AUTHOR-Dean W. Frischknecht
Ping American College Golf Guide
P.O. Box 1179
Hillsboro OR 97123
503/648-1333
FAX: 503/681-9615
Internet: http://www.collegegolf.com
COST-$14.95

Alphabetical listing by state of two and four year colleges with intercollegiate golf programs. Includes scholarship and financial aid information, resumes, ratings, and scores. 352 pages. Updated annually.

3745—PUBLICATIONS CATALOG

AUTHOR-
National Hemophilia Foundation
116 W. 32nd Street, 11th Floor
New York NY 10001
800/42-HANDI ext. 3734
FAX: 212/328-3777
E-mail: info@hemophilia.org
Internet: http://www.hemophilia.org
COST-Free

This catalog lists several publications that are available to those with a bleeding disorder and those doing research in this area. Some are available in both English and Spanish.

3746—PHYSICIAN ASSISTANT INTERNATIONAL DIRECTORY

AUTHOR-
Association of Physician Assistant Programs
1950 N. Washington Street
Alexandria VA 22314
Internet: http://www.daemen.edu
COST-$25.00

A catalog of of physician assistant educational programs, including addresses, admissions procedures and requirements, course outlines, length of program, university and institutional affiliations, tuition, and sources of financial assistance. Order from above location.

3747—POUR MAN'S FRIEND: A GUIDE AND REFERENCE FOR BAR PERSONNEL

AUTHOR-John C. Burton;
ISBN: 0-9624625-0-0
Pour Man's Friend (A Guide and Reference for Bar Personnel)
Aperitifs Publishing
1731 King Street
Santa Rosa CA 95404
707/523-4100 or 707/523-1611
FAX: 703/569-9855
E-mail: johncburton@ms.com
COST-$14.95 + shipping

Includes comprehensive bartending techniques, ways to achieve top industry standards with current regulations and guidelines.

3748—REPAIR YOUR OWN CREDIT

AUTHOR-Bob Hammond;
ISBN 1-56414-308-2
Career Press/New Page Books
3 Tice Road
P.O. Box 687
Franklin Lakes NJ 07417
800/227-3371
FAX: 201/848-1727
Internet: http://www.careerpress.com
COST-$11.99

Reveals the unethical and illegal secrets of the credit repair industry from an insider's point of view and explains how you can restore your own credit. 128 pages.

3749—SCHOLARSHIP LIST SERVICE

AUTHOR-
National Foundation for Advancement in the Arts
800 Brickell Ave., Suite 500
Miami FL 33131
800/970-ARTS or 305/377-1140
FAX: 305/377-1149
E-mail: info@nfaa.org
Internet: http://www.nfaa.org/sls/slsschools.htm
COST-Varies

A list of higher education institutions that offer opportunities for scholarships and financial to students in the arts. Available via E-mail address above. Contact organization for details. Can register online at above Web site.

3750—SCHOLARSHIPS & LOANS FOR NURSING EDUCATION

AUTHOR-National League for Nursing;
ISBN #0-88737-730-0
Jones and Bartlett Publishers
40 Tall Pine Drive
Sudbury MA 01776
978/443-5000
FAX: 978/443-8000
E-mail: info@jbpub.com
Internet: http://www.jbpub.com
COST-$23.95

Information on all types of scholarships, awards, grants, fellowships, and loans for launching or continuing your career in nursing. 125 pages. Other book available: NURSING: THE CAREER OF A LIFETIME ($29.95).

3751—SCHOOLS ABROAD OF INTEREST TO AMERICANS

AUTHOR-ISBN 0-87558-127-7
Porter Sargent Publishers, Inc.
11 Beacon Street, Suite 1400
Boston MA 02108-3099
617/523-1670
FAX: 617/523-1021
E-mail: info@portersargent.com
Internet: http://www.portersargent.com
COST-$45.00

This reference book for American students seeking preparatory schooling overseas, now in its 9th edition, can be found in most libraries. It describes approximately 650 elementary and secondary schools, in some 125 countries, that accept English-speaking students. 544 pages. Cloth.

3753—SMART WOMAN'S GUIDE TO INTERVIEWING AND SALARY NEGOTIATION

AUTHOR-Julie Adair King & Betsy Sheldon; ISBN 1-56414-206-X

Career Press/New Page Books
3 Tice Road
P.O. Box 687
Franklin Lakes NJ 07417
800/227-3371
FAX: 201/848-1727
Internet: http://www.careerpress.com
COST-$12.99

Covers the entire interview process, job applications, employment tests (including drug tests), evaluating job offers, negotiating your best deal, accepting or declining an offer, and how to ask for a raise-and get it. 224 pages.

3754—SMART WOMAN'S GUIDE TO RESUMES AND JOB HUNTING

AUTHOR-Julie Adair King; ISBN 1-56414-205-1
Career Press/New Page Books
3 Tice Road
P.O. Box 687
Franklin Lakes NJ 07417
800/227-3371
FAX: 201/848-1727
Internet: http://www.careerpress.com
COST-$9.99

Walks the reader through the resume-creating process step by step (including career worksheets and sample resumes). Addresses other key career issues of interest to women, including breaking through the glass ceiling and other gender barriers, commanding a fair salary, networking to find hidden job opportunities, using "power language," and more. 216 pages.

3755—SPANISH ABROAD

AUTHOR-
Spanish Abroad, Inc.
5112 N. 48th Street, Suite 103
Phoenix AZ 85018
888/722-7623 (toll-free U.S. & Canada) or 602/778-6791
FAX: 602/840-1545
E-mail: info@spanishabroad.com
Internet: http://www.spanishabroad.com
COST-Varies

This Web site is a vast source of opportunities for Spanish immersion programs in many countries around the world. Included is a page that has a list of financial aid and scholarships for this purpose. See Web site for details.

3756—SPORTS FOR HER

AUTHOR-Penny Hastings; ISBN 0-313-30551-X
Greenwood Publishing Group, Inc.
88 Post Road West
Westport CT 06881
800/225-5800 or 203/226-3571
FAX: 203/222-1502
Internet: http://www.greenwood.com
COST-$45.00

This reference guide for teenage girls explores high school sports from a girl's perspective and examines sports issues as they pertain to young women. Provides practical advice on training and practicing techniques, trying out for the team, and organizing school teams. Includes advice on possible sports-related problems for girls and information about sports-related careers. 264 pages.

3757—STUDENT FINANCIAL AID AND SCHOLARSHIPS AT WYOMING COLLEGES

AUTHOR-UW
University of Wyoming Office of Student Financial Aid
174 Knight Hall
Laramie WY 82071-3335
307/766-2116
FAX: 307/766-3800
Internet: http://siswww.uwyo.edu/sfa
COST-Free on the Internet

Describes postsecondary student aid and scholarship programs that are available to Wyoming students. Booklets can be obtained at all Wyoming high schools and colleges.

3758—STUDY ABROAD

AUTHOR-UNESCO
United Nations Educational, Scientific and Cultural Organization
Bernan Associates; UNESCO Agent
4611-F Assembly Drive
Lanham MD 20706
E-mail: publishing.promotion@unesco.org
Internet: http://llupo.unesco.org
COST-$29.95 + postage/handling

Printed in English, French, and Spanish, this volume lists 2,650 international study programs in all academic and professional fields in more than 124 countries.

3759—STUDY IN THE NETHERLANDS

AUTHOR-NUFFIC
Netherlands Organization for International Cooperation in Higher Education
Kortenaerkade 11; Postbus 29777
2502 LT Den Haag
THE NETHERLANDS
+31 070 426 02 00
FAX: +31 070 426 03 99
E-mail: nuffic@nuffic.nl
Internet: http://www.nuffic.nl
COST-Free on the Internet

Helpful info for students from foreign countries planning to study in The Netherlands. Includes details on applying for admission; practical matters such as money, housing, and scholarships; and courses and study programs conducted in English and Dutch.

3760—SUMMER FUN-LEARNING PROGRAMS

AUTHOR-ISBN: 0-7689-0448-X
Peterson's
Princeton Pike Corporate Center
2000 Lenox Drive
Lawrenceville NJ 08648
609/896-1800
Internet: http://www.petersons.com
COST-$6.97

Includes detailed listings of summer learning camps and programs, advice on how to pick the right program, secrets to handling homesickness, firsthand experiences from other kids, and more. 230 pages.

3761—STUDYING IN THE UK: SOURCES OF FUNDING FOR INTERNATIONAL STUDENTS

AUTHOR-Published by The British Council 1997
The British Council, International Student Service
Bridgewater House
58 Whitworth Street
Manchester M1 6BB ENGLAND
0161 957 7249
FAX: 0161 957 7319
E-mail: general.enquiries@britishcouncil.org
Internet: http://www.britishcouncil.org
COST-Free

A booklet describing various forms of student financial aid for study in the United Kingdom.

3762—CORPORATE GIVING DIRECTORY

AUTHOR-ISBN #0-56995-436-4
Gale
P.O. Box 9187
Farmington Hills MI 48333-9187

800/877-GALE
Internet: http://www.galegroup.com
COST-$505.00

This reference book is found in most major libraries. It contains comprehensive information on over 1,000 foundations sponsored by top corporations.

3763—TARGETING THE JOB YOU WANT

AUTHOR-Kate Wendleton;
ISBN 1-56414-449-6
Career Press/New Page Books
3 Tice Road
P.O. Box 687
Franklin Lakes NJ 07417
800/227-3371
FAX: 201/848-1727
Internet: http://www.careerpress.com
COST-$12.99

Includes strategies and tips that can help people figure out what they want to do with their lives. Readers learn to develop job targets, become industry leaders, discover new opportunities, and network more quickly and efficiently. 224 pages.

3764—TEN STEPS IN WRITING THE RESEARCH PAPER

AUTHOR-Roberta Markman, Peter Markman, and Marie Waddell;
ISBN 07641 13623
Barron's Educational Series Inc.
250 Wireless Boulevard
Hauppauge NY 11788
800/645-3476
Internet: http://www.barronseduc.com
COST-$10.95

Arranged to lead the student step-by-step through the writing of a research paper-from finding a suitable subject to checking the final copy. Easy enough for the beginner, complete enough for the graduate student. 160 pages.

3765—TEXAS MUSIC INDUSTRY DIRECTORY

AUTHOR-
Texas Music Office
P.O. Box 13246
Austin TX 78711
512/463-6666
FAX: 512/463-4114
E-mail: music@governor.state.tx.us
Internet: http://www.governor.state.tx.us/music
COST-$20.00

A publication of the Texas Governor's Office which lists more than 8,000 Texas music business contacts, including events, classical music, books, and texas colleges offering music and music business courses. Could be a valuable resource to anyone considering a career in the business of music. 424 pages.

3766—THE BUNTING & LYON BLUE BOOK: PRIVATE INDEPENDENT SCHOOLS 1998

AUTHOR-ISBN 0-913094-54-4
Bunting & Lyon, Inc.
238 North Main Street
Wallingford CT 06492
203/269-3333
FAX: 203/269-5697
E-mail: Bandlblubk@aol.com
Internet: http://www.acadia.net/bunting_lyon/
COST-$105.00

A comprehensive directory of independent elementary and secondary schools in the U.S. and abroad. Access Internet for an online search and/or more information. A counseling service (for which there is a charge) is also available. 1,122 listings; 656 pages.

3767—THE CAREER ATLAS

AUTHOR-Gail Kuenstler, Ph.D.;
ISBN 1-56414-225-6
Career Press/New Page Books
3 Tice Road
P.O. Box 687
Franklin Lakes NJ 07417
800/227-3371
FAX: 201/848-1727
Internet: http://www.careerpress.com
COST-$12.99

Details education and experience requirements for 400 career paths within 40 occupational areas. 256 pages.

3768—THE COLLEGE HANDBOOK

AUTHOR-CBP; ISBN #0-87447-590-2, 1998
The College Board Publications
Department CBO
P.O. Box 869010
Plano TX 75074
800/323-7155
FAX: 800/321-7183
Internet: http://www.collegeboard.org
COST-$26.95

Describes in detail more than 3,200 two- and four-year undergraduate institutions in the U.S. Includes information on admission requirements, costs, financial aid, majors, activities, enrollment, campus life, and more. 1,200 pages. Includes CD-ROM for Windows.

3769—THE FOUNDATION DIRECTORY

AUTHOR-ISBN #0-87954-449-6 (soft cover); 0-87954-484-8 (hard cover)
The Foundation Center
79 Fifth Ave.
New York NY 10003
800/424-9836
Internet: http://fdncenter.org
COST-$160.00 soft cover; $215.00 hard cover; + $5.50 shipping by UPS

Authoritative annual reference book found in most major libraries. Contains detailed information on over 6,300 of America's largest foundations. Indexes allow grantseekers; researchers; etc. to quickly locate foundations of interest.

3770—THE MEMORY KEY

AUTHOR-Dr. Fiona McPherson;
ISBN 1-56414-470-4
Career Press/New Page Books
3 Tice Road
P.O. Box 687
Franklin Lakes NJ 07417
800/227-3371
FAX: 201/848-1727
Internet: http://www.newpagebooks.com
COST-$12.99

Practical, easy-to-use handbook helps students with study skills and anyone dealing with information overload, shedding light on how memory works and what you need to do to achieve memory improvement.

3771—THERE ARE NO LIMITS

AUTHOR-Danny Cox;
ISBN 1-56414-340-6
Career Press/New Page Books
3 Tice Road
P.O. Box 687
Franklin Lakes NJ 07417
800/227-3371
FAX: 201/848-1727
Internet: http://www.careerpress.com
COST-$24.99

Helps students and others develop a plan for achieving goals, written for anyone who wants to make a change in his or her personal or professional life. 256 pages.

3772—TOP SECRET EXECUTIVE RESUMES

AUTHOR-Steven Provenzano;
ISBN 1-56414-431-3
Career Press/New Page Books
3 Tice Road
P.O. Box 687
Franklin Lakes NJ 07417
800/227-3371
FAX: 201/848-1727
Internet: http://www.careerpress.com
COST-$15.99

Presents the writing and most effective use of cover letters; executive networking; preparation and format of reference, support materials, and salary information sheets; using the Internet to expand your search; and more than 150 pages of sample resumes covering most major professions. 256 pages.

3773—UAA-102 COLLEGIATE AVIATION GUIDE

AUTHOR-Gary W. Kiteley, Executive Director
University Aviation Association
3410 Skyway Drive
Auburn AL 36830
334/844-2434
FAX: 334/844-2432
Internet: http://uaa.auburn.edu
COST-$30 non-members; $20 members

Guide to college level aviation study. Detailed state-by-state listings of aviation programs offered by U.S. colleges and universities.

3774—UAA-116 COLLEGIATE AVIATION SCHOLARSHIP LISTING

AUTHOR-Gary W. Kiteley, Executive Director
University Aviation Association
3410 Skyway Drive
Auburn AL 36830
334/844-2434
FAX: 334/844-2432
Internet: http://uaa.auburn.edu
COST-$8 members; $15 non-members

This guide includes a listing of financial aid sources, methods of applying for general purpose aid, and a listing of aviation scholarships arranged by broad classification.

3775—ULTIMATE HIGH SCHOOL SURVIVAL GUIDE

AUTHOR-Julianne Dueber;
ISBN: 0-7689-0241-X
Peterson's
Princeton Pike Corporate Center
2000 Lenox Drive
Lawrenceville NJ 08648
609/896-1800
Internet: http://www.petersons.com
COST-$10.47

Includes helpful information on getting along with teachers, dealing with pressure, preventing intimidation, taking tests, managing time, making friends, and developing creativity. This guide is packed with caring 'reality therapy' for improving skills and building confidence. 292 pages.

3776—WHAT COLOR IS YOUR PARACHUTE?

AUTHOR-Richard N. Bolles;
ISBN 1-58008-341-2
Ten Speed Press
P.O. Box 7123
Berkeley CA 94707
800/841-BOOK or 510/559-1600
FAX: 510/559-1629
E-mail: order@tenspeed.com
Internet: http://www.tenspeed.com
COST-$16.95

Step-by-step career planning guide now in its 30th Anniversary Edition. Highly recommended for anyone who is job hunting or changing careers. Contains valuable tips on assessing your skills, writing resumes, and handling job interviews. 368 pages.

3777—WHERE THE JOBS ARE

AUTHOR-Joyce Hadley Copeland;
ISBN 1-56414-422-4
Career Press/New Page Books
3 Tice Road
P.O. Box 687
Franklin Lakes NJ 07417
800/227-3371
FAX: 201/848-1727
Internet: http://www.careerpress.com
COST-$13.99

An in-depth look at today's job market reveals more about the most current trends and the hottest industries that offer the greatest career opportunities. 320 pages.

3778—WINNING SCHOLARSHIPS FOR COLLEGE-AN INSIDER'S GUIDE

AUTHOR-Marianne Ragins; Order Code: DSC999
The Scholarship Workshop
P.O. Box 176
Centreville VA 20122
478/755-8428
FAX: 703/803-9267
E-mail: feedback@scholarship workshop.com
Internet: http://www.scholarship workshop.com
COST-$12.95

Marianne Ragins, winner of more than $400,000 in scholarship funds, proves that it's not always those with the best grades or highest SAT scores who win scholarships. You'll see that rigorous research efforts, involvement in extracurricular activities, leadership potential, and special talents all combine to determine your chances of securing aid for college. Includes tips on using the Internet, scholarly resumes, selling yourself, test-taking tips, and writing essays.

3779—WORLD DIRECTORY OF MEDICAL SCHOOLS

AUTHOR-WHO
World Health Organization
(1211 Geneva 27; Switzerland)
WHO Publication Center
49 Sheridan Ave.
Albany NY 12210
518/436-9686
E-mail: qcorp@compuserve.com
Internet: http://www.who.int
COST-$40.50

Comprehensive book that describes the medical education programs and schools in each country. Arranged in order by country or area.

3780—WRITE YOUR WAY TO A HIGHER GPA

AUTHOR-Randall S. Hansen, Ph.D. & Katherine Hansen;
ISBN 0-89815-903-2
Ten Speed Press
P.O. Box 7123
Berkeley CA 94707
800/841-BOOK or 510/559-1600
FAX: 510/559-1629
E-mail: order@tenspeed.com
Internet: http://www.tenspeed.com
COST-$11.95

This book tells how any student can use writing skills to get the highest grade possible in any class. Special focus on the Internet and other new resources. 240 pages.

3781—WHERE THERE'S A WILL THERE'S AN "A" TO GET BETTER GRADES IN COLLEGE (or High School)

AUTHOR-
Where There's a Will There's an A
Olney "A" Seminars
P.O. Box 686
Scottsdale AZ 85252-0686
800/546-3883
Internet: http://www.wheretheresa will.com
COST-$46.95

Video tape seminars on how to get better grades.

Career Information

3782—Accounting

ACCOUNTING/NET
60 Orland Square Drive, Suite 101
Orland Park IL 60462
708/403-8333
FAX: 708/403-8770
E-mail: ccasson@accting.net
Internet: http://www.accting.net

3783—Accounting (Career Information)

AMERICAN INSTITUTE OF CERTIFIED PUBLIC ACCOUNTANTS
1211 Avenue of the Americas
New York NY 10036-8775
212/596-6200
FAX: 212/596-6213
Internet: http://www.aicpa.org

3784—Accounting (Career Information)

NATIONAL SOCIETY OF ACCOUNTANTS
1010 North Fairfax Street
Alexandria VA 22314-1574
703/549-6400
FAX: 703/549-2984
Internet: http://www.nsacct.org

3785—Accounting (Career Information)

INSTITUTE OF MANAGEMENT ACCOUNTANTS
10 Paragon Drive
Montvale NJ 07645
800/638-4427 ext.1565
201/474-1565
Internet: http://www.imanet.org

3786—Actuarial Science (Career Information)

SOCIETY OF ACTUARIES
475 N. Martingale Road, Suite 800
Schaumburg IL 60173-2226
847/706-3500
FAX: 847/706-3599
Internet: http://www.soa.org

3787—Acupuncture/Oriental Medicine & Drug/Alcoholism Recovery (Career Information)

NATIONAL ACUPUNCTURE DETOXIFICATION ASSOCIATION
P.O. Box 208
Manchester, M16 9YZ
TEL/FAX: 161/877-3375 (6 pm - 8 pm Monday-Friday) (answer machine outside these times)
E-mail: naduk@btinternet.com

3788—Acupuncture/Oriental Medicine (Career Information)

NATIONAL ACUPUNCTURE AND ORIENTAL MEDICINE ALLIANCE
14637 Starr Road SE
Olalla WA 98359
253/851-6896
FAX: 253/851-6883
Internet: http://www.Acupuncture Alliance.org

3789—Acupuncture/Oriental Medicine (Career Information)

CALIFORNIA SOCIETY FOR ORIENTAL MEDICINE (CSOM)
12926 Riverside Drive, #B
Sherman Oaks CA 91423
FAX: 818/981-2766
Internet: http://www.quickcom.net/csom/

3790—Advertising (Career Information)

AMERICAN ADVERTISING FEDERATION
Education Services
1101 Vermont Avenue NW, Suite 500
Washington DC 20005-6306
800/999-2231 or 202/898-0089
FAX: 202/898-0159
Internet: http://www.aaf.org
E-mail: aaf@aaf.org

3791—Aeronautics (Career Information)

AMERICAN INSTITUTE OF AERONAUTICS AND ASTRONAUTICS (Student Programs Department)
1801 Alexander Bell Drive, Suite 500
Reston VA 20191-4344
800/NEW-AIAA or 703/264-7500
FAX: 703/264-7551
Internet: http://www.aiaa.org

3792—Aerospace Education (Career Information)

AEROSPACE EDUCATION FOUNDATION
1501 Lee Highway
Arlington VA 22209-1198
800/291-8480
E-mail: aefstaff@aef.org Internet:
Internet: http://www.aef.org

3793—Agricultural & Biological Engineering (Career Information)

ASAE SOCIETY FOR ENGINEERING IN AGRICULTURAL FOOD AND BIOLOGICAL SYSTEMS
2950 Niles Road
St. Joseph MI 49085
616/429-0300
FAX: 616/429-3852
Internet: http://www.ASAE.org

3794—Agriculture (Career Information)

AMERICAN FARM BUREAU FEDERATION ("There's A New Challenge In Agriculture")
225 Touhy Avenue
Public Policy Division
Park Ridge IL 60068
847/685-8600
FAX: 847/685-8896
Internet: http://www.fb.com
E-mail: susan@fb.com

3795—Agronomny; Crops; Soils; Environment (Career Information)

AMERICAN SOCIETY OF AGRONOMY
677 S. Segoe Road
Madison WI 53711
608/273-8080
FAX: 608/273-2021
E-mail: headquarters@Agronomy.org
Internet: http://www.Agronomy.org

3796—Air Force Academy/AFROTC (Career Information)

DIRECTOR OF SELECTIONS
HQ USAFA/RRS
2304 Cadet Drive, Suite 200
USAF Academy CO 80840-5025
Internet: http://www.usafa.edu/rr/

3797—Airline (Career Information)

AIR TRANSPORT ASSOCIATION OF AMERICA
1301 Pennsylvania Avenue NW, Suite 1100
Washington DC 20004-1707
202/626-4000

3798—Animal Science (Career Information)

NATIONAL ASSOCIATION OF ANIMAL BREEDERS (NAAB)
P.O. Box 1033
Columbia MO 65205
573/445-4406
FAX: 573/446-2279
E-mail: naab-css@naab-css.org
Internet: http://www.naag-css.org//

3799—Animation (Career Information)

WOMEN IN ANIMATION (WIA)
P.O. Box 17706
Encino CA 91416
818/759-9596
E-mail: info@womeninanimation.org
Internet: http://www.women.in.animation.org

3800—Anthropology (Career Information)

AMERICAN ANTHROPOLOGICAL ASSOCIATION
4350 N. Fairfax Drive, Suite 640
Arlington VA 22203-1620
703/528-1902
FAX: 703/528-3546
Internet: http://www.aaanet.org

3801—Appraising (Career Information)

AMERICAN SOCIETY OF APPRAISERS
555 Herndon Parkway, Suite 125
Herndon VA 20170
703/478-2228
FAX: 703/742-8471
E-mail: asainfo@appraisers.org
Internet: http://www.appraisers.org

3802—Apprenticeship (Career Information)

U.S. DEPT OF LABOR; BUREAU OF APPRENTICESHIP AND TRAINING
200 Constitution Avenue NW
Washington DC 20210
202/693-3812
Internet: http://www.dol.gov

3803—ARCHAEOLOGY (Career Information)

ARCHAEOLOGICAL INSTITUTE OF AMERICA
Boston University
656 Beacon Street, 4th Floor
Boston MA 02215-2006
617/353-9361
FAX: 617/353-6550
E-mail: aia@aia.bu.edu
Internet: http://www.archaeological.org

3804—Architecture (Career Information)

AMERICAN ARCHITECTURAL FOUNDATION (AIA/AAF Scholarship Program)
1735 New York Avenue NW
Washington DC 20006-5292
202/626-7511
FAX: 202/626-7420
E-mail: mfelber@archfoundation.org
Internet: http://www.amerarchfoundation.com

3805—Astronomy & Astrophysics (Career Information for Women)

HARVARD-SMITHSONIAN CENTER FOR ASTROPHYSICS
Publication Dept., MS-28
60 Garden Street
Cambridge MA 02138
617/495-7461
E-mail: pubaffairs@cfa.harvard.edu
Internet: http://www.cfa-www.harvard.edu

3806—Astronomy (Career Information)

AMERICAN ASTRONOMICAL SOCIETY
2000 Florida Avenue NW, Suite 400
Washington DC 20009-1231
202/328-2010
FAX: 202/324-2560
E-mail: aas@aas.org
Internet: http://www.aas.org

3807—Audiology; Speech Pathology (Career Information)

AMERICAN SPEECH-LANGUAGE HEARING FOUNDATION
10801 Rockville Pike
Rockville MD 20852
301/897-5700 ext. 4203
FAX: 301/571-0457
E-mail: actioncenter@asha.org
Internet: http://www.asha.org

3808—Automotive Engineering (Career Information)

SOCIETY OF AUTOMOTIVE ENGINEERS (SAE)
400 Commonwealth Drive
Warrendale PA 15096-0001
724/776-4841
FAX: 724/776-1615
E-mail: foundation@sae.org
Internet: http://www.sae.org

3809—Aviation (Career Information)

AVIATION DISTRIBUTORS AND MANUFACTURERS ASSOCIATION
1900 Arch Street
Philadelphia PA 19103-1498
215/564-3484
FAX: 215/963-9784
E-mail: adma@fernley.com
Internet: http://www.adma.org

3810—Aviation (Career Information)

GENERAL AVIATION MANUFACTURERS ASSOCIATION
1400 K Street NW, Suite 801
Washington DC 20005
202/637-1378
FAX: 202/842-4063
E-mail: bmikula@generalaviation.org
Internet: http://www.generalaviation.org

3811—Aviation Maintenance (Career Information)

PROFESSIONAL AVIATION MAINTENANCE ASSOCIATION
1707 H Street NW, Suite 700
Washington DC 20006-3915
202/730-0260
FAX: 202/730-0259
E-mail: hq@pama.org
Internet: http://www.pama.org

3812—Bartending (Career Information)

PROFESSIONAL BARTENDING SCHOOLS OF AMERICA
See Web site
888/4-BARKIT
Internet: http://www.pbsa.com

3813—Bartending (Career Information)

BARTENDERS' SCHOOL OF SANTA ROSA
1050 Hopper Avenue
Santa Rosa CA 95403
707/523-1611

3814—Biologist (Career Information)

AMERICAN INSTITUTE OF BIOLOGICAL SCIENCES
1444 Eye Street NW, Suite 200
Washington DC 20005
202/628-1500 ext. 281
FAX: 202/628-1509
Internet: http://www.aibs.org
E-mail: admin@aibs.org

3815—Biotechnology (Career Information)

BIOTECHNOLOGY INDUSTRY ORGANIZATION
1625 K Street NW, Suite 1100
Washington DC 20006
202/857-0244
FAX: 202/857-0237
Internet: http://www.bio.org

3816—Broadcast News (Career Information)

RADIO AND TELEVISION NEWS DIRECTORS ASSOCIATION
1600 K Street NW, Suite 700
Washington DC 20036-2838
202/659-6510
FAX: 202/223-4007
E-mail: rtnaf@rtndf.org
Internet: http://www.rtndf.org

3817—Broadcasting (Career Information)

AMERICAN WOMEN IN RADIO & TELEVISION
c/o Nancy Cullen
1771 North Street NW
Washington DC 20036
202/429-5416
FAX: 202/429-5406
E-mail: info@awrt.org
Internet: http://www.awrt.org

3818—Careers in the Public Life (Information)

NATIONAL ASSOCIATION OF SCHOOLS OF PUBLIC AFFAIRS AND ADMINISTRATION
1120 G Street NW, Suite 730
Washington DC 20005-3801
202/628-8965
FAX: 202/626-4978
E-mail: publicservicecareers@naspaa.org
Internet: http://www.naspaa.org/publicservicecareers

3819—Cartooning (Career Information)

NEWSPAPER FEATURES COUNCIL
22 Byfield Lane
Greenwich CT 06830-3446
203/661-3386

3820—Cartooning (Career Information)

NATIONAL CARTOONISTS SOCIETY
10 Columbus Circle, Suite 1620
New York NY 10019
Internet: www.reuben.org

3821—Chemical Engineering (Career Information)

AMERICAN INSTITUTE OF CHEMICAL ENGINEERS
3 Park Avenue
New York NY 10016
212/591-7338
Internet: www.aiche.org/careers/

3822—Chiropractics (Career/College Information)

AMERICAN CHIROPRACTIC ASSOCIATION
1701 Clarendon Boulevard
Arlington VA 22209
800/986-4636 or 703/276-8800
FAX: 703/243-2593
Internet: http://www.amerchiro.org

3823—Chiropractics (Career/School Information)

INTERNATIONAL CHIROPRACTORS ASSOCIATION
1110 N. Glebe Road, Suite 1000
Arlington VA 22201
800/423-4690 or 703/528-5000
FAX: 703/528-5023
E-mail: chiro@chiropractic.org
Internet: http://www.chiropractic.org

3824—Civil Engineering (Career Information)

AMERICAN SOCIETY OF CIVIL ENGINEERS
1801 Alexander Bell Drive
Reston VA 20191-4400
800-548-ASCE or 703/295-6000
FAX: 703/295-6333
E-mail: student@asce.org
Internet: http://www.asce.org

3825—Clinical Chemist (Career Information)

AMERICAN ASSOCIATION FOR CLINICAL CHEMISTRY
2101 L Street NW, Suite 202
Washington DC 20037-1558
800/892-1400 or 202/857-0717
FAX: 202/887-5093
E-mail: info@aacc.org
Internet: http://www.aacc.org

3826—College Information

CALIFORNIA COMMUNITY COLLEGES
1102 Q Street
Sacramento CA 95814
916/445-8752
Internet: http://www.cccco.edu

3827—College Information

UNIVERSITY OF CALIFORNIA SYSTEM
300 Lakeside Drive, 17th Floor
Oakland CA 94612-3550

3828—College Information

CALIFORNIA STATE UNIVERSITY SYSTEM
401 Golden Shore
Long Beach CA 90802-4210
562/951-4000
Internet: http://www.calstate.edu

3829—College Information

ASSOCIATION OF INDEPENDENT COLLEGES AND UNIVERSITIES
1025 Connecticut Avenue NW, Suite 700
Washington DC 20036-5405
202/785-8866

FAX: 202/835-0003
Internet: http://www.naicu.edu/

3830—Computer Science (Career Information)

IEEE COMPUTER SOCIETY
1730 Massachusetts Avenue NW
Washington DC 20036-1992
202/371-0101
FAX: 202/728-9614
Internet: http://www.computer.org

3831—Computer Science (Career Information)

ASSOCIATION FOR COMPUTING MACHINERY
1515 Broadway, 17th Fl.
New York NY 10036-5701
212/869-7440
FAX: 212/944-1318
Internet: http://www.acm.org/membership/career/

3832—Construction (Career Information)

ASSOCIATED GENERAL CONTRACTORS OF AMERICA
333 John Carlyle Street, Suite 200
Alexandria VA 22314-5743
703/548-3118
FAX: 703/548-3119
E-mail: info@agc.org
Internet: http://www.agc.org

3833—Cosmetology (Career Information)

AMERICAN ASSOCIATION OF COSMETOLOGY SCHOOLS
15825 N. 71st Street, Suite 100
Scootsdale AZ 85254-1521
800/831-1086 or 480/281-0431
FAX: 480/905-0708
E-mail: jim@beautyschools.org
Internet: http://www2.beautyschools.org/index2.html

3834—Crafts (Career Information)

AMERICAN CRAFT COUNCIL LIBRARY
72 Spring Street
New York NY 10012
212/274-0630
FAX: 212/274-0650
E-mail: library@craftcouncil.org
Internet: http://www.craftcouncil.org

3835—Creative Writing (Career Information)

NATIONAL WRITERS ASSOCIATION
3140 S. Peoria, PMB 295
Aurora CO 80014
303/751-7844
FAX: 303/751-8593
E-mail: sandywrter@aol.com
Internet: www.nationalwriters.com

3836—Data Processing Management (Career Information)

ASSOCIATION OF INFORMATION TECHNOLOGY PROFESSIONALS
315 S. Northwest Highway, Suite 200
Park Ridge IL 60068-4278
847/825-8124
Internet: http://www.aitp.org

3837—Dental Assistant (Career Information)

AMERICAN DENTAL ASSISTANTS ASSOCIATION
203 N. LaSalle Street, Suite 1320
Chicago IL 60601
312/541-1550 or 800/733-2322
FAX: 312/541-1496
E-mail: adaa1@aol.com
Internet: http://www.dentalassistant.org

3838—Dental Laboratory Technology (Career Information)

NATIONAL ASSOCIATION OF DENTAL LABORATORIES
8201 Greensboro Drive, Suite 300
McLean VA 22102
703/610-9035
Internet: http://www.nadl.org

3839—Dental Profession (Career Information)

ADA ENDOWMENT AND ASSISTANCE FUND INC.
211 E. Chicago Avenue
Chicago IL 60611
312/440-2500
800/877-1600 x 4898
FAX: 312/440-2800
Internet: http://www.ada.org

3840—Dietitian (Career Information)

AMERICAN DIETETIC ASSOCIATION (ADA)
Attn: Networks Team
216 W. Jackson Boulevard
Chicago IL 60606-6995
312/899-0040
FAX: 312/899-0008
E-mail: network@eatright.org
Internet: www.eatright.org

3841—Drama/Acting (Career Information)

SCREEN ACTORS GUILD
5757 Wilshire Boulevard
Los Angeles CA 90036-3600
323/954-1600
FAX: 323/549-6603
Internet: http://www.eatright.org

3842—Education (Career Information)

AMERICAN FEDERATION OF TEACHERS
Public Affairs Dept.
555 New Jersey Avenue NW
Washington DC 20001-2079
202/879-4400
E-mail: online@aft.org
Internet: http://www.aft.org

3843—Electrical Engineering (Career Information)

INSTITUTE OF ELECTRICAL AND ELECTRONICS ENGINEERS-US ACTIVITIES
1828 L Street NW, Suite 1202
Washington DC 20036-5104
202/785-0017

3844—Engineering (Program/Career Information)

JUNIOR ENGINEERING TECHNICAL SOCIETY INC (JETS)
1420 King Street, Suite 405
Alexandria VA 22314
703/548-5387
FAX: 703/548-0769
Internet: http://www.jets.org

3845—Engineering (Career Information)

NATIONAL SOCIETY OF PROFESSIONAL ENGINEERS
1420 King Street
Alexandria VA 22314
703/684-2800

3846—Entomology (Career Information)

ENTOMOLOGICAL SOCIETY OF AMERICA
9301 Annapolis Road, Suite 300
Lanham MD 20706-3115
301/731-4535
FAX: 301/731-4538
E-mail: esa@entsoc.org
Internet: http://www.entsoc.org

3847—Environmental (Career/Studies Information)

U.S. ENVIRONMENTAL PROTECTION AGENCY
Office of Communications, Education, and Public Affairs
Environmental Education Division
401 M Street SW
Washington DC 20024
Internet: http://www.epa.gov

3848—FBI (Career Information)

FEDERAL BUREAU OF INVESTIGATION
J. Edgar Hoover Building
935 Pennsylvania Avenue NW
Washington DC 20535-0001
202/324-3000
Internet: http://www.fbi.gov

3849—Family & Consumer Science (Career Information)

AMERICAN ASSOCIATION OF FAMILY AND CONSUMER SCIENCES
1555 King Street
Alexandria VA 22314-2752
703/706-4600
FAX: 703/706-4663
E-mail: info@aafcs.org
Internet: http://www.aafcs.org

3850—Fashion Design (Educational Information)

FASHION INSTITUTE OF TECHNOLOGY
Seventh Avenue at 27th Street
New York NY 10001-5992
212/217-7999
E-mail: FITinfo@fitsuny.edu
Internet: http://www.fitnyc.suny.edu

3851—Film & Television (Career Information)

ACADEMY OF CANADIAN CINEMA AND TELEVISION
172 King Street East
Toronto Ontario M5A 1J3 CANADA
416/366-2227
FAX: 416/366-8454
E-mail: info@academy.ca
Internet: http://www.academy.ca

3852—Fire Service (Career Information)

NATIONAL FIRE PROTECTION ASSN. (Public Fire Protection)
1 Batterymarch Park
P.O. Box 9101
Quincy MA 02269-9101
617/770-3000
FAX: 617/770-0700
Internet: http://www.nfpa.org/Home/index.asp

3853—Fisheries (Career/University Information)

AMERICAN FISHERIES SOCIETY
5410 Grosvenor Lane, Suite 110
Bethesda MD 20814-2199
301/897-8616
FAX: 301/897-8096
E-mail: main@fisheries.org
Internet: http://www.fisheries.org

3854—Floristry (Career Information)

SOCIETY OF AMERICAN FLORISTS
1601 Duke Street
Alexandria VA 22314
703/836-8700 or 800/336-4743
Internet: http://www.safnow.org

3855—Food & Nutrition Service (Career Information)

U.S. DEPT OF AGRICULTURE FOOD AND NUTRITION SERVICE
Personnel Division, Rm. 620
3101 Park Center Drive
Alexandria VA 22302
Internet: http://www.fns.usda.gov/fncs/

3856—Food Service (Career Information)

NATIONAL RESTAURANT ASSOCIATION EDUCATIONAL FOUNDATION
175 West Jackson Boulevard, Suite 1500
Chicago IL 60604-2702
800/765-2122 ext. 733 or 312/715-1010
FAX: 312/715-1362
E-mail: info@foodtrain.org
Internet: http://www.edfound.org

3857—Forest Service (Career Information)

U.S. DEPT. OF AGRICULTURE
1400 Independence Avenue SW
Washington DC 20250
Internet: http://www.usda.gov

3858—Forestry (Career Information ONLY)

SOCIETY OF AMERICAN FORESTERS
5400 Grosvenor Lane
Bethesda MD 20814-2198
301/897-8720
FAX: 301/897-3690
E-mail: safweb@safnet.org
Internet: http://www.safnet.org

3859—Funeral Director (Career Information)

NATIONAL FUNERAL DIRECTORS ASSOCIATION
13625 Bishops Drive
Brookfield WI 53005
800/228-6332 or 262/789-1880
FAX: 262/789-6977
E-mail: nfda@nfda.org
Internet: www.nfda.org

3860—Gemology (Career Information)

GEMLINES.COM
1524 NW 52nd Street
Seattle WA 98107
FAX: 978/477-8361
E-mail: gemlines@yahoo.com
Internet: www.gemlines.com

3861—Geography (Career Information)

ASSOCIATION OF AMERICAN GEOGRAPHERS
1710 16th Street NW
Washington DC 20009-3198
202/234-1450
FAX: 202/234-2744
E-mail: gaia@aag.org
Internet: www.aag.org

3862—Geological Sciences (Career Information)

GEOLOGICAL SOCIETY OF AMERICA
3300 Penrose Place
P.O. Box 9140
Boulder CO 80301-9140
303/447-2020
FAX: 303/357-1070
E-mail: member@geosociety.org
Internet: http://www.geosociety.org/educate/index.htm

3863—Geological Sciences (Career Information)

AMERICAN GEOLOGICAL INSTITUTE
4220 King Street
Alexandria VA 22302
703/379-2480
FAX: 703/379-7563
E-mail: ehrinfo@agiweb.org
Internet: http://www.agiweb.org

3864—Geophysics (Career Information)

AMERICAN GEOPHYSICAL UNION
2000 Florida Avenue NW
Washington DC 20009-1277
202/462-6900 or 800/966-2481
FAX: 202/328-0566
E-mail: service@agu.org
Internet: http://www.agu.org

3865—Graphic Arts (Career Information)

AMERICAN INSTITUTE OF GRAPHIC ARTS
164 Fifth Avenue
New York NY 10010
212/807-1990

3866—Graphic Communications (Career/Education Information)

EDUCATION COUNCIL OF THE GRAPHIC ARTS INDUSTRY
1899 Preston White Drive
Reston VA 20191
703/648-1768
FAX: 703/620-0994

3867—Heating & Air Conditioning Engineer (Career Information)

REFRIGERATION SERVICE ENGINEERS SOCIETY
1666 Rand Road
Des Plaines IL 60016-3552
847/297-6464
FAX: 847-297-5038
E-mail: general@rses.org
Internet: www.rses.org

3868—Homeopathic Medicine (Career Information)

NATIONAL CENTER FOR HOMEOPATHY
801 N. Fairfax Street, Suite 306
Alexandria VA 22314-1757
703/548-7790
FAX: 703/548-7792
E-mail: info@homeopathic.org
Internet: http://www.homeopathic.org

3869—Homeopathic Medicine (Career Information)

HOMEOPATHIC EDUCATIONAL SERVICES
2124B Kittredge Street
Berkeley CA 94704
510/649-0294
FAX: 510/649-1955
E-mail: mail@homeopathic.com
Internet: http://www.homeopathic.com/ailments/hesdent.htm

3870—Horticulture (Career Information)

AMERICAN ASSOCIATION OF NURSERYMEN
1250 "Eye" Street NW
Washington DC 20005
202/789-2900
FAX: 202/789-1893
E-mail: aanhq@aol.com

3871—Hospital Administration (Career Information)

AMERICAN COLLEGE OF HEALTH CARE EXECUTIVES
One N. Franklin Street, Suite 1700
Chicago IL 60606-3491
312/424-2800
FAX: 312/424-0023
Internet: http://www.ache.org

3872—Hotel Management (Career Information)

AMERICAN HOTEL FOUNDATION
1201 New York Avenue NW, Suite 600
Washington DC 20005
202/289-3180
FAX: 202/289-3199
E-mail: ahlf@ahlf.org
Internet: http://www.ahlf.org

3873—Illuminating Engineering (Career Information)

ILLUMINATING ENGINEERING SOCIETY OF NORTH AMERICA
120 Wall Street 17th Floor
New York NY 10005
212/248-5000
FAX: 212/248-5017
E-mail: iesna@iesna.org
Internet: http://www.iesna.org

3874—Insurance (Career Information)

COLLEGE OF INSURANCE
101 Murray Street
New York NY 10007
212/962-4111
FAX: 212/964-3381

3875—Journalism (Career Information)

AMERICAN SOCIETY OF NEWSPAPER EDITORS
11690B Sunrise Valley Drive
Reston VA 20191-1409
703/453-1122
FAX: 703/453-1133
E-mail: asne@asne.org
Internet: http://www.asne.org

3876—Journalism (Online Career Information)

DOW JONES NEWSPAPER FUND
P.O. Box 300
Princeton NJ 08543-0300
609/452-2820
FAX: 609/520-5804
E-mail: newsfund@wsj.dowjones.com
Internet: http://www.dowjones.com/newsfund

3877—Law (Career Information Booklet)

AMERICAN BAR ASSOCIATION
750 N. Lake Shore Drive
Chicago IL 60611
312/988-5000
Internet: http://www.abanet.org

3878—Law Librarianship (Career Information)

AMERICAN ASSOCIATION OF LAW LIBRARIES
53 W. Jackson Boulevard, Suite 940
Chicago IL 60604
312/939-4764
FAX: 312/431-1097
E-mail: membership@aall.org
Internet: http://www.aallnet.org

3879—Learn to Fly (Career Information)

NATIONAL AIR TRANSPORTATION ASSOCIATION
4226 King Street
Alexandria VA 22302
703/845-9000

3880—Learning Disabled (Education/Career Information)

LEARNING DISABILITIES ASSN OF AMERICA
4156 Library Road
Pittsburgh PA 15234-1349
412/341-1515
FAX: 412/344-0224
E-mail: info@idaamerica.org
Internet: http://www.idanatl.org

3881—Management (Career Information)

AMERICAN MANAGEMENT ASSOCIATION
1601 Broadway
New York NY 10019-7420
212/586-8100
FAX: 212/903-8168
E-mail: customerservice@amanet.org
Internet: http://www.amanet.org

3882—Massage Therapy (Career Information)

CANADIAN MASSAGE THERAPIST ALLIANCE-CMTA
365 Bloor Street East, Suite 1807
Toronto Ontario M4W 3L4
CANADA
416/968-2149
FAX: 416/968-6818

3883—Massage Therapy (Career Information)

AMERICAN MASSAGE THERAPY ASSOCIATION-AMTA
820 Davis Street, Suite 100
Evanston IL 60201-4444
847/864-0123
FAX: 847/864-1178
Internet: http://www.amtamassage.org

3884—Massage Therapy (Career Information)

ASSOCIATION OF MASSAGE THERAPISTS-AUSTRALIA INCORPORATED
P.O. Box 358
Prahran Victoria AUSTRALIA 3181
613 9510 3930
FAX: 613 9521 3209
E-mail: amta@amta.asn.au
Internet: http://www.amta.asn.au

3885—Mathematical Sciences (Career Information)

MATHEMATICAL ASSOCIATION OF AMERICA
P.O. Box 91112
Washington DC 20090-1112
800/331-1622
FAX: 301/206-9789
Internet: http://www.maa.org

3886—Mathematics Teacher (Career Information)

NATIONAL COUNCIL OF TEACHERS OF MATHEMATICS
1906 Association Drive
Reston VA 22091-9988
703/620-9840
FAX: 703/476-2970
E-mail: infocentral@nctm.org;
Internet: http://www.nctm.org

3887—Mechanical Engineering (Career Information)

AMERICAN SOCIETY OF MECHANICAL ENGINEERS
Three Park Avenue
New York NY 10016-5990
212/591-7158
FAX: 212/591-7739
E-mail: infocentral@asme.org
Internet: http://www.asme.org

3888—Medical Laboratory Technology (Career Information)

AMERICAN SOCIETY OF CLINICAL PATHOLOGISTS
Careers
2100 W. Harrison
Chicago IL 60612
312/738-1336
Internet: http://www.ascp.org/index.asp

3889—Medical Records (Career Information)

AMERICAN HEALTH INFORMATION MANAGEMENT ASSOCIATION
233 N. Michigan Avenue, Suite 2150
Chicago IL 60601-5800
312/233-1100
FAX: 312/233-1090
E-mail: info@ahimo.org
Internet: http://www.ahima.org

3890—Medicine (Career Information)

ROYAL SOCIETY OF MEDICINE
1 Wimpole Street
London W1G 0AE ENGLAND UK
0207 290 2900
FAX: 0207 290 2992
E-mail: Membership@rsm.ac.uk
Internet: http://www.Roysocmed.ac.uk

3891—Medicine (Career Information)

AMERICAN MEDICAL ASSOCIATION
515 N. State Street
Chicago IL 60610
312/464-5000
Internet: http://www.ama-assn.org

3892—Metallurgy & Materials Science (Career Information)

ASM FOUNDATION FOR EDUCATION & RESEARCH
Scholarship Committee
ASM International
Materials Park OH 44073
216/338-5151
Internet: http://www.free-4u.com/asm.htm

3893—Microbiology (Career Information)

AMERICAN SOCIETY FOR MICROBIOLOGY (Office of Education & Training)
1752 N Street NW
Washington DC 20036
202/942-9283
FAX: 202/942-9329
Internet: http://www.asmusa.org/edusrc/edu2.htm

3894—Music Therapy (Career Information)

NATIONAL ASSN FOR MUSIC THERAPY
8455 Colesville Road, Suite 1000
Silver Spring MD 20910
301/589-3300
FAX 301/589-5175
E-mail: info@musictherapy.org
Internet: http://www.musictherapy.org

3895—Naturopathic Medicine (Career Information)

AMERICAN ASSOCIATION OF NATUROPATHIC PHYSICIANS
8201 Greensboro Drive, Suite 300
McLean VA 22102
703/610-9037
FAX: 703/610-9005
Internet: http://www.naturopathic.org

3896—Naval Architecture (Career Information)

SOCIETY OF NAVAL ARCHITECTS AND MARINE ENGINEERS
601 Pavonia Avenue
Jersey City NJ 07306
800/798-2188 or 201/798-4800
E-mail: ccali-poutre@sname
Internet: http://www.sname.org

3897—Naval/Marine Engineering (Career Information)

SOCIETY OF NAVAL ARCHITECTS AND MARINE ENGINEERS
601 Pavonia Avenue
Jersey City NJ 07306
800/798-2188 or 201/798-4800
E-mail: ccali-poutre@sname
Internet: http://www.sname.org

3898—Newspaper Industry (Career Information)

NEWSPAPER ASSN OF AMERICA
921 Gallows Road, Suite 600
Vienna VA 22182-3900
703/902-1861
Internet: http://www.NAA.org/newspapercareers

3899—Nurse Anesthetist (Career Information)

AMERICAN ASSOCIATION OF NURSE ANESTHETISTS
222 S. Prospect Avenue
Park Ridge IL 60068-4001
708/692-7050
Internet: http://www.aana.com

3900—Nursing (Career Information)

NATIONAL LEAGUE FOR NURSING
61 Broadway, 33rd Floor
New York NY 10006
800/669-1656 or 212/363-5555
FAX: 212/812-0393
E-mail: custhelp@nln.org
Internet: http://www.nln.org

3901—Oceanography & Marine Science (Career Information)

MARINE TECHNOLOGY SOCIETY
1828 L Street NW, Suite 906
Washington DC 20036
202/775-5966
Internet: http://www.mtsociety.org

3902—Operations Research & Management Science (Career Information)

INSTITUTE FOR OPERATIONS RESEARCH AND THE MANAGEMENT SCIENCES (INFORMS)
901 Elkridge Landing Road
Suite 400
Linthicum MD 21090-2909
800/4INFORMS
FAX: 410/684-2963
E-mail: informs@informs.org
Internet: www.informs.org/Edu/Career/booklet.html

3903—Optometry (Career Information)

NATIONAL OPTOMETRIC ASSOCIATION
P.O. Box F
E. Chicago IN 46312
219/398-1832
FAX: 219/398-1077
E-mail: info@natoptassoc.org
Internet: http://www.natoptassoc.org

3904—Optometry (Career Information)

AMERICAN OPTOMETRIC ASSOCIATION
243 N. Lindbergh Boulevard
St. Louis MO 63141-7881
314/991-4100
FAX: 314/991-4101
Internet: http://www.aoanet.org

3905—Osteopathic Medicine (Career Information)

AMERICAN OSTEOPATHIC ASSOCIATION
Dept. of Predoctoral Education
142 East Ontario
Chicago IL 60611
800/621-1773 ext. 7401
FAX: 312/202-8200
E-mail: info@aoa-net.org
Internet: http://www.aoa-net.org

3906—Paleontology (Career Information)

PALEONTOLOGICAL SOCIETY
Box 870338
Tuscaloosa AL 35487-0338
Internet: http://www.paleosoc.org

3907—Pathology as Career in Medicine (Career Information Brochure)

INTERSOCIETY COMMITTEE ON PATHOLOGY INFORMATION
9650 Rockville Pike
Bethesda MD 20814-3993
301/571-1880
FAX: 301/571-1879
Internet: http://pathologytraining.org
E-mail: ICPI@pathol.faseb.org

3908—Pediatrics (Career Information)

AMERICAN ACADEMY OF PEDIATRICS
141 NW Point Boulevard
Elk Grove Village IL 60007-1098
800/434-4000
FAX: 847/434-8000
E-mail: kidsdocs@aap.org
Internet: http://www.aap.org

3909—Petroleum Engineering (Career Information)

SOCIETY OF PETROLEUM ENGINEERS
P.O. Box 833836
Richardson TX 75083-3836
972/952-9393
FAX: 972/952-9435
E-mail: twhipple@spelink.spe.org
Internet: http://www.spe.org

3910—Pharmacology (Career Information)

AMERICAN SOCIETY FOR PHARMACOLOGY & EXPERIMENTAL THERAPEUTICS INC.
9650 Rockville Pike
Bethesda MD 20814-3995
301/530-7060
FAX: 301/530-7061
E-mail: info@aspet.org
Internet: http://www.aspet.org

3911—Pharmacy (Career Information)

AMERICAN ASSOCIATION OF COLLEGES OF PHARMACY
Office of Student Affairs
1426 Prince Street
Alexandria VA 22314
703/739-2330
FAX:703/836-8982
Internet: http://www.aacp.org

3912—Pharmacy (Career Information)

AMERICAN FOUNDATION FOR PHARMACEUTICAL EDUCATION
One Church Street, Suite 202
Rockville MD 20850
301/738-2160
FAX: 301/738-2161
E-mail: info@afpenet.orgInternet: http://www.afpenet.org

3913— Pharmacy (School Information Booklet)

AMERICAN COUNCIL ON PHARMACEUTICAL EDUCATION
20 North Clark Street, Suite 2500
Chicago IL 60602-5109
312/664-3577
FAX: 312/664-4652
Internet: http:// www.acpe-accredit.org

3914—Physical Therapy (Career Information)

AMERICAN PHYSICAL THERAPY ASS'N.
1111 N. Fairfax Street
Alexandria VA 22314-1488
703/684-2782
FAX: 703/684-7343
Internet: http://www.apta.org

3915—Physics (Career Information)

AMERICAN INSTITUTE OF PHYSICS STUDENTS
One Physics Ellipse
College Park MD 20740-3843
301/209-3100
FAX: 301/209-0843
E-mail: aipinfo@aip.org
Internet: http://www.aip.org

3916—Podiatry (Career Information)

FUND FOR PODIATRIC MEDICAL EDUCATION
9312 Old Georgetown Road
Bethesda MD 20814-1698
301/581-9200
FAX: 301/530-2752
Internet: http://www.apma.org

3917—Precision Machining Technology (Career Information)

NATIONAL TOOLING AND MACHINING ASSN
9300 Livingston Road
Ft. Washington MD 20744
301/248-6200
Internet: http://www.ntma.org

3918—Psychiatry (Career Information)

AMERICAN PSYCHIATRIC ASSN., DIVISION OF PUBLIC AFFAIRS
1400 K Street NW
Washington DC 20005
888/357-7924
FAX: 202/682-6850
Internet: http://www.psych.org

3919—Psychology (Career Information)

AMERICAN PSYCHOLOGICAL ASSOCIATION
750 First Street NE
Washington DC 20002-4242
202/336-5510
E-mail: mfp@apa.org
Internet: http://www.apa.org

3920—Public Administration (Career Information)

AMERICAN SOCIETY FOR PUBLIC ADMINISTRATION
1120 G Street NW, Suite 700
Washington DC 20005-3801
202/393-7878
FAX: 202/638-4952
E-mail: info@aspanet.org
Internet: http://www.aspanet.org

3921—Radiologic Technology (Career Information)

AMERICAN SOCIETY OF RADIOLOGIC TECHNOLOGISTS (ASRT)
15000 Central Avenue SE
Albuquerque NM 87123-3917
505/298-4500
FAX: 505/298-5063
Internet: http://www.asrt.org

3922—Range Management (Career Information)

SOCIETY FOR RANGE MANAGEMENT
445 Union Boulevard, Suite 230
Lakewood CO 80228
303/986-3309
FAX: 303/986-3892
E-mail: jburwell@ix.netcom.com
Internet: http://www.srm.org

3923—Rehabilitation Counseling (Career Information)

NATIONAL REHABILITATION COUNSELING ASSN.
8807 Sudley Road, #102
Manassas VA 22110-4719
703/361-2077
FAX: 703/361-2489
Internet: http://www.hrca-net.org

3924—Respiratory Therapy (Career Information)

AMERICAN RESPIRATORY CARE FOUNDATION
11030 Ables Lane
Dallas TX 75229-4593
972/243-2272
FAX: 972/484-2720
E-mail: info@aarc.org
Internet: http://www.aarc.org

3925—Safety Engineering (Career Information)

AMERICAN SOCIETY OF SAFETY ENGINEERS
1800 E. Oakton Street
Des Plaines IL 60018-2187
847/699-2929
FAX:847/768-3434
Internet: http://www.asse.org

3926—School Administration (Career Information)

AMERICAN ASSOCIATION OF SCHOOL ADMINISTRATORS
1801 North Moore Street
Arlington VA 22209-1813
703/528-070
FAX: 703/841-1543
Internet: www.aasa.org

3927—Science Teacher (Career Information)

NATIONAL SCIENCE TEACHERS ASSN
Attn Office of Public Information
1840 Wilson Boulevard
Arlington VA 22201
703/243-7100
Internet: http://www.nsta.org

3928—Secretary/Office Professional (Career Information)

PROFESSIONAL SECRETARIES INTERNATIONAL—THE ASSOCIATION FOR OFFICE PROFESSIONALS
10502 NW Ambassador Drive
Kansas City MO 64195-0404
816/891-6600
FAX: 816-891-9118
E-mail: service@psi.org
Internet: http://www.main.org/psi/

3929—Social Work (Career Information)

NATIONAL ASSN OF SOCIAL WORKERS
750 First Street NE, Suite 700
Washington DC 20002
202/408-8600
FAX: 202/336-8310
Internet: http://www.naswdc.org

3930—Sociology (Career Information)

AMERICAN SOCIOLOGICAL ASSOCIATION
1307 New York Avenue NW, Suite 700
Washington DC 20005
202/383-9005
FAX: 202/638-0882
E-mail: apap@asanet.org
Internet: http://www.asanet.org

3931—Soil Conservation (Career Information)

SOIL & WATER CONSERVATION SOCIETY
7515 NE Ankeny Road
Ankeny IA 50021-9764
515/289-2331 or 800/THE-SOIL
FAX: 515/289-1227
E-mail: charliep@secs.org
Internet: http://www.swcs.org

3932—Special Education Teaching (Career Information)

NATIONAL CLEARINGHOUSE FOR PROFESSIONS IN SPECIAL EDUCATION
The Council for Exceptional Children
1110 North Glebe Road, Suite 300
Arlington VA 22201
703/264-9446
FAX: 703/264-9494
E-mail: ncpse@cec.sped.org
Internet: http://www.cec.sped.org/ncpse.htm

3933—Speech & Hearing Therapy (Career Information-send SASE)

ALEXANDER GRAHAM BELL ASSOCIATION FOR THE DEAF
3417 Volta Place NW
Washington DC 20007-2778
202/337-5220
FAX: 202-337-8314
E-mail: Agbell2@aol.com
Internet: http://www.agbell.org

3934—Sports Industry (Online Career Information)

ESPN
Internet: http://espn.monster.com

3935—Teratology (Career Information)

TERATOLOGY SOCIETY
1767 Business Center Drive, Suite 200
Reston VA 20190-5332
703/438-3104
FAX: 703/438-3113
E-mail: tshq@teratology.org
Internet: http://www.teratology.org

3936—Truckdriving (Career Information)

LAYOVER.COM
See Web site
800/361-3081
FAX: 717/859-1524
E-mail: info@layover.com
Internet: http://www.layover.com

3937—Truckdriving (Career Information)

AMERICAN TRUCKING ASSOCIATIONS
2200 Mill Road
Alexandria VA 22314-4677
703/838-1700
Internet: http://www.trucking.org

3938—U.S. Navy Officer (Career Information)

U.S. NAVAL ACADEMY
121 Blake Road
Annapolis MD 21402-5000
800/638-9156
Internet: http://www.usna.edu

3939—U.S. Navy/Marine Corps (Career Information)

U.S. NAVAL ACADEMY
Candidate Guidance
117 Decatur Road
Annapolis MD 21402-5018

3940—U.S. Navy/Marine Corps (Career Information)

NAVY AND MARINE CORPS ROTC
COLLEGE SCHOLARSHIPS BULLETIN
Navy Recruiting Command Code 314
801 N. Randolph Street
Arlington VA 22203-1991
800/USA-NAVY
Internet: http://www.navyjobs.com

3941—United States Army (Career Information)

U.S. MILITARY ACADEMY
Director of Admissions
606 Thayer Road
West Point NY 10996

3942—United States Coast Guard (Career Information)

U.S. COAST GUARD ACADEMY
Director of Admissions
15 Mohegan Avenue
New London CT 06320
860/444-8500
FAX: 860/701-6700

3943—Urban Planning (Career Information)

AMERICAN PLANNING ASSOCIATION
122 South Michigan Avenue, Suite 1600
Chicago IL 60603
312/431-9100
FAX: 312/431-9985

3944—Veterinarian (Career Information)

AMERICAN VETERINARY MEDICAL ASSOCIATION
1931 N. Meacham Road, Suite 100
Schaumburg IL 60173
847/925-8070
FAX: 847/925-1329
Internet: http://www.avma.org

3945—Water Management (Career Information)

WATER ENVIRONMENT FEDERATION
Internet: http://www.bgca.org
601 Wythe Street
Alexandria VA 22314-1994
703/684-2400
Internet: http://www.wef.org

3946—Welding Technology (Career Information)

HOBART INSTITUTE OF WELDING TECHONOLOGY
Trade Square East
Troy OH 45373
800/332.9448
FAX: 513/332-5200
E-mail: hiwt@welding.org
Internet: http://www.welding.org

3947—Women Pilots (Career Information)

THE NINETY-NINES, INC.
Box 965, 7100 Terminal Drive
Oklahoma City OK 73159
405/685-7969
FAX: 405/685-7985
Internet: http://www.ninety-nines.org/contact.html

3948—Women in Airport Management (Career Information)

AIRPORTS COUNCIL INTERNATIONAL-NORTH AMERICA
1775 K Street NW, Suite 500
Washington DC 20006
202/293-8500
FAX: 202/331-1362
Internet: http://www.aci-na.org

3949—Writing (Career Information)

KIDZWRITE
To subscribe, send message: subscribe KidzWrite
E-mail Subscription: majordomo@userhome.com

3950—Youth Leadership (Career Information)

BOYS & GIRLS CLUBS OF AMERICA
1230 W. Peachtree Street NW
Atlanta GA 30309
404/487-5700

3951—Youth Leadership (Career Information)

BOY SCOUTS OF AMERICA
National Eagle Scout Association
1325 W. Walnut Hill Lane
P.O. Box 152079
Irving TX 75015
972/580-2431
Internet: http://www.scouting.org

Alphabetical Index